Almanac
of the
50 States

Comparative Data Profiles &
Guide to Government Data

2008 Edition

Almanac of the 50 States

Comparative Data Profiles &
Guide to Government Data

2008 Edition

State & Municipal Profiles Series

information
publications

Woodside, California

Books from Information Publications

State & Municipal Profiles Series

Almanac of the 50 States

California Cities, Towns & Counties   *Connecticut Municipal Profiles*
Florida Cities, Towns & Counties   *Massachusetts Municipal Profiles*
The New Jersey Municipal Data Book   *North Carolina Cities, Towns & Counties*

American Profiles Series

Asian Americans: A Statistical Sourcebook and Guide to Government Data
Black Americans: A Statistical Sourcebook and Guide to Government Data
Hispanic Americans: A Statistical Sourcebook and Guide to Government Data

Essential Topics Series

Energy, Transportation & the Environment:
A Statistical Sourcebook and Guide to Government Data

Almanac of the 50 States, 2008
ISBN 978-0-929960-47-0 Paper
ISBN 978-0-929960-46-3 Cloth

©2008 Information Publications, Inc.
Printed in the United States of America

All rights reserved. No part of this book may be reproduced or transmitted in any form or by any means, including but not limited to electronic or mechanical photocopying, recording, or any information storage and retrieval system without written permission from the publisher.

Data from *Hospital Statistics* is copyright © 2007 Health Forum LLC.,
a division of the American Hospital Association.
Data from *Physician Characteristics and Distribution in the US*
is copyright © 2007 American Medical Association.
Data from *Rankings of the States 2006* and *Estimates of School Statistics 2007* is used
with permission of the National Education Association © 2007.
Data on existing home sales is copyright © 2007 National Association of Realtors
Women in office data is copyright © 2007 the Center for American Women and Politics.
Data from *Black Elected Officials* is copyright © 2007 the Joint Center for Political and Economic Studies.
State Legislature data is copyright © 2007 the National Conference of State Legislatures.
Data from the *Fortune 500* is copyright © 2007 Time Inc.
Data from *Gas Facts* is copyright © 2007 the American Gas Association.
All Rights Reserved.

Information Publications, Inc.
2995 Woodside Rd., Suite 400-182
Woodside, CA 94062-2446

www.informationpublications.com
info@informationpublications.com

Toll Free Phone 877.544.INFO (4636)
Toll Free Fax 877.544.4635

Direct Dial Phone 650.568.6170
Direct Dial Fax 650.568.6150

Table of Contents

Introduction ix

Disclaimer. xxiv

State Profiles **3-418**

Alabama 3	Montana 211
Alaska 11	Nebraska 219
Arizona 19	Nevada 227
Arkansas. 27	New Hampshire 235
California 35	New Jersey 243
Colorado 43	New Mexico 251
Connecticut 51	New York. 259
Delaware. 59	North Carolina 267
District of Columbia. 67	North Dakota 275
Florida. 75	Ohio. 283
Georgia 83	Oklahoma. 291
Hawaii. 91	Oregon. 299
Idaho. 99	Pennsylvania 307
Illinois 107	Rhode Island 315
Indiana 115	South Carolina 323
Iowa. 123	South Dakota 331
Kansas 131	Tennessee. 339
Kentucky. 139	Texas 347
Louisiana 147	Utah. 355
Maine 155	Vermont 363
Maryland. 163	Virginia 371
Massachusetts. 171	Washington 379
Michigan. 179	West Virginia 387
Minnesota. 187	Wisconsin 395
Mississippi 195	Wyoming. 403
Missouri 203	US Summary 411

Comparative Tables **421-470**

©2008 Information Publications, Inc.
All rights reserved. Photocopying prohibited.
877-544-INFO (4636) or www.informationpublications.com

Table of Contents

Comparative Tables

Population, Demographics & Geography

1. Total Area (square miles)......................................421
2. Federally-Owned Land, 2004.............................421
3. Population, 2000 422
4. Population, 2007 (estimate) 422
5. Population, 2008 (projected)..............................423
6. Population, 2030 (projected)..............................423
7. Persons per Square Mile, 2007 (estimate) 424
8. Change in Population, 2000-2007 (estimate)...........424
9. Cities with over 100,000 Population, 2006.............425
10. Population Living in Group Quarters, 2006..............425
11. Core-Based Statistical Area Population, 2006 (x 1,000)..............426
12. Non-CBSA population, 2006 (x 1,000)...............426
13. Median Age, 2006 427
14. Households, 2006 427
15. Legal Permanent Residents Admitted, 2006 428
16. Naturalizations, 2006....................................428
17. Persons Born in State of Residence, 2006 429

Health and Vital Statistics

18. Adults who Smoke, 2006 429
19. Death Rate, 2005 (per 100,000 population, age-adjusted) 430
20. Infant Death Rate, 2004 (per 1,000 births) 430
21. Twin Birth Rate, 2005 (per 1,000 births)..............431
22. Triplet Birth Rate, 2005 (per 100,000 births)..........431
23. Overweight Persons, 2006 432
24. Obese Persons, 2006....................................432
25. People who Get No Regular Exercise, 2005 433
26. People who Regularly Get at Least Moderate Exercise, 2005 433
27. People who Regularly Get Vigorous Exercise, 2005...................434
28. Abortions Performed, 2004 434

Education

29. High School Graduates or higher, 2006................435
30. Bachelor's Degree or higher, 2006.....................435
31. NAEP – 4th Graders Scoring Basic or Better in Math, 2007.............436
32. NAEP – 4th Graders Scoring Proficient or Better in Math, 2007 436
33. NAEP – 4th Graders Scoring Basic or Better in Reading, 2007.........437
34. NAEP – 4th Graders Scoring Proficient or Better in Reading, 2007 437
35. NAEP – 8th Graders Scoring Basic or Better in Math, 2007.............438

©2008 Information Publications, Inc.
All rights reserved. Photocopying prohibited.
877-544-INFO (4636) or www.informationpublications.com

Table of Contents

Comparative Tables *(continued)*

Education *(con't)*

36. NAEP – 8th Graders Scoring Proficient or Better in Math, 2007 438
37. NAEP – 8th Graders Scoring Basic or Better in Reading, 2007 439
38. NAEP – 8th Graders Scoring Proficient or Better in Reading, 2007 439
39. SAT Participation, 2007 440
40. Average Public School Teacher Salary, 2006-07 440
41. Expenditures for Public Schools, per capita, 2006-07 441
42. Expenditures for Public Schools, per pupil, 2006-07 441
43. Public School Revenue, 2006-07 (x $1 million) 442
44. State Appropriations for Higher Education, 2006 (per FTE enrollment). . . 442
45. Library Visits per capita, 2006 443
46. Library Circulation per capita, 2006. 443

Social Insurance and Welfare

47. People without Health Insurance, 2006. 444
48. Children without Health Insurance, 2006 444
49. Health Care Expenditures, per capita, 2004 445
50. Social Security Beneficiaries, 2005 (x 1,000). 445
51. Medicare Enrollment, July 2005 (x 1,000) 446
52. Medicaid Beneficiaries, 2004 (x 1,000) 446

Housing and Construction

53. Median Home Value, 2006 447
54. Median Rent, 2006. 447
55. Home Ownership Rate, 2006 448

Government Finance

56. Federal Grants to State and Local Governments, 2005 (x 1,000) 448
57. State Government Revenues, per capita, 2006 449
58. State Government Expenditures, per capita, 2006 449

Crime and Law Enforcement

59. Violent Crime Rate, 2006 (per 100,000 residents) 450
60. Property Crime Rate, 2006 (per 100,000 residents). 450
61. Identity Theft Rate, 2006 (complaints per 100,000 residents) 451
62. Fraud Rate, 2006 (complaints per 100,000 residents). 451
63. Incarceration Rate, 2006 (per 100,000 residents) 452
64. Incarceration Rate, White, June 2005 (per 100,000 residents). 452
65. Incarceration Rate, Black, June 2005 (per 100,000 residents). 453
66. Incarceration Rate, Hispanic, June 2005 (per 100,000 residents) 453
67. Incarceration Rate, Men, June 2005 (per 100,000 residents) 454
68. Incarceration Rate, Women, June 2005 (per 100,000 residents) 454

©2008 Information Publications, Inc.
All rights reserved. Photocopying prohibited.
877-544-INFO (4636) or www.informationpublications.com

Table of Contents

Comparative Tables *(continued)*

Labor and Income

69. Civilian Labor Force, 2006 (x 1,000) 455
70. Unemployment Rate, 2006 455
71. Average Hourly Earnings – Production, 2006 456
72. Average Weekly Earnings – Production, 2006 456
73. Average Annual Pay, 2006 457
74. Median Household Income, 2006. 457
75. Personal Income, in Current Dollars, 2006 458
76. Personal Income, in Constant (2000) Dollars, 2006 458
77. Persons Below the Poverty Level, 2006 459

Economy, Business, Industry & Agriculture

78. Gross Domestic Product, 2006 (x $1 million) 459
79. Annual Payroll for Major Industry Groups, 2006 (x $1,000) 460
80. Paid Employees for Major Industry Groups, 2006 (x 1,000) 460
81. Number of Farms, 2006 461
82. Net Farm Income, 2006 (x $1 million) 461
83. Farm Marketing Receipts, 2006 (x $1 million) 462
84. Exports, Total Value, 2006 (x $1 million) 462

Communication, Energy & Transportation

85. Households with Computers, 2003 463
86. Households with Internet Access, 2003 463
87. Wireless Phone Customers, December 2006 464
88. FCC-Licensed TV Stations, January 1, 2008 464
89. Energy Spending, per capita, 2004 465
90. Price of Energy, 2004 (per million Btu) 465
91. Energy Consumption, per capita, 2005 (x 1 million Btu) 466
92. Electricity from Renewable Sources, 2005 (% of net generation) 466
93. Average Daily Commute, 2006 (minutes each way) 467
94. Workers who Drove to Work Alone, 2006 467
95. Workers who Carpooled, 2006 468
96. Workers who used Public Transit, 2006 468
97. Gasoline Consumption, per capita, 2006 (in gallons) 469
98. Automobile Registrations, 2006. 469
99. Vehicle-Miles Traveled, per capita, 2006 470
100. Motor Vehicle Deaths, 2006 470

©2008 Information Publications, Inc.
All rights reserved. Photocopying prohibited.
877-544-INFO (4636) or www.informationpublications.com

**State &
Municipal
Profiles
Series**

Introduction

The *Almanac of the Fifty States* is a comprehensive, easy to use statistical reference book, providing a general overview of every state and the District of Columbia, along with tables of comparative rankings.

The book is divided into two parts. The first, **State Profiles**, is comprised of 52 profile sections: one for each of the 50 states, one for the District of Columbia, and one for the US in summary. Each profile is eight pages long, utilizes the same format of 13 subject categories, and has been compiled from the same sources of information. The result is a set of basic data profiles that are readable, understandable, and provide a strong basis for comparative analysis.

The individual profiles are the heart of the book. They have been designed to include information that has the greatest appeal to the broadest cross-section of users. The information comes from the latest reports of federal government agencies, augmented with data from business and trade organizations. No original material or new surveys are included, as our objective is to provide the most vital and significant information about each state, from the most reliable and respected collectors of data. A discussion outlining the data sources for the profiles is provided below.

The second part of the book, **Comparative Tables**, is composed of 100 tables. Each ranks the 50 states, the District of Columbia, and the US as a whole, according to a selected characteristic from the profiles. The purpose here is to provide straightforward tabular data, grouped by subject, on how states compare with regard to a given characteristic.

Scope of this Book

The overall goal of the *Almanac of the 50 States* is to bring together into a single volume a wide variety of diverse information and present it, state by state, in a clear, comprehensible format. It is not intended as a detailed research tool, but rather as a ready reference source, the first place to turn to answer basic questions about the states. For readers requiring more depth of coverage or a different focus, the full range of federal government resources should be examined. The Bureau of the Census, beyond the Decennial Census for which it is best known, collects many other samples of data on a biennial, annual, or even monthly basis, depending on the subject matter. Most Census data has been published online and can be found by visiting www.census.gov and clicking on the appropriate topic. The Census website is relatively easy to navigate and contains a wealth of information.

One particularly useful publication is the Census Bureau's *Statistical Abstract*. This publication, updated annually, contains a summary of all the Bureau's programs (as well as other federal agencies'), and collectively presents a thorough profile of the United States and its population, economy, and government. The abstract is available online at

©2008 Information Publications, Inc.
All rights reserved. Photocopying prohibited.
877-544-INFO (4636) or www.informationpublications.com

Introduction

http://www.census.gov/prod/www/statistical-abstract.html. All information from the *Abstract* that appears in this book was taken from the 2008 edition. Besides *Statistical Abstract* (and its supplements *City and County Data Book* and *State and Metropolitan Area Data Book*), the annual reports and serial publications of individual departments and agencies merit some attention. The federal government is the largest publishing enterprise in the United States, and once the initial hurdle of access is overcome, the researcher is well rewarded: the available materials cover a wide range of topics in great depth and detail.

Additionally, the publications of various trade and professional associations provide an excellent source of state information. Most of these organizations produce monographs and annual reports which provide statistical information that is not available elsewhere. Such publications have been useful in compiling this book, and the most pertinent of proprietary information has been reprinted here with permission.

Finally, state governments are themselves publishers of note. Frequently they bring together and make available valuable information on a state and regional level. Most of their material is collected and made available by the respective state libraries.

The Profiles

All information in the profiles has been selected from federal government reports and publications, or from materials published by business and trade organizations. The use of such sources ensures an internal consistency and reliability of data, and enables the users of this book to go back to the more detailed original source materials for further information.

To enhance this consistency, all headings and terms used in the profiles have been carried over as they appear in the original sources. Those unfamiliar with government terminology may at times be puzzled by either the meaning of a specific term, or why the data was gathered in a certain way. We define a few unclear terms (as the data collection agency uses them) and present the original source for each item of information; readers seeking more detailed definitions and fuller explanations of data-collection procedures are referred there.

Each profile has been designed to be clear and stand on its own. The headings are clear, abbreviations have been avoided whenever possible, and indents have been used to indicate subgroups of the main heading. However, users are cautioned to pay attention to the wording of a heading, and to note whether a dollar amount, median (midway point), mean (average), rate, or percent is being provided. Additionally, not all subgroups add to the total shown. This may be due to rounding, or to only selected subgroups being displayed. Finally, while we strive to include the most complete set

©2008 Information Publications, Inc.
All rights reserved. Photocopying prohibited.
877-544-INFO (4636) or www.informationpublications.com

of information available, not all agencies are uniform in their data-tracking; in several cases, data is not available for all 50 states. In these cases, or when something does not apply (such as state government employees and payroll for Washington, DC, which is not a state), or when a sample size too small to produce a reliable estimate, "NA" appears in the place of the data item.

Note on Data Sources

Since the majority of the data presented here comes from the Census Bureau, one change in their data-collection methods warrants mentioning. The American Community Survey (ACS), a monthly sample of the population, is beginning to track much of the information previously only measured by the Decennial Census. Currently the ACS provides data on a nationwide and statewide level, as well as for individual communities with populations over 65,000. In 2008, the ACS coverage will expand to all communities with populations greater than 20,000. By 2010, the Bureau of the Census hopes to use the ACS to track all the information collected in the long form of the Decennial Census. One caution in using American Community Survey data is that, owing to the margin of error inherent in any sampling process, the ACS provides different figures for the total population from the Census Bureau's Population Division statistics. In order to avoid confusion, information obtained from the two sources should never be presented together; here, such data is kept under separate headings. You can find out more information about the ACS at http://www.census.gov/acs/www.

Categories, Headings & Terms

A review of the 13 categories that make up each of the profiles appears below. In addition to citing the source of origin, the paragraphs contain a brief identification of terms and some background methodology on the data collection.

State Summary

All information in this section is taken from the other 12 categories, and individual sources are identified in these sections' discussions.

Geography & Environment

General coastline data represents the length of the outline of the coast. Tidal shoreline data represents the shoreline of the outer coast, off-shore islands, sounds, bays, rivers, and creeks to the head of the tidewater. The original source of this information is *The Coastline of the United States, 1975.*

©2008 Information Publications, Inc.
All rights reserved. Photocopying prohibited.
877-544-INFO (4636) or www.informationpublications.com

Introduction

Federally-owned land data comes from the *Federal Real Property Profile*, published on September 30, 2004 by the US General Services Administration, Office of Governmentwide Policy, located online at www.gsa.gov.

Information on highest and lowest elevations, land and water area, and state parks comes from *Statistical Abstract*.

Cropland and forest land data comes from the *2003 National Resources Inventory (NRI) Land Use report*, from the National Resources Conservation Service (NRCS).

Number of cities with population over 100,000, and population data for the largest and capital cities come from the 1990 and 2000 Decennial Censuses, and the US Census Bureau Population Division's *Annual Population Estimates*.

National Forest System data comes from the US Department of Agriculture Forestry Service's 2007 *Land Area Reports*.

Demographics & Population Characteristics

All 1980, 1990, and 2000 items are from the 1980, 1990, and 2000 Decennial Censuses of Population, respectively, conducted by the Bureau of the Census. Figures for the 2006 and 2007 population, changes in population, and information on age, sex, and race & Hispanic origin, as well as projections and breakdowns for future years, come from ongoing reports published by the Bureau of the Census. Note that population projections were made in 2005 and do not reflect events that have happened since then. For example, population projections for Louisiana are now very different from the current figures due to the loss of population in the aftermath of hurricane Katrina.

Persons per square mile is calculated based on land size estimates and the 2007 population estimates.

Core-Based Statistical Area (CBSA) population information comes from the Bureau of Census' Annual Population Estimates, reprinted in *Statistical Abstract*. Core-Based Statistical Area populations encompass the all the people living in categories of Metropolitan and Micropolitan areas in the state. CBSAs, Metropolitan, and Micropolitan Areas are defined by the US Office of Management and Budget (OMB). The most recent definitions, effective June, 2003, are fairly complicated, but generally, each category consists of a large population nucleus, together with adjacent communities which have a high degree of economic and social integration with that nucleus. A Metropolitan Area must include at least one place with 50,000 or more inhabitants. A Micropolitan Area must include at least one place with a population of greater than 10,000, but less than 50,000. (In addition, states in New England use slightly different criteria due to their population distributions.) Non-CBSA area population is everyone not included

©2008 Information Publications, Inc.
All rights reserved. Photocopying prohibited.
877-544-INFO (4636) or www.informationpublications.com

in the Core-Based Statistical Area population of the state. The data presented here represents a change from previous editions of *Almanac of the 50 States*, which presented only metropolitan and non-metropolitan populations. Although the census no longer publishes data organized into metropolitan and non-metropolitan areas, this information can be found in the 2006 edition of *Almanac of the 50 States*, or in previous (2003 and earlier) editions of *Statistical Abstract*.

Racial statistics are provided, although they are a highly sensitive subject. The breakdown represents the self-identification of respondents in regard to pre-set Census categories, and does not in any way denote any scientific of biological notion of race. The terms used in this book, such as "Black," "Asian," and "Hispanic," are presented because they are the terms used by the Federal government for data collection purposes. Hispanic origin is not racial group as defined by the Bureau, and persons may be of any race and be of Hispanic origin as well. Readers should note that racial category information comes from the US Census Bureau's Population Division, while more specific breakdowns about the Asian and Hispanic populations comes from the American Community Survey. Because the Population Survey and American Community Survey are different estimates, they present different figures for the total population.

A household is defined as the person or persons occupying a housing unit. A housing unit is defined below, under "Housing & Construction." Briefly, a housing unit is a separate set of living quarters such as a house, apartment, mobile home, etc. A family is a type of household and consists of a householder and one or more other persons living in the same household who are related to the householder by birth, marriage, or adoption. Married couples, and female heads of household with dependent children and no husband present, are subgroups, or types of families. Data on households, languages spoken at home, marital status, and nativity within state of residence are all obtained from the 2006 American Community Survey. Under marital status, "married" includes all people who are currently separated. Data on the group quarters population (including people living in college dormitories, residential treatment centers, group homes, military barracks, correctional facilities, and workers' dormitories) are also taken from the ACS, and marks the first time this population has been included in the survey.

Immigration and naturalization data is from the *Yearbook of Immigration Statistics*, an annual publication of the US Department of Homeland Security (www.dhs.gov).

Vital Statistics & Health

Birth, death, infant death, marriage, and divorce data comes from *National Vital Statistics Reports*, publications from the National Center for Health Statistics, a division of the Department of Health & Human Services' Centers for Disease Control (www.cdc.gov/nchs). All death rates are age-adjusted.

©2008 Information Publications, Inc.
All rights reserved. Photocopying prohibited.
877-544-INFO (4636) or www.informationpublications.com

Introduction

Statistics on abortion come from *Morbidity and Mortality Weekly Report (MMWR)*, a publication of the Centers for Disease Control. Note that several states do not provide information on abortion, and the statistics provided cover only legal, reported abortions.

Percentages of adults who smoke, and those who are overweight and obese are from the CDC's Behavioral Risk Factor Surveillance Service (BRFSS). "Overweight" is defined as having a Body Mass Index (defined as kg/m²) greater than 25, and "obese" is defined by a Body Mass Index over 30. Data on exercise also comes from the BRFSS, published in MMWR's "Surveillance of Certain Health Behaviors Among States and Selected Local Areas" report for 2005. "Moderate" physical activity is defined as causing a small increase in heart rate and breathing for 30 minutes per day, at least 5 times per week. "Vigorous" activity is defined as causing a large increase in heart rate and breathing for 20 minutes per day, at least 3 times per week. For all BRFSS data, the US Summary figure is the median of the state values.

Data for physicians are counts of active, non-federally employed practitioners. Physicians exclude doctors of osteopathy. This information comes from the American Medical Association, reprinted in *Statistical Abstract*, and is reprinted here with permission.

Hospital data comes from the American Hospital Association, is reprinted in *Statistical Abstract*, and appears here with permission. Data reflects American Hospital Association member hospitals only. The average daily census refers to the average total number of inpatients receiving treatment each day, excluding newborns.

Information on disability status of the population comes from the 2006 American Community Survey.

Education

Educational attainment data comes from the 2006 American Community Survey.

Higher education enrollment, minority enrollment, institutions, and degrees conferred come from *Digest of Education Statistics 2005*, compiled by the National Center for Educational Statistics, US Department of Education (www.nces.ed.gov). Public elementary and secondary school enrollment, as well as high school graduates, also come from the NCES. Testing proficiency data for grades 4 and 8 comes from the NCES' *National Assessment of Educational Progress* (NAEP) report. Public library data is taken from the NCES' report *Public Libraries in the US* for Fiscal Year 2005.

Public school finance and teacher data is from the National Education Association's *Rankings & Estimates* report for 2006-07, and is reproduced here with permission. Per capita spending data was calculated using the NEA's estimate for total current expen-

©2008 Information Publications, Inc.
All rights reserved. Photocopying prohibited.
877-544-INFO (4636) or www.informationpublications.com

ditures (which do not count capital outlay or interest on school debt) and the Census' population estimate for July 1, 2006.

Information on state and local financial support for higher education comes from the State Higher Education Executive Officers' (SHEEO) report for the 2006 Fiscal Year.

SAT test scores and the percentage of high school graduates who take the test are from www.collegeboard.com.

Social Insurance & Welfare Programs

All Social Security information has been obtained from the Social Security Administration's *Annual Statistical Supplement, 2006*. Detail is provided for three major Social Security programs: those for the retired; for the survivors of enrollees; and for the disabled covered under the program. The current Statistical Supplement, as well as several older editions, can be found online at www.socialsecurity.gov, in the Office of Policy Data. Supplemental Security Income data also comes from the *Annual Statistical Supplement*.

Medicare and health care expenditure data are produced by the US Centers for Medicare and Medicaid Services, accessible online at www.cms.hhs.gov.

State Children's Health Insurance Program and Medicaid information is from the US Centers for Medicare and Medicaid Services, reprinted in *Statistical Abstract*.

Information on persons without health insurance is gathered by the Census Bureau's *Current Population Reports*.

State unemployment insurance data comes from the US Department of Labor, Employment and Training Administration's *Unemployment Insurance Financial Data Handbook*, reprinted in *Statistical Abstract*.

Information on Temporary Assistance for Needy Families comes from the Administration for Children & Families, a division of the US Department of Health & Human Services, and refers to the total recipients for the year.

Food Stamp program data is obtained from the US Department of Agriculture's Food and Nutrition Service.

Housing & Construction

The Bureau defines some key terms as follows: a housing unit is a house, apartment, mobile home or trailer, group of rooms, or single room occupied as separate living

©2008 Information Publications, Inc.
All rights reserved. Photocopying prohibited.
877-544-INFO (4636) or www.informationpublications.com

Introduction

quarter or, if vacant, intended as a separate living quarter. Separate living quarters are those in which occupants live and eat separately from any other persons in the building and which have direct access from the outside of the building or from a common hall.

Home ownership and vacancy rate data comes from the Census Bureau's Housing and Vacancy Survey.

Data for total housing units can be found at the Census' Population Division.

Owner- and renter-occupied, seasonally-occupied housing units, and median rent and home values, are obtained from the American Community Survey.

Figures for existing home sales come from the National Association of Realtors, and are reprinted here with permission.

New authorizations for housing unit construction are obtained from the Manufacuring, Mining, and Construction Statistics division of the US Census Bureau.

Information on new home construction comes from the National Association of Home Builders, reprinted in *Statistical Abstract.*

Government and Elections

Names of state officials have been obtained from websites for the National Governors Association, the National Lieutenant Governors Association, the National Association of Secretaries of State, the National Association of Attorneys General, and the Conference of Chief Justices. Party in majority information comes from the National Conference of State Legislatures (www.ncsl.org), and is reprinted with permission.

Information about the governorship and legislative structure of each state was obtained from respective legislative manuals and annual election reports, as well as the 2007 edition of *The Book of the States*, published by the Council of State Governments.

State and local employee data is from *State Government Employment and Payroll, 2006,* and *Local Government Employment and Payroll, 2006,* respectively, published by the Federal, State, and Local Government division of the Bureau of the Census. Figures represent March 2006, full-time equivalent employees, along with March payroll data. Federal government employment and payroll is taken from the US Office of Personnel Management's *Federal Employment Statistics: Employment and Trends* report for September 2006, and pertains to the fiscal year ending September 30, 2006.

Information on local governments comes from the 2002 *Census of Governments* (conducted every 5 years by the Bureau of the Census). Data provided concerns govern-

©2008 Information Publications, Inc.
All rights reserved. Photocopying prohibited.
877-544-INFO (4636) or www.informationpublications.com

mental units, as opposed to geographic entities. For example, in Connecticut there are eight counties, but no county governments, hence Connecticut's profile lists zero under "county."

Voting estimates for the 2006 election come from the November 2006 *Voting and Registration Survey* from Current Population Reports, a monthly sample of about 56,000 households published by the US Census Bureau of the Census. Note that the figures are estimates calculated from a survey performed the week after the election, in which respondents were asked whether they had voted in the election, and will differ from official vote tallies.

Women holding public office data comes from press releases provided by the Center for American Women and Politics at the Eagleton Institute of Rutgers University, and is reprinted with permission. More data can be found online at www.cawp.rutgers.edu.

Data concerning Black elected officials are from the Joint Center for Political & Economic Studies, printed in *Statistical Abstract*, and is reproduced here with permission.

Hispanic public officials information is from the National Association of Latino Elected and Appointed Officials, reprinted in *Statistical Abstract*.

Names, parties and terms of office for Senators come from the federal website, www.senate.gov. The number of Representatives by party, congressional election results, and vote totals come from the Clerk of the House of Representatives, clerkweb.house.gov. At press time, there were three vacancies in the House due to the deaths or resignations of representatives in Illinois, Indiana, and Mississippi. Special elections to fill these seats until the 2008 general election were to be held after this book went to press, so this edition reflects those vacant seats. Vote for president in 2004 is from the Federal Election Commission.

Governmental Finance

Revenue, expenditure and debt information comes from the *2006 State Government Finance Data* report. Federal government grants information comes from the *2005 Consolidated Federal Funds Report*. Finance data for the District of Columbia comes from the *State and Local Government Finance: 2004-05* report. All are publications from the Federal, State and Local Governments section of the US Census Bureau and are available on their website, www.census.gov/govs/www/index.html.

Federal budget data comes from the US Office of Management and Budget's annual report *Historical Tables, Budget of the United States Government, Fiscal Year 2008*. Per capita national debt was calculated using the Census' population estimate for 2007.

©2008 Information Publications, Inc.
All rights reserved. Photocopying prohibited.
877-544-INFO (4636) or www.informationpublications.com

Introduction

Crime & Law Enforcement

Information on crime, crime rates, police agencies, and arrests comes from *Crime in the United States, 2006*, published by the Uniform Crime Reports division of the Federal Bureau of Investigation (FBI). The information is located online at www.fbi.gov/ucr/ucr.htm. Readers are cautioned that crime information is based on crimes known to police, and may not include all crimes that have been committed. Hate crime data comes from the FBI's report *Hate Crime Statistics, 2006*.

Fraud and identity theft data come from the US Federal Trade Commission's report *Consumer Fraud and Identity Theft Complaint Data, January–December 2006*.

Information on the number of persons under sentence of death is as of January 1, 2008, and comes from *Sourcebook of Criminal Justice Statistics, 2003* with ongoing updates online.

Information on prisoners comes from *Prisoners in 2006* and *Prisoners at Mid-year 2005*. Data for adults on probation and parole comes from *Probation and Parole Statistics in the United States, 2006*. State court information comes from *State Court Organization 2004*. These sources are publications of the Bureau of Justice Statistics, US Department of Justice.

Labor & Income

Most of the civilian labor force and unemployment data comes from *Geographic Profile of Employment and Unemployment, 2003*, and the *Profile*'s *Annual Averages 2006*, published by the Department of Labor, Bureau of Labor Statistics. The Bureau of Labor Statistics can be found online at www.bls.gov. Civilian labor force includes all civilians who are either employed or unemployed.

Generally, employed persons are those who: 1) did any work as a paid employee; 2) worked 15 hours or more as an unpaid employee in a family enterprise; or 3) had jobs but were not working due to illness, vacation, etc. A full-time employee is one who works at least 35 hours per week. Unemployed persons are those who: 1) had no paid employment and were both available for and looking for work; or 2) were waiting to be recalled to a job; or 3) were waiting to report to a new job.

Labor union membership comes from *Union Members*, published in the Current Population Summary from the Bureau of Labor Statistics.

Experienced civilian labor force by occupation is from the *Occupational Employment Statistics Survey*, published by Bureau of Labor Statistics.

©2008 Information Publications, Inc.
All rights reserved. Photocopying prohibited.
877-544-INFO (4636) or www.informationpublications.com

Hours and earnings data comes from *Current Employment Statistics*, a division of the Bureau of Labor Statistics.

Average annual pay and experienced civilian labor force by private industry come from the Census of Employment and Wages' *Annual Averages 2006*, published by the Bureau of Labor Statistics. It includes the workers who are covered by state unemployment insurance laws, and federal civilian workers covered by federal unemployment. This represents approximately 98% of total civilian employment. It excludes members of the armed forces, elected officials in most states, railroad employees, most self-employed persons, and some others. Pay includes bonuses, the cash value of meals and lodging, and tips and other gratuities.

Household income and poverty information comes from *Income, Earnings, and Poverty Data from the 2006 American Community Survey*, published by the US Bureau of the Census.

Personal (per capita) income information was obtained from the Bureau of Economic Analysis, reprinted in *Statistical Abstract*.

Federal individual income tax data is from the Internal Revenue Service's latest *Statistics of Income Bulletin*. Further information can be found at www.irs.gov/taxstats/ Charitable contribution data also comes from the *Statistics of Income Bulletin*, reprinted in *Statistical Abstract*.

Economy, Business, Industry & Agriculture

Fortune 500 companies come from a count of listed corporations found in the annual directory issue of *Fortune*, reprinted here with permission.

Information on patents and trademarks issued is from the US Trademark Office's annual report.

Bankruptcy information is from statistical tables for the Federal Judiciary's bankruptcy courts (www.uscourts.gov).

Business firm ownership is from the *2002 Survey of Business Owners (SBO)*, published by Bureau of the Census as part of the 2002 Economic Census. The 2002 SBO can be found online at www.census.gov/csd/sbo.

Gross Domestic Product (formerly Gross State Product) is taken from the Department of Commerce's Bureau of Economic Analysis, available at www.bea.gov. The industries represented are major categories under the North American Industry Classification System (NAICS). The NAICS has replaced the US SIC (Standard Industrial Classification)

©2008 Information Publications, Inc.
All rights reserved. Photocopying prohibited.
877-544-INFO (4636) or www.informationpublications.com

Introduction

system, and was developed jointly by the US, Canada, and Mexico to provide new comparability in statistics about business activity across North America. For more information on NAICS and to understand the correspondence between NAICS and SIC, please visit the US Bureau of the Census website, www.census.gov, and search for NAICS.

Agricultural data comes from the US Department of Agriculture's Economic Research Service, www.ers.usda.gov.

Federal economic activity data is from the *Consolidated Federal Funds Report, 2005*.

Department of Defense expenditure information comes from *Atlas/Data Abstract for the United States and Selected Areas*, published annually by the department.

Homeland security information comes from the Department of Homeland Security, State and Local Government Coordination and Preparedness, Office for Domestic Preparedness, and is accessible at www.dhs.gov.

FDIC-insured institution data comes from US Federal Deposit Insurance Corporation, and was obtained directly from the agency.

Fishing data is from *Fisheries of the United States, 2006*, a publication of the National Oceanic and Atmospheric Administration (NOAA).

Mining statistics are from the US Geological Survey, obtained from the current *Mineral Commodity Summaries* report. It can be found at http://minerals.usgs.gov.

Establishment, annual payroll and paid employee data come from the 2005 *County Business Patterns*, a 52-volume report issued annually by the Bureau of the Census. Receipts data comes from the 2002 Economic Census. Both the Economic Census and *County Business Patterns* follow NAICS classifications; however, the two reports are separate (and measure different time periods), and their data should be treated separately. *In particular, the 2002 receipts data should not be combined with the 2005 establishment, employee, or payroll data in any calculations.*

Trade statistics and export information come from the *US International Trade in Goods and Services* report for December 2006, from the Census Bureau's Foreign Trade Statistics division.

Foreign investment in US affiliates refers to US business enterprises (excluding banks) with at least one foreign owner with a direct or indirect voting interest of at least 10%. Data shown here comes from the US Bureau of Economic Analysis' *Survey of Current Business* for August 2006 and *Foreign Direct Investment in the United States, Operations of US Affiliates of Foreign Companies* report, reprinted in *Statistical Abstract*.

©2008 Information Publications, Inc.
All rights reserved. Photocopying prohibited.
877-544-INFO (4636) or www.informationpublications.com

Introduction

Communication, Energy & Transportation

The percent of households with computers and internet access are from the US Department of Commerce's National Telecommunications and Information Division, reprinted in *Statistical Abstract*.

The number of FCC-licensed TV and radio stations comes from the FCC's database, which is updated daily. Data presented here is as of January 1, 2008. Wireless customer information comes from the FCC Industry Analysis and Technology Division's *Local Telephone Competition* report, which is based on reports from individual carriers. Data on high-speed internet providers comes from the FCC's report *High-Speed Services for Internet Access: Status as of December 31, 2006*.

All energy information except gas utility data has been obtained from the US Energy Information Administration, www.eia.doe.gov. Energy consumption data comes from the *State Energy Data Report*, electricity information from the *Electric Power Annual*, and renewable energy data from *Renewable Energy Consumption and Electricity Preliminary 2006 Statistics*, and nuclear power plant from the EIA's annual power plant report.

Natural gas utility information comes from the American Gas Association's *Gas Facts*, and is reprinted with permission.

All transportation information comes from *Highway Statistics, 2006*, an annual publication of the Department of Transportation. It can be accessed online at www.fhwa.dot.gov. For the purpose of registration figures, the definition of motor vehicles includes automobiles, buses, and trucks, but not motorcycles. Gasoline figures include gasohol, a mixture of gasoline and alcohol (usually ethanol). Road system statistics refer to public roads.

Commuting statistics are from the 2006 American Community Survey.

©2008 Information Publications, Inc.
All rights reserved. Photocopying prohibited.
877-544-INFO (4636) or www.informationpublications.com

Introduction

Disclaimer

The *Almanac of the 50 States* contains thousands of pieces of information. Every reasonable precaution, along with a good deal of care, was taken in its preparation. Despite all efforts, it is possible that some of the information contained in this book may not be accurate. Some errors may be due to errors in the original source materials, others may have been made by the compilers of this volume. An incorrect spelling may occur, a figure may be inverted and similar mistakes may exist. The compilers, editors, typist, printers, and others are all human, and in a work of this magnitude the possibility of error can never be fully eliminated. If any piece of information is believed to be inaccurate, please contact the publisher. We are eager to eliminate any errors from coming editions and we will be pleased to check a piece of information.

The publisher is also aware that some users may apply the data in this book in various remunerative projects. Although we have taken reasonable, responsible measures to insure total accuracy, we cannot take responsibility for liability or losses suffered by users of the data. The information provided here is believed to be correct at the time of publication. No other guarantees are made or implied.

The publisher assumes no liability for losses incurred by users, and warrants only that diligence and due care were used in the production of this volume.

A Final Word

In order to continue to meet its goals, *Almanac of the 50 States* is revised and updated on an annual basis. The best suggestions for improvement in a ready-reference source such as this come from the regular users of the work. Therefore, we actively solicit your comments and ideas. If you know how this book could become more useful to you, please contact us.

The Editors
Almanac of the 50 States
Information Publications, Inc.
2995 Woodside Road, Suite 400-182
Woodside, CA 94062

www.informationpublications.com
info@informationpublications.com

Toll Free Phone: 877-544-4636
Toll Free Fax: 877-544-4635

©2008 Information Publications, Inc.
All rights reserved. Photocopying prohibited.
877-544-INFO (4636) or www.informationpublications.com

State Profiles

[ip]
State &
Municipal
Profiles
Series

State Summary

Capital city . . . . .Montgomery
Governor . . . . .Bob Riley

State Capitol
600 Dexter Ave
Montgomery, AL 36130
334-242-7100

Admitted as a state 1819
Area (square miles) 52,419
Population, 2007 (estimate). 4,627,851
Largest city . . . . .Birmingham
Population, 2006 229,424
Personal income per capita, 2006
(in current dollars) $31,295
Gross domestic product, 2006 ($ mil) . . . $160,569

Leading industries by payroll, 2005

Manufacturing, Health care/Social assistance,
Professional/Scientific/Technical

**Leading agricultural commodities
by receipts, 2005**

Broilers, Cattle and calves, Greenhouse/nursery,
Chicken eggs, Cotton

Geography & Environment

Total area (square miles). 52,419
land 50,744
water 1,675
Federally-owned land, 2004 (acres) 513,913
percent. 1.6%
Highest point . . . . Cheaha Mountain
elevation (feet) 2,405
Lowest point . . . . Gulf of Mexico
elevation (feet) . . . . sea level
General coastline (miles) 53
Tidal shoreline (miles) 607
Cropland, 2003 (x 1,000 acres) 2,509
Forest land, 2003 (x 1,000 acres). 21,530
Capital city . . . . .Montgomery
Population 2000 201,568
Population 2006 201,998
Largest city . . . . .Birmingham
Population 2000 242,820
Population 2006 229,424

Number of cities with over 100,000 population

1990 4
2000 4
2006 4

State park and recreation areas, 2005

Area (x 1,000 acres) 48
Number of visitors (x 1,000) 2,961
Revenues ($1,000) $22,363
percent of operating expenditures. 66.6%

National forest system land, 2007

Acres 668,947

Demographics & Population Characteristics

Population

1980 3,893,800
1990 4,040,587
2000 4,447,351
2006 4,599,030
Male. 2,229,469
Female 2,369,561
Living in group quarters, 2006. 115,155
percent of total. 2.5%
2007 (estimate). 4,627,851
persons per square mile of land 91.2
2008 (projected). 4,568,983
2010 (projected). 4,596,330
2020 (projected). 4,728,915
2030 (projected). 4,874,243

**Population of Core-Based Statistical Areas
(formerly Metropolitan Areas), x 1,000**

	CBSA	Non-CBSA
1990	3,559	482
2000	3,945	503
2006	4,109	490

Change in population, 2000-2007

Number 180,500
percent. 4.1%
Natural increase (births minus deaths) 102,880
Net internal migration 59,843
Net international migration 30,650

Persons by age, 2006

Under 5 years 299,377
5 to 17 years 814,924
18 years and over 3,484,729
65 years and over 615,597
85 years and over 79,530
Median age 37.1

Persons by age, 2010 (projected)

Under 5 years 298,302
18 and over 3,504,146
65 and over 648,889
Median age 38.5

Race, 2006

One Race

White. 3,276,561
Black or African American 1,211,583
Asian 41,881
American Indian/Alaska Native. 23,799
Hawaiian Native/Pacific Islander. 1,749
Two or more races. 43,457

Persons of Hispanic origin, 2006

Total Hispanic or Latino 111,432
Mexican. 71,146
Puerto Rican 8,629
Cuban 5,312

©2008 Information Publications, Inc.
All rights reserved. Photocopying prohibited.
877-544-INFO (4636) or www.informationpublications.com

Persons of Asian origin, 2006

Total Asian	45,882
Asian Indian	10,184
Chinese	8,876
Filipino	2,682
Japanese	3,835
Korean	6,402
Vietnamese	8,761

Marital status, 2006

Population 15 years & over	3,682,816
Never married	988,715
Married	1,978,644
Separated	95,558
Widowed	272,160
Divorced	443,297

Language spoken at home, 2006

Population 5 years and older	4,305,303
English only	4,124,326
Spanish	107,806
French	8,932
German	9,180
Chinese	7,221

Households & families, 2006

Households	1,796,058
with persons under 18 years	612,801
with persons over 65 years	435,989
persons per household	2.50
Families	1,222,858
persons per family	3.06
Married couples	888,609
Female householder, no husband present	259,482
One-person households	496,850

Nativity, 2006

Number of residents born in state	3,261,356
percent of population	70.9%

Immigration & naturalization, 2006

Legal permanent residents admitted	4,278
Persons naturalized	1,946
Non-immigrant admissions	71,983

Vital Statistics and Health

Marriages

2004	42,536
2005	41,962
2006	39,627

Divorces

2004	22,405
2005	22,430
2006	22,054

Health risks, 2006

Percent of adults who are:

Smokers	23.2%
Overweight (BMI > 25)	65.0%
Obese (BMI > 30)	30.5%

Births

2005	60,453
Birthrate (per 1,000)	13.3
White	41,252
Black	18,136
Hispanic	4,020
Asian/Pacific Islander	875
Amer. Indian/Alaska Native	190
Low birth weight (2,500g or less)	10.7%
Cesarian births	31.8%
Preterm births	16.7%
To unmarried mothers	35.7%
Twin births (per 1,000)	32.2
Triplets or higher order (per 100,000)	198.3
2006 (preliminary)	63,235
rate per 1,000	13.7

Deaths

2004

All causes	46,121
rate per 100,000	992.5
Heart disease	12,774
rate per 100,000	276.3
Malignant neoplasms	9,756
rate per 100,000	203.7
Cerebrovascular disease	2,986
rate per 100,000	65.0
Chronic lower respiratory disease	2,361
rate per 100,000	50.0
Diabetes	1,449
rate per 100,000	30.7
2005 (preliminary)	47,088
rate per 100,000	997.9
2006 (provisional)	47,032

Infant deaths

2004	516
rate per 1,000	8.7
2005 (provisional)	546
rate per 1,000	9.1

Exercise routines, 2005

None	29.7%
Moderate or greater	42.8%
Vigorous	20.3%

Abortions, 2004

Total performed in state	11,370
rate per 1,000 women age 15-44	12
% obtained by out-of-state residents	15.2%

Physicians, 2005

Total	9,786
rate per 100,000 persons	215

Community hospitals, 2005

Number of hospitals	109
Beds (x 1,000)	15.5
Patients admitted (x 1,000)	706
Average daily census (x 1,000)	9.9
Average cost per day	$1,198
Outpatient visits (x 1 mil)	7.5

©2008 Information Publications, Inc.
All rights reserved. Photocopying prohibited.
877-544-INFO (4636) or www.informationpublications.com

Disability status of population, 2006

5 to 15 years 7.5%
16 to 64 years 17.5%
65 years and over 48.4%

Education

Educational attainment, 2006

Population over 25 years 3,022,878
   Less than 9th grade. 6.6%
   High school graduate or more 80.1%
   College graduate or more. 21.1%
   Graduate or professional degree. 7.7%

Public school enrollment, 2005-06

Total. 741,758
   Pre-kindergarten through grade 8. 527,479
   Grades 9 through 12 212,414

Graduating public high school seniors, 2004-05

Diplomas (incl. GED and others) 39,990

SAT scores, 2007

Average critical reading score 563
Average writing score 554
Average math score 556
Percent of graduates taking test 9%

Public school teachers, 2006-07 (estimate)

Total (x 1,000) 50.0
   Elementary 28.5
   Secondary 21.5
Average salary $43,389
   Elementary $43,055
   Secondary $43,800

State receipts & expenditures for
public schools, 2006-07 (estimate)

Revenue receipts ($ mil) $6,139
Expenditures
Total ($ mil) $6,444
   Per capita $1,234
   Per pupil $7,908

NAEP proficiency scores, 2007

	Reading		Math	
	Basic	Proficient	Basic	Proficient
Grade 4	61.6%	28.9%	70.2%	25.8%
Grade 8	62.3%	21.2%	55.3%	18.2%

Higher education enrollment, fall 2005

Total. 28,236
   Full-time men 10,151
   Full-time women 13,496
   Part-time men 1,783
   Part-time women. 2,806

Minority enrollment in institutions
of higher education, 2005

Black, non-Hispanic 74,968
Hispanic 3,717
Asian/Pacific Islander 3,577
American Indian/Alaska Native. 1,895

Institutions of higher education, 2005-06

Total. 66
   Public. 39
   Private 27

Earned degrees conferred, 2004-05

Associate's. 9,274
Bachelor's 21,616
Master's 9,993
First-professional. 1,100
Doctor's 571

Public Libraries, 2006

Number of libraries. 207
Number of outlets 302
Annual visits per capita 3.2
Circulation per capita. 4.1

State & local financial support for
higher education, FY 2006

Full-time equivalent enrollment (x 1,000) 181.0
Appropriations per FTE. $5,617

Social Insurance & Welfare Programs

Social Security benefits & beneficiaries, 2005

Beneficiaries (x 1,000) 904
   Retired & dependents. 546
   Survivors. 140
   Disabled & dependents. 218
Annual benefit payments ($ mil) $9,259
   Retired & dependents. $5,370
   Survivors. $1,741
   Disabled & dependents. $2,149
Average monthly benefit
   Retired & dependents. $960
   Disabled & dependents. $907
   Widowed. $897

Medicare, July 2005

Enrollment (x 1,000) 755
Payments ($ mil) $4,897

Medicaid, 2004

Beneficiaries (x 1,000). 118
Payments ($ mil) $905

State Children's Health Insurance Program, 2006

Enrollment (x 1,000). 84.3
Expenditures ($ mil) $111.1

Persons without health insurance, 2006

Number (x 1,000). 689
   percent. 15.2%
Number of children (x 1,000) 82
   percent of children 7.4%

Health care expenditures, 2004

Total expenditures. $23,199
   per capita $5,135

©2008 Information Publications, Inc.
All rights reserved. Photocopying prohibited.
877-544-INFO (4636) or www.informationpublications.com

Federal and state public aid

State unemployment insurance, 2006
Recipients, first payments (x 1,000) 105
Total payments ($ mil) $206
Average weekly benefit $184
Temporary Assistance for Needy Families, 2006
Recipients (x 1,000) 533.8
Families (x 1,000) 228.5
Supplemental Security Income, 2005
Recipients (x 1,000) .163.7
Payments ($ mil) $776.4
Food Stamp Program, 2006
Avg monthly participants (x 1,000) 546.7
Total benefits ($ mil) $593.7

Housing & Construction

Housing units
Total 2005 (estimate) 2,081,960
Total 2006 (estimate) 2,110,154
Seasonal or recreational use, 2006 65,853
Owner-occupied, 2006 1,289,272
    Median home value $107,000
    Homeowner vacancy rate 2.8%
Renter-occupied, 2006 506,786
    Median rent $573
    Rental vacancy rate 13.4%
Home ownership rate, 2005 . . . . 76.6%
Home ownership rate, 2006 . . . . 74.2%

New privately-owned housing units
Number authorized, 2006 (x 1,000) 32.0
Value ($ mil) $4,402.0
Started 2005 (x 1,000, estimate) 20.9
Started 2006 (x 1,000, estimate) 21.1

Existing home sales
2005 (x 1,000) 128.0
2006 (x 1,000) 125.8

Government & Elections

State officials 2008
Governor . . . . .Bob Riley
            Republican, term expires 1/11
Lieutenant Governor . . . . Jim Folsom Jr
Secretary of State . . . . Beth Chapman
Attorney General . . . . Troy King
Chief Justice .Sue Bell Cobb

Governorship
Minimum age 30
Length of term . . . . 4 years
Consecutive terms permitted 2
Who succeeds . . . . Lieutenant Governor

Local governments by type, 2002
Total 1,171
    County 67
    Municipal 451
    Township 0
    School District 128
    Special District 525

State legislature

Name . . . . Legislature
Upper chamber . . . . .Senate
    Number of members 35
    Length of term . . . . 4 years
    Party in majority, 2008 . . . . .Democratic
Lower chamber . . . . .House of Representatives
    Number of members 105
    Length of term . . . . 4 years
    Party in majority, 2008 . . . . .Democratic

Federal representation, 2008 (110th Congress)
Senator . . . . Jeff Sessions
    Party . . . . Republican
    Year term expires 2009
Senator . . . . .Richard Shelby
    Party . . . . Republican
    Year term expires 2011
Representatives, total 7
    Democrats 2
    Republicans 5

Voters in November 2006 election (estimate)
Total 1,667,457
    Male 792,343
    Female 875,113
    White 1,241,244
    Black 400,946
    Hispanic 8,488
    Asian . . . . NA

Presidential election, 2004
Total Popular Vote 1,883,449
    Kerry 693,933
    Bush 1,176,394
Total Electoral Votes 9

Votes cast for US Senators
2004
Total vote (x 1,000) .1,839
Leading party . . . . Republican
Percent for leading party 67.5%
2006
Total vote (x 1,000) . . . . NA
Leading party . . . . NA
Percent for leading party . . . . NA

Votes cast for US Representatives
2004
Total vote (x 1,000) .1,793
    Democratic 708
    Republican 1,080
Leading party . . . . Republican
Percent for leading party 60.2%
2006
Total vote (x 1,000) .1,140
    Democratic 502
    Republican 628
Leading party . . . . Republican
Percent for leading party 55.0%

©2008 Information Publications, Inc.
All rights reserved. Photocopying prohibited.
877-544-INFO (4636) or www.informationpublications.com

State government employment, 2006
Full-time equivalent employees 85,223
Payroll ($ mil) $304.2

Local government employment, 2006
Full-time equivalent employees 187,312
Payroll ($ mil) $534.9

Women holding public office, 2008
US Congress 0
Statewide elected office...................... 5
State legislature 18

Black public officials, 2002
Total....................................... 757
   US and state legislatures 36
   City/county/regional offices 569
   Judicial/law enforcement................. 56
   Education/school boards................. 96

Hispanic public officials, 2006
Total....................................... 0
   State executives & legislators 0
   City/county/regional offices 0
   Judicial/law enforcement................. 0
   Education/school boards................. 0

Governmental Finance

State government revenues, 2006
Total revenue (x $1,000)............$23,670,922
   per capita $5,156.79
General revenue (x $1,000) $20,306,022
   Intergovernmental 7,587,663
   Taxes 8,529,676
     general sales.................... 2,221,506
     individual income tax 2,766,239
     corporate income tax 558,768
   Current charges................... 2,831,624
   Miscellaneous 1,357,059

State government expenditure, 2006
Total expenditure (x $1,000) $22,260,824
   per capita $4,849.60
General expenditure (x $1,000) $20,010,410
   per capita, total.................... $4,359.34
     Education...................... 1,880.57
     Public welfare 1,116.88
     Health.......................... 208.62
     Hospitals....................... 242.78
     Highways 291.14
     Police protection.................. 35.26
     Corrections 98.44
     Natural resources 61.81
     Parks & recreation 8.22
     Governmental administration....... 106.93
     Interest on general debt............. 54.10

State debt & cash, 2006 ($ per capita)
Debt $1,388.38
Cash/security holdings.............. $8,425.34

Federal government grants to state & local government, 2005 (x $1,000)
Total.............................$7,346,245
by Federal agency
   Defense 62,908
   Education 613,336
   Energy........................... 32,674
   Environmental Protection Agency 53,366
   Health & Human Services. 3,934,254
   Homeland Security................ 510,384
   Housing & Urban Development...... 403,224
   Justice 65,806
   Labor 108,019
   Transportation 891,539
   Veterans Affairs................... 10,156

Crime & Law Enforcement

Crime, 2006 (rates per 100,000 residents)
Property crimes 181,021
   Burglary 44,571
   Larceny 121,610
   Motor vehicle theft 14,840
   Property crime rate................. 3,936.1
Violent crimes........................ 19,557
   Murder 382
   Forcible rape....................... 1,649
   Robbery.......................... 7,059
   Aggravated assault 10,467
   Violent crime rate 425.2
Hate crimes............................ 1

Fraud and identity theft, 2006
Fraud complaints...................... 4,708
   rate per 100,000 residents 102.4
Identity theft complaints 2,774
   rate per 100,000 residents 60.3

Law enforcement agencies, 2006
Total agencies.......................... 358
Total employees 15,697
   Officers 10,347
   Civilians 5,350

Prisoners, probation, and parole, 2006
Total prisoners........................ 28,241
   percent change, 12/31/05 to 12/31/06 .... 1.3%
   in private facilities 0%
   in local jails 4.1%
Sentenced to more than one year 27,526
   rate per 100,000 residents 595
Adults on probation 55,766
Adults on parole....................... 8,658

Prisoner demographics, June 30, 2005 (rate per 100,000 residents)
Male.................................. 1,665
Female................................ 161
White................................. 542
Black................................. 1,916
Hispanic .... NA

©2008 Information Publications, Inc.
All rights reserved. Photocopying prohibited.
877-544-INFO (4636) or www.informationpublications.com

Arrests, 2006

Total............................. 189,558
  Persons under 18 years of age.........11,577

Persons under sentence of death, 1/1/07

Total..................................... 195
  White..................................... 100
  Black 93
  Hispanic 2

State's highest court

Name ....Supreme Court
Number of members........................ 9
Length of term........................ 6 years
Intermediate appeals court? ....yes

Labor & Income

Civilian labor force, 2006 (x 1,000)

Total.....................................2,210
  Men 1,179
  Women 1,031
  Persons 16-19 years..................... 84
  White................................. 1,640
  Black 516
  Hispanic 53

Civilian labor force as a percent of civilian non-institutional population, 2006

Total................................. 62.1%
  Men 69.8
  Women 55.2
  Persons 16-19 years....................37.2
  White.................................63.1
  Black 59.0
  Hispanic 74.5

Employment, 2006 (x 1,000)

Total.....................................2,119
  Men 1,133
  Women 986
  Persons 16-19 years..................... 72
  White.................................1,590
  Black 478
  Hispanic 53

Unemployment rate, 2006

Total................................. 4.1%
  Men 3.9
  Women 4.4
  Persons 16-19 years...................14.4
  White.................................3.0
  Black 7.5
  Hispanic 1.1

Full-time/part-time labor force, 2003 (x 1,000)

Full-time labor force, employed 1,723
Part-time labor force, employed........... 299
Unemployed, looking for
  Full-time work........................ 108
  Part-time work........................ 16
*Mean duration of unemployment (weeks)......*20.0
  Median 10.6

Labor unions, 2006

Membership (x 1,000).................... 170
  percent of employed 8.8%

Experienced civilian labor force by private industry, 2006

Total.............................1,574,558
  Natural resources & mining 21,888
  Construction 110,025
  Manufacturing..................... 302,792
  Trade, transportation & utilities 383,473
  Information 30,305
  Finance 96,572
  Professional & business 213,949
  Education & health 197,774
  Leisure & hospitality.................169,709
  Other.......................... 48,070

Experienced civilian labor force by occupation, May 2006

Management......................... 77,880
Business & financial 61,520
Legal...................................10,160
Sales................................ 205,000
Office & admin. support................. 303,160
Computers & math 33,590
Architecture & engineering............. 40,360
Arts & entertainment 17,840
Education 106,540
Social services 18,150
Health care practitioner & technical.... 108,640
Health care support 47,670
Maintenance & repair................. 92,800
Construction 102,010
Transportation & moving 160,950
Production 227,380
Farming, fishing & forestry..............7,130

Hours and earnings of production workers on manufacturing payrolls, 2006

Average weekly hours.....................40.9
Average hourly earnings $15.56
Average weekly earnings $636.40

Income and poverty, 2006

Median household income............ $38,783
Personal income, per capita (current $)... $31,295
  in constant (2000) dollars $27,319
Persons below poverty level.............. 16.6%

Average annual pay

2006................................. $36,204
  increase from 2005 .... 4.6%

Federal individual income tax returns, 2005

Returns filed........................ 1,955,914
Adjusted gross income ($1,000) $88,628,735
Total tax liability ($1,000) $10,434,751

Charitable contributions, 2004

Number of contributions.................516.2
Total amount ($ mil).................$2,492.7

©2008 Information Publications, Inc.
All rights reserved. Photocopying prohibited.
877-544-INFO (4636) or www.informationpublications.com

Economy, Business, Industry & Agriculture

Fortune 500 companies, 2007................ 1
Bankruptcy cases filed, FY 2007.........23,176

Patents and trademarks issued, 2007

Patents................................. 386
Trademarks............................. 382

Business firm ownership, 2002

Women-owned.........................81,821
   Sales ($ mil) $11,435
Black-owned.......................... 28,666
   Sales ($ mil) $1,651
Hispanic-owned......................... 2,524
   Sales ($ mil) $748
Asian-owned 4,270
   Sales ($ mil) $1,491
Amer. Indian/Alaska Native-owned 2,908
   Sales ($ mil) $470
Hawaiian/Pacific Islander-owned 96
   Sales ($ mil) $5

Gross domestic product, 2006 ($ mil)

Total gross domestic product $160,569
   Agriculture, forestry, fishing and
     hunting 2,466
   Mining..............................2,574
   Utilities............................ 4,349
   Construction 8,085
   Manufacturing, durable goods....... 18,284
   Manufacturing, non-durable goods 11,687
   Wholesale trade.....................9,180
   Retail trade....................... 12,673
   Transportation & warehousing 4,476
   Information 4,609
   Finance & insurance................. 8,342
   Real estate, rental & leasing 15,388
   Professional and technical services 9,234
   Educational services.................. 751
   Health care and social assistance.......11,248
   Accommodation/food services..........3,629
   Other services, except government 3,881
   Government 24,185

Establishments, payroll, employees & receipts, by major industry group, 2005

Total...............................101,976
   Annual payroll ($1,000).........$53,365,320
   Paid employees 1,667,526
Forestry, fishing & agriculture............. 980
   Annual payroll ($1,000)........... $188,609
   Paid employees 6,955
Mining............................... 268
   Annual payroll ($1,000)........... $405,665
   Paid employees 7,427
   Receipts, 2002 ($1,000) $2,615,060

Utilities 413
   Annual payroll ($1,000)..........$1,329,504
   Paid employees 20,254
   Receipts, 2002 ($1,000) ....NA
Construction...........................9,952
   Annual payroll ($1,000)......... $3,597,814
   Paid employees 105,850
   Receipts, 2002 ($1,000) $15,582,292
Manufacturing........................4,953
   Annual payroll ($1,000).........$10,526,271
   Paid employees 282,136
   Receipts, 2002 ($1,000) $66,686,220
Wholesale trade 5,533
   Annual payroll ($1,000)......... $3,259,343
   Paid employees 78,099
   Receipts, 2002 ($1,000) $43,641,369
Retail trade 19,451
   Annual payroll ($1,000)...... $4,846,484
   Paid employees 237,503
   Receipts, 2002 ($1,000) $43,784,342
Transportation & warehousing 3,144
   Annual payroll ($1,000)..........$1,974,948
   Paid employees 58,881
   Receipts, 2002 ($1,000) $4,794,369
Information...........................1,702
   Annual payroll ($1,000)..........$1,717,058
   Paid employees 37,341
   Receipts, 2002 ($1,000) ....NA
Finance & insurance 6,743
   Annual payroll ($1,000)...... $4,040,625
   Paid employees 77,144
   Receipts, 2002 ($1,000) ....NA
Professional, scientific & technical 9,180
   Annual payroll ($1,000)........$4,919,444
   Paid employees 95,543
   Receipts, 2002 ($1,000) $8,757,629
Education 785
   Annual payroll ($1,000)........ $607,875
   Paid employees 25,390
   Receipts, 2002 ($1,000) $185,253
Health care & social assistance 9,820
   Annual payroll ($1,000)..........$7,920,889
   Paid employees 228,797
   Receipts, 2002 ($1,000) $16,594,961
Arts and entertainment 1,130
   Annual payroll ($1,000)........ $251,848
   Paid employees 16,286
   Receipts, 2002 ($1,000) $706,653
Real estate 4,055
   Annual payroll ($1,000)........... $671,937
   Paid employees 23,860
   Receipts, 2002 ($1,000) $2,636,384
Accommodation & food service...........7,529
   Annual payroll ($1,000)..........$1,591,435
   Paid employees 145,447
   Receipts, 2002 ($1,000) $4,692,297

©2008 Information Publications, Inc.
All rights reserved. Photocopying prohibited.
877-544-INFO (4636) or www.informationpublications.com

Exports, 2006
Value of exported goods ($ mil) $13,878
  Manufactured $12,142
  Non-manufactured. $1,436

Foreign direct investment in US affiliates, 2004
Property, plants & equipment ($ mil) . . . $16,857
Employment (x 1,000). 70.6

Agriculture, 2006
Number of farms 43,000
Farm acreage (x 1,000) 8,600
  Acres per farm 200
Farm marketings and income ($ mil)
Total $3,739.1
  Crops $695.9
  Livestock $3,043.1
Net farm income $1,579.8

Principal commodities, in order by marketing receipts, 2005
Broilers, Cattle and calves, Greenhouse/nursery, Chicken eggs, Cotton

Federal economic activity in state
Expenditures, 2005 ($ mil)
  Total. $42,061
    Per capita $9,247.55
  Defense $9,781
  Non-defense $32,280
Defense department, 2006 ($ mil)
  Payroll $3,503
  Contract awards $6,954
  Grants $64
Homeland security grants ($1,000)
  2006 . . . .$15,578
  2007 . . . .$11,574

FDIC-insured financial institutions, 2005
Number 159
Assets ($ billion) $233.3
Deposits ($ billion) $171.3

Fishing, 2006
Catch (x 1,000 lbs) 34,052
Value ($1,000). $48,566

Mining, 2006 ($ mil)
Total non-fuel mineral production $1,200
Percent of U.S. 1.86%

Communication, Energy & Transportation

Communication
Households with computers, 2003 . . . . 53.9%
Households with internet access, 2003 . . . . 45.7%
High-speed internet providers 63
Total high-speed internet lines 898,850
  Residential 616,392
  Business. 282,458
Wireless phone customers, 12/2006 3,374,701

FCC-licensed stations (as of January 1, 2008)
TV stations 43
FM radio stations. 193
AM radio stations 153

Energy
Energy consumption, 2004
  Total (trillion Btu). 2,160
  Per capita (million Btu) 478.1
By source of production (trillion Btu)
  Coal 854
  Natural gas 404
  Petroleum. 639
  Nuclear electric power 330
  Hydroelectric power 107
By end-use sector (trillion Btu)
  Residential 394
  Commercial 270
  Industrial 1,001
  Transportation 495
Electric energy, 2005
  Primary source of electricity. . . . . Coal
  Net generation (billion kWh) 137.9
    percent from renewable sources. 10.1%
  Net summer capability (million kW) 30.7
  CO_2 emitted from generation 83.8
Natural gas utilities, 2005
  Customers (x 1,000) 867
  Sales (trillion Btu). 226
  Revenues ($ mil) $1,294
Nuclear plants, 2007 5
Total CO_2 emitted (million metric tons). 136.0
Energy spending, 2004 ($ mil) $15,180
  per capita $3,360
  Price per million Btu $11.29

Transportation, 2006
Public road & street mileage 96,521
  Urban. 21,846
  Rural 74,675
  Interstate. 908
Vehicle miles of travel (millions) 60,414
  per capita 13,161.4
Total motor vehicle registrations 4,630,314
  Automobiles. .1,795,596
  Trucks 2,825,636
  Motorcycles 104,074
Licensed drivers 3,665,180
  19 years & under 216,227
Deaths from motor vehicle accidents 1,208
Gasoline consumed (x 1,000 gallons) 2,627,049
  per capita 572.3

Commuting Statistics, 2006
Average commute time (min) 23.6
  Drove to work alone 83.6%
  Carpooled. 11.3%
  Public transit 0.5%
  Walk to work 1.1%
  Work from home 2.5%

©2008 Information Publications, Inc.
All rights reserved. Photocopying prohibited.
877-544-INFO (4636) or www.informationpublications.com

State Summary

Capital city . . . . Juneau
Governor . . . . Sarah Palin

PO Box 110001
Juneau, AK 99811
907-465-3500

Admitted as a state 1959
Area (square miles) 663,267
Population, 2007 (estimate). 683,478
Largest city . . . . Anchorage
    Population, 2006. 278,700
Personal income per capita, 2006
    (in current dollars) $37,271
Gross domestic product, 2006 ($ mil) $41,105

Leading industries by payroll, 2005

Health care/Social assistance, Construction,
    Transportation & Warehousing

**Leading agricultural commodities
by receipts, 2005**

Greenhouse/nursery, Hay, Cattle and calves,
    Potatoes, Dairy products

Geography & Environment

Total area (square miles). 663,267
    land 571,951
    water 91,316
Federally-owned land, 2004 (acres) . .252,495,811
    percent. 69.1%
Highest point . . . . Mt. McKinley
    elevation (feet) 20,320
Lowest point . . . . Pacific Ocean
    elevation (feet) . . . . sea level
General coastline (miles) 6,568
Tidal shoreline (miles) 33,904
Cropland, 2003 (x 1,000 acres) . . . . NA
Forest land, 2003 (x 1,000 acres). . . . . NA
Capital city . . . . Juneau
    Population 2000 .30,711
    Population 2006 .30,737
Largest city . . . . Anchorage
    Population 2000 260,283
    Population 2006 278,700

Number of cities with over 100,000 population
1990 1
2000 1
2006 1

State park and recreation areas, 2005
Area (x 1,000 acres) .3,353
Number of visitors (x 1,000) 4,678
Revenues ($1,000) $2,511
    percent of operating expenditures 38.9%

National forest system land, 2007
Acres 21,972,605

Demographics & Population Characteristics

Population
1980 401,851
1990 550,043
2000 626,931
2006 670,053
    Male 346,411
    Female 323,642
Living in group quarters, 2006 23,100
    percent of total. 3.4%
2007 (estimate) 683,478
    persons per square mile of land 1.2
2008 (projected) 680,082
2010 (projected) 694,109
2020 (projected) 774,421
2030 (projected) 867,674

**Population of Core-Based Statistical Areas
(formerly Metropolitan Areas), x 1,000**

	CBSA	Non-CBSA
1990	398	152
2000	461	166
2006	503	167

Change in population, 2000-2007
Number 56,547
    percent. 9.0%
Natural increase (births minus deaths) 53,166
Net internal migration . . . . -5,125
Net international migration 4,236

Persons by age, 2006
Under 5 years 49,771
5 to 17 years 131,663
18 years and over 488,619
65 years and over 45,630
85 years and over 4,148
    Median age 33.4

Persons by age, 2010 (projected)
Under 5 years 58,380
18 and over 510,126
65 and over 56,548
    Median age 32.5

Race, 2006
One Race
    White. 473,645
    Black or African American 25,108
    Asian 31,113
    American Indian/Alaska Native. 103,497
    Hawaiian Native/Pacific Islander. 4,138
Two or more races. 32,552

Persons of Hispanic origin, 2006
Total Hispanic or Latino 37,498
    Mexican. 21,987
    Puerto Rican 2,495
    Cuban 510

©2008 Information Publications, Inc.
All rights reserved. Photocopying prohibited.
877-544-INFO (4636) or www.informationpublications.com

Persons of Asian origin, 2006

Total Asian 30,151
   Asian Indian............................ 689
   Chinese 2,447
   Filipino 16,885
   Japanese 1,267
   Korean............................3,211
   Vietnamese.........................1,537

Marital status, 2006

Population 15 years & over 524,378
   Never married 171,898
   Married....................... 274,300
   Separated 8,277
   Widowed........................ 20,329
   Divorced 57,851

Language spoken at home, 2006

Population 5 years and older.......... 622,572
   English only 526,829
   Spanish 22,649
   French 2,470
   German......................... 4,716
   Chinese 875

Households & families, 2006

Households....................... 229,878
   with persons under 18 years 90,661
   with persons over 65 years............30,161
   persons per household 2.81
Families......................157,939
   persons per family....................3.36
Married couples......................117,329
Female householder,
   no husband present.................. 28,062
One-person households 57,133

Nativity, 2006

Number of residents born in state 260,324
   percent of population 38.9%

Immigration & naturalization, 2006

Legal permanent residents admitted.......1,554
Persons naturalized 831
Non-immigrant admissions 100,647

Vital Statistics and Health

Marriages

2004 5,594
2005 5,446
2006 5,309

Divorces

2004 2,829
2005 2,865
2006 2,968

Health risks, 2006

Percent of adults who are:
   Smokers.......................24.0%
   Overweight (BMI > 25)................64.2%
   Obese (BMI > 30)....................26.2%

Births

2005 10,459
   Birthrate (per 1,000)..................15.8
   White......................... 6,536
   Black 422
   Hispanic 779
   Asian/Pacific Islander 778
   Amer. Indian/Alaska Native 2,723
   Low birth weight (2,500g or less)....... 6.1%
   Cesarian births 21.9%
   Preterm births..................... 10.6%
   To unmarried mothers.............. 36.0%
   Twin births (per 1,000)...............26.9
   Triplets or higher order (per 100,000).....68.0
2006 (preliminary)....................10,991
   rate per 1,000 ....16.4

Deaths

2004
All causes 3,051
   rate per 100,000......................750.5
Heart disease 589
   rate per 100,000......................158.3
Malignant neoplasms 728
   rate per 100,000......................183.8
Cerebrovascular disease.............. 172
   rate per 100,000......................52.1
Chronic lower respiratory disease 139
   rate per 100,000......................39.4
Diabetes................................. 93
   rate per 100,000......................22.5
2005 (preliminary)....................3,170
   rate per 100,000......................750.8
2006 (provisional) 3,318

Infant deaths

2004 69
   rate per 1,000 ....6.7
2005 (provisional) 54
   rate per 1,000 ....5.2

Exercise routines, 2005

None..................... 21.4%
Moderate or greater..................... 59.2%
Vigorous 35.9%

Abortions, 2004

Total performed in state.................1,937
   rate per 1,000 women age 15-44.......... 14
   % obtained by out-of-state residents 0.2%

Physicians, 2005

Total.................................1,515
   rate per 100,000 persons 228

Community hospitals, 2005

Number of hospitals 22
Beds (x 1,000)............................1.4
Patients admitted (x 1,000) 51
Average daily census (x 1,000) 0.8
Average cost per day $2,246
Outpatient visits (x 1 mil) 1.7

©2008 Information Publications, Inc.
All rights reserved. Photocopying prohibited.
877-544-INFO (4636) or www.informationpublications.com

Disability status of population, 2006

5 to 15 years 5.9%
16 to 64 years 14.1%
65 years and over 47.9%

Education

Educational attainment, 2006

Population over 25 years 415,630
  Less than 9th grade. 3.8%
  High school graduate or more 89.7%
  College graduate or more. 26.9%
  Graduate or professional degree. 9.5%

Public school enrollment, 2005-06

Total. 133,288
  Pre-kindergarten through grade 8. 91,225
  Grades 9 through 12 42,063

Graduating public high school seniors, 2004-05

Diplomas (incl. GED and others) 7,236

SAT scores, 2007

Average critical reading score 519
Average writing score 491
Average math score 517
Percent of graduates taking test 48%

Public school teachers, 2006-07 (estimate)

Total (x 1,000) 8.0
  Elementary 5.3
  Secondary 2.7
Average salary $54,658
  Elementary $54,658
  Secondary $54,658

State receipts & expenditures for public schools, 2006-07 (estimate)

Revenue receipts ($ mil) $1,346
Expenditures
Total ($ mil) $1,486
  Per capita $2,060
  Per pupil $11,900

NAEP proficiency scores, 2007

	Reading		Math	
	Basic	Proficient	Basic	Proficient
Grade 4	61.7%	28.7%	78.8%	37.9%
Grade 8	70.8%	27.1%	73.0%	32.2%

Higher education enrollment, fall 2005

Total. 1,365
  Full-time men 252
  Full-time women 432
  Part-time men 222
  Part-time women 459

Minority enrollment in institutions of higher education, 2005

Black, non-Hispanic .1,016
Hispanic 1,071
Asian/Pacific Islander 1,476
American Indian/Alaska Native. 4,078

Institutions of higher education, 2005-06

Total 8
  Public. 5
  Private 3

Earned degrees conferred, 2004-05

Associate's. 879
Bachelor's 1,427
Master's 655
First-professional. 0
Doctor's 25

Public Libraries, 2006

Number of libraries. 89
Number of outlets 107
Annual visits per capita 5.2
Circulation per capita. 6.1

State & local financial support for higher education, FY 2006

Full-time equivalent enrollment (x 1,000) 18.8
Appropriations per FTE. $12,097

Social Insurance & Welfare Programs

Social Security benefits & beneficiaries, 2005

Beneficiaries (x 1,000) 65
  Retired & dependents. 42
  Survivors. 10
  Disabled & dependents. 13
Annual benefit payments ($ mil) $659
  Retired & dependents. $415
  Survivors. $120
  Disabled & dependents. $124
Average monthly benefit
  Retired & dependents. $962
  Disabled & dependents. $912
  Widowed. $913

Medicare, July 2005

Enrollment (x 1,000). 52
Payments ($ mil) $343

Medicaid, 2004

Beneficiaries (x 1,000). 808
Payments ($ mil) $3,857

State Children's Health Insurance Program, 2006

Enrollment (x 1,000). 22.2
Expenditures ($ mil). $27.8

Persons without health insurance, 2006

Number (x 1,000). 109
  percent. 16.5%
Number of children (x 1,000) 19
  percent of children 10.5%

Health care expenditures, 2004

Total expenditures. $4,237
  per capita $6,450

©2008 Information Publications, Inc.
All rights reserved. Photocopying prohibited.
877-544-INFO (4636) or www.informationpublications.com

Federal and state public aid

State unemployment insurance, 2006
Recipients, first payments (x 1,000) 41
Total payments ($ mil) $110
Average weekly benefit $198
Temporary Assistance for Needy Families, 2006
Recipients (x 1,000) 114.8
Families (x 1,000) 42.5
Supplemental Security Income, 2005
Recipients (x 1,000) 11.0
Payments ($ mil) $53.2
Food Stamp Program, 2006
Avg monthly participants (x 1,000) 57.2
Total benefits ($ mil) $86.0

Housing & Construction

Housing units

Total 2005 (estimate) 274,182
Total 2006 (estimate) 276,571
Seasonal or recreational use, 2006 23,131
Owner-occupied, 2006 148,249
   Median home value $213,200
   Homeowner vacancy rate 1.7%
Renter-occupied, 2006 81,629
   Median rent $883
   Rental vacancy rate 8.5%
Home ownership rate, 2005 .... 66.0%
Home ownership rate, 2006 .... 67.2%

New privately-owned housing units

Number authorized, 2006 (x 1,000) 2.7
   Value ($ mil) $511.5
Started 2005 (x 1,000, estimate) 2.3
Started 2006 (x 1,000, estimate) 2.3

Existing home sales

2005 (x 1,000) 24.6
2006 (x 1,000) 30.7

Government & Elections

State officials 2008

Governor .... Sarah Palin
     Republican, term expires 12/10
Lieutenant Governor .... Sean Parnell
Secretary of State .... (no secretary of state)
Attorney General .... Talis Colberg
Chief Justice .... Dana Fabe

Governorship

Minimum age 30
Length of term .... 4 years
Consecutive terms permitted 2
Who succeeds .... Lieutenant Governor

Local governments by type, 2002

Total 175
   County 12
   Municipal 149
   Township 0
   School District 0
   Special District 14

State legislature

Name .... Legislature
Upper chamber .... Senate
   Number of members 20
   Length of term .... 4 years
   Party in majority, 2008 .... Republican
Lower chamber .... House of Representatives
   Number of members 40
   Length of term .... 2 years
   Party in majority, 2008 .... Republican

Federal representation, 2008 (110th Congress)

Senator .... Ted Stevens
   Party .... Republican
   Year term expires 2009
Senator .... Lisa Murkowski
   Party .... Republican
   Year term expires 2011
Representatives, total 1
   Democrats 0
   Republicans 1

Voters in November 2006 election (estimate)

Total 247,901
   Male 118,516
   Female 129,384
   White 202,045
   Black 5,753
   Hispanic 1,905
   Asian 3,908

Presidential election, 2004

Total Popular Vote 312,598
   Kerry 111,025
   Bush 190,889
Total Electoral Votes 3

Votes cast for US Senators

2004
Total vote (x 1,000) 308
Leading party .... Republican
Percent for leading party 48.6%

2006
Total vote (x 1,000) .... NA
Leading party .... NA
Percent for leading party .... NA

Votes cast for US Representatives

2004
Total vote (x 1,000) 300
   Democratic 67
   Republican 213
Leading party .... Republican
Percent for leading party 71.1%

2006
Total vote (x 1,000) 235
   Democratic 94
   Republican 133
Leading party .... Republican
Percent for leading party 56.6%

©2008 Information Publications, Inc.
All rights reserved. Photocopying prohibited.
877-544-INFO (4636) or www.informationpublications.com

State government employment, 2006
Full-time equivalent employees 25,151
Payroll ($ mil) $107.5

Local government employment, 2006
Full-time equivalent employees 27,480
Payroll ($ mil) $111.9

Women holding public office, 2008
US Congress 1
Statewide elected office. 1
State legislature 13

Black public officials, 2002
Total. 2
 US and state legislatures 1
 City/county/regional offices 1
 Judicial/law enforcement. 0
 Education/school boards 0

Hispanic public officials, 2006
Total. 1
 State executives & legislators 0
 City/county/regional offices 1
 Judicial/law enforcement. 0
 Education/school boards 0

Governmental Finance

State government revenues, 2006
Total revenue (x $1,000). $10,844,814
 per capita $16,008.29
General revenue (x $1,000) $8,920,140
 Intergovernmental 2,155,908
 Taxes 2,484,422
  general sales. 0
  individual income tax 0
  corporate income tax 821,664
 Current charges. 519,470
 Miscellaneous .3,760,340

State government expenditure, 2006
Total expenditure (x $1,000) $8,599,090
 per capita $12,693.32
General expenditure (x $1,000) $7,528,220
 per capita, total. *$11,112.58*
  Education 2,672.91
  Public welfare 2,147.40
  Health 303.76
  Hospitals. 45.70
  Highways 1,673.24
  Police protection. 105.75
  Corrections 310.29
  Natural resources 404.43
  Parks & recreation 15.93
  Governmental administration 729.13
  Interest on general debt 445.84

State debt & cash, 2006 ($ per capita)
Debt $9,240.46
Cash/security holdings. $76,637.60

Federal government grants to state & local government, 2005 (x $1,000)
Total. $3,131,207
by Federal agency
 Defense 42,948
 Education 306,817
 Energy 8,488
 Environmental Protection Agency 101,021
 Health & Human Services. 1,321,234
 Homeland Security. 16,181
 Housing & Urban Development. 187,412
 Justice 56,303
 Labor 47,501
 Transportation 537,548
 Veterans Affairs. 2,406

Crime & Law Enforcement

Crime, 2006 (rates per 100,000 residents)
Property crimes 24,155
 Burglary 4,136
 Larceny 17,490
 Motor vehicle theft 2,529
 Property crime rate. 688.0
Violent crimes. 4,610
 Murder 36
 Forcible rape. 509
 Robbery. 605
 Aggravated assault 3,460
 Violent crime rate 688.0
Hate crimes. 11

Fraud and identity theft, 2006
Fraud complaints. 1,079
 rate per 100,000 residents 161.0
Identity theft complaints 384
 rate per 100,000 residents 57.3

Law enforcement agencies, 2006
Total agencies. 42
Total employees 1,937
 Officers 1,220
 Civilians 717

Prisoners, probation, and parole, 2006
Total prisoners. 5,069
 percent change, 12/31/05 to 12/31/06 . . . . 5.3%
 in private facilities 33.2%
 in local jails . . . . NA
Sentenced to more than one year 3,116
 rate per 100,000 residents 462
Adults on probation 6,095
Adults on parole. 1,044

Prisoner demographics, June 30, 2005 (rate per 100,000 residents)
Male. 1,232
Female 141
White 500
Black. 2,163
Hispanic 380

©2008 Information Publications, Inc.
All rights reserved. Photocopying prohibited.
877-544-INFO (4636) or www.informationpublications.com

Arrests, 2006
Total 36,994
   Persons under 18 years of age 4,136

Persons under sentence of death, 1/1/07
Total 0
   White 0
   Black 0
   Hispanic 0

State's highest court
Name . . . . Supreme Court
Number of members 5
Length of term . . . . 10 years
Intermediate appeals court? . . . . .yes

Labor & Income

Civilian labor force, 2006 (x 1,000)
Total 349
   Men 187
   Women 162
   Persons 16-19 years 20
   White 273
   Black 11
   Hispanic 13

Civilian labor force as a percent of civilian non-institutional population, 2006
Total 72.0%
   Men 77.1
   Women 66.8
   Persons 16-19 years 50.0
   White 73.7
   Black 75.8
   Hispanic 77.9

Employment, 2006 (x 1,000)
Total 325
   Men 172
   Women 153
   Persons 16-19 years 17
   White 258
   Black 10
   Hispanic 12

Unemployment rate, 2006
Total 6.9%
   Men 8.0
   Women 5.7
   Persons 16-19 years 14.7
   White 5.3
   Black 10.7
   Hispanic 10.3

Full-time/part-time labor force, 2003 (x 1,000)
Full-time labor force, employed 250
Part-time labor force, employed 55
Unemployed, looking for
   Full-time work 22
   Part-time work 5
Mean duration of unemployment (weeks) 15.6
   Median 7.6

Labor unions, 2006
Membership (x 1,000) 62
   percent of employed 22.2%

Experienced civilian labor force by private industry, 2006
Total 231,542
   Natural resources & mining 13,196
   Construction 17,994
   Manufacturing 13,208
   Trade, transportation & utilities 63,780
   Information 6,947
   Finance 13,700
   Professional & business 24,342
   Education & health 37,054
   Leisure & hospitality 31,371
   Other 9,487

Experienced civilian labor force by occupation, May 2006
Management 23,980
Business & financial 9,660
Legal 2,090
Sales 25,760
Office & admin. support 50,970
Computers & math 3,930
Architecture & engineering 6,330
Arts & entertainment 3,010
Education 21,720
Social services 5,630
Health care practitioner & technical 13,150
Health care support 6,220
Maintenance & repair 16,260
Construction 20,810
Transportation & moving 23,200
Production 11,520
Farming, fishing & forestry 700

Hours and earnings of production workers on manufacturing payrolls, 2006
Average weekly hours .40.5
Average hourly earnings $14.30
Average weekly earnings $579.15

Income and poverty, 2006
Median household income $59,393
Personal income, per capita (current $) . . . $37,271
   in constant (2000) dollars $32,535
Persons below poverty level 10.9%

Average annual pay
2006 . . . . $41,750
   increase from 2005 . . . . 3.8%

Federal individual income tax returns, 2005
Returns filed 346,927
Adjusted gross income ($1,000) $16,725,880
Total tax liability ($1,000) $2,215,386

Charitable contributions, 2004
Number of contributions 69.7
Total amount ($ mil) $260.4

©2008 Information Publications, Inc.
All rights reserved. Photocopying prohibited.
877-544-INFO (4636) or www.informationpublications.com

Economy, Business, Industry & Agriculture

Fortune 500 companies, 2007 0
Bankruptcy cases filed, FY 2007 696

Patents and trademarks issued, 2007
Patents 27
Trademarks 74

Business firm ownership, 2002
Women-owned 16,308
  Sales ($ mil) $2,348
Black-owned 926
  Sales ($ mil) $81
Hispanic-owned 1,241
  Sales ($ mil) $171
Asian-owned 1,908
  Sales ($ mil) $421
Amer. Indian/Alaska Native-owned 5,019
  Sales ($ mil) $648
Hawaiian/Pacific Islander-owned 152
  Sales ($ mil) $10

Gross domestic product, 2006 ($ mil)
Total gross domestic product $41,105
  Agriculture, forestry, fishing and hunting 306
  Mining 12,133
  Utilities 416
  Construction 1,882
  Manufacturing, durable goods 153
  Manufacturing, non-durable goods 779
  Wholesale trade 805
  Retail trade 1,881
  Transportation & warehousing 3,561
  Information 910
  Finance & insurance 1,205
  Real estate, rental & leasing 3,301
  Professional and technical services 1,399
  Educational services 129
  Health care and social assistance 2,262
  Accommodation/food services 997
  Other services, except government 615
  Government 7,272

Establishments, payroll, employees & receipts, by major industry group, 2005

Total 19,808
  Annual payroll ($1,000) $9,774,285
  Paid employees 231,088
Forestry, fishing & agriculture 332
  Annual payroll ($1,000) .... NA
  Paid employees .... NA
Mining 123
  Annual payroll ($1,000) $620,607
  Paid employees 6,780
  Receipts, 2002 ($1,000) $8,254,126

Utilities 85
  Annual payroll ($1,000) $120,284
  Paid employees 1,721
  Receipts, 2002 ($1,000) .... NA
Construction 2,773
  Annual payroll ($1,000) $1,272,040
  Paid employees 19,353
  Receipts, 2002 ($1,000) $4,417,369
Manufacturing 514
  Annual payroll ($1,000) $402,806
  Paid employees 9,860
  Receipts, 2002 ($1,000) $3,832,024
Wholesale trade 736
  Annual payroll ($1,000) $386,296
  Paid employees 8,239
  Receipts, 2002 ($1,000) $3,616,674
Retail trade 2,675
  Annual payroll ($1,000) $911,704
  Paid employees 34,897
  Receipts, 2002 ($1,000) $7,437,071
Transportation & warehousing 1,149
  Annual payroll ($1,000) $961,489
  Paid employees 18,549
  Receipts, 2002 ($1,000) $3,205,233
Information 380
  Annual payroll ($1,000) $366,003
  Paid employees 7,824
  Receipts, 2002 ($1,000) .... NA
Finance & insurance 744
  Annual payroll ($1,000) $393,778
  Paid employees 7,836
  Receipts, 2002 ($1,000) .... NA
Professional, scientific & technical 1,832
  Annual payroll ($1,000) $676,383
  Paid employees 12,014
  Receipts, 2002 ($1,000) $1,362,539
Education 224
  Annual payroll ($1,000) $58,716
  Paid employees 2,709
  Receipts, 2002 ($1,000) $56,481
Health care & social assistance 1,959
  Annual payroll ($1,000) $1,627,019
  Paid employees 37,476
  Receipts, 2002 ($1,000) $3,393,974
Arts and entertainment 522
  Annual payroll ($1,000) $68,344
  Paid employees 4,215
  Receipts, 2002 ($1,000) $282,921
Real estate 876
  Annual payroll ($1,000) $145,988
  Paid employees 4,443
  Receipts, 2002 ($1,000) $675,209
Accommodation & food service 1,966
  Annual payroll ($1,000) $483,353
  Paid employees 23,939
  Receipts, 2002 ($1,000) $1,393,225

©2008 Information Publications, Inc.
All rights reserved. Photocopying prohibited.
877-544-INFO (4636) or www.informationpublications.com

Exports, 2006
Value of exported goods ($ mil) $4,044
   Manufactured $577
   Non-manufactured $3,400

Foreign direct investment in US affiliates, 2004
Property, plants & equipment ($ mil) $31,121
Employment (x 1,000)..................... 11.3

Agriculture, 2006
Number of farms 640
Farm acreage (x 1,000) 900
   Acres per farm 1,406
Farm marketings and income ($ mil)
Total $64.2
   Crops $24.9
   Livestock $39.4
Net farm income $20.0

Principal commodities, in order by marketing receipts, 2005
   Greenhouse/nursery, Hay, Cattle and calves,
      Potatoes, Dairy products

Federal economic activity in state
Expenditures, 2005 ($ mil)
   Total.............................. $9,230
     Per capita $13,915.75
   Defense $3,217
   Non-defense $6,012
Defense department, 2006 ($ mil)
   Payroll............................. $1,640
   Contract awards $1,656
   Grants $43
Homeland security grants ($1,000)
   2006............................... $8,294
   2007............................... $7,195

FDIC-insured financial institutions, 2005
Number 7
Assets ($ billion) $4.3
Deposits ($ billion) $3.1

Fishing, 2006
Catch (x 1,000 lbs)................... 5,421,263
Value ($1,000)..................... $1,342,294

Mining, 2006 ($ mil)
Total non-fuel mineral production $2,850
Percent of U.S. 4.43%

Communication, Energy & Transportation

Communication
Households with computers, 2003 .... 72.7%
Households with internet access, 2003 .... 67.6%
High-speed internet providers 18
Total high-speed internet lines......... 145,008
   Residential 123,538
   Business........................... 21,470
Wireless phone customers, 12/2006 412,112

FCC-licensed stations (as of January 1, 2008)
TV stations 17
FM radio stations......................... 80
AM radio stations 39

Energy
Energy consumption, 2004
   Total (trillion Btu)..................... 779
   Per capita (million Btu) 1,186.1
By source of production (trillion Btu)
   Coal 14
   Natural gas 412
   Petroleum 335
   Nuclear electric power 0
   Hydroelectric power 15
By end-use sector (trillion Btu)
   Residential 56
   Commercial 63
   Industrial 393
   Transportation 266
Electric energy, 2005
   Primary source of electricity............ Gas
   Net generation (billion kWh) 6.6
     percent from renewable sources...... 22.3%
   Net summer capability (million kW) 1.9
   CO_2 emitted from generation 4.3
Natural gas utilities, 2005
   Customers (x 1,000) 123
   Sales (trillion Btu)..................... 90
   Revenues ($ mil) $348
Nuclear plants, 2007 0
Total CO_2 emitted (million metric tons).... 44.8
Energy spending, 2004 ($ mil) $4,164
   per capita $6,339
   Price per million Btu $11.09

Transportation, 2006
Public road & street mileage 14,787
   Urban............................. 2,370
   Rural 12,417
   Interstate........................... 1,081
Vehicle miles of travel (millions) 4,967
   per capita 7,331.9
Total motor vehicle registrations........ 675,094
   Automobiles....................... 242,487
   Trucks 429,901
   Motorcycles 24,114
Licensed drivers 489,024
   19 years & under 23,645
Deaths from motor vehicle accidents 74
Gasoline consumed (x 1,000 gallons) 293,351
   per capita 433.0

Commuting Statistics, 2006
Average commute time (min) 17.7
   Drove to work alone 67.7%
   Carpooled.......................... 12.7%
   Public transit 1.1%
   Walk to work 9.1%
   Work from home 5.1%

©2008 Information Publications, Inc.
All rights reserved. Photocopying prohibited.
877-544-INFO (4636) or www.informationpublications.com

Arizona   1

State Summary

Capital city . . . . Phoenix
Governor . . . . Janet Napolitano
State Capitol
1700 W Washington
Phoenix, AZ 85007
602-542-4331
Admitted as a state 1912
Area (square miles) 113,998
Population, 2007 (estimate) 6,338,755
Largest city . . . . Phoenix
Population, 2006 1,512,986
Personal income per capita, 2006
(in current dollars) $31,458
Gross domestic product, 2006 ($ mil) . . . $232,463

Leading industries by payroll, 2005

Health care/Social assistance, Construction,
Manufacturing

**Leading agricultural commodities
by receipts, 2005**

Cattle and calves, Dairy products, Lettuce, Cotton, Hay

Geography & Environment

Total area (square miles) 113,998
land 113,635
water 364
Federally-owned land, 2004 (acres) . . .34,933,236
percent 48.1%
Highest point . . . . Humphreys Peak
elevation (feet) 12,633
Lowest point . . . . .Colorado River
elevation (feet) 70
General coastline (miles) 0
Tidal shoreline (miles) 0
Cropland, 2003 (x 1,000 acres) 934
Forest land, 2003 (x 1,000 acres) 4,141
Capital city . . . . Phoenix
Population 2000 1,321,045
Population 2006 1,512,986
Largest city . . . . Phoenix
Population 2000 1,321,045
Population 2006 1,512,986

Number of cities with over 100,000 population
1990 6
2000 9
2006 9

State park and recreation areas, 2005
Area (x 1,000 acres) 64
Number of visitors (x 1,000) 2,224
Revenues ($1,000) $9,188
percent of operating expenditures 43.3%

National forest system land, 2007
Acres 11,264,377

Demographics & Population Characteristics

Population
1980 2,718,215
1990 3,665,228
2000 5,130,632
2006 6,166,318
Male 3,085,755
Female 3,080,563
Living in group quarters, 2006 109,501
percent of total 1.8%
2007 (estimate) 6,338,755
persons per square mile of land 55.8
2008 (projected) 6,320,874
2010 (projected) 6,637,381
2020 (projected) 8,456,448
2030 (projected) 10,712,397

**Population of Core-Based Statistical Areas
(formerly Metropolitan Areas), x 1,000**

	CBSA	Non-CBSA
1990	3,512	153
2000	4,944	187
2006	5,964	203

Change in population, 2000-2007
Number 1,208,140
percent 23.5%
Natural increase (births minus deaths) 353,002
Net internal migration 655,354
Net international migration 214,014

Persons by age, 2006
Under 5 years 480,491
5 to 17 years 1,147,707
18 years and over 4,538,120
65 years and over 790,286
85 years and over 105,104
Median age 34.6

Persons by age, 2010 (projected)
Under 5 years 515,408
18 and over 4,948,917
65 and over 922,010
Median age 36.4

Race, 2006
One Race
White 5,380,815
Black or African American 231,677
Asian 146,725
American Indian/Alaska Native 294,118
Hawaiian Native/Pacific Islander 12,132
Two or more races 100,851

Persons of Hispanic origin, 2006
Total Hispanic or Latino 1,803,377
Mexican 1,601,082
Puerto Rican 31,273
Cuban 9,119

©2008 Information Publications, Inc.
All rights reserved. Photocopying prohibited.
877-544-INFO (4636) or www.informationpublications.com

Persons of Asian origin, 2006

Total Asian 144,858
  Asian Indian. 28,015
  Chinese 32,461
  Filipino 23,653
  Japanese 10,707
  Korean. 10,792
  Vietnamese. 26,308

Marital status, 2006

Population 15 years & over 4,806,252
  Never married 1,441,518
  Married. 2,518,326
  Separated 96,570
  Widowed. 277,749
  Divorced 568,659

Language spoken at home, 2006

Population 5 years and older. 5,687,173
  English only 4,094,302
  Spanish 1,244,012
  French 14,946
  German. 23,855
  Chinese 21,515

Households & families, 2006

Households. 2,224,992
  with persons under 18 years 760,124
  with persons over 65 years. 543,788
  persons per household 2.72
Families 1,476,269
  persons per family. 3.33
Married couples. 1,104,808
Female householder,
  no husband present. 256,384
One-person households 596,850

Nativity, 2006

Number of residents born in state 2,200,209
  percent of population. 35.7%

Immigration & naturalization, 2006

Legal permanent residents admitted 21,530
Persons naturalized .9,707
Non-immigrant admissions 769,491

Vital Statistics and Health

Marriages

2004 37,882
2005 38,308
2006 38,983

Divorces

2004 24,403
2005 24,535
2006 24,274

Health risks, 2006

Percent of adults who are:
  Smokers. 18.2%
  Overweight (BMI > 25). 59.6%
  Obese (BMI > 30). 22.9%

Births

2005 96,199
  Birthrate (per 1,000). 16.2
  White. 83,147
  Black 3,645
  Hispanic 42,852
  Asian/Pacific Islander 2,953
  Amer. Indian/Alaska Native 6,454
  Low birth weight (2,500g or less). 6.9%
  Cesarian births 24.7%
  Preterm births 13.2%
  To unmarried mothers. 43.1%
  Twin births (per 1,000) 26.5
  Triplets or higher order (per 100,000). . . .164.9
2006 (preliminary). 102,475
  rate per 1,000 . . . . .16.6

Deaths

2004
All causes 43,198
  rate per 100,000 .758.1
Heart disease 10,539
  rate per 100,000. . . . . .185.7
Malignant neoplasms 9,618
  rate per 100,000. . . . . .167.2
Cerebrovascular disease. 2,446
  rate per 100,000. .43.3
Chronic lower respiratory disease 2,416
  rate per 100,000. .42.4
Diabetes. 1,196
  rate per 100,000. .20.9
2005 (preliminary). 45,837
  rate per 100,000 .771.8
2006 (provisional) 46,073

Infant deaths

2004 630
  rate per 1,000 . . . . .6.7
2005 (provisional) 667
  rate per 1,000 . . . . .6.9

Exercise routines, 2005

None. 22.6%
Moderate or greater. 53.4%
Vigorous 28.9%

Abortions, 2004

Total performed in state. 12,690
  rate per 1,000 women age 15-44 11
  % obtained by out-of-state residents 3.0%

Physicians, 2005

Total. 12,503
  rate per 100,000 persons 210

Community hospitals, 2005

Number of hospitals 67
Beds (x 1,000). 11.8
Patients admitted (x 1,000) 665
Average daily census (x 1,000) 8.0
Average cost per day $1,769
Outpatient visits (x 1 mil) 6.8

©2008 Information Publications, Inc.
All rights reserved. Photocopying prohibited.
877-544-INFO (4636) or www.informationpublications.com

Disability status of population, 2006
5 to 15 years 5.9%
16 to 64 years 11.3%
65 years and over 38.9%

Education

Educational attainment, 2006
Population over 25 years 3,953,375
  Less than 9th grade..................... 7.1%
  High school graduate or more 83.8%
  College graduate or more............. 25.5%
  Graduate or professional degree........ 9.2%

Public school enrollment, 2005-06
Total.............................1,094,454
  Pre-kindergarten through grade 8.... 739,359
  Grades 9 through 12 354,901

Graduating public high school seniors, 2004-05
Diplomas (incl. GED and others) 59,498

SAT scores, 2007
Average critical reading score 519
Average writing score 502
Average math score 525
Percent of graduates taking test 32%

Public school teachers, 2006-07 (estimate)
Total (x 1,000) 47.1
  Elementary............................ 29.3
  Secondary............................. 17.8
Average salary $45,941
  Elementary....................... $45,941
  Secondary........................ $45,941

State receipts & expenditures for public schools, 2006-07 (estimate)
Revenue receipts ($ mil) $8,431
Expenditures
Total ($ mil) $7,173
  Per capita $955
  Per pupil $5,896

NAEP proficiency scores, 2007

	Reading		Math	
	Basic	Proficient	Basic	Proficient
Grade 4	55.9%	24.2%	73.7%	30.6%
Grade 8	64.9%	24.3%	66.5%	26.3%

Higher education enrollment, fall 2005
Total............................... 224,732
  Full-time men 81,214
  Full-time women................... 130,752
  Part-time men 4,392
  Part-time women.................... 8,374

Minority enrollment in institutions of higher education, 2005
Black, non-Hispanic 48,521
Hispanic 85,654
Asian/Pacific Islander 19,763
American Indian/Alaska Native......... 17,880

Institutions of higher education, 2005-06
Total..................................... 76
  Public................................. 25
  Private................................ 51

Earned degrees conferred, 2004-05
Associate's............................ 15,918
Bachelor's 29,133
Master's 19,882
First-professional....................... 788
Doctor's................................ 906

Public Libraries, 2006
Number of libraries...................... 86
Number of outlets 200
Annual visits per capita 4.0
Circulation per capita.................... 7.3

State & local financial support for higher education, FY 2006
Full-time equivalent enrollment (x 1,000).... 219.5
Appropriations per FTE................ $6,316

Social Insurance & Welfare Programs

Social Security benefits & beneficiaries, 2005
Beneficiaries (x 1,000) 919
  Retired & dependents................. 654
  Survivors............................ 110
  Disabled & dependents................. 155
Annual benefit payments ($ mil) $10,030
  Retired & dependents............... $6,887
  Survivors......................... $1,505
  Disabled & dependents.............. $1,638
Average monthly benefit
  Retired & dependents................ $1,023
  Disabled & dependents............... $970
  Widowed........................... $1,002

Medicare, July 2005
Enrollment (x 1,000).................... 794
Payments ($ mil) $3,906

Medicaid, 2004
Beneficiaries (x 1,000).................... 708
Payments ($ mil) $2,358

State Children's Health Insurance Program, 2006
Enrollment (x 1,000)..................... 96.7
Expenditures ($ mil)..................... $95.8

Persons without health insurance, 2006
Number (x 1,000)...................... 1,311
  percent............................ 20.9%
Number of children (x 1,000) 283
  percent of children 17.0%

Health care expenditures, 2004
Total expenditures.................... $23,576
  per capita $4,103

©2008 Information Publications, Inc.
All rights reserved. Photocopying prohibited.
877-544-INFO (4636) or www.informationpublications.com

Federal and state public aid

State unemployment insurance, 2006
Recipients, first payments (x 1,000) 68
Total payments ($ mil) $209
Average weekly benefit $198
Temporary Assistance for Needy Families, 2006
Recipients (x 1,000) 1,009.2
Families (x 1,000) 460.5
Supplemental Security Income, 2005
Recipients (x 1,000) 97.7
Payments ($ mil) $481.7
Food Stamp Program, 2006
Avg monthly participants (x 1,000) 540.8
Total benefits ($ mil) $626.3

Housing & Construction

Housing units
Total 2005 (estimate) 2,516,563
Total 2006 (estimate) 2,605,283
Seasonal or recreational use, 2006 160,512
Owner-occupied, 2006 1,523,041
  Median home value $236,500
  Homeowner vacancy rate 3.0%
Renter-occupied, 2006 701,951
  Median rent $762
  Rental vacancy rate 9.3%
Home ownership rate, 2005 . . . . 71.1%
Home ownership rate, 2006 . . . . 71.6%

New privately-owned housing units
Number authorized, 2006 (x 1,000) 65.4
  Value ($ mil) $11,203.1
Started 2005 (x 1,000, estimate) 61.9
Started 2006 (x 1,000, estimate) 60.1

Existing home sales
2005 (x 1,000) 199.2
2006 (x 1,000) 142.9

Government & Elections

State officials 2008
Governor . . . . Janet Napolitano
      Democratic, term expires 1/11
Lieutenant Governor . . (no Lieutenant Governor)
Secretary of State . . . . Jan Brewer
Attorney General . . . . Terry Goddard
Chief Justice . . . . Ruth McGregor

Governorship
Minimum age 25
Length of term . . . . 4 years
Consecutive terms permitted 2
Who succeeds . . . . Secretary of State

Local governments by type, 2002
Total 638
  County 15
  Municipal 87
  Township 0
  School District 231
  Special District 305

State legislature
Name . . . . Legislature
Upper chamber . . . . Senate
  Number of members 30
  Length of term . . . . 2 years
  Party in majority, 2008 . . . . Republican
Lower chamber . . . . House of Representatives
  Number of members 60
  Length of term . . . . 2 years
  Party in majority, 2008 . . . . Republican

Federal representation, 2008 (110th Congress)
Senator . . . . John McCain
  Party . . . . Republican
  Year term expires 2011
Senator . . . . Jon Kyl
  Party . . . . Republican
  Year term expires 2013
Representatives, total 8
  Democrats 4
  Republicans 4

Voters in November 2006 election (estimate)
Total 1,777,409
  Male 797,135
  Female 980,274
  White 1,669,501
  Black 35,422
  Hispanic 166,397
  Asian 11,775

Presidential election, 2004
Total Popular Vote 2,012,585
  Kerry 893,524
  Bush 1,104,294
Total Electoral Votes 10

Votes cast for US Senators
2004
Total vote (x 1,000) 1,962
Leading party . . . . Republican
Percent for leading party 76.7%
2006
Total vote (x 1,000) 1,527
Leading party . . . . Republican
Percent for leading party 53.3%

Votes cast for US Representatives
2004
Total vote (x 1,000) 1,871
  Democratic 598
  Republican 1,128
Leading party . . . . Republican
Percent for leading party 60.3%
2006
Total vote (x 1,000) 1,493
  Democratic 627
  Republican 771
Leading party . . . . Republican
Percent for leading party 51.7%

©2008 Information Publications, Inc.
All rights reserved. Photocopying prohibited.
877-544-INFO (4636) or www.informationpublications.com

State government employment, 2006
Full-time equivalent employees 66,858
Payroll ($ mil) $240.7

Local government employment, 2006
Full-time equivalent employees 218,226
Payroll ($ mil) $807.7

Women holding public office, 2008
US Congress 1
Statewide elected office 3
State legislature 30

Black public officials, 2002
Total 13
  US and state legislatures 1
  City/county/regional offices 1
  Judicial/law enforcement 6
  Education/school boards 5

Hispanic public officials, 2006
Total 357
  State executives & legislators 17
  City/county/regional offices 141
  Judicial/law enforcement 47
  Education/school boards 152

Governmental Finance

State government revenues, 2006
Total revenue (x $1,000) $27,834,655
  per capita $4,514.44
General revenue (x $1,000) $22,978,622
  Intergovernmental 8,093,916
  Taxes 11,713,167
    general sales 5,189,786
    individual income tax 3,253,279
    corporate income tax 890,004
  Current charges 1,419,649
  Miscellaneous 1,751,890

State government expenditure, 2006
Total expenditure (x $1,000) $25,731,467
  per capita $4,173.33
General expenditure (x $1,000) $23,284,278
  per capita, total *$3,776.43*
  Education 1,311.99
  Public welfare 1,091.53
  Health 219.04
  Hospitals 10.03
  Highways 325.03
  Police protection 36.12
  Corrections 142.72
  Natural resources 45.56
  Parks & recreation 36.18
  Governmental administration 99.68
  Interest on general debt 65.68

State debt & cash, 2006 ($ per capita)
Debt $1,364.01
Cash/security holdings $7,119.00

Federal government grants to state & local government, 2005 (x $1,000)
Total $8,603,017
by Federal agency
  Defense 68,647
  Education 855,247
  Energy 14,239
  Environmental Protection Agency 61,308
  Health & Human Services 5,457,773
  Homeland Security 33,270
  Housing & Urban Development 417,228
  Justice 107,311
  Labor 112,346
  Transportation 712,630
  Veterans Affairs 5,531

Crime & Law Enforcement

Crime, 2006 (rates per 100,000 residents)
Property crimes 285,370
  Burglary 57,055
  Larceny 173,466
  Motor vehicle theft 54,849
  Property crime rate 4,627.9
Violent crimes 30,916
  Murder 465
  Forcible rape 1,941
  Robbery 9,226
  Aggravated assault 19,284
  Violent crime rate 501.4
Hate crimes 215

Fraud and identity theft, 2006
Fraud complaints 9,222
  rate per 100,000 residents 149.6
Identity theft complaints 9,113
  rate per 100,000 residents 147.8

Law enforcement agencies, 2006
Total agencies 98
Total employees 21,434
  Officers 11,932
  Civilians 9,502

Prisoners, probation, and parole, 2006
Total prisoners 35,892
  percent change, 12/31/05 to 12/31/06 .... 6.9%
  in private facilities 14.5%
  in local jails 0.1%
Sentenced to more than one year 31,830
  rate per 100,000 residents 509
Adults on probation 73,265
Adults on parole 6,463

Prisoner demographics, June 30, 2005 (rate per 100,000 residents)
Male 1,443
Female 171
White 590
Black 3,294
Hispanic 1,075

©2008 Information Publications, Inc.
All rights reserved. Photocopying prohibited.
877-544-INFO (4636) or www.informationpublications.com

Arrests, 2006

Total................................ 307,695
  Persons under 18 years of age.........50,744

Persons under sentence of death, 1/1/07

Total.................................... 124
  White................................... 88
  Black.................................... 13
  Hispanic................................ 20

State's highest court

Name.......................Supreme Court
Number of members....................... 5
Length of term........................ 6 years
Intermediate appeals court?...............yes

Labor & Income

Civilian labor force, 2006 (x 1,000)

Total................................. 2,969
  Men..................................1,659
  Women................................1,310
  Persons 16-19 years.................... 170
  White.................................2,670
  Black................................... 113
  Hispanic............................... 848

Civilian labor force as a percent of civilian non-institutional population, 2006

Total................................64.7%
  Men..................................73.4
  Women...............................56.3
  Persons 16-19 years.................47.5
  White................................64.9
  Black................................70.6
  Hispanic.............................65.6

Employment, 2006 (x 1,000)

Total................................. 2,844
  Men..................................1,597
  Women................................1,247
  Persons 16-19 years.................... 148
  White................................ 2,563
  Black................................... 106
  Hispanic............................... 806

Unemployment rate, 2006

Total................................. 4.2%
  Men...................................3.7
  Women................................4.8
  Persons 16-19 years.................13.2
  White.................................4.0
  Black.................................6.1
  Hispanic..............................4.9

Full-time/part-time labor force, 2003 (x 1,000)

Full-time labor force, employed.......... 2,090
Part-time labor force, employed............ 450
Unemployed, looking for
  Full-time work........................ 117
  Part-time work......................... 34
Mean duration of unemployment (weeks)......17.8
  Median.................................8.4

Labor unions, 2006

Membership (x 1,000).................... 197
  percent of employed................... 7.6%

Experienced civilian labor force by private industry, 2006

Total.............................2,225,734
  Natural resources & mining...........37,927
  Construction...................... 239,650
  Manufacturing.....................187,057
  Trade, transportation & utilities..... 510,489
  Information........................ 44,885
  Finance...........................181,637
  Professional & business............ 394,485
  Education & health................. 284,407
  Leisure & hospitality.............. 266,285
  Other............................. 70,024

Experienced civilian labor force by occupation, May 2006

Management..........................122,110
Business & financial...................111,310
Legal............................... 16,000
Sales.............................. 273,050
Office & admin. support.............. 500,150
Computers & math.................... 51,500
Architecture & engineering............57,910
Arts & entertainment................. 26,940
Education.......................... 133,870
Social services..................... 25,960
Health care practitioner & technical.....107,110
Health care support..................58,410
Maintenance & repair................. 98,840
Construction....................... 203,180
Transportation & moving.............. 162,450
Production......................... 128,430
Farming, fishing & forestry............13,760

Hours and earnings of production workers on manufacturing payrolls, 2006

Average weekly hours....................40.6
Average hourly earnings..............$14.88
Average weekly earnings.............. $604.13

Income and poverty, 2006

Median household income............. $47,265
Personal income, per capita (current $)... $31,458
  in constant (2000) dollars...........$27,461
Persons below poverty level............. 14.2%

Average annual pay

2006................................ $40,019
  increase from 2005.................... 4.9%

Federal individual income tax returns, 2005

Returns filed......................2,474,093
Adjusted gross income ($1,000)....$135,510,440
Total tax liability ($1,000)........$17,288,262

Charitable contributions, 2004

Number of contributions................789.3
Total amount ($ mil).................$2,726.7

©2008 Information Publications, Inc.
All rights reserved. Photocopying prohibited.
877-544-INFO (4636) or www.informationpublications.com

Economy, Business, Industry & Agriculture

Fortune 500 companies, 2007 4
Bankruptcy cases filed, FY 2007 9,749

Patents and trademarks issued, 2007
Patents 1,814
Trademarks 1,597

Business firm ownership, 2002
Women-owned 109,748
  Sales ($ mil) $15,761
Black-owned 6,330
  Sales ($ mil) $530
Hispanic-owned 35,104
  Sales ($ mil) $4,295
Asian-owned 10,215
  Sales ($ mil) $2,396
Amer. Indian/Alaska Native-owned 6,614
  Sales ($ mil) $960
Hawaiian/Pacific Islander-owned 348
  Sales ($ mil) $38

Gross domestic product, 2006 ($ mil)
Total gross domestic product $232,463
  Agriculture, forestry, fishing and
    hunting 2,121
  Mining 3,343
  Utilities 4,214
  Construction 18,096
  Manufacturing, durable goods 15,834
  Manufacturing, non-durable goods 2,993
  Wholesale trade 13,575
  Retail trade 19,908
  Transportation & warehousing 6,021
  Information 6,519
  Finance & insurance 19,603
  Real estate, rental & leasing 33,555
  Professional and technical services 13,471
  Educational services 1,681
  Health care and social assistance 16,321
  Accommodation/food services 7,666
  Other services, except government 4,423
  Government 28,108

Establishments, payroll, employees & receipts, by major industry group, 2005

Total 131,651
  Annual payroll ($1,000) $76,340,525
  Paid employees 2,159,823
Forestry, fishing & agriculture 204
  Annual payroll ($1,000) $38,512
  Paid employees .1,531
Mining 229
  Annual payroll ($1,000) $443,346
  Paid employees 8,882
  Receipts, 2002 ($1,000) $2,180,922

Utilities 244
  Annual payroll ($1,000) $752,361
  Paid employees 10,415
  Receipts, 2002 ($1,000) . . . . .NA
Construction 15,082
  Annual payroll ($1,000) $7,954,878
  Paid employees 211,584
  Receipts, 2002 ($1,000) $28,926,214
Manufacturing 4,858
  Annual payroll ($1,000) $7,827,619
  Paid employees 167,886
  Receipts, 2002 ($1,000) $41,910,739
Wholesale trade 6,646
  Annual payroll ($1,000) $4,437,410
  Paid employees 95,027
  Receipts, 2002 ($1,000) $60,976,999
Retail trade 18,228
  Annual payroll ($1,000) $7,311,713
  Paid employees 306,113
  Receipts, 2002 ($1,000) $56,457,863
Transportation & warehousing 3,092
  Annual payroll ($1,000) $2,748,306
  Paid employees 72,724
  Receipts, 2002 ($1,000) $6,602,709
Information 2,224
  Annual payroll ($1,000) $2,478,510
  Paid employees 51,772
  Receipts, 2002 ($1,000) . . . . .NA
Finance & insurance 9,187
  Annual payroll ($1,000) $7,004,350
  Paid employees 131,283
  Receipts, 2002 ($1,000) . . . . .NA
Professional, scientific & technical 15,426
  Annual payroll ($1,000) $6,193,259
  Paid employees 118,943
  Receipts, 2002 ($1,000) $11,751,755
Education 1,625
  Annual payroll ($1,000) $1,152,769
  Paid employees 38,802
  Receipts, 2002 ($1,000) $616,930
Health care & social assistance 13,843
  Annual payroll ($1,000) $9,831,310
  Paid employees 252,401
  Receipts, 2002 ($1,000) $18,821,645
Arts and entertainment 1,782
  Annual payroll ($1,000) $1,222,715
  Paid employees 43,895
  Receipts, 2002 ($1,000) $3,416,701
Real estate 8,866
  Annual payroll ($1,000) $1,945,948
  Paid employees 48,118
  Receipts, 2002 ($1,000) . . . . .NA
Accommodation & food service 10,688
  Annual payroll ($1,000) $3,238,141
  Paid employees 238,838
  Receipts, 2002 ($1,000) $8,612,730

©2008 Information Publications, Inc.
All rights reserved. Photocopying prohibited.
877-544-INFO (4636) or www.informationpublications.com

8   Arizona

Exports, 2006
Value of exported goods ($ mil) $18,287
  Manufactured $12,960
  Non-manufactured...................$1,622

Foreign direct investment in US affiliates, 2004
Property, plants & equipment ($ mil) $9,333
Employment (x 1,000)....................62.9

Agriculture, 2006
Number of farms 10,000
Farm acreage (x 1,000) 26,100
  Acres per farm 2,610
Farm marketings and income ($ mil)
Total............................$2,879.2
  Crops.....................$1,558.5
  Livestock....................$1,320.7
Net farm income $773.7

Principal commodities, in order by
  marketing receipts, 2005
  Cattle and calves, Dairy products, Lettuce, Cotton, Hay

Federal economic activity in state
Expenditures, 2005 ($ mil)
  Total............................. $44,639
    Per capita $7,498.49
  Defense $12,001
  Non-defense $32,638
Defense department, 2006 ($ mil)
  Payroll.......................... $2,656
  Contract awards $9,696
  Grants $79
Homeland security grants ($1,000)
  2006..............................$20,171
  2007..............................$33,774

FDIC-insured financial institutions, 2005
Number 55
Assets ($ billion) $18.9
Deposits ($ billion) $14.2

Fishing, 2006
Catch (x 1,000 lbs)...................... NA
Value ($1,000)........................... NA

Mining, 2006 ($ mil)
Total non-fuel mineral production $6,710
Percent of U.S. 10.42%

Communication, Energy & Transportation

Communication
Households with computers, 2003........64.3%
Households with internet access, 2003 ....55.2%
High-speed internet providers 52
Total high-speed internet lines........1,832,564
  Residential 1,220,053
  Business.........................612,511
Wireless phone customers, 12/2006 4,405,032

FCC-licensed stations (as of January 1, 2008)
TV stations 31
FM radio stations......................... 143
AM radio stations 74

Energy
Energy consumption, 2004
  Total (trillion Btu)....................1,437
  Per capita (million Btu) 250.0
By source of production (trillion Btu)
  Coal 425
  Natural gas.......................... 355
  Petroleum........................... 563
  Nuclear electric power 293
  Hydroelectric power................... 70
By end-use sector (trillion Btu)
  Residential 369
  Commercial 326
  Industrial 231
  Transportation 511
Electric energy, 2005
  Primary source of electricity........... Coal
  Net generation (billion kWh) 101.5
    percent from renewable sources........ 6.4%
  Net summer capability (million kW) 24.9
  CO_2 emitted from generation 51.4
Natural gas utilities, 2005
  Customers (x 1,000) 1,100
  Sales (trillion Btu)..................... 87
  Revenues ($ mil) $915
Nuclear plants, 2007 4
Total CO_2 emitted (million metric tons).....88.8
Energy spending, 2004 ($ mil) $13,779
  per capita $2,398
  Price per million Btu $15.24

Transportation, 2006
Public road & street mileage 60,376
  Urban.............................. 22,560
  Rural 37,816
  Interstate..........................1,169
Vehicle miles of travel (millions) 62,468
  per capita 10,131.6
Total motor vehicle registrations.......4,182,332
  Automobiles.......................2,189,979
  Trucks 1,987,392
  Motorcycles 114,435
Licensed drivers 4,032,643
  19 years & under 165,665
Deaths from motor vehicle accidents 1,288
Gasoline consumed (x 1,000 gallons) 2,870,781
  per capita 465.6

Commuting Statistics, 2006
Average commute time (min) 25.0
  Drove to work alone 74.6%
  Carpooled...........................13.9%
  Public transit 2.1%
  Walk to work 2.3%
  Work from home 4.5%

©2008 Information Publications, Inc.
All rights reserved. Photocopying prohibited.
877-544-INFO (4636) or www.informationpublications.com

State Summary

Capital city . . . . Little Rock
Governor . . . . Mike Beebe

State Capitol
Room 250
Little Rock, AR 72201
501-682-2345

Admitted as a state 1836
Area (square miles) 53,179
Population, 2007 (estimate). 2,834,797
Largest city . . . . Little Rock
  Population, 2006 184,422
Personal income per capita, 2006
  (in current dollars) $27,935
Gross domestic product, 2006 ($ mil) $91,837

Leading industries by payroll, 2005

Manufacturing, Health care/Social assistance,
Retail trade

Leading agricultural commodities by receipts, 2005

Broilers, Rice, Cotton, Soybeans, Cattle and
calves

Geography & Environment

Total area (square miles). 53,179
  land 52,068
  water 1,110
Federally-owned land, 2004 (acres) 2,407,948
  percent. 7.2%
Highest point . . . . Magazine Mountain
  elevation (feet) .2,753
Lowest point . . . . .Ouachita River
  elevation (feet) 55
General coastline (miles) 0
Tidal shoreline (miles) 0
Cropland, 2003 (x 1,000 acres) 7,522
Forest land, 2003 (x 1,000 acres). 15,008
Capital city . . . . Little Rock
  Population 2000 183,133
  Population 2006 184,422
Largest city . . . . Little Rock
  Population 2000 183,133
  Population 2006 184,422

Number of cities with over 100,000 population

1990 1
2000 1
2006 1

State park and recreation areas, 2005

Area (x 1,000 acres). 53
Number of visitors (x 1,000) 9,751
Revenues ($1,000) $16,174
  percent of operating expenditures. 41.6%

National forest system land, 2007

Acres 3,598,417

Demographics & Population Characteristics

Population

1980 2,286,435
1990 2,350,725
2000 2,673,398
2006 2,810,872
  Male. 1,377,711
  Female 1,433,161
Living in group quarters, 2006 78,322
  percent of total. .2.8%
2007 (estimate). 2,834,797
  persons per square mile of land 54.4
2008 (projected). 2,836,580
2010 (projected) 2,875,039
2020 (projected) 3,060,219
2030 (projected) 3,240,208

Population of Core-Based Statistical Areas (formerly Metropolitan Areas), x 1,000

	CBSA	Non-CBSA
1990	1,802	549
2000	2,082	591
2006	2,224	587

Change in population, 2000-2007

Number 161,399
  percent. 6.0%
Natural increase (births minus deaths) 78,302
Net internal migration 62,982
Net international migration 27,119

Persons by age, 2006

Under 5 years 192,891
5 to 17 years 498,295
18 years and over 2,119,686
65 years and over 390,421
85 years and over 54,889
  Median age 36.8

Persons by age, 2010 (projected)

Under 5 years 194,806
18 and over 2,172,383
65 and over 412,152
  Median age 37.9

Race, 2006

One Race
  White. 2,279,839
  Black or African American 442,155
  Asian 29,312
  American Indian/Alaska Native. 21,635
  Hawaiian Native/Pacific Islander. 2,649
Two or more races. 35,282

Persons of Hispanic origin, 2006

Total Hispanic or Latino 138,283
  Mexican. 104,920
  Puerto Rican 2,615
  Cuban 650

©2008 Information Publications, Inc.
All rights reserved. Photocopying prohibited.
877-544-INFO (4636) or www.informationpublications.com

Persons of Asian origin, 2006

Total Asian 28,168
  Asian Indian........................ .5,279
  Chinese 4,672
  Filipino 3,839
  Japanese 793
  Korean............................. .3,431
  Vietnamese......................... 2,488

Marital status, 2006

Population 15 years & over 2,237,108
  Never married 538,460
  Married....................... 1,253,688
  Separated 53,052
  Widowed.......................... 167,095
  Divorced 277,865

Language spoken at home, 2006

Population 5 years and older......... 2,616,131
  English only 2,456,301
  Spanish 116,396
  French 4,352
  German 5,050
  Chinese 3,611

Households & families, 2006

Households........................ 1,103,428
  with persons under 18 years .... .379,411
  with persons over 65 years.......... 274,524
  persons per household 2.48
Families........................... 758,195
  persons per family................. .2.99
Married couples................... .567,229
Female householder,
  no husband present............... .142,145
One-person households 296,225

Nativity, 2006

Number of residents born in state 1,723,478
  percent of population 61.3%

Immigration & naturalization, 2006

Legal permanent residents admitted 2,926
Persons naturalized 1,133
Non-immigrant admissions 39,848

Vital Statistics and Health

Marriages

2004 36,806
2005 35,882
2006 34,261

Divorces

2004 .... .16,874
2005 .... .16,728
2006 .... .16,150

Health risks, 2006

Percent of adults who are:
  Smokers........................... 23.7%
  Overweight (BMI > 25)............. 63.8%
  Obese (BMI > 30).................. 26.9%

Births

2005 39,208
  Birthrate (per 1,000)............... 14.1
  White............................. 30,807
  Black 7,473
  Hispanic 4,038
  Asian/Pacific Islander 687
  Amer. Indian/Alaska Native 241
  Low birth weight (2,500g or less)....... 8.9%
  Cesarian births 31.5%
  Preterm births 13.4%
  To unmarried mothers.............. 40.2%
  Twin births (per 1,000) 29.4
  Triplets or higher order (per 100,000)....100.4
2006 (preliminary)................... 40,973
  rate per 1,000 .... .14.6

Deaths

2004

All causes .... .27,528
  rate per 100,000.................. 924.7
Heart disease 7,534
  rate per 100,000.................. .250.9
Malignant neoplasms 6,304
  rate per 100,000.................. 208.9
Cerebrovascular disease............. .1,948
  rate per 100,000.................. .65.0
Chronic lower respiratory disease 1,428
  rate per 100,000.................. .47.4
Diabetes........................... 838
  rate per 100,000.................. .28.0
2005 (preliminary)................. 28,055
  rate per 100,000.................. 930.2
2006 (provisional) 28,032

Infant deaths

2004 319
  rate per 1,000 .... .8.3
2005 (provisional) 294
  rate per 1,000 .... .7.5

Exercise routines, 2005

None............................... 30.6%
Moderate or greater................. 46.4%
Vigorous 24.8%

Abortions, 2004

Total performed in state............. 4,644
  rate per 1,000 women age 15-44............ 8
  % obtained by out-of-state residents 17.4%

Physicians, 2005

Total.............................. .5,619
  rate per 100,000 persons 202

Community hospitals, 2005

Number of hospitals 85
Beds (x 1,000)......................... .9.4
Patients admitted (x 1,000) 380
Average daily census (x 1,000) 5.5
Average cost per day $1,238
Outpatient visits (x 1 mil) 5.0

©2008 Information Publications, Inc.
All rights reserved. Photocopying prohibited.
877-544-INFO (4636) or www.informationpublications.com

Disability status of population, 2006
5 to 15 years 9.4%
16 to 64 years 18.7%
65 years and over 50.5%

Education

Educational attainment, 2006
Population over 25 years 1,847,325
   Less than 9th grade. 7.4%
   High school graduate or more 80.5%
   College graduate or more. 18.2%
   Graduate or professional degree. 6.2%

Public school enrollment, 2005-06
Total. 474,206
   Pre-kindergarten through grade 8. . . . 335,223
   Grades 9 through 12 138,237

Graduating public high school seniors, 2004-05
Diplomas (incl. GED and others) 26,698

SAT scores, 2007
Average critical reading score 578
Average writing score 565
Average math score 566
Percent of graduates taking test 5%

Public school teachers, 2006-07 (estimate)
Total (x 1,000) 34.1
   Elementary. 16.6
   Secondary. 17.5
Average salary $44,245
   Elementary. $44,245
   Secondary. $44,245

State receipts & expenditures for public schools, 2006-07 (estimate)
Revenue receipts ($ mil) $4,308
Expenditures
Total ($ mil) $4,515
   Per capita $1,441
   Per pupil $10,398

NAEP proficiency scores, 2007

	Reading		Math	
	Basic	Proficient	Basic	Proficient
Grade 4	63.5%	28.6%	80.7%	36.7%
Grade 8	69.6%	25.4%	64.7%	24.4%

Higher education enrollment, fall 2005
Total. 15,155
   Full-time men 5,652
   Full-time women. 6,833
   Part-time men 837
   Part-time women. 1,833

Minority enrollment in institutions of higher education, 2005
Black, non-Hispanic 26,242
Hispanic 2,913
Asian/Pacific Islander 2,059
American Indian/Alaska Native. 1,576

Institutions of higher education, 2005-06
Total. 48
   Public. 33
   Private 15

Earned degrees conferred, 2004-05
Associate's. 5,166
Bachelor's 11,191
Master's. 2,851
First-professional. 505
Doctor's. 249

Public Libraries, 2006
Number of libraries. 48
Number of outlets 216
Annual visits per capita 3.2
Circulation per capita. 4.4

State & local financial support for higher education, FY 2006
Full-time equivalent enrollment (x 1,000). . . .101.3
Appropriations per FTE. $5,899

Social Insurance & Welfare Programs

Social Security benefits & beneficiaries, 2005
Beneficiaries (x 1,000) 558
   Retired & dependents. 346
   Survivors. 80
   Disabled & dependents. 132
Annual benefit payments ($ mil) $5,564
   Retired & dependents. $3,332
   Survivors. $961
   Disabled & dependents. $1,271
Average monthly benefit
   Retired & dependents. $935
   Disabled & dependents. $887
   Widowed. $868

Medicare, July 2005
Enrollment (x 1,000). 472
Payments ($ mil) $3,132

Medicaid, 2004
Beneficiaries (x 1,000). 1,070
Payments ($ mil) $3,888

State Children's Health Insurance Program, 2006
Enrollment (x 1,000). .3.4
Expenditures ($ mil) $60.4

Persons without health insurance, 2006
Number (x 1,000). 521
   percent. 18.9%
Number of children (x 1,000) 65
   percent of children 9.3%

Health care expenditures, 2004
Total expenditures. $13,357
   per capita $4,863

©2008 Information Publications, Inc.
All rights reserved. Photocopying prohibited.
877-544-INFO (4636) or www.informationpublications.com

Federal and state public aid

State unemployment insurance, 2006
Recipients, first payments (x 1,000) 80
Total payments ($ mil) $243
Average weekly benefit $244
Temporary Assistance for Needy Families, 2006
Recipients (x 1,000) 219.8
Families (x 1,000) 99.8
Supplemental Security Income, 2005
Recipients (x 1,000) 91.0
Payments ($ mil) $406.6
Food Stamp Program, 2006
Avg monthly participants (x 1,000) 384.9
Total benefits ($ mil) $414.4

Housing & Construction

Housing units
Total 2005 (estimate) 1,248,831
Total 2006 (estimate) 1,273,615
Seasonal or recreational use, 2006 39,144
Owner-occupied, 2006 753,412
   Median home value $93,900
   Homeowner vacancy rate 1.9%
Renter-occupied, 2006 350,016
   Median rent $566
   Rental vacancy rate 13.5%
Home ownership rate, 2005 . . . . 69.2%
Home ownership rate, 2006 . . . . 70.8%

New privately-owned housing units
Number authorized, 2006 (x 1,000) 13.9
   Value ($ mil) $1,793.8
Started 2005 (x 1,000, estimate) 13.6
Started 2006 (x 1,000, estimate) 13.6

Existing home sales
2005 (x 1,000) 75.3
2006 (x 1,000) 82.6

Government & Elections

State officials 2008
Governor . . . . Mike Beebe
   Democratic, term expires 1/11
Lieutenant Governor . . . . Bill Halter
Secretary of State . . . . Charlie Daniels
Attorney General . . . . .Dustin McDaniel
Chief Justice . . . . Jim Hannah

Governorship
Minimum age 30
Length of term . . . . 4 years
Consecutive terms permitted 2
Who succeeds . . . . Lieutenant Governor

Local governments by type, 2002
Total 1,588
   County 75
   Municipal 499
   Township 0
   School District 310
   Special District 704

State legislature
Name . . . . General Assembly
Upper chamber . . . . .Senate
   Number of members 35
   Length of term . . . . 4 years
   Party in majority, 2008 . . . . .Democratic
Lower chamber . . . . .House of Representatives
   Number of members 100
   Length of term . . . . 2 years
   Party in majority, 2008 . . . . .Democratic

Federal representation, 2008 (110th Congress)
Senator . . . . Mark Pryor
   Party . . . . .Democratic
   Year term expires 2009
Senator . . . . .Blanche Lincoln
   Party . . . . .Democratic
   Year term expires 2011
Representatives, total 4
   Democrats 3
   Republicans 1

Voters in November 2006 election (estimate)
Total 910,565
Male 430,602
Female 479,963
White 792,177
Black 101,004
Hispanic 7,811
Asian . . . . NA

Presidential election, 2004
Total Popular Vote 1,054,945
   Kerry 469,953
   Bush 572,898
Total Electoral Votes 6

Votes cast for US Senators
2004
Total vote (x 1,000) 1,039
Leading party .Democratic
Percent for leading party 55.9%
2006
Total vote (x 1,000) . . . . NA
Leading party . . . . NA
Percent for leading party . . . . NA

Votes cast for US Representatives
2004
Total vote (x 1,000) 791
   Democratic 426
   Republican 358
Leading party .Democratic
Percent for leading party 53.9%
2006
Total vote (x 1,000) 763
   Democratic 457
   Republican 306
Leading party .Democratic
Percent for leading party 59.8%

©2008 Information Publications, Inc.
All rights reserved. Photocopying prohibited.
877-544-INFO (4636) or www.informationpublications.com

State government employment, 2006
Full-time equivalent employees 58,147
Payroll ($ mil) $177.8

Local government employment, 2006
Full-time equivalent employees 103,776
Payroll ($ mil) $277.4

Women holding public office, 2008
US Congress 1
Statewide elected office 1
State legislature 28

Black public officials, 2002
Total 535
   US and state legislatures 15
   City/county/regional offices 374
   Judicial/law enforcement 17
   Education/school boards 129

Hispanic public officials, 2006
Total 0
   State executives & legislators 0
   City/county/regional offices 0
   Judicial/law enforcement 0
   Education/school boards 0

Governmental Finance

State government revenues, 2006
Total revenue (x $1,000) $16,424,851
   per capita $5,846.99
General revenue (x $1,000) $13,644,838
   Intergovernmental 4,288,097
   Taxes 6,959,438
      general sales .2,772,131
      individual income tax 2,012,835
      corporate income tax 368,523
   Current charges 1,696,823
   Miscellaneous 700,480

State government expenditure, 2006
Total expenditure (x $1,000) $14,370,337
   per capita $5,115.62
General expenditure (x $1,000) $13,302,770
   per capita, total $4,735.58
      Education 2,017.23
      Public welfare 1,224.39
      Health 124.95
      Hospitals 237.19
      Highways 339.82
      Police protection 36.57
      Corrections .140.61
      Natural resources 81.42
      Parks & recreation 33.75
      Governmental administration 193.25
      Interest on general debt 55.96

State debt & cash, 2006 ($ per capita)
Debt $1,614.11
Cash/security holdings $8,496.33

Federal government grants to state & local government, 2005 (x $1,000)
Total $4,681,690
by Federal agency
   Defense 45,249
   Education 386,623
   Energy 5,503
   Environmental Protection Agency 31,133
   Health & Human Services 2,933,378
   Homeland Security 29,581
   Housing & Urban Development 249,928
   Justice 42,706
   Labor 69,227
   Transportation 435,771
   Veterans Affairs 6,457

Crime & Law Enforcement

Crime, 2006 (rates per 100,000 residents)
Property crimes 111,521
   Burglary 32,042
   Larceny 72,016
   Motor vehicle theft 7,463
   Property crime rate 3,967.5
Violent crimes 15,506
   Murder 205
   Forcible rape 1,308
   Robbery 2,766
   Aggravated assault 11,227
   Violent crime rate 551.6
Hate crimes 133

Fraud and identity theft, 2006
Fraud complaints 2,428
   rate per 100,000 residents 86.4
Identity theft complaints 1,537
   rate per 100,000 residents 54.7

Law enforcement agencies, 2006
Total agencies 264
Total employees 8,266
   Officers 5,405
   Civilians 2,861

Prisoners, probation, and parole, 2006
Total prisoners 13,729
   percent change, 12/31/05 to 12/31/06 . . . . 1.4%
   in private facilities 0%
   in local jails 6.1%
Sentenced to more than one year 13,713
   rate per 100,000 residents 485
Adults on probation 31,508
Adults on parole 18,405

Prisoner demographics, June 30, 2005 (rate per 100,000 residents)
Male 1,231
Female 136
White 478
Black 1,846
Hispanic 288

©2008 Information Publications, Inc.
All rights reserved. Photocopying prohibited.
877-544-INFO (4636) or www.informationpublications.com

Arrests, 2006
Total 113,791
    Persons under 18 years of age 11,389

Persons under sentence of death, 1/1/07
Total 37
    White 14
    Black 23
    Hispanic 0

State's highest court
Name .... Supreme Court
Number of members 7
Length of term .... 8 years
Intermediate appeals court? .... yes

Labor & Income

Civilian labor force, 2006 (x 1,000)
Total 1,374
    Men 724
    Women 650
    Persons 16-19 years 69
    White 1,137
    Black 194
    Hispanic 76

Civilian labor force as a percent of civilian non-institutional population, 2006
Total 63.5%
    Men 69.3
    Women 58.0
    Persons 16-19 years 45.3
    White 63.6
    Black 62.6
    Hispanic 74.9

Employment, 2006 (x 1,000)
Total 1,302
    Men 684
    Women 617
    Persons 16-19 years 57
    White 1,087
    Black 174
    Hispanic 72

Unemployment rate, 2006
Total 5.3%
    Men 5.4
    Women 5.1
    Persons 16-19 years 17.2
    White 4.4
    Black 10.3
    Hispanic 4.7

Full-time/part-time labor force, 2003 (x 1,000)
Full-time labor force, employed 996
Part-time labor force, employed 191
Unemployed, looking for
    Full-time work 67
    Part-time work 11
Mean duration of unemployment (weeks) ... 16.7
    Median 9.2

Labor unions, 2006
Membership (x 1,000) 58
    percent of employed 5.1%

Experienced civilian labor force by private industry, 2006
Total $973,615
    Natural resources & mining 18,550
    Construction 56,956
    Manufacturing 198,822
    Trade, transportation & utilities 244,917
    Information 19,911
    Finance 51,171
    Professional & business 114,216
    Education & health 145,778
    Leisure & hospitality 97,450
    Other 25,845

Experienced civilian labor force by occupation, May 2006
Management 44,020
Business & financial 34,560
Legal 5,620
Sales 117,740
Office & admin. support 184,070
Computers & math 14,430
Architecture & engineering 13,910
Arts & entertainment 8,670
Education 69,800
Social services 14,470
Health care practitioner & technical 64,750
Health care support 31,320
Maintenance & repair 52,420
Construction 49,700
Transportation & moving 126,680
Production 152,190
Farming, fishing & forestry 6,600

Hours and earnings of production workers on manufacturing payrolls, 2006
Average weekly hours 41.0
Average hourly earnings $13.35
Average weekly earnings $547.35

Income and poverty, 2006
Median household income $36,599
Personal income, per capita (current $) ... $27,935
    in constant (2000) dollars $24,385
Persons below poverty level 17.3%

Average annual pay
2006 .... $32,389
    increase from 2005 .... 3.6%

Federal individual income tax returns, 2005
Returns filed 1,153,654
Adjusted gross income ($1,000) $47,857,444
Total tax liability ($1,000) $5,382,410

Charitable contributions, 2004
Number of contributions 235.0
Total amount ($ mil) $1,224.1

©2008 Information Publications, Inc.
All rights reserved. Photocopying prohibited.
877-544-INFO (4636) or www.informationpublications.com

Economy, Business, Industry & Agriculture

Fortune 500 companies, 2007 5
Bankruptcy cases filed, FY 2007 11,494

Patents and trademarks issued, 2007
Patents 151
Trademarks 246

Business firm ownership, 2002
Women-owned 49,618
  Sales ($ mil) $6,339
Black-owned 8,942
  Sales ($ mil) $442
Hispanic-owned 2,094
  Sales ($ mil) $374
Asian-owned 2,013
  Sales ($ mil) $614
Amer. Indian/Alaska Native-owned 2,283
  Sales ($ mil) $317
Hawaiian/Pacific Islander-owned 61
  Sales ($ mil) $4

Gross domestic product, 2006 ($ mil)
Total gross domestic product $91,837
  Agriculture, forestry, fishing and
    hunting 2,306
  Mining 1,293
  Utilities 1,924
  Construction 4,079
  Manufacturing, durable goods 9,679
  Manufacturing, non-durable goods 8,350
  Wholesale trade 6,260
  Retail trade 6,847
  Transportation & warehousing 4,408
  Information 3,527
  Finance & insurance 3,585
  Real estate, rental & leasing 7,953
  Professional and technical services 3,423
  Educational services 395
  Health care and social assistance 6,866
  Accommodation/food services 2,099
  Other services, except government 2,074
  Government 12,492

Establishments, payroll, employees & receipts, by major industry group, 2005

Total 66,039
  Annual payroll ($1,000) $30,185,779
  Paid employees 1,017,424
Forestry, fishing & agriculture 829
  Annual payroll ($1,000) $157,170
  Paid employees 5,413
Mining 305
  Annual payroll ($1,000) $191,156
  Paid employees 3,999
  Receipts, 2002 ($1,000) $917,469

Utilities 370
  Annual payroll ($1,000) $420,862
  Paid employees 7,059
  Receipts, 2002 ($1,000) . . . . .NA
Construction 6,348
  Annual payroll ($1,000) $1,634,994
  Paid employees 49,959
  Receipts, 2002 ($1,000) $6,623,949
Manufacturing 3,105
  Annual payroll ($1,000) $6,577,058
  Paid employees 198,288
  Receipts, 2002 ($1,000) $46,721,413
Wholesale trade 3,473
  Annual payroll ($1,000) $1,904,796
  Paid employees 49,206
  Receipts, 2002 ($1,000) $34,470,795
Retail trade 11,880
  Annual payroll ($1,000) $2,724,653
  Paid employees 140,465
  Receipts, 2002 ($1,000) $25,611,630
Transportation & warehousing 2,596
  Annual payroll ($1,000) $2,037,033
  Paid employees 61,474
  Receipts, 2002 ($1,000) $5,222,960
Information 1,034
  Annual payroll ($1,000) $1,077,266
  Paid employees 24,579
  Receipts, 2002 ($1,000) . . . . .NA
Finance & insurance 4,304
  Annual payroll ($1,000) $1,496,807
  Paid employees 37,092
  Receipts, 2002 ($1,000) . . . . .NA
Professional, scientific & technical 5,474
  Annual payroll ($1,000) $1,455,707
  Paid employees 36,141
  Receipts, 2002 ($1,000) $2,599,015
Education 507
  Annual payroll ($1,000) $216,266
  Paid employees 12,572
  Receipts, 2002 ($1,000) $71,850
Health care & social assistance 6,828
  Annual payroll ($1,000) $5,001,545
  Paid employees 154,792
  Receipts, 2002 ($1,000) $9,675,926
Arts and entertainment 856
  Annual payroll ($1,000) . . . . NA
  Paid employees . . . . NA
  Receipts, 2002 ($1,000) $391,164
Real estate 2,983
  Annual payroll ($1,000) $321,152
  Paid employees 12,612
  Receipts, 2002 ($1,000) $1,397,076
Accommodation & food service 4,878
  Annual payroll ($1,000) $890,819
  Paid employees 86,916
  Receipts, 2002 ($1,000) $2,766,905

©2008 Information Publications, Inc.
All rights reserved. Photocopying prohibited.
877-544-INFO (4636) or www.informationpublications.com

8 Arkansas

Exports, 2006
Value of exported goods ($ mil) $4,265
  Manufactured $3,906
  Non-manufactured................... $203

Foreign direct investment in US affiliates, 2004
Property, plants & equipment ($ mil) $4,913
Employment (x 1,000)................... 32.0

Agriculture, 2006
Number of farms 46,500
Farm acreage (x 1,000) 14,300
  Acres per farm....................... 308
Farm marketings and income ($ mil)
Total.............................. $6,164.1
  Crops............................ $2,396.7
  Livestock........................ $3,767.4
Net farm income $1,950.9

Principal commodities, in order by marketing receipts, 2005
  Broilers, Rice, Cotton, Soybeans, Cattle and calves

Federal economic activity in state
Expenditures, 2005 ($ mil)
  Total.......................... $20,387
    Per capita $7,344.76
  Defense $1,862
  Non-defense...................... $18,525
Defense department, 2006 ($ mil)
  Payroll.......................... $1,080
  Contract awards $881
  Grants $64
Homeland security grants ($1,000)
  2006........................... $8,343
  2007........................... $7,238

FDIC-insured financial institutions, 2005
Number................................. 156
Assets ($ billion) $48.5
Deposits ($ billion) $39.3

Fishing, 2006
Catch (x 1,000 lbs)...................... NA
Value ($1,000).......................... NA

Mining, 2006 ($ mil)
Total non-fuel mineral production $617
Percent of U.S. 0.96%

Communication, Energy & Transportation

Communication
Households with computers, 2003........ 50.0%
Households with internet access, 2003 .... 42.4%
High-speed internet providers 45
Total high-speed internet lines........ 424,685
  Residential 385,669
  Business.......................... 39,016
Wireless phone customers, 12/2006 2,044,217

FCC-licensed stations (as of January 1, 2008)
TV stations 27
FM radio stations........................ 207
AM radio stations 84

Energy
Energy consumption, 2004
  Total (trillion Btu)................... 1,136
  Per capita (million Btu) 413.5
By source of production (trillion Btu)
  Coal 270
  Natural gas 229
  Petroleum........................... 388
  Nuclear electric power 161
  Hydroelectric power.................... 37
By end-use sector (trillion Btu)
  Residential 218
  Commercial 155
  Industrial 474
  Transportation 289
Electric energy, 2005
  Primary source of electricity........... Coal
  Net generation (billion kWh) 47.8
    percent from renewable sources...... 10.1%
  Net summer capability (million kW) 14.1
  CO_2 emitted from generation 26.4
Natural gas utilities, 2005
  Customers (x 1,000) 627
  Sales (trillion Btu)................... 159
  Revenues ($ mil) $741
Nuclear plants, 2007 2
Total CO_2 emitted (million metric tons)..... 62.4
Energy spending, 2004 ($ mil) $8,718
  per capita $3,174
  Price per million Btu $11.89

Transportation, 2006
Public road & street mileage 99,005
  Urban.............................. 11,272
  Rural 87,733
  Interstate.......................... 655
Vehicle miles of travel (millions) 33,007
  per capita 11,750.0
Total motor vehicle registrations....... 1,994,255
  Automobiles........................ 958,640
  Trucks 1,027,414
  Motorcycles 58,686
Licensed drivers 2,034,975
  19 years & under 105,116
Deaths from motor vehicle accidents 665
Gasoline consumed (x 1,000 gallons) 1,447,192
  per capita 515.2

Commuting Statistics, 2006
Average commute time (min) 20.7
  Drove to work alone 80.2%
  Carpooled........................... 12.9%
  Public transit 0.4%
  Walk to work 1.8%
  Work from home...................... 3.3%

©2008 Information Publications, Inc.
All rights reserved. Photocopying prohibited.
877-544-INFO (4636) or www.informationpublications.com

State Summary

Capital city . . . . .Sacramento
Governor. . . . . .Arnold Schwarzenegger
Office of the Governor
State Capitol
Sacramento, CA 95814
916-445-2841

Admitted as a state 1850
Area (square miles) 163,696
Population, 2007 (estimate). 36,553,215
Largest city . . . . .Los Angeles
   Population, 2006. 3,849,378
Personal income per capita, 2006
   (in current dollars) $38,956
Gross domestic product, 2006 ($ mil) . .$1,727,355

Leading industries by payroll, 2005

Professional/Scientific/Technical, Manufacturing, Health care/Social assistance

**Leading agricultural commodities
by receipts, 2005**

Dairy products, Greenhouse/nursery, Grapes,
Almonds, Cattle and calves

Geography & Environment

Total area (square miles). 163,696
   land 155,959
   water 7,736
Federally-owned land, 2004 (acres) . . .45,393,238
   percent. 45.3%
Highest point .Mt. Whitney
   elevation (feet) 14,494
Lowest point .Death Valley
   elevation (feet) . . . . -282
General coastline (miles) 840
Tidal shoreline (miles) 3,427
Cropland, 2003 (x 1,000 acres) 9,468
Forest land, 2003 (x 1,000 acres). 13,903
Capital city . . . . .Sacramento
   Population 2000 407,018
   Population 2006 453,781
Largest city .Los Angeles
   Population 2000 3,694,820
   Population 2006 3,849,378

Number of cities with over 100,000 population
1990 43
2000 56
2006 62

State park and recreation areas, 2005
Area (x 1,000 acres) 1,554
Number of visitors (x 1,000) 77,119
Revenues ($1,000) $82,819
   percent of operating expenditures. 17.8%

National forest system land, 2007
Acres 20,802,641

Demographics & Population Characteristics

Population
1980 23,667,902
1990 29,760,021
2000 33,871,653
2006 36,457,549
   Male. 18,224,444
   Female. 18,233,105
Living in group quarters, 2006. 863,207
   percent of total. 2.4%
2007 (estimate). 36,553,215
   persons per square mile of land 234.4
2008 (projected). 37,262,310
2010 (projected). 38,067,134
2020 (projected). 42,206,743
2030 (projected). 46,444,861

**Population of Core-Based Statistical Areas
(formerly Metropolitan Areas), x 1,000**

	CBSA	Non-CBSA
1990	29,540	218
2000	33,628	243
2006	36,195	262

Change in population, 2000-2007
Number 2,681,560
   percent. 7.9%
Natural increase (births minus deaths) . . 2,232,397
Net internal migration . . . . -1,223,992
Net international migration 1,807,426

Persons by age, 2006
Under 5 years 2,678,019
5 to 17 years 6,854,595
18 years and over 26,924,935
65 years and over 3,931,514
85 years and over 555,473
   Median age. 34.4

Persons by age, 2010 (projected)
Under 5 years 2,853,032
18 and over 28,570,156
65 and over 4,392,708
   Median age. 34.9

Race, 2006
One Race
   White. 28,043,733
   Black or African American 2,445,228
   Asian 4,510,534
   American Indian/Alaska Native. 421,346
   Hawaiian Native/Pacific Islander. 153,193
Two or more races. 883,515

Persons of Hispanic origin, 2006
Total Hispanic or Latino 13,074,155
   Mexican. 10,841,524
   Puerto Rican 160,130
   Cuban 85,992

©2008 Information Publications, Inc.
All rights reserved. Photocopying prohibited.
877-544-INFO (4636) or www.informationpublications.com

Persons of Asian origin, 2006

Total Asian 4,483,252
  Asian Indian. 475,118
  Chinese 1,165,605
  Filipino 1,100,767
  Japanese 300,355
  Korean. 430,913
  Vietnamese. 533,893

Marital status, 2006

Population 15 years & over 28,569,779
  Never married 9,732,918
  Married. 14,552,553
  Separated 709,120
  Widowed. 1,550,349
  Divorced 2,733,959

Language spoken at home, 2006

Population 5 years and older. 33,784,883
  English only 19,414,977
  Spanish 9,588,622
  French 136,449
  German 150,299
  Chinese 936,113

Households & families, 2006

Households. 12,151,227
  with persons under 18 years 4,696,427
  with persons over 65 years. 2,710,892
  persons per household 2.93
Families. 8,303,793
  persons per family. 3.54
Married couples. 6,051,701
Female householder,
  no husband present. 1,553,660
One-person households 2,994,372

Nativity, 2006

Number of residents born in state . . . 19,089,635
  percent of population. 52.4%

Immigration & naturalization, 2006

Legal permanent residents admitted. . . . 264,677
Persons naturalized 152,836
Non-immigrant admissions 5,573,588

Vital Statistics and Health

Marriages

2004 227,486
2005 228,762
2006 215,985

Divorces

2004 . . . . NA
2005 . . . . NA
2006 . . . . NA

Health risks, 2006

Percent of adults who are:
  Smokers. 14.9%
  Overweight (BMI > 25). 58.8%
  Obese (BMI > 30). 23.3%

Births

2005 548,882
  Birthrate (per 1,000). 15.2
  White. 445,277
  Black 32,252
  Hispanic 282,842
  Asian/Pacific Islander 68,232
  Amer. Indian/Alaska Native. 3,121
  Low birth weight (2,500g or less) 6.9%
  Cesarian births 30.7%
  Preterm births 10.7%
  To unmarried mothers. 35.7%
  Twin births (per 1,000) 29.0
  Triplets or higher order (per 100,000). . . .149.6
2006 (preliminary). 562,431
  rate per 1,000 . . . . .15.4

Deaths

2004
All causes 232,525
  rate per 100,000. . . . . .715.6
Heart disease 64,999
  rate per 100,000. . . . . .202.1
Malignant neoplasms 53,700
  rate per 100,000. . . . . .166.8
Cerebrovascular disease. 16,882
  rate per 100,000. . . . . .52.7
Chronic lower respiratory disease 12,522
  rate per 100,000. . . . . .39.7
Diabetes. 7,117
  rate per 100,000. . . . . .22.2
2005 (preliminary). 237,079
  rate per 100,000. . . . . .713.1
2006 (provisional) 238,011

Infant deaths

2004 2,811
  rate per 1,000 . . . . .5.2
2005 (provisional) 2,800
  rate per 1,000 . . . . .5.1

Exercise routines, 2005

None. 23.9%
Moderate or greater. 53.4%
Vigorous 36.2%

Abortions, 2004

Total performed in state. . . . . NA
  rate per 1,000 women age 15-44. . . . . NA
  % obtained by out-of-state residents . . . . . . NA

Physicians, 2005

Total. 94,341
  rate per 100,000 persons 261

Community hospitals, 2005

Number of hospitals 357
Beds (x 1,000). 70.2
Patients admitted (x 1,000) 3,434
Average daily census (x 1,000) 50.0
Average cost per day $1,994
Outpatient visits (x 1 mil) 49.0

©2008 Information Publications, Inc.
All rights reserved. Photocopying prohibited.
877-544-INFO (4636) or www.informationpublications.com

Disability status of population, 2006
5 to 15 years 4.8%
16 to 64 years 10.3%
65 years and over 41.1%

Education

Educational attainment, 2006
Population over 25 years 23,133,174
  Less than 9ᵗʰ grade................... 10.6%
  High school graduate or more 80.1%
  College graduate or more............. 29.0%
  Graduate or professional degree....... 10.4%

Public school enrollment, 2005-06
Total.............................6,437,202
  Pre-kindergarten through grade 8...4,431,994
  Grades 9 through 12..............1,953,077

Graduating public high school seniors, 2004-05
Diplomas (incl. GED and others) 355,217

SAT scores, 2007
Average critical reading score.............. 499
Average writing score..................... 498
Average math score....................... 516
Percent of graduates taking test 49%

Public school teachers, 2006-07 (estimate)
Total (x 1,000) 304.2
  Elementary.........................222.9
  Secondary...........................81.3
Average salary $63,640
  Elementary........................ $63,640
  Secondary......................... $63,640

State receipts & expenditures for public schools, 2006-07 (estimate)
Revenue receipts ($ mil) $67,460
Expenditures
Total ($ mil) $71,622
  Per capita $1,523
  Per pupil $9,156

NAEP proficiency scores, 2007

	Reading		Math	
	Basic	Proficient	Basic	Proficient
Grade 4	53.2%	22.9%	69.6%	29.7%
Grade 8	62.3%	21.5%	59.1%	23.9%

Higher education enrollment, fall 2005
Total................................391,678
  Full-time men 130,335
  Full-time women....................169,171
  Part-time men 39,913
  Part-time women.................... 52,259

Minority enrollment in institutions of higher education, 2005
Black, non-Hispanic 185,659
Hispanic 632,358
Asian/Pacific Islander 451,454
American Indian/Alaska Native........ 22,007

Institutions of higher education, 2005-06
Total.................................... 408
  Public................................ 146
  Private 262

Earned degrees conferred, 2004-05
Associate's.......................... 92,687
Bachelor's 146,959
Master's............................ 54,254
First-professional.....................9,188
Doctor's............................ 6,203

Public Libraries, 2006
Number of libraries...................... 179
Number of outlets 1,153
Annual visits per capita 4.1
Circulation per capita....................5.4

State & local financial support for higher education, FY 2006
Full-time equivalent enrollment (x 1,000).. 1,662.1
Appropriations per FTE................ $6,586

Social Insurance & Welfare Programs

Social Security benefits & beneficiaries, 2005
Beneficiaries (x 1,000) 4,460
  Retired & dependents..................3,193
  Survivors............................ 571
  Disabled & dependents................. 697
Annual benefit payments ($ mil) $48,106
  Retired & dependents.............$32,751
  Survivors.........................$7,946
  Disabled & dependents.............$7,409
Average monthly benefit
  Retired & dependents..................$1,003
  Disabled & dependents................. $955
  Widowed............................ $995

Medicare, July 2005
Enrollment (x 1,000)................... 4,201
Payments ($ mil) $22,477

Medicaid, 2004
Beneficiaries (x 1,000)..................10,015
Payments ($ mil) $27,444

State Children's Health Insurance Program, 2006
Enrollment (x 1,000)................... 1,391.4
Expenditures ($ mil)................. $1,801.1

Persons without health insurance, 2006
Number (x 1,000)......................6,791
  percent 18.8%
Number of children (x 1,000) 1,225
  percent of children 12.8%

Health care expenditures, 2004
Total expenditures................... $166,236
  per capita $4,638

©2008 Information Publications, Inc.
All rights reserved. Photocopying prohibited.
877-544-INFO (4636) or www.informationpublications.com

Federal and state public aid

State unemployment insurance, 2006
Recipients, first payments (x 1,000) 948
Total payments ($ mil) $4,485
Average weekly benefit $289
Temporary Assistance for Needy Families, 2006
Recipients (x 1,000) 12,874.3
Families (x 1,000) 5,451.5
Supplemental Security Income, 2005
Recipients (x 1,000) 1,212.1
Payments ($ mil) $8,146.4
Food Stamp Program, 2006
Avg monthly participants (x 1,000) 1,999.7
Total benefits ($ mil) $2,376.7

Housing & Construction

Housing units
Total 2005 (estimate) 12,993,870
Total 2006 (estimate) 13,174,378
Seasonal or recreational use, 2006 275,870
Owner-occupied, 2006 7,102,197
  Median home value $535,700
  Homeowner vacancy rate 1.9%
Renter-occupied, 2006 5,049,030
  Median rent $1,029
  Rental vacancy rate 5.8%
Home ownership rate, 2005 . . . . 59.7%
Home ownership rate, 2006 . . . . 60.2%

New privately-owned housing units
Number authorized, 2006 (x 1,000) 160.5
  Value ($ mil) $29,614.4
Started 2005 (x 1,000, estimate) 165.0
Started 2006 (x 1,000, estimate) 154.2

Existing home sales
2005 (x 1,000) 601.1
2006 (x 1,000) 459.9

Government & Elections

State officials 2008
Governor . . . . Arnold Schwarzenegger
      Republican, term expires 1/11
Lieutenant Governor . . . . John Garamendi
Secretary of State . . . . Debra Bowen
Attorney General . . . . Jerry Brown
Chief Justice . . . . Ronald George

Governorship
Minimum age 18
Length of term . . . . 4 years
Consecutive terms permitted 2
Who succeeds . . . . Lieutenant Governor

Local governments by type, 2002
Total 4,409
  County 57
  Municipal 475
  Township 0
  School District 1,047
  Special District 2,830

State legislature
Name . . . . Legislature
Upper chamber . . . . .Senate
  Number of members 40
  Length of term . . . . 4 years
  Party in majority, 2008 . . . . .Democratic
Lower chamber . . . . .Assembly
  Number of members 80
  Length of term . . . . 2 years
  Party in majority, 2008 . . . . .Democratic

Federal representation, 2008 (110th Congress)
Senator . . . . Barbara Boxer
  Party . . . . .Democratic
  Year term expires 2011
Senator .Dianne Feinstein
  Party . . . . .Democratic
  Year term expires 2013
Representatives, total 53
  Democrats 34
  Republicans 19

Voters in November 2006 election (estimate)
Total 10,103,659
  Male 4,806,091
  Female 5,297,568
  White 8,335,875
  Black 608,009
  Hispanic 868,190
  Asian 882,153

Presidential election, 2004
Total Popular Vote 12,421,852
  Kerry 6,745,485
  Bush 5,509,826
Total Electoral Votes 55

Votes cast for US Senators
2004
Total vote (x 1,000) 12,053
Leading party . . . . .Democratic
Percent for leading party 57.7%
2006
Total vote (x 1,000) 8,541
Leading party . . . . .Democratic
Percent for leading party 59.4%

Votes cast for US Representatives
2004
Total vote (x 1,000) 11,624
  Democratic 6,224
  Republican 5,031
Leading party . . . . .Democratic
Percent for leading party 53.5%
2006
Total vote (x 1,000) 8,296
  Democratic 4,720
  Republican 3,314
Leading party . . . . .Democratic
Percent for leading party 56.9%

©2008 Information Publications, Inc.
All rights reserved. Photocopying prohibited.
877-544-INFO (4636) or www.informationpublications.com

State government employment, 2006
Full-time equivalent employees 393,609
Payroll ($ mil) $2,051.1

Local government employment, 2006
Full-time equivalent employees 1,425,123
Payroll ($ mil) $6,931.5

Women holding public office, 2008
US Congress 21
Statewide elected office...................... 1
State legislature 34

Black public officials, 2002
Total...................................... 234
US and state legislatures 10
City/county/regional offices 78
Judicial/law enforcement................. 76
Education/school boards................. 70

Hispanic public officials, 2006
Total......................................1,059
State executives & legislators 30
City/county/regional offices 388
Judicial/law enforcement................. 41
Education/school boards............... 600

Governmental Finance

State government revenues, 2006
Total revenue (x $1,000)...........$263,764,713
per capita $7,276.29
General revenue (x $1,000) $188,443,700
Intergovernmental 53,685,005
Taxes 111,346,857
general sales...................32,199,800
individual income tax 51,219,823
corporate income tax 10,316,467
Current charges.................13,328,957
Miscellaneous 10,082,881

State government expenditure, 2006
Total expenditure (x $1,000) $225,317,442
per capita $6,215.68
General expenditure (x $1,000) $191,607,263
per capita, total.................... $5,285.74
Education 1,910.55
Public welfare 1,464.38
Health 270.05
Hospitals......................... 153.50
Highways 344.88
Police protection....................36.49
Corrections 187.48
Natural resources 117.91
Parks & recreation................14.15
Governmental administration.......218.90
Interest on general debt............145.79

State debt & cash, 2006 ($ per capita)
Debt...............................$3,018.40
Cash/security holdings..............$13,837.40

Federal government grants to state & local government, 2005 (x $1,000)
Total............................. $55,334,202
by Federal agency
Defense 375,279
Education 4,613,968
Energy.............................267,414
Environmental Protection Agency 312,186
Health & Human Services. 34,997,223
Homeland Security................ 367,844
Housing & Urban Development.... 4,344,298
Justice 640,662
Labor 533,832
Transportation 4,000,705
Veterans Affairs................... 35,877

Crime & Law Enforcement

Crime, 2006 (rates per 100,000 residents)
Property crimes 1,156,017
Burglary 246,464
Larceny 666,860
Motor vehicle theft 242,693
Property crime rate.................. 3,170.9
Violent crimes........................ 194,120
Murder 2,485
Forcible rape.......................9,212
Robbery.......................... 70,968
Aggravated assault 111,455
Violent crime rate 532.5
Hate crimes........................1,604

Fraud and identity theft, 2006
Fraud complaints.....................49,070
rate per 100,000 residents 134.6
Identity theft complaints 41,396
rate per 100,000 residents 113.5

Law enforcement agencies, 2006
Total agencies............................ 460
Total employees 115,912
Officers 75,483
Civilians 40,429

Prisoners, probation, and parole, 2006
Total prisoners.......................175,512
percent change, 12/31/05 to 12/31/06 ....2.8%
in private facilities 1.8%
in local jails 1.4%
Sentenced to more than one year 173,942
rate per 100,000 residents 475
Adults on probation 401,707
Adults on parole....................... 118,592

Prisoner demographics, June 30, 2005 (rate per 100,000 residents)
Male..................................... 1,246
Female 119
White................................... 460
Black.................................... 2,992
Hispanic 782

©2008 Information Publications, Inc.
All rights reserved. Photocopying prohibited.
877-544-INFO (4636) or www.informationpublications.com

6　California

Arrests, 2006

Total.................................1,543,797
　　Persons under 18 years of age.........231,735

Persons under sentence of death, 1/1/07

Total................................... 660
　　White............................. 254
　　Black 235
　　Hispanic 136

State's highest court

Name ....Supreme Court
Number of members...................... 7
Length of term..................... 12 years
Intermediate appeals court? ....yes

Labor & Income

Civilian labor force, 2006 (x 1,000)

Total...................................17,751
　　Men 9,876
　　Women 7,875
　　Persons 16-19 years.................... 740
　　White.............................13,833
　　Black 1,058
　　Hispanic 5,822

Civilian labor force as a percent of civilian non-institutional population, 2006

Total................................... 65.1%
　　Men 73.9
　　Women 56.7
　　Persons 16-19 years....................36.1
　　White.................................65.6
　　Black 61.1
　　Hispanic 68.4

Employment, 2006 (x 1,000)

Total................................. 16,892
　　Men 9,410
　　Women 7,482
　　Persons 16-19 years.................... 611
　　White.............................13,188
　　Black 959
　　Hispanic 5,493

Unemployment rate, 2006

Total................................... 4.8%
　　Men 4.7
　　Women 5.0
　　Persons 16-19 years....................17.5
　　White.................................4.7
　　Black 9.4
　　Hispanic 5.6

Full-time/part-time labor force, 2003 (x 1,000)

Full-time labor force, employed 13,408
Part-time labor force, employed.......... 2,875

Unemployed, looking for
　　Full-time work........................ 1,004
　　Part-time work........................ 173
*Mean duration of unemployment (weeks)......*19.8
　　Median 10.0

Labor unions, 2006

Membership (x 1,000)................. 2,273
　　percent of employed 15.7%

Experienced civilian labor force by private industry, 2006

Total..........................13,125,809
　　Natural resources & mining 402,871
　　Construction 929,950
　　Manufacturing....................1,495,034
　　Trade, transportation & utilities 2,854,723
　　Information 470,144
　　Finance 934,448
　　Professional & business 2,222,644
　　Education & health 1,576,182
　　Leisure & hospitality.............. 1,514,160
　　Other........................... 700,575

Experienced civilian labor force by occupation, May 2006

Management....................... 790,790
Business & financial 740,470
Legal..............................109,180
Sales.............................1,568,140
Office & admin. support.............2,713,590
Computers & math 391,960
Architecture & engineering........... 324,780
Arts & entertainment 308,110
Education 968,230
Social services 186,650
Health care practitioner & technical 615,630
Health care support 318,080
Maintenance & repair.................511,120
Construction 823,290
Transportation & moving 1,034,210
Production 974,890
Farming, fishing & forestry........... 182,520

Hours and earnings of production workers on manufacturing payrolls, 2006

Average weekly hours 40.4
Average hourly earnings $15.95
Average weekly earnings $644.38

Income and poverty, 2006

Median household income............ $56,645
Personal income, per capita (current $)... $38,956
　　in constant (2000) dollars $34,006
Persons below poverty level.............. 13.1%

Average annual pay

2006............................... $48,345
　　increase from 2005 .... 4.6%

Federal individual income tax returns, 2005

Returns filed.......................15,572,877
Adjusted gross income ($1,000) $970,448,917
Total tax liability ($1,000) $136,858,733

Charitable contributions, 2004

Number of contributions.............. 5,287.9
Total amount ($ mil)................ $21,867.9

©2008 Information Publications, Inc.
All rights reserved. Photocopying prohibited.
877-544-INFO (4636) or www.informationpublications.com

Economy, Business, Industry & Agriculture

Fortune 500 companies, 2007 52
Bankruptcy cases filed, FY 2007 62,951

Patents and trademarks issued, 2007

Patents 22,888
Trademarks 13,965

Business firm ownership, 2002

Women-owned 870,496
  Sales ($ mil) $137,692
Black-owned 112,815
  Sales ($ mil) $9,741
Hispanic-owned 427,678
  Sales ($ mil) $57,186
Asian-owned 371,530
  Sales ($ mil) $125,757
Amer. Indian/Alaska Native-owned 40,541
  Sales ($ mil) $4,387
Hawaiian/Pacific Islander-owned 7,074
  Sales ($ mil) $1,230

Gross domestic product, 2006 ($ mil)

Total gross domestic product $1,727,355
  Agriculture, forestry, fishing and
    hunting 24,222
  Mining 12,954
  Utilities 28,123
  Construction 82,664
  Manufacturing, durable goods 100,665
  Manufacturing, non-durable goods . . . 68,312
  Wholesale trade 101,757
  Retail trade 119,716
  Transportation & warehousing 38,813
  Information 103,269
  Finance & insurance 115,104
  Real estate, rental & leasing 292,786
  Professional and technical services 147,869
  Educational services 13,909
  Health care and social assistance 103,704
  Accommodation/food services 46,020
  Other services, except government 38,871
  Government 189,935

Establishments, payroll, employees & receipts, by major industry group, 2005

Total 860,866
  Annual payroll ($1,000) $588,450,315
  Paid employees 13,382,470
Forestry, fishing & agriculture 2,034
  Annual payroll ($1,000) $705,641
  Paid employees 23,719
Mining 819
  Annual payroll ($1,000) $1,420,222
  Paid employees 19,651
  Receipts, 2002 ($1,000) $7,293,240

Utilities 1,140
  Annual payroll ($1,000) $5,026,299
  Paid employees 59,422
  Receipts, 2002 ($1,000) . . . . .NA
Construction 75,151
  Annual payroll ($1,000) $39,863,707
  Paid employees 865,810
  Receipts, 2002 ($1,000) $150,527,556
Manufacturing 44,825
  Annual payroll ($1,000) $71,776,365
  Paid employees 1,450,372
  Receipts, 2002 ($1,000) $378,661,414
Wholesale trade .59,252
  Annual payroll ($1,000) $47,831,555
  Paid employees 816,186
  Receipts, 2002 ($1,000) $655,954,708
Retail trade 112,382
  Annual payroll ($1,000) $43,416,017
  Paid employees 1,651,973
  Receipts, 2002 ($1,000) $359,120,365
Transportation & warehousing 20,086
  Annual payroll ($1,000) $17,941,928
  Paid employees 448,607
  Receipts, 2002 ($1,000) $45,507,276
Information 20,837
  Annual payroll ($1,000) $40,284,426
  Paid employees 509,258
  Receipts, 2002 ($1,000) . . . . .NA
Finance & insurance 51,819
  Annual payroll ($1,000) $54,895,842
  Paid employees 703,282
  Receipts, 2002 ($1,000) . . . . .NA
Professional, scientific & technical 108,411
  Annual payroll ($1,000) $74,611,098
  Paid employees 1,192,324
  Receipts, 2002 ($1,000) $145,236,098
Education 10,492
  Annual payroll ($1,000) $9,169,034
  Paid employees 301,561
  Receipts, 2002 ($1,000) $4,270,794
Health care & social assistance 93,546
  Annual payroll ($1,000) $63,344,431
  Paid employees 1,507,717
  Receipts, 2002 ($1,000) $136,397,384
Arts and entertainment 18,817
  Annual payroll ($1,000) $11,677,810
  Paid employees 298,786
  Receipts, 2002 ($1,000) $26,292,138
Real estate 50,007
  Annual payroll ($1,000) $13,602,382
  Paid employees 317,240
  Receipts, 2002 ($1,000) $54,377,915
Accommodation & food service 71,625
  Annual payroll ($1,000) $19,887,731
  Paid employees 1,285,138
  Receipts, 2002 ($1,000) $55,559,669

©2008 Information Publications, Inc.
All rights reserved. Photocopying prohibited.
877-544-INFO (4636) or www.informationpublications.com

Exports, 2006
Value of exported goods ($ mil) $127,746
Manufactured $93,348
Non-manufactured. $12,109

Foreign direct investment in US affiliates, 2004
Property, plants & equipment ($ mil) . . . $90,622
Employment (x 1,000). 547.0

Agriculture, 2006
Number of farms 76,000
Farm acreage (x 1,000) 26,300
Acres per farm 346
Farm marketings and income ($ mil)
Total. $31,402.7
Crops $23,787.7
Livestock. $7,615.0
Net farm income $5,905.7

Principal commodities, in order by marketing receipts, 2005
Dairy products, Greenhouse/nursery, Grapes, Almonds, Cattle and calves

Federal economic activity in state
Expenditures, 2005 ($ mil)
Total. $242,023
Per capita $6,694.20
Defense $45,124
Non-defense. $196,900
Defense department, 2006 ($ mil)
Payroll. $15,270
Contract awards $32,126
Grants $350
Homeland security grants ($1,000)
2006. . . . .$231,951
2007. . . . .$242,245

FDIC-insured financial institutions, 2005
Number 304
Assets ($ billion) $573.6
Deposits ($ billion) $371.3

Fishing, 2006
Catch (x 1,000 lbs). 341,573
Value ($1,000). $129,929

Mining, 2006 ($ mil)
Total non-fuel mineral production $4,500
Percent of U.S. 6.99%

Communication, Energy & Transportation

Communication
Households with computers, 2003. . . . . . . .66.3%
Households with internet access, 2003 . . . . 59.6%
High-speed internet providers 77
Total high-speed internet lines. 11,753,765
Residential 7,707,939
Business. 4,045,826
Wireless phone customers, 12/2006 . . . 29,717,334

FCC-licensed stations (as of January 1, 2008)
TV stations 108
FM radio stations. 600
AM radio stations 251

Energy
Energy consumption, 2004
Total (trillion Btu). 8,365
Per capita (million Btu) 233.4
By source of production (trillion Btu)
Coal 69
Natural gas. 2,474
Petroleum. 3,788
Nuclear electric power 316
Hydroelectric power. 342
By end-use sector (trillion Btu)
Residential 1,556
Commercial 1,556
Industrial 2,053
Transportation 3,200
Electric energy, 2005
Primary source of electricity. . . . . Gas
Net generation (billion kWh) 200.3
percent from renewable sources. 31.6%
Net summer capability (million kW) 61.7
CO_2 emitted from generation 54.7
Natural gas utilities, 2005
Customers (x 1,000) 10,600
Sales (trillion Btu). 1,542
Revenues ($ mil) $7,922
Nuclear plants, 2007 4
Total CO_2 emitted (million metric tons). . . .388.9
Energy spending, 2004 ($ mil) $90,260
per capita $2,518
Price per million Btu $15.12

Transportation, 2006
Public road & street mileage 170,290
Urban. 86,565
Rural. 83,725
Interstate. 2,460
Vehicle miles of travel (millions) 327,478
per capita 9,033.9
Total motor vehicle registrations. 33,182,058
Automobiles. 19,835,554
Trucks 13,289,690
Motorcycles 726,096
Licensed drivers 23,021,279
19 years & under 938,414
Deaths from motor vehicle accidents 4,236
Gasoline consumed (x 1,000 gallons) . . .15,844,687
per capita 437.1

Commuting Statistics, 2006
Average commute time (min) 26.8
Drove to work alone 73.0%
Carpooled. 12.4%
Public transit 5.0%
Walk to work 2.7%
Work from home. 4.8%

©2008 Information Publications, Inc.
All rights reserved. Photocopying prohibited.
877-544-INFO (4636) or www.informationpublications.com

State Summary

Capital city . . . . Denver
Governor . . . . Bill Ritter

136 State Capitol
Denver, CO 80203
303-866-2471

Admitted as a state 1876
Area (square miles) 104,094
Population, 2007 (estimate). 4,861,515
Largest city . . . . Denver
   Population, 2006 566,974
Personal income per capita, 2006
   (in current dollars) $39,186
Gross domestic product, 2006 ($ mil) . . . $230,478

Leading industries by payroll, 2005

Professional/Scientific/Technical, Health care/
   Social assistance, Construction

Leading agricultural commodities by receipts, 2005

Cattle and calves, Dairy products, Greenhouse/
   nursery, Corn, Hay

Geography & Environment

Total area (square miles). 104,094
   land 103,718
   water 376
Federally-owned land, 2004 (acres) . . .24,354,713
   percent. 36.6%
Highest point . . . . Mt. Elbert
   elevation (feet) 14,433
Lowest point . . . . Arikaree River
   elevation (feet) 3,315
General coastline (miles) 0
Tidal shoreline (miles) 0
Cropland, 2003 (x 1,000 acres) 8,348
Forest land, 2003 (x 1,000 acres). 3,289
Capital city . . . . Denver
   Population 2000 554,636
   Population 2006 566,974
Largest city . . . . Denver
   Population 2000 554,636
   Population 2006 566,974

Number of cities with over 100,000 population

1990 4
2000 8
2006 9

State park and recreation areas, 2005

Area (x 1,000 acres) 410
Number of visitors (x 1,000) 11,377
Revenues ($1,000) $19,500
   percent of operating expenditures 67.1%

National forest system land, 2007

Acres 14,519,030

Demographics & Population Characteristics

Population

1980 2,889,964
1990 3,294,394
2000 4,302,015
2006 4,753,377
   Male 2,393,004
   Female 2,360,373
Living in group quarters, 2006 102,994
   percent of total. 2.2%
2007 (estimate). 4,861,515
   persons per square mile of land 46.9
2008 (projected). 4,746,528
2010 (projected) .4,831,554
2020 (projected) .5,278,867
2030 (projected) .5,792,357

Population of Core-Based Statistical Areas (formerly Metropolitan Areas), x 1,000

	CBSA	Non-CBSA
1990	2,989	306
2000	23,922	380
2006	4,356	397

Change in population, 2000-2007

Number 559,496
   percent 13.0%
Natural increase (births minus deaths) 291,317
Net internal migration 132,566
Net international migration 141,730

Persons by age, 2006

Under 5 years 341,069
5 to 17 years 828,232
18 years and over 3,584,076
65 years and over 477,186
85 years and over 61,232
   Median age 35.4

Persons by age, 2010 (projected)

Under 5 years 353,009
18 and over 3,642,971
65 and over 517,419
   Median age 35.7

Race, 2006

One Race
   White. 4,282,804
   Black or African American 195,978
   Asian 125,724
   American Indian/Alaska Native. 54,626
   Hawaiian Native/Pacific Islander. 6,755
Two or more races. 87,490

Persons of Hispanic origin, 2006

Total Hispanic or Latino 934,410
   Mexican. 671,341
   Puerto Rican 18,148
   Cuban 4,917

©2008 Information Publications, Inc.
All rights reserved. Photocopying prohibited.
877-544-INFO (4636) or www.informationpublications.com

2   Colorado

Persons of Asian origin, 2006
Total Asian 133,079
- Asian Indian........................15,144
- Chinese 28,753
- Filipino 12,537
- Japanese 13,166
- Korean...........................25,722
- Vietnamese........................ 19,646

Marital status, 2006
Population 15 years & over 3,778,016
- Never married 1,096,726
- Married......................... 2,065,116
- Separated 67,812
- Widowed......................... 181,840
- Divorced 434,334

Language spoken at home, 2006
Population 5 years and older........ 4,414,382
- English only 3,653,462
- Spanish 545,112
- French 19,827
- German.......................... 33,463
- Chinese 20,839

Households & families, 2006
Households.........................1,846,988
- with persons under 18 years 629,349
- with persons over 65 years.......... 335,325
- persons per household 2.52
Families..............................1,196,223
- persons per family...................3.11
Married couples...................... 934,148
Female householder,
- no husband present................ 181,646
One-person households 521,377

Nativity, 2006
Number of residents born in state 2,000,357
- percent of population 42.1%

Immigration & naturalization, 2006
Legal permanent residents admitted......12,714
Persons naturalized 5,526
Non-immigrant admissions 355,991

Vital Statistics and Health

Marriages
2004 33,826
2005 35,132
2006 36,121

Divorces
2004 20,230
2005 20,504
2006 21,138

Health risks, 2006
Percent of adults who are:
- Smokers........................... 17.9%
- Overweight (BMI > 25)..................54.9%
- Obese (BMI > 30)..................... 18.2%

Births
2005 68,944
- Birthrate (per 1,000)...................14.8
- White........................ 62,856
- Black 3,123
- Hispanic 21,785
- Asian/Pacific Islander 2,390
- Amer. Indian/Alaska Native........... 575
- Low birth weight (2,500g or less)........ 9.2%
- Cesarian births 24.6%
- Preterm births 12.3%
- To unmarried mothers................ 27.1%
- Twin births (per 1,000)................31.7
- Triplets or higher order (per 100,000)....153.8
2006 (preliminary)......................70,750
- rate per 1,000 ....14.9

Deaths
2004
All causes 28,309
- rate per 100,000.....................736.4
Heart disease 6,079
- rate per 100,000.....................162.7
Malignant neoplasms 6,196
- rate per 100,000.....................160.1
Cerebrovascular disease.................1,638
- rate per 100,000.......................44.6
Chronic lower respiratory disease 1,899
- rate per 100,000.......................51.7
Diabetes................................ 696
- rate per 100,000.......................18.2
2005 (preliminary)....................29,628
- rate per 100,000.....................742.8
2006 (provisional) 29,502

Infant deaths
2004 434
- rate per 1,000 ....6.3
2005 (provisional) 451
- rate per 1,000 ....6.5

Exercise routines, 2005
None............................... 17.3%
Moderate or greater..................... 54.4%
Vigorous 32.6%

Abortions, 2004
Total performed in state.................11,415
- rate per 1,000 women age 15-44.......... 11
- % obtained by out-of-state residents 9.2%

Physicians, 2005
Total..............................12,101
- rate per 100,000 persons 259

Community hospitals, 2005
Number of hospitals 71
Beds (x 1,000)..........................9.6
Patients admitted (x 1,000) 417
Average daily census (x 1,000) 5.8
Average cost per day $1,751
Outpatient visits (x 1 mil) 7.4

©2008 Information Publications, Inc.
All rights reserved. Photocopying prohibited.
877-544-INFO (4636) or www.informationpublications.com

Disability status of population, 2006
5 to 15 years 5.2%
16 to 64 years 10.5%
65 years and over 38.3%

Education

Educational attainment, 2006
Population over 25 years 3,118,500
  Less than 9th grade. 4.6%
  High school graduate or more 88.0%
  College graduate or more. 34.3%
  Graduate or professional degree. 12.4%

Public school enrollment, 2005-06
Total 779,826
  Pre-kindergarten through grade 8. ... 549,875
  Grades 9 through 12 229,951

Graduating public high school seniors, 2004-05
Diplomas (incl. GED and others) 45,058

SAT scores, 2007
Average critical reading score 560
Average writing score 549
Average math score 565
Percent of graduates taking test 24%

Public school teachers, 2006-07 (estimate)
Total (x 1,000) 47.0
  Elementary 24.0
  Secondary 23.0
Average salary $45,833
  Elementary $45,520
  Secondary $46,110

State receipts & expenditures for public schools, 2006-07 (estimate)
Revenue receipts ($ mil) $7,428
Expenditures
Total ($ mil) $8,516
  Per capita $1,486
  Per pupil $9,592

NAEP proficiency scores, 2007

	Reading		Math	
	Basic	Proficient	Basic	Proficient
Grade 4	70.0%	36.2%	81.8%	41.2%
Grade 8	78.7%	34.6%	75.1%	37.4%

Higher education enrollment, fall 2005
Total 68,163
  Full-time men 21,914
  Full-time women 27,752
  Part-time men 8,508
  Part-time women 9,989

Minority enrollment in institutions of higher education, 2005
Black, non-Hispanic 15,528
Hispanic 33,856
Asian/Pacific Islander 11,710
American Indian/Alaska Native 4,370

Institutions of higher education, 2005-06
Total 78
  Public 27
  Private 51

Earned degrees conferred, 2004-05
Associate's 9,788
Bachelor's 25,230
Master's 10,921
First-professional. 1,054
Doctor's 1,062

Public Libraries, 2006
Number of libraries. 115
Number of outlets 253
Annual visits per capita 6.2
Circulation per capita. 11.0

State & local financial support for higher education, FY 2006
Full-time equivalent enrollment (x 1,000) 158.9
Appropriations per FTE. $3,364

Social Insurance & Welfare Programs

Social Security benefits & beneficiaries, 2005
Beneficiaries (x 1,000) 588
  Retired & dependents. 419
  Survivors. 77
  Disabled & dependents. 92
Annual benefit payments ($ mil) $6,227
  Retired & dependents. $4,206
  Survivors. $1,065
  Disabled & dependents. $955
Average monthly benefit
  Retired & dependents. $982
  Disabled & dependents. $934
  Widowed. $977

Medicare, July 2005
Enrollment (x 1,000) 522
Payments ($ mil) $2,647

Medicaid, 2004
Beneficiaries (x 1,000). 503
Payments ($ mil) $2,399

State Children's Health Insurance Program, 2006
Enrollment (x 1,000) 70.0
Expenditures ($ mil) $77.1

Persons without health insurance, 2006
Number (x 1,000) 826
  percent. 17.2%
Number of children (x 1,000) 176
  percent of children 14.6%

Health care expenditures, 2004
Total expenditures. $21,691
  per capita $4,717

©2008 Information Publications, Inc.
All rights reserved. Photocopying prohibited.
877-544-INFO (4636) or www.informationpublications.com

Federal and state public aid

State unemployment insurance, 2006
Recipients, first payments (x 1,000) 69
Total payments ($ mil) $288
Average weekly benefit $312
Temporary Assistance for Needy Families, 2006
Recipients (x 1,000) 426.0
Families (x 1,000) 165.5
Supplemental Security Income, 2005
Recipients (x 1,000) 55.4
Payments ($ mil) $263.8
Food Stamp Program, 2006
Avg monthly participants (x 1,000) 251.4
Total benefits ($ mil) $321.0

Housing & Construction

Housing units
Total 2005 (estimate) 2,053,794
Total 2006 (estimate) 2,094,898
Seasonal or recreational use, 2006 95,893
Owner-occupied, 2006 1,269,421
   Median home value $232,900
   Homeowner vacancy rate 3.0%
Renter-occupied, 2006 577,567
   Median rent $780
   Rental vacancy rate 10.5%
Home ownership rate, 2005 . . . . 71.0%
Home ownership rate, 2006 . . . . 70.1%

New privately-owned housing units
Number authorized, 2006 (x 1,000) 38.3
   Value ($ mil) $7,769.5
Started 2005 (x 1,000, estimate) 36.8
Started 2006 (x 1,000, estimate) 37.7

Existing home sales
2005 (x 1,000) 130.4
2006 (x 1,000) 123.7

Government & Elections

State officials 2008
Governor . . . . Bill Ritter
     Democratic, term expires 1/11
Lieutenant Governor . . . . Barbara O'Brien
Secretary of State . . . . Mike Coffman
Attorney General . . . . .John Suthers
Chief Justice . . . . .Mary Mullarkey

Governorship
Minimum age 30
Length of term . . . . 4 years
Consecutive terms permitted 2
Who succeeds . . . . Lieutenant Governor

Local governments by type, 2002
Total 1,928
   County 62
   Municipal 270
   Township 0
   School District 182
   Special District 1,414

State legislature
Name . . . . General Assembly
Upper chamber . . . . .Senate
   Number of members 35
   Length of term . . . . 4 years
   Party in majority, 2008 . . . . .Democratic
Lower chamber . . . . . . .House of Representatives
   Number of members 65
   Length of term . . . . 2 years
   Party in majority, 2008 . . . . .Democratic

Federal representation, 2008 (110th Congress)
Senator . . . . Wayne Allard
   Party . . . . Republican
   Year term expires 2009
Senator . . . . .Ken Salazar
   Party . . . . .Democratic
   Year term expires 2011
Representatives, total 7
   Democrats 4
   Republicans 3

Voters in November 2006 election (estimate)
Total 1,729,916
   Male 805,406
   Female 924,510
   White 1,659,514
   Black 24,618
   Hispanic 85,614
   Asian 19,579

Presidential election, 2004
Total Popular Vote 2,130,330
   Kerry 1,001,732
   Bush 1,101,255
Total Electoral Votes 9

Votes cast for US Senators
2004
Total vote (x 1,000) .2,107
Leading party .Democratic
Percent for leading party 51.3%
2006
Total vote (x 1,000) . . . . NA
Leading party . . . . NA
Percent for leading party . . . . NA

Votes cast for US Representatives
2004
Total vote (x 1,000) 2,039
   Democratic 995
   Republican 992
Leading party .Democratic
Percent for leading party 48.8%
2006
Total vote (x 1,000) .1,539
   Democratic 833
   Republican 624
Leading party .Democratic
Percent for leading party 54.1%

©2008 Information Publications, Inc.
All rights reserved. Photocopying prohibited.
877-544-INFO (4636) or www.informationpublications.com

State government employment, 2006
Full-time equivalent employees 67,451
Payroll ($ mil) $290.9

Local government employment, 2006
Full-time equivalent employees 187,551
Payroll ($ mil) $691.2

Women holding public office, 2008
US Congress 2
Statewide elected office..................... 2
State legislature 35

Black public officials, 2002
Total..................................... 17
  US and state legislatures 4
  City/county/regional offices 5
  Judicial/law enforcement................... 8
  Education/school boards................. 0

Hispanic public officials, 2006
Total..................................... 145
  State executives & legislators 7
  City/county/regional offices 101
  Judicial/law enforcement................... 7
  Education/school boards................. 30

Governmental Finance

State government revenues, 2006
Total revenue (x $1,000)...........$23,466,755
  per capita $4,923.53
General revenue (x $1,000) $17,493,287
  Intergovernmental 4,725,831
  Taxes 8,522,307
    general sales.....................2,105,049
    individual income tax 4,258,944
    corporate income tax 457,673
  Current charges................. 2,404,244
  Miscellaneous 1,840,905

State government expenditure, 2006
Total expenditure (x $1,000) $20,150,921
  per capita $4,227.84
General expenditure (x $1,000) $16,965,585
  per capita, total................... $3,559.53
    Education......................1,465.92
    Public welfare 851.19
    Health 151.25
    Hospitals..........................74.55
    Highways 264.72
    Police protection.................. 23.20
    Corrections 171.56
    Natural resources..................59.34
    Parks & recreation 18.30
    Governmental administration...... 146.53
    Interest on general debt............137.88

State debt & cash, 2006 ($ per capita)
Debt $2,783.59
Cash/security holdings.............. $11,778.13

Federal government grants to state & local government, 2005 (x $1,000)
Total............................$5,433,177
by Federal agency
  Defense 45,419
  Education 475,650
  Energy........................ 64,729
  Environmental Protection Agency 63,271
  Health & Human Services. 2,682,837
  Homeland Security..................20,917
  Housing & Urban Development...... 403,828
  Justice 85,459
  Labor 110,307
  Transportation 595,647
  Veterans Affairs.................. 9,364

Crime & Law Enforcement

Crime, 2006 (rates per 100,000 residents)
Property crimes 164,054
  Burglary 32,422
  Larceny 110,837
  Motor vehicle theft 20,795
  Property crime rate...............3,451.3
Violent crimes........................18,616
  Murder 158
  Forcible rape......................2,076
  Robbery.........................3,835
  Aggravated assault 12,547
  Violent crime rate 391.6
Hate crimes............................ 174

Fraud and identity theft, 2006
Fraud complaints......................7,657
  rate per 100,000 residents 161.1
Identity theft complaints 4,395
  rate per 100,000 residents 92.5

Law enforcement agencies, 2006
Total agencies........................ 235
Total employees 16,471
  Officers 11,298
  Civilians 5,173

Prisoners, probation, and parole, 2006
Total prisoners...................... 22,481
  percent change, 12/31/05 to 12/31/06 ....4.8%
  in private facilities 21.6%
  in local jails 1.9%
Sentenced to more than one year 22,481
  rate per 100,000 residents 469
Adults on probation 63,032
Adults on parole......................9,551

Prisoner demographics, June 30, 2005 (rate per 100,000 residents)
Male.................................1,279
Female............................... 166
White 525
Black.................................3,491
Hispanic 1,042

©2008 Information Publications, Inc.
All rights reserved. Photocopying prohibited.
877-544-INFO (4636) or www.informationpublications.com

Arrests, 2006

Total................................ 247,536
  Persons under 18 years of age .... .44,178

Persons under sentence of death, 1/1/07

Total.................................... 2
  White.................................. 0
  Black 1
  Hispanic 1

State's highest court

Name ....Supreme Court
Number of members...................... 7
Length of term..................... 10 years
Intermediate appeals court? ....yes

Labor & Income

Civilian labor force, 2006 (x 1,000)

Total....................................2,610
  Men 1,424
  Women 1,186
  Persons 16-19 years................... 114
  White................................. 2,389
  Black 85
  Hispanic 428

Civilian labor force as a percent of civilian non-institutional population, 2006

Total....................................72.7%
  Men 80.0
  Women 65.6
  Persons 16-19 years...................47.8
  White.................................73.0
  Black 67.8
  Hispanic 71.4

Employment, 2006 (x 1,000)

Total.................................... 2,499
  Men 1,368
  Women 1,131
  Persons 16-19 years................... 96
  White................................. 2,294
  Black 79
  Hispanic 398

Unemployment rate, 2006

Total....................................4.2%
  Men 4.0
  Women 4.6
  Persons 16-19 years...................15.9
  White.................................4.0
  Black 6.6
  Hispanic 6.9

Full-time/part-time labor force, 2003 (x 1,000)

Full-time labor force, employed 1,899
Part-time labor force, employed............ 429
Unemployed, looking for
  Full-time work......................... 123
  Part-time work......................... 26
*Mean duration of unemployment (weeks)......*18.8
  Median 9.9

Labor unions, 2006

Membership (x 1,000).................... 165
  percent of employed 7.7%

Experienced civilian labor force by private industry, 2006

Total.................................1,890,640
  Natural resources & mining 35,514
  Construction 167,647
  Manufacturing.......................149,147
  Trade, transportation & utilities 415,032
  Information 75,633
  Finance 156,739
  Professional & business 331,871
  Education & health.................. 228,145
  Leisure & hospitality................ 264,980
  Other 65,664

Experienced civilian labor force by occupation, May 2006

Management...........................107,070
Business & financial 114,640
Legal.................................17,630
Sales.................................257,450
Office & admin. support............... 372,340
Computers & math 77,980
Architecture & engineering............ 54,890
Arts & entertainment 31,630
Education 120,890
Social services 26,380
Health care practitioner & technical..... 99,920
Health care support 41,610
Maintenance & repair.................. 89,030
Construction 141,740
Transportation & moving 137,740
Production 103,820
Farming, fishing & forestry.............3,450

Hours and earnings of production workers on manufacturing payrolls, 2006

Average weekly hours 39.2
Average hourly earnings $16.58
Average weekly earnings $649.94

Income and poverty, 2006

Median household income............ $52,015
Personal income, per capita (current $)... $39,186
  in constant (2000) dollars $34,207
Persons below poverty level............. 12.0%

Average annual pay

2006................................. $43,506
  increase from 2005 .... 4.6%

Federal individual income tax returns, 2005

Returns filed.......................2,160,153
Adjusted gross income ($1,000) ... $125,994,344
Total tax liability ($1,000) $16,946,987

Charitable contributions, 2004

Number of contributions.................758.9
Total amount ($ mil).................$2,790.8

©2008 Information Publications, Inc.
All rights reserved. Photocopying prohibited.
877-544-INFO (4636) or www.informationpublications.com

Economy, Business, Industry & Agriculture

Fortune 500 companies, 2007 12
Bankruptcy cases filed, FY 2007 14,238

Patents and trademarks issued, 2007
Patents 2,071
Trademarks 1,866

Business firm ownership, 2002
Women-owned 135,220
   Sales ($ mil) $16,359
Black-owned 7,066
   Sales ($ mil) $758
Hispanic-owned. 24,054
   Sales ($ mil) $5,114
Asian-owned 10,910
   Sales ($ mil) $2,451
Amer. Indian/Alaska Native-owned 3,950
   Sales ($ mil) $490
Hawaiian/Pacific Islander-owned 391
   Sales ($ mil) $35

Gross domestic product, 2006 ($ mil)
Total gross domestic product $230,478
   Agriculture, forestry, fishing and
     hunting 1,920
   Mining. 12,775
   Utilities 3,635
   Construction 14,278
   Manufacturing, durable goods. 9,221
   Manufacturing, non-durable goods 5,791
   Wholesale trade. 12,544
   Retail trade. 13,816
   Transportation & warehousing 5,533
   Information 19,534
   Finance & insurance. 13,669
   Real estate, rental & leasing 30,421
   Professional and technical services 20,589
   Educational services. 1,430
   Health care and social assistance. 13,192
   Accommodation/food services. 6,640
   Other services, except government 5,262
   Government 26,501

Establishments, payroll, employees & receipts, by major industry group, 2005

Total 151,070
   Annual payroll ($1,000) $75,525,841
   Paid employees 1,936,264
Forestry, fishing & agriculture 269
   Annual payroll ($1,000) $35,709
   Paid employees 1,418
Mining 1,011
   Annual payroll ($1,000) $1,227,392
   Paid employees .16,191
   Receipts, 2002 ($1,000) $5,342,881

Utilities 370
   Annual payroll ($1,000) $548,366
   Paid employees 8,013
   Receipts, 2002 ($1,000) . . . . .NA
Construction. 19,153
   Annual payroll ($1,000) $6,620,283
   Paid employees 152,212
   Receipts, 2002 ($1,000) $32,663,596
Manufacturing 5,189
   Annual payroll ($1,000) $6,279,451
   Paid employees 135,832
   Receipts, 2002 ($1,000) $34,661,144
Wholesale trade 7,269
   Annual payroll ($1,000) $5,635,317
   Paid employees 98,511
   Receipts, 2002 ($1,000) $92,092,155
Retail trade 19,208
   Annual payroll ($1,000) $6,046,900
   Paid employees 249,433
   Receipts, 2002 ($1,000) $52,226,983
Transportation & warehousing 3,285
   Annual payroll ($1,000). $2,216,693
   Paid employees 59,969
   Receipts, 2002 ($1,000) $4,357,611
Information. 3,222
   Annual payroll ($1,000) $4,934,931
   Paid employees 79,149
   Receipts, 2002 ($1,000) . . . . .NA
Finance & insurance 10,485
   Annual payroll ($1,000) $6,280,715
   Paid employees 102,599
   Receipts, 2002 ($1,000) . . . . .NA
Professional, scientific & technical 21,670
   Annual payroll ($1,000) $9,458,401
   Paid employees 155,267
   Receipts, 2002 ($1,000) $20,547,273
Education 1,917
   Annual payroll ($1,000) $901,651
   Paid employees 35,311
   Receipts, 2002 ($1,000) $722,991
Health care & social assistance 12,686
   Annual payroll ($1,000) $8,294,247
   Paid employees 221,956
   Receipts, 2002 ($1,000) $17,499,334
Arts and entertainment 2,349
   Annual payroll ($1,000) $1,069,914
   Paid employees 44,714
   Receipts, 2002 ($1,000) $3,084,694
Real estate 9,702
   Annual payroll ($1,000) $1,755,618
   Paid employees 46,058
   Receipts, 2002 ($1,000) $6,686,060
Accommodation & food service 11,697
   Annual payroll ($1,000) $3,136,250
   Paid employees 222,283
   Receipts, 2002 ($1,000) $8,808,846

©2008 Information Publications, Inc.
All rights reserved. Photocopying prohibited.
877-544-INFO (4636) or www.informationpublications.com

8   Colorado

Exports, 2006
Value of exported goods ($ mil) $7,956
    Manufactured $6,056
    Non-manufactured. $310

Foreign direct investment in US affiliates, 2004
Property, plants & equipment ($ mil) $16,115
Employment (x 1,000). 71.4

Agriculture, 2006
Number of farms 30,700
Farm acreage (x 1,000) 30,700
    Acres per farm 1,000
Farm marketings and income ($ mil)
Total. $5,614.4
    Crops $1,552.5
    Livestock. $4,061.9
Net farm income $734.0

Principal commodities, in order by marketing receipts, 2005
Cattle and calves, Dairy products, Greenhouse/
    nursery, Corn, Hay

Federal economic activity in state
Expenditures, 2005 ($ mil)
    Total. $31,173
    Per capita $6,684.69
    Defense $6,691
    Non-defense. $24,481
Defense department, 2006 ($ mil)
    Payroll $3,210
    Contract awards $4,127
    Grants $46
Homeland security grants ($1,000)
    2006. . . . . $21,080
    2007. . . . . $19,899

FDIC-insured financial institutions, 2005
Number. 164
Assets ($ billion) $47.2
Deposits ($ billion) $39.2

Fishing, 2006
Catch (x 1,000 lbs). . . . . NA
Value ($1,000). . . . . NA

Mining, 2006 ($ mil)
Total non-fuel mineral production $1,670
Percent of U.S. 2.59%

Communication, Energy & Transportation

Communication
Households with computers, 2003. . . . . . . .70.0%
Households with internet access, 2003 . . . . 63.0%
High-speed internet providers 63
Total high-speed internet lines. 1,489,091
    Residential 1,018,006
    Business. 471,085
Wireless phone customers, 12/2006 3,608,209

FCC-licensed stations (as of January 1, 2008)
TV stations 31
FM radio stations. 179
AM radio stations 82

Energy
Energy consumption, 2004
    Total (trillion Btu). 1,384
    Per capita (million Btu) 300.9
By source of production (trillion Btu)
    Coal 390
    Natural gas 438
    Petroleum. 500
    Nuclear electric power 0
    Hydroelectric power. 12
By end-use sector (trillion Btu)
    Residential 308
    Commercial 285
    Industrial 373
    Transportation 417
Electric energy, 2005
    Primary source of electricity. . . . . Coal
    Net generation (billion kWh) 49.6
        percent from renewable sources. 4.5%
    Net summer capability (million kW) 11.1
    CO_2 emitted from generation 40.8
Natural gas utilities, 2005
    Customers (x 1,000) 1,667
    Sales (trillion Btu). 322
    Revenues ($ mil) $1,887
Nuclear plants, 2007 0
Total CO_2 emitted (million metric tons). 89.7
Energy spending, 2004 ($ mil) $11,805
    per capita $2,567
    Price per million Btu $12.54

Transportation, 2006
Public road & street mileage 88,021
    Urban. 19,066
    Rural 68,955
    Interstate. 954
Vehicle miles of travel (millions) 48,641
    per capita 10,205.3
Total motor vehicle registrations. 1,807,823
    Automobiles. 858,967
    Trucks 943,027
    Motorcycles 117,159
Licensed drivers 3,341,275
    19 years & under 155,126
Deaths from motor vehicle accidents 535
Gasoline consumed (x 1,000 gallons) 2,164,191
    per capita 454.1

Commuting Statistics, 2006
Average commute time (min) 23.9
    Drove to work alone 75.1%
    Carpooled. 10.6%
    Public transit 3.2%
    Walk to work 3.1%
    Work from home. 5.7%

©2008 Information Publications, Inc.
All rights reserved. Photocopying prohibited.
877-544-INFO (4636) or www.informationpublications.com

State Summary

Capital city . . . . Hartford
Governor . . . . .M. Jodi Rell

210 Capitol Ave
Hartford, CT 06106
800-406-1527

Admitted as a state 1788
Area (square miles) 5,543
Population, 2007 (estimate) 3,502,309
Largest city . . . . Bridgeport
  Population, 2006 137,912
Personal income per capita, 2006
  (in current dollars) $49,852
Gross domestic product, 2006 ($ mil) . . . $204,134

Leading industries by payroll, 2005

Finance & Insurance, Manufacturing, Health
    care/Social assistance

Leading agricultural commodities
by receipts, 2005

Greenhouse/nursery, Dairy products, Chicken
    eggs, Aquaculture, Tobacco

Geography & Environment

Total area (square miles). 5,543
  land 4,845
  water 699
Federally-owned land, 2004 (acres) 13,938
  percent. 0.4%
Highest point . . . . Mt. Frissell (south slope)
  elevation (feet) 2,380
Lowest point . . . . Long Island Sound
  elevation (feet) . . . . sea level
General coastline (miles) 0
Tidal shoreline (miles) 618
Cropland, 2003 (x 1,000 acres) 172
Forest land, 2003 (x 1,000 acres). 1,706
Capital city . . . . Hartford
  Population 2000 121,578
  Population 2006 124,512
Largest city . . . . Bridgeport
  Population 2000 139,529
  Population 2006 137,912

Number of cities with over 100,000 population

1990 5
2000 5
2006 5

State park and recreation areas, 2005

Area (x 1,000 acres) 204
Number of visitors (x 1,000) 6,235
Revenues ($1,000) $4,611
  percent of operating expenditures 32.0%

National forest system land, 2007

Acres 24

Demographics & Population
Characteristics

Population

1980 3,107,576
1990 3,287,116
2000 3,405,602
2006 3,504,809
  Male 1,706,188
  Female 1,798,621
Living in group quarters, 2006 113,079
  percent of total 3.2%
2007 (estimate) 3,502,309
  persons per square mile of land 722.9
2008 (projected) .3,550,416
2010 (projected) .3,577,490
2020 (projected) .3,675,650
2030 (projected) .3,688,630

Population of Core-Based Statistical Areas
(formerly Metropolitan Areas), x 1,000

	CBSA	Non-CBSA
1990	3,287	0
2000	3,406	0
2006	3,505	0

Change in population, 2000-2007

Number 96,707
  percent 2.8%
Natural increase (births minus deaths) 92,010
Net internal migration . . . . -78,064
Net international migration 97,695

Persons by age, 2006

Under 5 years 202,831
5 to 17 years 615,455
18 years and over 2,686,523
65 years and over 470,443
85 years and over 76,395
  Median age 39.0

Persons by age, 2010 (projected)

Under 5 years 217,712
18 and over 2,763,482
65 and over 515,621
  Median age 39.6

Race, 2006

One Race
  White 2,966,187
  Black or African American 358,210
  Asian 117,986
  American Indian/Alaska Native. 12,497
  Hawaiian Native/Pacific Islander. 2,597
Two or more races. 47,332

Persons of Hispanic origin, 2006

Total Hispanic or Latino 391,935
  Mexican. 37,155
  Puerto Rican 221,658
  Cuban 7,159

Persons of Asian origin, 2006

Total Asian 117,054
  Asian Indian........................ 40,394
  Chinese 26,493
  Filipino 12,352
  Japanese 3,623
  Korean 11,310
  Vietnamese.......................... 8,324

Marital status, 2006

Population 15 years & over 2,839,111
  Never married 879,704
  Married........................... 1,503,801
  Separated 44,462
  Widowed........................... 181,942
  Divorced 273,664

Language spoken at home, 2006

Population 5 years and older......... 3,302,738
  English only 2,639,307
  Spanish 308,863
  French 46,702
  German............................. 11,837
  Chinese 21,772

Households & families, 2006

Households........................1,325,443
  with persons under 18 years 460,658
  with persons over 65 years.......... 325,996
  persons per household 2.56
Families.............................. 894,348
  persons per family.......................3.13
Married couples..................... 680,656
Female householder,
  no husband present................ 160,504
One-person households 359,319

Nativity, 2006

Number of residents born in state 1,953,665
  percent of population................ 55.7%

Immigration & naturalization, 2006

Legal permanent residents admitted..... 18,700
Persons naturalized 7,231
Non-immigrant admissions 212,993

Vital Statistics and Health

Marriages

2004............................... 20,240
2005...............................20,514
2006...............................17,382

Divorces

2004............................... 10,942
2005...............................10,623
2006................................9,773

Health risks, 2006

Percent of adults who are:
  Smokers............................ 17.0%
  Overweight (BMI > 25).................58.8%
  Obese (BMI > 30)......................20.6%

Births

2005....................................41,718
  Birthrate (per 1,000)...................11.9
  White............................. 33,988
  Black 5,280
  Hispanic 8,004
  Asian/Pacific Islander 2,237
  Amer. Indian/Alaska Native............ 213
  Low birth weight (2,500g or less)....... 8.0%
  Cesarian births 32.4%
  Preterm births 10.4%
  To unmarried mothers................32.2%
  Twin births (per 1,000) 41.5
  Triplets or higher order (per 100,000)... 245.5
2006 (preliminary)..................... 41,807
  rate per 1,000 ....11.9

Deaths

2004
All causes 29,314
  rate per 100,000..................... 706.2
Heart disease 7,868
  rate per 100,000....................182.5
Malignant neoplasms 7,175
  rate per 100,000....................181.5
Cerebrovascular disease..............1,635
  rate per 100,000....................37.6
Chronic lower respiratory disease 1,432
  rate per 100,000....................34.7
Diabetes............................. 767
  rate per 100,000....................18.7
2005 (preliminary)..................... 29,466
  rate per 100,000..................... 696.0
2006 (provisional) 29,790

Infant deaths

2004 233
  rate per 1,000 ....5.5
2005 (provisional) 226
  rate per 1,000 ....5.4

Exercise routines, 2005

None................................ 21.2%
Moderate or greater.................... 51.2%
Vigorous 31.0%

Abortions, 2004

Total performed in state.................12,189
  rate per 1,000 women age 15-44.......... 17
  % obtained by out-of-state residents 3.7%

Physicians, 2005

Total................................ 12,780
  rate per 100,000 persons 365

Community hospitals, 2005

Number of hospitals 36
Beds (x 1,000)...........................7.7
Patients admitted (x 1,000) 405
Average daily census (x 1,000) 6.3
Average cost per day $1,714
Outpatient visits (x 1 mil) 7.1

©2008 Information Publications, Inc.
All rights reserved. Photocopying prohibited.
877-544-INFO (4636) or www.informationpublications.com

Disability status of population, 2006
5 to 15 years 5.4%
16 to 64 years 10.0%
65 years and over 36.3%

Education

Educational attainment, 2006
Population over 25 years 2,367,511
  Less than 9th grade..................... 4.8%
  High school graduate or more 88.0%
  College graduate or more.............. 33.7%
  Graduate or professional degree........ 14.4%

Public school enrollment, 2005-06
Total................................. 575,059
  Pre-kindergarten through grade 8.... 399,705
  Grades 9 through 12 175,354

Graduating public high school seniors, 2004-05
Diplomas (incl. GED and others) 35,560

SAT scores, 2007
Average critical reading score 510
Average writing score 511
Average math score 512
Percent of graduates taking test 84%

Public school teachers, 2006-07 (estimate)
Total (x 1,000) 42.5
  Elementary........................... 29.0
  Secondary............................ 13.5
Average salary $60,822
  Elementary........................ $60,822
  Secondary......................... $60,822

State receipts & expenditures for public schools, 2006-07 (estimate)
Revenue receipts ($ mil) $8,331
Expenditures
Total ($ mil) $8,339
  Per capita $2,129
  Per pupil $13,370

NAEP proficiency scores, 2007

	Reading		Math	
	Basic	Proficient	Basic	Proficient
Grade 4	72.6%	41.2%	83.9%	44.7%
Grade 8	76.7%	37.1%	72.8%	34.7%

Higher education enrollment, fall 2005
Total................................. 62,970
  Full-time men 21,391
  Full-time women..................... 27,075
  Part-time men 5,193
  Part-time women...................... 9,311

Minority enrollment in institutions of higher education, 2005
Black, non-Hispanic 18,528
Hispanic 14,285
Asian/Pacific Islander 7,877
American Indian/Alaska Native........... 672

Institutions of higher education, 2005-06
Total..................................... 44
  Public................................ 22
  Private 22

Earned degrees conferred, 2004-05
Associate's............................ 5,022
Bachelor's 16,617
Master's.............................. 8,851
First-professional..................... 1,014
Doctor's............................... 675

Public Libraries, 2006
Number of libraries..................... 194
Number of outlets 251
Annual visits per capita 6.4
Circulation per capita................... 9.0

State & local financial support for higher education, FY 2006
Full-time equivalent enrollment (x 1,000) 73.6
Appropriations per FTE............... $9,503

Social Insurance & Welfare Programs

Social Security benefits & beneficiaries, 2005
Beneficiaries (x 1,000) 585
  Retired & dependents.................. 435
  Survivors............................. 68
  Disabled & dependents................. 82
Annual benefit payments ($ mil) $6,917
  Retired & dependents................ $4,994
  Survivors........................... $1,029
  Disabled & dependents................ $894
Average monthly benefit
  Retired & dependents................ $1,096
  Disabled & dependents................ $981
  Widowed............................ $1,072

Medicare, July 2005
Enrollment (x 1,000)..................... 525
Payments ($ mil) $3,996

Medicaid, 2004
Beneficiaries (x 1,000)................... 501
Payments ($ mil) $3,696

State Children's Health Insurance Program, 2006
Enrollment (x 1,000)..................... 23.1
Expenditures ($ mil)................... $31.5

Persons without health insurance, 2006
Number (x 1,000)........................ 325
  percent............................ 9.4%
Number of children (x 1,000) 49
  percent of children 6.0%

Health care expenditures, 2004
Total expenditures.................... $22,167
  per capita $6,344

©2008 Information Publications, Inc.
All rights reserved. Photocopying prohibited.
877-544-INFO (4636) or www.informationpublications.com

4   Connecticut

Federal and state public aid

State unemployment insurance, 2006
Recipients, first payments (x 1,000) 119
Total payments ($ mil) $559
Average weekly benefit $304
Temporary Assistance for Needy Families, 2006
Recipients (x 1,000) 432.6
Families (x 1,000) 217.5
Supplemental Security Income, 2005
Recipients (x 1,000) 52.1
Payments ($ mil) $259.8
Food Stamp Program, 2006
Avg monthly participants (x 1,000) 210.3
Total benefits ($ mil) $239.1

Housing & Construction

Housing units
Total 2005 (estimate) 1,423,343
Total 2006 (estimate) 1,432,241
Seasonal or recreational use, 2006 22,144
Owner-occupied, 2006 921,382
  Median home value $298,900
  Homeowner vacancy rate 2.1%
Renter-occupied, 2006 404,061
  Median rent $886
  Rental vacancy rate 7.9%
Home ownership rate, 2005 . . . . 70.5%
Home ownership rate, 2006 . . . . 71.1%

New privately-owned housing units
Number authorized, 2006 (x 1,000) 9.2
  Value ($ mil) $1,874.2
Started 2005 (x 1,000, estimate) 8.5
Started 2006 (x 1,000, estimate) 8.5

Existing home sales
2005 (x 1,000) 80.4
2006 (x 1,000) 70.8

Government & Elections

State officials 2008
Governor . . . . M. Jodi Rell
        Republican, term expires 1/11
Lieutenant Governor . . . . Michael Fedele
Secretary of State . . . . Susan Bysiewicz
Attorney General . . . . Richard Blumenthal
Chief Justice . . . . Chase Rogers

Governorship
Minimum age 30
Length of term . . . . 4 years
Consecutive terms permitted . . . . . . not specified
Who succeeds . . . . Lieutenant Governor

Local governments by type, 2002
Total 580
  County 0
  Municipal 30
  Township 149
  School District 17
  Special District 384

State legislature
Name . . . . General Assembly
Upper chamber . . . . Senate
  Number of members 36
  Length of term . . . . 2 years
  Party in majority, 2008 . . . . Democratic
Lower chamber . . . . House of Representatives
  Number of members 151
  Length of term . . . . 2 years
  Party in majority, 2008 . . . . Democratic

Federal representation, 2008 (110th Congress)
Senator . . . . Christopher J. Dodd
  Party . . . . Democratic
  Year term expires 2011
Senator . . . . Joseph Lieberman
  Party . . . . Independent Democrat
  Year term expires 2013
Representatives, total 5
  Democrats 4
  Republicans 1

Voters in November 2006 election (estimate)
Total 1,219,997
  Male 571,821
  Female 648,176
  White 1,117,425
  Black 80,758
  Hispanic 29,616
  Asian 15,380

Presidential election, 2004
Total Popular Vote 1,578,769
  Kerry 857,488
  Bush 693,826
Total Electoral Votes 7

Votes cast for US Senators
2004
Total vote (x 1,000) 1,425
Leading party . . . . Democratic
Percent for leading party 66.4%
2006
Total vote (x 1,000) 1,135
Leading party . . . . Independent Democrat
Percent for leading party 49.8%

Votes cast for US Representatives
2004
Total vote (x 1,000) 1,429
  Democratic 786
  Republican 630
Leading party . . . . Democratic
Percent for leading party 55.0%
2006
Total vote (x 1,000) 1,075
  Democratic 649
  Republican 420
Leading party . . . . Democratic
Percent for leading party 48.9%

©2008 Information Publications, Inc.
All rights reserved. Photocopying prohibited.
877-544-INFO (4636) or www.informationpublications.com

State government employment, 2006
Full-time equivalent employees 61,971
Payroll ($ mil) $305.5

Local government employment, 2006
Full-time equivalent employees 126,251
Payroll ($ mil) $549.7

Women holding public office, 2008
US Congress............................... 1
Statewide elected office....................... 4
State legislature 53

Black public officials, 2002
Total....................................... 69
  US and state legislatures 14
  City/county/regional offices 46
  Judicial/law enforcement.................. 3
  Education/school boards.................. 6

Hispanic public officials, 2006
Total....................................... 29
  State executives & legislators 6
  City/county/regional offices 19
  Judicial/law enforcement.................. 0
  Education/school boards.................. 4

Governmental Finance

State government revenues, 2006
Total revenue (x $1,000).......... $22,896,537
  per capita $6,549.82
General revenue (x $1,000) $19,460,063
  Intergovernmental 4,176,892
  Taxes 12,131,894
    general sales....................3,040,683
    individual income tax 5,777,636
    corporate income tax 634,990
  Current charges...................1,573,469
  Miscellaneous 1,577,808

State government expenditure, 2006
Total expenditure (x $1,000) $20,674,608
  per capita $5,914.21
General expenditure (x $1,000) $17,771,850
  per capita, total.................. $5,083.84
    Education......................1,440.38
    Public welfare 1,407.69
    Health 219.97
    Hospitals.........................347.70
    Highways 229.12
    Police protection................. 56.57
    Corrections 176.78
    Natural resources 25.37
    Parks & recreation 16.56
    Governmental administration.......289.13
    Interest on general debt...........307.48

State debt & cash, 2006 ($ per capita)
Debt $6,875.68
Cash/security holdings..............$10,722.64

Federal government grants to state & local government, 2005 (x $1,000)
Total...............................$5,438,708
by Federal agency
  Defense 56,863
  Education 366,474
  Energy 47,693
  Environmental Protection Agency 34,677
  Health & Human Services. 3,377,354
  Homeland Security................... 25,469
  Housing & Urban Development...... 582,537
  Justice 63,904
  Labor 99,750
  Transportation 507,432
  Veterans Affairs...................7,247

Crime & Law Enforcement

Crime, 2006 (rates per 100,000 residents)
Property crimes 87,764
  Burglary 14,694
  Larceny 62,680
  Motor vehicle theft 10,390
  Property crime rate.................2,504.1
*Violent crimes.........................9,841
  Murder 108
  Forcible rape........................ 636
  Robbery......................... 4,241
  Aggravated assault 4,856
  Violent crime rate 280.8
Hate crimes............................ 180

Fraud and identity theft, 2006
Fraud complaints...................... 4,695
  rate per 100,000 residents 134.0
Identity theft complaints 2,305
  rate per 100,000 residents 65.8

Law enforcement agencies, 2006
Total agencies......................... 101
Total employees 9,703
  Officers 7,875
  Civilians 1,828

Prisoners, probation, and parole, 2006
Total prisoners........................ 20,566
  percent change, 12/31/05 to 12/31/06 ....5.8%
  in private facilities 0%
  in local jails .... NA
Sentenced to more than one year 13,746
  rate per 100,000 residents 392
Adults on probation 54,511
Adults on parole........................ 2,567

Prisoner demographics, June 30, 2005 (rate per 100,000 residents)
Male..................................1,030
Female 85
White................................. 211
Black..................................2,532
Hispanic 1,401

©2008 Information Publications, Inc.
All rights reserved. Photocopying prohibited.
877-544-INFO (4636) or www.informationpublications.com

Arrests, 2006

Total 96,616
   Persons under 18 years of age 15,185

Persons under sentence of death, 1/1/07

Total 8
   White 3
   Black 3
   Hispanic 2

State's highest court

Name . . . . .Supreme Court
Number of members 7
Length of term . . . . 8 years
Intermediate appeals court? . . . . .yes

Labor & Income

Civilian labor force, 2006 (x 1,000)

Total 1,858
   Men 982
   Women 876
   Persons 16-19 years 93
   White 1,592
   Black 182
   Hispanic 186

Civilian labor force as a percent of civilian non-institutional population, 2006

Total 67.9%
   Men 75.1
   Women 61.4
   Persons 16-19 years .48.3
   White 67.3
   Black 72.2
   Hispanic 70.1

Employment, 2006 (x 1,000)

Total 1,778
   Men 939
   Women 839
   Persons 16-19 years 80
   White 1,531
   Black 167
   Hispanic 170

Unemployment rate, 2006

Total 4.3%
   Men 4.4
   Women 4.2
   Persons 16-19 years .14.5
   White 3.8
   Black 8.1
   Hispanic 8.2

Full-time/part-time labor force, 2003 (x 1,000)

Full-time labor force, employed 1,346
Part-time labor force, employed 358
Unemployed, looking for
   Full-time work 80
   Part-time work 20
Mean duration of unemployment (weeks) 20.3
   Median 12.4

Labor unions, 2006

Membership (x 1,000) 247
   percent of employed 15.6%

Experienced civilian labor force by private industry, 2006

Total 1,425,174
   Natural resources & mining 5,868
   Construction 67,157
   Manufacturing 193,714
   Trade, transportation & utilities 307,295
   Information 37,730
   Finance 144,325
   Professional & business 205,869
   Education & health 272,738
   Leisure & hospitality 132,475
   Other 57,761

Experienced civilian labor force by occupation, May 2006

Management 90,860
Business & financial 84,160
Legal 12,760
Sales 179,080
Office & admin. support 294,610
Computers & math 46,360
Architecture & engineering 35,060
Arts & entertainment 20,600
Education 122,480
Social services 30,590
Health care practitioner & technical 89,820
Health care support 51,510
Maintenance & repair 55,590
Construction 55,190
Transportation & moving 94,760
Production 118,720
Farming, fishing & forestry 1,040

Hours and earnings of production workers on manufacturing payrolls, 2006

Average weekly hours 42.2
Average hourly earnings $19.78
Average weekly earnings $834.72

Income and poverty, 2006

Median household income $63,422
Personal income, per capita (current $) . . . $49,852
   in constant (2000) dollars $43,518
Persons below poverty level 8.3%

Average annual pay

2006 . . . . $54,814
   increase from 2005 . . . . 3.5%

Federal individual income tax returns, 2005

Returns filed 1,681,956
Adjusted gross income ($1,000) . . . $132,285,344
Total tax liability ($1,000) $22,513,429

Charitable contributions, 2004

Number of contributions 666.9
Total amount ($ mil) $2,690.0

©2008 Information Publications, Inc.
All rights reserved. Photocopying prohibited.
877-544-INFO (4636) or www.informationpublications.com

Economy, Business, Industry & Agriculture

Fortune 500 companies, 2007 11
Bankruptcy cases filed, FY 2007 5,572

Patents and trademarks issued, 2007
Patents 1,632
Trademarks 1,040

Business firm ownership, 2002
Women-owned 82,118
   Sales ($ mil) $12,216
Black-owned 10,309
   Sales ($ mil) $723
Hispanic-owned 9,408
   Sales ($ mil) $1,277
Asian-owned 7,170
   Sales ($ mil) $1,863
Amer. Indian/Alaska Native-owned 1,216
   Sales ($ mil) $148
Hawaiian/Pacific Islander-owned 167
   Sales ($ mil) $78

Gross domestic product, 2006 ($ mil)
Total gross domestic product $204,134
   Agriculture, forestry, fishing and
      hunting 353
   Mining 96
   Utilities 3,400
   Construction 6,726
   Manufacturing, durable goods 15,223
   Manufacturing, non-durable goods 8,324
   Wholesale trade .11,363
   Retail trade 11,725
   Transportation & warehousing 3,185
   Information 7,747
   Finance & insurance 33,640
   Real estate, rental & leasing 28,502
   Professional and technical services 15,369
   Educational services 3,102
   Health care and social assistance 15,295
   Accommodation/food services 3,672
   Other services, except government 4,039
   Government 18,347

Establishments, payroll, employees & receipts, by major industry group, 2005

Total 93,561
   Annual payroll ($1,000) $75,605,605
   Paid employees 1,529,827
Forestry, fishing & agriculture 81
   Annual payroll ($1,000) . . . . NA
   Paid employees . . . . NA
Mining 74
   Annual payroll ($1,000) $61,986
   Paid employees 911
   Receipts, 2002 ($1,000) $208,448

Utilities 140
   Annual payroll ($1,000) $1,000,312
   Paid employees 9,947
   Receipts, 2002 ($1,000) . . . . .NA
Construction 9,811
   Annual payroll ($1,000) $3,385,312
   Paid employees 62,362
   Receipts, 2002 ($1,000) $13,697,394
Manufacturing 5,037
   Annual payroll ($1,000) $9,766,644
   Paid employees 185,259
   Receipts, 2002 ($1,000) $45,053,345
Wholesale trade 4,671
   Annual payroll ($1,000) $4,873,666
   Paid employees 80,024
   Receipts, 2002 ($1,000) $86,932,049
Retail trade 13,928
   Annual payroll ($1,000) $5,083,890
   Paid employees 198,459
   Receipts, 2002 ($1,000) $41,952,682
Transportation & warehousing 1,694
   Annual payroll ($1,000) $1,436,078
   Paid employees 38,157
   Receipts, 2002 ($1,000) $4,014,398
Information 1,778
   Annual payroll ($1,000) $2,828,910
   Paid employees 41,534
   Receipts, 2002 ($1,000) . . . . .NA
Finance & insurance 6,145
   Annual payroll ($1,000) $15,586,173
   Paid employees 133,285
   Receipts, 2002 ($1,000) . . . . .NA
Professional, scientific & technical 10,224
   Annual payroll ($1,000) $6,581,420
   Paid employees 99,651
   Receipts, 2002 ($1,000) $14,610,345
Education 1,182
   Annual payroll ($1,000) $2,088,379
   Paid employees 58,583
   Receipts, 2002 ($1,000) $525,061
Health care & social assistance 9,651
   Annual payroll ($1,000) $9,326,294
   Paid employees 238,784
   Receipts, 2002 ($1,000) $18,512,454
Arts and entertainment 1,678
   Annual payroll ($1,000) $605,839
   Paid employees 23,250
   Receipts, 2002 ($1,000) $1,984,816
Real estate 3,544
   Annual payroll ($1,000) $1,081,044
   Paid employees 22,750
   Receipts, 2002 ($1,000) $4,603,410
Accommodation & food service 7,579
   Annual payroll ($1,000) $2,374,481
   Paid employees 128,777
   Receipts, 2002 ($1,000) $6,681,803

©2008 Information Publications, Inc.
All rights reserved. Photocopying prohibited.
877-544-INFO (4636) or www.informationpublications.com

Exports, 2006
Value of exported goods ($ mil) $12,238
   Manufactured $10,988
   Non-manufactured.................... $695

Foreign direct investment in US affiliates, 2004
Property, plants & equipment ($ mil) $12,517
Employment (x 1,000)..................102.7

Agriculture, 2006
Number of farms 4,200
Farm acreage (x 1,000) 360
   Acres per farm........................ 86
Farm marketings and income ($ mil)
Total................................$523.6
   Crops $372.3
   Livestock..........................$151.3
Net farm income $182.8

Principal commodities, in order by marketing receipts, 2005
Greenhouse/nursery, Dairy products, Chicken eggs, Aquaculture, Tobacco

Federal economic activity in state
Expenditures, 2005 ($ mil)
   Total............................. $30,774
      Per capita $8,790.67
   Defense $9,523
   Non-defense...................... $21,250
Defense department, 2006 ($ mil)
   Payroll $758
   Contract awards $7,781
   Grants $64
Homeland security grants ($1,000)
   2006.............................$13,521
   2007.............................$10,479

FDIC-insured financial institutions, 2005
Number................................ 57
Assets ($ billion) $63.3
Deposits ($ billion) $47.0

Fishing, 2006
Catch (x 1,000 lbs)....................11,746
Value ($1,000)....................... $36,892

Mining, 2006 ($ mil)
Total non-fuel mineral production $169
Percent of U.S. 0.26%

Communication, Energy & Transportation

Communication
Households with computers, 2003........ 69.2%
Households with internet access, 2003 .... 62.9%
High-speed internet providers 25
Total high-speed internet lines........ 1,251,241
   Residential 844,344
   Business.......................... 406,897
Wireless phone customers, 12/2006 2,705,023

FCC-licensed stations (as of January 1, 2008)
TV stations 13
FM radio stations......................... 61
AM radio stations 40

Energy
Energy consumption, 2004
   Total (trillion Btu)..................... 924
   Per capita (million Btu) 264.4
By source of production (trillion Btu)
   Coal 44
   Natural gas......................... 163
   Petroleum........................... 471
   Nuclear electric power 173
   Hydroelectric power.................... 5
By end-use sector (trillion Btu)
   Residential 304
   Commercial 211
   Industrial 123
   Transportation 285
Electric energy, 2005
   Primary source of electricity......... Nuclear
   Net generation (billion kWh) 33.5
      percent from renewable sources....... 3.7%
   Net summer capability (million kW) 8.0
   CO_2 emitted from generation 11.5
Natural gas utilities, 2005
   Customers (x 1,000) 531
   Sales (trillion Btu)................... 104
   Revenues ($ mil) $1,182
Nuclear plants, 2007 2
Total CO_2 emitted (million metric tons).....42.4
Energy spending, 2004 ($ mil) $10,595
   per capita $3,032
   Price per million Btu $15.86

Transportation, 2006
Public road & street mileage 21,249
   Urban...........................15,081
   Rural 6,168
   Interstate........................ 346
Vehicle miles of travel (millions) 31,743
   per capita 9,080.4
Total motor vehicle registrations....... 1,052,143
   Automobiles......................1,999,809
   Trucks 1,041,651
   Motorcycles 64,959
Licensed drivers 2,805,124
   19 years & under 104,155
Deaths from motor vehicle accidents 301
Gasoline consumed (x 1,000 gallons) 1,566,875
   per capita 448.2

Commuting Statistics, 2006
Average commute time (min) 24.1
   Drove to work alone 79.7%
   Carpooled........................... 8.4%
   Public transit 4.1%
   Walk to work 3.0%
   Work from home...................... 3.5%

©2008 Information Publications, Inc.
All rights reserved. Photocopying prohibited.
877-544-INFO (4636) or www.informationpublications.com

Delaware 1

State Summary

Capital city . . . . Dover
Governor. . . . . Ruth Ann Minner
Legislative Hall
Dover, DE 19902
302-577-3210
Admitted as a state 1787
Area (square miles) 2,489
Population, 2007 (estimate). 864,764
Largest city . . . . Wilmington
Population, 2006 72,826
Personal income per capita, 2006
(in current dollars) $39,022
Gross domestic product, 2006 ($ mil) $60,361

Leading industries by payroll, 2005

Finance & Insurance, Health care/Social assistance, Professional/Scientific/Technical

Leading agricultural commodities
by receipts, 2005

Broilers, Corn, Greenhouse/nursery, Soybeans,
Dairy products

Geography & Environment

Total area (square miles). 2,489
land 1,954
water 536
Federally-owned land, 2004 (acres) 25,874
percent. 2.0%
Highest point . . . . Ebright Road
elevation (feet) 442
Lowest point. . . . . .Atlantic Ocean
elevation (feet) . . . . sea level
General coastline (miles) 28
Tidal shoreline (miles) 381
Cropland, 2003 (x 1,000 acres) 458
Forest land, 2003 (x 1,000 acres). 341
Capital city . . . . Dover
Population 2000 .32,135
Population 2006 .34,745
Largest city . . . . Wilmington
Population 2000 72,664
Population 2006 72,826

Number of cities with over 100,000 population

1990 0
2000 0
2006 0

State park and recreation areas, 2005

Area (x 1,000 acres). 24
Number of visitors (x 1,000) 4,557
Revenues ($1,000) $11,366
percent of operating expenditures. 39.3%

National forest system land, 2007

Acres 0

Demographics & Population Characteristics

Population

1980 594,338
1990 666,168
2000 783,600
2006 853,476
Male. 414,244
Female 439,232
Living in group quarters, 2006. 24,915
percent of total. 2.9%
2007 (estimate). 864,764
persons per square mile of land 442.6
2008 (projected). 865,705
2010 (projected) 884,342
2020 (projected). 963,209
2030 (projected). 1,012,658

Population of Core-Based Statistical Areas
(formerly Metropolitan Areas), x 1,000

	CBSA	Non-CBSA
1990	666	0
2000	784	0
2006	853	0

Change in population, 2000-2007

Number 81,164
percent. 10.4%
Natural increase (births minus deaths) 31,157
Net internal migration 39,573
Net international migration 13,924

Persons by age, 2006

Under 5 years 56,692
5 to 17 years 146,674
18 years and over .650,110
65 years and over .114,574
85 years and over .14,553
Median age 37.5

Persons by age, 2010 (projected)

Under 5 years 58,179
18 and over 682,134
65 and over 124,972
Median age 39.4

Race, 2006

One Race
White. 636,116
Black or African American 178,201
Asian 23,680
American Indian/Alaska Native. 3,454
Hawaiian Native/Pacific Islander. 498
Two or more races. 11,527

Persons of Hispanic origin, 2006

Total Hispanic or Latino 53,836
Mexican. 24,631
Puerto Rican 14,715
Cuban 890

©2008 Information Publications, Inc.
All rights reserved. Photocopying prohibited.
877-544-INFO (4636) or www.informationpublications.com

Persons of Asian origin, 2006

Total Asian 24,413
  Asian Indian. 11,424
  Chinese 5,067
  Filipino 2,878
  Japanese 949
  Korean. 1,797
  Vietnamese. 1,314

Marital status, 2006

Population 15 years & over 685,569
  Never married 214,894
  Married. 351,482
  Separated 16,713
  Widowed. 44,350
  Divorced 74,843

Language spoken at home, 2006

Population 5 years and older. 796,385
  English only 700,255
  Spanish 51,762
  French 6,214
  German. 4,391
  Chinese 4,490

Households & families, 2006

Households. 320,110
  with persons under 18 years 107,624
  with persons over 65 years. 78,042
  persons per household 2.59
Families. 213,565
  persons per family. 3.15
Married couples. .157,209
Female householder,
  no husband present. 41,147
One-person households 86,967

Nativity, 2006

Number of residents born in state 400,956
  percent of population 47.0%

Immigration & naturalization, 2006

Legal permanent residents admitted 2,265
Persons naturalized .1,187
Non-immigrant admissions 34,511

Vital Statistics and Health

Marriages

2004 5,095
2005 5,015
2006 5,153

Divorces

2004 3,108
2005 3,251
2006 3,849

Health risks, 2006

Percent of adults who are:
  Smokers. 21.7%
  Overweight (BMI > 25). 63.8%
  Obese (BMI > 30). 26.0%

Births

2005 11,643
  Birthrate (per 1,000). 13.8
  White. 8,192
  Black 2,912
  Hispanic 1,652
  Asian/Pacific Islander 501
  Amer. Indian/Alaska Native 38
  Low birth weight (2,500g or less) 9.5%
  Cesarian births 30.0%
  Preterm births 14.0%
  To unmarried mothers. 44.3%
  Twin births (per 1,000) 35.6
  Triplets or higher order (per 100,000). . . .180.5
2006 (preliminary). .11,988
  rate per 1,000 . . . . .14.0

Deaths

2004
All causes 7,143
  rate per 100,000. . . . . .823.3
Heart disease 2,015
  rate per 100,000. 232.3
Malignant neoplasms 1,827
  rate per 100,000. . . . . .207.4
Cerebrovascular disease. 350
  rate per 100,000. . . . . .40.6
Chronic lower respiratory disease 345
  rate per 100,000. . . . . .39.8
Diabetes. 210
  rate per 100,000. . . . . .24.1
2005 (preliminary). .7,472
  rate per 100,000. . . . . 830.5
2006 (provisional) 7,111

Infant deaths

2004 98
  rate per 1,000 . . . . .8.6
2005 (provisional) 88
  rate per 1,000 . . . . .7.6

Exercise routines, 2005

None. 23.3%
Moderate or greater. 45.2%
Vigorous 24.9%

Abortions, 2004

Total performed in state. 4,588
  rate per 1,000 women age 15-44 26
  % obtained by out-of-state residents 28.9%

Physicians, 2005

Total. 2,090
  rate per 100,000 persons 248

Community hospitals, 2005

Number of hospitals 6
Beds (x 1,000). 2.0
Patients admitted (x 1,000) 104
Average daily census (x 1,000) 1.7
Average cost per day $1,715
Outpatient visits (x 1 mil) 1.9

©2008 Information Publications, Inc.
All rights reserved. Photocopying prohibited.
877-544-INFO (4636) or www.informationpublications.com

Disability status of population, 2006

5 to 15 years 6.7%
16 to 64 years 12.6%
65 years and over 38.8%

Education

Educational attainment, 2006

Population over 25 years 566,312
Less than 9th grade. 4.8%
High school graduate or more 85.5%
College graduate or more. 27.0%
Graduate or professional degree. 10.5%

Public school enrollment, 2005-06

Total 120,937
Pre-kindergarten through grade 8. 84,639
Grades 9 through 12 36,298

Graduating public high school seniors, 2004-05

Diplomas (incl. GED and others) 7,102

SAT scores, 2007

Average critical reading score 497
Average writing score 486
Average math score 496
Percent of graduates taking test 72%

Public school teachers, 2006-07 (estimate)

Total (x 1,000) 8.0
Elementary 4.0
Secondary 4.1
Average salary $54,680
Elementary $54,855
Secondary $54,509

State receipts & expenditures for public schools, 2006-07 (estimate)

Revenue receipts ($ mil) $1,676
Expenditures
Total ($ mil) $1,898
Per capita $1,800
Per pupil $13,380

NAEP proficiency scores, 2007

	Reading		Math	
	Basic	Proficient	Basic	Proficient
Grade 4	72.6%	33.8%	86.9%	40.0%
Grade 8	77.2%	30.5%	74.3%	31.3%

Higher education enrollment, fall 2005

Total 12,930
Full-time men 2,758
Full-time women 4,009
Part-time men 2,118
Part-time women 4,045

Minority enrollment in institutions of higher education, 2005

Black, non-Hispanic 10,169
Hispanic 1,818
Asian/Pacific Islander 1,500
American Indian/Alaska Native 154

Institutions of higher education, 2005-06

Total 10
Public 5
Private 5

Earned degrees conferred, 2004-05

Associate's 1,262
Bachelor's 5,247
Master's 2,031
First-professional 335
Doctor's 234

Public Libraries, 2006

Number of libraries 21
Number of outlets 35
Annual visits per capita 5.0
Circulation per capita 6.9

State & local financial support for higher education, FY 2006

Full-time equivalent enrollment (x 1,000) 31.3
Appropriations per FTE $6,632

Social Insurance & Welfare Programs

Social Security benefits & beneficiaries, 2005

Beneficiaries (x 1,000) 152
Retired & dependents 108
Survivors 19
Disabled & dependents 26
Annual benefit payments ($ mil) $1,725
Retired & dependents $1,173
Survivors $268
Disabled & dependents $284
Average monthly benefit
Retired & dependents $1,054
Disabled & dependents $984
Widowed $1,040

Medicare, July 2005

Enrollment (x 1,000) 128
Payments ($ mil) $1,021

Medicaid, 2004

Beneficiaries (x 1,000) 158
Payments ($ mil) $1,269

State Children's Health Insurance Program, 2006

Enrollment (x 1,000) 10.8
Expenditures ($ mil) $10.8

Persons without health insurance, 2006

Number (x 1,000) 105
percent 12.2%
Number of children (x 1,000) 24
percent of children 11.7%

Health care expenditures, 2004

Total expenditures $5,226
per capita $6,306

©2008 Information Publications, Inc.
All rights reserved. Photocopying prohibited.
877-544-INFO (4636) or www.informationpublications.com

4   Delaware

Federal and state public aid
State unemployment insurance, 2006
Recipients, first payments (x 1,000) 23
Total payments ($ mil) $97
Average weekly benefit $251
Temporary Assistance for Needy Families, 2006
Recipients (x 1,000) 142.3
Families (x 1,000) 64.4
Supplemental Security Income, 2005
Recipients (x 1,000) 13.7
Payments ($ mil) $65.7
Food Stamp Program, 2006
Avg monthly participants (x 1,000) 65.7
Total benefits ($ mil) $70.2

Housing & Construction

Housing units
Total 2005 (estimate) 374,872
Total 2006 (estimate) 382,828
Seasonal or recreational use, 2006 31,435
Owner-occupied, 2006 238,194
   Median home value $227,100
   Homeowner vacancy rate 2.6%
Renter-occupied, 2006 81,916
   Median rent $830
   Rental vacancy rate 12.2%
Home ownership rate, 2005 . . . . 75.8%
Home ownership rate, 2006 . . . . 76.8%

New privately-owned housing units
Number authorized, 2006 (x 1,000) 6.5
   Value ($ mil) $785.5
Started 2005 (x 1,000, estimate) 5.9
Started 2006 (x 1,000, estimate) 5.7

Existing home sales
2005 (x 1,000) 19.3
2006 (x 1,000) 17.8

Government & Elections

State officials 2008
Governor . . . . Ruth Ann Minner
          Democratic, term expires 1/09
Lieutenant Governor . . . . John Carney
Secretary of State . . . . . . Harriet Smith Windsor
Attorney General . . . . .Joseph Biden III
Chief Justice .Myron Steele

Governorship
Minimum age 30
Length of term . . . . 4 years
Consecutive terms permitted 2
Who succeeds . . . . Lieutenant Governor

Local governments by type, 2002
Total 339
   County 3
   Municipal 57
   Township 0
   School District 19
   Special District 260

State legislature
Name . . . . General Assembly
Upper chamber . . . . .Senate
   Number of members 21
   Length of term . . . . 4 years
   Party in majority, 2008 . . . . Democratic
Lower chamber . . . . House of Representatives
   Number of members 41
   Length of term . . . . 2 years
   Party in majority, 2008 . . . . Republican

Federal representation, 2008 (110th Congress)
Senator . . . . Joseph R. Biden Jr
   Party . . . . Democratic
   Year term expires 2009
Senator . . . . Thomas Carper
   Party . . . . Democratic
   Year term expires 2013
Representatives, total 1
   Democrats 0
   Republicans 1

Voters in November 2006 election (estimate)
Total 275,407
   Male 123,761
   Female 151,647
   White 219,948
   Black 47,276
   Hispanic 2,290
   Asian 5,417

Presidential election, 2004
Total Popular Vote 375,190
   Kerry 200,152
   Bush 171,660
Total Electoral Votes 3

Votes cast for US Senators
2004
Total vote (x 1,000) . . . . NA
Leading party . . . . NA
Percent for leading party . . . . NA
2006
Total vote (x 1,000) 243
Leading party . . . . Democratic
Percent for leading party 70.2%

Votes cast for US Representatives
2004
Total vote (x 1,000) 356
   Democratic 106
   Republican 246
Leading party . . . . Republican
Percent for leading party 69.1%
2006
Total vote (x 1,000) 252
   Democratic 98
   Republican 144
Leading party . . . . Republican
Percent for leading party 57.2%

©2008 Information Publications, Inc.
All rights reserved. Photocopying prohibited.
877-544-INFO (4636) or www.informationpublications.com

State government employment, 2006
Full-time equivalent employees 25,614
Payroll ($ mil) $98.8

Local government employment, 2006
Full-time equivalent employees 23,874
Payroll ($ mil) $92.7

Women holding public office, 2008
US Congress.............................. 0
Statewide elected office...................... 1
State legislature 19

Black public officials, 2002
Total...................................... 29
    US and state legislatures 4
    City/county/regional offices 18
    Judicial/law enforcement.................. 0
    Education/school boards.................. 7

Hispanic public officials, 2006
Total....................................... 2
    State executives & legislators 1
    City/county/regional offices 1
    Judicial/law enforcement.................. 0
    Education/school boards.................. 0

Governmental Finance

State government revenues, 2006
Total revenue (x $1,000)............\$6,839,982
    per capita \$8,021.12
General revenue (x $1,000) \$5,954,563
    Intergovernmental 1,218,950
    Taxes 2,860,749
        general sales............................ 0
        individual income tax 1,018,633
        corporate income tax 295,577
    Current charges................... 807,693
    Miscellaneous 1,067,171

State government expenditure, 2006
Total expenditure (x $1,000).........\$6,519,932
    per capita \$7,645.80
General expenditure (x $1,000) \$6,019,481
    per capita, total.................. \$7,058.93
    Education 2,414.19
    Public welfare 1,472.32
    Health............................391.50
    Hospitals..........................71.20
    Highways 590.88
    Police protection....................118.81
    Corrections 287.00
    Natural resources 98.75
    Parks & recreation 75.13
    Governmental administration.......569.02
    Interest on general debt 202.84

State debt & cash, 2006 ($ per capita)
Debt \$4,930.38
Cash/security holdings..............\$13,563.53

Federal government grants to state & local government, 2005 (x $1,000)
Total...............................\$1,265,225
by Federal agency
    Defense 22,524
    Education 119,362
    Energy 11,104
    Environmental Protection Agency 27,974
    Health & Human Services. 661,022
    Homeland Security.................3,478
    Housing & Urban Development....... 95,821
    Justice 26,491
    Labor............................ 23,423
    Transportation 140,992
    Veterans Affairs...................19,478

Crime & Law Enforcement

Crime, 2006 (rates per 100,000 residents)
Property crimes 29,171
    Burglary 6,189
    Larceny 20,166
    Motor vehicle theft 2,816
    Property crime rate................. 3,417.9
Violent crimes.........................5,817
    Murder 42
    Forcible rape....................... 400
    Robbery...........................1,735
    Aggravated assault 3,640
    Violent crime rate 681.6
Hate crimes............................. 72

Fraud and identity theft, 2006
Fraud complaints.......................1,119
    rate per 100,000 residents 131.1
Identity theft complaints 569
    rate per 100,000 residents 66.7

Law enforcement agencies, 2006
Total agencies............................. 53
Total employees 3,085
    Officers 2,247
    Civilians 838

Prisoners, probation, and parole, 2006
Total prisoners.........................7,206
    percent change, 12/31/05 to 12/31/06 .... 3.4%
    in private facilities 0%
    in local jails .... NA
Sentenced to more than one year 4,195
    rate per 100,000 residents 488
Adults on probation 16,958
Adults on parole......................... 544

Prisoner demographics, June 30, 2005 (rate per 100,000 residents)
Male....................................1,547
Female................................. 128
White................................. 396
Black..................................2,517
Hispanic 683

©2008 Information Publications, Inc.
All rights reserved. Photocopying prohibited.
877-544-INFO (4636) or www.informationpublications.com

6　Delaware

Arrests, 2006
Total 39,832
　　Persons under 18 years of age 7,448

Persons under sentence of death, 1/1/07
Total 18
　　White 8
　　Black 7
　　Hispanic 3

State's highest court
Name . . . . .Supreme Court
Number of members 5
Length of term . . . . 12 years
Intermediate appeals court? . . . . no

Labor & Income

Civilian labor force, 2006 (x 1,000)
Total 448
　　Men 233
　　Women 215
　　Persons 16-19 years 23
　　White 337
　　Black 91
　　Hispanic 29

Civilian labor force as a percent of civilian non-institutional population, 2006
Total 67.1%
　　Men 73.3
　　Women 61.5
　　Persons 16-19 years 48.3
　　White 66.0
　　Black 71.4
　　Hispanic 74.4

Employment, 2006 (x 1,000)
Total 432
　　Men 224
　　Women 208
　　Persons 16-19 years 21
　　White 327
　　Black 86
　　Hispanic 28

Unemployment rate, 2006
Total 3.5%
　　Men 3.8
　　Women 3.2
　　Persons 16-19 years 8.9
　　White 3.0
　　Black 5.5
　　Hispanic 4.0

Full-time/part-time labor force, 2003 (x 1,000)
Full-time labor force, employed 338
Part-time labor force, employed 61
Unemployed, looking for
　　Full-time work 16
　　Part-time work 2
Mean duration of unemployment (weeks) 16.3
　　Median 10.3

Labor unions, 2006
Membership (x 1,000) 43
　　percent of employed 10.8%

Experienced civilian labor force by private industry, 2006
Total 364,323
　　Natural resources & mining 1,406
　　Construction 29,247
　　Manufacturing 33,245
　　Trade, transportation & utilities 81,169
　　Information 6,710
　　Finance 44,031
　　Professional & business 62,212
　　Education & health 52,085
　　Leisure & hospitality 40,927
　　Other 13,291

Experienced civilian labor force by occupation, May 2006
Management 18,600
Business & financial 22,750
Legal 4,580
Sales 47,700
Office & admin. support 78,670
Computers & math 12,560
Architecture & engineering . . . . NA
Arts & entertainment 4,660
Education 21,980
Social services 6,490
Health care practitioner & technical 22,030
Health care support .9,770
Maintenance & repair 16,350
Construction 23,570
Transportation & moving 25,390
Production 26,730
Farming, fishing & forestry 930

Hours and earnings of production workers on manufacturing payrolls, 2006
Average weekly hours .39.9
Average hourly earnings $18.13
Average weekly earnings $723.39

Income and poverty, 2006
Median household income $52,833
Personal income, per capita (current $) . . . $39,022
　　in constant (2000) dollars $34,064
Persons below poverty level 11.1%

Average annual pay
2006 . . . . $46,285
　　increase from 2005 . . . . 3.7%

Federal individual income tax returns, 2005
Returns filed 402,938
Adjusted gross income ($1,000) $23,183,670
Total tax liability ($1,000) $3,086,150

Charitable contributions, 2004
Number of contributions 129.0
Total amount ($ mil) $483.3

©2008 Information Publications, Inc.
All rights reserved. Photocopying prohibited.
877-544-INFO (4636) or www.informationpublications.com

Economy, Business, Industry & Agriculture

Fortune 500 companies, 2007 1
Bankruptcy cases filed, FY 2007 1,897

Patents and trademarks issued, 2007
Patents 353
Trademarks 23,801

Business firm ownership, 2002
Women-owned 15,344
   Sales ($ mil) $2,021
Black-owned 4,258
   Sales ($ mil) $215
Hispanic-owned 879
   Sales ($ mil) $137
Asian-owned 1,895
   Sales ($ mil) $618
Amer. Indian/Alaska Native-owned 333
   Sales ($ mil) . . . . NA
Hawaiian/Pacific Islander-owned 17
   Sales ($ mil) . . . . NA

Gross domestic product, 2006 ($ mil)
Total gross domestic product $60,361
   Agriculture, forestry, fishing and
      hunting 398
   Mining . . . . NA
   Utilities 1,070
   Construction . . . . NA
   Manufacturing, durable goods 1,262
   Manufacturing, non-durable goods 3,292
   Wholesale trade 2,264
   Retail trade 2,504
   Transportation & warehousing 717
   Information 1,075
   Finance & insurance 19,818
   Real estate, rental & leasing 7,124
   Professional and technical services 3,545
   Educational services 328
   Health care and social assistance 3,083
   Accommodation/food services 919
   Other services, except government 1,034
   Government 5,168

Establishments, payroll, employees & receipts, by major industry group, 2005

Total 25,319
   Annual payroll ($1,000) $16,875,311
   Paid employees 392,840
Forestry, fishing & agriculture 44
   Annual payroll ($1,000) . . . . NA
   Paid employees . . . . NA
Mining 28
   Annual payroll ($1,000) . . . . NA
   Paid employees . . . . NA
   Receipts, 2002 ($1,000) $13,860

Utilities 47
   Annual payroll ($1,000) $205,557
   Paid employees 2,593
   Receipts, 2002 ($1,000) . . . . .NA
Construction 2,709
   Annual payroll ($1,000) $1,003,802
   Paid employees 23,925
   Receipts, 2002 ($1,000) $3,882,206
Manufacturing 652
   Annual payroll ($1,000) $1,661,304
   Paid employees 35,624
   Receipts, 2002 ($1,000) $16,417,927
Wholesale trade 999
   Annual payroll ($1,000) $1,399,099
   Paid employees 20,040
   Receipts, 2002 ($1,000) $17,292,794
Retail trade 3,842
   Annual payroll ($1,000) $1,298,046
   Paid employees 54,524
   Receipts, 2002 ($1,000) $10,912,971
Transportation & warehousing 740
   Annual payroll ($1,000) $475,939
   Paid employees 15,054
   Receipts, 2002 ($1,000) $749,566
Information 407
   Annual payroll ($1,000) $499,397
   Paid employees .9,510
   Receipts, 2002 ($1,000) . . . . .NA
Finance & insurance 2,082
   Annual payroll ($1,000) $2,896,158
   Paid employees 40,894
   Receipts, 2002 ($1,000) . . . . .NA
Professional, scientific & technical 2,460
   Annual payroll ($1,000) $1,895,569
   Paid employees .27,202
   Receipts, 2002 ($1,000) $3,135,436
Education 263
   Annual payroll ($1,000) $198,567
   Paid employees 6,426
   Receipts, 2002 ($1,000) $106,335
Health care & social assistance 2,242
   Annual payroll ($1,000) $2,085,645
   Paid employees 51,444
   Receipts, 2002 ($1,000) $3,792,091
Arts and entertainment 376
   Annual payroll ($1,000) $166,810
   Paid employees .6,702
   Receipts, 2002 ($1,000) $675,763
Real estate 1,215
   Annual payroll ($1,000) $243,068
   Paid employees 6,680
   Receipts, 2002 ($1,000) $6,948,051
Accommodation & food service 1,722
   Annual payroll ($1,000) $483,637
   Paid employees .31,094
   Receipts, 2002 ($1,000) $1,231,595

©2008 Information Publications, Inc.
All rights reserved. Photocopying prohibited.
877-544-INFO (4636) or www.informationpublications.com

8 Delaware

Exports, 2006
Value of exported goods ($ mil) $3,890
   Manufactured $3,593
   Non-manufactured..................... $39

Foreign direct investment in US affiliates, 2004
Property, plants & equipment ($ mil) $4,508
Employment (x 1,000)...................26.1

Agriculture, 2006
Number of farms 2,300
Farm acreage (x 1,000) 515
   Acres per farm 224
Farm marketings and income ($ mil)
Total $969.1
   Crops.............................$182.7
   Livestock.........................$786.4
Net farm income $388.2

**Principal commodities, in order by
  marketing receipts, 2005**
Broilers, Corn, Greenhouse/nursery, Soybeans,
         Dairy products

Federal economic activity in state
Expenditures, 2005 ($ mil)
  Total.............................. $5,495
    Per capita $6,527.79
  Defense $588
  Non-defense....................... $4,907
Defense department, 2006 ($ mil)
  Payroll............................. $420
  Contract awards $125
  Grants $21
Homeland security grants ($1,000)
  2006............................. $10,296
  2007.............................. $6,684

FDIC-insured financial institutions, 2005
Number.................................. 34
Assets ($ billion) $559.6
Deposits ($ billion) $255.1

Fishing, 2006
Catch (x 1,000 lbs)..................... 4,380
Value ($1,000)......................... $5,692

Mining, 2006 ($ mil)
Total non-fuel mineral production $22
Percent of U.S. 0.03%

Communication, Energy & Transportation

Communication
Households with computers, 2003........ 59.5%
Households with internet access, 2003 .... 53.2%
High-speed internet providers 22
Total high-speed internet lines........ 273,734
   Residential 169,563
   Business..........................104,171
Wireless phone customers, 12/2006 682,636

FCC-licensed stations (as of January 1, 2008)
TV stations 3
FM radio stations.......................... 21
AM radio stations 10

Energy
Energy consumption, 2004
  Total (trillion Btu)..................... 305
  Per capita (million Btu) 367.8
By source of production (trillion Btu)
  Coal 54
  Natural gas............................ 50
  Petroleum............................ 141
  Nuclear electric power 0
  Hydroelectric power................... 0
By end-use sector (trillion Btu)
  Residential 69
  Commercial 57
  Industrial 109
  Transportation 69
Electric energy, 2005
  Primary source of electricity........... Coal
  Net generation (billion kWh) 8.1
    percent from renewable sources........ NA
  Net summer capability (million kW) 3.4
  CO_2 emitted from generation 6.8
Natural gas utilities, 2005
  Customers (x 1,000) 149
  Sales (trillion Btu)...................... 35
  Revenues ($ mil) $262
Nuclear plants, 2007 0
Total CO_2 emitted (million metric tons)......17.2
Energy spending, 2004 ($ mil) $2,541
  per capita $3,066
  Price per million Btu $13.64

Transportation, 2006
Public road & street mileage 6,179
  Urban........................... 2,920
  Rural 3,259
  Interstate.......................... 41
Vehicle miles of travel (millions) 9,442
  per capita 11,072.5
Total motor vehicle registrations........813,188
  Automobiles...................... 432,509
  Trucks 378,512
  Motorcycles 22,786
Licensed drivers 619,877
  19 years & under 29,672
Deaths from motor vehicle accidents 148
Gasoline consumed (x 1,000 gallons) 458,885
  per capita 538.1

Commuting Statistics, 2006
Average commute time (min) 23.6
  Drove to work alone 80.8%
  Carpooled.......................... 9.4%
  Public transit 2.8%
  Walk to work 2.7%
  Work from home 2.6%

©2008 Information Publications, Inc.
All rights reserved. Photocopying prohibited.
877-544-INFO (4636) or www.informationpublications.com

District Summary

City...................... Washington, DC
Mayor........................ Adrian Fenty

John A. Wilson Building
1350 Pennsylvania Ave NW
Washington, DC 20004
202-727-1000

Founded............................... 1790
Area (square miles)........................ 68
Population, 2007 (estimate)............ 588,292
Largest city.................. Washington, DC
    Population, 2006.............. 581,530
Personal income per capita, 2006
    (in current dollars)................. $55,755
Gross domestic product, 2006 ($ mil) $87,664

Leading industries by payroll, 2005

Professional/Scientific/Technical, Health care/
    Social assistance, Information

Leading agricultural commodities by receipts, 2005

NA

Geography & Environment

Total area (square miles)................... 68
    land.................................. 61
    water 7
Federally-owned land, 2004 (acres) 9,631
    percent...............................24.7%
Highest point ....Tenleytown
    elevation (feet) 410
Lowest point.................. Potomac River
    elevation (feet) .... sea level
General coastline (miles) 0
Tidal shoreline (miles) 0
Cropland, 2003 (x 1,000 acres) .... NA
Forest land, 2003 (x 1,000 acres)........... NA
Capital city .... Washington, DC
    Population 2000 572,059
    Population 2006 581,530
Largest city .... Washington, DC
    Population 2000 572,059
    Population 2006 581,530

Number of cities with over 100,000 population

1990 1
2000 1
2006 1

State park and recreation areas, 2005

Area (x 1,000 acres)...................... NA
Number of visitors (x 1,000) .... NA
Revenues ($1,000) .... NA
    percent of operating expenditures........ NA

National forest system land, 2007

Acres 0

Demographics & Population Characteristics

Population

1980 638,333
1990 606,900
2000 572,059
2006 581,530
    Male.............................. 272,664
    Female............................ 308,866
Living in group quarters, 2006.......... 35,225
    percent of total...................... 6.1%
2007 (estimate)...................... 588,292
    persons per square mile of land 9,644.1
2008 (projected)..................... 538,487
2010 (projected).....................529,785
2020 (projected)..................... 480,540
2030 (projected).....................433,414

Population of Core-Based Statistical Areas (formerly Metropolitan Areas), x 1,000

	CBSA	Non-CBSA
1990	607	0
2000	572	0
2006	582	0

Change in population, 2000-2007

Number 16,233
    percent...............................2.8%
Natural increase (births minus deaths) 15,596
Net internal migration ....-43,431
Net international migration 25,783

Persons by age, 2006

Under 5 years 34,948
5 to 17 years 79,933
18 years and over 466,649
65 years and over 71,331
85 years and over 10,770
    Median age...........................35.0

Persons by age, 2010 (projected)

Under 5 years 41,737
18 and over 415,721
65 and over 61,036
    Median age...........................33.8

Race, 2006

One Race
    White............................ 223,033
    Black or African American 328,566
    Asian 18,871
    American Indian/Alaska Native.........2,161
    Hawaiian Native/Pacific Islander......... 511
Two or more races...................... 8,388

Persons of Hispanic origin, 2006

Total Hispanic or Latino 47,775
    Mexican 6,127
    Puerto Rican 2,744
    Cuban 2,346

©2008 Information Publications, Inc.
All rights reserved. Photocopying prohibited.
877-544-INFO (4636) or www.informationpublications.com

Persons of Asian origin, 2006

Total Asian 19,827
  Asian Indian........................5,430
  Chinese 5,261
  Filipino 2,652
  Japanese 382
  Korean............................1,327
  Vietnamese........................ 2,083

Marital status, 2006

Population 15 years & over 486,138
  Never married 262,607
  Married.......................... 147,417
  Separated 16,392
  Widowed.......................... 32,502
  Divorced 43,612

Language spoken at home, 2006

Population 5 years and older........... 546,550
  English only 462,774
  Spanish 45,023
  French 9,791
  German 2,325
  Chinese 3,022

Households & families, 2006

Households........................ 250,456
  with persons under 18 years 53,390
  with persons over 65 years........... 54,239
  persons per household 2.18
Families.......................... 108,759
  persons per family.....................3.24
Married couples.................... 55,871
Female householder,
  no husband present.................. 43,487
One-person households 118,150

Nativity, 2006

Number of residents born in district.... 232,943
  percent of population 40.1%

Immigration & naturalization, 2006

Legal permanent residents admitted.......3,775
Persons naturalized 1,089
Non-immigrant admissions 312,585

Vital Statistics and Health

Marriages

2004 2,925
2005 2,344
2006 2,276

Divorces

2004 1,043
2005 1,145
2006 1,254

Health risks, 2006

Percent of adults who are:
  Smokers........................... 17.9%
  Overweight (BMI > 25)..............54.6%
  Obese (BMI > 30).....................22.5%

Births

2005 7,971
  Birthrate (per 1,000)...................14.5
  White...........................2,401
  Black 5,368
  Hispanic 1,111
  Asian/Pacific Islander 195
  Amer. Indian/Alaska Native............. 7
  Low birth weight (2,500g or less)...... 11.2%
  Cesarian births 30.5%
  Preterm births....................... 15.9%
  To unmarried mothers.............. 56.0%
  Twin births (per 1,000) 34.5
  Triplets or higher order (per 100,000)..... NA
2006 (preliminary)..................... 8,529
  rate per 1,000 ....14.7

Deaths

2004
All causes 5,454
  rate per 100,000....................974.0
Heart disease 1,544
  rate per 100,000....................274.9
Malignant neoplasms 1,152
  rate per 100,000....................207.0
Cerebrovascular disease.................. 218
  rate per 100,000....................38.9
Chronic lower respiratory disease 165
  rate per 100,000....................29.5
Diabetes............................ 224
  rate per 100,000....................40.2
2005 (preliminary)....................5,483
  rate per 100,000....................971.4
2006 (provisional) 5,177

Infant deaths

2004 95
  rate per 1,000 ....12.0
2005 (provisional) 74
  rate per 1,000 ....10.2

Exercise routines, 2005

None............................22.5%
Moderate or greater.................... 53.1%
Vigorous 31.5%

Abortions, 2004

Total performed in district 2,401
  rate per 1,000 women age 15-44.......... 18
  % obtained by non-DC residents 52.6%

Physicians, 2005

Total................................ 4,483
  rate per 100,000 persons 770

Community hospitals, 2005

Number of hospitals 11
Beds (x 1,000)..........................3.5
Patients admitted (x 1,000) 141
Average daily census (x 1,000) 2.7
Average cost per day $1,910
Outpatient visits (x 1 mil) 1.6

©2008 Information Publications, Inc.
All rights reserved. Photocopying prohibited.
877-544-INFO (4636) or www.informationpublications.com

Disability status of population, 2006
5 to 15 years 7.9%
16 to 64 years 11.1%
65 years and over 37.6%

Education

Educational attainment, 2006
Population over 25 years 395,630
  Less than 9th grade................. 6.3%
  High school graduate or more 84.3%
  College graduate or more............. 45.9%
  Graduate or professional degree........ 25.4%

Public school enrollment, 2005-06
Total................................. 76,876
  Pre-kindergarten through grade 8...... 52,186
  Grades 9 through 12.................. 18,769

Graduating public high school seniors, 2004-05
Diplomas (incl. GED and others) 3,098

SAT scores, 2007
Average critical reading score............. 478
Average writing score 471
Average math score 462
Percent of graduates taking test 78%

Public school teachers, 2006-07 (estimate)
Total (x 1,000) 5.5
  Elementary........................ 3.6
  Secondary......................... 1.9
Average salary $59,000
  Elementary....................... $59,000
  Secondary........................ $59,000

District receipts & expenditures for public schools, 2006-07 (estimate)
Revenue receipts ($ mil) $882
Expenditures
Total ($ mil) $1,228
  Per capita $1,685
  Per pupil $18,260

NAEP proficiency scores, 2007
	Reading		Math	
	Basic	Proficient	Basic	Proficient
Grade 4	38.7%	13.8%	49.3%	13.5%
Grade 8	47.9%	12.1%	34.1%	8.0%

Higher education enrollment, fall 2005
Total................................. 99,302
  Full-time men 24,900
  Full-time women.................... 34,850
  Part-time men 15,586
  Part-time women.................... 23,966

Minority enrollment in institutions of higher education, 2005
Black, non-Hispanic 36,007
Hispanic 4,922
Asian/Pacific Islander 6,643
American Indian/Alaska Native........... 436

Institutions of higher education, 2005-06
Total................................. 15
  Public............................. 2
  Private 13

Earned degrees conferred, 2004-05
Associate's........................... 447
Bachelor's 9,199
Master's.............................. 8,536
First-professional..................... 2,950
Doctor's.............................. 613

Public Libraries, 2006
Number of libraries..................... 1
Number of outlets 24
Annual visits per capita 3.4
Circulation per capita 2.1

State & local financial support for higher education, FY 2006
Full-time equivalent enrollment (x 1,000)..... NA
Appropriations per FTE.................. NA

Social Insurance & Welfare Programs

Social Security benefits & beneficiaries, 2005
Beneficiaries (x 1,000) 71
  Retired & dependents................. 49
  Survivors.......................... 11
  Disabled & dependents................ 11
Annual benefit payments ($ mil) $674
  Retired & dependents................ $446
  Survivors.......................... $116
  Disabled & dependents............... $112
Average monthly benefit
  Retired & dependents................ $862
  Disabled & dependents............... $857
  Widowed.......................... $806

Medicare, July 2005
Enrollment (x 1,000)..................... 73
Payments ($ mil) $558

Medicaid, 2004
Beneficiaries (x 1,000)................... 157
Payments ($ mil) $800

State Children's Health Insurance Program, 2006
Enrollment (x 1,000).................... 6.3
Expenditures ($ mil)................... $9.9

Persons without health insurance, 2006
Number (x 1,000)....................... 66
  percent............................ 11.6%
Number of children (x 1,000) 10
  percent of children 8.7%

Health care expenditures, 2004
Total expenditures.................... $4,809
  per capita $8,295

©2008 Information Publications, Inc.
All rights reserved. Photocopying prohibited.
877-544-INFO (4636) or www.informationpublications.com

Federal and state public aid

State unemployment insurance, 2006
Recipients, first payments (x 1,000) 16
Total payments ($ mil) $93
Average weekly benefit $283
Temporary Assistance for Needy Families, 2006
Recipients (x 1,000) 380.5
Families (x 1,000) 157.1
Supplemental Security Income, 2005
Recipients (x 1,000) 21.2
Payments ($ mil) $113.4
Food Stamp Program, 2006
Avg monthly participants (x 1,000) 89.2
Total benefits ($ mil) $104.2

Housing & Construction

Housing units

Total 2005 (estimate) 280,044
Total 2006 (estimate) 282,894
Seasonal or recreational use, 2006 860
Owner-occupied, 2006 114,586
   Median home value $437,700
   Homeowner vacancy rate 3.7%
Renter-occupied, 2006 135,870
   Median rent $914
   Rental vacancy rate 7.8%
Home ownership rate, 2005 . . . . 45.8%
Home ownership rate, 2006 . . . . 45.9%

New privately-owned housing units

Number authorized, 2006 (x 1,000) 2.1
   Value ($ mil) $299.5
Started 2005 (x 1,000, estimate) 0.4
Started 2006 (x 1,000, estimate) 0.4

Existing home sales

2005 (x 1,000) 12.1
2006 (x 1,000) 10.1

Government & Elections

District officials 2008

Mayor . . . . Adrian Fenty
   Democratic, term expires 1/11
Secretary of the District . . . . Stephanie Scott
Attorney General . . . . Linda Singer
Chief Justice . . . . Eric Washington

Mayorship

Minimum age . . . . not specified
Length of term . . . . 4 years
Consecutive terms permitted . . . . yes
Who succeeds . . . . NA

Local governments by type, 2002

Total 2
   County 0
   Municipal 1
   Township 0
   School District 0
   Special District 1

District legislature

Name . . . . DC Council
   Number of members 13
     (1 each from 8 wards, 5 at-large)
   Length of term . . 2 years for at-large members,
   4 years for ward-elected members
   Party in majority, 2008 . . . . Democratic

Federal representation, 2008 (110th Congress)

Delegate . . . . Eleanor Holmes Norton
Shadow Representative . . . . Mike Panetta
Shadow Senator . . . . Paul Strauss
   Party . . . . Democratic
   Year term expires 2009
Shadow Senator . . . . Michael Brown
   Party . . . . Democratic
   Year term expires 2013
Representatives, total 1
   Democrats 1
   Republicans 0

Voters in November 2006 election (estimate)

Total 186,634
   Male 78,911
   Female 107,723
   White 80,727
   Black 98,324
   Hispanic 1,447
   Asian 5,375

Presidential election, 2004

Total Popular Vote 227,586
   Kerry 202,970
   Bush 21,256
Total Electoral Votes 3

Votes cast for US Senators

2004
Total vote (x 1,000) . . . . NA
Leading party . . . . NA
Percent for leading party . . . . NA

2006
Total vote (x 1,000) . . . . NA
Leading party . . . . Democratic
Percent for leading party . . . . NA

Votes cast for US Representatives

2004
Total vote (x 1,000) 195
   Democratic 169
   Republican . . . . NA
Leading party . . . . Democratic
Percent for leading party 86.3%

2006
Total vote (x 1,000) 115
   Democratic 112
   Republican 0
Leading party . . . . Democratic
Percent for leading party 97.3%

©2008 Information Publications, Inc.
All rights reserved. Photocopying prohibited.
877-544-INFO (4636) or www.informationpublications.com

District government employment, 2006
Full-time equivalent employees 46,611
Payroll ($ mil) $226.3

State government employment, 2006
Full-time equivalent employees . . . . NA
Payroll ($ mil) . . . . NA

Women holding public office, 2008
US Congress 1
Statewide elected office. . . . . NA
State legislature . . . . NA

Black public officials, 2002
Total. 174
  US and state legislatures 2
  City/county/regional offices 169
  Judicial/law enforcement. 0
  Education/school boards 3

Hispanic public officials, 2006
Total. 1
  State executives & legislators 0
  City/county/regional offices 0
  Judicial/law enforcement. 0
  Education/school boards 1

Governmental Finance

District government revenues, 2004-05
Total revenue (x $1,000) $9,326,744
  Revenue per capita $16,023.98
General Revenue (x $1,000) $13,924.89
  Intergovernmental 2,814,574
  Taxes 4,297,242
    general sales. 846,909
    individual income tax 1,147,940
    corporate income tax 199,310
  Current charges. 388,842
  Miscellaneous 604,313

District government expenditures, 2004-05
Total expenditure (x $1,000) $9,099,596
per capita. $15,633.73
Direct General Expend. (x $1,000). . . . $7,244,305
Expenditures per capita:
  Total. $12,446.21
  Education $2,295.85
  Public welfare. $2,902.42
  Health $782.84
  Hospitals. $449.51
  Highways $122.45
  Police protection $711.96
  Corrections. $282.41
  Natural resources $0.00
  Parks & recreation. $221.35
  Governmental administration $302.01
  Interest on general debt $479.32

District debt & cash, 2004-05 ($ per capita)
Debt $10,324.75
Cash/security holdings. $11,671.78

Federal government grants to district government, 2005 (x $1,000)
Total. $4,325,307
by Federal agency
  Defense 40,359
  Education 408,011
  Energy 29,452
  Environmental Protection Agency 73,527
  Health & Human Services. 1,682,697
  Homeland Security. 12,040
  Housing & Urban Development. 309,662
  Justice 201,903
  Labor 162,032
  Transportation 492,762
  Veterans Affairs. 915

Crime & Law Enforcement

Crime, 2006 (rates per 100,000 residents)
Property crimes 27,063
  Burglary 3,835
  Larceny 15,907
  Motor vehicle theft 7,321
  Property crime rate. 4,653.8
Violent crimes. 8,772
  Murder 169
  Forcible rape. 185
  Robbery. 3,829
  Aggravated assault 4,589
  Violent crime rate 1,508.4
Hate crimes. 64

Fraud and identity theft, 2006
Fraud complaints. .1,139
  rate per 100,000 residents 195.9
Identity theft complaints 765
  rate per 100,000 residents 131.5

Law enforcement agencies, 2006
Total agencies. 3
Total employees 4,880
  Officers 4,196
  Civilians 684

Prisoners, probation, and parole, 2006
Total prisoners. . . . . NA
(District of Columbia
prisoners have been housed
in federal jails since 2001)
Sentenced to more than one year . . . . NA
  rate per 100,000 residents . . . . NA
Adults on probation 6,883
Adults on parole. .5,387

Prisoner demographics, June 30, 2005 (rate per 100,000 residents)
Male. 1,202
Female 145
White. 56
Black. 1,065
Hispanic 267

©2008 Information Publications, Inc.
All rights reserved. Photocopying prohibited.
877-544-INFO (4636) or www.informationpublications.com

Arrests, 2006
Total 5,681
   Persons under 18 years of age 437

Persons under sentence of death, 1/1/07
Total 0
   White 0
   Black 0
   Hispanic 0

District's highest court
Name .... Court of Appeals
Number of members 9
Length of term .... 15 years
Intermediate appeals court? .... no

Labor & Income

Civilian labor force, 2006 (x 1,000)
Total 291
   Men 141
   Women 151
   Persons 16-19 years 6
   White 144
   Black 131
   Hispanic 30

Civilian labor force as a percent of civilian non-institutional population, 2006
Total 67.1%
   Men 70.4
   Women 64.3
   Persons 16-19 years 27.4
   White 78.4
   Black 57.2
   Hispanic 81.1

Employment, 2006 (x 1,000)
Total 274
   Men 133
   Women 141
   Persons 16-19 years 4
   White 140
   Black 118
   Hispanic 28

Unemployment rate, 2006
Total 5.8%
   Men 5.4
   Women 6.2
   Persons 16-19 years 29.8
   White 2.3
   Black 10.0
   Hispanic 4.2

Full-time/part-time labor force, 2003 (x 1,000)
Full-time labor force, employed 254
Part-time labor force, employed 27
Unemployed, looking for
   Full-time work 19
   Part-time work 2
Mean duration of unemployment (weeks) 26.8
   Median 14.1

Labor unions, 2006
Membership (x 1,000) 25
   percent of employed 10.3%

Experienced civilian labor force by private industry, 2006
Total 440,694
   Natural resources & mining .... NA
   Construction 12,575
   Manufacturing 1,755
   Trade, transportation & utilities 27,524
   Information 22,219
   Finance 26,950
   Professional & business 144,118
   Education & health 86,729
   Leisure & hospitality 54,126
   Other 56,496

Experienced civilian labor force by occupation, May 2006
Management 64,190
Business & financial 69,820
Legal 37,520
Sales 28,110
Office & admin. support 104,340
Computers & math 33,710
Architecture & engineering 11,820
Arts & entertainment 27,950
Education 32,220
Social services 8,420
Health care practitioner & technical 25,040
Health care support 7,420
Maintenance & repair 8,100
Construction 11,510
Transportation & moving 13,290
Production 6,770
Farming, fishing & forestry .... NA

Hours and earnings of production workers on manufacturing payrolls, 2006
Average weekly hours 38.7
Average hourly earnings $17.30
Average weekly earnings $669.51

Income and poverty, 2006
Median household income $51,847
Personal income, per capita (current $) ... $55,755
   in constant (2000) dollars $48,671
Persons below poverty level 19.6%

Average annual pay
2006 .... $70,151
   increase from 2005 .... 5.2%

Federal individual income tax returns, 2005
Returns filed 282,474
Adjusted gross income ($1,000) $19,712,600
Total tax liability ($1,000) $3,164,453

Charitable contributions, 2004
Number of contributions 104.3
Total amount ($ mil) $663.5

©2008 Information Publications, Inc.
All rights reserved. Photocopying prohibited.
877-544-INFO (4636) or www.informationpublications.com

Economy, Business, Industry & Agriculture

Fortune 500 companies, 2007 2
Bankruptcy cases filed, FY 2007 670

Patents and trademarks issued, 2007
Patents 67
Trademarks 782

Business firm ownership, 2002
Women-owned 15,675
  Sales ($ mil) $2,403
Black-owned 12,198
  Sales ($ mil) $1,568
Hispanic-owned .2,169
  Sales ($ mil) $548
Asian-owned 2,411
  Sales ($ mil) $1,003
Amer. Indian/Alaska Native-owned 217
  Sales ($ mil) $42
Hawaiian/Pacific Islander-owned 48
  Sales ($ mil) . . . . NA

Gross domestic product, 2006 ($ mil)
Total gross domestic product $87,664
  Agriculture, forestry, fishing and
    hunting 1
  Mining . . . . NA
  Utilities 831
  Construction . . . . NA
  Manufacturing, durable goods 70
  Manufacturing, non-durable goods 111
  Wholesale trade 765
  Retail trade 1,152
  Transportation & warehousing 415
  Information 5,130
  Finance & insurance 4,033
  Real estate, rental & leasing 9,616
  Professional and technical services 17,975
  Educational services 2,321
  Health care and social assistance 3,746
  Accommodation/food services 2,503
  Other services, except government 5,315
  Government 28,932

Establishments, payroll, employees & receipts, by major industry group, 2005
Total 20,481
  Annual payroll ($1,000) $25,152,741
  Paid employees .439,610
Forestry, fishing & agriculture 1
  Annual payroll ($1,000) . . . . NA
  Paid employees . . . . NA
Mining 5
  Annual payroll ($1,000) . . . . NA
  Paid employees . . . . NA
  Receipts, 2002 ($1,000) . . . . .NA

Utilities 33
  Annual payroll ($1,000) $97,551
  Paid employees .1,164
  Receipts, 2002 ($1,000) . . . . .NA
Construction 376
  Annual payroll ($1,000) $305,069
  Paid employees .5,798
  Receipts, 2002 ($1,000) *$1,380,689*
Manufacturing 142
  Annual payroll ($1,000) $75,172
  Paid employees .1,739
  Receipts, 2002 ($1,000) $246,237
Wholesale trade 448
  Annual payroll ($1,000) $358,165
  Paid employees .6,431
  Receipts, 2002 ($1,000) *$2,971,507*
Retail trade 1,913
  Annual payroll ($1,000) $481,963
  Paid employees 20,049
  Receipts, 2002 ($1,000) *$3,061,401*
Transportation & warehousing 188
  Annual payroll ($1,000) $124,179
  Paid employees .3,597
  Receipts, 2002 ($1,000) $905,612
Information 723
  Annual payroll ($1,000) $2,037,549
  Paid employees 24,445
  Receipts, 2002 ($1,000) . . . . .NA
Finance & insurance 954
  Annual payroll ($1,000) $1,786,209
  Paid employees 18,548
  Receipts, 2002 ($1,000) . . . . .NA
Professional, scientific & technical 4,579
  Annual payroll ($1,000) $8,206,840
  Paid employees 88,139
  Receipts, 2002 ($1,000) *$17,967,225*
Education 492
  Annual payroll ($1,000) $1,769,081
  Paid employees .47,816
  Receipts, 2002 ($1,000) $715,092
Health care & social assistance 2,092
  Annual payroll ($1,000) $2,865,767
  Paid employees 60,171
  Receipts, 2002 ($1,000) *$5,772,971*
Arts and entertainment 285
  Annual payroll ($1,000) $250,532
  Paid employees .6,081
  Receipts, 2002 ($1,000) $620,458
Real estate 985
  Annual payroll ($1,000) $600,351
  Paid employees .9,697
  Receipts, 2002 ($1,000) . . . . .NA
Accommodation & food service 1,956
  Annual payroll ($1,000) $1,161,792
  Paid employees 49,273
  Receipts, 2002 ($1,000) $2,943,078

©2008 Information Publications, Inc.
All rights reserved. Photocopying prohibited.
877-544-INFO (4636) or www.informationpublications.com

8   District of Columbia

Exports, 2006
Value of exported goods ($ mil) $1,040
   Manufactured $947
   Non-manufactured $50

Foreign direct investment in US affiliates, 2004
Property, plants & equipment ($ mil) $4,518
Employment (x 1,000). 15.7

Agriculture, 2006
Number of farms . . . . NA
Farm acreage (x 1,000) . . . . NA
   Acres per farm . . . . NA
Farm marketings and income ($ mil)
Total. . . . . NA
   Crops . . . . NA
   Livestock . . . . NA
Net farm income . . . . NA

Principal commodities, in order by marketing receipts, 2005
NA

Federal economic activity in district
Expenditures, 2005 ($ mil)
   Total. $37,859
    Per capita $65,044.63
   Defense $5,219
   Non-defense $32,640
Defense department, 2006 ($ mil)
   Payroll. $2,561
   Contract awards $4,067
   Grants $38
Homeland security grants ($1,000)
   2006. . . . . $54,015
   2007 . . . . $71,985

FDIC-insured financial institutions, 2005
Number 7
Assets ($ billion) $1.2
Deposits ($ billion) $1.0

Fishing, 2006
Catch (x 1,000 lbs) . . . . NA
Value ($1,000). . . . . NA

Mining, 2006 ($ mil)
Total non-fuel mineral production . . . . NA
Percent of U.S. . . . . NA

Communication, Energy & Transportation

Communication
Households with computers, 2003 . . . . .64.3%
Households with internet access, 2003 . . . .56.8%
High-speed internet providers 28
Total high-speed internet lines. 268,008
   Residential 144,289
   Business. 123,719
Wireless phone customers, 12/2006 880,077

FCC-licensed stations (as of January 1, 2008)
TV stations 8
FM radio stations. 14
AM radio stations 7

Energy
Energy consumption, 2004
   Total (trillion Btu). 190
   Per capita (million Btu) 328.3
By source of production (trillion Btu)
   Coal 1
   Natural gas 33
   Petroleum 31
   Nuclear electric power 0
   Hydroelectric power 0
By end-use sector (trillion Btu)
   Residential 38
   Commercial 121
   Industrial 4
   Transportation 27
Electric energy, 2005
   Primary source of electricity. . . . . . . Petroleum
   Net generation (billion kWh) 0.2
    percent from renewable sources. . . . . . . NA
   Net summer capability (million kW) 0.8
   CO_2 emitted from generation 0.2
Natural gas utilities, 2005
   Customers (x 1,000) 151
   Sales (trillion Btu). 32
   Revenues ($ mil) $247
Nuclear plants, 2007 0
Total CO_2 emitted (million metric tons). 3.9
Energy spending, 2004 ($ mil) $1,729
   per capita $2,983
   Price per million Btu $16.87

Transportation, 2006
Public road & street mileage 1,500
   Urban. 1,500
   Rural 0
   Interstate. 13
Vehicle miles of travel (millions) 3,623
   per capita 6,188.3
Total motor vehicle registrations. 219,105
   Automobiles. 168,916
   Trucks 47,300
   Motorcycles 1,372
Licensed drivers 357,569
   19 years & under 8,300
Deaths from motor vehicle accidents 37
Gasoline consumed (x 1,000 gallons) 131,963
   per capita 225.4

Commuting Statistics, 2006
Average commute time (min) 29.2
   Drove to work alone 35.4%
   Carpooled. 6.3%
   Public transit 39.0%
   Walk to work 11.8%
   Work from home. 4.0%

©2008 Information Publications, Inc.
All rights reserved. Photocopying prohibited.
877-544-INFO (4636) or www.informationpublications.com

Florida   1

State Summary

Capital city . . . . Tallahassee
Governor. . . . . .Charlie Crist

PL 05 The Capitol
400 S Monroe St
Tallahassee, FL 32399
850-488-4441

Admitted as a state 1845
Area (square miles) 65,755
Population, 2007 (estimate). 18,251,243
Largest city . . . . Jacksonville
   Population, 2006. 794,555
Personal income per capita, 2006
   (in current dollars) $35,798
Gross domestic product, 2006 ($ mil) . . . $713,505

Leading industries by payroll, 2005

Health care/Social assistance, Retail trade, Pro-
   fessional/Scientific/Technical

Leading agricultural commodities by receipts, 2005

Greenhouse/nursery, Oranges, Tomatoes, Cattle
   and calves, Cane for sugar

Geography & Environment

Total area (square miles). 65,755
   land 53,927
   water 11,828
Federally-owned land, 2004 (acres) 2,858,782
   percent. 8.2%
Highest point . . . . .Britton Hill
   elevation (feet) 345
Lowest point. . . . . .Atlantic Ocean
   elevation (feet) . . . . sea level
General coastline (miles) 1,650
Tidal shoreline (miles) 8,426
Cropland, 2003 (x 1,000 acres) 2,873
Forest land, 2003 (x 1,000 acres). 12,733
Capital city . . . . Tallahassee
   Population 2000 150,624
   Population 2006 159,012
Largest city . . . . Jacksonville
   Population 2000 735,617
   Population 2006 794,555

Number of cities with over 100,000 population

1990 9
2000 13
2006 17

State park and recreation areas, 2005

Area (x 1,000 acres). 696
Number of visitors (x 1,000) 18,202
Revenues ($1,000) $38,179
   percent of operating expenditures. 49.3%

National forest system land, 2007

Acres 1,160,324

Demographics & Population Characteristics

Population

1980 9,746,324
1990 12,937,926
2000 15,982,824
2006 18,089,888
   Male. 8,884,135
   Female. 9,205,753
Living in group quarters, 2006. 412,218
   percent of total. 2.3%
2007 (estimate). 18,251,243
   persons per square mile of land 338.4
2008 (projected). 18,533,980
2010 (projected) 19,251,691
2020 (projected) 23,406,525
2030 (projected). 28,685,769

Population of Core-Based Statistical Areas (formerly Metropolitan Areas), x 1,000

	CBSA	Non-CBSA
1990	12,645	293
2000	15,620	363
2006	17,692	398

Change in population, 2000-2007

Number. 2,268,419
   percent. 14.2%
Natural increase (births minus deaths) 360,972
Net internal migration 1,286,175
Net international migration 674,271

Persons by age, 2006

Under 5 years 1,122,849
5 to 17 years 2,898,706
18 years and over 14,068,333
65 years and over 3,037,704
85 years and over 462,545
   Median age 39.6

Persons by age, 2010 (projected)

Under 5 years 1,195,168
18 and over 15,165,568
65 and over 3,418,697
   Median age 41.9

Race, 2006

One Race
   White. 14,503,894
   Black or African American 2,864,423
   Asian 397,143
   American Indian/Alaska Native. 80,369
   Hawaiian Native/Pacific Islander. 15,401
Two or more races. 228,658

Persons of Hispanic origin, 2006

Total Hispanic or Latino 3,642,989
   Mexican. 563,110
   Puerto Rican 682,432
   Cuban 1,054,371

©2008 Information Publications, Inc.
All rights reserved. Photocopying prohibited.
877-544-INFO (4636) or www.informationpublications.com

Persons of Asian origin, 2006

Total Asian	393,427
Asian Indian	117,195
Chinese	65,743
Filipino	74,826
Japanese	13,391
Korean	24,980
Vietnamese	54,204

Marital status, 2006

Population 15 years & over	14,789,121
Never married	4,040,890
Married	7,859,691
Separated	355,551
Widowed	1,110,370
Divorced	1,778,170

Language spoken at home, 2006

Population 5 years and older	16,972,259
English only	12,610,892
Spanish	3,171,968
French	413,484
German	83,489
Chinese	47,727

Households & families, 2006

Households	7,106,042
with persons under 18 years	2,163,568
with persons over 65 years	2,088,025
persons per household	2.49
Families	4,632,974
persons per family	3.05
Married couples	3,452,127
Female householder, no husband present	861,237
One-person households	1,991,903

Nativity, 2006

Number of residents born in state	6,079,334
percent of population	33.6%

Immigration & naturalization, 2006

Legal permanent residents admitted	155,996
Persons naturalized	90,846
Non-immigrant admissions	4,942,206

Vital Statistics and Health

Marriages

2004	156,370
2005	157,976
2006	155,505

Divorces

2004	82,662
2005	81,285
2006	87,789

Health risks, 2006

Percent of adults who are:

Smokers	21.0%
Overweight (BMI > 25)	59.6%
Obese (BMI > 30)	23.1%

Births

2005	226,240
Birthrate (per 1,000)	12.7
White	161,478
Black	56,503
Hispanic	63,756
Asian/Pacific Islander	7,565
Amer. Indian/Alaska Native	694
Low birth weight (2,500g or less)	8.7%
Cesarian births	34.9%
Preterm births	13.8%
To unmarried mothers	42.8%
Twin births (per 1,000)	29.9
Triplets or higher order (per 100,000)	142.7
2006 (preliminary)	236,882
rate per 1,000	13.1

Deaths

2004

All causes	169,008
rate per 100,000	763.6
Heart disease	47,160
rate per 100,000	204.9
Malignant neoplasms	39,840
rate per 100,000	179.9
Cerebrovascular disease	9,715
rate per 100,000	42.0
Chronic lower respiratory disease	8,971
rate per 100,000	38.8
Diabetes	4,809
rate per 100,000	21.6
2005 (preliminary)	170,787
rate per 100,000	749.4
2006 (provisional)	170,007

Infant deaths

2004	1,537
rate per 1,000	7.1
2005 (provisional)	1,633
rate per 1,000	7.2

Exercise routines, 2005

None	26.9%
Moderate or greater	45.3%
Vigorous	24.6%

Abortions, 2004

Total performed in state	91,710
rate per 1,000 women age 15-44	27
% obtained by out-of-state residents	NA

Physicians, 2005

Total	43,314
rate per 100,000 persons	244

Community hospitals, 2005

Number of hospitals	205
Beds (x 1,000)	51.2
Patients admitted (x 1,000)	2,371
Average daily census (x 1,000)	33.9
Average cost per day	$1,497
Outpatient visits (x 1 mil)	22.3

©2008 Information Publications, Inc.
All rights reserved. Photocopying prohibited.
877-544-INFO (4636) or www.informationpublications.com

Disability status of population, 2006

5 to 15 years 6.1%
16 to 64 years 12.4%
65 years and over 38.4%

Education

Educational attainment, 2006

Population over 25 years 12,460,438
Less than 9th grade................. 5.7%
High school graduate or more 84.5%
College graduate or more............. 25.3%
Graduate or professional degree........ 8.9%

Public school enrollment, 2005-06

Total................................2,675,024
Pre-kindergarten through grade 8... 1,873,395
Grades 9 through 12................ 801,629

Graduating public high school seniors, 2004-05

Diplomas (incl. GED and others) 141,868

SAT scores, 2007

Average critical reading score.............. 497
Average writing score 479
Average math score 496
Percent of graduates taking test 65%

Public school teachers, 2006-07 (estimate)

Total (x 1,000) 167.8
Elementary............................ 84.8
Secondary............................ 83.0
Average salary $45,308
Elementary....................... $45,308
Secondary........................ $45,308

State receipts & expenditures for public schools, 2006-07 (estimate)

Revenue receipts ($ mil) $27,556
Expenditures
Total ($ mil) $29,798
Per capita $1,251
Per pupil $8,928

NAEP proficiency scores, 2007

	Reading		Math	
	Basic	Proficient	Basic	Proficient
Grade 4	70.4%	34.0%	86.2%	40.3%
Grade 8	71.5%	28.0%	68.1%	27.4%

Higher education enrollment, fall 2005

Total............................... 223,663
Full-time men 68,522
Full-time women..................... 91,021
Part-time men 28,062
Part-time women..................... 36,058

Minority enrollment in institutions of higher education, 2005

Black, non-Hispanic 155,357
Hispanic 159,572
Asian/Pacific Islander 29,827
American Indian/Alaska Native.......... 3,476

Institutions of higher education, 2005-06

Total.................................... 169
Public................................ 40
Private.............................. 129

Earned degrees conferred, 2004-05

Associate's........................... 60,441
Bachelor's 65,839
Master's.............................. 24,014
First-professional..................... 3,716
Doctor's.............................. 3,064

Public Libraries, 2006

Number of libraries....................... 78
Number of outlets 531
Annual visits per capita 4.1
Circulation per capita.................. 5.5

State & local financial support for higher education, FY 2006

Full-time equivalent enrollment (x 1,000).... 532.7
Appropriations per FTE................ $5,641

Social Insurance & Welfare Programs

Social Security benefits & beneficiaries, 2005

Beneficiaries (x 1,000) 3,424
Retired & dependents.................. 2,526
Survivors............................ 401
Disabled & dependents.................. 497
Annual benefit payments ($ mil) $36,891
Retired & dependents.............. $26,145
Survivors........................ $5,567
Disabled & dependents.............. $5,178
Average monthly benefit
Retired & dependents.............. $999
Disabled & dependents............. $943
Widowed......................... $993

Medicare, July 2005

Enrollment (x 1,000)................... 3,046
Payments ($ mil) $21,363

Medicaid, 2004

Beneficiaries (x 1,000).................. 2,952
Payments ($ mil) $12,834

State Children's Health Insurance Program, 2006

Enrollment (x 1,000).................... 303.6
Expenditures ($ mil).................. $300.6

Persons without health insurance, 2006

Number (x 1,000)...................... 3,828
percent......................... 21.2%
Number of children (x 1,000) 771
percent of children 18.9%

Health care expenditures, 2004

Total expenditures.................... $95,223
per capita $5,483

Federal and state public aid

State unemployment insurance, 2006
Recipients, first payments (x 1,000) 240
Total payments ($ mil) $719
Average weekly benefit $231
Temporary Assistance for Needy Families, 2006
Recipients (x 1,000) 995.8
Families (x 1,000) 610.3
Supplemental Security Income, 2005
Recipients (x 1,000) 422.5
Payments ($ mil) $2,031.4
Food Stamp Program, 2006
Avg monthly participants (x 1,000) 1,417.7
Total benefits ($ mil) $1,684.3

Housing & Construction

Housing units

Total 2005 (estimate) 8,260,451
Total 2006 (estimate) 8,533,419
Seasonal or recreational use, 2006 655,647
Owner-occupied, 2006 4,994,101
Median home value $230,600
Homeowner vacancy rate 4.3%
Renter-occupied, 2006 2,111,941
Median rent $872
Rental vacancy rate 10.7%
Home ownership rate, 2005 . . . . 72.4%
Home ownership rate, 2006 . . . . 72.4%

New privately-owned housing units

Number authorized, 2006 (x 1,000) 203.2
Value ($ mil) $35,716.3
Started 2005 (x 1,000, estimate) 173.6
Started 2006 (x 1,000, estimate) 165.4

Existing home sales

2005 (x 1,000) 547.1
2006 (x 1,000) 395.3

Government & Elections

State officials 2008

Governor . . . . .Charlie Crist
Republican, term expires 1/11
Lieutenant Governor . . . . .Jeff Kottkamp
Secretary of State . . . . .Kurt Browning
Attorney General . . . . Bill McCollum
Chief Justice . . . . R. Fred Lewis

Governorship

Minimum age 30
Length of term . . . . 4 years
Consecutive terms permitted 2
Who succeeds . . . . Lieutenant Governor

Local governments by type, 2002

Total 1,191
County 66
Municipal 404
Township 0
School District 95
Special District 626

State legislature

Name . . . . Legislature
Upper chamber . . . . .Senate
Number of members 40
Length of term . . . . 4 years
Party in majority, 2008 . . . . Republican
Lower chamber . . . . .House of Representatives
Number of members 120
Length of term . . . . 2 years
Party in majority, 2008 . . . . Republican

Federal representation, 2008 (110th Congress)

Senator . . . . Mel Martinez
Party . . . . Republican
Year term expires 2011
Senator . . . . Bill Nelson
Party . . . . .Democratic
Year term expires 2013
Representatives, total 25
Democrats 9
Republicans 16

Voters in November 2006 election (estimate)

Total 5,342,902
Male 2,538,342
Female 2,804,559
White 4,592,237
Black 642,099
Hispanic 270,298
Asian 44,294

Presidential election, 2004

Total Popular Vote 7,609,810
Kerry 3,583,544
Bush 3,964,522
Total Electoral Votes 27

Votes cast for US Senators

2004
Total vote (x 1,000) .7,430
Leading party . . . . Republican
Percent for leading party 49.4%
2006
Total vote (x 1,000) .4,794
Leading party .Democratic
Percent for leading party 60.3%

Votes cast for US Representatives

2004
Total vote (x 1,000) .5,627
Democratic 2,212
Republican 3,319
Leading party . . . . Republican
Percent for leading party 59.0%
2006
Total vote (x 1,000) .3,852
Democratic 1,600
Republican 2,183
Leading party . . . . Republican
Percent for leading party 56.7%

©2008 Information Publications, Inc.
All rights reserved. Photocopying prohibited.
877-544-INFO (4636) or www.informationpublications.com

State government employment, 2006
Full-time equivalent employees 191,215
Payroll ($ mil) $657.0

Local government employment, 2006
Full-time equivalent employees 676,044
Payroll ($ mil) $2,365.5

Women holding public office, 2008
US Congress................................. 5
Statewide elected office...................... 1
State legislature 37

Black public officials, 2002
Total...................................... 275
   US and state legislatures 25
   City/county/regional offices 180
   Judicial/law enforcement................. 43
   Education/school boards................. 27

Hispanic public officials, 2006
Total...................................... 121
   State executives & legislators 19
   City/county/regional offices 70
   Judicial/law enforcement................. 26
   Education/school boards................. 6

Governmental Finance

State government revenues, 2006
Total revenue (x $1,000)...........$83,807,587
   per capita $4,641.15
General revenue (x $1,000) $66,623,771
   Intergovernmental 20,003,686
   Taxes 37,201,518
     general sales...................20,788,525
     individual income tax 0
     corporate income tax...........2,405,863
   Current charges...................4,734,440
   Miscellaneous 4,684,127

State government expenditure, 2006
Total expenditure (x $1,000) $76,142,277
   per capita $4,216.65
General expenditure (x $1,000) $67,862,305
   per capita, total.................. *$3,758.12*
     Education 1,145.98
     Public welfare 943.10
     Health 165.85
     Hospitals..........................33.33
     Highways 353.94
     Police protection................... 26.07
     Corrections 135.17
     Natural resources 101.58
     Parks & recreation..................8.74
     Governmental administration.......145.33
     Interest on general debt.............62.83

State debt & cash, 2006 ($ per capita)
Debt $1,429.42
Cash/security holdings..............$9,492.24

Federal government grants to state & local government, 2005 (x $1,000)
Total......................... $22,552,241
by Federal agency
   Defense 94,808
   Education 1,851,893
   Energy.......................... 49,222
   Environmental Protection Agency ... 104,705
   Health & Human Services. 11,699,806
   Homeland Security................2,420,195
   Housing & Urban Development.....1,294,327
   Justice 290,884
   Labor 318,890
   Transportation 2,364,264
   Veterans Affairs....................27,931

Crime & Law Enforcement

Crime, 2006 (rates per 100,000 residents)
Property crimes 721,084
   Burglary 170,873
   Larceny.........................473,774
   Motor vehicle theft 76,437
   Property crime rate..................3,986.1
Violent crimes........................ 128,795
   Murder 1,129
   Forcible rape.......................6,475
   Robbery..........................34,147
   Aggravated assault 87,044
   Violent crime rate 712.0
Hate crimes 257

Fraud and identity theft, 2006
Fraud complaints...................... 25,902
   rate per 100,000 residents 143.2
Identity theft complaints 17,780
   rate per 100,000 residents 98.3

Law enforcement agencies, 2006
Total agencies........................... 450
Total employees 74,051
   Officers 45,723
   Civilians 28,328

Prisoners, probation, and parole, 2006
Total prisoners........................ 92,969
   percent change, 12/31/05 to 12/31/06 .... 3.6%
   in private facilities 6.8%
   in local jails 0%
Sentenced to more than one year 92,874
   rate per 100,000 residents 509
Adults on probation 272,977
Adults on parole........................4,790

Prisoner demographics, June 30, 2005 (rate per 100,000 residents)
Male.....................................1,541
Female 155
White...................................... 588
Black....................................2,615
Hispanic 382

©2008 Information Publications, Inc.
All rights reserved. Photocopying prohibited.
877-544-INFO (4636) or www.informationpublications.com

Arrests, 2006
Total...............................1,110,535
   Persons under 18 years of age.........121,173

Persons under sentence of death, 1/1/07
Total......................................397
   White...................................221
   Black 139
   Hispanic 35

State's highest court
Name ....Supreme Court
Number of members.......................7
Length of term.....................6 years
Intermediate appeals court? ....yes

Labor & Income

Civilian labor force, 2006 (x 1,000)
Total....................................9,054
   Men 4,800
   Women 4,254
   Persons 16-19 years....................356
   White.................................7,413
   Black 1,310
   Hispanic 1,954

Civilian labor force as a percent of civilian non-institutional population, 2006
Total....................................63.5%
   Men 70.1
   Women 57.5
   Persons 16-19 years...................40.2
   White.................................62.9
   Black 65.7
   Hispanic 67.5

Employment, 2006 (x 1,000)
Total....................................8,762
   Men 4,647
   Women 4,115
   Persons 16-19 years....................314
   White.................................7,206
   Black 1,232
   Hispanic 1,887

Unemployment rate, 2006
Total.....................................3.2%
   Men 3.2
   Women 3.3
   Persons 16-19 years...................11.6
   White..................................2.8
   Black 5.9
   Hispanic 3.4

Full-time/part-time labor force, 2003 (x 1,000)
Full-time labor force, employed 6,552
Part-time labor force, employed..........1,191
Unemployed, looking for
   Full-time work.........................355
   Part-time work..........................65
Mean duration of unemployment (weeks)......18.3
   Median 9.5

Labor unions, 2006
Membership (x 1,000)....................397
   percent of employed 5.2%

Experienced civilian labor force by private industry, 2006
Total..................................6,887,084
   Natural resources & mining 97,141
   Construction 634,751
   Manufacturing......................402,317
   Trade, transportation & utilities 1,593,327
   Information 167,289
   Finance 544,294
   Professional & business 1,347,000
   Education & health.................939,776
   Leisure & hospitality..............904,030
   Other 248,095

Experienced civilian labor force by occupation, May 2006
Management........................231,960
Business & financial 360,270
Legal..................................69,320
Sales 984,230
Office & admin. support..............1,508,910
Computers & math 149,660
Architecture & engineering............127,420
Arts & entertainment 94,400
Education 390,160
Social services 80,800
Health care practitioner & technical.....413,180
Health care support 200,440
Maintenance & repair.................322,170
Construction 513,750
Transportation & moving 515,490
Production 353,550
Farming, fishing & forestry.............38,740

Hours and earnings of production workers on manufacturing payrolls, 2006
Average weekly hours...................41.5
Average hourly earnings $14.75
Average weekly earnings $612.13

Income and poverty, 2006
Median household income............$45,495
Personal income, per capita (current $)...$35,798
   in constant (2000) dollars $31,249
Persons below poverty level.............12.6%

Average annual pay
2006 ....$38,485
   increase from 2005 ....4.6%

Federal individual income tax returns, 2005
Returns filed........................8,411,496
Adjusted gross income ($1,000) $481,888,152
Total tax liability ($1,000) $69,937,790

Charitable contributions, 2004
Number of contributions...............2,182.1
Total amount ($ mil).................$9,481.9

©2008 Information Publications, Inc.
All rights reserved. Photocopying prohibited.
877-544-INFO (4636) or www.informationpublications.com

Economy, Business, Industry & Agriculture

Fortune 500 companies, 2007.............. 12
Bankruptcy cases filed, FY 2007......... 36,572

Patents and trademarks issued, 2007
Patents.............................. 3,049
Trademarks...........................5,779

Business firm ownership, 2002
Women-owned........................437,355
  Sales ($ mil) $61,275
Black-owned........................ 102,053
  Sales ($ mil) $5,721
Hispanic-owned..................... 266,688
  Sales ($ mil) $40,892
Asian-owned 41,258
  Sales ($ mil) $11,222
Amer. Indian/Alaska Native-owned 10,105
  Sales ($ mil) $647
Hawaiian/Pacific Islander-owned 1,480
  Sales ($ mil) $72

Gross domestic product, 2006 ($ mil)
Total gross domestic product $713,505
  Agriculture, forestry, fishing and hunting 6,313
  Mining............................... 805
  Utilities 11,685
  Construction 55,839
  Manufacturing, durable goods........ 24,430
  Manufacturing, non-durable goods 11,430
  Wholesale trade.....................47,023
  Retail trade........................ 56,573
  Transportation & warehousing 18,194
  Information 28,841
  Finance & insurance................. 48,397
  Real estate, rental & leasing 122,221
  Professional and technical services.... 45,405
  Educational services..................5,011
  Health care and social assistance......51,299
  Accommodation/food services........ 26,032
  Other services, except government 17,954
  Government........................ 78,875

Establishments, payroll, employees & receipts, by major industry group, 2005
Total............................... 504,662
  Annual payroll ($1,000)........$239,197,889
  Paid employees 7,107,378
Forestry, fishing & agriculture.............1,029
  Annual payroll ($1,000)............ $353,729
  Paid employees 16,165
Mining................................ 275
  Annual payroll ($1,000)............ $287,568
  Paid employees 5,588
  Receipts, 2002 ($1,000) $1,562,949

Utilities 645
  Annual payroll ($1,000)..........$2,099,914
  Paid employees 32,240
  Receipts, 2002 ($1,000) ....NA
Construction.........................57,346
  Annual payroll ($1,000)........$18,452,509
  Paid employees 477,670
  Receipts, 2002 ($1,000) $79,384,681
Manufacturing....................... 14,286
  Annual payroll ($1,000)........$14,906,536
  Paid employees 371,432
  Receipts, 2002 ($1,000) $78,474,770
Wholesale trade......................31,709
  Annual payroll ($1,000)........$13,996,062
  Paid employees 311,270
  Receipts, 2002 ($1,000) $219,490,896
Retail trade......................... 72,469
  Annual payroll ($1,000).... $23,452,267
  Paid employees 987,307
  Receipts, 2002 ($1,000) $191,805,685
Transportation & warehousing.......... 12,668
  Annual payroll ($1,000)......... $8,020,002
  Paid employees 216,297
  Receipts, 2002 ($1,000) $25,805,912
Information........................... 8,693
  Annual payroll ($1,000)..........$8,829,908
  Paid employees 174,999
  Receipts, 2002 ($1,000) ....NA
Finance & insurance...................32,974
  Annual payroll ($1,000)..........$20,227,493
  Paid employees 370,990
  Receipts, 2002 ($1,000) ....NA
Professional, scientific & technical.......65,901
  Annual payroll ($1,000)........$21,899,141
  Paid employees 422,953
  Receipts, 2002 ($1,000) $42,457,665
Education 4,966
  Annual payroll ($1,000)..........$3,481,093
  Paid employees 119,169
  Receipts, 2002 ($1,000) $1,883,151
Health care & social assistance.......... 48,207
  Annual payroll ($1,000)..........$32,749,098
  Paid employees 866,420
  Receipts, 2002 ($1,000) $70,972,374
Arts and entertainment 7,515
  Annual payroll ($1,000)..........$4,081,454
  Paid employees 166,236
  Receipts, 2002 ($1,000) $11,319,842
Real estate........................... 33,946
  Annual payroll ($1,000).......... $6,466,526
  Paid employees 168,266
  Receipts, 2002 ($1,000) $22,785,030
Accommodation & food service.......... 33,049
  Annual payroll ($1,000)..........$10,738,660
  Paid employees 724,791
  Receipts, 2002 ($1,000) $29,366,940

©2008 Information Publications, Inc.
All rights reserved. Photocopying prohibited.
877-544-INFO (4636) or www.informationpublications.com

8   Florida

Exports, 2006
Value of exported goods ($ mil) $38,545
   Manufactured $31,638
   Non-manufactured. $2,233

Foreign direct investment in US affiliates, 2004
Property, plants & equipment ($ mil) . . . $26,819
Employment (x 1,000). 238.4

Agriculture, 2006
Number of farms 41,000
Farm acreage (x 1,000) 10,000
   Acres per farm 244
Farm marketings and income ($ mil)
Total. $6,974.2
   Crops $5,669.3
   Livestock. $1,304.9
Net farm income $2,340.4

Principal commodities, in order by marketing receipts, 2005
Greenhouse/nursery, Oranges, Tomatoes, Cattle
and calves, Cane for sugar

Federal economic activity in state
Expenditures, 2005 ($ mil)
   Total. $134,544
      Per capita $7,572.16
   Defense $18,590
   Non-defense $115,954
Defense department, 2006 ($ mil)
   Payroll. $8,864
   Contract awards $10,707
   Grants $131
Homeland security grants ($1,000)
   2006. . . . . $100,122
   2007 . . . . $84,743

FDIC-insured financial institutions, 2005
Number 306
Assets ($ billion) $165.8
Deposits ($ billion) $120.0

Fishing, 2006
Catch (x 1,000 lbs). 95,255
Value ($1,000). $237,130

Mining, 2006 ($ mil)
Total non-fuel mineral production $2,790
Percent of U.S. 4.33%

Communication, Energy & Transportation

Communication
Households with computers, 2003. . . . . 61.0%
Households with internet access, 2003 . . . . 55.6%
High-speed internet providers 60
Total high-speed internet lines. 5,346,321
   Residential 4,028,919
   Business. 1,317,402
Wireless phone customers, 12/2006 . . . 14,761,666

FCC-licensed stations (as of January 1, 2008)
TV stations 92
FM radio stations. 343
AM radio stations 226

Energy
Energy consumption, 2004
   Total (trillion Btu). 4,453
   Per capita (million Btu) 256.4
By source of production (trillion Btu)
   Coal 699
   Natural gas 755
   Petroleum. 2,120
   Nuclear electric power 326
   Hydroelectric power. 3
By end-use sector (trillion Btu)
   Residential 1,307
   Commercial 1,042
   Industrial 554
   Transportation 1,550
Electric energy, 2005
   Primary source of electricity. . . . . Gas
   Net generation (billion kWh) 220.3
     percent from renewable sources. 2.1%
   Net summer capability (million kW) 53.2
   CO_2 emitted from generation 130.3
Natural gas utilities, 2005
   Customers (x 1,000) 712
   Sales (trillion Btu). 141
   Revenues ($ mil) $665
Nuclear plants, 2007 5
Total CO_2 emitted (million metric tons). 243.9
Energy spending, 2004 ($ mil) $41,112
   per capita $2,367
   Price per million Btu $15.21

Transportation, 2006
Public road & street mileage 121,995
   Urban. 81,789
   Rural 40,206
   Interstate. 1,471
Vehicle miles of travel (millions) 203,741
   per capita 11,282.9
Total motor vehicle registrations. 16,373,565
   Automobiles. 7,425,148
   Trucks 8,899,488
   Motorcycles 588,900
Licensed drivers 13,988,630
   19 years & under 770,196
Deaths from motor vehicle accidents 3,374
Gasoline consumed (x 1,000 gallons) . . . 8,692,569
   per capita 481.4

Commuting Statistics, 2006
Average commute time (min) 25.9
   Drove to work alone 79.3%
   Carpooled. 10.9%
   Public transit 2.0%
   Walk to work 1.7%
   Work from home. 4.0%

©2008 Information Publications, Inc.
All rights reserved. Photocopying prohibited.
877-544-INFO (4636) or www.informationpublications.com

State Summary

Capital city . . . . .Atlanta
Governor. . . . . Sonny Perdue
203 State Capitol
Atlanta, GA 30334
404-656-1776
Admitted as a state 1788
Area (square miles) 59,425
Population, 2007 (estimate). 9,544,750
Largest city . . . . .Atlanta
Population, 2006. 486,411
Personal income per capita, 2006
(in current dollars) $31,891
Gross domestic product, 2006 ($ mil) . . . $379,550

Leading industries by payroll, 2005

Manufacturing, Health care/Social assistance,
Professional/Scientific/Technical

Leading agricultural commodities by receipts, 2005

Broilers, Cotton, Greenhouse/nursery, Chicken
eggs, Cattle and calves

Geography & Environment

Total area (square miles). 59,425
land 57,906
water 1,519
Federally-owned land, 2004 (acres) 1,409,406
percent. 3.8%
Highest point . . . . Brasstown Bald
elevation (feet) 4,784
Lowest point. . . . . .Atlantic Ocean
elevation (feet) . . . . sea level
General coastline (miles) 100
Tidal shoreline (miles) 2,344
Cropland, 2003 (x 1,000 acres) 4,152
Forest land, 2003 (x 1,000 acres). 21,893
Capital city . . . . .Atlanta
Population 2000 416,474
Population 2006 486,411
Largest city . . . . .Atlanta
Population 2000 416,474
Population 2006 486,411

Number of cities with over 100,000 population

1990 4
2000 5
2006 5

State park and recreation areas, 2005

Area (x 1,000 acres). 84
Number of visitors (x 1,000) 10,294
Revenues ($1,000) $32,834
percent of operating expenditures. 55.4%

National forest system land, 2007

Acres 866,024

Demographics & Population Characteristics

Population

1980 5,463,105
1990 6,478,216
2000 8,186,816
2006 9,363,941
Male. 4,611,078
Female. 4,752,863
Living in group quarters, 2006. 272,931
percent of total. 2.9%
2007 (estimate). 9,544,750
persons per square mile of land 164.8
2008 (projected). 9,325,827
2010 (projected). 9,589,080
2020 (projected). 10,843,753
2030 (projected). 12,017,838

Population of Core-Based Statistical Areas (formerly Metropolitan Areas), x 1,000

	CBSA	Non-CBSA
1990	5,822	656
2000	7,411	776
2006	8,534	830

Change in population, 2000-2007

Number. 1,357,934
percent. 16.6%
Natural increase (births minus deaths) 521,982
Net internal migration 484,919
Net international migration 240,814

Persons by age, 2006

Under 5 years 702,134
5 to 17 years 1,752,886
18 years and over 6,908,921
65 years and over 912,874
85 years and over 113,362
Median age. 34.6

Persons by age, 2010 (projected)

Under 5 years 730,521
18 and over 7,086,694
65 and over 980,824
Median age. 34.7

Race, 2006

One Race
White. 6,158,769
Black or African American 2,799,625
Asian 261,401
American Indian/Alaska Native. 30,893
Hawaiian Native/Pacific Islander. 7,396
Two or more races. 105,857

Persons of Hispanic origin, 2006

Total Hispanic or Latino 696,146
Mexican. 455,008
Puerto Rican 51,349
Cuban 18,448

©2008 Information Publications, Inc.
All rights reserved. Photocopying prohibited.
877-544-INFO (4636) or www.informationpublications.com

Persons of Asian origin, 2006

Total Asian 254,899
  Asian Indian. 74,525
  Chinese 37,017
  Filipino 14,562
  Japanese 6,774
  Korean. 45,846
  Vietnamese. 44,830

Marital status, 2006

Population 15 years & over 7,325,075
  Never married 2,308,808
  Married. 3,756,569
  Separated 183,167
  Widowed. 418,204
  Divorced 841,494

Language spoken at home, 2006

Population 5 years and older. 8,665,006
  English only 7,633,572
  Spanish 610,402
  French 51,396
  German. 26,723
  Chinese 32,902

Households & families, 2006

Households. 3,376,763
  with persons under 18 years 1,253,007
  with persons over 65 years. 636,235
  persons per household 2.69
Families. 2,296,694
  persons per family. 3.27
Married couples. 1,639,379
Female householder,
  no husband present. 492,332
One-person households 892,833

Nativity, 2006

Number of residents born in state 5,200,328
  percent of population. 55.5%

Immigration & naturalization, 2006

Legal permanent residents admitted. 32,202
Persons naturalized 19,785
Non-immigrant admissions 436,905

Vital Statistics and Health

Marriages

2004. 68,897
2005. 62,893
2006. 66,456

Divorces

2004. . . . . NA
2005. . . . . NA
2006. . . . . NA

Health risks, 2006

Percent of adults who are:
  Smokers. 19.9%
  Overweight (BMI > 25). 61.7%
  Obese (BMI > 30). 27.1%

Births

2005 142,200
  Birthrate (per 1,000). 15.7
  White. 90,958
  Black 46,027
  Hispanic 21,891
  Asian/Pacific Islander 4,953
  Amer. Indian/Alaska Native 262
  Low birth weight (2,500g or less). 9.5%
  Cesarian births 30.5%
  Preterm births 13.6%
  To unmarried mothers. 40.6%
  Twin births (per 1,000) 31.2
  Triplets or higher order (per 100,000). . . .149.6
2006 (preliminary). 148,619
  rate per 1,000 . . . . .15.9

Deaths

2004

All causes 65,818
  rate per 100,000. . . . . 924.6
Heart disease 16,557
  rate per 100,000. . . . . .239.7
Malignant neoplasms 14,313
  rate per 100,000. . . . . .196.3
Cerebrovascular disease. 4,063
  rate per 100,000. . . . . .60.5
Chronic lower respiratory disease 3,125
  rate per 100,000. . . . . .45.8
Diabetes. 1,623
  rate per 100,000. . . . . .22.5
2005 (preliminary). 66,735
  rate per 100,000. . . . . 905.8
2006 (provisional) 66,335

Infant deaths

2004 1,181
  rate per 1,000 . . . . .8.5
2005 (provisional) 1,108
  rate per 1,000 . . . . .7.8

Exercise routines, 2005

None. 27.2%
Moderate or greater. 42.0%
Vigorous 23.7%

Abortions, 2004

Total performed in state. 32,513
  rate per 1,000 women age 15-44. 16
  % obtained by out-of-state residents 12.5%

Physicians, 2005

Total. 19,997
  rate per 100,000 persons 219

Community hospitals, 2005

Number of hospitals 149
Beds (x 1,000). 25.0
Patients admitted (x 1,000) 961
Average daily census (x 1,000) 17.0
Average cost per day $1,202
Outpatient visits (x 1 mil) 13.8

©2008 Information Publications, Inc.
All rights reserved. Photocopying prohibited.
877-544-INFO (4636) or www.informationpublications.com

Disability status of population, 2006

5 to 15 years 5.6%
16 to 64 years 12.3%
65 years and over 45.1%

Education

Educational attainment, 2006

Population over 25 years 5,968,250
   Less than 9th grade..................... 6.4%
   High school graduate or more 82.2%
   College graduate or more.............. 26.6%
   Graduate or professional degree........ 9.2%

Public school enrollment, 2005-06

Total...............................1,598,461
   Pre-kindergarten through grade 8...1,145,446
   Grades 9 through 12 453,015

Graduating public high school seniors, 2004-05

Diplomas (incl. GED and others) 79,128

SAT scores, 2007

Average critical reading score............. 494
Average writing score 483
Average math score 495
Percent of graduates taking test 69%

Public school teachers, 2006-07 (estimate)

Total (x 1,000) 112.9
   Elementary...........................68.4
   Secondary........................... 44.5
Average salary $49,905
   Elementary........................ $49,357
   Secondary......................... $50,748

State receipts & expenditures for public schools, 2006-07 (estimate)

Revenue receipts ($ mil) $16,777
Expenditures
Total ($ mil) $16,333
   Per capita $1,531
   Per pupil $9,502

NAEP proficiency scores, 2007

	Reading		Math	
	Basic	Proficient	Basic	Proficient
Grade 4	65.6%	28.3%	78.6%	31.6%
Grade 8	70.1%	25.6%	64.2%	24.7%

Higher education enrollment, fall 2005

Total............................... 84,638
   Full-time men 28,317
   Full-time women.................... 42,432
   Part-time men 5,186
   Part-time women.....................8,703

Minority enrollment in institutions of higher education, 2005

Black, non-Hispanic 131,040
Hispanic 10,597
Asian/Pacific Islander 15,790
American Indian/Alaska Native..........1,187

Institutions of higher education, 2005-06

Total.................................. 132
   Public................................ 74
   Private............................... 58

Earned degrees conferred, 2004-05

Associate's......................... 12,705
Bachelor's 35,515
Master's 13,111
First-professional.................... 2,029
Doctor's.............................1,225

Public Libraries, 2006

Number of libraries.................... 58
Number of outlets 396
Annual visits per capita 3.7
Circulation per capita....................4.8

State & local financial support for higher education, FY 2006

Full-time equivalent enrollment (x 1,000)....292.7
Appropriations per FTE.................$7,824

Social Insurance & Welfare Programs

Social Security benefits & beneficiaries, 2005

Beneficiaries (x 1,000) 1,231
   Retired & dependents................... 799
   Survivors............................ 182
   Disabled & dependents................. 250
Annual benefit payments ($ mil) $12,846
   Retired & dependents............... $8,048
   Survivors......................... $2,261
   Disabled & dependents.............. $2,537
Average monthly benefit
   Retired & dependents.................. $978
   Disabled & dependents................. $924
   Widowed.............................. $913

Medicare, July 2005

Enrollment (x 1,000)....................1,039
Payments ($ mil) $7,143

Medicaid, 2004

Beneficiaries (x 1,000)..................1,929
Payments ($ mil) $6,944

State Children's Health Insurance Program, 2006

Enrollment (x 1,000)....................343.7
Expenditures ($ mil)................. $265.2

Persons without health insurance, 2006

Number (x 1,000).......................1,659
   percent............................. 17.7%
Number of children (x 1,000) 314
   percent of children 12.8%

Health care expenditures, 2004

Total expenditures.................... $41,097
   per capita $4,600

©2008 Information Publications, Inc.
All rights reserved. Photocopying prohibited.
877-544-INFO (4636) or www.informationpublications.com

Federal and state public aid

State unemployment insurance, 2006
Recipients, first payments (x 1,000) 198
Total payments ($ mil) $537
Average weekly benefit $256
Temporary Assistance for Needy Families, 2006
Recipients (x 1,000) .672.7
Families (x 1,000) 351.9
Supplemental Security Income, 2005
Recipients (x 1,000) 202.7
Payments ($ mil) $943.6
Food Stamp Program, 2006
Avg monthly participants (x 1,000) 946.8
Total benefits ($ mil) $1,098.3

Housing & Construction

Housing units

Total 2005 (estimate) 3,772,200
Total 2006 (estimate) 3,873,183
Seasonal or recreational use, 2006 75,646
Owner-occupied, 2006 2,285,179
Median home value $156,800
Homeowner vacancy rate 3.4%
Renter-occupied, 2006 1,091,584
Median rent $738
Rental vacancy rate 13.0%
Home ownership rate, 2005 . . . . 67.9%
Home ownership rate, 2006 . . . . 68.5%

New privately-owned housing units

Number authorized, 2006 (x 1,000) 104.2
Value ($ mil) $14,454.8
Started 2005 (x 1,000, estimate) 86.1
Started 2006 (x 1,000, estimate) 84.1

Existing home sales

2005 (x 1,000) 242.1
2006 (x 1,000) 248.8

Government & Elections

State officials 2008

Governor . . . . Sonny Perdue
Republican, term expires 1/11
Lieutenant Governor . . . . Casey Cagle
Secretary of State . . . . .Karen Handel
Attorney General . . . . Thurbert Baker
Chief Justice . . . . Leah Ward Sears

Governorship

Minimum age 30
Length of term . . . . 4 years
Consecutive terms permitted 2
Who succeeds . . . . Lieutenant Governor

Local governments by type, 2002

Total 1,448
County 156
Municipal 531
Township 0
School District 180
Special District 581

State legislature

Name . . . . General Assembly
Upper chamber . . . . .Senate
Number of members 56
Length of term . . . . 2 years
Party in majority, 2008 . . . . Republican
Lower chamber . . . . .House of Representatives
Number of members 180
Length of term . . . . 2 years
Party in majority, 2008 . . . . Republican

Federal representation, 2008 (110th Congress)

Senator . . . . Saxby Chambliss
Party . . . . Republican
Year term expires .2009
Senator . . . . Johnny Isakson
Party . . . . Republican
Year term expires 2011
Representatives, total 13
Democrats 6
Republicans 7

Voters in November 2006 election (estimate)

Total 2,671,578
Male 1,197,134
Female 1,474,444
White 1,904,631
Black 721,981
Hispanic 30,939
Asian 26,220

Presidential election, 2004

Total Popular Vote 3,301,875
Kerry 1,366,149
Bush 1,914,254
Total Electoral Votes 15

Votes cast for US Senators

2004
Total vote (x 1,000) 3,221
Leading party . . . . Republican
Percent for leading party 57.8%
2006
Total vote (x 1,000) . . . . NA
Leading party . . . . NA
Percent for leading party . . . . NA

Votes cast for US Representatives

2004
Total vote (x 1,000) 2,961
Democratic 1,141
Republican 1,820
Leading party . . . . Republican
Percent for leading party 61.5%
2006
Total vote (x 1,000) 2,070
Democratic 932
Republican 1,138
Leading party . . . . Republican
Percent for leading party 55.0%

©2008 Information Publications, Inc.
All rights reserved. Photocopying prohibited.
877-544-INFO (4636) or www.informationpublications.com

State government employment, 2006
Full-time equivalent employees 124,361
Payroll ($ mil) $420.6

Local government employment, 2006
Full-time equivalent employees 381,283
Payroll ($ mil) $1,203.9

Women holding public office, 2008
US Congress 0
Statewide elected office................. 3
State legislature 46

Black public officials, 2002
Total..................................... 640
   US and state legislatures 53
   City/county/regional offices 413
   Judicial/law enforcement............... 48
   Education/school boards............... 126

Hispanic public officials, 2006
Total..................................... 7
   State executives & legislators 3
   City/county/regional offices 2
   Judicial/law enforcement............... 2
   Education/school boards................ 0

Governmental Finance

State government revenues, 2006
Total revenue (x $1,000)............$37,594,200
   per capita $4,024.18
General revenue (x $1,000) $32,352,787
   Intergovernmental 10,609,465
   Taxes 17,033,651
      general sales...................5,802,913
      individual income tax 8,040,366
      corporate income tax............ 890,732
   Current charges...................2,790,463
   Miscellaneous 1,919,208

State government expenditure, 2006
Total expenditure (x $1,000) $34,944,785
   per capita ....,..$3,740.58
General expenditure (x $1,000) $31,300,124
   per capita, total...................$3,350.44
      Education.........................1,534.01
      Public welfare 946.84
      Health........................... 106.20
      Hospitals.........................74.82
      Highways 152.30
      Police protection.................27.53
      Corrections 148.08
      Natural resources.................47.46
      Parks & recreation................18.96
      Governmental administration.......69.59
      Interest on general debt..............47.99

State debt & cash, 2006 ($ per capita)
Debt $1,123.22
Cash/security holdings................$7,443.82

Federal government grants to state & local government, 2005 (x $1,000)
Total.............................$11,165,966
by Federal agency
   Defense 49,431
   Education 1,075,668
   Energy............................40,810
   Environmental Protection Agency 44,181
   Health & Human Services. 6,317,744
   Homeland Security.................47,492
   Housing & Urban Development...... 773,556
   Justice 211,135
   Labor 161,864
   Transportation...................1,373,966
   Veterans Affairs.................. 13,844

Crime & Law Enforcement

Crime, 2006 (rates per 100,000 residents)
Property crimes 364,183
   Burglary 85,117
   Larceny 235,903
   Motor vehicle theft 43,163
   Property crime rate................3,889.2
Violent crimes........................ 44,106
   Murder 600
   Forcible rape.......................2,173
   Robbery............................ 15,509
   Aggravated assault 25,824
   Violent crime rate 471.0
Hate crimes 16

Fraud and identity theft, 2006
Fraud complaints.......................11,941
   rate per 100,000 residents 127.5
Identity theft complaints 8,084
   rate per 100,000 residents 86.3

Law enforcement agencies, 2006
Total agencies......................... 436
Total employees 30,854
   Officers 22,162
   Civilians 8,692

Prisoners, probation, and parole, 2006
Total prisoners....................... 52,792
   percent change, 12/31/05 to 12/31/06 ....8.3%
   in private facilities 9.6%
   in local jails 9.4%
Sentenced to more than one year 52,781
   rate per 100,000 residents 558
Adults on probation 422,790
Adults on parole..................... 22,958

Prisoner demographics, June 30, 2005 (rate per 100,000 residents)
Male..................................1,877
Female................................ 184
White................................. 623
Black................................. 2,068
Hispanic 576

©2008 Information Publications, Inc.
All rights reserved. Photocopying prohibited.
877-544-INFO (4636) or www.informationpublications.com

Arrests, 2006
Total. 234,735
    Persons under 18 years of age 24,368

Persons under sentence of death, 1/1/07
Total. 107
    White. 53
    Black 50
    Hispanic 3

State's highest court
Name . . . . .Supreme Court
Number of members. 7
Length of term . . . . 6 years
Intermediate appeals court? . . . . .yes

Labor & Income

Civilian labor force, 2006 (x 1,000)
Total. 4,694
    Men 2,511
    Women 2,183
    Persons 16-19 years. 184
    White. 3,177
    Black 1,342
    Hispanic 379

Civilian labor force as a percent of civilian non-institutional population, 2006
Total. 67.9%
    Men 75.5
    Women 60.9
    Persons 16-19 years. 35.9
    White. 67.7
    Black 68.1
    Hispanic 76.9

Employment, 2006 (x 1,000)
Total. 4,476
    Men 2,398
    Women 2,078
    Persons 16-19 years. 146
    White. 3,072
    Black 1,236
    Hispanic 361

Unemployment rate, 2006
Total. 4.6%
    Men 4.5
    Women 4.8
    Persons 16-19 years. 20.5
    White. 3.3
    Black 7.9
    Hispanic 4.8

Full-time/part-time labor force, 2003 (x 1,000)
Full-time labor force, employed 3,654
Part-time labor force, employed. 553
Unemployed, looking for
    Full-time work. 187
    Part-time work. 21
*Mean duration of unemployment (weeks). *20.9
    Median 13.0

Labor unions, 2006
Membership (x 1,000). 176
    percent of employed 4.4%

Experienced civilian labor force by private industry, 2006
Total. 3,367,178
    Natural resources & mining 33,050
    Construction 218,511
    Manufacturing. 447,903
    Trade, transportation & utilities 862,887
    Information 115,966
    Finance 227,061
    Professional & business 550,357
    Education & health 414,017
    Leisure & hospitality. 383,810
    Other 98,918

Experienced civilian labor force by occupation, May 2006
Management. 228,460
Business & financial 167,100
Legal. 24,370
Sales 422,650
Office & admin. support. 710,350
Computers & math 92,900
Architecture & engineering. 54,170
Arts & entertainment 35,700
Education 251,300
Social services 42,990
Health care practitioner & technical. . . . 184,650
Health care support 79,160
Maintenance & repair. 188,270
Construction 175,830
Transportation & moving 331,340
Production 345,950
Farming, fishing & forestry. 13,470

Hours and earnings of production workers on manufacturing payrolls, 2006
Average weekly hours 39.5
Average hourly earnings $14.74
Average weekly earnings $582.23

Income and poverty, 2006
Median household income. $46,832
Personal income, per capita (current $). . . $31,891
    in constant (2000) dollars $27,839
Persons below poverty level. 14.7%

Average annual pay
2006 . . . . $40,370
    increase from 2005 . . . . 3.3%

Federal individual income tax returns, 2005
Returns filed. 3,917,976
Adjusted gross income ($1,000) $199,214,881
Total tax liability ($1,000) $24,999,408

Charitable contributions, 2004
Number of contributions 1,318.1
Total amount ($ mil). $5,889.9

©2008 Information Publications, Inc.
All rights reserved. Photocopying prohibited.
877-544-INFO (4636) or www.informationpublications.com

Economy, Business, Industry & Agriculture

Fortune 500 companies, 2007.............. 15
Bankruptcy cases filed, FY 2007........ 48,104

Patents and trademarks issued, 2007

Patents.................................1,614
Trademarks............................ 2,050

Business firm ownership, 2002

Women-owned........................ 196,195
  Sales ($ mil) $30,027
Black-owned.......................... 90,461
  Sales ($ mil) $5,665
Hispanic-owned.......................18,310
  Sales ($ mil) $4,200
Asian-owned 26,925
  Sales ($ mil) $7,984
Amer. Indian/Alaska Native-owned 4,472
  Sales ($ mil) $662
Hawaiian/Pacific Islander-owned 176
  Sales ($ mil) $25

Gross domestic product, 2006 ($ mil)

Total gross domestic product $379,550
  Agriculture, forestry, fishing and
    hunting 3,255
  Mining..............................1,030
  Utilities............................ 8,055
  Construction 19,793
  Manufacturing, durable goods........19,437
  Manufacturing, non-durable goods ... 29,564
  Wholesale trade..................... 30,236
  Retail trade........................ 25,370
  Transportation & warehousing 12,601
  Information 23,434
  Finance & insurance................. 22,328
  Real estate, rental & leasing 45,616
  Professional and technical services.... 24,674
  Educational services..................3,332
  Health care and social assistance.......22,171
  Accommodation/food services.........9,988
  Other services, except government 7,620
  Government 48,859

Establishments, payroll, employees & receipts, by major industry group, 2005

Total............................. 220,528
  Annual payroll ($1,000).........$128,827,270
  Paid employees 3,489,046
*Forestry, fishing & agriculture.............*1,081
  Annual payroll ($1,000)............ $239,929
  Paid employees 8,178
Mining................................ 219
  Annual payroll ($1,000)............ $331,858
  Paid employees 6,494
  Receipts, 2002 ($1,000) $1,635,358

Utilities 572
  Annual payroll ($1,000)..........$1,693,241
  Paid employees 27,291
  Receipts, 2002 ($1,000) ....NA
Construction......................... 22,466
  Annual payroll ($1,000).......... $7,901,149
  Paid employees 201,496
  Receipts, 2002 ($1,000) $41,366,986
Manufacturing........................8,623
  Annual payroll ($1,000).........$16,218,823
  Paid employees 428,467
  Receipts, 2002 ($1,000) $126,156,636
Wholesale trade 13,973
  Annual payroll ($1,000)..........$10,510,976
  Paid employees 200,693
  Receipts, 2002 ($1,000) $201,091,040
Retail trade 35,023
  Annual payroll ($1,000)..........$10,225,754
  Paid employees 474,458
  Receipts, 2002 ($1,000) $90,098,578
Transportation & warehousing...........5,986
  Annual payroll ($1,000)..........$6,188,812
  Paid employees 152,508
  Receipts, 2002 ($1,000) $10,586,256
Information..........................4,198
  Annual payroll ($1,000)..........$7,432,375
  Paid employees 121,905
  Receipts, 2002 ($1,000) ....NA
Finance & insurance 14,779
  Annual payroll ($1,000)..........$10,044,949
  Paid employees 174,282
  Receipts, 2002 ($1,000) ....NA
Professional, scientific & technical 26,284
  Annual payroll ($1,000)..........$11,815,810
  Paid employees 209,548
  Receipts, 2002 ($1,000) $25,165,914
Education 2,197
  Annual payroll ($1,000)..........$1,996,873
  Paid employees 67,298
  Receipts, 2002 ($1,000) $748,348
Health care & social assistance 19,446
  Annual payroll ($1,000)......... $14,800,306
  Paid employees 398,607
  Receipts, 2002 ($1,000) $31,478,319
Arts and entertainment 2,693
  Annual payroll ($1,000)..........$1,095,981
  Paid employees 40,022
  Receipts, 2002 ($1,000) $2,449,690
Real estate...........................11,540
  Annual payroll ($1,000)..........$2,599,140
  Paid employees 62,813
  Receipts, 2002 ($1,000) $9,574,062
Accommodation & food service..........17,218
  Annual payroll ($1,000)..........$4,341,413
  Paid employees 336,804
  Receipts, 2002 ($1,000) $12,740,423

©2008 Information Publications, Inc.
All rights reserved. Photocopying prohibited.
877-544-INFO (4636) or www.informationpublications.com

8   Georgia

Exports, 2006
Value of exported goods ($ mil) $20,073
   Manufactured $16,996
   Non-manufactured $1,619

Foreign direct investment in US affiliates, 2004
Property, plants & equipment ($ mil) . . . $23,574
Employment (x 1,000). 175.9

Agriculture, 2006
Number of farms 49,000
Farm acreage (x 1,000) 10,800
   Acres per farm 220
Farm marketings and income ($ mil)
Total $6,005.1
   Crops $2,240.2
   Livestock $3,764.9
Net farm income $2,387.6

Principal commodities, in order by marketing receipts, 2005
Broilers, Cotton, Greenhouse/nursery, Chicken
eggs, Cattle and calves

Federal economic activity in state
Expenditures, 2005 ($ mil)
   Total. $59,846
      Per capita $6,553.09
   Defense $11,868
   Non-defense $47,979
Defense department, 2006 ($ mil)
   Payroll $7,409
   Contract awards $5,515
   Grants $54
Homeland security grants ($1,000)
   2006 . . . . $44,406
   2007 . . . . $39,959

FDIC-insured financial institutions, 2005
Number 352
Assets ($ billion) $284.7
Deposits ($ billion) $205.8

Fishing, 2006
Catch (x 1,000 lbs) 7,747
Value ($1,000). $10,798

Mining, 2006 ($ mil)
Total non-fuel mineral production $1,970
Percent of U.S. 3.06%

Communication, Energy & Transportation

Communication
Households with computers, 2003 . . . . 60.6%
Households with internet access, 2003 . . . . 53.5%
High-speed internet providers 81
Total high-speed internet lines 2,651,349
   Residential 1,869,159
   Business. 782,190
Wireless phone customers, 12/2006 7,281,724

FCC-licensed stations (as of January 1, 2008)
TV stations 47
FM radio stations. 266
AM radio stations 185

Energy
Energy consumption, 2004
   Total (trillion Btu). 3,141
   Per capita (million Btu) 351.5
By source of production (trillion Btu)
   Coal 835
   Natural gas 410
   Petroleum 1,118
   Nuclear electric power 352
   Hydroelectric power 37
By end-use sector (trillion Btu)
   Residential 720
   Commercial 534
   Industrial 960
   Transportation 928
Electric energy, 2005
   Primary source of electricity. . . . . Coal
   Net generation (billion kWh) 136.7
      percent from renewable sources. 5.3%
   Net summer capability (million kW) 36.5
   CO_2 emitted from generation 89.3
Natural gas utilities, 2005
   Customers (x 1,000) 1,902
   Sales (trillion Btu). 341
   Revenues ($ mil) $656
Nuclear plants, 2007 4
Total CO_2 emitted (million metric tons). 168.0
Energy spending, 2004 ($ mil) $25,659
   per capita $2,872
   Price per million Btu $12.42

Transportation, 2006
Public road & street mileage 118,199
   Urban. 37,325
   Rural 80,874
   Interstate. 1,244
Vehicle miles of travel (millions) 113,532
   per capita 12,152.8
Total motor vehicle registrations 8,286,454
   Automobiles. 4,141,179
   Trucks 4,123,932
   Motorcycles 142,239
Licensed drivers .5,906,834
   19 years & under 286,654
Deaths from motor vehicle accidents 1,693
Gasoline consumed (x 1,000 gallons) 4,982,331
   per capita 533.3

Commuting Statistics, 2006
Average commute time (min) 27.3
   Drove to work alone 78.2%
   Carpooled. 11.5%
   Public transit 2.4%
   Walk to work 1.7%
   Work from home 4.2%

©2008 Information Publications, Inc.
All rights reserved. Photocopying prohibited.
877-544-INFO (4636) or www.informationpublications.com

State Summary

Capital city . . . . Honolulu
Governor . . . . Linda Lingle

Executive Chambers
State Capitol
Honolulu, HI 96813
808-586-0034

Admitted as a state 1959
Area (square miles) 10,931
Population, 2007 (estimate). 1,283,388
Largest city . . . . Honolulu
   Population, 2006 377,357
Personal income per capita, 2006
   (in current dollars) $36,299
Gross domestic product, 2006 ($ mil) $58,307

Leading industries by payroll, 2005

Health care/Social assistance, Accommodation &
Food services, Retail trade

**Leading agricultural commodities
by receipts, 2005**

Greenhouse/nursery, Pineapples, Cane for sugar,
Macadamia nuts, Coffee

Geography & Environment

Total area (square miles). 10,931
   land 6,423
   water 4,508
Federally-owned land, 2004 (acres) 796,726
   percent. 19.4%
Highest point . . . . Mauna Kea
   elevation (feet) 13,796
Lowest point . . . . Pacific Ocean
   elevation (feet) . . . . sea level
General coastline (miles) 750
Tidal shoreline (miles) 1,052
Cropland, 2003 (x 1,000 acres) . . . . NA
Forest land, 2003 (x 1,000 acres). . . . . NA
Capital city . . . . Honolulu
   Population 2000 371,657
   Population 2006 377,357
Largest city . . . . Honolulu
   Population 2000 371,657
   Population 2006 377,357

Number of cities with over 100,000 population

1990 1
2000 1
2006 1

State park and recreation areas, 2005

Area (x 1,000 acres) 27
Number of visitors (x 1,000) . . . . NA
Revenues ($1,000) $2,111
   percent of operating expenditures 28.2%

National forest system land, 2007

Acres 1

Demographics & Population Characteristics

Population

1980 964,691
1990 1,108,229
2000 1,211,537
2006 1,285,498
   Male 643,328
   Female 642,170
Living in group quarters, 2006 37,547
   percent of total. 2.9%
2007 (estimate). 1,283,388
   persons per square mile of land 199.8
2008 (projected). 1,317,607
2010 (projected). 1,340,674
2020 (projected). 1,412,373
2030 (projected). 1,466,046

**Population of Core-Based Statistical Areas
(formerly Metropolitan Areas), x 1,000**

	CBSA	Non-CBSA
1990	1,108	0
2000	1,211	0
2006	1,285	0

Change in population, 2000-2007

Number 71,851
   percent. 5.9%
Natural increase (births minus deaths) 66,781
Net internal migration . . . . -20,583
Net international migration 30,891

Persons by age, 2006

Under 5 years 87,321
5 to 17 years 210,760
18 years and over .987,417
65 years and over .179,370
85 years and over 26,888
   Median age 37.3

Persons by age, 2010 (projected)

Under 5 years 101,347
18 and over 1,024,411
65 and over 191,065
   Median age 37.4

Race, 2006

One Race
   White 367,230
   Black or African American 31,761
   Asian 514,395
   American Indian/Alaska Native. 6,378
   Hawaiian Native/Pacific Islander. 116,967
Two or more races. 248,767

Persons of Hispanic origin, 2006

Total Hispanic or Latino 99,664
   Mexican. 24,385
   Puerto Rican 37,862
   Cuban 771

©2008 Information Publications, Inc.
All rights reserved. Photocopying prohibited.
877-544-INFO (4636) or www.informationpublications.com

Persons of Asian origin, 2006

Total Asian 512,995
- Asian Indian. 1,722
- Chinese 56,288
- Filipino 182,767
- Japanese 194,208
- Korean. 20,823
- Vietnamese. 9,564

Marital status, 2006

Population 15 years & over 1,039,527
- Never married 332,193
- Married. 544,426
- Separated 12,620
- Widowed. 65,080
- Divorced 97,828

Language spoken at home, 2006

Population 5 years and older. 1,198,319
- English only 917,085
- Spanish 17,442
- French 4,917
- German. 3,875
- Chinese 28,201

Households & families, 2006

Households. 432,632
- with persons under 18 years 149,125
- with persons over 65 years. 121,910
- persons per household 2.88
Families. 301,102
- persons per family. 3.45
Married couples. 222,725
Female householder,
- no husband present. 54,111
One-person households 106,013

Nativity, 2006

Number of residents born in state 709,105
- percent of population. 55.2%

Immigration & naturalization, 2006

Legal permanent residents admitted. 7,501
Persons naturalized .5,276
Non-immigrant admissions 1,669,783

Vital Statistics and Health

Marriages

2004 28,843
2005 29,271
2006 28,662

Divorces

2004 . . . . NA
2005 . . . . NA
2006 . . . . NA

Health risks, 2006

Percent of adults who are:
- Smokers. 17.5%
- Overweight (BMI > 25). 56.1%
- Obese (BMI > 30). 20.6%

Births

2005 17,924
- Birthrate (per 1,000). 14.1
- White. 5,115
- Black 487
- Hispanic 2,789
- Asian/Pacific Islander 12,205
- Amer. Indian/Alaska Native. 117
- Low birth weight (2,500g or less). 8.2%
- Cesarian births 25.6%
- Preterm births 12.2%
- To unmarried mothers. 36.3%
- Twin births (per 1,000) 28.0
- Triplets or higher order (per 100,000). 88.4
2006 (preliminary). 18,982
- rate per 1,000 . . . . .14.8

Deaths

2004
All causes 9,030
- rate per 100,000. . . . . .623.1
Heart disease 2,457
- rate per 100,000. . . . . .167.3
Malignant neoplasms 2,088
- rate per 100,000. . . . . .147.8
Cerebrovascular disease. 714
- rate per 100,000. . . . . .47.1
Chronic lower respiratory disease 307
- rate per 100,000. . . . . .21.0
Diabetes. 194
- rate per 100,000. . . . . .13.4
2005 (preliminary). 9,137
- rate per 100,000. . . . . .609.1
2006 (provisional) .9,384

Infant deaths

2004 104
- rate per 1,000 . . . . .5.7
2005 (provisional) 123
- rate per 1,000 . . . . .6.9

Exercise routines, 2005

None. 19.5%
Moderate or greater. 52.2%
Vigorous 30.2%

Abortions, 2004

Total performed in state. 3,467
- rate per 1,000 women age 15-44. 14
- % obtained by out-of-state residents 0.3%

Physicians, 2005

Total. 3,964
- rate per 100,000 persons 311

Community hospitals, 2005

Number of hospitals 25
Beds (x 1,000). 3.0
Patients admitted (x 1,000) 114
Average daily census (x 1,000) 2.3
Average cost per day $1,310
Outpatient visits (x 1 mil) 1.9

©2008 Information Publications, Inc.
All rights reserved. Photocopying prohibited.
877-544-INFO (4636) or www.informationpublications.com

Disability status of population, 2006
5 to 15 years 4.9%
16 to 64 years 9.6%
65 years and over 38.2%

Education

Educational attainment, 2006
Population over 25 years 863,019
  Less than 9th grade. 5.3%
  High school graduate or more 89.0%
  College graduate or more. 29.7%
  Graduate or professional degree. 9.8%

Public school enrollment, 2005-06
Total. 182,818
  Pre-kindergarten through grade 8. 127,379
  Grades 9 through 12. 55,258

Graduating public high school seniors, 2004-05
Diplomas (incl. GED and others) 11,014

SAT scores, 2007
Average critical reading score. 484
Average writing score 473
Average math score 506
Percent of graduates taking test 61%

Public school teachers, 2006-07 (estimate)
Total (x 1,000) 11.5
  Elementary. 6.1
  Secondary. 5.3
Average salary $51,922
  Elementary. $51,922
  Secondary. $51,922

State receipts & expenditures for public schools, 2006-07 (estimate)
Revenue receipts ($ mil) $2,801
Expenditures
Total ($ mil) $2,103
  Per capita $1,466
  Per pupil $11,529

NAEP proficiency scores, 2007

	Reading		Math	
	Basic	Proficient	Basic	Proficient
Grade 4	59.0%	25.7%	76.9%	33.3%
Grade 8	62.5%	20.3%	59.1%	21.2%

Higher education enrollment, fall 2005
Total. 16,926
  Full-time men 4,275
  Full-time women. .7,587
  Part-time men 2,274
  Part-time women. 2,790

Minority enrollment in institutions of higher education, 2005
Black, non-Hispanic .1,534
Hispanic 2,040
Asian/Pacific Islander 40,352
American Indian/Alaska Native. 379

Institutions of higher education, 2005-06
Total. 23
  Public. 10
  Private 13

Earned degrees conferred, 2004-05
Associate's. 3,423
Bachelor's 5,300
Master's 2,025
First-professional. 155
Doctor's 172

Public Libraries, 2006
Number of libraries. 1
Number of outlets 53
Annual visits per capita 4.4
Circulation per capita. 5.1

State & local financial support for higher education, FY 2006
Full-time equivalent enrollment (x 1,000). 35.3
Appropriations per FTE. $10,893

Social Insurance & Welfare Programs

Social Security benefits & beneficiaries, 2005
Beneficiaries (x 1,000) 203
  Retired & dependents. 157
  Survivors. 23
  Disabled & dependents. 23
Annual benefit payments ($ mil) $2,162
  Retired & dependents. $1,607
  Survivors. $302
  Disabled & dependents. $253
Average monthly benefit
  Retired & dependents. $990
  Disabled & dependents. $964
  Widowed. $945

Medicare, July 2005
Enrollment (x 1,000). 182
Payments ($ mil) $628

Medicaid, 2004
Beneficiaries (x 1,000). 218
Payments ($ mil) $862

State Children's Health Insurance Program, 2006
Enrollment (x 1,000). 22.0
Expenditures ($ mil) $19.3

Persons without health insurance, 2006
Number (x 1,000). 110
  percent. 8.8%
Number of children (x 1,000) 19
  percent of children 6.4%

Health care expenditures, 2004
Total expenditures. $6,222
  per capita $4,941

©2008 Information Publications, Inc.
All rights reserved. Photocopying prohibited.
877-544-INFO (4636) or www.informationpublications.com

Federal and state public aid

State unemployment insurance, 2006
Recipients, first payments (x 1,000) 21
Total payments ($ mil) $97
Average weekly benefit $365
Temporary Assistance for Needy Families, 2006
Recipients (x 1,000) 203.4
Families (x 1,000) 81.6
Supplemental Security Income, 2005
Recipients (x 1,000) 22.7
Payments ($ mil) $119.1
Food Stamp Program, 2006
Avg monthly participants (x 1,000) 87.9
Total benefits ($ mil) $147.8

Housing & Construction

Housing units
Total 2005 (estimate) 491,071
Total 2006 (estimate) 500,036
Seasonal or recreational use, 2006 33,334
Owner-occupied, 2006 257,599
   Median home value $529,700
   Homeowner vacancy rate 1.0%
Renter-occupied, 2006 175,033
   Median rent $1,116
   Rental vacancy rate 5.5%
Home ownership rate, 2005 . . . . 59.8%
Home ownership rate, 2006 . . . . 59.9%

New privately-owned housing units
Number authorized, 2006 (x 1,000) 7.5
   Value ($ mil) $1,761.2
Started 2005 (x 1,000, estimate) 6.5
Started 2006 (x 1,000, estimate) 6.2

Existing home sales
2005 (x 1,000) 36.8
2006 (x 1,000) 31.5

Government & Elections

State officials 2008
Governor . . . . Linda Lingle
      Republican, term expires 12/10
Lieutenant Governor . . . . James Aiona
Secretary of State . . . . (no secretary of state)
Attorney General . . . . Mark Bennett
Chief Justice . . . . Ronald Moon

Governorship
Minimum age 30
Length of term . . . . 4 years
Consecutive terms permitted 2
Who succeeds . . . . Lieutenant Governor

Local governments by type, 2002
Total 19
   County 3
   Municipal 1
   Township 0
   School District 0
   Special District 15

State legislature

Name . . . . Legislature
Upper chamber . . . . .Senate
   Number of members 25
   Length of term . . . . 4 years
   Party in majority, 2008 . . . . Democratic
Lower chamber . . . . House of Representatives
   Number of members 51
   Length of term . . . . 2 years
   Party in majority, 2008 . . . . Democratic

Federal representation, 2008 (110ᵗʰ Congress)
Senator . . . . .Daniel Inouye
   Party . . . . .Democratic
   Year term expires 2011
Senator . . . . Daniel Akaka
   Party . . . . .Democratic
   Year term expires 2013
Representatives, total 2
   Democrats 2
   Republicans 0

Voters in November 2006 election (estimate)
Total 387,520
   Male 178,218
   Female 209,302
   White 97,342
   Black 2,881
   Hispanic 9,187
   Asian 201,645

Presidential election, 2004
Total Popular Vote 429,013
   Kerry 231,708
   Bush 194,191
Total Electoral Votes 4

Votes cast for US Senators
2004
Total vote (x 1,000) 415
Leading party .Democratic
Percent for leading party 75.5%
2006
Total vote (x 1,000) 343
Leading party .Democratic
Percent for leading party 61.3%

Votes cast for US Representatives
2004
Total vote (x 1,000) 417
   Democratic 262
   Republican 148
Leading party .Democratic
Percent for leading party 62.9%
2006
Total vote (x 1,000) 338
   Democratic 220
   Republican 118
Leading party .Democratic
Percent for leading party 65.0%

©2008 Information Publications, Inc.
All rights reserved. Photocopying prohibited.
877-544-INFO (4636) or www.informationpublications.com

State government employment, 2006
Full-time equivalent employees 54,958
Payroll ($ mil) $207.3

Local government employment, 2006
Full-time equivalent employees 14,636
Payroll ($ mil) $61.4

Women holding public office, 2008
US Congress............................... 1
Statewide elected office...................... 1
State legislature 25

Black public officials, 2002
Total...................................... 1
US and state legislatures 1
City/county/regional offices 0
Judicial/law enforcement.................. 0
Education/school boards 0

Hispanic public officials, 2006
Total...................................... 1
State executives & legislators 1
City/county/regional offices 0
Judicial/law enforcement.................. 0
Education/school boards.................. 0

Governmental Finance

State government revenues, 2006
Total revenue (x $1,000).............$9,856,552
per capita $7,708.65
General revenue (x $1,000) $8,551,896
Intergovernmental 1,834,393
Taxes 4,918,655
general sales....................2,355,316
individual income tax 1,550,757
corporate income tax............ 148,084
Current charges..................1,142,090
Miscellaneous 656,758

State government expenditure, 2006
Total expenditure (x $1,000) $8,913,697
per capita $6,971.26
General expenditure (x $1,000) $8,090,272
per capita, total................... $6,327.27
Education 2,277.91
Public welfare 1,116.21
Health 389.80
Hospitals........................318.94
Highways 209.78
Police protection....................11.43
Corrections 140.24
Natural resources 93.26
Parks & recreation 56.81
Governmental administration...... 303.86
Interest on general debt........... 338.00

State debt & cash, 2006 ($ per capita)
Debt................................$4,529.66
Cash/security holdings.............$14,327.06

Federal government grants to state & local government, 2005 (x $1,000)
Total............................$2,167,856
by Federal agency
Defense 37,635
Education 213,383
Energy 7,986
Environmental Protection Agency 29,597
Health & Human Services. 1,022,177
Homeland Security.................. 10,223
Housing & Urban Development...... 153,043
Justice 47,471
Labor 41,913
Transportation 309,643
Veterans Affairs...................20,916

Crime & Law Enforcement

Crime, 2006 (rates per 100,000 residents)
Property crimes 54,382
Burglary 8,709
Larceny 37,910
Motor vehicle theft 7,763
Property crime rate..................4,230.4
Violent crimes..........................3,615
Murder 21
Forcible rape........................ 355
Robbery............................1,143
Aggravated assault 2,096
Violent crime rate 281.2
Hate crimes............................ NA

Fraud and identity theft, 2006
Fraud complaints...................... 2,020
rate per 100,000 residents 157.1
Identity theft complaints 615
rate per 100,000 residents 47.8

Law enforcement agencies, 2006
Total agencies............................ 4
Total employees 3,654
Officers 2,896
Civilians 758

Prisoners, probation, and parole, 2006
Total prisoners.......................5,967
percent change, 12/31/05 to 12/31/06 .. -2.9%
in private facilities 32.1%
in local jails .... NA
Sentenced to more than one year 4,373
rate per 100,000 residents 338
Adults on probation 18,598
Adults on parole......................2,316

Prisoner demographics, June 30, 2005 (rate per 100,000 residents)
Male..................................... 787
Female 109
White.................................... 453
Black.................................... 851
Hispanic 185

©2008 Information Publications, Inc.
All rights reserved. Photocopying prohibited.
877-544-INFO (4636) or www.informationpublications.com

Arrests, 2006
Total...................................48,018
    Persons under 18 years of age..........10,315

Persons under sentence of death, 1/1/07
Total.......................................0
    White....................................0
    Black....................................0
    Hispanic.................................0

State's highest court
Name.........................Supreme Court
Number of members........................5
Length of term.......................10 years
Intermediate appeals court?...............yes

Labor & Income

Civilian labor force, 2006 (x 1,000)
Total.....................................657
    Men....................................342
    Women..................................315
    Persons 16-19 years.....................23
    White..................................147
    Black...................................NA
    Hispanic................................40

Civilian labor force as a percent of civilian non-institutional population, 2006
Total....................................66.5%
    Men....................................72.6
    Women..................................61.0
    Persons 16-19 years....................42.0
    White..................................67.1
    Black...................................NA
    Hispanic...............................72.5

Employment, 2006 (x 1,000)
Total.....................................639
    Men....................................333
    Women..................................307
    Persons 16-19 years.....................20
    White..................................144
    Black...................................NA
    Hispanic................................39

Unemployment rate, 2006
Total.....................................2.7%
    Men....................................2.8
    Women..................................2.5
    Persons 16-19 years....................14.8
    White..................................2.6
    Black...................................NA
    Hispanic................................4.4

Full-time/part-time labor force, 2003 (x 1,000)
Full-time labor force, employed...........487
Part-time labor force, employed...........105
Unemployed, looking for
    Full-time work..........................22
    Part-time work...........................5
Mean duration of unemployment (weeks)......15.9
    Median..................................8.9

Labor unions, 2006
Membership (x 1,000)....................139
    percent of employed..................24.7%

Experienced civilian labor force by private industry, 2006
Total................................500,515
    Natural resources & mining............7,587
    Construction.........................35,723
    Manufacturing........................15,149
    Trade, transportation & utilities....120,758
    Information..........................10,706
    Finance..............................29,922
    Professional & business..............78,275
    Education & health...................69,697
    Leisure & hospitality...............107,807
    Other................................24,686

Experienced civilian labor force by occupation, May 2006
Management...........................28,520
Business & financial.................23,180
Legal.................................3,860
Sales................................62,240
Office & admin. support.............103,830
Computers & math.....................8,500
Architecture & engineering...........8,750
Arts & entertainment.................9,790
Education............................38,710
Social services......................9,420
Health care practitioner & technical...24,650
Health care support..................13,290
Maintenance & repair.................22,570
Construction.........................30,560
Transportation & moving..............41,870
Production...........................17,930
Farming, fishing & forestry...........1,070

Hours and earnings of production workers on manufacturing payrolls, 2006
Average weekly hours....................38.6
Average hourly earnings..............$15.89
Average weekly earnings.............$613.35

Income and poverty, 2006
Median household income.............$61,160
Personal income, per capita (current $)...$36,299
    in constant (2000) dollars...........$31,687
Persons below poverty level.............9.3%

Average annual pay
2006.................................$37,799
    increase from 2005....................4.0%

Federal individual income tax returns, 2005
Returns filed.......................621,014
Adjusted gross income ($1,000).....$31,284,219
Total tax liability ($1,000)..........$3,785,802

Charitable contributions, 2004
Number of contributions...............178.4
Total amount ($ mil).................$560.9

©2008 Information Publications, Inc.
All rights reserved. Photocopying prohibited.
877-544-INFO (4636) or www.informationpublications.com

Economy, Business, Industry & Agriculture

Fortune 500 companies, 2007 0
Bankruptcy cases filed, FY 2007 1,281

Patents and trademarks issued, 2007

Patents 83
Trademarks 264

Business firm ownership, 2002

Women-owned 29,943
  Sales ($ mil) $4,594
Black-owned 817
  Sales ($ mil) $81
Hispanic-owned 3,095
  Sales ($ mil) $483
Asian-owned 44,924
  Sales ($ mil) $12,556
Amer. Indian/Alaska Native-owned 953
  Sales ($ mil) $114
Hawaiian/Pacific Islander-owned 8,359
  Sales ($ mil) $1,436

Gross domestic product, 2006 ($ mil)

Total gross domestic product $58,307
  Agriculture, forestry, fishing and
    hunting 348
  Mining 39
  Utilities 997
  Construction 3,465
  Manufacturing, durable goods 330
  Manufacturing, non-durable goods 668
  Wholesale trade 1,998
  Retail trade 4,279
  Transportation & warehousing 1,997
  Information 1,461
  Finance & insurance 2,645
  Real estate, rental & leasing 10,457
  Professional and technical services 2,653
  Educational services 605
  Health care and social assistance 3,902
  Accommodation/food services 4,887
  Other services, except government 1,427
  Government 12,844

Establishments, payroll, employees & receipts, by major industry group, 2005

Total 32,244
  Annual payroll ($1,000) $16,163,137
  Paid employees 490,682
Forestry, fishing & agriculture 46
  Annual payroll ($1,000) $7,001
  Paid employees 350
Mining 9
  Annual payroll ($1,000) . . . . NA
  Paid employees . . . . NA
  Receipts, 2002 ($1,000) $25,581

Utilities 46
  Annual payroll ($1,000) $187,927
  Paid employees 2,730
  Receipts, 2002 ($1,000) . . . . .NA
Construction 2,753
  Annual payroll ($1,000) $1,556,880
  Paid employees 29,480
  Receipts, 2002 ($1,000) $5,640,054
Manufacturing 946
  Annual payroll ($1,000) $478,722
  Paid employees .14,923
  Receipts, 2002 ($1,000) $3,460,199
Wholesale trade 1,861
  Annual payroll ($1,000) $763,702
  Paid employees 19,978
  Receipts, 2002 ($1,000) $9,986,355
Retail trade 4,924
  Annual payroll ($1,000) $1,645,587
  Paid employees 69,323
  Receipts, 2002 ($1,000) $13,008,182
Transportation & warehousing 850
  Annual payroll ($1,000) $926,945
  Paid employees 26,490
  Receipts, 2002 ($1,000) $1,293,826
Information 631
  Annual payroll ($1,000) $471,448
  Paid employees 10,291
  Receipts, 2002 ($1,000) . . . . .NA
Finance & insurance 1,600
  Annual payroll ($1,000) $1,060,036
  Paid employees 19,707
  Receipts, 2002 ($1,000) . . . . .NA
Professional, scientific & technical 3,257
  Annual payroll ($1,000) $1,218,103
  Paid employees 24,724
  Receipts, 2002 ($1,000) $2,290,675
Education 516
  Annual payroll ($1,000) $480,968
  Paid employees 16,801
  Receipts, 2002 ($1,000) $107,844
Health care & social assistance 3,389
  Annual payroll ($1,000) $2,358,932
  Paid employees 61,005
  Receipts, 2002 ($1,000) $4,686,323
Arts and entertainment 490
  Annual payroll ($1,000) $231,148
  Paid employees .11,854
  Receipts, 2002 ($1,000) $605,862
Real estate 2,111
  Annual payroll ($1,000) $564,209
  Paid employees 15,047
  Receipts, 2002 ($1,000) $2,372,266
Accommodation & food service 3,393
  Annual payroll ($1,000) $2,308,858
  Paid employees 99,886
  Receipts, 2002 ($1,000) $5,551,380

©2008 Information Publications, Inc.
All rights reserved. Photocopying prohibited.
877-544-INFO (4636) or www.informationpublications.com

8   Hawaii

Exports, 2006
Value of exported goods ($ mil) $706
  Manufactured $477
  Non-manufactured $91

Foreign direct investment in US affiliates, 2004
Property, plants & equipment ($ mil) $6,948
Employment (x 1,000). .31.6

Agriculture, 2006
Number of farms 5,500
Farm acreage (x 1,000) 1,300
  Acres per farm 236
Farm marketings and income ($ mil)
Total $554.6
  Crops $466.9
  Livestock $87.7
Net farm income $105.5

Principal commodities, in order by
  marketing receipts, 2005
Greenhouse/nursery, Pineapples, Cane for sugar,
      Macadamia nuts, Coffee

Federal economic activity in state
Expenditures, 2005 ($ mil)
  Total. $12,699
    Per capita $9,973.72
  Defense $5,015
  Non-defense $7,684
Defense department, 2006 ($ mil)
  Payroll $4,064
  Contract awards $1,963
  Grants $77
Homeland security grants ($1,000)
  2006 . . . . $12,935
  2007 . . . .$12,114

FDIC-insured financial institutions, 2005
Number 9
Assets ($ billion) $37.5
Deposits ($ billion) $27.5

Fishing, 2006
Catch (x 1,000 lbs) 26,021
Value ($1,000). $66,780

Mining, 2006 ($ mil)
Total non-fuel mineral production $107
Percent of U.S. 0.17%

Communication, Energy & Transportation

Communication
Households with computers, 2003 . . . . 63.3%
Households with internet access, 2003 . . . . 55.0%
High-speed internet providers 14
Total high-speed internet lines 417,674
  Residential 294,863
  Business. 122,811
Wireless phone customers, 12/2006 1,034,788

FCC-licensed stations (as of January 1, 2008)
TV stations 27
FM radio stations. 58
AM radio stations 31

Energy
Energy consumption, 2004
  Total (trillion Btu). 324
  Per capita (million Btu) 256.9
By source of production (trillion Btu)
  Coal 19
  Natural gas 3
  Petroleum 283
  Nuclear electric power 0
  Hydroelectric power 1
By end-use sector (trillion Btu)
  Residential 35
  Commercial 47
  Industrial 69
  Transportation 172
Electric energy, 2005
  Primary source of electricity. . . . . . . Petroleum
  Net generation (billion kWh) 11.5
    percent from renewable sources. 5.5%
  Net summer capability (million kW) 2.4
  CO_2 emitted from generation 9.0
Natural gas utilities, 2005
  Customers (x 1,000) 29
  Sales (trillion Btu) 3
  Revenues ($ mil) $70
Nuclear plants, 2007 0
Total CO_2 emitted (million metric tons) 21.5
Energy spending, 2004 ($ mil) $4,038
  per capita $3,207
  Price per million Btu $18.05

Transportation, 2006
Public road & street mileage 4,330
  Urban. 2,290
  Rural 2,040
  Interstate. 55
Vehicle miles of travel (millions) 10,182
  per capita 7,963.2
Total motor vehicle registrations 1,008,540
  Automobiles. 538,581
  Trucks 464,288
  Motorcycles 31,223
Licensed drivers 867,375
  19 years & under 29,602
Deaths from motor vehicle accidents 161
Gasoline consumed (x 1,000 gallons) 483,136
  per capita 377.9

Commuting Statistics, 2006
Average commute time (min) 25.5
  Drove to work alone 67.0%
  Carpooled. 16.0%
  Public transit 5.4%
  Walk to work 4.8%
  Work from home 4.3%

©2008 Information Publications, Inc.
All rights reserved. Photocopying prohibited.
877-544-INFO (4636) or www.informationpublications.com

State Summary

Capital city . . . . .Boise
Governor. . . . . C.L. "Butch" Otter
700 West Jefferson
Second Floor
Boise, ID 83702
208-334-2100
Admitted as a state 1890
Area (square miles) 83,570
Population, 2007 (estimate). 1,499,402
Largest city . . . . .Boise
    Population, 2006. 198,638
Personal income per capita, 2006
    (in current dollars) $29,952
Gross domestic product, 2006 ($ mil) $49,907

Leading industries by payroll, 2005

Manufacturing, Health care/Social assistance,
Retail trade

**Leading agricultural commodities
by receipts, 2005**

Dairy products, Cattle and calves, Potatoes,
Wheat, Hay

Geography & Environment

Total area (square miles). 83,570
    land 82,747
    water 823
Federally-owned land, 2004 (acres) . . .26,565,412
    percent. 50.2%
Highest point . . . . Borah Peak
    elevation (feet) 12,662
Lowest point . . . . .Snake River
    elevation (feet) 710
General coastline (miles) 0
Tidal shoreline (miles) 0
Cropland, 2003 (x 1,000 acres) 5,453
Forest land, 2003 (x 1,000 acres). 4,007
Capital city . . . . .Boise
    Population 2000 185,787
    Population 2006 198,638
Largest city . . . . .Boise
    Population 2000 185,787
    Population 2006 198,638

Number of cities with over 100,000 population

1990 1
2000 1
2006 1

State park and recreation areas, 2005

Area (x 1,000 acres). 46
Number of visitors (x 1,000) . . . . NA
Revenues ($1,000) $3,241
    percent of operating expenditures. 21.2%

National forest system land, 2007

Acres 20,466,617

Demographics & Population Characteristics

Population

1980 943,935
1990 1,006,749
2000 1,293,956
2006 1,466,465
    Male. 738,366
    Female 728,099
Living in group quarters, 2006. 33,801
    percent of total. .2.3%
2007 (estimate). 1,499,402
    persons per square mile of land 18.1
2008 (projected). 1,472,584
2010 (projected). 1,517,291
2020 (projected). 1,741,333
2030 (projected). 1,969,624

**Population of Core-Based Statistical Areas
(formerly Metropolitan Areas), x 1,000**

	CBSA	Non-CBSA
1990	846	161
2000	1,103	191
2006	1,267	200

Change in population, 2000-2007

Number. 205,446
    percent. 15.9%
Natural increase (births minus deaths) 88,483
Net internal migration 100,415
Net international migration 17,520

Persons by age, 2006

Under 5 years 112,963
5 to 17 years 281,317
18 years and over 1,072,185
65 years and over 169,173
85 years and over 23,384
    Median age. 34.2

Persons by age, 2010 (projected)

Under 5 years 115,880
18 and over 1,117,054
65 and over 181,416
    Median age. 34.8

Race, 2006

One Race

White. 1,396,543
Black or African American 9,534
Asian 15,918
American Indian/Alaska Native. 20,897
Hawaiian Native/Pacific Islander. 1,841
Two or more races. .21,732

Persons of Hispanic origin, 2006

Total Hispanic or Latino 138,871
    Mexican. 120,107
    Puerto Rican 1,607
    Cuban 1,011

©2008 Information Publications, Inc.
All rights reserved. Photocopying prohibited.
877-544-INFO (4636) or www.informationpublications.com

Persons of Asian origin, 2006

Total Asian	15,335
Asian Indian	1,269
Chinese	4,281
Filipino	2,077
Japanese	2,560
Korean	1,129
Vietnamese	1,671

Marital status, 2006

Population 15 years & over	1,140,486
Never married	272,985
Married	669,856
Separated	15,659
Widowed	60,335
Divorced	137,310

Language spoken at home, 2006

Population 5 years and older	1,354,099
English only	1,217,344
Spanish	103,686
French	2,365
German	5,356
Chinese	2,488

Households & families, 2006

Households	548,555
with persons under 18 years	197,141
with persons over 65 years	115,908
persons per household	2.61
Families	382,686
persons per family	3.11
Married couples	313,995
Female householder, no husband present	47,130
One-person households	130,887

Nativity, 2006

Number of residents born in state	661,708
percent of population	45.1%

Immigration & naturalization, 2006

Legal permanent residents admitted	2,377
Persons naturalized	980
Non-immigrant admissions	26,975

Vital Statistics and Health

Marriages

2004	14,997
2005	14,935
2006	14,811

Divorces

2004	6,922
2005	7,126
2006	7,500

Health risks, 2006

Percent of adults who are:

Smokers	16.8%
Overweight (BMI > 25)	59.7%
Obese (BMI > 30)	24.1%

Births

2005	23,062
Birthrate (per 1,000)	16.1
White	22,112
Black	146
Hispanic	3,488
Asian/Pacific Islander	392
Amer. Indian/Alaska Native	412
Low birth weight (2,500g or less)	6.7%
Cesarian births	22.6%
Preterm births	11.4%
To unmarried mothers	22.9%
Twin births (per 1,000)	29.5
Triplets or higher order (per 100,000)	178.1
2006 (preliminary)	24,184
rate per 1,000	16.5

Deaths

2004

All causes	10,028
rate per 100,000	753.5
Heart disease	2,450
rate per 100,000	184.3
Malignant neoplasms	2,227
rate per 100,000	169.3
Cerebrovascular disease	712
rate per 100,000	53.8
Chronic lower respiratory disease	572
rate per 100,000	44.4
Diabetes	344
rate per 100,000	26.4
2005 (preliminary)	10,554
rate per 100,000	766.4
2006 (provisional)	10,703

Infant deaths

2004	139
rate per 1,000	6.2
2005 (provisional)	154
rate per 1,000	6.7

Exercise routines, 2005

None	21.6%
Moderate or greater	54.0%
Vigorous	31.1%

Abortions, 2004

Total performed in state	963
rate per 1,000 women age 15-44	3
% obtained by out-of-state residents	3.6%

Physicians, 2005

Total	2,429
rate per 100,000 persons	170

Community hospitals, 2005

Number of hospitals	39
Beds (x 1,000)	3.3
Patients admitted (x 1,000)	130
Average daily census (x 1,000)	1.8
Average cost per day	$1,484
Outpatient visits (x 1 mil)	2.7

©2008 Information Publications, Inc.
All rights reserved. Photocopying prohibited.
877-544-INFO (4636) or www.informationpublications.com

Disability status of population, 2006
5 to 15 years 5.9%
16 to 64 years 12.8%
65 years and over 41.4%

Education

Educational attainment, 2006
Population over 25 years 919,203
  Less than 9th grade 4.5%
  High school graduate or more 87.3%
  College graduate or more 23.3%
  Graduate or professional degree 7.1%

Public school enrollment, 2005-06
Total 261,982
  Pre-kindergarten through grade 8 182,829
  Grades 9 through 12 79,153

Graduating public high school seniors, 2004-05
Diplomas (incl. GED and others) 15,877

SAT scores, 2007
Average critical reading score 541
Average writing score 519
Average math score 539
Percent of graduates taking test 19%

Public school teachers, 2006-07 (estimate)
Total (x 1,000) 14.8
  Elementary 7.7
  Secondary 7.1
Average salary $42,798
  Elementary $42,837
  Secondary $42,756

State receipts & expenditures for public schools, 2006-07 (estimate)
Revenue receipts ($ mil) $1,963
Expenditures
Total ($ mil) $2,130
  Per capita $1,309
  Per pupil $7,649

NAEP proficiency scores, 2007

	Reading		Math	
	Basic	Proficient	Basic	Proficient
Grade 4	70.3%	35.1%	84.5%	40.1%
Grade 8	78.5%	31.6%	74.7%	34.1%

Higher education enrollment, fall 2005
Total 17,405
  Full-time men 6,860
  Full-time women .8,514
  Part-time men 885
  Part-time women .1,146

Minority enrollment in institutions of higher education, 2005
Black, non-Hispanic 651
Hispanic 3,594
Asian/Pacific Islander 1,472
American Indian/Alaska Native 1,022

Institutions of higher education, 2005-06
Total 14
  Public 7
  Private 7

Earned degrees conferred, 2004-05
Associate's 3,189
Bachelor's 7,295
Master's 1,623
First-professional 163
Doctor's 139

Public Libraries, 2006
Number of libraries 104
Number of outlets 146
Annual visits per capita 6.0
Circulation per capita 8.3

State & local financial support for higher education, FY 2006
Full-time equivalent enrollment (x 1,000) 44.6
Appropriations per FTE $7,303

Social Insurance & Welfare Programs

Social Security benefits & beneficiaries, 2005
Beneficiaries (x 1,000) 228
  Retired & dependents 162
  Survivors 28
  Disabled & dependents 37
Annual benefit payments ($ mil) $2,379
  Retired & dependents $1,618
  Survivors $388
  Disabled & dependents $373
Average monthly benefit
  Retired & dependents $980
  Disabled & dependents $913
  Widowed $985

Medicare, July 2005
Enrollment (x 1,000) 192
Payments ($ mil) $1,005

Medicaid, 2004
Beneficiaries (x 1,000) 383
Payments ($ mil) $2,206

State Children's Health Insurance Program, 2006
Enrollment (x 1,000) 24.7
Expenditures ($ mil) $23.0

Persons without health insurance, 2006
Number (x 1,000) 227
  percent 15.4%
Number of children (x 1,000) 52
  percent of children 12.9%

Health care expenditures, 2004
Total expenditures $6,197
  per capita $4,444

©2008 Information Publications, Inc.
All rights reserved. Photocopying prohibited.
877-544-INFO (4636) or www.informationpublications.com

Federal and state public aid

State unemployment insurance, 2006
Recipients, first payments (x 1,000) 40
Total payments ($ mil) $101
Average weekly benefit $241
Temporary Assistance for Needy Families, 2006
Recipients (x 1,000) 35.3
Families (x 1,000) 21.4
Supplemental Security Income, 2005
Recipients (x 1,000) 22.2
Payments ($ mil) $105.6
Food Stamp Program, 2006
Avg monthly participants (x 1,000) 91.1
Total benefits ($ mil) $100.2

Housing & Construction

Housing units

Total 2005 (estimate) 595,623
Total 2006 (estimate) 615,624
Seasonal or recreational use, 2006 31,591
Owner-occupied, 2006 390,982
    Median home value $163,900
    Homeowner vacancy rate 2.2%
Renter-occupied, 2006 157,573
    Median rent $623
    Rental vacancy rate 7.4%
Home ownership rate, 2005 . . . . 74.2%
Home ownership rate, 2006 . . . . 75.1%

New privately-owned housing units

Number authorized, 2006 (x 1,000) 17.1
    Value ($ mil) $2,987.3
Started 2005 (x 1,000, estimate) 13.1
Started 2006 (x 1,000, estimate) 12.8

Existing home sales

2005 (x 1,000) . . . . NA
2006 (x 1,000) 37.0

Government & Elections

State officials 2008

Governor . . . . C.L. "Butch" Otter
            Republican, term expires 1/11
Lieutenant Governor . . . . .Jim Risch
Secretary of State . . . . Ben Ysursa
Attorney General . . . . Lawrence Wasden
Chief Justice . . . . Daniel Eismann

Governorship

Minimum age 30
Length of term . . . . 4 years
Consecutive terms permitted . . . . . . not specified
Who succeeds . . . . Lieutenant Governor

Local governments by type, 2002

Total 1,158
    County 44
    Municipal 200
    Township 0
    School District 116
    Special District 798

State legislature

Name . . . . Legislature
Upper chamber . . . . .Senate
    Number of members 35
    Length of term . . . . 2 years
    Party in majority, 2008 . . . . Republican
Lower chamber . . . . . . .House of Representatives
    Number of members 70
    Length of term . . . . 2 years
    Party in majority, 2008 . . . . Republican

Federal representation, 2008 (110th Congress)

Senator . . . . .Larry Craig
    Party . . . . Republican
    Year term expires 2009
Senator . . . . .Mike Crapo
    Party . . . . Republican
    Year term expires 2011
Representatives, total 2
    Democrats 0
    Republicans 2

Voters in November 2006 election (estimate)

Total 522,807
    Male 249,300
    Female 273,506
    White 515,271
    Black . . . . NA
    Hispanic 5,904
    Asian 2,553

Presidential election, 2004

Total Popular Vote 598,447
    Kerry 181,098
    Bush 409,235
Total Electoral Votes 4

Votes cast for US Senators

2004
Total vote (x 1,000) 504
Leading party . . . . Republican
Percent for leading party 99.2%
2006
Total vote (x 1,000) . . . . NA
Leading party . . . . NA
Percent for leading party . . . . NA

Votes cast for US Representatives

2004
Total vote (x 1,000) 572
    Democratic 171
    Republican 401
Leading party . . . . Republican
Percent for leading party 70.1%
2006
Total vote (x 1,000) 445
    Democratic 177
    Republican 248
Leading party . . . . Republican
Percent for leading party 55.7%

©2008 Information Publications, Inc.
All rights reserved. Photocopying prohibited.
877-544-INFO (4636) or www.informationpublications.com

State government employment, 2006
Full-time equivalent employees 22,259
Payroll ($ mil) $74.5

Local government employment, 2006
Full-time equivalent employees 57,154
Payroll ($ mil) $161.4

Women holding public office, 2008
US Congress 0
Statewide elected office..................... 1
State legislature 25

Black public officials, 2002
Total....................................... 1
   US and state legislatures 0
   City/county/regional offices 1
   Judicial/law enforcement.................. 0
   Education/school boards 0

Hispanic public officials, 2006
Total....................................... 2
   State executives & legislators 1
   City/county/regional offices 1
   Judicial/law enforcement.................. 0
   Education/school boards.................. 0

Governmental Finance

State government revenues, 2006
Total revenue (x $1,000)............. $7,785,621
   per capita $5,318.49
General revenue (x $1,000) $5,978,897
   Intergovernmental 1,836,357
   Taxes 3,142,663
      general sales....................1,078,543
      individual income tax 1,222,569
      corporate income tax 198,302
   Current charges.................... 532,248
   Miscellaneous 467,629

State government expenditure, 2006
Total expenditure (x $1,000) $6,352,876
   per capita $4,339.76
General expenditure (x $1,000) $5,659,741
   per capita, total................... $3,866.27
      Education 1,477.30
      Public welfare 982.72
      Health 93.94
      Hospitals.........................31.00
      Highways 410.52
      Police protection...................31.04
      Corrections 136.50
      Natural resources 132.28
      Parks & recreation 24.12
      Governmental administration.......185.97
      Interest on general debt.............83.96

State debt & cash, 2006 ($ per capita)
Debt $1,677.25
Cash/security holdings...............$10,008.78

Federal government grants to state & local government, 2005 (x $1,000)
Total............................. $2,092,900
by Federal agency
   Defense 26,313
   Education 178,209
   Energy 17,226
   Environmental Protection Agency 41,443
   Health & Human Services. 1,039,421
   Homeland Security....................8,013
   Housing & Urban Development....... 86,303
   Justice 33,407
   Labor 44,478
   Transportation 335,979
   Veterans Affairs......................6,075

Crime & Law Enforcement

Crime, 2006 (rates per 100,000 residents)
Property crimes 35,471
   Burglary 7,526
   Larceny 25,516
   Motor vehicle theft 2,429
   Property crime rate..................2,418.8
Violent crimes.........................3,625
   Murder 36
   Forcible rape......................... 587
   Robbery............................. 301
   Aggravated assault 2,701
   Violent crime rate 247.2
Hate crimes............................ 25

Fraud and identity theft, 2006
Fraud complaints......................2,012
   rate per 100,000 residents 137.2
Identity theft complaints 718
   rate per 100,000 residents 49.0

Law enforcement agencies, 2006
Total agencies.......................... 107
Total employees 3,896
   Officers 2,594
   Civilians 1,302

Prisoners, probation, and parole, 2006
Total prisoners........................7,124
   percent change, 12/31/05 to 12/31/06 ....4.5%
   in private facilities 27.0%
   in local jails 6.4%
Sentenced to more than one year 7,124
   rate per 100,000 residents 480
Adults on probation 48,609
Adults on parole.......................2,732

Prisoner demographics, June 30, 2005
   (rate per 100,000 residents)
Male....................................1,379
Female 185
White.................................. 675
Black.................................. 2,869
Hispanic 1,654

©2008 Information Publications, Inc.
All rights reserved. Photocopying prohibited.
877-544-INFO (4636) or www.informationpublications.com

Arrests, 2006
Total 65,945
   Persons under 18 years of age 14,339

Persons under sentence of death, 1/1/07
Total 20
   White 20
   Black 0
   Hispanic 0

State's highest court
Name . . . . .Supreme Court
Number of members 5
Length of term . . . . 6 years
Intermediate appeals court? . . . . .yes

Labor & Income

Civilian labor force, 2006 (x 1,000)
Total 759
   Men 416
   Women 343
   Persons 16-19 years 48
   White 724
   Black . . . . NA
   Hispanic 63

Civilian labor force as a percent of civilian non-institutional population, 2006
Total 68.9%
   Men 76.4
   Women 61.5
   Persons 16-19 years 52.4
   White 69.1
   Black . . . . NA
   Hispanic 71.3

Employment, 2006 (x 1,000)
Total 732
   Men 403
   Women 329
   Persons 16-19 years 43
   White 699
   Black . . . . NA
   Hispanic 60

Unemployment rate, 2006
Total 3.5%
   Men 3.1
   Women 4.0
   Persons 16-19 years 11.4
   White 3.3
   Black . . . . NA
   Hispanic 4.5

Full-time/part-time labor force, 2003 (x 1,000)
Full-time labor force, employed 510
Part-time labor force, employed 145
Unemployed, looking for
   Full-time work 31
   Part-time work 7
Mean duration of unemployment (weeks) 14.1
   Median 7.0

Labor unions, 2006
Membership (x 1,000) 37
   percent of employed 6.0%

Experienced civilian labor force by private industry, 2006
Total 532,929
   Natural resources & mining 24,096
   Construction 52,113
   Manufacturing 65,981
   Trade, transportation & utilities 126,344
   Information 10,592
   Finance 29,828
   Professional & business 81,598
   Education & health 66,979
   Leisure & hospitality 59,727
   Other 15,628

Experienced civilian labor force by occupation, May 2006
Management 43,590
Business & financial 20,750
Legal 3,640
Sales 61,090
Office & admin. support 104,050
Computers & math 10,760
Architecture & engineering 15,080
Arts & entertainment 7,440
Education 34,830
Social services 9,050
Health care practitioner & technical 28,050
Health care support 16,590
Maintenance & repair 28,090
Construction 41,440
Transportation & moving 46,990
Production 40,890
Farming, fishing & forestry 6,520

Hours and earnings of production workers on manufacturing payrolls, 2006
Average weekly hours 41.7
Average hourly earnings $16.89
Average weekly earnings $704.31

Income and poverty, 2006
Median household income $42,865
Personal income, per capita (current $) . . . $29,952
   in constant (2000) dollars $26,146
Persons below poverty level 12.6%

Average annual pay
2006 . . . . $32,580
   increase from 2005 . . . . 5.9%

Federal individual income tax returns, 2005
Returns filed 613,932
Adjusted gross income ($1,000) $28,226,440
Total tax liability ($1,000) $3,288,355

Charitable contributions, 2004
Number of contributions 175.0
Total amount ($ mil) $707.0

©2008 Information Publications, Inc.
All rights reserved. Photocopying prohibited.
877-544-INFO (4636) or www.informationpublications.com

Economy, Business, Industry & Agriculture

Fortune 500 companies, 2007 2
Bankruptcy cases filed, FY 2007 3,716

Patents and trademarks issued, 2007

Patents 1,478
Trademarks 260

Business firm ownership, 2002

Women-owned 28,824
   Sales ($ mil) $3,216
Black-owned 373
   Sales ($ mil) $58
Hispanic-owned 2,775
   Sales ($ mil) $352
Asian-owned 1,111
   Sales ($ mil) $284
Amer. Indian/Alaska Native-owned 1,143
   Sales ($ mil) $204
Hawaiian/Pacific Islander-owned 99
   Sales ($ mil) $9

Gross domestic product, 2006 ($ mil)

Total gross domestic product $49,907
   Agriculture, forestry, fishing and
      hunting 2,253
   Mining 302
   Utilities 903
   Construction 3,357
   Manufacturing, durable goods 5,584
   Manufacturing, non-durable goods 1,609
   Wholesale trade 2,716
   Retail trade 4,307
   Transportation & warehousing 1,393
   Information 1,126
   Finance & insurance 2,283
   Real estate, rental & leasing 5,760
   Professional and technical services 3,444
   Educational services 276
   Health care and social assistance 3,326
   Accommodation/food services 1,248
   Other services, except government 964
   Government 6,303

Establishments, payroll, employees & receipts, by major industry group, 2005

Total 43,346
   Annual payroll ($1,000) $15,397,889
   Paid employees .519,319

Forestry, fishing & agriculture 543
   Annual payroll ($1,000) $110,786
   Paid employees .3,742

Mining 134
   Annual payroll ($1,000) $104,826
   Paid employees 2,071
   Receipts, 2002 ($1,000) $284,619

Utilities 184
   Annual payroll ($1,000) $200,283
   Paid employees .3,451
   Receipts, 2002 ($1,000) . . . . .NA

Construction 7,697
   Annual payroll ($1,000) $1,622,096
   Paid employees 44,658
   Receipts, 2002 ($1,000) $5,507,211

Manufacturing 1,849
   Annual payroll ($1,000) $2,393,039
   Paid employees .61,167
   Receipts, 2002 ($1,000) $15,174,196

Wholesale trade 1,983
   Annual payroll ($1,000) $907,831
   Paid employees 23,602
   Receipts, 2002 ($1,000) $11,458,012

Retail trade 6,064
   Annual payroll ($1,000) $1,673,120
   Paid employees .75,716
   Receipts, 2002 ($1,000) $13,540,952

Transportation & warehousing 1,645
   Annual payroll ($1,000) $455,008
   Paid employees .15,533
   Receipts, 2002 ($1,000) $1,183,968

Information 698
   Annual payroll ($1,000) $458,656
   Paid employees 12,575
   Receipts, 2002 ($1,000) . . . . .NA

Finance & insurance 2,670
   Annual payroll ($1,000) $907,058
   Paid employees 20,924
   Receipts, 2002 ($1,000) . . . . .NA

Professional, scientific & technical 3,805
   Annual payroll ($1,000) $1,411,856
   Paid employees .35,126
   Receipts, 2002 ($1,000) $2,309,182

Education 361
   Annual payroll ($1,000) $147,680
   Paid employees 8,349
   Receipts, 2002 ($1,000) $54,738

Health care & social assistance 4,153
   Annual payroll ($1,000) $2,146,695
   Paid employees 68,820
   Receipts, 2002 ($1,000) $4,251,492

Arts and entertainment 670
   Annual payroll ($1,000) $104,488
   Paid employees .7,326
   Receipts, 2002 ($1,000) $274,384

Real estate 2,133
   Annual payroll ($1,000) $199,311
   Paid employees .7,287
   Receipts, 2002 ($1,000) $700,380

Accommodation & food service 3,256
   Annual payroll ($1,000) $571,584
   Paid employees .51,670
   Receipts, 2002 ($1,000) $1,653,671

©2008 Information Publications, Inc.
All rights reserved. Photocopying prohibited.
877-544-INFO (4636) or www.informationpublications.com

8   Idaho

Exports, 2006
Value of exported goods ($ mil) $3,721
   Manufactured $2,849
   Non-manufactured. $259

Foreign direct investment in US affiliates, 2004
Property, plants & equipment ($ mil) $2,187
Employment (x 1,000). 12.9

Agriculture, 2006
Number of farms 25,000
Farm acreage (x 1,000) 11,800
   Acres per farm 472
Farm marketings and income ($ mil)
Total $4,415.6
   Crops $1,999.6
   Livestock. $2,416.0
Net farm income $758.4

Principal commodities, in order by marketing receipts, 2005
   Dairy products, Cattle and calves, Potatoes,
         Wheat, Hay

Federal economic activity in state
Expenditures, 2005 ($ mil)
   Total. $9,598
      Per capita $6,714.69
   Defense $678
   Non-defense $8,920
Defense department, 2006 ($ mil)
   Payroll. $541
   Contract awards $168
   Grants $37
Homeland security grants ($1,000)
   2006. . . . .$11,759
   2007 . . . .$6,701

FDIC-insured financial institutions, 2005
Number 19
Assets ($ billion) $6.9
Deposits ($ billion) $5.4

Fishing, 2006
Catch (x 1,000 lbs) . . . . NA
Value ($1,000). . . . . NA

Mining, 2006 ($ mil)
Total non-fuel mineral production $810
Percent of U.S. 1.26%

Communication, Energy & Transportation

Communication
Households with computers, 2003 . . . . 69.2%
Households with internet access, 2003 . . . . 56.4%
High-speed internet providers 45
Total high-speed internet lines. 381,583
   Residential 242,163
   Business. 139,420
Wireless phone customers, 12/2006 972,825

FCC-licensed stations (as of January 1, 2008)
TV stations 21
FM radio stations. 102
AM radio stations 47

Energy
Energy consumption, 2004
   Total (trillion Btu). 500
   Per capita (million Btu) 358.4
By source of production (trillion Btu)
   Coal 12
   Natural gas 77
   Petroleum. 157
   Nuclear electric power 0
   Hydroelectric power. 85
By end-use sector (trillion Btu)
   Residential 110
   Commercial 78
   Industrial 190
   Transportation 122
Electric energy, 2005
   Primary source of electricity. . . . Hydroelectric
   Net generation (billion kWh) 10.8
      percent from renewable sources. 84.2%
   Net summer capability (million kW) 3.2
   CO_2 emitted from generation 1.3
Natural gas utilities, 2005
   Customers (x 1,000) 335
   Sales (trillion Btu). 59
   Revenues ($ mil) $345
Nuclear plants, 2007 0
Total CO_2 emitted (million metric tons). . . .14.2
Energy spending, 2004 ($ mil) $3,736
   per capita $2,679
   Price per million Btu $11.82

Transportation, 2006
Public road & street mileage 47,105
   Urban. 4,755
   Rural 42,350
   Interstate 612
Vehicle miles of travel (millions) 15,198
   per capita 10,382.0
Total motor vehicle registrations. 1,275,115
   Automobiles. 541,487
   Trucks 729,861
   Motorcycles 50,536
Licensed drivers 1,008,016
   19 years & under 66,038
Deaths from motor vehicle accidents 267
Gasoline consumed (x 1,000 gallons) 658,019
   per capita 449.5

Commuting Statistics, 2006
Average commute time (min) 20.1
   Drove to work alone 77.2%
   Carpooled. 11.7%
   Public transit 0.8%
   Walk to work 3.4%
   Work from home 5.0%

©2008 Information Publications, Inc.
All rights reserved. Photocopying prohibited.
877-544-INFO (4636) or www.informationpublications.com

State Summary

Capital city . . . . Springfield
Governor . . . . Rod Blagojevich
State Capitol
207 Statehouse
Springfield, IL 62706
217-782-6830
Admitted as a state 1818
Area (square miles) 57,914
Population, 2007 (estimate). 12,852,548
Largest city . . . . Chicago
Population, 2006 2,833,321
Personal income per capita, 2006
(in current dollars) $38,215
Gross domestic product, 2006 ($ mil) . . . $589,598

Leading industries by payroll, 2005

Manufacturing, Health care/Social assistance,
Finance & Insurance

Leading agricultural commodities by receipts, 2005

Corn, Soybeans, Hogs, Cattle and calves, Green-house/nursery

Geography & Environment

Total area (square miles). 57,914
land 55,584
water 2,331
Federally-owned land, 2004 (acres) 641,959
percent. 1.8%
Highest point . . . . Charles Mound
elevation (feet) .1,235
Lowest point . . . . Mississippi River
elevation (feet) 279
General coastline (miles) 0
Tidal shoreline (miles) 0
Cropland, 2003 (x 1,000 acres) 23,981
Forest land, 2003 (x 1,000 acres). 3,949
Capital city . . . . Springfield
Population 2000 111,454
Population 2006 116,482
Largest city . . . . Chicago
Population 2000 2,896,016
Population 2006 2,833,321

Number of cities with over 100,000 population

1990 4
2000 7
2006 8

State park and recreation areas, 2005

Area (x 1,000 acres). 481
Number of visitors (x 1,000) 44,950
Revenues ($1,000) $7,336
percent of operating expenditures. 14.0%

National forest system land, 2007

Acres 297,077

Demographics & Population Characteristics

Population

1980 11,426,518
1990 11,430,602
2000 12,419,647
2006 12,831,970
Male. 6,317,460
Female. 6,514,510
Living in group quarters, 2006. 323,647
percent of total. 2.5%
2007 (estimate). 12,852,548
persons per square mile of land 231.2
2008 (projected) 12,835,851
2010 (projected) 12,916,894
2020 (projected). 13,236,720
2030 (projected). 13,432,892

Population of Core-Based Statistical Areas (formerly Metropolitan Areas), x 1,000

	CBSA	Non-CBSA
1990	10,809	622
2000	11,796	624
2006	12,218	614

Change in population, 2000-2007

Number 432,901
percent. 3.5%
Natural increase (births minus deaths) 564,091
Net internal migration . . . . -551,311
Net international migration 420,052

Persons by age, 2006

Under 5 years 887,605
5 to 17 years 2,327,639
18 years and over 9,616,726
65 years and over 1,534,476
85 years and over .227,074
Median age 35.7

Persons by age, 2010 (projected)

Under 5 years 926,650
18 and over 9,719,988
65 and over 1,600,863
Median age 36.0

Race, 2006

One Race
White. 10,169,966
Black or African American 1,928,153
Asian 541,218
American Indian/Alaska Native. 41,231
Hawaiian Native/Pacific Islander. 8,448
Two or more races. 142,954

Persons of Hispanic origin, 2006

Total Hispanic or Latino 1,888,439
Mexican. 1,486,386
Puerto Rican 169,955
Cuban 19,515

©2008 Information Publications, Inc.
All rights reserved. Photocopying prohibited.
877-544-INFO (4636) or www.informationpublications.com

Persons of Asian origin, 2006

Total Asian	536,992
Asian Indian	166,870
Chinese	104,266
Filipino	114,266
Japanese	20,602
Korean	58,026
Vietnamese	24,365

Marital status, 2006

Population 15 years & over	10,169,211
Never married	3,318,202
Married	5,244,153
Separated	189,423
Widowed	657,856
Divorced	949,000

Language spoken at home, 2006

Population 5 years and older	11,942,632
English only	9,341,064
Spanish	1,516,560
French	36,856
German	60,726
Chinese	81,702

Households & families, 2006

Households	4,724,252
with persons under 18 years	1,661,252
with persons over 65 years	1,067,221
persons per household	2.65
Families	3,146,342
persons per family	3.29
Married couples	2,355,451
Female householder, no husband present	587,369
One-person households	1,329,813

Nativity, 2006

Number of residents born in state	8,580,066
percent of population	66.9%

Immigration & naturalization, 2006

Legal permanent residents admitted	52,459
Persons naturalized	30,156
Non-immigrant admissions	791,277

Vital Statistics and Health

Marriages

2004	77,845
2005	74,065
2006	77,981

Divorces

2004	33,076
2005	32,408
2006	32,158

Health risks, 2006

Percent of adults who are:

Smokers	20.5%
Overweight (BMI > 25)	61.7%
Obese (BMI > 30)	25.1%

Births

2005	179,020
Birthrate (per 1,000)	14.0
White	138,884
Black	30,710
Hispanic	43,441
Asian/Pacific Islander	9,139
Amer. Indian/Alaska Native	287
Low birth weight (2,500g or less)	8.5%
Cesarian births	28.8%
Preterm births	13.1%
To unmarried mothers	37.1%
Twin births (per 1,000)	35.9
Triplets or higher order (per 100,000)	234.6
2006 (preliminary)	180,583
rate per 1,000	14.1

Deaths

2004

All causes	102,670
rate per 100,000	801.4
Heart disease	28,284
rate per 100,000	219.1
Malignant neoplasms	24,289
rate per 100,000	193.2
Cerebrovascular disease	6,489
rate per 100,000	50.0
Chronic lower respiratory disease	4,723
rate per 100,000	37.5
Diabetes	3,069
rate per 100,000	24.2
2005 (preliminary)	103,977
rate per 100,000	798.2
2006 (provisional)	101,922

Infant deaths

2004	1,349
rate per 1,000	7.5
2005 (provisional)	1,261
rate per 1,000	7.1

Exercise routines, 2005

None	25.6%
Moderate or greater	47.1%
Vigorous	25.7%

Abortions, 2004

Total performed in state	43,537
rate per 1,000 women age 15-44	16
% obtained by out-of-state residents	7.8%

Physicians, 2005

Total	34,826
rate per 100,000 persons	273

Community hospitals, 2005

Number of hospitals	191
Beds (x 1,000)	34.5
Patients admitted (x 1,000)	1,583
Average daily census (x 1,000)	22.6
Average cost per day	$1,637
Outpatient visits (x 1 mil)	28.7

©2008 Information Publications, Inc.
All rights reserved. Photocopying prohibited.
877-544-INFO (4636) or www.informationpublications.com

Disability status of population, 2006

5 to 15 years 5.6%
16 to 64 years 9.9%
65 years and over 39.6%

Education

Educational attainment, 2006

Population over 25 years 8,326,130
   Less than 9th grade. 6.6%
   High school graduate or more 85.0%
   College graduate or more. 28.9%
   Graduate or professional degree. 10.8%

Public school enrollment, 2005-06

Total. 2,111,706
   Pre-kindergarten through grade 8. . .1,480,047
   Grades 9 through 12 631,198

Graduating public high school seniors, 2004-05

Diplomas (incl. GED and others) 123,615

SAT scores, 2007

Average critical reading score 594
Average writing score 588
Average math score 611
Percent of graduates taking test 8%

Public school teachers, 2006-07 (estimate)

Total (x 1,000) 131.9
   Elementary 89.8
   Secondary 42.2
Average salary $58,246
   Elementary $55,775
   Secondary $64,061

State receipts & expenditures for public schools, 2006-07 (estimate)

Revenue receipts ($ mil) $21,566
Expenditures
Total ($ mil) $24,071
   Per capita $1,717
   Per pupil $11,489

NAEP proficiency scores, 2007

	Reading		Math	
	Basic	Proficient	Basic	Proficient
Grade 4	65.0%	32.2%	78.6%	36.3%
Grade 8	74.9%	29.8%	70.3%	30.8%

Higher education enrollment, fall 2005

Total. 277,818
   Full-time men 87,050
   Full-time women .116,432
   Part-time men 28,458
   Part-time women. 45,878

Minority enrollment in institutions of higher education, 2005

Black, non-Hispanic 118,905
Hispanic 95,542
Asian/Pacific Islander 48,336
American Indian/Alaska Native. 3,109

Institutions of higher education, 2005-06

Total. 172
   Public. 60
   Private 112

Earned degrees conferred, 2004-05

Associate's. 34,715
Bachelor's 63,913
Master's 35,992
First-professional. .4,573
Doctor's 2,752

Public Libraries, 2006

Number of libraries. 623
Number of outlets 811
Annual visits per capita 5.8
Circulation per capita. 8.6

State & local financial support for higher education, FY 2006

Full-time equivalent enrollment (x 1,000) 385.3
Appropriations per FTE. $6,689

Social Insurance & Welfare Programs

Social Security benefits & beneficiaries, 2005

Beneficiaries (x 1,000) 1,898
   Retired & dependents. 1,347
   Survivors. 271
   Disabled & dependents. 281
Annual benefit payments ($ mil) $21,364
   Retired & dependents. $14,497
   Survivors. $3,899
   Disabled & dependents. $2,967
Average monthly benefit
   Retired & dependents. $1,040
   Disabled & dependents. $966
   Widowed. $1,031

Medicare, July 2005

Enrollment (x 1,000). 1,691
Payments ($ mil) $12,468

Medicaid, 2004

Beneficiaries (x 1,000). 206
Payments ($ mil) $990

State Children's Health Insurance Program, 2006

Enrollment (x 1,000). 316.8
Expenditures ($ mil). $312.1

Persons without health insurance, 2006

Number (x 1,000). 1,776
   percent. 14.0%
Number of children (x 1,000) 302
   percent of children 9.5%

Health care expenditures, 2004

Total expenditures. $67,292
   per capita $5,293

©2008 Information Publications, Inc.
All rights reserved. Photocopying prohibited.
877-544-INFO (4636) or www.informationpublications.com

Federal and state public aid

State unemployment insurance, 2006
Recipients, first payments (x 1,000) 335
Total payments ($ mil) $1,649
Average weekly benefit $292
Temporary Assistance for Needy Families, 2006
Recipients (x 1,000) .1,042.1
Families (x 1,000) 422.0
Supplemental Security Income, 2005
Recipients (x 1,000) 258.6
Payments ($ mil) $1,336.6
Food Stamp Program, 2006
Avg monthly participants (x 1,000) 1,225.1
Total benefits ($ mil) $1,503.2

Housing & Construction

Housing units
Total 2005 (estimate) 5,144,625
Total 2006 (estimate) 5,199,589
Seasonal or recreational use, 2006 36,049
Owner-occupied, 2006 3,301,367
  Median home value $200,200
  Homeowner vacancy rate 2.3%
Renter-occupied, 2006 1,422,885
  Median rent $761
  Rental vacancy rate 12.6%
Home ownership rate, 2005 . . . . 70.9%
Home ownership rate, 2006 . . . . 70.4%

New privately-owned housing units
Number authorized, 2006 (x 1,000) 58.8
  Value ($ mil) $9,470.3
Started 2005 (x 1,000, estimate) 58.5
Started 2006 (x 1,000, estimate) 56.6

Existing home sales
2005 (x 1,000) 315.3
2006 (x 1,000) 289.0

Government & Elections

State officials 2008
Governor . . . . .Rod Blagojevich
       Democratic, term expires 1/11
Lieutenant Governor . . . . Patrick Quinn
Secretary of State . . . . .Jesse White
Attorney General . . . . Lisa Madigan
Chief Justice . . . . .Robert Thomas

Governorship
Minimum age 25
Length of term . . . . 4 years
Consecutive terms permitted . . . . . . not specified
Who succeeds . . . . Lieutenant Governor

Local governments by type, 2002
Total 6,903
  County 102
  Municipal 1,291
  Township 1,431
  School District 934
  Special District 3,145

State legislature
Name . . . . General Assembly
Upper chamber . . . . .Senate
  Number of members 59
  Length of term . . . . 4 years
  Party in majority, 2008 . . . . Democratic
Lower chamber . . . . House of Representatives
  Number of members 118
  Length of term . . . . 2 years
  Party in majority, 2008 . . . . .Democratic

Federal representation, 2008 (110ᵗʰ Congress)
Senator . . . . Richard Durbin
  Party . . . . .Democratic
  Year term expires 2009
Senator . . . . Barack Obama
  Party . . . . .Democratic
  Year term expires 2011
Representatives, total . . . . 19 (1 vacant)
  Democrats 10
  Republicans 8

Voters in November 2006 election (estimate)
Total 3,967,614
  Male 1,805,445
  Female 2,162,169
  White 3,261,613
  Black 601,554
  Hispanic 100,349
  Asian 79,456

Presidential election, 2004
Total Popular Vote 5,274,322
  Kerry 2,891,550
  Bush 2,345,946
Total Electoral Votes 21

Votes cast for US Senators
2004
Total vote (x 1,000) 5,142
Leading party .Democratic
Percent for leading party 70.0%
2006
Total vote (x 1,000) . . . . NA
Leading party . . . . NA
Percent for leading party . . . . NA

Votes cast for US Representatives
2004
Total vote (x 1,000) 4,989
  Democratic 2,675
  Republican 2,272
Leading party .Democratic
Percent for leading party 53.6%
2006
Total vote (x 1,000) .3,453
  Democratic 1,986
  Republican 1,443
Leading party .Democratic
Percent for leading party 57.5%

©2008 Information Publications, Inc.
All rights reserved. Photocopying prohibited.
877-544-INFO (4636) or www.informationpublications.com

State government employment, 2006
Full-time equivalent employees 131,859
Payroll ($ mil) $537.3

Local government employment, 2006
Full-time equivalent employees 503,131
Payroll ($ mil) $1,941.6

Women holding public office, 2008
US Congress 3
Statewide elected office 1
State legislature 48

Black public officials, 2002
Total 619
US and state legislatures 28
City/county/regional offices 327
Judicial/law enforcement 59
Education/school boards 205

Hispanic public officials, 2006
Total 96
State executives & legislators 11
City/county/regional offices 63
Judicial/law enforcement 6
Education/school boards 16

Governmental Finance

State government revenues, 2006
Total revenue (x $1,000) $62,728,922
per capita $4,909.50
General revenue (x $1,000) $49,271,484
Intergovernmental 13,387,270
Taxes 28,128,749
general sales .7,760,590
individual income tax 8,635,104
corporate income tax 2,400,270
Current charges 3,885,325
Miscellaneous 3,870,140

State government expenditure, 2006
Total expenditure (x $1,000) $55,767,569
per capita $4,364.67
General expenditure (x $1,000) $48,051,530
per capita, total. *$3,760.77*
Education 1,162.93
Public welfare 1,154.07
Health 164.70
Hospitals. 72.54
Highways 285.79
Police protection 33.72
Corrections 90.06
Natural resources 21.54
Parks & recreation 20.58
Governmental administration 89.63
Interest on general debt 184.74

State debt & cash, 2006 ($ per capita)
Debt $4,199.36
Cash/security holdings. $9,820.59

Federal government grants to state & local government, 2005 (x $1,000)
Total $16,634,795
by Federal agency
Defense 100,879
Education 1,531,680
Energy 94,897
Environmental Protection Agency . . . 129,838
Health & Human Services. 9,636,578
Homeland Security 46,143
Housing & Urban Development 1,866,308
Justice 206,139
Labor 401,598
Transportation 1,241,528
Veterans Affairs 24,619

Crime & Law Enforcement

Crime, 2006 (rates per 100,000 residents)
Property crimes 387,478
Burglary 77,259
Larceny 272,578
Motor vehicle theft 37,641
Property crime rate. 3,019.6
Violent crimes. 69,498
Murder 780
Forcible rape. 4,078
Robbery. 23,782
Aggravated assault 40,858
Violent crime rate 541.6
Hate crimes. 188

Fraud and identity theft, 2006
Fraud complaints 13,908
rate per 100,000 residents 108.4
Identity theft complaints 10,080
rate per 100,000 residents 78.6

Law enforcement agencies, 2006
Total agencies 757
Total employees 52,055
Officers 37,229
Civilians 14,826

Prisoners, probation, and parole, 2006
Total prisoners 45,106
percent change, 12/31/05 to 12/31/06 . . . . 0.4%
in private facilities 0%
in local jails 0%
Sentenced to more than one year 45,106
rate per 100,000 residents 350
Adults on probation 141,000
Adults on parole. . . . . NA

Prisoner demographics, June 30, 2005 (rate per 100,000 residents)
Male 951
Female 79
White 223
Black. 2,020
Hispanic 415

©2008 Information Publications, Inc.
All rights reserved. Photocopying prohibited.
877-544-INFO (4636) or www.informationpublications.com

6 Illinois

Arrests, 2006
Total..................................191,165
  Persons under 18 years of age.........33,775

Persons under sentence of death, 1/1/07
Total....................................... 11
  White....................................... 5
  Black 3
  Hispanic 3

State's highest court
Name........................Supreme Court
Number of members........................ 7
Length of term...................... 10 years
Intermediate appeals court?................yes

Labor & Income

Civilian labor force, 2006 (x 1,000)
Total.................................. 6,584
  Men 3,569
  Women 3,015
  Persons 16-19 years.................. 307
  White................................5,358
  Black 846
  Hispanic 734

Civilian labor force as a percent of civilian non-institutional population, 2006
Total................................... 67.4%
  Men 75.4
  Women 59.8
  Persons 16-19 years..................41.8
  White................................68.2
  Black 62.3
  Hispanic 72.3

Employment, 2006 (x 1,000)
Total.................................. 6,289
  Men 3,408
  Women 2,882
  Persons 16-19 years................. 272
  White................................5,162
  Black 761
  Hispanic 694

Unemployment rate, 2006
Total.................................... 4.5%
  Men 4.5
  Women 4.4
  Persons 16-19 years..................11.4
  White................................3.7
  Black 10.0
  Hispanic 5.5

Full-time/part-time labor force, 2003 (x 1,000)
Full-time labor force, employed......... 4,907
Part-time labor force, employed......... 1,000
Unemployed, looking for
  Full-time work....................... 366
  Part-time work....................... 57
Mean duration of unemployment (weeks)......20.9
  Median 11.5

Labor unions, 2006
Membership (x 1,000).................... 931
  percent of employed 16.4%

Experienced civilian labor force by private industry, 2006
Total..............................5,012,850
  Natural resources & mining 25,835
  Construction 275,205
  Manufacturing...................... 682,715
  Trade, transportation & utilities 1,181,726
  Information 116,813
  Finance 399,344
  Professional & business 855,136
  Education & health 750,330
  Leisure & hospitality............... 522,867
  Other............................... 195,835

Experienced civilian labor force by occupation, May 2006
Management......................... 250,790
Business & financial 305,860
Legal................................47,560
Sales 622,590
Office & admin. support.............1,004,380
Computers & math 136,450
Architecture & engineering........... 82,850
Arts & entertainment 66,650
Education 371,910
Social services 66,650
Health care practitioner & technical.....297,370
Health care support 137,740
Maintenance & repair................210,810
Construction 240,910
Transportation & moving 478,240
Production 530,540
Farming, fishing & forestry............. 5,000

Hours and earnings of production workers on manufacturing payrolls, 2006
Average weekly hours 41.1
Average hourly earnings $16.03
Average weekly earnings $658.83

Income and poverty, 2006
Median household income............ $52,006
Personal income, per capita (current $)... $38,215
  in constant (2000) dollars $33,359
Persons below poverty level............. 12.3%

Average annual pay
2006 .... $45,650
  increase from 2005 .... 4.4%

Federal individual income tax returns, 2005
Returns filed........................5,836,193
Adjusted gross income ($1,000) $335,321,455
Total tax liability ($1,000) $46,753,758

Charitable contributions, 2004
Number of contributions..............1,840.4
Total amount ($ mil)................. $7,054.5

©2008 Information Publications, Inc.
All rights reserved. Photocopying prohibited.
877-544-INFO (4636) or www.informationpublications.com

Economy, Business, Industry & Agriculture

Fortune 500 companies, 2007 33
Bankruptcy cases filed, FY 2007 39,147

Patents and trademarks issued, 2007
Patents 3,795
Trademarks 3,910

Business firm ownership, 2002
Women-owned 284,954
  Sales ($ mil) $46,862
Black-owned 68,699
  Sales ($ mil) $4,980
Hispanic-owned 39,539
  Sales ($ mil) $7,389
Asian-owned 44,477
  Sales ($ mil) $14,545
Amer. Indian/Alaska Native-owned 3,393
  Sales ($ mil) $452
Hawaiian/Pacific Islander-owned 656
  Sales ($ mil) . . . . NA

Gross domestic product, 2006 ($ mil)
Total gross domestic product $589,598
  Agriculture, forestry, fishing and
    hunting 1,996
  Mining 1,765
  Utilities 13,223
  Construction 28,041
  Manufacturing, durable goods 44,275
  Manufacturing, non-durable goods . . . 33,366
  Wholesale trade 42,284
  Retail trade 33,874
  Transportation & warehousing 20,691
  Information 21,078
  Finance & insurance 55,049
  Real estate, rental & leasing 77,914
  Professional and technical services 49,639
  Educational services 6,183
  Health care and social assistance 38,404
  Accommodation/food services 13,641
  Other services, except government 13,872
  Government 56,823

Establishments, payroll, employees & receipts, by major industry group, 2005
Total 318,927
  Annual payroll ($1,000) $217,221,786
  Paid employees 5,235,866
Forestry, fishing & agriculture 324
  Annual payroll ($1,000) $56,494
  Paid employees .1,598
Mining 603
  Annual payroll ($1,000) $556,295
  Paid employees .9,934
  Receipts, 2002 ($1,000) $2,276,094

Utilities 481
  Annual payroll ($1,000) $2,437,078
  Paid employees 27,688
  Receipts, 2002 ($1,000) . . . . .NA
Construction 32,551
  Annual payroll ($1,000) $13,615,634
  Paid employees 250,157
  Receipts, 2002 ($1,000) $55,308,836
Manufacturing 16,073
  Annual payroll ($1,000) $30,078,477
  Paid employees 676,298
  Receipts, 2002 ($1,000) $188,365,216
Wholesale trade 20,001
  Annual payroll ($1,000) $17,770,519
  Paid employees 322,342
  Receipts, 2002 ($1,000) $317,467,059
Retail trade 43,169
  Annual payroll ($1,000) $14,365,019
  Paid employees 629,286
  Receipts, 2002 ($1,000) $131,469,518
Transportation & warehousing 10,924
  Annual payroll ($1,000) $8,717,147
  Paid employees 218,771
  Receipts, 2002 ($1,000) $19,329,778
Information 5,697
  Annual payroll ($1,000) $7,685,997
  Paid employees 133,241
  Receipts, 2002 ($1,000) . . . . .NA
Finance & insurance 23,108
  Annual payroll ($1,000) $24,867,356
  Paid employees 341,884
  Receipts, 2002 ($1,000) . . . . .NA
Professional, scientific & technical 38,478
  Annual payroll ($1,000) $22,464,307
  Paid employees 350,082
  Receipts, 2002 ($1,000) $45,533,746
Education 3,294
  Annual payroll ($1,000) $4,239,205
  Paid employees 132,528
  Receipts, 2002 ($1,000) $1,233,194
Health care & social assistance 29,475
  Annual payroll ($1,000) $25,360,320
  Paid employees 677,927
  Receipts, 2002 ($1,000) $52,394,634
Arts and entertainment 4,537
  Annual payroll ($1,000) $1,930,647
  Paid employees 71,638
  Receipts, 2002 ($1,000) $5,737,943
Real estate 13,673
  Annual payroll ($1,000) $3,885,579
  Paid employees 84,839
  Receipts, 2002 ($1,000) $16,942,947
Accommodation & food service 25,595
  Annual payroll ($1,000) $6,277,520
  Paid employees 446,724
  Receipts, 2002 ($1,000) $19,072,168

©2008 Information Publications, Inc.
All rights reserved. Photocopying prohibited.
877-544-INFO (4636) or www.informationpublications.com

Exports, 2006

Value of exported goods ($ mil) $42,085
   Manufactured $36,288
   Non-manufactured $2,039

Foreign direct investment in US affiliates, 2004

Property, plants & equipment ($ mil) $39,276
Employment (x 1,000). 235.6

Agriculture, 2006

Number of farms 72,400
Farm acreage (x 1,000) 27,300
   Acres per farm 377
Farm marketings and income ($ mil)
Total. $8,635.7
   Crops $6,840.8
   Livestock. $1,794.9
Net farm income $1,511.0

Principal commodities, in order by marketing receipts, 2005

Corn, Soybeans, Hogs, Cattle and calves, Green-
house/nursery

Federal economic activity in state

Expenditures, 2005 ($ mil)
   Total. $80,778
      Per capita $6,327.91
   Defense $6,412
   Non-defense $74,367
Defense department, 2006 ($ mil)
   Payroll $2,838
   Contract awards $3,274
   Grants $107
Homeland security grants ($1,000)
   2006 . . . . $90,405
   2007 . . . . $86,248

FDIC-insured financial institutions, 2005

Number 685
Assets ($ billion) $380.9
Deposits ($ billion) $284.0

Fishing, 2006

Catch (x 1,000 lbs) . . . . NA
Value ($1,000). . . . . NA

Mining, 2006 ($ mil)

Total non-fuel mineral production $1,280
Percent of U.S. 1.99%

Communication, Energy & Transportation

Communication

Households with computers, 2003 . . . . .60.0%
Households with internet access, 2003 . . . . 51.1%
High-speed internet providers 121
Total high-speed internet lines 3,317,065
   Residential 2,401,478
   Business. 915,587
Wireless phone customers, 12/2006 9,588,517

FCC-licensed stations (as of January 1, 2008)

TV stations 47
FM radio stations. 334
AM radio stations 135

Energy

Energy consumption, 2004
   Total (trillion Btu). 3,961
   Per capita (million Btu) 311.5
By source of production (trillion Btu)
   Coal 1,070
   Natural gas 956
   Petroleum 1,375
   Nuclear electric power 960
   Hydroelectric power 2
By end-use sector (trillion Btu)
   Residential 958
   Commercial 746
   Industrial 1,253
   Transportation 1,004
Electric energy, 2005
   Primary source of electricity. . . . . Nuclear
   Net generation (billion kWh) 194.1
      percent from renewable sources. 0.5%
   Net summer capability (million kW) 42.5
   CO_2 emitted from generation 100.8
Natural gas utilities, 2005
   Customers (x 1,000) 4,092
   Sales (trillion Btu) 911
   Revenues ($ mil) $5,620
Nuclear plants, 2007 11
Total CO_2 emitted (million metric tons). 230.0
Energy spending, 2004 ($ mil) $34,067
   per capita $2,680
   Price per million Btu $12.46

Transportation, 2006

Public road & street mileage 138,997
   Urban. 40,403
   Rural 98,594
   Interstate. 2,169
Vehicle miles of travel (millions) 106,869
   per capita 8,364.1
Total motor vehicle registrations. 9,876,246
   Automobiles. 5,947,468
   Trucks 5,965,504
   Motorcycles 293,052
Licensed drivers .8,071,253
   19 years & under 455,823
Deaths from motor vehicle accidents 1,254
Gasoline consumed (x 1,000 gallons) 5,189,824
   per capita 406.2

Commuting Statistics, 2006

Average commute time (min) 27.9
   Drove to work alone 74.3%
   Carpooled. 9.3%
   Public transit 8.4%
   Walk to work 2.9%
   Work from home 3.6%

©2008 Information Publications, Inc.
All rights reserved. Photocopying prohibited.
877-544-INFO (4636) or www.informationpublications.com

State Summary

Capital city . . . . Indianapolis
Governor . . . . Mitch Daniels

State House
Room 206
Indianapolis, IN 46204
317-232-4567

Admitted as a state 1816
Area (square miles) .36,418
Population, 2007 (estimate) 6,345,289
Largest city . . . . Indianapolis
   Population, 2006 785,597
Personal income per capita, 2006
   (in current dollars) $32,526
Gross domestic product, 2006 ($ mil) . . . $248,915

Leading industries by payroll, 2005

Manufacturing, Health care/Social assistance,
Retail trade

**Leading agricultural commodities
by receipts, 2005**

Corn, Soybeans, Hogs, Dairy products, Cattle
and calves

Geography & Environment

Total area (square miles) 36,418
   land 35,867
   water 551
Federally-owned land, 2004 (acres) 463,245
   percent 2.0%
Highest point . . . . Hoosier Hill
   elevation (feet) 1,257
Lowest point . . . . Ohio River
   elevation (feet) 320
General coastline (miles) 0
Tidal shoreline (miles) 0
Cropland, 2003 (x 1,000 acres) 13,316
Forest land, 2003 (x 1,000 acres) 3,817
Capital city . . . . Indianapolis
   Population 2000 781,870
   Population 2006 785,597
Largest city . . . . Indianapolis
   Population 2000 781,870
   Population 2006 785,597

Number of cities with over 100,000 population

1990 5
2000 5
2006 4

State park and recreation areas, 2005

Area (x 1,000 acres) 178
Number of visitors (x 1,000) 19,674
Revenues ($1,000) $39,855
   percent of operating expenditures 83.7%

National forest system land, 2007

Acres 201,467

Demographics & Population Characteristics

Population

1980 5,490,224
1990 5,544,159
2000 6,080,517
2006 6,313,520
   Male 3,110,503
   Female 3,203,017
Living in group quarters, 2006 178,789
   percent of total 2.8%
2007 (estimate) 6,345,289
   persons per square mile of land 176.9
2008 (projected) 6,337,404
2010 (projected) 6,392,139
2020 (projected) 6,627,008
2030 (projected) 6,810,108

**Population of Core-Based Statistical Areas
(formerly Metropolitan Areas), x 1,000**

	CBSA	Non-CBSA
1990	5,198	346
2000	5,715	366
2006	5,946	367

Change in population, 2000-2007

Number 264,768
   percent 4.4%
Natural increase (births minus deaths) 229,514
Net internal migration . . . . -16,431
Net international migration 69,836

Persons by age, 2006

Under 5 years 431,089
5 to 17 years 1,146,540
18 years and over 4,735,891
65 years and over 784,219
85 years and over 111,190
   Median age 36.3

Persons by age, 2010 (projected)

Under 5 years 436,614
18 and over 4,795,954
65 and over 811,290
   Median age 36.5

Race, 2006

One Race

White 5,575,402
Black or African American 563,037
Asian 83,583
American Indian/Alaska Native 18,603
Hawaiian Native/Pacific Islander 2,850
Two or more races 70,045

Persons of Hispanic origin, 2006

Total Hispanic or Latino 299,398
   Mexican 228,457
   Puerto Rican 23,907
   Cuban 1,899

©2008 Information Publications, Inc.
All rights reserved. Photocopying prohibited.
877-544-INFO (4636) or www.informationpublications.com

Persons of Asian origin, 2006

Total Asian 81,054
  Asian Indian. 16,204
  Chinese 23,020
  Filipino 9,296
  Japanese 5,284
  Korean. 8,351
  Vietnamese. 7,210

Marital status, 2006

Population 15 years & over 5,010,795
  Never married 1,386,975
  Married. 2,694,647
  Separated 79,300
  Widowed. 322,019
  Divorced 607,154

Language spoken at home, 2006

Population 5 years and older. 5,879,940
  English only 5,434,897
  Spanish 254,219
  French 17,184
  German. 52,813
  Chinese 17,662

Households & families, 2006

Households. 2,435,274
  with persons under 18 years 839,268
  with persons over 65 years. 539,677
  persons per household 2.52
Families. 1,645,031
  persons per family. 3.06
Married couples. 1,248,625
Female householder,
  no husband present. 283,854
One-person households 661,365

Nativity, 2006

Number of residents born in state 4,329,973
  percent of population. 68.6%

Immigration & naturalization, 2006

Legal permanent residents admitted. 8,125
Persons naturalized 3,885
Non-immigrant admissions 127,523

Vital Statistics and Health

Marriages

2004. 48,354
2005. 43,496
2006. 50,854

Divorces

2004. . . . . NA
2005. . . . . NA
2006. . . . . NA

Health risks, 2006

Percent of adults who are:
  Smokers. 24.1%
  Overweight (BMI > 25). 62.8%
  Obese (BMI > 30). 27.8%

Births

2005 87,193
  Birthrate (per 1,000). 13.9
  White. 75,733
  Black 9,878
  Hispanic 8,039
  Asian/Pacific Islander 1,435
  Amer. Indian/Alaska Native. 147
  Low birth weight (2,500g or less). 8.3%
  Cesarian births 28.2%
  Preterm births 13.5%
  To unmarried mothers. 40.2%
  Twin births (per 1,000) 31.9
  Triplets or higher order (per 100,000). . . 234.3
2006 (preliminary). 88,674
  rate per 1,000 . . . . .14.0

Deaths

2004
All causes 54,211
  rate per 100,000. . . . . .849.4
Heart disease 14,636
  rate per 100,000. . . . . 228.0
Malignant neoplasms 12,552
  rate per 100,000. . . . . .198.2
Cerebrovascular disease. 3,454
  rate per 100,000. . . . . .53.7
Chronic lower respiratory disease 3,145
  rate per 100,000. . . . . .49.8
Diabetes. 1,673
  rate per 100,000. . . . . .26.3
2005 (preliminary). 55,676
  rate per 100,000. . . . . .858.7
2006 (provisional) 55,652

Infant deaths

2004 700
  rate per 1,000 . . . . .8.0
2005 (provisional) 676
  rate per 1,000 . . . . .7.7

Exercise routines, 2005

None. 26.9%
Moderate or greater. 47.7%
Vigorous 27.1%

Abortions, 2004

Total performed in state. 10,514
  rate per 1,000 women age 15-44. 8
  % obtained by out-of-state residents 3.9%

Physicians, 2005

Total. 13,448
  rate per 100,000 persons 215

Community hospitals, 2005

Number of hospitals 113
Beds (x 1,000). 17.8
Patients admitted (x 1,000) 717
Average daily census (x 1,000) 10.3
Average cost per day $1,569
Outpatient visits (x 1 mil) 16.5

©2008 Information Publications, Inc.
All rights reserved. Photocopying prohibited.
877-544-INFO (4636) or www.informationpublications.com

Disability status of population, 2006
5 to 15 years 7.4%
16 to 64 years 12.7%
65 years and over 41.8%

Education

Educational attainment, 2006
Population over 25 years 4,110,754
Less than 9th grade.................... 4.6%
High school graduate or more 85.2%
College graduate or more............. 21.7%
Graduate or professional degree........ 8.0%

Public school enrollment, 2005-06
Total.............................. 1,035,074
Pre-kindergarten through grade 8.... 724,467
Grades 9 through 12 310,607

Graduating public high school seniors, 2004-05
Diplomas (incl. GED and others) 57,021

SAT scores, 2007
Average critical reading score.............. 497
Average writing score..................... 483
Average math score....................... 507
Percent of graduates taking test 62%

Public school teachers, 2006-07 (estimate)
Total (x 1,000) 61.2
Elementary........................... 32.8
Secondary............................ 28.4
Average salary $47,831
Elementary......................... $49,079
Secondary.......................... $47,744

State receipts & expenditures for public schools, 2006-07 (estimate)
Revenue receipts ($ mil) $10,948
Expenditures
Total ($ mil) $11,575
Per capita $1,530
Per pupil $10,044

NAEP proficiency scores, 2007

	Reading		Math	
	Basic	Proficient	Basic	Proficient
Grade 4	68.2%	33.0%	88.9%	46.3%
Grade 8	76.1%	31.1%	75.7%	35.1%

Higher education enrollment, fall 2005
Total.................................. 93,955
Full-time men 34,182
Full-time women..................... 43,430
Part-time men 5,817
Part-time women.................... 10,526

Minority enrollment in institutions of higher education, 2005
Black, non-Hispanic 30,315
Hispanic 10,366
Asian/Pacific Islander 7,443
American Indian/Alaska Native.......... 1,343

Institutions of higher education, 2005-06
Total................................... 100
Public............................... 29
Private.............................. 71

Earned degrees conferred, 2004-05
Associate's......................... 13,836
Bachelor's 36,655
Master's............................ 11,087
First-professional.................... 1,764
Doctor's............................ 1,306

Public Libraries, 2006
Number of libraries...................... 239
Number of outlets 476
Annual visits per capita 6.9
Circulation per capita.................... 12.2

State & local financial support for higher education, FY 2006
Full-time equivalent enrollment (x 1,000).... 218.7
Appropriations per FTE................ $5,390

Social Insurance & Welfare Programs

Social Security benefits & beneficiaries, 2005
Beneficiaries (x 1,000) 1,055
Retired & dependents.................. 728
Survivors............................ 145
Disabled & dependents................ 182
Annual benefit payments ($ mil) $11,872
Retired & dependents................ $7,937
Survivors.......................... $2,083
Disabled & dependents.............. $1,852
Average monthly benefit
Retired & dependents................ $1,053
Disabled & dependents.............. $938
Widowed........................... $1,030

Medicare, July 2005
Enrollment (x 1,000)..................... 905
Payments ($ mil) $6,310

Medicaid, 2004
Beneficiaries (x 1,000)................... 2,032
Payments ($ mil) $10,796

State Children's Health Insurance Program, 2006
Enrollment (x 1,000)................... 133.7
Expenditures ($ mil)................. $106.3

Persons without health insurance, 2006
Number (x 1,000)....................... 748
percent............................ 11.8%
Number of children (x 1,000) 123
percent of children 7.8%

Health care expenditures, 2004
Total expenditures.................... $32,951
per capita $5,295

©2008 Information Publications, Inc.
All rights reserved. Photocopying prohibited.
877-544-INFO (4636) or www.informationpublications.com

Federal and state public aid

State unemployment insurance, 2006
Recipients, first payments (x 1,000) 187
Total payments ($ mil) $731
Average weekly benefit $286
Temporary Assistance for Needy Families, 2006
Recipients (x 1,000) 1,432.3
Families (x 1,000) 506.4
Supplemental Security Income, 2005
Recipients (x 1,000) 98.6
Payments ($ mil) $488.1
Food Stamp Program, 2006
Avg monthly participants (x 1,000) 574.7
Total benefits ($ mil) $648.1

Housing & Construction

Housing units
Total 2005 (estimate) 2,724,479
Total 2006 (estimate) 2,756,331
Seasonal or recreational use, 2006 38,051
Owner-occupied, 2006 1,756,328
  Median home value $120,700
  Homeowner vacancy rate 3.2%
Renter-occupied, 2006 678,946
  Median rent $638
  Rental vacancy rate 14.0%
Home ownership rate, 2005 . . . . .75.0%
Home ownership rate, 2006 . . . . 74.2%

New privately-owned housing units
Number authorized, 2006 (x 1,000) 29.1
  Value ($ mil) $4,687.9
Started 2005 (x 1,000, estimate) 39.4
Started 2006 (x 1,000, estimate) 38.8

Existing home sales
2005 (x 1,000) 138.3
2006 (x 1,000) 147.4

Government & Elections

State officials 2008
Governor . . . . .Mitch Daniels
           Republican, term expires 1/09
Lieutenant Governor . . . . Becky Skillman
Secretary of State . . . . Todd Rokita
Attorney General . . . . Steve Carter
Chief Justice . . . . Randall Shepard

Governorship
Minimum age 30
Length of term . . . . 4 years
Consecutive terms permitted . 8 out of any 12 yrs
Who succeeds . . . . Lieutenant Governor

Local governments by type, 2002
Total 3,085
  County 91
  Municipal 567
  Township 1,008
  School District 294
  Special District 1,125

State legislature
Name . . . . General Assembly
Upper chamber . . . . .Senate
  Number of members 50
  Length of term . . . . 4 years
  Party in majority, 2008 . . . . Republican
Lower chamber . . . . House of Representatives
  Number of members 100
  Length of term . . . . 2 years
  Party in majority, 2008 . . . . .Democratic

Federal representation, 2008 (110th Congress)
Senator . . . . Even Bayh
  Party . . . . .Democratic
  Year term expires 2011
Senator . . . . Richard Lugar
  Party . . . . Republican
  Year term expires 2013
Representatives, total . . . . 9 (1 vacant)
  Democrats 4
  Republicans 4

Voters in November 2006 election (estimate)
Total 2,052,579
  Male 1,024,420
  Female 1,028,160
  White 1,901,436
  Black 139,539
  Hispanic 11,356
  Asian 9,074

Presidential election, 2004
Total Popular Vote 2,468,002
  Kerry 969,011
  Bush 1,479,438
Total Electoral Votes 11

Votes cast for US Senators
2004
Total vote (x 1,000) 2,428
Leading party .Democratic
Percent for leading party 61.6%
2006
Total vote (x 1,000) .1,341
Leading party .Democratic
Percent for leading party 87.4%

Votes cast for US Representatives
2004
Total vote (x 1,000) .2,416
  Democratic 999
  Republican 1,382
Leading party . . . . Republican
Percent for leading party 57.2%
2006
Total vote (x 1,000) .1,667
  Democratic 812
  Republican 832
Leading party . . . . Republican
Percent for leading party 49.9%

©2008 Information Publications, Inc.
All rights reserved. Photocopying prohibited.
877-544-INFO (4636) or www.informationpublications.com

State government employment, 2006
Full-time equivalent employees 89,799
Payroll ($ mil) $303.7

Local government employment, 2006
Full-time equivalent employees 243,050
Payroll ($ mil) $789.8

Women holding public office, 2008
US Congress 0
Statewide elected office..................... 2
State legislature 29

Black public officials, 2002
Total.................................... 94
   US and state legislatures 13
   City/county/regional offices 54
   Judicial/law enforcement................. 13
   Education/school boards................. 14

Hispanic public officials, 2006
Total.................................... 13
   State executives & legislators 1
   City/county/regional offices 8
   Judicial/law enforcement.................. 3
   Education/school boards................. 1

Governmental Finance

State government revenues, 2006
Total revenue (x $1,000)........... $32,854,548
   per capita $5,212.82
General revenue (x $1,000) $29,603,636
   Intergovernmental 7,270,493
   Taxes 13,625,667
      general sales....................5,334,275
      individual income tax 4,381,548
      corporate income tax 1,043,873
   Current charges..................6,861,100
   Miscellaneous 1,846,376

State government expenditure, 2006
Total expenditure (x $1,000) $26,958,772
   per capita $4,277.37
General expenditure (x $1,000) $24,955,887
   per capita, total................... *$3,959.59*
      Education.......................1,568.00
      Public welfare 985.50
      Health 86.05
      Hospitals........................41.56
      Highways 281.34
      Police protection..................31.77
      Corrections 99.58
      Natural resources 46.60
      Parks & recreation 9.47
      Governmental administration.......92.81
      Interest on general debt........... 120.24

State debt & cash, 2006 ($ per capita)
Debt $2,748.45
Cash/security holdings............. $8,804.52

Federal government grants to state & local government, 2005 (x $1,000)
Total........................... $8,064,847
by Federal agency
   Defense 31,177
   Education 652,897
   Energy 45,264
   Environmental Protection Agency 67,649
   Health & Human Services. 4,905,919
   Homeland Security................. 76,665
   Housing & Urban Development...... 526,459
   Justice 76,039
   Labor 156,966
   Transportation 937,807
   Veterans Affairs....................5,891

Crime & Law Enforcement

Crime, 2006 (rates per 100,000 residents)
Property crimes 221,127
   Burglary 46,168
   Larceny 153,093
   Motor vehicle theft 21,866
   Property crime rate.................3,502.4
Violent crimes........................19,876
   Murder 369
   Forcible rape......................1,835
   Robbery.........................7,243
   Aggravated assault 10,429
   Violent crime rate 314.8
Hate crimes............................ 43

Fraud and identity theft, 2006
Fraud complaints.......................7,863
   rate per 100,000 residents 124.5
Identity theft complaints 3,928
   rate per 100,000 residents 62.2

Law enforcement agencies, 2006
Total agencies............................ 208
Total employees 15,934
   Officers 10,197
   Civilians 5,737

Prisoners, probation, and parole, 2006
Total prisoners....................... 26,091
   percent change, 12/31/05 to 12/31/06 .... 6.7%
   in private facilities 4.9%
   in local jails 4.5%
Sentenced to more than one year 26,055
   rate per 100,000 residents 411
Adults on probation 120,421
Adults on parole.......................7,950

Prisoner demographics, June 30, 2005 (rate per 100,000 residents)
Male..................................1,165
Female................................. 126
White................................. 463
Black................................. 2,526
Hispanic 579

©2008 Information Publications, Inc.
All rights reserved. Photocopying prohibited.
877-544-INFO (4636) or www.informationpublications.com

Arrests, 2006
Total................................ 170,293
    Persons under 18 years of age 27,770

Persons under sentence of death, 1/1/07
Total..................................... 23
    White.................................. 16
    Black 7
    Hispanic 0

State's highest court
Name ....Supreme Court
Number of members....................... 5
Length of term .... 10 years
Intermediate appeals court? ....yes

Labor & Income

Civilian labor force, 2006 (x 1,000)
Total....................................3,253
    Men 1,751
    Women 1,502
    Persons 16-19 years.................... 162
    White................................2,947
    Black 258
    Hispanic 138

Civilian labor force as a percent of civilian non-institutional population, 2006
Total................................... 67.7%
    Men 74.9
    Women 60.8
    Persons 16-19 years....................45.7
    White.................................67.8
    Black 66.5
    Hispanic 73.6

Employment, 2006 (x 1,000)
Total.................................... 3,090
    Men 1,672
    Women 1,417
    Persons 16-19 years.................... 137
    White................................2,815
    Black 230
    Hispanic 130

Unemployment rate, 2006
Total.................................... 5.0%
    Men 4.5
    Women 5.6
    Persons 16-19 years...................15.5
    White.................................4.5
    Black 10.9
    Hispanic 5.3

Full-time/part-time labor force, 2003 (x 1,000)
Full-time labor force, employed 2,488
Part-time labor force, employed........... 537
Unemployed, looking for
    Full-time work........................ 140
    Part-time work......................... 23
Mean duration of unemployment (weeks)......21.7
    Median 12.0

Labor unions, 2006
Membership (x 1,000).................... 334
    percent of employed 12.0%

Experienced civilian labor force by private industry, 2006
Total.................................2,494,391
    Natural resources & mining 18,788
    Construction 150,648
    Manufacturing...................... 565,032
    Trade, transportation & utilities 578,299
    Information 39,875
    Finance 136,601
    Professional & business 279,986
    Education & health...................359,759
    Leisure & hospitality................ 280,923
    Other 83,846

Experienced civilian labor force by occupation, May 2006
Management........................ 109,250
Business & financial 90,470
Legal................................ 12,630
Sales 289,780
Office & admin. support............... 453,900
Computers & math 38,660
Architecture & engineering............ 45,780
Arts & entertainment 30,150
Education 163,890
Social services 33,720
Health care practitioner & technical.... 154,870
Health care support 67,190
Maintenance & repair................. 134,980
Construction 142,420
Transportation & moving 263,630
Production 398,820
Farming, fishing & forestry.............2,760

Hours and earnings of production workers on manufacturing payrolls, 2006
Average weekly hours 41.7
Average hourly earnings $18.57
Average weekly earnings $774.37

Income and poverty, 2006
Median household income............ $45,394
Personal income, per capita (current $)... $32,526
    in constant (2000) dollars $28,393
Persons below poverty level.............. 12.7%

Average annual pay
2006 .... $36,553
    increase from 2005 .... 3.2%

Federal individual income tax returns, 2005
Returns filed........................2,883,701
Adjusted gross income ($1,000) $134,324,776
Total tax liability ($1,000) $15,673,118

Charitable contributions, 2004
Number of contributions................ 724.5
Total amount ($ mil)..................$2,660.3

©2008 Information Publications, Inc.
All rights reserved. Photocopying prohibited.
877-544-INFO (4636) or www.informationpublications.com

Economy, Business, Industry & Agriculture

Fortune 500 companies, 2007 5
Bankruptcy cases filed, FY 2007 29,656

Patents and trademarks issued, 2007

Patents 1,350
Trademarks 1,236

Business firm ownership, 2002

Women-owned 118,857
   Sales ($ mil) $16,481
Black-owned 14,056
   Sales ($ mil) $1,688
Hispanic-owned 5,482
   Sales ($ mil) $792
Asian-owned 6,078
   Sales ($ mil) $2,584
Amer. Indian/Alaska Native-owned 1,974
   Sales ($ mil) $288
Hawaiian/Pacific Islander-owned 114
   Sales ($ mil) $77

Gross domestic product, 2006 ($ mil)

Total gross domestic product $248,915
   Agriculture, forestry, fishing and
      hunting 1,788
   Mining 898
   Utilities 5,816
   Construction 10,835
   Manufacturing, durable goods 43,930
   Manufacturing, non-durable goods 26,110
   Wholesale trade .14,078
   Retail trade 15,804
   Transportation & warehousing 8,826
   Information 5,328
   Finance & insurance 14,065
   Real estate, rental & leasing 24,351
   Professional and technical services 9,397
   Educational services 1,925
   Health care and social assistance 18,005
   Accommodation/food services 5,358
   Other services, except government 5,664
   Government 24,439

Establishments, payroll, employees & receipts, by major industry group, 2005

Total 149,871
   Annual payroll ($1,000) $88,145,224
   Paid employees 2,610,899
Forestry, fishing & agriculture 250
   Annual payroll ($1,000) $46,597
   Paid employees 1,408
Mining 329
   Annual payroll ($1,000) $300,784
   Paid employees 5,591
   Receipts, 2002 ($1,000) $1,359,560

Utilities 529
   Annual payroll ($1,000) $918,875
   Paid employees .14,401
   Receipts, 2002 ($1,000) . . . . .NA
Construction 16,442
   Annual payroll ($1,000) $5,963,039
   Paid employees 139,661
   Receipts, 2002 ($1,000) $23,435,911
Manufacturing 8,970
   Annual payroll ($1,000) $24,191,908
   Paid employees 554,273
   Receipts, 2002 ($1,000) $160,924,188
Wholesale trade 8,153
   Annual payroll ($1,000) $5,206,097
   Paid employees 117,305
   Receipts, 2002 ($1,000) $79,806,006
Retail trade 23,494
   Annual payroll ($1,000) $6,912,064
   Paid employees 346,073
   Receipts, 2002 ($1,000) $67,261,298
Transportation & warehousing 5,090
   Annual payroll ($1,000) $3,531,963
   Paid employees 106,149
   Receipts, 2002 ($1,000) $10,601,332
Information 2,334
   Annual payroll ($1,000) $2,010,861
   Paid employees 47,493
   Receipts, 2002 ($1,000) . . . . .NA
Finance & insurance 10,077
   Annual payroll ($1,000) $5,324,071
   Paid employees 107,628
   Receipts, 2002 ($1,000) . . . . .NA
Professional, scientific & technical 12,797
   Annual payroll ($1,000) $5,022,670
   Paid employees 110,046
   Receipts, 2002 ($1,000) $9,154,500
Education 1,372
   Annual payroll ($1,000) $1,189,334
   Paid employees 49,491
   Receipts, 2002 ($1,000) $340,184
Health care & social assistance 14,280
   Annual payroll ($1,000) $12,213,877
   Paid employees 354,481
   Receipts, 2002 ($1,000) $25,539,903
Arts and entertainment 2,103
   Annual payroll ($1,000) $839,422
   Paid employees 33,431
   Receipts, 2002 ($1,000) $2,725,191
Real estate 6,121
   Annual payroll ($1,000) $1,047,878
   Paid employees 35,169
   Receipts, 2002 ($1,000) $4,491,668
Accommodation & food service 12,316
   Annual payroll ($1,000) $2,934,176
   Paid employees 245,467
   Receipts, 2002 ($1,000) $9,409,270

©2008 Information Publications, Inc.
All rights reserved. Photocopying prohibited.
877-544-INFO (4636) or www.informationpublications.com

Exports, 2006

Value of exported goods ($ mil) $22,620
   Manufactured $20,660
   Non-manufactured $460

Foreign direct investment in US affiliates, 2004

Property, plants & equipment ($ mil) . . . $30,904
Employment (x 1,000). 132.5

Agriculture, 2006

Number of farms 59,000
Farm acreage (x 1,000) 15,000
   Acres per farm 254
Farm marketings and income ($ mil)
Total. $5,973.2
   Crops $3,918.9
   Livestock. $2,054.3
Net farm income $1,545.4

Principal commodities, in order by marketing receipts, 2005

Corn, Soybeans, Hogs, Dairy products, Cattle
and calves

Federal economic activity in state

Expenditures, 2005 ($ mil)
   Total. $42,347
     Per capita $6,758.14
   Defense $5,633
   Non-defense $36,714
Defense department, 2006 ($ mil)
   Payroll $1,361
   Contract awards $4,627
   Grants $64
Homeland security grants ($1,000)
   2006 . . . .$21,129
   2007 . . . . $23,397

FDIC-insured financial institutions, 2005

Number 172
Assets ($ billion) $71.8
Deposits ($ billion) $54.7

Fishing, 2006

Catch (x 1,000 lbs) . . . . NA
Value ($1,000). . . . . NA

Mining, 2006 ($ mil)

Total non-fuel mineral production $963
Percent of U.S. 1.50%

Communication, Energy & Transportation

Communication

Households with computers, 2003 . . . . 59.6%
Households with internet access, 2003 . . . . 51.0%
High-speed internet providers 81
Total high-speed internet lines 1,586,501
   Residential 1,077,595
   Business. 508,906
Wireless phone customers, 12/2006 4,271,412

FCC-licensed stations (as of January 1, 2008)

TV stations 40
FM radio stations. 256
AM radio stations 86

Energy

Energy consumption, 2004
   Total (trillion Btu). 2,946
   Per capita (million Btu) 473.3
By source of production (trillion Btu)
   Coal 1,614
   Natural gas 543
   Petroleum 885
   Nuclear electric power 0
   Hydroelectric power 4
By end-use sector (trillion Btu)
   Residential 532
   Commercial 373
   Industrial 1,400
   Transportation 641
Electric energy, 2005
   Primary source of electricity. . . . . Coal
   Net generation (billion kWh) 130.4
     percent from renewable sources. 0.4%
   Net summer capability (million kW) 27.0
   CO_2 emitted from generation 122.1
Natural gas utilities, 2005
   Customers (x 1,000) 1,866
   Sales (trillion Btu). 502
   Revenues ($ mil) $2,635
Nuclear plants, 2007 0
Total CO_2 emitted (million metric tons). 235.1
Energy spending, 2004 ($ mil) $20,932
   per capita $3,364
   Price per million Btu $10.19

Transportation, 2006

Public road & street mileage 96,250
   Urban. 21,780
   Rural 74,470
   Interstate. 1,169
Vehicle miles of travel (millions) 71,215
   per capita 11,299.2
Total motor vehicle registrations 4,955,434
   Automobiles. .2,694,901
   Trucks 2,228,559
   Motorcycles 147,544
Licensed drivers .4,246,189
   19 years & under 232,326
Deaths from motor vehicle accidents 899
Gasoline consumed (x 1,000 gallons) 3,221,758
   per capita 511.2

Commuting Statistics, 2006

Average commute time (min) 22.3
   Drove to work alone 82.4%
   Carpooled. 9.9%
   Public transit 1.0%
   Walk to work 2.2%
   Work from home 3.2%

©2008 Information Publications, Inc.
All rights reserved. Photocopying prohibited.
877-544-INFO (4636) or www.informationpublications.com

State Summary

Capital city . . . . Des Moines
Governor. . . . . .Chet Culver

State Capitol
Des Moines, IA 50319
515-281-5211

Admitted as a state 1846
Area (square miles) 56,272
Population, 2007 (estimate). 2,988,046
Largest city . . . . Des Moines
  Population, 2006. 193,886
Personal income per capita, 2006
  (in current dollars) $33,236
Gross domestic product, 2006 ($ mil) . . . $123,970

Leading industries by payroll, 2005

Manufacturing, Health care/Social assistance,
Finance & Insurance

Leading agricultural commodities by receipts, 2005

Corn, Hogs, Soybeans, Cattle and calves, Dairy
products

Geography & Environment

Total area (square miles). 56,272
  land 55,869
  water 402
Federally-owned land, 2004 (acres) 273,954
  percent. 0.8%
Highest point . . . . Hawkeye Point
  elevation (feet) 1,670
Lowest point . . . . Mississippi River
  elevation (feet) 480
General coastline (miles) 0
Tidal shoreline (miles) 0
Cropland, 2003 (x 1,000 acres) 25,511
Forest land, 2003 (x 1,000 acres). 2,301
Capital city . . . . Des Moines
  Population 2000 198,682
  Population 2006 193,886
Largest city . . . . Des Moines
  Population 2000 198,682
  Population 2006 193,886

Number of cities with over 100,000 population

1990 2
2000 2
2006 2

State park and recreation areas, 2005

Area (x 1,000 acres). 68
Number of visitors (x 1,000) 13,580
Revenues ($1,000) $4,070
  percent of operating expenditures. 29.6%

National forest system land, 2007

Acres 0

Demographics & Population Characteristics

Population

1980 2,913,808
1990 2,776,755
2000 2,926,382
2006 2,982,085
  Male. 1,472,810
  Female 1,509,275
Living in group quarters, 2006. 104,071
  percent of total. 3.5%
2007 (estimate). 2,988,046
  persons per square mile of land 53.5
2008 (projected). 2,997,608
2010 (projected) .3,009,907
2020 (projected). 3,020,496
2030 (projected). 2,955,172

Population of Core-Based Statistical Areas (formerly Metropolitan Areas), x 1,000

	CBSA	Non-CBSA
1990	1,939	838
2000	2,090	836
2006	2,167	816

Change in population, 2000-2007

Number 61,664
  percent. 2.1%
Natural increase (births minus deaths) 81,489
Net internal migration . . . .-50,248
Net international migration 36,217

Persons by age, 2006

Under 5 years 192,055
5 to 17 years 518,139
18 years and over 2,271,891
65 years and over 435,657
85 years and over .75,180
  Median age. 37.8

Persons by age, 2010 (projected)

Under 5 years 193,313
18 and over 2,298,851
65 and over 449,887
  Median age. 38.3

Race, 2006

One Race
  White. 2,820,425
  Black or African American 73,086
  Asian 46,553
  American Indian/Alaska Native. 11,145
  Hawaiian Native/Pacific Islander. 1,400
Two or more races. .29,476

Persons of Hispanic origin, 2006

Total Hispanic or Latino 112,987
  Mexican. 89,751
  Puerto Rican 2,836
  Cuban 1,197

©2008 Information Publications, Inc.
All rights reserved. Photocopying prohibited.
877-544-INFO (4636) or www.informationpublications.com

Persons of Asian origin, 2006

Total Asian	45,647
Asian Indian	8,695
Chinese	8,093
Filipino	4,638
Japanese	1,897
Korean	5,105
Vietnamese	8,274

Marital status, 2006

Population 15 years & over	2,397,350
Never married	639,253
Married	1,355,795
Separated	28,739
Widowed	162,063
Divorced	240,239

Language spoken at home, 2006

Population 5 years and older	2,790,958
English only	2,612,625
Spanish	97,876
French	5,260
German	17,127
Chinese	7,064

Households & families, 2006

Households	1,208,765
with persons under 18 years	386,758
with persons over 65 years	294,264
persons per household	2.38
Families	796,970
persons per family	2.92
Married couples	641,334
Female householder, no husband present	110,569
One-person households	337,390

Nativity, 2006

Number of residents born in state	2,156,469
percent of population	72.3%

Immigration & naturalization, 2006

Legal permanent residents admitted	4,086
Persons naturalized	805
Non-immigrant admissions	43,543

Vital Statistics and Health

Marriages

2004	20,455
2005	20,419
2006	20,024

Divorces

2004	8,305
2005	8,148
2006	8,024

Health risks, 2006

Percent of adults who are:

Smokers	21.4%
Overweight (BMI > 25)	62.9%
Obese (BMI > 30)	25.7%

Births

2005	39,311
Birthrate (per 1,000)	13.3
White	36,603
Black	1,508
Hispanic	3,115
Asian/Pacific Islander	946
Amer. Indian/Alaska Native	254
Low birth weight (2,500g or less)	7.2%
Cesarian births	26.7%
Preterm births	11.8%
To unmarried mothers	32.5%
Twin births (per 1,000)	33.2
Triplets or higher order (per 100,000)	154.4
2006 (preliminary)	40,610
rate per 1,000	13.6

Deaths

2004

All causes	26,897
rate per 100,000	729.4
Heart disease	7,299
rate per 100,000	191.9
Malignant neoplasms	6,340
rate per 100,000	181.8
Cerebrovascular disease	1,960
rate per 100,000	49.5
Chronic lower respiratory disease	1,547
rate per 100,000	42.5
Diabetes	700
rate per 100,000	19.4
2005 (preliminary)	27,812
rate per 100,000	742.0
2006 (provisional)	27,493

Infant deaths

2004	195
rate per 1,000	5.1
2005 (provisional)	202
rate per 1,000	5.2

Exercise routines, 2005

None	24.7%
Moderate or greater	46.2%
Vigorous	22.9%

Abortions, 2004

Total performed in state	6,022
rate per 1,000 women age 15-44	10
% obtained by out-of-state residents	11.4%

Physicians, 2005

Total	5,503
rate per 100,000 persons	186

Community hospitals, 2005

Number of hospitals	116
Beds (x 1,000)	10.8
Patients admitted (x 1,000)	363
Average daily census (x 1,000)	6.4
Average cost per day	$1,036
Outpatient visits (x 1 mil)	10.1

©2008 Information Publications, Inc.
All rights reserved. Photocopying prohibited.
877-544-INFO (4636) or www.informationpublications.com

Disability status of population, 2006
5 to 15 years 6.7%
16 to 64 years 11.3%
65 years and over 36.0%

Education

Educational attainment, 2006
Population over 25 years 1,952,026
   Less than 9th grade. 4.4%
   High school graduate or more 88.9%
   College graduate or more. 24.0%
   Graduate or professional degree. 7.4%

Public school enrollment, 2005-06
Total. 483,482
   Pre-kindergarten through grade 8. . . . 326,160
   Grades 9 through 12 157,322

Graduating public high school seniors, 2004-05
Diplomas (incl. GED and others) 33,641

SAT scores, 2007
Average critical reading score. 608
Average writing score 586
Average math score 613
Percent of graduates taking test 4%

Public school teachers, 2006-07 (estimate)
Total (x 1,000) 35.4
   Elementary. 23.3
   Secondary. 12.1
Average salary $43,130
   Elementary. $43,308
   Secondary. $42,787

State receipts & expenditures for
   public schools, 2006-07 (estimate)
Revenue receipts ($ mil) $4,814
Expenditures
Total ($ mil) $4,580
   Per capita $1,319
   Per pupil $8,684

NAEP proficiency scores, 2007

	Reading		Math	
	Basic	Proficient	Basic	Proficient
Grade 4	73.7%	36.1%	86.6%	43.0%
Grade 8	79.8%	35.7%	77.2%	35.2%

Higher education enrollment, fall 2005
Total. 78,815
   Full-time men 21,724
   Full-time women. 31,493
   Part-time men 7,434
   Part-time women. 18,164

Minority enrollment in institutions
   of higher education, 2005
Black, non-Hispanic 11,660
Hispanic 6,423
Asian/Pacific Islander 4,804
American Indian/Alaska Native. 1,045

Institutions of higher education, 2005-06
Total. 65
   Public. 19
   Private. 46

Earned degrees conferred, 2004-05
Associate's. 12,199
Bachelor's 20,786
Master's 4,316
First-professional. .1,683
Doctor's. 672

Public Libraries, 2006
Number of libraries. 540
Number of outlets 568
Annual visits per capita 5.8
Circulation per capita. 9.4

State & local financial support for
   higher education, FY 2006
Full-time equivalent enrollment (x 1,000) 112.3
Appropriations per FTE. $5,809

Social Insurance & Welfare Programs

Social Security benefits & beneficiaries, 2005
Beneficiaries (x 1,000) 548
   Retired & dependents. 397
   Survivors. 76
   Disabled & dependents. 75
Annual benefit payments ($ mil) $5,946
   Retired & dependents. $4,102
   Survivors. $1,087
   Disabled & dependents. $757
Average monthly benefit
   Retired & dependents. $1,000
   Disabled & dependents. $896
   Widowed. $992

Medicare, July 2005
Enrollment (x 1,000). 490
Payments ($ mil) $2,818

Medicaid, 2004
Beneficiaries (x 1,000). 946
Payments ($ mil) $4,343

State Children's Health Insurance Program, 2006
Enrollment (x 1,000). 49.6
Expenditures ($ mil) $64.2

Persons without health insurance, 2006
Number (x 1,000). 307
   percent. 10.5%
Number of children (x 1,000) 44
   percent of children 6.2%

Health care expenditures, 2004
Total expenditures. $15,892
   per capita $5,380

©2008 Information Publications, Inc.
All rights reserved. Photocopying prohibited.
877-544-INFO (4636) or www.informationpublications.com

4   Iowa

Federal and state public aid

State unemployment insurance, 2006
Recipients, first payments (x 1,000) 93
Total payments ($ mil) $310
Average weekly benefit $282
Temporary Assistance for Needy Families, 2006
Recipients (x 1,000) 470.1
Families (x 1,000) 195.7
Supplemental Security Income, 2005
Recipients (x 1,000) 43.4
Payments ($ mil) $193.2
Food Stamp Program, 2006
Avg monthly participants (x 1,000) 225.7
Total benefits ($ mil) $244.2

Housing & Construction

Housing units
Total 2005 (estimate) 1,306,516
Total 2006 (estimate) 1,320,331
Seasonal or recreational use, 2006 18,443
Owner-occupied, 2006 885,969
   Median home value $112,600
   Homeowner vacancy rate 2.7%
Renter-occupied, 2006 322,796
   Median rent $584
   Rental vacancy rate 13.5%
Home ownership rate, 2005 . . . . 73.9%
Home ownership rate, 2006 . . . . 74.0%

New privately-owned housing units
Number authorized, 2006 (x 1,000) 13.4
   Value ($ mil) $2,006.0
Started 2005 (x 1,000, estimate) 14.6
Started 2006 (x 1,000, estimate) 14.1

Existing home sales
2005 (x 1,000) 74.9
2006 (x 1,000) 74.6

Government & Elections

State officials 2008
Governor . . . . Chet Culver
         Democratic, term expires 1/11
Lieutenant Governor . . . . Patty Judge
Secretary of State . . . . Michael Mauro
Attorney General . . . . Tom Miller
Chief Justice . . . . Marsha Ternus

Governorship
Minimum age 30
Length of term . . . . 4 years
Consecutive terms permitted . . . . . not specified
Who succeeds . . . . Lieutenant Governor

Local governments by type, 2002
Total 1,975
   County 99
   Municipal 948
   Township 0
   School District 386
   Special District 542

State legislature
Name . . . . General Assembly
Upper chamber . . . . Senate
   Number of members 50
   Length of term . . . . 4 years
   Party in majority, 2008 . . . . Democratic
Lower chamber . . . . House of Representatives
   Number of members 100
   Length of term . . . . 2 years
   Party in majority, 2008 . . . . Democratic

Federal representation, 2008 (110th Congress)
Senator . . . . Tom Harkin
   Party . . . . Democratic
   Year term expires 2009
Senator . . . . Charles Grassley
   Party . . . . Republican
   Year term expires 2011
Representatives, total 5
   Democrats 3
   Republicans 2

Voters in November 2006 election (estimate)
Total 1,179,795
   Male 544,951
   Female 634,844
   White 1,148,860
   Black 14,313
   Hispanic 2,309
   Asian 10,816

Presidential election, 2004
Total Popular Vote 1,506,908
   Kerry 741,898
   Bush 751,957
Total Electoral Votes 7

Votes cast for US Senators
2004
Total vote (x 1,000) 1,479
Leading party . . . . Republican
Percent for leading party 70.2%
2006
Total vote (x 1,000) . . . . NA
Leading party . . . . NA
Percent for leading party . . . . NA

Votes cast for US Representatives
2004
Total vote (x 1,000) 1,458
   Democratic 625
   Republican 823
Leading party . . . . Republican
Percent for leading party 56.4%
2006
Total vote (x 1,000) 1,033
   Democratic 493
   Republican 522
Leading party . . . . Republican
Percent for leading party 50.6%

©2008 Information Publications, Inc.
All rights reserved. Photocopying prohibited.
877-544-INFO (4636) or www.informationpublications.com

State government employment, 2006
Full-time equivalent employees 53,258
Payroll ($ mil) $230.0

Local government employment, 2006
Full-time equivalent employees 132,663
Payroll ($ mil) $398.3

Women holding public office, 2008
US Congress 0
Statewide elected office................... 1
State legislature 34

Black public officials, 2002
Total.................................... 12
US and state legislatures 1
City/county/regional offices 8
Judicial/law enforcement................... 1
Education/school boards................... 2

Hispanic public officials, 2006
Total..................................... 0
State executives & legislators 0
City/county/regional offices 0
Judicial/law enforcement................... 0
Education/school boards................... 0

Governmental Finance

State government revenues, 2006
Total revenue (x $1,000)............$16,808,578
per capita $5,654.57
General revenue (x $1,000) $13,434,028
Intergovernmental 4,296,014
Taxes 6,118,897
general sales....................1,800,829
individual income tax 2,413,775
corporate income tax 284,976
Current charges..................2,017,249
Miscellaneous 1,001,868

State government expenditure, 2006
Total expenditure (x $1,000) $14,941,961
per capita $5,026.62
General expenditure (x $1,000) $13,470,126
per capita, total................... $4,531.48
Education 1,741.32
Public welfare 1,229.15
Health 65.70
Hospitals.........................311.19
Highways 491.46
Police protection..................29.31
Corrections 80.95
Natural resources 83.44
Parks & recreation 8.09
Governmental administration...... 166.85
Interest on general debt.............87.85

State debt & cash, 2006 ($ per capita)
Debt $2,219.75
Cash/security holdings.............. $11,053.74

Federal government grants to state & local government, 2005 (x $1,000)
Total...............................$4,035,419
by Federal agency
Defense 36,812
Education 329,551
Energy 27,127
Environmental Protection Agency 73,047
Health & Human Services. 2,358,362
Homeland Security..................21,736
Housing & Urban Development...... 241,726
Justice 59,283
Labor 73,056
Transportation 392,421
Veterans Affairs................... 14,598

Crime & Law Enforcement

Crime, 2006 (rates per 100,000 residents)
Property crimes 83,579
Burglary 18,017
Larceny 60,556
Motor vehicle theft 5,006
Property crime rate................2,802.7
Violent crimes...................... 8,455
Murder 55
Forcible rape...................... 828
Robbery...........................1,298
Aggravated assault 6,274
Violent crime rate 283.5
Hate crimes........................ 42

Fraud and identity theft, 2006
Fraud complaints..................... 2,666
rate per 100,000 residents 89.4
Identity theft complaints 1,041
rate per 100,000 residents 34.9

Law enforcement agencies, 2006
Total agencies......................... 231
Total employees 7,615
Officers 5,040
Civilians 2,575

Prisoners, probation, and parole, 2006
Total prisoners.......................8,875
percent change, 12/31/05 to 12/31/06 .... 1.6%
in private facilities 0%
in local jails 0%
Sentenced to more than one year 8,838
rate per 100,000 residents 296
Adults on probation 22,622
Adults on parole......................3,578

Prisoner demographics, June 30, 2005 (rate per 100,000 residents)
Male..................................... 751
Female................................... 83
White.................................... 309
Black.................................... 4,200
Hispanic 764

©2008 Information Publications, Inc.
All rights reserved. Photocopying prohibited.
877-544-INFO (4636) or www.informationpublications.com

6   Iowa

Arrests, 2006
Total................................ 109,230
    Persons under 18 years of age........ 19,605

Persons under sentence of death, 1/1/07
Total...................................... 0
    White.................................... 0
    Black.................................... 0
    Hispanic................................. 0

State's highest court
Name.....................Supreme Court
Number of members....................... 7
Length of term....................... 8 years
Intermediate appeals court?...............yes

Labor & Income

Civilian labor force, 2006 (x 1,000)
Total..................................1,701
    Men................................... 896
    Women................................. 806
    Persons 16-19 years.................... 108
    White.................................1,619
    Black................................. 34
    Hispanic.............................. 69

Civilian labor force as a percent of civilian non-institutional population, 2006
Total.................................72.7%
    Men...................................78.4
    Women.................................67.2
    Persons 16-19 years...................64.6
    White.................................72.9
    Black.................................73.0
    Hispanic..............................76.9

Employment, 2006 (x 1,000)
Total..................................1,641
    Men................................... 864
    Women................................. 776
    Persons 16-19 years.................... 97
    White................................. 1,566
    Black................................. 28
    Hispanic.............................. 65

Unemployment rate, 2006
Total..................................3.6%
    Men...................................3.5
    Women.................................3.6
    Persons 16-19 years...................10.1
    White.................................3.2
    Black.................................16.5
    Hispanic..............................4.8

Full-time/part-time labor force, 2003 (x 1,000)
Full-time labor force, employed..........1,217
Part-time labor force, employed........ 323
Unemployed, looking for
    Full-time work........................ 55
    Part-time work........................ 17
*Mean duration of unemployment (weeks)......*15.4
    Median...............................8.0

Labor unions, 2006
Membership (x 1,000).................... 161
    percent of employed...................11.3%

Experienced civilian labor force by private industry, 2006
Total..............................1,240,335
    Natural resources & mining.......... 16,294
    Construction.........................74,412
    Manufacturing.......................231,162
    Trade, transportation & utilities..... 305,731
    Information.......................... 32,965
    Finance.............................. 100,719
    Professional & business..............116,974
    Education & health...................187,376
    Leisure & hospitality............... 134,072
    Other................................ 40,631

Experienced civilian labor force by occupation, May 2006
Management........................... 54,900
Business & financial................... 58,980
Legal.................................6,770
Sales.................................157,080
Office & admin. support.............. 232,640
Computers & math.................... 26,130
Architecture & engineering.............17,070
Arts & entertainment..................17,430
Education............................ 90,290
Social services...................... 22,580
Health care practitioner & technical......74,160
Health care support.................. 43,990
Maintenance & repair................. 60,720
Construction......................... 68,140
Transportation & moving............. 126,620
Production........................... 166,660
Farming, fishing & forestry.............4,510

Hours and earnings of production workers on manufacturing payrolls, 2006
Average weekly hours....................41.9
Average hourly earnings...............$16.40
Average weekly earnings...............$687.16

Income and poverty, 2006
Median household income............ $44,491
Personal income, per capita (current $)... $33,236
    in constant (2000) dollars...........$29,013
Persons below poverty level............. 11.0%

Average annual pay
2006.............................. $34,320
    increase from 2005................... 3.8%

Federal individual income tax returns, 2005
Returns filed......................1,346,535
Adjusted gross income ($1,000).... $61,643,860
Total tax liability ($1,000)..........$6,917,573

Charitable contributions, 2004
Number of contributions................ 364.8
Total amount ($ mil).................. $1,159.7

©2008 Information Publications, Inc.
All rights reserved. Photocopying prohibited.
877-544-INFO (4636) or www.informationpublications.com

Economy, Business, Industry & Agriculture

Fortune 500 companies, 2007 1
Bankruptcy cases filed, FY 2007 6,660

Patents and trademarks issued, 2007

Patents 665
Trademarks 715

Business firm ownership, 2002

Women-owned 63,821
   Sales ($ mil) $7,399
Black-owned 1,609
   Sales ($ mil) $258
Hispanic-owned 1,536
   Sales ($ mil) $289
Asian-owned 1,786
   Sales ($ mil) $456
Amer. Indian/Alaska Native-owned 644
   Sales ($ mil) $86
Hawaiian/Pacific Islander-owned 17
   Sales ($ mil) $7

Gross domestic product, 2006 ($ mil)

Total gross domestic product $123,970
   Agriculture, forestry, fishing and
     hunting 4,051
   Mining. 205
   Utilities 2,451
   Construction 5,191
   Manufacturing, durable goods 15,078
   Manufacturing, non-durable goods 10,991
   Wholesale trade. .7,177
   Retail trade. 7,537
   Transportation & warehousing 4,429
   Information 3,670
   Finance & insurance 15,055
   Real estate, rental & leasing 11,312
   Professional and technical services 3,764
   Educational services 1,010
   Health care and social assistance 8,184
   Accommodation/food services 2,455
   Other services, except government 2,558
   Government 14,266

Establishments, payroll, employees & receipts, by major industry group, 2005

Total 82,087
   Annual payroll ($1,000) $39,420,961
   Paid employees 1,261,108
Forestry, fishing & agriculture 259
   Annual payroll ($1,000) $55,239
   Paid employees 1,501
Mining 205
   Annual payroll ($1,000) $91,551
   Paid employees 1,942
   Receipts, 2002 ($1,000) $333,227

Utilities 255
   Annual payroll ($1,000) $500,719
   Paid employees .7,963
   Receipts, 2002 ($1,000) . . . . .NA
Construction 9,055
   Annual payroll ($1,000) $2,573,372
   Paid employees 62,855
   Receipts, 2002 ($1,000) $9,940,503
Manufacturing 3,800
   Annual payroll ($1,000) $9,025,961
   Paid employees 225,567
   Receipts, 2002 ($1,000) $65,042,043
Wholesale trade 4,815
   Annual payroll ($1,000) $2,558,534
   Paid employees .63,167
   Receipts, 2002 ($1,000) $33,546,948
Retail trade 13,643
   Annual payroll ($1,000) $3,494,449
   Paid employees .178,216
   Receipts, 2002 ($1,000) $31,195,012
Transportation & warehousing 3,702
   Annual payroll ($1,000) $1,698,170
   Paid employees .49,876
   Receipts, 2002 ($1,000) $5,063,344
Information 1,582
   Annual payroll ($1,000) $1,418,993
   Paid employees 36,695
   Receipts, 2002 ($1,000) . . . . .NA
Finance & insurance 5,945
   Annual payroll ($1,000) $4,380,754
   Paid employees .91,727
   Receipts, 2002 ($1,000) . . . . .NA
Professional, scientific & technical 6,103
   Annual payroll ($1,000) $1,759,551
   Paid employees 42,486
   Receipts, 2002 ($1,000) $3,580,073
Education 700
   Annual payroll ($1,000) $625,473
   Paid employees .33,121
   Receipts, 2002 ($1,000) $263,404
Health care & social assistance 7,513
   Annual payroll ($1,000) $5,921,736
   Paid employees 188,242
   Receipts, 2002 ($1,000) $11,441,141
Arts and entertainment 1,441
   Annual payroll ($1,000) $379,634
   Paid employees .21,811
   Receipts, 2002 ($1,000) $1,229,803
Real estate 2,848
   Annual payroll ($1,000) $387,079
   Paid employees 14,006
   Receipts, 2002 ($1,000) $1,702,144
Accommodation & food service 6,771
   Annual payroll ($1,000) $1,105,219
   Paid employees 108,439
   Receipts, 2002 ($1,000) $3,698,955

©2008 Information Publications, Inc.
All rights reserved. Photocopying prohibited.
877-544-INFO (4636) or www.informationpublications.com

8   Iowa

Exports, 2006
Value of exported goods ($ mil)	$8,410
Manufactured	$7,559
Non-manufactured.	$581

Foreign direct investment in US affiliates, 2004
Property, plants & equipment ($ mil)	$6,391
Employment (x 1,000).	36.2

Agriculture, 2006
Number of farms	88,600
Farm acreage (x 1,000)	31,500
Acres per farm	356
Farm marketings and income ($ mil)	
Total.	$15,108.3
Crops	$7,229.1
Livestock.	$7,879.1
Net farm income	$3,274.8

Principal commodities, in order by marketing receipts, 2005
Corn, Hogs, Soybeans, Cattle and calves, Dairy products

Federal economic activity in state
Expenditures, 2005 ($ mil)
Total.	$20,345
Per capita	$6,860.47
Defense	$1,355
Non-defense	$18,990

Defense department, 2006 ($ mil)
Payroll	$445
Contract awards	$944
Grants	$42

Homeland security grants ($1,000)
2006.	$13,480
2007.	$7,043

FDIC-insured financial institutions, 2005
Number	401
Assets ($ billion)	$56.6
Deposits ($ billion)	$44.8

Fishing, 2006
Catch (x 1,000 lbs)	NA
Value ($1,000).	NA

Mining, 2006 ($ mil)
Total non-fuel mineral production	$704
Percent of U.S.	1.09%

Communication, Energy & Transportation

Communication
Households with computers, 2003	64.7%
Households with internet access, 2003	57.1%
High-speed internet providers	182
Total high-speed internet lines	654,694
Residential	452,699
Business.	201,995
Wireless phone customers, 12/2006	2,009,826

FCC-licensed stations (as of January 1, 2008)
TV stations	33
FM radio stations.	186
AM radio stations	84

Energy
Energy consumption, 2004
Total (trillion Btu).	1,206
Per capita (million Btu)	408.2

By source of production (trillion Btu)
Coal	443
Natural gas	229
Petroleum	439
Nuclear electric power	51
Hydroelectric power	10

By end-use sector (trillion Btu)
Residential	230
Commercial	182
Industrial	496
Transportation	297

Electric energy, 2005
Primary source of electricity.	Coal
Net generation (billion kWh)	44.2
percent from renewable sources.	6.2%
Net summer capability (million kW)	11.1
CO_2 emitted from generation	40.2

Natural gas utilities, 2005
Customers (x 1,000)	950
Sales (trillion Btu).	215
Revenues ($ mil)	$1,299
Nuclear plants, 2007	1
Total CO_2 emitted (million metric tons).	78.9
Energy spending, 2004 ($ mil)	$10,111
per capita	$3,423
Price per million Btu	$11.80

Transportation, 2006
Public road & street mileage	114,084
Urban.	11,197
Rural	102,887
Interstate.	781
Vehicle miles of travel (millions)	31,355
per capita	10,548.1
Total motor vehicle registrations	3,345,951
Automobiles.	1,744,519
Trucks	1,593,003
Motorcycles	161,106
Licensed drivers	2,040,873
19 years & under	123,970
Deaths from motor vehicle accidents	439
Gasoline consumed (x 1,000 gallons)	1,673,188
per capita	562.9

Commuting Statistics, 2006
Average commute time (min)	18.2
Drove to work alone	78.5%
Carpooled.	10.8%
Public transit	1.0%
Walk to work	3.7%
Work from home	4.7%

©2008 Information Publications, Inc.
All rights reserved. Photocopying prohibited.
877-544-INFO (4636) or www.informationpublications.com

State Summary

Capital city . . . . Topeka
Governor . . . . Kathleen Sebelius

Capitol
300 SW 10th Ave, Suite 212S
Topeka, KS 66612
785-296-3232

Admitted as a state 1861
Area (square miles) 82,277
Population, 2007 (estimate) 2,775,997
Largest city . . . . Wichita
    Population, 2006 357,698
Personal income per capita, 2006
    (in current dollars) $34,743
Gross domestic product, 2006 ($ mil) . . . $111,699

Leading industries by payroll, 2005

Manufacturing, Health care/Social assistance,
Retail trade

**Leading agricultural commodities
by receipts, 2005**

Cattle and calves, Wheat, Corn, Soybeans, Hogs

Geography & Environment

Total area (square miles) 82,277
    land 81,815
    water 462
Federally-owned land, 2004 (acres) 631,351
    percent 1.2%
Highest point . . . . Mt. Sunflower
    elevation (feet) 4,039
Lowest point . . . . Verdigris River
    elevation (feet) 679
General coastline (miles) 0
Tidal shoreline (miles) 0
Cropland, 2003 (x 1,000 acres) 26,466
Forest land, 2003 (x 1,000 acres) 1,549
Capital city . . . . Topeka
    Population 2000 122,377
    Population 2006 122,113
Largest city . . . . Wichita
    Population 2000 344,284
    Population 2006 357,698

Number of cities with over 100,000 population

1990 4
2000 4
2006 5

State park and recreation areas, 2005

Area (x 1,000 acres) 33
Number of visitors (x 1,000) 7,310
Revenues ($1,000) $5,967
    percent of operating expenditures 58.6%

National forest system land, 2007

Acres 108,175

Demographics & Population Characteristics

Population

1980 2,363,679
1990 2,477,574
2000 2,688,824
2006 2,764,075
    Male 1,371,446
    Female 1,392,629
Living in group quarters, 2006 82,162
    percent of total 3.0%
2007 (estimate) 2,775,997
    persons per square mile of land 33.9
2008 (projected) 2,784,728
2010 (projected) 2,805,470
2020 (projected) 2,890,566
2030 (projected) 2,940,084

**Population of Core-Based Statistical Areas
(formerly Metropolitan Areas), x 1,000**

	CBSA	Non-CBSA
1990	2,029	448
2000	2,248	440
2006	2,349	415

Change in population, 2000-2007

Number 87,173
    percent 3.2%
Natural increase (births minus deaths) 109,842
Net internal migration . . . . -67,315
Net international migration 46,314

Persons by age, 2006

Under 5 years 194,100
5 to 17 years 501,737
18 years and over 2,068,238
65 years and over 357,709
85 years and over 59,518
    Median age 36.0

Persons by age, 2010 (projected)

Under 5 years 199,534
18 and over 2,106,474
65 and over 375,315
    Median age 36.4

Race, 2006

One Race
    White 2,462,232
    Black or African American 164,507
    Asian 60,870
    American Indian/Alaska Native 27,374
    Hawaiian Native/Pacific Islander 1,863
Two or more races 47,229

Persons of Hispanic origin, 2006

Total Hispanic or Latino 236,351
    Mexican 193,309
    Puerto Rican 6,241
    Cuban 785

©2008 Information Publications, Inc.
All rights reserved. Photocopying prohibited.
877-544-INFO (4636) or www.informationpublications.com

Persons of Asian origin, 2006

Total Asian 60,646
    Asian Indian. 15,295
    Chinese 9,646
    Filipino 3,743
    Japanese 1,352
    Korean. 5,068
    Vietnamese. 12,525

Marital status, 2006

Population 15 years & over 2,190,376
    Never married 582,595
    Married. 1,229,547
    Separated 31,025
    Widowed. 138,334
    Divorced 239,900

Language spoken at home, 2006

Population 5 years and older. 2,569,373
    English only 2,304,997
    Spanish 169,376
    French 4,647
    German. 16,736
    Chinese 8,159

Households & families, 2006

Households. 1,088,288
    with persons under 18 years 371,279
    with persons over 65 years. 241,992
    persons per household 2.46
Families. 724,553
    persons per family. 3.02
Married couples. 571,689
Female householder,
    no husband present. 111,874
One-person households 303,157

Nativity, 2006

Number of residents born in state 1,633,671
    percent of population. 59.1%

Immigration & naturalization, 2006

Legal permanent residents admitted. 4,280
Persons naturalized 2,509
Non-immigrant admissions 61,161

Vital Statistics and Health

Marriages

2004 19,072
2005 18,804
2006 18,862

Divorces

2004 9,102
2005 8,512
2006 9,158

Health risks, 2006

Percent of adults who are:
    Smokers. 20.0%
    Overweight (BMI > 25). 62.3%
    Obese (BMI > 30). 25.9%

Births

2005 39,888
    Birthrate (per 1,000). 14.5
    White. 35,116
    Black 3,127
    Hispanic 6,121
    Asian/Pacific Islander 1,214
    Amer. Indian/Alaska Native 431
    Low birth weight (2,500g or less). 7.2%
    Cesarian births 28.9%
    Preterm births 12.2%
    To unmarried mothers. 34.2%
    Twin births (per 1,000) 30.3
    Triplets or higher order (per 100,000). . . .158.8
2006 (preliminary). 40,964
    rate per 1,000 . . . . .14.8

Deaths

2004
All causes 23,818
    rate per 100,000. . . . . .793.5
Heart disease 6,048
    rate per 100,000. . . . . .197.3
Malignant neoplasms 5,312
    rate per 100,000. . . . . .183.2
Cerebrovascular disease. 1,611
    rate per 100,000. . . . . .51.8
Chronic lower respiratory disease 1,316
    rate per 100,000. . . . . .44.9
Diabetes. 690
    rate per 100,000. . . . . .23.5
2005 (preliminary). 24,684
    rate per 100,000. . . . . 806.8
2006 (provisional) 24,473

Infant deaths

2004 284
    rate per 1,000 . . . . .7.2
2005 (provisional) 280
    rate per 1,000 . . . . .6.9

Exercise routines, 2005

None. 24.4%
Moderate or greater. 48.7%
Vigorous 25.0%

Abortions, 2004

Total performed in state. 11,357
    rate per 1,000 women age 15-44. 20
    % obtained by out-of-state residents 48.2%

Physicians, 2005

Total. 6,070
    rate per 100,000 persons 221

Community hospitals, 2005

Number of hospitals 131
Beds (x 1,000). 10.1
Patients admitted (x 1,000) 330
Average daily census (x 1,000) 5.7
Average cost per day $1,055
Outpatient visits (x 1 mil) 5.9

©2008 Information Publications, Inc.
All rights reserved. Photocopying prohibited.
877-544-INFO (4636) or www.informationpublications.com

Disability status of population, 2006

5 to 15 years 6.9%
16 to 64 years 11.8%
65 years and over 40.5%

Education

Educational attainment, 2006

Population over 25 years 1,771,185
    Less than 9th grade. 4.3%
    High school graduate or more 88.5%
    College graduate or more. 28.6%
    Graduate or professional degree. 9.8%

Public school enrollment, 2005-06

Total. 467,285
    Pre-kindergarten through grade 8. . . . 309,555
    Grades 9 through 12 142,349

Graduating public high school seniors, 2004-05

Diplomas (incl. GED and others) 30,355

SAT scores, 2007

Average critical reading score. 583
Average writing score 569
Average math score 590
Percent of graduates taking test 8%

Public school teachers, 2006-07 (estimate)

Total (x 1,000) 34.4
    Elementary. 16.9
    Secondary. 17.4
Average salary $43,334
    Elementary. $43,334
    Secondary. $43,334

State receipts & expenditures for
public schools, 2006-07 (estimate)

Revenue receipts ($ mil) $4,923
Expenditures
Total ($ mil) $4,957
    Per capita $1,500
    Per pupil $10,119

NAEP proficiency scores, 2007

	Reading		Math	
	Basic	Proficient	Basic	Proficient
Grade 4	71.8%	36.1%	89.4%	51.1%
Grade 8	80.6%	35.2%	81.4%	40.2%

Higher education enrollment, fall 2005

Total. 21,433
    Full-time men 6,844
    Full-time women. 8,206
    Part-time men 2,380
    Part-time women. 4,003

Minority enrollment in institutions
of higher education, 2005

Black, non-Hispanic 11,230
Hispanic 8,618
Asian/Pacific Islander 7,279
American Indian/Alaska Native. 3,194

Institutions of higher education, 2005-06

Total. 62
    Public. 35
    Private 27

Earned degrees conferred, 2004-05

Associate's. 7,954
Bachelor's 16,221
Master's 5,668
First-professional. 767
Doctor's 413

Public Libraries, 2006

Number of libraries. 325
Number of outlets 379
Annual visits per capita 6.4
Circulation per capita 10.9

State & local financial support for
higher education, FY 2006

Full-time equivalent enrollment (x 1,000). . . .127.6
Appropriations per FTE. $5,792

Social Insurance &
Welfare Programs

Social Security benefits & beneficiaries, 2005

Beneficiaries (x 1,000) 451
    Retired & dependents. 320
    Survivors. 61
    Disabled & dependents. 70
Annual benefit payments ($ mil) $4,974
    Retired & dependents. $3,406
    Survivors. $879
    Disabled & dependents. $690
Average monthly benefit
    Retired & dependents. $1,027
    Disabled & dependents. $909
    Widowed. $1,025

Medicare, July 2005

Enrollment (x 1,000). 402
Payments ($ mil) $2,661

Medicaid, 2004

Beneficiaries (x 1,000). 365
Payments ($ mil) $1,860

State Children's Health Insurance Program, 2006

Enrollment (x 1,000). 48.9
Expenditures ($ mil) $67.2

Persons without health insurance, 2006

Number (x 1,000). 335
    percent. 12.3%
Number of children (x 1,000) 51
    percent of children 7.3%

Health care expenditures, 2004

Total expenditures. $14,736
    per capita $5,382

©2008 Information Publications, Inc.
All rights reserved. Photocopying prohibited.
877-544-INFO (4636) or www.informationpublications.com

Federal and state public aid

State unemployment insurance, 2006
Recipients, first payments (x 1,000) 54
Total payments ($ mil) $210
Average weekly benefit $287
Temporary Assistance for Needy Families, 2006
Recipients (x 1,000) 525.5
Families (x 1,000) 201.9
Supplemental Security Income, 2005
Recipients (x 1,000) 39.2
Payments ($ mil) $186.7
Food Stamp Program, 2006
Avg monthly participants (x 1,000) 183.1
Total benefits ($ mil) $188.3

Housing & Construction

Housing units
Total 2005 (estimate) 1,196,732
Total 2006 (estimate) 1,207,987
Seasonal or recreational use, 2006 11,864
Owner-occupied, 2006 761,022
Median home value $114,400
Homeowner vacancy rate 2.1%
Renter-occupied, 2006 327,266
Median rent $609
Rental vacancy rate 11.3%
Home ownership rate, 2005 . . . . 69.5%
Home ownership rate, 2006 . . . . 70.0%

New privately-owned housing units
Number authorized, 2006 (x 1,000) 14.6
Value ($ mil) $1,995.5
Started 2005 (x 1,000, estimate) 13.8
Started 2006 (x 1,000, estimate) 13.8

Existing home sales
2005 (x 1,000) 77.9
2006 (x 1,000) 76.1

Government & Elections

State officials 2008
Governor . . . . Kathleen Sebelius
Democratic, term expires 1/11
Lieutenant Governor . . . . .Mark Parkinson
Secretary of State . . . . Ron Thornburgh
Attorney General . . . . (vacant)
Chief Justice . . . . .Kay McFarland

Governorship
Minimum age . . . . not specified
Length of term . . . . 4 years
Consecutive terms permitted 2
Who succeeds . . . . Lieutenant Governor

Local governments by type, 2002
Total 3,887
County 104
Municipal 627
Township 1,299
School District 324
Special District 1,533

State legislature
Name . . . . Legislature
Upper chamber . . . . .Senate
Number of members 40
Length of term . . . . 4 years
Party in majority, 2008 . . . . Republican
Lower chamber . . . . .House of Representatives
Number of members 125
Length of term . . . . 2 years
Party in majority, 2008 . . . . Republican

Federal representation, 2008 (110ᵗʰ Congress)
Senator . . . . .Pat Roberts
Party . . . . Republican
Year term expires 2009
Senator . . . . Sam Brownback
Party . . . . Republican
Year term expires 2011
Representatives, total 4
Democrats 2
Republicans 2

Voters in November 2006 election (estimate)
Total 900,638
Male 417,509
Female 483,129
White 854,991
Black 36,468
Hispanic 13,112
Asian . . . . NA

Presidential election, 2004
Total Popular Vote 1,187,756
Kerry 434,993
Bush 736,456
Total Electoral Votes 6

Votes cast for US Senators
2004
Total vote (x 1,000) .1,129
Leading party . . . . Republican
Percent for leading party 69.2%
2006
Total vote (x 1,000) . . . . NA
Leading party . . . . NA
Percent for leading party . . . . NA

Votes cast for US Representatives
2004
Total vote (x 1,000) .1,156
Democratic 387
Republican 724
Leading party . . . . Republican
Percent for leading party 62.6%
2006
Total vote (x 1,000) 845
Democratic 369
Republican 459
Leading party . . . . Republican
Percent for leading party 54.3%

©2008 Information Publications, Inc.
All rights reserved. Photocopying prohibited.
877-544-INFO (4636) or www.informationpublications.com

State government employment, 2006
Full-time equivalent employees 44,393
Payroll ($ mil) $153.8

Local government employment, 2006
Full-time equivalent employees 140,550
Payroll ($ mil) $413.3

Women holding public office, 2008
US Congress 1
Statewide elected office...................... 3
State legislature 48

Black public officials, 2002
Total..................................... 16
  US and state legislatures 7
  City/county/regional offices 4
  Judicial/law enforcement.................. 3
  Education/school boards 2

Hispanic public officials, 2006
Total..................................... 11
  State executives & legislators 4
  City/county/regional offices 6
  Judicial/law enforcement.................. 0
  Education/school boards.................. 1

Governmental Finance

State government revenues, 2006
Total revenue (x $1,000)...........$13,615,302
  per capita $4,940.57
General revenue (x $1,000) $11,448,515
  Intergovernmental 3,314,770
  Taxes 6,275,075
    general sales.................... 2,127,597
    individual income tax 2,401,128
    corporate income tax 381,259
  Current charges.................... 1,135,185
  Miscellaneous 723,485

State government expenditure, 2006
Total expenditure (x $1,000).......$12,553,494
  per capita $4,555.27
General expenditure (x $1,000) $11,439,941
  per capita, total................... $4,151.20
    Education....................... 1,876.44
    Public welfare 1,020.56
    Health 71.10
    Hospitals....................... 44.35
    Highways 455.24
    Police protection................ 43.64
    Corrections 113.63
    Natural resources 69.19
    Parks & recreation 9.40
    Governmental administration...... 160.49
    Interest on general debt........... 103.35

State debt & cash, 2006 ($ per capita)
Debt...................................$2,084.14
Cash/security holdings...............$6,043.97

Federal government grants to state & local government, 2005 (x $1,000)
Total.............................. $3,617,795
by Federal agency
  Defense 26,874
  Education 354,695
  Energy 12,065
  Environmental Protection Agency 44,838
  Health & Human Services. 1,869,708
  Homeland Security................ 101,898
  Housing & Urban Development...... 194,646
  Justice 49,069
  Labor 54,289
  Transportation 401,699
  Veterans Affairs.................. 4,810

Crime & Law Enforcement

Crime, 2006 (rates per 100,000 residents)
Property crimes 103,658
  Burglary 19,992
  Larceny 74,963
  Motor vehicle theft 8,703
  Property crime rate............... 3,750.2
Violent crimes....................... 11,748
  Murder 127
  Forcible rape..................... 1,238
  Robbery........................... 1,877
  Aggravated assault 8,506
  Violent crime rate 425.0
Hate crimes........................... 135

Fraud and identity theft, 2006
Fraud complaints...................... 3,068
  rate per 100,000 residents 111.0
Identity theft complaints 1,626
  rate per 100,000 residents 58.8

Law enforcement agencies, 2006
Total agencies........................ 327
Total employees 10,451
  Officers 7,085
  Civilians 3,366

Prisoners, probation, and parole, 2006
Total prisoners....................... 8,816
  percent change, 12/31/05 to 12/31/06 ... -2.8%
  in private facilities 0%
  in local jails 0%
Sentenced to more than one year 8,816
  rate per 100,000 residents 318
Adults on probation 15,518
Adults on parole...................... 4,886

Prisoner demographics, June 30, 2005 (rate per 100,000 residents)
Male.................................. 1,054
Female 117
White................................. 443
Black................................. 3,096
Hispanic .... NA

©2008 Information Publications, Inc.
All rights reserved. Photocopying prohibited.
877-544-INFO (4636) or www.informationpublications.com

Arrests, 2006

Total 70,057
   Persons under 18 years of age 10,036

Persons under sentence of death, 1/1/07

Total 9
   White 5
   Black 4
   Hispanic 0

State's highest court

Name .... Supreme Court
Number of members 7
Length of term .... 6 years
Intermediate appeals court? .... yes

Labor & Income

Civilian labor force, 2006 (x 1,000)

Total 1,480
   Men 787
   Women 693
   Persons 16-19 years 84
   White 1,338
   Black 67
   Hispanic 90

Civilian labor force as a percent of civilian non-institutional population, 2006

Total 70.4%
   Men 76.5
   Women 64.5
   Persons 16-19 years 51.9
   White 70.7
   Black 63.8
   Hispanic 75.8

Employment, 2006 (x 1,000)

Total 1,414
   Men 755
   Women 659
   Persons 16-19 years 71
   White 1,288
   Black 59
   Hispanic 85

Unemployment rate, 2006

Total 4.4%
   Men 4.0
   Women 4.9
   Persons 16-19 years 15.3
   White 3.7
   Black 12.4
   Hispanic 5.6

Full-time/part-time labor force, 2003 (x 1,000)

Full-time labor force, employed 1,073
Part-time labor force, employed 284
Unemployed, looking for
   Full-time work 63
   Part-time work 14
Mean duration of unemployment (weeks) 15.2
   Median 8.3

Labor unions, 2006

Membership (x 1,000) 99
   percent of employed 8.0%

Experienced civilian labor force by private industry, 2006

Total 1,085,952
   Natural resources & mining 18,260
   Construction 64,867
   Manufacturing 182,714
   Trade, transportation & utilities 256,056
   Information 39,382
   Finance 71,826
   Professional & business 139,661
   Education & health 161,184
   Leisure & hospitality 115,277
   Other 36,704

Experienced civilian labor force by occupation, May 2006

Management 57,470
Business & financial 54,490
Legal 7,410
Sales 133,930
Office & admin. support 229,540
Computers & math 24,870
Architecture & engineering 25,800
Arts & entertainment 16,120
Education 87,860
Social services 16,870
Health care practitioner & technical 65,150
Health care support 39,880
Maintenance & repair 56,470
Construction 65,320
Transportation & moving 91,660
Production 126,420
Farming, fishing & forestry 2,260

Hours and earnings of production workers on manufacturing payrolls, 2006

Average weekly hours 43.0
Average hourly earnings $17.68
Average weekly earnings $760.24

Income and poverty, 2006

Median household income $45,478
Personal income, per capita (current $) ... $34,743
   in constant (2000) dollars $30,328
Persons below poverty level 12.4%

Average annual pay

2006 .... $35,696
   increase from 2005 .... 5.4%

Federal individual income tax returns, 2005

Returns filed 1,241,568
Adjusted gross income ($1,000) $60,483,659
Total tax liability ($1,000) $7,427,755

Charitable contributions, 2004

Number of contributions 328.8
Total amount ($ mil) $1,347.6

©2008 Information Publications, Inc.
All rights reserved. Photocopying prohibited.
877-544-INFO (4636) or www.informationpublications.com

Economy, Business, Industry & Agriculture

Fortune 500 companies, 2007 1
Bankruptcy cases filed, FY 2007 7,730

Patents and trademarks issued, 2007

Patents 544
Trademarks 557

Business firm ownership, 2002

Women-owned 59,635
  Sales ($ mil) $6,949
Black-owned 4,468
  Sales ($ mil) $376
Hispanic-owned 4,176
  Sales ($ mil) $660
Asian-owned 3,547
  Sales ($ mil) $896
Amer. Indian/Alaska Native-owned 1,727
  Sales ($ mil) $353
Hawaiian/Pacific Islander-owned 44
  Sales ($ mil) $20

Gross domestic product, 2006 ($ mil)

Total gross domestic product $111,699
  Agriculture, forestry, fishing and
    hunting 3,092
  Mining 2,578
  Utilities 2,494
  Construction 4,465
  Manufacturing, durable goods 8,757
  Manufacturing, non-durable goods 6,552
  Wholesale trade .7,055
  Retail trade 7,566
  Transportation & warehousing 3,951
  Information 6,798
  Finance & insurance 6,555
  Real estate, rental & leasing 10,775
  Professional and technical services 5,682
  Educational services 622
  Health care and social assistance 7,802
  Accommodation/food services 2,675
  Other services, except government 2,575
  Government 16,622

Establishments, payroll, employees & receipts, by major industry group, 2005

Total 76,173
  Annual payroll ($1,000) $36,646,065
  Paid employees 1,116,216
Forestry, fishing & agriculture 188
  Annual payroll ($1,000) $16,298
  Paid employees 670
Mining 941
  Annual payroll ($1,000) $381,069
  Paid employees 8,004
  Receipts, 2002 ($1,000) $3,247,527

Utilities 254
  Annual payroll ($1,000) $429,864
  Paid employees 6,545
  Receipts, 2002 ($1,000) . . . . .NA
Construction 8,032
  Annual payroll ($1,000) $2,465,977
  Paid employees 62,331
  Receipts, 2002 ($1,000) $10,341,081
Manufacturing 3,128
  Annual payroll ($1,000) $7,221,614
  Paid employees 177,170
  Receipts, 2002 ($1,000) $50,897,796
Wholesale trade 4,541
  Annual payroll ($1,000) $2,345,990
  Paid employees 54,461
  Receipts, 2002 ($1,000) $44,117,100
Retail trade 11,562
  Annual payroll ($1,000) $2,952,196
  Paid employees 148,988
  Receipts, 2002 ($1,000) $26,505,396
Transportation & warehousing 2,632
  Annual payroll ($1,000) $1,393,651
  Paid employees 42,533
  Receipts, 2002 ($1,000) $3,963,169
Information 1,519
  Annual payroll ($1,000) $2,395,081
  Paid employees 43,002
  Receipts, 2002 ($1,000) . . . . .NA
Finance & insurance 5,708
  Annual payroll ($1,000) $2,786,136
  Paid employees 58,675
  Receipts, 2002 ($1,000) . . . . .NA
Professional, scientific & technical 7,087
  Annual payroll ($1,000) $2,418,500
  Paid employees 56,793
  Receipts, 2002 ($1,000) $6,285,201
Education 699
  Annual payroll ($1,000) $375,781
  Paid employees 18,026
  Receipts, 2002 ($1,000) $309,700
Health care & social assistance 7,412
  Annual payroll ($1,000) $5,487,089
  Paid employees 169,777
  Receipts, 2002 ($1,000) $11,162,607
Arts and entertainment 1,109
  Annual payroll ($1,000) $196,594
  Paid employees 13,536
  Receipts, 2002 ($1,000) $694,248
Real estate 3,203
  Annual payroll ($1,000) $465,149
  Paid employees 15,558
  Receipts, 2002 ($1,000) $2,028,027
Accommodation & food service 5,776
  Annual payroll ($1,000) $1,101,854
  Paid employees 101,824
  Receipts, 2002 ($1,000) $3,196,947

©2008 Information Publications, Inc.
All rights reserved. Photocopying prohibited.
877-544-INFO (4636) or www.informationpublications.com

8   Kansas

Exports, 2006
Value of exported goods ($ mil) $8,626
    Manufactured $7,591
    Non-manufactured $598

Foreign direct investment in US affiliates, 2004
Property, plants & equipment ($ mil) $5,322
Employment (x 1,000). 32.2

Agriculture, 2006
Number of farms 64,000
Farm acreage (x 1,000) 47,200
    Acres per farm 738
Farm marketings and income ($ mil)
Total $10,335.8
    Crops $3,365.1
    Livestock $6,970.7
Net farm income $1,614.3

Principal commodities, in order by marketing receipts, 2005
Cattle and calves, Wheat, Corn, Soybeans, Hogs

Federal economic activity in state
Expenditures, 2005 ($ mil)
    Total. $20,492
        Per capita $7,456.72
    Defense $3,269
    Non-defense $17,224
Defense department, 2006 ($ mil)
    Payroll $1,827
    Contract awards $1,706
    Grants $46
Homeland security grants ($1,000)
    2006 . . . .$14,274
    2007 . . . . $8,375

FDIC-insured financial institutions, 2005
Number 362
Assets ($ billion) $59.2
Deposits ($ billion) $44.0

Fishing, 2006
Catch (x 1,000 lbs) . . . . NA
Value ($1,000). . . . . NA

Mining, 2006 ($ mil)
Total non-fuel mineral production $913
Percent of U.S. 1.42%

Communication, Energy & Transportation

Communication
Households with computers, 2003 . . . . 63.8%
Households with internet access, 2003 . . . . 54.3%
High-speed internet providers 83
Total high-speed internet lines 755,922
    Residential 600,073
    Business. 155,849
Wireless phone customers, 12/2006 2,046,542

FCC-licensed stations (as of January 1, 2008)
TV stations 25
FM radio stations. 165
AM radio stations 62

Energy
Energy consumption, 2004
    Total (trillion Btu). 1,104
    Per capita (million Btu) 403.0
By source of production (trillion Btu)
    Coal 386
    Natural gas 273
    Petroleum 428
    Nuclear electric power 106
    Hydroelectric power 0
By end-use sector (trillion Btu)
    Residential 217
    Commercial 197
    Industrial 408
    Transportation 281
Electric energy, 2005
    Primary source of electricity. . . . . Coal
    Net generation (billion kWh) 45.9
        percent from renewable sources 1.0%
    Net summer capability (million kW) 11.0
    CO_2 emitted from generation 37.6
Natural gas utilities, 2005
    Customers (x 1,000) 950
    Sales (trillion Btu). 198
    Revenues ($ mil) $1,059
Nuclear plants, 2007 1
Total CO_2 emitted (million metric tons). 79.9
Energy spending, 2004 ($ mil) $8,954
    per capita $3,270
    Price per million Btu $12.44

Transportation, 2006
Public road & street mileage 140,381
    Urban. 12,790
    Rural. 127,591
    Interstate. 874
Vehicle miles of travel (millions) 30,215
    per capita 10,964.1
Total motor vehicle registrations 2,389,192
    Automobiles. 872,878
    Trucks 1,512,396
    Motorcycles 72,072
Licensed drivers 2,003,112
    19 years & under 166,663
Deaths from motor vehicle accidents 468
Gasoline consumed (x 1,000 gallons) 1,329,522
    per capita 482.4

Commuting Statistics, 2006
Average commute time (min) 18.5
    Drove to work alone 81.8%
    Carpooled. 9.2%
    Public transit 0.6%
    Walk to work 2.6%
    Work from home 4.3%

©2008 Information Publications, Inc.
All rights reserved. Photocopying prohibited.
877-544-INFO (4636) or www.informationpublications.com

Kentucky 1

State Summary

Capital city . . . . Frankfort
Governor . . . . Steve Beshar
700 Capitol Ave
Suite 100
Frankfort, KY 40601
502-564-2611
Admitted as a state 1792
Area (square miles) 40,409
Population, 2007 (estimate) 4,241,474
Largest city . . . . Louisville
Population, 2006 554,496
Personal income per capita, 2006
(in current dollars) $29,352
Gross domestic product, 2006 ($ mil) . . . $145,959

Leading industries by payroll, 2005

Manufacturing, Health care/Social assistance,
Retail trade

**Leading agricultural commodities
by receipts, 2005**

Horses/mules, Cattle and calves, Broilers, Corn,
Soybeans

Geography & Environment

Total area (square miles) 40,409
land 39,728
water 681
Federally-owned land, 2004 (acres) 1,378,677
percent 5.4%
Highest point . . . . Black Mountain
elevation (feet) 4,139
Lowest point . . . . Mississippi River
elevation (feet) 257
General coastline (miles) 0
Tidal shoreline (miles) 0
Cropland, 2003 (x 1,000 acres) 5,479
Forest land, 2003 (x 1,000 acres) 10,510
Capital city . . . . Frankfort
Population 2000 27,741
Population 2006 27,077
Largest city . . . . Louisville
Population 2000 551,284
Population 2006 554,496

Number of cities with over 100,000 population

1990 2
2000 2
2006 2

State park and recreation areas, 2005

Area (x 1,000 acres) 58
Number of visitors (x 1,000) 7,037
Revenues ($1,000) $52,143
percent of operating expenditures 61.7%

National forest system land, 2007

Acres 814,045

Demographics & Population Characteristics

Population

1980 3,660,777
1990 3,685,296
2000 4,042,285
2006 4,206,074
Male 2,061,310
Female 2,144,764
Living in group quarters, 2006 114,777
percent of total 2.7%
2007 (estimate) 4,241,474
persons per square mile of land 106.8
2008 (projected) 4,226,659
2010 (projected) 4,265,117
2020 (projected) 4,424,431
2030 (projected) 4,554,998

**Population of Core-Based Statistical Areas
(formerly Metropolitan Areas), x 1,000**

	CBSA	Non-CBSA
1990	2,734	953
2000	3,036	1,006
2006	3,184	1,022

Change in population, 2000-2007

Number 199,193
percent 4.9%
Natural increase (births minus deaths) 110,877
Net internal migration 63,791
Net international migration 30,881

Persons by age, 2006

Under 5 years 275,751
5 to 17 years 723,780
18 years and over 3,206,543
65 years and over 537,294
85 years and over 69,463
Median age 37.2

Persons by age, 2010 (projected)

Under 5 years 275,053
18 and over 3,262,810
65 and over 557,471
Median age 38.0

Race, 2006

One Race
White 3,793,438
Black or African American 316,945
Asian 41,752
American Indian/Alaska Native 9,988
Hawaiian Native/Pacific Islander 1,765
Two or more races 42,186

Persons of Hispanic origin, 2006

Total Hispanic or Latino 83,015
Mexican 55,761
Puerto Rican 6,785
Cuban 6,421

©2008 Information Publications, Inc.
All rights reserved. Photocopying prohibited.
877-544-INFO (4636) or www.informationpublications.com

Persons of Asian origin, 2006

Total Asian	38,835
Asian Indian	10,912
Chinese	7,306
Filipino	3,843
Japanese	5,040
Korean	3,056
Vietnamese	5,394

Marital status, 2006

Population 15 years & over	3,381,302
Never married	879,970
Married	1,828,798
Separated	69,732
Widowed	243,830
Divorced	428,704

Language spoken at home, 2006

Population 5 years and older	3,929,110
English only	3,769,097
Spanish	80,450
French	9,056
German	16,243
Chinese	6,259

Households & families, 2006

Households	1,651,911
with persons under 18 years	550,811
with persons over 65 years	378,261
persons per household	2.48
Families	1,106,404
persons per family	3.04
Married couples	832,504
Female householder, no husband present	205,540
One-person households	465,843

Nativity, 2006

Number of residents born in state	3,019,808
percent of population	71.8%

Immigration & naturalization, 2006

Legal permanent residents admitted	5,506
Persons naturalized	2,049
Non-immigrant admissions	70,731

Vital Statistics and Health

Marriages

2004	36,391
2005	36,251
2006	36,905

Divorces

2004	20,298
2005	19,342
2006	21,489

Health risks, 2006

Percent of adults who are:

Smokers	28.5%
Overweight (BMI > 25)	66.4%
Obese (BMI > 30)	28.0%

Births

2005	56,444
Birthrate (per 1,000)	13.5
White	50,445
Black	5,094
Hispanic	2,509
Asian/Pacific Islander	823
Amer. Indian/Alaska Native	82
Low birth weight (2,500g or less)	9.1%
Cesarian births	33.9%
Preterm births	15.2%
To unmarried mothers	35.5%
Twin births (per 1,000)	30.6
Triplets or higher order (per 100,000)	234.8
2006 (preliminary)	58,291
rate per 1,000	13.9

Deaths

2004

All causes	38,646
rate per 100,000	935.1
Heart disease	10,465
rate per 100,000	254.9
Malignant neoplasms	9,159
rate per 100,000	215.4
Cerebrovascular disease	2,339
rate per 100,000	58.0
Chronic lower respiratory disease	2,265
rate per 100,000	54.7
Diabetes	1,195
rate per 100,000	28.6
2005 (preliminary)	40,223
rate per 100,000	958.4
2006 (provisional)	40,066

Infant deaths

2004	378
rate per 1,000	6.8
2005 (provisional)	367
rate per 1,000	6.5

Exercise routines, 2005

None	31.5%
Moderate or greater	34.7%
Vigorous	16.8%

Abortions, 2004

Total performed in state	3,557
rate per 1,000 women age 15-44	4
% obtained by out-of-state residents	NA

Physicians, 2005

Total	9,608
rate per 100,000 persons	230

Community hospitals, 2005

Number of hospitals	105
Beds (x 1,000)	14.9
Patients admitted (x 1,000)	618
Average daily census (x 1,000)	9.3
Average cost per day	$1,194
Outpatient visits (x 1 mil)	8.8

©2008 Information Publications, Inc.
All rights reserved. Photocopying prohibited.
877-544-INFO (4636) or www.informationpublications.com

Disability status of population, 2006
5 to 15 years 8.5%
16 to 64 years 19.2%
65 years and over 47.9%

Education

Educational attainment, 2006
Population over 25 years 2,812,772
  Less than 9th grade. 8.6%
  High school graduate or more 79.6%
  College graduate or more. 20.0%
  Graduate or professional degree. 8.2%

Public school enrollment, 2005-06
Total. 679,878
  Pre-kindergarten through grade 8. . . . 483,797
  Grades 9 through 12 190,975

Graduating public high school seniors, 2004-05
Diplomas (incl. GED and others) 38,782

SAT scores, 2007
Average critical reading score 567
Average writing score 553
Average math score 565
Percent of graduates taking test 10%

Public school teachers, 2006-07 (estimate)
Total (x 1,000) 41.3
  Elementary. 29.3
  Secondary. 12.0
Average salary $43,646
  Elementary. $43,432
  Secondary. $44,175

State receipts & expenditures for public schools, 2006-07 (estimate)
Revenue receipts ($ mil) $6,061
Expenditures
Total ($ mil) $5,984
  Per capita $1,300
  Per pupil $9,214

NAEP proficiency scores, 2007

	Reading		Math	
	Basic	Proficient	Basic	Proficient
Grade 4	68.4%	33.5%	79.3%	30.8%
Grade 8	73.3%	27.7%	69.0%	27.3%

Higher education enrollment, fall 2005
Total. 43,390
  Full-time men 12,392
  Full-time women. 19,606
  Part-time men 4,024
  Part-time women. 7,368

Minority enrollment in institutions of higher education, 2005
Black, non-Hispanic 21,322
Hispanic 2,834
Asian/Pacific Islander 2,995
American Indian/Alaska Native. 748

Institutions of higher education, 2005-06
Total. 76
  Public. 31
  Private 45

Earned degrees conferred, 2004-05
Associate's. 9,009
Bachelor's 17,862
Master's 6,564
First-professional. .1,111
Doctor's 511

Public Libraries, 2006
Number of libraries. 116
Number of outlets 277
Annual visits per capita 4.0
Circulation per capita. 6.0

State & local financial support for higher education, FY 2006
Full-time equivalent enrollment (x 1,000). . . .144.3
Appropriations per FTE. $6,753

Social Insurance & Welfare Programs

Social Security benefits & beneficiaries, 2005
Beneficiaries (x 1,000) 799
  Retired & dependents. 468
  Survivors. 123
  Disabled & dependents. 207
Annual benefit payments ($ mil) $8,129
  Retired & dependents. $4,509
  Survivors. $1,547
  Disabled & dependents. $2,073
Average monthly benefit
  Retired & dependents. $949
  Disabled & dependents. $924
  Widowed. $881

Medicare, July 2005
Enrollment (x 1,000) 678
Payments ($ mil) $4,581

Medicaid, 2004
Beneficiaries (x 1,000). 861
Payments ($ mil) $3,924

State Children's Health Insurance Program, 2006
Enrollment (x 1,000). 64.9
Expenditures ($ mil). $98.3

Persons without health insurance, 2006
Number (x 1,000). 639
  percent. 15.6%
Number of children (x 1,000) 98
  percent of children 9.7%

Health care expenditures, 2004
Total expenditures. $22,662
  per capita $5,473

©2008 Information Publications, Inc.
All rights reserved. Photocopying prohibited.
877-544-INFO (4636) or www.informationpublications.com

Federal and state public aid

State unemployment insurance, 2006
Recipients, first payments (x 1,000) 111
Total payments ($ mil) $382
Average weekly benefit $271
Temporary Assistance for Needy Families, 2006
Recipients (x 1,000) 816.7
Families (x 1,000) 389.6
Supplemental Security Income, 2005
Recipients (x 1,000) 180.2
Payments ($ mil) $861.9
Food Stamp Program, 2006
Avg monthly participants (x 1,000) 589.1
Total benefits ($ mil) $645.4

Housing & Construction

Housing units
Total 2005 (estimate) 1,865,387
Total 2006 (estimate) 1,888,164
Seasonal or recreational use, 2006 31,449
Owner-occupied, 2006 1,167,081
    Median home value $111,000
    Homeowner vacancy rate 3.4%
Renter-occupied, 2006 484,830
    Median rent $548
    Rental vacancy rate 9.8%
Home ownership rate, 2005 . . . . 71.6%
Home ownership rate, 2006 . . . . 71.7%

New privately-owned housing units
Number authorized, 2006 (x 1,000) 16.6
    Value ($ mil) $2,260.8
Started 2005 (x 1,000, estimate) 20.4
Started 2006 (x 1,000, estimate) 20.5

Existing home sales
2005 (x 1,000) 96.2
2006 (x 1,000) 96.9

Government & Elections

State officials 2008
Governor . . . . Steve Beshar
        Democratic, term expires 12/11
Lieutenant Governor . . . . Daniel Mongiardo
Secretary of State . . . . Trey Grayson
Attorney General . . . . Jack Conway
Chief Justice . . . . Joseph Lambert

Governorship
Minimum age 30
Length of term . . . . 4 years
Consecutive terms permitted 2
Who succeeds . . . . Lieutenant Governor

Local governments by type, 2002
Total 1,439
    County 119
    Municipal 424
    Township 0
    School District 176
    Special District 720

State legislature
Name . . . . General Assembly
Upper chamber . . . . .Senate
    Number of members 38
    Length of term . . . . 4 years
    Party in majority, 2008 . . . . Republican
Lower chamber . . . . House of Representatives
    Number of members 100
    Length of term . . . . 2 years
    Party in majority, 2008 . . . . Democratic

Federal representation, 2008 (110ᵗʰ Congress)
Senator . . . . Mitch McConnell
    Party . . . . Republican
    Year term expires 2009
Senator . . . . .Jim Bunning
    Party . . . . Republican
    Year term expires 2011
Representatives, total 6
    Democrats 2
    Republicans 4

Voters in November 2006 election (estimate)
Total 1,508,207
    Male 742,986
    Female 765,220
    White 1,412,696
    Black 86,321
    Hispanic 1,605
    Asian . . . . NA

Presidential election, 2004
Total Popular Vote 1,795,882
    Kerry 712,733
    Bush 1,069,439
Total Electoral Votes 8

Votes cast for US Senators
2004
Total vote (x 1,000) .1,724
Leading party . . . . Republican
Percent for leading party 50.7%
2006
Total vote (x 1,000) . . . . NA
Leading party . . . . NA
Percent for leading party . . . . NA

Votes cast for US Representatives
2004
Total vote (x 1,000) .1,635
    Democratic 602
    Republican 1,017
Leading party . . . . Republican
Percent for leading party 62.2%
2006
Total vote (x 1,000) .1,254
    Democratic 602
    Republican 612
Leading party . . . . Republican
Percent for leading party 48.8%

©2008 Information Publications, Inc.
All rights reserved. Photocopying prohibited.
877-544-INFO (4636) or www.informationpublications.com

State government employment, 2006
Full-time equivalent employees 79,266
Payroll ($ mil) $270.8

Local government employment, 2006
Full-time equivalent employees 164,532
Payroll ($ mil) $453.2

Women holding public office, 2008
US Congress 0
Statewide elected office 1
State legislature 17

Black public officials, 2002
Total 62
   US and state legislatures 5
   City/county/regional offices 45
   Judicial/law enforcement 6
   Education/school boards 6

Hispanic public officials, 2006
Total 0
   State executives & legislators 0
   City/county/regional offices 0
   Judicial/law enforcement 0
   Education/school boards 0

Governmental Finance

State government revenues, 2006
Total revenue (x $1,000) $23,542,502
   per capita $5,599.43
General revenue (x $1,000) $20,061,184
   Intergovernmental 6,374,951
   Taxes 9,953,098
      general sales 2,748,643
      individual income tax 2,918,536
      corporate income tax 1,001,619
   Current charges 2,335,402
   Miscellaneous 1,397,733

State government expenditure, 2006
Total expenditure (x $1,000) $21,992,340
   per capita $5,230.74
General expenditure (x $1,000) $19,335,386
   per capita, total *$4,598.80*
      Education 1,679.24
      Public welfare 1,368.91
      Health 131.20
      Hospitals 206.31
      Highways 400.15
      Police protection 44.52
      Corrections 109.13
      Natural resources 90.21
      Parks & recreation 34.25
      Governmental administration 189.96
      Interest on general debt 102.63

State debt & cash, 2006 ($ per capita)
Debt $2,324.93
Cash/security holdings $9,319.50

Federal government grants to state & local government, 2005 (x $1,000)
Total $6,633,970
by Federal agency
   Defense 19,895
   Education 562,013
   Energy 21,183
   Environmental Protection Agency 52,212
   Health & Human Services 4,111,657
   Homeland Security 51,381
   Housing & Urban Development 476,266
   Justice 95,194
   Labor 118,606
   Transportation 591,543
   Veterans Affairs 11,921

Crime & Law Enforcement

Crime, 2006 (rates per 100,000 residents)
Property crimes 107,023
   Burglary 27,122
   Larceny 70,658
   Motor vehicle theft 9,243
   Property crime rate 2,544.5
Violent crimes 11,063
   Murder 168
   Forcible rape 1,297
   Robbery 3,626
   Aggravated assault 5,972
   Violent crime rate 263.0
Hate crimes 70

Fraud and identity theft, 2006
Fraud complaints 4,477
   rate per 100,000 residents 106.4
Identity theft complaints 1,766
   rate per 100,000 residents 42.0

Law enforcement agencies, 2006
Total agencies 391
Total employees 10,194
   Officers 8,028
   Civilians 2,166

Prisoners, probation, and parole, 2006
Total prisoners 20,000
   percent change, 12/31/05 to 12/31/06 . . . . 1.7%
   in private facilities 12.5%
   in local jails 29.6%
Sentenced to more than one year 19,514
   rate per 100,000 residents 462
Adults on probation 41,162
Adults on parole 11,867

Prisoner demographics, June 30, 2005 (rate per 100,000 residents)
Male 1,287
Female 173
White 561
Black 2,793
Hispanic 757

©2008 Information Publications, Inc.
All rights reserved. Photocopying prohibited.
877-544-INFO (4636) or www.informationpublications.com

Arrests, 2006
Total 73,504
   Persons under 18 years of age 8,746

Persons under sentence of death, 1/1/07
Total 41
   White 31
   Black 9
   Hispanic 1

State's highest court
Name . . . . .Supreme Court
Number of members 7
Length of term . . . . 8 years
Intermediate appeals court? . . . . .yes

Labor & Income

Civilian labor force, 2006 (x 1,000)
Total 2,042
   Men 1,077
   Women 965
   Persons 16-19 years 103
   White 1,870
   Black 132
   Hispanic 34

Civilian labor force as a percent of civilian non-institutional population, 2006
Total 62.8%
   Men 68.8
   Women 57.2
   Persons 16-19 years 45.4
   White 62.8
   Black 64.2
   Hispanic 79.3

Employment, 2006 (x 1,000)
Total 1,927
   Men 1,017
   Women 910
   Persons 16-19 years 82
   White 1,771
   Black 117
   Hispanic 32

Unemployment rate, 2006
Total 5.6%
   Men 5.5
   Women 5.7
   Persons 16-19 years 19.8
   White 5.3
   Black 10.8
   Hispanic 4.4

Full-time/part-time labor force, 2003 (x 1,000)
Full-time labor force, employed 1,510
Part-time labor force, employed 326
Unemployed, looking for
   Full-time work 98
   Part-time work 22
Mean duration of unemployment (weeks) 18.0
   Median 9.7

Labor unions, 2006
Membership (x 1,000) 172
   percent of employed 9.8%

Experienced civilian labor force by private industry, 2006
Total 1,483,314
   Natural resources & mining 30,094
   Construction 83,184
   Manufacturing 260,876
   Trade, transportation & utilities 375,694
   Information 29,707
   Finance 89,973
   Professional & business 178,880
   Education & health 218,722
   Leisure & hospitality 168,410
   Other 45,202

Experienced civilian labor force by occupation, May 2006
Management 77,480
Business & financial 52,270
Legal 10,000
Sales 180,770
Office & admin. support 292,820
Computers & math 23,970
Architecture & engineering 22,110
Arts & entertainment 16,350
Education 107,220
Social services 21,300
Health care practitioner & technical 101,600
Health care support 47,880
Maintenance & repair 79,610
Construction 84,710
Transportation & moving 158,120
Production 209,360
Farming, fishing & forestry 4,510

Hours and earnings of production workers on manufacturing payrolls, 2006
Average weekly hours .41.1
Average hourly earnings $16.92
Average weekly earnings $695.41

Income and poverty, 2006
Median household income $39,372
Personal income, per capita (current $) . . . $29,352
   in constant (2000) dollars $25,622
Persons below poverty level 17.0%

Average annual pay
2006 . . . . $35,201
   increase from 2005 . . . . 3.6%

Federal individual income tax returns, 2005
Returns filed 1,779,856
Adjusted gross income ($1,000) $77,639,797
Total tax liability ($1,000) $8,758,762

Charitable contributions, 2004
Number of contributions 461.1
Total amount ($ mil) $1,642.6

©2008 Information Publications, Inc.
All rights reserved. Photocopying prohibited.
877-544-INFO (4636) or www.informationpublications.com

Economy, Business, Industry & Agriculture

Fortune 500 companies, 2007................ 6
Bankruptcy cases filed, FY 2007.........16,216

Patents and trademarks issued, 2007

Patents..................................... 500
Trademarks................................. 475

Business firm ownership, 2002

Women-owned.........................77,159
   Sales ($ mil) $9,451
Black-owned..........................7,592
   Sales ($ mil) $1,106
Hispanic-owned..................... 2,094
   Sales ($ mil) $770
Asian-owned 3,236
   Sales ($ mil) $1,363
Amer. Indian/Alaska Native-owned 1,324
   Sales ($ mil) $79
Hawaiian/Pacific Islander-owned 60
   Sales ($ mil) .... NA

Gross domestic product, 2006 ($ mil)

Total gross domestic product $145,959
   Agriculture, forestry, fishing and
      hunting 2,400
   Mining............................3,788
   Utilities 2,460
   Construction 6,118
   Manufacturing, durable goods........ 16,458
   Manufacturing, non-durable goods 10,870
   Wholesale trade.....................9,140
   Retail trade....................10,115
   Transportation & warehousing 6,734
   Information 3,937
   Finance & insurance.................7,145
   Real estate, rental & leasing 13,631
   Professional and technical services.....5,923
   Educational services.................. 815
   Health care and social assistance.......11,811
   Accommodation/food services..........3,818
   Other services, except government 3,167
   Government....................... 21,448

Establishments, payroll, employees & receipts, by major industry group, 2005

Total..................................92,176
   Annual payroll ($1,000).......... $47,983,162
   Paid employees 1,514,199
Forestry, fishing & agriculture.............. 299
   Annual payroll ($1,000)............. $44,803
   Paid employees 1,680
Mining................................ 667
   Annual payroll ($1,000)..........$1,074,803
   Paid employees 20,198
   Receipts, 2002 ($1,000) $4,948,381

Utilities 330
   Annual payroll ($1,000)........... $530,266
   Paid employees 8,179
   Receipts, 2002 ($1,000) ....NA
Construction.........................9,318
   Annual payroll ($1,000)..........$2,974,769
   Paid employees 82,815
   Receipts, 2002 ($1,000) $12,644,444
Manufacturing........................4,152
   Annual payroll ($1,000)..........$10,625,628
   Paid employees 253,804
   Receipts, 2002 ($1,000) $88,513,497
Wholesale trade 4,560
   Annual payroll ($1,000)........... $2,992,997
   Paid employees 69,769
   Receipts, 2002 ($1,000) $51,838,719
Retail trade 16,566
   Annual payroll ($1,000)..........$4,340,765
   Paid employees 223,666
   Receipts, 2002 ($1,000) $40,062,561
Transportation & warehousing............3,167
   Annual payroll ($1,000)..........$3,071,746
   Paid employees 75,975
   Receipts, 2002 ($1,000) $8,249,830
Information...........................1,688
   Annual payroll ($1,000)..........$1,127,912
   Paid employees 31,102
   Receipts, 2002 ($1,000) ....NA
Finance & insurance 6,189
   Annual payroll ($1,000)..........$2,940,416
   Paid employees 66,124
   Receipts, 2002 ($1,000) ....NA
Professional, scientific & technical 8,004
   Annual payroll ($1,000)..........$2,395,720
   Paid employees 60,829
   Receipts, 2002 ($1,000) $5,190,416
Education 865
   Annual payroll ($1,000).......... $564,572
   Paid employees 28,076
   Receipts, 2002 ($1,000) $258,040
Health care & social assistance 10,083
   Annual payroll ($1,000)..........$7,623,152
   Paid employees 224,193
   Receipts, 2002 ($1,000) $16,633,446
Arts and entertainment 1,301
   Annual payroll ($1,000)...........$317,393
   Paid employees 17,294
   Receipts, 2002 ($1,000) $1,005,610
Real estate...........................3,734
   Annual payroll ($1,000).......... $513,704
   Paid employees 19,162
   Receipts, 2002 ($1,000) $2,470,137
Accommodation & food service.......... 6,965
   Annual payroll ($1,000)..........$1,676,868
   Paid employees 147,371
   Receipts, 2002 ($1,000) $4,908,331

©2008 Information Publications, Inc.
All rights reserved. Photocopying prohibited.
877-544-INFO (4636) or www.informationpublications.com

Exports, 2006
Value of exported goods ($ mil) $17,232
    Manufactured $14,800
    Non-manufactured. $589

Foreign direct investment in US affiliates, 2004
Property, plants & equipment ($ mil) . . . $26,919
Employment (x 1,000). 84.7

Agriculture, 2006
Number of farms 84,000
Farm acreage (x 1,000) 13,700
    Acres per farm 163
Farm marketings and income ($ mil)
Total. $4,007.2
    Crops. $1,299.2
    Livestock. $2,708.0
Net farm income $1,741.5

Principal commodities, in order by marketing receipts, 2005
Horses/mules, Cattle and calves, Broilers, Corn, Soybeans

Federal economic activity in state
Expenditures, 2005 ($ mil)
    Total. $34,653
        Per capita $8,304.85
    Defense $6,665
    Non-defense $27,988
Defense department, 2006 ($ mil)
    Payroll. $2,959
    Contract awards $5,395
    Grants $18
Homeland security grants ($1,000)
    2006. . . . .$24,119
    2007. . . . .$11,757

FDIC-insured financial institutions, 2005
Number 220
Assets ($ billion) $45.7
Deposits ($ billion) $36.0

Fishing, 2006
Catch (x 1,000 lbs). . . . . NA
Value ($1,000). . . . . NA

Mining, 2006 ($ mil)
Total non-fuel mineral production $918
Percent of U.S. 1.43%

Communication, Energy & Transportation

Communication
Households with computers, 2003 . . . . 58.1%
Households with internet access, 2003 . . . . 49.6%
High-speed internet providers 66
Total high-speed internet lines. 774,736
    Residential 612,529
    Business. 162,207
Wireless phone customers, 12/2006 2,966,195

FCC-licensed stations (as of January 1, 2008)
TV stations 38
FM radio stations. 211
AM radio stations 132

Energy
Energy consumption, 2004
    Total (trillion Btu). 1,956
    Per capita (million Btu) 472.5
By source of production (trillion Btu)
    Coal 962
    Natural gas 232
    Petroleum. 728
    Nuclear electric power 0
    Hydroelectric power 38
By end-use sector (trillion Btu)
    Residential 354
    Commercial 255
    Industrial 863
    Transportation 485
Electric energy, 2005
    Primary source of electricity. . . . . Coal
    Net generation (billion kWh) 97.8
        percent from renewable sources. 3.5%
    Net summer capability (million kW) 20.0
    CO_2 emitted from generation 90.3
Natural gas utilities, 2005
    Customers (x 1,000) 857
    Sales (trillion Btu). 211
    Revenues ($ mil) $1,246
Nuclear plants, 2007 0
Total CO_2 emitted (million metric tons). 143.0
Energy spending, 2004 ($ mil) $13,882
    per capita $3,353
    Price per million Btu $11.30

Transportation, 2006
Public road & street mileage 78,231
    Urban. 12,325
    Rural 65,906
    Interstate. 762
Vehicle miles of travel (millions) 47,742
    per capita 11,355.1
Total motor vehicle registrations. 3,558,122
    Automobiles. 1,969,142
    Trucks 1,574,731
    Motorcycles 58,959
Licensed drivers 2,896,460
    19 years & under 132,217
Deaths from motor vehicle accidents 913
Gasoline consumed (x 1,000 gallons) 2,228,724
    per capita 530.1

Commuting Statistics, 2006
Average commute time (min) 22.4
    Drove to work alone 81.5%
    Carpooled. 11.3%
    Public transit 1.0%
    Walk to work 2.0%
    Work from home 3.2%

©2008 Information Publications, Inc.
All rights reserved. Photocopying prohibited.
877-544-INFO (4636) or www.informationpublications.com

State Summary

Capital city . . . . Baton Rouge
Governor . . . . Bobby Jindal

PO Box 94004
Baton Rouge, LA 70804
225-342-0991

Admitted as a state 1812
Area (square miles) 51,840
Population, 2007 (estimate) 4,293,204
Largest city . . . . Baton Rouge
    Population, 2006 229,553
Personal income per capita, 2006
    (in current dollars) $30,952
Gross domestic product, 2006 ($ mil) . . . $193,138

Leading industries by payroll, 2005

Health care/Social assistance, Manufacturing,
Retail trade

**Leading agricultural commodities
by receipts, 2005**

Cotton, Cane for sugar, Rice, Cattle and calves,
Soybeans

Geography & Environment

Total area (square miles) 51,840
    land 43,562
    water 8,278
Federally-owned land, 2004 (acres) 1,474,788
    percent 5.1%
Highest point . . . . Driskill Mountain
    elevation (feet) 535
Lowest point . . . . New Orleans
    elevation (feet) . . . .-8
General coastline (miles) 397
Tidal shoreline (miles) 7,721
Cropland, 2003 (x 1,000 acres) 5,435
Forest land, 2003 (x 1,000 acres) 13,338
Capital city . . . . Baton Rouge
    Population 2000 227,818
    Population 2006 229,553
Largest city . . . . Baton Rouge
    Population 2000 227,818
    Population 2006 229,553

Number of cities with over 100,000 population

1990 4
2000 4
2006 4

State park and recreation areas, 2005

Area (x 1,000 acres) 41
Number of visitors (x 1,000) 1,598
Revenues ($1,000) $4,821
    percent of operating expenditures 16.8%

National forest system land, 2007

Acres 604,373

Demographics & Population Characteristics

Population

1980 4,205,900
1990 4,219,973
2000 4,468,958
2006 4,287,768
    Male 2,085,761
    Female 2,202,007
Living in group quarters, 2006 122,467
    percent of total 2.9%
2007 (estimate) .4,293,204
    persons per square mile of land 98.6
2008 (projected) .4,583,733
2010 (projected) .4,612,679
2020 (projected) .4,719,160
2030 (projected) .4,802,633

**Population of Core-Based Statistical Areas
(formerly Metropolitan Areas), x 1,000**

	CBSA	Non-CBSA
1990	3,917	303
2000	4,156	312
2006	3,979	309

Change in population, 2000-2007

Number . . . .-175,754
    percent . . . . - 3.9%
Natural increase (births minus deaths) 156,595
Net internal migration . . . .-335,216
Net international migration 22,477

Persons by age, 2006

Under 5 years 301,375
5 to 17 years 788,626
18 years and over 3,197,767
65 years and over 523,346
85 years and over 67,599
    Median age 35.7

Persons by age, 2010 (projected)

Under 5 years 337,954
18 and over 3,441,177
65 and over 582,340
    Median age 35.7

Race, 2006

One Race

    White 2,802,347
    Black or African American 1,357,661
    Asian 60,455
    American Indian/Alaska Native 27,042
    Hawaiian Native/Pacific Islander 1,610
Two or more races 38,653

Persons of Hispanic origin, 2006

Total Hispanic or Latino 123,281
    Mexican 50,280
    Puerto Rican 8,165
    Cuban 8,808

©2008 Information Publications, Inc.
All rights reserved. Photocopying prohibited.
877-544-INFO (4636) or www.informationpublications.com

Persons of Asian origin, 2006

Total Asian 57,084
  Asian Indian. 8,069
  Chinese 9,438
  Filipino 3,599
  Japanese 2,076
  Korean. 1,785
  Vietnamese. 24,887

Marital status, 2006

Population 15 years & over 3,386,670
  Never married 1,069,428
  Married. 1,688,642
  Separated 84,330
  Widowed. 255,167
  Divorced 373,433

Language spoken at home, 2006

Population 5 years and older. 3,986,570
  English only 3,650,061
  Spanish 106,872
  French 155,975
  German. 6,371
  Chinese 7,446

Households & families, 2006

Households. 1,564,978
  with persons under 18 years 556,956
  with persons over 65 years. 369,047
  persons per household 2.66
Families. 1,072,568
  persons per family. 3.25
Married couples. 748,396
Female householder,
  no husband present. 251,656
One-person households 415,423

Nativity, 2006

Number of residents born in state 3,420,568
  percent of population. 79.8%

Immigration & naturalization, 2006

Legal permanent residents admitted. 2,693
Persons naturalized 1,336
Non-immigrant admissions 87,185

Vital Statistics and Health

Marriages

2004 36,282
2005 36,569
2006 . . . . NA

Divorces

2004 . . . . NA
2005 . . . . NA
2006 . . . . NA

Health risks, 2006

Percent of adults who are:
  Smokers. 23.4%
  Overweight (BMI > 25). 63.0%
  Obese (BMI > 30). 27.1%

Births

2005 60,937
  Birthrate (per 1,000). 13.5
  White. 35,374
  Black 24,145
  Hispanic 1,897
  Asian/Pacific Islander 1,040
  Amer. Indian/Alaska Native 378
  Low birth weight (2,500g or less). 11.5%
  Cesarian births 36.8%
  Preterm births 16.5%
  To unmarried mothers. 48.0%
  Twin births (per 1,000) 31.3
  Triplets or higher order (per 100,000). . . .154.7
2006 (preliminary). 63,399
  rate per 1,000 . . . . .14.8

Deaths

2004

All causes 42,215
  rate per 100,000. . . . . .986.1
Heart disease 10,852
  rate per 100,000. . . . . 256.6
Malignant neoplasms 9,434
  rate per 100,000. . . . . 216.7
Cerebrovascular disease. 2,489
  rate per 100,000. . . . . .59.4
Chronic lower respiratory disease 1,615
  rate per 100,000. . . . . .38.2
Diabetes. 1,717
  rate per 100,000. . . . . .39.9
2005 (preliminary). 44,333
  rate per 100,000. . . . . .1,020.6
2006 (provisional) 38,376

Infant deaths

2004 684
  rate per 1,000 . . . . .10.5
2005 (provisional) 632
  rate per 1,000 . . . . .9.7

Exercise routines, 2005

None. 33.4%
Moderate or greater. 38.3%
Vigorous 20.7%

Abortions, 2004

Total performed in state. 11,224
  rate per 1,000 women age 15-44. 11
  % obtained by out-of-state residents . . . . . . NA

Physicians, 2005

Total. 11,481
  rate per 100,000 persons 255

Community hospitals, 2005

Number of hospitals 128
Beds (x 1,000). 15.5
Patients admitted (x 1,000) 620
Average daily census (x 1,000) 9.5
Average cost per day $1,293
Outpatient visits (x 1 mil) 9.8

©2008 Information Publications, Inc.
All rights reserved. Photocopying prohibited.
877-544-INFO (4636) or www.informationpublications.com

Disability status of population, 2006
5 to 15 years 7.8%
16 to 64 years 16.0%
65 years and over 48.1%

Education

Educational attainment, 2006
Population over 25 years 2,734,518
    Less than 9th grade...................... 7.3%
    High school graduate or more 79.4%
    College graduate or more.............. 20.3%
    Graduate or professional degree........ 6.8%

Public school enrollment, 2005-06
Total................................ 654,526
    Pre-kindergarten through grade 8.... 482,082
    Grades 9 through 12 172,444

Graduating public high school seniors, 2004-05
Diplomas (incl. GED and others) 37,785

SAT scores, 2007
Average critical reading score 569
Average writing score 563
Average math score 567
Percent of graduates taking test 7%

Public school teachers, 2006-07 (estimate)
Total (x 1,000) 46.4
    Elementary............................ 32.7
    Secondary............................. 13.7
Average salary $42,816
    Elementary......................... $42,816
    Secondary.......................... $42,816

State receipts & expenditures for public schools, 2006-07 (estimate)
Revenue receipts ($ mil) $7,115
Expenditures
Total ($ mil) $6,849
    Per capita $1,365
    Per pupil $9,355

NAEP proficiency scores, 2007

	Reading		Math	
	Basic	Proficient	Basic	Proficient
Grade 4	51.9%	20.4%	72.9%	24.4%
Grade 8	64.2%	19.4%	63.9%	19.0%

Higher education enrollment, fall 2005
Total................................. 16,670
    Full-time men 3,949
    Full-time women.................... 10,053
    Part-time men 773
    Part-time women.................... 1,895

Minority enrollment in institutions of higher education, 2005
Black, non-Hispanic 59,974
Hispanic 3,589
Asian/Pacific Islander 3,657
American Indian/Alaska Native.......... 1,220

Institutions of higher education, 2005-06
Total.................................... 90
    Public................................. 58
    Private................................ 32

Earned degrees conferred, 2004-05
Associate's........................... 5,734
Bachelor's 21,494
Master's............................. 6,874
First-professional.................... 1,651
Doctor's.............................. 562

Public Libraries, 2006
Number of libraries..................... 67
Number of outlets 363
Annual visits per capita 3.1
Circulation per capita................... 3.9

State & local financial support for higher education, FY 2006
Full-time equivalent enrollment (x 1,000).... 170.8
Appropriations per FTE............... $5,583

Social Insurance & Welfare Programs

Social Security benefits & beneficiaries, 2005
Beneficiaries (x 1,000) 716
    Retired & dependents.................. 429
    Survivors............................ 140
    Disabled & dependents................ 146
Annual benefit payments ($ mil) $7,378
    Retired & dependents................ $4,109
    Survivors.......................... $1,782
    Disabled & dependents.............. $1,488
Average monthly benefit
    Retired & dependents................ $937
    Disabled & dependents............... $937
    Widowed........................... $891

Medicare, July 2005
Enrollment (x 1,000)..................... 610
Payments ($ mil) $4,883

Medicaid, 2004
Beneficiaries (x 1,000)................. 1,108
Payments ($ mil) $4,039

State Children's Health Insurance Program, 2006
Enrollment (x 1,000)................... 142.4
Expenditures ($ mil)................... $122.4

Persons without health insurance, 2006
Number (x 1,000)........................ 921
    percent.............................. 21.9%
Number of children (x 1,000) 170
    percent of children 15.9%

Health care expenditures, 2004
Total expenditures.................... $22,658
    per capita $5,040

©2008 Information Publications, Inc.
All rights reserved. Photocopying prohibited.
877-544-INFO (4636) or www.informationpublications.com

Federal and state public aid

State unemployment insurance, 2006
Recipients, first payments (x 1,000) 60
Total payments ($ mil) $294
Average weekly benefit $191
Temporary Assistance for Needy Families, 2006
Recipients (x 1,000) 297.1
Families (x 1,000) 133.3
Supplemental Security Income, 2005
Recipients (x 1,000) 155.8
Payments ($ mil) $771.3
Food Stamp Program, 2006
Avg monthly participants (x 1,000) 829.9
Total benefits ($ mil) $1,031.6

Housing & Construction

Housing units
Total 2005 (estimate) 1,940,006
Total 2006 (estimate) 1,830,073
Seasonal or recreational use, 2006 42,431
Owner-occupied, 2006 1,071,667
  Median home value $114,700
  Homeowner vacancy rate 1.4%
Renter-occupied, 2006 493,311
  Median rent $618
  Rental vacancy rate 7.9%
Home ownership rate, 2005 . . . . .72.5%
Home ownership rate, 2006 . . . . .71.3%

New privately-owned housing units
Number authorized, 2006 (x 1,000) 28.7
  Value ($ mil) $3,818.3
Started 2005 (x 1,000, estimate) 18.0
Started 2006 (x 1,000, estimate) 17.7

Existing home sales
2005 (x 1,000) 87.7
2006 (x 1,000) 92.3

Government & Elections

State officials 2008
Governor . . . . .Bobby Jindal
          Republican, term expires 1/12
Lieutenant Governor . . . . Mitch Landrieu
Secretary of State . . . . Jay Dardenne
Attorney General . . . . .James Caldwell
Chief Justice . . . . .Pascal Calogero Jr

Governorship
Minimum age 25
Length of term . . . . 4 years
Consecutive terms permitted 2
Who succeeds . . . . Lieutenant Governor

Local governments by type, 2002
Total 473
  County 60
  Municipal 302
  Township 0
  School District 66
  Special District 45

State legislature
Name . . . . Legislature
Upper chamber . . . . .Senate
  Number of members 39
  Length of term . . . . 4 years
  Party in majority, 2008 . . . . .Democratic
Lower chamber . . . . . . .House of Representatives
  Number of members 105
  Length of term . . . . 4 years
  Party in majority, 2008 . . . . .Democratic

Federal representation, 2008 (110th Congress)
Senator . . . . .Mary Landrieu
  Party . . . . .Democratic
  Year term expires 2009
Senator . . . . David Vitter
  Party . . . . Republican
  Year term expires 2011
Representatives, total 7
  Democrats 2
  Republicans 5

Voters in November 2006 election (estimate)
Total 1,201,499
Male 551,100
Female 650,399
White 864,705
Black 319,176
Hispanic 15,008
Asian 15,474

Presidential election, 2004
Total Popular Vote 1,943,106
  Kerry 820,299
  Bush 1,102,169
Total Electoral Votes 9

Votes cast for US Senators
2004
Total vote (x 1,000) 1,848
Leading party . . . . Republican
Percent for leading party 51.0%
2006
Total vote (x 1,000) . . . . NA
Leading party . . . . NA
Percent for leading party . . . . NA

Votes cast for US Representatives
2004
Total vote (x 1,000) .1,259
  Democratic 478
  Republican 780
Leading party . . . . Republican
Percent for leading party 62.0%
2006
Total vote (x 1,000) 916
  Democratic 309
  Republican 580
Leading party . . . . Republican
Percent for leading party 63.3%

©2008 Information Publications, Inc.
All rights reserved. Photocopying prohibited.
877-544-INFO (4636) or www.informationpublications.com

State government employment, 2006
Full-time equivalent employees 83,358
Payroll ($ mil) $284.1

Local government employment, 2006
Full-time equivalent employees .... NA
Payroll ($ mil) .... NA

Women holding public office, 2008
US Congress 1
Statewide elected office...................... 0
State legislature 25

Black public officials, 2002
Total.................................... 739
US and state legislatures 32
City/county/regional offices 408
Judicial/law enforcement................ 132
Education/school boards 167

Hispanic public officials, 2006
Total..................................... 3
State executives & legislators 0
City/county/regional offices 1
Judicial/law enforcement.................. 2
Education/school boards.................. 0

Governmental Finance

State government revenues, 2006
Total revenue (x $1,000)........... $27,679,632
per capita $6,523.16
General revenue (x $1,000) $22,925,700
Intergovernmental 9,079,426
Taxes 9,651,457
general sales.................... 3,427,486
individual income tax 2,501,120
corporate income tax 506,174
Current charges.................. 2,360,563
Miscellaneous 1,834,254

State government expenditure, 2006
Total expenditure (x $1,000) $24,220,667
per capita $5,708.00
General expenditure (x $1,000) $21,026,980
per capita, total................... $4,955.35
Education....................... 1,618.26
Public welfare 1,090.67
Health.......................... 131.21
Hospitals....................... 364.93
Highways 373.95
Police protection................ 70.73
Corrections 154.45
Natural resources 102.01
Parks & recreation 61.71
Governmental administration...... 152.09
Interest on general debt.......... 156.24

State debt & cash, 2006 ($ per capita)
Debt.............................. $2,765.64
Cash/security holdings............. $11,505.15

Federal government grants to state & local government, 2005 (x $1,000)
Total............................ $11,388,684
by Federal agency
Defense 55,252
Education 716,375
Energy........................... 10,417
Environmental Protection Agency 49,283
Health & Human Services. 5,082,396
Homeland Security................3,380,689
Housing & Urban Development...... 468,531
Justice 109,550
Labor 140,643
Transportation 646,107
Veterans Affairs.................. 39,657

Crime & Law Enforcement

Crime, 2006 (rates per 100,000 residents)
Property crimes 171,239
Burglary 44,986
Larceny......................... 110,613
Motor vehicle theft 15,640
Property crime rate.............. 3,993.7
Violent crimes........................ 29,919
Murder 530
Forcible rape.................... 1,562
Robbery......................... 5,729
Aggravated assault 22,098
Violent crime rate 697.8
Hate crimes....................... 27

Fraud and identity theft, 2006
Fraud complaints................... 3,981
rate per 100,000 residents 92.8
Identity theft complaints 2,256
rate per 100,000 residents 52.6

Law enforcement agencies, 2006
Total agencies........................ 171
Total employees 18,969
Officers 14,779
Civilians 4,190

Prisoners, probation, and parole, 2006
Total prisoners...................... 37,012
percent change, 12/31/05 to 12/31/06 .... 2.6%
in private facilities 8.3%
in local jails 43.9%
Sentenced to more than one year 36,376
rate per 100,000 residents 846
Adults on probation 38,057
Adults on parole..................... 24,663

Prisoner demographics, June 30, 2005 (rate per 100,000 residents)
Male............................... 2,134
Female 195
White.............................. 523
Black.............................. 2,452
Hispanic 244

©2008 Information Publications, Inc.
All rights reserved. Photocopying prohibited.
877-544-INFO (4636) or www.informationpublications.com

Arrests, 2006

Total	161,316
Persons under 18 years of age	22,355

Persons under sentence of death, 1/1/07

Total	88
White	30
Black	55
Hispanic	2

State's highest court

Name	Supreme Court
Number of members	7
Length of term	10 years
Intermediate appeals court?	yes

Labor & Income

Civilian labor force, 2006 (x 1,000)

Total	1,960
Men	1,041
Women	919
Persons 16-19 years	102
White	1,370
Black	539
Hispanic	53

Civilian labor force as a percent of civilian non-institutional population, 2006

Total	61.8%
Men	69.4
Women	55.0
Persons 16-19 years	39.8
White	63.1
Black	58.5
Hispanic	69.6

Employment, 2006 (x 1,000)

Total	1,870
Men	995
Women	875
Persons 16-19 years	89
White	1,333
Black	490
Hispanic	50

Unemployment rate, 2006

Total	4.6%
Men	4.4
Women	4.8
Persons 16-19 years	13.0
White	2.7
Black	9.1
Hispanic	5.7

Full-time/part-time labor force, 2003 (x 1,000)

Full-time labor force, employed	1,617
Part-time labor force, employed	287

Unemployed, looking for

Full-time work	120
Part-time work	14

Mean duration of unemployment (weeks) 16.7

Median	9.9

Labor unions, 2006

Membership (x 1,000)	107
percent of employed	6.4%

Experienced civilian labor force by private industry, 2006

Total	1,474,800
Natural resources & mining	56,549
Construction	130,424
Manufacturing	152,076
Trade, transportation & utilities	369,758
Information	27,012
Finance	91,285
Professional & business	194,141
Education & health	220,252
Leisure & hospitality	184,162
Other	46,441

Experienced civilian labor force by occupation, May 2006

Management	89,060
Business & financial	56,890
Legal	12,530
Sales	188,670
Office & admin. support	296,390
Computers & math	17,590
Architecture & engineering	28,280
Arts & entertainment	16,660
Education	98,460
Social services	22,890
Health care practitioner & technical	104,430
Health care support	49,440
Maintenance & repair	92,120
Construction	118,900
Transportation & moving	152,880
Production	121,040
Farming, fishing & forestry	5,220

Hours and earnings of production workers on manufacturing payrolls, 2006

Average weekly hours	43.0
Average hourly earnings	$17.94
Average weekly earnings	$771.42

Income and poverty, 2006

Median household income	$39,337
Personal income, per capita (current $)	$30,952
in constant (2000) dollars	$27,019
Persons below poverty level	19.0%

Average annual pay

2006	$36,604
increase from 2005	9.1%

Federal individual income tax returns, 2005

Returns filed	1,770,050
Adjusted gross income ($1,000)	$77,629,149
Total tax liability ($1,000)	$9,031,225

Charitable contributions, 2004

Number of contributions	347.9
Total amount ($ mil)	$1,476.7

©2008 Information Publications, Inc.
All rights reserved. Photocopying prohibited.
877-544-INFO (4636) or www.informationpublications.com

Economy, Business, Industry & Agriculture

Fortune 500 companies, 2007 3
Bankruptcy cases filed, FY 2007 13,534

Patents and trademarks issued, 2007
Patents 293
Trademarks 391

Business firm ownership, 2002
Women-owned 86,876
   Sales ($ mil) $12,253
Black-owned 40,243
   Sales ($ mil) $1,934
Hispanic-owned 7,645
   Sales ($ mil) $1,945
Asian-owned 8,218
   Sales ($ mil) $1,794
Amer. Indian/Alaska Native-owned 2,707
   Sales ($ mil) $283
Hawaiian/Pacific Islander-owned 80
   Sales ($ mil) $9

Gross domestic product, 2006 ($ mil)
Total gross domestic product $193,138
   Agriculture, forestry, fishing and
      hunting 1,326
   Mining 27,431
   Utilities 4,915
   Construction 8,939
   Manufacturing, durable goods 8,014
   Manufacturing, non-durable goods . . . 32,500
   Wholesale trade .8,773
   Retail trade 12,826
   Transportation & warehousing 6,318
   Information 4,140
   Finance & insurance 6,261
   Real estate, rental & leasing 15,286
   Professional and technical services 7,338
   Educational services 1,146
   Health care and social assistance 10,404
   Accommodation/food services 4,947
   Other services, except government 3,706
   Government 19,899

Establishments, payroll, employees & receipts, by major industry group, 2005
Total 102,790
   Annual payroll ($1,000) $50,657,624
   Paid employees 1,617,507
Forestry, fishing & agriculture 704
   Annual payroll ($1,000) $138,320
   Paid employees 4,448
Mining 1,390
   Annual payroll ($1,000) $2,743,845
   Paid employees 44,247
   Receipts, 2002 ($1,000) $30,181,037

Utilities 567
   Annual payroll ($1,000) $738,018
   Paid employees 11,382
   Receipts, 2002 ($1,000) . . . . .NA
Construction 8,615
   Annual payroll ($1,000) $4,080,813
   Paid employees 117,564
   Receipts, 2002 ($1,000) $15,288,176
Manufacturing 3,377
   Annual payroll ($1,000) $7,074,264
   Paid employees 145,173
   Receipts, 2002 ($1,000) $89,540,799
Wholesale trade 5,604
   Annual payroll ($1,000) $2,990,452
   Paid employees 72,586
   Receipts, 2002 ($1,000) $47,192,153
Retail trade 17,426
   Annual payroll ($1,000) $4,572,205
   Paid employees 227,856
   Receipts, 2002 ($1,000) $41,885,192
Transportation & warehousing 3,652
   Annual payroll ($1,000) $2,489,818
   Paid employees 62,936
   Receipts, 2002 ($1,000) $7,847,325
Information 1,498
   Annual payroll ($1,000) $1,376,922
   Paid employees 32,639
   Receipts, 2002 ($1,000) . . . . .NA
Finance & insurance 7,618
   Annual payroll ($1,000) $3,054,677
   Paid employees 67,802
   Receipts, 2002 ($1,000) . . . . .NA
Professional, scientific & technical 11,047
   Annual payroll ($1,000) $3,535,206
   Paid employees 85,308
   Receipts, 2002 ($1,000) $8,243,267
Education 981
   Annual payroll ($1,000) $914,885
   Paid employees 36,448
   Receipts, 2002 ($1,000) $230,627
Health care & social assistance 11,332
   Annual payroll ($1,000) $7,940,735
   Paid employees 264,664
   Receipts, 2002 ($1,000) $18,169,655
Arts and entertainment 1,329
   Annual payroll ($1,000) $755,662
   Paid employees 33,279
   Receipts, 2002 ($1,000) $2,248,731
Real estate 4,491
   Annual payroll ($1,000) $1,042,231
   Paid employees 31,196
   Receipts, 2002 ($1,000) $3,942,696
Accommodation & food service 7,886
   Annual payroll ($1,000) $2,194,457
   Paid employees 180,353
   Receipts, 2002 ($1,000) $7,411,702

©2008 Information Publications, Inc.
All rights reserved. Photocopying prohibited.
877-544-INFO (4636) or www.informationpublications.com

Exports, 2006
Value of exported goods ($ mil) $23,503
   Manufactured $13,788
   Non-manufactured $9,415

Foreign direct investment in US affiliates, 2004
Property, plants & equipment ($ mil) $27,962
Employment (x 1,000) 49.9

Agriculture, 2006
Number of farms 26,800
Farm acreage (x 1,000) 7,800
   Acres per farm 291
Farm marketings and income ($ mil)
Total $2,186.2
   Crops $1,321.9
   Livestock $864.3
Net farm income $765.7

Principal commodities, in order by marketing receipts, 2005
Cotton, Cane for sugar, Rice, Cattle and calves,
Soybeans

Federal economic activity in state
Expenditures, 2005 ($ mil)
   Total $39,628
      Per capita $8,791.94
   Defense $4,693
   Non-defense $34,935
Defense department, 2006 ($ mil)
   Payroll $1,734
   Contract awards $5,154
   Grants $311
Homeland security grants ($1,000)
   2006 . . . . $30,437
   2007 . . . .$21,873

FDIC-insured financial institutions, 2005
Number 166
Assets ($ billion) $76.4
Deposits ($ billion) $59.6

Fishing, 2006
Catch (x 1,000 lbs) 844,027
Value ($1,000) $201,742

Mining, 2006 ($ mil)
Total non-fuel mineral production $362
Percent of U.S. 0.56%

Communication, Energy & Transportation

Communication
Households with computers, 2003 . . . . .52.3%
Households with internet access, 2003 . . . . 44.1%
High-speed internet providers 51
Total high-speed internet lines 892,835
   Residential 689,828
   Business 203,007
Wireless phone customers, 12/2006 3,492,358

FCC-licensed stations (as of January 1, 2008)
TV stations 38
FM radio stations 179
AM radio stations 83

Energy
Energy consumption, 2004
   Total (trillion Btu) 3,816
   Per capita (million Btu) 848.9
By source of production (trillion Btu)
   Coal 257
   Natural gas 1,400
   Petroleum 1,651
   Nuclear electric power 178
   Hydroelectric power 11
By end-use sector (trillion Btu)
   Residential 369
   Commercial 286
   Industrial 2,403
   Transportation 758
Electric energy, 2005
   Primary source of electricity . . . . Gas
   Net generation (billion kWh) 92.6
      percent from renewable sources 3.8%
   Net summer capability (million kW) 26.8
   CO_2 emitted from generation 57.1
Natural gas utilities, 2005
   Customers (x 1,000) 956
   Sales (trillion Btu) 893
   Revenues ($ mil) $3,010
Nuclear plants, 2007 2
Total CO_2 emitted (million metric tons) 179.1
Energy spending, 2004 ($ mil) $24,402
   per capita $5,428
   Price per million Btu $10.09

Transportation, 2006
Public road & street mileage 60,925
   Urban 15,932
   Rural 44,993
   Interstate 903
Vehicle miles of travel (millions) 45,417
   per capita 10,703.3
Total motor vehicle registrations 3,872,744
   Automobiles 1,950,372
   Trucks 1,900,270
   Motorcycles 61,117
Licensed drivers 3,014,191
   19 years & under 120,282
Deaths from motor vehicle accidents 982
Gasoline consumed (x 1,000 gallons) 2,621,024
   per capita 617.7

Commuting Statistics, 2006
Average commute time (min) 25.1
   Drove to work alone 81.6%
   Carpooled 11.6%
   Public transit 1.1%
   Walk to work 1.8%
   Work from home 2.2%

©2008 Information Publications, Inc.
All rights reserved. Photocopying prohibited.
877-544-INFO (4636) or www.informationpublications.com

State Summary

Capital city . . . . Augusta
Governor . . . . John Baldacci

#1 State House Station
Augusta, ME 04333
207-287-3531

Admitted as a state 1820
Area (square miles) 35,385
Population, 2007 (estimate) 1,317,207
Largest city . . . . Portland
    Population, 2006 63,011
Personal income per capita, 2006
    (in current dollars) $32,348
Gross domestic product, 2006 ($ mil) $46,973

Leading industries by payroll, 2005

Health care/Social assistance, Manufacturing,
Retail trade

**Leading agricultural commodities
by receipts, 2005**

Potatoes, Dairy products, Blueberries, Chicken
eggs, Greenhouse/nursery

Geography & Environment

Total area (square miles) 35,385
    land 30,862
    water 4,523
Federally-owned land, 2004 (acres) 208,422
    percent 1.1%
Highest point . . . . Mount Katahdin
    elevation (feet) 5,268
Lowest point . . . . Atlantic Ocean
    elevation (feet) . . . . sea level
General coastline (miles) 228
Tidal shoreline (miles) 3,478
Cropland, 2003 (x 1,000 acres) 385
Forest land, 2003 (x 1,000 acres) 17,620
Capital city . . . . Augusta
    Population 2000 18,560
    Population 2006 18,560
Largest city . . . . Portland
    Population 2000 64,249
    Population 2006 63,011

Number of cities with over 100,000 population

1990 0
2000 0
2006 0

State park and recreation areas, 2005

Area (x 1,000 acres) 100
Number of visitors (x 1,000) 2,006
Revenues ($1,000) $3,146
    percent of operating expenditures 37.7%

National forest system land, 2007

Acres 53,042

Demographics & Population Characteristics

Population

1980 1,124,660
1990 1,227,928
2000 1,274,923
2006 1,321,574
    Male 646,427
    Female 675,147
Living in group quarters, 2006 37,484
    percent of total 2.8%
2007 (estimate) 1,317,207
    persons per square mile of land 42.7
2008 (projected) 1,342,286
2010 (projected) 1,357,134
2020 (projected) 1,408,665
2030 (projected) 1,411,097

**Population of Core-Based Statistical Areas
(formerly Metropolitan Areas), x 1,000**

	CBSA	Non-CBSA
1990	845	383
2000	893	382
2006	931	391

Change in population, 2000-2007

Number 42,286
    percent 3.3%
Natural increase (births minus deaths) 10,644
Net internal migration 31,390
Net international migration 5,275

Persons by age, 2006

Under 5 years 70,245
5 to 17 years 210,749
18 years and over 1,040,580
65 years and over 192,639
85 years and over 27,012
    Median age 41.1

Persons by age, 2010 (projected)

Under 5 years 72,829
18 and over 1,087,902
65 and over 212,278
    Median age 42.2

Race, 2006

One Race
    White 1,278,398
    Black or African American 10,918
    Asian 11,490
    American Indian/Alaska Native 7,582
    Hawaiian Native/Pacific Islander 433
Two or more races 12,753

Persons of Hispanic origin, 2006

Total Hispanic or Latino 12,622
    Mexican 3,262
    Puerto Rican 3,913
    Cuban 447

©2008 Information Publications, Inc.
All rights reserved. Photocopying prohibited.
877-544-INFO (4636) or www.informationpublications.com

Persons of Asian origin, 2006

Total Asian	12,004
Asian Indian	1,805
Chinese	2,764
Filipino	1,990
Japanese	714
Korean	1,843
Vietnamese	1,369

Marital status, 2006

Population 15 years & over	1,096,285
Never married	294,724
Married	592,562
Separated	12,522
Widowed	72,887
Divorced	136,112

Language spoken at home, 2006

Population 5 years and older	1,251,347
English only	1,154,615
Spanish	12,576
French	58,273
German	4,314
Chinese	2,081

Households & families, 2006

Households	548,247
with persons under 18 years	166,980
with persons over 65 years	136,742
persons per household	2.34
Families	358,314
persons per family	2.82
Married couples	276,972
Female householder, no husband present	57,724
One-person households	149,229

Nativity, 2006

Number of residents born in state	859,105
percent of population	65.0%

Immigration & naturalization, 2006

Legal permanent residents admitted	1,719
Persons naturalized	802
Non-immigrant admissions	46,993

Vital Statistics and Health

Marriages

2004	11,234
2005	10,879
2006	9,740

Divorces

2004	5,677
2005	5,443
2006	4,752

Health risks, 2006

Percent of adults who are:

Smokers	20.9%
Overweight (BMI > 25)	59.7%
Obese (BMI > 30)	23.1%

Births

2005	14,112
Birthrate (per 1,000)	10.7
White	13,508
Black	264
Hispanic	181
Asian/Pacific Islander	226
Amer. Indian/Alaska Native	114
Low birth weight (2,500g or less)	6.8%
Cesarian births	28.3%
Preterm births	10.7%
To unmarried mothers	35.0%
Twin births (per 1,000)	32.8
Triplets or higher order (per 100,000)	138.4
2006 (preliminary)	14,151
rate per 1,000	10.7

Deaths

2004

All causes	12,443
rate per 100,000	806.3
Heart disease	2,948
rate per 100,000	188.3
Malignant neoplasms	3,124
rate per 100,000	200.8
Cerebrovascular disease	801
rate per 100,000	51.0
Chronic lower respiratory disease	766
rate per 100,000	49.3
Diabetes	382
rate per 100,000	24.5
2005 (preliminary)	12,871
rate per 100,000	813.2
2006 (provisional)	12,280

Infant deaths

2004	79
rate per 1,000	5.7
2005 (provisional)	97
rate per 1,000	6.8

Exercise routines, 2005

None	22.3%
Moderate or greater	54.1%
Vigorous	30.8%

Abortions, 2004

Total performed in state	2,593
rate per 1,000 women age 15-44	10
% obtained by out-of-state residents	4.2%

Physicians, 2005

Total	3,520
rate per 100,000 persons	267

Community hospitals, 2005

Number of hospitals	37
Beds (x 1,000)	3.5
Patients admitted (x 1,000)	151
Average daily census (x 1,000)	2.3
Average cost per day	$1,528
Outpatient visits (x 1 mil)	4.3

©2008 Information Publications, Inc.
All rights reserved. Photocopying prohibited.
877-544-INFO (4636) or www.informationpublications.com

Disability status of population, 2006
5 to 15 years 10.1%
16 to 64 years 16.8%
65 years and over 40.6%

Education

Educational attainment, 2006
Population over 25 years 923,328
  Less than 9ᵗʰ grade. 4.2%
  High school graduate or more 88.7%
  College graduate or more. 25.8%
  Graduate or professional degree. 8.9%

Public school enrollment, 2005-06
Total. 195,498
  Pre-kindergarten through grade 8. 133,491
  Grades 9 through 12. 62,007

Graduating public high school seniors, 2004-05
Diplomas (incl. GED and others) 13,407

SAT scores, 2007
Average critical reading score. 466
Average writing score 457
Average math score 465
Percent of graduates taking test 100%

Public school teachers, 2006-07 (estimate)
Total (x 1,000) 16.4
  Elementary. 11.0
  Secondary. 5.4
Average salary $41,596
  Elementary. $41,596
  Secondary. $41,596

State receipts & expenditures for public schools, 2006-07 (estimate)
Revenue receipts ($ mil) $2,425
Expenditures
Total ($ mil) $2,584
  Per capita $1,787
  Per pupil $13,025

NAEP proficiency scores, 2007

	Reading		Math	
	Basic	Proficient	Basic	Proficient
Grade 4	73.1%	35.8%	85.5%	41.8%
Grade 8	82.8%	36.9%	78.3%	34.1%

Higher education enrollment, fall 2005
Total. 18,032
  Full-time men 5,610
  Full-time women. 7,633
  Part-time men 1,359
  Part-time women. 3,430

Minority enrollment in institutions of higher education, 2005
Black, non-Hispanic 1,279
Hispanic 832
Asian/Pacific Islander 1,101
American Indian/Alaska Native. 975

Institutions of higher education, 2005-06
Total. 30
  Public. 15
  Private 15

Earned degrees conferred, 2004-05
Associate's 2,374
Bachelor's 6,500
Master's. 1,648
First-professional. 217
Doctor's 40

Public Libraries, 2006
Number of libraries. 272
Number of outlets 278
Annual visits per capita 5.7
Circulation per capita. 7.5

State & local financial support for higher education, FY 2006
Full-time equivalent enrollment (x 1,000). . . .35.2
Appropriations per FTE. $6,096

Social Insurance & Welfare Programs

Social Security benefits & beneficiaries, 2005
Beneficiaries (x 1,000) 269
  Retired & dependents. 178
  Survivors. 33
  Disabled & dependents. 59
Annual benefit payments ($ mil) $2,686
  Retired & dependents. $1,702
  Survivors. $435
  Disabled & dependents. $549
Average monthly benefit
  Retired & dependents. $926
  Disabled & dependents. $863
  Widowed. $924

Medicare, July 2005
Enrollment (x 1,000). 235
Payments ($ mil) $1,429

Medicaid, 2004
Beneficiaries (x 1,000). 1,074
Payments ($ mil) $7,776

State Children's Health Insurance Program, 2006
Enrollment (x 1,000). 31.1
Expenditures ($ mil). $33.1

Persons without health insurance, 2006
Number (x 1,000). 122
  percent. 9.3%
Number of children (x 1,000) 18
  percent of children 6.3%

Health care expenditures, 2004
Total expenditures. $8,593
  per capita $6,540

©2008 Information Publications, Inc.
All rights reserved. Photocopying prohibited.
877-544-INFO (4636) or www.informationpublications.com

Federal and state public aid

State unemployment insurance, 2006
Recipients, first payments (x 1,000) 31
Total payments ($ mil) $106
Average weekly benefit $246
Temporary Assistance for Needy Families, 2006
Recipients (x 1,000) 296.4
Families (x 1,000) 111.1
Supplemental Security Income, 2005
Recipients (x 1,000) 32.0
Payments ($ mil) $145.9
Food Stamp Program, 2006
Avg monthly participants (x 1,000) 160.3
Total benefits ($ mil) $169.3

Housing & Construction

Housing units
Total 2005 (estimate) 683,802
Total 2006 (estimate) 691,132
Seasonal or recreational use, 2006 99,118
Owner-occupied, 2006 399,076
    Median home value $170,500
    Homeowner vacancy rate 1.9%
Renter-occupied, 2006 149,171
    Median rent $636
    Rental vacancy rate 6.8%
Home ownership rate, 2005 . . . . .73.9%
Home ownership rate, 2006 . . . . .75.3%

New privately-owned housing units
Number authorized, 2006 (x 1,000) 7.3
    Value ($ mil) $1,125.3
Started 2005 (x 1,000, estimate) 6.8
Started 2006 (x 1,000, estimate) 6.5

Existing home sales
2005 (x 1,000) 33.3
2006 (x 1,000) 30.7

Government & Elections

State officials 2008
Governor . . . . John Baldacci
            Democratic, term expires 1/11
Lieutenant Governor . . . . Beth Edmonds
Secretary of State . . . . Matthew Dunlap
Attorney General . . . . .G. Steven Rowe
Chief Justice . . . . Leigh Saufley

Governorship
Minimum age 30
Length of term . . . . 4 years
Consecutive terms permitted 2
Who succeeds . . . . President of the Senate

Local governments by type, 2002
Total 826
    County 16
    Municipal 22
    Township 467
    School District 99
    Special District 222

State legislature
Name . . . . Legislature
Upper chamber . . . . .Senate
    Number of members 35
    Length of term . . . . 2 years
    Party in majority, 2008 . . . . .Democratic
Lower chamber . . . . House of Representatives
    Number of members 151
    Length of term . . . . 2 years
    Party in majority, 2008 . . . . .Democratic

Federal representation, 2008 (110th Congress)
Senator . . . . Susan Collins
    Party . . . . Republican
    Year term expires 2009
Senator . . . . Olympia Snowe
    Party . . . . Republican
    Year term expires 2013
Representatives, total 2
    Democrats 2
    Republicans 0

Voters in November 2006 election (estimate)
Total 594,723
    Male 286,075
    Female 308,648
    White 584,519
    Black 1,961
    Hispanic 607
    Asian . . . . NA

Presidential election, 2004
Total Popular Vote 740,752
    Kerry 396,842
    Bush 330,201
Total Electoral Votes 4

Votes cast for US Senators
2004
Total vote (x 1,000) . . . . NA
Leading party . . . . NA
Percent for leading party . . . . NA
2006
Total vote (x 1,000) 545
Leading party . . . . Republican
Percent for leading party 74.4%

Votes cast for US Representatives
2004
Total vote (x 1,000) 710
    Democratic 418
    Republican 283
Leading party .Democratic
Percent for leading party 58.9%
2006
Total vote (x 1,000) 536
    Democratic 351
    Republican 163
Leading party .Democratic
Percent for leading party 65.4%

©2008 Information Publications, Inc.
All rights reserved. Photocopying prohibited.
877-544-INFO (4636) or www.informationpublications.com

State government employment, 2006
Full-time equivalent employees 21,680
Payroll ($ mil) $78.8

Local government employment, 2006
Full-time equivalent employees 55,925
Payroll ($ mil) $165.8

Women holding public office, 2008
US Congress 2
Statewide elected office...................... 0
State legislature 56

Black public officials, 2002
Total..................................... 2
  US and state legislatures 0
  City/county/regional offices 1
  Judicial/law enforcement.................. 0
  Education/school boards.................. 1

Hispanic public officials, 2006
Total..................................... 0
  State executives & legislators 0
  City/county/regional offices 0
  Judicial/law enforcement.................. 0
  Education/school boards.................. 0

Governmental Finance

State government revenues, 2006
Total revenue (x $1,000)............ $8,630,865
  per capita $6,563.84
General revenue (x $1,000) $7,565,287
  Intergovernmental 2,580,118
  Taxes 3,590,334
    general sales.....................1,041,216
    individual income tax 1,368,927
    corporate income tax 188,016
  Current charges.....................649,911
  Miscellaneous 744,924

State government expenditure, 2006
Total expenditure (x $1,000).........$7,854,687
  per capita $5,973.55
General expenditure (x $1,000) $7,231,514
  per capita, total.................. *$5,499.63*
    Education 1,419.79
    Public welfare 1,893.11
    Health 359.43
    Hospitals..........................40.88
    Highways 429.52
    Police protection...................50.46
    Corrections 96.37
    Natural resources 133.40
    Parks & recreation 8.98
    Governmental administration.......215.29
    Interest on general debt............173.95

State debt & cash, 2006 ($ per capita)
Debt $3,802.77
Cash/security holdings.............$12,038.51

Federal government grants to state & local government, 2005 (x $1,000)
Total..............................$2,773,126
by Federal agency
  Defense 3,340
  Education 174,123
  Energy.............................5,161
  Environmental Protection Agency 32,484
  Health & Human Services. 1,891,964
  Homeland Security................. 29,992
  Housing & Urban Development...... 194,443
  Justice 32,399
  Labor 57,551
  Transportation 171,509
  Veterans Affairs...................8,671

Crime & Law Enforcement

Crime, 2006 (rates per 100,000 residents)
Property crimes 33,286
  Burglary 6,779
  Larceny 25,167
  Motor vehicle theft 1,340
  Property crime rate.................2,518.7
Violent crimes..........................1,526
  Murder 23
  Forcible rape....................... 339
  Robbery............................ 384
  Aggravated assault 780
  Violent crime rate 115.5
Hate crimes........................... 74

Fraud and identity theft, 2006
Fraud complaints......................1,791
  rate per 100,000 residents 135.5
Identity theft complaints 525
  rate per 100,000 residents 39.7

Law enforcement agencies, 2006
Total agencies......................... 133
Total employees 2,933
  Officers 2,202
  Civilians 731

Prisoners, probation, and parole, 2006
Total prisoners........................2,120
  percent change, 12/31/05 to 12/31/06 .... 4.8%
  in private facilities 0.9%
  in local jails 0%
Sentenced to more than one year 1,997
  rate per 100,000 residents 151
Adults on probation 7,919
Adults on parole........................ 31

Prisoner demographics, June 30, 2005 (rate per 100,000 residents)
Male................................. 513
Female............................... 44
White................................ 262
Black................................1,992
Hispanic .... NA

©2008 Information Publications, Inc.
All rights reserved. Photocopying prohibited.
877-544-INFO (4636) or www.informationpublications.com

Arrests, 2006

Total...................................57,351
   Persons under 18 years of age..........7,765

Persons under sentence of death, 1/1/07

Total.. 0
   White..................................... 0
   Black..................................... 0
   Hispanic.................................. 0

State's highest court

Name................ Supreme Judicial Court
Number of members....................... 7
Length of term...................... 7 years
Intermediate appeals court?.............. no

Labor & Income

Civilian labor force, 2006 (x 1,000)

Total...................................... 715
   Men 373
   Women 342
   Persons 16-19 years..................... 42
   White.................................. 695
   Black .... NA
   Hispanic .... NA

Civilian labor force as a percent of civilian non-institutional population, 2006

Total...................................66.7%
   Men 72.1
   Women 61.6
   Persons 16-19 years....................52.4
   White..................................67.0
   Black .... NA
   Hispanic .... NA

Employment, 2006 (x 1,000)

Total...................................... 683
   Men 355
   Women 328
   Persons 16-19 years..................... 35
   White.................................. 664
   Black .... NA
   Hispanic .... NA

Unemployment rate, 2006

Total......................................4.6%
   Men 4.9
   Women 4.2
   Persons 16-19 years....................15.0
   White..................................4.5
   Black .... NA
   Hispanic .... NA

Full-time/part-time labor force, 2003 (x 1,000)

Full-time labor force, employed........... 509
Part-time labor force, employed........... 149
Unemployed, looking for
   Full-time work.......................... 29
   Part-time work.......................... 6
Mean duration of unemployment (weeks)......16.0
   Median 8.8

Labor unions, 2006

Membership (x 1,000)..................... 69
   percent of employed 11.9%

Experienced civilian labor force by private industry, 2006

Total................................ 498,942
   Natural resources & mining 5,842
   Construction 31,310
   Manufacturing........................60,188
   Trade, transportation & utilities 125,001
   Information 11,267
   Finance 32,352
   Professional & business 51,776
   Education & health..................105,170
   Leisure & hospitality.................59,736
   Other 16,209

Experienced civilian labor force by occupation, May 2006

Management...........................31,130
Business & financial 21,000
Legal.................................. 3,380
Sales................................. 58,260
Office & admin. support............... 102,660
Computers & math 8,010
Architecture & engineering.............8,930
Arts & entertainment 7,330
Education 42,040
Social services 13,950
Health care practitioner & technical......35,120
Health care support 19,340
Maintenance & repair................. 25,840
Construction 32,230
Transportation & moving 42,120
Production 41,740
Farming, fishing & forestry............. 2,900

Hours and earnings of production workers on manufacturing payrolls, 2006

Average weekly hours....................41.4
Average hourly earnings $18.57
Average weekly earnings $768.80

Income and poverty, 2006

Median household income............ $43,439
Personal income, per capita (current $)... $32,348
   in constant (2000) dollars $28,238
Persons below poverty level............. 12.9%

Average annual pay

2006 .... $33,794
   increase from 2005 .... 3.3%

Federal individual income tax returns, 2005

Returns filed.........................621,150
Adjusted gross income ($1,000) $27,763,882
Total tax liability ($1,000) $3,137,737

Charitable contributions, 2004

Number of contributions................163.5
Total amount ($ mil)................. $421.0

©2008 Information Publications, Inc.
All rights reserved. Photocopying prohibited.
877-544-INFO (4636) or www.informationpublications.com

Economy, Business, Industry & Agriculture

Fortune 500 companies, 2007 1
Bankruptcy cases filed, FY 2007 2,143

Patents and trademarks issued, 2007

Patents 133
Trademarks 362

Business firm ownership, 2002

Women-owned 32,512
  Sales ($ mil) $3,282
Black-owned 327
  Sales ($ mil) $32
Hispanic-owned 731
  Sales ($ mil) $113
Asian-owned 833
  Sales ($ mil) $205
Amer. Indian/Alaska Native-owned 680
  Sales ($ mil) $47
Hawaiian/Pacific Islander-owned 29
  Sales ($ mil) $5

Gross domestic product, 2006 ($ mil)

Total gross domestic product $46,973
  Agriculture, forestry, fishing and
    hunting 653
  Mining 8
  Utilities 998
  Construction 2,535
  Manufacturing, durable goods 2,726
  Manufacturing, non-durable goods 2,641
  Wholesale trade .2,514
  Retail trade 4,169
  Transportation & warehousing 1,038
  Information 1,236
  Finance & insurance 3,195
  Real estate, rental & leasing 6,484
  Professional and technical services 2,214
  Educational services 483
  Health care and social assistance 5,070
  Accommodation/food services 1,462
  Other services, except government 1,016
  Government 6,603

Establishments, payroll, employees & receipts, by major industry group, 2005

Total 41,933
  Annual payroll ($1,000) $15,873,419
  Paid employees 497,387
Forestry, fishing & agriculture 773
  Annual payroll ($1,000) . . . . NA
  Paid employees . . . . NA
Mining 30
  Annual payroll ($1,000) . . . . NA
  Paid employees . . . . NA
  Receipts, 2002 ($1,000) . . . . .NA

Utilities 109
  Annual payroll ($1,000) $130,042
  Paid employees 2,345
  Receipts, 2002 ($1,000) . . . . .NA
Construction 5,536
  Annual payroll ($1,000) $1,060,191
  Paid employees .27,065
  Receipts, 2002 ($1,000) $4,256,279
Manufacturing 1,850
  Annual payroll ($1,000) $2,496,875
  Paid employees 60,995
  Receipts, 2002 ($1,000) $13,851,915
Wholesale trade 1,669
  Annual payroll ($1,000) $809,605
  Paid employees .19,456
  Receipts, 2002 ($1,000) $10,371,084
Retail trade 6,980
  Annual payroll ($1,000) $1,850,083
  Paid employees 85,352
  Receipts, 2002 ($1,000) $16,053,515
Transportation & warehousing 1,274
  Annual payroll ($1,000) $463,365
  Paid employees .14,071
  Receipts, 2002 ($1,000) $1,118,787
Information 770
  Annual payroll ($1,000) $467,386
  Paid employees .11,729
  Receipts, 2002 ($1,000) . . . . .NA
Finance & insurance 1,921
  Annual payroll ($1,000) $1,293,728
  Paid employees .29,421
  Receipts, 2002 ($1,000) . . . . .NA
Professional, scientific & technical 3,503
  Annual payroll ($1,000) $1,028,862
  Paid employees 22,199
  Receipts, 2002 ($1,000) $2,252,787
Education 466
  Annual payroll ($1,000) $337,530
  Paid employees 12,501
  Receipts, 2002 ($1,000) $112,910
Health care & social assistance 4,620
  Annual payroll ($1,000) $3,260,097
  Paid employees .97,973
  Receipts, 2002 ($1,000) $6,237,132
Arts and entertainment 899
  Annual payroll ($1,000) $127,790
  Paid employees .6,783
  Receipts, 2002 ($1,000) $392,456
Real estate 1,744
  Annual payroll ($1,000) $205,083
  Paid employees 6,807
  Receipts, 2002 ($1,000) $761,069
Accommodation & food service 3,909
  Annual payroll ($1,000) $717,503
  Paid employees 45,484
  Receipts, 2002 ($1,000) $2,045,841

©2008 Information Publications, Inc.
All rights reserved. Photocopying prohibited.
877-544-INFO (4636) or www.informationpublications.com

8   Maine

Exports, 2006
Value of exported goods ($ mil) $2,627
   Manufactured $2,077
   Non-manufactured.................... $471

Foreign direct investment in US affiliates, 2004
Property, plants & equipment ($ mil) $5,313
Employment (x 1,000)....................29.0

Agriculture, 2006
Number of farms 7,100
Farm acreage (x 1,000) 1,360
   Acres per farm........................ 192
Farm marketings and income ($ mil)
Total..................................$591.7
   Crops.............................. $302.8
   Livestock........................... $288.9
Net farm income $216.8

Principal commodities, in order by marketing receipts, 2005
Potatoes, Dairy products, Blueberries, Chicken eggs, Greenhouse/nursery

Federal economic activity in state
Expenditures, 2005 ($ mil)
   Total..............................$11,356
     Per capita $8,614.55
   Defense $2,374
   Non-defense....................... $8,982
Defense department, 2006 ($ mil)
   Payroll............................ $827
   Contract awards $1,020
   Grants $19
Homeland security grants ($1,000)
   2006...............................$7,785
   2007............................... $6,697

FDIC-insured financial institutions, 2005
Number 36
Assets ($ billion) $56.3
Deposits ($ billion) $39.4

Fishing, 2006
Catch (x 1,000 lbs).................... 234,275
Value ($1,000)........................ $361,862

Mining, 2006 ($ mil)
Total non-fuel mineral production $155
Percent of U.S. 0.24%

Communication, Energy & Transportation

Communication
Households with computers, 2003........ 67.8%
Households with internet access, 2003 .... 57.9%
High-speed internet providers 25
Total high-speed internet lines......... 305,883
   Residential.......................247,991
   Business.........................57,892
Wireless phone customers, 12/2006 844,537

FCC-licensed stations (as of January 1, 2008)
TV stations 15
FM radio stations......................... 89
AM radio stations 29

Energy
Energy consumption, 2004
   Total (trillion Btu)..................... 480
   Per capita (million Btu)...............365.5
By source of production (trillion Btu)
   Coal 7
   Natural gas........................... 76
   Petroleum............................ 261
   Nuclear electric power 0
   Hydroelectric power.................... 34
By end-use sector (trillion Btu)
   Residential 123
   Commercial 81
   Industrial 154
   Transportation 122
Electric energy, 2005
   Primary source of electricity............ Gas
   Net generation (billion kWh)...........18.8
     percent from renewable sources...... 43.3%
   Net summer capability (million kW) 4.2
   CO_2 emitted from generation 7.1
Natural gas utilities, 2005
   Customers (x 1,000) 27
   Sales (trillion Btu)...................... 9
   Revenues ($ mil) $63
Nuclear plants, 2007 0
Total CO_2 emitted (million metric tons).....23.3
Energy spending, 2004 ($ mil) $4,471
   per capita $3,403
   Price per million Btu $12.80

Transportation, 2006
Public road & street mileage 22,783
   Urban........................... 2,972
   Rural............................19,811
   Interstate.......................... 367
Vehicle miles of travel (millions) 15,044
   per capita 11,441.1
Total motor vehicle registrations...... 1,071,876
   Automobiles.......................581,797
   Trucks 486,680
   Motorcycles 45,482
Licensed drivers 1,005,160
   19 years & under 45,890
Deaths from motor vehicle accidents 188
Gasoline consumed (x 1,000 gallons) 704,463
   per capita 535.7

Commuting Statistics, 2006
Average commute time (min) 22.3
   Drove to work alone 77.6%
   Carpooled.......................... 11.0%
   Public transit 0.7%
   Walk to work 4.2%
   Work from home 4.9%

©2008 Information Publications, Inc.
All rights reserved. Photocopying prohibited.
877-544-INFO (4636) or www.informationpublications.com

Maryland 1

State Summary

Capital city . . . . Annapolis
Governor . . . . Martin O'Malley

100 State Circle
Annapolis, MD 21401
410-974-3591

Admitted as a state 1788
Area (square miles) 12,407
Population, 2007 (estimate) 5,618,344
Largest city . . . . Baltimore
    Population, 2006 631,366
Personal income per capita, 2006
    (in current dollars) $44,077
Gross domestic product, 2006 ($ mil) . . . $257,815

Leading industries by payroll, 2005

Professional/Scientific/Technical, Health care/
    Social assistance, Construction

Leading agricultural commodities
by receipts, 2005

Broilers, Greenhouse/nursery, Dairy products,
    Corn, Soybeans

Geography & Environment

Total area (square miles) 12,407
    land 9,774
    water 2,633
Federally-owned land, 2004 (acres) 178,527
    percent 2.8%
Highest point . . Hoye Crest, Backbone Mountain
    elevation (feet) 3,360
Lowest point . . . . Atlantic Ocean
    elevation (feet) . . . . sea level
General coastline (miles) 31
Tidal shoreline (miles) 3,190
Cropland, 2003 (x 1,000 acres) 1,517
Forest land, 2003 (x 1,000 acres) 2,370
Capital city . . . . Annapolis
    Population 2000 35,838
    Population 2006 36,408
Largest city . . . . Baltimore
    Population 2000 651,154
    Population 2006 631,366

Number of cities with over 100,000 population

1990 1
2000 1
2006 1

State park and recreation areas, 2005

Area (x 1,000 acres) 137
Number of visitors (x 1,000) 11,186
Revenues ($1,000) $13,811
    percent of operating expenditures 38.5%

National forest system land, 2007

Acres 0

Demographics & Population Characteristics

Population

1980 4,216,975
1990 4,781,468
2000 5,296,506
2006 5,615,727
    Male 2,716,854
    Female 2,898,873
Living in group quarters, 2006 141,501
    percent of total 2.5%
2007 (estimate) .5,618,344
    persons per square mile of land 574.8
2008 (projected) 5,783,344
2010 (projected) 5,904,970
2020 (projected) 6,497,626
2030 (projected) 7,022,251

Population of Core-Based Statistical Areas
(formerly Metropolitan Areas), x 1,000

	CBSA	Non-CBSA
1990	4,708	73
2000	5,218	79
2006	5,533	82

Change in population, 2000-2007

Number 321,836
    percent 6.1%
Natural increase (births minus deaths) 227,910
Net internal migration . . . . -54,415
Net international migration 135,800

Persons by age, 2006

Under 5 years 368,199
5 to 17 years 992,332
18 years and over 4,255,196
65 years and over 650,568
85 years and over 85,783
    Median age 37.2

Persons by age, 2010 (projected)

Under 5 years 412,152
18 and over 4,498,676
65 and over 717,987
    Median age 36.8

Race, 2006

One Race
    White 3,573,922
    Black or African American 1,656,615
    Asian 277,697
    American Indian/Alaska Native 18,584
    Hawaiian Native/Pacific Islander 3,515
Two or more races 85,394

Persons of Hispanic origin, 2006

Total Hispanic or Latino 336,390
    Mexican 64,374
    Puerto Rican 36,592
    Cuban 7,862

©2008 Information Publications, Inc.
All rights reserved. Photocopying prohibited.
877-544-INFO (4636) or www.informationpublications.com

Persons of Asian origin, 2006

Total Asian 276,362
  Asian Indian. 64,142
  Chinese 67,351
  Filipino 33,812
  Japanese 8,876
  Korean. 48,516
  Vietnamese. 22,736

Marital status, 2006

Population 15 years & over 4,501,537
  Never married 1,456,369
  Married. 2,339,736
  Separated 135,688
  Widowed. 278,321
  Divorced 427,111

Language spoken at home, 2006

Population 5 years and older. 5,247,226
  English only 4,467,027
  Spanish 298,072
  French 62,022
  German. 26,722
  Chinese 55,704

Households & families, 2006

Households. 2,089,031
  with persons under 18 years 744,133
  with persons over 65 years. 458,675
  persons per household 2.62
Families. 1,405,655
  persons per family. .3.19
Married couples. 1,018,096
Female householder,
  no husband present. 290,453
One-person households 557,622

Nativity, 2006

Number of residents born in state 2,685,350
  percent of population 47.8%

Immigration & naturalization, 2006

Legal permanent residents admitted. 30,204
Persons naturalized 14,465
Non-immigrant admissions 300,318

Vital Statistics and Health

Marriages

2004 38,318
2005 38,475
2006 36,495

Divorces

2004 17,802
2005 17,233
2006 17,012

Health risks, 2006

Percent of adults who are:
  Smokers. 17.7%
  Overweight (BMI > 25). 60.7%
  Obese (BMI > 30). 24.9%

Births

2005 74,980
  Birthrate (per 1,000). 13.4
  White. 43,285
  Black 26,526
  Hispanic 8,681
  Asian/Pacific Islander 4,980
  Amer. Indian/Alaska Native. 189
  Low birth weight (2,500g or less). 9.1%
  Cesarian births 31.1%
  Preterm births 13.3%
  To unmarried mothers. 37.1%
  Twin births (per 1,000) 37.1
  Triplets or higher order (per 100,000). . . .193.7
2006 (preliminary). 77,478
  rate per 1,000 . . . . .13.8

Deaths

2004
All causes 43,232
  rate per 100,000. 806.0
Heart disease 11,346
  rate per 100,000. . . . . .212.4
Malignant neoplasms 10,168
  rate per 100,000. . . . . .188.6
Cerebrovascular disease. 2,718
  rate per 100,000. .51.5
Chronic lower respiratory disease 1,910
  rate per 100,000. .36.5
Diabetes. 1,417
  rate per 100,000. .26.4
2005 (preliminary). 43,893
  rate per 100,000. . . . . .796.4
2006 (provisional) 43,566

Infant deaths

2004 630
  rate per 1,000 . . . . .8.4
2005 (provisional) 602
  rate per 1,000 . . . . .7.9

Exercise routines, 2005

None. 22.9%
Moderate or greater. 49.1%
Vigorous 29.6%

Abortions, 2004

Total performed in state. 10,096
  rate per 1,000 women age 15-44. 8
  % obtained by out-of-state residents 12.6%

Physicians, 2005

Total. 23,128
  rate per 100,000 persons 414

Community hospitals, 2005

Number of hospitals 50
Beds (x 1,000). 11.4
Patients admitted (x 1,000) 680
Average daily census (x 1,000) 8.7
Average cost per day $1,831
Outpatient visits (x 1 mil) 6.8

©2008 Information Publications, Inc.
All rights reserved. Photocopying prohibited.
877-544-INFO (4636) or www.informationpublications.com

Disability status of population, 2006

5 to 15 years 6.0%
16 to 64 years 10.2%
65 years and over 37.7%

Education

Educational attainment, 2006

Population over 25 years 3,717,512
    Less than 9th grade...................... 4.2%
    High school graduate or more 87.1%
    College graduate or more.............. 35.1%
    Graduate or professional degree....... 15.7%

Public school enrollment, 2005-06

Total............................... 860,020
    Pre-kindergarten through grade 8.... 588,571
    Grades 9 through 12................ 271,449

Graduating public high school seniors, 2004-05

Diplomas (incl. GED and others) 54,750

SAT scores, 2007

Average critical reading score.............. 500
Average writing score 496
Average math score 502
Percent of graduates taking test 70%

Public school teachers, 2006-07 (estimate)

Total (x 1,000) 59.3
    Elementary.............................34.4
    Secondary..............................24.9
Average salary $56,927
    Elementary........................ $56,678
    Secondary..........................$57,228

State receipts & expenditures for public schools, 2006-07 (estimate)

Revenue receipts ($ mil) $10,523
Expenditures
Total ($ mil) $9,771
    Per capita $1,561
    Per pupil $10,824

NAEP proficiency scores, 2007

	Reading		Math	
	Basic	Proficient	Basic	Proficient
Grade 4	68.9%	35.9%	80.0%	40.1%
Grade 8	75.6%	33.2%	73.6%	36.5%

Higher education enrollment, fall 2005

Total................................ 58,078
    Full-time men 15,076
    Full-time women.....................21,168
    Part-time men 8,494
    Part-time women.................... 13,340

Minority enrollment in institutions of higher education, 2005

Black, non-Hispanic 86,984
Hispanic 12,063
Asian/Pacific Islander 20,185
American Indian/Alaska Native..........1,292

Institutions of higher education, 2005-06

Total................................... 58
    Public................................ 29
    Private 29

Earned degrees conferred, 2004-05

Associate's...........................9,834
Bachelor's 25,018
Master's.............................13,163
First-professional....................1,080
Doctor's.............................1,228

Public Libraries, 2006

Number of libraries...................... 24
Number of outlets 193
Annual visits per capita 5.0
Circulation per capita....................9.4

State & local financial support for higher education, FY 2006

Full-time equivalent enrollment (x 1,000)....192.6
Appropriations per FTE............... $6,427

Social Insurance & Welfare Programs

Social Security benefits & beneficiaries, 2005

Beneficiaries (x 1,000) 772
    Retired & dependents................... 549
    Survivors........................... 110
    Disabled & dependents............... 113
Annual benefit payments ($ mil) $8,512
    Retired & dependents.................$5,766
    Survivors...........................$1,516
    Disabled & dependents...............$1,231
Average monthly benefit
    Retired & dependents.................$1,012
    Disabled & dependents............... $967
    Widowed............................ $986

Medicare, July 2005

Enrollment (x 1,000)..................... 695
Payments ($ mil) $5,832

Medicaid, 2004

Beneficiaries (x 1,000).................. 750
Payments ($ mil) $4,594

State Children's Health Insurance Program, 2006

Enrollment (x 1,000)..................136.0
Expenditures ($ mil)..................$212.4

Persons without health insurance, 2006

Number (x 1,000)........................ 776
    percent............................13.8%
Number of children (x 1,000) 137
    percent of children 9.9%

Health care expenditures, 2004

Total expenditures.................... $31,044
    per capita $5,590

©2008 Information Publications, Inc.
All rights reserved. Photocopying prohibited.
877-544-INFO (4636) or www.informationpublications.com

Federal and state public aid

State unemployment insurance, 2006
Recipients, first payments (x 1,000) 96
Total payments ($ mil) $391
Average weekly benefit $274
Temporary Assistance for Needy Families, 2006
Recipients (x 1,000) 535.1
Families (x 1,000) 234.5
Supplemental Security Income, 2005
Recipients (x 1,000) 94.4
Payments ($ mil) $480.9
Food Stamp Program, 2006
Avg monthly participants (x 1,000) 305.4
Total benefits ($ mil) $336.1

Housing & Construction

Housing units

Total 2005 (estimate) 2,274,307
Total 2006 (estimate) 2,300,567
Seasonal or recreational use, 2006 49,654
Owner-occupied, 2006 1,450,411
      Median home value $334,700
      Homeowner vacancy rate 2.1%
Renter-occupied, 2006 638,620
      Median rent $953
      Rental vacancy rate 10.2%
Home ownership rate, 2005 . . . . 71.2%
Home ownership rate, 2006 . . . . 72.6%

New privately-owned housing units

Number authorized, 2006 (x 1,000) 23.3
      Value ($ mil) $3,889.9
Started 2005 (x 1,000, estimate) 27.1
Started 2006 (x 1,000, estimate) 27.0

Existing home sales

2005 (x 1,000) 135.5
2006 (x 1,000) 113.2

Government & Elections

State officials 2008

Governor . . . . Martin O'Malley
            Democratic, term expires 1/11
Lieutenant Governor . . . . Anthony Brown
Secretary of State . . . . Dennis Schnepfe
Attorney General . . . . Douglas Gansler
Chief Justice . . . . Robert Bell

Governorship

Minimum age 30
Length of term . . . . 4 years
Consecutive terms permitted 2
Who succeeds . . . . Lieutenant Governor

Local governments by type, 2002

Total 265
      County 23
      Municipal 157
      Township 0
      School District 0
      Special District 85

State legislature

Name . . . . General Assembly
Upper chamber . . . . .Senate
      Number of members 47
      Length of term . . . . 4 years
      Party in majority, 2008 . . . . .Democratic
Lower chamber . . . . House of Delegates
      Number of members 141
      Length of term . . . . 4 years
      Party in majority, 2008 . . . . .Democratic

Federal representation, 2008 (110th Congress)

Senator . . . . Barbara Mikulski
      Party . . . . .Democratic
      Year term expires 2011
Senator . . . . Ben Cardin
      Party . . . . .Democratic
      Year term expires 2013
Representatives, total 8
      Democrats 6
      Republicans 2

Voters in November 2006 election (estimate)

Total 2,144,913
      Male 982,029
      Female 1,162,884
      White 1,512,616
      Black 584,152
      Hispanic 35,174
      Asian 25,102

Presidential election, 2004

Total Popular Vote 2,386,678
      Kerry 1,334,493
      Bush 1,024,703
Total Electoral Votes 10

Votes cast for US Senators

2004
Total vote (x 1,000) 2,322
Leading party .Democratic
Percent for leading party 64.8%

2006
Total vote (x 1,000) 1,781
Leading party .Democratic
Percent for leading party 54.2%

Votes cast for US Representatives

2004
Total vote (x 1,000) 2,254
      Democratic 1,311
      Republican 896
Leading party .Democratic
Percent for leading party 58.2%

2006
Total vote (x 1,000) 1,701
      Democratic 1,099
      Republican 547
Leading party .Democratic
Percent for leading party 64.6%

©2008 Information Publications, Inc.
All rights reserved. Photocopying prohibited.
877-544-INFO (4636) or www.informationpublications.com

State government employment, 2006
Full-time equivalent employees 90,262
Payroll ($ mil) $379.8

Local government employment, 2006
Full-time equivalent employees 200,878
Payroll ($ mil) $857.1

Women holding public office, 2008
US Congress 1
Statewide elected office 0
State legislature 61

Black public officials, 2002
Total 192
   US and state legislatures 40
   City/county/regional offices 101
   Judicial/law enforcement 41
   Education/school boards 10

Hispanic public officials, 2006
Total 13
   State executives & legislators 4
   City/county/regional offices 7
   Judicial/law enforcement 0
   Education/school boards 2

Governmental Finance

State government revenues, 2006
Total revenue (x $1,000) $31,006,534
   per capita $5,534.89
General revenue (x $1,000) $26,272,398
   Intergovernmental 6,967,769
   Taxes 14,626,889
      general sales 3,381,694
      individual income tax 6,151,365
      corporate income tax 846,863
   Current charges 2,642,009
   Miscellaneous .2,035,731

State government expenditure, 2006
Total expenditure (x $1,000) $28,965,977
   per capita $5,170.63
General expenditure (x $1,000) $25,721,600
   per capita, total *$4,591.49*
      Education 1,585.19
      Public welfare 1,141.98
      Health 307.09
      Hospitals 81.48
      Highways 383.88
      Police protection 69.33
      Corrections 212.28
      Natural resources 72.56
      Parks & recreation 28.00
      Governmental administration 205.96
      Interest on general debt 139.43

State debt & cash, 2006 ($ per capita)
Debt $2,838.58
Cash/security holdings $9,804.63

Federal government grants to state & local government, 2005 (x $1,000)
Total $8,643,028
by Federal agency
   Defense 206,636
   Education 589,413
   Energy 28,233
   Environmental Protection Agency 95,172
   Health & Human Services 5,350,761
   Homeland Security 29,555
   Housing & Urban Development 683,496
   Justice 129,369
   Labor 179,134
   Transportation 654,638
   Veterans Affairs 4,493

Crime & Law Enforcement

Crime, 2006 (rates per 100,000 residents)
Property crimes 195,476
   Burglary 37,457
   Larceny 127,497
   Motor vehicle theft 30,522
   Property crime rate 3,480.9
Violent crimes 38,110
   Murder 546
   Forcible rape 1,178
   Robbery 14,375
   Aggravated assault 22,011
   Violent crime rate 678.6
Hate crimes 218

Fraud and identity theft, 2006
Fraud complaints 8,653
   rate per 100,000 residents 154.1
Identity theft complaints 4,656
   rate per 100,000 residents 82.9

Law enforcement agencies, 2006
Total agencies 149
Total employees 20,097
   Officers 15,048
   Civilians 5,049

Prisoners, probation, and parole, 2006
Total prisoners 22,945
   percent change, 12/31/05 to 12/31/06 . . . . 0.9%
   in private facilities 0.5%
   in local jails 0.7%
Sentenced to more than one year 22,316
   rate per 100,000 residents 396
Adults on probation 75,698
Adults on parole 14,351

Prisoner demographics, June 30, 2005
   (rate per 100,000 residents)
Male 1,219
Female 88
White 288
Black 1,579
Hispanic . . . . NA

©2008 Information Publications, Inc.
All rights reserved. Photocopying prohibited.
877-544-INFO (4636) or www.informationpublications.com

Arrests, 2006

Total................................ 297,530
    Persons under 18 years of age 49,359

Persons under sentence of death, 1/1/07

Total...................................... 8
    White..................................... 3
    Black 5
    Hispanic 0

State's highest court

Name .... Court of Appeals
Number of members 7
Length of term .... 10 years
Intermediate appeals court? ....yes

Labor & Income

Civilian labor force, 2006 (x 1,000)

Total...................................3,001
    Men 1,548
    Women 1,453
    Persons 16-19 years.................... 131
    White.................................1,990
    Black 825
    Hispanic 242

Civilian labor force as a percent of civilian non-institutional population, 2006

Total................................. 69.5%
    Men 76.0
    Women 63.7
    Persons 16-19 years...................45.6
    White.................................69.8
    Black 68.1
    Hispanic 80.4

Employment, 2006 (x 1,000)

Total................................. 2,885
    Men 1,489
    Women 1,395
    Persons 16-19 years.................... 115
    White.................................1,932
    Black 773
    Hispanic 233

Unemployment rate, 2006

Total................................... 3.9%
    Men 3.8
    Women 4.0
    Persons 16-19 years...................12.1
    White..................................2.9
    Black 6.3
    Hispanic 3.5

Full-time/part-time labor force, 2003 (x 1,000)

Full-time labor force, employed 2,336
Part-time labor force, employed........... 438
Unemployed, looking for
    Full-time work......................... 111
    Part-time work......................... 20
*Mean duration of unemployment (weeks)......*18.4
    Median 9.1

Labor unions, 2006

Membership (x 1,000).................... 342
    percent of employed 13.1%

Experienced civilian labor force by private industry, 2006

Total.............................2,074,499
    Natural resources & mining 6,825
    Construction 188,310
    Manufacturing..................... 136,253
    Trade, transportation & utilities 470,261
    Information 50,774
    Finance 157,614
    Professional & business 394,712
    Education & health 349,186
    Leisure & hospitality................229,611
    Other 89,690

Experienced civilian labor force by occupation, May 2006

Management........................ 138,520
Business & financial 137,050
Legal................................. 19,280
Sales 265,160
Office & admin. support............. 439,730
Computers & math 96,090
Architecture & engineering.............56,170
Arts & entertainment 31,270
Education 165,270
Social services 33,170
Health care practitioner & technical.....133,010
Health care support 63,670
Maintenance & repair................. 103,270
Construction 148,130
Transportation & moving 150,040
Production 102,080
Farming, fishing & forestry............. 2,530

Hours and earnings of production workers on manufacturing payrolls, 2006

Average weekly hours 40.6
Average hourly earnings $17.87
Average weekly earnings $725.52

Income and poverty, 2006

Median household income............ $65,144
Personal income, per capita (current $)... $44,077
    in constant (2000) dollars $38,476
Persons below poverty level.............. 7.8%

Average annual pay

2006 .... $46,162
    increase from 2005 .... 4.0%

Federal individual income tax returns, 2005

Returns filed.......................2,674,329
Adjusted gross income ($1,000) $170,124,868
Total tax liability ($1,000) $22,826,143

Charitable contributions, 2004

Number of contributions 1,177.5
Total amount ($ mil)................. $4,887.2

©2008 Information Publications, Inc.
All rights reserved. Photocopying prohibited.
877-544-INFO (4636) or www.informationpublications.com

Economy, Business, Industry & Agriculture

Fortune 500 companies, 2007 6
Bankruptcy cases filed, FY 2007 12,509

Patents and trademarks issued, 2007

Patents 1,435
Trademarks 1,511

Business firm ownership, 2002

Women-owned 137,410
  Sales ($ mil) $17,295
Black-owned 69,410
  Sales ($ mil) $4,655
Hispanic-owned 15,353
  Sales ($ mil) $2,398
Asian-owned 26,184
  Sales ($ mil) $7,062
Amer. Indian/Alaska Native-owned 3,634
  Sales ($ mil) $344
Hawaiian/Pacific Islander-owned 83
  Sales ($ mil) . . . . NA

Gross domestic product, 2006 ($ mil)

Total gross domestic product $257,815
  Agriculture, forestry, fishing and
    hunting 760
  Mining 299
  Utilities 7,014
  Construction 15,876
  Manufacturing, durable goods 6,591
  Manufacturing, non-durable goods 7,469
  Wholesale trade 13,231
  Retail trade 16,202
  Transportation & warehousing 5,090
  Information 9,134
  Finance & insurance 16,549
  Real estate, rental & leasing 43,786
  Professional and technical services 26,340
  Educational services 3,204
  Health care and social assistance 18,988
  Accommodation/food services 6,886
  Other services, except government 6,529
  Government 42,428

Establishments, payroll, employees & receipts, by major industry group, 2005

Total 138,481
  Annual payroll ($1,000) $88,964,728
  Paid employees 2,167,999
Forestry, fishing & agriculture 217
  Annual payroll ($1,000) $28,949
  Paid employees 991
Mining 92
  Annual payroll ($1,000) $88,289
  Paid employees 1,999
  Receipts, 2002 ($1,000) $417,336

Utilities 108
  Annual payroll ($1,000) $888,039
  Paid employees .10,181
  Receipts, 2002 ($1,000) . . . . .NA
Construction 16,888
  Annual payroll ($1,000) $8,298,193
  Paid employees 181,735
  Receipts, 2002 ($1,000) $29,735,639
Manufacturing 3,742
  Annual payroll ($1,000) $6,717,027
  Paid employees 135,120
  Receipts, 2002 ($1,000) $36,363,340
Wholesale trade 6,043
  Annual payroll ($1,000) $5,215,987
  Paid employees 97,350
  Receipts, 2002 ($1,000) $60,679,602
Retail trade 19,561
  Annual payroll ($1,000) $7,225,671
  Paid employees 299,658
  Receipts, 2002 ($1,000) $60,039,971
Transportation & warehousing 3,712
  Annual payroll ($1,000) $2,264,039
  Paid employees 62,663
  Receipts, 2002 ($1,000) $4,635,726
Information 2,631
  Annual payroll ($1,000) $3,941,341
  Paid employees 66,195
  Receipts, 2002 ($1,000) . . . . .NA
Finance & insurance 8,130
  Annual payroll ($1,000) $8,071,435
  Paid employees 121,374
  Receipts, 2002 ($1,000) . . . . .NA
Professional, scientific & technical 19,132
  Annual payroll ($1,000) $13,706,692
  Paid employees 221,269
  Receipts, 2002 ($1,000) $28,059,470
Education 1,805
  Annual payroll ($1,000) $2,132,329
  Paid employees 63,413
  Receipts, 2002 ($1,000) $904,718
Health care & social assistance 14,622
  Annual payroll ($1,000) $11,855,818
  Paid employees 300,272
  Receipts, 2002 ($1,000) $23,785,022
Arts and entertainment 2,172
  Annual payroll ($1,000) $864,554
  Paid employees 35,698
  Receipts, 2002 ($1,000) $2,143,001
Real estate 6,549
  Annual payroll ($1,000) $2,123,783
  Paid employees 49,532
  Receipts, 2002 ($1,000) $8,482,853
Accommodation & food service 10,230
  Annual payroll ($1,000) $2,710,753
  Paid employees 188,835
  Receipts, 2002 ($1,000) $7,832,268

©2008 Information Publications, Inc.
All rights reserved. Photocopying prohibited.
877-544-INFO (4636) or www.informationpublications.com

Exports, 2006

Value of exported goods ($ mil) $7,598
   Manufactured $6,035
   Non-manufactured $907

Foreign direct investment in US affiliates, 2004

Property, plants & equipment ($ mil) $11,172
Employment (x 1,000). 101.1

Agriculture, 2006

Number of farms 12,000
Farm acreage (x 1,000) 2,035
   Acres per farm 170
Farm marketings and income ($ mil)
Total. $1,597.7
   Crops $725.6
   Livestock $872.1
Net farm income $594.6

Principal commodities, in order by marketing receipts, 2005

   Broilers, Greenhouse/nursery, Dairy products,
       Corn, Soybeans

Federal economic activity in state

Expenditures, 2005 ($ mil)
   Total. $66,720
      Per capita $11,936.47
   Defense $15,256
   Non-defense $51,464
Defense department, 2006 ($ mil)
   Payroll. $5,334
   Contract awards $10,244
   Grants $215
Homeland security grants ($1,000)
   2006. . . . . $24,291
   2007 . . . . $32,670

FDIC-insured financial institutions, 2005

Number 112
Assets ($ billion) $54.2
Deposits ($ billion) $40.7

Fishing, 2006

Catch (x 1,000 lbs) 51,216
Value ($1,000). $53,546

Mining, 2006 ($ mil)

Total non-fuel mineral production $596
Percent of U.S. 0.93%

Communication, Energy & Transportation

Communication

Households with computers, 2003 . . . . 66.0%
Households with internet access, 2003 . . . . 59.2%
High-speed internet providers 43
Total high-speed internet lines 1,813,960
   Residential 1,347,366
   Business. 466,594
Wireless phone customers, 12/2006 4,691,026

FCC-licensed stations (as of January 1, 2008)

TV stations 16
FM radio stations. 75
AM radio stations 53

Energy

Energy consumption, 2004
   Total (trillion Btu). 1,527
   Per capita (million Btu) 274.9
By source of production (trillion Btu)
   Coal 327
   Natural gas 199
   Petroleum 582
   Nuclear electric power 152
   Hydroelectric power 25
By end-use sector (trillion Btu)
   Residential 437
   Commercial 281
   Industrial 368
   Transportation 440
Electric energy, 2005
   Primary source of electricity. . . . . Coal
   Net generation (billion kWh) 52.7
      percent from renewable sources. 4.4%
   Net summer capability (million kW) 12.5
   CO_2 emitted from generation 33.3
Natural gas utilities, 2005
   Customers (x 1,000) 1,100
   Sales (trillion Btu) 185
   Revenues ($ mil) $1,385
Nuclear plants, 2007 2
Total CO_2 emitted (million metric tons). 78.8
Energy spending, 2004 ($ mil) $14,167
   per capita $2,551
   Price per million Btu $14.11

Transportation, 2006

Public road & street mileage 31,099
   Urban. 17,099
   Rural 14,000
   Interstate. 481
Vehicle miles of travel (millions) 56,302
   per capita 10,050.3
Total motor vehicle registrations 4,488,397
   Automobiles. 2,656,597
   Trucks 1,819,645
   Motorcycles 72,626
Licensed drivers 3,694,290
   19 years & under 160,482
Deaths from motor vehicle accidents 651
Gasoline consumed (x 1,000 gallons) 2,770,954
   per capita 494.6

Commuting Statistics, 2006

Average commute time (min) 30.6
   Drove to work alone 72.8%
   Carpooled. 10.7%
   Public transit 8.8%
   Walk to work 2.6%
   Work from home 3.6%

©2008 Information Publications, Inc.
All rights reserved. Photocopying prohibited.
877-544-INFO (4636) or www.informationpublications.com

State Summary

Capital city .... Boston
Governor...................... Deval Patrick

State House
Office of the Governor, Room 360
Boston, MA 02133
617-727-6250

Admitted as a state 1788
Area (square miles) 10,555
Population, 2007 (estimate)..........6,449,755
Largest city .... Boston
   Population, 2006.................. 590,763
Personal income per capita, 2006
   (in current dollars) $45,877
Gross domestic product, 2006 ($ mil) ... $337,570

Leading industries by payroll, 2005

Health care/Social assistance, Finance & Insurance, Professional/Scientific/Technical

Leading agricultural commodities by receipts, 2005

Greenhouse/nursery, Cranberries, Dairy products, Sweet corn, Apples

Geography & Environment

Total area (square miles)............... 10,555
   land 7,840
   water 2,715
Federally-owned land, 2004 (acres) 93,950
   percent............................. 1.9%
Highest point ....Mt. Greylock
   elevation (feet) 3,491
Lowest point..................Atlantic Ocean
   elevation (feet) .... sea level
General coastline (miles) 192
Tidal shoreline (miles) 1,519
Cropland, 2003 (x 1,000 acres) 252
Forest land, 2003 (x 1,000 acres)......... 2,665
Capital city .... Boston
   Population 2000 589,141
   Population 2006 590,763
Largest city .... Boston
   Population 2000 589,141
   Population 2006 590,763

Number of cities with over 100,000 population

1990 3
2000 5
2006 5

State park and recreation areas, 2005

Area (x 1,000 acres) 336
Number of visitors (x 1,000) 33,162
Revenues ($1,000) $13,898
   percent of operating expenditures...... 22.9%

National forest system land, 2007

Acres 0

Demographics & Population Characteristics

Population

1980 5,737,037
1990 6,016,425
2000 6,349,105
2006 6,437,193
   Male.............................3,117,205
   Female...........................3,319,988
Living in group quarters, 2006......... 215,883
   percent of total...................... 3.4%
2007 (estimate).....................6,449,755
   persons per square mile of land 822.7
2008 (projected)....................6,601,235
2010 (projected)....................6,649,441
2020 (projected)....................6,855,546
2030 (projected)....................7,012,009

Population of Core-Based Statistical Areas (formerly Metropolitan Areas), x 1,000

	CBSA	Non-CBSA
1990	5,999	18
2000	6,325	25
2006	6,411	26

Change in population, 2000-2007

Number............................ 100,650
   percent............................. 1.6%
Natural increase (births minus deaths) 172,254
Net internal migration ....-305,690
Net international migration 206,438

Persons by age, 2006

Under 5 years 387,863
5 to 17 years 1,061,021
18 years and over 4,988,309
65 years and over 855,962
85 years and over 137,022
   Median age 38.2

Persons by age, 2010 (projected)

Under 5 years 400,704
18 and over 5,165,588
65 and over 908,565
   Median age 38.8

Race, 2006

One Race
   White..........................5,568,643
   Black or African American 446,721
   Asian 313,942
   American Indian/Alaska Native....... 19,044
   Hawaiian Native/Pacific Islander.......5,126
Two or more races.....................83,717

Persons of Hispanic origin, 2006

Total Hispanic or Latino 510,482
   Mexican........................... 35,659
   Puerto Rican 226,892
   Cuban 8,012

©2008 Information Publications, Inc.
All rights reserved. Photocopying prohibited.
877-544-INFO (4636) or www.informationpublications.com

Persons of Asian origin, 2006

Total Asian 310,441
Asian Indian. 61,042
Chinese 114,638
Filipino 10,823
Japanese 8,218
Korean 21,840
Vietnamese. 47,121

Marital status, 2006

Population 15 years & over 5,249,776
Never married 1,804,439
Married. 2,634,715
Separated 107,866
Widowed. 341,245
Divorced 469,377

Language spoken at home, 2006

Population 5 years and older. 6,049,574
English only 4,827,632
Spanish 411,192
French 125,209
German. 19,443
Chinese 94,615

Households & families, 2006

Households. 2,446,485
with persons under 18 years 792,164
with persons over 65 years. 590,012
persons per household 2.54
Families. 1,565,973
persons per family. 3.17
Married couples. 1,175,784
Female householder,
no husband present. 290,102
One-person households 707,650

Nativity, 2006

Number of residents born in state 4,126,291
percent of population. 64.1%

Immigration & naturalization, 2006

Legal permanent residents admitted. 35,560
Persons naturalized 22,932
Non-immigrant admissions 716,538

Vital Statistics and Health

Marriages

2004. 41,549
2005. 39,507
2006. 38,494

Divorces

2004. 14,148
2005. 14,354
2006. 14,607

Health risks, 2006

Percent of adults who are:
Smokers. 17.8%
Overweight (BMI > 25). 55.5%
Obese (BMI > 30). 20.3%

Births

2005 76,865
Birthrate (per 1,000). 12.0
White. 62,406
Black 8,800
Hispanic 10,125
Asian/Pacific Islander 5,482
Amer. Indian/Alaska Native 177
Low birth weight (2,500g or less). 7.9%
Cesarian births 32.2%
Preterm births 11.3%
To unmarried mothers. 30.2%
Twin births (per 1,000) 44.5
Triplets or higher order (per 100,000). . . .290.4
2006 (preliminary). 77,769
rate per 1,000 . . . . .12.1

Deaths

2004
All causes 54,511
rate per 100,000 . . . . .740.6
Heart disease 13,824
rate per 100,000. . . . . .183.3
Malignant neoplasms 13,337
rate per 100,000 . . . . .188.7
Cerebrovascular disease. 3,254
rate per 100,000 . . . . .42.5
Chronic lower respiratory disease 2,574
rate per 100,000 . . . . .35.2
Diabetes. 1,329
rate per 100,000 . . . . .18.4
2005 (preliminary). 53,872
rate per 100,000 . . . . .721.9
2006 (provisional) 53,631

Infant deaths

2004 380
rate per 1,000 . . . . .4.8
2005 (provisional) 395
rate per 1,000 . . . . .5.1

Exercise routines, 2005

None. 23.3%
Moderate or greater. 52.6%
Vigorous 29.7%

Abortions, 2004

Total performed in state. 24,366
rate per 1,000 women age 15-44. 18
% obtained by out-of-state residents 4.6%

Physicians, 2005

Total. 29,343
rate per 100,000 persons 456

Community hospitals, 2005

Number of hospitals 80
Beds (x 1,000). 16.2
Patients admitted (x 1,000) 800
Average daily census (x 1,000) 12.0
Average cost per day (x 1,000) $1,751
Outpatient visits (x 1 mil) 18.9

©2008 Information Publications, Inc.
All rights reserved. Photocopying prohibited.
877-544-INFO (4636) or www.informationpublications.com

Disability status of population, 2006
5 to 15 years 6.6%
16 to 64 years 10.9%
65 years and over 37.7%

Education

Educational attainment, 2006
Population over 25 years 4,345,561
  Less than 9th grade..................... 5.0%
  High school graduate or more 87.9%
  College graduate or more.............. 37.0%
  Graduate or professional degree........ 15.6%

Public school enrollment, 2005-06
Total.............................. 971,909
  Pre-kindergarten through grade 8.... 675,398
  Grades 9 through 12 296,511

Graduating public high school seniors, 2004-05
Diplomas (incl. GED and others) 60,653

SAT scores, 2007
Average critical reading score.............. 513
Average writing score 511
Average math score 522
Percent of graduates taking test 85%

Public school teachers, 2006-07 (estimate)
Total (x 1,000) 73.2
  Elementary 29.2
  Secondary 44.0
Average salary $58,624
  Elementary $58,624
  Secondary $58,624

State receipts & expenditures for public schools, 2006-07 (estimate)
Revenue receipts ($ mil) $14,585
Expenditures
Total ($ mil) $14,945
  Per capita $1,999
  Per pupil $14,125

NAEP proficiency scores, 2007

	Reading		Math	
	Basic	Proficient	Basic	Proficient
Grade 4	81.1%	49.2%	93.2%	57.6%
Grade 8	83.9%	43.0%	85.0%	50.7%

Higher education enrollment, fall 2005
Total................................. 255,021
  Full-time men 88,824
  Full-time women..................... 109,755
  Part-time men 21,292
  Part-time women..................... 35,150

Minority enrollment in institutions of higher education, 2005
Black, non-Hispanic 34,986
Hispanic 27,174
Asian/Pacific Islander 32,061
American Indian/Alaska Native.......... 1,885

Institutions of higher education, 2005-06
Total.................................... 121
  Public................................. 31
  Private................................. 90

Earned degrees conferred, 2004-05
Associate's.......................... 11,595
Bachelor's 45,714
Master's............................. 27,663
First-professional..................... 4,305
Doctor's............................. 2,676

Public Libraries, 2006
Number of libraries..................... 370
Number of outlets 488
Annual visits per capita 5.9
Circulation per capita................... 7.8

State & local financial support for higher education, FY 2006
Full-time equivalent enrollment (x 1,000).... 139.9
Appropriations per FTE............... $8,372

Social Insurance & Welfare Programs

Social Security benefits & beneficiaries, 2005
Beneficiaries (x 1,000) 1,072
  Retired & dependents................ 748
  Survivors........................... 128
  Disabled & dependents................ 196
Annual benefit payments ($ mil) $11,691
  Retired & dependents................ $7,865
  Survivors........................... $1,829
  Disabled & dependents................ $1,997
Average monthly benefit
  Retired & dependents................ $1,009
  Disabled & dependents................ $924
  Widowed............................ $1,001

Medicare, July 2005
Enrollment (x 1,000)..................... 971
Payments ($ mil) $6,699

Medicaid, 2004
Beneficiaries (x 1,000)................... 294
Payments ($ mil) $2,366

State Children's Health Insurance Program, 2006
Enrollment (x 1,000)..................... 190.6
Expenditures ($ mil) $233.5

Persons without health insurance, 2006
Number (x 1,000)........................ 657
  percent 10.4%
Number of children (x 1,000) 103
  percent of children 7.0%

Health care expenditures, 2004
Total expenditures.................... $43,009
  per capita $6,683

©2008 Information Publications, Inc.
All rights reserved. Photocopying prohibited.
877-544-INFO (4636) or www.informationpublications.com

Federal and state public aid

State unemployment insurance, 2006
Recipients, first payments (x 1,000) 210
Total payments ($ mil) $1,255
Average weekly benefit $366
Temporary Assistance for Needy Families, 2006
Recipients (x 1,000) .1,104.8
Families (x 1,000) .552.6
Supplemental Security Income, 2005
Recipients (x 1,000) .171.5
Payments ($ mil) $902.3
Food Stamp Program, 2006
Avg monthly participants (x 1,000) 431.5
Total benefits ($ mil) $421.5

Housing & Construction

Housing units

Total 2005 (estimate) 2,691,111
Total 2006 (estimate) 2,708,986
Seasonal or recreational use, 2006 103,599
Owner-occupied, 2006 1,588,359
  Median home value $370,400
  Homeowner vacancy rate 1.8%
Renter-occupied, 2006 858,126
  Median rent $933
  Rental vacancy rate 6.2%
Home ownership rate, 2005 . . . . 63.4%
Home ownership rate, 2006 . . . . 65.2%

New privately-owned housing units

Number authorized, 2006 (x 1,000) 19.6
  Value ($ mil) $3,249.2
Started 2005 (x 1,000, estimate) 16.0
Started 2006 (x 1,000, estimate) 16.0

Existing home sales

2005 (x 1,000) 148.6
2006 (x 1,000) 128.1

Government & Elections

State officials 2008

Governor . . . . Deval Patrick
        Democratic, term expires 1/11
Lieutenant Governor . . . . Tim Murray
Secretary of State . . . . William Galvin
Attorney General . . . . .Martha Coakley
Chief Justice . . . . Margaret Marshall

Governorship

Minimum age . . . . not specified
Length of term . . . . 4 years
Consecutive terms permitted . . . . . . not specified
Who succeeds . . . . Lieutenant Governor

Local governments by type, 2002

Total 841
  County 5
  Municipal 45
  Township 306
  School District 82
  Special District 403

State legislature

Name . . . . General Court
Upper chamber . . . . .Senate
  Number of members 40
  Length of term . . . . 2 years
  Party in majority, 2008 . . . . .Democratic
Lower chamber . . . . . .House of Representatives
  Number of members 160
  Length of term . . . . 2 years
  Party in majority, 2008 . . . . .Democratic

Federal representation, 2008 (110th Congress)

Senator . . . . John Kerry
  Party . . . . .Democratic
  Year term expires 2009
Senator . . . . Edward M. Kennedy
  Party . . . . .Democratic
  Year term expires 2013
Representatives, total 10
  Democrats 10
  Republicans 0

Voters in November 2006 election (estimate)

Total 2,434,432
  Male 1,110,863
  Female 1,323,569
  White 2,274,168
  Black 97,096
  Hispanic 44,032
  Asian 42,590

Presidential election, 2004

Total Popular Vote 2,912,388
  Kerry 1,803,800
  Bush 1,071,109
Total Electoral Votes 12

Votes cast for US Senators

2004
Total vote (x 1,000) . . . . NA
Leading party . . . . NA
Percent for leading party . . . . NA
2006
Total vote (x 1,000) 2,244
Leading party .Democratic
Percent for leading party 66.9%

Votes cast for US Representatives

2004
Total vote (x 1,000) 2,927
  Democratic 2,060
  Republican 435
Leading party .Democratic
Percent for leading party 70.4%
2006
Total vote (x 1,000) 2,244
  Democratic 1,632
  Republican 199
Leading party .Democratic
Percent for leading party 72.7%

©2008 Information Publications, Inc.
All rights reserved. Photocopying prohibited.
877-544-INFO (4636) or www.informationpublications.com

State government employment, 2006
Full-time equivalent employees 90,989
Payroll ($ mil) $414.9

Local government employment, 2006
Full-time equivalent employees 241,083
Payroll ($ mil) $979.9

Women holding public office, 2008
US Congress 1
Statewide elected office...................... 1
State legislature 49

Black public officials, 2002
Total..................................... 79
US and state legislatures 6
City/county/regional offices 60
Judicial/law enforcement.................. 2
Education/school boards 11

Hispanic public officials, 2006
Total..................................... 19
State executives & legislators 4
City/county/regional offices 10
Judicial/law enforcement.................. 0
Education/school boards 5

Governmental Finance

State government revenues, 2006
Total revenue (x $1,000)...........$45,499,157
per capita $7,071.25
General revenue (x $1,000) $36,522,412
Intergovernmental 8,801,349
Taxes 19,395,270
general sales....................4,009,371
individual income tax 10,483,437
corporate income tax 1,859,009
Current charges..................3,265,387
Miscellaneous 5,060,406

State government expenditure, 2006
Total expenditure (x $1,000) $39,880,324
per capita $6,198.00
General expenditure (x $1,000) $36,036,961
per capita, total..................$5,600.68
Education.......................1,401.12
Public welfare 1,843.16
Health 116.77
Hospitals........................70.47
Highways 261.30
Police protection................81.11
Corrections 166.52
Natural resources 48.27
Parks & recreation...............32.70
Governmental administration......233.22
Interest on general debt...........486.73

State debt & cash, 2006 ($ per capita)
Debt $10,150.18
Cash/security holdings..............$14,001.75

Federal government grants to state & local government, 2005 (x $1,000)
Total.............................$13,748,662
by Federal agency
Defense 148,664
Education 747,337
Energy 146,497
Environmental Protection Agency ... 112,379
Health & Human Services. 8,822,429
Homeland Security.................72,177
Housing & Urban Development.....1,674,041
Justice 112,513
Labor 183,753
Transportation 653,233
Veterans Affairs................... 29,049

Crime & Law Enforcement

Crime, 2006 (rates per 100,000 residents)
Property crimes 153,913
Burglary 35,181
Larceny 100,771
Motor vehicle theft 17,961
Property crime rate................2,391.0
Violent crimes......................... 28,775
Murder 186
Forcible rape......................1,742
Robbery........................... 8,047
Aggravated assault 18,800
Violent crime rate 447.0
Hate crimes............................. 448

Fraud and identity theft, 2006
Fraud complaints......................7,333
rate per 100,000 residents 113.9
Identity theft complaints 4,102
rate per 100,000 residents 63.7

Law enforcement agencies, 2006
Total agencies......................... 340
Total employees 20,410
Officers 17,032
Civilians 3,378

Prisoners, probation, and parole, 2006
Total prisoners.......................11,032
percent change, 12/31/05 to 12/31/06 .... 3.1%
in private facilities 0%
in local jails 1.6%
Sentenced to more than one year 9,472
rate per 100,000 residents 243
Adults on probation 169,522
Adults on parole.......................3,223

Prisoner demographics, June 30, 2005
(rate per 100,000 residents)
Male 687
Female 45
White 201
Black 1,635
Hispanic 1,229

©2008 Information Publications, Inc.
All rights reserved. Photocopying prohibited.
877-544-INFO (4636) or www.informationpublications.com

Arrests, 2006
Total.................................. 130,219
    Persons under 18 years of age..........17,862

Persons under sentence of death, 1/1/07
Total...................................... 0
    White..................................... 0
    Black..................................... 0
    Hispanic.................................. 0

State's highest court
Name.................. Supreme Judicial Court
Number of members........................ 7
Length of term......................to age 70
Intermediate appeals court?................yes

Labor & Income

Civilian labor force, 2006 (x 1,000)
Total................................... 3,368
    Men...................................1,770
    Women.................................1,598
    Persons 16-19 years..................... 163
    White.................................2,976
    Black..................................... 192
    Hispanic................................. 215

Civilian labor force as a percent of civilian non-institutional population, 2006
Total.................................. 67.0%
    Men....................................73.5
    Women..................................61.0
    Persons 16-19 years....................44.0
    White..................................67.4
    Black..................................61.9
    Hispanic...............................66.4

Employment, 2006 (x 1,000)
Total...................................3,198
    Men...................................1,670
    Women.................................1,528
    Persons 16-19 years..................... 144
    White.................................2,836
    Black..................................... 175
    Hispanic................................. 192

Unemployment rate, 2006
Total.................................... 5.1%
    Men.....................................5.6
    Women...................................4.4
    Persons 16-19 years....................11.4
    White...................................4.7
    Black...................................9.0
    Hispanic...............................10.9

Full-time/part-time labor force, 2003 (x 1,000)
Full-time labor force, employed.......... 2,558
Part-time labor force, employed........... 659
Unemployed, looking for
    Full-time work......................... 163
    Part-time work.......................... 35
Mean duration of unemployment (weeks)......21.5
    Median.................................11.5

Labor unions, 2006
Membership (x 1,000).................... 414
    percent of employed.................. 14.5%

Experienced civilian labor force by private industry, 2006
Total...............................2,789,469
    Natural resources & mining.......... 8,360
    Construction...................... 140,883
    Manufacturing..................... 299,389
    Trade, transportation & utilities..... 566,900
    Information.........................87,184
    Finance........................... 224,146
    Professional & business............. 472,670
    Education & health................. 571,561
    Leisure & hospitality.............. 296,219
    Other............................. 122,157

Experienced civilian labor force by occupation, May 2006
Management........................ 185,530
Business & financial.................. 169,230
Legal................................. 24,210
Sales............................... 327,560
Office & admin. support...............547,190
Computers & math................... 113,890
Architecture & engineering.............74,130
Arts & entertainment..................47,630
Education........................... 213,600
Social services....................... 58,500
Health care practitioner & technical.....197,320
Health care support.................. 94,700
Maintenance & repair..................101,130
Construction........................ 115,860
Transportation & moving............. 165,900
Production..........................177,060
Farming, fishing & forestry............. 2,900

Hours and earnings of production workers on manufacturing payrolls, 2006
Average weekly hours....................40.7
Average hourly earnings...............$18.26
Average weekly earnings..............$743.18

Income and poverty, 2006
Median household income........... $59,963
Personal income, per capita (current $)... $45,877
    in constant (2000) dollars.......... $40,048
Persons below poverty level............. 9.9%

Average annual pay
2006................................. $52,435
    increase from 2005.................. 4.7%

Federal individual income tax returns, 2005
Returns filed.......................3,083,021
Adjusted gross income ($1,000)... $206,948,515
Total tax liability ($1,000)....... $30,926,389

Charitable contributions, 2004
Number of contributions.............. 1,134.3
Total amount ($ mil)..................$3,930.4

©2008 Information Publications, Inc.
All rights reserved. Photocopying prohibited.
877-544-INFO (4636) or www.informationpublications.com

Economy, Business, Industry & Agriculture

Fortune 500 companies, 2007.............. 10
Bankruptcy cases filed, FY 2007.........13,011

Patents and trademarks issued, 2007
Patents................................3,876
Trademarks.......................... 2,056

Business firm ownership, 2002
Women-owned.......................161,918
   Sales ($ mil) $23,134
Black-owned.........................12,819
   Sales ($ mil) $1,239
Hispanic-owned.....................15,933
   Sales ($ mil) $2,068
Asian-owned 18,081
   Sales ($ mil) $5,020
Amer. Indian/Alaska Native-owned 2,220
   Sales ($ mil) $340
Hawaiian/Pacific Islander-owned 208
   Sales ($ mil) $24

Gross domestic product, 2006 ($ mil)
Total gross domestic product $337,570
   Agriculture, forestry, fishing and
     hunting 821
   Mining............................. 191
   Utilities 4,571
   Construction 14,745
   Manufacturing, durable goods........ 23,204
   Manufacturing, non-durable goods 10,116
   Wholesale trade.....................20,715
   Retail trade.......................17,826
   Transportation & warehousing 5,280
   Information 16,619
   Finance & insurance.................33,316
   Real estate, rental & leasing 50,186
   Professional and technical services 36,855
   Educational services.................. 8,267
   Health care and social assistance...... 30,229
   Accommodation/food services......... 8,395
   Other services, except government 7,017
   Government 29,588

Establishments, payroll, employees & receipts, by major industry group, 2005

Total...............................175,291
   Annual payroll ($1,000)........$140,580,627
   Paid employees 2,996,347
Forestry, fishing & agriculture............. 425
   Annual payroll ($1,000)............. $30,052
   Paid employees 1,115
Mining............................. 103
   Annual payroll ($1,000)............. $92,120
   Paid employees 1,400
   Receipts, 2002 ($1,000) $297,738

Utilities 251
   Annual payroll ($1,000)........... $949,020
   Paid employees 11,601
   Receipts, 2002 ($1,000) ....NA
Construction..........................19,326
   Annual payroll ($1,000)......... $7,118,084
   Paid employees 126,481
   Receipts, 2002 ($1,000) $31,547,604
Manufacturing.......................7,915
   Annual payroll ($1,000)......... $15,570,158
   Paid employees 285,916
   Receipts, 2002 ($1,000) $77,996,586
Wholesale trade........................8,818
   Annual payroll ($1,000)......... $9,591,832
   Paid employees 149,283
   Receipts, 2002 ($1,000) $127,129,789
Retail trade 25,839
   Annual payroll ($1,000).........$8,908,761
   Paid employees 369,290
   Receipts, 2002 ($1,000) $73,903,837
Transportation & warehousing 3,675
   Annual payroll ($1,000)...........$2,857,806
   Paid employees 77,335
   Receipts, 2002 ($1,000) $5,919,533
Information...........................3,720
   Annual payroll ($1,000)......... $7,335,491
   Paid employees 118,772
   Receipts, 2002 ($1,000) ....NA
Finance & insurance 9,731
   Annual payroll ($1,000).........$19,344,901
   Paid employees 206,327
   Receipts, 2002 ($1,000) ....NA
Professional, scientific & technical 22,073
   Annual payroll ($1,000).........$18,513,912
   Paid employees 243,889
   Receipts, 2002 ($1,000) $37,329,788
Education 2,482
   Annual payroll ($1,000)......... $5,922,084
   Paid employees 185,539
   Receipts, 2002 ($1,000) $1,130,911
Health care & social assistance 17,298
   Annual payroll ($1,000).........$19,545,348
   Paid employees 485,617
   Receipts, 2002 ($1,000) $37,307,723
Arts and entertainment 3,058
   Annual payroll ($1,000).........$1,437,862
   Paid employees 47,509
   Receipts, 2002 ($1,000) $3,310,135
Real estate 6,962
   Annual payroll ($1,000).........$2,344,568
   Paid employees 48,932
   Receipts, 2002 ($1,000) $8,440,569
Accommodation & food service.......... 15,562
   Annual payroll ($1,000).........$4,045,039
   Paid employees 241,077
   Receipts, 2002 ($1,000) $11,789,582

©2008 Information Publications, Inc.
All rights reserved. Photocopying prohibited.
877-544-INFO (4636) or www.informationpublications.com

Exports, 2006
Value of exported goods ($ mil) $24,047
  Manufactured $20,910
  Non-manufactured...................$1,383

Foreign direct investment in US affiliates, 2004
Property, plants & equipment ($ mil) ... $22,834
Employment (x 1,000)...................182.9

Agriculture, 2006
Number of farms 6,100
Farm acreage (x 1,000) 520
  Acres per farm......................... 85
Farm marketings and income ($ mil)
Total................................. $433.0
  Crops $343.6
  Livestock.............................$89.4
Net farm income $115.4

Principal commodities, in order by marketing receipts, 2005
Greenhouse/nursery, Cranberries, Dairy products, Sweet corn, Apples

Federal economic activity in state
Expenditures, 2005 ($ mil)
  Total............................. $55,830
    Per capita $8,678.17
  Defense $9,457
  Non-defense $46,373
Defense department, 2006 ($ mil)
  Payroll.............................$1,098
  Contract awards $9,077
  Grants $155
Homeland security grants ($1,000)
  2006............................. $41,246
  2007............................. $35,509

FDIC-insured financial institutions, 2005
Number 194
Assets ($ billion) $244.7
Deposits ($ billion) $173.9

Fishing, 2006
Catch (x 1,000 lbs)................... 383,466
Value ($1,000)...................... $436,903

Mining, 2006 ($ mil)
Total non-fuel mineral production $262
Percent of U.S. 0.41%

Communication, Energy & Transportation

Communication
Households with computers, 2003........ 64.1%
Households with internet access, 2003 .... 58.1%
High-speed internet providers 37
Total high-speed internet lines........2,243,743
  Residential 1,577,555
  Business........................... 666,188
Wireless phone customers, 12/2006 5,128,860

FCC-licensed stations (as of January 1, 2008)
TV stations 22
FM radio stations......................... 125
AM radio stations 73

Energy
Energy consumption, 2004
  Total (trillion Btu)....................1,543
  Per capita (million Btu) 239.7
By source of production (trillion Btu)
  Coal 105
  Natural gas.......................... 387
  Petroleum........................... 749
  Nuclear electric power 62
  Hydroelectric power.................. 10
By end-use sector (trillion Btu)
  Residential 468
  Commercial 395
  Industrial 205
  Transportation 475
Electric energy, 2005
  Primary source of electricity............ Gas
  Net generation (billion kWh) 47.5
    percent from renewable sources....... 4.8%
  Net summer capability (million kW) 14.0
  CO_2 emitted from generation 26.8
Natural gas utilities, 2005
  Customers (x 1,000) 1,430
  Sales (trillion Btu)................... 230
  Revenues ($ mil) $2,637
Nuclear plants, 2007 1
Total CO_2 emitted (million metric tons)......87.0
Energy spending, 2004 ($ mil) $17,855
  per capita $2,774
  Price per million Btu $16.18

Transportation, 2006
Public road & street mileage 35,938
  Urban..............................27,977
  Rural 7,961
  Interstate.......................... 573
Vehicle miles of travel (millions) 55,136
  per capita 8,569.0
Total motor vehicle registrations.......5,385,215
  Automobiles.......................3,310,725
  Trucks 2,063,283
  Motorcycles 143,853
Licensed drivers 4,711,735
  19 years & under 197,165
Deaths from motor vehicle accidents 430
Gasoline consumed (x 1,000 gallons) ... 2,826,663
  per capita 439.3

Commuting Statistics, 2006
Average commute time (min) 26.6
  Drove to work alone 73.7%
  Carpooled........................... 8.5%
  Public transit 8.6%
  Walk to work 4.2%
  Work from home..................... 3.6%

©2008 Information Publications, Inc.
All rights reserved. Photocopying prohibited.
877-544-INFO (4636) or www.informationpublications.com

State Summary

Capital city . . . . Lansing
Governor . . . . Jennifer Granholm
PO Box 30013
Lansing, MI 48909
517-335-7858
Admitted as a state 1837
Area (square miles) .96,716
Population, 2007 (estimate) 10,071,822
Largest city . . . . Detroit
    Population, 2006 .871,121
Personal income per capita, 2006
    (in current dollars) $33,847
Gross domestic product, 2006 ($ mil) . . . $381,003

Leading industries by payroll, 2005

Manufacturing, Health care/Social assistance,
    Professional/Scientific/Technical

**Leading agricultural commodities
by receipts, 2005**

Dairy products, Greenhouse/nursery, Corn,
    Soybeans, Cattle and calves

Geography & Environment

Total area (square miles) 96,716
    land 56,804
    water 39,912
Federally-owned land, 2004 (acres) 3,637,873
    percent 10.0%
Highest point . . . . Mt. Avron
    elevation (feet) 1,979
Lowest point . . . . .Lake Erie
    elevation (feet) 571
General coastline (miles) 0
Tidal shoreline (miles) 0
Cropland, 2003 (x 1,000 acres) 8,097
Forest land, 2003 (x 1,000 acres) 16,708
Capital city . . . . Lansing
    Population 2000 119,128
    Population 2006 114,276
Largest city . . . . .Detroit
    Population 2000 951,270
    Population 2006 871,121

Number of cities with over 100,000 population

1990 7
2000 8
2006 7

State park and recreation areas, 2005

Area (x 1,000 acres) 273
Number of visitors (x 1,000) 23,057
Revenues ($1,000) $36,095
    percent of operating expenditures 81.7%

National forest system land, 2007

Acres 2,872,833

Demographics & Population Characteristics

Population

1980 9,262,078
1990 9,295,297
2000 9,938,480
2006 10,095,643
    Male 4,969,692
    Female 5,125,951
Living in group quarters, 2006 255,247
    percent of total 2.5%
2007 (estimate) .10,071,822
    persons per square mile of land 177.3
2008 (projected) .10,345,033
2010 (projected) .10,428,683
2020 (projected) .10,695,993
2030 (projected) .10,694,172

**Population of Core-Based Statistical Areas
(formerly Metropolitan Areas), x 1,000**

	CBSA	Non-CBSA
1990	8,601	694
2000	9,153	785
2006	9,302	794

Change in population, 2000-2007

Number 133,340
    percent 1.3%
Natural increase (births minus deaths) 319,389
Net internal migration . . . . -359,758
Net international migration 155,686

Persons by age, 2006

Under 5 years 638,195
5 to 17 years 1,840,161
18 years and over 7,617,287
65 years and over 1,260,864
85 years and over .174,758
    Median age 37.2

Persons by age, 2010 (projected)

Under 5 years 681,154
18 and over 7,941,625
65 and over 1,334,491
    Median age 37.4

Race, 2006

One Race
    White 8,198,927
    Black or African American 1,444,451
    Asian 237,389
    American Indian/Alaska Native 60,820
    Hawaiian Native/Pacific Islander 3,757
Two or more races 150,299

Persons of Hispanic origin, 2006

Total Hispanic or Latino 392,770
    Mexican 281,856
    Puerto Rican 34,284
    Cuban 10,197

©2008 Information Publications, Inc.
All rights reserved. Photocopying prohibited.
877-544-INFO (4636) or www.informationpublications.com

Persons of Asian origin, 2006

Total Asian 236,972
  Asian Indian. 71,757
  Chinese 41,810
  Filipino 23,718
  Japanese 14,711
  Korean............................. 26,291
  Vietnamese.........................21,854

Marital status, 2006

Population 15 years & over 8,076,640
  Never married 2,478,408
  Married......................... 4,192,545
  Separated 119,967
  Widowed......................... 505,129
  Divorced 900,558

Language spoken at home, 2006

Population 5 years and older......... 9,456,404
  English only 8,607,334
  Spanish 292,996
  French 33,089
  German........................... 53,317
  Chinese 35,232

Households & families, 2006

Households........................ 3,869,117
  with persons under 18 years 1,301,031
  with persons over 65 years.......... 887,504
  persons per household 2.54
Families........................... 2,579,201
  persons per family.................... 3.13
Married couples..................... 1,938,688
Female householder,
  no husband present................. 475,035
One-person households 1,082,712

Nativity, 2006

Number of residents born in state 7,638,467
  percent of population................. 75.7%

Immigration & naturalization, 2006

Legal permanent residents admitted......20,911
Persons naturalized 11,675
Non-immigrant admissions 373,108

Vital Statistics and Health

Marriages

2004 61,932
2005 61,108
2006 59,162

Divorces

2004 34,701
2005 34,580
2006 35,596

Health risks, 2006

Percent of adults who are:
  Smokers......................... 22.4%
  Overweight (BMI > 25)............... 64.8%
  Obese (BMI > 30)................... 28.8%

Births

2005 127,706
  Birthrate (per 1,000).................. 12.6
  White........................... 100,039
  Black 22,509
  Hispanic 8,611
  Asian/Pacific Islander 4,429
  Amer. Indian/Alaska Native............ 729
  Low birth weight (2,500g or less)....... 8.3%
  Cesarian births 28.8%
  Preterm births 12.5%
  To unmarried mothers................ 36.6%
  Twin births (per 1,000) 34.2
  Triplets or higher order (per 100,000)....229.0
2006 (preliminary)................... 127,476
  rate per 1,000 .... 12.6

Deaths

2004
All causes 85,169
  rate per 100,000..................... 812.6
Heart disease 24,825
  rate per 100,000..................... 234.3
Malignant neoplasms 19,653
  rate per 100,000..................... 189.5
Cerebrovascular disease................ 5,290
  rate per 100,000..................... 49.9
Chronic lower respiratory disease 4,252
  rate per 100,000..................... 41.0
Diabetes............................ 2,953
  rate per 100,000..................... 28.4
2005 (preliminary)................... 86,868
  rate per 100,000..................... 812.3
2006 (provisional) 84,716

Infant deaths

2004 984
  rate per 1,000 .... 7.6
2005 (provisional) 1,014
  rate per 1,000 .... 7.9

Exercise routines, 2005

None............................. 22.5%
Moderate or greater.................. 49.5%
Vigorous 28.1%

Abortions, 2004

Total performed in state................ 26,269
  rate per 1,000 women age 15-44.......... 12
  % obtained by out-of-state residents 2.9%

Physicians, 2005

Total............................. 24,387
  rate per 100,000 persons 241

Community hospitals, 2005

Number of hospitals 146
Beds (x 1,000)........................ 26.2
Patients admitted (x 1,000) 1,198
Average daily census (x 1,000) 17.6
Average cost per day $1,460
Outpatient visits (x 1 mil) 26.1

©2008 Information Publications, Inc.
All rights reserved. Photocopying prohibited.
877-544-INFO (4636) or www.informationpublications.com

Disability status of population, 2006
5 to 15 years 7.3%
16 to 64 years 13.5%
65 years and over 40.2%

Education

Educational attainment, 2006
Population over 25 years 6,638,666
Less than 9th grade. 3.8%
High school graduate or more 87.2%
College graduate or more. 24.5%
Graduate or professional degree. 9.2%

Public school enrollment, 2005-06
Total 1,741,845
Pre-kindergarten through grade 8. . . 1,165,704
Grades 9 through 12 538,642

Graduating public high school seniors, 2004-05
Diplomas (incl. GED and others) 101,835

SAT scores, 2007
Average critical reading score 568
Average writing score 553
Average math score 579
Percent of graduates taking test 9%

Public school teachers, 2006-07 (estimate)
Total (x 1,000) 109.9
Elementary 60.9
Secondary 49.0
Average salary $54,895
Elementary $54,895
Secondary $54,895

State receipts & expenditures for public schools, 2006-07 (estimate)
Revenue receipts ($ mil) $19,580
Expenditures
Total ($ mil) $19,010
Per capita $1,754
Per pupil $11,149

NAEP proficiency scores, 2007

	Reading		Math	
	Basic	Proficient	Basic	Proficient
Grade 4	66.2%	32.4%	79.9%	37.1%
Grade 8	72.1%	28.2%	66.4%	28.9%

Higher education enrollment, fall 2005
Total 121,165
Full-time men 29,917
Full-time women 42,762
Part-time men 17,315
Part-time women 31,171

Minority enrollment in institutions of higher education, 2005
Black, non-Hispanic 83,007
Hispanic 17,520
Asian/Pacific Islander 20,819
American Indian/Alaska Native 5,271

Institutions of higher education, 2005-06
Total 104
Public. 45
Private 59

Earned degrees conferred, 2004-05
Associate's 23,509
Bachelor's 51,207
Master's 22,834
First-professional. 2,942
Doctor's 1,634

Public Libraries, 2006
Number of libraries. 383
Number of outlets 672
Annual visits per capita 4.8
Circulation per capita 6.6

State & local financial support for higher education, FY 2006
Full-time equivalent enrollment (x 1,000) 377.7
Appropriations per FTE $5,799

Social Insurance & Welfare Programs

Social Security benefits & beneficiaries, 2005
Beneficiaries (x 1,000) 1,743
Retired & dependents 1,189
Survivors 247
Disabled & dependents. 306
Annual benefit payments ($ mil) $20,106
Retired & dependents. $13,193
Survivors $3,599
Disabled & dependents. $3,315
Average monthly benefit
Retired & dependents $1,080
Disabled & dependents. $994
Widowed $1,043

Medicare, July 2005
Enrollment (x 1,000) 1,483
Payments ($ mil) $11,693

Medicaid, 2004
Beneficiaries (x 1,000). 1,799
Payments ($ mil) $7,697

State Children's Health Insurance Program, 2006
Enrollment (x 1,000) 118.5
Expenditures ($ mil) $95.5

Persons without health insurance, 2006
Number (x 1,000) 1,043
percent 10.5%
Number of children (x 1,000) 116
percent of children 4.7%

Health care expenditures, 2004
Total expenditures. $51,048
per capita $5,058

Federal and state public aid

State unemployment insurance, 2006
Recipients, first payments (x 1,000) 476
Total payments ($ mil) $1,960
Average weekly benefit $294
Temporary Assistance for Needy Families, 2006
Recipients (x 1,000) 2,560.0
Families (x 1,000) 970.4
Supplemental Security Income, 2005
Recipients (x 1,000) 222.1
Payments ($ mil) $1,157.3
Food Stamp Program, 2006
Avg monthly participants (x 1,000) 1,133.8
Total benefits ($ mil) $1,238.8

Housing & Construction

Housing units

Total 2005 (estimate) 4,478,354
Total 2006 (estimate) 4,513,726
Seasonal or recreational use, 2006 246,759
Owner-occupied, 2006 2,908,273
  Median home value $153,300
  Homeowner vacancy rate 3.4%
Renter-occupied, 2006 960,844
  Median rent $675
  Rental vacancy rate 18.1%
Home ownership rate, 2005 . . . . 76.4%
Home ownership rate, 2006 . . . . 77.4%

New privately-owned housing units

Number authorized, 2006 (x 1,000) 29.2
  Value ($ mil) $4,492.9
Started 2005 (x 1,000, estimate) 51.7
Started 2006 (x 1,000, estimate) 50.7

Existing home sales

2005 (x 1,000) 208.6
2006 (x 1,000) 182.4

Government & Elections

State officials 2008

Governor . . . . Jennifer Granholm
    Democratic, term expires 1/11
Lieutenant Governor . . . . John Cherry
Secretary of State . . . . Terri Lynn Land
Attorney General . . . . Mike Cox
Chief Justice . . . . Clifford Taylor

Governorship

Minimum age 30
Length of term . . . . 4 years
Consecutive terms permitted 2
Who succeeds . . . . Lieutenant Governor

Local governments by type, 2002

Total 2,804
  County 83
  Municipal 533
  Township 1,242
  School District 580
  Special District 366

State legislature

Name . . . . Legislature
Upper chamber . . . . Senate
  Number of members 38
  Length of term . . . . 4 years
  Party in majority, 2008 . . . . Republican
Lower chamber . . . . House of Representatives
  Number of members 110
  Length of term . . . . 2 years
  Party in majority, 2008 . . . . Democratic

Federal representation, 2008 (110th Congress)

Senator . . . . Carl Levin
  Party . . . . Democratic
  Year term expires 2009
Senator . . . . Debbie Stabenow
  Party . . . . Democratic
  Year term expires 2013
Representatives, total 15
  Democrats 6
  Republicans 9

Voters in November 2006 election (estimate)

Total 4,087,790
Male 1,945,650
Female 2,142,140
White 3,412,356
Black 545,729
Hispanic 43,137
Asian 53,652

Presidential election, 2004

Total Popular Vote 4,839,252
  Kerry 2,479,183
  Bush 2,313,746
Total Electoral Votes 17

Votes cast for US Senators

2004
Total vote (x 1,000) . . . . NA
Leading party . . . . NA
Percent for leading party . . . . NA
2006
Total vote (x 1,000) 3,780
Leading party . . . . Democratic
Percent for leading party 56.9%

Votes cast for US Representatives

2004
Total vote (x 1,000) 4,631
  Democratic 2,242
  Republican 2,289
Leading party . . . . Republican
Percent for leading party 49.4%
2006
Total vote (x 1,000) 3,646
  Democratic 1,923
  Republican 1,625
Leading party . . . . Democratic
Percent for leading party 52.7%

©2008 Information Publications, Inc.
All rights reserved. Photocopying prohibited.
877-544-INFO (4636) or www.informationpublications.com

State government employment, 2006
Full-time equivalent employees 134,918
Payroll ($ mil) $560.3

Local government employment, 2006
Full-time equivalent employees 351,779
Payroll ($ mil) $1,328.2

Women holding public office, 2008
US Congress 3
Statewide elected office....................... 2
State legislature 29

Black public officials, 2002
Total..................................... 353
US and state legislatures 24
City/county/regional offices 153
Judicial/law enforcement................. 62
Education/school boards................ 114

Hispanic public officials, 2006
Total 16
State executives & legislators 3
City/county/regional offices 3
Judicial/law enforcement.................. 3
Education/school boards................. 7

Governmental Finance

State government revenues, 2006
Total revenue (x $1,000)...........$62,087,004
per capita $6,145.82
General revenue (x $1,000) $46,001,404
Intergovernmental 12,551,526
Taxes 23,714,514
general sales..................8,080,905
individual income tax 6,226,304
corporate income tax 1,886,168
Current charges...................5,896,047
Miscellaneous 3,839,317

State government expenditure, 2006
Total expenditure (x $1,000).......$53,087,424
per capita $5,254.97
General expenditure (x $1,000) $46,793,387
per capita, total.................. $4,631.94
Education.......................2,107.34
Public welfare 1,174.22
Health 97.92
Hospitals.........................201.75
Highways 274.27
Police protection................... 32.55
Corrections 170.34
Natural resources 35.45
Parks & recreation 8.51
Governmental administration.......117.43
Interest on general debt........... 105.85

State debt & cash, 2006 ($ per capita)
Debt $2,869.22
Cash/security holdings..............$9,909.08

Federal government grants to state & local government, 2005 (x $1,000)
Total..........................$13,313,206
by Federal agency
Defense 37,876
Education 1,168,870
Energy 117,557
Environmental Protection Agency ... 166,638
Health & Human Services. 8,220,031
Homeland Security................. 25,671
Housing & Urban Development...... 882,237
Justice 148,169
Labor 351,787
Transportation 1,185,101
Veterans Affairs...................17,199

Crime & Law Enforcement

Crime, 2006 (rates per 100,000 residents)
Property crimes 324,351
Burglary 76,107
Larceny 198,227
Motor vehicle theft 50,017
Property crime rate..................3,212.8
Violent crimes........................ 56,778
Murder 713
Forcible rape....................... 5,269
Robbery.......................... 14,208
Aggravated assault 36,588
Violent crime rate 562.4
Hate crimes........................... 739

Fraud and identity theft, 2006
Fraud complaints.....................11,665
rate per 100,000 residents 115.5
Identity theft complaints 6,784
rate per 100,000 residents 67.2

Law enforcement agencies, 2006
Total agencies............................ 600
Total employees...................... 25,896
Officers 19,228
Civilians 6,668

Prisoners, probation, and parole, 2006
Total prisoners........................51,577
percent change, 12/31/05 to 12/31/06 .... 4.1%
in private facilities 0%
in local jails 0.1%
Sentenced to more than one year 51,577
rate per 100,000 residents 511
Adults on probation 182,650
Adults on parole....................... 18,486

Prisoner demographics, June 30, 2005 (rate per 100,000 residents)
Male 1,262
Female 85
White 412
Black.................................. 2,262
Hispanic 397

©2008 Information Publications, Inc.
All rights reserved. Photocopying prohibited.
877-544-INFO (4636) or www.informationpublications.com

Arrests, 2006
Total............................... 324,698
  Persons under 18 years of age 44,002

Persons under sentence of death, 1/1/07
Total.. 0
  White....................................... 0
  Black....................................... 0
  Hispanic 0

State's highest court
Name ....Supreme Court
Number of members...................... 7
Length of term........................ 8 years
Intermediate appeals court? ....yes

Labor & Income

Civilian labor force, 2006 (x 1,000)
Total................................. 5,086
  Men 2,699
  Women 2,387
  Persons 16-19 years.................... 272
  White................................ 4,232
  Black 610
  Hispanic 178

Civilian labor force as a percent of civilian non-institutional population, 2006
Total................................. 65.1%
  Men 71.4
  Women 59.2
  Persons 16-19 years...................46.5
  White.................................65.7
  Black 59.3
  Hispanic 69.9

Employment, 2006 (x 1,000)
Total.................................4,732
  Men 2,502
  Women 2,230
  Persons 16-19 years................... 220
  White................................3,970
  Black 532
  Hispanic 168

Unemployment rate, 2006
Total................................. 7.0%
  Men 7.3
  Women 6.6
  Persons 16-19 years...................19.2
  White.................................6.2
  Black 12.8
  Hispanic 5.5

Full-time/part-time labor force, 2003 (x 1,000)
Full-time labor force, employed 3,694
Part-time labor force, employed........... 980
Unemployed, looking for
  Full-time work......................... 304
  Part-time work.......................... 64
Mean duration of unemployment (weeks)......20.1
  Median 10.4

Labor unions, 2006
Membership (x 1,000).................... 842
  percent of employed 19.6%

Experienced civilian labor force by private industry, 2006
Total.............................3,613,440
  Natural resources & mining 31,028
  Construction 175,278
  Manufacturing..................... 649,203
  Trade, transportation & utilities 786,053
  Information 65,252
  Finance 210,249
  Professional & business 581,769
  Education & health 562,870
  Leisure & hospitality............... 403,143
  Other 130,914

Experienced civilian labor force by occupation, May 2006
Management......................... 175,640
Business & financial 197,100
Legal................................ 22,970
Sales.............................. 448,050
Office & admin. support............. 687,690
Computers & math 94,090
Architecture & engineering........... 134,900
Arts & entertainment 53,150
Education 261,730
Social services 51,700
Health care practitioner & technical.... 233,860
Health care support 124,550
Maintenance & repair................ 173,840
Construction 162,550
Transportation & moving 295,220
Production 462,350
Farming, fishing & forestry..............5,770

Hours and earnings of production workers on manufacturing payrolls, 2006
Average weekly hours 42.2
Average hourly earnings $21.83
Average weekly earnings $921.23

Income and poverty, 2006
Median household income.............$47,182
Personal income, per capita (current $)... $33,847
  in constant (2000) dollars $29,546
Persons below poverty level.............. 13.5%

Average annual pay
2006 .... $42,157
  increase from 2005 .... 2.3%

Federal individual income tax returns, 2005
Returns filed.......................4,562,770
Adjusted gross income ($1,000) ... $226,438,921
Total tax liability ($1,000) $27,538,094

Charitable contributions, 2004
Number of contributions............... 1,483.1
Total amount ($ mil).................$5,273.9

©2008 Information Publications, Inc.
All rights reserved. Photocopying prohibited.
877-544-INFO (4636) or www.informationpublications.com

Economy, Business, Industry & Agriculture

Fortune 500 companies, 2007 22
Bankruptcy cases filed, FY 2007 43,806

Patents and trademarks issued, 2007

Patents 3,797
Trademarks 2,140

Business firm ownership, 2002

Women-owned 217,673
   Sales ($ mil) $29,217
Black-owned 44,366
   Sales ($ mil) $4,294
Hispanic-owned 9,841
   Sales ($ mil) $3,184
Asian-owned 15,337
   Sales ($ mil) $5,111
Amer. Indian/Alaska Native-owned 5,365
   Sales ($ mil) $773
Hawaiian/Pacific Islander-owned 196
   Sales ($ mil) $37

Gross domestic product, 2006 ($ mil)

Total gross domestic product $381,003
   Agriculture, forestry, fishing and
      hunting 2,123
   Mining 1,585
   Utilities 8,754
   Construction 15,958
   Manufacturing, durable goods 53,768
   Manufacturing, non-durable goods . . . 14,587
   Wholesale trade 23,441
   Retail trade 25,881
   Transportation & warehousing 9,102
   Information 10,837
   Finance & insurance 23,336
   Real estate, rental & leasing 47,141
   Professional and technical services 29,644
   Educational services 2,470
   Health care and social assistance 29,649
   Accommodation/food services 8,603
   Other services, except government 8,780
   Government 41,127

Establishments, payroll, employees & receipts, by major industry group, 2005

Total 237,523
   Annual payroll ($1,000) $148,456,286
   Paid employees 3,796,876
Forestry, fishing & agriculture 604
   Annual payroll ($1,000) $93,514
   Paid employees 3,103
Mining 442
   Annual payroll ($1,000) $327,428
   Paid employees 5,464
   Receipts, 2002 ($1,000) $1,427,350

Utilities 401
   Annual payroll ($1,000) $1,608,841
   Paid employees .23,935
   Receipts, 2002 ($1,000) . . . . .NA
Construction 26,168
   Annual payroll ($1,000) $7,589,911
   Paid employees 160,493
   Receipts, 2002 ($1,000) $36,536,275
Manufacturing 14,033
   Annual payroll ($1,000) $31,631,273
   Paid employees 635,234
   Receipts, 2002 ($1,000) $221,433,262
Wholesale trade 11,981
   Annual payroll ($1,000) $9,277,616
   Paid employees 172,853
   Receipts, 2002 ($1,000) $165,958,945
Retail trade 38,675
   Annual payroll ($1,000) $10,364,568
   Paid employees 499,121
   Receipts, 2002 ($1,000) $109,350,139
Transportation & warehousing 5,557
   Annual payroll ($1,000) $4,040,167
   Paid employees .99,822
   Receipts, 2002 ($1,000) $9,189,132
Information 3,895
   Annual payroll ($1,000) $4,514,440
   Paid employees .84,575
   Receipts, 2002 ($1,000) . . . . .NA
Finance & insurance 13,915
   Annual payroll ($1,000) $8,744,903
   Paid employees 163,807
   Receipts, 2002 ($1,000) . . . . .NA
Professional, scientific & technical 22,701
   Annual payroll ($1,000) $18,336,119
   Paid employees 291,171
   Receipts, 2002 ($1,000) $24,220,096
Education 2,081
   Annual payroll ($1,000) $1,445,064
   Paid employees .64,882
   Receipts, 2002 ($1,000) $687,578
Health care & social assistance 25,348
   Annual payroll ($1,000) $19,567,164
   Paid employees 528,673
   Receipts, 2002 ($1,000) $39,441,794
Arts and entertainment 3,647
   Annual payroll ($1,000) $1,525,685
   Paid employees .55,389
   Receipts, 2002 ($1,000) $4,715,019
Real estate 9,200
   Annual payroll ($1,000) $1,813,884
   Paid employees .59,018
   Receipts, 2002 ($1,000) . . . . .NA
Accommodation & food service 19,297
   Annual payroll ($1,000) $3,861,399
   Paid employees 331,065
   Receipts, 2002 ($1,000) $12,248,269

©2008 Information Publications, Inc.
All rights reserved. Photocopying prohibited.
877-544-INFO (4636) or www.informationpublications.com

8   Michigan

Exports, 2006
Value of exported goods ($ mil) $40,405
   Manufactured $35,342
   Non-manufactured................. $2,738

Foreign direct investment in US affiliates, 2004
Property, plants & equipment ($ mil) ... $38,886
Employment (x 1,000)..................201.0

Agriculture, 2006
Number of farms 53,000
Farm acreage (x 1,000) 10,100
   Acres per farm........................ 191
Farm marketings and income ($ mil)
Total................................$4,487.8
   Crops.............................$2,833.4
   Livestock.........................$1,654.4
Net farm income $1,321.2

Principal commodities, in order by marketing receipts, 2005
   Dairy products, Greenhouse/nursery, Corn,
     Soybeans, Cattle and calves

Federal economic activity in state
Expenditures, 2005 ($ mil)
   Total............................. $64,787
     Per capita $6,414.02
   Defense $5,026
   Non-defense...................... $59,760
Defense department, 2006 ($ mil)
   Payroll..........................$1,307
   Contract awards $3,898
   Grants $98
Homeland security grants ($1,000)
   2006........................... $46,899
   2007........................... $39,237

FDIC-insured financial institutions, 2005
Number............................... 171
Assets ($ billion) $231.5
Deposits ($ billion) $163.1

Fishing, 2006
Catch (x 1,000 lbs)......................9,351
Value ($1,000)....................... $5,977

Mining, 2006 ($ mil)
Total non-fuel mineral production $2,010
Percent of U.S....................... 3.12%

Communication, Energy & Transportation

Communication
Households with computers, 2003........ 59.9%
Households with internet access, 2003 .... 52.0%
High-speed internet providers 67
Total high-speed internet lines........2,416,451
   Residential 1,734,686
   Business.........................681,765
Wireless phone customers, 12/2006 7,093,721

FCC-licensed stations (as of January 1, 2008)
TV stations 54
FM radio stations....................... 304
AM radio stations 133

Energy
Energy consumption, 2004
   Total (trillion Btu)....................3,119
   Per capita (million Btu) 309.1
By source of production (trillion Btu)
   Coal 774
   Natural gas........................... 918
   Petroleum...........................1,034
   Nuclear electric power 319
   Hydroelectric power.................... 15
By end-use sector (trillion Btu)
   Residential 799
   Commercial 629
   Industrial 885
   Transportation 807
Electric energy, 2005
   Primary source of electricity........... Coal
   Net generation (billion kWh) 121.6
     percent from renewable sources....... 3.3%
   Net summer capability (million kW) 30.4
   CO_2 emitted from generation 78.7
Natural gas utilities, 2005
   Customers (x 1,000) 3,451
   Sales (trillion Btu)..................... 767
   Revenues ($ mil) $4,947
Nuclear plants, 2007 4
Total CO_2 emitted (million metric tons).....184.9
Energy spending, 2004 ($ mil) $27,063
   per capita $2,681
   Price per million Btu $12.24

Transportation, 2006
Public road & street mileage 121,722
   Urban...............................35,619
   Rural 86,103
   Interstate............................1,241
Vehicle miles of travel (millions) 104,184
   per capita 10,312.9
Total motor vehicle registrations.......8,154,235
   Automobiles......................4,765,547
   Trucks 3,362,440
   Motorcycles 247,988
Licensed drivers 7,112,992
   19 years & under 373,957
Deaths from motor vehicle accidents 1,085
Gasoline consumed (x 1,000 gallons) 4,879,874
   per capita 483.0

Commuting Statistics, 2006
Average commute time (min) 23.4
   Drove to work alone 82.9%
   Carpooled............................ 9.1%
   Public transit 1.2%
   Walk to work 2.2%
   Work from home...................... 3.4%

©2008 Information Publications, Inc.
All rights reserved. Photocopying prohibited.
877-544-INFO (4636) or www.informationpublications.com

State Summary

Capital city . . . . St. Paul
Governor . . . . Tim Pawlenty

130 State Capitol
75 Rev Dr MLK Jr Blvd
St Paul, MN 55155
651-296-3391

Admitted as a state 1858
Area (square miles) 86,939
Population, 2007 (estimate) 5,197,621
Largest city . . . . Minneapolis
Population, 2006 372,833
Personal income per capita, 2006
(in current dollars) $38,712
Gross domestic product, 2006 ($ mil) . . . $244,546

Leading industries by payroll, 2005

Manufacturing, Health care/Social assistance,
Finance & Insurance

**Leading agricultural commodities
by receipts, 2005**

Corn, Hogs, Soybeans, Dairy products, Cattle
and calves

Geography & Environment

Total area (square miles). 86,939
land 79,610
water 7,329
Federally-owned land, 2004 (acres) 2,873,517
percent 5.6%
Highest point . . . . Eagle Mountain
elevation (feet) 2,301
Lowest point . . . . Lake Superior
elevation (feet) 601
General coastline (miles) 0
Tidal shoreline (miles) 0
Cropland, 2003 (x 1,000 acres) 21,100
Forest land, 2003 (x 1,000 acres). 16,357
Capital city . . . . St. Paul
Population 2000 .287,151
Population 2006 273,535
Largest city . . . . Minneapolis
Population 2000 382,618
Population 2006 372,833

Number of cities with over 100,000 population

1990 2
2000 2
2006 2

State park and recreation areas, 2005

Area (x 1,000 acres) 220
Number of visitors (x 1,000) 8,245
Revenues ($1,000) $15,025
percent of operating expenditures 46.0%

National forest system land, 2007

Acres 2,840,746

Demographics & Population Characteristics

Population

1980 4,075,970
1990 4,375,099
2000 4,919,492
2006 5,167,101
Male 2,568,869
Female 2,598,232
Living in group quarters, 2006 141,703
percent of total 2.7%
2007 (estimate) 5,197,621
persons per square mile of land 65.3
2008 (projected) .5,321,587
2010 (projected) .5,420,636
2020 (projected) .5,900,769
2030 (projected) .6,306,130

**Population of Core-Based Statistical Areas
(formerly Metropolitan Areas), x 1,000**

	CBSA	Non-CBSA
1990	3,750	626
2000	4,266	654
2006	4,510	657

Change in population, 2000-2007

Number 278,129
percent 5.7%
Natural increase (births minus deaths) 238,111
Net internal migration . . . . -34,997
Net international migration 89,636

Persons by age, 2006

Under 5 years 345,250
5 to 17 years 912,014
18 years and over 3,909,837
65 years and over .627,394
85 years and over .101,634
Median age 36.8

Persons by age, 2010 (projected)

Under 5 years 369,571
18 and over 4,130,673
65 and over 670,429
Median age 36.5

Race, 2006

One Race
White 4,615,613
Black or African American 231,053
Asian 181,065
American Indian/Alaska Native 60,491
Hawaiian Native/Pacific Islander 2,766
Two or more races. 76,113

Persons of Hispanic origin, 2006

Total Hispanic or Latino 195,138
Mexican 138,368
Puerto Rican 8,813
Cuban 1,902

©2008 Information Publications, Inc.
All rights reserved. Photocopying prohibited.
877-544-INFO (4636) or www.informationpublications.com

Persons of Asian origin, 2006

Total Asian 179,295
  Asian Indian. 28,669
  Chinese 20,540
  Filipino 7,828
  Japanese 2,936
  Korean. 14,450
  Vietnamese. 23,563

Marital status, 2006

Population 15 years & over 4,134,380
  Never married 1,251,658
  Married. 2,267,495
  Separated 48,648
  Widowed. 230,610
  Divorced 384,617

Language spoken at home, 2006

Population 5 years and older. 4,819,697
  English only 4,356,565
  Spanish 171,042
  French 15,622
  German. 29,438
  Chinese 15,296

Households & families, 2006

Households. 2,042,297
  with persons under 18 years 679,983
  with persons over 65 years. 426,838
  persons per household 2.46
Families. 1,330,451
  persons per family. 3.03
Married couples. 1,064,699
Female householder,
  no husband present. 185,465
One-person households 573,640

Nativity, 2006

Number of residents born in state 3,570,653
  percent of population. 69.1%

Immigration & naturalization, 2006

Legal permanent residents admitted. 18,254
Persons naturalized 9,137
Non-immigrant admissions 158,805

Vital Statistics and Health

Marriages

2004 30,359
2005 30,515
2006 30,916

Divorces

2004 14,235
2005 . . . . NA
2006 . . . . NA

Health risks, 2006

Percent of adults who are:
  Smokers. 18.3%
  Overweight (BMI > 25). 62.7%
  Obese (BMI > 30). 24.7%

Births

2005 70,919
  Birthrate (per 1,000). 13.8
  White. 57,776
  Black 6,898
  Hispanic 5,509
  Asian/Pacific Islander 4,777
  Amer. Indian/Alaska Native 1,468
  Low birth weight (2,500g or less). 6.5%
  Cesarian births 25.3%
  Preterm births 10.7%
  To unmarried mothers. 29.8%
  Twin births (per 1,000) 33.5
  Triplets or higher order (per 100,000). . . 208.9
2006 (preliminary). 73,559
  rate per 1,000 . . . . .14.2

Deaths

2004
All causes 37,034
  rate per 100,000. . . . . .691.2
Heart disease 7,891
  rate per 100,000. . . . . .144.3
Malignant neoplasms 9,093
  rate per 100,000. . . . . .176.4
Cerebrovascular disease. 2,542
  rate per 100,000. .46.2
Chronic lower respiratory disease 1,839
  rate per 100,000. .35.4
Diabetes. 1,130
  rate per 100,000. .21.4
2005 (preliminary). 37,537
  rate per 100,000. . . . . .683.9
2006 (provisional) 36,982

Infant deaths

2004 332
  rate per 1,000 . . . . .4.7
2005 (provisional) 370
  rate per 1,000 . . . . .5.2

Exercise routines, 2005

None. 16.2%
Moderate or greater. 51.0%
Vigorous 28.3%

Abortions, 2004

Total performed in state. 13,791
  rate per 1,000 women age 15-44. 13
  % obtained by out-of-state residents 7.5%

Physicians, 2005

Total. 14,595
  rate per 100,000 persons 285

Community hospitals, 2005

Number of hospitals 133
Beds (x 1,000). 16.0
Patients admitted (x 1,000) 635
Average daily census (x 1,000) 11.0
Average cost per day $1,300
Outpatient visits (x 1 mil) 9.4

©2008 Information Publications, Inc.
All rights reserved. Photocopying prohibited.
877-544-INFO (4636) or www.informationpublications.com

Disability status of population, 2006
5 to 15 years 6.1%
16 to 64 years 10.1%
65 years and over 34.8%

Education

Educational attainment, 2006
Population over 25 years 3,387,448
  Less than 9th grade..................... 3.8%
  High school graduate or more 90.7%
  College graduate or more............. 30.4%
  Graduate or professional degree........ 9.6%

Public school enrollment, 2005-06
Total.............................. 839,243
  Pre-kindergarten through grade 8..... 557,493
  Grades 9 through 12 281,486

Graduating public high school seniors, 2004-05
Diplomas (incl. GED and others) 58,391

SAT scores, 2007
Average critical reading score 596
Average writing score 577
Average math score 603
Percent of graduates taking test 9%

Public school teachers, 2006-07 (estimate)
Total (x 1,000) 50.2
  Elementary............................ 25.1
  Secondary............................. 25.1
Average salary $49,634
  Elementary........................ $49,634
  Secondary......................... $49,634

State receipts & expenditures for public schools, 2006-07 (estimate)
Revenue receipts ($ mil) $9,429
Expenditures
Total ($ mil) $10,623
  Per capita $1,627
  Per pupil $10,809

NAEP proficiency scores, 2007

	Reading		Math	
	Basic	Proficient	Basic	Proficient
Grade 4	72.8%	36.9%	87.5%	50.6%
Grade 8	80.2%	36.6%	81.0%	43.1%

Higher education enrollment, fall 2005
Total.............................. 120,848
  Full-time men 30,471
  Full-time women................... 50,523
  Part-time men 13,865
  Part-time women................... 25,989

Minority enrollment in institutions of higher education, 2005
Black, non-Hispanic 24,452
Hispanic 8,368
Asian/Pacific Islander 15,670
American Indian/Alaska Native.......... 4,253

Institutions of higher education, 2005-06
Total.................................. 109
  Public............................... 42
  Private 67

Earned degrees conferred, 2004-05
Associate's........................... 15,469
Bachelor's 28,275
Master's 13,052
First-professional...................... 1,759
Doctor's.............................. 1,239

Public Libraries, 2006
Number of libraries...................... 140
Number of outlets 373
Annual visits per capita 5.2
Circulation per capita.................... 9.9

State & local financial support for higher education, FY 2006
Full-time equivalent enrollment (x 1,000).... 189.0
Appropriations per FTE............... $5,907

Social Insurance & Welfare Programs

Social Security benefits & beneficiaries, 2005
Beneficiaries (x 1,000) 786
  Retired & dependents.................. 575
  Survivors............................ 100
  Disabled & dependents................. 112
Annual benefit payments ($ mil) $8,525
  Retired & dependents................ $5,959
  Survivors.......................... $1,425
  Disabled & dependents............... $1,140
Average monthly benefit
  Retired & dependents............... $1,004
  Disabled & dependents................. $922
  Widowed............................ $988

Medicare, July 2005
Enrollment (x 1,000).................... 698
Payments ($ mil) $3,861

Medicaid, 2004
Beneficiaries (x 1,000)................... 698
Payments ($ mil) $4,575

State Children's Health Insurance Program, 2006
Enrollment (x 1,000).................... 5.3
Expenditures ($ mil).................... $39.4

Persons without health insurance, 2006
Number (x 1,000)....................... 475
  percent............................ 9.2%
Number of children (x 1,000) 104
  percent of children 8.3%

Health care expenditures, 2004
Total expenditures.................... $29,524
  per capita $5,795

©2008 Information Publications, Inc.
All rights reserved. Photocopying prohibited.
877-544-INFO (4636) or www.informationpublications.com

Federal and state public aid

State unemployment insurance, 2006
Recipients, first payments (x 1,000) 141
Total payments ($ mil) $663
Average weekly benefit $333
Temporary Assistance for Needy Families, 2006
Recipients (x 1,000) 790.9
Families (x 1,000) 326.9
Supplemental Security Income, 2005
Recipients (x 1,000) 72.9
Payments ($ mil) $354.5
Food Stamp Program, 2006
Avg monthly participants (x 1,000) 264.0
Total benefits ($ mil) $282.4

Housing & Construction

Housing units
Total 2005 (estimate) 2,251,975
Total 2006 (estimate) 2,283,453
Seasonal or recreational use, 2006 110,451
Owner-occupied, 2006 1,558,206
  Median home value $208,200
  Homeowner vacancy rate 2.0%
Renter-occupied, 2006 484,091
  Median rent $701
  Rental vacancy rate 8.9%
Home ownership rate, 2005 . . . . 76.5%
Home ownership rate, 2006 . . . . 75.6%

New privately-owned housing units
Number authorized, 2006 (x 1,000) 26.4
  Value ($ mil) $4,842.7
Started 2005 (x 1,000, estimate) 39.0
Started 2006 (x 1,000, estimate) 37.1

Existing home sales
2005 (x 1,000) 134.9
2006 (x 1,000) 115.4

Government & Elections

State officials 2008
Governor . . . . Tim Pawlenty
    Republican, term expires 1/11
Lieutenant Governor . . . . Carol Molnau
Secretary of State . . . . .Mark Ritchie
Attorney General . . . . Lori Swanson
Chief Justice . . . . .Russell Anderson

Governorship
Minimum age 25
Length of term . . . . 4 years
Consecutive terms permitted . . . . . . not specified
Who succeeds . . . . Lieutenant Governor

Local governments by type, 2002
Total 3,482
  County 87
  Municipal 854
  Township 1,793
  School District 345
  Special District 403

State legislature
Name . . . . Legislature
Upper chamber . . . . .Senate
  Number of members 67
  Length of term . . . . 4 years
  Party in majority, 2008 . . . . .Democratic
Lower chamber . . . . . . .House of Representatives
  Number of members 134
  Length of term . . . . 2 years
  Party in majority, 2008 . . . . .Democratic

Federal representation, 2008 (110th Congress)
Senator . . . . Norm Coleman
  Party . . . . Republican
  Year term expires 2009
Senator . . . . Amy Klobuchar
  Party . . . . .Democratic
  Year term expires 2013
Representatives, total 8
  Democrats 5
  Republicans 3

Voters in November 2006 election (estimate)
Total 2,374,680
Male 1,173,376
Female 1,201,304
White 2,287,760
Black 53,199
Hispanic 11,895
Asian 16,222

Presidential election, 2004
Total Popular Vote 2,828,387
  Kerry 1,445,014
  Bush 1,346,695
Total Electoral Votes 10

Votes cast for US Senators
2004
Total vote (x 1,000) . . . . NA
Leading party . . . . NA
Percent for leading party . . . . NA
2006
Total vote (x 1,000) 2,203
Leading party .Democratic
Percent for leading party 58.1%

Votes cast for US Representatives
2004
Total vote (x 1,000) 2,722
  Democratic 1,400
  Republican 1,236
Leading party .Democratic
Percent for leading party 51.4%
2006
Total vote (x 1,000) 2,179
  Democratic 1,153
  Republican 925
Leading party .Democratic
Percent for leading party 52.9%

©2008 Information Publications, Inc.
All rights reserved. Photocopying prohibited.
877-544-INFO (4636) or www.informationpublications.com

State government employment, 2006
Full-time equivalent employees 76,795
Payroll ($ mil) $338.2

Local government employment, 2006
Full-time equivalent employees 195,599
Payroll ($ mil) $734.2

Women holding public office, 2008
US Congress 3
Statewide elected office. 3
State legislature 70

Black public officials, 2002
Total. 20
   US and state legislatures 2
   City/county/regional offices 4
   Judicial/law enforcement. 10
   Education/school boards 4

Hispanic public officials, 2006
Total. 3
   State executives & legislators 1
   City/county/regional offices 1
   Judicial/law enforcement. 1
   Education/school boards 0

Governmental Finance

State government revenues, 2006
Total revenue (x $1,000) $34,772,988
   per capita $6,746.03
General revenue (x $1,000) $27,690,770
   Intergovernmental 6,660,890
   Taxes 17,331,413
      general sales. 4,437,407
      individual income tax 6,862,953
      corporate income tax 1,071,884
   Current charges. 2,213,701
   Miscellaneous 1,484,766

State government expenditure, 2006
Total expenditure (x $1,000) $30,988,533
   per capita $6,011.84
General expenditure (x $1,000) $27,449,035
   per capita, total. *$5,325.17*
   Education 2,236.41
   Public welfare 1,604.47
   Health 99.60
   Hospitals. 56.91
   Highways 370.11
   Police protection. 50.94
   Corrections 85.76
   Natural resources 86.31
   Parks & recreation 31.74
   Governmental administration 167.35
   Interest on general debt 82.68

State debt & cash, 2006 ($ per capita)
Debt $1,442.40
Cash/security holdings. $11,491.48

Federal government grants to state & local government, 2005 (x $1,000)
Total. $7,483,670
by Federal agency
   Defense 67,750
   Education 545,652
   Energy 48,126
   Environmental Protection Agency 71,294
   Health & Human Services. 4,708,816
   Homeland Security. 33,689
   Housing & Urban Development 583,328
   Justice 84,958
   Labor 130,405
   Transportation 529,678
   Veterans Affairs. 14,268

Crime & Law Enforcement

Crime, 2006 (rates per 100,000 residents)
Property crimes 159,119
   Burglary 30,173
   Larceny 115,567
   Motor vehicle theft 13,379
   Property crime rate. 3,079.5
Violent crimes. 16,123
   Murder 125
   Forcible rape. .1,645
   Robbery. 5,433
   Aggravated assault 8,920
   Violent crime rate 312.0
Hate crimes. 162

Fraud and identity theft, 2006
Fraud complaints. 5,860
   rate per 100,000 residents 113.4
Identity theft complaints 2,872
   rate per 100,000 residents 55.6

Law enforcement agencies, 2006
Total agencies. 317
Total employees 13,179
   Officers 8,493
   Civilians 4,686

Prisoners, probation, and parole, 2006
Total prisoners. 9,108
   percent change, 12/31/05 to 12/31/06 . . . -1.9%
   in private facilities 10.7%
   in local jails 5.6%
Sentenced to more than one year 9,108
   rate per 100,000 residents 176
Adults on probation 127,289
Adults on parole. .4,431

Prisoner demographics, June 30, 2005 (rate per 100,000 residents)
Male 553
Female 52
White 212
Black. 1,937
Hispanic . . . . NA

©2008 Information Publications, Inc.
All rights reserved. Photocopying prohibited.
877-544-INFO (4636) or www.informationpublications.com

Arrests, 2006
Total.................................... NA
   Persons under 18 years of age .... NA

Persons under sentence of death, 1/1/07
Total..................................... 0
   White.................................. 0
   Black 0
   Hispanic 0

State's highest court
Name ....Supreme Court
Number of members...................... 7
Length of term....................... 6 years
Intermediate appeals court? ....yes

Labor & Income

Civilian labor force, 2006 (x 1,000)
Total...................................2,933
   Men 1,534
   Women 1,399
   Persons 16-19 years.................... 187
   White................................ 2,667
   Black 107
   Hispanic 115

Civilian labor force as a percent of civilian non-institutional population, 2006
Total.................................72.9%
   Men 77.5
   Women 68.3
   Persons 16-19 years...................59.3
   White................................72.8
   Black 71.3
   Hispanic 79.9

Employment, 2006 (x 1,000)
Total...................................2,815
   Men 1,462
   Women 1,353
   Persons 16-19 years.................... 160
   White................................2,571
   Black 95
   Hispanic 110

Unemployment rate, 2006
Total.................................. 4.0%
   Men 4.7
   Women 3.3
   Persons 16-19 years...................14.7
   White................................3.6
   Black 10.7
   Hispanic 4.7

Full-time/part-time labor force, 2003 (x 1,000)
Full-time labor force, employed 2,175
Part-time labor force, employed........... 602
Unemployed, looking for
   Full-time work......................... 114
   Part-time work......................... 32
Mean duration of unemployment (weeks)......14.4
   Median 8.0

Labor unions, 2006
Membership (x 1,000)................... 395
   percent of employed 16.0%

Experienced civilian labor force by private industry, 2006
Total...............................2,296,367
   Natural resources & mining 22,401
   Construction 126,393
   Manufacturing................... 345,757
   Trade, transportation & utilities 522,327
   Information 58,009
   Finance 178,417
   Professional & business 320,928
   Education & health................. 390,104
   Leisure & hospitality............. 244,200
   Other 87,129

Experienced civilian labor force by occupation, May 2006
Management....................... 132,070
Business & financial 150,620
Legal.................................17,950
Sales 280,330
Office & admin. support............... 434,080
Computers & math 74,630
Architecture & engineering............. 52,390
Arts & entertainment 35,540
Education 148,290
Social services 49,280
Health care practitioner & technical.... 142,160
Health care support 77,290
Maintenance & repair................ 92,770
Construction 116,700
Transportation & moving 174,660
Production 236,940
Farming, fishing & forestry............ 4,300

Hours and earnings of production workers on manufacturing payrolls, 2006
Average weekly hours 41.0
Average hourly earnings $17.23
Average weekly earnings $706.43

Income and poverty, 2006
Median household income............ $54,023
Personal income, per capita (current $)... $38,712
   in constant (2000) dollars $33,793
Persons below poverty level.............. 9.8%

Average annual pay
2006 .... $42,185
   increase from 2005 .... 3.4%

Federal individual income tax returns, 2005
Returns filed......................2,445,599
Adjusted gross income ($1,000) $137,232,136
Total tax liability ($1,000) $17,597,364

Charitable contributions, 2004
Number of contributions.................896.1
Total amount ($ mil)................. $3,161.7

©2008 Information Publications, Inc.
All rights reserved. Photocopying prohibited.
877-544-INFO (4636) or www.informationpublications.com

Economy, Business, Industry & Agriculture

Fortune 500 companies, 2007.............. 20
Bankruptcy cases filed, FY 2007.........11,139

Patents and trademarks issued, 2007

Patents................................ 2,992
Trademarks............................. 2,289

Business firm ownership, 2002

Women-owned...................... 123,905
    Sales ($ mil) $16,252
Black-owned........................7,837
    Sales ($ mil) $682
Hispanic-owned.................... 3,984
    Sales ($ mil) $463
Asian-owned 7,700
    Sales ($ mil) $1,776
Amer. Indian/Alaska Native-owned 2,742
    Sales ($ mil) $321
Hawaiian/Pacific Islander-owned 119
    Sales ($ mil) $11

Gross domestic product, 2006 ($ mil)

Total gross domestic product $244,546
    Agriculture, forestry, fishing and
        hunting 3,724
    Mining.............................1,094
    Utilities...........................3,419
    Construction 11,275
    Manufacturing, durable goods.........21,232
    Manufacturing, non-durable goods ... 12,644
    Wholesale trade.....................17,719
    Retail trade........................14,738
    Transportation & warehousing 6,408
    Information 8,441
    Finance & insurance................. 22,937
    Real estate, rental & leasing 32,014
    Professional and technical services.....14,591
    Educational services................. 2,086
    Health care and social assistance...... 20,300
    Accommodation/food services.........5,317
    Other services, except government 5,697
    Government....................... 25,509

Establishments, payroll, employees & receipts, by major industry group, 2005

Total............................ 150,231
    Annual payroll ($1,000).........$96,992,711
    Paid employees 2,430,853
Forestry, fishing & agriculture............. 446
    Annual payroll ($1,000)............. $61,339
    Paid employees 2,211
Mining............................ 156
    Annual payroll ($1,000)........... $373,043
    Paid employees 5,372
    Receipts, 2002 ($1,000) $1,649,882

Utilities 276
    Annual payroll ($1,000)........... $866,279
    Paid employees 11,988
    Receipts, 2002 ($1,000) ....NA
Construction........................ 18,284
    Annual payroll ($1,000)..........$6,555,958
    Paid employees 123,782
    Receipts, 2002 ($1,000) $29,296,756
Manufacturing........................7,957
    Annual payroll ($1,000)..........$15,434,841
    Paid employees 336,311
    Receipts, 2002 ($1,000) $80,623,873
Wholesale trade 8,743
    Annual payroll ($1,000) $8,262,854
    Paid employees 141,320
    Receipts, 2002 ($1,000) $108,388,816
Retail trade 20,950
    Annual payroll ($1,000)...........$7,063,822
    Paid employees 308,231
    Receipts, 2002 ($1,000) $60,015,531
Transportation & warehousing 4,666
    Annual payroll ($1,000)...........$3,125,684
    Paid employees 78,428
    Receipts, 2002 ($1,000) $6,735,513
Information............................2,725
    Annual payroll ($1,000)...........$3,385,894
    Paid employees 64,407
    Receipts, 2002 ($1,000) ....NA
Finance & insurance 9,949
    Annual payroll ($1,000) $10,175,833
    Paid employees 150,673
    Receipts, 2002 ($1,000) ....NA
Professional, scientific & technical 16,534
    Annual payroll ($1,000)...........$7,495,145
    Paid employees 127,953
    Receipts, 2002 ($1,000) $14,652,614
Education 1,676
    Annual payroll ($1,000)...........$1,268,128
    Paid employees 56,757
    Receipts, 2002 ($1,000) $645,269
Health care & social assistance 13,408
    Annual payroll ($1,000)..........$13,297,478
    Paid employees 377,267
    Receipts, 2002 ($1,000) $24,337,547
Arts and entertainment 2,668
    Annual payroll ($1,000)...........$1,004,347
    Paid employees 38,352
    Receipts, 2002 ($1,000) $2,252,664
Real estate 7,035
    Annual payroll ($1,000)...........$1,259,089
    Paid employees 37,646
    Receipts, 2002 ($1,000) $5,912,883
Accommodation & food service...........10,812
    Annual payroll ($1,000)...........$2,768,082
    Paid employees 214,543
    Receipts, 2002 ($1,000) $7,959,590

©2008 Information Publications, Inc.
All rights reserved. Photocopying prohibited.
877-544-INFO (4636) or www.informationpublications.com

Exports, 2006
Value of exported goods ($ mil) $16,309
  Manufactured $13,970
  Non-manufactured...................$1,047

Foreign direct investment in US affiliates, 2004
Property, plants & equipment ($ mil) ... $10,926
Employment (x 1,000)....................83.2

Agriculture, 2006
Number of farms 79,300
Farm acreage (x 1,000) 27,400
  Acres per farm 346
Farm marketings and income ($ mil)
Total................................$9,769.5
  Crops $5,127.6
  Livestock..........................$4,641.9
Net farm income $2,493.6

Principal commodities, in order by marketing receipts, 2005
  Corn, Hogs, Soybeans, Dairy products, Cattle and calves

Federal economic activity in state
Expenditures, 2005 ($ mil)
  Total..............................$31,067
    Per capita $6,059.76
  Defense $2,437
  Non-defense $28,630
Defense department, 2006 ($ mil)
  Payroll............................ $762
  Contract awards $1,526
  Grants $70
Homeland security grants ($1,000)
  2006............................ $13,395
  2007............................ $20,504

FDIC-insured financial institutions, 2005
Number............................... 448
Assets ($ billion) $80.0
Deposits ($ billion) $60.6

Fishing, 2006
Catch (x 1,000 lbs)..................... 308
Value ($1,000)......................... $178

Mining, 2006 ($ mil)
Total non-fuel mineral production $2,740
Percent of U.S. 4.25%

Communication, Energy & Transportation

Communication
Households with computers, 2003........ 67.9%
Households with internet access, 2003 .... 61.6%
High-speed internet providers 101
Total high-speed internet lines........ 1,312,911
  Residential 952,244
  Business........................... 360,667
Wireless phone customers, 12/2006 3,701,515

FCC-licensed stations (as of January 1, 2008)
TV stations 31
FM radio stations......................... 235
AM radio stations 103

Energy
Energy consumption, 2004
  Total (trillion Btu)....................1,826
  Per capita (million Btu) 358.5
By source of production (trillion Btu)
  Coal 379
  Natural gas......................... 363
  Petroleum........................... 715
  Nuclear electric power 139
  Hydroelectric power................... 7
By end-use sector (trillion Btu)
  Residential 402
  Commercial 335
  Industrial 559
  Transportation 530
Electric energy, 2005
  Primary source of electricity........... Coal
  Net generation (billion kWh) 53.0
    percent from renewable sources....... 6.5%
  Net summer capability (million kW) 12.1
  CO_2 emitted from generation 38.9
Natural gas utilities, 2005
  Customers (x 1,000) 1,492
  Sales (trillion Btu)..................... 329
  Revenues ($ mil) $2,734
Nuclear plants, 2007 3
Total CO_2 emitted (million metric tons).....102.4
Energy spending, 2004 ($ mil) $15,229
  per capita $2,989
  Price per million Btu $12.17

Transportation, 2006
Public road & street mileage 132,309
  Urban..............................16,756
  Rural 115,553
  Interstate.......................... 913
Vehicle miles of travel (millions) 56,518
  per capita 10,964.6
Total motor vehicle registrations.......4,704,914
  Automobiles......................2,512,491
  Trucks 2,174,813
  Motorcycles 215,665
Licensed drivers 3,086,610
  19 years & under 182,918
Deaths from motor vehicle accidents 494
Gasoline consumed (x 1,000 gallons) 2,691,672
  per capita 522.2

Commuting Statistics, 2006
Average commute time (min) 22.0
  Drove to work alone 78.1%
  Carpooled........................... 9.3%
  Public transit 3.0%
  Walk to work 3.1%
  Work from home 4.9%

©2008 Information Publications, Inc.
All rights reserved. Photocopying prohibited.
877-544-INFO (4636) or www.informationpublications.com

State Summary

Capital city . . . . Jackson
Governor. Haley Barbour

PO Box 139
Jackson, MS 39205
601-359-3100

Admitted as a state 1817
Area (square miles) 48,430
Population, 2007 (estimate). 2,918,785
Largest city . . . . Jackson
   Population, 2006 .176,614
Personal income per capita, 2006
   (in current dollars) $26,535
Gross domestic product, 2006 ($ mil) $84,225

Leading industries by payroll, 2005

Manufacturing, Health care/Social assistance,
Retail trade

Leading agricultural commodities by receipts, 2005

Broilers, Cotton, Soybeans, Aquaculture, Cattle
and calves

Geography & Environment

Total area (square miles). 48,430
   land 46,907
   water 1,523
Federally-owned land, 2004 (acres) 2,196,940
   percent. 7.3%
Highest point . . . . Woodall Mountain
   elevation (feet) 806
Lowest point . . . . Gulf of Mexico
   elevation (feet) . . . . sea level
General coastline (miles) 44
Tidal shoreline (miles) 359
Cropland, 2003 (x 1,000 acres) 4,976
Forest land, 2003 (x 1,000 acres). 16,755
Capital city . . . . Jackson
   Population 2000 184,256
   Population 2006 176,614
Largest city . . . . Jackson
   Population 2000 184,256
   Population 2006 176,614

Number of cities with over 100,000 population

1990 1
2000 1
2006 1

State park and recreation areas, 2005

Area (x 1,000 acres). 24
Number of visitors (x 1,000) 2,256
Revenues ($1,000) $7,865
   percent of operating expenditures. 74.4%

National forest system land, 2007

Acres 1,174,079

Demographics & Population Characteristics

Population

1980 2,520,638
1990 2,573,216
2000 2,844,656
2006 2,910,540
   Male. 1,409,348
   Female. 1,501,192
Living in group quarters, 2006 94,247
   percent of total. 3.2%
2007 (estimate) 2,918,785
   persons per square mile of land 62.2
2008 (projected). 2,950,652
2010 (projected) .2,971,412
2020 (projected) .3,044,812
2030 (projected) .3,092,410

Population of Core-Based Statistical Areas (formerly Metropolitan Areas), x 1,000

	CBSA	Non-CBSA
1990	1,969	606
2000	2,196	648
2006	2,263	647

Change in population, 2000-2007

Number 74,129
   percent. 2.6%
Natural increase (births minus deaths) 106,023
Net internal migration . . . . -30,039
Net international migration 10,429

Persons by age, 2006

Under 5 years 209,457
5 to 17 years 549,948
18 years and over 2,151,135
65 years and over 362,172
85 years and over 49,582
   Median age 35.3

Persons by age, 2010 (projected)

Under 5 years 211,215
18 and over 2,211,962
65 and over 379,025
   Median age 36.5

Race, 2006

One Race
   White. 1,771,596
   Black or African American 1,080,796
   Asian 22,399
   American Indian/Alaska Native. 13,816
   Hawaiian Native/Pacific Islander. 935
Two or more races. 20,998

Persons of Hispanic origin, 2006

Total Hispanic or Latino 46,348
   Mexican. 30,399
   Puerto Rican 2,205
   Cuban 1,182

©2008 Information Publications, Inc.
All rights reserved. Photocopying prohibited.
877-544-INFO (4636) or www.informationpublications.com

Persons of Asian origin, 2006

Total Asian 22,116
  Asian Indian........................ 5,220
  Chinese 4,325
  Filipino 3,391
  Japanese 1,261
  Korean.............................1,218
  Vietnamese......................... 4,835

Marital status, 2006

Population 15 years & over 2,284,716
  Never married 712,155
  Married........................... 1,147,068
  Separated 75,574
  Widowed.......................... 180,352
  Divorced 245,141

Language spoken at home, 2006

Population 5 years and older........ 2,704,451
  English only 2,619,420
  Spanish 46,561
  French 4,860
  German........................... 4,198
  Chinese 3,352

Households & families, 2006

Households........................1,075,521
  with persons under 18 years 401,497
  with persons over 65 years.......... 257,854
  persons per household 2.62
Families..........................741,988
  persons per family....................3.19
Married couples...................... 497,649
Female householder,
  no husband present................. 192,667
One-person households 294,381

Nativity, 2006

Number of residents born in state 2,115,526
  percent of population 72.7%

Immigration & naturalization, 2006

Legal permanent residents admitted 1,480
Persons naturalized 495
Non-immigrant admissions 25,197

Vital Statistics and Health

Marriages

2004 17,705
2005 16,868
2006 16,861

Divorces

2004 13,077
2005 12,798
2006 13,658

Health risks, 2006

Percent of adults who are:
  Smokers......................... 25.1%
  Overweight (BMI > 25)................. 66.7%
  Obese (BMI > 30)..................... 31.4%

Births

2005 42,395
  Birthrate (per 1,000)...................14.5
  White........................ 23,045
  Black 18,659
  Hispanic 1,170
  Asian/Pacific Islander 408
  Amer. Indian/Alaska Native 283
  Low birth weight (2,500g or less)....... 11.8%
  Cesarian births 35.1%
  Preterm births 18.8%
  To unmarried mothers............... 49.4%
  Twin births (per 1,000)................31.9
  Triplets or higher order (per 100,000)....130.9
2006 (preliminary).................... 46,069
  rate per 1,000 ....15.8

Deaths

2004
All causes 27,871
  rate per 100,000.................... 998.2
Heart disease 8,282
  rate per 100,000.....................300.1
Malignant neoplasms 5,983
  rate per 100,000.....................209.8
Cerebrovascular disease.................1,651
  rate per 100,000.....................60.1
Chronic lower respiratory disease 1,350
  rate per 100,000.....................48.4
Diabetes............................. 665
  rate per 100,000.....................23.6
2005 (preliminary)...................29,198
  rate per 100,000.................... 1,026.9
2006 (provisional) 28,656

Infant deaths

2004 420
  rate per 1,000 ....9.8
2005 (provisional) 465
  rate per 1,000 ....11.0

Exercise routines, 2005

None..................................... 32.4%
Moderate or greater......................40.0%
Vigorous 20.9%

Abortions, 2004

Total performed in state................. 3,500
  rate per 1,000 women age 15-44........... 6
  % obtained by out-of-state residents 2.8%

Physicians, 2005

Total.................................5,168
  rate per 100,000 persons 178

Community hospitals, 2005

Number of hospitals 94
Beds (x 1,000)...........................12.8
Patients admitted (x 1,000) 414
Average daily census (x 1,000) 7.3
Average cost per day $1,021
Outpatient visits (x 1 mil) 4.1

©2008 Information Publications, Inc.
All rights reserved. Photocopying prohibited.
877-544-INFO (4636) or www.informationpublications.com

Disability status of population, 2006
5 to 15 years 8.1%
16 to 64 years 19.0%
65 years and over 52.0%

Education

Educational attainment, 2006
Population over 25 years 1,839,682
  Less than 9th grade.................... 7.8%
  High school graduate or more 77.9%
  College graduate or more............. 18.8%
  Graduate or professional degree......... 6.1%

Public school enrollment, 2005-06
Total................................. 494,954
  Pre-kindergarten through grade 8.... 350,983
  Grades 9 through 12................ 132,192

Graduating public high school seniors, 2004-05
Diplomas (incl. GED and others) 25,180

SAT scores, 2007
Average critical reading score.............. 568
Average writing score...................... 560
Average math score........................ 549
Percent of graduates taking test 4%

Public school teachers, 2006-07 (estimate)
Total (x 1,000) 33.5
  Elementary.............................19.8
  Secondary.............................13.7
Average salary $40,182
  Elementary....................... $39,636
  Secondary........................ $40,851

State receipts & expenditures for public schools, 2006-07 (estimate)
Revenue receipts ($ mil) $3,933
Expenditures
Total ($ mil) $3,803
  Per capita $1,166
  Per pupil $7,189

NAEP proficiency scores, 2007

	Reading		Math	
	Basic	Proficient	Basic	Proficient
Grade 4	51.5%	18.7%	69.9%	21.3%
Grade 8	60.3%	17.4%	53.8%	13.6%

Higher education enrollment, fall 2005
Total.................................14,561
  Full-time men 4,371
  Full-time women.....................7,663
  Part-time men 684
  Part-time women..................... 1,843

Minority enrollment in institutions of higher education, 2005
Black, non-Hispanic 58,758
Hispanic 1,203
Asian/Pacific Islander 1,252
American Indian/Alaska Native........... 648

Institutions of higher education, 2005-06
Total.................................... 41
  Public................................. 26
  Private................................ 15

Earned degrees conferred, 2004-05
Associate's........................... 8,630
Bachelor's 11,681
Master's..............................3,877
First-professional...................... 607
Doctor's.............................. 373

Public Libraries, 2006
Number of libraries....................... 50
Number of outlets 243
Annual visits per capita 2.9
Circulation per capita 3.2

State & local financial support for higher education, FY 2006
Full-time equivalent enrollment (x 1,000).... 117.7
Appropriations per FTE............... $5,053

Social Insurance & Welfare Programs

Social Security benefits & beneficiaries, 2005
Beneficiaries (x 1,000) 552
  Retired & dependents................... 322
  Survivors............................ 88
  Disabled & dependents................. 142
Annual benefit payments ($ mil) $5,395
  Retired & dependents............... $3,052
  Survivors.........................$998
  Disabled & dependents.............. $1,344
Average monthly benefit
  Retired & dependents................. $920
  Disabled & dependents.............. $880
  Widowed........................... $838

Medicare, July 2005
Enrollment (x 1,000)..................... 454
Payments ($ mil) $3,488

Medicaid, 2004
Beneficiaries (x 1,000)..................1,140
Payments ($ mil) $4,887

State Children's Health Insurance Program, 2006
Enrollment (x 1,000)....................83.4
Expenditures ($ mil).................. $124.2

Persons without health insurance, 2006
Number (x 1,000)........................ 600
  percent........................... 20.7%
Number of children (x 1,000) 146
  percent of children 18.9%

Health care expenditures, 2004
Total expenditures.................... $14,634
  per capita $5,059

©2008 Information Publications, Inc.
All rights reserved. Photocopying prohibited.
877-544-INFO (4636) or www.informationpublications.com

Federal and state public aid

State unemployment insurance, 2006
Recipients, first payments (x 1,000) 53
Total payments ($ mil) $161
Average weekly benefit $186
Temporary Assistance for Needy Families, 2006
Recipients (x 1,000) 316.3
Families (x 1,000) 153.6
Supplemental Security Income, 2005
Recipients (x 1,000) 124.6
Payments ($ mil) $571.8
Food Stamp Program, 2006
Avg monthly participants (x 1,000) 447.7
Total benefits ($ mil) $507.1

Housing & Construction

Housing units

Total 2005 (estimate) 1,235,377
Total 2006 (estimate) 1,241,489
Seasonal or recreational use, 2006 29,187
Owner-occupied, 2006 760,318
    Median home value $88,600
    Homeowner vacancy rate 1.6%
Renter-occupied, 2006 315,203
    Median rent $584
    Rental vacancy rate 12.9%
Home ownership rate, 2005 . . . . 78.8%
Home ownership rate, 2006 . . . . 76.2%

New privately-owned housing units

Number authorized, 2006 (x 1,000) 16.6
    Value ($ mil) $2,011.2
Started 2005 (x 1,000, estimate) 12.8
Started 2006 (x 1,000, estimate) 12.9

Existing home sales

2005 (x 1,000) 61.2
2006 (x 1,000) 63.8

Government & Elections

State officials 2008

Governor . . . . Haley Barbour
          Republican, term expires 1/08
Lieutenant Governor . . . . Phil Bryant
Secretary of State . . . . Delbert Hosemann
Attorney General . . . . Jim Hood
Chief Justice . . . . James Smith Jr

Governorship

Minimum age 30
Length of term . . . . 4 years
Consecutive terms permitted 2
Who succeeds . . . . Lieutenant Governor

Local governments by type, 2002

Total 1,000
    County 82
    Municipal 296
    Township 0
    School District 164
    Special District 458

State legislature

Name . . . . Legislature
Upper chamber . . . . Senate
    Number of members 52
    Length of term . . . . 4 years
    Party in majority, 2008 . . . . Democratic
Lower chamber . . . . House of Representatives
    Number of members 122
    Length of term . . . . 4 years
    Party in majority, 2008 . . . . Democratic

Federal representation, 2008 (110ᵗʰ Congress)

Senator . . . . Roger Wicker
    Party . . . . Republican
    Year term expires . . . . . 2008 (special election)
Senator . . . . Thad Cochran
    Party . . . . Republican
    Year term expires 2009
Representatives, total . . . . 4 (1 vacant)
    Democrats 2
    Republicans 1

Voters in November 2006 election (estimate)

Total 878,567
    Male 378,883
    Female 499,684
    White 510,205
    Black 362,465
    Hispanic . . . . NA
    Asian . . . . NA

Presidential election, 2004

Total Popular Vote 1,152,145
    Kerry 458,094
    Bush 684,981
Total Electoral Votes 6

Votes cast for US Senators

2004
Total vote (x 1,000) . . . . NA
Leading party . . . . NA
Percent for leading party . . . . NA

2006
Total vote (x 1,000) 611
Leading party . . . . Republican
Percent for leading party 63.6%

Votes cast for US Representatives

2004
Total vote (x 1,000) 1,116
    Democratic 335
    Republican 659
Leading party . . . . Republican
Percent for leading party 59.0%

2006
Total vote (x 1,000) 601
    Democratic 260
    Republican 304
Leading party . . . . Republican
Percent for leading party 50.7%

©2008 Information Publications, Inc.
All rights reserved. Photocopying prohibited.
877-544-INFO (4636) or www.informationpublications.com

State government employment, 2006
Full-time equivalent employees 55,036
Payroll ($ mil) $169.5

Local government employment, 2006
Full-time equivalent employees .... NA
Payroll ($ mil) .... NA

Women holding public office, 2008
US Congress 0
Statewide elected office.................... 0
State legislature 26

Black public officials, 2002
Total.................................... 950
  US and state legislatures 46
  City/county/regional offices 646
  Judicial/law enforcement................ 121
  Education/school boards 137

Hispanic public officials, 2006
Total.................................... 0
  State executives & legislators 0
  City/county/regional offices 0
  Judicial/law enforcement.................. 0
  Education/school boards 0

Governmental Finance

State government revenues, 2006
Total revenue (x $1,000)........... $17,743,579
  per capita..........................$6,120.35
General revenue (x $1,000) $14,604,494
  Intergovernmental 6,973,204
  Taxes 5,989,603
    general sales....................3,047,837
    individual income tax 1,254,733
    corporate income tax 316,981
  Current charges..................1,174,397
  Miscellaneous 467,290

State government expenditure, 2006
Total expenditure (x $1,000) $16,293,095
  per capita $5,620.03
General expenditure (x $1,000) $14,554,388
  per capita, total................... *$5,020.29*
  Education 1,690.51
  Public welfare 1,334.74
  Health 105.13
  Hospitals........................ 264.16
  Highways 468.01
  Police protection.................35.04
  Corrections 106.84
  Natural resources 77.41
  Parks & recreation 13.40
  Governmental administration.......83.14
  Interest on general debt.............73.20

State debt & cash, 2006 ($ per capita)
Debt $1,679.99
Cash/security holdings..............$10,054.72

Federal government grants to state & local government, 2005 (x $1,000)
Total.............................$6,567,356
by Federal agency
  Defense 51,914
  Education 467,203
  Energy....................... 19,243
  Environmental Protection Agency 46,294
  Health & Human Services. 3,533,567
  Homeland Security................. 834,082
  Housing & Urban Development..... 274,465
  Justice 53,704
  Labor 109,356
  Transportation 588,248
  Veterans Affairs................. 13,988

Crime & Law Enforcement

Crime, 2006 (rates per 100,000 residents)
Property crimes 93,393
  Burglary 27,239
  Larceny 57,807
  Motor vehicle theft 8,347
  Property crime rate................3,208.8
Violent crimes........................8,691
  Murder 223
  Forcible rape..................... 1,000
  Robbery.........................3,118
  Aggravated assault 4,350
  Violent crime rate 298.6
Hate crimes............................. 0

Fraud and identity theft, 2006
Fraud complaints......................2,318
  rate per 100,000 residents 79.6
Identity theft complaints 1,494
  rate per 100,000 residents 51.3

Law enforcement agencies, 2006
Total agencies........................... 193
Total employees 9,200
  Officers 5,624
  Civilians 3,576

Prisoners, probation, and parole, 2006
Total prisoners....................... 21,068
  percent change, 12/31/05 to 12/31/06 .... 2.7%
  in private facilities 23.1%
  in local jails 22.2%
Sentenced to more than one year 19,219
  rate per 100,000 residents 658
Adults on probation 24,107
Adults on parole........................1,899

Prisoner demographics, June 30, 2005 (rate per 100,000 residents)
Male......................................1,790
Female 168
White 503
Black.....................................1,742
Hispanic 611

©2008 Information Publications, Inc.
All rights reserved. Photocopying prohibited.
877-544-INFO (4636) or www.informationpublications.com

Arrests, 2006
Total................................ 119,506
   Persons under 18 years of age 11,802

Persons under sentence of death, 1/1/07
Total...................................... 66
   White...................................... 30
   Black 35
   Hispanic 0

State's highest court
Name ....Supreme Court
Number of members........................ 9
Length of term........................ 8 years
Intermediate appeals court? ....yes

Labor & Income

Civilian labor force, 2006 (x 1,000)
Total....................................1,296
   Men 681
   Women 615
   Persons 16-19 years..................... 67
   White................................. 841
   Black 424
   Hispanic 43

Civilian labor force as a percent of civilian non-institutional population, 2006
Total...................................59.6%
   Men 66.4
   Women 53.6
   Persons 16-19 years....................36.7
   White.................................61.2
   Black 56.0
   Hispanic 76.5

Employment, 2006 (x 1,000)
Total....................................1,213
   Men 635
   Women 577
   Persons 16-19 years..................... 56
   White................................. 807
   Black 376
   Hispanic 42

Unemployment rate, 2006
Total..................................... 6.4%
   Men 6.6
   Women 6.2
   Persons 16-19 years....................17.4
   White..................................4.0
   Black 11.3
   Hispanic 4.5

Full-time/part-time labor force, 2003 (x 1,000)
Full-time labor force, employed 1,051
Part-time labor force, employed........... 178
Unemployed, looking for
   Full-time work......................... 73
   Part-time work......................... 11
*Mean duration of unemployment (weeks)......*24.1
   Median 12.0

Labor unions, 2006
Membership (x 1,000)..................... 60
   percent of employed 5.6%

Experienced civilian labor force by private industry, 2006
Total................................890,161
   Natural resources & mining 20,669
   Construction 57,448
   Manufacturing......................175,718
   Trade, transportation & utilities 224,844
   Information 13,701
   Finance 45,724
   Professional & business 93,880
   Education & health.................115,313
   Leisure & hospitality...............119,135
   Other 23,728

Experienced civilian labor force by occupation, May 2006
Management...........................47,580
Business & financial 24,900
Legal................................. 5,850
Sales............................... 118,040
Office & admin. support.............. 172,270
Computers & math 8,960
Architecture & engineering................ NA
Arts & entertainment...................8,780
Education 73,490
Social services 10,570
Health care practitioner & technical..... 65,380
Health care support 30,190
Maintenance & repair..................47,330
Construction 57,230
Transportation & moving 95,900
Production 130,850
Farming, fishing & forestry............5,330

Hours and earnings of production workers on manufacturing payrolls, 2006
Average weekly hours....................39.4
Average hourly earnings $13.78
Average weekly earnings $542.93

Income and poverty, 2006
Median household income............ $34,473
Personal income, per capita (current $)... $26,535
   in constant (2000) dollars $23,163
Persons below poverty level.............. 21.1%

Average annual pay
2006 ....$31,194
   increase from 2005 .... 4.8%

Federal individual income tax returns, 2005
Returns filed........................1,169,598
Adjusted gross income ($1,000) $45,340,179
Total tax liability ($1,000) $4,712,723

Charitable contributions, 2004
Number of contributions 235.5
Total amount ($ mil)................. $1,128.1

©2008 Information Publications, Inc.
All rights reserved. Photocopying prohibited.
877-544-INFO (4636) or www.informationpublications.com

Economy, Business, Industry & Agriculture

Fortune 500 companies, 2007.................. 0
Bankruptcy cases filed, FY 2007..........10,789

Patents and trademarks issued, 2007
Patents..................................... 169
Trademarks.............................. 176

Business firm ownership, 2002
Women-owned.........................47,102
  Sales ($ mil) $6,728
Black-owned.......................... 25,002
  Sales ($ mil) $1,314
Hispanic-owned.......................1,326
  Sales ($ mil) $213
Asian-owned 2,921
  Sales ($ mil) $1,216
Amer. Indian/Alaska Native-owned 689
  Sales ($ mil) $64
Hawaiian/Pacific Islander-owned 126
  Sales ($ mil) $7

Gross domestic product, 2006 ($ mil)
Total gross domestic product $84,225
  Agriculture, forestry, fishing and
    hunting 2,003
  Mining................................ 2,225
  Utilities 2,242
  Construction 4,281
  Manufacturing, durable goods..........7,847
  Manufacturing, non-durable goods 5,039
  Wholesale trade...................... 4,624
  Retail trade.........................7,505
  Transportation & warehousing 3,034
  Information 2,035
  Finance & insurance.................. 3,550
  Real estate, rental & leasing 7,570
  Professional and technical services..... 2,954
  Educational services.................... 483
  Health care and social assistance....... 6,080
  Accommodation/food services..........3,122
  Other services, except government 2,026
  Government...................... 14,230

Establishments, payroll, employees & receipts, by major industry group, 2005
Total................................ 60,542
  Annual payroll ($1,000)......... $25,796,066
  Paid employees 926,952
Forestry, fishing & agriculture.............. 820
  Annual payroll ($1,000)........... $153,849
  Paid employees 5,276
Mining.................................. 309
  Annual payroll ($1,000)........... $214,896
  Paid employees 4,246
  Receipts, 2002 ($1,000) $988,177

Utilities 576
  Annual payroll ($1,000)........... $496,075
  Paid employees 8,693
  Receipts, 2002 ($1,000) ....NA
Construction...........................4,976
  Annual payroll ($1,000)..........$1,665,301
  Paid employees 49,735
  Receipts, 2002 ($1,000) $7,212,182
Manufacturing.......................2,629
  Annual payroll ($1,000)..........$5,792,877
  Paid employees 176,767
  Receipts, 2002 ($1,000) $38,276,054
Wholesale trade..................... 2,853
  Annual payroll ($1,000)..........$1,307,500
  Paid employees 35,256
  Receipts, 2002 ($1,000) $19,215,751
Retail trade......................... 12,429
  Annual payroll ($1,000)......... $2,692,884
  Paid employees 140,119
  Receipts, 2002 ($1,000) $25,017,531
Transportation & warehousing.......... 2,342
  Annual payroll ($1,000)..........$1,067,633
  Paid employees 33,548
  Receipts, 2002 ($1,000) $2,801,650
Information...........................1,106
  Annual payroll ($1,000)........... $642,136
  Paid employees 17,519
  Receipts, 2002 ($1,000) ....NA
Finance & insurance 4,707
  Annual payroll ($1,000)..........$1,388,034
  Paid employees 35,616
  Receipts, 2002 ($1,000) ....NA
Professional, scientific & technical 4,597
  Annual payroll ($1,000)..........$1,256,427
  Paid employees 31,689
  Receipts, 2002 ($1,000) $2,922,664
Education 570
  Annual payroll ($1,000)........... $296,439
  Paid employees 16,435
  Receipts, 2002 ($1,000) $79,757
Health care & social assistance 5,599
  Annual payroll ($1,000)..........$4,674,594
  Paid employees 141,936
  Receipts, 2002 ($1,000) $10,092,701
Arts and entertainment 660
  Annual payroll ($1,000)........... $168,254
  Paid employees 10,021
  Receipts, 2002 ($1,000) $529,276
Real estate........................... 2,347
  Annual payroll ($1,000)........... $256,194
  Paid employees 10,396
  Receipts, 2002 ($1,000) $1,296,752
Accommodation & food service........... 4,649
  Annual payroll ($1,000)..........$1,598,053
  Paid employees 114,571
  Receipts, 2002 ($1,000) $5,486,105

©2008 Information Publications, Inc.
All rights reserved. Photocopying prohibited.
877-544-INFO (4636) or www.informationpublications.com

8   Mississippi

Exports, 2006
Value of exported goods ($ mil) $4,674
  Manufactured $3,696
  Non-manufactured $424

Foreign direct investment in US affiliates, 2004
Property, plants & equipment ($ mil) $6,777
Employment (x 1,000). 25.5

Agriculture, 2006
Number of farms 42,000
Farm acreage (x 1,000) 11,000
  Acres per farm 262
Farm marketings and income ($ mil)
Total. $3,788.5
  Crops $1,245.0
  Livestock $2,543.5
Net farm income $1,230.3

Principal commodities, in order by
marketing receipts, 2005
  Broilers, Cotton, Soybeans, Aquaculture, Cattle
      and calves

Federal economic activity in state
Expenditures, 2005 ($ mil)
  Total. $26,181
    Per capita $9,001.47
  Defense $4,869
  Non-defense $21,311
Defense department, 2006 ($ mil)
  Payroll. $1,702
  Contract awards $5,477
  Grants $126
Homeland security grants ($1,000)
  2006. . . . . $8,528
  2007 . . . .$7,002

FDIC-insured financial institutions, 2005
Number 98
Assets ($ billion) $50.6
Deposits ($ billion) $40.7

Fishing, 2006
Catch (x 1,000 lbs) 221,838
Value ($1,000). $21,751

Mining, 2006 ($ mil)
Total non-fuel mineral production $212
Percent of U.S. 0.33%

Communication, Energy & Transportation

Communication
Households with computers, 2003 . . . . .48.3%
Households with internet access, 2003 . . . .38.9%
High-speed internet providers 51
Total high-speed internet lines. 332,307
  Residential 275,423
  Business. 56,884
Wireless phone customers, 12/2006 2,029,916

FCC-licensed stations (as of January 1, 2008)
TV stations 29
FM radio stations. 191
AM radio stations 92

Energy
Energy consumption, 2004
  Total (trillion Btu). 1,214
  Per capita (million Btu) 419.8
By source of production (trillion Btu)
  Coal 185
  Natural gas 294
  Petroleum 488
  Nuclear electric power 107
  Hydroelectric power 0
By end-use sector (trillion Btu)
  Residential 230
  Commercial 167
  Industrial 452
  Transportation 365
Electric energy, 2005
  Primary source of electricity. . . . . Coal
  Net generation (billion kWh) 45.1
      percent from renewable sources. 3.4%
  Net summer capability (million kW) 16.9
  CO_2 emitted from generation 25.1
Natural gas utilities, 2005
  Customers (x 1,000) 495
  Sales (trillion Btu). 142
  Revenues ($ mil) $912
Nuclear plants, 2007 1
Total CO_2 emitted (million metric tons). 62.1
Energy spending, 2004 ($ mil) $9,453
  per capita $3,268
  Price per million Btu $12.51

Transportation, 2006
Public road & street mileage 74,408
  Urban. 10,681
  Rural 63,727
  Interstate. 685
Vehicle miles of travel (millions) 41,498
  per capita 14,314.0
Total motor vehicle registrations. 1,997,581
  Automobiles. 1,118,200
  Trucks 869,860
  Motorcycles 27,553
Licensed drivers 1,929,636
  19 years & under 123,579
Deaths from motor vehicle accidents 911
Gasoline consumed (x 1,000 gallons) 1,678,003
  per capita 578.8

Commuting Statistics, 2006
Average commute time (min) 24.0
  Drove to work alone 82.2%
  Carpooled. 12.1%
  Public transit 0.4%
  Walk to work 1.8%
  Work from home 2.1%

©2008 Information Publications, Inc.
All rights reserved. Photocopying prohibited.
877-544-INFO (4636) or www.informationpublications.com

State Summary

Capital city . . . . Jefferson City
Governor. . . . . .Matt Blunt

Capitol Building
Room 218, PO Box 720
Jefferson City, MO 65102
573-751-3222

Admitted as a state 1821
Area (square miles) 69,704
Population, 2007 (estimate). 5,878,415
Largest city .Kansas City
    Population, 2006 447,306
Personal income per capita, 2006
    (in current dollars) $32,705
Gross domestic product, 2006 ($ mil) . . . $225,876

Leading industries by payroll, 2005

Health care/Social assistance, Manufacturing,
Finance & Insurance

**Leading agricultural commodities
by receipts, 2005**

Cattle and calves, Soybeans, Corn, Hogs, Turkeys

Geography & Environment

Total area (square miles). 69,704
    land 68,886
    water 818
Federally-owned land, 2004 (acres) 2,224,788
    percent. 5.0%
Highest point . . . . .Taum Sauk Mountain
    elevation (feet) .1,772
Lowest point . . . . .St. Francis River
    elevation (feet) 230
General coastline (miles) 0
Tidal shoreline (miles) 0
Cropland, 2003 (x 1,000 acres) 13,678
Forest land, 2003 (x 1,000 acres). 12,550
Capital city . . . . Jefferson City
    Population 2000 .39,636
    Population 2006 39,274
Largest city .Kansas City
    Population 2000 441,545
    Population 2006 447,306

Number of cities with over 100,000 population

1990 4
2000 4
2006 4

State park and recreation areas, 2005

Area (x 1,000 acres) 202
Number of visitors (x 1,000) 16,695
Revenues ($1,000) $7,406
    percent of operating expenditures. 26.6%

National forest system land, 2007

Acres 1,491,811

Demographics & Population Characteristics

Population

1980 4,916,686
1990 5,117,073
2000 5,596,683
2006 5,842,713
    Male. 2,854,715
    Female. 2,987,998
Living in group quarters, 2006. 167,076
    percent of total. 2.9%
2007 (estimate). 5,878,415
    persons per square mile of land 85.3
2008 (projected). 5,860,326
2010 (projected) 5,922,078
2020 (projected). 6,199,882
2030 (projected). 6,430,173

**Population of Core-Based Statistical Areas
(formerly Metropolitan Areas), x 1,000**

	CBSA	Non-CBSA
1990	4,392	725
2000	4,810	787
2006	5,043	800

Change in population, 2000-2007

Number 281,732
    percent. 5.0%
Natural increase (births minus deaths) 168,856
Net internal migration 41,079
Net international migration 51,809

Persons by age, 2006

Under 5 years 386,752
5 to 17 years 1,029,840
18 years and over 4,426,121
65 years and over 778,891
85 years and over .113,789
    Median age 37.1

Persons by age, 2010 (projected)

Under 5 years 394,878
18 and over 4,510,684
65 and over 821,645
    Median age 37.6

Race, 2006

One Race

    White. 4,974,983
    Black or African American 673,075
    Asian 83,216
    American Indian/Alaska Native. 28,332
    Hawaiian Native/Pacific Islander. 4,373
Two or more races. 78,734

Persons of Hispanic origin, 2006

Total Hispanic or Latino 160,898
    Mexican. 110,119
    Puerto Rican 10,033
    Cuban 3,129

©2008 Information Publications, Inc.
All rights reserved. Photocopying prohibited.
877-544-INFO (4636) or www.informationpublications.com

Persons of Asian origin, 2006
Total Asian 86,010
  Asian Indian........................18,152
  Chinese 19,513
  Filipino 11,858
  Japanese 2,620
  Korean..............................9,256
  Vietnamese........................ 16,849

Marital status, 2006
Population 15 years & over 4,674,246
  Never married 1,300,189
  Married.......................... 2,513,178
  Separated 91,782
  Widowed........................ 316,307
  Divorced 544,572

Language spoken at home, 2006
Population 5 years and older........ 5,451,998
  English only 5,146,967
  Spanish 129,329
  French 16,725
  German......................... 32,547
  Chinese 15,890

Households & families, 2006
Households........................2,305,027
  with persons under 18 years 769,181
  with persons over 65 years...........541,314
  persons per household 2.46
Families...........................1,518,860
  persons per family..................3.04
Married couples......................1,154,259
Female householder,
  no husband present................ 273,870
One-person households 662,944

Nativity, 2006
Number of residents born in state 3,875,492
  percent of population.................66.3%

Immigration & naturalization, 2006
Legal permanent residents admitted...... 6,857
Persons naturalized 3,711
Non-immigrant admissions 101,566

Vital Statistics and Health

Marriages
2004............................... 40,824
2005............................... 40,675
2006...............................40,746

Divorces
2004...............................21,700
2005...............................21,013
2006............................... 22,935

Health risks, 2006
Percent of adults who are:
  Smokers.........................23.2%
  Overweight (BMI > 25)...............62.9%
  Obese (BMI > 30)....................27.2%

Births
2005...................................78,618
  Birthrate (per 1,000)....................13.6
  White........................ 64,729
  Black 11,686
  Hispanic 4,271
  Asian/Pacific Islander 1,760
  Amer. Indian/Alaska Native........... 443
  Low birth weight (2,500g or less)....... 8.1%
  Cesarian births 29.7%
  Preterm births 13.3%
  To unmarried mothers.............. 37.8%
  Twin births (per 1,000)...............32.5
  Triplets or higher order (per 100,000)....170.1
2006 (preliminary).....................81,388
  rate per 1,000 ....13.9

Deaths
2004
All causes 53,950
  rate per 100,000.......................872.0
Heart disease 15,500
  rate per 100,000...................... 248.4
Malignant neoplasms 12,450
  rate per 100,000......................201.2
Cerebrovascular disease.............. 3,503
  rate per 100,000......................56.0
Chronic lower respiratory disease 2,731
  rate per 100,000......................44.1
Diabetes............................1,461
  rate per 100,000......................23.6
2005 (preliminary)................. 54,658
  rate per 100,000......................869.4
2006 (provisional) 54,913

Infant deaths
2004................................. 584
  rate per 1,000 ....7.5
2005 (provisional) 580
  rate per 1,000 ....7.4

Exercise routines, 2005
None................................ 25.4%
Moderate or greater................... 46.4%
Vigorous 25.3%

Abortions, 2004
Total performed in state................ 8,072
  rate per 1,000 women age 15-44........... 7
  % obtained by out-of-state residents 10.0%

Physicians, 2005
Total............................... 13,965
  rate per 100,000 persons 241

Community hospitals, 2005
Number of hospitals 119
Beds (x 1,000)..........................19.1
Patients admitted (x 1,000) 836
Average daily census (x 1,000) 12.0
Average cost per day $1,560
Outpatient visits (x 1 mil) 17.2

©2008 Information Publications, Inc.
All rights reserved. Photocopying prohibited.
877-544-INFO (4636) or www.informationpublications.com

Disability status of population, 2006

5 to 15 years 7.0%
16 to 64 years 14.2%
65 years and over 43.3%

Education

Educational attainment, 2006

Population over 25 years 3,849,275
  Less than 9th grade. 5.2%
  High school graduate or more 84.8%
  College graduate or more. 24.3%
  Graduate or professional degree. 8.7%

Public school enrollment, 2005-06

Total. 917,705
  Pre-kindergarten through grade 8. 635,142
  Grades 9 through 12 282,563

Graduating public high school seniors, 2004-05

Diplomas (incl. GED and others) 57,841

SAT scores, 2007

Average critical reading score. 594
Average writing score 587
Average math score 594
Percent of graduates taking test 6%

Public school teachers, 2006-07 (estimate)

Total (x 1,000) 66.8
  Elementary 34.4
  Secondary 32.4
Average salary $41,839
  Elementary $41,879
  Secondary $41,797

State receipts & expenditures for public schools, 2006-07 (estimate)

Revenue receipts ($ mil) $9,242
Expenditures
Total ($ mil) $8,540
  Per capita $1,256
  Per pupil $8,857

NAEP proficiency scores, 2007

	Reading		Math	
	Basic	Proficient	Basic	Proficient
Grade 4	67.1%	31.8%	82.0%	38.4%
Grade 8	74.9%	31.0%	72.2%	29.9%

Higher education enrollment, fall 2005

Total. 156,723
  Full-time men 40,125
  Full-time women. 53,442
  Part-time men 26,708
  Part-time women. 36,448

Minority enrollment in institutions of higher education, 2005

Black, non-Hispanic 46,582
Hispanic 10,624
Asian/Pacific Islander 9,516
American Indian/Alaska Native. 2,293

Institutions of higher education, 2005-06

Total. 128
  Public. 33
  Private 95

Earned degrees conferred, 2004-05

Associate's. 13,451
Bachelor's 34,352
Master's 17,180
First-professional. 2,625
Doctor's 1,363

Public Libraries, 2006

Number of libraries. 149
Number of outlets 387
Annual visits per capita 5.0
Circulation per capita. 8.9

State & local financial support for higher education, FY 2006

Full-time equivalent enrollment (x 1,000). . . .170.7
Appropriations per FTE. $5,846

Social Insurance & Welfare Programs

Social Security benefits & beneficiaries, 2005

Beneficiaries (x 1,000) 1,064
  Retired & dependents. 712
  Survivors. 144
  Disabled & dependents. 207
Annual benefit payments ($ mil) $11,281
  Retired & dependents. $7,289
  Survivors. $1,929
  Disabled & dependents. $2,063
Average monthly benefit
  Retired & dependents. $990
  Disabled & dependents. $913
  Widowed. $968

Medicare, July 2005

Enrollment (x 1,000). 912
Payments ($ mil) $5,734

Medicaid, 2004

Beneficiaries (x 1,000). 726
Payments ($ mil) $3,312

State Children's Health Insurance Program, 2006

Enrollment (x 1,000) 106.6
Expenditures ($ mil) $106.4

Persons without health insurance, 2006

Number (x 1,000). 772
  percent. 13.3%
Number of children (x 1,000) 127
  percent of children 9.1%

Health care expenditures, 2004

Total expenditures. $31,317
  per capita $5,444

©2008 Information Publications, Inc.
All rights reserved. Photocopying prohibited.
877-544-INFO (4636) or www.informationpublications.com

Federal and state public aid

State unemployment insurance, 2006
Recipients, first payments (x 1,000) 135
Total payments ($ mil) $411
Average weekly benefit $212
Temporary Assistance for Needy Families, 2006
Recipients (x 1,000).................... 1,110.9
Families (x 1,000) 459.9
Supplemental Security Income, 2005
Recipients (x 1,000)..................... 117.6
Payments ($ mil) $573.1
Food Stamp Program, 2006
Avg monthly participants (x 1,000) 796.4
Total benefits ($ mil)...................$740.1

Housing & Construction

Housing units
Total 2005 (estimate) 2,595,306
Total 2006 (estimate) 2,623,094
Seasonal or recreational use, 2006.......70,472
Owner-occupied, 2006...............1,628,838
   Median home value................ $131,900
   Homeowner vacancy rate.............. 2.8%
Renter-occupied, 2006 676,189
   Median rent $607
   Rental vacancy rate................. 11.3%
Home ownership rate, 2005.............72.3%
Home ownership rate, 2006 .... 71.9%

New privately-owned housing units
Number authorized, 2006 (x 1,000)........29.2
   Value ($ mil).......................$4,086.7
Started 2005 (x 1,000, estimate)...........27.5
Started 2006 (x 1,000, estimate)...........27.5

Existing home sales
2005 (x 1,000)..........................142.9
2006 (x 1,000)..........................135.3

Government & Elections

State officials 2008
Governor.........................Matt Blunt
   Republican, term expires 1/09
Lieutenant Governor.............. Peter Kinder
Secretary of State............ Robin Carnahan
Attorney General.............. Jeremiah Nixon
Chief Justice .... Laura Denvir Stith

Governorship
Minimum age........................... 30
Length of term .... 4 years
Consecutive terms permitted 2
Who succeeds........... Lieutenant Governor

Local governments by type, 2002
Total..................................3,422
   County................................ 114
   Municipal 946
   Township 312
   School District........................ 536
   Special District 1,514

State legislature
Name .... General Assembly
Upper chamber ....Senate
   Number of members................... 34
   Length of term.................... 4 years
   Party in majority, 2008 .... Republican
Lower chamber....... House of Representatives
   Number of members.................. 163
   Length of term.................... 2 years
   Party in majority, 2008 .... Republican

Federal representation, 2008 (110th Congress)
Senator.................... Christopher Bond
   Party .... Republican
   Year term expires 2011
Senator...................... Claire McCaskill
   Party ....Democratic
   Year term expires 2013
Representatives, total 9
   Democrats......................... 4
   Republicans 5

Voters in November 2006 election (estimate)
Total...............................2,310,214
   Male...............................1,094,660
   Female.............................1,215,554
   White..............................2,052,974
   Black 208,591
   Hispanic 14,568
   Asian 8,421

Presidential election, 2004
Total Popular Vote 2,731,364
   Kerry 1,259,171
   Bush...........................1,455,713
Total Electoral Votes....................... 11

Votes cast for US Senators
2004
Total vote (x 1,000) 2,706
Leading party..................... Republican
Percent for leading party 56.1%
2006
Total vote (x 1,000) 2,128
Leading party...................Democratic
Percent for leading party 49.6%

Votes cast for US Representatives
2004
Total vote (x 1,000) 2,667
   Democratic.......................1,193
   Republican 1,430
Leading party.................... Republican
Percent for leading party 53.6%
2006
Total vote (x 1,000) 2,097
   Democratic........................ 992
   Republican 1,049
Leading party.................... Republican
Percent for leading party 50.0%

©2008 Information Publications, Inc.
All rights reserved. Photocopying prohibited.
877-544-INFO (4636) or www.informationpublications.com

State government employment, 2006
Full-time equivalent employees 90,228
Payroll ($ mil) $271.9

Local government employment, 2006
Full-time equivalent employees 229,855
Payroll ($ mil) $689.7

Women holding public office, 2008
US Congress 2
Statewide elected office...................... 3
State legislature 38

Black public officials, 2002
Total................................... 206
  US and state legislatures 19
  City/county/regional offices 145
  Judicial/law enforcement................. 17
  Education/school boards................. 25

Hispanic public officials, 2006
Total..................................... 1
  State executives & legislators 0
  City/county/regional offices 1
  Judicial/law enforcement................. 0
  Education/school boards................. 0

Governmental Finance

State government revenues, 2006
Total revenue (x $1,000) $28,760,284
  per capita $4,926.70
General revenue (x $1,000) $22,372,539
  Intergovernmental 7,936,489
  Taxes 10,180,045
    general sales...................3,100,045
    individual income tax 4,491,428
    corporate income tax 343,689
  Current charges..................2,166,823
  Miscellaneous 2,089,182

State government expenditure, 2006
Total expenditure (x $1,000) $24,355,850
  per capita $4,172.21
General expenditure (x $1,000) $21,721,267
  per capita, total................... *$3,720.90*
  Education......................1,294.61
  Public welfare 1,027.15
  Health 179.98
  Hospitals........................197.86
  Highways 341.55
  Police protection.................. 32.56
  Corrections 103.74
  Natural resources 59.55
  Parks & recreation 7.09
  Governmental administration.......92.75
  Interest on general debt............159.18

State debt & cash, 2006 ($ per capita)
Debt................................$3,026.67
Cash/security holdings..............$12,236.65

Federal government grants to state & local government, 2005 (x $1,000)
Total.......................... $8,930,488
by Federal agency
  Defense 35,476
  Education 645,758
  Energy 30,594
  Environmental Protection Agency 101,748
  Health & Human Services. 5,799,930
  Homeland Security................. 34,853
  Housing & Urban Development...... 518,222
  Justice 99,156
  Labor 129,596
  Transportation 880,629
  Veterans Affairs....................31,942

Crime & Law Enforcement

Crime, 2006 (rates per 100,000 residents)
Property crimes 223,570
  Burglary 44,647
  Larceny 153,490
  Motor vehicle theft 25,433
  Property crime rate..................3,826.5
Violent crimes........................ 31,880
  Murder 368
  Forcible rape.......................1,764
  Robbery...........................7,587
  Aggravated assault 22,161
  Violent crime rate 545.6
Hate crimes............................. 97

Fraud and identity theft, 2006
Fraud complaints.......................7,331
  rate per 100,000 residents 125.5
Identity theft complaints 3,753
  rate per 100,000 residents 64.2

Law enforcement agencies, 2006
Total agencies............................ 552
Total employees 19,378
  Officers 13,584
  Civilians 5,794

Prisoners, probation, and parole, 2006
Total prisoners........................30,167
  percent change, 12/31/05 to 12/31/06 ... -2.1%
  in private facilities 0%
  in local jails 0%
Sentenced to more than one year 30,146
  rate per 100,000 residents 514
Adults on probation 54,963
Adults on parole........................19,063

Prisoner demographics, June 30, 2005 (rate per 100,000 residents)
Male.................................1,323
Female 133
White................................. 487
Black................................. 2,556
Hispanic 587

©2008 Information Publications, Inc.
All rights reserved. Photocopying prohibited.
877-544-INFO (4636) or www.informationpublications.com

Arrests, 2006
```
Total.................................372,182
    Persons under 18 years of age........ 49,659
```

Persons under sentence of death, 1/1/07
```
Total................................... 51
    White................................ 30
    Black ............................... 21
    Hispanic ............................. 0
```

State's highest court
```
Name.......................Supreme Court
Number of members...................... 7
Length of term..................... 12 years
Intermediate appeals court? ...............yes
```

Labor & Income

Civilian labor force, 2006 (x 1,000)
```
Total..................................3,069
    Men .................................1,604
    Women ...............................1,465
    Persons 16-19 years................... 169
    White............................. 2,634
    Black .............................. 339
    Hispanic ............................ 79
```

Civilian labor force as a percent of civilian non-institutional population, 2006
```
Total................................. 67.8%
    Men ................................ 73.8
    Women .............................. 62.3
    Persons 16-19 years................. 51.4
    White............................... 67.4
    Black .............................. 71.9
    Hispanic ........................... 71.7
```

Employment, 2006 (x 1,000)
```
Total..................................2,921
    Men .................................1,529
    Women ...............................1,391
    Persons 16-19 years................. 144
    White...............................2,532
    Black .............................. 298
    Hispanic ............................ 74
```

Unemployment rate, 2006
```
Total................................... 4.8%
    Men .................................4.6
    Women ...............................5.0
    Persons 16-19 years.................14.6
    White................................3.9
    Black ..............................12.2
    Hispanic ............................7.3
```

Full-time/part-time labor force, 2003 (x 1,000)
```
Full-time labor force, employed ..........2,351
Part-time labor force, employed............ 500
```
Unemployed, looking for
```
    Full-time work........................ 147
    Part-time work........................ 23
```
Mean duration of unemployment (weeks)......19.0
```
    Median ..............................8.6
```

Labor unions, 2006
```
Membership (x 1,000)................... 284
    percent of employed ................. 10.9%
```

Experienced civilian labor force by private industry, 2006
```
Total........................... 2,280,566
    Natural resources & mining ..........16,619
    Construction .....................147,806
    Manufacturing.................... 306,961
    Trade, transportation & utilities ..... 540,284
    Information ....................... 62,984
    Finance .......................... 158,719
    Professional & business .............331,395
    Education & health ................. 353,375
    Leisure & hospitality.............. 278,385
    Other ............................ 84,038
```

Experienced civilian labor force by occupation, May 2006
```
Management......................... 84,290
Business & financial .................. 108,800
Legal...............................17,340
Sales.............................. 297,480
Office & admin. support.............. 478,600
Computers & math ................... 62,880
Architecture & engineering.............37,270
Arts & entertainment ................. 32,970
Education ......................... 155,260
Social services ...................... 30,060
Health care practitioner & technical.... 160,030
Health care support ................. 72,730
Maintenance & repair.................115,740
Construction ...................... 133,820
Transportation & moving ............. 204,350
Production ........................ 229,100
Farming, fishing & forestry............ 4,550
```

Hours and earnings of production workers on manufacturing payrolls, 2006
```
Average weekly hours ...................39.3
Average hourly earnings ............... $17.16
Average weekly earnings .............. $674.39
```

Income and poverty, 2006
```
Median household income............ $42,841
Personal income, per capita (current $)... $32,705
    in constant (2000) dollars .......... $28,549
Persons below poverty level............. 13.6%
```

Average annual pay
```
2006 ................................$37,143
    increase from 2005 .................. 3.3%
```

Federal individual income tax returns, 2005
```
Returns filed......................2,610,839
Adjusted gross income ($1,000) ....$122,774,783
Total tax liability ($1,000)........$14,859,837
```

Charitable contributions, 2004
```
Number of contributions.................687.9
Total amount ($ mil)..................$2,595.7
```

©2008 Information Publications, Inc.
All rights reserved. Photocopying prohibited.
877-544-INFO (4636) or www.informationpublications.com

Economy, Business, Industry & Agriculture

Fortune 500 companies, 2007 10
Bankruptcy cases filed, FY 2007 20,141

Patents and trademarks issued, 2007

Patents 858
Trademarks 1,543

Business firm ownership, 2002

Women-owned 120,443
  Sales ($ mil) $18,605
Black-owned 16,750
  Sales ($ mil) $1,345
Hispanic-owned 3,652
  Sales ($ mil) $682
Asian-owned 6,376
  Sales ($ mil) $1,883
Amer. Indian/Alaska Native-owned 3,298
  Sales ($ mil) $340
Hawaiian/Pacific Islander-owned 96
  Sales ($ mil) $34

Gross domestic product, 2006 ($ mil)

Total gross domestic product $225,876
  Agriculture, forestry, fishing and
    hunting 1,946
  Mining 945
  Utilities 3,968
  Construction 10,835
  Manufacturing, durable goods 18,543
  Manufacturing, non-durable goods 15,742
  Wholesale trade .14,749
  Retail trade 15,527
  Transportation & warehousing 7,795
  Information 10,802
  Finance & insurance 13,541
  Real estate, rental & leasing 24,077
  Professional and technical services 13,416
  Educational services 2,864
  Health care and social assistance 16,858
  Accommodation/food services 5,792
  Other services, except government 5,551
  Government 26,133

Establishments, payroll, employees & receipts, by major industry group, 2005

Total 154,306
  Annual payroll ($1,000) $82,340,359
  Paid employees 2,425,403
Forestry, fishing & agriculture 261
  Annual payroll ($1,000) $32,435
  Paid employees 1,386
Mining 257
  Annual payroll ($1,000) $183,533
  Paid employees 4,257
  Receipts, 2002 ($1,000) $773,258

Utilities 384
  Annual payroll ($1,000) $1,065,504
  Paid employees .15,112
  Receipts, 2002 ($1,000) . . . . .NA
Construction 17,050
  Annual payroll ($1,000) $6,218,667
  Paid employees 148,881
  Receipts, 2002 ($1,000) $26,103,729
Manufacturing 6,935
  Annual payroll ($1,000) $11,640,421
  Paid employees 298,117
  Receipts, 2002 ($1,000) $92,909,173
Wholesale trade 8,276
  Annual payroll ($1,000) $5,291,381
  Paid employees 130,004
  Receipts, 2002 ($1,000) $95,603,561
Retail trade 23,507
  Annual payroll ($1,000) $6,780,597
  Paid employees 321,615
  Receipts, 2002 ($1,000) $61,861,163
Transportation & warehousing 5,114
  Annual payroll ($1,000) $3,046,865
  Paid employees 87,366
  Receipts, 2002 ($1,000) $9,216,811
Information 2,570
  Annual payroll ($1,000) $3,612,077
  Paid employees 74,233
  Receipts, 2002 ($1,000) . . . . .NA
Finance & insurance 10,742
  Annual payroll ($1,000) $7,067,143
  Paid employees 136,316
  Receipts, 2002 ($1,000) . . . . .NA
Professional, scientific & technical 13,570
  Annual payroll ($1,000) $6,968,986
  Paid employees 133,171
  Receipts, 2002 ($1,000) $14,379,844
Education 1,460
  Annual payroll ($1,000) $1,874,297
  Paid employees 66,197
  Receipts, 2002 ($1,000) $335,325
Health care & social assistance 15,229
  Annual payroll ($1,000) $11,730,526
  Paid employees 355,301
  Receipts, 2002 ($1,000) $24,944,155
Arts and entertainment 2,134
  Annual payroll ($1,000) $1,119,419
  Paid employees 36,856
  Receipts, 2002 ($1,000) $2,747,690
Real estate 6,873
  Annual payroll ($1,000) $1,330,721
  Paid employees 41,101
  Receipts, 2002 ($1,000) $5,654,672
Accommodation & food service 11,811
  Annual payroll ($1,000) $2,867,580
  Paid employees 234,662
  Receipts, 2002 ($1,000) $8,607,025

©2008 Information Publications, Inc.
All rights reserved. Photocopying prohibited.
877-544-INFO (4636) or www.informationpublications.com

8   Missouri

Exports, 2006
Value of exported goods ($ mil) $12,776
   Manufactured $11,361
   Non-manufactured. $1,087

Foreign direct investment in US affiliates, 2004
Property, plants & equipment ($ mil) $16,027
Employment (x 1,000). 84.2

Agriculture, 2006
Number of farms 105,000
Farm acreage (x 1,000) 30,100
   Acres per farm 287
Farm marketings and income ($ mil)
Total. $5,621.3
   Crops $2,627.6
   Livestock. $2,993.7
Net farm income $1,697.3

Principal commodities, in order by marketing receipts, 2005
Cattle and calves, Soybeans, Corn, Hogs, Turkeys

Federal economic activity in state
Expenditures, 2005 ($ mil)
   Total. $48,273
      Per capita $8,326.24
   Defense $8,975
   Non-defense $39,298
Defense department, 2006 ($ mil)
   Payroll. $2,432
   Contract awards $9,393
   Grants $46
Homeland security grants ($1,000)
   2006 . . . . $42,861
   2007 . . . . $31,244

FDIC-insured financial institutions, 2005
Number 368
Assets ($ billion) $106.9
Deposits ($ billion) $83.8

Fishing, 2006
Catch (x 1,000 lbs). . . . . NA
Value ($1,000). . . . . NA

Mining, 2006 ($ mil)
Total non-fuel mineral production $2,130
Percent of U.S. 3.31%

Communication, Energy & Transportation

Communication
Households with computers, 2003 . . . . .60.7%
Households with internet access, 2003 . . . .53.0%
High-speed internet providers 83
Total high-speed internet lines. 1,266,504
   Residential 1,024,388
   Business. 242,116
Wireless phone customers, 12/2006 4,322,458

FCC-licensed stations (as of January 1, 2008)
TV stations 35
FM radio stations. 253
AM radio stations 117

Energy
Energy consumption, 2004
   Total (trillion Btu). 1,849
   Per capita (million Btu) 321.5
By source of production (trillion Btu)
   Coal 808
   Natural gas 268
   Petroleum. 747
   Nuclear electric power 82
   Hydroelectric power. 15
By end-use sector (trillion Btu)
   Residential 489
   Commercial 391
   Industrial 390
   Transportation 578
Electric energy, 2005
   Primary source of electricity. . . . . Coal
   Net generation (billion kWh) 90.8
      percent from renewable sources. 1.3%
   Net summer capability (million kW) 20.5
   CO_2 emitted from generation 79.8
Natural gas utilities, 2005
   Customers (x 1,000) 1,494
   Sales (trillion Btu). 241
   Revenues ($ mil) $2,006
Nuclear plants, 2007 1
Total CO_2 emitted (million metric tons). . . . 137.2
Energy spending, 2004 ($ mil) $16,370
   per capita $2,846
   Price per million Btu $12.89

Transportation, 2006
Public road & street mileage 127,205
   Urban. 19,244
   Rural 107,961
   Interstate. 1,181
Vehicle miles of travel (millions) 68,834
   per capita 11,791.4
Total motor vehicle registrations. 4,957,172
   Automobiles. .2,715,297
   Trucks 2,230,390
   Motorcycles 85,464
Licensed drivers .4,139,632
   19 years & under 226,221
Deaths from motor vehicle accidents 1,096
Gasoline consumed (x 1,000 gallons) 3,221,159
   per capita 551.8

Commuting Statistics, 2006
Average commute time (min) 22.9
   Drove to work alone 80.8%
   Carpooled. 10.4%
   Public transit 1.4%
   Walk to work 2.1%
   Work from home 4.1%

©2008 Information Publications, Inc.
All rights reserved. Photocopying prohibited.
877-544-INFO (4636) or www.informationpublications.com

State Summary

Capital city . . . . Helena
Governor . . . . Brian Schweitzer

State Capitol
Helena, MT 59620
406-444-3111

Admitted as a state 1889
Area (square miles) .147,042
Population, 2007 (estimate). 957,861
Largest city . . . . Billings
Population, 2006 100,148
Personal income per capita, 2006
(in current dollars) $30,688
Gross domestic product, 2006 ($ mil) $32,322

Leading industries by payroll, 2005

Health care/Social assistance, Retail trade,
Construction

**Leading agricultural commodities
by receipts, 2005**

Cattle and calves, Wheat, Barley, Hay, Sugar
beets

Geography & Environment

Total area (square miles). 147,042
land 145,552
water 1,490
Federally-owned land, 2004 (acres) . . . 27,910,152
percent. 29.9%
Highest point .Granite Peak
elevation (feet) 12,799
Lowest point . . . . .Kootenai River
elevation (feet) 1,800
General coastline (miles) 0
Tidal shoreline (miles) 0
Cropland, 2003 (x 1,000 acres) 14,527
Forest land, 2003 (x 1,000 acres). 5,402
Capital city . . . . Helena
Population 2000 25,780
Population 2006 27,885
Largest city . . . . Billings
Population 2000 89,847
Population 2006 100,148

Number of cities with over 100,000 population

1990 0
2000 0
2006 1

State park and recreation areas, 2005

Area (x 1,000 acres) 55
Number of visitors (x 1,000) 5,671
Revenues ($1,000) $5,214
percent of operating expenditures 66.4%

National forest system land, 2007

Acres 1,692,737

Demographics & Population Characteristics

Population

1980 786,690
1990 799,065
2000 902,195
2006 944,632
Male. 472,660
Female 471,972
Living in group quarters, 2006 25,102
percent of total. 2.7%
2007 (estimate). 957,861
persons per square mile of land 6.6
2008 (projected). 954,653
2010 (projected) 968,598
2020 (projected) 1,022,735
2030 (projected) 1,044,898

**Population of Core-Based Statistical Areas
(formerly Metropolitan Areas), x 1,000**

	CBSA	Non-CBSA
1990	495	304
2000	574	328
2006	615	330

Change in population, 2000-2007

Number 55,666
percent 6.2%
Natural increase (births minus deaths) 23,847
Net internal migration 30,446
Net international migration 2,099

Persons by age, 2006

Under 5 years 57,916
5 to 17 years 159,932
18 years and over 726,784
65 years and over 130,592
85 years and over 19,000
Median age 39.2

Persons by age, 2010 (projected)

Under 5 years 59,714
18 and over 756,286
65 and over 144,961
Median age 40.4

Race, 2006

One Race
White. 858,140
Black or African American 4,094
Asian 5,699
American Indian/Alaska Native. 60,725
Hawaiian Native/Pacific Islander. 527
Two or more races. 15,447

Persons of Hispanic origin, 2006

Total Hispanic or Latino 20,513
Mexican. 12,835
Puerto Rican 2,429
Cuban 929

©2008 Information Publications, Inc.
All rights reserved. Photocopying prohibited.
877-544-INFO (4636) or www.informationpublications.com

Persons of Asian origin, 2006

Total Asian	5,525
Asian Indian	473
Chinese	646
Filipino	1,433
Japanese	923
Korean	1,208
Vietnamese	581

Marital status, 2006

Population 15 years & over	769,036
Never married	206,878
Married	424,273
Separated	10,318
Widowed	48,890
Divorced	88,995

Language spoken at home, 2006

Population 5 years and older	887,055
English only	845,089
Spanish	13,458
French	2,018
German	9,671
Chinese	303

Households & families, 2006

Households	372,190
with persons under 18 years	112,207
with persons over 65 years	90,662
persons per household	2.47
Families	240,412
persons per family	3.05
Married couples	197,345
Female householder, no husband present	30,098
One-person households	107,392

Nativity, 2006

Number of residents born in state	505,296
percent of population	53.5%

Immigration & naturalization, 2006

Legal permanent residents admitted	505
Persons naturalized	225
Non-immigrant admissions	34,791

Vital Statistics and Health

Marriages

2004	6,946
2005	6,964
2006	6,757

Divorces

2004	3,516
2005	4,203
2006	3,372

Health risks, 2006

Percent of adults who are:

Smokers	18.9%
Overweight (BMI > 25)	59.3%
Obese (BMI > 30)	21.2%

Births

2005	11,583
Birthrate (per 1,000)	12.4
White	9,914
Black	63
Hispanic	396
Asian/Pacific Islander	119
Amer. Indian/Alaska Native	1,487
Low birth weight (2,500g or less)	6.6%
Cesarian births	25.8%
Preterm births	11.4%
To unmarried mothers	34.6%
Twin births (per 1,000)	27.6
Triplets or higher order (per 100,000)	95.6
2006 (preliminary)	12,506
rate per 1,000	13.2

Deaths

2004

All causes	8,094
rate per 100,000	778.6
Heart disease	1,838
rate per 100,000	173.6
Malignant neoplasms	1,867
rate per 100,000	180.2
Cerebrovascular disease	484
rate per 100,000	45.7
Chronic lower respiratory disease	578
rate per 100,000	56.1
Diabetes	237
rate per 100,000	22.6
2005 (preliminary)	8,529
rate per 100,000	798.4
2006 (provisional)	8,488

Infant deaths

2004	52
rate per 1,000	4.5
2005 (provisional)	71
rate per 1,000	6.3

Exercise routines, 2005

None	22.4%
Moderate or greater	56.5%
Vigorous	33.1%

Abortions, 2004

Total performed in state	2,256
rate per 1,000 women age 15-44	12
% obtained by out-of-state residents	8.6%

Physicians, 2005

Total	2,084
rate per 100,000 persons	223

Community hospitals, 2005

Number of hospitals	54
Beds (x 1,000)	4.3
Patients admitted (x 1,000)	106
Average daily census (x 1,000)	2.8
Average cost per day	$814
Outpatient visits (x 1 mil)	2.9

©2008 Information Publications, Inc.
All rights reserved. Photocopying prohibited.
877-544-INFO (4636) or www.informationpublications.com

Disability status of population, 2006
5 to 15 years 6.6%
16 to 64 years 14.6%
65 years and over 42.1%

Education

Educational attainment, 2006
Population over 25 years 630,680
　　Less than 9th grade. 3.6%
　　High school graduate or more 90.1%
　　College graduate or more. 27.4%
　　Graduate or professional degree. 8.4%

Public school enrollment, 2005-06
Total. 145,416
　　Pre-kindergarten through grade 8. 97,575
　　Grades 9 through 12 47,562

Graduating public high school seniors, 2004-05
Diplomas (incl. GED and others) 10,335

SAT scores, 2007
Average critical reading score. 538
Average writing score 522
Average math score 543
Percent of graduates taking test 28%

Public school teachers, 2006-07 (estimate)
Total (x 1,000) 10.5
　　Elementary. 7.0
　　Secondary. 3.6
Average salary $41,225
　　Elementary. $41,225
　　Secondary. $41,225

State receipts & expenditures for public schools, 2006-07 (estimate)
Revenue receipts ($ mil) $1,372
Expenditures
Total ($ mil) $1,306
　　Per capita $1,327
　　Per pupil $10,119

NAEP proficiency scores, 2007

	Reading		Math	
	Basic	Proficient	Basic	Proficient
Grade 4	75.0%	38.5%	87.7%	44.4%
Grade 8	84.5%	38.9%	79.1%	37.6%

Higher education enrollment, fall 2005
Total. 4,853
　　Full-time men 1,585
　　Full-time women .2,215
　　Part-time men 360
　　Part-time women. 693

Minority enrollment in institutions of higher education, 2005
Black, non-Hispanic 270
Hispanic 791
Asian/Pacific Islander 536
American Indian/Alaska Native. 4,588

Institutions of higher education, 2005-06
Total. 23
　　Public. 18
　　Private 5

Earned degrees conferred, 2004-05
Associate's. 1,782
Bachelor's 5,177
Master's 1,122
First-professional. 129
Doctor's 117

Public Libraries, 2006
Number of libraries. 79
Number of outlets 112
Annual visits per capita 4.1
Circulation per capita. 6.2

State & local financial support for higher education, FY 2006
Full-time equivalent enrollment (x 1,000). 35.4
Appropriations per FTE. $4,409

Social Insurance & Welfare Programs

Social Security benefits & beneficiaries, 2005
Beneficiaries (x 1,000) 169
　　Retired & dependents. 122
　　Survivors. 23
　　Disabled & dependents. 25
Annual benefit payments ($ mil) $1,748
　　Retired & dependents. $1,193
　　Survivors. $305
　　Disabled & dependents. $250
Average monthly benefit
　　Retired & dependents. $959
　　Disabled & dependents. $903
　　Widowed. $955

Medicare, July 2005
Enrollment (x 1,000). 148
Payments ($ mil) $847

Medicaid, 2004
Beneficiaries (x 1,000). 113
Payments ($ mil) $585

State Children's Health Insurance Program, 2006
Enrollment (x 1,000). 17.3
Expenditures ($ mil). $21.8

Persons without health insurance, 2006
Number (x 1,000). 160
　　percent. 17.2%
Number of children (x 1,000) 31
　　percent of children 14.6%

Health care expenditures, 2004
Total expenditures. $4,706
　　per capita $5,080

©2008 Information Publications, Inc.
All rights reserved.　Photocopying prohibited.
877-544-INFO (4636) or www.informationpublications.com

Federal and state public aid

State unemployment insurance, 2006
Recipients, first payments (x 1,000) 20
Total payments ($ mil) $63
Average weekly benefit $204
Temporary Assistance for Needy Families, 2006
Recipients (x 1,000) 112.7
Families (x 1,000) 43.7
Supplemental Security Income, 2005
Recipients (x 1,000) 14.8
Payments ($ mil) $69.9
Food Stamp Program, 2006
Avg monthly participants (x 1,000) 81.6
Total benefits ($ mil) $90.0

Housing & Construction

Housing units
Total 2005 (estimate) 428,300
Total 2006 (estimate) 432,023
Seasonal or recreational use, 2006 27,992
Owner-occupied, 2006 260,137
  Median home value $155,500
  Homeowner vacancy rate 1.9%
Renter-occupied, 2006 112,053
  Median rent $571
  Rental vacancy rate 7.9%
Home ownership rate, 2005 . . . . 70.4%
Home ownership rate, 2006 . . . . 69.5%

New privately-owned housing units
Number authorized, 2006 (x 1,000) 4.5
  Value ($ mil) $723.1
Started 2005 (x 1,000, estimate) 2.9
Started 2006 (x 1,000, estimate) 2.8

Existing home sales
2005 (x 1,000) 25.4
2006 (x 1,000) 26.8

Government & Elections

State officials 2008
Governor . . . . Brian Schweitzer
    Democratic, term expires 1/09
Lieutenant Governor . . . . John Bohlinger
Secretary of State . . . . Brad Johnson
Attorney General . . . . Mike McGrath
Chief Justice . . . . Karla Gray

Governorship
Minimum age 25
Length of term . . . . 4 years
Consecutive terms permitted . . . . . 8 out of 16 yrs
Who succeeds . . . . Lieutenant Governor

Local governments by type, 2002
Total 1,127
  County 54
  Municipal 129
  Township 0
  School District 352
  Special District 592

State legislature
Name . . . . Legislature
Upper chamber . . . . Senate
  Number of members 50
  Length of term . . . . 4 years
  Party in majority, 2008 . . . . Democratic
Lower chamber . . . . House of Representatives
  Number of members 100
  Length of term . . . . 2 years
  Party in majority, 2008 . . . . Republican

Federal representation, 2008 (110th Congress)
Senator . . . . Max Baucus
  Party . . . . Democratic
  Year term expires 2009
Senator . . . . Jon Tester
  Party . . . . Democratic
  Year term expires 2013
Representatives, total 1
  Democrats 0
  Republicans 1

Voters in November 2006 election (estimate)
Total 435,025
  Male 220,871
  Female 214,154
  White 413,480
  Black 393
  Hispanic 1,524
  Asian 1,571

Presidential election, 2004
Total Popular Vote 450,445
  Kerry 173,710
  Bush 266,063
Total Electoral Votes 3

Votes cast for US Senators
2004
Total vote (x 1,000) . . . . NA
Leading party . . . . NA
Percent for leading party . . . . NA
2006
Total vote (x 1,000) 407
Leading party . . . . Democratic
Percent for leading party 49.2%

Votes cast for US Representatives
2004
Total vote (x 1,000) 444
  Democratic 146
  Republican 286
Leading party . . . . Republican
Percent for leading party 64.4%
2006
Total vote (x 1,000) 406
  Democratic 159
  Republican 239
Leading party . . . . Republican
Percent for leading party 58.9%

©2008 Information Publications, Inc.
All rights reserved. Photocopying prohibited.
877-544-INFO (4636) or www.informationpublications.com

State government employment, 2006
Full-time equivalent employees 18,933
Payroll ($ mil) $64.2

Local government employment, 2006
Full-time equivalent employees 35,255
Payroll ($ mil) $100.5

Women holding public office, 2008
US Congress............................... 0
Statewide elected office.................. 1
State legislature 38

Black public officials, 2002
Total..................................... 0
   US and state legislatures 0
   City/county/regional offices 0
   Judicial/law enforcement................... 0
   Education/school boards.................. 0

Hispanic public officials, 2006
Total..................................... 1
   State executives & legislators 0
   City/county/regional offices 0
   Judicial/law enforcement................... 1
   Education/school boards.................. 0

Governmental Finance

State government revenues, 2006
Total revenue (x $1,000)............$6,130,467
   per capita $6,474.97
General revenue (x $1,000) $4,935,220
   Intergovernmental 1,825,693
   Taxes 2,126,324
      general sales........................... 0
      individual income tax 768,911
      corporate income tax 153,675
   Current charges................... 476,860
   Miscellaneous 506,343

State government expenditure, 2006
Total expenditure (x $1,000).........$5,194,561
   per capita $5,486.47
General expenditure (x $1,000) $4,583,636
   per capita, total.................. *$4,841.21*
      Education 1,607.32
      Public welfare 900.26
      Health 306.03
      Hospitals....................... 42.82
      Highways 616.01
      Police protection.................... 42.47
      Corrections 151.53
      Natural resources 215.99
      Parks & recreation 16.15
      Governmental administration..... 298.78
      Interest on general debt.............165.03

State debt & cash, 2006 ($ per capita)
Debt $4,598.43
Cash/security holdings..............$15,249.00

Federal government grants to state & local government, 2005 (x $1,000)
Total.............................$2,139,765
by Federal agency
   Defense 47,326
   Education 213,571
   Energy............................8,415
   Environmental Protection Agency 44,436
   Health & Human Services. 883,416
   Homeland Security.................10,731
   Housing & Urban Development...... 106,990
   Justice 34,289
   Labor 32,473
   Transportation 404,448
   Veterans Affairs...................3,539

Crime & Law Enforcement

Crime, 2006 (rates per 100,000 residents)
Property crimes 25,387
   Burglary 2,935
   Larceny 20,704
   Motor vehicle theft 1,748
   Property crime rate.................2,687.5
Violent crimes........................ 2,397
   Murder 17
   Forcible rape...................... 269
   Robbery.......................... 164
   Aggravated assault 1,947
   Violent crime rate 253.7
Hate crimes........................ 29

Fraud and identity theft, 2006
Fraud complaints......................1,289
   rate per 100,000 residents 136.5
Identity theft complaints 434
   rate per 100,000 residents 45.9

Law enforcement agencies, 2006
Total agencies........................ 109
Total employees 2,753
   Officers 1,679
   Civilians 1,074

Prisoners, probation, and parole, 2006
Total prisoners........................3,572
   percent change, 12/31/05 to 12/31/06 .... 1.1%
   in private facilities 26.9%
   in local jails 19.1%
Sentenced to more than one year 3,547
   rate per 100,000 residents 374
Adults on probation 8,770
Adults on parole....................... 844

Prisoner demographics, June 30, 2005 (rate per 100,000 residents)
Male...................................... 926
Female 129
White.................................... 433
Black.................................... 3,569
Hispanic 846

©2008 Information Publications, Inc.
All rights reserved. Photocopying prohibited.
877-544-INFO (4636) or www.informationpublications.com

Arrests, 2006

Total .... NA
    Persons under 18 years of age .... NA

Persons under sentence of death, 1/1/07

Total 2
    White 2
    Black 0
    Hispanic 0

State's highest court

Name .... Supreme Court
Number of members 7
Length of term .... 8 years
Intermediate appeals court? .... no

Labor & Income

Civilian labor force, 2006 (x 1,000)

Total 505
    Men 265
    Women 240
    Persons 16-19 years 29
    White 475
    Black .... NA
    Hispanic 10

Civilian labor force as a percent of civilian non-institutional population, 2006

Total 67.2%
    Men 71.5
    Women 63.1
    Persons 16-19 years 53.1
    White 67.6
    Black .... NA
    Hispanic 76.4

Employment, 2006 (x 1,000)

Total 487
    Men 255
    Women 232
    Persons 16-19 years 26
    White 460
    Black .... NA
    Hispanic 9

Unemployment rate, 2006

Total 3.6%
    Men 3.7
    Women 3.5
    Persons 16-19 years 10.5
    White 3.2
    Black .... NA
    Hispanic 5.1

Full-time/part-time labor force, 2003 (x 1,000)

Full-time labor force, employed 354
Part-time labor force, employed 99
Unemployed, looking for
    Full-time work 18
    Part-time work 5
Mean duration of unemployment (weeks) 15.1
    Median 8.3

Labor unions, 2006

Membership (x 1,000) 48
    percent of employed 12.2%

Experienced civilian labor force by private industry, 2006

Total 346,275
    Natural resources & mining 11,726
    Construction 30,136
    Manufacturing 20,168
    Trade, transportation & utilities 86,444
    Information 7,736
    Finance 22,008
    Professional & business 38,016
    Education & health 57,184
    Leisure & hospitality 56,759
    Other 15,833

Experienced civilian labor force by occupation, May 2006

Management 19,210
Business & financial 14,290
Legal 2,970
Sales 43,990
Office & admin. support 72,280
Computers & math 6,000
Architecture & engineering 6,210
Arts & entertainment 5,980
Education 27,460
Social services 7,240
Health care practitioner & technical 21,710
Health care support 10,960
Maintenance & repair 19,050
Construction 29,210
Transportation & moving 29,400
Production 18,450
Farming, fishing & forestry 2,560

Hours and earnings of production workers on manufacturing payrolls, 2006

Average weekly hours 40.0
Average hourly earnings $15.90
Average weekly earnings $636.00

Income and poverty, 2006

Median household income $40,627
Personal income, per capita (current $) ... $30,688
    in constant (2000) dollars $26,789
Persons below poverty level 13.6%

Average annual pay

2006 .... $30,596
    increase from 2005 .... 5.0%

Federal individual income tax returns, 2005

Returns filed 448,050
Adjusted gross income ($1,000) $18,315,335
Total tax liability ($1,000) $2,063,735

Charitable contributions, 2004

Number of contributions 111.8
Total amount ($ mil) $348.8

©2008 Information Publications, Inc.
All rights reserved. Photocopying prohibited.
877-544-INFO (4636) or www.informationpublications.com

Economy, Business, Industry & Agriculture

Fortune 500 companies, 2007 0
Bankruptcy cases filed, FY 2007 1,934

Patents and trademarks issued, 2007
Patents 123
Trademarks 198

Business firm ownership, 2002
Women-owned 24,519
　Sales ($ mil) $2,139
Black-owned 220
　Sales ($ mil) $12
Hispanic-owned 964
　Sales ($ mil) $99
Asian-owned 511
　Sales ($ mil) $100
Amer. Indian/Alaska Native-owned 1,990
　Sales ($ mil) $215
Hawaiian/Pacific Islander-owned 40
　Sales ($ mil) $2

Gross domestic product, 2006 ($ mil)
Total gross domestic product $32,322
　Agriculture, forestry, fishing and
　　hunting 1,281
　Mining 1,838
　Utilities 1,181
　Construction 2,160
　Manufacturing, durable goods 907
　Manufacturing, non-durable goods 566
　Wholesale trade 1,729
　Retail trade 2,296
　Transportation & warehousing 1,364
　Information 907
　Finance & insurance 1,601
　Real estate, rental & leasing 3,800
　Professional and technical services 1,511
　Educational services 137
　Health care and social assistance 2,923
　Accommodation/food services 1,034
　Other services, except government 725
　Government 5,166

Establishments, payroll, employees & receipts, by major industry group, 2005

Total 35,736
　Annual payroll ($1,000) $8,950,520
　Paid employees 326,887
Forestry, fishing & agriculture 405
　Annual payroll ($1,000) $50,741
　Paid employees 1,602
Mining 294
　Annual payroll ($1,000) $325,011
　Paid employees 5,552
　Receipts, 2002 ($1,000) $1,226,555

Utilities 217
　Annual payroll ($1,000) $170,688
　Paid employees 2,645
　Receipts, 2002 ($1,000) . . . . NA
Construction 5,367
　Annual payroll ($1,000) $876,686
　Paid employees 23,795
　Receipts, 2002 ($1,000) $3,372,837
Manufacturing 1,283
　Annual payroll ($1,000) $739,644
　Paid employees 19,470
　Receipts, 2002 ($1,000) $4,987,577
Wholesale trade 1,491
　Annual payroll ($1,000) $488,131
　Paid employees 13,931
　Receipts, 2002 ($1,000) $7,223,420
Retail trade 5,192
　Annual payroll ($1,000) $1,165,388
　Paid employees 56,287
　Receipts, 2002 ($1,000) $10,122,625
Transportation & warehousing 1,237
　Annual payroll ($1,000) $311,031
　Paid employees 10,647
　Receipts, 2002 ($1,000) $996,647
Information 613
　Annual payroll ($1,000) $295,958
　Paid employees 7,915
　Receipts, 2002 ($1,000) . . . . NA
Finance & insurance 1,937
　Annual payroll ($1,000) $618,820
　Paid employees 16,096
　Receipts, 2002 ($1,000) . . . . NA
Professional, scientific & technical 3,274
　Annual payroll ($1,000) $727,538
　Paid employees 21,555
　Receipts, 2002 ($1,000) $1,249,057
Education 278
　Annual payroll ($1,000) $96,852
　Paid employees 5,342
　Receipts, 2002 ($1,000) $39,674
Health care & social assistance 3,216
　Annual payroll ($1,000) $1,665,581
　Paid employees 54,114
　Receipts, 2002 ($1,000) $3,432,698
Arts and entertainment 1,034
　Annual payroll ($1,000) $135,631
　Paid employees 9,723
　Receipts, 2002 ($1,000) $486,116
Real estate 1,727
　Annual payroll ($1,000) $149,727
　Paid employees 5,933
　Receipts, 2002 ($1,000) $520,932
Accommodation & food service 3,375
　Annual payroll ($1,000) $474,679
　Paid employees 42,447
　Receipts, 2002 ($1,000) $1,537,986

©2008 Information Publications, Inc.
All rights reserved. Photocopying prohibited.
877-544-INFO (4636) or www.informationpublications.com

8   Montana

Exports, 2006
Value of exported goods ($ mil) $887
  Manufactured $685
  Non-manufactured. $176

Foreign direct investment in US affiliates, 2004
Property, plants & equipment ($ mil) $2,233
Employment (x 1,000). 6.4

Agriculture, 2006
Number of farms 28,100
Farm acreage (x 1,000) 60,100
  Acres per farm 2,139
Farm marketings and income ($ mil)
Total. $2,349.2
  Crops. $1,070.0
  Livestock. $1,279.2
Net farm income $256.8

Principal commodities, in order by marketing receipts, 2005
  Cattle and calves, Wheat, Barley, Hay, Sugar
      beets

Federal economic activity in state
Expenditures, 2005 ($ mil)
  Total. $7,814
    Per capita $8,359.11
  Defense $663
  Non-defense $7,151
Defense department, 2006 ($ mil)
  Payroll. $407
  Contract awards $247
  Grants $32
Homeland security grants ($1,000)
  2006. . . . .$7,930
  2007. . . . .$6,686

FDIC-insured financial institutions, 2005
Number 83
Assets ($ billion) $17.1
Deposits ($ billion) $13.2

Fishing, 2006
Catch (x 1,000 lbs). . . . . NA
Value ($1,000). . . . . NA

Mining, 2006 ($ mil)
Total non-fuel mineral production $1,040
Percent of U.S. 1.61%

Communication, Energy & Transportation

Communication
Households with computers, 2003 . . . . 59.5%
Households with internet access, 2003 . . . . 50.4%
High-speed internet providers 38
Total high-speed internet lines. 264,121
  Residential 146,276
  Business. 117,845
Wireless phone customers, 12/2006 619,620

FCC-licensed stations (as of January 1, 2008)
TV stations 26
FM radio stations. 123
AM radio stations 52

Energy
Energy consumption, 2004
  Total (trillion Btu). 403
  Per capita (million Btu) 434.9
By source of production (trillion Btu)
  Coal 196
  Natural gas 67
  Petroleum 186
  Nuclear electric power 0
  Hydroelectric power 89
By end-use sector (trillion Btu)
  Residential 74
  Commercial 66
  Industrial 153
  Transportation 110
Electric energy, 2005
  Primary source of electricity. . . . . Coal
  Net generation (billion kWh) 27.9
    percent from renewable sources. 34.5%
  Net summer capability (million kW) 5.3
  CO_2 emitted from generation 19.5
Natural gas utilities, 2005
  Customers (x 1,000) 273
  Sales (trillion Btu). 57
  Revenues ($ mil) $325
Nuclear plants, 2007 0
*Total CO_2 emitted (million metric tons). 32.7
Energy spending, 2004 ($ mil) $3,182
  per capita $3,435
  Price per million Btu $12.12

Transportation, 2006
Public road & street mileage 73,148
  Urban. 2,973
  Rural. 70,175
  Interstate. 1,192
Vehicle miles of travel (millions) 11,265
  per capita 11,898.0
*Total motor vehicle registrations. 1,066,562
  Automobiles. 447,446
  Trucks 616,613
  Motorcycles 85,873
Licensed drivers 723,976
  19 years & under 46,810
Deaths from motor vehicle accidents 263
Gasoline consumed (x 1,000 gallons) 498,343
  per capita 526.3

Commuting Statistics, 2006
Average commute time (min) 17.6
  Drove to work alone 72.7%
  Carpooled. 12.0%
  Public transit 0.9%
  Walk to work 5.3%
  Work from home 6.7%

©2008 Information Publications, Inc.
All rights reserved. Photocopying prohibited.
877-544-INFO (4636) or www.informationpublications.com

State Summary

Capital city . . . . Lincoln
Governor . . . . Dave Heineman

PO Box 94848
Lincoln, NE 68509
402-471-2244

Admitted as a state 1867
Area (square miles) .77,354
Population, 2007 (estimate). 1,774,571
Largest city . . . . Omaha
    Population, 2006 419,545
Personal income per capita, 2006
    (in current dollars) $34,397
Gross domestic product, 2006 ($ mil) $75,700

Leading industries by payroll, 2005

Manufacturing, Health care/Social assistance,
Finance & Insurance

Leading agricultural commodities
by receipts, 2005

Cattle and calves, Corn, Soybeans, Hogs, Wheat

Geography & Environment

Total area (square miles). 77,354
    land 76,872
    water 481
Federally-owned land, 2004 (acres) 665,481
    percent. 1.4%
Highest point . . . . Panorama Point
    elevation (feet) 5,424
Lowest point . . . Missouri River (Richardson Co.)
    elevation (feet) 840
General coastline (miles) 0
Tidal shoreline (miles) 0
Cropland, 2003 (x 1,000 acres) 19,552
Forest land, 2003 (x 1,000 acres). 812
Capital city . . . . Lincoln
    Population 2000 225,581
    Population 2006 241,167
Largest city . . . . Omaha
    Population 2000 390,007
    Population 2006 419,545

Number of cities with over 100,000 population

1990 2
2000 2
2006 2

State park and recreation areas, 2005

Area (x 1,000 acres). 135
Number of visitors (x 1,000) 9,998
Revenues ($1,000) $16,044
    percent of operating expenditures. 86.8%

National forest system land, 2007

Acres 352,289

Demographics & Population Characteristics

Population

1980 1,569,825
1990 1,578,385
2000 1,711,265
2006 1,768,331
    Male 876,754
    Female 891,577
Living in group quarters, 2006 52,087
    percent of total. 2.9%
2007 (estimate). 1,774,571
    persons per square mile of land 23.1
2008 (projected) 1,759,829
2010 (projected) 1,768,997
2020 (projected) 1,802,678
2030 (projected). 1,820,247

Population of Core-Based Statistical Areas
(formerly Metropolitan Areas), x 1,000

	CBSA	Non-CBSA
1990	1,198	381
2000	1,339	373
2006	1,415	354

Change in population, 2000-2007

Number 63,306
    percent. 3.7%
Natural increase (births minus deaths) 77,995
Net internal migration . . . .-36,717
Net international migration 27,398

Persons by age, 2006

Under 5 years 127,665
5 to 17 years 317,368
18 years and over 1,323,298
65 years and over 234,655
85 years and over .39,128
    Median age 36.0

Persons by age, 2010 (projected)

Under 5 years 127,806
18 and over 1,322,741
65 and over 243,313
    Median age 36.7

Race, 2006

One Race
    White. 1,622,682
    Black or African American 77,636
    Asian 29,253
    American Indian/Alaska Native. 17,103
    Hawaiian Native/Pacific Islander. 1,225
Two or more races. 20,432

Persons of Hispanic origin, 2006

Total Hispanic or Latino 130,230
    Mexican. 102,180
    Puerto Rican 2,645
    Cuban 625

©2008 Information Publications, Inc.
All rights reserved. Photocopying prohibited.
877-544-INFO (4636) or www.informationpublications.com

Persons of Asian origin, 2006

Total Asian 29,815
- Asian Indian. 5,558
- Chinese 6,465
- Filipino 1,667
- Japanese 1,626
- Korean. 1,917
- Vietnamese. 9,163

Marital status, 2006

Population 15 years & over 1,400,725
- Never married 384,010
- Married. 790,764
- Separated 18,404
- Widowed. 89,291
- Divorced 136,660

Language spoken at home, 2006

Population 5 years and older. 1,640,024
- English only 1,491,321
- Spanish 98,211
- French 4,576
- German. 6,614
- Chinese 5,553

Households & families, 2006

Households. 700,888
- with persons under 18 years 235,508
- with persons over 65 years. 158,988
- persons per household 2.45
Families. 462,408
- persons per family. 3.02
Married couples. .371,052
Female householder,
- no husband present. 65,408
One-person households 198,674

Nativity, 2006

Number of residents born in state 1,158,794
- percent of population 65.5%

Immigration & naturalization, 2006

Legal permanent residents admitted 3,795
Persons naturalized .1,797
Non-immigrant admissions 25,483

Vital Statistics and Health

Marriages

2004 12,489
2005 12,256
2006 12,037

Divorces

2004 5,962
2005 5,864
2006 6,173

Health risks, 2006

Percent of adults who are:
- Smokers. 18.7%
- Overweight (BMI > 25). 63.9%
- Obese (BMI > 30). 26.9%

Births

2005 26,145
- Birthrate (per 1,000). 14.9
- White. 23,233
- Black 1,718
- Hispanic 3,854
- Asian/Pacific Islander 697
- Amer. Indian/Alaska Native 497
- Low birth weight (2,500g or less) 7.0%
- Cesarian births .28.6%
- Preterm births 12.2%
- To unmarried mothers. 30.9%
- Twin births (per 1,000) 32.1
- Triplets or higher order (per 100,000). . . .269.2
2006 (preliminary). 26,733
- rate per 1,000 . . . . .15.1

Deaths

2004
All causes 14,657
- rate per 100,000. . . . . .746.9
Heart disease 3,738
- rate per 100,000. . . . . .185.3
Malignant neoplasms 3,270
- rate per 100,000. . . . . .173.6
Cerebrovascular disease. 978
- rate per 100,000. . . . . .48.0
Chronic lower respiratory disease 815
- rate per 100,000. . . . . .42.0
Diabetes. 395
- rate per 100,000. . . . . .20.4
2005 (preliminary). 14,964
- rate per 100,000. . . . . .749.5
2006 (provisional) 14,952

Infant deaths

2004 173
- rate per 1,000 . . . . .6.6
2005 (provisional) 149
- rate per 1,000 . . . . .5.7

Exercise routines, 2005

None. 23.8%
Moderate or greater. 47.3%
Vigorous 24.7%

Abortions, 2004

Total performed in state. 3,584
- rate per 1,000 women age 15-44. 10
- % obtained by out-of-state residents 14.3%

Physicians, 2005

Total. 4,209
- rate per 100,000 persons 239

Community hospitals, 2005

Number of hospitals 87
Beds (x 1,000). 7.6
Patients admitted (x 1,000) 214
Average daily census (x 1,000) 4.8
Average cost per day $1,066
Outpatient visits (x 1 mil) 3.9

©2008 Information Publications, Inc.
All rights reserved. Photocopying prohibited.
877-544-INFO (4636) or www.informationpublications.com

Nebraska   3

Disability status of population, 2006
5 to 15 years 6.0%
16 to 64 years 10.7%
65 years and over 37.3%

Education

Educational attainment, 2006
Population over 25 years 1,135,868
    Less than 9th grade.................... 4.2%
    High school graduate or more 89.5%
    College graduate or more.............. 26.9%
    Graduate or professional degree........ 8.4%

Public school enrollment, 2005-06
Total.................................. 286,646
    Pre-kindergarten through grade 8.... 195,055
    Grades 9 through 12 91,591

Graduating public high school seniors, 2004-05
Diplomas (incl. GED and others) 20,089

SAT scores, 2007
Average critical reading score.............. 579
Average writing score 562
Average math score 585
Percent of graduates taking test 6%

Public school teachers, 2006-07 (estimate)
Total (x 1,000) 21.3
    Elementary............................13.6
    Secondary.............................7.7
Average salary $42,044
    Elementary........................ $42,044
    Secondary......................... $42,044

State receipts & expenditures for public schools, 2006-07 (estimate)
Revenue receipts ($ mil) $2,620
Expenditures
Total ($ mil) $2,577
    Per capita $1,349
    Per pupil $9,028

NAEP proficiency scores, 2007

	Reading		Math	
	Basic	Proficient	Basic	Proficient
Grade 4	70.8%	34.6%	80.1%	37.9%
Grade 8	78.8%	35.0%	74.3%	34.6%

Higher education enrollment, fall 2005
Total................................. 28,055
    Full-time men 9,449
    Full-time women.................... 12,828
    Part-time men 2,016
    Part-time women....................3,762

Minority enrollment in institutions of higher education, 2005
Black, non-Hispanic 5,094
Hispanic 4,224
Asian/Pacific Islander 2,827
American Indian/Alaska Native........... 908

Institutions of higher education, 2005-06
Total..................................... 39
    Public.................................. 15
    Private................................. 24

Earned degrees conferred, 2004-05
Associate's........................... 4,630
Bachelor's 11,999
Master's..............................3,936
First-professional...................... 864
Doctor's.............................. 492

Public Libraries, 2006
Number of libraries...................... 270
Number of outlets 294
Annual visits per capita 6.5
Circulation per capita..................10.1

State & local financial support for higher education, FY 2006
Full-time equivalent enrollment (x 1,000).....72.6
Appropriations per FTE................ $6,999

Social Insurance & Welfare Programs

Social Security benefits & beneficiaries, 2005
Beneficiaries (x 1,000) 294
    Retired & dependents.................. 212
    Survivors............................. 39
    Disabled & dependents.................. 43
Annual benefit payments ($ mil) $3,120
    Retired & dependents.................$2,153
    Survivors............................$549
    Disabled & dependents................ $418
Average monthly benefit
    Retired & dependents................. $985
    Disabled & dependents................ $889
    Widowed............................ $994

Medicare, July 2005
Enrollment (x 1,000).................... 261
Payments ($ mil) $1,716

Medicaid, 2004
Beneficiaries (x 1,000)..................1,513
Payments ($ mil) $7,388

State Children's Health Insurance Program, 2006
Enrollment (x 1,000).....................45.0
Expenditures ($ mil)...................$29.9

Persons without health insurance, 2006
Number (x 1,000)........................ 217
    percent..............................12.3%
Number of children (x 1,000) 45
    percent of children 10.1%

Health care expenditures, 2004
Total expenditures.....................$9,782
    per capita $5,599

©2008 Information Publications, Inc.
All rights reserved. Photocopying prohibited.
877-544-INFO (4636) or www.informationpublications.com

Federal and state public aid

State unemployment insurance, 2006
Recipients, first payments (x 1,000) 33
Total payments ($ mil) $93
Average weekly benefit $231
Temporary Assistance for Needy Families, 2006
Recipients (x 1,000) 283.7
Families (x 1,000) 118.1
Supplemental Security Income, 2005
Recipients (x 1,000) 22.3
Payments ($ mil) $103.2
Food Stamp Program, 2006
Avg monthly participants (x 1,000) 119.7
Total benefits ($ mil) $124.3

Housing & Construction

Housing units
Total 2005 (estimate) 767,070
Total 2006 (estimate) 774,843
Seasonal or recreational use, 2006 14,506
Owner-occupied, 2006 475,899
  Median home value $119,200
  Homeowner vacancy rate 2.6%
Renter-occupied, 2006 224,989
  Median rent $593
  Rental vacancy rate 10.2%
Home ownership rate, 2005 . . . . 70.2%
Home ownership rate, 2006 . . . . 67.6%

New privately-owned housing units
Number authorized, 2006 (x 1,000) 8.2
  Value ($ mil) $1,064.9
Started 2005 (x 1,000, estimate) 10.0
Started 2006 (x 1,000, estimate) 9.7

Existing home sales
2005 (x 1,000) 41.2
2006 (x 1,000) 38.7

Government & Elections

State officials 2008
Governor . . . . Dave Heineman
      Republican, term expires 1/11
Lieutenant Governor . . . . Rick Sheehy
Secretary of State . . . . John Gale
Attorney General . . . . Jon Bruning
Chief Justice . . . . Michael Heavican

Governorship
Minimum age 30
Length of term . . . . 4 years
Consecutive terms permitted 2
Who succeeds . . . . Lieutenant Governor

Local governments by type, 2002
Total 2,791
  County 93
  Municipal 531
  Township 446
  School District 575
  Special District 1,146

State legislature
Name . . . . Unicameral Legislature
Upper chamber . . . . NA
  Number of members 49
  Length of term . . . . 4 year
  Party in majority, 2008 . . . . Nonpartisan
Lower chamber . . . . NA
  Number of members . . . . NA
  Length of term . . . . NA
  Party in majority, 2008 . . . . Nonpartisan

Federal representation, 2008 (110th Congress)
Senator . . . . .Charles Hagel
  Party . . . . Republican
  Year term expires 2009
Senator . . . . Benjamin Nelson
  Party . . . . Democratic
  Year term expires 2013
Representatives, total 3
  Democrats 0
  Republicans 3

Voters in November 2006 election (estimate)
Total 634,194
Male 295,008
Female 339,186
White 614,024
Black 12,381
Hispanic 6,243
Asian . . . . NA

Presidential election, 2004
Total Popular Vote 778,186
  Kerry 254,328
  Bush 512,814
Total Electoral Votes 5

Votes cast for US Senators
2004
Total vote (x 1,000) . . . . NA
Leading party . . . . NA
Percent for leading party . . . . NA
2006
Total vote (x 1,000) 592
Leading party . . . . Democratic
Percent for leading party 63.9%

Votes cast for US Representatives
2004
Total vote (x 1,000) 765
  Democratic 231
  Republican 515
Leading party . . . . Republican
Percent for leading party 67.3%
2006
Total vote (x 1,000) 596
  Democratic 262
  Republican 334
Leading party . . . . Republican
Percent for leading party 56.1%

©2008 Information Publications, Inc.
All rights reserved. Photocopying prohibited.
877-544-INFO (4636) or www.informationpublications.com

State government employment, 2006
Full-time equivalent employees 32,904
Payroll ($ mil) $101.8

Local government employment, 2006
Full-time equivalent employees 84,592
Payroll ($ mil) $285.9

Women holding public office, 2008
US Congress............................ 0
Statewide elected office....................... 1
State legislature 9

Black public officials, 2002
Total.. 9
   US and state legislatures 1
   City/county/regional offices 5
   Judicial/law enforcement.................. 0
   Education/school boards................... 3

Hispanic public officials, 2006
Total.. 3
   State executives & legislators 1
   City/county/regional offices 1
   Judicial/law enforcement................... 0
   Education/school boards................... 1

Governmental Finance

State government revenues, 2006
Total revenue (x $1,000)............$9,103,340
   per capita $5,161.31
General revenue (x $1,000) $8,045,282
   Intergovernmental 2,472,030
   Taxes 3,961,093
      general sales....................1,409,015
      individual income tax 1,545,024
      corporate income tax 262,296
   Current charges................... 769,908
   Miscellaneous 842,251

State government expenditure, 2006
Total expenditure (x $1,000) $7,702,325
   per capita $4,366.98
General expenditure (x $1,000) $7,357,894
   per capita, total.................. *$4,171.70*
   Education 1,456.47
   Public welfare 1,117.40
   Health 239.98
   Hospitals........................ 124.59
   Highways 365.00
   Police protection.................43.63
   Corrections 112.74
   Natural resources 89.70
   Parks & recreation 16.66
   Governmental administration...... 104.09
   Interest on general debt.............45.33

State debt & cash, 2006 ($ per capita)
Debt $1,045.69
Cash/security holdings...............$6,788.04

Federal government grants to state & local government, 2005 (x $1,000)
Total...............................$2,595,784
by Federal agency
   Defense 23,349
   Education 220,723
   Energy..............................6,195
   Environmental Protection Agency 31,951
   Health & Human Services. 1,428,059
   Homeland Security....................19,512
   Housing & Urban Development...... 146,764
   Justice 43,590
   Labor 34,888
   Transportation 293,236
   Veterans Affairs................... 24,423

Crime & Law Enforcement

Crime, 2006 (rates per 100,000 residents)
Property crimes 59,075
   Burglary 9,452
   Larceny 44,585
   Motor vehicle theft 5,038
   Property crime rate.................3,340.7
Violent crimes.........................4,983
   Murder 50
   Forcible rape........................ 548
   Robbery.............................1,129
   Aggravated assault 3,256
   Violent crime rate 281.8
Hate crimes........................... 62

Fraud and identity theft, 2006
Fraud complaints......................1,968
   rate per 100,000 residents 111.3
Identity theft complaints 868
   rate per 100,000 residents 49.1

Law enforcement agencies, 2006
Total agencies......................... 156
Total employees 4,774
   Officers 3,453
   Civilians 1,321

Prisoners, probation, and parole, 2006
Total prisoners........................ 4,407
   percent change, 12/31/05 to 12/31/06 ....-1.1%
   in private facilities 0%
   in local jails 0%
Sentenced to more than one year 4,204
   rate per 100,000 residents 237
Adults on probation 18,731
Adults on parole........................ 797

Prisoner demographics, June 30, 2005 (rate per 100,000 residents)
Male.................................... 756
Female................................... 93
White 290
Black.................................2,418
Hispanic 739

©2008 Information Publications, Inc.
All rights reserved. Photocopying prohibited.
877-544-INFO (4636) or www.informationpublications.com

6   Nebraska

Arrests, 2006
Total 88,602
   Persons under 18 years of age 14,967

Persons under sentence of death, 1/1/07
Total 9
   White 5
   Black 1
   Hispanic 3

State's highest court
Name .... Supreme Court
Number of members 7
Length of term .... 6 years
Intermediate appeals court? .... yes

Labor & Income

Civilian labor force, 2006 (x 1,000)
Total 982
   Men 524
   Women 458
   Persons 16-19 years 59
   White 906
   Black 34
   Hispanic 69

Civilian labor force as a percent of civilian non-institutional population, 2006
Total 72.5%
   Men 79.2
   Women 66.1
   Persons 16-19 years 58.3
   White 72.8
   Black 63.8
   Hispanic 70.6

Employment, 2006 (x 1,000)
Total 951
   Men 506
   Women 446
   Persons 16-19 years 53
   White 882
   Black 31
   Hispanic 66

Unemployment rate, 2006
Total 3.1%
   Men 3.5
   Women 2.7
   Persons 16-19 years 9.5
   White 2.7
   Black 9.2
   Hispanic 4.5

Full-time/part-time labor force, 2003 (x 1,000)
Full-time labor force, employed 750
Part-time labor force, employed 187
Unemployed, looking for
   Full-time work 31
   Part-time work 8
Mean duration of unemployment (weeks) 16.4
   Median 8.1

Labor unions, 2006
Membership (x 1,000) 66
   percent of employed 7.9%

Experienced civilian labor force by private industry, 2006
Total 748,399
   Natural resources & mining 11,852
   Construction 47,201
   Manufacturing 101,484
   Trade, transportation & utilities 188,043
   Information 19,502
   Finance 62,814
   Professional & business 101,326
   Education & health 110,267
   Leisure & hospitality 80,553
   Other 25,359

Experienced civilian labor force by occupation, May 2006
Management 29,590
Business & financial 38,110
Legal 4,470
Sales 95,210
Office & admin. support 159,330
Computers & math 21,240
Architecture & engineering 10,870
Arts & entertainment 10,900
Education 53,660
Social services 12,960
Health care practitioner & technical ... 48,680
Health care support 25,090
Maintenance & repair 41,850
Construction 43,490
Transportation & moving 79,450
Production 80,910
Farming, fishing & forestry 2,860

Hours and earnings of production workers on manufacturing payrolls, 2006
Average weekly hours 40.9
Average hourly earnings $15.04
Average weekly earnings $615.14

Income and poverty, 2006
Median household income $45,474
Personal income, per capita (current $) ... $34,397
   in constant (2000) dollars $30,026
Persons below poverty level 11.5%

Average annual pay
2006 .... $33,814
   increase from 2005 .... 4.3%

Federal individual income tax returns, 2005
Returns filed 816,053
Adjusted gross income ($1,000) $37,830,701
Total tax liability ($1,000) $4,433,778

Charitable contributions, 2004
Number of contributions 218.6
Total amount ($ mil) $848.8

©2008 Information Publications, Inc.
All rights reserved. Photocopying prohibited.
877-544-INFO (4636) or www.informationpublications.com

Economy, Business, Industry & Agriculture

Fortune 500 companies, 2007 5
Bankruptcy cases filed, FY 2007 5,204

Patents and trademarks issued, 2007

Patents 245
Trademarks 429

Business firm ownership, 2002

Women-owned 38,679
  Sales ($ mil) $5,765
Black-owned 2,091
  Sales ($ mil) $141
Hispanic-owned 1,966
  Sales ($ mil) $434
Asian-owned 1,456
  Sales ($ mil) $686
Amer. Indian/Alaska Native-owned 425
  Sales ($ mil) $47
Hawaiian/Pacific Islander-owned 9
  Sales ($ mil) . . . . NA

Gross domestic product, 2006 ($ mil)

Total gross domestic product $75,700
  Agriculture, forestry, fishing and
    hunting 3,496
  Mining 113
  Utilities 1,425
  Construction 3,270
  Manufacturing, durable goods 4,857
  Manufacturing, non-durable goods 4,065
  Wholesale trade 4,458
  Retail trade 4,775
  Transportation & warehousing 5,635
  Information 2,323
  Finance & insurance 7,514
  Real estate, rental & leasing 7,102
  Professional and technical services 3,484
  Educational services 624
  Health care and social assistance 5,461
  Accommodation/food services 1,502
  Other services, except government 1,665
  Government 10,427

Establishments, payroll, employees & receipts, by major industry group, 2005

Total 51,440
  Annual payroll ($1,000) $24,180,753
  Paid employees 773,082
Forestry, fishing & agriculture 162
  Annual payroll ($1,000) . . . . NA
  Paid employees . . . . NA
Mining 128
  Annual payroll ($1,000) $37,616
  Paid employees 943
  Receipts, 2002 ($1,000) $163,244

Utilities 128
  Annual payroll ($1,000) $93,103
  Paid employees .1,172
  Receipts, 2002 ($1,000) . . . . .NA
Construction 6,078
  Annual payroll ($1,000) $1,576,751
  Paid employees 43,088
  Receipts, 2002 ($1,000) $6,700,924
Manufacturing 1,985
  Annual payroll ($1,000) $3,662,922
  Paid employees 102,367
  Receipts, 2002 ($1,000) $30,610,970
Wholesale trade 2,905
  Annual payroll ($1,000) $1,625,672
  Paid employees 37,932
  Receipts, 2002 ($1,000) $26,155,770
Retail trade 8,080
  Annual payroll ($1,000) $2,134,208
  Paid employees 107,366
  Receipts, 2002 ($1,000) $20,249,200
Transportation & warehousing 2,330
  Annual payroll ($1,000) $1,102,031
  Paid employees 30,150
  Receipts, 2002 ($1,000) $4,452,719
Information 899
  Annual payroll ($1,000) $812,644
  Paid employees 19,818
  Receipts, 2002 ($1,000) . . . . .NA
Finance & insurance 3,993
  Annual payroll ($1,000) $2,915,960
  Paid employees 59,858
  Receipts, 2002 ($1,000) . . . . .NA
Professional, scientific & technical 4,139
  Annual payroll ($1,000) $1,997,798
  Paid employees 44,813
  Receipts, 2002 ($1,000) $3,020,944
Education 483
  Annual payroll ($1,000) $378,634
  Paid employees 16,136
  Receipts, 2002 ($1,000) $74,932
Health care & social assistance 4,634
  Annual payroll ($1,000) $3,633,981
  Paid employees 109,104
  Receipts, 2002 ($1,000) $7,492,496
Arts and entertainment 839
  Annual payroll ($1,000) $149,189
  Paid employees 10,528
  Receipts, 2002 ($1,000) $468,527
Real estate 1,971
  Annual payroll ($1,000) $287,835
  Paid employees 10,049
  Receipts, 2002 ($1,000) $1,194,332
Accommodation & food service 4,108
  Annual payroll ($1,000) $696,713
  Paid employees 66,768
  Receipts, 2002 ($1,000) $2,088,710

©2008 Information Publications, Inc.
All rights reserved. Photocopying prohibited.
877-544-INFO (4636) or www.informationpublications.com

8 Nebraska

Exports, 2006
Value of exported goods ($ mil) $3,625
   Manufactured $2,903
   Non-manufactured.................. $584

Foreign direct investment in US affiliates, 2004
Property, plants & equipment ($ mil) $2,021
Employment (x 1,000)....................20.0

Agriculture, 2006
Number of farms 47,600
Farm acreage (x 1,000) 45,700
   Acres per farm......................... 960
Farm marketings and income ($ mil)
Total...........................$12,042.3
   Crops...........................$4,359.0
   Livestock.......................$7,683.4
Net farm income $2,297.0

Principal commodities, in order by marketing receipts, 2005
Cattle and calves, Corn, Soybeans, Hogs, Wheat

Federal economic activity in state
Expenditures, 2005 ($ mil)
   Total...................... $12,785
    Per capita $7,272.04
   Defense $1,351
   Non-defense.......................$11,434
Defense department, 2006 ($ mil)
   Payroll.............................. $961
   Contract awards $718
   Grants $11
Homeland security grants ($1,000)
   2006.............................$21,746
   2007..............................$7,226

FDIC-insured financial institutions, 2005
Number 254
Assets ($ billion) $39.6
Deposits ($ billion) $30.4

Fishing, 2006
Catch (x 1,000 lbs) .... NA
Value ($1,000)........................... NA

Mining, 2006 ($ mil)
Total non-fuel mineral production $112
Percent of U.S. 0.17%

Communication, Energy & Transportation

Communication
Households with computers, 2003........ 66.1%
Households with internet access, 2003 .... 55.4%
High-speed internet providers 67
Total high-speed internet lines..........470,118
   Residential 352,387
   Business........................... 117,731
Wireless phone customers, 12/2006 1,272,067

FCC-licensed stations (as of January 1, 2008)
TV stations 27
FM radio stations....................... 109
AM radio stations 53

Energy
Energy consumption, 2004
   Total (trillion Btu)...................... 652
   Per capita (million Btu) 373.2
By source of production (trillion Btu)
   Coal 224
   Natural gas........................... 115
   Petroleum............................ 238
   Nuclear electric power 107
   Hydroelectric power..................... 9
By end-use sector (trillion Btu)
   Residential 144
   Commercial 128
   Industrial 206
   Transportation 174
Electric energy, 2005
   Primary source of electricity........... Coal
   Net generation (billion kWh) 31.5
    percent from renewable sources....... 3.2%
   Net summer capability (million kW) 7.0
   CO_2 emitted from generation 22.1
Natural gas utilities, 2005
   Customers (x 1,000) 567
   Sales (trillion Btu)..................... 110
   Revenues ($ mil) $586
Nuclear plants, 2007 2
Total CO_2 emitted (million metric tons)....43.2
Energy spending, 2004 ($ mil) $5,404
   per capita $3,093
   Price per million Btu $12.18

Transportation, 2006
Public road & street mileage 93,379
   Urban........................... .6,191
   Rural 87,188
   Interstate........................... 482
Vehicle miles of travel (millions) 19,415
   per capita 11,007.7
Total motor vehicle registrations....... 1,733,133
   Automobiles.................... 832,511
   Trucks 893,627
   Motorcycles 36,951
Licensed drivers 1,327,916
   19 years & under 85,217
Deaths from motor vehicle accidents 269
Gasoline consumed (x 1,000 gallons) 836,683
   per capita 474.4

Commuting Statistics, 2006
Average commute time (min) 17.7
   Drove to work alone 79.1%
   Carpooled........................... 10.4%
   Public transit 0.5%
   Walk to work 3.5%
   Work from home...................... 5.0%

©2008 Information Publications, Inc.
All rights reserved. Photocopying prohibited.
877-544-INFO (4636) or www.informationpublications.com

State Summary

Capital city . . . . .Carson City
Governor . . . . Jim Gibbons

Capitol Building
Carson City, NV 89701
775-684-5670

Admitted as a state 1864
Area (square miles) 110,561
Population, 2007 (estimate). 2,565,382
Largest city .Las Vegas
　Population, 2006 552,539
Personal income per capita, 2006
　(in current dollars) $37,089
Gross domestic product, 2006 ($ mil) . . . $118,399

Leading industries by payroll, 2005

Accommodation & Food services, Construction,
Health care/Social assistance

**Leading agricultural commodities
by receipts, 2005**

Cattle and calves, Hay, Dairy products, Onions,
Potatoes

Geography & Environment

Total area (square miles). 110,561
　land 109,826
　water 735
Federally-owned land, 2004 (acres) . . .59,362,643
　percent. 84.5%
Highest point . . . . Boundary Peak
　elevation (feet) 13,140
Lowest point . . . . .Colorado River
　elevation (feet) 479
General coastline (miles) 0
Tidal shoreline (miles) 0
Cropland, 2003 (x 1,000 acres) 636
Forest land, 2003 (x 1,000 acres). 314
Capital city . . . . .Carson City
　Population 2000 52,457
　Population 2006 55,289
Largest city . . . . .Las Vegas
　Population 2000 478,434
　Population 2006 552,539

Number of cities with over 100,000 population
1990 3
2000 4
2006 4

State park and recreation areas, 2005
Area (x 1,000 acres). 133
Number of visitors (x 1,000) 3,178
Revenues ($1,000) $2,565
　percent of operating expenditures. 23.9%

National forest system land, 2007
Acres 5,853,963

Demographics & Population Characteristics

Population
1980 800,493
1990 1,201,833
2000 1,998,257
2006 2,495,529
　Male. 1,268,894
　Female. 1,226,635
Living in group quarters, 2006. 33,434
　percent of total. 1.3%
2007 (estimate). 2,565,382
　persons per square mile of land 23.4
2008 (projected) 2,551,889
2010 (projected) 2,690,531
2020 (projected) 3,452,283
2030 (projected) 4,282,102

**Population of Core-Based Statistical Areas
(formerly Metropolitan Areas), x 1,000**

	CBSA	Non-CBSA
1990	1,157	44
2000	1,950	48
2006	2,447	49

Change in population, 2000-2007
Number. 567,125
　percent. 28.4%
Natural increase (births minus deaths) 124,490
Net internal migration 364,683
Net international migration 84,578

Persons by age, 2006
Under 5 years 183,588
5 to 17 years 450,932
18 years and over 1,861,009
65 years and over 276,943
85 years and over 27,841
　Median age 35.5

Persons by age, 2010 (projected)
Under 5 years 196,094
18 and over 2,025,446
65 and over 329,621
　Median age 37.8

Race, 2006
One Race
　White. 2,038,372
　Black or African American 196,075
　Asian 149,621
　American Indian/Alaska Native. 34,813
　Hawaiian Native/Pacific Islander. 12,441
Two or more races. 64,207

Persons of Hispanic origin, 2006
Total Hispanic or Latino 610,051
　Mexican. 475,390
　Puerto Rican 19,020
　Cuban 15,120

©2008 Information Publications, Inc.
All rights reserved. Photocopying prohibited.
877-544-INFO (4636) or www.informationpublications.com

Persons of Asian origin, 2006

Total Asian	147,363
Asian Indian	6,524
Chinese	23,700
Filipino	73,261
Japanese	12,678
Korean	8,886
Vietnamese	9,238

Marital status, 2006

Population 15 years & over	1,965,437
Never married	566,781
Married	1,026,022
Separated	42,362
Widowed	111,826
Divorced	260,808

Language spoken at home, 2006

Population 5 years and older	2,312,092
English only	1,691,109
Spanish	445,622
French	7,654
German	11,722
Chinese	18,553

Households & families, 2006

Households	936,828
with persons under 18 years	325,947
with persons over 65 years	199,099
persons per household	2.63
Families	612,349
persons per family	3.20
Married couples	443,841
Female householder,	
no husband present	108,682
One-person households	248,784

Nativity, 2006

Number of residents born in state	575,422
percent of population	23.1%

Immigration & naturalization, 2006

Legal permanent residents admitted	14,714
Persons naturalized	8,202
Non-immigrant admissions	1,067,921

Vital Statistics and Health

Marriages

2004	145,763
2005	139,572
2006	131,826

Divorces

2004	14,828
2005	18,084
2006	16,737

Health risks, 2006

Percent of adults who are:

Smokers	22.2%
Overweight (BMI > 25)	63.6%
Obese (BMI > 30)	25.0%

Births

2005	37,268
Birthrate (per 1,000)	15.4
White	30,664
Black	3,219
Hispanic	14,090
Asian/Pacific Islander	2,906
Amer. Indian/Alaska Native	479
Low birth weight (2,500g or less)	8.3%
Cesarian births	31.0%
Preterm births	13.9%
To unmarried mothers	40.9%
Twin births (per 1,000)	29.0
Triplets or higher order (per 100,000)	147.0
2006 (preliminary)	40,085
rate per 1,000	16.1

Deaths

2004

All causes	17,929
rate per 100,000	880.5
Heart disease	4,693
rate per 100,000	236.6
Malignant neoplasms	4,119
rate per 100,000	193.4
Cerebrovascular disease	1,030
rate per 100,000	53.4
Chronic lower respiratory disease	1,124
rate per 100,000	56.8
Diabetes	290
rate per 100,000	13.9
2005 (preliminary)	19,037
rate per 100,000	892.3
2006 (provisional)	18,295

Infant deaths

2004	225
rate per 1,000	6.4
2005 (provisional)	210
rate per 1,000	5.8

Exercise routines, 2005

None	26.8%
Moderate or greater	50.7%
Vigorous	32.6%

Abortions, 2004

Total performed in state	9,856
rate per 1,000 women age 15-44	20
% obtained by out-of-state residents	6.6%

Physicians, 2005

Total	4,519
rate per 100,000 persons	187

Community hospitals, 2005

Number of hospitals	32
Beds (x 1,000)	4.7
Patients admitted (x 1,000)	241
Average daily census (x 1,000)	3.5
Average cost per day	$1,685
Outpatient visits (x 1 mil)	2.6

©2008 Information Publications, Inc.
All rights reserved. Photocopying prohibited.
877-544-INFO (4636) or www.informationpublications.com

Disability status of population, 2006

5 to 15 years 3.7%
16 to 64 years 10.4%
65 years and over 38.7%

Education

Educational attainment, 2006

Population over 25 years 1,644,320
  Less than 9th grade. 6.3%
  High school graduate or more 83.9%
  College graduate or more. 20.8%
  Graduate or professional degree. 7.2%

Public school enrollment, 2005-06

Total. 412,395
  Pre-kindergarten through grade 8. 295,011
  Grades 9 through 12 116,375

Graduating public high school seniors, 2004-05

Diplomas (incl. GED and others) 18,236

SAT scores, 2007

Average critical reading score 500
Average writing score 480
Average math score 506
Percent of graduates taking test 41%

Public school teachers, 2006-07 (estimate)

Total (x 1,000) 22.1
  Elementary 12.9
  Secondary 9.2
Average salary $45,342
  Elementary $45,342
  Secondary $45,342

State receipts & expenditures for
public schools, 2006-07 (estimate)

Revenue receipts ($ mil) $3,104
Expenditures
Total ($ mil) $3,912
  Per capita $1,190
  Per pupil $7,060

NAEP proficiency scores, 2007

	Reading		Math	
	Basic	Proficient	Basic	Proficient
Grade 4	57.1%	24.4%	73.7%	30.1%
Grade 8	63.1%	21.5%	60.2%	23.0%

Higher education enrollment, fall 2005

Total. 10,662
  Full-time men 4,102
  Full-time women 5,906
  Part-time men 276
  Part-time women. 378

Minority enrollment in institutions
of higher education, 2005

Black, non-Hispanic .8,651
Hispanic 15,515
Asian/Pacific Islander 11,877
American Indian/Alaska Native. 1,658

Institutions of higher education, 2005-06

Total. 23
  Public. 7
  Private 16

Earned degrees conferred, 2004-05

Associate's. 3,236
Bachelor's 5,608
Master's 2,042
First-professional. 180
Doctor's 126

Public Libraries, 2006

Number of libraries. 22
Number of outlets 89
Annual visits per capita 4.1
Circulation per capita. 6.2

State & local financial support for
higher education, FY 2006

Full-time equivalent enrollment (x 1,000). 60.9
Appropriations per FTE. $8,919

Social Insurance &
Welfare Programs

Social Security benefits & beneficiaries, 2005

Beneficiaries (x 1,000) 348
  Retired & dependents. 254
  Survivors. 38
  Disabled & dependents. 55
Annual benefit payments ($ mil) $3,830
  Retired & dependents. $2,666
  Survivors. $538
  Disabled & dependents. $626
Average monthly benefit
  Retired & dependents. $1,008
  Disabled & dependents. $1,008
  Widowed $1,012

Medicare, July 2005

Enrollment (x 1,000). 297
Payments ($ mil) $1,539

Medicaid, 2004

Beneficiaries (x 1,000). 78
Payments ($ mil) $477

State Children's Health Insurance Program, 2006

Enrollment (x 1,000). 39.3
Expenditures ($ mil). $40.2

Persons without health insurance, 2006

Number (x 1,000). 496
  percent. 19.6%
Number of children (x 1,000) 122
  percent of children 18.8%

Health care expenditures, 2004

Total expenditures. $10,656
  per capita $4,569

©2008 Information Publications, Inc.
All rights reserved. Photocopying prohibited.
877-544-INFO (4636) or www.informationpublications.com

Federal and state public aid

State unemployment insurance, 2006
Recipients, first payments (x 1,000) 64
Total payments ($ mil) $246
Average weekly benefit $274
Temporary Assistance for Needy Families, 2006
Recipients (x 1,000) 153.1
Families (x 1,000) 66.6
Supplemental Security Income, 2005
Recipients (x 1,000) 33.0
Payments ($ mil) $163.0
Food Stamp Program, 2006
Avg monthly participants (x 1,000) 117.9
Total benefits ($ mil) $124.3

Housing & Construction

Housing units
Total 2005 (estimate) 1,019,435
Total 2006 (estimate) 1,065,197
Seasonal or recreational use, 2006 30,879
Owner-occupied, 2006 580,705
   Median home value $315,200
   Homeowner vacancy rate 3.0%
Renter-occupied, 2006 356,123
   Median rent $917
   Rental vacancy rate 9.1%
Home ownership rate, 2005 . . . . 63.4%
Home ownership rate, 2006 . . . . 65.7%

New privately-owned housing units
Number authorized, 2006 (x 1,000) 39.4
   Value ($ mil) $5,383.2
Started 2005 (x 1,000, estimate) 36.1
Started 2006 (x 1,000, estimate) 35.0

Existing home sales
2005 (x 1,000) 98.0
2006 (x 1,000) 70.2

Government & Elections

State officials 2008
Governor . . . . Jim Gibbons
          Republican, term expires 1/11
Lieutenant Governor . . . . Brian Krolicki
Secretary of State . . . . Ross Miller
Attorney General . . . . Catherine Masto
Chief Justice . . . . .A. William Maupin

Governorship
Minimum age 25
Length of term . . . . 4 years
Consecutive terms permitted 2
Who succeeds . . . . Lieutenant Governor

Local governments by type, 2002
Total 210
   County 16
   Municipal 19
   Township 0
   School District 17
   Special District 158

State legislature

Name . . . . Legislature
Upper chamber . . . . .Senate
   Number of members 21
   Length of term . . . . 4 years
   Party in majority, 2008 . . . . Republican
Lower chamber .Assembly
   Number of members 42
   Length of term . . . . 2 years
   Party in majority, 2008 . . . . Democratic

Federal representation, 2008 (110th Congress)
Senator . . . . Harry Reid
   Party . . . . .Democratic
   Year term expires 2011
Senator . . . . John Ensign
   Party . . . . Republican
   Year term expires 2013
Representatives, total 3
   Democrats 1
   Republicans 2

Voters in November 2006 election (estimate)
Total 686,199
   Male 331,614
   Female 354,584
   White 595,064
   Black 41,124
   Hispanic 27,210
   Asian 37,267

Presidential election, 2004
Total Popular Vote 829,587
   Kerry 397,190
   Bush 418,690
Total Electoral Votes 5

Votes cast for US Senators
2004
Total vote (x 1,000) 810
Leading party .Democratic
Percent for leading party 61.1%
2006
Total vote (x 1,000) 583
Leading party . . . . Republican
Percent for leading party 55.4%

Votes cast for US Representatives
2004
Total vote (x 1,000) 791
   Democratic 334
   Republican 421
Leading party . . . . Republican
Percent for leading party 53.2%
2006
Total vote (x 1,000) 575
   Democratic 288
   Republican 260
Leading party .Democratic
Percent for leading party 50.1%

©2008 Information Publications, Inc.
All rights reserved. Photocopying prohibited.
877-544-INFO (4636) or www.informationpublications.com

State government employment, 2006
Full-time equivalent employees 25,859
Payroll ($ mil) $104.5

Local government employment, 2006
Full-time equivalent employees 77,445
Payroll ($ mil) $331.3

Women holding public office, 2008
US Congress 1
Statewide elected office 3
State legislature 19

Black public officials, 2002
Total 13
  US and state legislatures 5
  City/county/regional offices 4
  Judicial/law enforcement 2
  Education/school boards 2

Hispanic public officials, 2006
Total 11
  State executives & legislators 2
  City/county/regional offices 5
  Judicial/law enforcement 3
  Education/school boards 1

Governmental Finance

State government revenues, 2006
Total revenue (x $1,000) $12,341,503
  per capita $4,951.60
General revenue (x $1,000) $9,461,111
  Intergovernmental 1,980,326
  Taxes 6,152,980
    general sales 3,163,832
    individual income tax 0
    corporate income tax 0
  Current charges 632,196
  Miscellaneous 695,609

State government expenditure, 2006
Total expenditure (x $1,000) $10,341,683
  per capita $4,149.24
General expenditure (x $1,000) $9,152,975
  per capita, total *$3,672.31*
    Education 1,420.13
    Public welfare 654.10
    Health 75.55
    Hospitals 83.31
    Highways 303.87
    Police protection 39.26
    Corrections 105.47
    Natural resources 57.43
    Parks & recreation 9.73
    Governmental administration 134.86
    Interest on general debt 72.51

State debt & cash, 2006 ($ per capita)
Debt $1,625.01
Cash/security holdings $10,867.20

Federal government grants to state & local government, 2005 (x $1,000)
Total $2,925,545
by Federal agency
  Defense 32,254
  Education 231,079
  Energy 86,742
  Environmental Protection Agency 49,961
  Health & Human Services 1,079,572
  Homeland Security 22,047
  Housing & Urban Development 159,706
  Justice 66,360
  Labor 53,895
  Transportation 275,037
  Veterans Affairs .9,608

Crime & Law Enforcement

Crime, 2006 (rates per 100,000 residents)
Property crimes 102,036
  Burglary 24,820
  Larceny 50,255
  Motor vehicle theft 26,961
  Property crime rate 4,088.8
Violent crimes 18,508
  Murder 224
  Forcible rape 1,079
  Robbery 7,027
  Aggravated assault 10,178
  Violent crime rate 741.6
Hate crimes 142

Fraud and identity theft, 2006
Fraud complaints 4,222
  rate per 100,000 residents 169.2
Identity theft complaints 2,994
  rate per 100,000 residents 120.0

Law enforcement agencies, 2006
Total agencies 37
Total employees 9,080
  Officers 5,262
  Civilians 3,818

Prisoners, probation, and parole, 2006
Total prisoners 12,901
  percent change, 12/31/05 to 12/31/06 . . . . 9.5%
  in private facilities .0%
  in local jails 1.1%
Sentenced to more than one year 12,753
  rate per 100,000 residents 503
Adults on probation 13,208
Adults on parole 3,824

Prisoner demographics, June 30, 2005 (rate per 100,000 residents)
Male 1,319
Female 173
White 627
Black 2,916
Hispanic 621

©2008 Information Publications, Inc.
All rights reserved. Photocopying prohibited.
877-544-INFO (4636) or www.informationpublications.com

Arrests, 2006

Total 163,109
    Persons under 18 years of age 20,725

Persons under sentence of death, 1/1/07

Total 80
    White 42
    Black 29
    Hispanic 8

State's highest court

Name . . . . .Supreme Court
Number of members 7
Length of term . . . . 6 years
Intermediate appeals court? . . . . no

Labor & Income

Civilian labor force, 2006 (x 1,000)

Total 1,296
    Men 716
    Women 580
    Persons 16-19 years 62
    White 1,052
    Black 92
    Hispanic 300

Civilian labor force as a percent of civilian non-institutional population, 2006

Total 68.3%
    Men 74.9
    Women 61.5
    Persons 16-19 years 45.7
    White 67.9
    Black 68.3
    Hispanic 76.5

Employment, 2006 (x 1,000)

Total 1,243
    Men 686
    Women 557
    Persons 16-19 years 52
    White 1,012
    Black 86
    Hispanic 285

Unemployment rate, 2006

Total 4.1%
    Men 4.2
    Women 4.0
    Persons 16-19 years 16.2
    White 3.8
    Black 6.8
    Hispanic 4.9

Full-time/part-time labor force, 2003 (x 1,000)

Full-time labor force, employed 941
Part-time labor force, employed 141
Unemployed, looking for
    Full-time work 51
    Part-time work 8
Mean duration of unemployment (weeks) 16.3
    Median 8.5

Labor unions, 2006

Membership (x 1,000) 167
    percent of employed 14.8%

Experienced civilian labor force by private industry, 2006

Total 1,125,197
    Natural resources & mining 13,812
    Construction 142,815
    Manufacturing. 50,252
    Trade, transportation & utilities 225,743
    Information 15,161
    Finance 65,576
    Professional & business 158,250
    Education & health 87,356
    Leisure & hospitality. 336,970
    Other 28,465

Experienced civilian labor force by occupation, May 2006

Management 50,570
Business & financial 38,760
Legal 8,410
Sales 131,840
Office & admin. support 197,350
Computers & math 13,260
Architecture & engineering. 17,010
Arts & entertainment 16,680
Education 47,750
Social services 8,430
Health care practitioner & technical 39,540
Health care support 19,440
Maintenance & repair. 51,380
Construction 121,920
Transportation & moving 100,300
Production 45,370
Farming, fishing & forestry 790

Hours and earnings of production workers on manufacturing payrolls, 2006

Average weekly hours 39.4
Average hourly earnings $15.47
Average weekly earnings $609.52

Income and poverty, 2006

Median household income $52,998
Personal income, per capita (current $) . . . $37,089
    in constant (2000) dollars $32,376
Persons below poverty level 10.3%

Average annual pay

2006 . . . . $40,070
    increase from 2005 . . . . 3.4%

Federal individual income tax returns, 2005

Returns filed 1,150,204
Adjusted gross income ($1,000) $72,209,472
Total tax liability ($1,000) $10,495,210

Charitable contributions, 2004

Number of contributions 346.7
Total amount ($ mil) $1,500.6

©2008 Information Publications, Inc.
All rights reserved. Photocopying prohibited.
877-544-INFO (4636) or www.informationpublications.com

Economy, Business, Industry & Agriculture

Fortune 500 companies, 2007 2
Bankruptcy cases filed, FY 2007 9,445

Patents and trademarks issued, 2007

Patents 451
Trademarks 2,777

Business firm ownership, 2002

Women-owned 47,675
   Sales ($ mil) $8,643
Black-owned 4,343
   Sales ($ mil) $434
Hispanic-owned .9,741
   Sales ($ mil) $1,643
Asian-owned 8,872
   Sales ($ mil) $1,989
Amer. Indian/Alaska Native-owned 1,915
   Sales ($ mil) $218
Hawaiian/Pacific Islander-owned 313
   Sales ($ mil) $55

Gross domestic product, 2006 ($ mil)

Total gross domestic product $118,399
   Agriculture, forestry, fishing and
     hunting 243
   Mining 2,047
   Utilities 1,969
   Construction .11,881
   Manufacturing, durable goods 4,307
   Manufacturing, non-durable goods 1,453
   Wholesale trade 5,005
   Retail trade 9,067
   Transportation & warehousing 3,268
   Information 2,161
   Finance & insurance 8,134
   Real estate, rental & leasing 17,611
   Professional and technical services 6,042
   Educational services 303
   Health care and social assistance 5,724
   Accommodation/food services 16,506
   Other services, except government 2,080
   Government 11,776

Establishments, payroll, employees & receipts, by major industry group, 2005

Total 58,561
   Annual payroll ($1,000) $39,261,902
   Paid employees 1,089,422
Forestry, fishing & agriculture 52
   Annual payroll ($1,000) $5,608
   Paid employees 210
Mining 198
   Annual payroll ($1,000) $570,033
   Paid employees 9,483
   Receipts, 2002 ($1,000) $2,570,066

Utilities 103
   Annual payroll ($1,000) $448,209
   Paid employees 5,324
   Receipts, 2002 ($1,000) . . . . .NA
Construction 5,713
   Annual payroll ($1,000) $5,267,935
   Paid employees 122,231
   Receipts, 2002 ($1,000) $16,100,809
Manufacturing 1,863
   Annual payroll ($1,000) $1,897,233
   Paid employees 45,068
   Receipts, 2002 ($1,000) $8,466,212
Wholesale trade .2,812
   Annual payroll ($1,000) $1,726,773
   Paid employees 36,417
   Receipts, 2002 ($1,000) $16,513,814
Retail trade 8,006
   Annual payroll ($1,000) $3,583,275
   Paid employees 135,522
   Receipts, 2002 ($1,000) $26,999,899
Transportation & warehousing 1,447
   Annual payroll ($1,000) $1,159,454
   Paid employees 39,281
   Receipts, 2002 ($1,000) $1,842,072
Information 1,155
   Annual payroll ($1,000) $757,260
   Paid employees 15,689
   Receipts, 2002 ($1,000) . . . . .NA
Finance & insurance 4,444
   Annual payroll ($1,000) $1,946,376
   Paid employees 38,672
   Receipts, 2002 ($1,000) . . . . .NA
Professional, scientific & technical 7,477
   Annual payroll ($1,000) $2,854,612
   Paid employees 53,317
   Receipts, 2002 ($1,000) $5,665,309
Education 552
   Annual payroll ($1,000) $188,865
   Paid employees 6,649
   Receipts, 2002 ($1,000) $159,673
Health care & social assistance 5,256
   Annual payroll ($1,000) $3,649,668
   Paid employees 88,200
   Receipts, 2002 ($1,000) $7,553,145
Arts and entertainment 1,286
   Annual payroll ($1,000) $726,470
   Paid employees 28,290
   Receipts, 2002 ($1,000) $2,392,612
Real estate 4,426
   Annual payroll ($1,000) $1,050,710
   Paid employees 28,812
   Receipts, 2002 ($1,000) $3,432,258
Accommodation & food service 4,915
   Annual payroll ($1,000) $7,733,195
   Paid employees 290,919
   Receipts, 2002 ($1,000) $19,537,592

©2008 Information Publications, Inc.
All rights reserved. Photocopying prohibited.
877-544-INFO (4636) or www.informationpublications.com

8 Nevada

Exports, 2006
Value of exported goods ($ mil) $5,493
    Manufactured $4,475
    Non-manufactured $463

Foreign direct investment in US affiliates, 2004
Property, plants & equipment ($ mil) $6,530
Employment (x 1,000) 27.0

Agriculture, 2006
Number of farms 3,000
Farm acreage (x 1,000) 6,300
    Acres per farm 2,100
Farm marketings and income ($ mil)
Total $446.6
    Crops $166.2
    Livestock $280.4
Net farm income $84.6

Principal commodities, in order by marketing receipts, 2005
Cattle and calves, Hay, Dairy products, Onions, Potatoes

Federal economic activity in state
Expenditures, 2005 ($ mil)
Total $14,089
    Per capita $5,840.47
    Defense $1,625
    Non-defense $12,464
Defense department, 2006 ($ mil)
    Payroll $1,146
    Contract awards $750
    Grants $20
Homeland security grants ($1,000)
    2006 . . . . $20,509
    2007 . . . . $19,357

FDIC-insured financial institutions, 2005
Number 38
Assets ($ billion) $1,416.3
Deposits ($ billion) $917.8

Fishing, 2006
Catch (x 1,000 lbs) . . . . NA
Value ($1,000) . . . . NA

Mining, 2006 ($ mil)
Total non-fuel mineral production $5,240
Percent of U.S. 8.14%

Communication, Energy & Transportation

Communication
Households with computers, 2003 . . . . 61.3%
Households with internet access, 2003 . . . . 55.2%
High-speed internet providers 32
Total high-speed internet lines 782,840
    Residential 550,643
    Business 232,197
Wireless phone customers, 12/2006 1,990,215

FCC-licensed stations (as of January 1, 2008)
TV stations 21
FM radio stations 66
AM radio stations 30

Energy
Energy consumption, 2004
    Total (trillion Btu) 694
    Per capita (million Btu) 297.4
By source of production (trillion Btu)
    Coal 194
    Natural gas 220
    Petroleum 264
    Nuclear electric power 0
    Hydroelectric power 16
By end-use sector (trillion Btu)
    Residential 159
    Commercial 121
    Industrial 186
    Transportation 228
Electric energy, 2005
    Primary source of electricity . . . . Gas
    Net generation (billion kWh) 40.2
        percent from renewable sources 7.4%
    Net summer capability (million kW) . . .8.7
    CO_2 emitted from generation 26.0
Natural gas utilities, 2005
    Customers (x 1,000) 725
    Sales (trillion Btu) 79
    Revenues ($ mil) $872
Nuclear plants, 2007 0
Total CO_2 emitted (million metric tons) 43.3
Energy spending, 2004 ($ mil) $6,878
    per capita $2,949
    Price per million Btu $15.43

Transportation, 2006
Public road & street mileage 33,703
    Urban 7,143
    Rural 26,560
    Interstate 571
Vehicle miles of travel (millions) 21,824
    per capita 8,756.1
Total motor vehicle registrations 1,366,557
    Automobiles 679,828
    Trucks 684,806
    Motorcycles 56,971
Licensed drivers .1,626,021
    19 years & under 58,743
Deaths from motor vehicle accidents 432
Gasoline consumed (x 1,000 gallons) 1,173,077
    per capita 470.7

Commuting Statistics, 2006
Average commute time (min) 24.2
    Drove to work alone 76.7%
    Carpooled 12.3%
    Public transit 3.6%
    Walk to work 2.1%
    Work from home 3.1%

©2008 Information Publications, Inc.
All rights reserved. Photocopying prohibited.
877-544-INFO (4636) or www.informationpublications.com

State Summary

Capital city . . . . .Concord
Governor. . . . . John Lynch

Office of the Governor
25 Capitol St, Room 212
Concord, NH 03301
603-271-7532

Admitted as a state 1788
Area (square miles) 9,350
Population, 2007 (estimate). 1,315,828
Largest city . . . . .Manchester
    Population, 2006 109,497
Personal income per capita, 2006
    (in current dollars) $39,311
Gross domestic product, 2006 ($ mil) $56,276

Leading industries by payroll, 2005

Manufacturing, Health care/Social assistance,
Retail trade

Leading agricultural commodities by receipts, 2005

Greenhouse/nursery, Dairy products, Cattle and
calves, Apples, Hay

Geography & Environment

Total area (square miles). 9,350
    land 8,968
    water 382
Federally-owned land, 2004 (acres) 775,665
    percent. 13.5%
Highest point . . . . .Mt. Washington
    elevation (feet) 6,288
Lowest point . . . . .Atlantic Ocean
    elevation (feet) . . . . sea level
General coastline (miles) 13
Tidal shoreline (miles) 131
Cropland, 2003 (x 1,000 acres) 125
Forest land, 2003 (x 1,000 acres). 3,899
Capital city . . . . .Concord
    Population 2000 40,687
    Population 2006 42,378
Largest city . . . . .Manchester
    Population 2000 107,006
    Population 2006 109,497

Number of cities with over 100,000 population

1990 0
2000 1
2006 1

State park and recreation areas, 2005

Area (x 1,000 acres) 232
Number of visitors (x 1,000) . . . . NA
Revenues ($1,000) . . . . NA
    percent of operating expenditures . . . . NA

National forest system land, 2007

Acres 734,798

Demographics & Population Characteristics

Population

1980 920,610
1990 1,109,252
2000 1,235,786
2006 1,314,895
    Male. 648,568
    Female 666,327
Living in group quarters, 2006 37,347
    percent of total. .2.8%
2007 (estimate). 1,315,828
    persons per square mile of land 146.7
2008 (projected). 1,357,216
2010 (projected). 1,385,560
2020 (projected). 1,524,751
2030 (projected). 1,646,471

Population of Core-Based Statistical Areas (formerly Metropolitan Areas), x 1,000

	CBSA	Non-CBSA
1990	1,074	35
2000	1,192	44
2006	1,267	47

Change in population, 2000-2007

Number 80,042
    percent 6.5%
Natural increase (births minus deaths) 35,461
Net internal migration 35,682
Net international migration 13,928

Persons by age, 2006

Under 5 years 73,575
5 to 17 years 224,050
18 years and over 1,017,270
65 years and over 162,629
85 years and over 23,118
    Median age 39.4

Persons by age, 2010 (projected)

Under 5 years 82,238
18 and over 1,081,396
65 and over 178,823
    Median age 39.6

Race, 2006

One Race
    White. 1,259,738
    Black or African American 13,905
    Asian 24,389
    American Indian/Alaska Native. 3,458
    Hawaiian Native/Pacific Islander. 514
Two or more races. 12,891

Persons of Hispanic origin, 2006

Total Hispanic or Latino 29,721
    Mexican 5,354
    Puerto Rican 11,123
    Cuban 783

©2008 Information Publications, Inc.
All rights reserved. Photocopying prohibited.
877-544-INFO (4636) or www.informationpublications.com

Persons of Asian origin, 2006

Total Asian	26,136
Asian Indian	6,823
Chinese	6,267
Filipino	1,535
Japanese	1,486
Korean	2,996
Vietnamese	2,720

Marital status, 2006

Population 15 years & over	1,075,279
Never married	308,733
Married	584,486
Separated	14,698
Widowed	62,527
Divorced	119,533

Language spoken at home, 2006

Population 5 years and older	1,241,415
English only	1,139,278
Spanish	26,607
French	28,134
German	4,207
Chinese	5,144

Households & families, 2006

Households	504,503
with persons under 18 years	162,731
with persons over 65 years	110,236
persons per household	2.53
Families	335,509
persons per family	3.05
Married couples	267,935
Female householder, no husband present	45,983
One-person households	129,310

Nativity, 2006

Number of residents born in state	549,491
percent of population	41.8%

Immigration & naturalization, 2006

Legal permanent residents admitted	2,990
Persons naturalized	2,483
Non-immigrant admissions	57,196

Vital Statistics and Health

Marriages

2004	10,383
2005	9,488
2006	9,328

Divorces

2004	5,131
2005	5,028
2006	5,258

Health risks, 2006

Percent of adults who are:

Smokers	18.7%
Overweight (BMI > 25)	60.7%
Obese (BMI > 30)	22.4%

Births

2005	14,420
Birthrate (per 1,000)	11.0
White	13,572
Black	232
Hispanic	522
Asian/Pacific Islander	587
Amer. Indian/Alaska Native	29
Low birth weight (2,500g or less)	7.0%
Cesarian births	28.0%
Preterm births	10.5%
To unmarried mothers	27.3%
Twin births (per 1,000)	37.2
Triplets or higher order (per 100,000)	214.4
2006 (preliminary)	14,380
rate per 1,000	10.9

Deaths

2004

All causes	10,111
rate per 100,000	761.1
Heart disease	2,639
rate per 100,000	197.6
Malignant neoplasms	2,554
rate per 100,000	192.1
Cerebrovascular disease	586
rate per 100,000	44.2
Chronic lower respiratory disease	600
rate per 100,000	45.8
Diabetes	313
rate per 100,000	23.5
2005 (preliminary)	10,194
rate per 100,000	732.3
2006 (provisional)	9,901

Infant deaths

2004	81
rate per 1,000	5.6
2005 (provisional)	75
rate per 1,000	5.2

Exercise routines, 2005

None	21.6%
Moderate or greater	56.0%
Vigorous	32.9%

Abortions, 2004

Total performed in state	NA
rate per 1,000 women age 15-44	NA
% obtained by out-of-state residents	NA

Physicians, 2005

Total	3,440
rate per 100,000 persons	263

Community hospitals, 2005

Number of hospitals	28
Beds (x 1,000)	2.8
Patients admitted (x 1,000)	117
Average daily census (x 1,000)	1.8
Average cost per day	$1,627
Outpatient visits (x 1 mil)	3.8

©2008 Information Publications, Inc.
All rights reserved. Photocopying prohibited.
877-544-INFO (4636) or www.informationpublications.com

Disability status of population, 2006

5 to 15 years 6.6%
16 to 64 years 11.5%
65 years and over 37.9%

Education

Educational attainment, 2006

Population over 25 years 896,872
　Less than 9th grade.................... 3.2%
　High school graduate or more 89.9%
　College graduate or more............. 31.9%
　Graduate or professional degree....... 11.2%

Public school enrollment, 2005-06

Total............................... 205,767
　Pre-kindergarten through grade 8.... 138,043
　Grades 9 through 12 67,112

Graduating public high school seniors, 2004-05

Diplomas (incl. GED and others) 13,847

SAT scores, 2007

Average critical reading score.............. 521
Average writing score 512
Average math score 521
Percent of graduates taking test 83%

Public school teachers, 2006-07 (estimate)

Total (x 1,000) 15.8
　Elementary........................... 10.9
　Secondary............................ 4.9
Average salary $46,527
　Elementary....................... $46,527
　Secondary........................ $46,527

**State receipts & expenditures for
public schools, 2006-07 (estimate)**

Revenue receipts ($ mil) $2,401
Expenditures
Total ($ mil) $2,438
　Per capita $1,690
　Per pupil $11,879

NAEP proficiency scores, 2007

	Reading		Math	
	Basic	Proficient	Basic	Proficient
Grade 4	76.0%	41.1%	91.3%	51.8%
Grade 8	81.9%	37.2%	77.6%	37.9%

Higher education enrollment, fall 2005

Total............................... 28,886
　Full-time men 9,891
　Full-time women..................... 12,166
　Part-time men 2,171
　Part-time women.................... 4,658

**Minority enrollment in institutions
of higher education, 2005**

Black, non-Hispanic 1,418
Hispanic 1,742
Asian/Pacific Islander 1,775
American Indian/Alaska Native........... 382

Institutions of higher education, 2005-06

Total............................... 26
　Public............................ 9
　Private........................... 17

Earned degrees conferred, 2004-05

Associate's........................... 3,498
Bachelor's 8,107
Master's.............................. 2,751
First-professional..................... 183
Doctor's.............................. 167

Public Libraries, 2006

Number of libraries..................... 230
Number of outlets 238
Annual visits per capita 4.9
Circulation per capita................... 7.7

**State & local financial support for
higher education, FY 2006**

Full-time equivalent enrollment (x 1,000)..... 31.7
Appropriations per FTE................. $3,193

Social Insurance & Welfare Programs

Social Security benefits & beneficiaries, 2005

Beneficiaries (x 1,000) 226
　Retired & dependents.................. 157
　Survivors............................ 26
　Disabled & dependents................. 42
Annual benefit payments ($ mil) $2,485
　Retired & dependents................ $1,686
　Survivors.......................... $369
　Disabled & dependents............... $430
Average monthly benefit
　Retired & dependents................ $1,028
　Disabled & dependents............... $943
　Widowed........................... $1,023

Medicare, July 2005

Enrollment (x 1,000)..................... 192
Payments ($ mil) $1,206

Medicaid, 2004

Beneficiaries (x 1,000).................... 244
Payments ($ mil) $1,346

State Children's Health Insurance Program, 2006

Enrollment (x 1,000).................... 12.4
Expenditures ($ mil).................... $11.6

Persons without health insurance, 2006

Number (x 1,000)....................... 150
　percent............................ 11.5%
Number of children (x 1,000) 22
　percent of children 7.3%

Health care expenditures, 2004

Total expenditures..................... $7,050
　per capita $5,432

©2008 Information Publications, Inc.
All rights reserved. Photocopying prohibited.
877-544-INFO (4636) or www.informationpublications.com

Federal and state public aid

State unemployment insurance, 2006
Recipients, first payments (x 1,000) 25
Total payments ($ mil) $78
Average weekly benefit $256
Temporary Assistance for Needy Families, 2006
Recipients (x 1,000) 159.3
Families (x 1,000) 71.4
Supplemental Security Income, 2005
Recipients (x 1,000) 13.6
Payments ($ mil) $66.5
Food Stamp Program, 2006
Avg monthly participants (x 1,000) 56.3
Total benefits ($ mil) $57.9

Housing & Construction

Housing units
Total 2005 (estimate) 583,318
Total 2006 (estimate) 589,812
Seasonal or recreational use, 2006 56,722
Owner-occupied, 2006 363,652
   Median home value $253,200
   Homeowner vacancy rate 1.4%
Renter-occupied, 2006 140,851
   Median rent $861
   Rental vacancy rate 6.0%
Home ownership rate, 2005 . . . . 74.0%
Home ownership rate, 2006 . . . . 74.2%

New privately-owned housing units
Number authorized, 2006 (x 1,000) 5.7
   Value ($ mil) $1,036.6
Started 2005 (x 1,000, estimate) 7.0
Started 2006 (x 1,000, estimate) 6.6

Existing home sales
2005 (x 1,000) . . . . NA
2006 (x 1,000) . . . . NA

Government & Elections

State officials 2008
Governor . . . . John Lynch
      Democratic, term expires 1/09
Lieutenant Governor . . (no Lieutenant Governor)
Secretary of State . . . . William Gardner
Attorney General . . . . Kelly Ayotte
Chief Justice . . . . John Broderick Jr

Governorship
Minimum age 30
Length of term . . . . 2 years
Consecutive terms permitted . . . . . . not specified
Who succeeds . . . . President of Senate

Local governments by type, 2002
Total 559
   County 10
   Municipal 13
   Township 221
   School District 167
   Special District 148

State legislature
Name . . . . General Court
Upper chamber . . . . .Senate
   Number of members 24
   Length of term . . . . 2 years
   Party in majority, 2008 . . . . Democratic
Lower chamber . . . . House of Representatives
   Number of members 400
   Length of term . . . . 2 years
   Party in majority, 2008 . . . . Democratic

Federal representation, 2008 (110th Congress)
Senator . . . . John Sununu
   Party . . . . Republican
   Year term expires 2009
Senator . . . . Judd Gregg
   Party . . . . Republican
   Year term expires 2011
Representatives, total 2
   Democrats 2
   Republicans 0

Voters in November 2006 election (estimate)
Total 477,037
   Male 229,479
   Female 247,557
   White 462,517
   Black 2,979
   Hispanic 1,500
   Asian 5,602

Presidential election, 2004
Total Popular Vote 677,738
   Kerry 340,511
   Bush 331,237
Total Electoral Votes 4

Votes cast for US Senators
2004
Total vote (x 1,000) 657
Leading party . . . . Republican
Percent for leading party 66.2%
2006
Total vote (x 1,000) . . . . NA
Leading party . . . . NA
Percent for leading party . . . . NA

Votes cast for US Representatives
2004
Total vote (x 1,000) 652
   Democratic 244
   Republican 396
Leading party . . . . Republican
Percent for leading party 60.8%
2006
Total vote (x 1,000) 403
   Democratic 209
   Republican 190
Leading party . . . . Democratic
Percent for leading party 52.0%

©2008 Information Publications, Inc.
All rights reserved. Photocopying prohibited.
877-544-INFO (4636) or www.informationpublications.com

State government employment, 2006
Full-time equivalent employees 19,076
Payroll ($ mil) $70.4

Local government employment, 2006
Full-time equivalent employees 50,701
Payroll ($ mil) $163.9

Women holding public office, 2008
US Congress 1
Statewide elected office 0
State legislature 152

Black public officials, 2002
Total 5
  US and state legislatures 5
  City/county/regional offices 0
  Judicial/law enforcement 0
  Education/school boards 0

Hispanic public officials, 2006
Total 3
  State executives & legislators 2
  City/county/regional offices 1
  Judicial/law enforcement 0
  Education/school boards 0

Governmental Finance

State government revenues, 2006
Total revenue (x $1,000) $6,373,151
  per capita $4,858.25
General revenue (x $1,000) $5,186,159
  Intergovernmental 1,717,500
  Taxes 2,080,573
    general sales 0
    individual income tax 80,931
    corporate income tax 542,644
  Current charges 689,445
  Miscellaneous 698,641

State government expenditure, 2006
Total expenditure (x $1,000) $5,987,952
  per capita $4,564.61
General expenditure (x $1,000) $5,212,161
  per capita, total *$3,973.23*
    Education 1,440.06
    Public welfare 1,066.19
    Health 100.60
    Hospitals 41.81
    Highways 340.26
    Police protection 34.85
    Corrections 89.04
    Natural resources 48.58
    Parks & recreation 10.62
    Governmental administration 149.74
    Interest on general debt 262.51

State debt & cash, 2006 ($ per capita)
Debt $5,666.35
Cash/security holdings $9,040.18

Federal government grants to state & local government, 2005 (x $1,000)
Total $1,795,266
by Federal agency
  Defense 20,176
  Education 147,320
  Energy 6,469
  Environmental Protection Agency 37,510
  Health & Human Services 981,105
  Homeland Security 14,131
  Housing & Urban Development 143,170
  Justice 52,624
  Labor 27,795
  Transportation .171,780
  Veterans Affairs .5,759

Crime & Law Enforcement

Crime, 2006 (rates per 100,000 residents)
Property crimes 24,642
  Burglary 4,358
  Larceny 18,862
  Motor vehicle theft 1,422
  Property crime rate 1,874.1
Violent crimes 1,824
  Murder 13
  Forcible rape 344
  Robbery 423
  Aggravated assault 1,044
  Violent crime rate 138.7
Hate crimes 39

Fraud and identity theft, 2006
Fraud complaints 1,964
  rate per 100,000 residents 149.4
Identity theft complaints 606
  rate per 100,000 residents 46.1

Law enforcement agencies, 2006
Total agencies 148
Total employees 3,197
  Officers 2,414
  Civilians 783

Prisoners, probation, and parole, 2006
Total prisoners 2,805
  percent change, 12/31/05 to 12/31/06 . . . 10.9%
  in private facilities .0%
  in local jails 0.5%
Sentenced to more than one year 2,737
  rate per 100,000 residents 207
Adults on probation 4,590
Adults on parole 1,621

Prisoner demographics, June 30, 2005 (rate per 100,000 residents)
Male 590
Female 56
White 289
Black 2,666
Hispanic 1,063

©2008 Information Publications, Inc.
All rights reserved. Photocopying prohibited.
877-544-INFO (4636) or www.informationpublications.com

Arrests, 2006

Total................................ 46,100
　Persons under 18 years of age 8,314

Persons under sentence of death, 1/1/07

Total..................................... 0
　White..................................... 0
　Black 0
　Hispanic 0

State's highest court

Name ....Supreme Court
Number of members........................ 5
Length of term .... 5 years
Intermediate appeals court? .... no

Labor & Income

Civilian labor force, 2006 (x 1,000)

Total.................................... 741
　Men 392
　Women 349
　Persons 16-19 years.................... 38
　White.................................. 710
　Black .... NA
　Hispanic 13

Civilian labor force as a percent of civilian non-institutional population, 2006

Total....................................70.9%
　Men 76.9
　Women 65.3
　Persons 16-19 years....................52.2
　White..................................70.8
　Black .... NA
　Hispanic...............................76.8

Employment, 2006 (x 1,000)

Total.................................... 716
　Men 378
　Women 338
　Persons 16-19 years.................... 34
　White.................................. 687
　Black .... NA
　Hispanic 12

Unemployment rate, 2006

Total.................................... 3.4%
　Men 3.5
　Women 3.1
　Persons 16-19 years....................11.8
　White.................................. 3.3
　Black .... NA
　Hispanic 3.6

Full-time/part-time labor force, 2003 (x 1,000)

Full-time labor force, employed 550
Part-time labor force, employed........... 139
Unemployed, looking for
　Full-time work......................... 23
　Part-time work......................... 7
*Mean duration of unemployment (weeks)......*20.6
　Median 10.0

Labor unions, 2006

Membership (x 1,000)..................... 63
　percent of employed 10.1%

Experienced civilian labor force by private industry, 2006

Total............................... 541,506
　Natural resources & mining 2,416
　Construction 29,443
　Manufacturing...................... 78,363
　Trade, transportation & utilities 141,903
　Information 12,531
　Finance 37,541
　Professional & business 61,507
　Education & health 94,072
　Leisure & hospitality................63,975
　Other 19,274

Experienced civilian labor force by occupation, May 2006

Management........................... 32,890
Business & financial 27,490
Legal................................. 3,280
Sales................................. 80,560
Office & admin. support.............. 108,740
Computers & math 16,620
Architecture & engineering............ 12,420
Arts & entertainment 5,700
Education 45,530
Social services 7,560
Health care practitioner & technical 31,900
Health care support 14,860
Maintenance & repair................. 26,390
Construction 25,950
Transportation & moving 35,820
Production 49,780
Farming, fishing & forestry............ 840

Hours and earnings of production workers on manufacturing payrolls, 2006

Average weekly hours 41.2
Average hourly earnings $16.56
Average weekly earnings $682.27

Income and poverty, 2006

Median household income............ $59,683
Personal income, per capita (current $)... $39,311
　in constant (2000) dollars $34,316
Persons below poverty level.............. 8.0%

Average annual pay

2006 .... $42,447
　increase from 2005 .... 4.7%

Federal individual income tax returns, 2005

Returns filed........................ 650,233
Adjusted gross income ($1,000) $37,533,740
Total tax liability ($1,000) $5,094,192

Charitable contributions, 2004

Number of contributions 196.9
Total amount ($ mil)...................$547.5

©2008 Information Publications, Inc.
All rights reserved. Photocopying prohibited.
877-544-INFO (4636) or www.informationpublications.com

Economy, Business, Industry & Agriculture

Fortune 500 companies, 2007............... 0
Bankruptcy cases filed, FY 2007......... 2,804

Patents and trademarks issued, 2007
Patents.................................. 609
Trademarks.............................. 334

Business firm ownership, 2002
Women-owned.........................31,024
   Sales ($ mil)...................... $4,665
Black-owned............................. 470
   Sales ($ mil)...................... $68
Hispanic-owned......................... 913
   Sales ($ mil)...................... $194
Asian-owned 1,528
   Sales ($ mil)...................... $404
Amer. Indian/Alaska Native-owned 535
   Sales ($ mil)...................... $59
Hawaiian/Pacific Islander-owned 17
   Sales ($ mil)...................... NA

Gross domestic product, 2006 ($ mil)
Total gross domestic product $56,276
   Agriculture, forestry, fishing and
     hunting 221
   Mining............................... 63
   Utilities 2,089
   Construction 2,733
   Manufacturing, durable goods......... 4,924
   Manufacturing, non-durable goods 1,678
   Wholesale trade......................3,634
   Retail trade.........................4,714
   Transportation & warehousing 872
   Information 1,958
   Finance & insurance.................. 4,607
   Real estate, rental & leasing 8,251
   Professional and technical services.....3,739
   Educational services..................1,041
   Health care and social assistance....... 4,808
   Accommodation/food services......... 1,664
   Other services, except government 1,349
   Government 5,182

Establishments, payroll, employees & receipts, by major industry group, 2005

Total............................... 39,224
   Annual payroll ($1,000).........$21,026,773
   Paid employees 562,398

Forestry, fishing & agriculture.............. 153
   Annual payroll ($1,000).............$19,217
   Paid employees 691

Mining................................. 46
   Annual payroll ($1,000).............$18,910
   Paid employees 326
   Receipts, 2002 ($1,000) $61,093

Utilities 103
   Annual payroll ($1,000)........... $233,759
   Paid employees 3,434
   Receipts, 2002 ($1,000) ....NA

Construction..........................4,913
   Annual payroll ($1,000)...........$1,349,971
   Paid employees 27,877
   Receipts, 2002 ($1,000) $5,222,133

Manufacturing........................2,155
   Annual payroll ($1,000)...........$3,549,995
   Paid employees 75,837
   Receipts, 2002 ($1,000) $15,235,144

Wholesale trade 2,018
   Annual payroll ($1,000)...........$1,383,024
   Paid employees 24,728
   Receipts, 2002 ($1,000) $13,741,876

Retail trade 6,687
   Annual payroll ($1,000)...........$2,359,255
   Paid employees 99,693
   Receipts, 2002 ($1,000) $20,830,057

Transportation & warehousing............. 839
   Annual payroll ($1,000)........... $389,185
   Paid employees 12,244
   Receipts, 2002 ($1,000) $1,297,644

Information.............................. 777
   Annual payroll ($1,000)........... $785,703
   Paid employees 13,392
   Receipts, 2002 ($1,000) ....NA

Finance & insurance 1,942
   Annual payroll ($1,000)...........$1,678,378
   Paid employees 28,136
   Receipts, 2002 ($1,000) ....NA

Professional, scientific & technical 4,032
   Annual payroll ($1,000)...........$1,715,627
   Paid employees 29,619
   Receipts, 2002 ($1,000) $2,866,611

Education 588
   Annual payroll ($1,000)........... $702,695
   Paid employees 21,659
   Receipts, 2002 ($1,000) $200,819

Health care & social assistance 3,334
   Annual payroll ($1,000)...........$2,936,765
   Paid employees 79,240
   Receipts, 2002 ($1,000) $5,518,477

Arts and entertainment 747
   Annual payroll ($1,000)........... $199,301
   Paid employees 10,530
   Receipts, 2002 ($1,000) $601,029

Real estate............................1,592
   Annual payroll ($1,000)........... $278,452
   Paid employees 7,943
   Receipts, 2002 ($1,000) $1,117,115

Accommodation & food service 3,369
   Annual payroll ($1,000)........... $803,288
   Paid employees 56,070
   Receipts, 2002 ($1,000) $2,082,145

©2008 Information Publications, Inc.
All rights reserved. Photocopying prohibited.
877-544-INFO (4636) or www.informationpublications.com

Exports, 2006
Value of exported goods ($ mil) $2,811
   Manufactured $2,307
   Non-manufactured.................... $258

Foreign direct investment in US affiliates, 2004
Property, plants & equipment ($ mil) $4,693
Employment (x 1,000)..................... 41.0

Agriculture, 2006
Number of farms 3,400
Farm acreage (x 1,000) 450
   Acres per farm....................... 132
Farm marketings and income ($ mil)
Total................................... $161.8
   Crops $97.8
   Livestock............................ $64.0
Net farm income $42.6

Principal commodities, in order by marketing receipts, 2005
Greenhouse/nursery, Dairy products, Cattle and calves, Apples, Hay

Federal economic activity in state
Expenditures, 2005 ($ mil)
   Total.............................. $8,331
     Per capita $6,374.82
   Defense............................ $1,293
   Non-defense........................ $7,038
Defense department, 2006 ($ mil)
   Payroll.............................. $324
   Contract awards $1,106
   Grants $32
Homeland security grants ($1,000)
   2006............................... $7,887
   2007............................... $6,955

FDIC-insured financial institutions, 2005
Number 26
Assets ($ billion) $19.7
Deposits ($ billion) $13.4

Fishing, 2006
Catch (x 1,000 lbs)..................... 10,295
Value ($1,000)......................... $18,970

Mining, 2006 ($ mil)
Total non-fuel mineral production $100
Percent of U.S. 0.16%

Communication, Energy & Transportation

Communication
Households with computers, 2003 .... 71.5%
Households with internet access, 2003 .... 65.2%
High-speed internet providers 36
Total high-speed internet lines........ 443,137
   Residential 304,594
   Business........................... 138,543
Wireless phone customers, 12/2006 943,330

FCC-licensed stations (as of January 1, 2008)
TV stations 7
FM radio stations........................... 59
AM radio stations 27

Energy
Energy consumption, 2004
   Total (trillion Btu)..................... 341
   Per capita (million Btu) 262.5
By source of production (trillion Btu)
   Coal 43
   Natural gas.............................. 65
   Petroleum............................... 205
   Nuclear electric power 106
   Hydroelectric power..................... 13
By end-use sector (trillion Btu)
   Residential 100
   Commercial 76
   Industrial 56
   Transportation 109
Electric energy, 2005
   Primary source of electricity......... Nuclear
   Net generation (billion kWh) 24.5
     percent from renewable sources...... 11.2%
   Net summer capability (million kW) 4.3
   CO_2 emitted from generation 8.2
Natural gas utilities, 2005
   Customers (x 1,000) 111
   Sales (trillion Btu)..................... 25
   Revenues ($ mil) $228
Nuclear plants, 2007 1
Total CO_2 emitted (million metric tons).....20.5
Energy spending, 2004 ($ mil) $3,928
   per capita $3,026
   Price per million Btu $15.52

Transportation, 2006
Public road & street mileage 15,647
   Urban................................4,733
   Rural 10,914
   Interstate 225
Vehicle miles of travel (millions) 13,614
   per capita 10,377.9
Total motor vehicle registrations...... 1,059,963
   Automobiles........................ 585,455
   Trucks 472,635
   Motorcycles 70,778
Licensed drivers 1,027,582
   19 years & under 57,114
Deaths from motor vehicle accidents 127
Gasoline consumed (x 1,000 gallons) 717,750
   per capita 547.1

Commuting Statistics, 2006
Average commute time (min) 24.6
   Drove to work alone 81.7%
   Carpooled............................ 8.6%
   Public transit 0.7%
   Walk to work 3.4%
   Work from home 4.3%

©2008 Information Publications, Inc.
All rights reserved. Photocopying prohibited.
877-544-INFO (4636) or www.informationpublications.com

State Summary

Capital city . . . . Trenton
Governor . . . . Jon Corzine

The State House
PO Box 001
Trenton, NJ 08625
609-292-6000

Admitted as a state 1787
Area (square miles) 8,721
Population, 2007 (estimate) 8,685,920
Largest city . . . . Newark
  Population, 2006 281,402
Personal income per capita, 2006
  (in current dollars) $46,344
Gross domestic product, 2006 ($ mil) . . . $453,177

Leading industries by payroll, 2005

Professional/Scientific/Technical, Health care/
  Social assistance, Wholesale trade

**Leading agricultural commodities
  by receipts, 2005**

Greenhouse/nursery, Horses/mules, Blueberries,
  Peaches, Dairy products

Geography & Environment

Total area (square miles) 8,721
  land 7,417
  water 1,304
Federally-owned land, 2004 (acres) 148,441
  percent 3.1%
Highest point . . . . High Point
  elevation (feet) 1,803
Lowest point . . . . Atlantic Ocean
  elevation (feet) . . . . sea level
General coastline (miles) 130
Tidal shoreline (miles) 1,792
Cropland, 2003 (x 1,000 acres) 528
Forest land, 2003 (x 1,000 acres) 1,605
Capital city . . . . Trenton
  Population 2000 85,403
  Population 2006 83,923
Largest city . . . . Newark
  Population 2000 273,546
  Population 2006 281,402

Number of cities with over 100,000 population

1990 4
2000 4
2006 4

State park and recreation areas, 2005

Area (x 1,000 acres) 397
Number of visitors (x 1,000) 15,791
Revenues ($1,000) $10,176
  percent of operating expenditures 27.6%

National forest system land, 2007

Acres 0

Demographics & Population Characteristics

Population

1980 7,364,823
1990 7,730,188
2000 8,414,347
2006 8,724,560
  Male 4,262,291
  Female 4,462,269
Living in group quarters, 2006 197,712
  percent of total 2.3%
2007 (estimate) .8,685,920
  persons per square mile of land 1,171.1
2008 (projected) .8,915,495
2010 (projected) .9,018,231
2020 (projected) .9,461,635
2030 (projected) .9,802,440

**Population of Core-Based Statistical Areas
  (formerly Metropolitan Areas), x 1,000**

	CBSA	Non-CBSA
1990	7,730	0
2000	8,414	0
2006	8,725	0

Change in population, 2000-2007

Number 271,573
  percent 3.2%
Natural increase (births minus deaths) 291,260
Net internal migration . . . . -377,159
Net international migration 376,519

Persons by age, 2006

Under 5 years 558,994
5 to 17 years 1,530,344
18 years and over 6,635,222
65 years and over 1,127,742
85 years and over 166,529
  Median age 38.2

Persons by age, 2010 (projected)

Under 5 years 587,220
18 and over 6,930,007
65 and over 1,231,585
  Median age 38.9

Race, 2006

One Race
  White 6,665,390
  Black or African American 1,264,681
  Asian 647,986
  American Indian/Alaska Native 27,970
  Hawaiian Native/Pacific Islander 6,878
Two or more races 111,655

Persons of Hispanic origin, 2006

Total Hispanic or Latino 1,364,699
  Mexican 186,918
  Puerto Rican 392,619
  Cuban 73,024

Persons of Asian origin, 2006

Total Asian 652,378
  Asian Indian. 256,965
  Chinese 129,896
  Filipino 105,806
  Japanese 16,681
  Korean 86,356
  Vietnamese. 24,251

Marital status, 2006

Population 15 years & over 7,006,178
  Never married 2,222,005
  Married. 3,723,172
  Separated 160,006
  Widowed. 483,310
  Divorced 577,691

Language spoken at home, 2006

Population 5 years and older 8,164,688
  English only 5,907,177
  Spanish 1,134,033
  French 68,457
  German. 32,276
  Chinese 104,226

Households & families, 2006

Households. 3,135,490
  with persons under 18 years 1,146,672
  with persons over 65 years. 783,466
  persons per household 2.72
Families. 2,180,404
  persons per family. 3.29
Married couples. 1,631,340
Female householder,
  no husband present. 404,348
One-person households 803,445

Nativity, 2006

Number of residents born in state 4,573,613
  percent of population 52.4%

Immigration & naturalization, 2006

Legal permanent residents admitted 65,934
Persons naturalized 39,801
Non-immigrant admissions 771,060

Vital Statistics and Health

Marriages

2004 50,662
2005 49,305
2006 42,398

Divorces

2004 25,981
2005 25,343
2006 25,794

Health risks, 2006

Percent of adults who are:
  Smokers. 18.0%
  Overweight (BMI > 25). 59.9%
  Obese (BMI > 30). 22.6%

Births

2005 113,776
  Birthrate (per 1,000). 13.1
  White. 82,659
  Black 19,990
  Hispanic 27,959
  Asian/Pacific Islander 10,949
  Amer. Indian/Alaska Native 178
  Low birth weight (2,500g or less) 8.2%
  Cesarian births 36.3%
  Preterm births 12.5%
  To unmarried mothers. 31.4%
  Twin births (per 1,000) 41.8
  Triplets or higher order (per 100,000). . . 288.7
2006 (preliminary). 115,006
  rate per 1,000 . . . . 13.2

Deaths

2004
All causes 71,371
  rate per 100,000. . . . . 752.7
Heart disease 20,560
  rate per 100,000. . . . . 213.0
Malignant neoplasms 17,208
  rate per 100,000. . . . . 184.4
Cerebrovascular disease. 3,781
  rate per 100,000. . . . . 39.2
Chronic lower respiratory disease 3,031
  rate per 100,000. . . . . 32.1
Diabetes. 2,595
  rate per 100,000. . . . . 27.6
2005 (preliminary) 71,970
  rate per 100,000. . . . . 745.9
2006 (provisional) 71,809

Infant deaths

2004 651
  rate per 1,000 . . . . 5.7
2005 (provisional) 586
  rate per 1,000 . . . . 5.1

Exercise routines, 2005

None. 29.2%
Moderate or greater. 45.9%
Vigorous 25.5%

Abortions, 2004

Total performed in state. 32,642
  rate per 1,000 women age 15-44 18
  % obtained by out-of-state residents 4.8%

Physicians, 2005

Total. 26,918
  rate per 100,000 persons 309

Community hospitals, 2005

Number of hospitals 80
Beds (x 1,000). 22.1
Patients admitted (x 1,000) 1,110
Average daily census (x 1,000) 16.2
Average cost per day $1,797
Outpatient visits (x 1 mil) 16.8

©2008 Information Publications, Inc.
All rights reserved. Photocopying prohibited.
877-544-INFO (4636) or www.informationpublications.com

Disability status of population, 2006

5 to 15 years 5.3%
16 to 64 years 9.3%
65 years and over 36.5%

Education

Educational attainment, 2006

Population over 25 years 5,871,240
   Less than 9th grade. 5.9%
   High school graduate or more 86.1%
   College graduate or more. 33.4%
   Graduate or professional degree. 12.4%

Public school enrollment, 2005-06

Total 1,395,602
   Pre-kindergarten through grade 8. . . . 926,870
   Grades 9 through 12 407,314

Graduating public high school seniors, 2004-05

Diplomas (incl. GED and others) 86,502

SAT scores, 2007

Average critical reading score 495
Average writing score 494
Average math score 510
Percent of graduates taking test 82%

Public school teachers, 2006-07 (estimate)

Total (x 1,000) 115.0
   Elementary 44.4
   Secondary 70.6
Average salary $59,920
   Elementary $58,866
   Secondary $61,373

State receipts & expenditures for public schools, 2006-07 (estimate)

Revenue receipts ($ mil) $21,167
Expenditures
Total ($ mil) $21,096
   Per capita $2,336
   Per pupil $14,824

NAEP proficiency scores, 2007

	Reading		Math	
	Basic	Proficient	Basic	Proficient
Grade 4	77.2%	43.1%	89.6%	51.8%
Grade 8	81.1%	39.0%	77.5%	40.4%

Higher education enrollment, fall 2005

Total 75,443
   Full-time men 25,388
   Full-time women 26,707
   Part-time men 9,601
   Part-time women 13,747

Minority enrollment in institutions of higher education, 2005

Black, non-Hispanic 53,971
Hispanic 50,502
Asian/Pacific Islander 32,409
American Indian/Alaska Native 1,170

Institutions of higher education, 2005-06

Total 59
   Public. 33
   Private 26

Earned degrees conferred, 2004-05

Associate's. 14,726
Bachelor's 31,987
Master's 12,386
First-professional. 1,817
Doctor's 1,142

Public Libraries, 2006

Number of libraries. 306
Number of outlets 467
Annual visits per capita 5.4
Circulation per capita. 6.4

State & local financial support for higher education, FY 2006

Full-time equivalent enrollment (x 1,000) 228.1
Appropriations per FTE. $8,145

Social Insurance & Welfare Programs

Social Security benefits & beneficiaries, 2005

Beneficiaries (x 1,000) 1,379
   Retired & dependents 1,012
   Survivors. 169
   Disabled & dependents. 197
Annual benefit payments ($ mil) $16,474
   Retired & dependents $11,675
   Survivors. $2,565
   Disabled & dependents. $2,234
Average monthly benefit
   Retired & dependents $1,105
   Disabled & dependents. $1,023
   Widowed. $1,065

Medicare, July 2005

Enrollment (x 1,000). 1,227
Payments ($ mil) $9,860

Medicaid, 2004

Beneficiaries (x 1,000). 119
Payments ($ mil) $822

State Children's Health Insurance Program, 2006

Enrollment (x 1,000) 120.9
Expenditures ($ mil) $190.6

Persons without health insurance, 2006

Number (x 1,000) 1,341
   percent 15.5%
Number of children (x 1,000) 277
   percent of children 13.3%

Health care expenditures, 2004

Total expenditures. $50,384
   per capita $5,807

©2008 Information Publications, Inc.
All rights reserved. Photocopying prohibited.
877-544-INFO (4636) or www.informationpublications.com

Federal and state public aid

State unemployment insurance, 2006
Recipients, first payments (x 1,000) 305
Total payments ($ mil) $1,775
Average weekly benefit $344
Temporary Assistance for Needy Families, 2006
Recipients (x 1,000)..................... 1,157.4
Families (x 1,000) 472.1
Supplemental Security Income, 2005
Recipients (x 1,000).......................152.4
Payments ($ mil) $763.4
Food Stamp Program, 2006
Avg monthly participants (x 1,000) 405.7
Total benefits ($ mil)..................$455.9

Housing & Construction

Housing units
Total 2005 (estimate) 3,443,194
Total 2006 (estimate) 3,472,643
Seasonal or recreational use, 2006......119,636
Owner-occupied, 2006...............2,110,308
  Median home value.............. $366,600
  Homeowner vacancy rate.............. 1.6%
Renter-occupied, 2006 1,025,182
  Median rent $974
  Rental vacancy rate................... 7.3%
Home ownership rate, 2005.............. 70.1%
Home ownership rate, 2006.............. 69.0%

New privately-owned housing units
Number authorized, 2006 (x 1,000)....34.3
  Value ($ mil)......................$4,382.7
Started 2005 (x 1,000, estimate)...........26.5
Started 2006 (x 1,000, estimate)...........26.1

Existing home sales
2005 (x 1,000).........................184.4
2006 (x 1,000).........................154.1

Government & Elections

State officials 2008
Governor........................Jon Corzine
  Democratic, term expires 1/10
Lieutenant Governor.. (no Lieutenant Governor)
Secretary of State................. Nina Wells
Attorney General...............Anne Milgram
Chief Justice ....Stuart Rabner

Governorship
Minimum age............................ 30
Length of term....................... 4 years
Consecutive terms permitted 2
Who succeeds.............. President of Senate

Local governments by type, 2002
Total....................................1,412
  County.................................. 21
  Municipal............................. 324
  Township 242
  School District....................... 549
  Special District 276

State legislature
Name .... Legislature
Upper chamber ....Senate
  Number of members.................... 40
  Length of term.................... 4 years
  Party in majority, 2008 ....Democratic
Lower chamber............. General Assembly
  Number of members.................... 80
  Length of term.................... 2 years
  Party in majority, 2008 ....Democratic

Federal representation, 2008 (110th Congress)
Senator.................... Frank Lautenberg
  Party ....Democratic
  Year term expires 2009
Senator.................... Robert Menendez
  Party ....Democratic
  Year term expires 2013
Representatives, total 13
  Democrats.............................. 7
  Republicans 6

Voters in November 2006 election (estimate)
Total....................2,406,132
  Male....................1,121,355
  Female....................1,284,777
  White....................2,036,979
  Black 266,563
  Hispanic 83,157
  Asian 96,283

Presidential election, 2004
Total Popular Vote 3,611,691
  Kerry 1,911,430
  Bush.....................1,670,003
Total Electoral Votes..................... 15

Votes cast for US Senators
2004
Total vote (x 1,000) .... NA
Leading party........................... NA
Percent for leading party .... NA
2006
Total vote (x 1,000) 102
Leading party...................Democratic
Percent for leading party 57.2%

Votes cast for US Representatives
2004
Total vote (x 1,000) 3,285
  Democratic.....................1,721
  Republican 1,515
Leading party...................Democratic
Percent for leading party 52.4%
2006
Total vote (x 1,000) 2,137
  Democratic..................... 1,208
  Republican 903
Leading party...................Democratic
Percent for leading party 56.5%

©2008 Information Publications, Inc.
All rights reserved. Photocopying prohibited.
877-544-INFO (4636) or www.informationpublications.com

State government employment, 2006
Full-time equivalent employees 156,768
Payroll ($ mil) $767.5

Local government employment, 2006
Full-time equivalent employees 354,987
Payroll ($ mil) $1,608.8

Women holding public office, 2008
US Congress 0
Statewide elected office..................... 0
State legislature 34

Black public officials, 2002
Total.................................... 269
   US and state legislatures 18
   City/county/regional offices 162
   Judicial/law enforcement.................. 0
   Education/school boards.................. 89

Hispanic public officials, 2006
Total.................................... 109
   State executives & legislators 5
   City/county/regional offices 61
   Judicial/law enforcement.................. 0
   Education/school boards................. 43

Governmental Finance

State government revenues, 2006
Total revenue (x $1,000)............ $57,610,331
   per capita $6,647.80
General revenue (x $1,000) $46,445,905
   Intergovernmental 11,378,454
   Taxes 26,266,187
     general sales....................6,853,418
     individual income tax 10,506,565
     corporate income tax........... 2,508,428
   Current charges...................4,682,195
   Miscellaneous 4,119,069

State government expenditure, 2006
Total expenditure (x $1,000).......$54,073,301
   per capita $6,239.65
General expenditure (x $1,000) $43,349,868
   per capita, total...................$5,002.25
     Education 1,632.60
     Public welfare 1,442.60
     Health 92.11
     Hospitals.......................197.67
     Highways 301.83
     Police protection.................61.54
     Corrections 164.02
     Natural resources 66.60
     Parks & recreation 52.12
     Governmental administration...... 204.17
     Interest on general debt............175.17

State debt & cash, 2006 ($ per capita)
Debt $5,515.84
Cash/security holdings.............. $11,192.67

Federal government grants to state & local government, 2005 (x $1,000)
Total............................$11,124,122
by Federal agency
   Defense 68,094
   Education 890,179
   Energy 39,441
   Environmental Protection Agency 89,819
   Health & Human Services. 6,397,656
   Homeland Security....................33,108
   Housing & Urban Development.....1,273,098
   Justice 130,135
   Labor 243,616
   Transportation 1,216,468
   Veterans Affairs.................. 22,569

Crime & Law Enforcement

Crime, 2006 (rates per 100,000 residents)
Property crimes 199,958
   Burglary 39,433
   Larceny 135,801
   Motor vehicle theft 24,724
   Property crime rate................2,291.9
Violent crimes........................ 30,672
   Murder 428
   Forcible rape......................1,237
   Robbery...........................13,357
   Aggravated assault 15,650
   Violent crime rate 351.6
Hate crimes 802

Fraud and identity theft, 2006
Fraud complaints.......................11,284
   rate per 100,000 residents 129.3
Identity theft complaints 6,394
   rate per 100,000 residents 73.3

Law enforcement agencies, 2006
Total agencies......................... 529
Total employees 36,456
   Officers 29,013
   Civilians 7,443

Prisoners, probation, and parole, 2006
Total prisoners.......................27,371
   percent change, 12/31/05 to 12/31/06 ....0.0%
   in private facilities 9.5%
   in local jails 6.7%
Sentenced to more than one year 27,371
   rate per 100,000 residents 313
Adults on probation 132,636
Adults on parole....................... 14,405

Prisoner demographics, June 30, 2005 (rate per 100,000 residents)
Male..................................1,019
Female.................................. 70
White.................................. 190
Black.................................. 2,352
Hispanic 630

©2008 Information Publications, Inc.
All rights reserved. Photocopying prohibited.
877-544-INFO (4636) or www.informationpublications.com

Arrests, 2006

Total.................................388,116

    Persons under 18 years of age........ 60,840

Persons under sentence of death, 1/1/07

Total..................................... 11

    White..................................... 5

    Black..................................... 6

    Hispanic................................. 0

State's highest court

Name.......................Supreme Court

Number of members........................ 7

Length of term........................ 7 years

Intermediate appeals court?.................yes

Labor & Income

Civilian labor force, 2006 (x 1,000)

Total.................................. 4,490

    Men 2,428

    Women 2,063

    Persons 16-19 years................... 187

    White.................................3,473

    Black 599

    Hispanic 722

Civilian labor force as a percent of civilian non-institutional population, 2006

Total.................................66.6%

    Men 75.2

    Women 58.7

    Persons 16-19 years.................38.1

    White................................66.2

    Black 66.5

    Hispanic 70.6

Employment, 2006 (x 1,000)

Total.................................4,273

    Men 2,312

    Women 1,961

    Persons 16-19 years................... 162

    White................................3,328

    Black 541

    Hispanic 676

Unemployment rate, 2006

Total..................................4.8%

    Men 4.8

    Women 4.9

    Persons 16-19 years.................13.3

    White................................4.2

    Black 9.7

    Hispanic 6.4

Full-time/part-time labor force, 2003 (x 1,000)

Full-time labor force, employed.......... 3,454

Part-time labor force, employed............ 664

Unemployed, looking for

    Full-time work........................ 222

    Part-time work......................... 35

Mean duration of unemployment (weeks)......20.4

    Median 12.0

Labor unions, 2006

Membership (x 1,000)..................... 770

    percent of employed 20.1%

Experienced civilian labor force by private industry, 2006

Total.............................3,340,229

    Natural resources & mining 12,073

    Construction 172,909

    Manufacturing...................... 321,825

    Trade, transportation & utilities 864,235

    Information 97,150

    Finance 266,608

    Professional & business 596,296

    Education & health 522,312

    Leisure & hospitality............... 335,325

    Other............................. 124,190

Experienced civilian labor force by occupation, May 2006

Management........................185,110

Business & financial 200,310

Legal............................. 32,750

Sales............................. 418,290

Office & admin. support............. 761,070

Computers & math 119,890

Architecture & engineering........... 56,210

Arts & entertainment................ 44,720

Education 265,780

Social services 54,890

Health care practitioner & technical.... 201,670

Health care support 106,650

Maintenance & repair.................147,460

Construction 144,050

Transportation & moving 318,750

Production 223,550

Farming, fishing & forestry........... 4,620

Hours and earnings of production workers on manufacturing payrolls, 2006

Average weekly hours....................42.1

Average hourly earnings $16.55

Average weekly earnings $696.76

Income and poverty, 2006

Median household income............ $64,470

Personal income, per capita (current $).. $46,344

    in constant (2000) dollars $40,455

Persons below poverty level.............. 8.7%

Average annual pay

2006 .... $51,645

    increase from 2005 .... 4.4%

Federal individual income tax returns, 2005

Returns filed....................... 4,152,741

Adjusted gross income ($1,000) ... $282,306,218

Total tax liability ($1,000) $42,460,858

Charitable contributions, 2004

Number of contributions.............. 1,683.8

Total amount ($ mil)................. $5,533.7

©2008 Information Publications, Inc.
All rights reserved. Photocopying prohibited.
877-544-INFO (4636) or www.informationpublications.com

Economy, Business, Industry & Agriculture

Fortune 500 companies, 2007 24
Bankruptcy cases filed, FY 2007 18,702

Patents and trademarks issued, 2007

Patents 3,185
Trademarks 2,691

Business firm ownership, 2002

Women-owned 185,197
   Sales ($ mil) $35,573
Black-owned 36,280
   Sales ($ mil) $3,202
Hispanic-owned 49,841
   Sales ($ mil) $7,245
Asian-owned 51,957
   Sales ($ mil) $18,495
Amer. Indian/Alaska Native-owned 2,645
   Sales ($ mil) $284
Hawaiian/Pacific Islander-owned 448
   Sales ($ mil) $37

Gross domestic product, 2006 ($ mil)

Total gross domestic product $453,177
   Agriculture, forestry, fishing and
     hunting 642
   Mining 226
   Utilities 8,917
   Construction 19,068
   Manufacturing, durable goods 13,915
   Manufacturing, non-durable goods 27,644
   Wholesale trade 36,464
   Retail trade 28,413
   Transportation & warehousing 13,119
   Information 21,541
   Finance & insurance 37,327
   Real estate, rental & leasing 78,182
   Professional and technical services 38,536
   Educational services 3,994
   Health care and social assistance 32,062
   Accommodation/food services 11,176
   Other services, except government 9,208
   Government 45,003

Establishments, payroll, employees & receipts, by major industry group, 2005

Total 242,128
   Annual payroll ($1,000) $166,018,238
   Paid employees 3,594,862
Forestry, fishing & agriculture 243
   Annual payroll ($1,000) $26,847
   Paid employees 751
Mining 110
   Annual payroll ($1,000) $137,556
   Paid employees 2,305
   Receipts, 2002 ($1,000) $379,558

Utilities 340
   Annual payroll ($1,000) $1,545,619
   Paid employees .18,164
   Receipts, 2002 ($1,000) . . . .*NA*
Construction 25,455
   Annual payroll ($1,000) $9,240,445
   Paid employees 175,322
   Receipts, 2002 ($1,000) $37,867,759
Manufacturing 9,575
   Annual payroll ($1,000) $15,352,555
   Paid employees 304,976
   Receipts, 2002 ($1,000) $96,599,807
Wholesale trade 16,347
   Annual payroll ($1,000) $17,375,975
   Paid employees 274,063
   Receipts, 2002 ($1,000) $256,925,492
Retail trade 35,263
   Annual payroll ($1,000) $11,303,325
   Paid employees 454,878
   Receipts, 2002 ($1,000) $102,153,833
Transportation & warehousing 7,228
   Annual payroll ($1,000) $6,443,091
   Paid employees 169,118
   Receipts, 2002 ($1,000) $16,421,043
Information 4,059
   Annual payroll ($1,000) $7,846,435
   Paid employees 122,177
   Receipts, 2002 ($1,000) . . . .*NA*
Finance & insurance 12,543
   Annual payroll ($1,000) $16,995,391
   Paid employees 216,384
   Receipts, 2002 ($1,000) . . . .*NA*
Professional, scientific & technical 31,669
   Annual payroll ($1,000) $20,504,746
   Paid employees 304,803
   Receipts, 2002 ($1,000) $36,005,523
Education 3,021
   Annual payroll ($1,000) $2,702,816
   Paid employees 84,880
   Receipts, 2002 ($1,000) $1,662,096
Health care & social assistance 24,772
   Annual payroll ($1,000) $19,367,540
   Paid employees 479,536
   Receipts, 2002 ($1,000) $38,708,974
Arts and entertainment 3,601
   Annual payroll ($1,000) $1,162,942
   Paid employees 46,240
   Receipts, 2002 ($1,000) $3,303,069
Real estate 9,584
   Annual payroll ($1,000) $2,841,714
   Paid employees 61,965
   Receipts, 2002 ($1,000) $12,262,786
Accommodation & food service 18,872
   Annual payroll ($1,000) $4,978,755
   Paid employees 274,639
   Receipts, 2002 ($1,000) $15,715,595

©2008 Information Publications, Inc.
All rights reserved. Photocopying prohibited.
877-544-INFO (4636) or www.informationpublications.com

Exports, 2006

Value of exported goods ($ mil) $27,002
  Manufactured $20,112
  Non-manufactured. $1,862

Foreign direct investment in US affiliates, 2004

Property, plants & equipment ($ mil) . . . $33,846
Employment (x 1,000). 219.7

Agriculture, 2006

Number of farms 9,800
Farm acreage (x 1,000) 790
  Acres per farm 81
Farm marketings and income ($ mil)
Total. $923.9
  Crops. $762.6
  Livestock. $161.3
Net farm income $305.4

Principal commodities, in order by marketing receipts, 2005

Greenhouse/nursery, Horses/mules, Blueberries,
Peaches, Dairy products

Federal economic activity in state

Expenditures, 2005 ($ mil)
  Total. $58,617
    Per capita $6,735.11
  Defense $7,645
  Non-defense. $50,972
Defense department, 2006 ($ mil)
  Payroll. $2,004
  Contract awards $6,151
  Grants $77
Homeland security grants ($1,000)
  2006. . . . .$51,983
  2007. . . . .$61,109

FDIC-insured financial institutions, 2005

Number. 131
Assets ($ billion) $139.7
Deposits ($ billion) $90.8

Fishing, 2006

Catch (x 1,000 lbs). 175,759
Value ($1,000). $145,850

Mining, 2006 ($ mil)

Total non-fuel mineral production $369
Percent of U.S. 0.57%

Communication, Energy & Transportation

Communication

Households with computers, 2003. . . . . . . .65.5%
Households with internet access, 2003 . . . .60.5%
High-speed internet providers 41
Total high-speed internet lines. 3,392,607
  Residential 2,109,126
  Business. 1,283,481
Wireless phone customers, 12/2006 7,207,018

FCC-licensed stations (as of January 1, 2008)

TV stations 15
FM radio stations. 97
AM radio stations 41

Energy

Energy consumption, 2004
  Total (trillion Btu). 2,630
  Per capita (million Btu) 303.2
By source of production (trillion Btu)
  Coal 113
  Natural gas. 647
  Petroleum. 1,270
  Nuclear electric power 282
  Hydroelectric power. 0
By end-use sector (trillion Btu)
  Residential 626
  Commercial 617
  Industrial 484
  Transportation 903
Electric energy, 2005
  Primary source of electricity. . . . . Nuclear
  Net generation (billion kWh) 60.5
    percent from renewable sources. 1.5%
  Net summer capability (million kW) 17.5
  CO_2 emitted from generation 21.1
Natural gas utilities, 2005
  Customers (x 1,000) 2,775
  Sales (trillion Btu). 490
  Revenues ($ mil) $4,795
Nuclear plants, 2007 4
Total CO_2 emitted (million metric tons). 123.7
Energy spending, 2004 ($ mil) $27,060
  per capita $3,119
  Price per million Btu $14.07

Transportation, 2006

Public road & street mileage 38,561
  Urban. 31,252
  Rural 7,309
  Interstate. 431
Vehicle miles of travel (millions) 75,371
  per capita 8,697.2
Total motor vehicle registrations. 5,957,988
  Automobiles. .3,692,966
  Trucks 2,241,195
  Motorcycles 163,609
Licensed drivers 5,834,227
  19 years & under 244,542
Deaths from motor vehicle accidents 772
Gasoline consumed (x 1,000 gallons) 4,281,216
  per capita 494.0

Commuting Statistics, 2006

Average commute time (min) 29.1
  Drove to work alone 71.9%
  Carpooled. 9.3%
  Public transit 10.3%
  Walk to work 3.4%
  Work from home. 3.2%

©2008 Information Publications, Inc.
All rights reserved. Photocopying prohibited.
877-544-INFO (4636) or www.informationpublications.com

State Summary

Capital city . . . . .Santa Fe
Governor. Bill Richardson

State Capitol
Fourth Floor
Santa Fe, NM 87300
505-827-3000

Admitted as a state 1912
Area (square miles) 121,590
Population, 2007 (estimate). 1,969,915
Largest city . . . . .Albuquerque
Population, 2006. 504,949
Personal income per capita, 2006
(in current dollars) $29,673
Gross domestic product, 2006 ($ mil) $75,910

Leading industries by payroll, 2005

Health care/Social assistance, Retail trade, Pro-
fessional/Scientific/Technical

**Leading agricultural commodities
by receipts, 2005**

Dairy products, Cattle and calves, Hay, Pecans,
Greenhouse/nursery

Geography & Environment

Total area (square miles). 121,590
land 121,356
water 234
Federally-owned land, 2004 (acres) . . .32,483,877
percent. 41.8%
Highest point . . . . Wheeler Peak
elevation (feet) 13,161
Lowest point . . . . .Red Bluff Reservoir
elevation (feet) 2,842
General coastline (miles) 0
Tidal shoreline (miles) 0
Cropland, 2003 (x 1,000 acres) 1,549
Forest land, 2003 (x 1,000 acres). 5,478
Capital city . . . . .Santa Fe
Population 2000 62,203
Population 2006 72,056
Largest city . . . . .Albuquerque
Population 2000 448,607
Population 2006 504,949

Number of cities with over 100,000 population
1990 1
2000 1
2006 1

State park and recreation areas, 2005
Area (x 1,000 acres). 93
Number of visitors (x 1,000) 4,157
Revenues ($1,000) $4,097
percent of operating expenditures. . . . . . . NA

National forest system land, 2007
Acres 9,413,211

Demographics & Population Characteristics

Population
1980 1,302,894
1990 1,515,069
2000 1,819,046
2006 1,954,599
Male. 964,808
Female. 989,791
Living in group quarters, 2006. 40,752
percent of total. 2.1%
2007 (estimate). 1,969,915
persons per square mile of land 16.2
2008 (projected). 1,951,229
2010 (projected) 1,980,225
2020 (projected). 2,084,341
2030 (projected). 2,099,708

**Population of Core-Based Statistical Areas
(formerly Metropolitan Areas), x 1,000**

	CBSA	Non-CBSA
1990	1,442	73
2000	1,737	82
2006	1,876	78

Change in population, 2000-2007
Number. 150,869
percent. 8.3%
Natural increase (births minus deaths) 99,615
Net internal migration 24,955
Net international migration 33,790

Persons by age, 2006
Under 5 years 141,969
5 to 17 years 366,961
18 years and over 1,445,669
65 years and over 242,600
85 years and over 31,309
Median age 35.3

Persons by age, 2010 (projected)
Under 5 years 145,063
18 and over 1,500,820
65 and over 278,967
Median age 38.3

Race, 2006
One Race
White. 1,653,876
Black or African American 49,161
Asian 26,140
American Indian/Alaska Native. 190,826
Hawaiian Native/Pacific Islander. 2,655
Two or more races. .31,941

Persons of Hispanic origin, 2006
Total Hispanic or Latino 860,687
Mexican. 448,714
Puerto Rican 9,632
Cuban 4,352

©2008 Information Publications, Inc.
All rights reserved. Photocopying prohibited.
877-544-INFO (4636) or www.informationpublications.com

Persons of Asian origin, 2006

Total Asian 25,983
  Asian Indian. 4,883
  Chinese 5,798
  Filipino 3,285
  Japanese 3,072
  Korean 3,269
  Vietnamese. 3,834

Marital status, 2006

Population 15 years & over 1,533,025
  Never married 483,436
  Married. 777,336
  Separated 29,699
  Widowed. 89,626
  Divorced 182,627

Language spoken at home, 2006

Population 5 years and older. 1,812,867
  English only 1,150,760
  Spanish 521,599
  French 4,673
  German. 8,606
  Chinese 4,227

Households & families, 2006

Households. 726,033
  with persons under 18 years 251,407
  with persons over 65 years. 168,577
  persons per household 2.64
Families. 477,430
  persons per family. 3.26
Married couples. 345,376
Female householder,
  no husband present. 92,088
One-person households 206,276

Nativity, 2006

Number of residents born in state 994,202
  percent of population 50.9%

Immigration & naturalization, 2006

Legal permanent residents admitted 3,805
Persons naturalized .1,538
Non-immigrant admissions 176,951

Vital Statistics and Health

Marriages

2004 14,067
2005 12,821
2006 13,423

Divorces

2004 8,829
2005 8,837
2006 8,383

Health risks, 2006

Percent of adults who are:
  Smokers. 20.1%
  Overweight (BMI > 25). 59.8%
  Obese (BMI > 30). 22.9%

Births

2005 28,835
  Birthrate (per 1,000). 15.0
  White. 24,119
  Black 540
  Hispanic 15,823
  Asian/Pacific Islander 460
  Amer. Indian/Alaska Native 3,716
  Low birth weight (2,500g or less). 8.5%
  Cesarian births 22.2%
  Preterm births 13.1%
  To unmarried mothers. 50.8%
  Twin births (per 1,000) 24.2
  Triplets or higher order (per 100,000). 65.9
2006 (preliminary). 29,937
  rate per 1,000 . . . . 15.3

Deaths

2004
All causes 14,298
  rate per 100,000. . . . . .778.9
Heart disease 3,264
  rate per 100,000. . . . . .180.4
Malignant neoplasms 3,036
  rate per 100,000. . . . . .161.9
Cerebrovascular disease. 721
  rate per 100,000. .40.5
Chronic lower respiratory disease 753
  rate per 100,000. .41.7
Diabetes. 590
  rate per 100,000. .31.7
2005 (preliminary). 14,984
  rate per 100,000. . . . . .795.0
2006 (provisional) 14,962

Infant deaths

2004 179
  rate per 1,000 . . . . .6.3
2005 (provisional) 177
  rate per 1,000 . . . . .6.2

Exercise routines, 2005

None. 23.3%
Moderate or greater. 51.0%
Vigorous 29.0%

Abortions, 2004

Total performed in state. 6,070
  rate per 1,000 women age 15-44. 15
  % obtained by out-of-state residents 6.2%

Physicians, 2005

Total. 4,622
  rate per 100,000 persons 240

Community hospitals, 2005

Number of hospitals 37
Beds (x 1,000). 3.5
Patients admitted (x 1,000) 172
Average daily census (x 1,000) 2.2
Average cost per day $1,780
Outpatient visits (x 1 mil) 4.7

©2008 Information Publications, Inc.
All rights reserved. Photocopying prohibited.
877-544-INFO (4636) or www.informationpublications.com

Disability status of population, 2006
5 to 15 years 6.3%
16 to 64 years 14.0%
65 years and over 43.1%

Education

Educational attainment, 2006
Population over 25 years 1,239,433
   Less than 9th grade. 8.3%
   High school graduate or more 81.5%
   College graduate or more. 25.3%
   Graduate or professional degree. 10.9%

Public school enrollment, 2005-06
Total. 326,758
   Pre-kindergarten through grade 8. . . . 229,552
   Grades 9 through 12 97,206

Graduating public high school seniors, 2004-05
Diplomas (incl. GED and others) 17,837

SAT scores, 2007
Average critical reading score 555
Average writing score 540
Average math score 546
Percent of graduates taking test 12%

Public school teachers, 2006-07 (estimate)
Total (x 1,000) 21.7
   Elementary 14.8
   Secondary 6.9
Average salary $42,780
   Elementary $42,634
   Secondary $43,130

State receipts & expenditures for public schools, 2006-07 (estimate)
Revenue receipts ($ mil) $3,277
Expenditures
Total ($ mil) $3,426
   Per capita $1,519
   Per pupil $10,106

NAEP proficiency scores, 2007

	Reading		Math	
	Basic	Proficient	Basic	Proficient
Grade 4	57.6%	24.0%	70.3%	24.5%
Grade 8	62.5%	17.3%	56.6%	17.4%

Higher education enrollment, fall 2005
Total. 10,361
   Full-time men 3,329
   Full-time women. 5,305
   Part-time men 665
   Part-time women. 1,062

Minority enrollment in institutions of higher education, 2005
Black, non-Hispanic 3,844
Hispanic 54,271
Asian/Pacific Islander 2,602
American Indian/Alaska Native. 11,272

Institutions of higher education, 2005-06
Total. 42
   Public. 28
   Private. 14

Earned degrees conferred, 2004-05
Associate's. 4,590
Bachelor's 7,342
Master's 3,219
First-professional. 250
Doctor's 313

Public Libraries, 2006
Number of libraries. 87
Number of outlets 117
Annual visits per capita 4.6
Circulation per capita 6.5

State & local financial support for higher education, FY 2006
Full-time equivalent enrollment (x 1,000) 79.5
Appropriations per FTE. $9,299

Social Insurance & Welfare Programs

Social Security benefits & beneficiaries, 2005
Beneficiaries (x 1,000) 311
   Retired & dependents. 209
   Survivors. 44
   Disabled & dependents. 58
Annual benefit payments ($ mil) $3,079
   Retired & dependents. $1,983
   Survivors. $526
   Disabled & dependents. $570
Average monthly benefit
   Retired & dependents. $935
   Disabled & dependents. $902
   Widowed. $895

Medicare, July 2005
Enrollment (x 1,000) 267
Payments ($ mil) $1,279

Medicaid, 2004
Beneficiaries (x 1,000). 960
Payments ($ mil) $6,623

State Children's Health Insurance Program, 2006
Enrollment (x 1,000). 25.2
Expenditures ($ mil) $23.8

Persons without health insurance, 2006
Number (x 1,000). 445
   percent. 22.9%
Number of children (x 1,000) 93
   percent of children 17.9%

Health care expenditures, 2004
Total expenditures. $8,498
   per capita $4,471

©2008 Information Publications, Inc.
All rights reserved. Photocopying prohibited.
877-544-INFO (4636) or www.informationpublications.com

Federal and state public aid

State unemployment insurance, 2006
Recipients, first payments (x 1,000) 25
Total payments ($ mil) $105
Average weekly benefit $238
Temporary Assistance for Needy Families, 2006
Recipients (x 1,000) 497.4
Families (x 1,000) 196.1
Supplemental Security Income, 2005
Recipients (x 1,000) 53.8
Payments ($ mil) $247.9
Food Stamp Program, 2006
Avg monthly participants (x 1,000) 244.7
Total benefits ($ mil) $253.4

Housing & Construction

Housing units
Total 2005 (estimate) 838,050
Total 2006 (estimate) 850,095
Seasonal or recreational use, 2006 42,091
Owner-occupied, 2006 505,915
  Median home value $141,200
  Homeowner vacancy rate 1.7%
Renter-occupied, 2006 220,118
  Median rent $617
  Rental vacancy rate 8.1%
Home ownership rate, 2005 . . . . 71.4%
Home ownership rate, 2006 . . . . 72.0%

New privately-owned housing units
Number authorized, 2006 (x 1,000) 13.6
  Value ($ mil) $2,315.5
Started 2005 (x 1,000, estimate) 10.3
Started 2006 (x 1,000, estimate) 10.1

Existing home sales
2005 (x 1,000) 57.5
2006 (x 1,000) 58.2

Government & Elections

State officials 2008
Governor . . . . Bill Richardson
  Democratic, term expires 1/11
Lieutenant Governor . . . . Diane Denish
Secretary of State . . . . Mary Herrera
Attorney General . . . . Gary King
Chief Justice . . . . Edward Chávez

Governorship
Minimum age 30
Length of term . . . . 4 years
Consecutive terms permitted 2
Who succeeds . . . . Lieutenant Governor

Local governments by type, 2002
Total 858
  County 33
  Municipal 101
  Township 0
  School District 96
  Special District 628

State legislature
Name . . . . Legislature
Upper chamber . . . . .Senate
  Number of members 42
  Length of term . . . . 4 years
  Party in majority, 2008 . . . . Democratic
Lower chamber . . . . House of Representatives
  Number of members 70
  Length of term . . . . 2 years
  Party in majority, 2008 . . . . Democratic

Federal representation, 2008 (110th Congress)
Senator . . . . Pete V. Dolmenici
  Party . . . . Republican
  Year term expires 2009
Senator . . . . .Jeff Bingaman
  Party . . . . Democratic
  Year term expires 2013
Representatives, total 3
  Democrats 1
  Republicans 2

Voters in November 2006 election (estimate)
Total 730,909
  Male 343,429
  Female 387,481
  White 641,173
  Black 10,040
  Hispanic 117,873
  Asian 6,141

Presidential election, 2004
Total Popular Vote 756,304
  Kerry 370,942
  Bush 376,930
Total Electoral Votes 5

Votes cast for US Senators
2004
Total vote (x 1,000) . . . . NA
Leading party . . . . NA
Percent for leading party . . . . NA
2006
Total vote (x 1,000) 559
Leading party .Democratic
Percent for leading party 70.6%

Votes cast for US Representatives
2004
Total vote (x 1,000) 743
  Democratic 385
  Republican 358
Leading party .Democratic
Percent for leading party 51.8%
2006
Total vote (x 1,000) 561
  Democratic 313
  Republican 248
Leading party .Democratic
Percent for leading party 55.8%

©2008 Information Publications, Inc.
All rights reserved. Photocopying prohibited.
877-544-INFO (4636) or www.informationpublications.com

State government employment, 2006
Full-time equivalent employees 50,783
Payroll ($ mil) $162.8

Local government employment, 2006
Full-time equivalent employees 77,146
Payroll ($ mil) $223.6

Women holding public office, 2008
US Congress.............................. 1
Statewide elected office..................... 3
State legislature 34

Black public officials, 2002
Total.. 4
  US and state legislatures 1
  City/county/regional offices 0
  Judicial/law enforcement.................. 2
  Education/school boards.................. 1

Hispanic public officials, 2006
Total...................................... 649
  State executives & legislators 48
  City/county/regional offices 337
  Judicial/law enforcement................. 111
  Education/school boards............... 144

Governmental Finance

State government revenues, 2006
Total revenue (x $1,000)...........$14,733,656
  per capita $7,585.67
General revenue (x $1,000) $12,116,954
  Intergovernmental 3,854,734
  Taxes 5,110,683
    general sales.....................1,741,673
    individual income tax 1,123,954
    corporate income tax..............377,185
  Current charges....................911,084
  Miscellaneous 2,240,453

State government expenditure, 2006
Total expenditure (x $1,000) $13,399,021
  per capita $6,898.53
General expenditure (x $1,000) $12,278,379
  per capita, total.................. $6,321.56
  Education........................2,305.87
  Public welfare 1,436.18
  Health 180.87
  Hospitals.........................353.12
  Highways 457.42
  Police protection.....................59.82
  Corrections 149.91
  Natural resources 114.48
  Parks & recreation 29.26
  Governmental administration...... 236.83
  Interest on general debt........... 160.26

State debt & cash, 2006 ($ per capita)
Debt $3,251.83
Cash/security holdings............. $21,277.77

Federal government grants to state & local government, 2005 (x $1,000)
Total........................... $4,564,332
by Federal agency
  Defense 20,223
  Education 508,571
  Energy 62,125
  Environmental Protection Agency 38,779
  Health & Human Services.........2,473,963
  Homeland Security................. 8,982
  Housing & Urban Development......159,018
  Justice 69,063
  Labor 61,116
  Transportation 305,766
  Veterans Affairs................... 3,608

Crime & Law Enforcement

Crime, 2006 (rates per 100,000 residents)
Property crimes 76,956
  Burglary 20,909
  Larceny 46,822
  Motor vehicle theft 9,225
  Property crime rate................. 3,937.2
Violent crimes...................... 12,572
  Murder 132
  Forcible rape......................1,094
  Robbery.........................2,105
  Aggravated assault 9,241
  Violent crime rate 643.2
Hate crimes........................ 22

Fraud and identity theft, 2006
Fraud complaints.................... 2,406
  rate per 100,000 residents 123.1
Identity theft complaints 1,621
  rate per 100,000 residents 82.9

Law enforcement agencies, 2006
Total agencies....................... 75
Total employees 4,731
  Officers 3,421
  Civilians 1,310

Prisoners, probation, and parole, 2006
Total prisoners......................6,639
  percent change, 12/31/05 to 12/31/06 .... 1.0%
  in private facilities 44.1%
  in local jails 2.1%
Sentenced to more than one year 6,361
  rate per 100,000 residents 323
Adults on probation 16,493
Adults on parole....................... 2,922

Prisoner demographics, June 30, 2005 (rate per 100,000 residents)
Male.................................1,421
Female 163
White................................ NA
Black................................. NA
Hispanic .... NA

©2008 Information Publications, Inc.
All rights reserved. Photocopying prohibited.
877-544-INFO (4636) or www.informationpublications.com

Arrests, 2006

Total 72,114
    Persons under 18 years of age 8,466

Persons under sentence of death, 1/1/07

Total 2
    White 2
    Black 0
    Hispanic 0

State's highest court

Name .... Supreme Court
Number of members 5
Length of term .... 8 years
Intermediate appeals court? .... yes

Labor & Income

Civilian labor force, 2006 (x 1,000)

Total 944
    Men 499
    Women 445
    Persons 16-19 years 51
    White 814
    Black 24
    Hispanic 354

Civilian labor force as a percent of civilian non-institutional population, 2006

Total 63.1%
    Men 69.2
    Women 57.5
    Persons 16-19 years 43.1
    White 63.8
    Black 70.7
    Hispanic 61.9

Employment, 2006 (x 1,000)

Total 903
    Men 477
    Women 425
    Persons 16-19 years 45
    White 779
    Black 23
    Hispanic 335

Unemployment rate, 2006

Total 4.4%
    Men 4.3
    Women 4.4
    Persons 16-19 years 13.0
    White 4.3
    Black 5.5
    Hispanic 5.3

Full-time/part-time labor force, 2003 (x 1,000)

Full-time labor force, employed 666
Part-time labor force, employed 174
Unemployed, looking for
    Full-time work 48
    Part-time work 9
Mean duration of unemployment (weeks) 16.5
    Median 9.0

Labor unions, 2006

Membership (x 1,000) 62
    percent of employed 7.8%

Experienced civilian labor force by private industry, 2006

Total 623,628
    Natural resources & mining 29,966
    Construction 59,191
    Manufacturing 37,659
    Trade, transportation & utilities 139,875
    Information 15,859
    Finance 33,870
    Professional & business 102,361
    Education & health 96,060
    Leisure & hospitality 86,621
    Other 21,817

Experienced civilian labor force by occupation, May 2006

Management 39,890
Business & financial 23,750
Legal 5,270
Sales 80,960
Office & admin. support 132,970
Computers & math 11,790
Architecture & engineering 21,170
Arts & entertainment 7,780
Education 54,630
Social services 13,920
Health care practitioner & technical 39,150
Health care support 20,640
Maintenance & repair 33,140
Construction 62,110
Transportation & moving 45,520
Production 33,940
Farming, fishing & forestry 4,250

Hours and earnings of production workers on manufacturing payrolls, 2006

Average weekly hours 39.2
Average hourly earnings $14.06
Average weekly earnings $551.15

Income and poverty, 2006

Median household income $40,629
Personal income, per capita (current $) ... $29,673
    in constant (2000) dollars $25,903
Persons below poverty level 18.5%

Average annual pay

2006 .... $34,567
    increase from 2005 .... 6.0%

Federal individual income tax returns, 2005

Returns filed 843,476
Adjusted gross income ($1,000) $35,785,778
Total tax liability ($1,000) $4,119,263

Charitable contributions, 2004

Number of contributions 182.6
Total amount ($ mil) $597.8

©2008 Information Publications, Inc.
All rights reserved. Photocopying prohibited.
877-544-INFO (4636) or www.informationpublications.com

Economy, Business, Industry & Agriculture

Fortune 500 companies, 2007 0
Bankruptcy cases filed, FY 2007 3,232

Patents and trademarks issued, 2007

Patents 313
Trademarks 246

Business firm ownership, 2002

Women-owned 42,254
   Sales ($ mil) $4,714
Black-owned 1,541
   Sales ($ mil) $255
Hispanic-owned 29,708
   Sales ($ mil) $4,678
Asian-owned 2,364
   Sales ($ mil) $631
Amer. Indian/Alaska Native-owned 6,819
   Sales ($ mil) $792
Hawaiian/Pacific Islander-owned 140
   Sales ($ mil) $17

Gross domestic product, 2006 ($ mil)

Total gross domestic product $75,910
   Agriculture, forestry, fishing and
      hunting 1,187
   Mining. 12,040
   Utilities 1,632
   Construction 3,637
   Manufacturing, durable goods 6,257
   Manufacturing, non-durable goods 1,080
   Wholesale trade. 2,581
   Retail trade. 4,683
   Transportation & warehousing 1,802
   Information 1,917
   Finance & insurance. 2,323
   Real estate, rental & leasing 7,136
   Professional and technical services 5,276
   Educational services. 365
   Health care and social assistance 4,722
   Accommodation/food services. 2,068
   Other services, except government 1,453
   Government 12,984

Establishments, payroll, employees & receipts, by major industry group, 2005

Total 45,006
   Annual payroll ($1,000) $18,171,120
   Paid employees 595,249
Forestry, fishing & agriculture. 93
   Annual payroll ($1,000). $9,897
   Paid employees 378
Mining 629
   Annual payroll ($1,000) $835,555
   Paid employees 15,516
   Receipts, 2002 ($1,000) $9,803,360

Utilities 225
   Annual payroll ($1,000). $255,416
   Paid employees 4,134
   Receipts, 2002 ($1,000) . . . . .NA
Construction 5,456
   Annual payroll ($1,000). $1,691,385
   Paid employees 50,027
   Receipts, 2002 ($1,000) $6,017,501
Manufacturing 1,531
   Annual payroll ($1,000). $1,391,868
   Paid employees 34,520
   Receipts, 2002 ($1,000) $10,168,130
Wholesale trade 1,960
   Annual payroll ($1,000). $824,284
   Paid employees 20,589
   Receipts, 2002 ($1,000) $8,993,729
Retail trade 7,232
   Annual payroll ($1,000). $2,132,370
   Paid employees 95,043
   Receipts, 2002 ($1,000) $18,328,637
Transportation & warehousing 1,281
   Annual payroll ($1,000). $502,221
   Paid employees 15,710
   Receipts, 2002 ($1,000) $1,655,584
Information. 793
   Annual payroll ($1,000). $471,028
   Paid employees 13,054
   Receipts, 2002 ($1,000) . . . . .NA
Finance & insurance 2,779
   Annual payroll ($1,000). $1,022,546
   Paid employees 24,666
   Receipts, 2002 ($1,000) . . . . .NA
Professional, scientific & technical 4,704
   Annual payroll ($1,000). $1,719,953
   Paid employees 35,769
   Receipts, 2002 ($1,000) $3,272,378
Education 543
   Annual payroll ($1,000). $229,797
   Paid employees 9,445
   Receipts, 2002 ($1,000) $138,081
Health care & social assistance 4,439
   Annual payroll ($1,000). $3,332,669
   Paid employees 95,623
   Receipts, 2002 ($1,000) $6,103,864
Arts and entertainment 666
   Annual payroll ($1,000). $284,729
   Paid employees 14,445
   Receipts, 2002 ($1,000) $1,228,882
Real estate 2,399
   Annual payroll ($1,000). $287,554
   Paid employees 10,216
   Receipts, 2002 ($1,000) $1,269,230
Accommodation & food service 3,944
   Annual payroll ($1,000). $933,609
   Paid employees 77,487
   Receipts, 2002 ($1,000) $2,771,474

©2008 Information Publications, Inc.
All rights reserved. Photocopying prohibited.
877-544-INFO (4636) or www.informationpublications.com

8　New Mexico

Exports, 2006
Value of exported goods ($ mil) $2,892
   Manufactured $2,605
   Non-manufactured.................. $117

Foreign direct investment in US affiliates, 2004
Property, plants & equipment ($ mil) $3,792
Employment (x 1,000)..................... 12.6

Agriculture, 2006
Number of farms 17,500
Farm acreage (x 1,000) 44,500
   Acres per farm 2,543
Farm marketings and income ($ mil)
Total............................... $2,463.5
   Crops $602.4
   Livestock........................ $1,861.1
Net farm income $423.0

Principal commodities, in order by marketing receipts, 2005
Dairy products, Cattle and calves, Hay, Pecans, Greenhouse/nursery

Federal economic activity in state
Expenditures, 2005 ($ mil)
   Total............................. $20,604
     Per capita $10,697.88
   Defense $2,451
   Non-defense...................... $18,152
Defense department, 2006 ($ mil)
   Payroll $1,466
   Contract awards $1,075
   Grants $30
Homeland security grants ($1,000)
   2006............................. $8,270
   2007............................. $6,973

FDIC-insured financial institutions, 2005
Number.................................. 54
Assets ($ billion) $17.7
Deposits ($ billion) $13.9

Fishing, 2006
Catch (x 1,000 lbs)...................... NA
Value ($1,000)........................... NA

Mining, 2006 ($ mil)
Total non-fuel mineral production $1,460
Percent of U.S. 2.27%

Communication, Energy & Transportation

Communication
Households with computers, 2003........ 53.9%
Households with internet access, 2003 .... 44.5%
High-speed internet providers 38
Total high-speed internet lines........ 422,964
   Residential 264,814
   Business......................... 158,150
Wireless phone customers, 12/2006 1,333,210

FCC-licensed stations (as of January 1, 2008)
TV stations 26
FM radio stations........................ 139
AM radio stations 63

Energy
Energy consumption, 2004
   Total (trillion Btu)...................... 682
   Per capita (million Btu) 359.0
By source of production (trillion Btu)
   Coal 309
   Natural gas.......................... 230
   Petroleum........................... 260
   Nuclear electric power 0
   Hydroelectric power.................... 1
By end-use sector (trillion Btu)
   Residential 107
   Commercial 121
   Industrial 228
   Transportation 226
Electric energy, 2005
   Primary source of electricity............ Coal
   Net generation (billion kWh) 35.1
     percent from renewable sources....... 2.7%
   Net summer capability (million kW) 6.5
   CO_2 emitted from generation 32.7
Natural gas utilities, 2005
   Customers (x 1,000) 579
   Sales (trillion Btu)...................... 85
   Revenues ($ mil) $544
Nuclear plants, 2007 0
Total CO_2 emitted (million metric tons)...... 57.6
Energy spending, 2004 ($ mil) $5,217
   per capita $2,745
   Price per million Btu $13.48

Transportation, 2006
Public road & street mileage 63,796
   Urban............................. 7,996
   Rural 55,800
   Interstate........................... 1,000
Vehicle miles of travel (millions) 25,787
   per capita 13,276.5
Total motor vehicle registrations....... 1,580,820
   Automobiles...................... 699,312
   Trucks 877,956
   Motorcycles 43,489
Licensed drivers 1,338,246
   19 years & under 49,485
Deaths from motor vehicle accidents 484
Gasoline consumed (x 1,000 gallons) 966,209
   per capita 497.5

Commuting Statistics, 2006
Average commute time (min) 20.9
   Drove to work alone 78.2%
   Carpooled.......................... 12.5%
   Public transit 0.9%
   Walk to work 2.2%
   Work from home...................... 4.6%

©2008 Information Publications, Inc.
All rights reserved. Photocopying prohibited.
877-544-INFO (4636) or www.informationpublications.com

State Summary

Capital city . . . . Albany
Governor . . . . Eliot Spitzer

State Capitol
Albany, NY 12224
518-474-7516

Admitted as a state 1788
Area (square miles) 54,556
Population, 2007 (estimate). 19,297,729
Largest city . . . . New York
  Population, 2006 8,214,426
Personal income per capita, 2006
  (in current dollars) $42,392
Gross domestic product, 2006 ($ mil) . . $1,021,944

Leading industries by payroll, 2005

Finance & Insurance, Health care/Social assistance, Professional/Scientific/Technical

**Leading agricultural commodities
by receipts, 2005**

Dairy products, Greenhouse/nursery, Apples,
Cattle and calves, Hay

Geography & Environment

Total area (square miles). 54,556
  land 47,214
  water 7,342
Federally-owned land, 2004 (acres) 233,533
  percent. 0.8%
Highest point . . . . Mt. Marcy
  elevation (feet) 5,344
Lowest point . . . . Atlantic Ocean
  elevation (feet) . . . . sea level
General coastline (miles) 127
Tidal shoreline (miles) 1,850
Cropland, 2003 (x 1,000 acres) 5,359
Forest land, 2003 (x 1,000 acres). 17,599
Capital city . . . . Albany
  Population 2000 95,658
  Population 2006 93,963
Largest city . . . . New York
  Population 2000 8,008,278
  Population 2006 8,214,426

Number of cities with over 100,000 population

1990 5
2000 5
2006 5

State park and recreation areas, 2005

Area (x 1,000 acres) 1,367
Number of visitors (x 1,000) 56,405
Revenues ($1,000) $83,000
  percent of operating expenditures. 41.3%

National forest system land, 2007

Acres 16,211

Demographics & Population Characteristics

Population

1980 17,558,072
1990 17,990,455
2000 18,976,821
2006 19,306,183
  Male. 9,355,020
  Female 9,951,163
Living in group quarters, 2006 603,275
  percent of total. 3.1%
2007 (estimate). 19,297,729
  persons per square mile of land 408.7
2008 (projected) 19,383,109
2010 (projected) 19,443,672
2020 (projected) 19,576,920
2030 (projected) 19,477,429

**Population of Core-Based Statistical Areas
(formerly Metropolitan Areas), x 1,000**

	CBSA	Non-CBSA
1990	17,574	417
2000	18,547	430
2006	18,873	433

Change in population, 2000-2007

Number 320,908
  percent. 1.7%
Natural increase (births minus deaths) 698,971
Net internal migration . . . . -1,449,169
Net international migration 859,994

Persons by age, 2006

Under 5 years 1,220,468
5 to 17 years 3,293,874
18 years and over 14,791,841
65 years and over 2,522,686
85 years and over 371,667
  Median age 37.3

Persons by age, 2010 (projected)

Under 5 years 1,250,867
18 and over 15,022,796
65 and over 2,651,655
  Median age 37.9

Race, 2006

One Race
  White. 14,220,047
  Black or African American 3,352,874
  Asian 1,326,089
  American Indian/Alaska Native. 104,936
  Hawaiian Native/Pacific Islander. 19,163
Two or more races. 283,074

Persons of Hispanic origin, 2006

Total Hispanic or Latino 3,139,590
  Mexican. 373,247
  Puerto Rican 1,071,394
  Cuban 64,899

Persons of Asian origin, 2006
```
Total Asian ........................1,322,971
    Asian Indian. ..................... 349,290
    Chinese ............................519,672
    Filipino ...........................107,418
    Japanese ........................... 39,350
    Korean ............................ 139,282
    Vietnamese........................ 40,523
```

Marital status, 2006
```
Population 15 years & over ........ 15,606,628
    Never married ................... 5,566,776
    Married......................... 7,674,884
    Separated ....................... 465,872
    Widowed......................... 1,049,212
    Divorced ....................... 1,315,756
```

Language spoken at home, 2006
```
Population 5 years and older........ 18,085,173
    English only .................... 12,875,365
    Spanish ......................... 2,574,121
    French .......................... 270,131
    German.......................... 84,763
    Chinese ......................... 447,602
```

Households & families, 2006
```
Households.........................7,088,376
    with persons under 18 years .......2,362,278
    with persons over 65 years.......... 1,775,976
    persons per household .................2.64
Families...........................4,573,941
    persons per family......................3.31
Married couples.................... 3,200,366
Female householder,
    no husband present................1,035,127
One-person households .............2,086,857
```

Nativity, 2006
```
Number of residents born in state ... 12,446,607
    percent of population.................64.5%
```

Immigration & naturalization, 2006
```
Legal permanent residents admitted.....180,165
Persons naturalized ................. 103,870
Non-immigrant admissions .........4,243,472
```

Vital Statistics and Health

Marriages
```
2004 ............................. 130,813
2005 ............................. 130,409
2006 .............................127,401
```

Divorces
```
2004 .............................57,830
2005 ............................. 54,708
2006 .............................55,627
```

Health risks, 2006
```
Percent of adults who are:
    Smokers...........................18.2%
    Overweight (BMI > 25)................58.3%
    Obese (BMI > 30)....................22.9%
```

Births
```
2005 ............................. 246,351
    Birthrate (per 1,000).................12.8
    White...........................170,021
    Black ........................... 54,360
    Hispanic .........................57,419
    Asian/Pacific Islander .............21,297
    Amer. Indian/Alaska Native............ 673
    Low birth weight (2,500g or less)....... 8.3%
    Cesarian births ..................... 31.5%
    Preterm births ...................... 12.1%
    To unmarried mothers..............38.7%
    Twin births (per 1,000)...............36.0
    Triplets or higher order (per 100,000)....229.9
2006 (preliminary).................... 250,091
    rate per 1,000 .....................13.0
```

Deaths
```
2004
All causes .......................... 152,681
    rate per 100,000.....................733.9
Heart disease ....................... 52,480
    rate per 100,000.....................247.9
Malignant neoplasms .................. 36,100
    rate per 100,000.....................176.2
Cerebrovascular disease................6,927
    rate per 100,000.....................32.9
Chronic lower respiratory disease ........6,786
    rate per 100,000.....................32.8
Diabetes...........................3,913
    rate per 100,000.....................19.0
2005 (preliminary)................... 152,427
    rate per 100,000.....................718.0
2006 (provisional) ................... 150,329
```

Infant deaths
```
2004 .............................1,518
    rate per 1,000 .........................6.1
2005 (provisional) ....................1,499
    rate per 1,000 .........................6.0
```

Exercise routines, 2005
```
None............................... 27.1%
Moderate or greater..................... 48.1%
Vigorous .......................... 27.3%
```

Abortions, 2004
```
Total performed in state............. 126,002
    rate per 1,000 women age 15-44........... 30
    % obtained by out-of-state residents ...... NA
```

Physicians, 2005
```
Total...............................74,945
    rate per 100,000 persons ............... 388
```

Community hospitals, 2005
```
Number of hospitals ...................... 203
Beds (x 1,000)..........................63.1
Patients admitted (x 1,000) .............. 2,538
Average daily census (x 1,000) ...........50.1
Average cost per day ..................$1,539
Outpatient visits (x 1 mil) ...............51.5
```

©2008 Information Publications, Inc.
All rights reserved. Photocopying prohibited.
877-544-INFO (4636) or www.informationpublications.com

Disability status of population, 2006

5 to 15 years	6.1%
16 to 64 years	10.9%
65 years and over	38.7%

Education

Educational attainment, 2006

Population over 25 years	12,845,882
Less than 9th grade	6.9%
High school graduate or more	84.1%
College graduate or more	31.2%
Graduate or professional degree	13.3%

Public school enrollment, 2005-06

Total	2,815,581
Pre-kindergarten through grade 8	1,857,165
Grades 9 through 12	851,404

Graduating public high school seniors, 2004-05

Diplomas (incl. GED and others)	158,880

SAT scores, 2007

Average critical reading score	491
Average writing score	482
Average math score	505
Percent of graduates taking test	.89%

Public school teachers, 2006-07 (estimate)

Total (x 1,000)	229.3
Elementary	112.9
Secondary	116.4
Average salary	$58,537
Elementary	$58,537
Secondary	$58,537

State receipts & expenditures for public schools, 2006-07 (estimate)

Revenue receipts ($ mil)	$43,033
Expenditures	
Total ($ mil)	$44,833
Per capita	$2,067
Per pupil	$15,263

NAEP proficiency scores, 2007

	Reading		Math	
	Basic	Proficient	Basic	Proficient
Grade 4	69.3%	36.0%	85.1%	43.3%
Grade 8	75.1%	32.2%	70.3%	30.2%

Higher education enrollment, fall 2005

Total	525,859
Full-time men	175,479
Full-time women	230,204
Part-time men	42,938
Part-time women	77,238

Minority enrollment in institutions of higher education, 2005

Black, non-Hispanic	160,007
Hispanic	130,198
Asian/Pacific Islander	89,927
American Indian/Alaska Native	4,144

Institutions of higher education, 2005-06

Total	308
Public	78
Private	230

Earned degrees conferred, 2004-05

Associate's	56,877
Bachelor's	109,852
Master's	60,505
First-professional	8,732
Doctor's	4,350

Public Libraries, 2006

Number of libraries	754
Number of outlets	1,076
Annual visits per capita	5.7
Circulation per capita	7.5

State & local financial support for higher education, FY 2006

Full-time equivalent enrollment (x 1,000)	501.8
Appropriations per FTE	$7,784

Social Insurance & Welfare Programs

Social Security benefits & beneficiaries, 2005

Beneficiaries (x 1,000)	3,064
Retired & dependents	2,170
Survivors	378
Disabled & dependents	516
Annual benefit payments ($ mil)	$34,797
Retired & dependents	$23,800
Survivors	$5,427
Disabled & dependents	$5,570
Average monthly benefit	
Retired & dependents	$1,059
Disabled & dependents	$989
Widowed	$1,020

Medicare, July 2005

Enrollment (x 1,000)	2,776
Payments ($ mil)	$19,430

Medicaid, 2004

Beneficiaries (x 1,000)	474
Payments ($ mil)	$2,278

State Children's Health Insurance Program, 2006

Enrollment (x 1,000)	688.4
Expenditures ($ mil)	$505.4

Persons without health insurance, 2006

Number (x 1,000)	2,662
percent	14.0%
Number of children (x 1,000)	380
percent of children	8.4%

Health care expenditures, 2004

Total expenditures	$126,076
per capita	$6,535

©2008 Information Publications, Inc.
All rights reserved. Photocopying prohibited.
877-544-INFO (4636) or www.informationpublications.com

Federal and state public aid

State unemployment insurance, 2006
Recipients, first payments (x 1,000) 454
Total payments ($ mil) $2,278
Average weekly benefit $277
Temporary Assistance for Needy Families, 2006
Recipients (x 1,000) .3,570.9
Families (x 1,000) 1,578.9
Supplemental Security Income, 2005
Recipients (x 1,000) .635.1
Payments ($ mil) $3,561.2
Food Stamp Program, 2006
Avg monthly participants (x 1,000) 1,785.9
Total benefits ($ mil) $2,240.0

Housing & Construction

Housing units
Total 2005 (estimate) 7,866,117
Total 2006 (estimate) 7,907,420
Seasonal or recreational use, 2006 255,667
Owner-occupied, 2006 3,940,942
   Median home value $303,400
   Homeowner vacancy rate 1.8%
Renter-occupied, 2006 3,147,434
   Median rent $875
   Rental vacancy rate 5.8%
Home ownership rate, 2005 . . . . 55.9%
Home ownership rate, 2006 . . . . 55.7%

New privately-owned housing units
Number authorized, 2006 (x 1,000) 54.4
   Value ($ mil) $7,078.0
Started 2005 (x 1,000, estimate) 38.8
Started 2006 (x 1,000, estimate) 37.5

Existing home sales
2005 (x 1,000) 319.8
2006 (x 1,000) 303.4

Government & Elections

State officials 2008
Governor . . . . Eliot Spitzer
         Democratic, term expires 1/11
Lieutenant Governor . . . . .David Paterson
Secretary of State . . . . . .Lorraine Cortes-Vasquez
Attorney General . . . . Andrew Cuomo
Chief Justice . . . . .Judith Kaye

Governorship
Minimum age 25
Length of term . . . . 4 years
Consecutive terms permitted . . . . . . not specified
Who succeeds . . . . Lieutenant Governor

Local governments by type, 2002
Total 3,420
   County 57
   Municipal 616
   Township 929
   School District 683
   Special District 1,135

State legislature
Name . . . . Legislature
Upper chamber . . . . .Senate
   Number of members 62
   Length of term . . . . 2 years
   Party in majority, 2008 . . . . Republican
Lower chamber .Assembly
   Number of members 150
   Length of term . . . . 2 years
   Party in majority, 2008 . . . . .Democratic

Federal representation, 2008 (110th Congress)
Senator . . . . Charles Schumer
   Party . . . . .Democratic
   Year term expires 2011
Senator . . . . Hillary Rodham Clinton
   Party . . . . .Democratic
   Year term expires 2013
Representatives, total 29
   Democrats 23
   Republicans 6

Voters in November 2006 election (estimate)
Total 5,402,247
   Male 2,494,729
   Female 2,907,517
   White 4,397,320
   Black 742,073
   Hispanic 246,015
   Asian 217,105

Presidential election, 2004
Total Popular Vote 7,391,036
   Kerry 4,314,280
   Bush 2,962,567
Total Electoral Votes 31

Votes cast for US Senators
2004
Total vote (x 1,000) .7,448
Leading party .Democratic
Percent for leading party 58.9%
2006
Total vote (x 1,000) .4,701
Leading party .Democratic
Percent for leading party 57.4%

Votes cast for US Representatives
2004
Total vote (x 1,000) .7,448
   Democratic 3,457
   Republican 2,209
Leading party .Democratic
Percent for leading party 46.4%
2006
Total vote (x 1,000) 4,687
   Democratic 2,538
   Republican 1,160
Leading party .Democratic
Percent for leading party 54.1%

©2008 Information Publications, Inc.
All rights reserved. Photocopying prohibited.
877-544-INFO (4636) or www.informationpublications.com

State government employment, 2006
Full-time equivalent employees 249,208
Payroll ($ mil) $1,183.8

Local government employment, 2006
Full-time equivalent employees 941,079
Payroll ($ mil) $4,222.4

Women holding public office, 2008
US Congress 8
Statewide elected office................... 0
State legislature 51

Black public officials, 2002
Total.................................... 328
   US and state legislatures 34
   City/county/regional offices 90
   Judicial/law enforcement................. 84
   Education/school boards............... 120

Hispanic public officials, 2006
Total.................................... 63
   State executives & legislators 16
   City/county/regional offices 30
   Judicial/law enforcement................. 15
   Education/school boards................. 2

Governmental Finance

State government revenues, 2006
Total revenue (x $1,000)........... $166,001,915
   per capita $8,609.17
General revenue (x $1,000) $123,484,906
   Intergovernmental 45,772,844
   Taxes 57,326,481
      general sales.................. 11,263,576
      individual income tax 30,812,924
      corporate income tax 4,018,199
   Current charges................. 8,051,582
   Miscellaneous 12,333,999

State government expenditure, 2006
Total expenditure (x $1,000) $142,853,305
   per capita $7,408.64
General expenditure (x $1,000) $115,453,948
   per capita, total.................... $5,987.66
      Education 1,744.60
      Public welfare 2,268.57
      Health 310.55
      Hospitals........................ 225.48
      Highways 200.46
      Police protection.................. 41.05
      Corrections 140.64
      Natural resources 21.83
      Parks & recreation................ 28.17
      Governmental administration...... 246.37
      Interest on general debt............ 184.91

State debt & cash, 2006 ($ per capita)
Debt.................................. $5,461.38
Cash/security holdings.............. $15,799.31

Federal government grants to state & local government, 2005 (x $1,000)
Total..........................$45,631,397
by Federal agency
   Defense 150,766
   Education 2,674,829
   Energy 173,620
   Environmental Protection Agency ... 293,632
   Health & Human Services. 32,364,871
   Homeland Security................ 160,435
   Housing & Urban Development.....3,720,291
   Justice 555,099
   Labor 391,649
   Transportation 2,642,815
   Veterans Affairs.................. 25,382

Crime & Law Enforcement

Crime, 2006 (rates per 100,000 residents)
Property crimes 396,304
   Burglary 68,565
   Larceny 295,605
   Motor vehicle theft 32,134
   Property crime rate................2,052.7
Violent crimes....................... 83,966
   Murder 921
   Forcible rape......................3,169
   Robbery......................... 34,489
   Aggravated assault 45,387
   Violent crime rate 434.9
Hate crimes........................... 537

Fraud and identity theft, 2006
Fraud complaints......................21,129
   rate per 100,000 residents 109.4
Identity theft complaints 16,452
   rate per 100,000 residents 85.2

Law enforcement agencies, 2006
Total agencies......................... 402
Total employees 86,053
   Officers 62,176
   Civilians 23,877

Prisoners, probation, and parole, 2006
Total prisoners.......................63,315
   percent change, 12/31/05 to 12/31/06 .... 0.9%
   in private facilities 0%
   in local jails 0%
Sentenced to more than one year 62,974
   rate per 100,000 residents 326
Adults on probation 123,418
Adults on parole...................... 53,001

Prisoner demographics, June 30, 2005 (rate per 100,000 residents)
Male.................................. 935
Female 57
White.................................. 174
Black...................................1,627
Hispanic 778

©2008 Information Publications, Inc.
All rights reserved. Photocopying prohibited.
877-544-INFO (4636) or www.informationpublications.com

6   New York

Arrests, 2006
Total................................ 345,357
   Persons under 18 years of age 48,209

Persons under sentence of death, 1/1/07
Total...................................... 1
   White..................................... 0
   Black 1
   Hispanic 0

State's highest court
Name .... Court of Appeals
Number of members....................... 7
Length of term...................... 14 years
Intermediate appeals court? ....yes

Labor & Income

Civilian labor force, 2006 (x 1,000)
Total....................................9,464
   Men 4,967
   Women 4,497
   Persons 16-19 years..................... 367
   White................................7,187
   Black 1,451
   Hispanic 1,379

Civilian labor force as a percent of civilian non-institutional population, 2006
Total.................................. 63.2%
   Men 69.6
   Women 57.3
   Persons 16-19 years.....................34.7
   White.................................64.2
   Black 59.6
   Hispanic 62.2

Employment, 2006 (x 1,000)
Total....................................9,043
   Men 4,726
   Women 4,317
   Persons 16-19 years..................... 296
   White................................ 6,905
   Black 1,338
   Hispanic 1,300

Unemployment rate, 2006
Total.................................... 4.4%
   Men 4.8
   Women 4.0
   Persons 16-19 years....................19.2
   White..................................3.9
   Black 7.8
   Hispanic 5.7

Full-time/part-time labor force, 2003 (x 1,000)
Full-time labor force, employed 7,215
Part-time labor force, employed...........1,511
Unemployed, looking for
   Full-time work......................... 502
   Part-time work......................... 87
*Mean duration of unemployment (weeks).......*23.4
   Median 12.8

Labor unions, 2006
Membership (x 1,000)....................1,981
   percent of employed 24.4%

Experienced civilian labor force by private industry, 2006
Total............................. 7,011,126
   Natural resources & mining 26,838
   Construction 335,333
   Manufacturing...................... 564,564
   Trade, transportation & utilities 1,493,355
   Information 266,721
   Finance 721,725
   Professional & business 1,100,828
   Education & health 1,462,019
   Leisure & hospitality.............. 675,009
   Other 315,962

Experienced civilian labor force by occupation, May 2006
Management.........................391,110
Business & financial 385,840
Legal................................ 104,430
Sales................................ 884,170
Office & admin. support.............1,616,450
Computers & math 193,190
Architecture & engineering........... 108,130
Arts & entertainment 169,990
Education 654,000
Social services 175,030
Health care practitioner & technical 444,180
Health care support 308,290
Maintenance & repair................. 304,930
Construction 314,280
Transportation & moving 451,870
Production 420,220
Farming, fishing & forestry..............7,420

Hours and earnings of production workers on manufacturing payrolls, 2006
Average weekly hours 41.1
Average hourly earnings $18.29
Average weekly earnings $751.72

Income and poverty, 2006
Median household income............ $51,384
Personal income, per capita (current $)... $42,392
   in constant (2000) dollars $37,005
Persons below poverty level.............. 14.2%

Average annual pay
2006 .... $55,479
   increase from 2005 .... 6.8%

Federal individual income tax returns, 2005
Returns filed........................ 8,715,913
Adjusted gross income ($1,000) ... $552,244,486
Total tax liability ($1,000) $84,125,598

Charitable contributions, 2004
Number of contributions............... 3,059.6
Total amount ($ mil)................$14,454.8

©2008 Information Publications, Inc.
All rights reserved. Photocopying prohibited.
877-544-INFO (4636) or www.informationpublications.com

Economy, Business, Industry & Agriculture

Fortune 500 companies, 2007 57
Bankruptcy cases filed, FY 2007........ 38,823

Patents and trademarks issued, 2007
Patents 6,007
Trademarks............................7,064

Business firm ownership, 2002
Women-owned...................... 505,077
　Sales ($ mil) $70,838
Black-owned........................ 129,329
　Sales ($ mil) $7,481
Hispanic-owned.................... 163,588
　Sales ($ mil) $12,326
Asian-owned 145,108
　Sales ($ mil) $30,408
Amer. Indian/Alaska Native-owned 12,307
　Sales ($ mil) $897
Hawaiian/Pacific Islander-owned 3,005
　Sales ($ mil) $123

Gross domestic product, 2006 ($ mil)
Total gross domestic product $1,021,944
　Agriculture, forestry, fishing and
　　hunting 2,093
　Mining.............................. 955
　Utilities 18,670
　Construction 32,181
　Manufacturing, durable goods........30,132
　Manufacturing, non-durable goods 34,010
　Wholesale trade.....................51,691
　Retail trade....................... 54,378
　Transportation & warehousing 17,041
　Information 73,142
　Finance & insurance............... 158,598
　Real estate, rental & leasing 156,865
　Professional and technical services.....88,137
　Educational services................ 15,665
　Health care and social assistance.......77,127
　Accommodation/food services........ 23,044
　Other services, except government 21,074
　Government........................101,956

Establishments, payroll, employees & receipts, by major industry group, 2005
Total............................... 514,265
　Annual payroll ($1,000)....... $370,842,630
　Paid employees 7,417,463
Forestry, fishing & agriculture.............. 608
　Annual payroll ($1,000)............$147,297
　Paid employees 4,983
Mining.............................. 390
　Annual payroll ($1,000)........... $234,876
　Paid employees 4,095
　Receipts, 2002 ($1,000) $813,202

Utilities 584
　Annual payroll ($1,000)..........$3,296,369
　Paid employees 40,341
　Receipts, 2002 ($1,000) ....NA
Construction......................... 46,448
　Annual payroll ($1,000)....... $15,792,641
　Paid employees 308,934
　Receipts, 2002 ($1,000) $65,368,319
Manufacturing....................... 19,349
　Annual payroll ($1,000)....... $24,908,069
　Paid employees 571,986
　Receipts, 2002 ($1,000) $147,317,463
Wholesale trade 35,437
　Annual payroll ($1,000)....... $22,824,939
　Paid employees 409,023
　Receipts, 2002 ($1,000) $343,663,041
Retail trade 78,134
　Annual payroll ($1,000)....... $21,139,844
　Paid employees 877,803
　Receipts, 2002 ($1,000) $178,067,530
Transportation & warehousing.......... 12,004
　Annual payroll ($1,000).......$8,140,912
　Paid employees 228,585
　Receipts, 2002 ($1,000) $18,845,179
Information..........................11,199
　Annual payroll ($1,000).........$20,214,888
　Paid employees 287,231
　Receipts, 2002 ($1,000) ....NA
Finance & insurance 27,567
　Annual payroll ($1,000)......... $83,556,622
　Paid employees 579,827
　Receipts, 2002 ($1,000) ....NA
Professional, scientific & technical 58,105
　Annual payroll ($1,000).....$39,540,151
　Paid employees 578,103
　Receipts, 2002 ($1,000) $83,549,043
Education 6,214
　Annual payroll ($1,000)..........$10,861,885
　Paid employees 340,497
　Receipts, 2002 ($1,000) $3,040,735
Health care & social assistance 52,246
　Annual payroll ($1,000).......$50,393,418
　Paid employees 1,297,637
　Receipts, 2002 ($1,000) $98,966,149
Arts and entertainment 10,837
　Annual payroll ($1,000).........$5,039,508
　Paid employees 138,313
　Receipts, 2002 ($1,000) $13,738,916
Real estate 32,262
　Annual payroll ($1,000)..........$7,535,087
　Paid employees 170,820
　Receipts, 2002 ($1,000) $35,629,134
Accommodation & food service.......... 42,300
　Annual payroll ($1,000)..........$10,007,371
　Paid employees 558,057
　Receipts, 2002 ($1,000) $27,835,952

Exports, 2006
Value of exported goods ($ mil) $57,369
  Manufactured $38,091
  Non-manufactured $7,260

Foreign direct investment in US affiliates, 2004
Property, plants & equipment ($ mil) . . . $60,572
Employment (x 1,000). 377.0

Agriculture, 2006
Number of farms 35,000
Farm acreage (x 1,000) 7,500
  Acres per farm 214
Farm marketings and income ($ mil)
Total $3,509.0
  Crops $1,527.3
  Livestock $1,981.7
Net farm income $868.7

Principal commodities, in order by marketing receipts, 2005
  Dairy products, Greenhouse/nursery, Apples,
         Cattle and calves, Hay

Federal economic activity in state
Expenditures, 2005 ($ mil)
  Total. $144,876
    Per capita $7,500.42
  Defense $8,568
  Non-defense $136,308
Defense department, 2006 ($ mil)
  Payroll $2,669
  Contract awards $8,020
  Grants $150
Homeland security grants ($1,000)
  2006 . . . . $183,674
  2007 . . . . $208,039

FDIC-insured financial institutions, 2005
Number 199
Assets ($ billion) $523.5
Deposits ($ billion) $362.5

Fishing, 2006
Catch (x 1,000 lbs) 32,834
Value ($1,000). $57,668

Mining, 2006 ($ mil)
Total non-fuel mineral production $1,330
Percent of U.S. 2.07%

Communication, Energy & Transportation

Communication
Households with computers, 2003 . . . . .60.0%
Households with internet access, 2003 . . . .53.3%
High-speed internet providers 72
Total high-speed internet lines 5,669,523
  Residential 4,129,160
  Business. 1,540,363
Wireless phone customers, 12/2006 . . . 15,261,760

FCC-licensed stations (as of January 1, 2008)
TV stations 55
FM radio stations. 377
AM radio stations 169

Energy
Energy consumption, 2004
  Total (trillion Btu). 4,254
  Per capita (million Btu) 220.5
By source of production (trillion Btu)
  Coal 277
  Natural gas 1,120
  Petroleum 1,885
  Nuclear electric power 424
  Hydroelectric power 240
By end-use sector (trillion Btu)
  Residential 1,215
  Commercial 1,399
  Industrial 535
  Transportation 1,105
Electric energy, 2005
  Primary source of electricity. . . . . Nuclear
  Net generation (billion kWh) 146.9
    percent from renewable sources. 18.9%
  Net summer capability (million kW) 39.1
  CO_2 emitted from generation 60.4
Natural gas utilities, 2005
  Customers (x 1,000) 4,611
  Sales (trillion Btu). 867
  Revenues ($ mil) $7,304
Nuclear plants, 2007 6
Total CO_2 emitted (million metric tons). 214.3
Energy spending, 2004 ($ mil) $48,504
  per capita $2,514
  Price per million Btu $15.65

Transportation, 2006
Public road & street mileage 113,617
  Urban. 47,744
  Rural 65,873
  Interstate. 1,697
Vehicle miles of travel (millions) 141,348
  per capita 7,330.6
Total motor vehicle registrations 11,283,896
  Automobiles. 8,528,457
  Trucks 2,685,424
  Motorcycles 203,207
Licensed drivers .11,146,367
  19 years & under 413,587
Deaths from motor vehicle accidents 1,456
Gasoline consumed (x 1,000 gallons) 5,784,552
  per capita 300.0

Commuting Statistics, 2006
Average commute time (min) 30.9
  Drove to work alone 54.4%
  Carpooled. 7.6%
  Public transit 26.1%
  Walk to work 6.3%
  Work from home 3.8%

©2008 Information Publications, Inc.
All rights reserved. Photocopying prohibited.
877-544-INFO (4636) or www.informationpublications.com

State Summary

Capital city . . . . Raleigh
Governor . . . . Michael Easley
Office of the Governor
20301 Mail Service Center
Raleigh, NC 27699
919-733-4240
Admitted as a state 1789
Area (square miles) 53,819
Population, 2007 (estimate) 9,061,032
Largest city . . . . .Charlotte
Population, 2006 630,478
Personal income per capita, 2006
(in current dollars) $32,234
Gross domestic product, 2006 ($ mil) . . . $374,525

Leading industries by payroll, 2005
Manufacturing, Health care/Social assistance,
Finance & Insurance

**Leading agricultural commodities
by receipts, 2005**
Broilers, Hogs, Greenhouse/nursery, Turkeys,
Tobacco

Geography & Environment

Total area (square miles). 53,819
land 48,711
water 5,108
Federally-owned land, 2004 (acres) 3,710,338
percent. 11.8%
Highest point . . . . Mt. Mitchell
elevation (feet) 6,684
Lowest point . . . . .Atlantic Ocean
elevation (feet) . . . . sea level
General coastline (miles) 301
Tidal shoreline (miles) 3,375
Cropland, 2003 (x 1,000 acres) 5,513
Forest land, 2003 (x 1,000 acres). 15,456
Capital city . . . . Raleigh
Population 2000 276,093
Population 2006 356,321
Largest city . . . . .Charlotte
Population 2000 540,828
Population 2006 630,478

Number of cities with over 100,000 population
1990 5
2000 6
2006 7

State park and recreation areas, 2005
Area (x 1,000 acres) 187
Number of visitors (x 1,000) 12,674
Revenues ($1,000) $5,132
percent of operating expenditures. 16.5%

National forest system land, 2007
Acres 1,255,167

Demographics & Population Characteristics

Population
1980 5,881,766
1990 6,628,637
2000 8,046,491
2006 8,856,505
Male 4,341,298
Female 4,515,207
Living in group quarters, 2006 270,572
percent of total 3.1%
2007 (estimate) 9,061,032
persons per square mile of land 186.0
2008 (projected) 9,086,527
2010 (projected) 9,345,823
2020 (projected) 10,709,289
2030 (projected) 12,227,739

**Population of Core-Based Statistical Areas
(formerly Metropolitan Areas), x 1,000**

	CBSA	Non-CBSA
1990	6,030	602
2000	7,352	695
2006	8,135	722

Change in population, 2000-2007
Number 1,014,541
percent 12.6%
Natural increase (births minus deaths) 352,899
Net internal migration 490,907
Net international migration 188,925

Persons by age, 2006
Under 5 years 611,110
5 to 17 years 1,544,277
18 years and over 6,701,118
65 years and over 1,076,951
85 years and over 136,229
Median age 36.6

Persons by age, 2010 (projected)
Under 5 years 645,144
18 and over 7,076,985
65 and over 1,161,164
Median age 36.9

Race, 2006
One Race
White 6,558,154
Black or African American 1,921,307
Asian 164,111
American Indian/Alaska Native 111,148
Hawaiian Native/Pacific Islander 5,755
Two or more races 96,030

Persons of Hispanic origin, 2006
Total Hispanic or Latino 597,382
Mexican 397,971
Puerto Rican 44,707
Cuban 10,530

©2008 Information Publications, Inc.
All rights reserved. Photocopying prohibited.
877-544-INFO (4636) or www.informationpublications.com

Persons of Asian origin, 2006

Total Asian	162,578
Asian Indian	45,291
Chinese	23,780
Filipino	16,721
Japanese	7,958
Korean	14,107
Vietnamese	22,698

Marital status, 2006

Population 15 years & over	7,072,249
Never married	2,021,960
Married	3,878,605
Separated	236,344
Widowed	456,182
Divorced	715,502

Language spoken at home, 2006

Population 5 years and older	8,253,772
English only	7,465,526
Spanish	532,553
French	29,080
German	23,168
Chinese	19,170

Households & families, 2006

Households	3,454,068
with persons under 18 years	1,170,646
with persons over 65 years	755,875
persons per household	2.49
Families	2,310,456
persons per family	3.04
Married couples	1,706,840
Female householder, no husband present	454,809
One-person households	959,166

Nativity, 2006

Number of residents born in state	5,286,411
percent of population	59.7%

Immigration & naturalization, 2006

Legal permanent residents admitted	18,989
Persons naturalized	12,592
Non-immigrant admissions	235,417

Vital Statistics and Health

Marriages

2004	62,235
2005	63,384
2006	55,343

Divorces

2004	35,926
2005	35,684
2006	36,378

Health risks, 2006

Percent of adults who are:

Smokers	22.1%
Overweight (BMI > 25)	62.8%
Obese (BMI > 30)	26.6%

Births

2005	123,096
Birthrate (per 1,000)	14.2
White	89,636
Black	28,433
Hispanic	19,519
Asian/Pacific Islander	3,342
Amer. Indian/Alaska Native	1,685
Low birth weight (2,500g or less)	9.2%
Cesarian births	29.3%
Preterm births	13.7%
To unmarried mothers	38.4%
Twin births (per 1,000)	31.9
Triplets or higher order (per 100,000)	150.0
2006 (preliminary)	127,841
rate per 1,000	14.4

Deaths

2004

All causes	72,384
rate per 100,000	874.9
Heart disease	17,607
rate per 100,000	214.4
Malignant neoplasms	16,477
rate per 100,000	195.4
Cerebrovascular disease	4,955
rate per 100,000	61.1
Chronic lower respiratory disease	3,625
rate per 100,000	44.0
Diabetes	2,253
rate per 100,000	27.0
2005 (preliminary)	74,639
rate per 100,000	876.0
2006 (provisional)	74,734

Infant deaths

2004	1,053
rate per 1,000	8.8
2005 (provisional)	1,058
rate per 1,000	8.6

Exercise routines, 2005

None	25.6%
Moderate or greater	42.1%
Vigorous	22.2%

Abortions, 2004

Total performed in state	33,954
rate per 1,000 women age 15-44	19
% obtained by out-of-state residents	15.5%

Physicians, 2005

Total	21,972
rate per 100,000 persons	253

Community hospitals, 2005

Number of hospitals	115
Beds (x 1,000)	23.3
Patients admitted (x 1,000)	1,013
Average daily census (x 1,000)	16.7
Average cost per day	$1,320
Outpatient visits (x 1 mil)	16.8

©2008 Information Publications, Inc.
All rights reserved. Photocopying prohibited.
877-544-INFO (4636) or www.informationpublications.com

Disability status of population, 2006

5 to 15 years 7.2%
16 to 64 years 14.4%
65 years and over 43.5%

Education

Educational attainment, 2006

Population over 25 years 5,845,235
   Less than 9th grade................... 6.6%
   High school graduate or more 82.0%
   College graduate or more............. 24.8%
   Graduate or professional degree........ 8.3%

Public school enrollment, 2005-06

Total...............................1,416,436
   Pre-kindergarten through grade 8... 1,003,118
   Grades 9 through 12 413,318

Graduating public high school seniors, 2004-05

Diplomas (incl. GED and others) 76,663

SAT scores, 2007

Average critical reading score.............. 495
Average writing score 482
Average math score 509
Percent of graduates taking test 71%

Public school teachers, 2006-07 (estimate)

Total (x 1,000) 95.5
   Elementary...........................71.8
   Secondary............................23.7
Average salary $46,410
   Elementary....................... $46,410
   Secondary........................ $46,410

State receipts & expenditures for public schools, 2006-07 (estimate)

Revenue receipts ($ mil) $11,281
Expenditures
Total ($ mil) $12,940
   Per capita $1,267
   Per pupil $8,544

NAEP proficiency scores, 2007

	Reading		Math	
	Basic	Proficient	Basic	Proficient
Grade 4	63.9%	29.1%	84.9%	41.0%
Grade 8	71.0%	28.0%	72.9%	34.5%

Higher education enrollment, fall 2005

Total..................................87,637
   Full-time men 31,956
   Full-time women.................... 42,309
   Part-time men 4,731
   Part-time women.................... 8,641

Minority enrollment in institutions of higher education, 2005

Black, non-Hispanic 116,786
Hispanic 12,052
Asian/Pacific Islander 11,740
American Indian/Alaska Native.......... 6,096

Institutions of higher education, 2005-06

Total................................... 128
   Public.............................. 75
   Private 53

Earned degrees conferred, 2004-05

Associate's.......................... 18,460
Bachelor's 39,303
Master's.............................11,534
First-professional......................1,925
Doctor's..............................1,355

Public Libraries, 2006

Number of libraries...................... 75
Number of outlets 423
Annual visits per capita 4.0
Circulation per capita 5.5

State & local financial support for higher education, FY 2006

Full-time equivalent enrollment (x 1,000)....338.6
Appropriations per FTE................$7,522

Social Insurance & Welfare Programs

Social Security benefits & beneficiaries, 2005

Beneficiaries (x 1,000) 1,511
   Retired & dependents................. 1,006
   Survivors........................... 192
   Disabled & dependents................. 313
Annual benefit payments ($ mil) $15,856
   Retired & dependents................ $10,269
   Survivors.......................... $2,400
   Disabled & dependents................$3,187
Average monthly benefit
   Retired & dependents................ $984
   Disabled & dependents............... $921
   Widowed............................$907

Medicare, July 2005

Enrollment (x 1,000)....................1,277
Payments ($ mil) $8,551

Medicaid, 2004

Beneficiaries (x 1,000)................... 237
Payments ($ mil) $806

State Children's Health Insurance Program, 2006

Enrollment (x 1,000)................... 248.0
Expenditures ($ mil) $271.9

Persons without health insurance, 2006

Number (x 1,000)......................1,585
   percent............................ 17.9%
Number of children (x 1,000) 307
   percent of children 14.0%

Health care expenditures, 2004

Total expenditures.................... $44,281
   per capita $5,191

©2008 Information Publications, Inc.
All rights reserved. Photocopying prohibited.
877-544-INFO (4636) or www.informationpublications.com

Federal and state public aid

State unemployment insurance, 2006
Recipients, first payments (x 1,000) 239
Total payments ($ mil) $720
Average weekly benefit $265
Temporary Assistance for Needy Families, 2006
Recipients (x 1,000) 677.8
Families (x 1,000) 350.3
Supplemental Security Income, 2005
Recipients (x 1,000) 199.3
Payments ($ mil) $894.2
Food Stamp Program, 2006
Avg monthly participants (x 1,000) 854.4
Total benefits ($ mil) $921.0

Housing & Construction

Housing units
Total 2005 (estimate) 3,940,154
Total 2006 (estimate) 4,028,959
Seasonal or recreational use, 2006 166,866
Owner-occupied, 2006 2,350,798
   Median home value $137,200
   Homeowner vacancy rate 2.2%
Renter-occupied, 2006 1,103,270
   Median rent $656
   Rental vacancy rate 11.7%
Home ownership rate, 2005 . . . . 70.9%
Home ownership rate, 2006 . . . . 70.2%

New privately-owned housing units
Number authorized, 2006 (x 1,000) 100.0
   Value ($ mil) $16,074.3
Started 2005 (x 1,000, estimate) 71.1
Started 2006 (x 1,000, estimate) 70.2

Existing home sales
2005 (x 1,000) 215.7
2006 (x 1,000) 234.8

Government & Elections

State officials 2008
Governor . . . . Michael Easley
         Democratic, term expires 1/09
Lieutenant Governor . . . . Beverly Perdue
Secretary of State . . . . Elaine Marshall
Attorney General . . . . Roy Cooper
Chief Justice . . . . .Sarah Parker

Governorship
Minimum age 30
Length of term . . . . 4 years
Consecutive terms permitted 2
Who succeeds . . . . Lieutenant Governor

Local governments by type, 2002
Total 960
   County 100
   Municipal 541
   Township 0
   School District 0
   Special District 319

State legislature
Name . . . . General Assembly
Upper chamber . . . . .Senate
   Number of members 50
   Length of term . . . . 2 years
   Party in majority, 2008 . . . . .Democratic
Lower chamber . . . . House of Representatives
   Number of members 120
   Length of term . . . . 2 years
   Party in majority, 2008 . . . . .Democratic

Federal representation, 2008 (110th Congress)
Senator . . . . Elizabeth Dole
   Party . . . . Republican
   Year term expires 2009
Senator . . . . Richard Burr
   Party . . . . Republican
   Year term expires 2011
Representatives, total 13
   Democrats 7
   Republicans 6

Voters in November 2006 election (estimate)
Total 2,422,170
   Male 1,180,136
   Female 1,242,034
   White 1,994,343
   Black 407,932
   Hispanic 5,874
   Asian 8,936

Presidential election, 2004
Total Popular Vote 3,501,007
   Kerry 1,525,849
   Bush 1,961,166
Total Electoral Votes 15

Votes cast for US Senators
2004
Total vote (x 1,000) .3,472
Leading party . . . . Republican
Percent for leading party 51.6%
2006
Total vote (x 1,000) . . . . NA
Leading party . . . . NA
Percent for leading party . . . . NA

Votes cast for US Representatives
2004
Total vote (x 1,000) .3,413
   Democratic 1,670
   Republican 1,743
Leading party . . . . Republican
Percent for leading party 51.1%
2006
Total vote (x 1,000) .1,941
   Democratic 1,027
   Republican 914
Leading party . . . . .Democratic
Percent for leading party 52.9%

©2008 Information Publications, Inc.
All rights reserved. Photocopying prohibited.
877-544-INFO (4636) or www.informationpublications.com

State government employment, 2006
Full-time equivalent employees 139,117
Payroll ($ mil) $495.4

Local government employment, 2006
Full-time equivalent employees 372,146
Payroll ($ mil) $1,154.0

Women holding public office, 2008
US Congress 3
Statewide elected office 4
State legislature 44

Black public officials, 2002
Total 523
US and state legislatures 28
City/county/regional offices 369
Judicial/law enforcement. 31
Education/school boards 95

Hispanic public officials, 2006
Total 3
State executives & legislators 2
City/county/regional offices 1
Judicial/law enforcement. 0
Education/school boards 0

Governmental Finance

State government revenues, 2006
Total revenue (x $1,000) $45,473,975
per capita $5,127.04
General revenue (x $1,000) $38,883,961
Intergovernmental 12,905,941
Taxes 20,602,549
general sales 5,021,648
individual income tax 9,467,278
corporate income tax 1,308,022
Current charges 3,285,975
Miscellaneous 2,089,496

State government expenditure, 2006
Total expenditure (x $1,000) $41,107,916
per capita $4,634.78
General expenditure (x $1,000) $37,179,612
per capita, total. $4,191.88
Education 1,715.53
Public welfare 1,131.94
Health 166.88
Hospitals. 142.19
Highways 343.81
Police protection 64.16
Corrections 129.72
Natural resources 53.39
Parks & recreation 23.84
Governmental administration 107.13
Interest on general debt 63.47

State debt & cash, 2006 ($ per capita)
Debt $2,001.18
Cash/security holdings. $9,678.41

Federal government grants to state & local government, 2005 (x $1,000)
Total $12,958,870
by Federal agency
Defense 75,636
Education 951,450
Energy 29,755
Environmental Protection Agency 82,040
Health & Human Services. 8,428,677
Homeland Security 117,937
Housing & Urban Development 707,344
Justice 118,814
Labor 305,327
Transportation 1,032,462
Veterans Affairs. 4,813

Crime & Law Enforcement

Crime, 2006 (rates per 100,000 residents)
Property crimes 364,960
Burglary 107,407
Larceny 227,427
Motor vehicle theft 30,126
Property crime rate. 4,120.8
Violent crimes. 42,124
Murder 540
Forcible rape. 2,495
Robbery. 13,484
Aggravated assault 25,605
Violent crime rate 475.6
Hate crimes. 141

Fraud and identity theft, 2006
Fraud complaints. 10,300
rate per 100,000 residents 116.3
Identity theft complaints 5,748
rate per 100,000 residents 64.9

Law enforcement agencies, 2006
Total agencies 512
Total employees 30,671
Officers 21,419
Civilians 9,252

Prisoners, probation, and parole, 2006
Total prisoners 37,460
percent change, 12/31/05 to 12/31/06 . . . . 3.0%
in private facilities 0.5%
in local jails 0%
Sentenced to more than one year 32,219
rate per 100,000 residents 360
Adults on probation 110,419
Adults on parole. 3,236

Prisoner demographics, June 30, 2005 (rate per 100,000 residents)
Male 1,154
Female 104
White. 320
Black. 1,727
Hispanic . . . . NA

©2008 Information Publications, Inc.
All rights reserved. Photocopying prohibited.
877-544-INFO (4636) or www.informationpublications.com

Arrests, 2006

Total 436,676

   Persons under 18 years of age 44,691

Persons under sentence of death, 1/1/07

Total 185

   White 72

   Black 98

   Hispanic 4

State's highest court

Name .... Supreme Court

Number of members 7

Length of term .... 8 years

Intermediate appeals court? .... yes

Labor & Income

Civilian labor force, 2006 (x 1,000)

Total 4,426

   Men 2,353

   Women 2,073

   Persons 16-19 years 204

   White 3,344

   Black 902

   Hispanic 362

Civilian labor force as a percent of civilian non-institutional population, 2006

Total 66.1%

   Men 73.4

   Women 59.5

   Persons 16-19 years 43.6

   White 66.3

   Black 66.0

   Hispanic 81.1

Employment, 2006 (x 1,000)

Total 4,218

   Men 2,250

   Women 1,967

   Persons 16-19 years 163

   White 3,228

   Black 821

   Hispanic 351

Unemployment rate, 2006

Total 4.7%

   Men 4.4

   Women 5.1

   Persons 16-19 years 20.0

   White 3.5

   Black 9.0

   Hispanic 3.1

Full-time/part-time labor force, 2003 (x 1,000)

Full-time labor force, employed 3,286

Part-time labor force, employed 671

Unemployed, looking for

   Full-time work 238

   Part-time work 35

Mean duration of unemployment (weeks) 20.6

   Median 11.3

Labor unions, 2006

Membership (x 1,000) 126

   percent of employed 3.3%

Experienced civilian labor force by private industry, 2006

Total 3,305,395

   Natural resources & mining 32,999

   Construction 244,888

   Manufacturing 553,483

   Trade, transportation & utilities 756,723

   Information 73,172

   Finance 202,415

   Professional & business 477,384

   Education & health 467,884

   Leisure & hospitality 376,394

   Other 99,206

Experienced civilian labor force by occupation, May 2006

Management 178,650

Business & financial 138,000

Legal 19,410

Sales 415,100

Office & admin. support 612,240

Computers & math 82,190

Architecture & engineering 53,420

Arts & entertainment 35,260

Education 250,300

Social services 47,540

Health care practitioner & technical 198,840

Health care support 126,360

Maintenance & repair 172,200

Construction 192,160

Transportation & moving 307,430

Production 407,640

Farming, fishing & forestry 8,270

Hours and earnings of production workers on manufacturing payrolls, 2006

Average weekly hours 40.0

Average hourly earnings $14.57

Average weekly earnings $582.80

Income and poverty, 2006

Median household income $42,625

Personal income, per capita (current $) ... $32,234

   in constant (2000) dollars $28,138

Persons below poverty level 14.7%

Average annual pay

2006 .... $37,439

   increase from 2005 .... 4.3%

Federal individual income tax returns, 2005

Returns filed 3,879,609

Adjusted gross income ($1,000) $186,047,795

Total tax liability ($1,000) $22,000,566

Charitable contributions, 2004

Number of contributions 1,202.0

Total amount ($ mil) $4,951.1

©2008 Information Publications, Inc.
All rights reserved. Photocopying prohibited.
877-544-INFO (4636) or www.informationpublications.com

Economy, Business, Industry & Agriculture

Fortune 500 companies, 2007 14
Bankruptcy cases filed, FY 2007 19,420

Patents and trademarks issued, 2007

Patents 1,935
Trademarks 1,492

Business firm ownership, 2002

Women-owned 173,874
  Sales ($ mil) $26,743
Black-owned 52,122
  Sales ($ mil) $3,549
Hispanic-owned 9,043
  Sales ($ mil) $1,789
Asian-owned 13,695
  Sales ($ mil) $3,506
Amer. Indian/Alaska Native-owned 5,973
  Sales ($ mil) $592
Hawaiian/Pacific Islander-owned 191
  Sales ($ mil) $13

Gross domestic product, 2006 ($ mil)

Total gross domestic product $374,525
  Agriculture, forestry, fishing and
    hunting 3,570
  Mining. 426
  Utilities 6,587
  Construction 18,703
  Manufacturing, durable goods 27,743
  Manufacturing, non-durable goods . . . 46,271
  Wholesale trade 20,833
  Retail trade 23,992
  Transportation & warehousing 8,238
  Information 12,684
  Finance & insurance 41,736
  Real estate, rental & leasing 36,656
  Professional and technical services 17,764
  Educational services 3,030
  Health care and social assistance 23,097
  Accommodation/food services 8,450
  Other services, except government 7,389
  Government 46,827

Establishments, payroll, employees & receipts, by major industry group, 2005

Total 216,994
  Annual payroll ($1,000) $115,740,410
  Paid employees 3,409,968
Forestry, fishing & agriculture 917
  Annual payroll ($1,000) . . . . NA
  Paid employees . . . . NA
Mining 210
  Annual payroll ($1,000) $173,076
  Paid employees .3,518
  Receipts, 2002 ($1,000) $815,465

Utilities 368
  Annual payroll ($1,000) $1,383,746
  Paid employees 19,722
  Receipts, 2002 ($1,000) . . . . .NA
Construction 27,202
  Annual payroll ($1,000) $7,970,603
  Paid employees 221,783
  Receipts, 2002 ($1,000) $34,385,593
Manufacturing 10,138
  Annual payroll ($1,000) $20,681,882
  Paid employees 554,442
  Receipts, 2002 ($1,000) $156,821,943
Wholesale trade 11,866
  Annual payroll ($1,000) $7,794,777
  Paid employees 163,867
  Receipts, 2002 ($1,000) $104,331,152
Retail trade 35,875
  Annual payroll ($1,000) $9,707,125
  Paid employees 449,870
  Receipts, 2002 ($1,000) $88,821,486
Transportation & warehousing 5,819
  Annual payroll ($1,000) $3,924,521
  Paid employees 115,901
  Receipts, 2002 ($1,000) $7,895,233
Information 3,356
  Annual payroll ($1,000) $3,812,515
  Paid employees 74,729
  Receipts, 2002 ($1,000) . . . . .NA
Finance & insurance 12,930
  Annual payroll ($1,000) $10,265,446
  Paid employees 178,306
  Receipts, 2002 ($1,000) . . . . .NA
Professional, scientific & technical 21,169
  Annual payroll ($1,000) $9,503,601
  Paid employees 174,892
  Receipts, 2002 ($1,000) $17,622,547
Education 2,054
  Annual payroll ($1,000) $2,311,554
  Paid employees 75,013
  Receipts, 2002 ($1,000) $747,826
Health care & social assistance 19,846
  Annual payroll ($1,000) $16,282,077
  Paid employees 470,820
  Receipts, 2002 ($1,000) $32,026,359
Arts and entertainment 3,232
  Annual payroll ($1,000) $1,196,776
  Paid employees 48,713
  Receipts, 2002 ($1,000) $3,058,898
Real estate 10,059
  Annual payroll ($1,000) $1,772,769
  Paid employees 50,364
  Receipts, 2002 ($1,000) $7,088,267
Accommodation & food service 16,903
  Annual payroll ($1,000) $3,894,008
  Paid employees 315,212
  Receipts, 2002 ($1,000) $11,237,386

©2008 Information Publications, Inc.
All rights reserved. Photocopying prohibited.
877-544-INFO (4636) or www.informationpublications.com

8   North Carolina

Exports, 2006
Value of exported goods ($ mil) $21,218
  Manufactured $18,320
  Non-manufactured. $1,236

Foreign direct investment in US affiliates, 2004
Property, plants & equipment ($ mil) $23,917
Employment (x 1,000). 198.0

Agriculture, 2006
Number of farms 48,000
Farm acreage (x 1,000) 8,800
  Acres per farm. 183
Farm marketings and income ($ mil)
Total. $8,199.3
  Crops $2,925.3
  Livestock. $5,274.0
Net farm income $3,702.2

Principal commodities, in order by marketing receipts, 2005
  Broilers, Hogs, Greenhouse/nursery, Turkeys,
             Tobacco

Federal economic activity in state
Expenditures, 2005 ($ mil)
  Total. $59,162
    Per capita $6,821.87
  Defense $9,404
  Non-defense $49,758
Defense department, 2006 ($ mil)
  Payroll. $7,132
  Contract awards $2,690
  Grants $100
Homeland security grants ($1,000)
  2006. . . . . $30,484
  2007. . . . . $25,256

FDIC-insured financial institutions, 2005
Number 110
Assets ($ billion) $1,913.6
Deposits ($ billion) $1,258.8

Fishing, 2006
Catch (x 1,000 lbs). 68,641
Value ($1,000). $71,886

Mining, 2006 ($ mil)
Total non-fuel mineral production $872
Percent of U.S. 1.35%

Communication, Energy & Transportation

Communication
Households with computers, 2003 . . . . 57.7%
Households with internet access, 2003 . . . . 51.1%
High-speed internet providers 60
Total high-speed internet lines. 2,366,079
  Residential 1,659,657
  Business. 706,422
Wireless phone customers, 12/2006 6,626,582

FCC-licensed stations (as of January 1, 2008)
TV stations 50
FM radio stations. 222
AM radio stations 219

Energy
Energy consumption, 2004
  Total (trillion Btu). 2,716
  Per capita (million Btu) 318.3
By source of production (trillion Btu)
  Coal 783
  Natural gas 233
  Petroleum 993
  Nuclear electric power 418
  Hydroelectric power 55
By end-use sector (trillion Btu)
  Residential 702
  Commercial 554
  Industrial 723
  Transportation 738
Electric energy, 2005
  Primary source of electricity. . . . . Coal
  Net generation (billion kWh) 129.7
    percent from renewable sources. 5.6%
  Net summer capability (million kW) 27.1
  CO_2 emitted from generation 75.9
Natural gas utilities, 2005
  Customers (x 1,000) 1,105
  Sales (trillion Btu). 204
  Revenues ($ mil) $1,782
Nuclear plants, 2007 5
Total CO_2 emitted (million metric tons). 146.2
Energy spending, 2004 ($ mil) $23,225
  per capita $2,722
  Price per million Btu $13.60

Transportation, 2006
Public road & street mileage 103,500
  Urban. 32,310
  Rural. 71,190
  Interstate. 1,082
Vehicle miles of travel (millions) 101,515
  per capita 11,445.5
Total motor vehicle registrations. 6,301,436
  Automobiles. .3,659,926
  Trucks 2,607,790
  Motorcycles 110,628
Licensed drivers 6,315,667
  19 years & under 214,442
Deaths from motor vehicle accidents 1,559
Gasoline consumed (x 1,000 gallons) 4,443,067
  per capita 500.9

Commuting Statistics, 2006
Average commute time (min) 23.4
  Drove to work alone 79.8%
  Carpooled. 12.5%
  Public transit 1.0%
  Walk to work 1.8%
  Work from home 3.6%

©2008 Information Publications, Inc.
All rights reserved. Photocopying prohibited.
877-544-INFO (4636) or www.informationpublications.com

State Summary

Capital city . . . . Bismarck
Governor . . . . John Hoeven

Dept 101
600 E Boulevard Ave
Bismarck, ND 58505
701-328-2200

Admitted as a state 1889
Area (square miles) 70,700
Population, 2007 (estimate) 639,715
Largest city . . . . Fargo
  Population, 2006 90,056
Personal income per capita, 2006
  (in current dollars) $32,552
Gross domestic product, 2006 ($ mil) $26,385

Leading industries by payroll, 2005

Health care/Social assistance, Retail trade,
Manufacturing

**Leading agricultural commodities
by receipts, 2005**

Wheat, Cattle and calves, Soybeans, Corn, Sugar
beets

Geography & Environment

Total area (square miles) 70,700
  land 68,976
  water 1,724
Federally-owned land, 2004 (acres) 1,185,777
  percent 2.7%
Highest point . . . . White Butte
  elevation (feet) 3,506
Lowest point . . . . .Red River
  elevation (feet) 750
General coastline (miles) 0
Tidal shoreline (miles) 0
Cropland, 2003 (x 1,000 acres) 24,267
Forest land, 2003 (x 1,000 acres) 467
Capital city . . . . Bismarck
  Population 2000 55,532
  Population 2006 58,333
Largest city . . . . Fargo
  Population 2000 90,599
  Population 2006 90,056

Number of cities with over 100,000 population

1990 0
2000 0
2006 0

State park and recreation areas, 2005

Area (x 1,000 acres) 18
Number of visitors (x 1,000) 948
Revenues ($1,000) $1,514
  percent of operating expenditures 47.3%

National forest system land, 2007

Acres 1,111,177

Demographics & Population Characteristics

Population

1980 652,717
1990 638,800
2000 642,204
2006 635,867
  Male 319,427
  Female 316,440
Living in group quarters, 2006 27,521
  percent of total 4.3%
2007 (estimate) .639,715
  persons per square mile of land 9.3
2008 (projected) 636,452
2010 (projected) 636,623
2020 (projected) .630,112
2030 (projected) 606,566

**Population of Core-Based Statistical Areas
(formerly Metropolitan Areas), x 1,000**

	CBSA	Non-CBSA
1990	410	228
2000	435	208
2006	442	194

Change in population, 2000-2007

Number . . . .-2,485
  percent . . . . -0.4%
Natural increase (births minus deaths) 16,608
Net internal migration . . . .-19,531
Net international migration 3,184

Persons by age, 2006

Under 5 years 39,556
5 to 17 years 105,378
18 years and over 490,933
65 years and over 92,874
85 years and over 16,797
  Median age 37.2

Persons by age, 2010 (projected)

Under 5 years 38,869
18 and over 494,659
65 and over 97,108
  Median age 38.4

Race, 2006

One Race
  White 584,116
  Black or African American 5,262
  Asian 4,743
  American Indian/Alaska Native 34,190
  Hawaiian Native/Pacific Islander 297
Two or more races .7,259

Persons of Hispanic origin, 2006

Total Hispanic or Latino 9,332
  Mexican 6,072
  Puerto Rican 667
  Cuban 80

©2008 Information Publications, Inc.
All rights reserved. Photocopying prohibited.
877-544-INFO (4636) or www.informationpublications.com

Persons of Asian origin, 2006

Total Asian	4,348
Asian Indian	536
Chinese	573
Filipino	776
Japanese	194
Korean	653
Vietnamese	291

Marital status, 2006

Population 15 years & over	519,296
Never married	153,251
Married	285,270
Separated	3,469
Widowed	36,278
Divorced	44,497

Language spoken at home, 2006

Population 5 years and older	596,773
English only	565,565
Spanish	8,853
French	1,204
German	10,299
Chinese	449

Households & families, 2006

Households	272,352
with persons under 18 years	80,213
with persons over 65 years	63,993
persons per household	2.23
Families	169,022
persons per family	2.82
Married couples	138,355
Female householder, no husband present	21,352
One-person households	83,357

Nativity, 2006

Number of residents born in state	451,804
percent of population	71.1%

Immigration & naturalization, 2006

Legal permanent residents admitted	649
Persons naturalized	329
Non-immigrant admissions	14,643

Vital Statistics and Health

Marriages

2004	4,424
2005	4,388
2006	4,331

Divorces

2004	1,979
2005	1,905
2006	1,673

Health risks, 2006

Percent of adults who are:

Smokers	19.5%
Overweight (BMI > 25)	64.5%
Obese (BMI > 30)	25.4%

Births

2005	8,390
Birthrate (per 1,000)	13.2
White	7,195
Black	129
Hispanic	179
Asian/Pacific Islander	106
Amer. Indian/Alaska Native	960
Low birth weight (2,500g or less)	6.4%
Cesarian births	26.4%
Preterm births	11.5%
To unmarried mothers	32.2%
Twin births (per 1,000)	32.6
Triplets or higher order (per 100,000)	240.3
2006 (preliminary)	8,622
rate per 1,000	13.6

Deaths

2004

All causes	5,601
rate per 100,000	697.1
Heart disease	1,470
rate per 100,000	175.8
Malignant neoplasms	1,265
rate per 100,000	166.9
Cerebrovascular disease	475
rate per 100,000	54.6
Chronic lower respiratory disease	273
rate per 100,000	34.7
Diabetes	209
rate per 100,000	26.5
2005 (preliminary)	5,744
rate per 100,000	699.1
2006 (provisional)	5,917

Infant deaths

2004	46
rate per 1,000	5.6
2005 (provisional)	53
rate per 1,000	6.3

Exercise routines, 2005

None	23.1%
Moderate or greater	48.4%
Vigorous	27.5%

Abortions, 2004

Total performed in state	1,357
rate per 1,000 women age 15-44	10
% obtained by out-of-state residents	37.5%

Physicians, 2005

Total	1,523
rate per 100,000 persons	240

Community hospitals, 2005

Number of hospitals	40
Beds (x 1,000)	3.5
Patients admitted (x 1,000)	87
Average daily census (x 1,000)	2.1
Average cost per day	$898
Outpatient visits (x 1 mil)	1.9

©2008 Information Publications, Inc.
All rights reserved. Photocopying prohibited.
877-544-INFO (4636) or www.informationpublications.com

Disability status of population, 2006

5 to 15 years 6.7%
16 to 64 years 10.1%
65 years and over 40.1%

Education

Educational attainment, 2006

Population over 25 years 409,865
  Less than 9th grade. 6.2%
  High school graduate or more 88.1%
  College graduate or more. 25.6%
  Graduate or professional degree. 6.5%

Public school enrollment, 2005-06

Total. 98,283
  Pre-kindergarten through grade 8. 65,638
  Grades 9 through 12 32,645

Graduating public high school seniors, 2004-05

Diplomas (incl. GED and others) 7,555

SAT scores, 2007

Average critical reading score 584
Average writing score 562
Average math score 596
Percent of graduates taking test 4%

Public school teachers, 2006-07 (estimate)

Total (x 1,000) 7.6
  Elementary. 5.1
  Secondary. 2.4
Average salary $38,822
  Elementary. $39,141
  Secondary. $38,144

State receipts & expenditures for public schools, 2006-07 (estimate)

Revenue receipts ($ mil) $967
Expenditures
Total ($ mil) $973
  Per capita $1,237
  Per pupil $9,036

NAEP proficiency scores, 2007

	Reading		Math	
	Basic	Proficient	Basic	Proficient
Grade 4	75.3%	35.3%	90.8%	45.7%
Grade 8	83.6%	32.2%	85.5%	41.0%

Higher education enrollment, fall 2005

Total. 6,581
  Full-time men 2,017
  Full-time women 3,362
  Part-time men 323
  Part-time women. 879

Minority enrollment in institutions of higher education, 2005

Black, non-Hispanic 682
Hispanic 489
Asian/Pacific Islander 530
American Indian/Alaska Native. 3,075

Institutions of higher education, 2005-06

Total. 22
  Public. 14
  Private 8

Earned degrees conferred, 2004-05

Associate's. 2,213
Bachelor's 5,161
Master's. 1,104
First-professional. 178
Doctor's 189

Public Libraries, 2006

Number of libraries. 83
Number of outlets 105
Annual visits per capita 4.8
Circulation per capita. 7.4

State & local financial support for higher education, FY 2006

Full-time equivalent enrollment (x 1,000) 35.9
Appropriations per FTE. $4,683

Social Insurance & Welfare Programs

Social Security benefits & beneficiaries, 2005

Beneficiaries (x 1,000) 115
  Retired & dependents. 82
  Survivors. 19
  Disabled & dependents. 14
Annual benefit payments ($ mil) $1,174
  Retired & dependents. $780
  Survivors. $257
  Disabled & dependents. $137
Average monthly benefit
  Retired & dependents. $935
  Disabled & dependents. $873
  Widowed. $927

Medicare, July 2005

Enrollment (x 1,000) 104
Payments ($ mil) $615

Medicaid, 2004

Beneficiaries (x 1,000). 4,712
Payments ($ mil) $37,273

State Children's Health Insurance Program, 2006

Enrollment (x 1,000). .6.3
Expenditures ($ mil) $14.1

Persons without health insurance, 2006

Number (x 1,000). 75
  percent. 12.2%
Number of children (x 1,000) 15
  percent of children 10.4%

Health care expenditures, 2004

Total expenditures. $3,693
  per capita $5,808

©2008 Information Publications, Inc.
All rights reserved. Photocopying prohibited.
877-544-INFO (4636) or www.informationpublications.com

Federal and state public aid

State unemployment insurance, 2006
Recipients, first payments (x 1,000) 14
Total payments ($ mil) $42
Average weekly benefit $255
Temporary Assistance for Needy Families, 2006
Recipients (x 1,000) 76.9
Families (x 1,000) 30.4
Supplemental Security Income, 2005
Recipients (x 1,000) 7.9
Payments ($ mil) $33.5
Food Stamp Program, 2006
Avg monthly participants (x 1,000) 42.6
Total benefits ($ mil) $46.2

Housing & Construction

Housing units
Total 2005 (estimate) 304,477
Total 2006 (estimate) 307,802
Seasonal or recreational use, 2006 11,805
Owner-occupied, 2006 181,666
   Median home value $99,700
   Homeowner vacancy rate 1.1%
Renter-occupied, 2006 90,686
   Median rent $497
   Rental vacancy rate 8.9%
Home ownership rate, 2005 . . . . .68.5%
Home ownership rate, 2006 . . . . .68.3%

New privately-owned housing units
Number authorized, 2006 (x 1,000) 3.5
   Value ($ mil) $462.3
Started 2005 (x 1,000, estimate) 3.4
Started 2006 (x 1,000, estimate) 3.3

Existing home sales
2005 (x 1,000) 15.8
2006 (x 1,000) 14.1

Government & Elections

State officials 2008
Governor . . . . John Hoeven
   Republican, term expires 12/08
Lieutenant Governor . . . . Jack Dalrymple
Secretary of State . . . . Al Jaeger
Attorney General . . . . Wayne Stenehjem
Chief Justice . . . . Gerald VandeWalle

Governorship
Minimum age 30
Length of term . . . . 4 years
Consecutive terms permitted . . . . . . not specified
Who succeeds . . . . Lieutenant Governor

Local governments by type, 2002
Total 2,735
   County 53
   Municipal 360
   Township 1,332
   School District 226
   Special District 764

State legislature

Name .Legislative Assembly
Upper chamber . . . . .Senate
   Number of members 47
   Length of term . . . . 4 years
   Party in majority, 2008 . . . . Republican
Lower chamber . . . . .House of Representatives
   Number of members 94
   Length of term . . . . 4 years
   Party in majority, 2008 . . . . Republican

Federal representation, 2008 (110th Congress)
Senator . . . . Byron Dorgan
   Party . . . . .Democratic
   Year term expires 2011
Senator . . . . .Kent Conrad
   Party . . . . .Democratic
   Year term expires 2013
Representatives, total 1
   Democrats 1
   Republicans 0

Voters in November 2006 election (estimate)
Total 258,566
   Male 126,807
   Female 131,759
   White 240,170
   Black 405
   Hispanic 562
   Asian 341

Presidential election, 2004
Total Popular Vote 312,833
   Kerry 111,052
   Bush 196,651
Total Electoral Votes 3

Votes cast for US Senators
2004
Total vote (x 1,000) 311
Leading party .Democratic
Percent for leading party 68.3%
2006
Total vote (x 1,000) 218
Leading party .Democratic
Percent for leading party 68.8%

Votes cast for US Representatives
2004
Total vote (x 1,000) 311
   Democratic 185
   Republican 126
Leading party .Democratic
Percent for leading party 59.6%
2006
Total vote (x 1,000) 218
   Democratic 143
   Republican 75
Leading party .Democratic
Percent for leading party 65.7%

©2008 Information Publications, Inc.
All rights reserved. Photocopying prohibited.
877-544-INFO (4636) or www.informationpublications.com

State government employment, 2006
Full-time equivalent employees 18,127
Payroll ($ mil) $57.6

Local government employment, 2006
Full-time equivalent employees 23,046
Payroll ($ mil) $75.7

Women holding public office, 2008
US Congress 0
Statewide elected office. 2
State legislature 25

Black public officials, 2002
Total. 1
   US and state legislatures 0
   City/county/regional offices 1
   Judicial/law enforcement 0
   Education/school boards 0

Hispanic public officials, 2006
Total. 1
   State executives & legislators 0
   City/county/regional offices 1
   Judicial/law enforcement. 0
   Education/school boards 0

Governmental Finance

State government revenues, 2006
Total revenue (x $1,000) $4,369,763
   per capita $6,854.96
General revenue (x $1,000) $3,667,407
   Intergovernmental 1,213,472
   Taxes 1,621,912
      general sales 427,487
      individual income tax 275,630
      corporate income tax 120,113
   Current charges 532,676
   Miscellaneous 299,347

State government expenditure, 2006
Total expenditure (x $1,000) $3,633,349
   per capita $5,699.73
General expenditure (x $1,000) $3,360,266
   per capita, total. *$5,271.34*
      Education 1,850.26
      Public welfare 1,103.83
      Health 90.53
      Hospitals. 35.49
      Highways 745.56
      Police protection. 39.22
      Corrections 89.13
      Natural resources 236.83
      Parks & recreation 25.50
      Governmental administration 202.67
      Interest on general debt 162.59

State debt & cash, 2006 ($ per capita)
Debt $2,777.16
Cash/security holdings. $15,550.53

Federal government grants to state & local government, 2005 (x $1,000)
Total $1,666,287
by Federal agency
   Defense 24,304
   Education 138,017
   Energy 17,124
   Environmental Protection Agency 40,308
   Health & Human Services. 570,013
   Homeland Security. 18,631
   Housing & Urban Development 102,556
   Justice 34,050
   Labor 25,973
   Transportation 257,349
   Veterans Affairs. 4,476

Crime & Law Enforcement

Crime, 2006 (rates per 100,000 residents)
Property crimes 12,719
   Burglary 2,393
   Larceny 9,314
   Motor vehicle theft 1,012
   Property crime rate. 2,000.3
Violent crimes. 813
   Murder 8
   Forcible rape. 193
   Robbery. 72
   Aggravated assault 540
   Violent crime rate 127.9
Hate crimes. 16

Fraud and identity theft, 2006
Fraud complaints. 544
   rate per 100,000 residents 85.6
Identity theft complaints 189
   rate per 100,000 residents 29.7

Law enforcement agencies, 2006
Total agencies. 93
Total employees 1,619
   Officers 1,178
   Civilians 441

Prisoners, probation, and parole, 2006
Total prisoners 1,363
   percent change, 12/31/05 to 12/31/06 . . . -1.6%
   in private facilities 0%
   in local jails 3.5%
Sentenced to more than one year 1,363
   rate per 100,000 residents 214
Adults on probation 4,303
Adults on parole. 370

Prisoner demographics, June 30, 2005 (rate per 100,000 residents)
Male 632
Female 87
White 267
Black. 2,683
Hispanic 848

©2008 Information Publications, Inc.
All rights reserved. Photocopying prohibited.
877-544-INFO (4636) or www.informationpublications.com

Arrests, 2006

Total.................................. 28,597
    Persons under 18 years of age 6,769

Persons under sentence of death, 1/1/07

Total...................................... 0
    White..................................... 0
    Black 0
    Hispanic 0

State's highest court

Name .... Supreme Court
Number of members 5
Length of term .... 10 years
Intermediate appeals court? .... no

Labor & Income

Civilian labor force, 2006 (x 1,000)

Total.................................... 368
    Men 192
    Women 176
    Persons 16-19 years..................... 21
    White.................................. 338
    Black .... NA
    Hispanic .... NA

Civilian labor force as a percent of civilian non-institutional population, 2006

Total................................. 73.2%
    Men 77.4
    Women 69.0
    Persons 16-19 years.................... 56.3
    White.................................. 73.9
    Black .... NA
    Hispanic .... NA

Employment, 2006 (x 1,000)

Total.................................... 355
    Men 185
    Women 171
    Persons 16-19 years..................... 19
    White.................................. 329
    Black .... NA
    Hispanic .... NA

Unemployment rate, 2006

Total.................................... 3.3%
    Men 3.8
    Women 2.9
    Persons 16-19 years.................... 10.6
    White................................... 2.6
    Black .... NA
    Hispanic .... NA

Full-time/part-time labor force, 2003 (x 1,000)

Full-time labor force, employed 264
Part-time labor force, employed............. 69

Unemployed, looking for
    Full-time work........................... 11
    Part-time work........................... 2
Mean duration of unemployment (weeks)...... 13.5
    Median 7.8

Labor unions, 2006

Membership (x 1,000)...................... 20
    percent of employed 6.8%

Experienced civilian labor force by private industry, 2006

Total................................. 271,603
    Natural resources & mining 7,574
    Construction 18,265
    Manufacturing...................... 26,009
    Trade, transportation & utilities 74,431
    Information 7,489
    Finance 18,707
    Professional & business 28,323
    Education & health................... 48,078
    Leisure & hospitality................. 31,573
    Other 11,154

Experienced civilian labor force by occupation, May 2006

Management........................... 13,520
Business & financial 11,070
Legal................................. 1,410
Sales................................ 37,210
Office & admin. support................ 56,420
Computers & math 4,760
Architecture & engineering.............. 4,960
Arts & entertainment 3,980
Education 20,900
Social services 4,840
Health care practitioner & technical 19,160
Health care support 11,590
Maintenance & repair.................. 15,580
Construction 19,620
Transportation & moving 26,460
Production 21,590
Farming, fishing & forestry.............. 1,140

Hours and earnings of production workers on manufacturing payrolls, 2006

Average weekly hours 39.0
Average hourly earnings $14.97
Average weekly earnings $583.83

Income and poverty, 2006

Median household income............. $41,919
Personal income, per capita (current $)... $32,552
    in constant (2000) dollars $28,416
Persons below poverty level............. 11.4%

Average annual pay

2006 .... $31,316
    increase from 2005 .... 4.5%

Federal individual income tax returns, 2005

Returns filed......................... 307,235
Adjusted gross income ($1,000) $12,970,269
Total tax liability ($1,000) $1,515,289

Charitable contributions, 2004

Number of contributions................. 47.5
Total amount ($ mil).................. $177.3

©2008 Information Publications, Inc.
All rights reserved. Photocopying prohibited.
877-544-INFO (4636) or www.informationpublications.com

Economy, Business, Industry & Agriculture

Fortune 500 companies, 2007................ 0
Bankruptcy cases filed, FY 2007...........1,090

Patents and trademarks issued, 2007

Patents................................ 92
Trademarks............................. 91

Business firm ownership, 2002

Women-owned..................... 13,203
   Sales ($ mil) $1,318
Black-owned............................ 78
   Sales ($ mil) $14
Hispanic-owned........................ 230
   Sales ($ mil) $16
Asian-owned 277
   Sales ($ mil) $108
Amer. Indian/Alaska Native-owned 853
   Sales ($ mil) $121
Hawaiian/Pacific Islander-owned 2
   Sales ($ mil) .... NA

Gross domestic product, 2006 ($ mil)

Total gross domestic product $26,385
   Agriculture, forestry, fishing and
      hunting 1,655
   Mining.............................1,020
   Utilities............................ 679
   Construction 1,250
   Manufacturing, durable goods.........1,801
   Manufacturing, non-durable goods 697
   Wholesale trade.....................2,076
   Retail trade........................1,883
   Transportation & warehousing 1,063
   Information 904
   Finance & insurance..................1,567
   Real estate, rental & leasing 2,458
   Professional and technical services 933
   Educational services.................... 116
   Health care and social assistance 2,238
   Accommodation/food services........... 615
   Other services, except government 564
   Government......................... 4,046

Establishments, payroll, employees & receipts, by major industry group, 2005

Total...............................21,061
   Annual payroll ($1,000)........... $7,779,322
   Paid employees 270,479
Forestry, fishing & agriculture.............. 144
   Annual payroll ($1,000).................. NA
   Paid employees .... NA
Mining............................... 182
   Annual payroll ($1,000)............. $273,613
   Paid employees 4,368
   Receipts, 2002 ($1,000) $1,250,027

Utilities 115
   Annual payroll ($1,000)........... $230,061
   Paid employees 3,250
   Receipts, 2002 ($1,000) ....NA
Construction......................... 2,299
   Annual payroll ($1,000)........... $641,985
   Paid employees 15,128
   Receipts, 2002 ($1,000) $2,338,220
Manufacturing........................ 748
   Annual payroll ($1,000)........... $827,442
   Paid employees 24,604
   Receipts, 2002 ($1,000) $6,856,653
Wholesale trade.......................1,452
   Annual payroll ($1,000)........... $668,191
   Paid employees 17,233
   Receipts, 2002 ($1,000) $8,806,340
Retail trade..........................3,435
   Annual payroll ($1,000)........... $854,201
   Paid employees 43,548
   Receipts, 2002 ($1,000) $7,723,945
Transportation & warehousing............1,040
   Annual payroll ($1,000)........... $296,518
   Paid employees 9,473
   Receipts, 2002 ($1,000) $1,021,195
Information........................... 374
   Annual payroll ($1,000)........... $292,650
   Paid employees 7,409
   Receipts, 2002 ($1,000) ....NA
Finance & insurance.....................1,582
   Annual payroll ($1,000)........... $563,818
   Paid employees 14,990
   Receipts, 2002 ($1,000) ....NA
Professional, scientific & technical.........1,397
   Annual payroll ($1,000).............$417,841
   Paid employees 11,561
   Receipts, 2002 ($1,000) $871,152
Education 147
   Annual payroll ($1,000).............$79,618
   Paid employees 4,659
   Receipts, 2002 ($1,000) $41,636
Health care & social assistance.............1,691
   Annual payroll ($1,000)...........$1,609,606
   Paid employees 50,372
   Receipts, 2002 ($1,000) $3,027,796
Arts and entertainment 395
   Annual payroll ($1,000)................ NA
   Paid employees .... NA
   Receipts, 2002 ($1,000) $242,898
Real estate............................ 751
   Annual payroll ($1,000)........... $82,551
   Paid employees 3,664
   Receipts, 2002 ($1,000) $463,572
Accommodation & food service...........1,795
   Annual payroll ($1,000)........... $290,993
   Paid employees 28,662
   Receipts, 2002 ($1,000) $854,656

©2008 Information Publications, Inc.
All rights reserved. Photocopying prohibited.
877-544-INFO (4636) or www.informationpublications.com

8   North Dakota

©2008 Information Publications, Inc.
All rights reserved. Photocopying prohibited.
877-544-INFO (4636) or www.informationpublications.com

Exports, 2006

Value of exported goods ($ mil)	$1,509
Manufactured	$1,206
Non-manufactured	$243

Foreign direct investment in US affiliates, 2004

Property, plants & equipment ($ mil)	$1,416
Employment (x 1,000)	NA

Agriculture, 2006

Number of farms 30,300
Farm acreage (x 1,000) 39,400
  Acres per farm 1,300
Farm marketings and income ($ mil)
Total $3,980.7
  Crops $3,088.4
  Livestock $892.4
Net farm income $605.9

Principal commodities, in order by marketing receipts, 2005

Wheat, Cattle and calves, Soybeans, Corn, Sugar beets

Federal economic activity in state

Expenditures, 2005 ($ mil)
  Total $6,608
    Per capita $10,412.83
  Defense $776
  Non-defense $5,832
Defense department, 2006 ($ mil)
  Payroll $501
  Contract awards $240
  Grants $37
Homeland security grants ($1,000)
  2006 .... $10,788
  2007 .... $6,678

FDIC-insured financial institutions, 2005

Number	96
Assets ($ billion)	$18.4
Deposits ($ billion)	$11.4

Fishing, 2006

Catch (x 1,000 lbs)	NA
Value ($1,000)	NA

Mining, 2006 ($ mil)

Total non-fuel mineral production	$56
Percent of U.S.	0.09%

Communication, Energy & Transportation

Communication

Households with computers, 2003 .... 61.2%
Households with internet access, 2003 .... 53.2%
High-speed internet providers 40
Total high-speed internet lines 131,348
  Residential 116,643
  Business 14,705
Wireless phone customers, 12/2006 472,799

FCC-licensed stations (as of January 1, 2008)

TV stations	27
FM radio stations	63
AM radio stations	34

Energy

Energy consumption, 2004
  Total (trillion Btu) 402
  Per capita (million Btu) 632.7
By source of production (trillion Btu)
  Coal 398
  Natural gas 60
  Petroleum 134
  Nuclear electric power 0
  Hydroelectric power 16
By end-use sector (trillion Btu)
  Residential 63
  Commercial 59
  Industrial 188
  Transportation 92
Electric energy, 2005
  Primary source of electricity .... Coal
  Net generation (billion kWh) 31.9
    percent from renewable sources 4.9%
  Net summer capability (million kW) 4.8
  CO_2 emitted from generation 32.8
Natural gas utilities, 2005
  Customers (x 1,000) 131
  Sales (trillion Btu) 33
  Revenues ($ mil) $247
Nuclear plants, 2007 0
Total CO_2 emitted (million metric tons) 50.7
Energy spending, 2004 ($ mil) $2,650
  per capita $4,167
  Price per million Btu $9.18

Transportation, 2006

Public road & street mileage 86,839
  Urban 1,870
  Rural 84,969
  Interstate 571
Vehicle miles of travel (millions) 7,890
  per capita 12,377.2
Total motor vehicle registrations 712,169
  Automobiles 345,502
  Trucks 364,080
  Motorcycles 25,353
Licensed drivers 468,711
  19 years & under 33,533
Deaths from motor vehicle accidents 111
Gasoline consumed (x 1,000 gallons) 352,308
  per capita 552.7

Commuting Statistics, 2006

Average commute time (min) 15.5
  Drove to work alone 79.3%
  Carpooled 9.2%
  Public transit 0.4%
  Walk to work 4.1%
  Work from home 5.8%

State Summary

Capital city . . . . Columbus
Governor. . . . . Ted Strickland

30th Floor
77 South High St
Columbus, OH 43215
614-466-3555

Admitted as a state 1803
Area (square miles) 44,825
Population, 2007 (estimate). 11,466,917
Largest city . . . . Columbus
Population, 2006. 733,203
Personal income per capita, 2006
(in current dollars) $33,338
Gross domestic product, 2006 ($ mil) . . . $461,302

Leading industries by payroll, 2005

Manufacturing, Health care/Social assistance,
Finance & Insurance

**Leading agricultural commodities
by receipts, 2005**

Soybeans, Corn, Dairy products, Greenhouse/
nursery, Cattle and calves

Geography & Environment

Total area (square miles). 44,825
land 40,948
water 3,877
Federally-owned land, 2004 (acres) 448,381
percent. 1.7%
Highest point . . . . Campbell Hill
elevation (feet) 1,550
Lowest point. Ohio River
elevation (feet) 455
General coastline (miles) 0
Tidal shoreline (miles) 0
Cropland, 2003 (x 1,000 acres) 11,243
Forest land, 2003 (x 1,000 acres). 7,225
Capital city . . . . Columbus
Population 2000 .711,470
Population 2006 733,203
Largest city . . . . Columbus
Population 2000 .711,470
Population 2006 733,203

Number of cities with over 100,000 population

1990 6
2000 6
2006 6

State park and recreation areas, 2005

Area (x 1,000 acres). 174
Number of visitors (x 1,000) 50,166
Revenues ($1,000) $27,667
percent of operating expenditures. 40.1%

National forest system land, 2007

Acres 238,984

Demographics & Population Characteristics

Population

1980 10,797,630
1990 10,847,115
2000 11,353,145
2006 11,478,006
Male. 5,597,677
Female. 5,880,329
Living in group quarters, 2006. 308,323
percent of total. 2.7%
2007 (estimate). 11,466,917
persons per square mile of land 280.0
2008 (projected). 11,541,279
2010 (projected). 11,576,181
2020 (projected). 11,644,058
2030 (projected). 11,550,528

**Population of Core-Based Statistical Areas
(formerly Metropolitan Areas), x 1,000**

	CBSA	Non-CBSA
1990	10,377	470
2000	10,849	504
2006	10,966	512

Change in population, 2000-2007

Number. 113,772
percent. 1.0%
Natural increase (births minus deaths) 302,012
Net internal migration . . . .-301,848
Net international migration 94,461

Persons by age, 2006

Under 5 years 734,735
5 to 17 years 2,035,300
18 years and over 8,707,971
65 years and over 1,531,994
85 years and over 216,992
Median age. 37.6

Persons by age, 2010 (projected)

Under 5 years 760,100
18 and over 8,831,750
65 and over 1,586,981
Median age. 38.1

Race, 2006

One Race
White. 9,747,752
Black or African American 1,377,161
Asian 177,215
American Indian/Alaska Native. 27,546
Hawaiian Native/Pacific Islander. 3,787
Two or more races. 144,545

Persons of Hispanic origin, 2006

Total Hispanic or Latino 265,762
Mexican. 137,456
Puerto Rican 69,657
Cuban 4,296

©2008 Information Publications, Inc.
All rights reserved. Photocopying prohibited.
877-544-INFO (4636) or www.informationpublications.com

Persons of Asian origin, 2006

Total Asian	175,000
Asian Indian	56,619
Chinese	43,167
Filipino	14,528
Japanese	9,117
Korean	12,036
Vietnamese	18,635

Marital status, 2006

Population 15 years & over	9,205,208
Never married	2,705,608
Married	4,797,458
Separated	164,304
Widowed	634,611
Divorced	1,067,531

Language spoken at home, 2006

Population 5 years and older	10,741,831
English only	10,079,739
Spanish	230,476
French	31,279
German	90,179
Chinese	35,071

Households & families, 2006

Households	4,499,506
with persons under 18 years	1,481,163
with persons over 65 years	1,068,490
persons per household	2.48
Families	2,953,361
persons per family	3.08
Married couples	2,202,145
Female householder, no husband present	563,407
One-person households	1,311,490

Nativity, 2006

Number of residents born in state	8,622,617
percent of population	75.1%

Immigration & naturalization, 2006

Legal permanent residents admitted	16,592
Persons naturalized	8,796
Non-immigrant admissions	243,902

Vital Statistics and Health

Marriages

2004	75,287
2005	74,453
2006	73,100

Divorces

2004	40,770
2005	40,181
2006	41,035

Health risks, 2006

Percent of adults who are:

Smokers	22.4%
Overweight (BMI > 25)	63.9%
Obese (BMI > 30)	28.4%

Births

2005	148,388
Birthrate (per 1,000)	12.9
White	120,507
Black	24,120
Hispanic	6,070
Asian/Pacific Islander	3,468
Amer. Indian/Alaska Native	293
Low birth weight (2,500g or less)	8.7%
Cesarian births	28.1%
Preterm births	13.0%
To unmarried mothers	38.9%
Twin births (per 1,000)	33.4
Triplets or higher order (per 100,000)	238.2
2006 (preliminary)	150,590
rate per 1,000	13.1

Deaths

2004

All causes	106,288
rate per 100,000	848.0
Heart disease	29,078
rate per 100,000	229.0
Malignant neoplasms	24,940
rate per 100,000	200.6
Cerebrovascular disease	6,501
rate per 100,000	50.9
Chronic lower respiratory disease	5,896
rate per 100,000	47.0
Diabetes	3,615
rate per 100,000	28.9
2005 (preliminary)	109,030
rate per 100,000	856.8
2006 (provisional)	106,977

Infant deaths

2004	1,143
rate per 1,000	7.7
2005 (provisional)	1,208
rate per 1,000	8.2

Exercise routines, 2005

None	25.6%
Moderate or greater	49.2%
Vigorous	27.2%

Abortions, 2004

Total performed in state	34,242
rate per 1,000 women age 15-44	14
% obtained by out-of-state residents	7.9%

Physicians, 2005

Total	30,096
rate per 100,000 persons	262

Community hospitals, 2005

Number of hospitals	170
Beds (x 1,000)	33.3
Patients admitted (x 1,000)	1,511
Average daily census (x 1,000)	21.4
Average cost per day	$1,673
Outpatient visits (x 1 mil)	31.3

©2008 Information Publications, Inc.
All rights reserved. Photocopying prohibited.
877-544-INFO (4636) or www.informationpublications.com

Disability status of population, 2006
5 to 15 years 7.4%
16 to 64 years 13.4%
65 years and over 39.8%

Education

Educational attainment, 2006
Population over 25 years 7,602,462
  Less than 9th grade. 3.6%
  High school graduate or more 86.2%
  College graduate or more. 23.0%
  Graduate or professional degree. 8.3%

Public school enrollment, 2005-06
Total 1,839,683
  Pre-kindergarten through grade 8. . . 1,261,331
  Grades 9 through 12 578,352

Graduating public high school seniors, 2004-05
Diplomas (incl. GED and others) 116,702

SAT scores, 2007
Average critical reading score 536
Average writing score 522
Average math score 542
Percent of graduates taking test 27%

Public school teachers, 2006-07 (estimate)
Total (x 1,000) 119.3
  Elementary 81.2
  Secondary 38.0
Average salary $51,937
  Elementary $51,937
  Secondary $51,937

State receipts & expenditures for public schools, 2006-07 (estimate)
Revenue receipts ($ mil) $21,510
Expenditures
Total ($ mil) $22,393
  Per capita $1,717
  Per pupil $11,947

NAEP proficiency scores, 2007
	Reading		Math	
	Basic	Proficient	Basic	Proficient
Grade 4	73.3%	36.3%	87.5%	45.9%
Grade 8	79.4%	35.9%	76.4%	35.4%

Higher education enrollment, fall 2005
Total 163,349
  Full-time men 53,803
  Full-time women 71,345
  Part-time men 13,676
  Part-time women. 24,525

Minority enrollment in institutions of higher education, 2005
Black, non-Hispanic 74,590
Hispanic 12,361
Asian/Pacific Islander 13,008
American Indian/Alaska Native. 2,439

Institutions of higher education, 2005-06
Total 200
  Public 61
  Private 139

Earned degrees conferred, 2004-05
Associate's 22,674
Bachelor's 56,969
Master's 20,360
First-professional. 3,398
Doctor's 2,018

Public Libraries, 2006
Number of libraries. 251
Number of outlets 788
Annual visits per capita 7.2
Circulation per capita. 15.0

State & local financial support for higher education, FY 2006
Full-time equivalent enrollment (x 1,000) 381.9
Appropriations per FTE. $4,690

Social Insurance & Welfare Programs

Social Security benefits & beneficiaries, 2005
Beneficiaries (x 1,000) 1,965
  Retired & dependents 1,352
  Survivors. 308
  Disabled & dependents. 305
Annual benefit payments ($ mil) $21,546
  Retired & dependents $14,077
  Survivors. $4,377
  Disabled & dependents. $3,091
Average monthly benefit
  Retired & dependents $1,016
  Disabled & dependents. $914
  Widowed. $1,000

Medicare, July 2005
Enrollment (x 1,000). 1,754
Payments ($ mil) $11,698

Medicaid, 2004
Beneficiaries (x 1,000). 1,896
Payments ($ mil) $11,375

State Children's Health Insurance Program, 2006
Enrollment (x 1,000). 218.5
Expenditures ($ mil) $236.1

Persons without health insurance, 2006
Number (x 1,000). 1,138
  percent. 10.1%
Number of children (x 1,000) 157
  percent of children 5.6%

Health care expenditures, 2004
Total expenditures. $65,622
  per capita $5,725

©2008 Information Publications, Inc.
All rights reserved. Photocopying prohibited.
877-544-INFO (4636) or www.informationpublications.com

Federal and state public aid

State unemployment insurance, 2006
Recipients, first payments (x 1,000) 275
Total payments ($ mil) $1,096
Average weekly benefit $287
Temporary Assistance for Needy Families, 2006
Recipients (x 1,000) .2,025.5
Families (x 1,000) 949.2
Supplemental Security Income, 2005
Recipients (x 1,000) 250.3
Payments ($ mil) $1,295.0
Food Stamp Program, 2006
Avg monthly participants (x 1,000) 1,063.9
Total benefits ($ mil) $1,266.2

Housing & Construction

Housing units
Total 2005 (estimate) 5,008,801
Total 2006 (estimate) 5,044,709
Seasonal or recreational use, 2006 47,088
Owner-occupied, 2006 3,150,239
   Median home value $135,200
   Homeowner vacancy rate 2.7%
Renter-occupied, 2006 1,349,267
   Median rent $627
   Rental vacancy rate 12.3%
Home ownership rate, 2005 . . . . 73.3%
Home ownership rate, 2006 . . . . 72.1%

New privately-owned housing units
Number authorized, 2006 (x 1,000) 34.4
   Value ($ mil) $5,920.0
Started 2005 (x 1,000, estimate) 49.7
Started 2006 (x 1,000, estimate) 48.8

Existing home sales
2005 (x 1,000) 286.9
2006 (x 1,000) 275.4

Government & Elections

State officials 2008
Governor . . . . Ted Strickland
   Democratic, term expires 1/11
Lieutenant Governor . . . . Lee Fisher
Secretary of State . . . . Jennifer Brunner
Attorney General . . . . Marc Dann
Chief Justice . . . . Thomas Moyer

Governorship
Minimum age 18
Length of term . . . . 4 years
Consecutive terms permitted . 8 out of any 12 yrs
Who succeeds . . . . Lieutenant Governor

Local governments by type, 2002
Total 3,636
   County 88
   Municipal 942
   Township 1,308
   School District 667
   Special District 631

State legislature

Name . . . . General Assembly
Upper chamber . . . . .Senate
   Number of members 33
   Length of term . . . . 4 years
   Party in majority, 2008 . . . . Republican
Lower chamber . . . . House of Representatives
   Number of members 99
   Length of term . . . . 2 years
   Party in majority, 2008 . . . . Republican

Federal representation, 2008 (110th Congress)
Senator . . . . George Voinovich
   Party . . . . Republican
   Year term expires 2011
Senator . . . . .Sherrod Brown
   Party . . . . .Democratic
   Year term expires 2013
Representatives, total 18
   Democrats 7
   Republicans 11

Voters in November 2006 election (estimate)
Total 4,408,448
   Male 2,051,155
   Female 2,357,293
   White 3,935,906
   Black 396,929
   Hispanic 38,736
   Asian 24,911

Presidential election, 2004
Total Popular Vote 5,627,908
   Kerry 2,741,167
   Bush 2,859,768
Total Electoral Votes 20

Votes cast for US Senators
2004
Total vote (x 1,000) 5,426
Leading party . . . . Republican
Percent for leading party 63.8%
2006
Total vote (x 1,000) .4,019
Leading party .Democratic
Percent for leading party 56.2%

Votes cast for US Representatives
2004
Total vote (x 1,000) .5,184
   Democratic 2,515
   Republican 2,650
Leading party . . . . Republican
Percent for leading party 51.1%
2006
Total vote (x 1,000) .3,961
   Democratic 2,082
   Republican 1,870
Leading party .Democratic
Percent for leading party 52.6%

©2008 Information Publications, Inc.
All rights reserved. Photocopying prohibited.
877-544-INFO (4636) or www.informationpublications.com

State government employment, 2006
Full-time equivalent employees 136,840
Payroll ($ mil) $520.5

Local government employment, 2006
Full-time equivalent employees 479,899
Payroll ($ mil) $1,680.1

Women holding public office, 2008
US Congress 5
Statewide elected office..................... 2
State legislature 22

Black public officials, 2002
Total.................................... 305
  US and state legislatures 21
  City/county/regional offices 197
  Judicial/law enforcement................. 35
  Education/school boards................. 52

Hispanic public officials, 2006
Total..................................... 4
  State executives & legislators 0
  City/county/regional offices 3
  Judicial/law enforcement.................. 1
  Education/school boards.................. 0

Governmental Finance

State government revenues, 2006
Total revenue (x $1,000)............$75,405,477
  per capita $6,577.87
General revenue (x $1,000) $51,349,846
  Intergovernmental 16,524,695
  Taxes 24,636,910
    general sales.................... 7,733,133
    individual income tax 9,859,712
    corporate income tax 1,102,351
  Current charges.................... 6,210,835
  Miscellaneous 3,977,406

State government expenditure, 2006
Total expenditure (x $1,000) $64,928,716
  per capita $5,663.95
General expenditure (x $1,000) $52,719,823
  per capita, total................... $4,598.92
    Education....................... 1,633.78
    Public welfare 1,397.69
    Health 213.02
    Hospitals....................... 170.18
    Highways 295.36
    Police protection.................. 20.97
    Corrections 140.01
    Natural resources 33.55
    Parks & recreation 9.38
    Governmental administration...... 170.62
    Interest on general debt........... 112.68

State debt & cash, 2006 ($ per capita)
Debt................................. $2,155.80
Cash/security holdings.............. $15,983.00

Federal government grants to state & local government, 2005 (x $1,000)
Total............................ $17,151,707
by Federal agency
  Defense 89,030
  Education 1,239,866
  Energy 79,687
  Environmental Protection Agency 157,037
  Health & Human Services......... 11,057,199
  Homeland Security............... 212,049
  Housing & Urban Development..... 1,323,892
  Justice 159,344
  Labor 324,831
  Transportation 1,363,161
  Veterans Affairs.................. 17,134

Crime & Law Enforcement

Crime, 2006 (rates per 100,000 residents)
Property crimes 422,235
  Burglary 104,426
  Larceny 280,384
  Motor vehicle theft 37,425
  Property crime rate................. 3,678.6
Violent crimes........................ 40,209
  Murder 539
  Forcible rape...................... 4,548
  Robbery......................... 19,149
  Aggravated assault 15,973
  Violent crime rate 350.3
Hate crimes........................... 350

Fraud and identity theft, 2006
Fraud complaints..................... 14,241
  rate per 100,000 residents 124.1
Identity theft complaints 6,878
  rate per 100,000 residents 59.9

Law enforcement agencies, 2006
Total agencies........................ 563
Total employees 29,607
  Officers 21,289
  Civilians 8,318

Prisoners, probation, and parole, 2006
Total prisoners........................ 49,166
  percent change, 12/31/05 to 12/31/06 .... 7.2%
  in private facilities 4.2%
  in local jails 0%
Sentenced to more than one year 49,166
  rate per 100,000 residents 428
Adults on probation 243,956
Adults on parole....................... 17,603

Prisoner demographics, June 30, 2005 (rate per 100,000 residents)
Male.................................. 1,040
Female 103
White................................. 344
Black................................. 2,196
Hispanic 613

©2008 Information Publications, Inc.
All rights reserved. Photocopying prohibited.
877-544-INFO (4636) or www.informationpublications.com

6   Ohio

Arrests, 2006
Total.............................. 235,005
   Persons under 18 years of age 38,509

Persons under sentence of death, 1/1/07
Total.................................. 191
   White.................................. 88
   Black 96
   Hispanic 3

State's highest court
Name ....Supreme Court
Number of members...................... 7
Length of term...................... 6 years
Intermediate appeals court? ....yes

Labor & Income

Civilian labor force, 2006 (x 1,000)
Total..................................5,975
   Men 3,121
   Women 2,854
   Persons 16-19 years.................. 344
   White................................5,163
   Black 649
   Hispanic 155

Civilian labor force as a percent of civilian non-institutional population, 2006
Total................................. 67.2%
   Men 73.1
   Women 61.7
   Persons 16-19 years.................53.0
   White................................67.3
   Black 66.7
   Hispanic 70.6

Employment, 2006 (x 1,000)
Total..................................5,652
   Men 2,938
   Women 2,714
   Persons 16-19 years................. 284
   White................................4,929
   Black 569
   Hispanic 144

Unemployment rate, 2006
Total................................. 5.4%
   Men 5.9
   Women 4.9
   Persons 16-19 years.................17.6
   White................................4.5
   Black 12.3
   Hispanic 7.2

Full-time/part-time labor force, 2003 (x 1,000)
Full-time labor force, employed 4,402
Part-time labor force, employed..........1,149
Unemployed, looking for
   Full-time work........................ 287
   Part-time work........................ 76
*Mean duration of unemployment (weeks)......*18.7
   Median 9.7

Labor unions, 2006
Membership (x 1,000)................... 734
   percent of employed 14.2%

Experienced civilian labor force by private industry, 2006
Total.............................4,562,713
   Natural resources & mining 24,906
   Construction 230,174
   Manufacturing......................795,610
   Trade, transportation & utilities 1,037,823
   Information 88,633
   Finance 298,788
   Professional & business 655,844
   Education & health 764,367
   Leisure & hospitality............... 500,612
   Other.......................... 163,682

Experienced civilian labor force by occupation, May 2006
Management.........................196,910
Business & financial 228,210
Legal................................. 32,050
Sales................................547,770
Office & admin. support............. 892,490
Computers & math 104,110
Architecture & engineering............89,730
Arts & entertainment................. 53,560
Education 316,110
Social services 58,530
Health care practitioner & technical.... 299,840
Health care support 175,320
Maintenance & repair................216,170
Construction 211,660
Transportation & moving 439,170
Production 589,000
Farming, fishing & forestry.............6,190

Hours and earnings of production workers on manufacturing payrolls, 2006
Average weekly hours 41.4
Average hourly earnings $19.16
Average weekly earnings $793.22

Income and poverty, 2006
Median household income............ $44,532
Personal income, per capita (current $)... $33,338
   in constant (2000) dollars $29,102
Persons below poverty level.............. 13.3%

Average annual pay
2006 .... $38,568
   increase from 2005 .... 3.3%

Federal individual income tax returns, 2005
Returns filed........................5,459,548
Adjusted gross income ($1,000) ... $252,434,762
Total tax liability ($1,000) $29,798,934

Charitable contributions, 2004
Number of contributions.............. 1,549.0
Total amount ($ mil)................$4,899.6

©2008 Information Publications, Inc.
All rights reserved. Photocopying prohibited.
877-544-INFO (4636) or www.informationpublications.com

Economy, Business, Industry & Agriculture

Fortune 500 companies, 2007 28
Bankruptcy cases filed, FY 2007 48,527

Patents and trademarks issued, 2007

Patents 3,058
Trademarks 2,869

Business firm ownership, 2002

Women-owned 229,972
 Sales ($ mil) $32,315
Black-owned 35,658
 Sales ($ mil) $3,600
Hispanic-owned 7,109
 Sales ($ mil) $1,263
Asian-owned 13,740
 Sales ($ mil) $5,106
Amer. Indian/Alaska Native-owned 3,123
 Sales ($ mil) $500
Hawaiian/Pacific Islander-owned 229
 Sales ($ mil) $28

Gross domestic product, 2006 ($ mil)

Total gross domestic product $461,302
 Agriculture, forestry, fishing and
  hunting 2,023
 Mining 2,173
 Utilities 9,822
 Construction 18,230
 Manufacturing, durable goods 60,493
 Manufacturing, non-durable goods . . . 28,827
 Wholesale trade 28,561
 Retail trade 30,957
 Transportation & warehousing 14,675
 Information 12,076
 Finance & insurance 38,331
 Real estate, rental & leasing 49,137
 Professional and technical services 25,444
 Educational services 3,521
 Health care and social assistance 37,037
 Accommodation/food services 9,979
 Other services, except government 10,579
 Government 49,507

Establishments, payroll, employees & receipts, by major industry group, 2005

Total 270,968
 Annual payroll ($1,000) $168,350,499
 Paid employees .4,762,618
Forestry, fishing & agriculture 298
 Annual payroll ($1,000) . . . . NA
 Paid employees . . . . NA
Mining 789
 Annual payroll ($1,000) $495,414
 Paid employees 10,051
 Receipts, 2002 ($1,000) $2,421,333

Utilities 593
 Annual payroll ($1,000) $2,039,541
 Paid employees .27,291
 Receipts, 2002 ($1,000) . . . . .NA
Construction 26,322
 Annual payroll ($1,000) $9,261,274
 Paid employees 214,948
 Receipts, 2002 ($1,000) $40,273,765
Manufacturing 16,617
 Annual payroll ($1,000) $35,677,361
 Paid employees 792,783
 Receipts, 2002 ($1,000) $243,903,865
Wholesale trade 15,545
 Annual payroll ($1,000) $11,276,311
 Paid employees 237,889
 Receipts, 2002 ($1,000) $166,446,529
Retail trade 40,949
 Annual payroll ($1,000) $12,465,820
 Paid employees 620,869
 Receipts, 2002 ($1,000) $119,778,409
Transportation & warehousing 7,583
 Annual payroll ($1,000) $6,118,482
 Paid employees 166,815
 Receipts, 2002 ($1,000) $15,546,563
Information 4,216
 Annual payroll ($1,000) $5,107,245
 Paid employees 99,458
 Receipts, 2002 ($1,000) . . . . .NA
Finance & insurance 18,403
 Annual payroll ($1,000) $13,685,220
 Paid employees 263,129
 Receipts, 2002 ($1,000) . . . . .NA
Professional, scientific & technical 25,597
 Annual payroll ($1,000) $12,704,427
 Paid employees 244,577
 Receipts, 2002 ($1,000) $24,241,958
Education 2,825
 Annual payroll ($1,000) $2,486,828
 Paid employees 103,175
 Receipts, 2002 ($1,000) $776,310
Health care & social assistance 26,961
 Annual payroll ($1,000) $24,680,904
 Paid employees 715,021
 Receipts, 2002 ($1,000) $50,262,849
Arts and entertainment 4,080
 Annual payroll ($1,000) $1,613,178
 Paid employees 59,680
 Receipts, 2002 ($1,000) $4,544,038
Real estate 10,581
 Annual payroll ($1,000) $2,272,201
 Paid employees 68,081
 Receipts, 2002 ($1,000) $9,768,869
Accommodation & food service 23,337
 Annual payroll ($1,000) $4,799,826
 Paid employees 430,134
 Receipts, 2002 ($1,000) $14,875,890

©2008 Information Publications, Inc.
All rights reserved. Photocopying prohibited.
877-544-INFO (4636) or www.informationpublications.com

Exports, 2006

Value of exported goods ($ mil) $37,833
   Manufactured $34,588
   Non-manufactured $1,257

Foreign direct investment in US affiliates, 2004

Property, plants & equipment ($ mil) . . . $32,898
Employment (x 1,000) 203.6

Agriculture, 2006

Number of farms 76,200
Farm acreage (x 1,000) 14,300
   Acres per farm 188
Farm marketings and income ($ mil)
Total $5,479.7
   Crops $3,448.4
   Livestock $2,031.3
Net farm income $1,614.4

Principal commodities, in order by marketing receipts, 2005

Soybeans, Corn, Dairy products, Greenhouse/
   nursery, Cattle and calves

Federal economic activity in state

Expenditures, 2005 ($ mil)
   Total $77,881
      Per capita $6,789.55
   Defense $8,243
   Non-defense $69,638
Defense department, 2006 ($ mil)
   Payroll $3,030
   Contract awards $5,980
   Grants $97
Homeland security grants ($1,000)
   2006 . . . . $41,347
   2007 . . . . $46,321

FDIC-insured financial institutions, 2005

Number 276
Assets ($ billion) $1,874.7
Deposits ($ billion) $1,105.5

Fishing, 2006

Catch (x 1,000 lbs) 4,242
Value ($1,000) $4,169

Mining, 2006 ($ mil)

Total non-fuel mineral production $1,260
Percent of U.S. 1.96%

Communication, Energy & Transportation

Communication

Households with computers, 2003 . . . . .58.8%
Households with internet access, 2003 . . . . 52.5%
High-speed internet providers 81
Total high-speed internet lines 3,186,537
   Residential 2,141,752
   Business 1,044,785
Wireless phone customers, 12/2006 8,380,138

FCC-licensed stations (as of January 1, 2008)

TV stations 52
FM radio stations 307
AM radio stations 124

Energy

Energy consumption, 2004
   Total (trillion Btu) 4,023
   Per capita (million Btu) 351.0
By source of production (trillion Btu)
   Coal 1,391
   Natural gas 845
   Petroleum 1,368
   Nuclear electric power 166
   Hydroelectric power 7
By end-use sector (trillion Btu)
   Residential 942
   Commercial 705
   Industrial 1,360
   Transportation .1,016
Electric energy, 2005
   Primary source of electricity . . . . Coal
   Net generation (billion kWh) 157.0
      percent from renewable sources 0.6%
   Net summer capability (million kW) 33.9
   CO_2 emitted from generation 131.8
Natural gas utilities, 2005
   Customers (x 1,000) 3,558
   Sales (trillion Btu) 807
   Revenues ($ mil) $3,605
Nuclear plants, 2007 2
Total CO_2 emitted (million metric tons) 265.5
Energy spending, 2004 ($ mil) $34,944
   per capita $3,049
   Price per million Btu $12.85

Transportation, 2006

Public road & street mileage 125,107
   Urban 44,594
   Rural 80,513
   Interstate 1,574
Vehicle miles of travel (millions) 111,247
   per capita 9,704.4
Total motor vehicle registrations 10,828,843
   Automobiles 6,438,988
   Trucks 4,345,371
   Motorcycles 332,275
Licensed drivers 7,739,410
   19 years & under 379,645
Deaths from motor vehicle accidents 1,238
Gasoline consumed (x 1,000 gallons) . . . 5,204,068
   per capita 454.0

Commuting Statistics, 2006

Average commute time (min) 22.1
   Drove to work alone 83.1%
   Carpooled 8.3%
   Public transit 2.0%
   Walk to work 2.5%
   Work from home 3.1%

©2008 Information Publications, Inc.
All rights reserved. Photocopying prohibited.
877-544-INFO (4636) or www.informationpublications.com

State Summary

Capital city . . . . Oklahoma City
Governor . . . . Brad Henry

Capitol Building
2300 N Lincoln Blvd, Room 212
Oklahoma City, OK 73105
405-521-2342

Admitted as a state 1907
Area (square miles) 69,898
Population, 2007 (estimate). 3,617,316
Largest city . . . . Oklahoma City
  Population, 2006 537,734
Personal income per capita, 2006
  (in current dollars) $32,210
Gross domestic product, 2006 ($ mil) . . . $134,651

Leading industries by payroll, 2005

  Health care/Social assistance, Manufacturing,
  Retail trade

**Leading agricultural commodities
by receipts, 2005**

  Cattle and calves, Hogs, Broilers, Wheat, Dairy
  products

Geography & Environment

Total area (square miles) 69,898
  land 68,667
  water 1,231
Federally-owned land, 2004 (acres) 1,586,148
  percent 3.6%
Highest point . . . . Black Mesa
  elevation (feet) 4,973
Lowest point . . . . Little River
  elevation (feet) 289
General coastline (miles) 0
Tidal shoreline (miles) 0
Cropland, 2003 (x 1,000 acres) 8,971
Forest land, 2003 (x 1,000 acres) 7,368
Capital city . . . . Oklahoma City
  Population 2000 506,132
  Population 2006 537,734
Largest city . . . . Oklahoma City
  Population 2000 506,132
  Population 2006 537,734

Number of cities with over 100,000 population

1990 2
2000 2
2006 3

State park and recreation areas, 2005

Area (x 1,000 acres) 72
Number of visitors (x 1,000) 13,282
Revenues ($1,000) $23,260
  percent of operating expenditures 58.9%

National forest system land, 2007

Acres 400,768

Demographics & Population Characteristics

Population

1980 3,025,290
1990 3,145,585
2000 3,450,652
2006 3,579,212
  Male 1,764,514
  Female 1,814,698
Living in group quarters, 2006 111,393
  percent of total 3.1%
2007 (estimate) 3,617,316
  persons per square mile of land 52.7
2008 (projected) 3,563,865
2010 (projected) 3,591,516
2020 (projected) 3,735,690
2030 (projected) 3,913,251

**Population of Core-Based Statistical Areas
(formerly Metropolitan Areas), x 1,000**

	CBSA	Non-CBSA
1990	2,610	536
2000	2,891	560
2006	3,018	561

Change in population, 2000-2007

Number 166,662
  percent 4.8%
Natural increase (births minus deaths) 120,981
Net internal migration 11,901
Net international migration 42,146

Persons by age, 2006

Under 5 years 254,718
5 to 17 years 639,316
18 years and over 2,685,178
65 years and over 473,545
85 years and over 65,571
  Median age 36.0

Persons by age, 2010 (projected)

Under 5 years 254,682
18 and over 2,696,443
65 and over 494,966
  Median age 36.8

Race, 2006

One Race
  White 2,803,755
  Black or African American 278,849
  Asian 60,201
  American Indian/Alaska Native 287,728
  Hawaiian Native/Pacific Islander 3,429
Two or more races 145,250

Persons of Hispanic origin, 2006

Total Hispanic or Latino 244,822
  Mexican 201,317
  Puerto Rican 8,349
  Cuban 1,727

©2008 Information Publications, Inc.
All rights reserved. Photocopying prohibited.
877-544-INFO (4636) or www.informationpublications.com

Persons of Asian origin, 2006

Total Asian 59,164
  Asian Indian. 11,196
  Chinese 8,292
  Filipino 5,142
  Japanese 2,694
  Korean. 5,812
  Vietnamese. 16,678

Marital status, 2006

Population 15 years & over 2,839,257
  Never married 721,736
  Married. 1,551,528
  Separated 62,155
  Widowed. 201,617
  Divorced 364,376

Language spoken at home, 2006

Population 5 years and older. 3,327,159
  English only 3,050,113
  Spanish 173,552
  French 5,359
  German. 11,900
  Chinese 6,325

Households & families, 2006

Households. 1,385,300
  with persons under 18 years 474,844
  with persons over 65 years. 334,153
  persons per household 2.50
Families. 927,086
  persons per family. 3.07
Married couples. 699,421
Female householder,
  no husband present. 164,547
One-person households 392,304

Nativity, 2006

Number of residents born in state 2,207,194
  percent of population. 61.7%

Immigration & naturalization, 2006

Legal permanent residents admitted 4,591
Persons naturalized 2,246
Non-immigrant admissions 65,802

Vital Statistics and Health

Marriages

2004 22,812
2005 25,755
2006 26,266

Divorces

2004 17,146
2005 19,966
2006 19,023

Health risks, 2006

Percent of adults who are:
  Smokers. 25.1%
  Overweight (BMI > 25). 64.8%
  Obese (BMI > 30). 28.8%

Births

2005 51,801
  Birthrate (per 1,000). 14.6
  White. 40,036
  Black 4,821
  Hispanic 6,275
  Asian/Pacific Islander 1,090
  Amer. Indian/Alaska Native 5,854
  Low birth weight (2,500g or less) 8.0%
  Cesarian births 32.5%
  Preterm births 13.1%
  To unmarried mothers. 39.1%
  Twin births (per 1,000) 27.4
  Triplets or higher order (per 100,000). 92.8
2006 (preliminary). 54,018
  rate per 1,000 . . . . .15.1

Deaths

2004
All causes 34,483
  rate per 100,000. . . . . .947.7
Heart disease 10,335
  rate per 100,000. . . . . 284.3
Malignant neoplasms 7,269
  rate per 100,000. . . . . .196.2
Cerebrovascular disease. 2,183
  rate per 100,000. . . . . .60.6
Chronic lower respiratory disease 1,985
  rate per 100,000. . . . . .54.0
Diabetes. 1,139
  rate per 100,000. . . . . .31.0
2005 (preliminary). 36,181
  rate per 100,000. . . . . 980.8
2006 (provisional) 35,585

Infant deaths

2004 411
  rate per 1,000 . . . . .8.0
2005 (provisional) 422
  rate per 1,000 . . . . .8.1

Exercise routines, 2005

None. 30.6%
Moderate or greater. 42.3%
Vigorous 22.5%

Abortions, 2004

Total performed in state. 6,712
  rate per 1,000 women age 15-44. 9
  % obtained by out-of-state residents 7.2%

Physicians, 2005

Total. 6,041
  rate per 100,000 persons 170

Community hospitals, 2005

Number of hospitals 110
Beds (x 1,000). 10.8
Patients admitted (x 1,000) 457
Average daily census (x 1,000) 6.4
Average cost per day $1,332
Outpatient visits (x 1 mil) 5.4

©2008 Information Publications, Inc.
All rights reserved. Photocopying prohibited.
877-544-INFO (4636) or www.informationpublications.com

Disability status of population, 2006

5 to 15 years 7.5%
16 to 64 years 17.0%
65 years and over 46.8%

Education

Educational attainment, 2006

Population over 25 years 2,312,121
   Less than 9th grade. 5.2%
   High school graduate or more 84.3%
   College graduate or more. 22.1%
   Graduate or professional degree. 7.2%

Public school enrollment, 2005-06

Total. 634,739
   Pre-kindergarten through grade 8. . . . 454,254
   Grades 9 through 12 176,683

Graduating public high school seniors, 2004-05

Diplomas (incl. GED and others) 36,227

SAT scores, 2007

Average critical reading score 578
Average writing score 559
Average math score 571
Percent of graduates taking test 6%

Public school teachers, 2006-07 (estimate)

Total (x 1,000) 42.2
   Elementary 21.2
   Secondary 21.0
Average salary $42,379
   Elementary $41,597
   Secondary $43,166

State receipts & expenditures for public schools, 2006-07 (estimate)

Revenue receipts ($ mil) $5,054
Expenditures
Total ($ mil) $5,041
   Per capita $1,265
   Per pupil $7,593

NAEP proficiency scores, 2007

	Reading		Math	
	Basic	Proficient	Basic	Proficient
Grade 4	65.0%	26.8%	82.4%	32.6%
Grade 8	72.1%	26.1%	66.1%	21.3%

Higher education enrollment, fall 2005

Total. 28,828
   Full-time men 11,370
   Full-time women 12,717
   Part-time men 2,142
   Part-time women. 2,599

Minority enrollment in institutions of higher education, 2005

Black, non-Hispanic 19,039
Hispanic 7,272
Asian/Pacific Islander 4,742
American Indian/Alaska Native. 21,158

Institutions of higher education, 2005-06

Total. 57
   Public. 29
   Private 28

Earned degrees conferred, 2004-05

Associate's. 9,243
Bachelor's 18,266
Master's 5,719
First-professional. 1,094
Doctor's 413

Public Libraries, 2006

Number of libraries. 113
Number of outlets 208
Annual visits per capita 4.6
Circulation per capita. 6.9

State & local financial support for higher education, FY 2006

Full-time equivalent enrollment (x 1,000) 134.9
Appropriations per FTE. $5,638

Social Insurance & Welfare Programs

Social Security benefits & beneficiaries, 2005

Beneficiaries (x 1,000) 635
   Retired & dependents. 427
   Survivors. 94
   Disabled & dependents. 114
Annual benefit payments ($ mil) $6,606
   Retired & dependents. $4,226
   Survivors. $1,227
   Disabled & dependents. $1,152
Average monthly benefit
   Retired & dependents. $962
   Disabled & dependents. $924
   Widowed. $939

Medicare, July 2005

Enrollment (x 1,000). 541
Payments ($ mil) $3,769

Medicaid, 2004

Beneficiaries (x 1,000). 654
Payments ($ mil) $2,335

State Children's Health Insurance Program, 2006

Enrollment (x 1,000) 116.0
Expenditures ($ mil) $105.0

Persons without health insurance, 2006

Number (x 1,000). 661
   percent. 18.9%
Number of children (x 1,000) 114
   percent of children 12.5%

Health care expenditures, 2004

Total expenditures. $17,323
   per capita $4,917

©2008 Information Publications, Inc.
All rights reserved. Photocopying prohibited.
877-544-INFO (4636) or www.informationpublications.com

Federal and state public aid

State unemployment insurance, 2006
Recipients, first payments (x 1,000) 41
Total payments ($ mil) $140
Average weekly benefit $233
Temporary Assistance for Needy Families, 2006
Recipients (x 1,000) 257.8
Families (x 1,000) 118.1
Supplemental Security Income, 2005
Recipients (x 1,000) 79.6
Payments ($ mil) $380.6
Food Stamp Program, 2006
Avg monthly participants (x 1,000) 435.5
Total benefits ($ mil) $467.3

Housing & Construction

Housing units

Total 2005 (estimate) 1,589,349
Total 2006 (estimate) 1,607,349
Seasonal or recreational use, 2006 34,345
Owner-occupied, 2006 950,407
   Median home value $94,500
   Homeowner vacancy rate 2.4%
Renter-occupied, 2006 434,893
   Median rent $580
   Rental vacancy rate 11.2%
Home ownership rate, 2005 . . . . .72.9%
Home ownership rate, 2006 . . . . 71.6%

New privately-owned housing units

Number authorized, 2006 (x 1,000) 15.8
   Value ($ mil) $2,322.2
Started 2005 (x 1,000, estimate) 14.3
Started 2006 (x 1,000, estimate) 14.2

Existing home sales

2005 (x 1,000) 104.6
2006 (x 1,000) 106.0

Government & Elections

State officials 2008

Governor . . . . .Brad Henry
          Democratic, term expires 1/11
Lieutenant Governor . . . . Jari Askins
Secretary of State . . . . M. Susan Savage
Attorney General . . . . . . W. A. Drew Edmondson
Chief Justice . . . . James Winchester

Governorship

Minimum age 31
Length of term . . . . 4 years
Consecutive terms permitted 2
Who succeeds . . . . Lieutenant Governor

Local governments by type, 2002

Total 1,798
   County 77
   Municipal 590
   Township 0
   School District 571
   Special District 560

State legislature

Name . . . . Legislature
Upper chamber . . . . .Senate
   Number of members 48
   Length of term . . . . 4 years
   Party in majority, 2008 . . . . 50/50
Lower chamber . . . . House of Representatives
   Number of members 101
   Length of term . . . . 2 years
   Party in majority, 2008 . . . . Republican

Federal representation, 2008 (110th Congress)

Senator . . . . .James Inhofe
   Party . . . . Republican
   Year term expires 2009
Senator . . . . .Tom Coburn
   Party . . . . Republican
   Year term expires 2011
Representatives, total 5
   Democrats 1
   Republicans 4

Voters in November 2006 election (estimate)

Total 1,173,627
   Male 560,684
   Female 612,943
   White 994,791
   Black 71,533
   Hispanic 14,169
   Asian 2,411

Presidential election, 2004

Total Popular Vote 1,463,758
   Kerry 503,966
   Bush 959,792
Total Electoral Votes 7

Votes cast for US Senators

2004
Total vote (x 1,000) 1,447
Leading party . . . . Republican
Percent for leading party 52.8%
2006
Total vote (x 1,000) . . . . NA
Leading party . . . . NA
Percent for leading party . . . . NA

Votes cast for US Representatives

2004
Total vote (x 1,000) 1,375
   Democratic 389
   Republican 875
Leading party . . . . Republican
Percent for leading party 63.7%
2006
Total vote (x 1,000) 905
   Democratic 373
   Republican 518
Leading party . . . . Republican
Percent for leading party 57.2%

©2008 Information Publications, Inc.
All rights reserved. Photocopying prohibited.
877-544-INFO (4636) or www.informationpublications.com

State government employment, 2006
Full-time equivalent employees 67,424
Payroll ($ mil) $217.8

Local government employment, 2006
Full-time equivalent employees 146,919
Payroll ($ mil) $389.9

Women holding public office, 2008
US Congress.............................. 1
Statewide elected office..................... 3
State legislature........................... 19

Black public officials, 2002
Total................................... 115
　US and state legislatures 6
　City/county/regional offices 85
　Judicial/law enforcement.................. 4
　Education/school boards 20

Hispanic public officials, 2006
Total.................................... 1
　State executives & legislators 0
　City/county/regional offices 0
　Judicial/law enforcement.................. 0
　Education/school boards.................. 1

Governmental Finance

State government revenues, 2006
Total revenue (x $1,000)........... $19,617,971
　per capita $5,483.65
General revenue (x $1,000) $16,233,400
　Intergovernmental 5,150,393
　Taxes 7,784,453
　　general sales....................1,799,947
　　individual income tax 2,658,272
　　corporate income tax............. 231,206
　Current charges....................1,813,668
　Miscellaneous 1,484,886

State government expenditure, 2006
Total expenditure (x $1,000) $16,882,365
　per capita $4,718.99
General expenditure (x $1,000) $14,766,688
　per capita, total.................. *$4,127.61*
　　Education 1,708.78
　　Public welfare 1,146.91
　　Health 167.52
　　Hospitals........................ 48.06
　　Highways 333.43
　　Police protection.................40.72
　　Corrections 156.32
　　Natural resources 61.17
　　Parks & recreation................27.51
　　Governmental administration.......133.99
　　Interest on general debt............139.62

State debt & cash, 2006 ($ per capita)
Debt $2,274.76
Cash/security holdings...............$9,026.85

Federal government grants to state & local government, 2005 (x $1,000)
Total.............................$5,501,741
by Federal agency
　Defense 31,135
　Education 538,914
　Energy............................. 10,508
　Environmental Protection Agency 79,502
　Health & Human Services. 2,947,723
　Homeland Security....................21,093
　Housing & Urban Development.......391,628
　Justice 87,181
　Labor 72,326
　Transportation 731,787
　Veterans Affairs.................... 30,470

Crime & Law Enforcement

Crime, 2006 (rates per 100,000 residents)
Property crimes 129,002
　Burglary 34,377
　Larceny 81,267
　Motor vehicle theft 13,358
　Property crime rate.................3,604.2
Violent crimes.........................17,803
　Murder 207
　Forcible rape........................1,488
　Robbery...........................3,133
　Aggravated assault 12,975
　Violent crime rate 497.4
Hate crimes 76

Fraud and identity theft, 2006
Fraud complaints......................3,711
　rate per 100,000 residents 103.7
Identity theft complaints 2,254
　rate per 100,000 residents 63.0

Law enforcement agencies, 2006
Total agencies........................... 296
Total employees 11,001
　Officers 7,058
　Civilians 3,943

Prisoners, probation, and parole, 2006
Total prisoners....................... 26,243
　percent change, 12/31/05 to 12/31/06 ... -1.6%
　in private facilities 21.8%
　in local jails 7.4%
Sentenced to more than one year 23,889
　rate per 100,000 residents 664
Adults on probation 27,415
Adults on parole......................3,072

Prisoner demographics, June 30, 2005 (rate per 100,000 residents)
Male.................................1,645
Female.............................. 209
White 740
Black...............................3,252
Hispanic 832

©2008 Information Publications, Inc.
All rights reserved. Photocopying prohibited.
877-544-INFO (4636) or www.informationpublications.com

6   Oklahoma

Arrests, 2006
Total.................................145,171
   Persons under 18 years of age.........20,192

Persons under sentence of death, 1/1/07
Total.................................. 88
   White.............................. 48
   Black 33
   Hispanic 3

State's highest court
Name ....Supreme Court
Number of members....................... 9
Length of term........................ 6 years
Intermediate appeals court? ....yes

Labor & Income

Civilian labor force, 2006 (x 1,000)
Total.................................1,733
   Men 936
   Women 797
   Persons 16-19 years.................. 98
   White.............................1,380
   Black 113
   Hispanic 91

Civilian labor force as a percent of civilian non-institutional population, 2006
Total................................ 63.4%
   Men 70.8
   Women 56.4
   Persons 16-19 years..................43.8
   White............................. 64.3
   Black 58.9
   Hispanic 71.9

Employment, 2006 (x 1,000)
Total.................................1,666
   Men 894
   Women 771
   Persons 16-19 years................. 86
   White.............................1,334
   Black 104
   Hispanic 85

Unemployment rate, 2006
Total................................. 3.9%
   Men 4.4
   Women 3.2
   Persons 16-19 years.................12.1
   White.............................3.3
   Black 8.2
   Hispanic 6.2

Full-time/part-time labor force, 2003 (x 1,000)
Full-time labor force, employed 1,324
Part-time labor force, employed............ 276
Unemployed, looking for
   Full-time work......................... 82
   Part-time work........................ 14
*Mean duration of unemployment (weeks)......*18.0
   Median 9.0

Labor unions, 2006
Membership (x 1,000)..................... 93
   percent of employed 6.4%

Experienced civilian labor force by private industry, 2006
Total.............................1,192,548
   Natural resources & mining 49,326
   Construction 70,437
   Manufacturing....................149,313
   Trade, transportation & utilities 282,549
   Information 29,884
   Finance 80,656
   Professional & business 175,854
   Education & health 180,309
   Leisure & hospitality................137,104
   Other............................ 36,164

Experienced civilian labor force by occupation, May 2006
Management.........................80,110
Business & financial 56,130
Legal.................................10,180
Sales................................149,190
Office & admin. support.............. 261,290
Computers & math 26,760
Architecture & engineering.............22,810
Arts & entertainment 14,350
Education 99,830
Social services 17,540
Health care practitioner & technical..... 82,680
Health care support 45,060
Maintenance & repair................. 72,460
Construction 82,550
Transportation & moving 104,700
Production 121,690
Farming, fishing & forestry............. 4,980

Hours and earnings of production workers on manufacturing payrolls, 2006
Average weekly hours.....................39.9
Average hourly earnings $14.77
Average weekly earnings $589.32

Income and poverty, 2006
Median household income............ $38,770
Personal income, per capita (current $)... $32,210
   in constant (2000) dollars $28,117
Persons below poverty level.............. 17.0%

Average annual pay
2006 .... $34,022
   increase from 2005 .... 7.3%

Federal individual income tax returns, 2005
Returns filed.......................1,495,579
Adjusted gross income ($1,000) $66,783,183
Total tax liability ($1,000) $8,223,215

Charitable contributions, 2004
Number of contributions................ 384.8
Total amount ($ mil)..................$1,848.9

©2008 Information Publications, Inc.
All rights reserved. Photocopying prohibited.
877-544-INFO (4636) or www.informationpublications.com

Economy, Business, Industry & Agriculture

Fortune 500 companies, 2007 4
Bankruptcy cases filed, FY 2007 8,966

Patents and trademarks issued, 2007

Patents 578
Trademarks 525

Business firm ownership, 2002

Women-owned 75,025
  Sales ($ mil) $9,255
Black-owned 7,441
  Sales ($ mil) $458
Hispanic-owned 5,442
  Sales ($ mil) $1,140
Asian-owned 4,583
  Sales ($ mil) $929
Amer. Indian/Alaska Native-owned 17,112
  Sales ($ mil) $2,531
Hawaiian/Pacific Islander-owned 282
  Sales ($ mil) $9

Gross domestic product, 2006 ($ mil)

Total gross domestic product $134,651
  Agriculture, forestry, fishing and
    hunting 2,035
  Mining 20,882
  Utilities 3,404
  Construction 5,162
  Manufacturing, durable goods 9,090
  Manufacturing, non-durable goods 4,909
  Wholesale trade 6,430
  Retail trade 8,967
  Transportation & warehousing 3,834
  Information 4,111
  Finance & insurance 5,818
  Real estate, rental & leasing 12,509
  Professional and technical services 5,478
  Educational services 647
  Health care and social assistance 8,545
  Accommodation/food services 2,852
  Other services, except government 2,849
  Government 20,551

Establishments, payroll, employees & receipts, by major industry group, 2005

Total 88,548
  Annual payroll ($1,000) $37,620,071
  Paid employees 1,220,285
Forestry, fishing & agriculture 179
  Annual payroll ($1,000) $26,964
  Paid employees 1,025
Mining 2,363
  Annual payroll ($1,000) $1,899,124
  Paid employees 31,155
  Receipts, 2002 ($1,000) $9,123,846

Utilities 390
  Annual payroll ($1,000) $513,603
  Paid employees 8,833
  Receipts, 2002 ($1,000) . . . . .NA
Construction 8,255
  Annual payroll ($1,000) $2,036,409
  Paid employees 61,415
  Receipts, 2002 ($1,000) $9,590,154
Manufacturing 3,865
  Annual payroll ($1,000) $5,556,517
  Paid employees 140,428
  Receipts, 2002 ($1,000) $39,924,050
Wholesale trade 4,616
  Annual payroll ($1,000) $2,311,890
  Paid employees 55,771
  Receipts, 2002 ($1,000) $30,799,789
Retail trade 13,727
  Annual payroll ($1,000) $3,350,298
  Paid employees 168,914
  Receipts, 2002 ($1,000) $32,112,960
Transportation & warehousing 2,591
  Annual payroll ($1,000) $1,280,244
  Paid employees 36,737
  Receipts, 2002 ($1,000) $4,649,332
Information 1,540
  Annual payroll ($1,000) $1,431,092
  Paid employees 34,298
  Receipts, 2002 ($1,000) . . . . .NA
Finance & insurance 6,309
  Annual payroll ($1,000) $2,359,868
  Paid employees 58,568
  Receipts, 2002 ($1,000) . . . . .NA
Professional, scientific & technical 8,926
  Annual payroll ($1,000) $2,718,604
  Paid employees 65,621
  Receipts, 2002 ($1,000) $5,833,528
Education 680
  Annual payroll ($1,000) $374,652
  Paid employees 17,960
  Receipts, 2002 ($1,000) $257,581
Health care & social assistance 9,753
  Annual payroll ($1,000) $5,821,233
  Paid employees 187,899
  Receipts, 2002 ($1,000) $12,432,870
Arts and entertainment 1,057
  Annual payroll ($1,000) $287,639
  Paid employees 15,758
  Receipts, 2002 ($1,000) $1,055,444
Real estate 3,795
  Annual payroll ($1,000) $641,194
  Paid employees 21,343
  Receipts, 2002 ($1,000) $2,381,396
Accommodation & food service 6,676
  Annual payroll ($1,000) $1,279,470
  Paid employees 121,362
  Receipts, 2002 ($1,000) $3,901,754

©2008 Information Publications, Inc.
All rights reserved. Photocopying prohibited.
877-544-INFO (4636) or www.informationpublications.com

8 Oklahoma

Exports, 2006
Value of exported goods ($ mil) $4,375
    Manufactured $3,803
    Non-manufactured $247

Foreign direct investment in US affiliates, 2004
Property, plants & equipment ($ mil) $8,222
Employment (x 1,000) 31.7

Agriculture, 2006
Number of farms 83,000
Farm acreage (x 1,000) 33,700
    Acres per farm 406
Farm marketings and income ($ mil)
Total $5,093.6
    Crops $974.1
    Livestock $4,119.5
Net farm income $876.5

Principal commodities, in order by marketing receipts, 2005
Cattle and calves, Hogs, Broilers, Wheat, Dairy
products

Federal economic activity in state
Expenditures, 2005 ($ mil)
    Total $27,637
        Per capita $7,799.37
    Defense $4,674
    Non-defense $22,963
Defense department, 2006 ($ mil)
    Payroll $3,260
    Contract awards $2,070
    Grants $33
Homeland security grants ($1,000)
    2006 . . . . $19,497
    2007 . . . . $14,198

FDIC-insured financial institutions, 2005
Number 264
Assets ($ billion) $67.3
Deposits ($ billion) $46.3

Fishing, 2006
Catch (x 1,000 lbs) . . . . NA
Value ($1,000) . . . . NA

Mining, 2006 ($ mil)
Total non-fuel mineral production $622
Percent of U.S. 0.97%

Communication, Energy & Transportation

Communication
Households with computers, 2003 . . . . 55.4%
Households with internet access, 2003 . . . . 48.4%
High-speed internet providers 69
Total high-speed internet lines 652,296
    Residential 585,745
    Business 66,551
Wireless phone customers, 12/2006 2,479,877

FCC-licensed stations (as of January 1, 2008)
TV stations 27
FM radio stations 169
AM radio stations 68

Energy
Energy consumption, 2004
    Total (trillion Btu) 1,486
    Per capita (million Btu) 421.8
By source of production (trillion Btu)
    Coal 372
    Natural gas 556
    Petroleum 533
    Nuclear electric power 0
    Hydroelectric power 30
By end-use sector (trillion Btu)
    Residential 289
    Commercial 230
    Industrial 554
    Transportation 413
Electric energy, 2005
    Primary source of electricity . . . . Coal
    Net generation (billion kWh) 68.6
        percent from renewable sources 5.5%
    Net summer capability (million kW) 19.8
    CO_2 emitted from generation 51.5
Natural gas utilities, 2005
    Customers (x 1,000) 962
    Sales (trillion Btu) 253
    Revenues ($ mil) $1,023
Nuclear plants, 2007 0
Total CO_2 emitted (million metric tons) 103.3
Energy spending, 2004 ($ mil) $11,274
    per capita $3,200
    Price per million Btu $12.24

Transportation, 2006
Public road & street mileage 113,085
    Urban 15,640
    Rural 97,445
    Interstate 933
Vehicle miles of travel (millions) 48,689
    per capita 13,609.6
Total motor vehicle registrations 3,201,831
    Automobiles 1,606,517
    Trucks 1,576,680
    Motorcycles 94,280
Licensed drivers 2,264,151
    19 years & under 159,696
Deaths from motor vehicle accidents 765
Gasoline consumed (x 1,000 gallons) 1,868,948
    per capita 522.4

Commuting Statistics, 2006
Average commute time (min) 20.0
    Drove to work alone 80.4%
    Carpooled 11.6%
    Public transit 0.5%
    Walk to work 2.1%
    Work from home 3.7%

©2008 Information Publications, Inc.
All rights reserved. Photocopying prohibited.
877-544-INFO (4636) or www.informationpublications.com

State Summary

Capital city . . . . Salem
Governor . . . . Ted Kulongoski

State Capitol
Room 160, 900 Court St N
Salem, OR 97301
503-378-4582

Admitted as a state 1859
Area (square miles) 98,381
Population, 2007 (estimate) 3,747,455
Largest city . . . . Portland
Population, 2006 537,081
Personal income per capita, 2006
(in current dollars) $33,666
Gross domestic product, 2006 ($ mil) . . . $151,301

Leading industries by payroll, 2005

Manufacturing, Health care/Social assistance,
Retail trade

Leading agricultural commodities by receipts, 2005

Greenhouse/nursery, Cattle and calves, Dairy
products, Hay, Ryegrass

Geography & Environment

Total area (square miles) 98,381
land 95,997
water 2,384
Federally-owned land, 2004 (acres) . . . 32,715,514
percent 53.1%
Highest point . . . . Mt. Hood
elevation (feet) 11,239
Lowest point . . . . Pacific Ocean
elevation (feet) . . . . sea level
General coastline (miles) 26
Tidal shoreline (miles) 1,410
Cropland, 2003 (x 1,000 acres) 3,701
Forest land, 2003 (x 1,000 acres) 12,734
Capital city . . . . Salem
Population 2000 136,924
Population 2006 152,239
Largest city . . . . Portland
Population 2000 529,121
Population 2006 537,081

Number of cities with over 100,000 population

1990 3
2000 3
2006 3

State park and recreation areas, 2005

Area (x 1,000 acres) 97
Number of visitors (x 1,000) 42,420
Revenues ($1,000) $15,384
percent of operating expenditures 37.0%

National forest system land, 2007

Acres 15,667,657

Demographics & Population Characteristics

Population

1980 2,633,105
1990 2,842,321
2000 3,421,436
2006 3,700,758
Male 1,839,688
Female 1,861,070
Living in group quarters, 2006 79,987
percent of total 2.2%
2007 (estimate) 3,747,455
persons per square mile of land 39.0
2008 (projected) 3,709,778
2010 (projected) 3,790,996
2020 (projected) 4,260,393
2030 (projected) 4,833,918

Population of Core-Based Statistical Areas (formerly Metropolitan Areas), x 1,000

	CBSA	Non-CBSA
1990	2,719	123
2000	3,281	140
2006	3,559	142

Change in population, 2000-2007

Number 326,019
percent 9.5%
Natural increase (births minus deaths) 113,876
Net internal migration 136,376
Net international migration 91,629

Persons by age, 2006

Under 5 years 230,660
5 to 17 years 625,599
18 years and over 2,844,499
65 years and over 478,180
85 years and over 70,969
Median age 37.5

Persons by age, 2010 (projected)

Under 5 years 249,899
18 and over 2,927,830
65 and over 494,328
Median age 37.6

Race, 2006

One Race
White 3,348,473
Black or African American 68,610
Asian 133,740
American Indian/Alaska Native 51,209
Hawaiian Native/Pacific Islander 10,277
Two or more races 88,449

Persons of Hispanic origin, 2006

Total Hispanic or Latino 379,034
Mexican 317,961
Puerto Rican 5,811
Cuban 2,320

©2008 Information Publications, Inc.
All rights reserved. Photocopying prohibited.
877-544-INFO (4636) or www.informationpublications.com

Persons of Asian origin, 2006
Total Asian 135,746
   Asian Indian. 13,454
   Chinese 29,717
   Filipino 17,776
   Japanese 14,254
   Korean. 19,910
   Vietnamese. 23,875

Marital status, 2006
Population 15 years & over 2,998,516
   Never married 854,994
   Married. 1,586,184
   Separated 55,623
   Widowed. 172,577
   Divorced 384,761

Language spoken at home, 2006
Population 5 years and older. 3,470,802
   English only 2,979,226
   Spanish 293,840
   French 10,909
   German. 21,410
   Chinese 24,046

Households & families, 2006
Households. 1,449,662
   with persons under 18 years 452,328
   with persons over 65 years. 330,756
   persons per household 2.50
Families. 927,071
   persons per family. 3.07
Married couples. 719,045
Female householder,
   no husband present. 147,864
One-person households 405,897

Nativity, 2006
Number of residents born in state 1,666,564
   percent of population. 45.0%

Immigration & naturalization, 2006
Legal permanent residents admitted. 9,192
Persons naturalized 4,332
Non-immigrant admissions 127,637

Vital Statistics and Health

Marriages
2004 29,040
2005 26,471
2006 26,888

Divorces
2004 14,774
2005 15,033
2006 14,214

Health risks, 2006
Percent of adults who are:
   Smokers. 18.5%
   Overweight (BMI > 25). 60.7%
   Obese (BMI > 30). 24.8%

Births
2005 45,922
   Birthrate (per 1,000). 12.6
   White. 41,561
   Black 1,011
   Hispanic 9,165
   Asian/Pacific Islander 2,502
   Amer. Indian/Alaska Native 848
   Low birth weight (2,500g or less) 6.1%
   Cesarian births 27.6%
   Preterm births 10.2%
   To unmarried mothers. 33.3%
   Twin births (per 1,000) 29.8
   Triplets or higher order (per 100,000). . . .104.0
2006 (preliminary). 48,717
   rate per 1,000 . . . . .13.2

Deaths
2004
All causes 30,313
   rate per 100,000 .777.7
Heart disease 6,725
   rate per 100,000 .169.3
Malignant neoplasms 7,236
   rate per 100,000 .189.6
Cerebrovascular disease. 2,328
   rate per 100,000 . . . . .58.2
Chronic lower respiratory disease 1,778
   rate per 100,000 . . . . .46.7
Diabetes. 1,073
   rate per 100,000 . . . . .27.9
2005 (preliminary). 31,099
   rate per 100,000 .773.7
2006 (provisional) .31,361

Infant deaths
2004 251
   rate per 1,000 . . . . .5.5
2005 (provisional) 265
   rate per 1,000 . . . . .5.8

Exercise routines, 2005
None. 18.6%
Moderate or greater. 56.4%
Vigorous 30.7%

Abortions, 2004
Total performed in state. 11,443
   rate per 1,000 women age 15-44 16
   % obtained by out-of-state residents 10.9%

Physicians, 2005
Total. 9,684
   rate per 100,000 persons 266

Community hospitals, 2005
Number of hospitals 58
Beds (x 1,000). 6.5
Patients admitted (x 1,000) 336
Average daily census (x 1,000) 4.1
Average cost per day $2,062
Outpatient visits (x 1 mil) 8.0

©2008 Information Publications, Inc.
All rights reserved. Photocopying prohibited.
877-544-INFO (4636) or www.informationpublications.com

Disability status of population, 2006
5 to 15 years 6.5%
16 to 64 years 13.8%
65 years and over 41.0%

Education

Educational attainment, 2006
Population over 25 years 2,501,372
   Less than 9th grade................... 4.7%
   High school graduate or more 87.6%
   College graduate or more............. 27.5%
   Graduate or professional degree....... 10.0%

Public school enrollment, 2005-06
Total............................... 552,194
   Pre-kindergarten through grade 8.... 378,892
   Grades 9 through 12 172,185

Graduating public high school seniors, 2004-05
Diplomas (incl. GED and others) 36,868

SAT scores, 2007
Average critical reading score.............. 522
Average writing score 502
Average math score 526
Percent of graduates taking test 54%

Public school teachers, 2006-07 (estimate)
Total (x 1,000) 29.3
   Elementary...........................18.9
   Secondary............................10.4
Average salary $50,911
   Elementary........................ $50,679
   Secondary......................... $51,349

State receipts & expenditures for public schools, 2006-07 (estimate)
Revenue receipts ($ mil) $5,742
Expenditures
Total ($ mil) $5,839
   Per capita $1,367
   Per pupil $10,251

NAEP proficiency scores, 2007

	Reading		Math	
	Basic	Proficient	Basic	Proficient
Grade 4	61.9%	28.3%	78.6%	35.0%
Grade 8	77.2%	34.0%	73.0%	34.8%

Higher education enrollment, fall 2005
Total............................... 36,281
   Full-time men 12,147
   Full-time women.....................16,798
   Part-time men 2,965
   Part-time women.....................4,371

Minority enrollment in institutions of higher education, 2005
Black, non-Hispanic 4,788
Hispanic 11,103
Asian/Pacific Islander 12,591
American Indian/Alaska Native..........3,330

Institutions of higher education, 2005-06
Total............................... 60
   Public............................ 26
   Private........................... 34

Earned degrees conferred, 2004-05
Associate's.......................... 8,506
Bachelor's 16,867
Master's...............................6,148
First-professional......................1,147
Doctor's............................ 477

Public Libraries, 2006
Number of libraries...................... 125
Number of outlets 223
Annual visits per capita 6.2
Circulation per capita...................14.9

State & local financial support for higher education, FY 2006
Full-time equivalent enrollment (x 1,000)....126.4
Appropriations per FTE............... $4,466

Social Insurance & Welfare Programs

Social Security benefits & beneficiaries, 2005
Beneficiaries (x 1,000) 625
   Retired & dependents................... 455
   Survivors............................ 76
   Disabled & dependents................. 94
Annual benefit payments ($ mil) $6,837
   Retired & dependents.................$4,741
   Survivors...........................$1,095
   Disabled & dependents...............$1,001
Average monthly benefit
   Retired & dependents.................$1,011
   Disabled & dependents................ $939
   Widowed............................$1,017

Medicare, July 2005
Enrollment (x 1,000)..................... 540
Payments ($ mil) $2,216

Medicaid, 2004
Beneficiaries (x 1,000)................... 559
Payments ($ mil) $2,153

State Children's Health Insurance Program, 2006
Enrollment (x 1,000)...................59.0
Expenditures ($ mil).................... $72.5

Persons without health insurance, 2006
Number (x 1,000)....................... 665
   percent............................. 17.9%
Number of children (x 1,000) 114
   percent of children 13.1%

Health care expenditures, 2004
Total expenditures....................$17,516
   per capita $4,880

©2008 Information Publications, Inc.
All rights reserved. Photocopying prohibited.
877-544-INFO (4636) or www.informationpublications.com

Federal and state public aid

State unemployment insurance, 2006
Recipients, first payments (x 1,000) 126
Total payments ($ mil) $470
Average weekly benefit $270
Temporary Assistance for Needy Families, 2006
Recipients (x 1,000) .495.8
Families (x 1,000) 218.9
Supplemental Security Income, 2005
Recipients (x 1,000) 60.6
Payments ($ mil) $297.5
Food Stamp Program, 2006
Avg monthly participants (x 1,000) 434.2
Total benefits ($ mil) $463.3

Housing & Construction

Housing units

Total 2005 (estimate) 1,558,414
Total 2006 (estimate) 1,586,498
Seasonal or recreational use, 2006 47,959
Owner-occupied, 2006 939,123
   Median home value $236,600
   Homeowner vacancy rate 1.7%
Renter-occupied, 2006 510,539
   Median rent $714
   Rental vacancy rate 7.5%
Home ownership rate, 2005 . . . . .68.2%
Home ownership rate, 2006 . . . . .68.1%

New privately-owned housing units

Number authorized, 2006 (x 1,000) 26.6
   Value ($ mil) $4,941.6
Started 2005 (x 1,000, estimate) 19.6
Started 2006 (x 1,000, estimate) 20.0

Existing home sales

2005 (x 1,000) 100.5
2006 (x 1,000) 85.8

Government & Elections

State officials 2008

Governor . . . . Ted Kulongoski
        Democratic, term expires 1/11
Lieutenant Governor . . (no Lieutenant Governor)
Secretary of State . . . . Bill Bradbury
Attorney General . . . . .Hardy Meyers
Chief Justice . . . . .Paul De Muniz

Governorship

Minimum age 30
Length of term . . . . 4 years
Consecutive terms permitted 2
Who succeeds . . . . .Secretary of State

Local governments by type, 2002

Total 1,439
   County 36
   Municipal 240
   Township 0
   School District 236
   Special District 927

State legislature

Name . . . . Legislature Assembly
Upper chamber . . . . .Senate
   Number of members 30
   Length of term . . . . 4 years
   Party in majority, 2008 . . . . .Democratic
Lower chamber . . . . .House of Representatives
   Number of members 60
   Length of term . . . . 2 years
   Party in majority, 2008 . . . . .Democratic

Federal representation, 2008 (110th Congress)

Senator . . . . Gordon Smith
   Party . . . . Republican
   Year term expires 2009
Senator . . . . .Ron Wyden
   Party . . . . .Democratic
   Year term expires 2011
Representatives, total 5
   Democrats 4
   Republicans 1

Voters in November 2006 election (estimate)

Total 1,600,533
   Male 749,052
   Female 851,482
   White 1,517,739
   Black 16,337
   Hispanic 24,798
   Asian 17,940

Presidential election, 2004

Total Popular Vote 1,836,782
   Kerry 943,163
   Bush 866,831
Total Electoral Votes 7

Votes cast for US Senators

2004
Total vote (x 1,000) 1,781
Leading party . . . . .Democratic
Percent for leading party 63.4%
2006
Total vote (x 1,000) . . . . NA
Leading party . . . . NA
Percent for leading party . . . . NA

Votes cast for US Representatives

2004
Total vote (x 1,000) 1,772
   Democratic 952
   Republican 762
Leading party . . . . .Democratic
Percent for leading party 53.7%
2006
Total vote (x 1,000) 1,357
   Democratic 766
   Republican 557
Leading party . . . . .Democratic
Percent for leading party 56.4%

©2008 Information Publications, Inc.
All rights reserved. Photocopying prohibited.
877-544-INFO (4636) or www.informationpublications.com

State government employment, 2006
Full-time equivalent employees 57,485
Payroll ($ mil) $219.2

Local government employment, 2006
Full-time equivalent employees 124,226
Payroll ($ mil) $463.7

Women holding public office, 2008
US Congress 1
Statewide elected office................. 1
State legislature 28

Black public officials, 2002
Total................................ 5
  US and state legislatures 3
  City/county/regional offices 1
  Judicial/law enforcement.................. 1
  Education/school boards 0

Hispanic public officials, 2006
Total................................ 17
  State executives & legislators 3
  City/county/regional offices 9
  Judicial/law enforcement................. 5
  Education/school boards 0

Governmental Finance

State government revenues, 2006
Total revenue (x $1,000)............$25,742,792
  per capita $6,974.32
General revenue (x $1,000) $16,495,371
  Intergovernmental 4,639,898
  Taxes 7,590,306
    general sales........................... 0
    individual income tax 5,416,466
    corporate income tax 438,255
  Current charges..................2,430,684
  Miscellaneous 1,834,483

State government expenditure, 2006
Total expenditure (x $1,000).......$20,070,629
  per capita $5,437.60
General expenditure (x $1,000) $16,564,827
per capita, total................... $4,487.79
  Education 1,605.37
  Public welfare 1,073.00
  Health 107.47
  Hospitals........................ 294.81
  Highways 390.94
  Police protection................... 72.85
  Corrections 173.28
  Natural resources 109.08
  Parks & recreation 23.24
  Governmental administration 237.36
  Interest on general debt 129.64

State debt & cash, 2006 ($ per capita)
Debt $2,981.99
Cash/security holdings..............$18,681.64

Federal government grants to state & local government, 2005 (x $1,000)
Total..............................$5,466,310
by Federal agency
  Defense 58,429
  Education 454,015
  Energy 24,183
  Environmental Protection Agency 68,276
  Health & Human Services. 2,945,329
  Homeland Security.................27,327
  Housing & Urban Development.......355,169
  Justice 74,803
  Labor 148,528
  Transportation 399,255
  Veterans Affairs.................... 3,889

Crime & Law Enforcement

Crime, 2006 (rates per 100,000 residents)
Property crimes 135,895
  Burglary 23,879
  Larceny 97,556
  Motor vehicle theft 14,460
  Property crime rate................. 3,672.1
Violent crimes..........................10,373
  Murder 86
  Forcible rape.......................1,195
  Robbery........................... 2,689
  Aggravated assault 6,403
  Violent crime rate 280.3
Hate crimes........................ 174

Fraud and identity theft, 2006
Fraud complaints.....................5,583
  rate per 100,000 residents 150.9
Identity theft complaints 2,815
  rate per 100,000 residents 76.1

Law enforcement agencies, 2006
Total agencies........................... 171
Total employees 7,471
  Officers 4,556
  Civilians 2,915

Prisoners, probation, and parole, 2006
Total prisoners.......................13,707
  percent change, 12/31/05 to 12/31/06 .... 2.2%
  in private facilities 0%
  in local jails 0.4%
Sentenced to more than one year 13,667
  rate per 100,000 residents 367
Adults on probation 45,250
Adults on parole....................... 22,396

Prisoner demographics, June 30, 2005 (rate per 100,000 residents)
Male 965
Female 101
White.................................. 502
Black.................................. 2,930
Hispanic 573

©2008 Information Publications, Inc.
All rights reserved. Photocopying prohibited.
877-544-INFO (4636) or www.informationpublications.com

6   Oregon

Arrests, 2006
Total............................... 124,612
   Persons under 18 years of age 24,723

Persons under sentence of death, 1/1/07
Total..................................... 33
   White.................................. 26
   Black 3
   Hispanic 2

State's highest court
Name ....Supreme Court
Number of members...................... 7
Length of term....................... 6 years
Intermediate appeals court? ....yes

Labor & Income

Civilian labor force, 2006 (x 1,000)
Total...................................1,897
   Men 1,033
   Women 865
   Persons 16-19 years.................. 93
   White................................1,719
   Black 28
   Hispanic 148

Civilian labor force as a percent of civilian non-institutional population, 2006
Total................................. 65.6%
   Men 72.7
   Women 58.7
   Persons 16-19 years.................47.3
   White................................65.5
   Black 62.5
   Hispanic 73.7

Employment, 2006 (x 1,000)
Total...................................1,795
   Men 978
   Women 816
   Persons 16-19 years................ 77
   White................................1,631
   Black 23
   Hispanic 139

Unemployment rate, 2006
Total................................. 5.4%
   Men 5.2
   Women 5.6
   Persons 16-19 years................17.3
   White................................5.1
   Black 16.1
   Hispanic 6.3

Full-time/part-time labor force, 2003 (x 1,000)
Full-time labor force, employed 1,360
Part-time labor force, employed............ 347
Unemployed, looking for
   Full-time work....................... 126
   Part-time work....................... 26
Mean duration of unemployment (weeks)......18.1
   Median 9.7

Labor unions, 2006
Membership (x 1,000).................... 211
   percent of employed 13.8%

Experienced civilian labor force by private industry, 2006
Total.............................1,433,342
   Natural resources & mining 49,945
   Construction 99,825
   Manufacturing...................... 206,697
   Trade, transportation & utilities 332,890
   Information 34,846
   Finance 89,239
   Professional & business 194,271
   Education & health 198,677
   Leisure & hospitality............... 164,615
   Other 61,659

Experienced civilian labor force by occupation, May 2006
Management.........................73,510
Business & financial 69,450
Legal................................9,250
Sales.............................. 176,950
Office & admin. support................277,520
Computers & math 35,180
Architecture & engineering............. 33,830
Arts & entertainment 21,100
Education 103,910
Social services 31,530
Health care practitioner & technical 72,260
Health care support 40,640
Maintenance & repair.................. 65,850
Construction 79,640
Transportation & moving 134,370
Production 135,470
Farming, fishing & forestry............12,810

Hours and earnings of production workers on manufacturing payrolls, 2006
Average weekly hours 40.5
Average hourly earnings $15.57
Average weekly earnings $630.59

Income and poverty, 2006
Median household income............ $46,230
Personal income, per capita (current $)... $33,666
   in constant (2000) dollars $29,388
Persons below poverty level.............. 13.3%

Average annual pay
2006 .... $38,077
   increase from 2005 .... 4.1%

Federal individual income tax returns, 2005
Returns filed.......................1,645,481
Adjusted gross income ($1,000) $81,023,741
Total tax liability ($1,000) $9,585,060

Charitable contributions, 2004
Number of contributions 558.1
Total amount ($ mil)................. $1,837.0

©2008 Information Publications, Inc.
All rights reserved. Photocopying prohibited.
877-544-INFO (4636) or www.informationpublications.com

Economy, Business, Industry & Agriculture

Fortune 500 companies, 2007................ 1
Bankruptcy cases filed, FY 2007......... 8,993

Patents and trademarks issued, 2007

Patents.................................... 2,398
Trademarks...............................1,196

Business firm ownership, 2002

Women-owned..........................88,317
  Sales ($ mil) $10,608
Black-owned............................. 2,222
  Sales ($ mil) $371
Hispanic-owned......................... 6,360
  Sales ($ mil) $1,416
Asian-owned 9,046
  Sales ($ mil) $2,182
Amer. Indian/Alaska Native-owned 3,070
  Sales ($ mil) $302
Hawaiian/Pacific Islander-owned 350
  Sales ($ mil) $52

Gross domestic product, 2006 ($ mil)

Total gross domestic product $151,301
  Agriculture, forestry, fishing and
    hunting 3,768
  Mining............................... 162
  Utilities............................ 2,232
  Construction 7,273
  Manufacturing, durable goods........21,627
  Manufacturing, non-durable goods 4,867
  Wholesale trade......................10,161
  Retail trade........................ 8,662
  Transportation & warehousing 4,196
  Information 4,776
  Finance & insurance..................8,493
  Real estate, rental & leasing 20,402
  Professional and technical services 7,156
  Educational services.................1,007
  Health care and social assistance.......11,309
  Accommodation/food services.........3,702
  Other services, except government 3,264
  Government 20,529

Establishments, payroll, employees & receipts, by major industry group, 2005

Total............................. 108,571
  Annual payroll ($1,000).........$50,019,294
  Paid employees 1,409,576
Forestry, fishing & agriculture............1,472
  Annual payroll ($1,000)........... $445,133
  Paid employees 13,106
Mining 161
  Annual payroll ($1,000)................. NA
  Paid employees .... NA
  Receipts, 2002 ($1,000) $270,239

Utilities 263
  Annual payroll ($1,000)........... $559,805
  Paid employees 8,051
  Receipts, 2002 ($1,000) ....NA
Construction...........................13,818
  Annual payroll ($1,000)...........$3,532,998
  Paid employees 85,319
  Receipts, 2002 ($1,000) $13,772,785
Manufacturing 5,559
  Annual payroll ($1,000)...........$7,987,583
  Paid employees 184,708
  Receipts, 2002 ($1,000) $45,864,552
Wholesale trade 5,637
  Annual payroll ($1,000)...........$3,629,651
  Paid employees 75,899
  Receipts, 2002 ($1,000) $56,855,958
Retail trade 14,488
  Annual payroll ($1,000)...........$4,708,601
  Paid employees 199,261
  Receipts, 2002 ($1,000) $37,896,022
Transportation & warehousing 3,106
  Annual payroll ($1,000)...........$1,996,733
  Paid employees 55,229
  Receipts, 2002 ($1,000) $4,892,472
Information...........................1,953
  Annual payroll ($1,000)........... $1,819,915
  Paid employees 35,185
  Receipts, 2002 ($1,000) ....NA
Finance & insurance 6,382
  Annual payroll ($1,000)........... $3,586,248
  Paid employees 68,114
  Receipts, 2002 ($1,000) ....NA
Professional, scientific & technical 10,983
  Annual payroll ($1,000)...........$3,692,635
  Paid employees 75,596
  Receipts, 2002 ($1,000) $6,956,805
Education 1,210
  Annual payroll ($1,000) $903,163
  Paid employees 36,795
  Receipts, 2002 ($1,000) $279,716
Health care & social assistance 10,601
  Annual payroll ($1,000)...........$6,773,806
  Paid employees 180,291
  Receipts, 2002 ($1,000) $13,860,847
Arts and entertainment 1,564
  Annual payroll ($1,000) $483,181
  Paid employees 23,234
  Receipts, 2002 ($1,000) $1,186,835
Real estate 6,055
  Annual payroll ($1,000)........... $965,246
  Paid employees 31,269
  Receipts, 2002 ($1,000) $3,561,488
Accommodation & food service............9,433
  Annual payroll ($1,000)...........$1,944,540
  Paid employees 140,934
  Receipts, 2002 ($1,000) $5,527,223

©2008 Information Publications, Inc.
All rights reserved. Photocopying prohibited.
877-544-INFO (4636) or www.informationpublications.com

Exports, 2006

Value of exported goods ($ mil) $15,288
    Manufactured $12,032
    Non-manufactured $1,953

Foreign direct investment in US affiliates, 2004

Property, plants & equipment ($ mil) $11,749
Employment (x 1,000). 47.6

Agriculture, 2006

Number of farms 39,300
Farm acreage (x 1,000) 17,100
    Acres per farm 435
Farm marketings and income ($ mil)
Total $3,990.6
    Crops $2,960.6
    Livestock $1,030.0
Net farm income $875.6

Principal commodities, in order by marketing receipts, 2005

    Greenhouse/nursery, Cattle and calves, Dairy
        products, Hay, Ryegrass

Federal economic activity in state

Expenditures, 2005 ($ mil)
    Total. $22,792
        Per capita $6,263.47
    Defense $1,316
    Non-defense $21,476
Defense department, 2006 ($ mil)
    Payroll $760
    Contract awards $562
    Grants $47
Homeland security grants ($1,000)
    2006 . . . .$17,956
    2007 . . . .$16,033

FDIC-insured financial institutions, 2005

Number 40
Assets ($ billion) $35.4
Deposits ($ billion) $17.1

Fishing, 2006

Catch (x 1,000 lbs) 300,670
Value ($1,000). $107,421

Mining, 2006 ($ mil)

Total non-fuel mineral production $428
Percent of U.S. 0.66%

Communication, Energy & Transportation

Communication

Households with computers, 2003 . . . . 67.0%
Households with internet access, 2003 . . . . 61.0%
High-speed internet providers 61
Total high-speed internet lines 1,055,986
    Residential 775,041
    Business. 280,945
Wireless phone customers, 12/2006 2,655,905

FCC-licensed stations (as of January 1, 2008)

TV stations 33
FM radio stations. 184
AM radio stations 95

Energy

Energy consumption, 2004
    Total (trillion Btu). 1,094
    Per capita (million Btu) 304.7
By source of production (trillion Btu)
    Coal 37
    Natural gas 243
    Petroleum 391
    Nuclear electric power 0
    Hydroelectric power 332
By end-use sector (trillion Btu)
    Residential 261
    Commercial 207
    Industrial 301
    Transportation 324
Electric energy, 2005
    Primary source of electricity. . . . Hydroelectric
    Net generation (billion kWh) 49.3
        percent from renewable sources. 66.1%
    Net summer capability (million kW) 12.2
    CO_2 emitted from generation 9.0
Natural gas utilities, 2005
    Customers (x 1,000) 701
    Sales (trillion Btu). 141
    Revenues ($ mil) $975
Nuclear plants, 2007 0
Total CO_2 emitted (million metric tons). 40.4
Energy spending, 2004 ($ mil) $9,129
    per capita $2,544
    Price per million Btu $12.85

Transportation, 2006

Public road & street mileage 64,358
    Urban. 12,698
    Rural 51,660
    Interstate. 728
Vehicle miles of travel (millions) 35,483
    per capita 9,613.2
Total motor vehicle registrations. 2,981,379
    Automobiles. .1,427,597
    Trucks 1,538,960
    Motorcycles 83,983
Licensed drivers .2,767,291
    19 years & under 108,571
Deaths from motor vehicle accidents 477
Gasoline consumed (x 1,000 gallons) 1,577,746
    per capita 427.4

Commuting Statistics, 2006

Average commute time (min) 21.8
    Drove to work alone 71.4%
    Carpooled. 11.7%
    Public transit 4.4%
    Walk to work 3.9%
    Work from home 6.0%

©2008 Information Publications, Inc.
All rights reserved. Photocopying prohibited.
877-544-INFO (4636) or www.informationpublications.com

Pennsylvania   1

State Summary

Capital city . . . . Harrisburg
Governor. . . . . .Ed Rendell

Room 225
Main Capitol Building
Harrisburg, PA 17120
717-787-2500

Admitted as a state 1787
Area (square miles) 46,055
Population, 2007 (estimate). 12,432,792
Largest city . . . . Philadelphia
Population, 2006 1,448,394
Personal income per capita, 2006
(in current dollars) $36,680
Gross domestic product, 2006 ($ mil) . . . $510,293

Leading industries by payroll, 2005

Health care/Social assistance, Manufacturing,
Professional/Scientific/Technical

**Leading agricultural commodities
by receipts, 2005**

Dairy products, Cattle and calves, Greenhouse/
nursery, Agaricus mushrooms, Broilers

Geography & Environment

Total area (square miles). 46,055
land 44,817
water 1,239
Federally-owned land, 2004 (acres) 719,864
percent. 2.5%
Highest point . . . . .Mt. Davis
elevation (feet) .3,213
Lowest point. . . . . .Delaware River
elevation (feet) . . . . sea level
General coastline (miles) 0
Tidal shoreline (miles) 83
Cropland, 2003 (x 1,000 acres) 5,124
Forest land, 2003 (x 1,000 acres). 15,631
Capital city . . . . Harrisburg
Population 2000 48,950
Population 2006 47,164
Largest city . . . . Philadelphia
Population 2000 1,517,550
Population 2006 1,448,394

Number of cities with over 100,000 population
1990 4
2000 4
2006 4

State park and recreation areas, 2005
Area (x 1,000 acres). 291
Number of visitors (x 1,000) 36,263
Revenues ($1,000) $13,893
percent of operating expenditures. 17.9%

National forest system land, 2007
Acres 513,428

Demographics & Population Characteristics

Population
1980 11,863,895
1990 11,881,643
2000 12,281,054
2006 12,440,621
Male. 6,047,537
Female. 6,393,084
Living in group quarters, 2006. 455,673
percent of total. 3.7%
2007 (estimate). 12,432,792
persons per square mile of land 277.4
2008 (projected). 12,525,118
2010 (projected). 12,584,487
2020 (projected). 12,787,354
2030 (projected). 12,768,184

**Population of Core-Based Statistical Areas
(formerly Metropolitan Areas), x 1,000**

	CBSA	Non-CBSA
1990	11,518	365
2000	11,899	382
2006	12,056	385

Change in population, 2000-2007
Number 151,738
percent. 1.2%
Natural increase (births minus deaths) 114,795
Net internal migration . . . .-44,416
Net international migration 128,305

Persons by age, 2006
Under 5 years 724,687
5 to 17 years 2,080,186
18 years and over 9,635,748
65 years and over 1,885,323
85 years and over 294,824
Median age. 39.5

Persons by age, 2010 (projected)
Under 5 years 746,518
18 and over 9,836,892
65 and over 1,956,235
Median age. 40.0

Race, 2006
One Race
White. 10,660,136
Black or African American 1,336,278
Asian 292,507
American Indian/Alaska Native. 24,077
Hawaiian Native/Pacific Islander. 5,446
Two or more races. 122,177

Persons of Hispanic origin, 2006
Total Hispanic or Latino 527,142
Mexican. 85,699
Puerto Rican 290,568
Cuban 11,704

©2008 Information Publications, Inc.
All rights reserved. Photocopying prohibited.
877-544-INFO (4636) or www.informationpublications.com

Persons of Asian origin, 2006

Total Asian	289,289
Asian Indian	84,111
Chinese	72,622
Filipino	18,671
Japanese	6,959
Korean	36,228
Vietnamese	35,004

Marital status, 2006

Population 15 years & over	10,164,450
Never married	3,150,116
Married	5,300,946
Separated	226,797
Widowed	793,730
Divorced	919,658

Language spoken at home, 2006

Population 5 years and older	11,716,171
English only	10,639,372
Spanish	436,254
French	55,002
German	106,931
Chinese	62,241

Households & families, 2006

Households	4,845,603
with persons under 18 years	1,498,721
with persons over 65 years	1,294,224
persons per household	2.47
Families	3,174,335
persons per family	3.07
Married couples	2,402,123
Female householder, no husband present	567,179
One-person households	1,421,285

Nativity, 2006

Number of residents born in state	9,399,122
percent of population	75.6%

Immigration & naturalization, 2006

Legal permanent residents admitted	25,958
Persons naturalized	15,846
Non-immigrant admissions	386,193

Vital Statistics and Health

Marriages

2004	73,599
2005	71,933
2006	68,584

Divorces

2004	36,692
2005	29,143
2006	27,357

Health risks, 2006

Percent of adults who are:

Smokers	21.5%
Overweight (BMI > 25)	61.3%
Obese (BMI > 30)	24.0%

Births

2005	145,383
Birthrate (per 1,000)	11.7
White	115,899
Black	23,294
Hispanic	12,208
Asian/Pacific Islander	5,829
Amer. Indian/Alaska Native	361
Low birth weight (2,500g or less)	8.4%
Cesarian births	28.9%
Preterm births	11.9%
To unmarried mothers	36.5%
Twin births (per 1,000)	33.7
Triplets or higher order (per 100,000)	192.9
2006 (preliminary)	149,082
rate per 1,000	12.0

Deaths

2004

All causes	127,640
rate per 100,000	814.6
Heart disease	36,434
rate per 100,000	223.7
Malignant neoplasms	29,424
rate per 100,000	193.8
Cerebrovascular disease	7,792
rate per 100,000	47.1
Chronic lower respiratory disease	5,978
rate per 100,000	37.6
Diabetes	3,579
rate per 100,000	23.1
2005 (preliminary)	129,536
rate per 100,000	814.8
2006 (provisional)	125,151

Infant deaths

2004	1,049
rate per 1,000	7.3
2005 (provisional)	1,036
rate per 1,000	7.2

Exercise routines, 2005

None	25.8%
Moderate or greater	48.7%
Vigorous	27.4%

Abortions, 2004

Total performed in state	36,030
rate per 1,000 women age 15-44	14
% obtained by out-of-state residents	4.2%

Physicians, 2005

Total	36,429
rate per 100,000 persons	294

Community hospitals, 2005

Number of hospitals	191
Beds (x 1,000)	39.6
Patients admitted (x 1,000)	1,863
Average daily census (x 1,000)	27.9
Average cost per day	$1,500
Outpatient visits (x 1 mil)	34.9

©2008 Information Publications, Inc.
All rights reserved. Photocopying prohibited.
877-544-INFO (4636) or www.informationpublications.com

Disability status of population, 2006

5 to 15 years 7.3%
16 to 64 years 13.0%
65 years and over 39.3%

Education

Educational attainment, 2006

Population over 25 years 8,431,859
   Less than 9th grade................. 4.2%
   High school graduate or more 86.2%
   College graduate or more............. 25.4%
   Graduate or professional degree........ 9.6%

Public school enrollment, 2005-06

Total.............................. 1,830,684
   Pre-kindergarten through grade 8... 1,225,383
   Grades 9 through 12 600,857

Graduating public high school seniors, 2004-05

Diplomas (incl. GED and others) 124,758

SAT scores, 2007

Average critical reading score.............. 493
Average writing score 482
Average math score 499
Percent of graduates taking test 75%

Public school teachers, 2006-07 (estimate)

Total (x 1,000) 123.2
   Elementary............................ 60.1
   Secondary............................. 63.0
Average salary $54,970
   Elementary...................... $54,970
   Secondary....................... $54,970

State receipts & expenditures for public schools, 2006-07 (estimate)

Revenue receipts ($ mil) $23,871

Expenditures
Total ($ mil) $23,836
   Per capita $1,655
   Per pupil $12,121

NAEP proficiency scores, 2007

	Reading		Math	
	Basic	Proficient	Basic	Proficient
Grade 4	72.6%	40.2%	85.1%	47.0%
Grade 8	78.6%	36.4%	76.9%	38.3%

Higher education enrollment, fall 2005

Total............................... 312,069
   Full-time men 107,097
   Full-time women................... 130,337
   Part-time men 26,626
   Part-time women.................... 48,009

Minority enrollment in institutions of higher education, 2005

Black, non-Hispanic 71,463
Hispanic 20,824
Asian/Pacific Islander 29,203
American Indian/Alaska Native.......... 1,839

Institutions of higher education, 2005-06

Total................................. 259
   Public............................. 65
   Private............................ 194

Earned degrees conferred, 2004-05

Associate's......................... 25,619
Bachelor's 77,765
Master's............................ 26,450
First-professional.................... 4,890
Doctor's............................ 2,959

Public Libraries, 2006

Number of libraries...................... 458
Number of outlets 670
Annual visits per capita 3.6
Circulation per capita..................... 5.3

State & local financial support for higher education, FY 2006

Full-time equivalent enrollment (x 1,000).... 327.2
Appropriations per FTE............... $5,660

Social Insurance & Welfare Programs

Social Security benefits & beneficiaries, 2005

Beneficiaries (x 1,000) 2,425
   Retired & dependents.................. 1,708
   Survivors........................... 341
   Disabled & dependents................. 375
Annual benefit payments ($ mil) $27,072
   Retired & dependents............... $18,227
   Survivors........................ $4,953
   Disabled & dependents.............. $3,892
Average monthly benefit
   Retired & dependents................. $1,030
   Disabled & dependents................ $954
   Widowed........................... $1,014

Medicare, July 2005

Enrollment (x 1,000)................... 2,132
Payments ($ mil) $12,179

Medicaid, 2004

Beneficiaries (x 1,000)................. 1,835
Payments ($ mil) $10,055

State Children's Health Insurance Program, 2006

Enrollment (x 1,000)................... 188.8
Expenditures ($ mil).................. $239.8

Persons without health insurance, 2006

Number (x 1,000)..................... 1,237
   percent......................... 10.0%
Number of children (x 1,000) 203
   percent of children 7.3%

Health care expenditures, 2004

Total expenditures................... $73,441
   per capita $5,933

©2008 Information Publications, Inc.
All rights reserved. Photocopying prohibited.
877-544-INFO (4636) or www.informationpublications.com

Federal and state public aid

State unemployment insurance, 2006
Recipients, first payments (x 1,000) 447
Total payments ($ mil) $2,030
Average weekly benefit $301
Temporary Assistance for Needy Families, 2006
Recipients (x 1,000) 2,824.8
Families (x 1,000) 1,097.2
Supplemental Security Income, 2005
Recipients (x 1,000) 317.5
Payments ($ mil) $1,658.8
Food Stamp Program, 2006
Avg monthly participants (x 1,000) 1,092.3
Total benefits ($ mil) $1,182.2

Housing & Construction

Housing units
Total 2005 (estimate) 5,422,584
Total 2006 (estimate) 5,453,228
Seasonal or recreational use, 2006 160,989
Owner-occupied, 2006 3,475,105
  Median home value $145,200
  Homeowner vacancy rate 1.6%
Renter-occupied, 2006 1,370,498
  Median rent $664
  Rental vacancy rate 10.6%
Home ownership rate, 2005 . . . . 73.3%
Home ownership rate, 2006 . . . . 73.2%

New privately-owned housing units
Number authorized, 2006 (x 1,000) 39.1
  Value ($ mil) $6,354.2
Started 2005 (x 1,000, estimate) 39.4
Started 2006 (x 1,000, estimate) 39.0

Existing home sales
2005 (x 1,000) 255.2
2006 (x 1,000) 234.5

Government & Elections

State officials 2008
Governor . . . . .Ed Rendell
    Democratic, term expires 1/11
Lieutenant Governor . . . . . Catherine Baker Knoll
Secretary of State . . . . .Pedro Cortes
Attorney General . . . . .Tom Corbett
Chief Justice .Ralph Cappy

Governorship
Minimum age 30
Length of term . . . . 4 years
Consecutive terms permitted 2
Who succeeds . . . . Lieutenant Governor

Local governments by type, 2002
Total 5,031
  County 66
  Municipal 1,018
  Township 1,546
  School District 516
  Special District .1,885

State legislature
Name . . . . General Assembly
Upper chamber . . . . .Senate
  Number of members 50
  Length of term . . . . 4 years
  Party in majority, 2008 . . . . Republican
Lower chamber . . . . .House of Representatives
  Number of members 203
  Length of term . . . . 2 years
  Party in majority, 2008 . . . . .Democratic

Federal representation, 2008 (110th Congress)
Senator . . . . Arlen Specter
  Party . . . . Republican
  Year term expires 2011
Senator . . . . Bob Casey Jr
  Party . . . . .Democratic
  Year term expires 2013
Representatives, total 19
  Democrats 11
  Republicans 8

Voters in November 2006 election (estimate)
Total 4,393,536
  Male 2,091,398
  Female 2,302,138
  White 4,026,589
  Black 304,598
  Hispanic 49,349
  Asian 36,490

Presidential election, 2004
Total Popular Vote 5,769,590
  Kerry 2,938,095
  Bush 2,793,847
Total Electoral Votes 21

Votes cast for US Senators
2004
Total vote (x 1,000) .5,559
Leading party . . . . Republican
Percent for leading party 52.6%
2006
Total vote (x 1,000) .4,081
Leading party .Democratic
Percent for leading party 58.6%

Votes cast for US Representatives
2004
Total vote (x 1,000) .5,151
  Democratic 2,478
  Republican 2,565
Leading party . . . . Republican
Percent for leading party 49.8%
2006
Total vote (x 1,000) .4,013
  Democratic 2,229
  Republican 1,732
Leading party .Democratic
Percent for leading party 55.5%

©2008 Information Publications, Inc.
All rights reserved. Photocopying prohibited.
877-544-INFO (4636) or www.informationpublications.com

State government employment, 2006
Full-time equivalent employees 161,136
Payroll ($ mil) $622.5

Local government employment, 2006
Full-time equivalent employees 407,214
Payroll ($ mil) $1,548.1

Women holding public office, 2008
US Congress 1
Statewide elected office. 2
State legislature 37

Black public officials, 2002
Total. 215
US and state legislatures 19
City/county/regional offices 85
Judicial/law enforcement. 75
Education/school boards 36

Hispanic public officials, 2006
Total. 12
State executives & legislators 1
City/county/regional offices 7
Judicial/law enforcement. 2
Education/school boards 2

Governmental Finance

State government revenues, 2006
Total revenue (x $1,000) $73,134,243
per capita $5,896.58
General revenue (x $1,000) $55,418,674
Intergovernmental 15,326,716
Taxes 29,050,577
general sales. 8,403,283
individual income tax 9,021,917
corporate income tax 2,116,954
Current charges. 6,426,381
Miscellaneous 4,615,000

State government expenditure, 2006
Total expenditure (x $1,000) $64,917,023
per capita $5,234.05
General expenditure (x $1,000) $55,565,739
per capita, total. *$4,480.09*
Education 1,378.46
Public welfare 1,535.03
Health 137.69
Hospitals. 196.92
Highways 465.47
Police protection. 53.51
Corrections 126.38
Natural resources 46.62
Parks & recreation 18.60
Governmental administration 185.81
Interest on general debt. 114.19

State debt & cash, 2006 ($ per capita)
Debt $2,589.85
Cash/security holdings. $10,167.92

Federal government grants to state & local government, 2005 (x $1,000)
Total. $19,868,667
by Federal agency
Defense 189,076
Education 1,338,208
Energy 138,266
Environmental Protection Agency 55,599
Health & Human Services. 12,866,514
Homeland Security. 230,647
Housing & Urban Development. 1,524,175
Justice 206,035
Labor 304,300
Transportation 1,777,051
Veterans Affairs. 33,669

Crime & Law Enforcement

Crime, 2006 (rates per 100,000 residents)
Property crimes 303,988
Burglary 57,623
Larceny 216,825
Motor vehicle theft 29,540
Property crime rate. 2,443.5
Violent crimes. 54,665
Murder 736
Forcible rape. .3,401
Robbery. 20,974
Aggravated assault 29,554
Violent crime rate 439.4
Hate crimes. 113

Fraud and identity theft, 2006
Fraud complaints. 16,242
rate per 100,000 residents 130.6
Identity theft complaints 8,080
rate per 100,000 residents 64.9

Law enforcement agencies, 2006
Total agencies. 783
Total employees 27,811
Officers 23,414
Civilians 4,397

Prisoners, probation, and parole, 2006
Total prisoners 44,397
percent change, 12/31/05 to 12/31/06 . . . . 4.8%
in private facilities 2.2%
in local jails 0%
Sentenced to more than one year 43,998
rate per 100,000 residents 353
Adults on probation 172,184
Adults on parole. 76,386

Prisoner demographics, June 30, 2005 (rate per 100,000 residents)
Male 1,155
Female 92
White 305
Black. 2,792
Hispanic 1,714

©2008 Information Publications, Inc.
All rights reserved. Photocopying prohibited.
877-544-INFO (4636) or www.informationpublications.com

Arrests, 2006

Total 457,514
    Persons under 18 years of age 106,572

Persons under sentence of death, 1/1/07

Total 226
    White 68
    Black 137
    Hispanic 19

State's highest court

Name . . . . .Supreme Court
Number of members 7
Length of term . . . . 10 years
Intermediate appeals court? . . . . .yes

Labor & Income

Civilian labor force, 2006 (x 1,000)

Total 6,308
    Men 3,360
    Women 2,948
    Persons 16-19 years 311
    White 5,606
    Black 558
    Hispanic 213

Civilian labor force as a percent of civilian non-institutional population, 2006

Total 64.4%
    Men 71.8
    Women 57.6
    Persons 16-19 years 45.2
    White 65.0
    Black 59.8
    Hispanic 64.4

Employment, 2006 (x 1,000)

Total 6,015
    Men 3,200
    Women 2,814
    Persons 16-19 years 268
    White 5,367
    Black 512
    Hispanic 194

Unemployment rate, 2006

Total 4.7%
    Men 4.7
    Women 4.5
    Persons 16-19 years 13.9
    White 4.3
    Black 8.2
    Hispanic 8.8

Full-time/part-time labor force, 2003 (x 1,000)

Full-time labor force, employed 4,707
Part-time labor force, employed 1,119
Unemployed, looking for
    Full-time work 276
    Part-time work 68
*Mean duration of unemployment (weeks) *18.7
    Median 11.2

Labor unions, 2006

Membership (x 1,000) 745
    percent of employed 13.6%

Experienced civilian labor force by private industry, 2006

Total 4,890,795
    Natural resources & mining 42,999
    Construction 261,541
    Manufacturing 672,365
    Trade, transportation & utilities 1,117,725
    Information 108,596
    Finance 335,179
    Professional & business 677,753
    Education & health 994,934
    Leisure & hospitality 491,168
    Other 188,338

Experienced civilian labor force by occupation, May 2006

Management 190,620
Business & financial 251,170
Legal 40,630
Sales 606,190
Office & admin. support 981,000
Computers & math 114,090
Architecture & engineering 93,950
Arts & entertainment 59,380
Education 343,020
Social services 102,090
Health care practitioner & technical 342,010
Health care support 175,450
Maintenance & repair 232,360
Construction 239,160
Transportation & moving 437,710
Production 467,590
Farming, fishing & forestry 5,720

Hours and earnings of production workers on manufacturing payrolls, 2006

Average weekly hours 40.8
Average hourly earnings $15.37
Average weekly earnings $627.10

Income and poverty, 2006

Median household income $46,259
Personal income, per capita (current $) . . . $36,680
    in constant (2000) dollars $32,019
Persons below poverty level 12.1%

Average annual pay

2006 . . . . $41,349
    increase from 2005 . . . . 4.3%

Federal individual income tax returns, 2005

Returns filed 5,867,052
Adjusted gross income ($1,000) $299,493,501
Total tax liability ($1,000) $38,771,971

Charitable contributions, 2004

Number of contributions 1,640.8
Total amount ($ mil) $5,687.3

©2008 Information Publications, Inc.
All rights reserved. Photocopying prohibited.
877-544-INFO (4636) or www.informationpublications.com

Economy, Business, Industry & Agriculture

Fortune 500 companies, 2007 25
Bankruptcy cases filed, FY 2007 29,111

Patents and trademarks issued, 2007
Patents 2,980
Trademarks 2,452

Business firm ownership, 2002
Women-owned 227,117
   Sales ($ mil) $38,998
Black-owned 24,757
   Sales ($ mil) $2,118
Hispanic-owned 11,023
   Sales ($ mil) $1,729
Asian-owned 22,631
   Sales ($ mil) $6,540
Amer. Indian/Alaska Native-owned 2,362
   Sales ($ mil) .... NA
Hawaiian/Pacific Islander-owned 291
   Sales ($ mil) $41

Gross domestic product, 2006 ($ mil)
Total gross domestic product $510,293
   Agriculture, forestry, fishing and
     hunting 2,809
   Mining 3,659
   Utilities 12,819
   Construction 23,957
   Manufacturing, durable goods 38,949
   Manufacturing, non-durable goods ... 36,423
   Wholesale trade 30,915
   Retail trade 32,475
   Transportation & warehousing 15,930
   Information 17,799
   Finance & insurance 37,155
   Real estate, rental & leasing 60,361
   Professional and technical services 37,387
   Educational services 9,813
   Health care and social assistance 48,035
   Accommodation/food services 10,954
   Other services, except government 12,598
   Government 49,752

Establishments, payroll, employees & receipts, by major industry group, 2005

Total 303,333
   Annual payroll ($1,000) $189,692,284
   Paid employees 5,082,630
Forestry, fishing & agriculture 563
   Annual payroll ($1,000) $68,327
   Paid employees 2,538
Mining 882
   Annual payroll ($1,000) $905,500
   Paid employees 17,451
   Receipts, 2002 ($1,000) $3,408,913

Utilities 709
   Annual payroll ($1,000) $2,724,637
   Paid employees 33,510
   Receipts, 2002 ($1,000) ....NA
Construction 29,828
   Annual payroll ($1,000) $11,463,841
   Paid employees 242,100
   Receipts, 2002 ($1,000) $46,642,336
Manufacturing 15,624
   Annual payroll ($1,000) ... $28,643,809
   Paid employees 663,605
   Receipts, 2002 ($1,000) $181,462,443
Wholesale trade 15,890
   Annual payroll ($1,000) $11,945,383
   Paid employees 238,710
   Receipts, 2002 ($1,000) $183,741,873
Retail trade 47,223
   Annual payroll ($1,000) $14,205,271
   Paid employees 668,973
   Receipts, 2002 ($1,000) $130,713,197
Transportation & warehousing 7,779
   Annual payroll ($1,000) $6,288,931
   Paid employees 195,581
   Receipts, 2002 ($1,000) $13,774,754
Information 5,315
   Annual payroll ($1,000) $6,965,474
   Paid employees 133,519
   Receipts, 2002 ($1,000) ....NA
Finance & insurance 18,645
   Annual payroll ($1,000) $17,612,704
   Paid employees 295,538
   Receipts, 2002 ($1,000) ....NA
Professional, scientific & technical 29,777
   Annual payroll ($1,000) $18,452,450
   Paid employees 304,291
   Receipts, 2002 ($1,000) $36,708,036
Education 3,242
   Annual payroll ($1,000) $6,634,848
   Paid employees 220,531
   Receipts, 2002 ($1,000) $1,444,570
Health care & social assistance 34,222
   Annual payroll ($1,000) $29,533,070
   Paid employees 837,643
   Receipts, 2002 ($1,000) $59,086,822
Arts and entertainment 4,749
   Annual payroll ($1,000) $1,902,342
   Paid employees 74,435
   Receipts, 2002 ($1,000) $4,702,320
Real estate 9,747
   Annual payroll ($1,000) $2,506,857
   Paid employees 69,248
   Receipts, 2002 ($1,000) $9,830,222
Accommodation & food service 26,115
   Annual payroll ($1,000) $5,053,740
   Paid employees 404,683
   Receipts, 2002 ($1,000) $15,305,402

©2008 Information Publications, Inc.
All rights reserved. Photocopying prohibited.
877-544-INFO (4636) or www.informationpublications.com

Exports, 2006

Value of exported goods ($ mil) $26,334
   Manufactured $23,339
   Non-manufactured.................$1,333

Foreign direct investment in US affiliates, 2004

Property, plants & equipment ($ mil) ... $30,237
Employment (x 1,000)..................225.6

Agriculture, 2006

Number of farms 58,200
Farm acreage (x 1,000) 7,650
   Acres per farm........................ 131
Farm marketings and income ($ mil)
Total................................$4,691.7
   Crops.............................$1,723.3
   Livestock.........................$2,968.3
Net farm income $1,516.4

Principal commodities, in order by marketing receipts, 2005

Dairy products, Cattle and calves, Greenhouse/
nursery, Agaricus mushrooms, Broilers

Federal economic activity in state

Expenditures, 2005 ($ mil)
   Total............................. $99,503
   Per capita $8,020.94
   Defense $10,244
   Non-defense..................... $89,259
Defense department, 2006 ($ mil)
   Payroll........................... $3,077
   Contract awards $7,515
   Grants $300
Homeland security grants ($1,000)
   2006.......................... $49,335
   2007.......................... $61,306

FDIC-insured financial institutions, 2005

Number 251
Assets ($ billion) $415.2
Deposits ($ billion) $294.9

Fishing, 2006

Catch (x 1,000 lbs)...................... 38
Value ($1,000).......................... $96

Mining, 2006 ($ mil)

Total non-fuel mineral production $1,670
Percent of U.S. 2.59%

Communication, Energy & Transportation

Communication

Households with computers, 2003........60.2%
Households with internet access, 2003 ....54.7%
High-speed internet providers 75
Total high-speed internet lines........3,374,313
   Residential 2,279,971
   Business.........................1,094,342
Wireless phone customers, 12/2006 8,831,238

FCC-licensed stations (as of January 1, 2008)

TV stations 46
FM radio stations....................... 325
AM radio stations 181

Energy

Energy consumption, 2004
   Total (trillion Btu)................... 4,049
   Per capita (million Btu) 327.2
By source of production (trillion Btu)
   Coal...............................1,474
   Natural gas......................... 733
   Petroleum..........................1,519
   Nuclear electric power 808
   Hydroelectric power................. 32
By end-use sector (trillion Btu)
   Residential 995
   Commercial 707
   Industrial 1,328
   Transportation 1,019
Electric energy, 2005
   Primary source of electricity........... Coal
   Net generation (billion kWh) 218.1
      percent from renewable sources...... 2.1%
   Net summer capability (million kW) 44.9
   CO_2 emitted from generation 126.7
Natural gas utilities, 2005
   Customers (x 1,000) 2,839
   Sales (trillion Btu)................... 592
   Revenues ($ mil) $4,572
Nuclear plants, 2007 9
Total CO_2 emitted (million metric tons).....271.4
Energy spending, 2004 ($ mil) $36,069
   per capita $2,914
   Price per million Btu $13.05

Transportation, 2006

Public road & street mileage 121,292
   Urban........................... 44,923
   Rural........................... 76,369
   Interstate.........................1,758
Vehicle miles of travel (millions) 108,278
   per capita 8,730.1
Total motor vehicle registrations.......9,894,163
   Automobiles.....................5,842,819
   Trucks 4,013,315
   Motorcycles 330,938
Licensed drivers 8,526,204
   19 years & under 348,567
Deaths from motor vehicle accidents 1,525
Gasoline consumed (x 1,000 gallons) 5,102,928
   per capita 411.4

Commuting Statistics, 2006

Average commute time (min) 25.0
   Drove to work alone 76.4%
   Carpooled............................ 9.9%
   Public transit 5.2%
   Walk to work 4.1%
   Work from home...................... 3.2%

©2008 Information Publications, Inc.
All rights reserved. Photocopying prohibited.
877-544-INFO (4636) or www.informationpublications.com

State Summary

Capital city . . . . Providence
Governor . . . . Don Carcieri

State House
Providence, RI 02903
401-222-2080

Admitted as a state 1790
Area (square miles) .1,545
Population, 2007 (estimate). 1,057,832
Largest city . . . . Providence
    Population, 2006 175,255
Personal income per capita, 2006
    (in current dollars) $37,388
Gross domestic product, 2006 ($ mil) $45,660

Leading industries by payroll, 2005

Health care/Social assistance, Manufacturing,
Finance & Insurance

**Leading agricultural commodities
by receipts, 2005**

Greenhouse/nursery, Dairy products, Sweet corn,
Aquaculture, Potatoes

Geography & Environment

Total area (square miles). 1,545
    land 1,045
    water 500
Federally-owned land, 2004 (acres) 2,923
    percent. 0.4%
Highest point . . . . Jerimoth Hill
    elevation (feet) 812
Lowest point . . . . Atlantic Ocean
    elevation (feet) . . . . sea level
General coastline (miles) 40
Tidal shoreline (miles) 384
Cropland, 2003 (x 1,000 acres) 20
Forest land, 2003 (x 1,000 acres). 374
Capital city . . . . Providence
    Population 2000 173,618
    Population 2006 175,255
Largest city . . . . Providence
    Population 2000 173,618
    Population 2006 175,255

Number of cities with over 100,000 population

1990 1
2000 1
2006 1

State park and recreation areas, 2005

Area (x 1,000 acres) 9
Number of visitors (x 1,000) 5,853
Revenues ($1,000) $3,515
    percent of operating expenditures. 39.3%

National forest system land, 2007

Acres 0

Demographics & Population Characteristics

Population

1980 947,154
1990 1,003,464
2000 1,048,319
2006 1,067,610
    Male 516,213
    Female 551,397
Living in group quarters, 2006 43,088
    percent of total. 4.0%
2007 (estimate) 1,057,832
    persons per square mile of land 1,012.3
2008 (projected) 1,105,525
2010 (projected) 1,116,652
2020 (projected) 1,154,230
2030 (projected) 1,152,941

**Population of Core-Based Statistical Areas
(formerly Metropolitan Areas), x 1,000**

	CBSA	Non-CBSA
1990	1,003	0
2000	1,048	0
2006	1,068	0

Change in population, 2000-2007

Number 9,513
    percent. 0.9%
Natural increase (births minus deaths) 20,554
Net internal migration . . . .-30,249
Net international migration 23,874

Persons by age, 2006

Under 5 years 61,961
5 to 17 years 175,490
18 years and over 830,159
65 years and over 147,966
85 years and over .25,123
    Median age 38.2

Persons by age, 2010 (projected)

Under 5 years 66,193
18 and over 867,379
65 and over 157,358
    Median age 38.2

Race, 2006

One Race

White. 947,030
Black or African American 67,328
Asian 29,177
American Indian/Alaska Native. 6,574
Hawaiian Native/Pacific Islander. 1,287
Two or more races. 16,214

Persons of Hispanic origin, 2006

Total Hispanic or Latino 117,708
    Mexican. 8,313
    Puerto Rican 33,685
    Cuban 2,502

©2008 Information Publications, Inc.
All rights reserved. Photocopying prohibited.
877-544-INFO (4636) or www.informationpublications.com

Persons of Asian origin, 2006

Total Asian	29,406
Asian Indian	5,545
Chinese	7,869
Filipino	3,558
Japanese	483
Korean	1,883
Vietnamese	1,017

Marital status, 2006

Population 15 years & over	873,859
Never married	299,121
Married	423,737
Separated	15,172
Widowed	59,563
Divorced	91,438

Language spoken at home, 2006

Population 5 years and older	1,005,812
English only	800,162
Spanish	100,227
French	23,281
German	2,774
Chinese	6,266

Households & families, 2006

Households	405,627
with persons under 18 years	130,032
with persons over 65 years	101,089
persons per household	2.53
Families	262,352
persons per family	3.13
Married couples	190,694
Female householder, no husband present	54,502
One-person households	116,234

Nativity, 2006

Number of residents born in state	631,785
percent of population	59.2%

Immigration & naturalization, 2006

Legal permanent residents admitted	4,778
Persons naturalized	2,266
Non-immigrant admissions	45,648

Vital Statistics and Health

Marriages

2004	8,243
2005	7,525
2006	6,916

Divorces

2004	3,287
2005	3,159
2006	3,115

Health risks, 2006

Percent of adults who are:

Smokers	19.2%
Overweight (BMI > 25)	61.0%
Obese (BMI > 30)	21.4%

Births

2005	12,697
Birthrate (per 1,000)	11.8
White	10,705
Black	1,288
Hispanic	2,559
Asian/Pacific Islander	555
Amer. Indian/Alaska Native	149
Low birth weight (2,500g or less)	7.8%
Cesarian births	30.3%
Preterm births	12.1%
To unmarried mothers	38.5%
Twin births (per 1,000)	38.9
Triplets or higher order (per 100,000)	178.4
2006 (preliminary)	12,379
rate per 1,000	11.6

Deaths

2004

All causes	9,769
rate per 100,000	741.1
Heart disease	2,969
rate per 100,000	216.0
Malignant neoplasms	2,418
rate per 100,000	194.1
Cerebrovascular disease	522
rate per 100,000	38.1
Chronic lower respiratory disease	463
rate per 100,000	35.3
Diabetes	280
rate per 100,000	21.9
2005 (preliminary)	10,007
rate per 100,000	747.3
2006 (provisional)	9,731

Infant deaths

2004	68
rate per 1,000	5.3
2005 (provisional)	74
rate per 1,000	5.9

Exercise routines, 2005

None	25.9%
Moderate or greater	51.1%
Vigorous	29.9%

Abortions, 2004

Total performed in state	5,587
rate per 1,000 women age 15-44	24
% obtained by out-of-state residents	23.9%

Physicians, 2005

Total	3,866
rate per 100,000 persons	360

Community hospitals, 2005

Number of hospitals	11
Beds (x 1,000)	2.4
Patients admitted (x 1,000)	127
Average daily census (x 1,000)	1.9
Average cost per day	$1,719
Outpatient visits (x 1 mil)	2.5

©2008 Information Publications, Inc.
All rights reserved. Photocopying prohibited.
877-544-INFO (4636) or www.informationpublications.com

Disability status of population, 2006
5 to 15 years 7.2%
16 to 64 years 12.9%
65 years and over 39.4%

Education

Educational attainment, 2006
Population over 25 years 712,984
    Less than 9th grade................... 7.3%
    High school graduate or more 82.4%
    College graduate or more............. 29.6%
    Graduate or professional degree....... 11.3%

Public school enrollment, 2005-06
Total............................... 153,422
    Pre-kindergarten through grade 8.... 103,870
    Grades 9 through 12 49,552

Graduating public high school seniors, 2004-05
Diplomas (incl. GED and others) 9,903

SAT scores, 2007
Average critical reading score.............. 496
Average writing score 492
Average math score 498
Percent of graduates taking test 68%

Public school teachers, 2006-07 (estimate)
Total (x 1,000) 14.9
    Elementary............................ 9.3
    Secondary............................ 5.6
Average salary $55,956
    Elementary...................... $55,956
    Secondary....................... $55,956

State receipts & expenditures for public schools, 2006-07 (estimate)
Revenue receipts ($ mil) $1,636
Expenditures
Total ($ mil) $1,952
    Per capita $1,748
    Per pupil $12,095

NAEP proficiency scores, 2007

	Reading		Math	
	Basic	Proficient	Basic	Proficient
Grade 4	65.4%	30.8%	79.6%	34.0%
Grade 8	69.3%	27.2%	65.5%	27.7%

Higher education enrollment, fall 2005
Total.................................. 41,374
    Full-time men 17,731
    Full-time women..................... 18,460
    Part-time men 2,434
    Part-time women..................... 2,749

Minority enrollment in institutions of higher education, 2005
Black, non-Hispanic 4,897
Hispanic 5,246
Asian/Pacific Islander 3,468
American Indian/Alaska Native........... 351

Institutions of higher education, 2005-06
Total..................................... 14
    Public................................. 3
    Private 11

Earned degrees conferred, 2004-05
Associate's............................. 3,573
Bachelor's 9,472
Master's............................... 2,223
First-professional...................... 318
Doctor's............................... 243

Public Libraries, 2006
Number of libraries....................... 49
Number of outlets 75
Annual visits per capita 5.9
Circulation per capita.................... 6.8

State & local financial support for higher education, FY 2006
Full-time equivalent enrollment (x 1,000)..... 28.1
Appropriations per FTE................ $6,413

Social Insurance & Welfare Programs

Social Security benefits & beneficiaries, 2005
Beneficiaries (x 1,000) 192
    Retired & dependents................. 134
    Survivors............................ 21
    Disabled & dependents................. 36
Annual benefit payments ($ mil) $2,089
    Retired & dependents............... $1,418
    Survivors........................ $302
    Disabled & dependents.............. $368
Average monthly benefit
    Retired & dependents............... $1,006
    Disabled & dependents.............. $913
    Widowed........................... $1,013

Medicare, July 2005
Enrollment (x 1,000)..................... 172
Payments ($ mil) $832

Medicaid, 2004
Beneficiaries (x 1,000)................... 208
Payments ($ mil) $1,531

State Children's Health Insurance Program, 2006
Enrollment (x 1,000)..................... 25.5
Expenditures ($ mil)................... $42.1

Persons without health insurance, 2006
Number (x 1,000)........................ 91
    percent............................ 8.6%
Number of children (x 1,000) 10
    percent of children 4.2%

Health care expenditures, 2004
Total expenditures..................... $6,682
    per capita $6,193

©2008 Information Publications, Inc.
All rights reserved. Photocopying prohibited.
877-544-INFO (4636) or www.informationpublications.com

Federal and state public aid

State unemployment insurance, 2006
Recipients, first payments (x 1,000) 38
Total payments ($ mil) $196
Average weekly benefit $342
Temporary Assistance for Needy Families, 2006
Recipients (x 1,000) 275.0
Families (x 1,000) 112.3
Supplemental Security Income, 2005
Recipients (x 1,000) 30.2
Payments ($ mil) $160.8
Food Stamp Program, 2006
Avg monthly participants (x 1,000) 73.2
Total benefits ($ mil) $80.9

Housing & Construction

Housing units
Total 2005 (estimate) 447,810
Total 2006 (estimate) 449,582
Seasonal or recreational use, 2006 14,856
Owner-occupied, 2006 255,495
  Median home value $295,700
  Homeowner vacancy rate 1.3%
Renter-occupied, 2006 150,132
  Median rent $840
  Rental vacancy rate 7.5%
Home ownership rate, 2005 . . . . 63.1%
Home ownership rate, 2006 . . . . 64.6%

New privately-owned housing units
Number authorized, 2006 (x 1,000) 2.4
  Value ($ mil) $383.8
Started 2005 (x 1,000, estimate) 2.4
Started 2006 (x 1,000, estimate) 2.4

Existing home sales
2005 (x 1,000) 19.8
2006 (x 1,000) 17.4

Government & Elections

State officials 2008
Governor . . . . .Don Carcieri
      Republican, term expires 1/11
Lieutenant Governor . . . . Elizabeth Roberts
Secretary of State . . . . .Ralph Mollis
Attorney General . . . . .Patrick Lynch
Chief Justice . . . . Frank Williams

Governorship
Minimum age 18
Length of term . . . . 4 years
Consecutive terms permitted 2
Who succeeds . . . . Lieutenant Governor

Local governments by type, 2002
Total 118
  County 0
  Municipal 8
  Township 31
  School District 4
  Special District 75

State legislature
Name . . . . General Assembly
Upper chamber . . . . .Senate
  Number of members 38
  Length of term . . . . 2 years
  Party in majority, 2008 . . . . .Democratic
Lower chamber . . . . .House of Representatives
  Number of members 75
  Length of term . . . . 2 years
  Party in majority, 2008 . . . . .Democratic

Federal representation, 2008 (110th Congress)
Senator . . . . John Reed
  Party . . . . .Democratic
  Year term expires 2009
Senator . . . . .Sheldon Whitehouse
  Party . . . . .Democratic
  Year term expires 2013
Representatives, total 2
  Democrats 2
  Republicans 0

Voters in November 2006 election (estimate)
Total 430,706
  Male 197,035
  Female 233,672
  White 400,636
  Black 17,165
  Hispanic 12,059
  Asian 4,455

Presidential election, 2004
Total Popular Vote .437,134
  Kerry 259,765
  Bush 169,046
Total Electoral Votes 4

Votes cast for US Senators
2004
Total vote (x 1,000) . . . . NA
Leading party . . . . NA
Percent for leading party . . . . NA
2006
Total vote (x 1,000) 385
Leading party .Democratic
Percent for leading party 53.5%

Votes cast for US Representatives
2004
Total vote (x 1,000) 402
  Democratic 279
  Republican 113
Leading party .Democratic
Percent for leading party 69.5%
2006
Total vote (x 1,000) 373
  Democratic 265
  Republican 42
Leading party .Democratic
Percent for leading party 71.0%

©2008 Information Publications, Inc.
All rights reserved. Photocopying prohibited.
877-544-INFO (4636) or www.informationpublications.com

State government employment, 2006
Full-time equivalent employees 20,594
Payroll ($ mil) $93.3

Local government employment, 2006
Full-time equivalent employees 30,638
Payroll ($ mil) $133.5

Women holding public office, 2008
US Congress 0
Statewide elected office...................... 1
State legislature 22

Black public officials, 2002
Total.. 8
   US and state legislatures 7
   City/county/regional offices 1
   Judicial/law enforcement.................. 0
   Education/school boards................... 0

Hispanic public officials, 2006
Total.. 7
   State executives & legislators 4
   City/county/regional offices 3
   Judicial/law enforcement.................. 0
   Education/school boards................... 0

Governmental Finance

State government revenues, 2006
Total revenue (x $1,000)............$7,670,233
   per capita $7,224.88
General revenue (x $1,000) $6,194,471
   Intergovernmental 2,148,174
   Taxes 2,741,734
      general sales..................... 854,257
      individual income tax 1,019,482
      corporate income tax 169,865
   Current charges.....................511,429
   Miscellaneous 793,134

State government expenditure, 2006
Total expenditure (x $1,000).........$6,955,860
   per capita $6,551.99
General expenditure (x $1,000) $5,872,054
   per capita, total................. *$5,531.11*
      Education.......................1,560.49
      Public welfare 2,048.86
      Health 143.44
      Hospitals....................... 108.22
      Highways 284.15
      Police protection.................52.27
      Corrections 162.17
      Natural resources 37.53
      Parks & recreation 13.73
      Governmental administration...... 336.54
      Interest on general debt.......... 260.04

State debt & cash, 2006 ($ per capita)
Debt $6,559.82
Cash/security holdings............. $13,777.71

Federal government grants to state & local government, 2005 (x $1,000)
Total..............................$2,325,111
by Federal agency
   Defense 17,441
   Education 146,373
   Energy 6,054
   Environmental Protection Agency 29,749
   Health & Human Services........ 1,467,433
   Homeland Security................ 8,946
   Housing & Urban Development.......233,411
   Justice 37,889
   Labor 37,320
   Transportation 190,408
   Veterans Affairs.................. 3,999

Crime & Law Enforcement

Crime, 2006 (rates per 100,000 residents)
Property crimes 27,618
   Burglary 5,415
   Larceny 18,621
   Motor vehicle theft 3,582
   Property crime rate.................2,586.9
Violent crimes........................ 2,429
   Murder 28
   Forcible rape...................... 285
   Robbery.......................... 735
   Aggravated assault 1,381
   Violent crime rate 227.5
Hate crimes........................... 20

Fraud and identity theft, 2006
Fraud complaints.......................1,153
   rate per 100,000 residents 108.0
Identity theft complaints 615
   rate per 100,000 residents 57.6

Law enforcement agencies, 2006
Total agencies........................ 47
Total employees 3,223
   Officers 2,561
   Civilians 662

Prisoners, probation, and parole, 2006
Total prisoners........................3,996
   percent change, 12/31/05 to 12/31/06 .... 9.4%
   in private facilities 0%
   in local jails .... NA
Sentenced to more than one year 2,149
   rate per 100,000 residents 202
Adults on probation 26,017
Adults on parole........................ 364

Prisoner demographics, June 30, 2005 (rate per 100,000 residents)
Male 607
Female 38
White 191
Black..................................1,838
Hispanic 631

©2008 Information Publications, Inc.
All rights reserved. Photocopying prohibited.
877-544-INFO (4636) or www.informationpublications.com

Arrests, 2006

Total	35,999
Persons under 18 years of age	4,900

Persons under sentence of death, 1/1/07

Total	0
White	0
Black	0
Hispanic	0

State's highest court

Name	Supreme Court
Number of members	5
Length of term	life
Intermediate appeals court?	no

Labor & Income

Civilian labor force, 2006 (x 1,000)

Total	577
Men	300
Women	278
Persons 16-19 years	32
White	519
Black	33
Hispanic	56

Civilian labor force as a percent of civilian non-institutional population, 2006

Total	68.6%
Men	74.8
Women	63.0
Persons 16-19 years	53.0
White	68.3
Black	71.9
Hispanic	67.7

Employment, 2006 (x 1,000)

Total	547
Men	284
Women	263
Persons 16-19 years	27
White	493
Black	30
Hispanic	51

Unemployment rate, 2006

Total	5.2%
Men	5.1
Women	5.3
Persons 16-19 years	14.9
White	4.9
Black	7.2
Hispanic	8.5

Full-time/part-time labor force, 2003 (x 1,000)

Full-time labor force, employed	422
Part-time labor force, employed	121

Unemployed, looking for

Full-time work	25
Part-time work	6

Mean duration of unemployment (weeks) 18.6

Median	9.7

Labor unions, 2006

Membership (x 1,000)	76
percent of employed	15.3%

Experienced civilian labor force by private industry, 2006

Total	417,683
Natural resources & mining	1,121
Construction	22,791
Manufacturing	52,730
Trade, transportation & utilities	79,256
Information	10,995
Finance	33,368
Professional & business	56,141
Education & health	92,656
Leisure & hospitality	50,234
Other	18,140

Experienced civilian labor force by occupation, May 2006

Management	23,270
Business & financial	20,950
Legal	3,410
Sales	45,370
Office & admin. support	84,260
Computers & math	9,770
Architecture & engineering	8,320
Arts & entertainment	6,730
Education	33,630
Social services	9,990
Health care practitioner & technical	29,010
Health care support	17,520
Maintenance & repair	15,410
Construction	22,000
Transportation & moving	27,630
Production	37,910
Farming, fishing & forestry	210

Hours and earnings of production workers on manufacturing payrolls, 2006

Average weekly hours	38.9
Average hourly earnings	$13.42
Average weekly earnings	$522.04

Income and poverty, 2006

Median household income	$51,814
Personal income, per capita (current $)	$37,388
in constant (2000) dollars	$32,637
Persons below poverty level	11.1%

Average annual pay

2006	$40,454
increase from 2005	4.4%

Federal individual income tax returns, 2005

Returns filed	502,440
Adjusted gross income ($1,000)	$26,529,043
Total tax liability ($1,000)	$3,414,395

Charitable contributions, 2004

Number of contributions	170.4
Total amount ($ mil)	$463.2

©2008 Information Publications, Inc.
All rights reserved. Photocopying prohibited.
877-544-INFO (4636) or www.informationpublications.com

Economy, Business, Industry & Agriculture

Fortune 500 companies, 2007 2
Bankruptcy cases filed, FY 2007 2,521

Patents and trademarks issued, 2007

Patents 381
Trademarks 348

Business firm ownership, 2002

Women-owned 23,195
  Sales ($ mil) $3,641
Black-owned .... NA
  Sales ($ mil) .... NA
Hispanic-owned 3,415
  Sales ($ mil) $214
Asian-owned 1,529
  Sales ($ mil) $326
Amer. Indian/Alaska Native-owned 446
  Sales ($ mil) $27
Hawaiian/Pacific Islander-owned 45
  Sales ($ mil) $3

Gross domestic product, 2006 ($ mil)

Total gross domestic product $45,660
  Agriculture, forestry, fishing and
    hunting 96
  Mining 24
  Utilities 917
  Construction 2,307
  Manufacturing, durable goods 3,270
  Manufacturing, non-durable goods 1,234
  Wholesale trade 2,319
  Retail trade 2,832
  Transportation & warehousing 630
  Information 1,700
  Finance & insurance 5,319
  Real estate, rental & leasing 6,856
  Professional and technical services 2,612
  Educational services 997
  Health care and social assistance 4,241
  Accommodation/food services 1,250
  Other services, except government 979
  Government 5,511

Establishments, payroll, employees & receipts, by major industry group, 2005

Total 30,331
  Annual payroll ($1,000) $15,756,079
  Paid employees 442,291
Forestry, fishing & agriculture 54
  Annual payroll ($1,000) .... NA
  Paid employees .... NA
Mining 25
  Annual payroll ($1,000) .... NA
  Paid employees .... NA
  Receipts, 2002 ($1,000) $34,173

Utilities 34
  Annual payroll ($1,000) $110,220
  Paid employees 1,444
  Receipts, 2002 ($1,000) .... NA
Construction 3,697
  Annual payroll ($1,000) $993,532
  Paid employees 20,041
  Receipts, 2002 ($1,000) $4,356,409
Manufacturing 1,956
  Annual payroll ($1,000) $2,366,601
  Paid employees 58,738
  Receipts, 2002 ($1,000) $10,818,058
Wholesale trade 1,419
  Annual payroll ($1,000) $857,371
  Paid employees 18,260
  Receipts, 2002 ($1,000) $8,566,430
Retail trade 4,201
  Annual payroll ($1,000) $1,284,483
  Paid employees 54,724
  Receipts, 2002 ($1,000) $10,342,351
Transportation & warehousing 703
  Annual payroll ($1,000) $300,350
  Paid employees 11,531
  Receipts, 2002 ($1,000) $723,864
Information 403
  Annual payroll ($1,000) $398,220
  Paid employees 8,164
  Receipts, 2002 ($1,000) .... NA
Finance & insurance 1,560
  Annual payroll ($1,000) $1,989,292
  Paid employees 33,032
  Receipts, 2002 ($1,000) .... NA
Professional, scientific & technical 3,114
  Annual payroll ($1,000) $1,141,686
  Paid employees 22,718
  Receipts, 2002 ($1,000) $2,158,832
Education 375
  Annual payroll ($1,000) $688,237
  Paid employees 22,070
  Receipts, 2002 ($1,000) $76,337
Health care & social assistance 3,118
  Annual payroll ($1,000) $2,825,111
  Paid employees 82,286
  Receipts, 2002 ($1,000) $5,186,163
Arts and entertainment 536
  Annual payroll ($1,000) $181,748
  Paid employees 6,909
  Receipts, 2002 ($1,000) $489,588
Real estate 1,218
  Annual payroll ($1,000) $235,339
  Paid employees 6,866
  Receipts, 2002 ($1,000) $849,718
Accommodation & food service 2,901
  Annual payroll ($1,000) $611,147
  Paid employees 42,638
  Receipts, 2002 ($1,000) $1,731,799

©2008 Information Publications, Inc.
All rights reserved. Photocopying prohibited.
877-544-INFO (4636) or www.informationpublications.com

Exports, 2006

Value of exported goods ($ mil) $1,531
   Manufactured $1,028
   Non-manufactured....................$329

Foreign direct investment in US affiliates, 2004

Property, plants & equipment ($ mil) $3,381
Employment (x 1,000)....................26.1

Agriculture, 2006

Number of farms 850
Farm acreage (x 1,000) 60
   Acres per farm 71
Farm marketings and income ($ mil)
Total..................................$65.6
   Crops....................................$55.6
   Livestock...........................$10.1
Net farm income $26.0

Principal commodities, in order by marketing receipts, 2005

Greenhouse/nursery, Dairy products, Sweet corn,
     Aquaculture, Potatoes

Federal economic activity in state

Expenditures, 2005 ($ mil)
   Total............................. $8,423
     Per capita $7,846.07
   Defense $959
   Non-defense......................$7,464
Defense department, 2006 ($ mil)
   Payroll.............................. $678
   Contract awards $431
   Grants $17
Homeland security grants ($1,000)
   2006.............................$7,838
   2007.............................$12,119

FDIC-insured financial institutions, 2005

Number 13
Assets ($ billion) $29.6
Deposits ($ billion) $13.9

Fishing, 2006

Catch (x 1,000 lbs) 112,605
Value ($1,000)...................... $100,049

Mining, 2006 ($ mil)

Total non-fuel mineral production $38
Percent of U.S. 0.06%

Communication, Energy & Transportation

Communication

Households with computers, 2003........62.3%
Households with internet access, 2003 ....55.7%
High-speed internet providers 19
Total high-speed internet lines........349,994
   Residential 235,663
   Business.........................114,331
Wireless phone customers, 12/2006 797,603

FCC-licensed stations (as of January 1, 2008)

TV stations 5
FM radio stations.......................... 21
AM radio stations 15

Energy

Energy consumption, 2004
   Total (trillion Btu)..................... 226
   Per capita (million Btu) 209.8
By source of production (trillion Btu)
   Coal 0
   Natural gas............................ 75
   Petroleum............................. 99
   Nuclear electric power 0
   Hydroelectric power.................... 0
By end-use sector (trillion Btu)
   Residential 79
   Commercial 59
   Industrial 26
   Transportation 62
Electric energy, 2005
   Primary source of electricity............ Gas
   Net generation (billion kWh) 6.1
     percent from renewable sources....... 0.1%
   Net summer capability (million kW) 1.7
   CO_2 emitted from generation 2.6
Natural gas utilities, 2005
   Customers (x 1,000) 248
   Sales (trillion Btu)..................... 37
   Revenues ($ mil) $402
Nuclear plants, 2007 0
*Total CO_2 emitted (million metric tons).....*11.4
Energy spending, 2004 ($ mil) $2,634
   per capita $2,442
   Price per million Btu $15.95

Transportation, 2006

Public road & street mileage 6,528
   Urban........................5,261
   Rural 1,267
   Interstate........................ 71
Vehicle miles of travel (millions) 8,300
   per capita 7,818.1
Total motor vehicle registrations....... 805,548
   Automobiles..................... 508,389
   Trucks 295,433
   Motorcycles 31,125
Licensed drivers 741,921
   19 years & under 30,695
Deaths from motor vehicle accidents 81
Gasoline consumed (x 1,000 gallons) 418,396
   per capita 394.1

Commuting Statistics, 2006

Average commute time (min) 22.3
   Drove to work alone 81.1%
   Carpooled......................... 8.9%
   Public transit 2.6%
   Walk to work 3.0%
   Work from home..................... 2.7%

©2008 Information Publications, Inc.
All rights reserved. Photocopying prohibited.
877-544-INFO (4636) or www.informationpublications.com

State Summary

Capital city . . . . Columbia
Governor . . . . Mark Sanford
PO Box 11829
Columbia, SC 29211
803-734-9400
Admitted as a state 1788
Area (square miles) 32,020
Population, 2007 (estimate) 4,407,709
Largest city . . . . Columbia
Population, 2006 119,961
Personal income per capita, 2006
(in current dollars) $29,515
Gross domestic product, 2006 ($ mil) . . . $149,214

Leading industries by payroll, 2005

Manufacturing, Health care/Social assistance,
Retail trade

Leading agricultural commodities
by receipts, 2005

Broilers, Greenhouse/nursery, Turkeys, Cattle
and calves, Cotton

Geography & Environment

Total area (square miles) 32,020
land 30,110
water 1,911
Federally-owned land, 2004 (acres) 560,956
percent 2.9%
Highest point . . . . Sassafras Mountain
elevation (feet) 3,560
Lowest point . . . . Atlantic Ocean
elevation (feet) . . . . sea level
General coastline (miles) 187
Tidal shoreline (miles) 2,876
Cropland, 2003 (x 1,000 acres) 2,368
Forest land, 2003 (x 1,000 acres) 11,161
Capital city . . . . Columbia
Population 2000 116,278
Population 2006 119,961
Largest city . . . . Columbia
Population 2000 116,278
Population 2006 119,961

Number of cities with over 100,000 population

1990 0
2000 1
2006 2

State park and recreation areas, 2005

Area (x 1,000 acres) 81
Number of visitors (x 1,000) 6,707
Revenues ($1,000) $18,304
percent of operating expenditures 73.5%

National forest system land, 2007

Acres 629,565

Demographics & Population Characteristics

Population

1980 3,121,820
1990 3,486,703
2000 4,011,816
2006 4,321,249
Male 2,103,713
Female 2,217,536
Living in group quarters, 2006 142,974
percent of total 3.3%
2007 (estimate) 4,407,709
persons per square mile of land 146.4
2008 (projected) 4,365,055
2010 (projected) 4,446,704
2020 (projected) 4,822,577
2030 (projected) 5,148,569

Population of Core-Based Statistical Areas
(formerly Metropolitan Areas), x 1,000

	CBSA	Non-CBSA
1990	3,230	256
2000	3,735	277
2006	4,046	275

Change in population, 2000-2007

Number 395,893
percent 9.9%
Natural increase (births minus deaths) 132,891
Net internal migration 228,133
Net international migration 40,959

Persons by age, 2006

Under 5 years 283,481
5 to 17 years 756,172
18 years and over 3,281,596
65 years and over 553,396
85 years and over 68,701
Median age 37.1

Persons by age, 2010 (projected)

Under 5 years 287,544
18 and over 3,410,355
65 and over 605,660
Median age 38.4

Race, 2006

One Race
White 2,958,982
Black or African American 1,253,131
Asian 49,681
American Indian/Alaska Native 16,849
Hawaiian Native/Pacific Islander 2,287
Two or more races 40,319

Persons of Hispanic origin, 2006

Total Hispanic or Latino 148,632
Mexican 93,660
Puerto Rican 15,083
Cuban 2,493

©2008 Information Publications, Inc.
All rights reserved. Photocopying prohibited.
877-544-INFO (4636) or www.informationpublications.com

Persons of Asian origin, 2006

Total Asian 46,939
　Asian Indian. 10,699
　Chinese 9,142
　Filipino 9,127
　Japanese 3,046
　Korean 2,585
　Vietnamese. 6,493

Marital status, 2006

Population 15 years & over 3,470,748
　Never married 1,044,564
　Married. 1,829,675
　Separated 126,529
　Widowed. 253,598
　Divorced 342,911

Language spoken at home, 2006

Population 5 years and older. 4,036,541
　English only 3,795,110
　Spanish 148,345
　French 14,435
　German. 14,706
　Chinese 6,586

Households & families, 2006

Households. 1,656,978
　with persons under 18 years 567,601
　with persons over 65 years. 390,775
　persons per household 2.52
Families. 1,122,724
　persons per family. 3.07
Married couples. 798,196
Female householder,
　no husband present. 253,002
One-person households 451,584

Nativity, 2006

Number of residents born in state 2,627,072
　percent of population 60.8%

Immigration & naturalization, 2006

Legal permanent residents admitted 5,292
Persons naturalized 2,940
Non-immigrant admissions 108,650

Vital Statistics and Health

Marriages

2004 34,546
2005 35,351
2006 32,846

Divorces

2004 13,448
2005 12,423
2006 12,821

Health risks, 2006

Percent of adults who are:
　Smokers. 22.3%
　Overweight (BMI > 25). 65.4%
　Obese (BMI > 30). 29.4%

Births

2005 57,711
　Birthrate (per 1,000). 13.6
　White. 36,098
　Black 20,369
　Hispanic 4,990
　Asian/Pacific Islander 1,028
　Amer. Indian/Alaska Native. 216
　Low birth weight (2,500g or less) 10.2%
　Cesarian births 32.7%
　Preterm births 15.6%
　To unmarried mothers. 43.3%
　Twin births (per 1,000) 31.5
　Triplets or higher order (per 100,000). . . .141.8
2006 (preliminary). 62,271
　rate per 1,000 . . . . .14.4

Deaths

2004

All causes 37,276
　rate per 100,000. . . . . 898.0
Heart disease 9,182
　rate per 100,000. . . . . 222.0
Malignant neoplasms 8,348
　rate per 100,000. . . . . .195.5
Cerebrovascular disease. 2,643
　rate per 100,000. . . . . .65.2
Chronic lower respiratory disease 1,792
　rate per 100,000. . . . . .43.1
Diabetes. 1,165
　rate per 100,000. . . . . .27.6
2005 (preliminary). 38,483
　rate per 100,000. . . . . .899.1
2006 (provisional) 36,652

Infant deaths

2004 525
　rate per 1,000 . . . . .9.3
2005 (provisional) 516
　rate per 1,000 . . . . .8.9

Exercise routines, 2005

None. 26.3%
Moderate or greater. 45.3%
Vigorous 24.6%

Abortions, 2004

Total performed in state. 6,565
　rate per 1,000 women age 15-44. 7
　% obtained by out-of-state residents 3.9%

Physicians, 2005

Total. 9,769
　rate per 100,000 persons 230

Community hospitals, 2005

Number of hospitals 63
Beds (x 1,000). 11.5
Patients admitted (x 1,000) 528
Average daily census (x 1,000) 8.4
Average cost per day $1,465
Outpatient visits (x 1 mil) 5.8

©2008 Information Publications, Inc.
All rights reserved. Photocopying prohibited.
877-544-INFO (4636) or www.informationpublications.com

Disability status of population, 2006
5 to 15 years 6.5%
16 to 64 years 14.9%
65 years and over 43.7%

Education

Educational attainment, 2006
Population over 25 years 2,845,744
  Less than 9th grade.................... 6.4%
  High school graduate or more 81.3%
  College graduate or more............. 22.7%
  Graduate or professional degree........ 7.9%

Public school enrollment, 2005-06
Total............................... 701,544
  Pre-kindergarten through grade 8.... 498,030
  Grades 9 through 12................ 203,514

Graduating public high school seniors, 2004-05
Diplomas (incl. GED and others) 36,192

SAT scores, 2007
Average critical reading score.............. 488
Average writing score..................... 475
Average math score 496
Percent of graduates taking test 62%

Public school teachers, 2006-07 (estimate)
Total (x 1,000) 47.0
  Elementary...........................33.2
  Secondary............................13.8
Average salary $44,133
  Elementary....................... $44,133
  Secondary........................ $44,133

State receipts & expenditures for public schools, 2006-07 (estimate)
Revenue receipts ($ mil) $6,870
Expenditures
Total ($ mil) $7,897
  Per capita $1,480
  Per pupil $9,891

NAEP proficiency scores, 2007

	Reading		Math	
	Basic	Proficient	Basic	Proficient
Grade 4	58.9%	25.8%	79.7%	35.9%
Grade 8	68.7%	24.6%	70.9%	31.9%

Higher education enrollment, fall 2005
Total...................................35,758
  Full-time men 11,957
  Full-time women.....................17,477
  Part-time men 1,966
  Part-time women..................... 4,358

Minority enrollment in institutions of higher education, 2005
Black, non-Hispanic....................57,941
Hispanic 3,374
Asian/Pacific Islander 3,272
American Indian/Alaska Native........... 868

Institutions of higher education, 2005-06
Total................................... 64
  Public............................... 33
  Private.............................. 31

Earned degrees conferred, 2004-05
Associate's............................8,123
Bachelor's 18,795
Master's............................. 5,007
First-professional...................... 857
Doctor's............................. 466

Public Libraries, 2006
Number of libraries....................... 42
Number of outlets 220
Annual visits per capita 3.6
Circulation per capita.....................5.0

State & local financial support for higher education, FY 2006
Full-time equivalent enrollment (x 1,000)....144.0
Appropriations per FTE............... $5,822

Social Insurance & Welfare Programs

Social Security benefits & beneficiaries, 2005
Beneficiaries (x 1,000) 774
  Retired & dependents.................. 505
  Survivors............................ 104
  Disabled & dependents................ 164
Annual benefit payments ($ mil) $8,100
  Retired & dependents.................$5,139
  Survivors.............................$1,283
  Disabled & dependents...............$1,677
Average monthly benefit
  Retired & dependents.................. $982
  Disabled & dependents................. $932
  Widowed.............................. $904

Medicare, July 2005
Enrollment (x 1,000)..................... 651
Payments ($ mil) $4,541

Medicaid, 2004
Beneficiaries (x 1,000).................... 857
Payments ($ mil) $4,015

State Children's Health Insurance Program, 2006
Enrollment (x 1,000)....................68.9
Expenditures ($ mil).................... $62.6

Persons without health insurance, 2006
Number (x 1,000)........................ 672
  percent............................. 15.9%
Number of children (x 1,000) 112
  percent of children 10.7%

Health care expenditures, 2004
Total expenditures.................... $21,450
  per capita $5,114

©2008 Information Publications, Inc.
All rights reserved. Photocopying prohibited.
877-544-INFO (4636) or www.informationpublications.com

Federal and state public aid

State unemployment insurance, 2006
Recipients, first payments (x 1,000) 112
Total payments ($ mil) $326
Average weekly benefit $223
Temporary Assistance for Needy Families, 2006
Recipients (x 1,000) 432.5
Families (x 1,000) 190.2
Supplemental Security Income, 2005
Recipients (x 1,000) 105.3
Payments ($ mil) $488.2
Food Stamp Program, 2006
Avg monthly participants (x 1,000) 534.3
Total benefits ($ mil) $589.4

Housing & Construction

Housing units

Total 2005 (estimate) 1,927,864
Total 2006 (estimate) 1,975,638
Seasonal or recreational use, 2006 93,096
Owner-occupied, 2006 1,165,464
  Median home value $122,400
  Homeowner vacancy rate 2.4%
Renter-occupied, 2006 491,514
  Median rent $640
  Rental vacancy rate 10.6%
Home ownership rate, 2005 . . . . 73.9%
Home ownership rate, 2006 . . . . 74.2%

New privately-owned housing units

Number authorized, 2006 (x 1,000) 50.8
  Value ($ mil) $7,592.1
Started 2005 (x 1,000, estimate) 33.4
Started 2006 (x 1,000, estimate) 32.3

Existing home sales

2005 (x 1,000) 114.6
2006 (x 1,000) 115.2

Government & Elections

State officials 2008

Governor . . . . .Mark Sanford
      Republican, term expires 1/11
Lieutenant Governor . . . . R. André Bauer
Secretary of State . . . . Mark Hammond
Attorney General . . . . Henry McMaster
Chief Justice . . . . Jean Hoefer Toal

Governorship

Minimum age 30
Length of term . . . . 4 years
Consecutive terms permitted 2
Who succeeds . . . . Lieutenant Governor

Local governments by type, 2002

Total 701
  County 46
  Municipal 269
  Township 0
  School District 85
  Special District 301

State legislature

Name . . . . General Assembly
Upper chamber . . . . .Senate
  Number of members 46
  Length of term . . . . 4 years
  Party in majority, 2008 . . . . Republican
Lower chamber . . . . . . .House of Representatives
  Number of members 124
  Length of term . . . . 2 years
  Party in majority, 2008 . . . . Republican

Federal representation, 2008 (110ᵗʰ Congress)

Senator . . . . Lindsay Graham
  Party . . . . Republican
  Year term expires .2009
Senator . . . . .Jim DeMint
  Party . . . . Republican
  Year term expires .2011
Representatives, total 6
  Democrats 2
  Republicans 4

Voters in November 2006 election (estimate)

Total 1,375,545
  Male 604,681
  Female 770,864
  White 935,354
  Black 419,066
  Hispanic 2,388
  Asian 1,638

Presidential election, 2004

Total Popular Vote 1,617,730
  Kerry 661,699
  Bush 937,974
Total Electoral Votes 8

Votes cast for US Senators

2004
Total vote (x 1,000) .1,597
Leading party . . . . Republican
Percent for leading party 53.7%
2006
Total vote (x 1,000) . . . . NA
Leading party . . . . NA
Percent for leading party . . . . NA

Votes cast for US Representatives

2004
Total vote (x 1,000) .1,439
  Democratic 486
  Republican 913
Leading party . . . . Republican
Percent for leading party 63.5%
2006
Total vote (x 1,000) .1,086
  Democratic 473
  Republican 600
Leading party . . . . Republican
Percent for leading party 55.2%

©2008 Information Publications, Inc.
All rights reserved. Photocopying prohibited.
877-544-INFO (4636) or www.informationpublications.com

State government employment, 2006
Full-time equivalent employees 76,468
Payroll ($ mil) $245.8

Local government employment, 2006
Full-time equivalent employees 172,498
Payroll ($ mil) $517.3

Women holding public office, 2008
US Congress 0
Statewide elected office..................... 0
State legislature 15

Black public officials, 2002
Total.................................... 547
   US and state legislatures 32
   City/county/regional offices 345
   Judicial/law enforcement................. 12
   Education/school boards 158

Hispanic public officials, 2006
Total..................................... 1
   State executives & legislators 1
   City/county/regional offices 0
   Judicial/law enforcement................. 0
   Education/school boards 0

Governmental Finance

State government revenues, 2006
Total revenue (x $1,000)........... $23,719,970
   per capita $5,477.92
General revenue (x $1,000) $19,435,908
   Intergovernmental 6,867,415
   Taxes 7,759,797
      general sales.................... 3,186,306
      individual income tax 2,727,251
      corporate income tax 296,753
   Current charges................... 3,305,309
   Miscellaneous 1,503,387

State government expenditure, 2006
Total expenditure (x $1,000) $23,430,743
   per capita $5,411.12
General expenditure (x $1,000) $19,785,364
   per capita, total.................. $4,569.25
      Education 1,633.33
      Public welfare 1,116.46
      Health 198.06
      Hospitals........................ 280.93
      Highways 345.87
      Police protection................. 45.08
      Corrections 101.76
      Natural resources................. 47.53
      Parks & recreation 21.13
      Governmental administration...... 214.85
      Interest on general debt........... 120.30

State debt & cash, 2006 ($ per capita)
Debt $3,172.47
Cash/security holdings.............. $8,956.94

Federal government grants to state & local government, 2005 (x $1,000)
Total............................. $6,323,699
by Federal agency
   Defense 61,136
   Education 543,606
   Energy 33,300
   Environmental Protection Agency 48,379
   Health & Human Services. 3,810,768
   Homeland Security................. 43,945
   Housing & Urban Development...... 337,899
   Justice 105,121
   Labor 126,872
   Transportation 675,414
   Veterans Affairs................... 5,569

Crime & Law Enforcement

Crime, 2006 (rates per 100,000 residents)
Property crimes 183,322
   Burglary 42,772
   Larceny 124,148
   Motor vehicle theft 16,402
   Property crime rate................ 4,242.3
Violent crimes........................ 33,078
   Murder 359
   Forcible rape...................... 1,762
   Robbery........................... 5,899
   Aggravated assault 25,058
   Violent crime rate 765.5
Hate crimes 128

Fraud and identity theft, 2006
Fraud complaints...................... 4,841
   rate per 100,000 residents 112.0
Identity theft complaints 2,408
   rate per 100,000 residents 55.7

Law enforcement agencies, 2006
Total agencies.......................... 365
Total employees 14,332
   Officers 10,597
   Civilians 3,735

Prisoners, probation, and parole, 2006
Total prisoners....................... 23,616
   percent change, 12/31/05 to 12/31/06 .... 2.0%
   in private facilities 0.1%
   in local jails 1.6%
Sentenced to more than one year 22,861
   rate per 100,000 residents 525
Adults on probation 38,353
Adults on parole....................... 2,735

Prisoner demographics, June 30, 2005 (rate per 100,000 residents)
Male................................. 1,558
Female 137
White 415
Black................................. 1,856
Hispanic 476

©2008 Information Publications, Inc.
All rights reserved. Photocopying prohibited.
877-544-INFO (4636) or www.informationpublications.com

Arrests, 2006

Total 187,578
    Persons under 18 years of age 23,565

Persons under sentence of death, 1/1/07

Total 67
    White 29
    Black 38
    Hispanic 0

State's highest court

Name . . . . .Supreme Court
Number of members 5
Length of term . . . . 10 years
Intermediate appeals court? . . . . .yes

Labor & Income

Civilian labor force, 2006 (x 1,000)

Total 2,124
    Men 1,115
    Women 1,009
    Persons 16-19 years 101
    White 1,492
    Black 592
    Hispanic 82

Civilian labor force as a percent of civilian non-institutional population, 2006

Total 64.2%
    Men 71.3
    Women 57.9
    Persons 16-19 years 44.2
    White 63.9
    Black 65.7
    Hispanic 72.2

Employment, 2006 (x 1,000)

Total 1,987
    Men 1,043
    Women 944
    Persons 16-19 years 78
    White 1,417
    Black 532
    Hispanic 78

Unemployment rate, 2006

Total 6.5%
    Men 6.5
    Women 6.5
    Persons 16-19 years 22.7
    White 5.0
    Black 10.2
    Hispanic 5.5

Full-time/part-time labor force, 2003 (x 1,000)

Full-time labor force, employed 1,566
Part-time labor force, employed 300

Unemployed, looking for
    Full-time work 112
    Part-time work 24
Mean duration of unemployment (weeks) 19.4
    Median 10.6

Labor unions, 2006

Membership (x 1,000) 59
    percent of employed 3.3%

Experienced civilian labor force by private industry, 2006

Total 1,534,903
    Natural resources & mining 14,111
    Construction 126,275
    Manufacturing 253,811
    Trade, transportation & utilities 368,720
    Information 27,631
    Finance 97,552
    Professional & business 214,788
    Education & health 170,190
    Leisure & hospitality 209,467
    Other 48,908

Experienced civilian labor force by occupation, May 2006

Management 84,000
Business & financial .55,470
Legal 11,420
Sales 196,950
Office & admin. support 288,670
Computers & math 24,280
Architecture & engineering 35,960
Arts & entertainment 15,210
Education 108,030
Social services 21,260
Health care practitioner & technical 91,210
Health care support 43,310
Maintenance & repair 87,930
Construction 97,300
Transportation & moving 145,750
Production 202,980
Farming, fishing & forestry 4,720

Hours and earnings of production workers on manufacturing payrolls, 2006

Average weekly hours 41.0
Average hourly earnings $15.03
Average weekly earnings $616.23

Income and poverty, 2006

Median household income $41,100
Personal income, per capita (current $) . . . $29,515
    in constant (2000) dollars $25,765
Persons below poverty level 15.7%

Average annual pay

2006 . . . . $34,281
    increase from 2005 . . . . 4.1%

Federal individual income tax returns, 2005

Returns filed 1,885,351
Adjusted gross income ($1,000) $84,321,938
Total tax liability ($1,000) $9,567,240

Charitable contributions, 2004

Number of contributions 533.0
Total amount ($ mil) $2,360.2

©2008 Information Publications, Inc.
All rights reserved. Photocopying prohibited.
877-544-INFO (4636) or www.informationpublications.com

Economy, Business, Industry & Agriculture

Fortune 500 companies, 2007 1
Bankruptcy cases filed, FY 2007 7,139

Patents and trademarks issued, 2007
Patents 588
Trademarks 552

Business firm ownership, 2002
Women-owned 76,831
  Sales ($ mil) $10,891
Black-owned 28,613
  Sales ($ mil) $1,597
Hispanic-owned 3,015
  Sales ($ mil) $691
Asian-owned 4,414
  Sales ($ mil) $2,061
Amer. Indian/Alaska Native-owned 1,445
  Sales ($ mil) $157
Hawaiian/Pacific Islander-owned 41
  Sales ($ mil) $10

Gross domestic product, 2006 ($ mil)
Total gross domestic product $149,214
  Agriculture, forestry, fishing and
    hunting 1,152
  Mining 242
  Utilities 4,086
  Construction 9,146
  Manufacturing, durable goods 14,693
  Manufacturing, non-durable goods 11,561
  Wholesale trade 9,056
  Retail trade 11,996
  Transportation & warehousing 3,596
  Information 4,098
  Finance & insurance 7,431
  Real estate, rental & leasing 16,901
  Professional and technical services 6,624
  Educational services 786
  Health care and social assistance 8,663
  Accommodation/food services 5,025
  Other services, except government 3,436
  Government 23,357

Establishments, payroll, employees & receipts, by major industry group, 2005
Total 103,416
  Annual payroll ($1,000) $49,450,267
  Paid employees 1,584,914
Forestry, fishing & agriculture 608
  Annual payroll ($1,000) $174,973
  Paid employees 4,971
Mining 79
  Annual payroll ($1,000) $55,707
  Paid employees 1,266
  Receipts, 2002 ($1,000) $266,806

Utilities 302
  Annual payroll ($1,000) $664,361
  Paid employees 11,279
  Receipts, 2002 ($1,000) . . . . .NA
Construction 12,285
  Annual payroll ($1,000) $3,594,290
  Paid employees 108,276
  Receipts, 2002 ($1,000) $15,285,860
Manufacturing 4,289
  Annual payroll ($1,000) $10,958,564
  Paid employees 271,326
  Receipts, 2002 ($1,000) $81,132,781
Wholesale trade 4,795
  Annual payroll ($1,000) $2,822,820
  Paid employees 63,718
  Receipts, 2002 ($1,000) $32,988,974
Retail trade 18,590
  Annual payroll ($1,000) $4,511,411
  Paid employees 220,737
  Receipts, 2002 ($1,000) $40,629,089
Transportation & warehousing 2,688
  Annual payroll ($1,000) $1,693,198
  Paid employees 51,146
  Receipts, 2002 ($1,000) $4,296,475
Information 1,354
  Annual payroll ($1,000) $1,276,632
  Paid employees 29,044
  Receipts, 2002 ($1,000) . . . . .NA
Finance & insurance 6,827
  Annual payroll ($1,000) $2,784,533
  Paid employees 65,591
  Receipts, 2002 ($1,000) . . . . .NA
Professional, scientific & technical 9,140
  Annual payroll ($1,000) $3,778,332
  Paid employees 76,896
  Receipts, 2002 ($1,000) $7,494,425
Education 917
  Annual payroll ($1,000) $505,894
  Paid employees 24,797
  Receipts, 2002 ($1,000) $144,059
Health care & social assistance 8,908
  Annual payroll ($1,000) $6,935,358
  Paid employees 196,457
  Receipts, 2002 ($1,000) $14,823,456
Arts and entertainment 1,512
  Annual payroll ($1,000) $356,010
  Paid employees 22,115
  Receipts, 2002 ($1,000) $1,114,283
Real estate 4,918
  Annual payroll ($1,000) $874,069
  Paid employees 27,204
  Receipts, 2002 ($1,000) $3,138,683
Accommodation & food service 8,913
  Annual payroll ($1,000) $2,150,063
  Paid employees 173,653
  Receipts, 2002 ($1,000) $6,104,316

©2008 Information Publications, Inc.
All rights reserved. Photocopying prohibited.
877-544-INFO (4636) or www.informationpublications.com

Exports, 2006
Value of exported goods ($ mil) $13,615
   Manufactured $11,889
   Non-manufactured $495

Foreign direct investment in US affiliates, 2004
Property, plants & equipment ($ mil) . . . $21,844
Employment (x 1,000). 121.7

Agriculture, 2006
Number of farms 24,600
Farm acreage (x 1,000) 4,850
   Acres per farm 197
Farm marketings and income ($ mil)
Total. $1,890.7
   Crops $788.1
   Livestock. $1,102.6
Net farm income $722.2

Principal commodities, in order by marketing receipts, 2005
   Broilers, Greenhouse/nursery, Turkeys, Cattle
      and calves, Cotton

Federal economic activity in state
Expenditures, 2005 ($ mil)
   Total. $32,044
     Per capita $7,545.10
   Defense $5,105
   Non-defense $26,939
Defense department, 2006 ($ mil)
   Payroll. $3,431
   Contract awards $2,197
   Grants $45
Homeland security grants ($1,000)
   2006 . . . .$14,679
   2007 . . . .$11,001

FDIC-insured financial institutions, 2005
Number 95
Assets ($ billion) $45.5
Deposits ($ billion) $35.1

Fishing, 2006
Catch (x 1,000 lbs) .11,112
Value ($1,000). $24,088

Mining, 2006 ($ mil)
Total non-fuel mineral production $730
Percent of U.S. 1.13%

Communication, Energy & Transportation

Communication
Households with computers, 2003 . . . . .54.9%
Households with internet access, 2003 . . . . 45.6%
High-speed internet providers 42
Total high-speed internet lines 1,041,762
   Residential 673,468
   Business. 368,294
Wireless phone customers, 12/2006 3,208,504

FCC-licensed stations (as of January 1, 2008)
TV stations 34
FM radio stations. 145
AM radio stations 101

Energy
Energy consumption, 2004
   Total (trillion Btu). 1,718
   Per capita (million Btu) 409.4
By source of production (trillion Btu)
   Coal 434
   Natural gas 164
   Petroleum. 595
   Nuclear electric power 534
   Hydroelectric power 25
By end-use sector (trillion Btu)
   Residential 354
   Commercial 252
   Industrial 663
   Transportation 449
Electric energy, 2005
   Primary source of electricity. . . . . Nuclear
   Net generation (billion kWh) 102.5
     percent from renewable sources. 4.6%
   Net summer capability (million kW) 22.6
   CO_2 emitted from generation 40.9
Natural gas utilities, 2005
   Customers (x 1,000) 600
   Sales (trillion Btu). 128
   Revenues ($ mil) $1,302
Nuclear plants, 2007 7
Total CO_2 emitted (million metric tons). 79.2
Energy spending, 2004 ($ mil) $13,397
   per capita $3,194
   Price per million Btu $12.53

Transportation, 2006
Public road & street mileage 66,242
   Urban. 16,444
   Rural 49,798
   Interstate. 843
Vehicle miles of travel (millions) 50,199
   per capita 11,593.0
Total motor vehicle registrations 3,453,843
   Automobiles. .1,964,994
   Trucks 1,470,771
   Motorcycles 87,769
Licensed drivers .3,067,747
   19 years & under 216,125
Deaths from motor vehicle accidents 1,037
Gasoline consumed (x 1,000 gallons) 2,556,418
   per capita 590.4

Commuting Statistics, 2006
Average commute time (min) 22.9
   Drove to work alone 81.1%
   Carpooled. 11.3%
   Public transit 0.6%
   Walk to work 1.8%
   Work from home 3.4%

©2008 Information Publications, Inc.
All rights reserved. Photocopying prohibited.
877-544-INFO (4636) or www.informationpublications.com

State Summary

Capital city . . . . Pierre
Governor . . . . Michael Rounds

500 East Capitol St
Pierre, SD 57501
605-773-3212

Admitted as a state 1889
Area (square miles) 77,117
Population, 2007 (estimate) 796,214
Largest city . . . . Sioux Falls
  Population, 2006 142,396
Personal income per capita, 2006
  (in current dollars) $33,929
Gross domestic product, 2006 ($ mil) $32,330

Leading industries by payroll, 2005

Health care/Social assistance, Manufacturing,
Retail trade

Leading agricultural commodities
by receipts, 2005

Cattle and calves, Corn, Soybeans, Hogs, Wheat

Geography & Environment

Total area (square miles) 77,117
  land 75,885
  water 1,232
Federally-owned land, 2004 (acres) 3,028,003
  percent 6.2%
Highest point . . . . Harney Peak
  elevation (feet) 7,242
Lowest point . . . . Big Stone Lake
  elevation (feet) 966
General coastline (miles) 0
Tidal shoreline (miles) 0
Cropland, 2003 (x 1,000 acres) 17,087
Forest land, 2003 (x 1,000 acres) 503
Capital city . . . . Pierre
  Population 2000 13,876
  Population 2006 14,095
Largest city . . . . Sioux Falls
  Population 2000 123,975
  Population 2006 142,396

Number of cities with over 100,000 population

1990 0
2000 1
2006 1

State park and recreation areas, 2005

Area (x 1,000 acres) 103
Number of visitors (x 1,000) 7,399
Revenues ($1,000) $9,951
  percent of operating expenditures 77.4%

National forest system land, 2007

Acres 2,016,889

Demographics & Population Characteristics

Population

1980 690,768
1990 696,004
2000 754,840
2006 781,919
  Male 390,578
  Female 391,341
Living in group quarters, 2006 29,816
  percent of total 3.8%
2007 (estimate) 796,214
  persons per square mile of land 10.5
2008 (projected) 780,947
2010 (projected) 786,399
2020 (projected) 801,939
2030 (projected) 800,462

Population of Core-Based Statistical Areas
(formerly Metropolitan Areas), x 1,000

	CBSA	Non-CBSA
1990	469	227
2000	527	228
2006	560	222

Change in population, 2000-2007

Number 41,370
  percent 5.5%
Natural increase (births minus deaths) 31,062
Net internal migration 2,516
Net international migration 4,461

Persons by age, 2006

Under 5 years 54,828
5 to 17 years 139,853
18 years and over 587,238
65 years and over 111,183
85 years and over 19,075
  Median age 36.9

Persons by age, 2010 (projected)

Under 5 years 54,618
18 and over 592,247
65 and over 114,459
  Median age 37.5

Race, 2006

One Race

  White 691,100
  Black or African American 7,389
  Asian 5,808
  American Indian/Alaska Native 66,665
  Hawaiian Native/Pacific Islander 381
Two or more races 10,576

Persons of Hispanic origin, 2006

Total Hispanic or Latino 15,544
  Mexican 9,444
  Puerto Rican 1,152
  Cuban 205

©2008 Information Publications, Inc.
All rights reserved. Photocopying prohibited.
877-544-INFO (4636) or www.informationpublications.com

Persons of Asian origin, 2006

Total Asian 7,064
 Asian Indian......................... 742
 Chinese 1,187
 Filipino 978
 Japanese 583
 Korean............................... 856
 Vietnamese...........................1,883

Marital status, 2006

Population 15 years & over 621,618
 Never married 173,914
 Married........................... 349,648
 Separated 5,983
 Widowed........................... 40,118
 Divorced 57,938

Language spoken at home, 2006

Population 5 years and older.......... 728,218
 English only 680,816
 Spanish 14,403
 French 699
 German............................ 11,841
 Chinese 1,152

Households & families, 2006

Households........................... 312,477
 with persons under 18 years 98,546
 with persons over 65 years........... 74,690
 persons per household 2.41
Families............................. 205,964
 persons per family....................2.97
Married couples.......................166,211
Female householder,
 no husband present..................27,788
One-person households 88,494

Nativity, 2006

Number of residents born in state 509,909
 percent of population 65.2%

Immigration & naturalization, 2006

Legal permanent residents admitted.......1,013
Persons naturalized 342
Non-immigrant admissions 10,120

Vital Statistics and Health

Marriages

2004................................. 6,485
2005.................................6,551
2006................................. 6,272

Divorces

2004................................. 2,364
2005.................................2,159
2006................................. 2,502

Health risks, 2006

Percent of adults who are:
 Smokers............................20.3%
 Overweight (BMI > 25)..............64.1%
 Obese (BMI > 30)...................25.4%

Births

2005 11,462
 Birthrate (per 1,000)..................14.8
 White.................................9,267
 Black 145
 Hispanic 392
 Asian/Pacific Islander 111
 Amer. Indian/Alaska Native 1,939
 Low birth weight (2,500g or less)....... 6.6%
 Cesarian births 25.1%
 Preterm births 11.5%
 To unmarried mothers................ 36.2%
 Twin births (per 1,000) 28.9
 Triplets or higher order (per 100,000).....91.6
2006 (preliminary)......................11,917
 rate per 1,000 ....15.2

Deaths

2004
All causes 6,833
 rate per 100,000....................746.4
Heart disease 1,783
 rate per 100,000....................187.1
Malignant neoplasms 1,555
 rate per 100,000....................176.8
Cerebrovascular disease.............. 469
 rate per 100,000....................48.1
Chronic lower respiratory disease 391
 rate per 100,000....................42.7
Diabetes............................. 229
 rate per 100,000....................25.2
2005 (preliminary)....................7,087
 rate per 100,000....................757.0
2006 (provisional) 7,043

Infant deaths

2004 93
 rate per 1,000 ....8.2
2005 (provisional) 75
 rate per 1,000 ....6.5

Exercise routines, 2005

None............................... 22.5%
Moderate or greater................. 47.6%
Vigorous 23.5%

Abortions, 2004

Total performed in state.................. 814
 rate per 1,000 women age 15-44........... 5
 % obtained by out-of-state residents 17.7%

Physicians, 2005

Total...............................1,698
 rate per 100,000 persons 219

Community hospitals, 2005

Number of hospitals 52
Beds (x 1,000)........................4.3
Patients admitted (x 1,000) 102
Average daily census (x 1,000) 2.8
Average cost per day $733
Outpatient visits (x 1 mil) 1.6

©2008 Information Publications, Inc.
All rights reserved. Photocopying prohibited.
877-544-INFO (4636) or www.informationpublications.com

Disability status of population, 2006

5 to 15 years 5.5%
16 to 64 years 10.3%
65 years and over 38.1%

Education

Educational attainment, 2006

Population over 25 years 505,237
 Less than 9ᵗʰ grade. 5.5%
 High school graduate or more 88.3%
 College graduate or more. 24.8%
 Graduate or professional degree. 7.2%

Public school enrollment, 2005-06

Total 122,012
 Pre-kindergarten through grade 8. 83,530
 Grades 9 through 12 38,482

Graduating public high school seniors, 2004-05

Diplomas (incl. GED and others) 8,585

SAT scores, 2007

Average critical reading score 589
Average writing score 567
Average math score 602
Percent of graduates taking test 3%

Public school teachers, 2006-07 (estimate)

Total (x 1,000) 9.0
 Elementary 6.3
 Secondary 2.7
Average salary $35,378
 Elementary $35,473
 Secondary $35,156

State receipts & expenditures for public schools, 2006-07 (estimate)

Revenue receipts ($ mil) $1,144
Expenditures
Total ($ mil) $1,121
 Per capita $1,267
 Per pupil $8,741

NAEP proficiency scores, 2007

	Reading		Math	
	Basic	Proficient	Basic	Proficient
Grade 4	70.9%	33.7%	86.1%	40.6%
Grade 8	83.5%	36.8%	81.2%	39.1%

Higher education enrollment, fall 2005

Total 11,220
 Full-time men 2,564
 Full-time women 4,283
 Part-time men 1,559
 Part-time women 2,814

Minority enrollment in institutions of higher education, 2005

Black, non-Hispanic 642
Hispanic 518
Asian/Pacific Islander 592
American Indian/Alaska Native 3,196

Institutions of higher education, 2005-06

Total 24
 Public. 12
 Private 12

Earned degrees conferred, 2004-05

Associate's. 2,225
Bachelor's 4,771
Master's 1,217
First-professional. 210
Doctor's 89

Public Libraries, 2006

Number of libraries. 124
Number of outlets 152
Annual visits per capita 6.2
Circulation per capita. 9.1

State & local financial support for higher education, FY 2006

Full-time equivalent enrollment (x 1,000) 29.3
Appropriations per FTE. $4,499

Social Insurance & Welfare Programs

Social Security benefits & beneficiaries, 2005

Beneficiaries (x 1,000) 142
 Retired & dependents. 103
 Survivors. 21
 Disabled & dependents. 19
Annual benefit payments ($ mil) $1,415
 Retired & dependents. $966
 Survivors. $269
 Disabled & dependents. $180
Average monthly benefit
 Retired & dependents. $920
 Disabled & dependents. $877
 Widowed. $916

Medicare, July 2005

Enrollment (x 1,000) 125
Payments ($ mil) $687

Medicaid, 2004

Beneficiaries (x 1,000). 128
Payments ($ mil) $580

State Children's Health Insurance Program, 2006

Enrollment (x 1,000) 14.6
Expenditures ($ mil) $14.0

Persons without health insurance, 2006

Number (x 1,000). 91
 percent. 11.8%
Number of children (x 1,000) 18
 percent of children 9.3%

Health care expenditures, 2004

Total expenditures. $4,103
 per capita $5,327

©2008 Information Publications, Inc.
All rights reserved. Photocopying prohibited.
877-544-INFO (4636) or www.informationpublications.com

Federal and state public aid

State unemployment insurance, 2006
Recipients, first payments (x 1,000) 8
Total payments ($ mil) $22
Average weekly benefit $219
Temporary Assistance for Needy Families, 2006
Recipients (x 1,000) 73.6
Families (x 1,000) 34.2
Supplemental Security Income, 2005
Recipients (x 1,000) 12.6
Payments ($ mil) $54.7
Food Stamp Program, 2006
Avg monthly participants (x 1,000) 58.5
Total benefits ($ mil) $66.2

Housing & Construction

Housing units
Total 2005 (estimate) 347,952
Total 2006 (estimate) 352,813
Seasonal or recreational use, 2006 12,362
Owner-occupied, 2006 216,212
   Median home value $112,600
   Homeowner vacancy rate 2.0%
Renter-occupied, 2006 96,265
   Median rent $522
   Rental vacancy rate 8.3%
Home ownership rate, 2005 . . . . 68.4%
Home ownership rate, 2006 . . . . 70.6%

New privately-owned housing units
Number authorized, 2006 (x 1,000) 5.3
   Value ($ mil) $658.8
Started 2005 (x 1,000, estimate) 4.9
Started 2006 (x 1,000, estimate) 4.8

Existing home sales
2005 (x 1,000) 18.3
2006 (x 1,000) 18.3

Government & Elections

State officials 2008
Governor . . . . Michael Rounds
   Republican, term expires 1/11
Lieutenant Governor . . . . Dennis Daugaard
Secretary of State . . . . .Chris Nelson
Attorney General . . . . Larry Long
Chief Justice . . . . .David Gilbertson

Governorship
Minimum age 18
Length of term . . . . 4 years
Consecutive terms permitted 2
Who succeeds . . . . Lieutenant Governor

Local governments by type, 2002
Total 1,866
   County 66
   Municipal 308
   Township 940
   School District 176
   Special District 376

State legislature
Name . . . . Legislature
Upper chamber . . . . .Senate
   Number of members 35
   Length of term . . . . 2 years
   Party in majority, 2008 . . . . Republican
Lower chamber . . . . House of Representatives
   Number of members 70
   Length of term . . . . 2 years
   Party in majority, 2008 . . . . Republican

Federal representation, 2008 (110th Congress)
Senator . . . . Tim Johnson
   Party . . . . Democratic
   Year term expires 2009
Senator . . . . John Thune
   Party . . . . Republican
   Year term expires 2011
Representatives, total 1
   Democrats 1
   Republicans 0

Voters in November 2006 election (estimate)
Total 358,388
   Male 166,916
   Female 191,472
   White 345,890
   Black 404
   Hispanic 1,753
   Asian . . . . NA

Presidential election, 2004
Total Popular Vote 388,215
   Kerry 149,244
   Bush 232,584
Total Electoral Votes 3

Votes cast for US Senators
2004
Total vote (x 1,000) 391
Leading party . . . . Republican
Percent for leading party 50.6%
2006
Total vote (x 1,000) . . . . NA
Leading party . . . . NA
Percent for leading party . . . . NA

Votes cast for US Representatives
2004
Total vote (x 1,000) 389
   Democratic 208
   Republican 179
Leading party . . . . Democratic
Percent for leading party 53.4%
2006
Total vote (x 1,000) 334
   Democratic 230
   Republican 98
Leading party . . . . Democratic
Percent for leading party 69.1%

©2008 Information Publications, Inc.
All rights reserved. Photocopying prohibited.
877-544-INFO (4636) or www.informationpublications.com

State government employment, 2006
Full-time equivalent employees 13,905
Payroll ($ mil) $44.2

Local government employment, 2006
Full-time equivalent employees 31,281
Payroll ($ mil) $90.5

Women holding public office, 2008
US Congress............................. 1
Statewide elected office...................... 0
State legislature 18

Black public officials, 2002
Total....................................... 0
US and state legislatures 0
City/county/regional offices 0
Judicial/law enforcement.................. 0
Education/school boards.................. 0

Hispanic public officials, 2006
Total....................................... 0
State executives & legislators 0
City/county/regional offices 0
Judicial/law enforcement.................. 0
Education/school boards.................. 0

Governmental Finance

State government revenues, 2006
Total revenue (x $1,000)............. $4,175,073
per capita $5,295.18
General revenue (x $1,000) $3,212,568
Intergovernmental 1,251,314
Taxes 1,182,027
general sales...................... 679,162
individual income tax 0
corporate income tax 61,865
Current charges.................... 245,597
Miscellaneous 533,630

State government expenditure, 2006
Total expenditure (x $1,000) $3,465,272
per capita $4,394.95
General expenditure (x $1,000) $3,175,403
per capita, total................... $4,027.31
Education 1,226.77
Public welfare 949.03
Health 127.18
Hospitals......................... 67.10
Highways 639.18
Police protection.................... 38.81
Corrections 135.83
Natural resources 151.90
Parks & recreation 33.77
Governmental administration...... 192.66
Interest on general debt............ 143.98

State debt & cash, 2006 ($ per capita)
Debt................................ $3,990.10
Cash/security holdings............. $14,560.47

Federal government grants to state & local government, 2005 (x $1,000)
Total............................. $1,741,877
by Federal agency
Defense 26,964
Education 173,836
Energy 4,040
Environmental Protection Agency 28,481
Health & Human Services. 664,026
Homeland Security.................. 7,501
Housing & Urban Development....... 114,485
Justice 33,087
Labor 27,542
Transportation 292,855
Veterans Affairs.................... 3,704

Crime & Law Enforcement

Crime, 2006 (rates per 100,000 residents)
Property crimes 12,664
Burglary 2,650
Larceny 9,296
Motor vehicle theft 718
Property crime rate.................. 1,619.6
Violent crimes........................ 1,340
Murder 9
Forcible rape........................ 336
Robbery........................... 119
Aggravated assault 876
Violent crime rate 171.4
Hate crimes........................... 79

Fraud and identity theft, 2006
Fraud complaints..................... 618
rate per 100,000 residents 79.0
Identity theft complaints 236
rate per 100,000 residents 30.2

Law enforcement agencies, 2006
Total agencies.......................... 141
Total employees....................... 2,070
Officers 1,231
Civilians 839

Prisoners, probation, and parole, 2006
Total prisoners........................ 3,359
percent change, 12/31/05 to 12/31/06 ... -3.0%
in private facilities 0.4%
in local jails 1.8%
Sentenced to more than one year 3,350
rate per 100,000 residents 426
Adults on probation 5,661
Adults on parole....................... 2,767

Prisoner demographics, June 30, 2005 (rate per 100,000 residents)
Male.............................. 1,092
Female 157
White 470
Black............................. 4,710
Hispanic .... NA

©2008 Information Publications, Inc.
All rights reserved. Photocopying prohibited.
877-544-INFO (4636) or www.informationpublications.com

Arrests, 2006

Total................................ 13,677
    Persons under 18 years of age 2,214

Persons under sentence of death, 1/1/07

Total....................................... 4
    White..................................... 4
    Black 0
    Hispanic 0

State's highest court

Name ....Supreme Court
Number of members........................ 5
Length of term .... 8 years
Intermediate appeals court? .... no

Labor & Income

Civilian labor force, 2006 (x 1,000)

Total..................................... 434
    Men 229
    Women 206
    Persons 16-19 years..................... 28
    White................................... 408
    Black .... NA
    Hispanic 9

Civilian labor force as a percent of civilian non-institutional population, 2006

Total...................................72.5%
    Men 78.2
    Women 67.1
    Persons 16-19 years.....................63.2
    White...................................73.2
    Black .... NA
    Hispanic 72.6

Employment, 2006 (x 1,000)

Total..................................... 421
    Men 222
    Women 199
    Persons 16-19 years..................... 25
    White................................... 398
    Black .... NA
    Hispanic 8

Unemployment rate, 2006

Total.................................... 3.1%
    Men 2.9
    Women 3.3
    Persons 16-19 years.....................8.9
    White...................................2.4
    Black .... NA
    Hispanic 6.7

Full-time/part-time labor force, 2003 (x 1,000)

Full-time labor force, employed 332
Part-time labor force, employed............. 77

Unemployed, looking for
    Full-time work........................... 13
    Part-time work........................... 3
Mean duration of unemployment (weeks)......15.1
    Median 7.3

Labor unions, 2006

Membership (x 1,000)..................... 21
    percent of employed 5.9%

Experienced civilian labor force by private industry, 2006

Total..............................314,784
    Natural resources & mining 4,099
    Construction 21,833
    Manufacturing.......................41,395
    Trade, transportation & utilities 79,334
    Information 6,953
    Finance 29,158
    Professional & business 25,633
    Education & health 53,601
    Leisure & hospitality. 42,467
    Other 10,312

Experienced civilian labor force by occupation, May 2006

Management...........................11,430
Business & financial 14,020
Legal.................................1,580
Sales................................41,370
Office & admin. support............... 66,640
Computers & math 5,290
Architecture & engineering............. 4,340
Arts & entertainment 4,920
Education 22,030
Social services 4,940
Health care practitioner & technical......23,310
Health care support 10,500
Maintenance & repair.................. 15,290
Construction 21,260
Transportation & moving 28,750
Production 30,130
Farming, fishing & forestry.............1,450

Hours and earnings of production workers on manufacturing payrolls, 2006

Average weekly hours 42.1
Average hourly earnings $13.75
Average weekly earnings $578.88

Income and poverty, 2006

Median household income............ $42,791
Personal income, per capita (current $)... $33,929
    in constant (2000) dollars $29,618
Persons below poverty level.............. 13.6%

Average annual pay

2006 .... $30,291
    increase from 2005 .... 3.9%

Federal individual income tax returns, 2005

Returns filed........................367,105
Adjusted gross income ($1,000) $16,165,957
Total tax liability ($1,000) $2,032,903

Charitable contributions, 2004

Number of contributions 55.5
Total amount ($ mil)................. $262.7

©2008 Information Publications, Inc.
All rights reserved. Photocopying prohibited.
877-544-INFO (4636) or www.informationpublications.com

Economy, Business, Industry & Agriculture

Fortune 500 companies, 2007 0
Bankruptcy cases filed, FY 2007 1,302

Patents and trademarks issued, 2007

Patents 72
Trademarks 175

Business firm ownership, 2002

Women-owned 15,573
   Sales ($ mil) $1,547
Black-owned 122
   Sales ($ mil) $61
Hispanic-owned 355
   Sales ($ mil) $122
Asian-owned 300
   Sales ($ mil) $88
Amer. Indian/Alaska Native-owned 1,304
   Sales ($ mil) $137
Hawaiian/Pacific Islander-owned 13
   Sales ($ mil) . . . . NA

Gross domestic product, 2006 ($ mil)

Total gross domestic product $32,330
   Agriculture, forestry, fishing and
     hunting 1,947
   Mining 119
   Utilities 582
   Construction 1,371
   Manufacturing, durable goods 2,509
   Manufacturing, non-durable goods 866
   Wholesale trade .1,817
   Retail trade 2,317
   Transportation & warehousing 894
   Information 887
   Finance & insurance 5,544
   Real estate, rental & leasing 2,811
   Professional and technical services 830
   Educational services 239
   Health care and social assistance 2,817
   Accommodation/food services 843
   Other services, except government 734
   Government 4,156

Establishments, payroll, employees & receipts, by major industry group, 2005

Total 25,205
   Annual payroll ($1,000) $8,860,458
   Paid employees 310,802
Forestry, fishing & agriculture 137
   Annual payroll ($1,000) . . . . NA
   Paid employees . . . . NA
Mining 63
   Annual payroll ($1,000) . . . . NA
   Paid employees . . . . NA
   Receipts, 2002 ($1,000) $206,689

Utilities 155
   Annual payroll ($1,000) $108,961
   Paid employees 2,018
   Receipts, 2002 ($1,000) . . . . NA
Construction 3,251
   Annual payroll ($1,000) $628,966
   Paid employees 17,683
   Receipts, 2002 ($1,000) $2,643,417
Manufacturing 964
   Annual payroll ($1,000) $1,313,973
   Paid employees 39,397
   Receipts, 2002 ($1,000) $10,710,187
Wholesale trade 1,278
   Annual payroll ($1,000) $520,909
   Paid employees 14,318
   Receipts, 2002 ($1,000) $7,845,096
Retail trade 4,282
   Annual payroll ($1,000) $982,171
   Paid employees 49,526
   Receipts, 2002 ($1,000) $9,601,175
Transportation & warehousing 1,055
   Annual payroll ($1,000) $242,009
   Paid employees 8,110
   Receipts, 2002 ($1,000) $904,994
Information 422
   Annual payroll ($1,000) $240,919
   Paid employees 6,868
   Receipts, 2002 ($1,000) . . . . NA
Finance & insurance 1,843
   Annual payroll ($1,000) $907,331
   Paid employees 23,964
   Receipts, 2002 ($1,000) . . . . NA
Professional, scientific & technical 1,703
   Annual payroll ($1,000) $331,875
   Paid employees 9,716
   Receipts, 2002 ($1,000) $934,637
Education 201
   Annual payroll ($1,000) $149,156
   Paid employees 8,024
   Receipts, 2002 ($1,000) $15,790
Health care & social assistance 2,172
   Annual payroll ($1,000) $1,947,125
   Paid employees 55,631
   Receipts, 2002 ($1,000) $3,467,289
Arts and entertainment 643
   Annual payroll ($1,000) $96,698
   Paid employees 6,245
   Receipts, 2002 ($1,000) $361,537
Real estate 892
   Annual payroll ($1,000) $92,243
   Paid employees 4,057
   Receipts, 2002 ($1,000) $377,363
Accommodation & food service 2,285
   Annual payroll ($1,000) $383,876
   Paid employees 34,689
   Receipts, 2002 ($1,000) $1,226,459

©2008 Information Publications, Inc.
All rights reserved. Photocopying prohibited.
877-544-INFO (4636) or www.informationpublications.com

Exports, 2006
Value of exported goods ($ mil) $1,185
  Manufactured $1,088
  Non-manufactured. $67

Foreign direct investment in US affiliates, 2004
Property, plants & equipment ($ mil) $750
Employment (x 1,000). 5.5

Agriculture, 2006
Number of farms 31,300
Farm acreage (x 1,000) 43,700
  Acres per farm. 1,396
Farm marketings and income ($ mil)
Total. $4,716.2
  Crops. $2,064.6
  Livestock. $2,651.6
Net farm income $741.5

Principal commodities, in order by marketing receipts, 2005
Cattle and calves, Corn, Soybeans, Hogs, Wheat

Federal economic activity in state
Expenditures, 2005 ($ mil)
  Total. $7,481
    Per capita $9,654.69
  Defense $777
  Non-defense. $6,704
Defense department, 2006 ($ mil)
  Payroll. $358
  Contract awards $372
  Grants $21
Homeland security grants ($1,000)
  2006. . . . .$7,734
  2007. . . . .$6,682

FDIC-insured financial institutions, 2005
Number. 89
Assets ($ billion) $499.0
Deposits ($ billion) $352.5

Fishing, 2006
Catch (x 1,000 lbs). . . . . NA
Value ($1,000). . . . . NA

Mining, 2006 ($ mil)
Total non-fuel mineral production $204
Percent of U.S. 0.32%

Communication, Energy & Transportation

Communication
Households with computers, 2003. . . . . 62.1%
Households with internet access, 2003 . . . . 53.6%
High-speed internet providers 42
Total high-speed internet lines. 154,738
  Residential 137,156
  Business. 17,582
Wireless phone customers, 12/2006 547,812

FCC-licensed stations (as of January 1, 2008)
TV stations 26
FM radio stations. 79
AM radio stations 36

Energy
Energy consumption, 2004
  Total (trillion Btu). 264
  Per capita (million Btu) 342.3
By source of production (trillion Btu)
  Coal 44
  Natural gas. 43
  Petroleum. 115
  Nuclear electric power 0
  Hydroelectric power. 36
By end-use sector (trillion Btu)
  Residential 61
  Commercial 53
  Industrial 63
  Transportation 87
Electric energy, 2005
  Primary source of electricity. . . . Hydroelectric
  Net generation (billion kWh) 6.5
    percent from renewable sources. 49.6%
  Net summer capability (million kW) 2.8
  CO_2 emitted from generation 3.3
Natural gas utilities, 2005
  Customers (x 1,000) 179
  Sales (trillion Btu). 34
  Revenues ($ mil) $253
Nuclear plants, 2007 0
Total CO_2 emitted (million metric tons). 13.7
Energy spending, 2004 ($ mil) $2,317
  per capita $3,008
  Price per million Btu $12.54

Transportation, 2006
Public road & street mileage 84,229
  Urban. 2,828
  Rural 81,401
  Interstate. 679
Vehicle miles of travel (millions) 9,168
  per capita 11,627.6
Total motor vehicle registrations. 843,984
  Automobiles. 375,760
  Trucks 465,580
  Motorcycles 53,477
Licensed drivers 582,517
  19 years & under 47,517
Deaths from motor vehicle accidents 191
Gasoline consumed (x 1,000 gallons) 428,785
  per capita 543.8

Commuting Statistics, 2006
Average commute time (min) 15.9
  Drove to work alone 77.5%
  Carpooled. 9.6%
  Public transit 0.4%
  Walk to work 4.3%
  Work from home. 6.6%

©2008 Information Publications, Inc.
All rights reserved. Photocopying prohibited.
877-544-INFO (4636) or www.informationpublications.com

State Summary

Capital city . . . . Nashville
Governor . . . . Phil Bredesen

Tennessee State Capitol
Nashville, TN 37243
615-741-2001

Admitted as a state 1796
Area (square miles) 42,143
Population, 2007 (estimate). 6,156,719
Largest city . . . . Memphis
Population, 2006 670,902
Personal income per capita, 2006
(in current dollars) $32,304
Gross domestic product, 2006 ($ mil) . . . $238,029

Leading industries by payroll, 2005

Manufacturing, Health care/Social assistance,
Retail trade

Leading agricultural commodities by receipts, 2005

Cattle and calves, Broilers, Cotton, Greenhouse/
nursery, Soybeans

Geography & Environment

Total area (square miles). 42,143
land 41,217
water 926
Federally-owned land, 2004 (acres) 865,837
percent. 3.2%
Highest point . . . . Clingmans Dome
elevation (feet) 6,643
Lowest point . . . . Mississippi River
elevation (feet) 178
General coastline (miles) 0
Tidal shoreline (miles) 0
Cropland, 2003 (x 1,000 acres) 4,750
Forest land, 2003 (x 1,000 acres). 11,959
Capital city . . . . Nashville
Population 2000 545,524
Population 2006 552,120
Largest city . . . . Memphis
Population 2000 650,100
Population 2006 670,902

Number of cities with over 100,000 population

1990 4
2000 5
2006 5

State park and recreation areas, 2005

Area (x 1,000 acres) 141
Number of visitors (x 1,000) 29,038
Revenues ($1,000) $34,865
percent of operating expenditures 50.8%

National forest system land, 2007

Acres 707,387

Demographics & Population Characteristics

Population

1980 4,591,120
1990 4,877,185
2000 5,689,262
2006 6,038,803
Male 2,950,890
Female 3,087,913
Living in group quarters, 2006 152,407
percent of total. 2.5%
2007 (estimate). .6,156,719
persons per square mile of land 149.4
2008 (projected) .6,124,341
2010 (projected) .6,230,852
2020 (projected). 6,780,670
2030 (projected). 7,380,634

Population of Core-Based Statistical Areas (formerly Metropolitan Areas), x 1,000

	CBSA	Non-CBSA
1990	4,350	527
2000	5,080	610
2006	5,412	627

Change in population, 2000-2007

Number 467,457
percent. 8.2%
Natural increase (births minus deaths) 168,757
Net internal migration 217,129
Net international migration 60,929

Persons by age, 2006

Under 5 years 398,252
5 to 17 years 1,044,341
18 years and over 4,596,210
65 years and over 769,222
85 years and over 97,712
Median age. 37.1

Persons by age, 2010 (projected)

Under 5 years 412,075
18 and over 4,751,937
65 and over 829,023
Median age 37.9

Race, 2006

One Race
White. 4,855,937
Black or African American 1,019,528
Asian 79,665
American Indian/Alaska Native. 18,733
Hawaiian Native/Pacific Islander. 3,078
Two or more races. 61,862

Persons of Hispanic origin, 2006

Total Hispanic or Latino 187,747
Mexican. 126,694
Puerto Rican 12,923
Cuban 3,155

©2008 Information Publications, Inc.
All rights reserved. Photocopying prohibited.
877-544-INFO (4636) or www.informationpublications.com

Persons of Asian origin, 2006

Total Asian 76,208
Asian Indian. 17,070
Chinese 16,270
Filipino 5,911
Japanese 3,655
Korean. 9,462
Vietnamese. .7,854

Marital status, 2006

Population 15 years & over 4,846,989
Never married 1,293,537
Married. 2,607,959
Separated 116,088
Widowed. 336,451
Divorced 609,042

Language spoken at home, 2006

Population 5 years and older. 5,639,797
English only 5,330,469
Spanish 171,646
French 13,389
German. 15,994
Chinese 13,448

Households & families, 2006

Households. 2,375,123
with persons under 18 years 807,349
with persons over 65 years. 543,746
persons per household 2.48
Families. 1,597,016
persons per family. 3.03
Married couples. 1,178,105
Female householder,
no husband present. 311,624
One-person households 659,600

Nativity, 2006

Number of residents born in state 3,781,851
percent of population 62.6%

Immigration & naturalization, 2006

Legal permanent residents admitted 10,042
Persons naturalized 3,334
Non-immigrant admissions 127,584

Vital Statistics and Health

Marriages

2004 67,104
2005 65,426
2006 64,028

Divorces

2004 28,858
2005 27,823
2006 25,886

Health risks, 2006

Percent of adults who are:
Smokers. 22.6%
Overweight (BMI > 25). 65.3%
Obese (BMI > 30). 28.8%

Births

2005 81,747
Birthrate (per 1,000). 13.7
White. 61,409
Black 18,484
Hispanic 7,000
Asian/Pacific Islander 1,697
Amer. Indian/Alaska Native 157
Low birth weight (2,500g or less). 9.5%
Cesarian births 31.1%
Preterm births 14.7%
To unmarried mothers. 40.2%
Twin births (per 1,000) 31.1
Triplets or higher order (per 100,000). . . .153.2
2006 (preliminary). 84,345
rate per 1,000 . . . . .14.0

Deaths

2004
All causes 55,829
rate per 100,000. . . . . 954.0
Heart disease 15,038
rate per 100,000. . . . . .259.1
Malignant neoplasms 12,586
rate per 100,000. . . . . 208.6
Cerebrovascular disease. 3,680
rate per 100,000. . . . . .64.7
Chronic lower respiratory disease 2,987
rate per 100,000. . . . . .50.9
Diabetes. 1,882
rate per 100,000. . . . . .31.6
2005 (preliminary). 57,270
rate per 100,000. . . . . .959.9
2006 (provisional) 56,687

Infant deaths

2004 687
rate per 1,000 . . . . .8.6
2005 (provisional) 737
rate per 1,000 . . . . .9.0

Exercise routines, 2005

None. 33.1%
Moderate or greater. 36.1%
Vigorous 17.4%

Abortions, 2004

Total performed in state. 16,400
rate per 1,000 women age 15-44. 13
% obtained by out-of-state residents 21.1%

Physicians, 2005

Total. 15,683
rate per 100,000 persons 263

Community hospitals, 2005

Number of hospitals 130
Beds (x 1,000). 20.6
Patients admitted (x 1,000) 829
Average daily census (x 1,000) 13.1
Average cost per day $1,234
Outpatient visits (x 1 mil) 11.7

©2008 Information Publications, Inc.
All rights reserved. Photocopying prohibited.
877-544-INFO (4636) or www.informationpublications.com

Disability status of population, 2006

5 to 15 years 7.0%
16 to 64 years 16.4%
65 years and over 46.0%

Education

Educational attainment, 2006

Population over 25 years 4,037,826
   Less than 9th grade. 7.6%
   High school graduate or more 80.9%
   College graduate or more. 21.7%
   Graduate or professional degree. 7.5%

Public school enrollment, 2005-06

Total. 953,928
   Pre-kindergarten through grade 8. ... 662,219
   Grades 9 through 12 277,352

Graduating public high school seniors, 2004-05

Diplomas (incl. GED and others) 51,165

SAT scores, 2007

Average critical reading score 574
Average writing score 568
Average math score 569
Percent of graduates taking test 13%

Public school teachers, 2006-07 (estimate)

Total (x 1,000) 61.8
   Elementary. 43.3
   Secondary. 18.5
Average salary $43,816
   Elementary. $43,238
   Secondary. $44,679

State receipts & expenditures for public schools, 2006-07 (estimate)

Revenue receipts ($ mil) $7,422
Expenditures
Total ($ mil) $7,329
   Per capita $1,142
   Per pupil $7,773

NAEP proficiency scores, 2007

	Reading		Math	
	Basic	Proficient	Basic	Proficient
Grade 4	60.6%	26.9%	76.1%	28.7%
Grade 8	71.3%	25.6%	63.9%	23.1%

Higher education enrollment, fall 2005

Total. 82,676
   Full-time men 29,954
   Full-time women. 39,693
   Part-time men 4,929
   Part-time women. 8,100

Minority enrollment in institutions of higher education, 2005

Black, non-Hispanic 55,288
Hispanic 5,142
Asian/Pacific Islander 5,277
American Indian/Alaska Native. 1,192

Institutions of higher education, 2005-06

Total. 98
   Public. 22
   Private. 76

Earned degrees conferred, 2004-05

Associate's. 9,707
Bachelor's 26,032
Master's. 8,530
First-professional. 1,402
Doctor's. 891

Public Libraries, 2006

Number of libraries. 186
Number of outlets 294
Annual visits per capita 3.2
Circulation per capita. 4.1

State & local financial support for higher education, FY 2006

Full-time equivalent enrollment (x 1,000). ... 170.4
Appropriations per FTE. $6,275

Social Insurance & Welfare Programs

Social Security benefits & beneficiaries, 2005

Beneficiaries (x 1,000) 1,098
   Retired & dependents. 708
   Survivors. 159
   Disabled & dependents. 231
Annual benefit payments ($ mil) $11,406
   Retired & dependents. $7,109
   Survivors. $2,010
   Disabled & dependents. $2,288
Average monthly benefit
   Retired & dependents. $978
   Disabled & dependents. $904
   Widowed. $923

Medicare, July 2005

Enrollment (x 1,000) 922
Payments ($ mil) $6,028

Medicaid, 2004

Beneficiaries (x 1,000). 1,730
Payments ($ mil) $6,945

State Children's Health Insurance Program, 2006

Enrollment (x 1,000). 0.0
Expenditures ($ mil) $0.0

Persons without health insurance, 2006

Number (x 1,000). 809
   percent. 13.7%
Number of children (x 1,000) 94
   percent of children 6.4%

Health care expenditures, 2004

Total expenditures. $32,161
   per capita $5,464

©2008 Information Publications, Inc.
All rights reserved. Photocopying prohibited.
877-544-INFO (4636) or www.informationpublications.com

Federal and state public aid

State unemployment insurance, 2006
Recipients, first payments (x 1,000) 143
Total payments ($ mil) $408
Average weekly benefit $216
Temporary Assistance for Needy Families, 2006
Recipients (x 1,000) 2,115.4
Families (x 1,000) 803.6
Supplemental Security Income, 2005
Recipients (x 1,000) 161.1
Payments ($ mil) $752.1
Food Stamp Program, 2006
Avg monthly participants (x 1,000) 870.4
Total benefits ($ mil) $976.0

Housing & Construction

Housing units
Total 2005 (estimate) 2,637,092
Total 2006 (estimate) 2,681,150
Seasonal or recreational use, 2006 53,185
Owner-occupied, 2006 1,660,152
  Median home value $123,100
  Homeowner vacancy rate 1.8%
Renter-occupied, 2006 714,971
  Median rent $613
  Rental vacancy rate 10.5%
Home ownership rate, 2005 . . . . .72.4%
Home ownership rate, 2006 . . . . .71.3%

New privately-owned housing units
Number authorized, 2006 (x 1,000) 46.0
  Value ($ mil) $6,781.7
Started 2005 (x 1,000, estimate) 34.2
Started 2006 (x 1,000, estimate) 34.3

Existing home sales
2005 (x 1,000) 170.9
2006 (x 1,000) 173.6

Government & Elections

State officials 2008
Governor . . . . Phil Bredesen
  Democratic, term expires 1/11
Lieutenant Governor . . . . Ron Ramsey
Secretary of State . . . . Riley Darnell
Attorney General . . . . Robert Cooper Jr
Chief Justice . . . . Mickey Barker

Governorship
Minimum age 30
Length of term . . . . 4 years
Consecutive terms permitted 2
Who succeeds . . . . Speaker of Senate

Local governments by type, 2002
Total 930
  County 92
  Municipal 349
  Township 0
  School District 14
  Special District 475

State legislature
Name . . . . General Assembly
Upper chamber . . . . .Senate
  Number of members 33
  Length of term . . . . 4 years
  Party in majority, 2008 . . . . Republican
Lower chamber . . . . House of Representatives
  Number of members 99
  Length of term . . . . 2 years
  Party in majority, 2008 . . . . Democratic

Federal representation, 2008 (110th Congress)
Senator .Lamar Alexander
  Party . . . . Republican
  Year term expires 2009
Senator . . . . Bob Corker
  Party . . . . Republican
  Year term expires 2013
Representatives, total 9
  Democrats 5
  Republicans 4

Voters in November 2006 election (estimate)
Total 2,003,441
  Male 927,249
  Female 1,076,192
  White 1,723,048
  Black 268,473
  Hispanic . . . . NA
  Asian 2,975

Presidential election, 2004
Total Popular Vote 2,437,319
  Kerry 1,036,477
  Bush 1,384,375
Total Electoral Votes 11

Votes cast for US Senators
2004
Total vote (x 1,000) . . . . NA
Leading party . . . . NA
Percent for leading party . . . . NA
2006
Total vote (x 1,000) .1,834
Leading party . . . . Republican
Percent for leading party 50.7%

Votes cast for US Representatives
2004
Total vote (x 1,000) .2,219
  Democratic 1,032
  Republican 1,161
Leading party . . . . Republican
Percent for leading party 52.3%
2006
Total vote (x 1,000) .1,715
  Democratic 861
  Republican 800
Leading party . . . . Democratic
Percent for leading party 50.2%

©2008 Information Publications, Inc.
All rights reserved. Photocopying prohibited.
877-544-INFO (4636) or www.informationpublications.com

State government employment, 2006
Full-time equivalent employees 83,117
Payroll ($ mil) $269.4

Local government employment, 2006
Full-time equivalent employees 240,556
Payroll ($ mil) $731.5

Women holding public office, 2008
US Congress 1
Statewide elected office................. 0
State legislature 22

Black public officials, 2002
Total.................................. 195
US and state legislatures 18
City/county/regional offices 118
Judicial/law enforcement................ 28
Education/school boards................ 31

Hispanic public officials, 2006
Total.................................... 2
State executives & legislators 1
City/county/regional offices 1
Judicial/law enforcement................. 0
Education/school boards................. 0

Governmental Finance

State government revenues, 2006
Total revenue (x $1,000)............ $26,315,890
per capita $4,331.90
General revenue (x $1,000) $23,644,213
Intergovernmental 8,202,128
Taxes 10,650,350
general sales..................... 6,451,838
individual income tax 192,764
corporate income tax............. 928,349
Current charges.................. 1,793,514
Miscellaneous 2,998,221

State government expenditure, 2006
Total expenditure (x $1,000)........ $23,967,779
per capita $3,945.37
General expenditure (x $1,000) $22,412,778
per capita, total.................... $3,689.40
Education..................... 1,208.08
Public welfare 1,335.62
Health........................ 187.69
Hospitals..................... 68.54
Highways 306.58
Police protection................ 24.66
Corrections 112.06
Natural resources 40.32
Parks & recreation 22.89
Governmental administration....... 114.94
Interest on general debt............. 31.97

State debt & cash, 2006 ($ per capita)
Debt.............................. $629.03
Cash/security holdings.............. $5,631.55

Federal government grants to state & local government, 2005 (x $1,000)
Total............................ $9,985,336
by Federal agency
Defense 37,458
Education 678,739
Energy........................... 27,564
Environmental Protection Agency 44,316
Health & Human Services.......... 6,814,522
Homeland Security................ 37,723
Housing & Urban Development...... 515,507
Justice 102,005
Labor 124,103
Transportation 734,789
Veterans Affairs................... 24,635

Crime & Law Enforcement

Crime, 2006 (rates per 100,000 residents)
Property crimes 249,297
Burglary 62,859
Larceny 163,845
Motor vehicle theft 22,593
Property crime rate.............. 4,128.3
Violent crimes. 45,907
Murder 409
Forcible rape..................... 2,142
Robbery......................... 11,129
Aggravated assault 32,227
Violent crime rate 760.2
Hate crimes............................ 241

Fraud and identity theft, 2006
Fraud complaints..................... 6,871
rate per 100,000 residents 113.8
Identity theft complaints 3,700
rate per 100,000 residents 61.3

Law enforcement agencies, 2006
Total agencies........................ 450
Total employees...................... 24,121
Officers 14,984
Civilians 9,137

Prisoners, probation, and parole, 2006
Total prisoners...................... 25,745
percent change, 12/31/05 to 12/31/06 ... -2.4%
in private facilities 19.9%
in local jails 25.1%
Sentenced to more than one year 25,745
rate per 100,000 residents 423
Adults on probation 52,558
Adults on parole..................... 9,702

Prisoner demographics, June 30, 2005 (rate per 100,000 residents)
Male................................ 1,339
Female.............................. 151
White............................... 487
Black................................ 2,006
Hispanic 561

©2008 Information Publications, Inc.
All rights reserved. Photocopying prohibited.
877-544-INFO (4636) or www.informationpublications.com

Arrests, 2006

Total 285,475
    Persons under 18 years of age 35,228

Persons under sentence of death, 1/1/07

Total 107
    White 59
    Black 43
    Hispanic 1

State's highest court

Name . . . . .Supreme Court
Number of members 5
Length of term . . . . 8 years
Intermediate appeals court? . . . . .yes

Labor & Income

Civilian labor force, 2006 (x 1,000)

Total 3,028
    Men 1,640
    Women 1,388
    Persons 16-19 years 157
    White 2,483
    Black 460
    Hispanic 127

Civilian labor force as a percent of civilian non-institutional population, 2006

Total 64.4%
    Men 72.5
    Women 56.9
    Persons 16-19 years 46.0
    White 64.3
    Black 63.5
    Hispanic 82.5

Employment, 2006 (x 1,000)

Total 2,872
    Men 1,557
    Women 1,315
    Persons 16-19 years 137
    White 2,377
    Black 415
    Hispanic 123

Unemployment rate, 2006

Total 5.2%
    Men 5.1
    Women 5.3
    Persons 16-19 years 12.7
    White 4.3
    Black 10.0
    Hispanic 3.5

Full-time/part-time labor force, 2003 (x 1,000)

Full-time labor force, employed 2,312
Part-time labor force, employed 429

Unemployed, looking for
    Full-time work 142
    Part-time work 27
Mean duration of unemployment (weeks) 18.6
    Median 9.0

Labor unions, 2006

Membership (x 1,000) 153
    percent of employed 6.0%

Experienced civilian labor force by private industry, 2006

Total 2,325,551
    Natural resources & mining 10,195
    Construction 130,251
    Manufacturing 399,213
    Trade, transportation & utilities 603,477
    Information 49,085
    Finance 142,411
    Professional & business 320,065
    Education & health 328,328
    Leisure & hospitality 270,190
    Other 70,464

Experienced civilian labor force by occupation, May 2006

Management 153,090
Business & financial .81,520
Legal 11,930
Sales 263,490
Office & admin. support 461,040
Computers & math 38,100
Architecture & engineering 35,010
Arts & entertainment 27,300
Education 141,680
Social services 29,420
Health care practitioner & technical 155,570
Health care support 65,620
Maintenance & repair 119,330
Construction 114,000
Transportation & moving 263,560
Production 322,630
Farming, fishing & forestry 4,120

Hours and earnings of production workers on manufacturing payrolls, 2006

Average weekly hours .39.4
Average hourly earnings $14.04
Average weekly earnings $553.18

Income and poverty, 2006

Median household income $40,315
Personal income, per capita (current $) . . . $32,304
    in constant (2000) dollars $28,199
Persons below poverty level 16.2%

Average annual pay

2006 . . . . $37,564
    increase from 2005 . . . . 4.7%

Federal individual income tax returns, 2005

Returns filed 2,657,790
Adjusted gross income ($1,000) $123,251,823
Total tax liability ($1,000) $15,663,355

Charitable contributions, 2004

Number of contributions 563.7
Total amount ($ mil) $3,027.3

©2008 Information Publications, Inc.
All rights reserved. Photocopying prohibited.
877-544-INFO (4636) or www.informationpublications.com

Economy, Business, Industry & Agriculture

Fortune 500 companies, 2007 9

Bankruptcy cases filed, FY 2007 37,779

Patents and trademarks issued, 2007

Patents 807
Trademarks 1,049

Business firm ownership, 2002

Women-owned 117,935
   Sales ($ mil) $17,641
Black-owned 26,811
   Sales ($ mil) $1,755
Hispanic-owned 4,301
   Sales ($ mil) $1,004
Asian-owned 7,241
   Sales ($ mil) $2,183
Amer. Indian/Alaska Native-owned 3,567
   Sales ($ mil) $619
Hawaiian/Pacific Islander-owned 94
   Sales ($ mil) $21

Gross domestic product, 2006 ($ mil)

Total gross domestic product $238,029
  Agriculture, forestry, fishing and
    hunting 1,392
  Mining 503
  Utilities 994
  Construction 10,465
  Manufacturing, durable goods 26,205
  Manufacturing, non-durable goods 16,178
  Wholesale trade 16,246
  Retail trade 19,852
  Transportation & warehousing 11,854
  Information 7,520
  Finance & insurance 12,938
  Real estate, rental & leasing 24,796
  Professional and technical services 12,285
  Educational services 2,410
  Health care and social assistance 20,836
  Accommodation/food services 7,480
  Other services, except government 6,084
  Government 25,131

Establishments, payroll, employees & receipts, by major industry group, 2005

Total 133,098
  Annual payroll ($1,000) $80,959,818
  Paid employees 2,378,754
Forestry, fishing & agriculture 281
  Annual payroll ($1,000) $38,712
  Paid employees 1,345
Mining 217
  Annual payroll ($1,000) $120,558
  Paid employees .2,768
  Receipts, 2002 ($1,000) $684,682

Utilities 163
  Annual payroll ($1,000) $156,536
  Paid employees .3,183
  Receipts, 2002 ($1,000) . . . . .NA
Construction 11,418
  Annual payroll ($1,000) $4,298,881
  Paid employees 112,611
  Receipts, 2002 ($1,000) $19,761,128
Manufacturing 6,671
  Annual payroll ($1,000) $15,564,711
  Paid employees 396,245
  Receipts, 2002 ($1,000) $109,293,454
Wholesale trade 7,336
  Annual payroll ($1,000) $5,574,316
  Paid employees 116,259
  Receipts, 2002 ($1,000) $97,792,030
Retail trade 23,798
  Annual payroll ($1,000) $6,874,676
  Paid employees 320,100
  Receipts, 2002 ($1,000) $60,136,403
Transportation & warehousing 4,259
  Annual payroll ($1,000) $4,315,420
  Paid employees 121,632
  Receipts, 2002 ($1,000) $11,650,494
Information 2,574
  Annual payroll ($1,000) $2,356,578
  Paid employees 55,151
  Receipts, 2002 ($1,000) . . . . .NA
Finance & insurance 9,740
  Annual payroll ($1,000) $6,237,489
  Paid employees 116,540
  Receipts, 2002 ($1,000) . . . . .NA
Professional, scientific & technical 11,082
  Annual payroll ($1,000) $5,320,454
  Paid employees 110,585
  Receipts, 2002 ($1,000) $11,022,883
Education 1,086
  Annual payroll ($1,000) $1,204,322
  Paid employees 44,848
  Receipts, 2002 ($1,000) $407,836
Health care & social assistance 13,696
  Annual payroll ($1,000) $12,325,142
  Paid employees 332,418
  Receipts, 2002 ($1,000) $24,475,539
Arts and entertainment 2,257
  Annual payroll ($1,000) $951,157
  Paid employees 29,339
  Receipts, 2002 ($1,000) $2,117,808
Real estate 5,588
  Annual payroll ($1,000) $1,274,377
  Paid employees 37,642
  Receipts, 2002 ($1,000) $4,635,964
Accommodation & food service 10,892
  Annual payroll ($1,000) $2,724,314
  Paid employees 219,970
  Receipts, 2002 ($1,000) $8,024,900

©2008 Information Publications, Inc.
All rights reserved. Photocopying prohibited.
877-544-INFO (4636) or www.informationpublications.com

8   Tennessee

Exports, 2006
Value of exported goods ($ mil) $22,020
   Manufactured $16,943
   Non-manufactured $1,981

Foreign direct investment in US affiliates, 2004
Property, plants & equipment ($ mil) . . . $19,890
Employment (x 1,000). 126.9

Agriculture, 2006
Number of farms 82,000
Farm acreage (x 1,000) 11,400
   Acres per farm 139
Farm marketings and income ($ mil)
Total. $2,564.9
   Crops $1,373.3
   Livestock $1,191.6
Net farm income $721.8

Principal commodities, in order by marketing receipts, 2005
Cattle and calves, Broilers, Cotton, Greenhouse/
   nursery, Soybeans

Federal economic activity in state
Expenditures, 2005 ($ mil)
   Total. $48,288
      Per capita $8,107.72
   Defense $4,298
   Non-defense $43,989
Defense department, 2006 ($ mil)
   Payroll. $1,520
   Contract awards $2,866
   Grants $56
Homeland security grants ($1,000)
   2006. . . . .$13,762
   2007 . . . . $20,045

FDIC-insured financial institutions, 2005
Number 201
Assets ($ billion) $88.6
Deposits ($ billion) $61.8

Fishing, 2006
Catch (x 1,000 lbs) . . . . NA
Value ($1,000). . . . . NA

Mining, 2006 ($ mil)
Total non-fuel mineral production $807
Percent of U.S. 1.25%

Communication, Energy & Transportation

Communication
Households with computers, 2003 . . . . .56.7%
Households with internet access, 2003 . . . .48.9%
High-speed internet providers 58
Total high-speed internet lines 1,573,992
   Residential 969,096
   Business. 604,896
Wireless phone customers, 12/2006 5,126,510

FCC-licensed stations (as of January 1, 2008)
TV stations 40
FM radio stations. 222
AM radio stations 187

Energy
Energy consumption, 2004
   Total (trillion Btu). 2,298
   Per capita (million Btu) 390.4
By source of production (trillion Btu)
   Coal 648
   Natural gas 239
   Petroleum 800
   Nuclear electric power 298
   Hydroelectric power 104
By end-use sector (trillion Btu)
   Residential 512
   Commercial 378
   Industrial 776
   Transportation 632
Electric energy, 2005
   Primary source of electricity. . . . . Coal
   Net generation (billion kWh) 97.1
      percent from renewable sources. 10.2%
   Net summer capability (million kW) 20.7
   CO_2 emitted from generation 59.9
Natural gas utilities, 2005
   Customers (x 1,000) 1,176
   Sales (trillion Btu). 222
   Revenues ($ mil) $1,923
Nuclear plants, 2007 3
Total CO_2 emitted (million metric tons). 120.1
Energy spending, 2004 ($ mil) $17,666
   per capita $3,001
   Price per million Btu $12.16

Transportation, 2006
Public road & street mileage 91,416
   Urban. 21,639
   Rural. 69,777
   Interstate. 1,104
Vehicle miles of travel (millions) 70,596
   per capita 11,620.9
Total motor vehicle registrations 5,091,328
   Automobiles. 2,878,136
   Trucks 2,193,213
   Motorcycles 134,123
Licensed drivers 4,387,883
   19 years & under 258,702
Deaths from motor vehicle accidents 1,287
Gasoline consumed (x 1,000 gallons) 3,128,807
   per capita 515.0

Commuting Statistics, 2006
Average commute time (min) 23.5
   Drove to work alone 83.3%
   Carpooled. 10.2%
   Public transit 0.7%
   Walk to work 1.4%
   Work from home 3.2%

©2008 Information Publications, Inc.
All rights reserved. Photocopying prohibited.
877-544-INFO (4636) or www.informationpublications.com

State Summary

Capital city . . . . Austin
Governor . . . . Rick Perry

PO Box 12428
Austin, TX 78711
512-463-2000

Admitted as a state 1845
Area (square miles) 268,581
Population, 2007 (estimate). 23,904,380
Largest city . . . . Houston
Population, 2006 2,144,491
Personal income per capita, 2006
(in current dollars) $34,257
Gross domestic product, 2006 ($ mil) . . $1,065,891

Leading industries by payroll, 2005

Manufacturing, Health care/Social assistance,
Professional/Scientific/Technical

**Leading agricultural commodities
by receipts, 2005**

Cattle and calves, Cotton, Greenhouse/nursery,
Broilers, Dairy products

Geography & Environment

Total area (square miles). 268,581
land 261,797
water 6,784
Federally-owned land, 2004 (acres) 3,130,345
percent. 1.9%
Highest point . . . . Gaudalupe Peak
elevation (feet) 8,749
Lowest point . . . . Gulf of Mexico
elevation (feet) . . . . sea level
General coastline (miles) 367
Tidal shoreline (miles) 3,359
Cropland, 2003 (x 1,000 acres) 25,562
Forest land, 2003 (x 1,000 acres). 10,613
Capital city . . . . Austin
Population 2000 656,562
Population 2006 709,893
Largest city . . . . Houston
Population 2000 1,953,631
Population 2006 2,144,491

Number of cities with over 100,000 population

1990 17
2000 24
2006 27

State park and recreation areas, 2005

Area (x 1,000 acres). 589
Number of visitors (x 1,000) 10,189
Revenues ($1,000) $33,955
percent of operating expenditures. 60.5%

National forest system land, 2007

Acres 755,365

Demographics & Population Characteristics

Population

1980 14,229,191
1990 16,986,510
2000 20,851,792
2006 23,507,783
Male 11,714,068
Female 11,793,715
Living in group quarters, 2006 594,214
percent of total. 2.5%
2007 (estimate). 23,904,380
persons per square mile of land 91.3
2008 (projected). 23,898,665
2010 (projected). 24,648,888
2020 (projected). 28,634,896
2030 (projected). 33,317,744

**Population of Core-Based Statistical Areas
(formerly Metropolitan Areas), x 1,000**

	CBSA	Non-CBSA
1990	15,723	1,264
2000	19,465	1,386
2006	22,090	1,418

Change in population, 2000-2007

Number 3,052,581
percent. 14.6%
Natural increase (births minus deaths) . . 1,635,015
Net internal migration 582,078
Net international migration 842,595

Persons by age, 2006

Under 5 years 1,925,197
5 to 17 years 4,568,768
18 years and over 17,013,818
65 years and over 2,334,459
85 years and over 302,646
Median age 33.1

Persons by age, 2010 (projected)

Under 5 years 2,077,328
18 and over 17,863,480
65 and over 2,587,383
Median age 33.4

Race, 2006

One Race
White. 19,452,577
Black or African American 2,804,949
Asian 788,356
American Indian/Alaska Native. 163,455
Hawaiian Native/Pacific Islander. 26,903
Two or more races. 271,543

Persons of Hispanic origin, 2006

Total Hispanic or Latino 8,385,118
Mexican. 7,024,667
Puerto Rican 96,034
Cuban 35,792

©2008 Information Publications, Inc.
All rights reserved. Photocopying prohibited.
877-544-INFO (4636) or www.informationpublications.com

Persons of Asian origin, 2006

Total Asian 787,208
  Asian Indian. 194,908
  Chinese 136,377
  Filipino 95,436
  Japanese 18,581
  Korean. 60,078
  Vietnamese. 184,096

Marital status, 2006

Population 15 years & over 18,066,247
  Never married 5,332,034
  Married. 9,790,299
  Separated 526,317
  Widowed. 1,014,640
  Divorced 1,929,274

Language spoken at home, 2006

Population 5 years and older. 21,585,556
  English only 14,289,136
  Spanish 6,278,980
  French 59,435
  German. 80,770
  Chinese 114,855

Households & families, 2006

Households. 8,109,388
  with persons under 18 years 3,239,101
  with persons over 65 years. 1,598,468
  persons per household 2.83
Families. 5,686,517
  persons per family. 3.41
Married couples. 4,173,567
Female householder,
  no husband present. 1,113,815
One-person households 2,015,666

Nativity, 2006

Number of residents born in state . . . 14,320,902
  percent of population 60.9%

Immigration & naturalization, 2006

Legal permanent residents admitted. 89,037
Persons naturalized 37,835
Non-immigrant admissions 2,450,389

Vital Statistics and Health

Marriages

2004 178,512
2005 176,768
2006 174,989

Divorces

2004 81,324
2005 75,980
2006 78,072

Health risks, 2006

Percent of adults who are:
  Smokers. 17.9%
  Overweight (BMI > 25). 62.4%
  Obese (BMI > 30). 26.1%

Births

2005 385,915
  Birthrate (per 1,000). 16.9
  White. 327,298
  Black 44,076
  Hispanic 191,445
  Asian/Pacific Islander 13,645
  Amer. Indian/Alaska Native. 896
  Low birth weight (2,500g or less). 8.3%
  Cesarian births 32.6%
  Preterm births 13.6%
  To unmarried mothers. 37.6%
  Twin births (per 1,000) 28.1
  Triplets or higher order (per 100,000). . . .143.4
2006 (preliminary). 399,612
  rate per 1,000 . . . . .17.0

Deaths

2004
All causes 152,870
  rate per 100,000. . . . . .835.6
Heart disease 40,196
  rate per 100,000. . . . . .227.0
Malignant neoplasms 33,937
  rate per 100,000. . . . . .182.2
Cerebrovascular disease. 9,853
  rate per 100,000. . . . . .56.9
Chronic lower respiratory disease 7,402
  rate per 100,000. . . . . .41.9
Diabetes. 5,435
  rate per 100,000. . . . . .29.7
2005 (preliminary). 156,474
  rate per 100,000. . . . . 828.8
2006 (provisional) 152,461

Infant deaths

2004 2,407
  rate per 1,000 . . . . .6.3
2005 (provisional) 2,480
  rate per 1,000 . . . . .6.4

Exercise routines, 2005

None. 27.4%
Moderate or greater. 46.7%
Vigorous 25.3%

Abortions, 2004

Total performed in state. 74,801
  rate per 1,000 women age 15-44. 15
  % obtained by out-of-state residents 3.3%

Physicians, 2005

Total. 48,776
  rate per 100,000 persons 213

Community hospitals, 2005

Number of hospitals 415
Beds (x 1,000). 58.2
Patients admitted (x 1,000) 2,509
Average daily census (x 1,000) 36.0
Average cost per day $1,636
Outpatient visits (x 1 mil) 32.3

©2008 Information Publications, Inc.
All rights reserved. Photocopying prohibited.
877-544-INFO (4636) or www.informationpublications.com

Disability status of population, 2006

5 to 15 years	6.7%
16 to 64 years	12.1%
65 years and over	45.5%

Education

Educational attainment, 2006

Population over 25 years	14,551,694
Less than 9th grade	10.5%
High school graduate or more	78.6%
College graduate or more	24.7%
Graduate or professional degree	8.0%

Public school enrollment, 2005-06

Total	4,525,394
Pre-kindergarten through grade 8	3,268,339
Grades 9 through 12	1,257,055

Graduating public high school seniors, 2004-05

Diplomas (incl. GED and others)	239,717

SAT scores, 2007

Average critical reading score	492
Average writing score	482
Average math score	507
Percent of graduates taking test	52%

Public school teachers, 2006-07 (estimate)

Total (x 1,000)	311.7
Elementary	159.9
Secondary	151.8
Average salary	$44,897
Elementary	$44,462
Secondary	$45,356

State receipts & expenditures for public schools, 2006-07 (estimate)

Revenue receipts ($ mil)	$44,267
Expenditures	
Total ($ mil)	$45,157
Per capita	$1,567
Per pupil	$8,573

NAEP proficiency scores, 2007

	Reading		Math	
	Basic	Proficient	Basic	Proficient
Grade 4	65.8%	29.6%	87.4%	40.2%
Grade 8	73.0%	27.5%	77.6%	34.7%

Higher education enrollment, fall 2005

Total	159,372
Full-time men	53,730
Full-time women	65,978
Part-time men	18,075
Part-time women	21,589

Minority enrollment in institutions of higher education, 2005

Black, non-Hispanic	153,416
Hispanic	324,803
Asian/Pacific Islander	62,688
American Indian/Alaska Native	6,401

Institutions of higher education, 2005-06

Total	213
Public	109
Private	104

Earned degrees conferred, 2004-05

Associate's	41,778
Bachelor's	88,757
Master's	32,391
First-professional	5,398
Doctor's	2,974

Public Libraries, 2006

Number of libraries	553
Number of outlets	863
Annual visits per capita	3.3
Circulation per capita	4.8

State & local financial support for higher education, FY 2006

Full-time equivalent enrollment (x 1,000)	820.8
Appropriations per FTE	$6,276

Social Insurance & Welfare Programs

Social Security benefits & beneficiaries, 2005

Beneficiaries (x 1,000)	2,955
Retired & dependents	1,990
Survivors	475
Disabled & dependents	490
Annual benefit payments ($ mil)	$30,684
Retired & dependents	$19,643
Survivors	$6,178
Disabled & dependents	$4,864
Average monthly benefit	
Retired & dependents	$975
Disabled & dependents	$924
Widowed	$940

Medicare, July 2005

Enrollment (x 1,000)	2,545
Payments ($ mil)	$20,020

Medicaid, 2004

Beneficiaries (x 1,000)	3,604
Payments ($ mil)	$13,214

State Children's Health Insurance Program, 2006

Enrollment (x 1,000)	585.5
Expenditures ($ mil)	$371.8

Persons without health insurance, 2006

Number (x 1,000)	5,704
percent	24.5%
Number of children (x 1,000)	1,392
percent of children	21.2%

Health care expenditures, 2004

Total expenditures	$103,600
per capita	$4,601

©2008 Information Publications, Inc.
All rights reserved. Photocopying prohibited.
877-544-INFO (4636) or www.informationpublications.com

Federal and state public aid

State unemployment insurance, 2006
Recipients, first payments (x 1,000) 297
Total payments ($ mil) $1,070
Average weekly benefit $271
Temporary Assistance for Needy Families, 2006
Recipients (x 1,000) 1,836.2
Families (x 1,000) 811.4
Supplemental Security Income, 2005
Recipients (x 1,000) .501.8
Payments ($ mil) $2,190.6
Food Stamp Program, 2006
Avg monthly participants (x 1,000) 2,622.5
Total benefits ($ mil) $2,939.3

Housing & Construction

Housing units

Total 2005 (estimate) 9,025,865
Total 2006 (estimate) 9,224,361
Seasonal or recreational use, 2006 193,708
Owner-occupied, 2006 5,291,045
  Median home value $114,000
  Homeowner vacancy rate 2.2%
Renter-occupied, 2006 2,818,343
  Median rent $711
  Rental vacancy rate 13.5%
Home ownership rate, 2005 . . . . 65.9%
Home ownership rate, 2006 . . . . 66.0%

New privately-owned housing units

Number authorized, 2006 (x 1,000) 216.6
  Value ($ mil) $29,206.1
Started 2005 (x 1,000, estimate) 154.9
Started 2006 (x 1,000, estimate) 149.1

Existing home sales

2005 (x 1,000) 532.5
2006 (x 1,000) 578.6

Government & Elections

State officials 2008

Governor . . . . .Rick Perry
    Republican, term expires 1/11
Lieutenant Governor . . . . .David Dewhurst
Secretary of State . . . . Roger Williams
Attorney General . . . . Greg Abbott
Chief Justice . . . . .Wallace Jefferson

Governorship

Minimum age 30
Length of term . . . . 4 years
Consecutive terms permitted . . . . . . not specified
Who succeeds . . . . Lieutenant Governor

Local governments by type, 2002

Total 4,784
  County 254
  Municipal 1,196
  Township 0
  School District 1,089
  Special District 2,245

State legislature

Name . . . . Legislature
Upper chamber . . . . .Senate
  Number of members 31
  Length of term . . . . 4 years
  Party in majority, 2008 . . . . Republican
Lower chamber . . . . .House of Representatives
  Number of members 150
  Length of term . . . . 2 years
  Party in majority, 2008 . . . . Republican

Federal representation, 2008 (110th Congress)

Senator . . . . .John Cornyn
  Party . . . . Republican
  Year term expires 2009
Senator . . . . .Kay Bailey Hutchinson
  Party . . . . Republican
  Year term expires 2013
Representatives, total 32
  Democrats 13
  Republicans 19

Voters in November 2006 election (estimate)

Total 5,525,824
  Male 2,568,765
  Female 2,957,059
  White 4,711,085
  Black 654,982
  Hispanic 503,503
  Asian 76,928

Presidential election, 2004

Total Popular Vote 7,410,765
  Kerry 2,832,704
  Bush 4,526,917
Total Electoral Votes 34

Votes cast for US Senators

2004
Total vote (x 1,000) . . . . NA
Leading party . . . . NA
Percent for leading party . . . . NA
2006
Total vote (x 1,000) .4,315
Leading party . . . . Republican
Percent for leading party 61.7%

Votes cast for US Representatives

2004
Total vote (x 1,000) .6,959
  Democratic 2,714
  Republican 4,013
Leading party . . . . Republican
Percent for leading party 57.7%
2006
Total vote (x 1,000) .4,141
  Democratic 1,831
  Republican 2,094
Leading party . . . . Republican
Percent for leading party 50.9%

©2008 Information Publications, Inc.
All rights reserved. Photocopying prohibited.
877-544-INFO (4636) or www.informationpublications.com

State government employment, 2006
Full-time equivalent employees 281,722
Payroll ($ mil) $1,008.2

Local government employment, 2006
Full-time equivalent employees 1,033,284
Payroll ($ mil) $3,184.4

Women holding public office, 2008
US Congress 4
Statewide elected office.................2
State legislature 35

Black public officials, 2002
Total....................................466
   US and state legislatures 19
   City/county/regional offices 306
   Judicial/law enforcement...............47
   Education/school boards...............94

Hispanic public officials, 2006
Total..................................2,109
   State executives & legislators 38
   City/county/regional offices 851
   Judicial/law enforcement...............413
   Education/school boards..............807

Governmental Finance

State government revenues, 2006
Total revenue (x $1,000) $103,964,436
   per capita $4,441.48
General revenue (x $1,000) $83,471,066
   Intergovernmental 28,708,710
   Taxes..........................36,591,749
      general sales...............18,275,210
      individual income tax 0
      corporate income tax 0
   Current charges.................8,614,238
   Miscellaneous 9,556,369

State government expenditure, 2006
Total expenditure (x $1,000) $85,513,928
   per capita $3,653.25
General expenditure (x $1,000) $75,895,975
   per capita, total..................$3,242.36
      Education......................1,344.37
      Public welfare 888.04
      Health 43.77
      Hospitals.....................106.27
      Highways 335.41
      Police protection 24.34
      Corrections 130.03
      Natural resources 36.17
      Parks & recreation 5.01
      Governmental administration.......61.99
      Interest on general debt.............43.53

State debt & cash, 2006 ($ per capita)
Debt $1,046.73
Cash/security holdings..............$10,303.13

Federal government grants to state & local government, 2005 (x $1,000)
Total........................... $28,912,208
by Federal agency
   Defense 131,561
   Education 3,221,991
   Energy...........................79,637
   Environmental Protection Agency ... 257,803
   Health & Human Services. 15,901,213
   Homeland Security 527,260
   Housing & Urban Development.....1,733,050
   Justice 425,793
   Labor 590,326
   Transportation 2,989,307
   Veterans Affairs...................32,452

Crime & Law Enforcement

Crime, 2006 (rates per 100,000 residents)
Property crimes 959,460
   Burglary 215,647
   Larceny 648,384
   Motor vehicle theft 95,429
   Property crime rate.................4,081.5
Violent crimes.........................121,378
   Murder 1,384
   Forcible rape......................8,372
   Robbery.........................37,254
   Aggravated assault 74,368
   Violent crime rate 516.3
Hate crimes........................... 292

Fraud and identity theft, 2006
Fraud complaints.....................25,425
   rate per 100,000 residents 108.2
Identity theft complaints 26,006
   rate per 100,000 residents 110.6

Law enforcement agencies, 2006
Total agencies............................981
Total employees 81,462
   Officers 49,470
   Civilians 31,992

Prisoners, probation, and parole, 2006
Total prisoners.......................172,116
   percent change, 12/31/05 to 12/31/06 ....1.8%
   in private facilities 10.8%
   in local jails 8.8%
Sentenced to more than one year 162,193
   rate per 100,000 residents 683
Adults on probation 431,967
Adults on parole......................100,053

Prisoner demographics, June 30, 2005 (rate per 100,000 residents)
Male...................................1,772
Female 186
White 667
Black.................................3,162
Hispanic 830

©2008 Information Publications, Inc.
All rights reserved. Photocopying prohibited.
877-544-INFO (4636) or www.informationpublications.com

6   Texas

Arrests, 2006
Total.............................1,078,961
    Persons under 18 years of age 169,460

Persons under sentence of death, 1/1/07
Total................................... 393
    White.............................. 121
    Black 161
    Hispanic 107

State's highest court
Name ....Supreme Court
Number of members 9
Length of term .... 6 years
Intermediate appeals court? ....yes

Labor & Income

Civilian labor force, 2006 (x 1,000)
Total................................11,465
    Men 6,390
    Women 5,075
    Persons 16-19 years................ 552
    White.............................9,509
    Black 1,286
    Hispanic 3,909

Civilian labor force as a percent of civilian non-institutional population, 2006
Total...................................66.8%
    Men 76.4
    Women 57.7
    Persons 16-19 years...............40.6
    White.............................66.7
    Black 65.6
    Hispanic 66.9

Employment, 2006 (x 1,000)
Total................................10,913
    Men 6,103
    Women 4,810
    Persons 16-19 years................ 460
    White.............................9,116
    Black 1,149
    Hispanic 3,728

Unemployment rate, 2006
Total...................................4.8%
    Men 4.5
    Women 5.2
    Persons 16-19 years...............16.7
    White.............................4.1
    Black 10.7
    Hispanic 4.6

Full-time/part-time labor force, 2003 (x 1,000)
Full-time labor force, employed 8,602
Part-time labor force, employed..........1,570
Unemployed, looking for
    Full-time work....................... 624
    Part-time work....................... 113
Mean duration of unemployment (weeks)...... 17.1
    Median 8.9

Labor unions, 2006
Membership (x 1,000)..................... 476
    percent of employed 4.9%

Experienced civilian labor force by private industry, 2006
Total...............................8,241,727
    Natural resources & mining 247,356
    Construction 605,600
    Manufacturing..................... 926,610
    Trade, transportation & utilities ...2,034,037
    Information 222,814
    Finance 619,559
    Professional & business 1,229,932
    Education & health 1,116,081
    Leisure & hospitality.............. 942,155
    Other 278,929

Experienced civilian labor force by occupation, May 2006
Management........................ 444,540
Business & financial 393,790
Legal................................69,970
Sales 1,052,990
Office & admin. support............. 1,740,210
Computers & math 231,420
Architecture & engineering........... 207,350
Arts & entertainment 97,710
Education 647,030
Social services 88,020
Health care practitioner & technical.... 463,810
Health care support 231,520
Maintenance & repair............. 428,020
Construction 513,910
Transportation & moving 697,490
Production 716,600
Farming, fishing & forestry............17,650

Hours and earnings of production workers on manufacturing payrolls, 2006
Average weekly hours 40.9
Average hourly earnings $14.01
Average weekly earnings $573.01

Income and poverty, 2006
Median household income............ $44,922
Personal income, per capita (current $)... $34,257
    in constant (2000) dollars $29,904
Persons below poverty level............. 16.9%

Average annual pay
2006 .... $42,458
    increase from 2005 .... 5.7%

Federal individual income tax returns, 2005
Returns filed........................ 9,727,703
Adjusted gross income ($1,000) $507,165,219
Total tax liability ($1,000) $71,420,283

Charitable contributions, 2004
Number of contributions.............. 1,991.6
Total amount ($ mil)................$9,927.6

©2008 Information Publications, Inc.
All rights reserved. Photocopying prohibited.
877-544-INFO (4636) or www.informationpublications.com

Economy, Business, Industry & Agriculture

Fortune 500 companies, 2007............... 56
Bankruptcy cases filed, FY 2007......... 42,487

Patents and trademarks issued, 2007
Patents...................................6,316
Trademarks..............................4,410

Business firm ownership, 2002
Women-owned........................ 468,705
  Sales ($ mil) $65,817
Black-owned.......................... 88,768
  Sales ($ mil) $6,419
Hispanic-owned..................... 319,340
  Sales ($ mil) $42,214
Asian-owned 77,834
  Sales ($ mil) $20,728
Amer. Indian/Alaska Native-owned 16,863
  Sales ($ mil) $3,321
Hawaiian/Pacific Islander-owned 1,391
  Sales ($ mil) $78

Gross domestic product, 2006 ($ mil)
Total gross domestic product $1,065,891
  Agriculture, forestry, fishing and
    hunting 8,339
  Mining........................... 100,653
  Utilities.............................33,135
  Construction 57,804
  Manufacturing, durable goods....... 72,498
  Manufacturing, non-durable goods 67,188
  Wholesale trade......................70,755
  Retail trade.........................67,262
  Transportation & warehousing 34,728
  Information 42,490
  Finance & insurance..................58,714
  Real estate, rental & leasing 101,262
  Professional and technical services.... 68,038
  Educational services................. 5,689
  Health care and social assistance...... 61,484
  Accommodation/food services.........25,691
  Other services, except government 21,971
  Government 112,861

Establishments, payroll, employees & receipts, by major industry group, 2005
Total...............................497,758
  Annual payroll ($1,000).........$315,809,126
  Paid employees 8,305,102
Forestry, fishing & agriculture.............1,188
  Annual payroll ($1,000)........... $231,834
  Paid employees 8,020
Mining............................... 6,343
  Annual payroll ($1,000)..........$9,071,718
  Paid employees 126,966
  Receipts, 2002 ($1,000) $50,406,285

Utilities 2,207
  Annual payroll ($1,000)..........$2,889,362
  Paid employees 41,610
  Receipts, 2002 ($1,000) ....NA
*Construction..........................*39,632
  Annual payroll ($1,000).........$19,869,823
  Paid employees 501,694
  Receipts, 2002 ($1,000) $94,067,369
Manufacturing...................... 20,552
  Annual payroll ($1,000)........ $38,224,668
  Paid employees 816,221
  Receipts, 2002 ($1,000) $310,815,965
*Wholesale trade......................*31,133
  Annual payroll ($1,000).........$23,894,136
  Paid employees 450,206
  Receipts, 2002 ($1,000) $397,405,111
Retail trade.......................... 76,335
  Annual payroll ($1,000).........$24,317,534
  Paid employees 1,080,932
  Receipts, 2002 ($1,000) $228,694,755
Transportation & warehousing.......... 15,245
  Annual payroll ($1,000) $13,537,995
  Paid employees 336,526
  Receipts, 2002 ($1,000) $32,254,393
*Information...........................*9,486
  Annual payroll ($1,000).........$14,311,499
  Paid employees 251,496
  Receipts, 2002 ($1,000) ....NA
Finance & insurance................... 35,277
  Annual payroll ($1,000)......... $24,080,494
  Paid employees 441,384
  Receipts, 2002 ($1,000) ....NA
*Professional, scientific & technical *55,618
  Annual payroll ($1,000)...........$31,442,127
  Paid employees 519,075
  Receipts, 2002 ($1,000) $62,549,237
*Education *4,878
  Annual payroll ($1,000)..........$3,678,489
  Paid employees 129,348
  Receipts, 2002 ($1,000) $1,944,319
*Health care & social assistance *51,460
  Annual payroll ($1,000).........$38,168,221
  Paid employees 1,097,308
  Receipts, 2002 ($1,000) $81,493,532
*Arts and entertainment *6,117
  Annual payroll ($1,000)..........$2,518,194
  Paid employees 105,477
  Receipts, 2002 ($1,000) $7,480,834
Real estate........................... 24,868
  Annual payroll ($1,000)..........$5,995,928
  Paid employees 160,838
  Receipts, 2002 ($1,000) $24,304,610
*Accommodation & food service..........*39,989
  Annual payroll ($1,000).........$10,304,662
  Paid employees 800,903
  Receipts, 2002 ($1,000) $29,914,774

©2008 Information Publications, Inc.
All rights reserved. Photocopying prohibited.
877-544-INFO (4636) or www.informationpublications.com

Exports, 2006

Value of exported goods ($ mil) $150,888
   Manufactured $123,094
   Non-manufactured $6,877

Foreign direct investment in US affiliates, 2004

Property, plants & equipment ($ mil) . . . $83,739
Employment (x 1,000). 341.2

Agriculture, 2006

Number of farms 230,000
Farm acreage (x 1,000) 129,700
   Acres per farm 564
Farm marketings and income ($ mil)
Total. $16,026.8
   Crops $5,703.0
   Livestock. $10,323.7
Net farm income $4,866.3

Principal commodities, in order by marketing receipts, 2005

Cattle and calves, Cotton, Greenhouse/nursery,
Broilers, Dairy products

Federal economic activity in state

Expenditures, 2005 ($ mil)
   Total. $148,683
      Per capita $6,484.63
   Defense $30,782
   Non-defense $117,901
Defense department, 2006 ($ mil)
   Payroll. $11,908
   Contract awards $27,102
   Grants $168
Homeland security grants ($1,000)
   2006 . . . . $89,880
   2007 . . . . $121,629

FDIC-insured financial institutions, 2005

Number 650
Assets ($ billion) $255.9
Deposits ($ billion) $193.4

Fishing, 2006

Catch (x 1,000 lbs) 116,860
Value ($1,000). $196,856

Mining, 2006 ($ mil)

Total non-fuel mineral production $2,910
Percent of U.S. 4.52%

Communication, Energy & Transportation

Communication

Households with computers, 2003 . . . . 59.0%
Households with internet access, 2003 . . . . 51.8%
High-speed internet providers 138
Total high-speed internet lines 5,452,666
   Residential 4,247,541
   Business. 1,205,125
Wireless phone customers, 12/2006 . . . 17,822,230

FCC-licensed stations (as of January 1, 2008)

TV stations 135
FM radio stations. 623
AM radio stations 304

Energy

Energy consumption, 2004
   Total (trillion Btu). 11,971
   Per capita (million Btu) 531.6
By source of production (trillion Btu)
   Coal 1,626
   Natural gas 3,941
   Petroleum 5,801
   Nuclear electric power 422
   Hydroelectric power 13
By end-use sector (trillion Btu)
   Residential 1,555
   Commercial 1,315
   Industrial 6,400
   Transportation .2,701
Electric energy, 2005
   Primary source of electricity. . . . . Gas
   Net generation (billion kWh) 396.7
      percent from renewable sources. 1.7%
   Net summer capability (million kW) 101.0
   CO_2 emitted from generation 258.7
Natural gas utilities, 2005
   Customers (x 1,000) 4,311
   Sales (trillion Btu). 1,866
   Revenues ($ mil) $12,466
Nuclear plants, 2007 4
Total CO_2 emitted (million metric tons). 670.2
Energy spending, 2004 ($ mil) $95,122
   per capita $4,224
   Price per million Btu $11.50

Transportation, 2006

Public road & street mileage 305,270
   Urban. 83,683
   Rural 221,587
   Interstate. 3,233
Vehicle miles of travel (millions) 238,256
   per capita 10,178.6
Total motor vehicle registrations 17,538,388
   Automobiles. 8,805,316
   Trucks 8,642,899
   Motorcycles 355,825
Licensed drivers 14,906,701
   19 years & under 685,314
Deaths from motor vehicle accidents 3,475
Gasoline consumed (x 1,000 gallons) . . .11,841,488
   per capita 505.9

Commuting Statistics, 2006

Average commute time (min) 24.6
   Drove to work alone 78.5%
   Carpooled. 12.7%
   Public transit 1.7%
   Walk to work 1.9%
   Work from home 3.5%

©2008 Information Publications, Inc.
All rights reserved. Photocopying prohibited.
877-544-INFO (4636) or www.informationpublications.com

State Summary

Capital city . . . . Salt Lake City
Governor . . . . Jon Huntsman Jr
210 State Capitol
Salt Lake City, UT 84114
801-538-1000
Admitted as a state 1896
Area (square miles) 84,899
Population, 2007 (estimate). 2,645,330
Largest city . . . . Salt Lake City
Population, 2006 178,858
Personal income per capita, 2006
(in current dollars) $29,108
Gross domestic product, 2006 ($ mil) $97,749

Leading industries by payroll, 2005

Manufacturing, Health care/Social assistance,
Retail trade

**Leading agricultural commodities
by receipts, 2005**

Cattle and calves, Dairy products, Hogs, Hay,
Greenhouse/nursery

Geography & Environment

Total area (square miles). 84,899
land 82,144
water 2,755
Federally-owned land, 2004 (acres) . . .30,271,905
percent. 57.5%
Highest point . . . . Kings Peak
elevation (feet) 13,528
Lowest point . . . . Beaverdam Wash
elevation (feet) 2,000
General coastline (miles) 0
Tidal shoreline (miles) 0
Cropland, 2003 (x 1,000 acres) 1,682
Forest land, 2003 (x 1,000 acres). 1,876
Capital city . . . . Salt Lake City
Population 2000 181,743
Population 2006 178,858
Largest city . . . . Salt Lake City
Population 2000 181,743
Population 2006 178,858

Number of cities with over 100,000 population

1990 1
2000 3
2006 3

State park and recreation areas, 2005

Area (x 1,000 acres) 150
Number of visitors (x 1,000) 4,552
Revenues ($1,000) $10,622
percent of operating expenditures. 39.9%

National forest system land, 2007

Acres 8,200,161

Demographics & Population Characteristics

Population

1980 1,461,037
1990 1,722,850
2000 2,233,198
2006 2,550,063
Male. 1,282,401
Female. 1,267,662
Living in group quarters, 2006. 42,646
percent of total. 1.7%
2007 (estimate). 2,645,330
persons per square mile of land 32.2
2008 (projected). 2,523,394
2010 (projected) 2,595,013
2020 (projected). 2,990,094
2030 (projected). 3,485,367

**Population of Core-Based Statistical Areas
(formerly Metropolitan Areas), x 1,000**

	CBSA	Non-CBSA
1990	1,618	105
2000	2,107	126
2006	2,420	130

Change in population, 2000-2007

Number. 412,132
percent. 18.5%
Natural increase (births minus deaths) 272,134
Net internal migration 30,709
Net international migration 63,278

Persons by age, 2006

Under 5 years 247,801
5 to 17 years 543,397
18 years and over 1,758,865
65 years and over 225,539
85 years and over 29,235
Median age 28.3

Persons by age, 2010 (projected)

Under 5 years 240,868
18 and over 1,776,028
65 and over 234,798
Median age 29.5

Race, 2006

One Race

White. 2,383,544
Black or African American 25,838
Asian 50,230
American Indian/Alaska Native. 33,663
Hawaiian Native/Pacific Islander. 19,277
Two or more races. .37,511

Persons of Hispanic origin, 2006

Total Hispanic or Latino 286,113
Mexican. 219,599
Puerto Rican 5,174
Cuban 790

©2008 Information Publications, Inc.
All rights reserved. Photocopying prohibited.
877-544-INFO (4636) or www.informationpublications.com

Persons of Asian origin, 2006

Total Asian	49,079
Asian Indian	4,125
Chinese	13,653
Filipino	3,513
Japanese	6,074
Korean	5,727
Vietnamese	6,944

Marital status, 2006

Population 15 years & over	1,881,043
Never married	528,268
Married	1,111,133
Separated	23,667
Widowed	73,433
Divorced	168,209

Language spoken at home, 2006

Population 5 years and older	2,302,896
English only	1,973,532
Spanish	216,327
French	9,734
German	13,116
Chinese	12,569

Households & families, 2006

Households	814,028
with persons under 18 years	351,192
with persons over 65 years	150,020
persons per household	3.08
Families	614,705
persons per family	3.56
Married couples	503,636
Female householder, no husband present	77,116
One-person households	155,746

Nativity, 2006

Number of residents born in state	1,607,096
percent of population	63.0%

Immigration & naturalization, 2006

Legal permanent residents admitted	5,749
Persons naturalized	2,740
Non-immigrant admissions	104,196

Vital Statistics and Health

Marriages

2004	23,796
2005	24,109
2006	23,678

Divorces

2004	9,811
2005	9,982
2006	9,890

Health risks, 2006

Percent of adults who are:

Smokers	9.8%
Overweight (BMI > 25)	54.9%
Obese (BMI > 30)	21.9%

Births

2005	51,556
Birthrate (per 1,000)	20.9
White	48,934
Black	482
Hispanic	7,566
Asian/Pacific Islander	1,500
Amer. Indian/Alaska Native	640
Low birth weight (2,500g or less)	6.8%
Cesarian births	21.6%
Preterm births	11.4%
To unmarried mothers	17.7%
Twin births (per 1,000)	26.5
Triplets or higher order (per 100,000)	134.8
2006 (preliminary)	53,499
rate per 1,000	21.0

Deaths

2004

All causes	13,331
rate per 100,000	760.4
Heart disease	2,942
rate per 100,000	175.0
Malignant neoplasms	2,445
rate per 100,000	141.2
Cerebrovascular disease	790
rate per 100,000	47.7
Chronic lower respiratory disease	595
rate per 100,000	35.5
Diabetes	485
rate per 100,000	28.6
2005 (preliminary)	13,434
rate per 100,000	731.3
2006 (provisional)	13,772

Infant deaths

2004	264
rate per 1,000	5.2
2005 (provisional)	226
rate per 1,000	4.4

Exercise routines, 2005

None	18.5%
Moderate or greater	55.0%
Vigorous	34.3%

Abortions, 2004

Total performed in state	3,665
rate per 1,000 women age 15-44	7
% obtained by out-of-state residents	7.8%

Physicians, 2005

Total	5,221
rate per 100,000 persons	210

Community hospitals, 2005

Number of hospitals	43
Beds (x 1,000)	4.6
Patients admitted (x 1,000)	223
Average daily census (x 1,000)	2.6
Average cost per day	$1,823
Outpatient visits (x 1 mil)	4.8

©2008 Information Publications, Inc.
All rights reserved. Photocopying prohibited.
877-544-INFO (4636) or www.informationpublications.com

Disability status of population, 2006

5 to 15 years 5.5%
16 to 64 years 10.6%
65 years and over 38.9%

Education

Educational attainment, 2006

Population over 25 years 1,437,561
    Less than 9th grade. 3.4%
    High school graduate or more 90.2%
    College graduate or more. 28.6%
    Graduate or professional degree. 9.4%

Public school enrollment, 2005-06

Total. 508,430
    Pre-kindergarten through grade 8. . . . 357,644
    Grades 9 through 12 150,786

Graduating public high school seniors, 2004-05

Diplomas (incl. GED and others) 30,399

SAT scores, 2007

Average critical reading score. 558
Average writing score 544
Average math score 556
Percent of graduates taking test 6%

Public school teachers, 2006-07 (estimate)

Total (x 1,000) 21.8
    Elementary. 11.8
    Secondary. 10.0
Average salary $40,566
    Elementary. $40,566
    Secondary. $40,566

State receipts & expenditures for public schools, 2006-07 (estimate)

Revenue receipts ($ mil) $3,470
Expenditures
Total ($ mil) $3,377
    Per capita $1,058
    Per pupil $6,060

NAEP proficiency scores, 2007

	Reading		Math	
	Basic	Proficient	Basic	Proficient
Grade 4	68.6%	33.9%	82.7%	39.4%
Grade 8	75.0%	30.1%	72.1%	32.4%

Higher education enrollment, fall 2005

Total. 51,731
    Full-time men 21,817
    Full-time women. 22,684
    Part-time men 3,431
    Part-time women. 3,799

Minority enrollment in institutions of higher education, 2005

Black, non-Hispanic 2,298
Hispanic 9,680
Asian/Pacific Islander 6,049
American Indian/Alaska Native. 2,269

Institutions of higher education, 2005-06

Total. 31
    Public. 13
    Private 18

Earned degrees conferred, 2004-05

Associate's. 9,915
Bachelor's 20,799
Master's 4,210
First-professional. 423
Doctor's 373

Public Libraries, 2006

Number of libraries. 71
Number of outlets 135
Annual visits per capita 6.9
Circulation per capita. 12.9

State & local financial support for higher education, FY 2006

Full-time equivalent enrollment (x 1,000). . . .104.3
Appropriations per FTE. $5,941

Social Insurance & Welfare Programs

Social Security benefits & beneficiaries, 2005

Beneficiaries (x 1,000) 272
    Retired & dependents. 198
    Survivors. 36
    Disabled & dependents. 39
Annual benefit payments ($ mil) $2,913
    Retired & dependents. $2,037
    Survivors. $495
    Disabled & dependents. $380
Average monthly benefit
    Retired & dependents. $1,009
    Disabled & dependents. $928
    Widowed. $1,033

Medicare, July 2005

Enrollment (x 1,000). 237
Payments ($ mil) $1,312

Medicaid, 2004

Beneficiaries (x 1,000). 307
Payments ($ mil) $1,356

State Children's Health Insurance Program, 2006

Enrollment (x 1,000). 52.0
Expenditures ($ mil). $56.9

Persons without health insurance, 2006

Number (x 1,000). 442
    percent. 17.4%
Number of children (x 1,000) 120
    percent of children 15.0%

Health care expenditures, 2004

Total expenditures. $9,618
    per capita $3,972

©2008 Information Publications, Inc.
All rights reserved. Photocopying prohibited.
877-544-INFO (4636) or www.informationpublications.com

Federal and state public aid

State unemployment insurance, 2006
Recipients, first payments (x 1,000) 23
Total payments ($ mil) $92
Average weekly benefit $274
Temporary Assistance for Needy Families, 2006
Recipients (x 1,000) 196.4
Families (x 1,000) 81.8
Supplemental Security Income, 2005
Recipients (x 1,000) 22.6
Payments ($ mil) $109.8
Food Stamp Program, 2006
Avg monthly participants (x 1,000) 131.8
Total benefits ($ mil) $140.4

Housing & Construction

Housing units
Total 2005 (estimate) 874,068
Total 2006 (estimate) 901,283
Seasonal or recreational use, 2006 36,886
Owner-occupied, 2006 585,929
   Median home value $188,500
   Homeowner vacancy rate 2.1%
Renter-occupied, 2006 228,099
   Median rent $697
   Rental vacancy rate 5.7%
Home ownership rate, 2005 . . . . 73.9%
Home ownership rate, 2006 . . . . 73.5%

New privately-owned housing units
Number authorized, 2006 (x 1,000) 25.9
   Value ($ mil) $4,847.4
Started 2005 (x 1,000, estimate) 19.9
Started 2006 (x 1,000, estimate) 19.8

Existing home sales
2005 (x 1,000) 51.7
2006 (x 1,000) 51.7

Government & Elections

State officials 2008
Governor . . . . Jon Huntsman Jr
    Republican, term expires 1/09
Lieutenant Governor . . . . Gary Herbert
Secretary of State . . . . (no Secretary of State)
Attorney General . . . . Mike Shurtleff
Chief Justice . . . . .Christine Durham

Governorship
Minimum age 30
Length of term . . . . 4 years
Consecutive terms permitted 3
Who succeeds . . . . Lieutenant Governor

Local governments by type, 2002
Total 605
   County 29
   Municipal 236
   Township 0
   School District 40
   Special District 300

State legislature
Name . . . . Legislature
Upper chamber . . . . .Senate
   Number of members 29
   Length of term . . . . 4 years
   Party in majority, 2008 . . . . Republican
Lower chamber . . . . House of Representatives
   Number of members 75
   Length of term . . . . 2 years
   Party in majority, 2008 . . . . Republican

Federal representation, 2008 (110ᵗʰ Congress)
Senator . . . . .Robert Bennett
   Party . . . . Republican
   Year term expires 2011
Senator . . . . Orrin Hatch
   Party . . . . Republican
   Year term expires 2013
Representatives, total 3
   Democrats 1
   Republicans 2

Voters in November 2006 election (estimate)
Total 602,690
   Male 293,992
   Female 308,698
   White 588,180
   Black 1,625
   Hispanic 13,066
   Asian 3,025

Presidential election, 2004
Total Popular Vote 927,844
   Kerry 241,199
   Bush 663,742
Total Electoral Votes 5

Votes cast for US Senators
2004
Total vote (x 1,000) 912
Leading party . . . . Republican
Percent for leading party 68.7%
2006
Total vote (x 1,000) 571
Leading party . . . . Republican
Percent for leading party 62.4%

Votes cast for US Representatives
2004
Total vote (x 1,000) 909
   Democratic 362
   Republican 520
Leading party . . . . Republican
Percent for leading party 57.3%
2006
Total vote (x 1,000) 570
   Democratic 244
   Republican 292
Leading party . . . . Republican
Percent for leading party 51.3%

©2008 Information Publications, Inc.
All rights reserved. Photocopying prohibited.
877-544-INFO (4636) or www.informationpublications.com

State government employment, 2006
Full-time equivalent employees 50,277
Payroll ($ mil) $171.5

Local government employment, 2006
Full-time equivalent employees 78,508
Payroll ($ mil) $246.0

Women holding public office, 2008
US Congress 0
Statewide elected office..................... 0
State legislature 18

Black public officials, 2002
Total....................................... 5
US and state legislatures 1
City/county/regional offices 3
Judicial/law enforcement.................. 1
Education/school boards.................. 0

Hispanic public officials, 2006
Total....................................... 5
State executives & legislators 2
City/county/regional offices 3
Judicial/law enforcement................. 0
Education/school boards................. 0

Governmental Finance

State government revenues, 2006
Total revenue (x $1,000)...........$14,163,297
per capita $5,490.64
General revenue (x $1,000) $11,786,469
Intergovernmental 3,235,660
Taxes 5,459,091
general sales...................1,890,793
individual income tax 2,277,478
corporate income tax 348,129
Current charges................. 2,200,608
Miscellaneous 891,110

State government expenditure, 2006
Total expenditure (x $1,000) $12,044,631
per capita $4,669.30
General expenditure (x $1,000) $10,966,239
per capita, total.................. $4,251.25
Education 1,868.24
Public welfare 893.57
Health 128.99
Hospitals........................ 260.49
Highways 315.03
Police protection................ 54.22
Corrections 116.73
Natural resources 67.42
Parks & recreation 15.38
Governmental administration...... 292.03
Interest on general debt............92.71

State debt & cash, 2006 ($ per capita)
Debt $2,299.44
Cash/security holdings..............$9,606.67

Federal government grants to state & local government, 2005 (x $1,000)
Total............................$3,038,268
by Federal agency
Defense 28,501
Education 296,118
Energy 25,388
Environmental Protection Agency 36,723
Health & Human Services. 1,640,721
Homeland Security.................27,715
Housing & Urban Development..... 146,293
Justice 43,047
Labor 69,148
Transportation 289,912
Veterans Affairs.................. 3,206

Crime & Law Enforcement

Crime, 2006 (rates per 100,000 residents)
Property crimes 89,671
Burglary 14,701
Larceny 66,671
Motor vehicle theft 8,299
Property crime rate................. 3,516.4
Violent crimes.........................5,722
Murder 46
Forcible rape....................... 869
Robbery........................... 1,245
Aggravated assault 3,562
Violent crime rate 224.4
Hate crimes............................. 45

Fraud and identity theft, 2006
Fraud complaints...................... 4,563
rate per 100,000 residents 178.9
Identity theft complaints 1,577
rate per 100,000 residents 61.8

Law enforcement agencies, 2006
Total agencies........................... 129
Total employees 7,502
Officers 4,495
Civilians 3,007

Prisoners, probation, and parole, 2006
Total prisoners....................... 6,430
percent change, 12/31/05 to 12/31/06 ....0.8%
in private facilities 0%
in local jails 20.7%
Sentenced to more than one year 6,339
rate per 100,000 residents 246
Adults on probation 10,426
Adults on parole........................3,374

Prisoner demographics, June 30, 2005 (rate per 100,000 residents)
Male...................................... 803
Female 127
White.................................... 392
Black.................................... 3,588
Hispanic 838

©2008 Information Publications, Inc.
All rights reserved. Photocopying prohibited.
877-544-INFO (4636) or www.informationpublications.com

6   Utah

Arrests, 2006
Total 109,762
   Persons under 18 years of age 23,519

Persons under sentence of death, 1/1/07
Total 9
   White 6
   Black 1
   Hispanic 1

State's highest court
Name . . . . .Supreme Court
Number of members 5
Length of term . . . . 10 years
Intermediate appeals court? . . . . .yes

Labor & Income

Civilian labor force, 2006 (x 1,000)
Total 1,309
   Men 735
   Women 574
   Persons 16-19 years 92
   White 1,231
   Black . . . . NA
   Hispanic 148

Civilian labor force as a percent of civilian non-institutional population, 2006
Total 72.3%
   Men 82.0
   Women 62.8
   Persons 16-19 years 56.9
   White 72.7
   Black . . . . NA
   Hispanic 77.3

Employment, 2006 (x 1,000)
Total 1,271
   Men 715
   Women 556
   Persons 16-19 years 83
   White 1,197
   Black . . . . NA
   Hispanic 143

Unemployment rate, 2006
Total 2.9%
   Men 2.8
   Women 3.0
   Persons 16-19 years 9.9
   White 2.8
   Black . . . . NA
   Hispanic 3.5

Full-time/part-time labor force, 2003 (x 1,000)
Full-time labor force, employed 834
Part-time labor force, employed 284
Unemployed, looking for
   Full-time work 46
   Part-time work 20
Mean duration of unemployment (weeks) 13.8
   Median 6.1

Labor unions, 2006
Membership (x 1,000) 61
   percent of employed 5.4%

Experienced civilian labor force by private industry, 2006
Total 978,130
   Natural resources & mining 14,456
   Construction 95,115
   Manufacturing 122,215
   Trade, transportation & utilities 232,209
   Information 31,306
   Finance 71,413
   Professional & business 152,788
   Education & health 120,815
   Leisure & hospitality 108,363
   Other 29,188

Experienced civilian labor force by occupation, May 2006
Management 46,280
Business & financial 48,810
Legal 6,440
Sales 130,550
Office & admin. support 210,570
Computers & math 30,680
Architecture & engineering 22,170
Arts & entertainment 16,170
Education 65,060
Social services 16,910
Health care practitioner & technical 49,740
Health care support 25,860
Maintenance & repair 49,690
Construction 84,850
Transportation & moving 79,160
Production 92,370
Farming, fishing & forestry 1,280

Hours and earnings of production workers on manufacturing payrolls, 2006
Average weekly hours .41.1
Average hourly earnings $15.25
Average weekly earnings $626.78

Income and poverty, 2006
Median household income $51,309
Personal income, per capita (current $) . . . $29,108
   in constant (2000) dollars $25,409
Persons below poverty level 10.6%

Average annual pay
2006 . . . . $35,130
   increase from 2005 . . . . 5.4%

Federal individual income tax returns, 2005
Returns filed 1,030,683
Adjusted gross income ($1,000) $51,060,650
Total tax liability ($1,000) $5,732,106

Charitable contributions, 2004
Number of contributions 363.1
Total amount ($ mil) $2,323.8

©2008 Information Publications, Inc.
All rights reserved. Photocopying prohibited.
877-544-INFO (4636) or www.informationpublications.com

Economy, Business, Industry & Agriculture

Fortune 500 companies, 2007 1
Bankruptcy cases filed, FY 2007 6,182

Patents and trademarks issued, 2007

Patents 790
Trademarks 905

Business firm ownership, 2002

Women-owned 48,475
   Sales ($ mil) $5,920
Black-owned 649
   Sales ($ mil) $188
Hispanic-owned 5,177
   Sales ($ mil) $555
Asian-owned 2,824
   Sales ($ mil) $707
Amer. Indian/Alaska Native-owned 1,148
   Sales ($ mil) $83
Hawaiian/Pacific Islander-owned 429
   Sales ($ mil) $152

Gross domestic product, 2006 ($ mil)

Total gross domestic product $97,749
   Agriculture, forestry, fishing and
      hunting 592
   Mining 3,108
   Utilities 1,310
   Construction 6,247
   Manufacturing, durable goods 7,824
   Manufacturing, non-durable goods 3,156
   Wholesale trade .4,935
   Retail trade 7,242
   Transportation & warehousing 3,282
   Information 3,661
   Finance & insurance 8,453
   Real estate, rental & leasing 10,662
   Professional and technical services 6,432
   Educational services 1,019
   Health care and social assistance 5,736
   Accommodation/food services 2,463
   Other services, except government 3,099
   Government 13,161

Establishments, payroll, employees & receipts, by major industry group, 2005

Total 65,549
   Annual payroll ($1,000) $30,970,696
   Paid employees 974,686
Forestry, fishing & agriculture 73
   Annual payroll ($1,000) . . . . NA
   Paid employees . . . . NA
Mining 373
   Annual payroll ($1,000) $476,697
   Paid employees .7,753
   Receipts, 2002 ($1,000) $2,455,982

Utilities 208
   Annual payroll ($1,000) $314,586
   Paid employees .4,725
   Receipts, 2002 ($1,000) . . . . .NA
Construction 10,006
   Annual payroll ($1,000) $2,485,740
   Paid employees 70,587
   Receipts, 2002 ($1,000) $10,792,051
Manufacturing 3,165
   Annual payroll ($1,000) $4,624,262
   Paid employees 116,003
   Receipts, 2002 ($1,000) $25,104,045
Wholesale trade 3,434
   Annual payroll ($1,000) $2,009,505
   Paid employees 45,994
   Receipts, 2002 ($1,000) $22,905,100
Retail trade 8,454
   Annual payroll ($1,000) $2,840,452
   Paid employees 130,073
   Receipts, 2002 ($1,000) $23,675,432
Transportation & warehousing 1,851
   Annual payroll ($1,000) $1,512,233
   Paid employees 42,063
   Receipts, 2002 ($1,000) $4,053,466
Information 1,349
   Annual payroll ($1,000) $1,452,188
   Paid employees 31,089
   Receipts, 2002 ($1,000) . . . . .NA
Finance & insurance 4,819
   Annual payroll ($1,000) $2,181,880
   Paid employees 48,763
   Receipts, 2002 ($1,000) . . . . .NA
Professional, scientific & technical 7,460
   Annual payroll ($1,000) $2,761,145
   Paid employees 64,467
   Receipts, 2002 ($1,000) $4,878,861
Education 737
   Annual payroll ($1,000) $657,061
   Paid employees 29,845
   Receipts, 2002 ($1,000) $264,917
Health care & social assistance 5,920
   Annual payroll ($1,000) $3,475,642
   Paid employees 108,171
   Receipts, 2002 ($1,000) $7,237,756
Arts and entertainment 802
   Annual payroll ($1,000) $259,806
   Paid employees 15,433
   Receipts, 2002 ($1,000) $1,910,635
Real estate 4,105
   Annual payroll ($1,000) $500,593
   Paid employees 17,266
   Receipts, 2002 ($1,000) $1,820,526
Accommodation & food service 4,360
   Annual payroll ($1,000) $1,016,166
   Paid employees 87,672
   Receipts, 2002 ($1,000) $2,984,632

©2008 Information Publications, Inc.
All rights reserved. Photocopying prohibited.
877-544-INFO (4636) or www.informationpublications.com

Exports, 2006

Value of exported goods ($ mil) $6,798
   Manufactured $5,871
   Non-manufactured.................... $764

Foreign direct investment in US affiliates, 2004

Property, plants & equipment ($ mil) $11,402
Employment (x 1,000)..................... 30.9

Agriculture, 2006

Number of farms 15,100
Farm acreage (x 1,000) 11,600
   Acres per farm 768
Farm marketings and income ($ mil)
Total............................... $1,243.7
   Crops $312.8
   Livestock.......................... $930.8
Net farm income $263.6

Principal commodities, in order by marketing receipts, 2005

Cattle and calves, Dairy products, Hogs, Hay,
       Greenhouse/nursery

Federal economic activity in state

Expenditures, 2005 ($ mil)
   Total........................... $14,823
      Per capita $5,952.33
   Defense $3,559
   Non-defense..................... $11,264
Defense department, 2006 ($ mil)
   Payroll.......................... $1,739
   Contract awards $2,304
   Grants $22
Homeland security grants ($1,000)
   2006............................. $8,271
   2007............................. $6,989

FDIC-insured financial institutions, 2005

Number.................................. 69
Assets ($ billion) $292.4
Deposits ($ billion) $168.5

Fishing, 2006

Catch (x 1,000 lbs)...................... NA
Value ($1,000).......................... NA

Mining, 2006 ($ mil)

Total non-fuel mineral production $3,990
Percent of U.S. 6.20%

Communication, Energy & Transportation

Communication

Households with computers, 2003........ 74.1%
Households with internet access, 2003 .... 62.6%
High-speed internet providers 40
Total high-speed internet lines......... 638,618
   Residential 393,338
   Business........................... 245,280
Wireless phone customers, 12/2006 1,774,755

FCC-licensed stations (as of January 1, 2008)

TV stations 17
FM radio stations........................ 73
AM radio stations 44

Energy

Energy consumption, 2004
   Total (trillion Btu)..................... 740
   Per capita (million Btu) 305.7
By source of production (trillion Btu)
   Coal 400
   Natural gas.......................... 165
   Petroleum 279
   Nuclear electric power 0
   Hydroelectric power.................. 5
By end-use sector (trillion Btu)
   Residential 150
   Commercial 144
   Industrial 212
   Transportation 233
Electric energy, 2005
   Primary source of electricity........... Coal
   Net generation (billion kWh) 38.2
      percent from renewable sources...... 2.6%
   Net summer capability (million kW) 6.5
   CO_2 emitted from generation 35.9
Natural gas utilities, 2005
   Customers (x 1,000) 799
   Sales (trillion Btu)................... 121
   Revenues ($ mil) $847
Nuclear plants, 2007 0
Total CO_2 emitted (million metric tons)...... 62.4
Energy spending, 2004 ($ mil) $5,673
   per capita $2,343
   Price per million Btu $11.39

Transportation, 2006

Public road & street mileage 43,769
   Urban................................ 10,610
   Rural 33,159
   Interstate........................... 936
Vehicle miles of travel (millions) 25,964
   per capita 10,065.4
Total motor vehicle registrations...... 2,236,088
   Automobiles......................... 1,079,455
   Trucks 1,155,325
   Motorcycles 50,895
Licensed drivers 1,619,085
   19 years & under 122,857
Deaths from motor vehicle accidents 287
Gasoline consumed (x 1,000 gallons) 1,061,532
   per capita 411.5

Commuting Statistics, 2006

Average commute time (min) 20.8
   Drove to work alone 75.2%
   Carpooled........................... 13.1%
   Public transit 2.6%
   Walk to work 2.8%
   Work from home 4.6%

©2008 Information Publications, Inc.
All rights reserved. Photocopying prohibited.
877-544-INFO (4636) or www.informationpublications.com

State Summary

Capital city . . . . Montpelier
Governor . . . . Jim Douglas

109 State St
Pavilion Office Building
Montpelier, VT 05609
802-828-3333

Admitted as a state 1791
Area (square miles) 9,614
Population, 2007 (estimate) 621,254
Largest city . . . . Burlington
  Population, 2006 38,358
Personal income per capita, 2006
  (in current dollars) $34,264
Gross domestic product, 2006 ($ mil) $24,213

Leading industries by payroll, 2005

Manufacturing, Health care/Social assistance,
Retail trade

**Leading agricultural commodities
by receipts, 2005**

Dairy products, Cattle and calves, Greenhouse/
nursery, Hay, Maple products

Geography & Environment

Total area (square miles) 9,614
  land 9,250
  water 365
Federally-owned land, 2004 (acres) 443,249
  percent 7.5%
Highest point . . . . Mt. Mansfield
  elevation (feet) 4,393
Lowest point . . . . Lake Champlain
  elevation (feet) 95
General coastline (miles) 0
Tidal shoreline (miles) 0
Cropland, 2003 (x 1,000 acres) 587
Forest land, 2003 (x 1,000 acres) 4,129
Capital city . . . . Montpelier
  Population 2000 .8,035
  Population 2006 .7,954
Largest city . . . . Burlington
  Population 2000 38,889
  Population 2006 38,358

Number of cities with over 100,000 population

1990 0
2000 0
2006 0

State park and recreation areas, 2005

Area (x 1,000 acres) 69
Number of visitors (x 1,000) 690
Revenues ($1,000) $6,638
  percent of operating expenditures 98.0%

National forest system land, 2007

Acres 398,529

Demographics & Population Characteristics

Population

1980 511,456
1990 562,758
2000 608,827
2006 623,908
  Male 307,023
  Female 316,885
Living in group quarters, 2006 20,760
  percent of total 3.3%
2007 (estimate) 621,254
  persons per square mile of land 67.2
2008 (projected) 643,905
2010 (projected) 652,512
2020 (projected) 690,686
2030 (projected) 711,867

**Population of Core-Based Statistical Areas
(formerly Metropolitan Areas), x 1,000**

	CBSA	Non-CBSA
1990	417	146
2000	449	159
2006	460	164

Change in population, 2000-2007

Number 12,427
  percent 2.0%
Natural increase (births minus deaths) 10,413
Net internal migration . . . .-379
Net international migration 5,046

Persons by age, 2006

Under 5 years 32,779
5 to 17 years 100,610
18 years and over 490,519
65 years and over 82,966
85 years and over .11,714
  Median age 40.4

Persons by age, 2010 (projected)

Under 5 years 34,303
18 and over 520,140
65 and over 93,442
  Median age 40.6

Race, 2006

One Race
  White 603,345
  Black or African American 4,329
  Asian 6,847
  American Indian/Alaska Native 2,386
  Hawaiian Native/Pacific Islander 172
Two or more races 6,829

Persons of Hispanic origin, 2006

Total Hispanic or Latino 6,644
  Mexican 1,802
  Puerto Rican 2,013
  Cuban 336

©2008 Information Publications, Inc.
All rights reserved. Photocopying prohibited.
877-544-INFO (4636) or www.informationpublications.com

Persons of Asian origin, 2006

Total Asian 5,693
- Asian Indian. 1,263
- Chinese 1,456
- Filipino 555
- Japanese 276
- Korean. 573
- Vietnamese. 950

Marital status, 2006

Population 15 years & over 517,561
- Never married 151,292
- Married. 274,387
- Separated 8,279
- Widowed. 29,846
- Divorced 62,036

Language spoken at home, 2006

Population 5 years and older. 590,894
- English only 559,412
- Spanish 5,950
- French 10,707
- German. 3,252
- Chinese 774

Households & families, 2006

Households. 253,808
- with persons under 18 years 79,330
- with persons over 65 years. 57,803
- persons per household 2.38
Families. 162,721
- persons per family. 2.90
Married couples. .127,054
Female householder,
- no husband present. 25,636
One-person households 69,822

Nativity, 2006

Number of residents born in state 328,764
- percent of population. 52.7%

Immigration & naturalization, 2006

Legal permanent residents admitted. 895
Persons naturalized 569
Non-immigrant admissions 46,098

Vital Statistics and Health

Marriages

2004 5,835
2005 5,525
2006 5,385

Divorces

2004 2,442
2005 2,215
2006 2,167

Health risks, 2006

Percent of adults who are:
- Smokers. 18.0%
- Overweight (BMI > 25). 56.0%
- Obese (BMI > 30). 21.2%

Births

2005 6,295
- Birthrate (per 1,000). 10.1
- White. 6,099
- Black 77
- Hispanic 72
- Asian/Pacific Islander 106
- Amer. Indian/Alaska Native. 13
- Low birth weight (2,500g or less). 6.2%
- Cesarian births 25.9%
- Preterm births 9.0%
- To unmarried mothers. 32.3%
- Twin births (per 1,000) 31.9
- Triplets or higher order (per 100,000). . . .107.8
2006 (preliminary). 6,509
- rate per 1,000 . . . . .10.4

Deaths

2004
All causes 4,995
- rate per 100,000. . . . . .731.0
Heart disease 1,289
- rate per 100,000. . . . . .186.6
Malignant neoplasms 1,212
- rate per 100,000. . . . . .176.3
Cerebrovascular disease. 302
- rate per 100,000. . . . . .43.5
Chronic lower respiratory disease 296
- rate per 100,000. . . . . .44.1
Diabetes. 150
- rate per 100,000. . . . . .22.3
2005 (preliminary). 5,066
- rate per 100,000. . . . . .728.4
2006 (provisional) 5,009

Infant deaths

2004 30
- rate per 1,000. . . . . .4.6
2005 (provisional) 39
- rate per 1,000. . . . . .6.1

Exercise routines, 2005

None. 19.2%
Moderate or greater. 57.7%
Vigorous 33.1%

Abortions, 2004

Total performed in state. 1,725
- rate per 1,000 women age 15-44. 14
- % obtained by out-of-state residents 13.4%

Physicians, 2005

Total. 2,269
- rate per 100,000 persons 365

Community hospitals, 2005

Number of hospitals 12
Beds (x 1,000). 0.9
Patients admitted (x 1,000) 51
Average daily census (x 1,000) 0.6
Average cost per day $1,166
Outpatient visits (x 1 mil) 2.3

©2008 Information Publications, Inc.
All rights reserved. Photocopying prohibited.
877-544-INFO (4636) or www.informationpublications.com

Disability status of population, 2006
5 to 15 years 8.1%
16 to 64 years 14.0%
65 years and over 39.9%

Education

Educational attainment, 2006
Population over 25 years 426,930
  Less than 9th grade..................... 3.5%
  High school graduate or more 89.8%
  College graduate or more............ 32.4%
  Graduate or professional degree....... 12.8%

Public school enrollment, 2005-06
Total................................. 96,638
  Pre-kindergarten through grade 8..... 64,662
  Grades 9 through 12 31,856

Graduating public high school seniors, 2004-05
Diplomas (incl. GED and others) 7,179

SAT scores, 2007
Average critical reading score 516
Average writing score 508
Average math score 518
Percent of graduates taking test 67%

Public school teachers, 2006-07 (estimate)
Total (x 1,000) 9.0
  Elementary 4.6
  Secondary 4.4
Average salary $48,370
  Elementary $48,370
  Secondary $48,370

State receipts & expenditures for public schools, 2006-07 (estimate)
Revenue receipts ($ mil) $1,397
Expenditures
Total ($ mil) $1,381
  Per capita $1,986
  Per pupil $15,940

NAEP proficiency scores, 2007

	Reading		Math	
	Basic	Proficient	Basic	Proficient
Grade 4	74.4%	40.9%	89.0%	49.0%
Grade 8	84.4%	42.1%	81.1%	41.4%

Higher education enrollment, fall 2005
Total................................. 15,825
  Full-time men 6,943
  Full-time women 6,409
  Part-time men 971
  Part-time women...................... 1,502

Minority enrollment in institutions of higher education, 2005
Black, non-Hispanic 725
Hispanic 827
Asian/Pacific Islander 857
American Indian/Alaska Native............ 254

Institutions of higher education, 2005-06
Total................................. 25
  Public............................... 6
  Private 19

Earned degrees conferred, 2004-05
Associate's............................ 1,271
Bachelor's 4,892
Master's 1,684
First-professional. 259
Doctor's.............................. 62

Public Libraries, 2006
Number of libraries...................... 184
Number of outlets 195
Annual visits per capita 5.7
Circulation per capita..................... 7.3

State & local financial support for higher education, FY 2006
Full-time equivalent enrollment (x 1,000).... 18.9
Appropriations per FTE............... $3,030

Social Insurance & Welfare Programs

Social Security benefits & beneficiaries, 2005
Beneficiaries (x 1,000) 112
  Retired & dependents................... 78
  Survivors............................ 14
  Disabled & dependents................. 20
Annual benefit payments ($ mil) $1,184
  Retired & dependents................. $802
  Survivors......................... $184
  Disabled & dependents............... $198
Average monthly benefit
  Retired & dependents................. $995
  Disabled & dependents............... $889
  Widowed.......................... $964

Medicare, July 2005
Enrollment (x 1,000)..................... 96
Payments ($ mil) $600

Medicaid, 2004
Beneficiaries (x 1,000)................... 732
Payments ($ mil) $3,574

State Children's Health Insurance Program, 2006
Enrollment (x 1,000)..................... 6.3
Expenditures ($ mil).................... $4.7

Persons without health insurance, 2006
Number (x 1,000)....................... 63
  percent........................... 10.2%
Number of children (x 1,000) 11
  percent of children 8.3%

Health care expenditures, 2004
Total expenditures..................... $3,768
  per capita $6,069

©2008 Information Publications, Inc.
All rights reserved. Photocopying prohibited.
877-544-INFO (4636) or www.informationpublications.com

Federal and state public aid

State unemployment insurance, 2006
Recipients, first payments (x 1,000) 22
Total payments ($ mil) $84
Average weekly benefit $275
Temporary Assistance for Needy Families, 2006
Recipients (x 1,000) 130.8
Families (x 1,000) 53.0
Supplemental Security Income, 2005
Recipients (x 1,000) 13.1
Payments ($ mil) $62.6
Food Stamp Program, 2006
Avg monthly participants (x 1,000) 47.2
Total benefits ($ mil) $50.1

Housing & Construction

Housing units

Total 2005 (estimate) 307,348
Total 2006 (estimate) 309,557
Seasonal or recreational use, 2006 44,144
Owner-occupied, 2006 182,389
    Median home value $193,000
    Homeowner vacancy rate 1.2%
Renter-occupied, 2006 71,419
    Median rent $716
    Rental vacancy rate 3.6%
Home ownership rate, 2005 . . . . 74.2%
Home ownership rate, 2006 . . . . 74.0%

New privately-owned housing units

Number authorized, 2006 (x 1,000) 2.6
    Value ($ mil) $421.9
Started 2005 (x 1,000, estimate) 2.7
Started 2006 (x 1,000, estimate) 2.6

Existing home sales

2005 (x 1,000) 15.3
2006 (x 1,000) 15.0

Government & Elections

State officials 2008

Governor . . . . Jim Douglas
        Republican, term expires 1/09
Lieutenant Governor . . . . Brian Dubie
Secretary of State . . . . Deborah Markowitz
Attorney General . . . . William Sorrell
Chief Justice . . . . Paul Reiber

Governorship

Minimum age 18
Length of term . . . . 2 years
Consecutive terms permitted . . . . . . not specified
Who succeeds . . . . Lieutenant Governor

Local governments by type, 2002

Total 733
    County 14
    Municipal 47
    Township 237
    School District 283
    Special District 152

State legislature

Name . . . . General Assembly
Upper chamber . . . . .Senate
    Number of members 30
    Length of term . . . . 2 years
    Party in majority, 2008 . . . . .Democratic
Lower chamber . . . . House of Representatives
    Number of members 150
    Length of term . . . . 2 years
    Party in majority, 2008 . . . . .Democratic

Federal representation, 2008 (110th Congress)

Senator . . . . Patrick Leahy
    Party . . . . .Democratic
    Year term expires 2011
Senator . . . . Bernard Sanders
    Party . . . . Independent
    Year term expires 2013
Representatives, total 1
    Democrats 1
    Republicans 0

Voters in November 2006 election (estimate)

Total 272,854
    Male 129,914
    Female 142,939
    White 266,764
    Black 657
    Hispanic . . . . NA
    Asian 450

Presidential election, 2004

Total Popular Vote 312,309
    Kerry 184,067
    Bush 121,180
Total Electoral Votes 3

Votes cast for US Senators

2004
Total vote (x 1,000) 307
Leading party .Democratic
Percent for leading party 70.6%
2006
Total vote (x 1,000) 262
Leading party . . . . Independent
Percent for leading party 66.1%

Votes cast for US Representatives

2004
Total vote (x 1,000) 305
    Democratic 22
    Republican 74
Leading party . . . . Independent
Percent for leading party 67.5%
2006
Total vote (x 1,000) 263
    Democratic 140
    Republican 117
Leading party .Democratic
Percent for leading party 53.2%

©2008 Information Publications, Inc.
All rights reserved. Photocopying prohibited.
877-544-INFO (4636) or www.informationpublications.com

State government employment, 2006
Full-time equivalent employees 14,615
Payroll ($ mil) $58.3

Local government employment, 2006
Full-time equivalent employees 25,527
Payroll ($ mil) $78.4

Women holding public office, 2008
US Congress 0
Statewide elected office 1
State legislature 68

Black public officials, 2002
Total 1
US and state legislatures 1
City/county/regional offices 0
Judicial/law enforcement 0
Education/school boards 0

Hispanic public officials, 2006
Total 0
State executives & legislators 0
City/county/regional offices 0
Judicial/law enforcement 0
Education/school boards 0

Governmental Finance

State government revenues, 2006
Total revenue (x $1,000) $4,880,873
per capita $7,862.51
General revenue (x $1,000) $4,459,078
Intergovernmental 1,288,175
Taxes 2,406,661
general sales 326,055
individual income tax 542,012
corporate income tax 86,083
Current charges 438,968
Miscellaneous .325,274

State government expenditure, 2006
Total expenditure (x $1,000) $4,647,719
per capita $7,486.93
General expenditure (x $1,000) $4,378,513
per capita, total $7,053.27
Education 3,264.01
Public welfare 1,817.53
Health 217.25
Hospitals 8.56
Highways 455.96
Police protection 136.53
Corrections 166.11
Natural resources 153.04
Parks & recreation 26.76
Governmental administration 233.58
Interest on general debt 234.60

State debt & cash, 2006 ($ per capita)
Debt $4,803.82
Cash/security holdings $9,828.00

Federal government grants to state & local government, 2005 (x $1,000)
Total $1,324,142
by Federal agency
Defense 10,979
Education 106,796
Energy 5,440
Environmental Protection Agency 20,674
Health & Human Services 795,922
Homeland Security 8,018
Housing & Urban Development 79,232
Justice 29,435
Labor 22,630
Transportation 143,265
Veterans Affairs 2,975

Crime & Law Enforcement

Crime, 2006 (rates per 100,000 residents)
Property crimes 14,379
Burglary 3,300
Larceny 10,493
Motor vehicle theft 586
Property crime rate 2,304.7
Violent crimes 852
Murder 12
Forcible rape 150
Robbery 110
Aggravated assault 580
Violent crime rate 136.6
Hate crimes 26

Fraud and identity theft, 2006
Fraud complaints 718
rate per 100,000 residents 115.1
Identity theft complaints 178
rate per 100,000 residents 28.5

Law enforcement agencies, 2006
Total agencies 69
Total employees 1,567
Officers 1,163
Civilians 404

Prisoners, probation, and parole, 2006
Total prisoners 2,215
percent change, 12/31/05 to 12/31/06 . . . . 6.6%
in private facilities 23.7%
in local jails . . . . NA
Sentenced to more than one year 1,634
rate per 100,000 residents 262
Adults on probation 7,631
Adults on parole 965

Prisoner demographics, June 30, 2005 (rate per 100,000 residents)
Male 598
Female 45
White 304
Black 3,797
Hispanic . . . . NA

©2008 Information Publications, Inc.
All rights reserved. Photocopying prohibited.
877-544-INFO (4636) or www.informationpublications.com

6   Vermont

Arrests, 2006
Total.................................13,798
   Persons under 18 years of age..........1,645

Persons under sentence of death, 1/1/07
Total..................................... 0
   White.................................. 0
   Black 0
   Hispanic 0

State's highest court
Name ....Supreme Court
Number of members....................... 5
Length of term .... 6 years
Intermediate appeals court? .... no

Labor & Income

Civilian labor force, 2006 (x 1,000)
Total................................... 365
   Men 189
   Women 176
   Persons 16-19 years..................... 21
   White................................. 352
   Black .... NA
   Hispanic .... NA

Civilian labor force as a percent of civilian non-institutional population, 2006
Total.................................. 72.1%
   Men 76.3
   Women 68.0
   Persons 16-19 years...................57.4
   White.................................72.0
   Black .... NA
   Hispanic .... NA

Employment, 2006 (x 1,000)
Total................................... 352
   Men 182
   Women 170
   Persons 16-19 years..................... 19
   White................................. 339
   Black .... NA
   Hispanic .... NA

Unemployment rate, 2006
Total................................... 3.6%
   Men 3.9
   Women 3.3
   Persons 16-19 years...................10.1
   White.................................3.6
   Black .... NA
   Hispanic .... NA

Full-time/part-time labor force, 2003 (x 1,000)
Full-time labor force, employed............ 263
Part-time labor force, employed............ 72
Unemployed, looking for
   Full-time work......................... 12
   Part-time work......................... 4
*Mean duration of unemployment (weeks)......*13.8
   Median 8.2

Labor unions, 2006
Membership (x 1,000).................... 34
   percent of employed 11.0%

Experienced civilian labor force by private industry, 2006
Total............................... 251,594
   Natural resources & mining 3,048
   Construction 17,334
   Manufacturing...................... 36,233
   Trade, transportation & utilities 59,331
   Information 6,056
   Finance 12,945
   Professional & business 22,243
   Education & health 52,015
   Leisure & hospitality...............33,419
   Other 8,970

Experienced civilian labor force by occupation, May 2006
Management.........................8,610
Business & financial 10,870
Legal.................................1,770
Sales................................ 30,760
Office & admin. support................49,870
Computers & math 6,100
Architecture & engineering.............5,920
Arts & entertainment 5,030
Education 27,060
Social services 6,790
Health care practitioner & technical.....16,510
Health care support 9,470
Maintenance & repair.................. 12,430
Construction 16,470
Transportation & moving 16,990
Production 24,150
Farming, fishing & forestry............. 890

Hours and earnings of production workers on manufacturing payrolls, 2006
Average weekly hours 39.6
Average hourly earnings $15.79
Average weekly earnings $625.28

Income and poverty, 2006
Median household income............ $47,665
Personal income, per capita (current $)... $34,264
   in constant (2000) dollars $29,910
Persons below poverty level............. 10.3%

Average annual pay
2006................................. $35,542
   increase from 2005 .... 3.9%

Federal individual income tax returns, 2005
Returns filed........................ 309,831
Adjusted gross income ($1,000) $14,703,594
Total tax liability ($1,000) $1,745,492

Charitable contributions, 2004
Number of contributions.................74.2
Total amount ($ mil)...................$212.7

©2008 Information Publications, Inc.
All rights reserved. Photocopying prohibited.
877-544-INFO (4636) or www.informationpublications.com

Economy, Business, Industry & Agriculture

Fortune 500 companies, 2007 0
Bankruptcy cases filed, FY 2007 849

Patents and trademarks issued, 2007

Patents 512
Trademarks 240

Business firm ownership, 2002

Women-owned 18,989
  Sales ($ mil) $1,454
Black-owned 211
  Sales ($ mil) $21
Hispanic-owned 452
  Sales ($ mil) $38
Asian-owned 434
  Sales ($ mil) $67
Amer. Indian/Alaska Native-owned 300
  Sales ($ mil) $44
Hawaiian/Pacific Islander-owned 43
  Sales ($ mil) $1

Gross domestic product, 2006 ($ mil)

Total gross domestic product $24,213
  Agriculture, forestry, fishing and
    hunting 342
  Mining 114
  Utilities 597
  Construction 1,295
  Manufacturing, durable goods 2,146
  Manufacturing, non-durable goods 784
  Wholesale trade 1,273
  Retail trade 2,010
  Transportation & warehousing 480
  Information 907
  Finance & insurance 1,479
  Real estate, rental & leasing 2,919
  Professional and technical services 1,448
  Educational services 518
  Health care and social assistance 2,355
  Accommodation/food services 1,037
  Other services, except government 561
  Government 3,251

Establishments, payroll, employees & receipts, by major industry group, 2005

Total 22,273
  Annual payroll ($1,000) $8,284,548
  Paid employees 261,656
Forestry, fishing & agriculture 127
  Annual payroll ($1,000) . . . . NA
  Paid employees . . . . NA
Mining 50
  Annual payroll ($1,000) . . . . NA
  Paid employees . . . . NA
  Receipts, 2002 ($1,000) $44,884

Utilities 54
  Annual payroll ($1,000) $131,472
  Paid employees .1,885
  Receipts, 2002 ($1,000) . . . . .NA
Construction 3,067
  Annual payroll ($1,000) $623,572
  Paid employees 15,083
  Receipts, 2002 ($1,000) $2,253,071
Manufacturing 1,126
  Annual payroll ($1,000) $1,655,015
  Paid employees 37,170
  Receipts, 2002 ($1,000) $9,660,529
Wholesale trade 875
  Annual payroll ($1,000) $444,784
  Paid employees 10,482
  Receipts, 2002 ($1,000) $5,094,373
Retail trade 3,905
  Annual payroll ($1,000) $930,372
  Paid employees 41,385
  Receipts, 2002 ($1,000) $7,623,872
Transportation & warehousing 536
  Annual payroll ($1,000) $189,337
  Paid employees 6,255
  Receipts, 2002 ($1,000) $405,598
Information 527
  Annual payroll ($1,000) $280,205
  Paid employees 6,737
  Receipts, 2002 ($1,000) . . . . .NA
Finance & insurance 983
  Annual payroll ($1,000) $482,077
  Paid employees 9,632
  Receipts, 2002 ($1,000) . . . . .NA
Professional, scientific & technical 2,099
  Annual payroll ($1,000) $587,749
  Paid employees 15,821
  Receipts, 2002 ($1,000) $1,100,405
Education 335
  Annual payroll ($1,000) $327,266
  Paid employees 13,692
  Receipts, 2002 ($1,000) $92,808
Health care & social assistance 2,082
  Annual payroll ($1,000) $1,291,378
  Paid employees 39,298
  Receipts, 2002 ($1,000) $2,526,933
Arts and entertainment 497
  Annual payroll ($1,000) $129,531
  Paid employees 8,619
  Receipts, 2002 ($1,000) $337,453
Real estate 807
  Annual payroll ($1,000) $97,136
  Paid employees 3,370
  Receipts, 2002 ($1,000) $340,163
Accommodation & food service 1,963
  Annual payroll ($1,000) $403,200
  Paid employees 29,634
  Receipts, 2002 ($1,000) $1,154,048

©2008 Information Publications, Inc.
All rights reserved. Photocopying prohibited.
877-544-INFO (4636) or www.informationpublications.com

8   Vermont

Exports, 2006
Value of exported goods ($ mil) $3,817
   Manufactured $2,300
   Non-manufactured.................... $83

Foreign direct investment in US affiliates, 2004
Property, plants & equipment ($ mil) $1,357
Employment (x 1,000)....................10.8

Agriculture, 2006
Number of farms 6,300
Farm acreage (x 1,000) 1,240
   Acres per farm....................... 197
Farm marketings and income ($ mil)
Total................................. $500.8
   Crops.............................$85.7
   Livestock..........................$415.1
Net farm income $103.2

Principal commodities, in order by marketing receipts, 2005
Dairy products, Cattle and calves, Greenhouse/ nursery, Hay, Maple products

Federal economic activity in state
Expenditures, 2005 ($ mil)
   Total............................... $4,645
   Per capita $7,462.63
   Defense $550
   Non-defense....................... $4,095
Defense department, 2006 ($ mil)
   Payroll............................. $168
   Contract awards $829
   Grants $21
Homeland security grants ($1,000)
   2006........................... $10,908
   2007............................ $6,677

FDIC-insured financial institutions, 2005
Number 19
Assets ($ billion) $8.6
Deposits ($ billion) $7.1

Fishing, 2006
Catch (x 1,000 lbs).................... NA
Value ($1,000)........................ NA

Mining, 2006 ($ mil)
Total non-fuel mineral production $101
Percent of U.S. 0.16%

Communication, Energy & Transportation

Communication
Households with computers, 2003........ 65.5%
Households with internet access, 2003 .... 58.1%
High-speed internet providers 27
Total high-speed internet lines......... 170,245
   Residential 135,596
   Business.......................... 34,649
Wireless phone customers, 12/2006 358,052

FCC-licensed stations (as of January 1, 2008)
TV stations 7
FM radio stations........................ 58
AM radio stations 19

Energy
Energy consumption, 2004
   Total (trillion Btu)..................... 169
   Per capita (million Btu) 272.7
By source of production (trillion Btu)
   Coal 0
   Natural gas............................ 9
   Petroleum............................ 95
   Nuclear electric power 40
   Hydroelectric power................... 12
By end-use sector (trillion Btu)
   Residential 51
   Commercial 33
   Industrial 32
   Transportation 54
Electric energy, 2005
   Primary source of electricity........ Nuclear
   Net generation (billion kWh) 5.7
     percent from renewable sources...... 28.6%
   Net summer capability (million kW) 1.0
   CO_2 emitted from generation 0.0
Natural gas utilities, 2005
   Customers (x 1,000) 38
   Sales (trillion Btu)..................... 9
   Revenues ($ mil) $80
Nuclear plants, 2007 1
Total CO_2 emitted (million metric tons).......6.5
Energy spending, 2004 ($ mil) $1,968
   per capita $3,170
   Price per million Btu $15.83

Transportation, 2006
Public road & street mileage 14,406
   Urban...............................1,421
   Rural 12,985
   Interstate............................ 320
*Vehicle miles of travel (millions) *7,832
   per capita 12,616.4
Total motor vehicle registrations....... 587,668
   Automobiles....................... 309,972
   Trucks 275,951
   Motorcycles 32,584
Licensed drivers 532,041
   19 years & under 23,962
Deaths from motor vehicle accidents 87
Gasoline consumed (x 1,000 gallons) 348,236
   per capita 561.0

Commuting Statistics, 2006
Average commute time (min) 21.2
   Drove to work alone 75.1%
   Carpooled........................... 11.2%
   Public transit 0.8%
   Walk to work 6.1%
   Work from home...................... 5.4%

©2008 Information Publications, Inc.
All rights reserved. Photocopying prohibited.
877-544-INFO (4636) or www.informationpublications.com

State Summary

Capital city . . . . Richmond
Governor. . . . . Tim Kaine

State Capitol
Third Floor
Richmond, VA 23219
804-786-2211

Admitted as a state 1788
Area (square miles) 42,774
Population, 2007 (estimate). 7,712,091
Largest city . . . . Virginia Beach
  Population, 2006. 435,619
Personal income per capita, 2006
  (in current dollars) $39,173
Gross domestic product, 2006 ($ mil) . . . $369,260

Leading industries by payroll, 2005

Professional/Scientific/Technical, Health care/
Social assistance, Manufacturing

Leading agricultural commodities by receipts, 2005

Broilers, Cattle and calves, Dairy products, Turkeys, Greenhouse/nursery

Geography & Environment

Total area (square miles). 42,774
  land 39,594
  water 3,180
Federally-owned land, 2004 (acres) 2,534,178
  percent. 9.9%
Highest point . . . . .Mt. Rogers
  elevation (feet) 5,729
Lowest point. . . . . .Atlantic Ocean
  elevation (feet) . . . . sea level
General coastline (miles) 112
Tidal shoreline (miles) 3,315
Cropland, 2003 (x 1,000 acres) 2,862
Forest land, 2003 (x 1,000 acres). 13,182
Capital city . . . . Richmond
  Population 2000 197,790
  Population 2006 192,913
Largest city . . . . Virginia Beach
  Population 2000 425,257
  Population 2006 435,619

Number of cities with over 100,000 population

1990 8
2000 8
2006 9

State park and recreation areas, 2005

Area (x 1,000 acres). 66
Number of visitors (x 1,000) 7,319
Revenues ($1,000) $10,643
  percent of operating expenditures. 43.3%

National forest system land, 2007

Acres 1,664,306

Demographics & Population Characteristics

Population

1980 5,346,818
1990 6,187,358
2000 7,079,030
2006 7,642,884
  Male. 3,756,771
  Female 3,886,113
Living in group quarters, 2006. 235,342
  percent of total. 3.1%
2007 (estimate). 7,712,091
  persons per square mile of land 194.8
2008 (projected). 7,827,657
2010 (projected). 8,010,245
2020 (projected). 8,917,395
2030 (projected). 9,825,019

Population of Core-Based Statistical Areas (formerly Metropolitan Areas), x 1,000

	CBSA	Non-CBSA
1990	5,434	755
2000	6,269	810
2006	6,814	829

Change in population, 2000-2007

Number 633,061
  percent. 8.9%
Natural increase (births minus deaths) . . . 324,115
Net internal migration 155,205
Net international migration 159,627

Persons by age, 2006

Under 5 years 508,965
5 to 17 years 1,297,882
18 years and over 5,836,037
65 years and over .887,768
85 years and over 112,129
  Median age 36.9

Persons by age, 2010 (projected)

Under 5 years 535,955
18 and over 6,130,061
65 and over 994,359
  Median age 37.2

Race, 2006

One Race
  White. 5,605,240
  Black or African American 1,519,812
  Asian 363,094
  American Indian/Alaska Native. 26,020
  Hawaiian Native/Pacific Islander. 5,624
Two or more races. 123,094

Persons of Hispanic origin, 2006

Total Hispanic or Latino 470,871
  Mexican. 118,264
  Puerto Rican 51,211
  Cuban 12,702

©2008 Information Publications, Inc.
All rights reserved. Photocopying prohibited.
877-544-INFO (4636) or www.informationpublications.com

Persons of Asian origin, 2006

Total Asian 365,515
  Asian Indian. 76,167
  Chinese 58,722
  Filipino 64,677
  Japanese 8,965
  Korean. 63,767
  Vietnamese. 48,729

Marital status, 2006

Population 15 years & over 6,153,763
  Never married 1,837,362
  Married. 3,341,125
  Separated 175,351
  Widowed 378,532
  Divorced 596,744

Language spoken at home, 2006

Population 5 years and older. 7,139,393
  English only 6,201,784
  Spanish 412,416
  French 40,008
  German. 33,000
  Chinese 47,179

Households & families, 2006

Households. 2,905,071
  with persons under 18 years 993,568
  with persons over 65 years. 625,955
  persons per household 2.55
Families. 1,939,891
  persons per family. 3.12
Married couples .1,466,223
Female householder,
  no husband present. 354,079
One-person households 806,999

Nativity, 2006

Number of residents born in state 3,879,738
  percent of population 50.8%

Immigration & naturalization, 2006

Legal permanent residents admitted 38,488
Persons naturalized 20,401
Non-immigrant admissions 377,462

Vital Statistics and Health

Marriages

2004 61,990
2005 62,023
2006 60,760

Divorces

2004 29,411
2005 30,052
2006 31,087

Health risks, 2006

Percent of adults who are:
  Smokers. 19.3%
  Overweight (BMI > 25). 61.8%
  Obese (BMI > 30). 25.1%

Births

2005 104,555
  Birthrate (per 1,000). 13.8
  White. 74,323
  Black 22,911
  Hispanic 13,058
  Asian/Pacific Islander 7,159
  Amer. Indian/Alaska Native 162
  Low birth weight (2,500g or less) 8.2%
  Cesarian births 31.4%
  Preterm births 12.3%
  To unmarried mothers. 32.2%
  Twin births (per 1,000) 33.6
  Triplets or higher order (per 100,000). . . .154.6
2006 (preliminary) 107,817
  rate per 1,000 . . . . .14.1

Deaths

2004
All causes 56,550
  rate per 100,000. . . . . .809.2
Heart disease 14,284
  rate per 100,000. . . . . 206.5
Malignant neoplasms 13,385
  rate per 100,000. . . . . .187.6
Cerebrovascular disease. 3,788
  rate per 100,000. . . . . .55.5
Chronic lower respiratory disease 2,730
  rate per 100,000. . . . . .39.9
Diabetes. 1,602
  rate per 100,000. . . . . .22.7
2005 (preliminary). 57,857
  rate per 100,000. . . . . .801.5
2006 (provisional) 57,571

Infant deaths

2004 776
  rate per 1,000 . . . . .7.5
2005 (provisional) 760
  rate per 1,000 . . . . .7.2

Exercise routines, 2005

None. 21.3%
Moderate or greater. 50.8%
Vigorous 30.4%

Abortions, 2004

Total performed in state. 26,117
  rate per 1,000 women age 15-44. 16
  % obtained by out-of-state residents 5.1%

Physicians, 2005

Total. 20,461
  rate per 100,000 persons 270

Community hospitals, 2005

Number of hospitals 87
Beds (x 1,000). 17.5
Patients admitted (x 1,000) 780
Average daily census (x 1,000) 12.3
Average cost per day $1,394
Outpatient visits (x 1 mil) 13.2

©2008 Information Publications, Inc.
All rights reserved. Photocopying prohibited.
877-544-INFO (4636) or www.informationpublications.com

Disability status of population, 2006

5 to 15 years 6.1%
16 to 64 years 11.0%
65 years and over 39.5%

Education

Educational attainment, 2006

Population over 25 years 5,068,993
   Less than 9th grade. 5.6%
   High school graduate or more 85.4%
   College graduate or more. 32.7%
   Graduate or professional degree. 13.2%

Public school enrollment, 2005-06

Total. 1,214,472
   Pre-kindergarten through grade 8. . . . 841,435
   Grades 9 through 12 373,037

Graduating public high school seniors, 2004-05

Diplomas (incl. GED and others) 76,860

SAT scores, 2007

Average critical reading score 511
Average writing score 498
Average math score 511
Percent of graduates taking test 73%

Public school teachers, 2006-07 (estimate)

Total (x 1,000) 93.6
   Elementary. 55.5
   Secondary. 38.0
Average salary $44,727
   Elementary. $44,727
   Secondary. $44,727

State receipts & expenditures for public schools, 2006-07 (estimate)

Revenue receipts ($ mil) $13,445
Expenditures
Total ($ mil) $15,333
   Per capita $1,574
   Per pupil $10,599

NAEP proficiency scores, 2007

	Reading		Math	
	Basic	Proficient	Basic	Proficient
Grade 4	74.4%	37.6%	87.3%	41.9%
Grade 8	78.7%	33.7%	77.0%	37.5%

Higher education enrollment, fall 2005

Total. 89,971
   Full-time men 29,658
   Full-time women. 42,887
   Part-time men 6,789
   Part-time women. 10,637

Minority enrollment in institutions of higher education, 2005

Black, non-Hispanic 85,096
Hispanic 16,615
Asian/Pacific Islander 24,429
American Indian/Alaska Native. 2,153

Institutions of higher education, 2005-06

Total. 107
   Public. 39
   Private 68

Earned degrees conferred, 2004-05

Associate's. 14,924
Bachelor's 36,970
Master's 12,736
First-professional. 2,496
Doctor's. 1,504

Public Libraries, 2006

Number of libraries. 91
Number of outlets 373
Annual visits per capita 4.6
Circulation per capita. 8.5

State & local financial support for higher education, FY 2006

Full-time equivalent enrollment (x 1,000). . . .265.6
Appropriations per FTE. $5,223

Social Insurance & Welfare Programs

Social Security benefits & beneficiaries, 2005

Beneficiaries (x 1,000) 1,139
   Retired & dependents. 772
   Survivors. 155
   Disabled & dependents. 212
Annual benefit payments ($ mil) $12,115
   Retired & dependents. $7,883
   Survivors. $2,045
   Disabled & dependents. $2,187
Average monthly benefit
   Retired & dependents. $989
   Disabled & dependents. $945
   Widowed. $930

Medicare, July 2005

Enrollment (x 1,000). 993
Payments ($ mil) $6,171

Medicaid, 2004

Beneficiaries (x 1,000). 149
Payments ($ mil) $744

State Children's Health Insurance Program, 2006

Enrollment (x 1,000). 137.2
Expenditures ($ mil) $145.9

Persons without health insurance, 2006

Number (x 1,000). 1,006
   percent. 13.3%
Number of children (x 1,000) 185
   percent of children 10.1%

Health care expenditures, 2004

Total expenditures. $36,032
   per capita $4,822

©2008 Information Publications, Inc.
All rights reserved. Photocopying prohibited.
877-544-INFO (4636) or www.informationpublications.com

Federal and state public aid

State unemployment insurance, 2006
Recipients, first payments (x 1,000) 107
Total payments ($ mil) $347
Average weekly benefit $256
Temporary Assistance for Needy Families, 2006
Recipients (x 1,000) 447.1
Families (x 1,000) 176.2
Supplemental Security Income, 2005
Recipients (x 1,000) .137.3
Payments ($ mil) $632.2
Food Stamp Program, 2006
Avg monthly participants (x 1,000) 506.7
Total benefits ($ mil) $525.7

Housing & Construction

Housing units
Total 2005 (estimate) 3,175,095
Total 2006 (estimate) 3,230,803
Seasonal or recreational use, 2006 73,931
Owner-occupied, 2006 2,030,284
    Median home value $244,200
    Homeowner vacancy rate 1.8%
Renter-occupied, 2006 874,787
    Median rent $846
    Rental vacancy rate 8.3%
Home ownership rate, 2005 . . . . 71.2%
Home ownership rate, 2006 . . . . 71.1%

New privately-owned housing units
Number authorized, 2006 (x 1,000) 47.7
    Value ($ mil) $7,706.8
Started 2005 (x 1,000, estimate) 51.8
Started 2006 (x 1,000, estimate) 50.6

Existing home sales
2005 (x 1,000) 182.5
2006 (x 1,000) 140.1

Government & Elections

State officials 2008
Governor . . . . .Tim Kaine
        Democratic, term expires 1/10
Lieutenant Governor . . . . Bill Bolling
Secretary of State . . . . Katherine Hanley
Attorney General . . . . Bob McDonnell
Chief Justice . . . . Leroy Rountree Hassell

Governorship
Minimum age 30
Length of term . . . . 4 years
Consecutive terms permitted . . . . none
Who succeeds . . . . Lieutenant Governor

Local governments by type, 2002
Total 521
    County 95
    Municipal 229
    Township 0
    School District 1
    Special District 196

State legislature

Name . . . . General Assembly
Upper chamber . . . . .Senate
    Number of members 40
    Length of term . . . . 4 years
    Party in majority, 2008 . . . . .Democratic
Lower chamber . . . . House of Delegates
    Number of members 100
    Length of term . . . . 2 years
    Party in majority, 2008 . . . . Republican

Federal representation, 2008 (110th Congress)
Senator . . . . .John Warner
    Party . . . . Republican
    Year term expires 2009
Senator . . . . .Jim Webb
    Party . . . . .Democratic
    Year term expires 2013
Representatives, total 11
    Democrats 3
    Republicans 8

Voters in November 2006 election (estimate)
Total 2,431,144
    Male 1,143,965
    Female 1,287,179
    White 2,017,169
    Black 355,052
    Hispanic 14,165
    Asian 35,261

Presidential election, 2004
Total Popular Vote 3,198,367
    Kerry 1,454,742
    Bush 1,716,959
Total Electoral Votes 13

Votes cast for US Senators
2004
Total vote (x 1,000) . . . . NA
Leading party . . . . NA
Percent for leading party . . . . NA
2006
Total vote (x 1,000) .2,370
Leading party . . . . .Democratic
Percent for leading party 49.6%

Votes cast for US Representatives
2004
Total vote (x 1,000) 3,004
    Democratic 1,023
    Republican 1,817
Leading party . . . . Republican
Percent for leading party 60.5%
2006
Total vote (x 1,000) 2,297
    Democratic 947
    Republican 1,223
Leading party . . . . Republican
Percent for leading party 53.2%

©2008 Information Publications, Inc.
All rights reserved. Photocopying prohibited.
877-544-INFO (4636) or www.informationpublications.com

State government employment, 2006

Full-time equivalent employees 122,634
Payroll ($ mil) $453.0

Local government employment, 2006

Full-time equivalent employees 307,987
Payroll ($ mil) $1,062.1

Women holding public office, 2008

US Congress 1
Statewide elected office...................... 0
State legislature 23

Black public officials, 2002

Total....................................... 248
  US and state legislatures 16
  City/county/regional offices 132
  Judicial/law enforcement.................. 16
  Education/school boards.................. 84

Hispanic public officials, 2006

Total....................................... 1
  State executives & legislators 0
  City/county/regional offices 1
  Judicial/law enforcement.................. 0
  Education/school boards.................. 0

Governmental Finance

State government revenues, 2006

Total revenue (x $1,000).......... $40,272,795
  per capita $5,271.14
General revenue (x $1,000) $32,619,477
  Intergovernmental 6,673,248
  Taxes 17,192,007
    general sales....................3,263,647
    individual income tax 9,073,077
    corporate income tax............. 863,320
  Current charges..................5,440,997
  Miscellaneous...................3,313,225

State government expenditure, 2006

Total expenditure (x $1,000) $34,776,228
  per capita $4,551.71
General expenditure (x $1,000) $31,831,209
  per capita, total................... $4,166.25
    Education......................1,622.73
    Public welfare 871.10
    Health.......................... 104.00
    Hospitals.........................315.00
    Highways.........................347.02
    Police protection....................83.53
    Corrections......................179.96
    Natural resources 27.46
    Parks & recreation 16.13
    Governmental administration.......138.31
    Interest on general debt.............97.72

State debt & cash, 2006 ($ per capita)

Debt $2,305.04
Cash/security holdings...............$9,616.80

Federal government grants to state & local government, 2005 (x $1,000)

Total.............................$7,745,362
by Federal agency
  Defense 73,940
  Education 799,341
  Energy........................... 60,569
  Environmental Protection Agency 97,253
  Health & Human Services......... 3,788,133
  Homeland Security................ 80,694
  Housing & Urban Development...... 652,898
  Justice 171,669
  Labor 265,859
  Transportation 847,605
  Veterans Affairs...................21,065

Crime & Law Enforcement

Crime, 2006 (rates per 100,000 residents)

Property crimes 189,406
  Burglary 31,913
  Larceny 142,679
  Motor vehicle theft 14,814
  Property crime rate..............2,478.2
Violent crimes...................... 21,568
  Murder 399
  Forcible rape.....................1,792
  Robbery 7,749
  Aggravated assault 11,628
  Violent crime rate 282.2
Hate crimes............................. 389

Fraud and identity theft, 2006

Fraud complaints..................... 12,039
  rate per 100,000 residents 157.5
Identity theft complaints 5,137
  rate per 100,000 residents 67.2

Law enforcement agencies, 2006

Total agencies.......................... 280
Total employees 22,872
  Officers 17,672
  Civilians 5,200

Prisoners, probation, and parole, 2006

Total prisoners...................... 36,688
  percent change, 12/31/05 to 12/31/06 .... 3.8%
  in private facilities 4.2%
  in local jails 16.3%
Sentenced to more than one year 36,688
  rate per 100,000 residents 477
Adults on probation 48,144
Adults on parole....................... 3,978

Prisoner demographics, June 30, 2005 (rate per 100,000 residents)

Male 1,393
Female 144
White................................... 396
Black...................................2,331
Hispanic 487

©2008 Information Publications, Inc.
All rights reserved. Photocopying prohibited.
877-544-INFO (4636) or www.informationpublications.com

Arrests, 2006

Total 276,305
    Persons under 18 years of age 34,797

Persons under sentence of death, 1/1/07

Total 20
    White 8
    Black 12
    Hispanic 0

State's highest court

Name . . . . Supreme Court
Number of members 7
Length of term . . . . 12 years
Intermediate appeals court? . . . . yes

Labor & Income

Civilian labor force, 2006 (x 1,000)

Total 3,971
    Men 2,076
    Women 1,895
    Persons 16-19 years 194
    White 2,973
    Black 761
    Hispanic 275

Civilian labor force as a percent of civilian non-institutional population, 2006

Total 68.4%
    Men 75.2
    Women 62.3
    Persons 16-19 years 45.2
    White 68.0
    Black 69.9
    Hispanic 75.1

Employment, 2006 (x 1,000)

Total 3,848
    Men 2,020
    Women 1,828
    Persons 16-19 years 171
    White 2,898
    Black 717
    Hispanic 267

Unemployment rate, 2006

Total 3.1%
    Men 2.7
    Women 3.5
    Persons 16-19 years 11.7
    White 2.5
    Black 5.7
    Hispanic 2.7

Full-time/part-time labor force, 2003 (x 1,000)

Full-time labor force, employed 3,055
Part-time labor force, employed 565
Unemployed, looking for
    Full-time work 127
    Part-time work 26
Mean duration of unemployment (weeks) 17.2
    Median 9.6

Labor unions, 2006

Membership (x 1,000) 139
    percent of employed 4.0%

Experienced civilian labor force by private industry, 2006

Total 2,976,895
    Natural resources & mining 22,092
    Construction 249,270
    Manufacturing 288,264
    Trade, transportation & utilities 657,061
    Information 91,782
    Finance 192,470
    Professional & business 629,471
    Education & health 377,108
    Leisure & hospitality 338,612
    Other 125,422

Experienced civilian labor force by occupation, May 2006

Management 118,720
Business & financial 202,700
Legal 31,200
Sales 415,380
Office & admin. support 591,390
Computers & math 176,240
Architecture & engineering 80,070
Arts & entertainment 48,250
Education 216,950
Social services 42,660
Health care practitioner & technical 159,520
Health care support 70,630
Maintenance & repair 156,630
Construction 216,400
Transportation & moving 245,660
Production 210,810
Farming, fishing & forestry 5,880

Hours and earnings of production workers on manufacturing payrolls, 2006

Average weekly hours 41.3
Average hourly earnings $16.75
Average weekly earnings $691.78

Income and poverty, 2006

Median household income $56,277
Personal income, per capita (current $) . . . $39,173
    in constant (2000) dollars $34,196
Persons below poverty level 9.6%

Average annual pay

2006 . . . . $44,051
    increase from 2005 . . . . 4.2%

Federal individual income tax returns, 2005

Returns filed 3,540,757
Adjusted gross income ($1,000) $214,671,763
Total tax liability ($1,000) $29,027,603

Charitable contributions, 2004

Number of contributions 1,239.9
Total amount ($ mil) $4,809.4

©2008 Information Publications, Inc.
All rights reserved. Photocopying prohibited.
877-544-INFO (4636) or www.informationpublications.com

Economy, Business, Industry & Agriculture

Fortune 500 companies, 2007 17

Bankruptcy cases filed, FY 2007 17,893

Patents and trademarks issued, 2007

Patents 1,192

Trademarks 1,905

Business firm ownership, 2002

Women-owned 157,030

   Sales ($ mil) $22,123

Black-owned 41,165

   Sales ($ mil) $3,719

Hispanic-owned 18,987

   Sales ($ mil) $3,452

Asian-owned 30,457

   Sales ($ mil) $7,709

Amer. Indian/Alaska Native-owned 2,692

   Sales ($ mil) $444

Hawaiian/Pacific Islander-owned 423

   Sales ($ mil) $142

Gross domestic product, 2006 ($ mil)

Total gross domestic product $369,260

   Agriculture, forestry, fishing and

      hunting 1,522

   Mining 1,783

   Utilities 6,835

   Construction 19,568

   Manufacturing, durable goods 15,590

   Manufacturing, non-durable goods 18,573

   Wholesale trade 16,182

   Retail trade 22,354

   Transportation & warehousing 8,508

   Information 18,749

   Finance & insurance 22,834

   Real estate, rental & leasing 49,674

   Professional and technical services 43,327

   Educational services 2,771

   Health care and social assistance 19,809

   Accommodation/food services 8,655

   Other services, except government 9,088

   Government 63,083

Establishments, payroll, employees & receipts, by major industry group, 2005

Total 193,067

   Annual payroll ($1,000) $121,801,479

   Paid employees 3,060,127

Forestry, fishing & agriculture 735

   Annual payroll ($1,000) $139,548

   Paid employees 3,783

Mining 356

   Annual payroll ($1,000) $564,203

   Paid employees 10,088

   Receipts, 2002 ($1,000) $2,277,885

Utilities 309

   Annual payroll ($1,000) $1,211,784

   Paid employees 15,625

   Receipts, 2002 ($1,000) . . . . .NA

Construction 24,527

   Annual payroll ($1,000) $9,166,257

   Paid employees 229,405

   Receipts, 2002 ($1,000) $33,667,129

Manufacturing 5,798

   Annual payroll ($1,000) $11,987,037

   Paid employees 290,052

   Receipts, 2002 ($1,000) $83,952,547

Wholesale trade 7,790

   Annual payroll ($1,000) $5,583,345

   Paid employees 110,990

   Receipts, 2002 ($1,000) $69,267,796

Retail trade 29,335

   Annual payroll ($1,000) $9,551,693

   Paid employees 424,451

   Receipts, 2002 ($1,000) $80,509,062

Transportation & warehousing 5,348

   Annual payroll ($1,000) $3,688,915

   Paid employees 104,237

   Receipts, 2002 ($1,000) $7,137,609

Information 4,099

   Annual payroll ($1,000) $7,107,890

   Paid employees 105,410

   Receipts, 2002 ($1,000) . . . . .NA

Finance & insurance 11,482

   Annual payroll ($1,000) $10,660,107

   Paid employees 163,718

   Receipts, 2002 ($1,000) . . . . .NA

Professional, scientific & technical 25,836

   Annual payroll ($1,000) $24,259,680

   Paid employees 355,406

   Receipts, 2002 ($1,000) $40,683,149

Education 2,280

   Annual payroll ($1,000) $1,532,308

   Paid employees 57,642

   Receipts, 2002 ($1,000) $989,795

Health care & social assistance 16,286

   Annual payroll ($1,000) $13,095,304

   Paid employees 346,082

   Receipts, 2002 ($1,000) $28,199,263

Arts and entertainment 2,650

   Annual payroll ($1,000) $996,562

   Paid employees 47,078

   Receipts, 2002 ($1,000) $2,781,488

Real estate 8,955

   Annual payroll ($1,000) $2,351,599

   Paid employees 60,741

   Receipts, 2002 ($1,000) $8,038,543

Accommodation & food service 14,670

   Annual payroll ($1,000) $3,927,633

   Paid employees 284,857

   Receipts, 2002 ($1,000) $10,929,429

©2008 Information Publications, Inc.
All rights reserved. Photocopying prohibited.
877-544-INFO (4636) or www.informationpublications.com

8 Virginia

Exports, 2006
Value of exported goods ($ mil) $14,104
    Manufactured $11,122
    Non-manufactured $2,005

Foreign direct investment in US affiliates, 2004
Property, plants & equipment ($ mil) . . . $16,422
Employment (x 1,000) 133.7

Agriculture, 2006
Number of farms 46,800
Farm acreage (x 1,000) 8,500
    Acres per farm 182
Farm marketings and income ($ mil)
Total $2,688.7
    Crops $834.1
    Livestock $1,854.6
Net farm income $678.0

Principal commodities, in order by marketing receipts, 2005
Broilers, Cattle and calves, Dairy products, Turkeys, Greenhouse/nursery

Federal economic activity in state
Expenditures, 2005 ($ mil)
    Total $95,097
        Per capita $12,571.83
    Defense $40,799
    Non-defense $54,298
Defense department, 2006 ($ mil)
    Payroll $16,693
    Contract awards $29,246
    Grants $85
Homeland security grants ($1,000)
    2006 . . . . $16,888
    2007 . . . . $33,278

FDIC-insured financial institutions, 2005
Number 126
Assets ($ billion) $247.3
Deposits ($ billion) $159.1

Fishing, 2006
Catch (x 1,000 lbs) 426,217
Value ($1,000) $110,024

Mining, 2006 ($ mil)
Total non-fuel mineral production $1,230
Percent of U.S. 1.91%

Communication, Energy & Transportation

Communication
Households with computers, 2003 . . . . 66.8%
Households with internet access, 2003 . . . . 60.3%
High-speed internet providers 66
Total high-speed internet lines 2,183,019
    Residential 1,451,016
    Business 732,003
Wireless phone customers, 12/2006 5,607,350

FCC-licensed stations (as of January 1, 2008)
TV stations 36
FM radio stations 208
AM radio stations 145

Energy
Energy consumption, 2004
    Total (trillion Btu) 2,558
    Per capita (million Btu) 342.4
By source of production (trillion Btu)
    Coal 453
    Natural gas 285
    Petroleum 1,039
    Nuclear electric power 295
    Hydroelectric power 16
By end-use sector (trillion Btu)
    Residential 617
    Commercial 578
    Industrial 591
    Transportation 772
Electric energy, 2005
    Primary source of electricity . . . . Coal
    Net generation (billion kWh) 78.9
        percent from renewable sources 5.0%
    Net summer capability (million kW) 22.6
    CO_2 emitted from generation 47.7
Natural gas utilities, 2005
    Customers (x 1,000) 1,158
    Sales (trillion Btu) 232
    Revenues ($ mil) $1,855
Nuclear plants, 2007 4
Total CO_2 emitted (million metric tons) 122.6
Energy spending, 2004 ($ mil) $21,298
    per capita $2,850
    Price per million Btu $12.64

Transportation, 2006
Public road & street mileage 72,331
    Urban 21,700
    Rural 50,631
    Interstate 1,117
Vehicle miles of travel (millions) 81,095
    per capita 10,614.2
Total motor vehicle registrations 6,635,976
    Automobiles 4,031,355
    Trucks 2,586,357
    Motorcycles 81,171
Licensed drivers .5,210,685
    19 years & under 219,680
Deaths from motor vehicle accidents 963
Gasoline consumed (x 1,000 gallons) 4,011,244
    per capita 525.0

Commuting Statistics, 2006
Average commute time (min) 26.9
    Drove to work alone 77.0%
    Carpooled 11.4%
    Public transit 4.1%
    Walk to work 2.3%
    Work from home 3.9%

©2008 Information Publications, Inc.
All rights reserved. Photocopying prohibited.
877-544-INFO (4636) or www.informationpublications.com

State Summary

Capital city . . . . Olympia
Governor . . . . Christine Gregoire

Office of the Governor
PO Box 40002
Olympia, WA 98504
360-902-4111

Admitted as a state 1889
Area (square miles) 71,300
Population, 2007 (estimate). 6,468,424
Largest city . . . . Seattle
Population, 2006 582,454
Personal income per capita, 2006
(in current dollars) $37,423
Gross domestic product, 2006 ($ mil) . . . $293,531

Leading industries by payroll, 2005

Manufacturing, Health care/Social assistance,
Professional/Scientific/Technical

**Leading agricultural commodities
by receipts, 2005**

Apples, Dairy products, Cattle and calves,
Wheat, Potatoes

Geography & Environment

Total area (square miles). 71,300
land 66,544
water 4,756
Federally-owned land, 2004 (acres) . . .12,949,662
percent. 30.3%
Highest point . . . . Mt. Rainier
elevation (feet) .14,411
Lowest point . . . . Pacific Ocean
elevation (feet) . . . . sea level
General coastline (miles) 157
Tidal shoreline (miles) 3,026
Cropland, 2003 (x 1,000 acres) 6,494
Forest land, 2003 (x 1,000 acres). 12,707
Capital city . . . . Olympia
Population 2000 .42,514
Population 2006 44,645
Largest city . . . . Seattle
Population 2000 563,374
Population 2006 582,454

Number of cities with over 100,000 population

1990 3
2000 5
2006 5

State park and recreation areas, 2005

Area (x 1,000 acres) 106
Number of visitors (x 1,000) 40,026
Revenues ($1,000) $17,627
percent of operating expenditures 31.2%

National forest system land, 2007

Acres 9,282,376

Demographics & Population Characteristics

Population

1980 4,132,156
1990 4,866,692
2000 5,894,140
2006 6,395,798
Male 3,189,630
Female 3,206,168
Living in group quarters, 2006 140,607
percent of total. 2.2%
2007 (estimate) 6,468,424
persons per square mile of land 97.2
2008 (projected) 6,399,035
2010 (projected) 6,541,963
2020 (projected) 7,432,136
2030 (projected) 8,624,801

**Population of Core-Based Statistical Areas
(formerly Metropolitan Areas), x 1,000**

	CBSA	Non-CBSA
1990	4,689	178
2000	5,678	216
2006	6,168	227

Change in population, 2000-2007

Number 574,284
percent 9.7%
Natural increase (births minus deaths) 267,052
Net internal migration 155,491
Net international migration 164,951

Persons by age, 2006

Under 5 years 408,158
5 to 17 years 1,118,109
18 years and over 4,869,531
65 years and over 738,369
85 years and over 107,032
Median age. 36.7

Persons by age, 2010 (projected)

Under 5 years 426,590
18 and over 5,053,540
65 and over 795,528
Median age. 37.3

Race, 2006

One Race
White. 5,420,961
Black or African American 227,926
Asian 422,039
American Indian/Alaska Native. 104,405
Hawaiian Native/Pacific Islander. 29,703
Two or more races 190,764

Persons of Hispanic origin, 2006

Total Hispanic or Latino 580,027
Mexican. 464,652
Puerto Rican 19,957
Cuban 6,746

©2008 Information Publications, Inc.
All rights reserved. Photocopying prohibited.
877-544-INFO (4636) or www.informationpublications.com

Persons of Asian origin, 2006

Total Asian	423,976
Asian Indian	44,271
Chinese	81,636
Filipino	80,896
Japanese	38,628
Korean	57,320
Vietnamese	68,308

Marital status, 2006

Population 15 years & over	5,142,602
Never married	1,511,538
Married	2,728,691
Separated	86,369
Widowed	270,178
Divorced	632,195

Language spoken at home, 2006

Population 5 years and older	5,988,982
English only	4,994,813
Spanish	431,021
French	21,683
German	39,134
Chinese	63,390

Households & families, 2006

Households	2,471,912
with persons under 18 years	819,840
with persons over 65 years	511,029
persons per household	2.53
Families	1,595,147
persons per family	3.11
Married couples	1,235,060
Female householder, no husband present	250,416
One-person households	698,549

Nativity, 2006

Number of residents born in state	3,019,592
percent of population	47.2%

Immigration & naturalization, 2006

Legal permanent residents admitted	23,805
Persons naturalized	12,762
Non-immigrant admissions	578,192

Vital Statistics and Health

Marriages

2004	40,169
2005	40,802
2006	40,967

Divorces

2004	26,674
2005	27,022
2006	24,014

Health risks, 2006

Percent of adults who are:

Smokers	17.1%
Overweight (BMI > 25)	60.7%
Obese (BMI > 30)	24.2%

Births

2005	82,703
Birthrate (per 1,000)	13.2
White	67,917
Black	4,230
Hispanic	15,013
Asian/Pacific Islander	8,473
Amer. Indian/Alaska Native	2,083
Low birth weight (2,500g or less)	6.1%
Cesarian births	27.8%
Preterm births	10.6%
To unmarried mothers	30.9%
Twin births (per 1,000)	29.4
Triplets or higher order (per 100,000)	92.7
2006 (preliminary)	86,848
rate per 1,000	13.6

Deaths

2004

All causes	44,770
rate per 100,000	738.3
Heart disease	10,644
rate per 100,000	174.7
Malignant neoplasms	10,989
rate per 100,000	183.6
Cerebrovascular disease	3,243
rate per 100,000	53.5
Chronic lower respiratory disease	2,549
rate per 100,000	43.3
Diabetes	1,508
rate per 100,000	25.0
2005 (preliminary)	46,212
rate per 100,000	738.2
2006 (provisional)	44,844

Infant deaths

2004	451
rate per 1,000	5.5
2005 (provisional)	414
rate per 1,000	5.0

Exercise routines, 2005

None	17.4%
Moderate or greater	54.7%
Vigorous	30.6%

Abortions, 2004

Total performed in state	24,664
rate per 1,000 women age 15-44	19
% obtained by out-of-state residents	5.0%

Physicians, 2005

Total	16,707
rate per 100,000 persons	266

Community hospitals, 2005

Number of hospitals	86
Beds (x 1,000)	11.0
Patients admitted (x 1,000)	543
Average daily census (x 1,000)	6.8
Average cost per day	$2,143
Outpatient visits (x 1 mil)	10.0

©2008 Information Publications, Inc.
All rights reserved. Photocopying prohibited.
877-544-INFO (4636) or www.informationpublications.com

Disability status of population, 2006
5 to 15 years 6.5%
16 to 64 years 13.6%
65 years and over 41.9%

Education

Educational attainment, 2006
Population over 25 years 4,253,582
    Less than 9th grade..................... 4.1%
    High school graduate or more 89.0%
    College graduate or more.............. 30.5%
    Graduate or professional degree....... 10.7%

Public school enrollment, 2005-06
Total........................... 1,031,985
    Pre-kindergarten through grade 8.... 699,482
    Grades 9 through 12................ 332,503

Graduating public high school seniors, 2004-05
Diplomas (incl. GED and others) 61,213

SAT scores, 2007
Average critical reading score.............. 526
Average writing score 510
Average math score 531
Percent of graduates taking test 53%

Public school teachers, 2006-07 (estimate)
Total (x 1,000) 54.0
    Elementary........................... 29.5
    Secondary............................ 24.4
Average salary $47,882
    Elementary......................... $47,926
    Secondary.......................... $47,828

State receipts & expenditures for public schools, 2006-07 (estimate)
Revenue receipts ($ mil) $10,395
Expenditures
Total ($ mil) $12,825
    Per capita $1,404
    Per pupil $9,334

NAEP proficiency scores, 2007

	Reading		Math	
	Basic	Proficient	Basic	Proficient
Grade 4	70.3%	36.3%	84.3%	43.8%
Grade 8	76.7%	34.1%	74.9%	35.9%

Higher education enrollment, fall 2005
Total.................................. 51,726
    Full-time men 17,651
    Full-time women..................... 23,792
    Part-time men 4,293
    Part-time women 5,990

Minority enrollment in institutions of higher education, 2005
Black, non-Hispanic 15,461
Hispanic 19,530
Asian/Pacific Islander 33,269
American Indian/Alaska Native.......... 6,236

Institutions of higher education, 2005-06
Total................................... 80
    Public................................ 43
    Private............................... 37

Earned degrees conferred, 2004-05
Associate's.......................... 22,338
Bachelor's 28,265
Master's.............................. 8,773
First-professional...................... 1,357
Doctor's............................... 793

Public Libraries, 2006
Number of libraries.................... 65
Number of outlets 354
Annual visits per capita 7.0
Circulation per capita.................. 11.1

State & local financial support for higher education, FY 2006
Full-time equivalent enrollment (x 1,000).... 213.1
Appropriations per FTE................ $6,437

Social Insurance & Welfare Programs

Social Security benefits & beneficiaries, 2005
Beneficiaries (x 1,000) 937
    Retired & dependents.................. 674
    Survivors............................ 113
    Disabled & dependents................. 150
Annual benefit payments ($ mil) $10,474
    Retired & dependents................. $7,218
    Survivors.......................... $1,646
    Disabled & dependents............... $1,611
Average monthly benefit
    Retired & dependents................. $1,042
    Disabled & dependents............... $952
    Widowed............................ $1,032

Medicare, July 2005
Enrollment (x 1,000)...................... 821
Payments ($ mil) $4,334

Medicaid, 2004
Beneficiaries (x 1,000)................. 1,109
Payments ($ mil) $4,930

State Children's Health Insurance Program, 2006
Enrollment (x 1,000)................... 15.0
Expenditures ($ mil).................. $40.3

Persons without health insurance, 2006
Number (x 1,000)...................... 746
    percent............................ 11.8%
Number of children (x 1,000) 105
    percent of children 6.9%

Health care expenditures, 2004
Total expenditures.................... $31,600
    per capita $5,092

©2008 Information Publications, Inc.
All rights reserved. Photocopying prohibited.
877-544-INFO (4636) or www.informationpublications.com

Federal and state public aid

State unemployment insurance, 2006
Recipients, first payments (x 1,000) 171
Total payments ($ mil) $710
Average weekly benefit $322
Temporary Assistance for Needy Families, 2006
Recipients (x 1,000) .1,504.6
Families (x 1,000) 637.5
Supplemental Security Income, 2005
Recipients (x 1,000) 115.6
Payments ($ mil) $616.1
Food Stamp Program, 2006
Avg monthly participants (x 1,000) 535.8
Total benefits ($ mil) $594.6

Housing & Construction

Housing units

Total 2005 (estimate) 2,651,323
Total 2006 (estimate) 2,699,333
Seasonal or recreational use, 2006 67,992
Owner-occupied, 2006 1,620,052
    Median home value $267,600
    Homeowner vacancy rate 1.3%
Renter-occupied, 2006 851,860
    Median rent $779
    Rental vacancy rate 6.3%
Home ownership rate, 2005 . . . . 67.6%
Home ownership rate, 2006 . . . . 66.7%

New privately-owned housing units

Number authorized, 2006 (x 1,000) 50.0
    Value ($ mil) $8,539.8
Started 2005 (x 1,000, estimate) 38.3
Started 2006 (x 1,000, estimate) 38.2

Existing home sales

2005 (x 1,000) 167.8
2006 (x 1,000) 154.2

Government & Elections

State officials 2008

Governor . . . . Christine Gregoire
            Democratic, term expires 1/09
Lieutenant Governor . . . . Brad Owen
Secretary of State . . . . .Sam Reed
Attorney General . . . . .Rob McKenna
Chief Justice . . . . Gerry Alexander

Governorship

Minimum age 18
Length of term . . . . 4 years
Consecutive terms permitted . . . . . . not specified
Who succeeds . . . . Lieutenant Governor

Local governments by type, 2002

Total 1,787
    County 39
    Municipal 279
    Township 0
    School District 296
    Special District .1,173

State legislature

Name . . . . Legislature
Upper chamber . . . . .Senate
    Number of members 49
    Length of term . . . . 4 years
    Party in majority, 2008 . . . . .Democratic
Lower chamber . . . . .House of Representatives
    Number of members 98
    Length of term . . . . 2 years
    Party in majority, 2008 . . . . .Democratic

Federal representation, 2008 (110th Congress)

Senator . . . . Patty Murray
    Party . . . . .Democratic
    Year term expires 2011
Senator . . . . Maria Cantwell
    Party . . . . .Democratic
    Year term expires 2013
Representatives, total 9
    Democrats 6
    Republicans 3

Voters in November 2006 election (estimate)

Total 2,346,002
    Male 1,103,061
    Female 1,242,940
    White 2,131,809
    Black 25,125
    Hispanic 36,988
    Asian 74,760

Presidential election, 2004

Total Popular Vote 2,859,084
    Kerry 1,510,201
    Bush 1,304,894
Total Electoral Votes 11

Votes cast for US Senators

2004
Total vote (x 1,000) 2,819
Leading party .Democratic
Percent for leading party 55.0%
2006
Total vote (x 1,000) 2,084
Leading party .Democratic
Percent for leading party 56.9%

Votes cast for US Representatives

2004
Total vote (x 1,000) 2,730
    Democratic 1,609
    Republican 1,095
Leading party .Democratic
Percent for leading party 58.9%
2006
Total vote (x 1,000) 2,054
    Democratic 1,244
    Republican 798
Leading party .Democratic
Percent for leading party 60.6%

©2008 Information Publications, Inc.
All rights reserved. Photocopying prohibited.
877-544-INFO (4636) or www.informationpublications.com

State government employment, 2006
Full-time equivalent employees 116,943
Payroll ($ mil) $468.6

Local government employment, 2006
Full-time equivalent employees 216,253
Payroll ($ mil) $936.6

Women holding public office, 2008
US Congress 3
Statewide elected office................... 2
State legislature 48

Black public officials, 2002
Total..................................... 24
   US and state legislatures 2
   City/county/regional offices 9
   Judicial/law enforcement................. 11
   Education/school boards 2

Hispanic public officials, 2006
Total..................................... 13
   State executives & legislators 3
   City/county/regional offices 4
   Judicial/law enforcement................. 0
   Education/school boards.................. 6

Governmental Finance

State government revenues, 2006
Total revenue (x $1,000)........... $40,832,013
  per capita $6,405.11
General revenue (x $1,000) $29,284,277
  Intergovernmental 7,729,139
  Taxes 16,410,977
    general sales.................. 10,048,349
    individual income tax 0
    corporate income tax 0
  Current charges...................3,280,139
  Miscellaneous 1,864,022

State government expenditure, 2006
Total expenditure (x $1,000) $33,914,746
  per capita $5,320.04
General expenditure (x $1,000) $29,056,032
per capita, total.................... $4,557.87
    Education 1,902.55
    Public welfare 1,047.85
    Health 227.95
    Hospitals..........................239.83
    Highways 362.45
    Police protection....................43.85
    Corrections 149.59
    Natural resources 103.71
    Parks & recreation 17.03
    Governmental administration........99.20
    Interest on general debt............131.14

State debt & cash, 2006 ($ per capita)
Debt $2,875.21
Cash/security holdings............. $13,174.72

Federal government grants to state & local government, 2005 (x $1,000)
Total..........................$9,046,698
by Federal agency
  Defense 59,745
  Education 695,425
  Energy 50,840
  Environmental Protection Agency ... 103,394
  Health & Human Services. 5,356,936
  Homeland Security.................. 41,241
  Housing & Urban Development...... 639,958
  Justice 130,674
  Labor 241,040
  Transportation 851,290
  Veterans Affairs.................... 12,777

Crime & Law Enforcement

Crime, 2006 (rates per 100,000 residents)
Property crimes 286,533
  Burglary 58,307
  Larceny 182,327
  Motor vehicle theft 45,899
  Property crime rate................4,480.0
Violent crimes......................... 22,120
  Murder 190
  Forcible rape.......................2,746
  Robbery........................... 6,405
  Aggravated assault 12,779
  Violent crime rate 345.9
Hate crimes 215

Fraud and identity theft, 2006
Fraud complaints.......................10,451
  rate per 100,000 residents 163.4
Identity theft complaints 5,336
  rate per 100,000 residents 83.4

Law enforcement agencies, 2006
Total agencies............................ 246
Total employees 14,420
  Officers 10,260
  Civilians 4,160

Prisoners, probation, and parole, 2006
Total prisoners.......................17,561
  percent change, 12/31/05 to 12/31/06 .... 1.0%
  in private facilities 5.4%
  in local jails 2.4%
Sentenced to more than one year 17,483
  rate per 100,000 residents 271
Adults on probation 108,076
Adults on parole.......................12,611

Prisoner demographics, June 30, 2005 (rate per 100,000 residents)
Male..................................... 831
Female 101
White.................................... 393
Black.................................... 2,522
Hispanic 527

©2008 Information Publications, Inc.
All rights reserved. Photocopying prohibited.
877-544-INFO (4636) or www.informationpublications.com

6   Washington

Arrests, 2006
Total................................ 246,388
   Persons under 18 years of age 34,902

Persons under sentence of death, 1/1/07
Total.................................... 9
   White................................. 5
   Black 4
   Hispanic 0

State's highest court
Name.........................Supreme Court
Number of members....................... 9
Length of term...................... 6 years
Intermediate appeals court? ....yes

Labor & Income

Civilian labor force, 2006 (x 1,000)
Total..................................3,335
   Men 1,792
   Women 1,543
   Persons 16-19 years................... 170
   White............................... 2,802
   Black 110
   Hispanic 216

Civilian labor force as a percent of civilian non-institutional population, 2006
Total.................................. 67.4%
   Men 73.9
   Women 61.1
   Persons 16-19 years..................47.6
   White................................66.8
   Black 67.1
   Hispanic 72.0

Employment, 2006 (x 1,000)
Total..................................3,168
   Men 1,701
   Women 1,467
   Persons 16-19 years.................. 140
   White............................... 2,664
   Black 102
   Hispanic 201

Unemployment rate, 2006
Total.................................. 5.0%
   Men 5.1
   Women 4.9
   Persons 16-19 years..................18.0
   White................................4.9
   Black 7.8
   Hispanic 7.2

Full-time/part-time labor force, 2003 (x 1,000)
Full-time labor force, employed 2,293
Part-time labor force, employed........... 610
Unemployed, looking for
   Full-time work....................... 196
   Part-time work....................... 41
*Mean duration of unemployment (weeks)......*19.6
   Median 10.3

Labor unions, 2006
Membership (x 1,000)................... 549
   percent of employed 19.8%

Experienced civilian labor force by private industry, 2006
Total.............................2,345,531
   Natural resources & mining 87,358
   Construction 182,170
   Manufacturing......................281,481
   Trade, transportation & utilities 526,402
   Information 97,725
   Finance 153,026
   Professional & business 320,487
   Education & health 317,865
   Leisure & hospitality............... 267,242
   Other 111,775

Experienced civilian labor force by occupation, May 2006
Management......................... 80,480
Business & financial 125,980
Legal................................ 20,240
Sales............................... 299,550
Office & admin. support.............. 457,550
Computers & math 93,500
Architecture & engineering........... 73,300
Arts & entertainment 39,350
Education 158,760
Social services 44,740
Health care practitioner & technical.... 128,730
Health care support 67,720
Maintenance & repair................113,700
Construction 151,670
Transportation & moving 206,540
Production 168,350
Farming, fishing & forestry............15,780

Hours and earnings of production workers on manufacturing payrolls, 2006
Average weekly hours.....................40.6
Average hourly earnings $19.90
Average weekly earnings $807.94

Income and poverty, 2006
Median household income............. $52,583
Personal income, per capita (current $)... $37,423
   in constant (2000) dollars $32,668
Persons below poverty level............. 11.8%

Average annual pay
2006 .... $42,897
   increase from 2005 .... 5.3%

Federal individual income tax returns, 2005
Returns filed........................ 2,931,911
Adjusted gross income ($1,000) ... $168,672,520
Total tax liability ($1,000) $22,605,158

Charitable contributions, 2004
Number of contributions 886.7
Total amount ($ mil)................. $3,435.4

©2008 Information Publications, Inc.
All rights reserved. Photocopying prohibited.
877-544-INFO (4636) or www.informationpublications.com

Economy, Business, Industry & Agriculture

Fortune 500 companies, 2007 10
Bankruptcy cases filed, FY 2007 14,632

Patents and trademarks issued, 2007

Patents 3,822
Trademarks 2,095

Business firm ownership, 2002

Women-owned 137,394
  Sales ($ mil) $17,368
Black-owned 6,982
  Sales ($ mil) $1,053
Hispanic-owned 10,261
  Sales ($ mil) $1,538
Asian-owned 26,890
  Sales ($ mil) $7,128
Amer. Indian/Alaska Native-owned 5,734
  Sales ($ mil) $938
Hawaiian/Pacific Islander-owned 728
  Sales ($ mil) $231

Gross domestic product, 2006 ($ mil)

Total gross domestic product $293,531
  Agriculture, forestry, fishing and
    hunting 5,355
  Mining 332
  Utilities 2,798
  Construction 14,713
  Manufacturing, durable goods 23,519
  Manufacturing, non-durable goods 9,401
  Wholesale trade 18,246
  Retail trade 21,392
  Transportation & warehousing 7,936
  Information 23,252
  Finance & insurance 16,573
  Real estate, rental & leasing 42,033
  Professional and technical services 17,677
  Educational services 1,599
  Health care and social assistance 19,305
  Accommodation/food services 7,747
  Other services, except government 6,565
  Government 39,465

Establishments, payroll, employees & receipts, by major industry group, 2005

Total 175,658
  Annual payroll ($1,000) $94,928,122
  Paid employees 2,316,296
Forestry, fishing & agriculture 1,580
  Annual payroll ($1,000) $530,207
  Paid employees 13,651
Mining 183
  Annual payroll ($1,000) $156,374
  Paid employees 2,983
  Receipts, 2002 ($1,000) $499,595

Utilities 305
  Annual payroll ($1,000) $374,928
  Paid employees 5,637
  Receipts, 2002 ($1,000) . . . . .NA
Construction 23,998
  Annual payroll ($1,000) $7,492,851
  Paid employees 164,391
  Receipts, 2002 ($1,000) $27,916,123
Manufacturing 7,404
  Annual payroll ($1,000) $12,547,603
  Paid employees 256,563
  Receipts, 2002 ($1,000) $79,313,884
Wholesale trade 9,494
  Annual payroll ($1,000) $6,384,947
  Paid employees 128,315
  Receipts, 2002 ($1,000) $84,634,499
Retail trade 22,791
  Annual payroll ($1,000) $8,064,049
  Paid employees 321,048
  Receipts, 2002 ($1,000) $65,262,333
Transportation & warehousing 4,767
  Annual payroll ($1,000) $3,513,449
  Paid employees 84,341
  Receipts, 2002 ($1,000) $7,592,392
Information 3,226
  Annual payroll ($1,000) $8,656,108
  Paid employees 105,314
  Receipts, 2002 ($1,000) . . . . .NA
Finance & insurance 10,422
  Annual payroll ($1,000) $6,460,604
  Paid employees 108,834
  Receipts, 2002 ($1,000) . . . . .NA
Professional, scientific & technical 18,399
  Annual payroll ($1,000) $9,140,640
  Paid employees 147,540
  Receipts, 2002 ($1,000) $16,730,409
Education 2,062
  Annual payroll ($1,000) $1,019,014
  Paid employees 44,690
  Receipts, 2002 ($1,000) $747,424
Health care & social assistance 17,528
  Annual payroll ($1,000) $12,130,929
  Paid employees 317,975
  Receipts, 2002 ($1,000) $24,707,761
Arts and entertainment 2,706
  Annual payroll ($1,000) $1,496,363
  Paid employees 57,737
  Receipts, 2002 ($1,000) $3,226,042
Real estate 10,031
  Annual payroll ($1,000) $1,734,609
  Paid employees 50,588
  Receipts, 2002 ($1,000) $7,660,742
Accommodation & food service 14,963
  Annual payroll ($1,000) $3,182,478
  Paid employees 214,805
  Receipts, 2002 ($1,000) $8,642,681

©2008 Information Publications, Inc.
All rights reserved. Photocopying prohibited.
877-544-INFO (4636) or www.informationpublications.com

8   Washington

Exports, 2006
Value of exported goods ($ mil) $53,075
   Manufactured $44,538
   Non-manufactured................. $6,530

Foreign direct investment in US affiliates, 2004
Property, plants & equipment ($ mil) $17,477
Employment (x 1,000)....................83.4

Agriculture, 2006
Number of farms 34,000
Farm acreage (x 1,000) 15,100
   Acres per farm 444
Farm marketings and income ($ mil)
Total..............................$6,139.0
   Crops $4,524.4
   Livestock........................$1,614.5
Net farm income $958.3

Principal commodities, in order by marketing receipts, 2005
   Apples, Dairy products, Cattle and calves,
      Wheat, Potatoes

Federal economic activity in state
Expenditures, 2005 ($ mil)
   Total............................. $46,338
     Per capita $7,364.77
   Defense $9,099
   Non-defense......................$37,239
Defense department, 2006 ($ mil)
   Payroll........................... $5,652
   Contract awards $4,766
   Grants $60
Homeland security grants ($1,000)
   2006.............................. $32,222
   2007.............................. $28,926

FDIC-insured financial institutions, 2005
Number 99
Assets ($ billion) $65.5
Deposits ($ billion) $48.3

Fishing, 2006
Catch (x 1,000 lbs)................... 538,791
Value ($1,000)........................$193,109

Mining, 2006 ($ mil)
Total non-fuel mineral production $720
Percent of U.S. 1.12%

Communication, Energy & Transportation

Communication
Households with computers, 2003........ 71.4%
Households with internet access, 2003 .... 62.3%
High-speed internet providers 63
Total high-speed internet lines........2,015,564
   Residential 1,360,776
   Business.......................... 654,788
Wireless phone customers, 12/2006 4,799,143

FCC-licensed stations (as of January 1, 2008)
TV stations 35
FM radio stations......................... 173
AM radio stations 109

Energy
Energy consumption, 2004
   Total (trillion Btu)................... 2,005
   Per capita (million Btu) 323.1
By source of production (trillion Btu)
   Coal 113
   Natural gas......................... 269
   Petroleum.......................... 842
   Nuclear electric power 94
   Hydroelectric power................. 717
By end-use sector (trillion Btu)
   Residential 469
   Commercial 371
   Industrial 559
   Transportation 605
Electric energy, 2005
   Primary source of electricity.... Hydroelectric
   Net generation (billion kWh) 102.0
     percent from renewable sources......72.8%
   Net summer capability (million kW) 27.8
   CO_2 emitted from generation 14.9
Natural gas utilities, 2005
   Customers (x 1,000) 1,062
   Sales (trillion Btu)...................... 196
   Revenues ($ mil) $1,451
Nuclear plants, 2007 1
Total CO_2 emitted (million metric tons)......78.7
Energy spending, 2004 ($ mil) $15,561
   per capita $2,508
   Price per million Btu $12.32

Transportation, 2006
Public road & street mileage 83,256
   Urban........................... 22,469
   Rural 60,787
   Interstate............................ 764
Vehicle miles of travel (millions) 56,517
   per capita 8,865.5
Total motor vehicle registrations.......5,689,497
   Automobiles......................3,087,818
   Trucks 2,590,014
   Motorcycles 194,109
Licensed drivers 4,790,864
   19 years & under 176,286
Deaths from motor vehicle accidents 630
Gasoline consumed (x 1,000 gallons) 2,730,776
   per capita 428.4

Commuting Statistics, 2006
Average commute time (min) 25.2
   Drove to work alone 72.8%
   Carpooled........................... 11.8%
   Public transit 5.2%
   Walk to work 3.3%
   Work from home...................... 5.1%

©2008 Information Publications, Inc.
All rights reserved. Photocopying prohibited.
877-544-INFO (4636) or www.informationpublications.com

State Summary

Capital city . . . . Charleston
Governor . . . . Joe Manchin III
1900 Kanawha St
Charleston, WV 25305
304-558-2000
Admitted as a state 1863
Area (square miles) 24,230
Population, 2007 (estimate) 1,812,035
Largest city . . . . Charleston
Population, 2006 50,846
Personal income per capita, 2006
(in current dollars) $27,897
Gross domestic product, 2006 ($ mil) $55,658

Leading industries by payroll, 2005
Health care/Social assistance, Manufacturing,
Retail trade

**Leading agricultural commodities
by receipts, 2005**
Broilers, Cattle and calves, Turkeys, Chicken
eggs, Dairy products

Geography & Environment

Total area (square miles) 24,230
land 24,078
water 152
Federally-owned land, 2004 (acres) 1,146,211
percent 7.4%
Highest point . . . . Spruce Knob
elevation (feet) 4,861
Lowest point . . . . Potomac River
elevation (feet) 240
General coastline (miles) 0
Tidal shoreline (miles) 0
Cropland, 2003 (x 1,000 acres) 821
Forest land, 2003 (x 1,000 acres) 10,556
Capital city . . . . Charleston
Population 2000 53,421
Population 2006 50,846
Largest city . . . . Charleston
Population 2000 53,421
Population 2006 50,846

Number of cities with over 100,000 population
1990 0
2000 0
2006 0

State park and recreation areas, 2005
Area (x 1,000 acres) 177
Number of visitors (x 1,000) 7,406
Revenues ($1,000) $19,602
percent of operating expenditures 58.4%

National forest system land, 2007
Acres 1,043,028

Demographics & Population Characteristics

Population
1980 1,949,644
1990 1,793,477
2000 1,808,350
2006 1,818,470
Male 890,588
Female 927,882
Living in group quarters, 2006 45,532
percent of total 2.5%
2007 (estimate) 1,812,035
persons per square mile of land 75.3
2008 (projected) 1,827,226
2010 (projected) 1,829,141
2020 (projected) 1,801,112
2030 (projected) 1,719,959

**Population of Core-Based Statistical Areas
(formerly Metropolitan Areas), x 1,000**

	CBSA	Non-CBSA
1990	1,315	478
2000	1,348	461
2006	1,366	453

Change in population, 2000-2007
Number 3,685
percent 0.2%
Natural increase (births minus deaths) . . . . . . -941
Net internal migration 7,802
Net international migration 4,246

Persons by age, 2006
Under 5 years 104,964
5 to 17 years 284,107
18 years and over 1,429,399
65 years and over 278,692
85 years and over 36,073
Median age 40.2

Persons by age, 2010 (projected)
Under 5 years 101,135
18 and over 1,446,830
65 and over 292,402
Median age 41.4

Race, 2006
One Race
White 1,725,687
Black or African American 60,196
Asian 11,778
American Indian/Alaska Native 4,045
Hawaiian Native/Pacific Islander 531
Two or more races 16,233

Persons of Hispanic origin, 2006
Total Hispanic or Latino 14,383
Mexican 5,756
Puerto Rican 1,816
Cuban 412

©2008 Information Publications, Inc.
All rights reserved. Photocopying prohibited.
877-544-INFO (4636) or www.informationpublications.com

Persons of Asian origin, 2006

Total Asian 10,479
   Asian Indian. 3,362
   Chinese 655
   Filipino 2,218
   Japanese 1,413
   Korean. 674
   Vietnamese. 1,210

Marital status, 2006

Population 15 years & over 1,499,797
   Never married 369,318
   Married. 838,050
   Separated 21,287
   Widowed. 119,259
   Divorced 173,170

Language spoken at home, 2006

Population 5 years and older. 1,714,041
   English only 1,675,050
   Spanish 18,207
   French 3,152
   German 2,126
   Chinese 1,111

Households & families, 2006

Households. 743,064
   with persons under 18 years 225,948
   with persons over 65 years. 202,011
   persons per household 2.39
Families. 502,381
   persons per family. 2.89
Married couples. 390,066
Female householder,
   no husband present. 80,983
One-person households 204,778

Nativity, 2006

Number of residents born in state 1,312,058
   percent of population 72.2%

Immigration & naturalization, 2006

Legal permanent residents admitted 764
Persons naturalized 390
Non-immigrant admissions 14,003

Vital Statistics and Health

Marriages

2004 13,621
2005 13,418
2006 13,129

Divorces

2004 9,148
2005 9,223
2006 8,541

Health risks, 2006

Percent of adults who are:
   Smokers. 25.7%
   Overweight (BMI > 25). 67.0%
   Obese (BMI > 30). 31.0%

Births

2005 20,836
   Birthrate (per 1,000). 11.5
   White. 19,935
   Black 707
   Hispanic 174
   Asian/Pacific Islander 178
   Amer. Indian/Alaska Native 16
   Low birth weight (2,500g or less). 9.6%
   Cesarian births. 34.2%
   Preterm births 14.4%
   To unmarried mothers. 36.5%
   Twin births (per 1,000) 27.2
   Triplets or higher order (per 100,000). . .105.3
2006 (preliminary). 20,928
   rate per 1,000 . . . . .11.5

Deaths

2004
All causes 20,793
   rate per 100,000. . . . . 966.0
Heart disease 5,674
   rate per 100,000. . . . . .260.9
Malignant neoplasms 4,694
   rate per 100,000. . . . . .211.7
Cerebrovascular disease. 1,178
   rate per 100,000. . . . . .54.1
Chronic lower respiratory disease 1,225
   rate per 100,000. . . . . .55.3
Diabetes. 840
   rate per 100,000. . . . . .38.1
2005 (preliminary). 20,780
   rate per 100,000. . . . . 960.4
2006 (provisional) 20,573

Infant deaths

2004 158
   rate per 1,000 . . . . .7.6
2005 (provisional) 169
   rate per 1,000 . . . . .8.2

Exercise routines, 2005

None. 28.5%
Moderate or greater. 39.4%
Vigorous 17.6%

Abortions, 2004

Total performed in state. . . . . NA
   rate per 1,000 women age 15-44. . . . . NA
   % obtained by out-of-state residents . . . . . NA

Physicians, 2005

Total. 4,190
   rate per 100,000 persons 231

Community hospitals, 2005

Number of hospitals 57
Beds (x 1,000). 7.2
Patients admitted (x 1,000) 292
Average daily census (x 1,000) 4.5
Average cost per day $1,113
Outpatient visits (x 1 mil) 6.1

©2008 Information Publications, Inc.
All rights reserved. Photocopying prohibited.
877-544-INFO (4636) or www.informationpublications.com

Disability status of population, 2006
5 to 15 years 8.6%
16 to 64 years 20.7%
65 years and over 48.1%

Education

Educational attainment, 2006
Population over 25 years 1,262,933
Less than 9th grade..................... 7.1%
High school graduate or more 81.0%
College graduate or more.............. 16.5%
Graduate or professional degree........ 6.6%

Public school enrollment, 2005-06
Total............................... 280,866
Pre-kindergarten through grade 8.... 196,988
Grades 9 through 12................. 83,677

Graduating public high school seniors, 2004-05
Diplomas (incl. GED and others) 17,137

SAT scores, 2007
Average critical reading score.............. 516
Average writing score..................... 505
Average math score...................... 507
Percent of graduates taking test 20%

Public school teachers, 2006-07 (estimate)
Total (x 1,000) 19.9
Elementary........................... 14.2
Secondary............................ 5.7
Average salary $40,531
Elementary......................... $40,350
Secondary.......................... $40,988

State receipts & expenditures for public schools, 2006-07 (estimate)
Revenue receipts ($ mil) $3,042
Expenditures
Total ($ mil) $3,288
Per capita $1,558
Per pupil $10,236

NAEP proficiency scores, 2007

	Reading		Math	
	Basic	Proficient	Basic	Proficient
Grade 4	62.6%	27.8%	81.2%	32.6%
Grade 8	68.4%	22.9%	61.2%	18.5%

Higher education enrollment, fall 2005
Total............................... 14,399
Full-time men 4,679
Full-time women..................... 7,453
Part-time men 770
Part-time women..................... 1,497

Minority enrollment in institutions of higher education, 2005
Black, non-Hispanic 5,220
Hispanic 1,108
Asian/Pacific Islander................. 1,151
American Indian/Alaska Native........... 371

Institutions of higher education, 2005-06
Total.................................... 44
Public................................ 23
Private............................... 21

Earned degrees conferred, 2004-05
Associate's............................ 3,738
Bachelor's 9,574
Master's.............................. 2,735
First-professional...................... 449
Doctor's.............................. 213

Public Libraries, 2006
Number of libraries...................... 97
Number of outlets 180
Annual visits per capita 3.3
Circulation per capita................... 4.3

State & local financial support for higher education, FY 2006
Full-time equivalent enrollment (x 1,000)..... 71.7
Appropriations per FTE................. $4,181

Social Insurance & Welfare Programs

Social Security benefits & beneficiaries, 2005
Beneficiaries (x 1,000) 413
Retired & dependents.................. 239
Survivors............................ 70
Disabled & dependents................. 104
Annual benefit payments ($ mil) $4,417
Retired & dependents................. $2,377
Survivors........................... $932
Disabled & dependents............... $1,108
Average monthly benefit
Retired & dependents................. $988
Disabled & dependents................. $981
Widowed............................ $927

Medicare, July 2005
Enrollment (x 1,000)..................... 355
Payments ($ mil) $2,262

Medicaid, 2004
Beneficiaries (x 1,000)................... 896
Payments ($ mil) $4,314

State Children's Health Insurance Program, 2006
Enrollment (x 1,000)..................... 39.9
Expenditures ($ mil)................... $41.6

Persons without health insurance, 2006
Number (x 1,000)........................ 245
percent............................ 13.5%
Number of children (x 1,000) 34
percent of children 8.6%

Health care expenditures, 2004
Total expenditures..................... $10,783
per capita $5,954

©2008 Information Publications, Inc.
All rights reserved. Photocopying prohibited.
877-544-INFO (4636) or www.informationpublications.com

Federal and state public aid

State unemployment insurance, 2006
Recipients, first payments (x 1,000) 40
Total payments ($ mil) $132
Average weekly benefit $231
Temporary Assistance for Needy Families, 2006
Recipients (x 1,000) 284.9
Families (x 1,000) 127.2
Supplemental Security Income, 2005
Recipients (x 1,000) 76.7
Payments ($ mil) $375.9
Food Stamp Program, 2006
Avg monthly participants (x 1,000) 267.6
Total benefits ($ mil) $266.4

Housing & Construction

Housing units
Total 2005 (estimate) 872,147
Total 2006 (estimate) 877,784
Seasonal or recreational use, 2006 41,805
Owner-occupied, 2006 554,791
  Median home value $89,700
  Homeowner vacancy rate 2.0%
Renter-occupied, 2006 188,273
  Median rent $499
  Rental vacancy rate 10.8%
Home ownership rate, 2005 . . . . 81.3%
Home ownership rate, 2006 . . . . 78.4%

New privately-owned housing units
Number authorized, 2006 (x 1,000) 5.6
  Value ($ mil) $944.4
Started 2005 (x 1,000, estimate) 5.4
Started 2006 (x 1,000, estimate) 5.4

Existing home sales
2005 (x 1,000) 38.6
2006 (x 1,000) 32.6

Government & Elections

State officials 2008
Governor . . . . Joe Manchin III
    Democratic, term expires 1/09
Lieutenant Governor . . . . Earl Ray Tomblin
Secretary of State . . . . Betty Ireland
Attorney General . . . . Darrell McGraw Jr
Chief Justice . . . . Robin Jean Davis

Governorship
Minimum age 30
Length of term . . . . 4 years
Consecutive terms permitted 2
Who succeeds . . . . President of Senate

Local governments by type, 2002
Total 686
  County 55
  Municipal 234
  Township 0
  School District 55
  Special District 342

State legislature
Name . . . . Legislature
Upper chamber . . . . Senate
  Number of members 34
  Length of term . . . . 4 years
  Party in majority, 2008 . . . . Democratic
Lower chamber . . . . House of Delegates
  Number of members 100
  Length of term . . . . 2 years
  Party in majority, 2008 . . . . Democratic

Federal representation, 2008 (110th Congress)
Senator . . . . John Rockefeller IV
  Party . . . . Democratic
  Year term expires 2009
Senator . . . . Robert Byrd
  Party . . . . Democratic
  Year term expires 2013
Representatives, total 3
  Democrats 2
  Republicans 1

Voters in November 2006 election (estimate)
Total 512,776
Male 245,029
Female 267,747
White 493,819
Black 11,402
Hispanic . . . . NA
Asian 1,085

Presidential election, 2004
Total Popular Vote 755,887
  Kerry 326,541
  Bush 423,778
Total Electoral Votes 5

Votes cast for US Senators
2004
Total vote (x 1,000) . . . . NA
Leading party . . . . NA
Percent for leading party . . . . NA
2006
Total vote (x 1,000) 207
Leading party . . . . Democratic
Percent for leading party 77.0%

Votes cast for US Representatives
2004
Total vote (x 1,000) 722
  Democratic 415
  Republican 303
Leading party . . . . Democratic
Percent for leading party 57.6%
2006
Total vote (x 1,000) 455
  Democratic 264
  Republican 191
Leading party . . . . Democratic
Percent for leading party 58.0%

©2008 Information Publications, Inc.
All rights reserved. Photocopying prohibited.
877-544-INFO (4636) or www.informationpublications.com

State government employment, 2006
Full-time equivalent employees 37,004
Payroll ($ mil) $113.4

Local government employment, 2006
Full-time equivalent employees 60,387
Payroll ($ mil) $167.6

Women holding public office, 2008
US Congress 1
Statewide elected office. 1
State legislature 19

Black public officials, 2002
Total. 19
   US and state legislatures 2
   City/county/regional offices 13
   Judicial/law enforcement. 3
   Education/school boards 1

Hispanic public officials, 2006
Total. 0
   State executives & legislators 0
   City/county/regional offices 0
   Judicial/law enforcement. 0
   Education/school boards 0

Governmental Finance

State government revenues, 2006
Total revenue (x $1,000) $11,435,205
   per capita $6,322.34
General revenue (x $1,000) $10,262,364
   Intergovernmental 3,224,309
   Taxes 4,558,219
      general sales. 1,125,766
      individual income tax 1,297,720
      corporate income tax 533,027
   Current charges. 1,100,687
   Miscellaneous 1,379,149

State government expenditure, 2006
Total expenditure (x $1,000) $9,791,417
   per capita $5,413.51
General expenditure (x $1,000) $9,199,607
per capita, total. *$5,086.31*
      Education 1,889.88
      Public welfare 1,316.28
      Health 166.28
      Hospitals. 44.91
      Highways 565.15
      Police protection. 30.02
      Corrections 118.71
      Natural resources 88.18
      Parks & recreation 28.88
      Governmental administration 305.76
      Interest on general debt 124.23

State debt & cash, 2006 ($ per capita)
Debt $2,989.10
Cash/security holdings. $6,136.06

Federal government grants to state & local government, 2005 (x $1,000)
Total. $3,808,971
by Federal agency
   Defense 17,876
   Education 272,646
   Energy. 10,653
   Environmental Protection Agency 82,613
   Health & Human Services. 2,191,826
   Homeland Security. 54,764
   Housing & Urban Development 173,549
   Justice 55,052
   Labor 59,814
   Transportation .617,930
   Veterans Affairs. .1,459

Crime & Law Enforcement

Crime, 2006 (rates per 100,000 residents)
Property crimes 47,672
   Burglary 11,531
   Larceny 32,220
   Motor vehicle theft 3,921
   Property crime rate. 2,621.5
Violent crimes. 5,087
   Murder 75
   Forcible rape. 389
   Robbery. 853
   Aggravated assault 3,770
   Violent crime rate 279.7
Hate crimes. 37

Fraud and identity theft, 2006
Fraud complaints. 2,058
   rate per 100,000 residents 113.2
Identity theft complaints 715
   rate per 100,000 residents 39.3

Law enforcement agencies, 2006
Total agencies. 339
Total employees 4,208
   Officers 3,333
   Civilians 875

Prisoners, probation, and parole, 2006
Total prisoners. 5,733
   percent change, 12/31/05 to 12/31/06 . . . . 7.9%
   in private facilities 0%
   in local jails 23.8%
Sentenced to more than one year 5,719
   rate per 100,000 residents 314
Adults on probation 7,668
Adults on parole. 1,523

Prisoner demographics, June 30, 2005 (rate per 100,000 residents)
Male 817
Female 84
White 392
Black. 2,188
Hispanic 211

©2008 Information Publications, Inc.
All rights reserved. Photocopying prohibited.
877-544-INFO (4636) or www.informationpublications.com

6   West Virginia

Arrests, 2006
Total 26,566
   Persons under 18 years of age 1,438

Persons under sentence of death, 1/1/07
Total 0
   White 0
   Black 0
   Hispanic 0

State's highest court
Name . . . . .Supreme Court of Appeals
Number of members 5
Length of term . . . . 12 years
Intermediate appeals court? . . . . no

Labor & Income

Civilian labor force, 2006 (x 1,000)
Total 815
   Men 433
   Women 382
   Persons 16-19 years 34
   White 782
   Black 23
   Hispanic . . . . NA

Civilian labor force as a percent of civilian non-institutional population, 2006
Total 55.9%
   Men 61.2
   Women 50.8
   Persons 16-19 years 35.0
   White 55.8
   Black 56.9
   Hispanic . . . . NA

Employment, 2006 (x 1,000)
Total 773
   Men 411
   Women 362
   Persons 16-19 years 28
   White 742
   Black 21
   Hispanic . . . . NA

Unemployment rate, 2006
Total 5.1%
   Men 5.1
   Women 5.2
   Persons 16-19 years 17.1
   White 5.1
   Black 6.7
   Hispanic . . . . NA

Full-time/part-time labor force, 2003 (x 1,000)
Full-time labor force, employed 622
Part-time labor force, employed 117
Unemployed, looking for
   Full-time work 42
   Part-time work 6
Mean duration of unemployment (weeks) 20.7
   Median 11.6

Labor unions, 2006
Membership (x 1,000) 101
   percent of employed 14.2%

Experienced civilian labor force by private industry, 2006
Total 567,898
   Natural resources & mining 28,995
   Construction 39,598
   Manufacturing 61,007
   Trade, transportation & utilities 138,992
   Information 11,513
   Finance 28,725
   Professional & business 59,633
   Education & health 106,329
   Leisure & hospitality 70,805
   Other 21,767

Experienced civilian labor force by occupation, May 2006
Management 26,400
Business & financial 20,470
Legal 5,690
Sales 77,790
Office & admin. support 117,080
Computers & math 7,330
Architecture & engineering 9,330
Arts & entertainment 5,530
Education 41,040
Social services 12,220
Health care practitioner & technical 46,120
Health care support 23,870
Maintenance & repair 37,290
Construction 51,010
Transportation & moving 61,510
Production 45,460
Farming, fishing & forestry 1,710

Hours and earnings of production workers on manufacturing payrolls, 2006
Average weekly hours 41.3
Average hourly earnings $17.89
Average weekly earnings $738.86

Income and poverty, 2006
Median household income $35,059
Personal income, per capita (current $) . . . $27,897
   in constant (2000) dollars $24,352
Persons below poverty level 17.3%

Average annual pay
2006 . . . . $32,728
   increase from 2005 . . . . 4.4%

Federal individual income tax returns, 2005
Returns filed 753,593
Adjusted gross income ($1,000) $30,318,090
Total tax liability ($1,000) $3,287,192

Charitable contributions, 2004
Number of contributions 105.1
Total amount ($ mil) $386.5

©2008 Information Publications, Inc.
All rights reserved. Photocopying prohibited.
877-544-INFO (4636) or www.informationpublications.com

Economy, Business, Industry & Agriculture

Fortune 500 companies, 2007 0
Bankruptcy cases filed, FY 2007 4,230

Patents and trademarks issued, 2007

Patents 118
Trademarks 115

Business firm ownership, 2002

Women-owned 31,301
   Sales ($ mil) $3,252
Black-owned 1,472
   Sales ($ mil) $92
Hispanic-owned 648
   Sales ($ mil) $187
Asian-owned 1,234
   Sales ($ mil) $435
Amer. Indian/Alaska Native-owned 405
   Sales ($ mil) $35
Hawaiian/Pacific Islander-owned 10
   Sales ($ mil) . . . . NA

Gross domestic product, 2006 ($ mil)

Total gross domestic product $55,658
   Agriculture, forestry, fishing and
      hunting 277
   Mining 3,834
   Utilities 2,847
   Construction 2,532
   Manufacturing, durable goods 3,393
   Manufacturing, non-durable goods 2,741
   Wholesale trade 2,864
   Retail trade 4,407
   Transportation & warehousing 1,874
   Information 1,405
   Finance & insurance 2,168
   Real estate, rental & leasing 5,243
   Professional and technical services 2,228
   Educational services 263
   Health care and social assistance 5,317
   Accommodation/food services 1,500
   Other services, except government 1,280
   Government 9,462

Establishments, payroll, employees & receipts, by major industry group, 2005

Total 40,735
   Annual payroll ($1,000) $16,323,457
   Paid employees 565,499
Forestry, fishing & agriculture 348
   Annual payroll ($1,000) $22,575
   Paid employees 1,253
Mining 631
   Annual payroll ($1,000) $1,329,536
   Paid employees 23,040
   Receipts, 2002 ($1,000) $5,429,555

Utilities 238
   Annual payroll ($1,000) $400,765
   Paid employees .6,251
   Receipts, 2002 ($1,000) . . . . .NA
Construction 4,625
   Annual payroll ($1,000) $1,045,632
   Paid employees 29,842
   Receipts, 2002 ($1,000) $3,393,385
Manufacturing 1,406
   Annual payroll ($1,000) $2,574,491
   Paid employees 62,972
   Receipts, 2002 ($1,000) $18,911,332
Wholesale trade 1,641
   Annual payroll ($1,000) $785,543
   Paid employees .21,134
   Receipts, 2002 ($1,000) $10,924,279
Retail trade 7,243
   Annual payroll ($1,000) $1,658,688
   Paid employees 92,369
   Receipts, 2002 ($1,000) $16,747,900
Transportation & warehousing 1,433
   Annual payroll ($1,000) $562,945
   Paid employees 15,944
   Receipts, 2002 ($1,000) $1,927,398
Information 718
   Annual payroll ($1,000) $416,302
   Paid employees 12,673
   Receipts, 2002 ($1,000) . . . . .NA
Finance & insurance 2,100
   Annual payroll ($1,000) $699,133
   Paid employees 20,338
   Receipts, 2002 ($1,000) . . . . .NA
Professional, scientific & technical 3,035
   Annual payroll ($1,000) $844,354
   Paid employees 23,323
   Receipts, 2002 ($1,000) $1,860,522
Education 260
   Annual payroll ($1,000) $129,775
   Paid employees .7,598
   Receipts, 2002 ($1,000) $60,628
Health care & social assistance 4,743
   Annual payroll ($1,000) $3,499,116
   Paid employees 112,764
   Receipts, 2002 ($1,000) $7,631,590
Arts and entertainment 688
   Annual payroll ($1,000) $180,831
   Paid employees 10,558
   Receipts, 2002 ($1,000) $934,176
Real estate 1,548
   Annual payroll ($1,000) $176,376
   Paid employees .6,975
   Receipts, 2002 ($1,000) $844,390
Accommodation & food service 3,501
   Annual payroll ($1,000) $652,685
   Paid employees 58,510
   Receipts, 2002 ($1,000) $1,974,851

©2008 Information Publications, Inc.
All rights reserved. Photocopying prohibited.
877-544-INFO (4636) or www.informationpublications.com

Exports, 2006

Value of exported goods ($ mil) $3,225
  Manufactured $2,575
  Non-manufactured................... $610

Foreign direct investment in US affiliates, 2004

Property, plants & equipment ($ mil) $5,716
Employment (x 1,000)..................... 19.0

Agriculture, 2006

Number of farms 21,200
Farm acreage (x 1,000) 3,600
  Acres per farm 170
Farm marketings and income ($ mil)
Total.................................... $449.6
  Crops................................... $79.7
  Livestock............................... $369.8
Net farm income $49.7

Principal commodities, in order by marketing receipts, 2005

Broilers, Cattle and calves, Turkeys, Chicken
    eggs, Dairy products

Federal economic activity in state

Expenditures, 2005 ($ mil)
  Total.............................. $16,087
    Per capita $8,868.07
  Defense $784
  Non-defense $15,304
Defense department, 2006 ($ mil)
  Payroll............................. $384
  Contract awards $392
  Grants $25
Homeland security grants ($1,000)
  2006............................. $13,294
  2007.............................. $6,712

FDIC-insured financial institutions, 2005

Number 70
Assets ($ billion) $21.3
Deposits ($ billion) $16.8

Fishing, 2006

Catch (x 1,000 lbs) .... NA
Value ($1,000)........................... NA

Mining, 2006 ($ mil)

Total non-fuel mineral production $211
Percent of U.S. 0.33%

Communication, Energy & Transportation

Communication

Households with computers, 2003........ 55.0%
Households with internet access, 2003 .... 47.6%
High-speed internet providers 24
Total high-speed internet lines........ 268,746
  Residential 248,611
  Business......................... 20,135
Wireless phone customers, 12/2006 1,040,224

FCC-licensed stations (as of January 1, 2008)

TV stations 18
FM radio stations......................... 118
AM radio stations 68

Energy

Energy consumption, 2004
  Total (trillion Btu)...................... 821
  Per capita (million Btu) 453.5
By source of production (trillion Btu)
  Coal.................................... 937
  Natural gas............................ 143
  Petroleum.............................. 280
  Nuclear electric power 0
  Hydroelectric power 13
By end-use sector (trillion Btu)
  Residential 165
  Commercial 113
  Industrial 361
  Transportation 182
Electric energy, 2005
  Primary source of electricity........... Coal
  Net generation (billion kWh) 93.6
    percent from renewable sources....... 1.7%
  Net summer capability (million kW) 16.5
  CO_2 emitted from generation 84.8
Natural gas utilities, 2005
  Customers (x 1,000) 411
  Sales (trillion Btu)..................... 91
  Revenues ($ mil) $625
Nuclear plants, 2007 0
Total CO_2 emitted (million metric tons)..... 114.4
Energy spending, 2004 ($ mil) $5,845
  per capita $3,228
  Price per million Btu $10.66

Transportation, 2006

Public road & street mileage 37,054
  Urban.................................. 4,514
  Rural 32,540
  Interstate............................. 555
Vehicle miles of travel (millions) 20,885
  per capita 11,547.0
Total motor vehicle registrations....... 1,441,099
  Automobiles........................ 734,599
  Trucks 703,706
  Motorcycles......................... 40,741
Licensed drivers 1,335,303
  19 years & under 60,611
Deaths from motor vehicle accidents 410
Gasoline consumed (x 1,000 gallons) 841,146
  per capita 465.1

Commuting Statistics, 2006

Average commute time (min) 25.6
  Drove to work alone 80.0%
  Carpooled........................... 12.1%
  Public transit 1.0%
  Walk to work 3.1%
  Work from home 2.4%

©2008 Information Publications, Inc.
All rights reserved. Photocopying prohibited.
877-544-INFO (4636) or www.informationpublications.com

State Summary

Capital city .... Madison
Governor.......................... Jim Doyle
115 East State Capitol
Madison, WI 53707
608-266-1212
Admitted as a state 1848
Area (square miles) 65,498
Population, 2007 (estimate)..........5,601,640
Largest city .... Milwaukee
Population, 2006 573,358
Personal income per capita, 2006
(in current dollars) $34,701
Gross domestic product, 2006 ($ mil) ... $227,230

Leading industries by payroll, 2005

Manufacturing, Health care/Social assistance,
Finance & Insurance

**Leading agricultural commodities
by receipts, 2005**

Dairy products, Cattle and calves, Corn, Soybeans, Greenhouse/nursery

Geography & Environment

Total area (square miles)................ 65,498
land 54,310
water 11,188
Federally-owned land, 2004 (acres) 1,971,902
percent............................. 5.6%
Highest point .... Timms Hil
elevation (feet) 1,951
Lowest point .... Lake Michigan
elevation (feet) 581
General coastline (miles) 0
Tidal shoreline (miles) 0
Cropland, 2003 (x 1,000 acres) 10,304
Forest land, 2003 (x 1,000 acres)......... 14,528
Capital city .... Madison
Population 2000 208,054
Population 2006 223,389
Largest city .... Milwaukee
Population 2000 596,974
Population 2006 573,358

Number of cities with over 100,000 population
1990 2
2000 3
2006 3

State park and recreation areas, 2005
Area (x 1,000 acres)...................... 135
Number of visitors (x 1,000) 14,964
Revenues ($1,000) $15,773
percent of operating expenditures...... 74.5%

National forest system land, 2007
Acres 1,530,686

Demographics & Population Characteristics

Population
1980 4,705,767
1990 4,891,769
2000 5,363,715
2006 5,556,506
Male......................2,760,942
Female 2,795,564
Living in group quarters, 2006......... 159,885
percent of total....................... 2.9%
2007 (estimate)....................5,601,640
persons per square mile of land 103.1
2008 (projected)....................5,659,640
2010 (projected) 5,727,426
2020 (projected)....................6,004,954
2030 (projected)...................6,150,764

**Population of Core-Based Statistical Areas
(formerly Metropolitan Areas), x 1,000**

	CBSA	Non-CBSA
1990	4,205	687
2000	4,604	759
2006	4,777	779

Change in population, 2000-2007
Number 237,925
percent............................ 4.4%
Natural increase (births minus deaths) 175,359
Net internal migration ....-5,618
Net international migration 58,366

Persons by age, 2006
Under 5 years 348,764
5 to 17 years 963,766
18 years and over 4,243,976
65 years and over 724,034
85 years and over 111,159
Median age 37.7

Persons by age, 2010 (projected)
Under 5 years 367,567
18 and over 4,408,282
65 and over 771,993
Median age 38.1

Race, 2006
One Race
White............................4,999,679
Black or African American 332,296
Asian 111,057
American Indian/Alaska Native........51,937
Hawaiian Native/Pacific Islander.......2,128
Two or more races..................... 59,409

Persons of Hispanic origin, 2006
Total Hispanic or Latino 256,304
Mexican........................ 178,638
Puerto Rican 43,500
Cuban 1,902

©2008 Information Publications, Inc.
All rights reserved. Photocopying prohibited.
877-544-INFO (4636) or www.informationpublications.com

Persons of Asian origin, 2006

Total Asian 110,778
   Asian Indian. 17,949
   Chinese 15,449
   Filipino 7,296
   Japanese 3,212
   Korean 6,677
   Vietnamese.........................4,953

Marital status, 2006

Population 15 years & over 4,483,075
   Never married 1,340,227
   Married........................ 2,435,425
   Separated 55,011
   Widowed......................... 268,374
   Divorced 439,049

Language spoken at home, 2006

Population 5 years and older........ 5,204,804
   English only 4,781,643
   Spanish 217,550
   French 13,372
   German.......................... 46,834
   Chinese 10,348

Households & families, 2006

Households.......................2,230,060
   with persons under 18 years 721,421
   with persons over 65 years........... 493,675
   persons per household 2.42
Families.........................1,456,314
   persons per family.....................2.98
Married couples.................... 1,147,656
Female householder,
   no husband present.................216,124
One-person households 628,248

Nativity, 2006

Number of residents born in state 4,007,850
   percent of population 72.1%

Immigration & naturalization, 2006

Legal permanent residents admitted...... 8,341
Persons naturalized 3,247
Non-immigrant admissions 119,990

Vital Statistics and Health

Marriages

2004 34,056
2005 33,876
2006 32,562

Divorces

2004 16,802
2005 16,297
2006 15,966

Health risks, 2006

Percent of adults who are:
   Smokers...........................20.8%
   Overweight (BMI > 25)................. 63.4%
   Obese (BMI > 30).....................26.6%

Births

2005 70,984
   Birthrate (per 1,000)..................12.8
   White...................... 60,461
   Black 6,794
   Hispanic 6,252
   Asian/Pacific Islander 2,612
   Amer. Indian/Alaska Native 1,117
   Low birth weight (2,500g or less)........ 7.0%
   Cesarian births 23.7%
   Preterm births 11.4%
   To unmarried mothers............... 32.5%
   Twin births (per 1,000)................30.8
   Triplets or higher order (per 100,000)....160.1
2006 (preliminary).................... 72,335
   rate per 1,000 ....13.0

Deaths

2004
All causes 45,600
   rate per 100,000......................749.8
Heart disease 11,909
   rate per 100,000......................191.8
Malignant neoplasms 10,861
   rate per 100,000......................184.4
Cerebrovascular disease.................3,071
   rate per 100,000......................48.8
Chronic lower respiratory disease 2,312
   rate per 100,000......................38.7
Diabetes.............................1,310
   rate per 100,000......................21.7
2005 (preliminary).................... 46,709
   rate per 100,000......................752.2
2006 (provisional) 46,188

Infant deaths

2004 420
   rate per 1,000 ....6.0
2005 (provisional) 468
   rate per 1,000 ....6.6

Exercise routines, 2005

None............................... 18.7%
Moderate or greater.................... 56.6%
Vigorous 32.8%

Abortions, 2004

Total performed in state.................9,943
   rate per 1,000 women age 15-44........... 9
   % obtained by out-of-state residents 2.3%

Physicians, 2005

Total................................14,093
   rate per 100,000 persons 255

Community hospitals, 2005

Number of hospitals 124
Beds (x 1,000)........................14.5
Patients admitted (x 1,000) 612
Average daily census (x 1,000) 9.0
Average cost per day $1,458
Outpatient visits (x 1 mil) 12.7

©2008 Information Publications, Inc.
All rights reserved. Photocopying prohibited.
877-544-INFO (4636) or www.informationpublications.com

Disability status of population, 2006
5 to 15 years 6.8%
16 to 64 years 10.7%
65 years and over 35.7%

Education

Educational attainment, 2006
Population over 25 years 3,682,631
  Less than 9th grade..................... 4.1%
  High school graduate or more 88.4%
  College graduate or more.............. 25.1%
  Graduate or professional degree........ 8.4%

Public school enrollment, 2005-06
Total................................875,174
  Pre-kindergarten through grade 8.... 583,998
  Grades 9 through 12.................291,176

Graduating public high school seniors, 2004-05
Diplomas (incl. GED and others) 64,160

SAT scores, 2007
Average critical reading score 587
Average writing score 575
Average math score 598
Percent of graduates taking test 6%

Public school teachers, 2006-07 (estimate)
Total (x 1,000) 59.3
  Elementary............................40.6
  Secondary.............................18.7
Average salary $47,901
  Elementary........................ $47,988
  Secondary......................... $47,712

State receipts & expenditures for public schools, 2006-07 (estimate)
Revenue receipts ($ mil) $10,130
Expenditures
Total ($ mil) $11,833
  Per capita $1,646
  Per pupil $11,019

NAEP proficiency scores, 2007

	Reading		Math	
	Basic	Proficient	Basic	Proficient
Grade 4	70.4%	35.6%	85.3%	46.9%
Grade 8	75.9%	33.2%	75.9%	37.0%

Higher education enrollment, fall 2005
Total..................................66,330
  Full-time men 18,922
  Full-time women.....................27,827
  Part-time men 6,530
  Part-time women.....................13,051

Minority enrollment in institutions of higher education, 2005
Black, non-Hispanic.....................17,185
Hispanic 9,605
Asian/Pacific Islander 9,691
American Indian/Alaska Native..........3,728

Institutions of higher education, 2005-06
Total..................................... 68
  Public................................. 31
  Private 37

Earned degrees conferred, 2004-05
Associate's...........................11,705
Bachelor's 31,144
Master's..............................8,716
First-professional.....................1,127
Doctor's.............................. 946

Public Libraries, 2006
Number of libraries...................... 381
Number of outlets 466
Annual visits per capita 6.0
Circulation per capita...................10.3

State & local financial support for higher education, FY 2006
Full-time equivalent enrollment (x 1,000)....212.2
Appropriations per FTE................ $6,226

Social Insurance & Welfare Programs

Social Security benefits & beneficiaries, 2005
Beneficiaries (x 1,000) 952
  Retired & dependents................ 694
  Survivors............................ 120
  Disabled & dependents................. 138
Annual benefit payments ($ mil) $10,551
  Retired & dependents.............. $7,395
  Survivors......................... $1,733
  Disabled & dependents.............. $1,423
Average monthly benefit
  Retired & dependents.............. $1,028
  Disabled & dependents............. $939
  Widowed........................... $1,020

Medicare, July 2005
Enrollment (x 1,000).................... 826
Payments ($ mil) $4,744

Medicaid, 2004
Beneficiaries (x 1,000).................... 377
Payments ($ mil) $2,020

State Children's Health Insurance Program, 2006
Enrollment (x 1,000)....................56.6
Expenditures ($ mil)...................$33.4

Persons without health insurance, 2006
Number (x 1,000)....................... 481
  percent............................8.8%
Number of children (x 1,000) 63
  percent of children 4.9%

Health care expenditures, 2004
Total expenditures.....................$31,177
  per capita $5,670

©2008 Information Publications, Inc.
All rights reserved. Photocopying prohibited.
877-544-INFO (4636) or www.informationpublications.com

Federal and state public aid

State unemployment insurance, 2006
Recipients, first payments (x 1,000) 259
Total payments ($ mil) $786
Average weekly benefit $259
Temporary Assistance for Needy Families, 2006
Recipients (x 1,000) 462.4
Families (x 1,000) 212.5
Supplemental Security Income, 2005
Recipients (x 1,000) .92.2
Payments ($ mil) $437.4
Food Stamp Program, 2006
Avg monthly participants (x 1,000) 367.9
Total benefits ($ mil) $346.6

Housing & Construction

Housing units
Total 2005 (estimate) 2,502,536
Total 2006 (estimate) 2,534,075
Seasonal or recreational use, 2006 152,256
Owner-occupied, 2006 1,571,129
   Median home value $163,500
   Homeowner vacancy rate 1.2%
Renter-occupied, 2006 658,931
   Median rent $658
   Rental vacancy rate 8.2%
Home ownership rate, 2005 . . . . 71.1%
Home ownership rate, 2006 . . . . 70.2%

New privately-owned housing units
Number authorized, 2006 (x 1,000) 27.3
   Value ($ mil) $4,424.4
Started 2005 (x 1,000, estimate) 36.7
Started 2006 (x 1,000, estimate) 35.8

Existing home sales
2005 (x 1,000) 122.8
2006 (x 1,000) 117.3

Government & Elections

State officials 2008
Governor . . . . Jim Doyle
   Democratic, term expires 1/11
Lieutenant Governor . . . . Barbara Lawton
Secretary of State . . . . Douglas La Follette
Attorney General . . . . J.B. Van Hollen
Chief Justice . . . . Shirley Abrahamson

Governorship
Minimum age 18
Length of term . . . . 4 years
Consecutive terms permitted . . . . . . not specified
Who succeeds . . . . Lieutenant Governor

Local governments by type, 2002
Total 3,048
   County 72
   Municipal 585
   Township 1,265
   School District 442
   Special District 684

State legislature
Name . . . . Legislature
Upper chamber . . . . .Senate
   Number of members 33
   Length of term . . . . 4 years
   Party in majority, 2008 . . . . .Democratic
Lower chamber .Assembly
   Number of members 99
   Length of term . . . . 2 years
   Party in majority, 2008 . . . . Republican

Federal representation, 2008 (110th Congress)
Senator . . . . .Russell Feingold
   Party . . . . .Democratic
   Year term expires 2011
Senator . . . . Herbert Kohl
   Party . . . . .Democratic
   Year term expires 2013
Representatives, total 8
   Democrats 5
   Republicans 3

Voters in November 2006 election (estimate)
Total 2,352,105
   Male 1,101,890
   Female 1,250,214
   White 2,201,274
   Black 89,424
   Hispanic 19,516
   Asian 9,382

Presidential election, 2004
Total Popular Vote 2,997,007
   Kerry 1,489,504
   Bush 1,478,120
Total Electoral Votes 10

Votes cast for US Senators
2004
Total vote (x 1,000) 2,950
Leading party . . . . .Democratic
Percent for leading party 55.4%
2006
Total vote (x 1,000) .2,138
Leading party . . . . .Democratic
Percent for leading party 67.3%

Votes cast for US Representatives
2004
Total vote (x 1,000) 2,822
   Democratic 1,369
   Republican 1,381
Leading party . . . . Republican
Percent for leading party 48.9%
2006
Total vote (x 1,000) 2,063
   Democratic 1,003
   Republican 1,040
Leading party . . . . Republican
Percent for leading party 50.4%

©2008 Information Publications, Inc.
All rights reserved. Photocopying prohibited.
877-544-INFO (4636) or www.informationpublications.com

State government employment, 2006
Full-time equivalent employees 68,143
Payroll ($ mil) $283.7

Local government employment, 2006
Full-time equivalent employees 219,930
Payroll ($ mil) $813.1

Women holding public office, 2008
US Congress..............................2
Statewide elected office...................3
State legislature.........................30

Black public officials, 2002
Total....................................33
    US and state legislatures 8
    City/county/regional offices 15
    Judicial/law enforcement.................5
    Education/school boards..................5

Hispanic public officials, 2006
Total....................................13
    State executives & legislators 1
    City/county/regional offices 5
    Judicial/law enforcement.................4
    Education/school boards..................3

Governmental Finance

State government revenues, 2006
Total revenue (x $1,000)...........$33,410,533
    per capita $5,995.44
General revenue (x $1,000) $25,707,505
    Intergovernmental 6,632,773
    Taxes 13,795,044
        general sales...................4,127,972
        individual income tax 5,906,515
        corporate income tax 808,200
    Current charges..................3,022,706
    Miscellaneous 2,256,982

State government expenditure, 2006
Total expenditure (x $1,000) $30,125,092
    per capita $5,405.87
General expenditure (x $1,000) $26,277,439
    per capita, total..................$4,715.42
        Education.......................1,754.82
        Public welfare 1,095.78
        Health 133.85
        Hospitals........................164.70
        Highways 334.14
        Police protection.................21.13
        Corrections 170.12
        Natural resources 105.60
        Parks & recreation................6.55
        Governmental administration......113.87
        Interest on general debt.........172.70

State debt & cash, 2006 ($ per capita)
Debt...............................$3,564.94
Cash/security holdings.............$15,877.40

Federal government grants to state & local government, 2005 (x $1,000)
Total...........................$7,538,150
by Federal agency
    Defense 39,029
    Education 610,854
    Energy............................71,947
    Environmental Protection Agency 57,456
    Health & Human Services. 4,579,319
    Homeland Security..................31,716
    Housing & Urban Development...... 475,502
    Justice 89,246
    Labor 179,275
    Transportation 695,710
    Veterans Affairs...................37,337

Crime & Law Enforcement

Crime, 2006 (rates per 100,000 residents)
Property crimes 156,571
    Burglary 26,994
    Larceny 115,546
    Motor vehicle theft 14,031
    Property crime rate................2,817.8
Violent crimes.........................15,783
    Murder 164
    Forcible rape.......................1,131
    Robbery............................5,567
    Aggravated assault 8,921
    Violent crime rate 284.0
Hate crimes............................ 103

Fraud and identity theft, 2006
Fraud complaints.......................6,724
    rate per 100,000 residents 121.0
Identity theft complaints 2,536
    rate per 100,000 residents 45.6

Law enforcement agencies, 2006
Total agencies......................... 370
Total employees 18,111
    Officers 13,038
    Civilians 5,073

Prisoners, probation, and parole, 2006
Total prisoners.......................23,431
    percent change, 12/31/05 to 12/31/06 ....3.2%
    in private facilities 0.1%
    in local jails 2.9%
Sentenced to more than one year 21,881
    rate per 100,000 residents 393
Adults on probation 55,806
Adults on parole......................16,206

Prisoner demographics, June 30, 2005 (rate per 100,000 residents)
Male................................. 1,209
Female.............................. 107
White............................... 415
Black................................4,416
Hispanic .... NA

©2008 Information Publications, Inc.
All rights reserved. Photocopying prohibited.
877-544-INFO (4636) or www.informationpublications.com

Arrests, 2006

Total 414,975
   Persons under 18 years of age 103,275

Persons under sentence of death, 1/1/07

Total 0
   White 0
   Black 0
   Hispanic 0

State's highest court

Name . . . . .Supreme Court
Number of members 7
Length of term . . . . 10 years
Intermediate appeals court? . . . . .yes

Labor & Income

Civilian labor force, 2006 (x 1,000)

Total 3,079
   Men 1,615
   Women 1,464
   Persons 16-19 years 195
   White 2,830
   Black 145
   Hispanic 113

Civilian labor force as a percent of civilian non-institutional population, 2006

Total 70.7%
   Men 75.8
   Women 65.8
   Persons 16-19 years 60.2
   White 70.9
   Black 69.3
   Hispanic 72.1

Employment, 2006 (x 1,000)

Total 2,931
   Men 1,531
   Women 1,400
   Persons 16-19 years 167
   White 2,707
   Black 127
   Hispanic 104

Unemployment rate, 2006

Total 4.8%
   Men 5.2
   Women 4.3
   Persons 16-19 years 14.3
   White 4.3
   Black 11.9
   Hispanic 7.8

Full-time/part-time labor force, 2003 (x 1,000)

Full-time labor force, employed 2,297
Part-time labor force, employed 607
Unemployed, looking for
   Full-time work 140
   Part-time work 33
*Mean duration of unemployment (weeks) *17.5
   Median 9.8

Labor unions, 2006

Membership (x 1,000) 386
   percent of employed 14.9%

Experienced civilian labor force by private industry, 2006

Total 2,389,062
   Natural resources & mining 22,043
   Construction 127,348
   Manufacturing 505,599
   Trade, transportation & utilities 541,211
   Information 49,302
   Finance 157,548
   Professional & business 270,595
   Education & health 359,597
   Leisure & hospitality 259,380
   Other 84,651

Experienced civilian labor force by occupation, May 2006

Management 95,960
Business & financial 114,390
Legal 12,530
Sales 270,760
Office & admin. support 443,110
Computers & math 48,250
Architecture & engineering 50,400
Arts & entertainment 32,510
Education 153,160
Social services 30,020
Health care practitioner & technical 136,670
Health care support 80,480
Maintenance & repair 105,980
Construction 116,370
Transportation & moving 225,040
Production 346,980
Farming, fishing & forestry 4,970

Hours and earnings of production workers on manufacturing payrolls, 2006

Average weekly hours .40.7
Average hourly earnings $16.54
Average weekly earnings $673.18

Income and poverty, 2006

Median household income $48,772
Personal income, per capita (current $) . . . $34,701
   in constant (2000) dollars $30,292
Persons below poverty level 11.0%

Average annual pay

2006 . . . . $36,821
   increase from 2005 . . . . 3.8%

Federal individual income tax returns, 2005

Returns filed 2,656,046
Adjusted gross income ($1,000) $132,137,153
Total tax liability ($1,000) $15,795,477

Charitable contributions, 2004

Number of contributions 861.0
Total amount ($ mil) $2,397.3

©2008 Information Publications, Inc.
All rights reserved. Photocopying prohibited.
877-544-INFO (4636) or www.informationpublications.com

Economy, Business, Industry & Agriculture

Fortune 500 companies, 2007 9
Bankruptcy cases filed, FY 2007 14,952

Patents and trademarks issued, 2007

Patents 1,973
Trademarks 1,673

Business firm ownership, 2002

Women-owned 104,170
   Sales ($ mil) $17,582
Black-owned 6,685
   Sales ($ mil) $633
Hispanic-owned 3,750
   Sales ($ mil) $975
Asian-owned 4,957
   Sales ($ mil) $1,499
Amer. Indian/Alaska Native-owned 2,530
   Sales ($ mil) $512
Hawaiian/Pacific Islander-owned 104
   Sales ($ mil) $4

Gross domestic product, 2006 ($ mil)

Total gross domestic product $227,230
   Agriculture, forestry, fishing and
      hunting 2,929
   Mining 322
   Utilities 3,829
   Construction 10,270
   Manufacturing, durable goods 28,059
   Manufacturing, non-durable goods 19,148
   Wholesale trade 13,365
   Retail trade 14,278
   Transportation & warehousing 7,183
   Information 6,601
   Finance & insurance 16,935
   Real estate, rental & leasing 27,783
   Professional and technical services 9,564
   Educational services 1,850
   Health care and social assistance 18,637
   Accommodation/food services 4,955
   Other services, except government 4,968
   Government 24,726

Establishments, payroll, employees & receipts, by major industry group, 2005

Total 145,159
   Annual payroll ($1,000) $85,781,279
   Paid employees 2,449,114
Forestry, fishing & agriculture 550
   Annual payroll ($1,000) $113,504
   Paid employees 3,169
Mining 159
   Annual payroll ($1,000) $238,052
   Paid employees 3,555
   Receipts, 2002 ($1,000) $518,984

Utilities 286
   Annual payroll ($1,000) $1,043,257
   Paid employees .14,874
   Receipts, 2002 ($1,000) . . . . .NA
Construction 17,364
   Annual payroll ($1,000) $5,668,227
   Paid employees 119,663
   Receipts, 2002 ($1,000) $23,477,496
Manufacturing 9,754
   Annual payroll ($1,000) $21,148,313
   Paid employees 493,661
   Receipts, 2002 ($1,000) $124,664,004
Wholesale trade 7,272
   Annual payroll ($1,000) $5,991,081
   Paid employees 124,033
   Receipts, 2002 ($1,000) $68,510,712
Retail trade 21,219
   Annual payroll ($1,000) $6,626,134
   Paid employees 317,423
   Receipts, 2002 ($1,000) $59,978,700
Transportation & warehousing 5,493
   Annual payroll ($1,000) $3,281,664
   Paid employees 95,390
   Receipts, 2002 ($1,000) $8,266,478
Information 2,284
   Annual payroll ($1,000) $2,558,853
   Paid employees 55,957
   Receipts, 2002 ($1,000) . . . . .NA
Finance & insurance 9,152
   Annual payroll ($1,000) $7,125,232
   Paid employees 135,409
   Receipts, 2002 ($1,000) . . . . .NA
Professional, scientific & technical 11,492
   Annual payroll ($1,000) $4,752,212
   Paid employees 96,891
   Receipts, 2002 ($1,000) $8,961,379
Education 1,403
   Annual payroll ($1,000) $1,188,516
   Paid employees 48,148
   Receipts, 2002 ($1,000) $431,985
Health care & social assistance 14,008
   Annual payroll ($1,000) $12,542,232
   Paid employees 348,275
   Receipts, 2002 ($1,000) $24,053,322
Arts and entertainment 2,620
   Annual payroll ($1,000) $852,241
   Paid employees 39,109
   Receipts, 2002 ($1,000) $2,145,020
Real estate 5,050
   Annual payroll ($1,000) $809,492
   Paid employees 27,250
   Receipts, 2002 ($1,000) $3,421,466
Accommodation & food service 13,972
   Annual payroll ($1,000) $2,382,706
   Paid employees 220,168
   Receipts, 2002 ($1,000) $6,885,765

©2008 Information Publications, Inc.
All rights reserved. Photocopying prohibited.
877-544-INFO (4636) or www.informationpublications.com

Exports, 2006
Value of exported goods ($ mil) $17,169
   Manufactured $15,103
   Non-manufactured.................. $1,263

Foreign direct investment in US affiliates, 2004
Property, plants & equipment ($ mil) ... $15,949
Employment (x 1,000)................... 86.9

Agriculture, 2006
Number of farms 76,000
Farm acreage (x 1,000) 15,300
   Acres per farm....................... 201
Farm marketings and income ($ mil)
Total............................... $6,791.3
   Crops.............................. $2,135.3
   Livestock.......................... $4,656.0
Net farm income $1,091.4

Principal commodities, in order by marketing receipts, 2005
Dairy products, Cattle and calves, Corn, Soybeans, Greenhouse/nursery

Federal economic activity in state
Expenditures, 2005 ($ mil)
   Total............................. $33,749
      Per capita $6,105.47
   Defense $3,191
   Non-defense....................... $30,558
Defense department, 2006 ($ mil)
   Payroll............................. $681
   Contract awards $2,165
   Grants $56
Homeland security grants ($1,000)
   2006.............................. $24,431
   2007.............................. $17,796

FDIC-insured financial institutions, 2005
Number 302
Assets ($ billion) $141.6
Deposits ($ billion) $103.6

Fishing, 2006
Catch (x 1,000 lbs)..................... 4,449
Value ($1,000)......................... $3,145

Mining, 2006 ($ mil)
Total non-fuel mineral production $591
Percent of U.S. 0.92%

Communication, Energy & Transportation

Communication
Households with computers, 2003........ 63.8%
Households with internet access, 2003 .... 57.4%
High-speed internet providers 79
Total high-speed internet lines........ 1,247,350
   Residential 1,012,294
   Business......................... 235,056
Wireless phone customers, 12/2006 3,509,528

FCC-licensed stations (as of January 1, 2008)
TV stations 43
FM radio stations......................... 221
AM radio stations 112

Energy
Energy consumption, 2004
   Total (trillion Btu).................... 1,848
   Per capita (million Btu) 336.0
By source of production (trillion Btu)
   Coal 499
   Natural gas......................... 385
   Petroleum.......................... 631
   Nuclear electric power 124
   Hydroelectric power................. 20
By end-use sector (trillion Btu)
   Residential 419
   Commercial 315
   Industrial 676
   Transportation 438
Electric energy, 2005
   Primary source of electricity........... Coal
   Net generation (billion kWh) 61.8
      percent from renewable sources....... 4.9%
   Net summer capability (million kW) 16.2
   CO_2 emitted from generation 54.0
Natural gas utilities, 2005
   Customers (x 1,000) 1,756
   Sales (trillion Btu)................... 358
   Revenues ($ mil) $2,639
Nuclear plants, 2007 3
Total CO_2 emitted (million metric tons).... 104.8
Energy spending, 2004 ($ mil) $16,069
   per capita $2,922
   Price per million Btu $12.69

Transportation, 2006
Public road & street mileage 114,485
   Urban............................. 21,998
   Rural 92,487
   Interstate.......................... 743
Vehicle miles of travel (millions) 59,398
   per capita 10,658.8
Total motor vehicle registrations....... 4,971,461
   Automobiles...................... 2,639,984
   Trucks 2,317,130
   Motorcycles 271,145
Licensed drivers 4,049,450
   19 years & under 221,157
Deaths from motor vehicle accidents 724
Gasoline consumed (x 1,000 gallons) 2,527,993
   per capita 453.6

Commuting Statistics, 2006
Average commute time (min) 20.8
   Drove to work alone 79.9%
   Carpooled.......................... 9.2%
   Public transit 1.9%
   Walk to work 3.5%
   Work from home 3.9%

©2008 Information Publications, Inc.
All rights reserved. Photocopying prohibited.
877-544-INFO (4636) or www.informationpublications.com

State Summary

Capital city . . . . Cheyenne
Governor . . . . David Freudenthal
State Capitol Building
Room 124
Cheyenne, WY 82002
307-777-7434
Admitted as a state 1890
Area (square miles) .97,814
Population, 2007 (estimate). 522,830
Largest city . . . . Cheyenne
Population, 2006 .55,314
Personal income per capita, 2006
(in current dollars) $40,676
Gross domestic product, 2006 ($ mil) $29,561

Leading industries by payroll, 2005

Mining, Health care/Social assistance, Retail
trade

**Leading agricultural commodities
by receipts, 2005**

Cattle and calves, Hay, Sugar beets, Hogs, Sheep
and lambs

Geography & Environment

Total area (square miles) 97,814
  land 97,100
  water 713
Federally-owned land, 2004 (acres) . . .26,391,487
  percent. 42.3%
Highest point . . . . Gannett Peak
  elevation (feet) 13,804
Lowest point . . . . .Belle Fourche River
  elevation (feet) 3,009
General coastline (miles) 0
Tidal shoreline (miles) 0
Cropland, 2003 (x 1,000 acres) 2,161
Forest land, 2003 (x 1,000 acres). 949
Capital city . . . . Cheyenne
  Population 2000 .53,011
  Population 2006 .55,314
Largest city . . . . Cheyenne
  Population 2000 .53,011
  Population 2006 .55,314

Number of cities with over 100,000 population

1990 0
2000 0
2006 0

State park and recreation areas, 2005

Area (x 1,000 acres) 121
Number of visitors (x 1,000) 2,114
Revenues ($1,000) $1,343
  percent of operating expenditures 8.0%

National forest system land, 2007

Acres 9,241,187

Demographics & Population Characteristics

Population

1980 469,557
1990 453,588
2000 493,782
2006 515,004
  Male. 261,002
  Female. 254,002
Living in group quarters, 2006 14,146
  percent of total. 2.7%
2007 (estimate). 522,830
  persons per square mile of land 5.4
2008 (projected) 515,408
2010 (projected) 519,886
2020 (projected) 530,948
2030 (projected) 522,979

**Population of Core-Based Statistical Areas
(formerly Metropolitan Areas), x 1,000**

	CBSA	Non-CBSA
1990	320	133
2000	352	142
2006	368	147

Change in population, 2000-2007

Number 29,048
  percent. 5.9%
Natural increase (births minus deaths) 19,423
Net internal migration 9,601
Net international migration 2,060

Persons by age, 2006

Under 5 years 33,553
5 to 17 years 88,241
18 years and over 393,210
65 years and over 62,750
85 years and over 8,367
  Median age 37.1

Persons by age, 2010 (projected)

Under 5 years 32,671
18 and over 403,613
65 and over 72,658
  Median age 39.5

Race, 2006

One Race
  White. 486,480
  Black or African American 4,867
  Asian 3,605
  American Indian/Alaska Native. 12,668
  Hawaiian Native/Pacific Islander. 385
Two or more races. 6,999

Persons of Hispanic origin, 2006

Total Hispanic or Latino 35,732
  Mexican. 26,247
  Puerto Rican 500
  Cuban . . . . NA

©2008 Information Publications, Inc.
All rights reserved. Photocopying prohibited.
877-544-INFO (4636) or www.informationpublications.com

Persons of Asian origin, 2006

Total Asian 4,656
　Asian Indian......................... 1,097
　Chinese 1,768
　Filipino 631
　Japanese 262
　Korean............................... 325
　Vietnamese........................... 265

Marital status, 2006

Population 15 years & over 416,436
　Never married 103,069
　Married............................ 235,541
　Separated 5,339
　Widowed 22,797
　Divorced 55,029

Language spoken at home, 2006

Population 5 years and older.......... 480,876
　English only 448,994
　Spanish 19,830
　French 2,624
　German............................. 1,566
　Chinese 1,045

Households & families, 2006

Households.......................... 207,302
　with persons under 18 years 65,571
　with persons over 65 years........... 43,317
　persons per household 2.42
Families............................ 136,835
　persons per family.................... 2.94
Married couples..................... 110,284
Female householder,
　no husband present.................. 17,301
One-person households 56,583

Nativity, 2006

Number of residents born in state 219,327
　percent of population............... 42.6%

Immigration & naturalization, 2006

Legal permanent residents admitted........ 376
Persons naturalized 169
Non-immigrant admissions 16,972

Vital Statistics and Health

Marriages

2004 4,740
2005 4,797
2006 5,027

Divorces

2004 2,656
2005 2,674
2006 2,749

Health risks, 2006

Percent of adults who are:
　Smokers............................ 21.6%
　Overweight (BMI > 25).............. 61.4%
　Obese (BMI > 30)................... 23.3%

Births

2005 7,239
　Birthrate (per 1,000)................. 14.2
　White............................... 6,770
　Black 63
　Hispanic 828
　Asian/Pacific Islander 70
　Amer. Indian/Alaska Native 336
　Low birth weight (2,500g or less)....... 8.6%
　Cesarian births 24.6%
　Preterm births...................... 13.1%
　To unmarried mothers................ 32.8%
　Twin births (per 1,000) 27.3
　Triplets or higher order (per 100,000).... 144.6
2006 (preliminary).................... 7,670
　rate per 1,000 .... 14.9

Deaths

2004
All causes 3,955
　rate per 100,000..................... 789.7
Heart disease 950
　rate per 100,000..................... 191.0
Malignant neoplasms 875
　rate per 100,000..................... 170.8
Cerebrovascular disease................. 214
　rate per 100,000..................... 43.9
Chronic lower respiratory disease 308
　rate per 100,000..................... 62.6
Diabetes.............................. 110
　rate per 100,000..................... 22.1
2005 (preliminary)................... 4,100
　rate per 100,000..................... 801.4
2006 (provisional) 4,281

Infant deaths

2004 60
　rate per 1,000 .... 8.8
2005 (provisional) 42
　rate per 1,000 .... 5.8

Exercise routines, 2005

None................................ 22.0%
Moderate or greater.................... 56.2%
Vigorous 33.1%

Abortions, 2004

Total performed in state................. 12
　rate per 1,000 women age 15-44......... NA
　% obtained by out-of-state residents 16.7%

Physicians, 2005

Total................................ 949
　rate per 100,000 persons 187

Community hospitals, 2005

Number of hospitals 24
Beds (x 1,000)......................... 2.1
Patients admitted (x 1,000) 51
Average daily census (x 1,000) 1.2
Average cost per day $805
Outpatient visits (x 1 mil) 1.0

©2008 Information Publications, Inc.
All rights reserved. Photocopying prohibited.
877-544-INFO (4636) or www.informationpublications.com

Disability status of population, 2006
5 to 15 years 7.3%
16 to 64 years 13.0%
65 years and over 40.9%

Education

Educational attainment, 2006
Population over 25 years 339,398
  Less than 9th grade..................... 3.0%
  High school graduate or more 90.2%
  College graduate or more.............. 22.7%
  Graduate or professional degree........ 7.4%

Public school enrollment, 2005-06
Total................................. 84,409
  Pre-kindergarten through grade 8......57,195
  Grades 9 through 12..................27,214

Graduating public high school seniors, 2004-05
Diplomas (incl. GED and others) 5,653

SAT scores, 2007
Average critical reading score.............. 565
Average writing score...................... 544
Average math score........................ 571
Percent of graduates taking test 8%

Public school teachers, 2006-07 (estimate)
Total (x 1,000) 6.5
  Elementary............................3.3
  Secondary............................3.2
Average salary $50,692
  Elementary........................ $50,428
  Secondary......................... $50,967

State receipts & expenditures for public schools, 2006-07 (estimate)
Revenue receipts ($ mil) $1,481
Expenditures
Total ($ mil) $1,395
  Per capita $2,190
  Per pupil $14,235

NAEP proficiency scores, 2007

	Reading		Math	
	Basic	Proficient	Basic	Proficient
Grade 4	73.5%	36.4%	88.5%	44.3%
Grade 8	79.7%	33.2%	79.8%	36.0%

Higher education enrollment, fall 2005
Total....................................2,723
  Full-time men 2,608
  Full-time women...................... 115
  Part-time men 0
  Part-time women........................ 0

Minority enrollment in institutions of higher education, 2005
Black, non-Hispanic 336
Hispanic 1,612
Asian/Pacific Islander 322
American Indian/Alaska Native........... 611

Institutions of higher education, 2005-06
Total..................................... 10
  Public............................... 8
  Private............................... 2

Earned degrees conferred, 2004-05
Associate's............................. 2,799
Bachelor's 1,695
Master's 455
First-professional...................... 125
Doctor's................................ 52

Public Libraries, 2006
Number of libraries.................... 23
Number of outlets 76
Annual visits per capita 6.2
Circulation per capita................... 9.1

State & local financial support for higher education, FY 2006
Full-time equivalent enrollment (x 1,000).....22.5
Appropriations per FTE.............. $13,425

Social Insurance & Welfare Programs

Social Security benefits & beneficiaries, 2005
Beneficiaries (x 1,000) 84
  Retired & dependents.................. 61
  Survivors............................. 11
  Disabled & dependents................. 13
Annual benefit payments ($ mil) $908
  Retired & dependents.................. $629
  Survivors............................. $149
  Disabled & dependents................. $130
Average monthly benefit
  Retired & dependents.................. $999
  Disabled & dependents................. $936
  Widowed............................. $1,009

Medicare, July 2005
Enrollment (x 1,000)...................... 71
Payments ($ mil) $429

Medicaid, 2004
Beneficiaries (x 1,000)..................... 68
Payments ($ mil) $363

State Children's Health Insurance Program, 2006
Enrollment (x 1,000).......................7.7
Expenditures ($ mil)......................$9.4

Persons without health insurance, 2006
Number (x 1,000)......................... 75
  percent............................. 14.5%
Number of children (x 1,000) 10
  percent of children 8.1%

Health care expenditures, 2004
Total expenditures...................... $2,662
  per capita $5,265

©2008 Information Publications, Inc.
All rights reserved. Photocopying prohibited.
877-544-INFO (4636) or www.informationpublications.com

Federal and state public aid

State unemployment insurance, 2006
Recipients, first payments (x 1,000) 10
Total payments ($ mil) $30
Average weekly benefit $253
Temporary Assistance for Needy Families, 2006
Recipients (x 1,000) 6.1
Families (x 1,000) 3.4
Supplemental Security Income, 2005
Recipients (x 1,000) 5.8
Payments ($ mil) $26.5
Food Stamp Program, 2006
Avg monthly participants (x 1,000) 24.2
Total benefits ($ mil) $26.3

Housing & Construction

Housing units
Total 2005 (estimate) 235,657
Total 2006 (estimate) 239,178
Seasonal or recreational use, 2006 14,167
Owner-occupied, 2006 144,117
    Median home value $148,900
    Homeowner vacancy rate 1.4%
Renter-occupied, 2006 63,185
    Median rent $601
    Rental vacancy rate 4.6%
Home ownership rate, 2005 . . . . .72.8%
Home ownership rate, 2006 . . . . 73.7%

New privately-owned housing units
Number authorized, 2006 (x 1,000) 3.5
    Value ($ mil) $638.8
Started 2005 (x 1,000, estimate) 2.2
Started 2006 (x 1,000, estimate) 2.3

Existing home sales
2005 (x 1,000) 14.3
2006 (x 1,000) 13.6

Government & Elections

State officials 2008
Governor . . . . David Freudenthal
    Democratic, term expires 1/11
Lieutenant Governor . . (no Lieutenant Governor)
Secretary of State . . . . Max Maxfield
Attorney General . . . . .Bruce Salzburg
Chief Justice .Barton Voigt

Governorship
Minimum age 30
Length of term . . . . 4 years
Consecutive terms permitted 2
Who succeeds . . . . .Secretary of State

Local governments by type, 2002
Total 722
    County 23
    Municipal 98
    Township 0
    School District 55
    Special District 546

State legislature
Name . . . . Legislature
Upper chamber . . . . .Senate
    Number of members 30
    Length of term . . . . 4 years
    Party in majority, 2008 . . . . Republican
Lower chamber . . . . .House of Representatives
    Number of members 60
    Length of term . . . . 2 years
    Party in majority, 2008 . . . . Republican

Federal representation, 2008 (110ᵗʰ Congress)
Senator . . . . .Michael Enzi
    Party . . . . Republican
    Year term expires 2009
Senator . . . . .John Barrasso
    Party . . . . Republican
    Year term expires 2013
Representatives, total 1
    Democrats 0
    Republicans 1

Voters in November 2006 election (estimate)
Total 199,387
    Male 93,951
    Female 105,436
    White 195,111
    Black 644
    Hispanic 4,684
    Asian 544

Presidential election, 2004
Total Popular Vote 243,428
    Kerry 70,776
    Bush 167,629
Total Electoral Votes 3

Votes cast for US Senators
2004
Total vote (x 1,000) . . . . NA
Leading party . . . . NA
Percent for leading party . . . . NA
2006
Total vote (x 1,000) 196
Leading party . . . . Republican
Percent for leading party 68.9%

Votes cast for US Representatives
2004
Total vote (x 1,000) 239
    Democratic 100
    Republican 132
Leading party . . . . Republican
Percent for leading party 55.2%
2006
Total vote (x 1,000) 196
    Democratic 92
    Republican 93
Leading party . . . . Republican
Percent for leading party 47.6%

©2008 Information Publications, Inc.
All rights reserved. Photocopying prohibited.
877-544-INFO (4636) or www.informationpublications.com

State government employment, 2006
Full-time equivalent employees 12,814
Payroll ($ mil) $43.1

Local government employment, 2006
Full-time equivalent employees 32,988
Payroll ($ mil) $103.0

Women holding public office, 2008
US Congress 1
Statewide elected office. 1
State legislature 21

Black public officials, 2002
Total. 1
US and state legislatures 0
City/county/regional offices 1
Judicial/law enforcement. 0
Education/school boards 0

Hispanic public officials, 2006
Total. 4
State executives & legislators 1
City/county/regional offices 3
Judicial/law enforcement. 0
Education/school boards 0

Governmental Finance

State government revenues, 2006
Total revenue (x $1,000) $5,616,758
per capita $10,954.03
General revenue (x $1,000) $4,897,206
Intergovernmental 2,009,304
Taxes 2,122,239
general sales. 624,924
individual income tax 0
corporate income tax 0
Current charges. 148,640
Miscellaneous 617,023

State government expenditure, 2006
Total expenditure (x $1,000) $4,011,496
per capita $7,823.39
General expenditure (x $1,000) $3,563,917
per capita, total. $6,950.50
Education 2,084.39
Public welfare 1,124.31
Health 351.77
Hospitals. 3.71
Highways 828.97
Police protection. 74.48
Corrections 247.14
Natural resources 420.21
Parks & recreation 68.60
Governmental administration 274.62
Interest on general debt. 86.48

State debt & cash, 2006 ($ per capita)
Debt $1,916.61
Cash/security holdings. $29,777.62

Federal government grants to state & local government, 2005 (x $1,000)
Total. $1,898,954
by Federal agency
Defense 13,439
Education 121,919
Energy. 7,743
Environmental Protection Agency 22,733
Health & Human Services. 373,094
Homeland Security. 2,943
Housing & Urban Development. 37,077
Justice 21,749
Labor 19,235
Transportation 220,533
Veterans Affairs. 1,321

Crime & Law Enforcement

Crime, 2006 (rates per 100,000 residents)
Property crimes 15,350
Burglary 2,320
Larceny 12,254
Motor vehicle theft 776
Property crime rate. 2,980.6
Violent crimes. 1,234
Murder 9
Forcible rape. 140
Robbery. 72
Aggravated assault 1,013
Violent crime rate 239.6
Hate crimes. 7

Fraud and identity theft, 2006
Fraud complaints. 657
rate per 100,000 residents 127.6
Identity theft complaints 218
rate per 100,000 residents 42.3

Law enforcement agencies, 2006
Total agencies. 65
Total employees .1,862
Officers 1,313
Civilians 549

Prisoners, probation, and parole, 2006
Total prisoners. 2,114
percent change, 12/31/05 to 12/31/06 . . . . 3.3%
in private facilities 37.0%
in local jails 1.0%
Sentenced to more than one year 2,114
rate per 100,000 residents 408
Adults on probation 5,225
Adults on parole. 674

Prisoner demographics, June 30, 2005 (rate per 100,000 residents)
Male. 1,189
Female 184
White. . . . . NA
Black. . . . . NA
Hispanic . . . . NA

©2008 Information Publications, Inc.
All rights reserved. Photocopying prohibited.
877-544-INFO (4636) or www.informationpublications.com

Arrests, 2006
Total................................... 38,780
  Persons under 18 years of age.......... 6,682

Persons under sentence of death, 1/1/07
Total... 2
  White....................................... 2
  Black....................................... 0
  Hispanic.................................... 0

State's highest court
Name........................Supreme Court
Number of members......................... 5
Length of term........................ 8 years
Intermediate appeals court?............... no

Labor & Income

Civilian labor force, 2006 (x 1,000)
Total...................................... 287
  Men..................................... 158
  Women................................... 130
  Persons 16-19 years...................... 17
  White................................... 275
  Black..................................... NA
  Hispanic................................. 17

Civilian labor force as a percent of civilian non-institutional population, 2006
Total..................................... 71.0%
  Men 78.3
  Women 63.8
  Persons 16-19 years..................... 53.8
  White................................... 71.1
  Black..................................... NA
  Hispanic................................. 69.5

Employment, 2006 (x 1,000)
Total...................................... 278
  Men..................................... 152
  Women................................... 126
  Persons 16-19 years...................... 15
  White................................... 267
  Black..................................... NA
  Hispanic................................. 16

Unemployment rate, 2006
Total...................................... 3.4%
  Men 3.5
  Women 3.2
  Persons 16-19 years..................... 12.0
  White..................................... 3.1
  Black..................................... NA
  Hispanic.................................. 8.2

Full-time/part-time labor force, 2003 (x 1,000)
Full-time labor force, employed............ 215
Part-time labor force, employed............ 52
Unemployed, looking for
  Full-time work........................... 10
  Part-time work............................ 2
Mean duration of unemployment (weeks)......13.3
  Median 6.5

Labor unions, 2006
Membership (x 1,000)...................... 19
  percent of employed 8.3%

Experienced civilian labor force by private industry, 2006
Total.................................. 207,465
  Natural resources & mining.......... 28,815
  Construction......................... 23,942
  Manufacturing........................ 10,146
  Trade, transportation & utilities...... 49,852
  Information............................ 4,173
  Finance.............................. 11,117
  Professional & business.............. 17,048
  Education & health................... 21,561
  Leisure & hospitality................ 32,611
  Other................................. 8,200

Experienced civilian labor force by occupation, May 2006
Management............................ 12,710
Business & financial................... 6,740
Legal................................. 1,430
Sales................................. 22,540
Office & admin. support............... 36,690
Computers & math....................... 2,070
Architecture & engineering............. 4,280
Arts & entertainment................... 2,500
Education............................. 17,090
Social services........................ 3,870
Health care practitioner & technical..... 10,860
Health care support.................... 6,350
Maintenance & repair.................. 15,640
Construction.......................... 30,180
Transportation & moving............... 25,020
Production................................ NA
Farming, fishing & forestry............. 430

Hours and earnings of production workers on manufacturing payrolls, 2006
Average weekly hours.................... 41.2
Average hourly earnings $17.44
Average weekly earnings $718.53

Income and poverty, 2006
Median household income............. $47,423
Personal income, per capita (current $)... $40,676
  in constant (2000) dollars........... $35,508
Persons below poverty level.............. 9.4%

Average annual pay
2006................................. $36,662
  increase from 2005................... 10.3%

Federal individual income tax returns, 2005
Returns filed........................ 248,212
Adjusted gross income ($1,000) $14,299,375
Total tax liability ($1,000)...........$2,051,817

Charitable contributions, 2004
Number of contributions................ 41.4
Total amount ($ mil).................. $322.2

©2008 Information Publications, Inc.
All rights reserved. Photocopying prohibited.
877-544-INFO (4636) or www.informationpublications.com

Economy, Business, Industry & Agriculture

Fortune 500 companies, 2007 0

Bankruptcy cases filed, FY 2007 784

Patents and trademarks issued, 2007

Patents 57

Trademarks 145

Business firm ownership, 2002

Women-owned 12,945

   Sales ($ mil) $1,130

Black-owned 149

   Sales ($ mil) $10

Hispanic-owned 1,320

   Sales ($ mil) $221

Asian-owned 401

   Sales ($ mil) $84

Amer. Indian/Alaska Native-owned 597

   Sales ($ mil) $60

Hawaiian/Pacific Islander-owned 23

   Sales ($ mil) $1

Gross domestic product, 2006 ($ mil)

Total gross domestic product $29,561

   Agriculture, forestry, fishing and

     hunting 441

   Mining 9,033

   Utilities 1,321

   Construction 1,763

   Manufacturing, durable goods 376

   Manufacturing, non-durable goods 618

   Wholesale trade 1,090

   Retail trade 1,629

   Transportation & warehousing 1,668

   Information 426

   Finance & insurance 678

   Real estate, rental & leasing 2,479

   Professional and technical services 856

   Educational services 64

   Health care and social assistance 1,193

   Accommodation/food services 953

   Other services, except government 507

   Government 3,817

Establishments, payroll, employees & receipts, by major industry group, 2005

Total 19,736

   Annual payroll ($1,000) $6,202,411

   Paid employees .191,934

Forestry, fishing & agriculture 89

   Annual payroll ($1,000) . . . . NA

   Paid employees . . . . NA

Mining 812

   Annual payroll ($1,000) $1,182,693

   Paid employees 19,443

   Receipts, 2002 ($1,000) $7,803,920

Utilities 117

   Annual payroll ($1,000) $150,897

   Paid employees 2,391

   Receipts, 2002 ($1,000) . . . . .NA

Construction 2,790

   Annual payroll ($1,000) $598,206

   Paid employees .16,372

   Receipts, 2002 ($1,000) $2,149,476

Manufacturing 543

   Annual payroll ($1,000) $463,053

   Paid employees 10,465

   Receipts, 2002 ($1,000) $4,061,516

Wholesale trade 770

   Annual payroll ($1,000) $288,683

   Paid employees .6,710

   Receipts, 2002 ($1,000) $3,331,043

Retail trade 2,975

   Annual payroll ($1,000) $655,186

   Paid employees .30,186

   Receipts, 2002 ($1,000) $5,783,756

Transportation & warehousing 858

   Annual payroll ($1,000) $309,655

   Paid employees .8,057

   Receipts, 2002 ($1,000) $746,816

Information 337

   Annual payroll ($1,000) $130,556

   Paid employees 4,038

   Receipts, 2002 ($1,000) . . . . .NA

Finance & insurance 919

   Annual payroll ($1,000) $264,363

   Paid employees .7,108

   Receipts, 2002 ($1,000) . . . . .NA

Professional, scientific & technical 1,745

   Annual payroll ($1,000) $300,600

   Paid employees .7,951

   Receipts, 2002 ($1,000) $654,070

Education 137

   Annual payroll ($1,000) $36,658

   Paid employees .1,730

   Receipts, 2002 ($1,000) $66,940

Health care & social assistance 1,627

   Annual payroll ($1,000) $908,285

   Paid employees 28,269

   Receipts, 2002 ($1,000) $1,621,193

Arts and entertainment 441

   Annual payroll ($1,000) . . . . NA

   Paid employees . . . . NA

   Receipts, 2002 ($1,000) $163,052

Real estate 979

   Annual payroll ($1,000) $104,965

   Paid employees 3,340

   Receipts, 2002 ($1,000) $398,649

Accommodation & food service 1,749

   Annual payroll ($1,000) $345,459

   Paid employees .25,765

   Receipts, 2002 ($1,000) $984,684

©2008 Information Publications, Inc.
All rights reserved. Photocopying prohibited.
877-544-INFO (4636) or www.informationpublications.com

Exports, 2006

Value of exported goods ($ mil) $830
   Manufactured $714
   Non-manufactured.................... $102

Foreign direct investment in US affiliates, 2004

Property, plants & equipment ($ mil) ... $12,444
Employment (x 1,000)..................... 8.5

Agriculture, 2006

Number of farms 9,100
Farm acreage (x 1,000) 34,400
   Acres per farm....................... 3,780
Farm marketings and income ($ mil)
Total.............................. $1,021.1
   Crops............................. $161.6
   Livestock.......................... $859.5
Net farm income $65.2

Principal commodities, in order by marketing receipts, 2005

Cattle and calves, Hay, Sugar beets, Hogs, Sheep and lambs

Federal economic activity in state

Expenditures, 2005 ($ mil)
   Total.............................. $4,782
      Per capita $9,399.02
   Defense $486
   Non-defense........................ $4,297
Defense department, 2006 ($ mil)
   Payroll............................. $306
   Contract awards $161
   Grants $12
Homeland security grants ($1,000)
   2006................................ $7,674
   2007................................ $6,674

FDIC-insured financial institutions, 2005

Number 45
Assets ($ billion) $7.1
Deposits ($ billion) $6.1

Fishing, 2006

Catch (x 1,000 lbs).................... NA
Value ($1,000)........................ NA

Mining, 2006 ($ mil)

Total non-fuel mineral production $1,250
Percent of U.S. 1.94%

Communication, Energy & Transportation

Communication

Households with computers, 2003........ 65.4%
Households with internet access, 2003 .... 57.7%
High-speed internet providers 28
Total high-speed internet lines......... 156,940
   Residential 89,719
   Business......................... 67,221
Wireless phone customers, 12/2006 387,164

FCC-licensed stations (as of January 1, 2008)

TV stations 17
FM radio stations....................... 92
AM radio stations 33

Energy

Energy consumption, 2004
   Total (trillion Btu)..................... 454
   Per capita (million Btu) 898.9
By source of production (trillion Btu)
   Coal 501
   Natural gas......................... 112
   Petroleum........................... 159
   Nuclear electric power 0
   Hydroelectric power 6
By end-use sector (trillion Btu)
   Residential 41
   Commercial 53
   Industrial 245
   Transportation 115
Electric energy, 2005
   Primary source of electricity........... Coal
   Net generation (billion kWh) 45.6
      percent from renewable sources...... 3.3%
   Net summer capability (million kW) 6.7
   CO_2 emitted from generation 45.4
Natural gas utilities, 2005
   Customers (x 1,000) 157
   Sales (trillion Btu).................... 66
   Revenues ($ mil) $122
Nuclear plants, 2007 0
Total CO_2 emitted (million metric tons)..... 62.9
Energy spending, 2004 ($ mil) $2,906
   per capita $5,749
   Price per million Btu $10.29

Transportation, 2006

Public road & street mileage 27,834
   Urban.............................. 2,618
   Rural.............................. 25,216
   Interstate.......................... 913
Vehicle miles of travel (millions) 9,415
   per capita 18,361.5
Total motor vehicle registrations........ 645,192
   Automobiles....................... 228,057
   Trucks 414,047
   Motorcycles 35,788
Licensed drivers 390,538
   19 years & under 24,355
Deaths from motor vehicle accidents 195
Gasoline consumed (x 1,000 gallons) 360,516
   per capita 703.1

Commuting Statistics, 2006

Average commute time (min) 17.9
   Drove to work alone 76.0%
   Carpooled.......................... 12.5%
   Public transit 1.3%
   Walk to work 3.1%
   Work from home 5.2%

©2008 Information Publications, Inc.
All rights reserved. Photocopying prohibited.
877-544-INFO (4636) or www.informationpublications.com

National Summary

Capital city . . . . Washington, DC
President . . . . George W. Bush

The White House
1600 Pennsylvania Ave NW
Washington DC, US 20500
202-456-1414

Founded. 1776
Area (square miles) 3,794,083
Population, 2007 (estimate). 301,621,157
Largest city . . . . New York City
Population, 2006 8,214,426
Personal income per capita, 2006
(in current dollars) $36,276
Gross domestic product, 2006 ($ mil). . .$13,149,033

Leading industries by payroll, 2005

Manufacturing, Health care/Social assistance,
Professional/Scientific/Technical

Leading agricultural commodities by receipts, 2005

Cattle and calves, Dairy products, Corn, Broilers,
Soybeans

Geography & Environment

Total area (square miles). 3,794,083
land 3,537,439
water 256,645
Federally-owned land, 2004 (acres). . . 653,299,090
percent. 28.8%
Highest point . . . . .Mt. McKinley
elevation (feet) 20,320
Lowest point .Death Valley
elevation (feet) . . . . -282
General coastline (miles) 12,383
Tidal shoreline (miles) 88,633
Cropland, 2003 (x 1,000 acres) 367,900
Forest land, 2003 (x 1,000 acres). 405,600
Capital city . . . . Washington, DC
Population 2000 572,059
Population 2006 581,530
Largest city . . . . New York City
Population 2000 8,008,278
Population 2006 8,214,426

Number of cities with over 100,000 population

1990 190
2000 239
2006 258

State park and recreation areas, 2005

Area (x 1,000 acres) 13,713
Number of visitors (x 1,000) 725,361
Revenues ($1,000) $847,117
percent of operating expenditures. 39.2%

National forest system land, 2007

Acres 192,794,673

Demographics & Population Characteristics

Population

1980 226,546,000
1990 248,709,873
2000 281,424,602
2006 299,398,484
Male 147,512,152
Female 151,886,332
Living in group quarters, 2006 8,065,644
percent of total. .2.7%
2007 (estimate). 301,621,157
persons per square mile of land 85.3
2008 (projected). 303,597,646
2010 (projected) 308,935,581
2020 (projected). 335,804,546
2030 (projected) 363,584,435

Population of Core-Based Statistical Areas (formerly Metropolitan Areas), x 1,000

	CBSA	Non-CBSA
1990	230,779	17,939
2000	262,114	19,310
2006	279,848	19,551

Change in population, 2000-2007

Number 20,196,555
percent. 7.2%
Natural increase (births minus deaths) . . 12,212,284
Net internal migration 0
Net international migration 7,984,271

Persons by age, 2006

Under 5 years 20,417,636
5 to 17 years 53,317,926
18 years and over 225,662,922
65 years and over 37,260,352
85 years and over 5,296,817
Median age 36.4

Persons by age, 2010 (projected)

Under 5 years 21,426,163
18 and over 234,504,070
65 and over 40,243,713
Median age 37.0

Race, 2006

One Race
White. 239,746,254
Black or African American 38,342,549
Asian 13,159,343
American Indian/Alaska Native. 2,902,851
Hawaiian Native/Pacific Islander. 528,818
Two or more races. 4,718,669

Persons of Hispanic origin, 2006

Total Hispanic or Latino 44,252,278
Mexican. 28,339,354
Puerto Rican 3,987,947
Cuban 1,520,276

©2008 Information Publications, Inc.
All rights reserved. Photocopying prohibited.
877-544-INFO (4636) or www.informationpublications.com

Persons of Asian origin, 2006

Total Asian	13,100,095
Asian Indian	2,482,141
Chinese	3,090,453
Filipino	2,328,097
Japanese	829,767
Korean	1,335,075
Vietnamese	1,475,798

Marital status, 2006

Population 15 years & over	238,585,682
Never married	72,787,209
Married	125,571,348
Separated	5,404,992
Widowed	15,182,891
Divorced	25,044,234

Language spoken at home, 2006

Population 5 years and older	279,012,712
English only	224,154,288
Spanish	34,044,945
French	1,997,618
German	1,391,413
Chinese	2,492,871

Households & families, 2006

Households	111,617,402
with persons under 18 years	38,628,743
with persons over 65 years	25,867,508
persons per household	2.61
Families	74,564,066
persons per family	3.20
Married couples	55,521,868
Female householder,	
no husband present	13,920,783
One-person households	30,496,588

Nativity, 2006

Persons born in state of residence	176,467,918
percent of population	58.9%

Immigration & naturalization, 2006

Legal permanent residents admitted	1,266,264
Persons naturalized	702,589
Non-immigrant admissions	33,667,328

Vital Statistics and Health

Marriages

2004	NA
2005	2,249,000
2006	2,160,000

Divorces

2004	NA
2005	NA
2006	NA

Health risks, 2006

Percent of adults who are:

Smokers	20.1%
Overweight (BMI > 25)	61.6%
Obese (BMI > 30)	25.1%

Births

2005	4,138,349
Birthrate (per 1,000)	14.0
White	3,229,294
Black	633,134
Hispanic	985,505
Asian/Pacific Islander	231,108
Amer. Indian/Alaska Native	44,813
Low birth weight (2,500g or less)	8.2%
Cesarian births	30.3%
Preterm births	12.7%
To unmarried mothers	36.9%
Twin births (per 1,000)	31.9
Triplets or higher order (per 100,000)	175.3
2006 (preliminary)	4,265,996
rate per 1,000	14.2

Deaths

2004

All causes	2,397,615
rate per 100,000	800.8
Heart disease	652,486
rate per 100,000	217.0
Malignant neoplasms	553,888
rate per 100,000	185.8
Cerebrovascular disease	150,074
rate per 100,000	50.0
Chronic lower respiratory disease	121,987
rate per 100,000	41.1
Diabetes	73,138
rate per 100,000	24.5
2005 (preliminary)	2,447,903
rate per 100,000	798.8
2006 (provisional)	2,416,000

Infant deaths

2004	27,936
rate per 1,000	6.8
2005 (provisional)	28,000
rate per 1,000	6.8

Exercise routines, 2005

None	23.9%
Moderate or greater	48.7%
Vigorous	27.4%

Abortions, 2004

Total performed in nation	839,226
rate per 1,000 women age 15-44	16
percent obtained in different state	8.2%

Physicians, 2005

Total	790,128
rate per 100,000 persons	266

Community hospitals, 2005

Number of hospitals	4,936
Beds (x 1,000)	802.3
Patients admitted (x 1,000)	35,239
Average daily census (x 1,000)	540.3
Average cost per day	$1,522
Outpatient visits (x 1 mil)	584.4

©2008 Information Publications, Inc.
All rights reserved. Photocopying prohibited.
877-544-INFO (4636) or www.informationpublications.com

Disability status of population, 2006

5 to 15 years 6.3%
16 to 64 years 12.3%
65 years and over 41.0%

Education

Educational attainment, 2006

Population over 25 years 195,932,824
    Less than 9th grade..................... 6.5%
    High school graduate or more 84.1%
    College graduate or more.............. 27.0%
    Graduate or professional degree........ 9.9%

Public school enrollment, 2005-06

Total............................. 49,113,474
    Pre-kindergarten through grade 8.. 33,998,903
    Grades 9 through 12..............14,788,672

Graduating public high school seniors, 2004-05

Diplomas (incl. GED and others) 2,853,262

SAT scores, 2007

Average critical reading score.............. 502
Average writing score..................... 494
Average math score....................... 515
Percent of graduates taking test 48%

Public school teachers, 2006-07 (estimate)

Total (x 1,000) 3,174.4
    Elementary.......................1,856.6
    Secondary......................... 1,317.8
Average salary $50,816
    Elementary....................... $50,684
    Secondary.........................$51,081

Total state receipts & expenditures for public schools, 2006-07 (estimate)

Revenue receipts ($ mil) $530,340
Expenditures
Total ($ mil) $552,375
    Per capita $1,561
    Per pupil $10,212

NAEP proficiency scores, 2007

	Reading		Math	
	Basic	Proficient	Basic	Proficient
Grade 4	67.0%	33.0%	82.0%	39.0%
Grade 8	74.0%	31.0%	71.0%	32.0%

Higher education enrollment, fall 2005

Total................................4,465,641
    Full-time men 1,452,903
    Full-time women..................1,935,347
    Part-time men 413,799
    Part-time women.................. 663,592

Minority enrollment in institutions of higher education, 2005

Black, non-Hispanic 2,214,561
Hispanic 1,881,975
Asian/Pacific Islander 1,134,382
American Indian/Alaska Native........ 176,303

Institutions of higher education, 2005-06

Total...............................4,276
    Public............................1,693
    Private.......................... 2,583

Earned degrees conferred, 2004-05

Associate's......................... 696,660
Bachelor's 1,439,264
Master's...........................574,618
First-professional...................87,289
Doctor's...........................52,631

Public Libraries, 2006

Number of libraries.....................9,198
Number of outlets 17,368
Annual visits per capita 4.7
Circulation per capita....................7.2

State & local financial support for higher education, FY 2006

Full-time equivalent enrollment (x 1,000) .. 10,189.8
Appropriations per FTE................ $6,325

Social Insurance & Welfare Programs

Social Security benefits & beneficiaries, 2005

Beneficiaries (x 1,000) 47,255
    Retired & dependents................ 32,727
    Survivors.........................6,431
    Disabled & dependents............... 8,097
Annual benefit payments ($ mil) $512,221
    Retired & dependents............. $340,499
    Survivors....................... $88,098
    Disabled & dependents............ $83,623
Average monthly benefit
    Retired & dependents.................. NA
    Disabled & dependents................. NA
    Widowed........................... NA

Medicare, July 2005

Enrollment (x 1,000)..................41,536
Payments ($ mil) $272,442

Medicaid, 2004

Beneficiaries (x 1,000)................ 55,078
Payments ($ mil) $257,722

State Children's Health Insurance Program, 2006

Enrollment (x 1,000)..................6,624.2
Expenditures ($ mil)................$7,034.3

Persons without health insurance, 2006

Number (x 1,000)..................... 46,995
    percent........................... 15.8%
Number of children (x 1,000) 8,661
    percent of children 11.7%

Health care expenditures, 2004

Total expenditures..................$1,551,255
    per capita $5,283

©2008 Information Publications, Inc.
All rights reserved. Photocopying prohibited.
877-544-INFO (4636) or www.informationpublications.com

Federal and state public aid

State unemployment insurance, 2006
Recipients, first payments (x 1,000)........7,349
Total payments ($ mil) $29,807
Average weekly benefit.................... $277

Temporary Assistance for Needy Families, 2006
Recipients (x 1,000)................... 49,999.9
Families (x 1,000) 21,376.9

Supplemental Security Income, 2005
Recipients (x 1,000).................. 7,113.9
Payments ($ mil) $37,235.8

Food Stamp Program, 2006
Avg monthly participants (x 1,000) 26,671.8
Total benefits ($ mil)................ $30,187.3

Housing & Construction

Housing units

Total 2005 (estimate) 124,528,801
Total 2006 (estimate) 126,316,181
Seasonal or recreational use, 2006..... 4,213,520
Owner-occupied, 2006............... 75,086,485
  Median home value............... $185,200
  Homeowner vacancy rate............... 2.4%
Renter-occupied, 2006 36,530,917
  Median rent $763
  Rental vacancy rate................... 9.7%
Home ownership rate, 2005............. 68.9%
Home ownership rate, 2006............. 68.8%

New privately-owned housing units

Number authorized, 2006 (x 1,000)...... 1,838.9
  Value ($ mil).................... $291,314.5
Started 2005 (x 1,000, estimate) 1,658.0
Started 2006 (x 1,000, estimate) 1,614.0

Existing home sales

2005 (x 1,000)...........................7,076
2006 (x 1,000)...........................6,478

Government & Elections

Federal officials 2008

President .... George W. Bush
       Republican, term expires 1/09
Vice President .... Richard Cheney
Secretary of State............ Condoleezza Rice
Attorney General......... Michael B. Mukasey
Chief Justice .... John G. Roberts

Presidency

Minimum age........................... 35
Length of term...................... 4 years
Consecutive terms permitted 2
Who succeeds................. Vice President

Local governments by type, 2002

Total................................. 87,525
  County............................. 3,034
  Municipal.......................... 19,429
  Township 16,504
  School District..................... 13,506
  Special District 35,052

Federal legislature

Name .... US Congress
Upper chamber .... US Senate
  Number of members.................. 100
  Length of term.................... 6 years
  Party in majority, 2008 .... Democratic
Lower chamber.....US House of Representatives
  Number of members.................... 435
  Length of term.................... 2 years
  Party in majority, 2008 .... Democratic

Federal representation, 2008 (110th Congress)

Senators, total........................... 100
  Democrats............................. 51
  Republicans 49
Representatives, total .... 435 (3 vacant)
  Democrats............................ 232
  Republicans 200

Voters in November 2006 election (estimate)

Total.............................96,118,886
  Male........................... 45,117,695
  Female......................... 51,001,191
  White.......................... 82,387,076
  Black 9,936,941
  Hispanic 3,006,370
  Asian 2,144,606

Presidential election, 2004

Total Popular Vote 122,295,345
  Kerry 59,028,444
  Bush.......................... 62,040,610
Total Electoral Votes................... 538

Votes cast for US Senators

2004
Total vote (x 1,000) 86,968
Leading party......................... NA
Percent for leading party .... NA

2006
Total vote (x 1,000) 60,839
Leading party.................. Democratic
Percent for leading party 53.2%

Votes cast for US Representatives

2004
Total vote (x 1,000) 113,192
  Democratic.....................52,745
  Republican 55,713
Leading party.................... Republican
Percent for leading party 49.2%

2006
Total vote (x 1,000) 80,976
  Democratic..................... 42,082
  Republican 35,675
Leading party.................. Democratic
Percent for leading party 52.0%

©2008 Information Publications, Inc.
All rights reserved. Photocopying prohibited.
877-544-INFO (4636) or www.informationpublications.com

Federal government employees, 2006

Total.................................2,700,0124
Payroll ($ mil) $160,498

State government employment, 2006

Full-time equivalent employees 4,250,554
Payroll ($ mil) $16,769.4

Local government employment, 2006

Full-time equivalent employees 11,885,145
Payroll ($ mil) $43,971.7

Women holding public office, 2008

US Congress............................. 86
Statewide elected office..................... 74
State legislature 1,744

Black public officials, 2002

Total...................................9,430
  US and state legislatures 636
  City/county/regional offices 5,753
  Judicial/law enforcement..............1,081
  Education/school boards.............1,960

Hispanic public officials, 2006

Total...................................4,932
  State executives & legislators 244
  City/county/regional offices 2,151
  Judicial/law enforcement............... 693
  Education/school boards.............1,835

Governmental Finance

Federal government finance, 2007 (estimate)

Total Receipts ($bil)..................$2,540.1
  Individual income taxes............. 1,168.8
  Corporate income texes............... 342.1
  Social Insurance and retirement receipts....873.4
  Excise taxes...........................57.1
Total Outlays ($bil) $2,784.3
  Agriculture...........................88.8
  Defense - military.................... 548.9
  Defense - civil programs 47.6
  Education 68.0
  Energy...............................22.0
  Health & Human Services.............671.3
  Homeland Security....................50.4
  Housing and Urban Development 42.8
  Justice 23.0
  Labor 47.4
  Transportation 63.8
  Treasury 490.5
  Social Security Administration:
    on-budget..........................55.7
    off-budget.........................567.2
Deficit ($bil) $244.2

Federal Budget debt, 2007 (estimate)

Gross debt ($bil) $9,007.8
  Held by the public...................5,083.3
  Federal government accounts.........3,924.5
  Gross national debt, per capita.......$29,865

Federal government grants to state & local governments, 2005 (x $1,000)

Total..........................$469,579,029
by Federal agency
  Defense 3,161,336
  Education 38,053,238
  Energy..........................2,271,238
  Environmental Protection Agency...3,972,392
  Health & Human Services....... 276,352,384
  Homeland Security..............10,454,170
  Housing & Urban Development....33,786,246
  Justice 6,074,154
  Labor 7,852,666
  Transportation 41,146,849
  Veterans Affairs................... 730,868

Crime & Law Enforcement

Crime, 2006 (rates per 100,000 residents)

Property crimes 9,983,568
  Burglary 2,183,746
  Larceny 6,607,013
  Motor vehicle theft 1,192,809
  Property crime rate..................3,334.5
Violent crimes...................... 1,417,745
  Murder 17,034
  Forcible rape....................... 92,455
  Robbery.......................... 447,403
  Aggravated assault 860,853
  Violent crime rate 473.5
Hate crimes..........................9,080

Fraud and identity theft, 2006

Fraud complaints................. 374,907
  rate per 100,000 residents 125.2
Identity theft complaints 239,313
  rate per 100,000 residents 79.9

Law enforcement agencies, 2006

Total agencies........................14,336
Total employees 987,125
  Officers 683,396
  Civilians 303,729

Prisoners, probation, and parole, 2006

Total prisoners.....................1,570,861
  percent change, 12/31/05 to 12/31/06 ....2.8%
  in private facilities 7.2%
  in local jails 5.0%
Sentenced to more than one year 1,502,179
  rate per 100,000 residents 501
Adults on probation 4,237,023
Adults on parole...................... 798,202

Prisoner demographics, June 30, 2005 (rate per 100,000 residents)

Male...............................1,249
Female 121
White.............................. 412
Black............................... 2,289
Hispanic 742

©2008 Information Publications, Inc.
All rights reserved. Photocopying prohibited.
877-544-INFO (4636) or www.informationpublications.com

6   US Summary

Arrests, 2006

Total.............................10,472,432
   Persons under 18 years of age 1,626,523

Persons under sentence of death, 1/1/07

Total................................. 3,350
   White.............................1,517
   Black 1,397
   Hispanic 359

Nation's highest court

Name ....Supreme Court
Number of members 9
Length of term ....life
Intermediate appeals court? ....yes

Labor & Income

Civilian labor force, 2006 (x 1,000)

Total............................... 151,428
   Men 81,255
   Women 70,173
   Persons 16-19 years...................7,281
   White............................ 123,834
   Black 17,314
   Hispanic 20,694

Civilian labor force as a percent of civilian non-institutional population, 2006

Total...............................66.2%
   Men 73.5
   Women 59.4
   Persons 16-19 years...................43.7
   White.............................66.5
   Black 64.1
   Hispanic 68.7

Employment, 2006 (x 1,000)

Total............................... 144,427
   Men 77,502
   Women 66,925
   Persons 16-19 years...................6,162
   White............................118,833
   Black 15,765
   Hispanic 19,613

Unemployment rate, 2006

Total................................. 4.6%
   Men 4.6
   Women 4.6
   Persons 16-19 years...................15.4
   White.............................4.0
   Black 8.9
   Hispanic 5.2

Full-time/part-time labor force, 2003 (x 1,000)

Full-time labor force, employed .... NA
Part-time labor force, employed........... NA
Unemployed, looking for
   Full-time work......................... NA
   Part-time work........................ NA
Mean duration of unemployment (weeks)...... NA
   Median .... NA

Labor unions, 2006

Membership (x 1,000)................. 15,359
   percent of employed 12.0%

Experienced civilian labor force by private industry, 2006

Total............................112,718,858
   Natural resources & mining 1,776,777
   Construction 7,602,148
   Manufacturing.................. 14,110,663
   Trade, transportation & utilities .. 26,006,269
   Information 3,040,577
   Finance 8,162,063
   Professional & business 17,469,679
   Education & health 16,916,228
   Leisure & hospitality.............13,024,615
   Other......................... 4,364,889

Experienced civilian labor force by occupation, May 2006

Management.....................5,892,900
Business & financial 5,826,140
Legal............................. 976,740
Sales............................14,114,860
Office & admin. support............23,077,190
Computers & math 3,076,200
Architecture & engineering..........2,430,250
Arts & entertainment 1,727,380
Education 8,206,440
Social services 1,749,210
Health care practitioner & technical...6,713,780
Health care support 3,483,270
Maintenance & repair................5,352,420
Construction 6,680,710
Transportation & moving 9,647,730
Production 10,268,510
Farming, fishing & forestry........... 450,040

Hours and earnings of production workers on manufacturing payrolls, 2006

Average weekly hours 41.1
Average hourly earnings $16.80
Average weekly earnings $690.83

Income and poverty, 2006

Median household income............ $48,451
Personal income, per capita (current $)... $36,276
   in constant (2000) dollars $31,667
Persons below poverty level.............. 13.3%

Average annual pay

2006 .... $42,535
   increase from 2005 .... 4.6%

Federal individual income tax returns, 2005

Returns filed.......................135,257,620
Adjusted gross income ($1,000)....$7,364,640,131
Total tax liability ($1,000) $989,191,350

Charitable contributions, 2004

Number of contributions.............40,426.9
Total amount ($ mil)...............$162,198.7

©2008 Information Publications, Inc.
All rights reserved. Photocopying prohibited.
877-544-INFO (4636) or www.informationpublications.com

Economy, Business, Industry & Agriculture

Fortune 500 companies, 2007 500
Bankruptcy cases filed, FY 2007 801,269

Patents and trademarks issued, 2007

Patents .... .94,618
Trademarks 122,266

Business firm ownership, 2002

Women-owned 6,489,259
  Sales ($ mil) $939,538
Black-owned 1,197,567
  Sales ($ mil) $88,642
Hispanic-owned 1,573,464
  Sales ($ mil) $221,927
Asian-owned 1,103,587
  Sales ($ mil) $326,663
Amer. Indian/Alaska Native-owned 206,125
  Sales ($ mil) $26,396
Hawaiian/Pacific Islander-owned 28,948
  Sales ($ mil) $4,280

Gross domestic product, 2006 ($ mil)

Total gross domestic product $13,149,033
  Agriculture, forestry, fishing and
    hunting 122,352
  Mining 256,049
  Utilities 262,604
  Construction 647,882
  Manufacturing, durable goods 915,677
  Manufacturing, non-durable goods .. 685,475
  Wholesale trade 788,674
  Retail trade 863,155
  Transportation & warehousing 363,678
  Information 579,232
  Finance & insurance 1,027,477
  Real estate, rental & leasing 1,731,115
  Professional and technical services ... .929,614
  Educational services 123,296
  Health care and social assistance ..... .911,681
  Accommodation/food services .... .349,915
  Other services, except government ... 295,704
  Government 1,538,624

Establishments, payroll, employees & receipts, by major industry group, 2005

Total 7,499,702
  Annual payroll ($1,000) $4,482,722,481
  Paid employees 116,317,003
Forestry, fishing & agriculture 24,102
  Annual payroll ($1,000) $5,095,741
  Paid employees 168,744
Mining 24,696
  Annual payroll ($1,000) $30,823,272
  Paid employees .... .497,272
  Receipts, 2002 ($1,000) $182,911,093

Utilities .... .17,326
  Annual payroll ($1,000) $46,292,766
  Paid employees 633,106
  Receipts, 2002 ($1,000) $398,907,044
Construction .... .787,672
  Annual payroll ($1,000) $292,519,343
  Paid employees 6,781,327
  Receipts, 2002 ($1,000) $1,196,555,587
Manufacturing 333,460
  Annual payroll ($1,000) $600,696,305
  Paid employees 13,667,337
  Receipts, 2002 ($1,000) $3,916,136,712
Wholesale trade 429,823
  Annual payroll ($1,000) $308,918,023
  Paid employees 5,968,929
  Receipts, 2002 ($1,000) $4,634,755,112
Retail trade 1,123,207
  Annual payroll ($1,000) $348,047,012
  Paid employees 15,338,672
  Receipts, 2002 ($1,000) $3,056,421,997
Transportation & warehousing .... .211,150
  Annual payroll ($1,000) $154,375,938
  Paid employees 4,168,016
  Receipts, 2002 ($1,000) $382,152,040
Information 141,290
  Annual payroll ($1,000) $203,129,725
  Paid employees 3,402,599
  Receipts, 2002 ($1,000) $891,845,956
Finance & insurance 476,806
  Annual payroll ($1,000) $446,739,512
  Paid employees 6,431,837
  Receipts, 2002 ($1,000) $2,803,854,868
Professional, scientific & technical ...... .826,101
  Annual payroll ($1,000) $456,455,965
  Paid employees 7,689,366
  Receipts, 2002 ($1,000) $886,801,038
Education 80,486
  Annual payroll ($1,000) $82,522,976
  Paid employees 2,879,374
  Receipts, 2002 ($1,000) $30,690,707
Health care & social assistance 746,600
  Annual payroll ($1,000) $589,654,273
  Paid employees 16,025,147
  Receipts, 2002 ($1,000) $1,207,299,734
Arts and entertainment .... .121,777
  Annual payroll ($1,000) $52,935,670
  Paid employees 1,936,484
  Receipts, 2002 ($1,000) $141,904,109
Real estate 370,651
  Annual payroll ($1,000) $81,790,239
  Paid employees 2,144,077
  Receipts, 2002 ($1,000) $335,587,706
Accommodation & food service 603,435
  Annual payroll ($1,000) $156,041,233
  Paid employees 11,025,909
  Receipts, 2002 ($1,000) $449,498,718

©2008 Information Publications, Inc.
All rights reserved. Photocopying prohibited.
877-544-INFO (4636) or www.informationpublications.com

Exports, 2006
Value of exported goods ($ mil) $1,037,320
  Manufactured $821,708
  Non-manufactured $107,955

Foreign direct investment in US affiliates, 2004
Property, plants & equipment ($ mil). . .$1,060,181
Employment (x 1,000). 5,116.4

Agriculture, 2006
Number of farms .2,089,790
Farm acreage (x 1,000) 932,430
  Acres per farm 446.18
Farm marketings and income ($ mil)
Total. $239,271.9
  Crops $119,951.5
  Livestock $119,320.4
Net farm income $59,005.5

Principal commodities, in order by
  marketing receipts, 2005
Cattle and calves, Dairy products, Corn, Broilers,
                  Soybeans

Federal economic activity in states
Expenditures, 2005 ($ mil)
  Total. $2,284,760
    Per capita $7,567.85
  Defense $374,203
  Non-defense $1,910,558
Defense department, 2006 ($ mil)
  Payroll. $146,858
  Contract awards $257,457
  Grants $3,934
Homeland security grants ($1,000)
  2006. . . . .$1,747,300
  2007 . . . .$1,666,460

FDIC-insured financial institutions, 2005
Number. 8,680
Assets ($ billion) $11,860.3
Deposits ($ billion) $7,825.2

Fishing, 2006
Catch (x 1,000 lbs) 9,489,031
Value ($1,000). $3,993,370

Mining, 2006 ($ mil)
Total non-fuel mineral production $64,400
Percent of U.S. 100%

Communication, Energy & Transportation

Communication
Households with computers, 2003 . . . . 61.8%
Households with internet access, 2003 . . . . 54.6%
High-speed internet providers 1,397
Total high-speed internet lines 82,547,651
  Residential 58,243,921
  Business. 24,303,730
Wireless phone customers, 12/2006 . . . 229,619,397

FCC-licensed stations (as of January 1, 2008)
TV stations 1,716
FM radio stations. 9,143
AM radio stations 4,740

Energy
Energy consumption, 2004
  Total (trillion Btu). 100,279
  Per capita (million Btu) 341.5
By source of production (trillion Btu)
  Coal 22,466
  Natural gas 22,902
  Petroleum. 40,593
  Nuclear electric power 8,222
  Hydroelectric power 2,690
By end-use sector (trillion Btu)
  Residential 21,243
  Commercial 17,721
  Industrial 33,415
  Transportation 27,900
Electric energy, 2005
  Primary source of electricity. . . . . Coal
  Net generation (billion kWh) 4,055.4
    percent from renewable sources. 8.8%
  Net summer capability (million kW) 978.0
  CO_2 emitted from generation 2,513.6
Natural gas utilities, 2005
  Customers (x 1,000) 68,785
  Sales (trillion Btu). 15,077
  Revenues ($ mil) $96,909
Nuclear plants, 2007 105
Total CO_2 emitted (million metric tons). . .5,800.5
Energy spending, 2004 ($ mil) $869,319
  per capita $2,961
  Price per million Btu $12.91

Transportation, 2006
Public road & street mileage 4,016,741
  Urban. 1,029,366
  Rural 2,987,375
  Interstate 46,630
Vehicle miles of travel (millions) 3,014,116
  per capita 10,088.9
Total motor vehicle registrations 244,165,686
  Automobiles. .135,399,945
  Trucks 107,943,782
  Motorcycles 6,686,147
Licensed drivers 202,810,438
  19 years & under 9,727,516
Deaths from motor vehicle accidents 42,642
Gasoline consumed (x 1,000 gallons). . . 140,320,089
  per capita 469.7

Commuting Statistics, 2006
Average commute time (min) 25.0
  Drove to work alone 76.0%
  Carpooled. 10.7%
  Public transit 4.8%
  Walk to work 2.9%
  Work from home 3.9%

©2008 Information Publications, Inc.
All rights reserved. Photocopying prohibited.
877-544-INFO (4636) or www.informationpublications.com

Comparative Tables

Note: Rankings that are tied are listed alphabetically, with the exception of the United States, which is always listed as the final item in a group of ties.

©2008 Information Publications, Inc.
All rights reserved. Photocopying prohibited.
877-544-INFO (4636) or www.informationpublications.com

Comparative Tables

1. Total Area (square miles)	
* UNITED STATES	3,794,083
1. Alaska	663,267
2. Texas	268,581
3. California	163,696
4. Montana	147,042
5. New Mexico	121,590
6. Arizona	113,998
7. Nevada	110,561
8. Colorado	104,094
9. Oregon	98,381
10. Wyoming	97,814
11. Michigan	96,716
12. Minnesota	86,939
13. Utah	84,899
14. Idaho	83,570
15. Kansas	82,277
16. Nebraska	77,354
17. South Dakota	77,117
18. Washington	71,300
19. North Dakota	70,700
20. Oklahoma	69,898
21. Missouri	69,704
22. Florida	65,755
23. Wisconsin	65,498
24. Georgia	59,425
25. Illinois	57,914
26. Iowa	56,272
27. New York	54,556
28. North Carolina	53,819
29. Arkansas	53,179
30. Alabama	52,419
31. Louisiana	51,840
32. Mississippi	48,430
33. Pennsylvania	46,055
34. Ohio	44,825
35. Virginia	42,774
36. Tennessee	42,143
37. Kentucky	40,409
38. Indiana	36,418
39. Maine	35,385
40. South Carolina	32,020
41. West Virginia	24,230
42. Maryland	12,407
43. Hawaii	10,931
44. Massachusetts	10,555
45. Vermont	9,614
46. New Hampshire	9,350
47. New Jersey	8,721
48. Connecticut	5,543
49. Delaware	2,489
50. Rhode Island	1,545
51. District of Columbia	68

2. Federally-Owned Land, 2004	
1. Nevada	84.5%
2. Alaska	69.1
3. Utah	57.5
4. Oregon	53.1
5. Idaho	50.2
6. Arizona	48.1
7. California	45.3
8. Wyoming	42.3
9. New Mexico	41.8
10. Colorado	36.6
11. Washington	30.3
12. Montana	29.9
* UNITED STATES	28.8
13. District of Columbia	24.7
14. Hawaii	19.4
15. New Hampshire	13.5
16. North Carolina	11.8
17. Michigan	10.0
18. Virginia	9.9
19. Florida	8.2
20. Vermont	7.5
21. West Virginia	7.4
22. Mississippi	7.3
23. Arkansas	7.2
24. South Dakota	6.2
25. Minnesota	5.6
26. Wisconsin	5.6
27. Kentucky	5.4
28. Louisiana	5.1
29. Missouri	5.0
30. Georgia	3.8
31. Oklahoma	3.6
32. Tennessee	3.2
33. New Jersey	3.1
34. South Carolina	2.9
35. Maryland	2.8
36. North Dakota	2.7
37. Pennsylvania	2.5
38. Delaware	2.0
39. Indiana	2.0
40. Massachusetts	1.9
41. Texas	1.9
42. Illinois	1.8
43. Ohio	1.7
44. Alabama	1.6
45. Nebraska	1.4
46. Kansas	1.2
47. Maine	1.1
48. Iowa	0.8
49. New York	0.8
50. Connecticut	0.4
51. Rhode Island	0.4

©2008 Information Publications, Inc.
All Rights Reserved. Photocopying prohibited.
877-544-INFO (4636) or www.informationpublications.com

Comparative Tables

3. Population, 2000

* UNITED STATES	281,424,602
1. California	33,871,653
2. Texas	20,851,792
3. New York	18,976,821
4. Florida	15,982,824
5. Illinois	12,419,647
6. Pennsylvania	12,281,054
7. Ohio	11,353,145
8. Michigan	9,938,480
9. New Jersey	8,414,347
10. Georgia	8,186,816
11. North Carolina	8,046,491
12. Virginia	7,079,030
13. Massachusetts	6,349,105
14. Indiana	6,080,517
15. Washington	5,894,140
16. Tennessee	5,689,262
17. Missouri	5,596,683
18. Wisconsin	5,363,715
19. Maryland	5,296,506
20. Arizona	5,130,632
21. Minnesota	4,919,492
22. Louisiana	4,468,958
23. Alabama	4,447,351
24. Colorado	4,302,015
25. Kentucky	4,042,285
26. South Carolina	4,011,816
27. Oklahoma	3,450,652
28. Oregon	3,421,436
29. Connecticut	3,405,602
30. Iowa	2,926,382
31. Mississippi	2,844,656
32. Kansas	2,688,824
33. Arkansas	2,673,398
34. Utah	2,233,198
35. Nevada	1,998,257
36. New Mexico	1,819,046
37. West Virginia	1,808,350
38. Nebraska	1,711,265
39. Idaho	1,293,956
40. Maine	1,274,923
41. New Hampshire	1,235,786
42. Hawaii	1,211,537
43. Rhode Island	1,048,319
44. Montana	902,195
45. Delaware	783,600
46. South Dakota	754,840
47. North Dakota	642,204
48. Alaska	626,931
49. Vermont	608,827
50. District of Columbia	572,059
51. Wyoming	493,782

4. Population, 2007 (estimate)

* UNITED STATES	301,621,157
1. California	36,553,215
2. Texas	23,904,380
3. New York	19,297,729
4. Florida	18,251,243
5. Illinois	12,852,548
6. Pennsylvania	12,432,792
7. Ohio	11,466,917
8. Michigan	10,071,822
9. Georgia	9,544,750
10. North Carolina	9,061,032
11. New Jersey	8,685,920
12. Virginia	7,712,091
13. Washington	6,468,424
14. Massachusetts	6,449,755
15. Indiana	6,345,289
16. Arizona	6,338,755
17. Tennessee	6,156,719
18. Missouri	5,878,415
19. Maryland	5,618,344
20. Wisconsin	5,601,640
21. Minnesota	5,197,621
22. Colorado	4,861,515
23. Alabama	4,627,851
24. South Carolina	4,407,709
25. Louisiana	4,293,204
26. Kentucky	4,241,474
27. Oregon	3,747,455
28. Oklahoma	3,617,316
29. Connecticut	3,502,309
30. Iowa	2,988,046
31. Mississippi	2,918,785
32. Arkansas	2,834,797
33. Kansas	2,775,997
34. Utah	2,645,330
35. Nevada	2,565,382
36. New Mexico	1,969,915
37. West Virginia	1,812,035
38. Nebraska	1,774,571
39. Idaho	1,499,402
40. Maine	1,317,207
41. New Hampshire	1,315,828
42. Hawaii	1,283,388
43. Rhode Island	1,057,832
44. Montana	957,861
45. Delaware	864,764
46. South Dakota	796,214
47. Alaska	683,478
48. North Dakota	639,715
49. Vermont	621,254
50. District of Columbia	588,292
51. Wyoming	522,830

©2008 Information Publications, Inc.
All Rights Reserved. Photocopying prohibited.
877-544-INFO (4636) or www.informationpublications.com

Comparative Tables

5. Population, 2008 (projected)

*	UNITED STATES	303,597,646
1.	California	37,262,310
2.	Texas	23,898,665
3.	New York	19,383,109
4.	Florida	18,533,980
5.	Illinois	12,835,851
6.	Pennsylvania	12,525,118
7.	Ohio	11,541,279
8.	Michigan	10,345,033
9.	Georgia	9,325,827
10.	North Carolina	9,086,527
11.	New Jersey	8,915,495
12.	Virginia	7,827,657
13.	Massachusetts	6,601,235
14.	Washington	6,399,035
15.	Indiana	6,337,404
16.	Arizona	6,320,874
17.	Tennessee	6,124,341
18.	Missouri	5,860,326
19.	Maryland	5,783,344
20.	Wisconsin	5,659,640
21.	Minnesota	5,321,587
22.	Colorado	4,746,528
23.	Louisiana	4,583,733
24.	Alabama	4,568,983
25.	South Carolina	4,365,055
26.	Kentucky	4,226,659
27.	Oregon	3,709,778
28.	Oklahoma	3,563,865
29.	Connecticut	3,550,416
30.	Iowa	2,997,608
31.	Mississippi	2,950,652
32.	Arkansas	2,836,580
33.	Kansas	2,784,728
34.	Nevada	2,551,889
35.	Utah	2,523,394
36.	New Mexico	1,951,229
37.	West Virginia	1,827,226
38.	Nebraska	1,759,829
39.	Idaho	1,472,584
40.	New Hampshire	1,357,216
41.	Maine	1,342,286
42.	Hawaii	1,317,607
43.	Rhode Island	1,105,525
44.	Montana	954,653
45.	Delaware	865,705
46.	South Dakota	780,947
47.	Alaska	680,082
48.	Vermont	643,905
49.	North Dakota	636,452
50.	District of Columbia	538,487
51.	Wyoming	515,408

6. Population, 2030 (projected)

*	UNITED STATES	363,584,435
1.	California	46,444,861
2.	Texas	33,317,744
3.	Florida	28,685,769
4.	New York	19,477,429
5.	Illinois	13,432,892
6.	Pennsylvania	12,768,184
7.	North Carolina	12,227,739
8.	Georgia	12,017,838
9.	Ohio	11,550,528
10.	Arizona	10,712,397
11.	Michigan	10,694,172
12.	Virginia	9,825,019
13.	New Jersey	9,802,440
14.	Washington	8,624,801
15.	Tennessee	7,380,634
16.	Maryland	7,022,251
17.	Massachusetts	7,012,009
18.	Indiana	6,810,108
19.	Missouri	6,430,173
20.	Minnesota	6,306,130
21.	Wisconsin	6,150,764
22.	Colorado	5,792,357
23.	South Carolina	5,148,569
24.	Alabama	4,874,243
25.	Oregon	4,833,918
26.	Louisiana	4,802,633
27.	Kentucky	4,554,998
28.	Nevada	4,282,102
29.	Oklahoma	3,913,251
30.	Connecticut	3,688,630
31.	Utah	3,485,367
32.	Arkansas	3,240,208
33.	Mississippi	3,092,410
34.	Iowa	2,955,172
35.	Kansas	2,940,084
36.	New Mexico	2,099,708
37.	Idaho	1,969,624
38.	Nebraska	1,820,247
39.	West Virginia	1,719,959
40.	New Hampshire	1,646,471
41.	Hawaii	1,466,046
42.	Maine	1,411,097
43.	Rhode Island	1,152,941
44.	Montana	1,044,898
45.	Delaware	1,012,658
46.	Alaska	867,674
47.	South Dakota	800,462
48.	Vermont	711,867
49.	North Dakota	606,566
50.	Wyoming	522,979
51.	District of Columbia	433,414

©2008 Information Publications, Inc.
All Rights Reserved. Photocopying prohibited.
877-544-INFO (4636) or www.informationpublications.com

Comparative Tables

7. Persons per Square Mile, 2007 (estimate)		8. Change in Population, 2000-2007 (estimate)	
1. District of Columbia	9,644.1	1. Nevada	28.4%
2. New Jersey	1,171.1	2. Arizona	23.5
3. Rhode Island	1,012.3	3. Utah	18.5
4. Massachusetts	822.7	4. Georgia	16.6
5. Connecticut	722.9	5. Idaho	15.9
6. Maryland	574.8	6. Texas	14.6
7. Delaware	442.6	7. Florida	14.2
8. New York	408.7	8. Colorado	13.0
9. Florida	338.4	9. North Carolina	12.6
10. Ohio	280.0	10. Delaware	10.4
11. Pennsylvania	277.4	11. South Carolina	9.9
12. California	234.4	12. Washington	9.7
13. Illinois	231.2	13. Oregon	9.5
14. Hawaii	199.8	14. Alaska	9.0
15. Virginia	194.8	15. Virginia	8.9
16. North Carolina	186.0	16. New Mexico	8.3
17. Michigan	177.3	17. Tennessee	8.2
18. Indiana	176.9	18. California	7.9
19. Georgia	164.8	* UNITED STATES	7.2
20. Tennessee	149.4	19. New Hampshire	6.5
21. New Hampshire	146.7	20. Montana	6.2
22. South Carolina	146.4	21. Maryland	6.1
23. Kentucky	106.8	22. Arkansas	6.0
24. Wisconsin	103.1	23. Hawaii	5.9
25. Louisiana	98.6	24. Wyoming	5.9
26. Washington	97.2	25. Minnesota	5.7
27. Texas	91.3	26. South Dakota	5.5
28. Alabama	91.2	27. Missouri	5.0
29. Missouri	85.3	28. Kentucky	4.9
* UNITED STATES	85.3	29. Oklahoma	4.8
30. West Virginia	75.3	30. Indiana	4.4
31. Vermont	67.2	31. Wisconsin	4.4
32. Minnesota	65.3	32. Alabama	4.1
33. Mississippi	62.2	33. Nebraska	3.7
34. Arizona	55.8	34. Illinois	3.5
35. Arkansas	54.4	35. Maine	3.3
36. Iowa	53.5	36. Kansas	3.2
37. Oklahoma	52.7	37. New Jersey	3.2
38. Colorado	46.9	38. Connecticut	2.8
39. Maine	42.7	39. District of Columbia	2.8
40. Oregon	39.0	40. Mississippi	2.6
41. Kansas	33.9	41. Iowa	2.1
42. Utah	32.2	42. Vermont	2.0
43. Nevada	23.4	43. New York	1.7
44. Nebraska	23.1	44. Massachusetts	1.6
45. Idaho	18.1	45. Michigan	1.3
46. New Mexico	16.2	46. Pennsylvania	1.2
47. South Dakota	10.5	47. Ohio	1.0
48. North Dakota	9.3	48. Rhode Island	0.9
49. Montana	6.6	49. West Virginia	0.2
50. Wyoming	5.4	50. North Dakota	-0.4
51. Alaska	1.2	51. Louisiana	-3.9

©2008 Information Publications, Inc.
All Rights Reserved. Photocopying prohibited.
877-544-INFO (4636) or www.informationpublications.com

Comparative Tables

9. Cities with over 100,000 Population, 2006

*	UNITED STATES	258
1.	California	62
2.	Texas	27
3.	Florida	17
4.	Arizona	9
5.	Colorado	9
6.	Virginia	9
7.	Illinois	8
8.	Michigan	7
9.	North Carolina	7
10.	Ohio	6
11.	Connecticut	5
12.	Georgia	5
13.	Kansas	5
14.	Massachusetts	5
15.	New York	5
16.	Tennessee	5
17.	Washington	5
18.	Alabama	4
19.	Indiana	4
20.	Louisiana	4
21.	Missouri	4
22.	Nevada	4
23.	New Jersey	4
24.	Pennsylvania	4
25.	Oklahoma	3
26.	Oregon	3
27.	Utah	3
28.	Wisconsin	3
29.	Iowa	2
30.	Kentucky	2
31.	Minnesota	2
32.	Nebraska	2
33.	South Carolina	2
34.	Alaska	1
35.	Arkansas	1
36.	District of Columbia	1
37.	Hawaii	1
38.	Idaho	1
39.	Maryland	1
40.	Mississippi	1
41.	Montana	1
42.	New Hampshire	1
43.	New Mexico	1
44.	Rhode Island	1
45.	South Dakota	1
46.	Delaware	0
47.	Maine	0
48.	North Dakota	0
49.	Vermont	0
50.	West Virginia	0
51.	Wyoming	0

10. Population Living in Group Quarters, 2006

1.	District of Columbia	6.1%
2.	North Dakota	4.3
3.	Rhode Island	4.0
4.	South Dakota	3.8
5.	Pennsylvania	3.7
6.	Iowa	3.5
7.	Alaska	3.4
8.	Massachusetts	3.4
9.	South Carolina	3.3
10.	Vermont	3.3
11.	Connecticut	3.2
12.	Mississippi	3.2
13.	New York	3.1
14.	North Carolina	3.1
15.	Oklahoma	3.1
16.	Virginia	3.1
17.	Kansas	3.0
18.	Delaware	2.9
19.	Georgia	2.9
20.	Hawaii	2.9
21.	Louisiana	2.9
22.	Missouri	2.9
23.	Nebraska	2.9
24.	Wisconsin	2.9
25.	Arkansas	2.8
26.	Indiana	2.8
27.	Maine	2.8
28.	New Hampshire	2.8
29.	Kentucky	2.7
30.	Minnesota	2.7
31.	Montana	2.7
32.	Ohio	2.7
33.	Wyoming	2.7
*	UNITED STATES	2.7
34.	Alabama	2.5
35.	Illinois	2.5
36.	Maryland	2.5
37.	Michigan	2.5
38.	Tennessee	2.5
39.	Texas	2.5
40.	West Virginia	2.5
41.	California	2.4
42.	Florida	2.3
43.	Idaho	2.3
44.	New Jersey	2.3
45.	Colorado	2.2
46.	Oregon	2.2
47.	Washington	2.2
48.	New Mexico	2.1
49.	Arizona	1.8
50.	Utah	1.7
51.	Nevada	1.3

©2008 Information Publications, Inc.
All Rights Reserved. Photocopying prohibited.
877-544-INFO (4636) or www.informationpublications.com

Comparative Tables

11. Core-Based Statistical Area Population, 2006 (x 1,000)	
* UNITED STATES	279,848
1. California	36,195
2. Texas	22,090
3. New York	18,873
4. Florida	17,692
5. Illinois	12,218
6. Pennsylvania	12,056
7. Ohio	10,966
8. Michigan	9,302
9. New Jersey	8,725
10. Georgia	8,534
11. North Carolina	8,135
12. Virginia	6,814
13. Massachusetts	6,411
14. Washington	6,168
15. Arizona	5,964
16. Indiana	5,946
17. Maryland	5,533
18. Tennessee	5,412
19. Missouri	5,043
20. Wisconsin	4,777
21. Minnesota	4,510
22. Colorado	4,356
23. Alabama	4,109
24. South Carolina	4,046
25. Louisiana	3,979
26. Oregon	3,559
27. Connecticut	3,505
28. Kentucky	3,184
29. Oklahoma	3,018
30. Nevada	2,447
31. Utah	2,420
32. Kansas	2,349
33. Mississippi	2,263
34. Arkansas	2,224
35. Iowa	2,167
36. New Mexico	1,876
37. Nebraska	1,415
38. West Virginia	1,366
39. Hawaii	1,285
40. Idaho	1,267
41. New Hampshire	1,267
42. Rhode Island	1,068
43. Maine	931
44. Delaware	853
45. Montana	615
46. District of Columbia	582
47. South Dakota	560
48. Alaska	503
49. Vermont	460
50. North Dakota	442
51. Wyoming	368

12. Non-CBSA population, 2006 (x 1,000)	
* UNITED STATES	19,551
1. Texas	1,418
2. Kentucky	1,022
3. Georgia	830
4. Virginia	829
5. Iowa	816
6. Missouri	800
7. Michigan	794
8. Wisconsin	779
9. North Carolina	722
10. Minnesota	657
11. Mississippi	647
12. Tennessee	627
13. Illinois	614
14. Arkansas	587
15. Oklahoma	561
16. Ohio	512
17. Alabama	490
18. West Virginia	453
19. New York	433
20. Kansas	415
21. Florida	398
22. Colorado	397
23. Maine	391
24. Pennsylvania	385
25. Indiana	367
26. Nebraska	354
27. Montana	330
28. Louisiana	309
29. South Carolina	275
30. California	262
31. Washington	227
32. South Dakota	222
33. Arizona	203
34. Idaho	200
35. North Dakota	194
36. Alaska	167
37. Vermont	164
38. Wyoming	147
39. Oregon	142
40. Utah	130
41. Maryland	82
42. New Mexico	78
43. Nevada	49
44. New Hampshire	47
45. Massachusetts	26
46. Connecticut	0
47. Delaware	0
48. District of Columbia	0
49. Hawaii	0
50. New Jersey	0
51. Rhode Island	0

©2008 Information Publications, Inc.
All Rights Reserved. Photocopying prohibited.
877-544-INFO (4636) or www.informationpublications.com

Comparative Tables

13. Median Age, 2006

1.	Maine	41.1
2.	Vermont	40.4
3.	West Virginia	40.2
4.	Florida	39.6
5.	Pennsylvania	39.5
6.	New Hampshire	39.4
7.	Montana	39.2
8.	Connecticut	39.0
9.	Massachusetts	38.2
10.	New Jersey	38.2
11.	Rhode Island	38.2
12.	Iowa	37.8
13.	Wisconsin	37.7
14.	Ohio	37.6
15.	Delaware	37.5
16.	Oregon	37.5
17.	Hawaii	37.3
18.	New York	37.3
19.	Kentucky	37.2
20.	Maryland	37.2
21.	Michigan	37.2
22.	North Dakota	37.2
23.	Alabama	37.1
24.	Missouri	37.1
25.	South Carolina	37.1
26.	Tennessee	37.1
27.	Wyoming	37.1
28.	South Dakota	36.9
29.	Virginia	36.9
30.	Arkansas	36.8
31.	Minnesota	36.8
32.	Washington	36.7
33.	North Carolina	36.6
*	UNITED STATES	36.4
34.	Indiana	36.3
35.	Kansas	36.0
36.	Nebraska	36.0
37.	Oklahoma	36.0
38.	Illinois	35.7
39.	Louisiana	35.7
40.	Nevada	35.5
41.	Colorado	35.4
42.	Mississippi	35.3
43.	New Mexico	35.3
44.	District of Columbia	35.0
45.	Arizona	34.6
46.	Georgia	34.6
47.	California	34.4
48.	Idaho	34.2
49.	Alaska	33.4
50.	Texas	33.1
51.	Utah	28.3

14. Households, 2006

*	UNITED STATES	111,617,402
1.	California	12,151,227
2.	Texas	8,109,388
3.	Florida	7,106,042
4.	New York	7,088,376
5.	Pennsylvania	4,845,603
6.	Illinois	4,724,252
7.	Ohio	4,499,506
8.	Michigan	3,869,117
9.	North Carolina	3,454,068
10.	Georgia	3,376,763
11.	New Jersey	3,135,490
12.	Virginia	2,905,071
13.	Washington	2,471,912
14.	Massachusetts	2,446,485
15.	Indiana	2,435,274
16.	Tennessee	2,375,123
17.	Missouri	2,305,027
18.	Wisconsin	2,230,060
19.	Arizona	2,224,992
20.	Maryland	2,089,031
21.	Minnesota	2,042,297
22.	Colorado	1,846,988
23.	Alabama	1,796,058
24.	South Carolina	1,656,978
25.	Kentucky	1,651,911
26.	Louisiana	1,564,978
27.	Oregon	1,449,662
28.	Oklahoma	1,385,300
29.	Connecticut	1,325,443
30.	Iowa	1,208,765
31.	Arkansas	1,103,428
32.	Kansas	1,088,288
33.	Mississippi	1,075,521
34.	Nevada	936,828
35.	Utah	814,028
36.	West Virginia	743,064
37.	New Mexico	726,033
38.	Nebraska	700,888
39.	Idaho	548,555
40.	Maine	548,247
41.	New Hampshire	504,503
42.	Hawaii	432,632
43.	Rhode Island	405,627
44.	Montana	372,190
45.	Delaware	320,110
46.	South Dakota	312,477
47.	North Dakota	272,352
48.	Vermont	253,808
49.	District of Columbia	250,456
50.	Alaska	229,878
51.	Wyoming	207,302

©2008 Information Publications, Inc.
All Rights Reserved. Photocopying prohibited.
877-544-INFO (4636) or www.informationpublications.com

Comparative Tables

15. Legal Permanent Residents Admitted, 2006

* UNITED STATES	1,266,264
1. California	264,677
2. New York	180,165
3. Florida	155,996
4. Texas	89,037
5. New Jersey	65,934
6. Illinois	52,459
7. Virginia	38,488
8. Massachusetts	35,560
9. Georgia	32,202
10. Maryland	30,204
11. Pennsylvania	25,958
12. Washington	23,805
13. Arizona	21,530
14. Michigan	20,911
15. North Carolina	18,989
16. Connecticut	18,700
17. Minnesota	18,254
18. Ohio	16,592
19. Nevada	14,714
20. Colorado	12,714
21. Tennessee	10,042
22. Oregon	9,192
23. Wisconsin	8,341
24. Indiana	8,125
25. Hawaii	7,501
26. Missouri	6,857
27. Utah	5,749
28. Kentucky	5,506
29. South Carolina	5,292
30. Rhode Island	4,778
31. Oklahoma	4,591
32. Kansas	4,280
33. Alabama	4,278
34. Iowa	4,086
35. New Mexico	3,805
36. Nebraska	3,795
37. District of Columbia	3,775
38. New Hampshire	2,990
39. Arkansas	2,926
40. Louisiana	2,693
41. Idaho	2,377
42. Delaware	2,265
43. Maine	1,719
44. Alaska	1,554
45. Mississippi	1,480
46. South Dakota	1,013
47. Vermont	895
48. West Virginia	764
49. North Dakota	649
50. Montana	505
51. Wyoming	376

16. Naturalizations, 2006

* UNITED STATES	702,589
1. California	152,836
2. New York	103,870
3. Florida	90,846
4. New Jersey	39,801
5. Texas	37,835
6. Illinois	30,156
7. Massachusetts	22,932
8. Virginia	20,401
9. Georgia	19,785
10. Pennsylvania	15,846
11. Maryland	14,465
12. Washington	12,762
13. North Carolina	12,592
14. Michigan	11,675
15. Arizona	9,707
16. Minnesota	9,137
17. Ohio	8,796
18. Nevada	8,202
19. Connecticut	7,231
20. Colorado	5,526
21. Hawaii	5,276
22. Oregon	4,332
23. Indiana	3,885
24. Missouri	3,711
25. Tennessee	3,334
26. Wisconsin	3,247
27. South Carolina	2,940
28. Utah	2,740
29. Kansas	2,509
30. New Hampshire	2,483
31. Rhode Island	2,266
32. Oklahoma	2,246
33. Kentucky	2,049
34. Alabama	1,946
35. Nebraska	1,797
36. New Mexico	1,538
37. Louisiana	1,336
38. Delaware	1,187
39. Arkansas	1,133
40. District of Columbia	1,089
41. Idaho	980
42. Alaska	831
43. Iowa	805
44. Maine	802
45. Vermont	569
46. Mississippi	495
47. West Virginia	390
48. South Dakota	342
49. North Dakota	329
50. Montana	225
51. Wyoming	169

©2008 Information Publications, Inc.
All Rights Reserved. Photocopying prohibited.
877-544-INFO (4636) or www.informationpublications.com

Comparative Tables

17. Persons Born in State of Residence, 2006

1.	Louisiana	79.8%
2.	Michigan	75.7
3.	Pennsylvania	75.6
4.	Ohio	75.1
5.	Mississippi	72.7
6.	Iowa	72.3
7.	West Virginia	72.2
8.	Wisconsin	72.1
9.	Kentucky	71.8
10.	North Dakota	71.1
11.	Alabama	70.9
12.	Minnesota	69.1
13.	Indiana	68.6
14.	Illinois	66.9
15.	Missouri	66.3
16.	Nebraska	65.5
17.	South Dakota	65.2
18.	Maine	65.0
19.	New York	64.5
20.	Massachusetts	64.1
21.	Utah	63.0
22.	Tennessee	62.6
23.	Oklahoma	61.7
24.	Arkansas	61.3
25.	Texas	60.9
26.	South Carolina	60.8
27.	North Carolina	59.7
28.	Rhode Island	59.2
29.	Kansas	59.1
*	UNITED STATES	58.9
30.	Connecticut	55.7
31.	Georgia	55.5
32.	Hawaii	55.2
33.	Montana	53.5
34.	Vermont	52.7
35.	California	52.4
36.	New Jersey	52.4
37.	New Mexico	50.9
38.	Virginia	50.8
39.	Maryland	47.8
40.	Washington	47.2
41.	Delaware	47.0
42.	Idaho	45.1
43.	Oregon	45.0
44.	Wyoming	42.6
45.	Colorado	42.1
46.	New Hampshire	41.8
47.	District of Columbia	40.1
48.	Alaska	38.9
49.	Arizona	35.7
50.	Florida	33.6
51.	Nevada	23.1

18. Adults who Smoke, 2006

1.	Kentucky	28.5%
2.	West Virginia	25.7
3.	Mississippi	25.1
4.	Oklahoma	25.1
5.	Indiana	24.1
6.	Alaska	24.0
7.	Arkansas	23.7
8.	Louisiana	23.4
9.	Alabama	23.2
10.	Missouri	23.2
11.	Tennessee	22.6
12.	Michigan	22.4
13.	Ohio	22.4
14.	South Carolina	22.3
15.	Nevada	22.2
16.	North Carolina	22.1
17.	Delaware	21.7
18.	Wyoming	21.6
19.	Pennsylvania	21.5
20.	Iowa	21.4
21.	Florida	21.0
22.	Maine	20.9
23.	Wisconsin	20.8
24.	Illinois	20.5
25.	South Dakota	20.3
26.	New Mexico	20.1
*	UNITED STATES	20.1
27.	Kansas	20.0
28.	Georgia	19.9
29.	North Dakota	19.5
30.	Virginia	19.3
31.	Rhode Island	19.2
32.	Montana	18.9
33.	Nebraska	18.7
34.	New Hampshire	18.7
35.	Oregon	18.5
36.	Minnesota	18.3
37.	Arizona	18.2
38.	New York	18.2
39.	New Jersey	18.0
40.	Vermont	18.0
41.	Colorado	17.9
42.	District of Columbia	17.9
43.	Texas	17.9
44.	Massachusetts	17.8
45.	Maryland	17.7
46.	Hawaii	17.5
47.	Washington	17.1
48.	Connecticut	17.0
49.	Idaho	16.8
50.	California	14.9
51.	Utah	9.8

©2008 Information Publications, Inc.
All Rights Reserved. Photocopying prohibited.
877-544-INFO (4636) or www.informationpublications.com

Comparative Tables

19. Death Rate, 2005 (per 100,000 population, age-adjusted)	
1. Mississippi	1,026.9
2. Louisiana	1,020.6
3. Alabama	997.9
4. Oklahoma	980.8
5. District of Columbia	971.4
6. West Virginia	960.4
7. Tennessee	959.9
8. Kentucky	958.4
9. Arkansas	930.2
10. Georgia	905.8
11. South Carolina	899.1
12. Nevada	892.3
13. North Carolina	876.0
14. Missouri	869.4
15. Indiana	858.7
16. Ohio	856.8
17. Delaware	830.5
18. Texas	828.8
19. Pennsylvania	814.8
20. Maine	813.2
21. Michigan	812.3
22. Kansas	806.8
23. Virginia	801.5
24. Wyoming	801.4
* UNITED STATES	798.8
25. Montana	798.4
26. Illinois	798.2
27. Maryland	796.4
28. New Mexico	795.0
29. Oregon	773.7
30. Arizona	771.8
31. Idaho	766.4
32. South Dakota	757.0
33. Wisconsin	752.2
34. Alaska	750.8
35. Nebraska	749.5
36. Florida	749.4
37. Rhode Island	747.3
38. New Jersey	745.9
39. Colorado	742.8
40. Iowa	742.0
41. Washington	738.2
42. New Hampshire	732.3
43. Utah	731.3
44. Vermont	728.4
45. Massachusetts	721.9
46. New York	718.0
47. California	713.1
48. North Dakota	699.1
49. Connecticut	696.0
50. Minnesota	683.9
51. Hawaii	609.1

20. Infant Death Rate, 2004 (per 1,000 births)	
1. District of Columbia	12.0
2. Louisiana	10.5
3. Mississippi	9.8
4. South Carolina	9.3
5. North Carolina	8.8
6. Wyoming	8.8
7. Alabama	8.7
8. Delaware	8.6
9. Tennessee	8.6
10. Georgia	8.5
11. Maryland	8.4
12. Arkansas	8.3
13. South Dakota	8.2
14. Indiana	8.0
15. Oklahoma	8.0
16. Ohio	7.7
17. Michigan	7.6
18. West Virginia	7.6
19. Illinois	7.5
20. Missouri	7.5
21. Virginia	7.5
22. Pennsylvania	7.3
23. Kansas	7.2
24. Florida	7.1
25. Kentucky	6.8
* UNITED STATES	6.8
26. Alaska	6.7
27. Arizona	6.7
28. Nebraska	6.6
29. Nevada	6.4
30. Colorado	6.3
31. New Mexico	6.3
32. Texas	6.3
33. Idaho	6.2
34. New York	6.1
35. Wisconsin	6.0
36. Hawaii	5.7
37. Maine	5.7
38. New Jersey	5.7
39. New Hampshire	5.6
40. North Dakota	5.6
41. Connecticut	5.5
42. Oregon	5.5
43. Washington	5.5
44. Rhode Island	5.3
45. California	5.2
46. Utah	5.2
47. Iowa	5.1
48. Massachusetts	4.8
49. Minnesota	4.7
50. Vermont	4.6
51. Montana	4.5

©2008 Information Publications, Inc.
All Rights Reserved. Photocopying prohibited.
877-544-INFO (4636) or www.informationpublications.com

Comparative Tables

21. Twin Birth Rate, 2005 (per 1,000 births)

1. Massachusetts	44.5
2. New Jersey	41.8
3. Connecticut	41.5
4. Rhode Island	38.9
5. New Hampshire	37.2
6. Maryland	37.1
7. New York	36.0
8. Illinois	35.9
9. Delaware	35.6
10. District of Columbia	34.5
11. Michigan	34.2
12. Pennsylvania	33.7
13. Virginia	33.6
14. Minnesota	33.5
15. Ohio	33.4
16. Iowa	33.2
17. Maine	32.8
18. North Dakota	32.6
19. Missouri	32.5
20. Alabama	32.2
21. Nebraska	32.1
22. Indiana	31.9
23. Mississippi	31.9
24. North Carolina	31.9
25. Vermont	31.9
* UNITED STATES	31.9
26. Colorado	31.7
27. South Carolina	31.5
28. Louisiana	31.3
29. Georgia	31.2
30. Tennessee	31.1
31. Wisconsin	30.8
32. Kentucky	30.6
33. Kansas	30.3
34. Florida	29.9
35. Oregon	29.8
36. Idaho	29.5
37. Arkansas	29.4
38. Washington	29.4
39. California	29.0
40. Nevada	29.0
41. South Dakota	28.9
42. Texas	28.1
43. Hawaii	28.0
44. Montana	27.6
45. Oklahoma	27.4
46. Wyoming	27.3
47. West Virginia	27.2
48. Alaska	26.9
49. Arizona	26.5
50. Utah	26.5
51. New Mexico	24.2

22. Triplet Birth Rate, 2005 (per 100,000 births)

1. Massachusetts	290.4
2. New Jersey	288.7
3. Nebraska	269.2
4. Connecticut	245.5
5. North Dakota	240.3
6. Ohio	238.2
7. Kentucky	234.8
8. Illinois	234.6
9. Indiana	234.3
10. New York	229.9
11. Michigan	229.0
12. New Hampshire	214.4
13. Minnesota	208.9
14. Alabama	198.3
15. Maryland	193.7
16. Pennsylvania	192.9
17. Delaware	180.5
18. Rhode Island	178.4
19. Idaho	178.1
* UNITED STATES	175.3
20. Missouri	170.1
21. Arizona	164.9
22. Wisconsin	160.1
23. Kansas	158.8
24. Louisiana	154.7
25. Virginia	154.6
26. Iowa	154.4
27. Colorado	153.8
28. Tennessee	153.2
29. North Carolina	150.0
30. California	149.6
31. Georgia	149.6
32. Nevada	147.0
33. Wyoming	144.6
34. Texas	143.4
35. Florida	142.7
36. South Carolina	141.8
37. Maine	138.4
38. Utah	134.8
39. Mississippi	130.9
40. Vermont	107.8
41. West Virginia	105.3
42. Oregon	104.0
43. Arkansas	100.4
44. Montana	95.6
45. Oklahoma	92.8
46. Washington	92.7
47. South Dakota	91.6
48. Hawaii	88.4
49. Alaska	68.0
50. New Mexico	65.9
51. District of Columbia	NA

©2008 Information Publications, inc.
All Rights Reserved. Photocopying prohibited.
877-544-INFO (4636) or www.informationpublications.com

Comparative Tables

23. Overweight Persons, 2006

1.	West Virginia	67.0%
2.	Mississippi	66.7
3.	Kentucky	66.4
4.	South Carolina	65.4
5.	Tennessee	65.3
6.	Alabama	65.0
7.	Michigan	64.8
8.	Oklahoma	64.8
9.	North Dakota	64.5
10.	Alaska	64.2
11.	South Dakota	64.1
12.	Nebraska	63.9
13.	Ohio	63.9
14.	Arkansas	63.8
15.	Delaware	63.8
16.	Nevada	63.6
17.	Wisconsin	63.4
18.	Louisiana	63.0
19.	Iowa	62.9
20.	Missouri	62.9
21.	Indiana	62.8
22.	North Carolina	62.8
23.	Minnesota	62.7
24.	Texas	62.4
25.	Kansas	62.3
26.	Virginia	61.8
27.	Georgia	61.7
28.	Illinois	61.7
*	UNITED STATES	61.6
29.	Wyoming	61.4
30.	Pennsylvania	61.3
31.	Rhode Island	61.0
32.	Maryland	60.7
33.	New Hampshire	60.7
34.	Oregon	60.7
35.	Washington	60.7
36.	New Jersey	59.9
37.	New Mexico	59.8
38.	Idaho	59.7
39.	Maine	59.7
40.	Arizona	59.6
41.	Florida	59.6
42.	Montana	59.3
43.	California	58.8
44.	Connecticut	58.8
45.	New York	58.3
46.	Hawaii	56.1
47.	Vermont	56.0
48.	Massachusetts	55.5
49.	Colorado	54.9
50.	Utah	54.9
51.	District of Columbia	54.6

24. Obese Persons, 2006

1.	Mississippi	31.4%
2.	West Virginia	31.0
3.	Alabama	30.5
4.	South Carolina	29.4
5.	Michigan	28.8
6.	Oklahoma	28.8
7.	Tennessee	28.8
8.	Ohio	28.4
9.	Kentucky	28.0
10.	Indiana	27.8
11.	Missouri	27.2
12.	Georgia	27.1
13.	Louisiana	27.1
14.	Arkansas	26.9
15.	Nebraska	26.9
16.	North Carolina	26.6
17.	Wisconsin	26.6
18.	Alaska	26.2
19.	Texas	26.1
20.	Delaware	26.0
21.	Kansas	25.9
22.	Iowa	25.7
23.	North Dakota	25.4
24.	South Dakota	25.4
25.	Illinois	25.1
26.	Virginia	25.1
*	UNITED STATES	25.1
27.	Nevada	25.0
28.	Maryland	24.9
29.	Oregon	24.8
30.	Minnesota	24.7
31.	Washington	24.2
32.	Idaho	24.1
33.	Pennsylvania	24.0
34.	California	23.3
35.	Wyoming	23.3
36.	Florida	23.1
37.	Maine	23.1
38.	Arizona	22.9
39.	New Mexico	22.9
40.	New York	22.9
41.	New Jersey	22.6
42.	District of Columbia	22.5
43.	New Hampshire	22.4
44.	Utah	21.9
45.	Rhode Island	21.4
46.	Montana	21.2
47.	Vermont	21.2
48.	Connecticut	20.6
49.	Hawaii	20.6
50.	Massachusetts	20.3
51.	Colorado	18.2

©2008 Information Publications, Inc.
All Rights Reserved. Photocopying prohibited.
877-544-INFO (4636) or www.informationpublications.com

Comparative Tables

<table>
<tr><td colspan="2">25. People who Get No Regular Exercise, 2005</td></tr>
<tr><td>1. Louisiana</td><td>33.4%</td></tr>
<tr><td>2. Tennessee</td><td>33.1</td></tr>
<tr><td>3. Mississippi</td><td>32.4</td></tr>
<tr><td>4. Kentucky</td><td>31.5</td></tr>
<tr><td>5. Arkansas</td><td>30.6</td></tr>
<tr><td>6. Oklahoma</td><td>30.6</td></tr>
<tr><td>7. Alabama</td><td>29.7</td></tr>
<tr><td>8. New Jersey</td><td>29.2</td></tr>
<tr><td>9. West Virginia</td><td>28.5</td></tr>
<tr><td>10. Texas</td><td>27.4</td></tr>
<tr><td>11. Georgia</td><td>27.2</td></tr>
<tr><td>12. New York</td><td>27.1</td></tr>
<tr><td>13. Florida</td><td>26.9</td></tr>
<tr><td>14. Indiana</td><td>26.9</td></tr>
<tr><td>15. Nevada</td><td>26.8</td></tr>
<tr><td>16. South Carolina</td><td>26.3</td></tr>
<tr><td>17. Rhode Island</td><td>25.9</td></tr>
<tr><td>18. Pennsylvania</td><td>25.8</td></tr>
<tr><td>19. Illinois</td><td>25.6</td></tr>
<tr><td>20. North Carolina</td><td>25.6</td></tr>
<tr><td>21. Ohio</td><td>25.6</td></tr>
<tr><td>22. Missouri</td><td>25.4</td></tr>
<tr><td>23. Iowa</td><td>24.7</td></tr>
<tr><td>24. Kansas</td><td>24.4</td></tr>
<tr><td>25. California</td><td>23.9</td></tr>
<tr><td>* UNITED STATES</td><td>23.9</td></tr>
<tr><td>26. Nebraska</td><td>23.8</td></tr>
<tr><td>27. Delaware</td><td>23.3</td></tr>
<tr><td>28. Massachusetts</td><td>23.3</td></tr>
<tr><td>29. New Mexico</td><td>23.3</td></tr>
<tr><td>30. North Dakota</td><td>23.1</td></tr>
<tr><td>31. Maryland</td><td>22.9</td></tr>
<tr><td>32. Arizona</td><td>22.6</td></tr>
<tr><td>33. District of Columbia</td><td>22.5</td></tr>
<tr><td>34. Michigan</td><td>22.5</td></tr>
<tr><td>35. South Dakota</td><td>22.5</td></tr>
<tr><td>36. Montana</td><td>22.4</td></tr>
<tr><td>37. Maine</td><td>22.3</td></tr>
<tr><td>38. Wyoming</td><td>22.0</td></tr>
<tr><td>39. Idaho</td><td>21.6</td></tr>
<tr><td>40. New Hampshire</td><td>21.6</td></tr>
<tr><td>41. Alaska</td><td>21.4</td></tr>
<tr><td>42. Virginia</td><td>21.3</td></tr>
<tr><td>43. Connecticut</td><td>21.2</td></tr>
<tr><td>44. Hawaii</td><td>19.5</td></tr>
<tr><td>45. Vermont</td><td>19.2</td></tr>
<tr><td>46. Wisconsin</td><td>18.7</td></tr>
<tr><td>47. Oregon</td><td>18.6</td></tr>
<tr><td>48. Utah</td><td>18.5</td></tr>
<tr><td>49. Washington</td><td>17.4</td></tr>
<tr><td>50. Colorado</td><td>17.3</td></tr>
<tr><td>51. Minnesota</td><td>16.2</td></tr>
</table>

<table>
<tr><td colspan="2">26. People who Regularly Get at Least Moderate Exercise, 2005</td></tr>
<tr><td>1. Alaska</td><td>59.2%</td></tr>
<tr><td>2. Vermont</td><td>57.7</td></tr>
<tr><td>3. Wisconsin</td><td>56.6</td></tr>
<tr><td>4. Montana</td><td>56.5</td></tr>
<tr><td>5. Oregon</td><td>56.4</td></tr>
<tr><td>6. Wyoming</td><td>56.2</td></tr>
<tr><td>7. New Hampshire</td><td>56.0</td></tr>
<tr><td>8. Utah</td><td>55.0</td></tr>
<tr><td>9. Washington</td><td>54.7</td></tr>
<tr><td>10. Colorado</td><td>54.4</td></tr>
<tr><td>11. Maine</td><td>54.1</td></tr>
<tr><td>12. Idaho</td><td>54.0</td></tr>
<tr><td>13. Arizona</td><td>53.4</td></tr>
<tr><td>14. California</td><td>53.4</td></tr>
<tr><td>15. District of Columbia</td><td>53.1</td></tr>
<tr><td>16. Massachusetts</td><td>52.6</td></tr>
<tr><td>17. Hawaii</td><td>52.2</td></tr>
<tr><td>18. Connecticut</td><td>51.2</td></tr>
<tr><td>19. Rhode Island</td><td>51.1</td></tr>
<tr><td>20. Minnesota</td><td>51.0</td></tr>
<tr><td>21. New Mexico</td><td>51.0</td></tr>
<tr><td>22. Virginia</td><td>50.8</td></tr>
<tr><td>23. Nevada</td><td>50.7</td></tr>
<tr><td>24. Michigan</td><td>49.5</td></tr>
<tr><td>25. Ohio</td><td>49.2</td></tr>
<tr><td>26. Maryland</td><td>49.1</td></tr>
<tr><td>27. Kansas</td><td>48.7</td></tr>
<tr><td>28. Pennsylvania</td><td>48.7</td></tr>
<tr><td>* UNITED STATES</td><td>48.7</td></tr>
<tr><td>29. North Dakota</td><td>48.4</td></tr>
<tr><td>30. New York</td><td>48.1</td></tr>
<tr><td>31. Indiana</td><td>47.7</td></tr>
<tr><td>32. South Dakota</td><td>47.6</td></tr>
<tr><td>33. Nebraska</td><td>47.3</td></tr>
<tr><td>34. Illinois</td><td>47.1</td></tr>
<tr><td>35. Texas</td><td>46.7</td></tr>
<tr><td>36. Arkansas</td><td>46.4</td></tr>
<tr><td>37. Missouri</td><td>46.4</td></tr>
<tr><td>38. Iowa</td><td>46.2</td></tr>
<tr><td>39. New Jersey</td><td>45.9</td></tr>
<tr><td>40. Florida</td><td>45.3</td></tr>
<tr><td>41. South Carolina</td><td>45.3</td></tr>
<tr><td>42. Delaware</td><td>45.2</td></tr>
<tr><td>43. Alabama</td><td>42.8</td></tr>
<tr><td>44. Oklahoma</td><td>42.3</td></tr>
<tr><td>45. North Carolina</td><td>42.1</td></tr>
<tr><td>46. Georgia</td><td>42.0</td></tr>
<tr><td>47. Mississippi</td><td>40.0</td></tr>
<tr><td>48. West Virginia</td><td>39.4</td></tr>
<tr><td>49. Louisiana</td><td>38.3</td></tr>
<tr><td>50. Tennessee</td><td>36.1</td></tr>
<tr><td>51. Kentucky</td><td>34.7</td></tr>
</table>

©2008 Information Publications, Inc.
All Rights Reserved. Photocopying prohibited.
877-544-INFO (4636) or www.informationpublications.com

Comparative Tables

27. People who Regularly Get Vigorous Exercise, 2005

1.	California	36.2%
2.	Alaska	35.9
3.	Utah	34.3
4.	Montana	33.1
5.	Vermont	33.1
6.	Wyoming	33.1
7.	New Hampshire	32.9
8.	Wisconsin	32.8
9.	Colorado	32.6
10.	Nevada	32.6
11.	District of Columbia	31.5
12.	Idaho	31.1
13.	Connecticut	31.0
14.	Maine	30.8
15.	Oregon	30.7
16.	Washington	30.6
17.	Virginia	30.4
18.	Hawaii	30.2
19.	Rhode Island	29.9
20.	Massachusetts	29.7
21.	Maryland	29.6
22.	New Mexico	29.0
23.	Arizona	28.9
24.	Minnesota	28.3
25.	Michigan	28.1
26.	North Dakota	27.5
27.	Pennsylvania	27.4
*	UNITED STATES	27.4
28.	New York	27.3
29.	Ohio	27.2
30.	Indiana	27.1
31.	Illinois	25.7
32.	New Jersey	25.5
33.	Missouri	25.3
34.	Texas	25.3
35.	Kansas	25.0
36.	Delaware	24.9
37.	Arkansas	24.8
38.	Nebraska	24.7
39.	Florida	24.6
40.	South Carolina	24.6
41.	Georgia	23.7
42.	South Dakota	23.5
43.	Iowa	22.9
44.	Oklahoma	22.5
45.	North Carolina	22.2
46.	Mississippi	20.9
47.	Louisiana	20.7
48.	Alabama	20.3
49.	West Virginia	17.6
50.	Tennessee	17.4
51.	Kentucky	16.8

28. Abortions Performed, 2004

*	UNITED STATES	839,226
1.	New York	126,002
2.	Florida	91,710
3.	Texas	74,801
4.	Illinois	43,537
5.	Pennsylvania	36,030
6.	Ohio	34,242
7.	North Carolina	33,954
8.	New Jersey	32,642
9.	Georgia	32,513
10.	Michigan	26,269
11.	Virginia	26,117
12.	Washington	24,664
13.	Massachusetts	24,366
14.	Tennessee	16,400
15.	Minnesota	13,791
16.	Arizona	12,690
17.	Connecticut	12,189
18.	Oregon	11,443
19.	Colorado	11,415
20.	Alabama	11,370
21.	Kansas	11,357
22.	Louisiana	11,224
23.	Indiana	10,514
24.	Maryland	10,096
25.	Wisconsin	9,943
26.	Nevada	9,856
27.	Missouri	8,072
28.	Oklahoma	6,712
29.	South Carolina	6,565
30.	New Mexico	6,070
31.	Iowa	6,022
32.	Rhode Island	5,587
33.	Arkansas	4,644
34.	Delaware	4,588
35.	Utah	3,665
36.	Nebraska	3,584
37.	Kentucky	3,557
38.	Mississippi	3,500
39.	Hawaii	3,467
40.	Maine	2,593
41.	District of Columbia	2,401
42.	Montana	2,256
43.	Alaska	1,937
44.	Vermont	1,725
45.	North Dakota	1,357
46.	Idaho	963
47.	South Dakota	814
48.	Wyoming	12
49.	California	NA
50.	New Hampshire	NA
51.	West Virginia	NA

434

©2008 Information Publications, Inc.
All Rights Reserved. Photocopying prohibited.
877-544-INFO (4636) or www.informationpublications.com

Comparative Tables

29. High School Graduates or higher, 2006

1.	Minnesota	90.7%
2.	Utah	90.2
3.	Wyoming	90.2
4.	Montana	90.1
5.	New Hampshire	89.9
6.	Vermont	89.8
7.	Alaska	89.7
8.	Nebraska	89.5
9.	Hawaii	89.0
10.	Washington	89.0
11.	Iowa	88.9
12.	Maine	88.7
13.	Kansas	88.5
14.	Wisconsin	88.4
15.	South Dakota	88.3
16.	North Dakota	88.1
17.	Colorado	88.0
18.	Connecticut	88.0
19.	Massachusetts	87.9
20.	Oregon	87.6
21.	Idaho	87.3
22.	Michigan	87.2
23.	Maryland	87.1
24.	Ohio	86.2
25.	Pennsylvania	86.2
26.	New Jersey	86.1
27.	Delaware	85.5
28.	Virginia	85.4
29.	Indiana	85.2
30.	Illinois	85.0
31.	Missouri	84.8
32.	Florida	84.5
33.	District of Columbia	84.3
34.	Oklahoma	84.3
35.	New York	84.1
*	UNITED STATES	84.1
36.	Nevada	83.9
37.	Arizona	83.8
38.	Rhode Island	82.4
39.	Georgia	82.2
40.	North Carolina	82.0
41.	New Mexico	81.5
42.	South Carolina	81.3
43.	West Virginia	81.0
44.	Tennessee	80.9
45.	Arkansas	80.5
46.	Alabama	80.1
47.	California	80.1
48.	Kentucky	79.6
49.	Louisiana	79.4
50.	Texas	78.6
51.	Mississippi	77.9

30. Bachelor's Degree or higher, 2006

1.	District of Columbia	45.9%
2.	Massachusetts	37.0
3.	Maryland	35.1
4.	Colorado	34.3
5.	Connecticut	33.7
6.	New Jersey	33.4
7.	Virginia	32.7
8.	Vermont	32.4
9.	New Hampshire	31.9
10.	New York	31.2
11.	Washington	30.5
12.	Minnesota	30.4
13.	Hawaii	29.7
14.	Rhode Island	29.6
15.	California	29.0
16.	Illinois	28.9
17.	Kansas	28.6
18.	Utah	28.6
19.	Oregon	27.5
20.	Montana	27.4
21.	Delaware	27.0
*	UNITED STATES	27.0
22.	Alaska	26.9
23.	Nebraska	26.9
24.	Georgia	26.6
25.	Maine	25.8
26.	North Dakota	25.6
27.	Arizona	25.5
28.	Pennsylvania	25.4
29.	Florida	25.3
30.	New Mexico	25.3
31.	Wisconsin	25.1
32.	North Carolina	24.8
33.	South Dakota	24.8
34.	Texas	24.7
35.	Michigan	24.5
36.	Missouri	24.3
37.	Iowa	24.0
38.	Idaho	23.3
39.	Ohio	23.0
40.	South Carolina	22.7
41.	Wyoming	22.7
42.	Oklahoma	22.1
43.	Indiana	21.7
44.	Tennessee	21.7
45.	Alabama	21.1
46.	Nevada	20.8
47.	Louisiana	20.3
48.	Kentucky	20.0
49.	Mississippi	18.8
50.	Arkansas	18.2
51.	West Virginia	16.5

©2008 Information Publications, Inc.
All Rights Reserved. Photocopying prohibited.
877-544-INFO (4636) or www.informationpublications.com

Comparative Tables

31. NAEP – 4th Graders Scoring Basic or Better in Math, 2007

1.	Massachusetts	93.2%
2.	New Hampshire	91.3
3.	North Dakota	90.8
4.	New Jersey	89.6
5.	Kansas	89.4
6.	Vermont	89.0
7.	Indiana	88.9
8.	Wyoming	88.5
9.	Montana	87.7
10.	Minnesota	87.5
11.	Ohio	87.5
12.	Texas	87.4
13.	Virginia	87.3
14.	Delaware	86.9
15.	Iowa	86.6
16.	Florida	86.2
17.	South Dakota	86.1
18.	Maine	85.5
19.	Wisconsin	85.3
20.	New York	85.1
21.	Pennsylvania	85.1
22.	North Carolina	84.9
23.	Idaho	84.5
24.	Washington	84.3
25.	Connecticut	83.9
26.	Utah	82.7
27.	Oklahoma	82.4
28.	Missouri	82.0
*	UNITED STATES	82.0
29.	Colorado	81.8
30.	West Virginia	81.2
31.	Arkansas	80.7
32.	Nebraska	80.1
33.	Maryland	80.0
34.	Michigan	79.9
35.	South Carolina	79.7
36.	Rhode Island	79.6
37.	Kentucky	79.3
38.	Alaska	78.8
39.	Georgia	78.6
40.	Illinois	78.6
41.	Oregon	78.6
42.	Hawaii	76.9
43.	Tennessee	76.1
44.	Arizona	73.7
45.	Nevada	73.7
46.	Louisiana	72.9
47.	New Mexico	70.3
48.	Alabama	70.2
49.	Mississippi	69.9
50.	California	69.6
51.	District of Columbia	49.3

32. NAEP – 4th Graders Scoring Proficient or Better in Math, 2007

1.	Massachusetts	57.6%
2.	New Hampshire	51.8
3.	New Jersey	51.8
4.	Kansas	51.1
5.	Minnesota	50.6
6.	Vermont	49.0
7.	Pennsylvania	47.0
8.	Wisconsin	46.9
9.	Indiana	46.3
10.	Ohio	45.9
11.	North Dakota	45.7
12.	Connecticut	44.7
13.	Montana	44.4
14.	Wyoming	44.3
15.	Washington	43.8
16.	New York	43.3
17.	Iowa	43.0
18.	Virginia	41.9
19.	Maine	41.8
20.	Colorado	41.2
21.	North Carolina	41.0
22.	South Dakota	40.6
23.	Florida	40.3
24.	Texas	40.2
25.	Idaho	40.1
26.	Maryland	40.1
27.	Delaware	40.0
28.	Utah	39.4
*	UNITED STATES	39.0
29.	Missouri	38.4
30.	Alaska	37.9
31.	Nebraska	37.9
32.	Michigan	37.1
33.	Arkansas	36.7
34.	Illinois	36.3
35.	South Carolina	35.9
36.	Oregon	35.0
37.	Rhode Island	34.0
38.	Hawaii	33.3
39.	Oklahoma	32.6
40.	West Virginia	32.6
41.	Georgia	31.6
42.	Kentucky	30.8
43.	Arizona	30.6
44.	Nevada	30.1
45.	California	29.7
46.	Tennessee	28.7
47.	Alabama	25.8
48.	New Mexico	24.5
49.	Louisiana	24.4
50.	Mississippi	21.3
51.	District of Columbia	13.5

©2008 Information Publications, Inc.
All Rights Reserved. Photocopying prohibited.
877-544-INFO (4636) or www.informationpublications.com

Comparative Tables

33. NAEP – 4th Graders Scoring Basic or Better in Reading, 2007

1.	Massachusetts	81.1%
2.	New Jersey	77.2
3.	New Hampshire	76.0
4.	North Dakota	75.3
5.	Montana	75.0
6.	Vermont	74.4
7.	Virginia	74.4
8.	Iowa	73.7
9.	Wyoming	73.5
10.	Ohio	73.3
11.	Maine	73.1
12.	Minnesota	72.8
13.	Connecticut	72.6
14.	Delaware	72.6
15.	Pennsylvania	72.6
16.	Kansas	71.8
17.	South Dakota	70.9
18.	Nebraska	70.8
19.	Florida	70.4
20.	Wisconsin	70.4
21.	Idaho	70.3
22.	Washington	70.3
23.	Colorado	70.0
24.	New York	69.3
25.	Maryland	68.9
26.	Utah	68.6
27.	Kentucky	68.4
28.	Indiana	68.2
29.	Missouri	67.1
*	UNITED STATES	67.0
30.	Michigan	66.2
31.	Texas	65.8
32.	Georgia	65.6
33.	Rhode Island	65.4
34.	Illinois	65.0
35.	Oklahoma	65.0
36.	North Carolina	63.9
37.	Arkansas	63.5
38.	West Virginia	62.6
39.	Oregon	61.9
40.	Alaska	61.7
41.	Alabama	61.6
42.	Tennessee	60.6
43.	Hawaii	59.0
44.	South Carolina	58.9
45.	New Mexico	57.6
46.	Nevada	57.1
47.	Arizona	55.9
48.	California	53.2
49.	Louisiana	51.9
50.	Mississippi	51.5
51.	District of Columbia	38.7

34. NAEP – 4th Graders Scoring Proficient or Better in Reading, 2007

1.	Massachusetts	49.2%
2.	New Jersey	43.1
3.	Connecticut	41.2
4.	New Hampshire	41.1
5.	Vermont	40.9
6.	Pennsylvania	40.2
7.	Montana	38.5
8.	Virginia	37.6
9.	Minnesota	36.9
10.	Wyoming	36.4
11.	Ohio	36.3
12.	Washington	36.3
13.	Colorado	36.2
14.	Iowa	36.1
15.	Kansas	36.1
16.	New York	36.0
17.	Maryland	35.9
18.	Maine	35.8
19.	Wisconsin	35.6
20.	North Dakota	35.3
21.	Idaho	35.1
22.	Nebraska	34.6
23.	Florida	34.0
24.	Utah	33.9
25.	Delaware	33.8
26.	South Dakota	33.7
27.	Kentucky	33.5
28.	Indiana	33.0
*	UNITED STATES	33.0
29.	Michigan	32.4
30.	Illinois	32.2
31.	Missouri	31.8
32.	Rhode Island	30.8
33.	Texas	29.6
34.	North Carolina	29.1
35.	Alabama	28.9
36.	Alaska	28.7
37.	Arkansas	28.6
38.	Georgia	28.3
39.	Oregon	28.3
40.	West Virginia	27.8
41.	Tennessee	26.9
42.	Oklahoma	26.8
43.	South Carolina	25.8
44.	Hawaii	25.7
45.	Nevada	24.4
46.	Arizona	24.2
47.	New Mexico	24.0
48.	California	22.9
49.	Louisiana	20.4
50.	Mississippi	18.7
51.	District of Columbia	13.8

©2008 Information Publications, Inc.
All Rights Reserved. Photocopying prohibited.
877-544-INFO (4636) or www.informationpublications.com

Comparative Tables

35. NAEP – 8th Graders Scoring Basic or Better in Math, 2007

1.	North Dakota	85.5%
2.	Massachusetts	85.0
3.	Kansas	81.4
4.	South Dakota	81.2
5.	Vermont	81.1
6.	Minnesota	81.0
7.	Wyoming	79.8
8.	Montana	79.1
9.	Maine	78.3
10.	New Hampshire	77.6
11.	Texas	77.6
12.	New Jersey	77.5
13.	Iowa	77.2
14.	Virginia	77.0
15.	Pennsylvania	76.9
16.	Ohio	76.4
17.	Wisconsin	75.9
18.	Indiana	75.7
19.	Colorado	75.1
20.	Washington	74.9
21.	Idaho	74.7
22.	Delaware	74.3
23.	Nebraska	74.3
24.	Maryland	73.6
25.	Alaska	73.0
26.	Oregon	73.0
27.	North Carolina	72.9
28.	Connecticut	72.8
29.	Missouri	72.2
30.	Utah	72.1
*	UNITED STATES	71.0
31.	South Carolina	70.9
32.	Illinois	70.3
33.	New York	70.3
34.	Kentucky	69.0
35.	Florida	68.1
36.	Arizona	66.5
37.	Michigan	66.4
38.	Oklahoma	66.1
39.	Rhode Island	65.5
40.	Arkansas	64.7
41.	Georgia	64.2
42.	Louisiana	63.9
43.	Tennessee	63.9
44.	West Virginia	61.2
45.	Nevada	60.2
46.	California	59.1
47.	Hawaii	59.1
48.	New Mexico	56.6
49.	Alabama	55.3
50.	Mississippi	53.8
51.	District of Columbia	34.1

36. NAEP – 8th Graders Scoring Proficient or Better in Math, 2007

1.	Massachusetts	50.7%
2.	Minnesota	43.1
3.	Vermont	41.4
4.	North Dakota	41.0
5.	New Jersey	40.4
6.	Kansas	40.2
7.	South Dakota	39.1
8.	Pennsylvania	38.3
9.	New Hampshire	37.9
10.	Montana	37.6
11.	Virginia	37.5
12.	Colorado	37.4
13.	Wisconsin	37.0
14.	Maryland	36.5
15.	Wyoming	36.0
16.	Washington	35.9
17.	Ohio	35.4
18.	Iowa	35.2
19.	Indiana	35.1
20.	Oregon	34.8
21.	Connecticut	34.7
22.	Texas	34.7
23.	Nebraska	34.6
24.	North Carolina	34.5
25.	Idaho	34.1
26.	Maine	34.1
27.	Utah	32.4
28.	Alaska	32.2
*	UNITED STATES	32.0
29.	South Carolina	31.9
30.	Delaware	31.3
31.	Illinois	30.8
32.	New York	30.2
33.	Missouri	29.9
34.	Michigan	28.9
35.	Rhode Island	27.7
36.	Florida	27.4
37.	Kentucky	27.3
38.	Arizona	26.3
39.	Georgia	24.7
40.	Arkansas	24.4
41.	California	23.9
42.	Tennessee	23.1
43.	Nevada	23.0
44.	Oklahoma	21.3
45.	Hawaii	21.2
46.	Louisiana	19.0
47.	West Virginia	18.5
48.	Alabama	18.2
49.	New Mexico	17.4
50.	Mississippi	13.6
51.	District of Columbia	8.0

©2008 Information Publications, Inc.
All Rights Reserved. Photocopying prohibited.
877-544-INFO (4636) or www.informationpublications.com

Comparative Tables

37. NAEP – 8th Graders Scoring Basic or Better in Reading, 2007

1. Montana	84.5%
2. Vermont	84.4
3. Massachusetts	83.9
4. North Dakota	83.6
5. South Dakota	83.5
6. Maine	82.8
7. New Hampshire	81.9
8. New Jersey	81.1
9. Kansas	80.6
10. Minnesota	80.2
11. Iowa	79.8
12. Wyoming	79.7
13. Ohio	79.4
14. Nebraska	78.8
15. Colorado	78.7
16. Virginia	78.7
17. Pennsylvania	78.6
18. Idaho	78.5
19. Delaware	77.2
20. Oregon	77.2
21. Connecticut	76.7
22. Washington	76.7
23. Indiana	76.1
24. Wisconsin	75.9
25. Maryland	75.6
26. New York	75.1
27. Utah	75.0
28. Illinois	74.9
29. Missouri	74.9
* UNITED STATES	74.0
30. Kentucky	73.3
31. Texas	73.0
32. Michigan	72.1
33. Oklahoma	72.1
34. Florida	71.5
35. Tennessee	71.3
36. North Carolina	71.0
37. Alaska	70.8
38. Georgia	70.1
39. Arkansas	69.6
40. Rhode Island	69.3
41. South Carolina	68.7
42. West Virginia	68.4
43. Arizona	64.9
44. Louisiana	64.2
45. Nevada	63.1
46. Hawaii	62.5
47. New Mexico	62.5
48. Alabama	62.3
49. California	62.3
50. Mississippi	60.3
51. District of Columbia	47.9

38. NAEP – 8th Graders Scoring Proficient or Better in Reading, 2007

1. Massachusetts	43.0%
2. Vermont	42.1
3. New Jersey	39.0
4. Montana	38.9
5. New Hampshire	37.2
6. Connecticut	37.1
7. Maine	36.9
8. South Dakota	36.8
9. Minnesota	36.6
10. Pennsylvania	36.4
11. Ohio	35.9
12. Iowa	35.7
13. Kansas	35.2
14. Nebraska	35.0
15. Colorado	34.6
16. Washington	34.1
17. Oregon	34.0
18. Virginia	33.7
19. Maryland	33.2
20. Wisconsin	33.2
21. Wyoming	33.2
22. New York	32.2
23. North Dakota	32.2
24. Idaho	31.6
25. Indiana	31.1
26. Missouri	31.0
* UNITED STATES	31.0
27. Delaware	30.5
28. Utah	30.1
29. Illinois	29.8
30. Michigan	28.2
31. Florida	28.0
32. North Carolina	28.0
33. Kentucky	27.7
34. Texas	27.5
35. Rhode Island	27.2
36. Alaska	27.1
37. Oklahoma	26.1
38. Georgia	25.6
39. Tennessee	25.6
40. Arkansas	25.4
41. South Carolina	24.6
42. Arizona	24.3
43. West Virginia	22.9
44. California	21.5
45. Nevada	21.5
46. Alabama	21.2
47. Hawaii	20.3
48. Louisiana	19.4
49. Mississippi	17.4
50. New Mexico	17.3
51. District of Columbia	12.1

©2008 Information Publications, Inc.
All Rights Reserved. Photocopying prohibited.
877-544-INFO (4636) or www.informationpublications.com

Comparative Tables

39. SAT Participation, 2007

1. Maine	100%
2. New York	89
3. Massachusetts	85
4. Connecticut	84
5. New Hampshire	83
6. New Jersey	82
7. District of Columbia	78
8. Pennsylvania	75
9. Virginia	73
10. Delaware	72
11. North Carolina	71
12. Maryland	70
13. Georgia	69
14. Rhode Island	68
15. Vermont	67
16. Florida	65
17. Indiana	62
18. South Carolina	62
19. Hawaii	61
20. Oregon	54
21. Washington	53
22. Texas	52
23. California	49
24. Alaska	48
* UNITED STATES	48
25. Nevada	41
26. Arizona	32
27. Montana	28
28. Ohio	27
29. Colorado	24
30. West Virginia	20
31. Idaho	19
32. Tennessee	13
33. New Mexico	12
34. Kentucky	10
35. Alabama	9
36. Michigan	9
37. Minnesota	9
38. Illinois	8
39. Kansas	8
40. Wyoming	8
41. Louisiana	7
42. Missouri	6
43. Nebraska	6
44. Oklahoma	6
45. Utah	6
46. Wisconsin	6
47. Arkansas	5
48. Iowa	4
49. Mississippi	4
50. North Dakota	4
51. South Dakota	3

40. Average Public School Teacher Salary, 2006-07

1. California	$63,640
2. Connecticut	60,822
3. New Jersey	59,920
4. District of Columbia	59,000
5. Massachusetts	58,624
6. New York	58,537
7. Illinois	58,246
8. Maryland	56,927
9. Rhode Island	55,956
10. Pennsylvania	54,970
11. Michigan	54,895
12. Delaware	54,680
13. Alaska	54,658
14. Ohio	51,937
15. Hawaii	51,922
16. Oregon	50,911
* UNITED STATES	50,816
17. Wyoming	50,692
18. Georgia	49,905
19. Minnesota	49,634
20. Vermont	48,370
21. Wisconsin	47,901
22. Washington	47,882
23. Indiana	47,831
24. New Hampshire	46,527
25. North Carolina	46,410
26. Arizona	45,941
27. Colorado	45,833
28. Nevada	45,342
29. Florida	45,308
30. Texas	44,897
31. Virginia	44,727
32. Arkansas	44,245
33. South Carolina	44,133
34. Tennessee	43,816
35. Kentucky	43,646
36. Alabama	43,389
37. Kansas	43,334
38. Iowa	43,130
39. Louisiana	42,816
40. Idaho	42,798
41. New Mexico	42,780
42. Oklahoma	42,379
43. Nebraska	42,044
44. Missouri	41,839
45. Maine	41,596
46. Montana	41,225
47. Utah	40,566
48. West Virginia	40,531
49. Mississippi	40,182
50. North Dakota	38,822
51. South Dakota	35,378

©2008 Information Publications, Inc.
All Rights Reserved. Photocopying prohibited.
877-544-INFO (4636) or www.informationpublications.com

Comparative Tables

41. Expenditures for Public Schools, per capita, 2006-07

1.	New Jersey	$2,336
2.	Wyoming	2,190
3.	Connecticut	2,129
4.	New York	2,067
5.	Alaska	2,060
6.	Massachusetts	1,999
7.	Vermont	1,986
8.	Delaware	1,800
9.	Maine	1,787
10.	Michigan	1,754
11.	Rhode Island	1,748
12.	Illinois	1,717
13.	Ohio	1,717
14.	New Hampshire	1,690
15.	District of Columbia	1,685
16.	Pennsylvania	1,655
17.	Wisconsin	1,646
18.	Minnesota	1,627
19.	Virginia	1,574
20.	Texas	1,567
21.	Maryland	1,561
*	UNITED STATES	1,561
22.	West Virginia	1,558
23.	Georgia	1,531
24.	Indiana	1,530
25.	California	1,523
26.	New Mexico	1,519
27.	Kansas	1,500
28.	Colorado	1,486
29.	South Carolina	1,480
30.	Hawaii	1,466
31.	Arkansas	1,441
32.	Washington	1,404
33.	Oregon	1,367
34.	Louisiana	1,365
35.	Nebraska	1,349
36.	Montana	1,327
37.	Iowa	1,319
38.	Idaho	1,309
39.	Kentucky	1,300
40.	North Carolina	1,267
41.	South Dakota	1,267
42.	Oklahoma	1,265
43.	Missouri	1,256
44.	Florida	1,251
45.	North Dakota	1,237
46.	Alabama	1,234
47.	Nevada	1,190
48.	Mississippi	1,166
49.	Tennessee	1,142
50.	Utah	1,058
51.	Arizona	955

(calculated using 7/1/2006 population est.)

42. Expenditures for Public Schools, per pupil, 2006-07

1.	District of Columbia	$18,260
2.	Vermont	15,940
3.	New York	15,263
4.	New Jersey	14,824
5.	Wyoming	14,235
6.	Massachusetts	14,125
7.	Delaware	13,380
8.	Connecticut	13,370
9.	Maine	13,025
10.	Pennsylvania	12,121
11.	Rhode Island	12,095
12.	Ohio	11,947
13.	Alaska	11,900
14.	New Hampshire	11,879
15.	Hawaii	11,529
16.	Illinois	11,489
17.	Michigan	11,149
18.	Wisconsin	11,019
19.	Maryland	10,824
20.	Minnesota	10,809
21.	Virginia	10,599
22.	Arkansas	10,398
23.	Oregon	10,251
24.	West Virginia	10,236
*	UNITED STATES	10,212
25.	Kansas	10,119
26.	Montana	10,119
27.	New Mexico	10,106
28.	Indiana	10,044
29.	South Carolina	9,891
30.	Colorado	9,592
31.	Georgia	9,502
32.	Louisiana	9,355
33.	Washington	9,334
34.	Kentucky	9,214
35.	California	9,156
36.	North Dakota	9,036
37.	Nebraska	9,028
38.	Florida	8,928
39.	Missouri	8,857
40.	South Dakota	8,741
41.	Iowa	8,684
42.	Texas	8,573
43.	North Carolina	8,544
44.	Alabama	7,908
45.	Tennessee	7,773
46.	Idaho	7,649
47.	Oklahoma	7,593
48.	Mississippi	7,189
49.	Nevada	7,060
50.	Utah	6,060
51.	Arizona	5,896

©2008 Information Publications, Inc.
All Rights Reserved. Photocopying prohibited.
877-544-INFO (4636) or www.informationpublications.com

Comparative Tables

43. Public School Revenue, 2006-07 (x $1 million)

*	UNITED STATES	$530,340
1.	California	67,460
2.	Texas	44,267
3.	New York	43,033
4.	Florida	27,556
5.	Pennsylvania	23,871
6.	Illinois	21,566
7.	Ohio	21,510
8.	New Jersey	21,167
9.	Michigan	19,580
10.	Georgia	16,777
11.	Massachusetts	14,585
12.	Virginia	13,445
13.	North Carolina	11,281
14.	Indiana	10,948
15.	Maryland	10,523
16.	Washington	10,395
17.	Wisconsin	10,130
18.	Minnesota	9,429
19.	Missouri	9,242
20.	Arizona	8,431
21.	Connecticut	8,331
22.	Colorado	7,428
23.	Tennessee	7,422
24.	Louisiana	7,115
25.	South Carolina	6,870
26.	Alabama	6,139
27.	Kentucky	6,061
28.	Oregon	5,742
29.	Oklahoma	5,054
30.	Kansas	4,923
31.	Iowa	4,814
32.	Arkansas	4,308
33.	Mississippi	3,933
34.	Utah	3,470
35.	New Mexico	3,277
36.	Nevada	3,104
37.	West Virginia	3,042
38.	Hawaii	2,801
39.	Nebraska	2,620
40.	Maine	2,425
41.	New Hampshire	2,401
42.	Idaho	1,963
43.	Delaware	1,676
44.	Rhode Island	1,636
45.	Wyoming	1,481
46.	Vermont	1,397
47.	Montana	1,372
48.	Alaska	1,346
49.	South Dakota	1,144
50.	North Dakota	967
51.	District of Columbia	882

44. State Appropriations for Higher Education, 2006 (per FTE enrollment)

1.	Wyoming	$13,425
2.	Alaska	12,097
3.	Hawaii	10,893
4.	Connecticut	9,503
5.	New Mexico	9,299
6.	Nevada	8,919
7.	Massachusetts	8,372
8.	New Jersey	8,145
9.	Georgia	7,824
10.	New York	7,784
11.	North Carolina	7,522
12.	Idaho	7,303
13.	Nebraska	6,999
14.	Kentucky	6,753
15.	Illinois	6,689
16.	Delaware	6,632
17.	California	6,586
18.	Washington	6,437
19.	Maryland	6,427
20.	Rhode Island	6,413
*	UNITED STATES	6,325
21.	Arizona	6,316
22.	Texas	6,276
23.	Tennessee	6,275
24.	Wisconsin	6,226
25.	Maine	6,096
26.	Utah	5,941
27.	Minnesota	5,907
28.	Arkansas	5,899
29.	Missouri	5,846
30.	South Carolina	5,822
31.	Iowa	5,809
32.	Michigan	5,799
33.	Kansas	5,792
34.	Pennsylvania	5,660
35.	Florida	5,641
36.	Oklahoma	5,638
37.	Alabama	5,617
38.	Louisiana	5,583
39.	Indiana	5,390
40.	Virginia	5,223
41.	Mississippi	5,053
42.	Ohio	4,690
43.	North Dakota	4,683
44.	South Dakota	4,499
45.	Oregon	4,466
46.	Montana	4,409
47.	West Virginia	4,181
48.	Colorado	3,364
49.	New Hampshire	3,193
50.	Vermont	3,030
51.	District of Columbia	NA

©2008 Information Publications, Inc.
All Rights Reserved. Photocopying prohibited.
877-544-INFO (4636) or www.informationpublications.com

Comparative Tables

45. Library Visits per capita, 2006

1. Ohio	7.2
2. Washington	7.0
3. Indiana	6.9
4. Utah	6.9
5. Nebraska	6.5
6. Connecticut	6.4
7. Kansas	6.4
8. Colorado	6.2
9. Oregon	6.2
10. South Dakota	6.2
11. Wyoming	6.2
12. Idaho	6.0
13. Wisconsin	6.0
14. Massachusetts	5.9
15. Rhode Island	5.9
16. Illinois	5.8
17. Iowa	5.8
18. Maine	5.7
19. New York	5.7
20. Vermont	5.7
21. New Jersey	5.4
22. Alaska	5.2
23. Minnesota	5.2
24. Delaware	5.0
25. Maryland	5.0
26. Missouri	5.0
27. New Hampshire	4.9
28. Michigan	4.8
29. North Dakota	4.8
* UNITED STATES	4.7
30. New Mexico	4.6
31. Oklahoma	4.6
32. Virginia	4.6
33. Hawaii	4.4
34. California	4.1
35. Florida	4.1
36. Montana	4.1
37. Nevada	4.1
38. Arizona	4.0
39. Kentucky	4.0
40. North Carolina	4.0
41. Georgia	3.7
42. Pennsylvania	3.6
43. South Carolina	3.6
44. District of Columbia	3.4
45. Texas	3.3
46. West Virginia	3.3
47. Alabama	3.2
48. Arkansas	3.2
49. Tennessee	3.2
50. Louisiana	3.1
51. Mississippi	2.9

46. Library Circulation per capita, 2006

1. Ohio	15.0
2. Oregon	14.9
3. Utah	12.9
4. Indiana	12.2
5. Washington	11.1
6. Colorado	11.0
7. Kansas	10.9
8. Wisconsin	10.3
9. Nebraska	10.1
10. Minnesota	9.9
11. Iowa	9.4
12. Maryland	9.4
13. South Dakota	9.1
14. Wyoming	9.1
15. Connecticut	9.0
16. Missouri	8.9
17. Illinois	8.6
18. Virginia	8.5
19. Idaho	8.3
20. Massachusetts	7.8
21. New Hampshire	7.7
22. Maine	7.5
23. New York	7.5
24. North Dakota	7.4
25. Arizona	7.3
26. Vermont	7.3
* UNITED STATES	7.2
27. Delaware	6.9
28. Oklahoma	6.9
29. Rhode Island	6.8
30. Michigan	6.6
31. New Mexico	6.5
32. New Jersey	6.4
33. Montana	6.2
34. Nevada	6.2
35. Alaska	6.1
36. Kentucky	6.0
37. Florida	5.5
38. North Carolina	5.5
39. California	5.4
40. Pennsylvania	5.3
41. Hawaii	5.1
42. South Carolina	5.0
43. Georgia	4.8
44. Texas	4.8
45. Arkansas	4.4
46. West Virginia	4.3
47. Alabama	4.1
48. Tennessee	4.1
49. Louisiana	3.9
50. Mississippi	3.2
51. District of Columbia	2.1

©2008 Information Publications, Inc.
All Rights Reserved. Photocopying prohibited.
877-544-INFO (4636) or www.informationpublications.com

Comparative Tables

47. People without Health Insurance, 2006	
1. Texas	24.5%
2. New Mexico	22.9
3. Louisiana	21.9
4. Florida	21.2
5. Arizona	20.9
6. Mississippi	20.7
7. Nevada	19.6
8. Arkansas	18.9
9. Oklahoma	18.9
10. California	18.8
11. North Carolina	17.9
12. Oregon	17.9
13. Georgia	17.7
14. Utah	17.4
15. Colorado	17.2
16. Montana	17.2
17. Alaska	16.5
18. South Carolina	15.9
* UNITED STATES	15.8
19. Kentucky	15.6
20. New Jersey	15.5
21. Idaho	15.4
22. Alabama	15.2
23. Wyoming	14.5
24. Illinois	14.0
25. New York	14.0
26. Maryland	13.8
27. Tennessee	13.7
28. West Virginia	13.5
29. Missouri	13.3
30. Virginia	13.3
31. Kansas	12.3
32. Nebraska	12.3
33. Delaware	12.2
34. North Dakota	12.2
35. Indiana	11.8
36. South Dakota	11.8
37. Washington	11.8
38. District of Columbia	11.6
39. New Hampshire	11.5
40. Iowa	10.5
41. Michigan	10.5
42. Massachusetts	10.4
43. Vermont	10.2
44. Ohio	10.1
45. Pennsylvania	10.0
46. Connecticut	9.4
47. Maine	9.3
48. Minnesota	9.2
49. Hawaii	8.8
50. Wisconsin	8.8
51. Rhode Island	8.6

48. Children without Health Insurance, 2006	
1. Texas	21.2%
2. Florida	18.9
3. Mississippi	18.9
4. Nevada	18.8
5. New Mexico	17.9
6. Arizona	17.0
7. Louisiana	15.9
8. Utah	15.0
9. Colorado	14.6
10. Montana	14.6
11. North Carolina	14.0
12. New Jersey	13.3
13. Oregon	13.1
14. Idaho	12.9
15. California	12.8
16. Georgia	12.8
17. Oklahoma	12.5
18. Delaware	11.7
* UNITED STATES	11.7
19. South Carolina	10.7
20. Alaska	10.5
21. North Dakota	10.4
22. Nebraska	10.1
23. Virginia	10.1
24. Maryland	9.9
25. Kentucky	9.7
26. Illinois	9.5
27. Arkansas	9.3
28. South Dakota	9.3
29. Missouri	9.1
30. District of Columbia	8.7
31. West Virginia	8.6
32. New York	8.4
33. Minnesota	8.3
34. Vermont	8.3
35. Wyoming	8.1
36. Indiana	7.8
37. Alabama	7.4
38. Kansas	7.3
39. New Hampshire	7.3
40. Pennsylvania	7.3
41. Massachusetts	7.0
42. Washington	6.9
43. Hawaii	6.4
44. Tennessee	6.4
45. Maine	6.3
46. Iowa	6.2
47. Connecticut	6.0
48. Ohio	5.6
49. Wisconsin	4.9
50. Michigan	4.7
51. Rhode Island	4.2

©2008 Information Publications, Inc.
All Rights Reserved. Photocopying prohibited.
877-544-INFO (4636) or www.informationpublications.com

Comparative Tables

49. Health Care Expenditures, per capita, 2004

1.	District of Columbia	$8,295
2.	Massachusetts	6,683
3.	Maine	6,540
4.	New York	6,535
5.	Alaska	6,450
6.	Connecticut	6,344
7.	Delaware	6,306
8.	Rhode Island	6,193
9.	Vermont	6,069
10.	West Virginia	5,954
11.	Pennsylvania	5,933
12.	North Dakota	5,808
13.	New Jersey	5,807
14.	Minnesota	5,795
15.	Ohio	5,725
16.	Wisconsin	5,670
17.	Nebraska	5,599
18.	Maryland	5,590
19.	Florida	5,483
20.	Kentucky	5,473
21.	Tennessee	5,464
22.	Missouri	5,444
23.	New Hampshire	5,432
24.	Kansas	5,382
25.	Iowa	5,380
26.	South Dakota	5,327
27.	Indiana	5,295
28.	Illinois	5,293
*	UNITED STATES	5,283
29.	Wyoming	5,265
30.	North Carolina	5,191
31.	Alabama	5,135
32.	South Carolina	5,114
33.	Washington	5,092
34.	Montana	5,080
35.	Mississippi	5,059
36.	Michigan	5,058
37.	Louisiana	5,040
38.	Hawaii	4,941
39.	Oklahoma	4,917
40.	Oregon	4,880
41.	Arkansas	4,863
42.	Virginia	4,822
43.	Colorado	4,717
44.	California	4,638
45.	Texas	4,601
46.	Georgia	4,600
47.	Nevada	4,569
48.	New Mexico	4,471
49.	Idaho	4,444
50.	Arizona	4,103
51.	Utah	3,972

50. Social Security Beneficiaries, 2005 (x 1,000)

*	UNITED STATES	47,255
1.	California	4,460
2.	Florida	3,424
3.	New York	3,064
4.	Texas	2,955
5.	Pennsylvania	2,425
6.	Ohio	1,965
7.	Illinois	1,898
8.	Michigan	1,743
9.	North Carolina	1,511
10.	New Jersey	1,379
11.	Georgia	1,231
12.	Virginia	1,139
13.	Tennessee	1,098
14.	Massachusetts	1,072
15.	Missouri	1,064
16.	Indiana	1,055
17.	Wisconsin	952
18.	Washington	937
19.	Arizona	919
20.	Alabama	904
21.	Kentucky	799
22.	Minnesota	786
23.	South Carolina	774
24.	Maryland	772
25.	Louisiana	716
26.	Oklahoma	635
27.	Oregon	625
28.	Colorado	588
29.	Connecticut	585
30.	Arkansas	558
31.	Mississippi	552
32.	Iowa	548
33.	Kansas	451
34.	West Virginia	413
35.	Nevada	348
36.	New Mexico	311
37.	Nebraska	294
38.	Utah	272
39.	Maine	269
40.	Idaho	228
41.	New Hampshire	226
42.	Hawaii	203
43.	Rhode Island	192
44.	Montana	169
45.	Delaware	152
46.	South Dakota	142
47.	North Dakota	115
48.	Vermont	112
49.	Wyoming	84
50.	District of Columbia	71
51.	Alaska	65

©2008 Information Publications, Inc.
All Rights Reserved. Photocopying prohibited.
877-544-INFO (4636) or www.informationpublications.com

Comparative Tables

51. Medicare Enrollment, July 2005 (x 1,000)	
* UNITED STATES	41,536
1. California	4,201
2. Florida	3,046
3. New York	2,776
4. Texas	2,545
5. Pennsylvania	2,132
6. Ohio	1,754
7. Illinois	1,691
8. Michigan	1,483
9. North Carolina	1,277
10. New Jersey	1,227
11. Georgia	1,039
12. Virginia	993
13. Massachusetts	971
14. Tennessee	922
15. Missouri	912
16. Indiana	905
17. Wisconsin	826
18. Washington	821
19. Arizona	794
20. Alabama	755
21. Minnesota	698
22. Maryland	695
23. Kentucky	678
24. South Carolina	651
25. Louisiana	610
26. Oklahoma	541
27. Oregon	540
28. Connecticut	525
29. Colorado	522
30. Iowa	490
31. Arkansas	472
32. Mississippi	454
33. Kansas	402
34. West Virginia	355
35. Nevada	297
36. New Mexico	267
37. Nebraska	261
38. Utah	237
39. Maine	235
40. Idaho	192
41. New Hampshire	192
42. Hawaii	182
43. Rhode Island	172
44. Montana	148
45. Delaware	128
46. South Dakota	125
47. North Dakota	104
48. Vermont	96
49. District of Columbia	73
50. Wyoming	71
51. Alaska	52

52. Medicaid Beneficiaries, 2004 (x 1,000)	
* UNITED STATES	55,078
1. California	10,015
2. North Dakota	4,712
3. Texas	3,604
4. Florida	2,952
5. Indiana	2,032
6. Georgia	1,929
7. Ohio	1,896
8. Pennsylvania	1,835
9. Michigan	1,799
10. Tennessee	1,730
11. Nebraska	1,513
12. Mississippi	1,140
13. Washington	1,109
14. Louisiana	1,108
15. Maine	1,074
16. Arkansas	1,070
17. New Mexico	960
18. Iowa	946
19. West Virginia	896
20. Kentucky	861
21. South Carolina	857
22. Alaska	808
23. Maryland	750
24. Vermont	732
25. Missouri	726
26. Arizona	708
27. Minnesota	698
28. Oklahoma	654
29. Oregon	559
30. Colorado	503
31. Connecticut	501
32. New York	474
33. Idaho	383
34. Wisconsin	377
35. Kansas	365
36. Utah	307
37. Massachusetts	294
38. New Hampshire	244
39. North Carolina	237
40. Hawaii	218
41. Rhode Island	208
42. Illinois	206
43. Delaware	158
44. District of Columbia	157
45. Virginia	149
46. South Dakota	128
47. New Jersey	119
48. Alabama	118
49. Montana	113
50. Nevada	78
51. Wyoming	68

©2008 Information Publications, Inc.
All Rights Reserved. Photocopying prohibited.
877-544-INFO (4636) or www.informationpublications.com

Comparative Tables

53. Median Home Value, 2006

1.	California	$535,700
2.	Hawaii	529,700
3.	District of Columbia	437,700
4.	Massachusetts	370,400
5.	New Jersey	366,600
6.	Maryland	334,700
7.	Nevada	315,200
8.	New York	303,400
9.	Connecticut	298,900
10.	Rhode Island	295,700
11.	Washington	267,600
12.	New Hampshire	253,200
13.	Virginia	244,200
14.	Oregon	236,600
15.	Arizona	236,500
16.	Colorado	232,900
17.	Florida	230,600
18.	Delaware	227,100
19.	Alaska	213,200
20.	Minnesota	208,200
21.	Illinois	200,200
22.	Vermont	193,000
23.	Utah	188,500
*	UNITED STATES	185,200
24.	Maine	170,500
25.	Idaho	163,900
26.	Wisconsin	163,500
27.	Georgia	156,800
28.	Montana	155,500
29.	Michigan	153,300
30.	Wyoming	148,900
31.	Pennsylvania	145,200
32.	New Mexico	141,200
33.	North Carolina	137,200
34.	Ohio	135,200
35.	Missouri	131,900
36.	Tennessee	123,100
37.	South Carolina	122,400
38.	Indiana	120,700
39.	Nebraska	119,200
40.	Louisiana	114,700
41.	Kansas	114,400
42.	Texas	114,000
43.	Iowa	112,600
44.	South Dakota	112,600
45.	Kentucky	111,000
46.	Alabama	107,000
47.	North Dakota	99,700
48.	Oklahoma	94,500
49.	Arkansas	93,900
50.	West Virginia	89,700
51.	Mississippi	88,600

54. Median Rent, 2006

1.	Hawaii	$1,116
2.	California	1,029
3.	New Jersey	974
4.	Maryland	953
5.	Massachusetts	933
6.	Nevada	917
7.	District of Columbia	914
8.	Connecticut	886
9.	Alaska	883
10.	New York	875
11.	Florida	872
12.	New Hampshire	861
13.	Virginia	846
14.	Rhode Island	840
15.	Delaware	830
16.	Colorado	780
17.	Washington	779
*	UNITED STATES	763
18.	Arizona	762
19.	Illinois	761
20.	Georgia	738
21.	Vermont	716
22.	Oregon	714
23.	Texas	711
24.	Minnesota	701
25.	Utah	697
26.	Michigan	675
27.	Pennsylvania	664
28.	Wisconsin	658
29.	North Carolina	656
30.	South Carolina	640
31.	Indiana	638
32.	Maine	636
33.	Ohio	627
34.	Idaho	623
35.	Louisiana	618
36.	New Mexico	617
37.	Tennessee	613
38.	Kansas	609
39.	Missouri	607
40.	Wyoming	601
41.	Nebraska	593
42.	Iowa	584
43.	Mississippi	584
44.	Oklahoma	580
45.	Alabama	573
46.	Montana	571
47.	Arkansas	566
48.	Kentucky	548
49.	South Dakota	522
50.	West Virginia	499
51.	North Dakota	497

©2008 Information Publications, Inc.
All Rights Reserved. Photocopying prohibited.
877-544-INFO (4636) or www.informationpublications.com

Comparative Tables

55. Home Ownership Rate, 2006

1.	West Virginia	78.4%
2.	Michigan	77.4
3.	Delaware	76.8
4.	Mississippi	76.2
5.	Minnesota	75.6
6.	Maine	75.3
7.	Idaho	75.1
8.	Alabama	74.2
9.	Indiana	74.2
10.	New Hampshire	74.2
11.	South Carolina	74.2
12.	Iowa	74.0
13.	Vermont	74.0
14.	Wyoming	73.7
15.	Utah	73.5
16.	Pennsylvania	73.2
17.	Maryland	72.6
18.	Florida	72.4
19.	Ohio	72.1
20.	New Mexico	72.0
21.	Missouri	71.9
22.	Kentucky	71.7
23.	Arizona	71.6
24.	Oklahoma	71.6
25.	Louisiana	71.3
26.	Tennessee	71.3
27.	Connecticut	71.1
28.	Virginia	71.1
29.	Arkansas	70.8
30.	South Dakota	70.6
31.	Illinois	70.4
32.	North Carolina	70.2
33.	Wisconsin	70.2
34.	Colorado	70.1
35.	Kansas	70.0
36.	Montana	69.5
37.	New Jersey	69.0
*	UNITED STATES	68.8
38.	Georgia	68.5
39.	North Dakota	68.3
40.	Oregon	68.1
41.	Nebraska	67.6
42.	Alaska	67.2
43.	Washington	66.7
44.	Texas	66.0
45.	Nevada	65.7
46.	Massachusetts	65.2
47.	Rhode Island	64.6
48.	California	60.2
49.	Hawaii	59.9
50.	New York	55.7
51.	District of Columbia	45.9

56. Federal Grants to State and Local Governments, 2005 (x 1,000)

*	UNITED STATES	$469,579,029
1.	California	55,334,202
2.	New York	45,631,397
3.	Texas	28,912,208
4.	Florida	22,552,241
5.	Pennsylvania	19,868,667
6.	Ohio	17,151,707
7.	Illinois	16,634,795
8.	Massachusetts	13,748,662
9.	Michigan	13,313,206
10.	North Carolina	12,958,870
11.	Louisiana	11,388,684
12.	Georgia	11,165,966
13.	New Jersey	11,124,122
14.	Tennessee	9,985,336
15.	Washington	9,046,698
16.	Missouri	8,930,488
17.	Maryland	8,643,028
18.	Arizona	8,603,017
19.	Indiana	8,064,847
20.	Virginia	7,745,362
21.	Wisconsin	7,538,150
22.	Minnesota	7,483,670
23.	Alabama	7,346,245
24.	Kentucky	6,633,970
25.	Mississippi	6,567,356
26.	South Carolina	6,323,699
27.	Oklahoma	5,501,741
28.	Oregon	5,466,310
29.	Connecticut	5,438,708
30.	Colorado	5,433,177
31.	Arkansas	4,681,690
32.	New Mexico	4,564,332
33.	District of Columbia	4,325,307
34.	Iowa	4,035,419
35.	West Virginia	3,808,971
36.	Kansas	3,617,795
37.	Alaska	3,131,207
38.	Utah	3,038,268
39.	Nevada	2,925,545
40.	Maine	2,773,126
41.	Nebraska	2,595,784
42.	Rhode Island	2,325,111
43.	Hawaii	2,167,856
44.	Montana	2,139,765
45.	Idaho	2,092,900
46.	Wyoming	1,898,954
47.	New Hampshire	1,795,266
48.	South Dakota	1,741,877
49.	North Dakota	1,666,287
50.	Vermont	1,324,142
51.	Delaware	1,265,225

448

©2008 Information Publications, Inc.
All Rights Reserved. Photocopying prohibited.
877-544-INFO (4636) or www.informationpublications.com

Comparative Tables

57. State Government Revenues, per capita, 2006	
1. District of Columbia	$16,023.98
2. Alaska	16,008.29
3. Wyoming	10,954.03
4. New York	8,609.17
5. Delaware	8,021.12
6. Vermont	7,862.51
7. Hawaii	7,708.65
8. New Mexico	7,585.67
9. California	7,276.29
10. Rhode Island	7,224.88
11. Massachusetts	7,071.25
12. Oregon	6,974.32
13. North Dakota	6,854.96
14. Minnesota	6,746.03
15. New Jersey	6,647.80
16. Ohio	6,577.87
17. Maine	6,563.84
18. Connecticut	6,549.82
19. Louisiana	6,523.16
20. Montana	6,474.97
21. Washington	6,405.11
22. West Virginia	6,322.34
23. Michigan	6,145.82
24. Mississippi	6,120.35
25. Wisconsin	5,995.44
* UNITED STATES	5,934.67
26. Pennsylvania	5,896.58
27. Arkansas	5,846.99
28. Iowa	5,654.57
29. Kentucky	5,599.43
30. Maryland	5,534.89
31. Utah	5,490.64
32. Oklahoma	5,483.65
33. South Carolina	5,477.92
34. Idaho	5,318.49
35. South Dakota	5,295.18
36. Virginia	5,271.14
37. Indiana	5,212.82
38. Nebraska	5,161.31
39. Alabama	5,156.79
40. North Carolina	5,127.04
41. Nevada	4,951.60
42. Kansas	4,940.57
43. Missouri	4,926.70
44. Colorado	4,923.53
45. Illinois	4,909.50
46. New Hampshire	4,858.25
47. Florida	4,641.15
48. Arizona	4,514.44
49. Texas	4,441.48
50. Tennessee	4,331.90
51. Georgia	4,024.18

58. State Government Expenditures, per capita, 2006	
1. District of Columbia	$15,633.73
2. Alaska	12,693.32
3. Wyoming	7,823.39
4. Delaware	7,645.80
5. Vermont	7,486.93
6. New York	7,408.64
7. Hawaii	6,971.26
8. New Mexico	6,898.53
9. Rhode Island	6,551.99
10. New Jersey	6,239.65
11. California	6,215.68
12. Massachusetts	6,198.00
13. Minnesota	6,011.84
14. Maine	5,973.55
15. Connecticut	5,914.21
16. Louisiana	5,708.00
17. North Dakota	5,699.73
18. Ohio	5,663.95
19. Mississippi	5,620.03
20. Montana	5,486.47
21. Oregon	5,437.60
22. West Virginia	5,413.51
23. South Carolina	5,411.12
24. Wisconsin	5,405.87
25. Washington	5,320.04
26. Michigan	5,254.97
27. Pennsylvania	5,234.05
28. Kentucky	5,230.74
* UNITED STATES	5,193.48
29. Maryland	5,170.63
30. Arkansas	5,115.62
31. Iowa	5,026.62
32. Alabama	4,849.60
33. Oklahoma	4,718.99
34. Utah	4,669.30
35. North Carolina	4,634.78
36. New Hampshire	4,564.61
37. Kansas	4,555.27
38. Virginia	4,551.71
39. South Dakota	4,394.95
40. Nebraska	4,366.98
41. Illinois	4,364.67
42. Idaho	4,339.76
43. Indiana	4,277.37
44. Colorado	4,227.84
45. Florida	4,216.65
46. Arizona	4,173.33
47. Missouri	4,172.21
48. Nevada	4,149.24
49. Tennessee	3,945.37
50. Georgia	3,740.58
51. Texas	3,653.25

©2008 Information Publications, Inc.
All Rights Reserved. Photocopying prohibited.
877-544-INFO (4636) or www.informationpublications.com

Comparative Tables

59. Violent Crime Rate, 2006
(per 100,000 residents)

1.	District of Columbia	1,508.4
2.	South Carolina	765.5
3.	Tennessee	760.2
4.	Nevada	741.6
5.	Florida	712.0
6.	Louisiana	697.8
7.	Alaska	688.0
8.	Delaware	681.6
9.	Maryland	678.6
10.	New Mexico	643.2
11.	Michigan	562.4
12.	Arkansas	551.6
13.	Missouri	545.6
14.	Illinois	541.6
15.	California	532.5
16.	Texas	516.3
17.	Arizona	501.4
18.	Oklahoma	497.4
19.	North Carolina	475.6
*	UNITED STATES	473.5
20.	Georgia	471.0
21.	Massachusetts	447.0
22.	Pennsylvania	439.4
23.	New York	434.9
24.	Alabama	425.2
25.	Kansas	425.0
26.	Colorado	391.6
27.	New Jersey	351.6
28.	Ohio	350.3
29.	Washington	345.9
30.	Indiana	314.8
31.	Minnesota	312.0
32.	Mississippi	298.6
33.	Wisconsin	284.0
34.	Iowa	283.5
35.	Virginia	282.2
36.	Nebraska	281.8
37.	Hawaii	281.2
38.	Connecticut	280.8
39.	Oregon	280.3
40.	West Virginia	279.7
41.	Kentucky	263.0
42.	Montana	253.7
43.	Idaho	247.2
44.	Wyoming	239.6
45.	Rhode Island	227.5
46.	Utah	224.4
47.	South Dakota	171.4
48.	New Hampshire	138.7
49.	Vermont	136.6
50.	North Dakota	127.9
51.	Maine	115.5

60. Property Crime Rate, 2006
(per 100,000 residents)

1.	District of Columbia	4,653.8
2.	Arizona	4,627.9
3.	Washington	4,480.0
4.	South Carolina	4,242.3
5.	Hawaii	4,230.4
6.	Tennessee	4,128.3
7.	North Carolina	4,120.8
8.	Nevada	4,088.8
9.	Texas	4,081.5
10.	Louisiana	3,993.7
11.	Florida	3,986.1
12.	Arkansas	3,967.5
13.	New Mexico	3,937.2
14.	Alabama	3,936.1
15.	Georgia	3,889.2
16.	Missouri	3,826.5
17.	Kansas	3,750.2
18.	Ohio	3,678.6
19.	Oregon	3,672.1
20.	Oklahoma	3,604.2
21.	Utah	3,516.4
22.	Indiana	3,502.4
23.	Maryland	3,480.9
24.	Colorado	3,451.3
25.	Delaware	3,417.9
26.	Nebraska	3,340.7
*	UNITED STATES	3,334.5
27.	Michigan	3,212.8
28.	Mississippi	3,208.8
29.	California	3,170.9
30.	Minnesota	3,079.5
31.	Illinois	3,019.6
32.	Wyoming	2,980.6
33.	Wisconsin	2,817.8
34.	Iowa	2,802.7
35.	Montana	2,687.5
36.	West Virginia	2,621.5
37.	Rhode Island	2,586.9
38.	Kentucky	2,544.5
39.	Maine	2,518.7
40.	Connecticut	2,504.1
41.	Virginia	2,478.2
42.	Pennsylvania	2,443.5
43.	Idaho	2,418.8
44.	Massachusetts	2,391.0
45.	Vermont	2,304.7
46.	New Jersey	2,291.9
47.	New York	2,052.7
48.	North Dakota	2,000.3
49.	New Hampshire	1,874.1
50.	South Dakota	1,619.6
51.	Alaska	688.0

©2008 Information Publications, Inc.
All Rights Reserved. Photocopying prohibited.
877-544-INFO (4636) or www.informationpublications.com

Comparative Tables

61. Identity Theft rate, 2006 (complaints per 100,000 residents)	
1. Arizona	147.8
2. District of Columbia	131.5
3. Nevada	120.0
4. California	113.5
5. Texas	110.6
6. Florida	98.3
7. Colorado	92.5
8. Georgia	86.3
9. New York	85.2
10. Washington	83.4
11. Maryland	82.9
12. New Mexico	82.9
* UNITED STATES	79.9
13. Illinois	78.6
14. Oregon	76.1
15. New Jersey	73.3
16. Michigan	67.2
17. Virginia	67.2
18. Delaware	66.7
19. Connecticut	65.8
20. North Carolina	64.9
21. Pennsylvania	64.9
22. Missouri	64.2
23. Massachusetts	63.7
24. Oklahoma	63.0
25. Indiana	62.2
26. Utah	61.8
27. Tennessee	61.3
28. Alabama	60.3
29. Ohio	59.9
30. Kansas	58.8
31. Rhode Island	57.6
32. Alaska	57.3
33. South Carolina	55.7
34. Minnesota	55.6
35. Arkansas	54.7
36. Louisiana	52.6
37. Mississippi	51.3
38. Nebraska	49.1
39. Idaho	49.0
40. Hawaii	47.8
41. New Hampshire	46.1
42. Montana	45.9
43. Wisconsin	45.6
44. Wyoming	42.3
45. Kentucky	42.0
46. Maine	39.7
47. West Virginia	39.3
48. Iowa	34.9
49. South Dakota	30.2
50. North Dakota	29.7
51. Vermont	28.5

62. Fraud Rate, 2006 (complaints per 100,000 residents)	
1. District of Columbia	195.9
2. Utah	178.9
3. Nevada	169.2
4. Washington	163.4
5. Colorado	161.1
6. Alaska	161.0
7. Virginia	157.5
8. Hawaii	157.1
9. Maryland	154.1
10. Oregon	150.9
11. Arizona	149.6
12. New Hampshire	149.4
13. Florida	143.2
14. Idaho	137.2
15. Montana	136.5
16. Maine	135.5
17. California	134.6
18. Connecticut	134.0
19. Delaware	131.1
20. Pennsylvania	130.6
21. New Jersey	129.3
22. Wyoming	127.6
23. Georgia	127.5
24. Missouri	125.5
* UNITED STATES	125.2
25. Indiana	124.5
26. Ohio	124.1
27. New Mexico	123.1
28. Wisconsin	121.0
29. North Carolina	116.3
30. Michigan	115.5
31. Vermont	115.1
32. Massachusetts	113.9
33. Tennessee	113.8
34. Minnesota	113.4
35. West Virginia	113.2
36. South Carolina	112.0
37. Nebraska	111.3
38. Kansas	111.0
39. New York	109.4
40. Illinois	108.4
41. Texas	108.2
42. Rhode Island	108.0
43. Kentucky	106.4
44. Oklahoma	103.7
45. Alabama	102.4
46. Louisiana	92.8
47. Iowa	89.4
48. Arkansas	86.4
49. North Dakota	85.6
50. Mississippi	79.6
51. South Dakota	79.0

©2008 Information Publications, Inc.
All Rights Reserved. Photocopying prohibited.
877-544-INFO (4636) or www.informationpublications.com

Comparative Tables

63. Incarceration Rate, 2006 (per 100,000 residents)		64. Incarceration Rate, White, June 2005 (per 100,000 residents)	
1. Louisiana	846	1. Oklahoma	740
2. Texas	683	2. Idaho	675
3. Oklahoma	664	3. Texas	667
4. Mississippi	658	4. Nevada	627
5. Alabama	595	5. Georgia	623
6. Georgia	558	6. Arizona	590
7. South Carolina	525	7. Florida	588
8. Missouri	514	8. Kentucky	561
9. Michigan	511	9. Alabama	542
10. Arizona	509	10. Colorado	525
11. Florida	509	11. Louisiana	523
12. Nevada	503	12. Mississippi	503
* UNITED STATES	501	13. Oregon	502
13. Delaware	488	14. Alaska	500
14. Arkansas	485	15. Missouri	487
15. Idaho	480	16. Tennessee	487
16. Virginia	477	17. Arkansas	478
17. California	475	18. South Dakota	470
18. Colorado	469	19. Indiana	463
19. Alaska	462	20. California	460
20. Kentucky	462	21. Hawaii	453
21. Ohio	428	22. Kansas	443
22. South Dakota	426	23. Montana	433
23. Tennessee	423	24. South Carolina	415
24. Indiana	411	25. Wisconsin	415
25. Wyoming	408	26. Michigan	412
26. Maryland	396	* UNITED STATES	412
27. Wisconsin	393	27. Delaware	396
28. Connecticut	392	28. Virginia	396
29. Montana	374	29. Washington	393
30. Oregon	367	30. Utah	392
31. North Carolina	360	31. West Virginia	392
32. Pennsylvania	353	32. Ohio	344
33. Illinois	350	33. North Carolina	320
34. Hawaii	338	34. Iowa	309
35. New York	326	35. Pennsylvania	305
36. New Mexico	323	36. Vermont	304
37. Kansas	318	37. Nebraska	290
38. West Virginia	314	38. New Hampshire	289
39. New Jersey	313	39. Maryland	288
40. Iowa	296	40. North Dakota	267
41. Washington	271	41. Maine	262
42. Vermont	262	42. Illinois	223
43. Utah	246	43. Minnesota	212
44. Massachusetts	243	44. Connecticut	211
45. Nebraska	237	45. Massachusetts	201
46. North Dakota	214	46. Rhode Island	191
47. New Hampshire	207	47. New Jersey	190
48. Rhode Island	202	48. New York	174
49. Minnesota	176	49. District of Columbia	56
50. Maine	151	50. New Mexico	NA
51. District of Columbia	NA	51. Wyoming	NA

©2008 Information Publications, Inc.
All Rights Reserved. Photocopying prohibited.
877-544-INFO (4636) or www.informationpublications.com

Comparative Tables

65. Incarceration Rate, Black, June 2005 (per 100,000 residents)

1.	South Dakota	4,710
2.	Wisconsin	4,416
3.	Iowa	4,200
4.	Vermont	3,797
5.	Utah	3,588
6.	Montana	3,569
7.	Colorado	3,491
8.	Arizona	3,294
9.	Oklahoma	3,252
10.	Texas	3,162
11.	Kansas	3,096
12.	California	2,992
13.	Oregon	2,930
14.	Nevada	2,916
15.	Idaho	2,869
16.	Kentucky	2,793
17.	Pennsylvania	2,792
18.	North Dakota	2,683
19.	New Hampshire	2,666
20.	Florida	2,615
21.	Missouri	2,556
22.	Connecticut	2,532
23.	Indiana	2,526
24.	Washington	2,522
25.	Delaware	2,517
26.	Louisiana	2,452
27.	Nebraska	2,418
28.	New Jersey	2,352
29.	Virginia	2,331
*	UNITED STATES	2,289
30.	Michigan	2,262
31.	Ohio	2,196
32.	West Virginia	2,188
33.	Alaska	2,163
34.	Georgia	2,068
35.	Illinois	2,020
36.	Tennessee	2,006
37.	Maine	1,992
38.	Minnesota	1,937
39.	Alabama	1,916
40.	South Carolina	1,856
41.	Arkansas	1,846
42.	Rhode Island	1,838
43.	Mississippi	1,742
44.	North Carolina	1,727
45.	Massachusetts	1,635
46.	New York	1,627
47.	Maryland	1,579
48.	District of Columbia	1,065
49.	Hawaii	851
50.	New Mexico	NA
51.	Wyoming	NA

66. Incarceration Rate, Hispanic, June 2005 (per 100,000 residents)

1.	Pennsylvania	1,714
2.	Idaho	1,654
3.	Connecticut	1,401
4.	Massachusetts	1,229
5.	Arizona	1,075
6.	New Hampshire	1,063
7.	Colorado	1,042
8.	North Dakota	848
9.	Montana	846
10.	Utah	838
11.	Oklahoma	832
12.	Texas	830
13.	California	782
14.	New York	778
15.	Iowa	764
16.	Kentucky	757
*	UNITED STATES	742
17.	Nebraska	739
18.	Delaware	683
19.	Rhode Island	631
20.	New Jersey	630
21.	Nevada	621
22.	Ohio	613
23.	Mississippi	611
24.	Missouri	587
25.	Indiana	579
26.	Georgia	576
27.	Oregon	573
28.	Tennessee	561
29.	Washington	527
30.	Virginia	487
31.	South Carolina	476
32.	Illinois	415
33.	Michigan	397
34.	Florida	382
35.	Alaska	380
36.	Arkansas	288
37.	District of Columbia	267
38.	Louisiana	244
39.	West Virginia	211
40.	Hawaii	185
41.	Alabama	NA
42.	Kansas	NA
43.	Maine	NA
44.	Maryland	NA
45.	Minnesota	NA
46.	New Mexico	NA
47.	North Carolina	NA
48.	South Dakota	NA
49.	Vermont	NA
50.	Wisconsin	NA
51.	Wyoming	NA

©2008 Information Publications, Inc.
All Rights Reserved. Photocopying prohibited.
877-544-INFO (4636) or www.informationpublications.com

Comparative Tables

67. Incarceration Rate, Men, June 2005 (per 100,000 residents)

1.	Louisiana	2,134
2.	Georgia	1,877
3.	Mississippi	1,790
4.	Texas	1,772
5.	Alabama	1,665
6.	Oklahoma	1,645
7.	South Carolina	1,558
8.	Delaware	1,547
9.	Florida	1,541
10.	Arizona	1,443
11.	New Mexico	1,421
12.	Virginia	1,393
13.	Idaho	1,379
14.	Tennessee	1,339
15.	Missouri	1,323
16.	Nevada	1,319
17.	Kentucky	1,287
18.	Colorado	1,279
19.	Michigan	1,262
*	UNITED STATES	1,249
20.	California	1,246
21.	Alaska	1,232
22.	Arkansas	1,231
23.	Maryland	1,219
24.	Wisconsin	1,209
25.	District of Columbia	1,202
26.	Wyoming	1,189
27.	Indiana	1,165
28.	Pennsylvania	1,155
29.	North Carolina	1,154
30.	South Dakota	1,092
31.	Kansas	1,054
32.	Ohio	1,040
33.	Connecticut	1,030
34.	New Jersey	1,019
35.	Oregon	965
36.	Illinois	951
37.	New York	935
38.	Montana	926
39.	Washington	831
40.	West Virginia	817
41.	Utah	803
42.	Hawaii	787
43.	Nebraska	756
44.	Iowa	751
45.	Massachusetts	687
46.	North Dakota	632
47.	Rhode Island	607
48.	Vermont	598
49.	New Hampshire	590
50.	Minnesota	553
51.	Maine	513

68. Incarceration Rate, Women, June 2005 (per 100,000 residents)

1.	Oklahoma	209
2.	Louisiana	195
3.	Texas	186
4.	Idaho	185
5.	Georgia	184
6.	Wyoming	184
7.	Kentucky	173
8.	Nevada	173
9.	Arizona	171
10.	Mississippi	168
11.	Colorado	166
12.	New Mexico	163
13.	Alabama	161
14.	South Dakota	157
15.	Florida	155
16.	Tennessee	151
17.	District of Columbia	145
18.	Virginia	144
19.	Alaska	141
20.	South Carolina	137
21.	Arkansas	136
22.	Missouri	133
23.	Montana	129
24.	Delaware	128
25.	Utah	127
26.	Indiana	126
*	UNITED STATES	121
27.	California	119
28.	Kansas	117
29.	Hawaii	109
30.	Wisconsin	107
31.	North Carolina	104
32.	Ohio	103
33.	Oregon	101
34.	Washington	101
35.	Nebraska	93
36.	Pennsylvania	92
37.	Maryland	88
38.	North Dakota	87
39.	Connecticut	85
40.	Michigan	85
41.	West Virginia	84
42.	Iowa	83
43.	Illinois	79
44.	New Jersey	70
45.	New York	57
46.	New Hampshire	56
47.	Minnesota	52
48.	Massachusetts	45
49.	Vermont	45
50.	Maine	44
51.	Rhode Island	38

©2008 Information Publications, Inc.
All Rights Reserved. Photocopying prohibited.
877-544-INFO (4636) or www.informationpublications.com

Comparative Tables

69. Civilian Labor Force, 2006 (x 1,000)	
* UNITED STATES	151,428
1. California	17,751
2. Texas	11,465
3. New York	9,464
4. Florida	9,054
5. Illinois	6,584
6. Pennsylvania	6,308
7. Ohio	5,975
8. Michigan	5,086
9. Georgia	4,694
10. New Jersey	4,490
11. North Carolina	4,426
12. Virginia	3,971
13. Massachusetts	3,368
14. Washington	3,335
15. Indiana	3,253
16. Wisconsin	3,079
17. Missouri	3,069
18. Tennessee	3,028
19. Maryland	3,001
20. Arizona	2,969
21. Minnesota	2,933
22. Colorado	2,610
23. Alabama	2,210
24. South Carolina	2,124
25. Kentucky	2,042
26. Louisiana	1,960
27. Oregon	1,897
28. Connecticut	1,858
29. Oklahoma	1,733
30. Iowa	1,701
31. Kansas	1,480
32. Arkansas	1,374
33. Utah	1,309
34. Mississippi	1,296
35. Nevada	1,296
36. Nebraska	982
37. New Mexico	944
38. West Virginia	815
39. Idaho	759
40. New Hampshire	741
41. Maine	715
42. Hawaii	657
43. Rhode Island	577
44. Montana	505
45. Delaware	448
46. South Dakota	434
47. North Dakota	368
48. Vermont	365
49. Alaska	349
50. District of Columbia	291
51. Wyoming	287

70. Unemployment Rate, 2006	
1. Michigan	7.0%
2. Alaska	6.9
3. South Carolina	6.5
4. Mississippi	6.4
5. District of Columbia	5.8
6. Kentucky	5.6
7. Ohio	5.4
8. Oregon	5.4
9. Arkansas	5.3
10. Rhode Island	5.2
11. Tennessee	5.2
12. Massachusetts	5.1
13. West Virginia	5.1
14. Indiana	5.0
15. Washington	5.0
16. California	4.8
17. Missouri	4.8
18. New Jersey	4.8
19. Texas	4.8
20. Wisconsin	4.8
21. North Carolina	4.7
22. Pennsylvania	4.7
23. Georgia	4.6
24. Louisiana	4.6
25. Maine	4.6
* UNITED STATES	4.6
26. Illinois	4.5
27. Kansas	4.4
28. New Mexico	4.4
29. New York	4.4
30. Connecticut	4.3
31. Arizona	4.2
32. Colorado	4.2
33. Alabama	4.1
34. Nevada	4.1
35. Minnesota	4.0
36. Maryland	3.9
37. Oklahoma	3.9
38. Iowa	3.6
39. Montana	3.6
40. Vermont	3.6
41. Delaware	3.5
42. Idaho	3.5
43. New Hampshire	3.4
44. Wyoming	3.4
45. North Dakota	3.3
46. Florida	3.2
47. Nebraska	3.1
48. South Dakota	3.1
49. Virginia	3.1
50. Utah	2.9
51. Hawaii	2.7

©2008 Information Publications, Inc.
All Rights Reserved. Photocopying prohibited.
877-544-INFO (4636) or www.informationpublications.com

Comparative Tables

71. Average Hourly Earnings – Production, 2006

1.	Michigan	$21.83
2.	Washington	19.90
3.	Connecticut	19.78
4.	Ohio	19.16
5.	Indiana	18.57
6.	Maine	18.57
7.	New York	18.29
8.	Massachusetts	18.26
9.	Delaware	18.13
10.	Louisiana	17.94
11.	West Virginia	17.89
12.	Maryland	17.87
13.	Kansas	17.68
14.	Wyoming	17.44
15.	District of Columbia	17.30
16.	Minnesota	17.23
17.	Missouri	17.16
18.	Kentucky	16.92
19.	Idaho	16.89
*	UNITED STATES	16.80
20.	Virginia	16.75
21.	Colorado	16.58
22.	New Hampshire	16.56
23.	New Jersey	16.55
24.	Wisconsin	16.54
25.	Iowa	16.40
26.	Illinois	16.03
27.	California	15.95
28.	Montana	15.90
29.	Hawaii	15.89
30.	Vermont	15.79
31.	Oregon	15.57
32.	Alabama	15.56
33.	Nevada	15.47
34.	Pennsylvania	15.37
35.	Utah	15.25
36.	Nebraska	15.04
37.	South Carolina	15.03
38.	North Dakota	14.97
39.	Arizona	14.88
40.	Oklahoma	14.77
41.	Florida	14.75
42.	Georgia	14.74
43.	North Carolina	14.57
44.	Alaska	14.30
45.	New Mexico	14.06
46.	Tennessee	14.04
47.	Texas	14.01
48.	Mississippi	13.78
49.	South Dakota	13.75
50.	Rhode Island	13.42
51.	Arkansas	13.35

72. Average Weekly Earnings – Production, 2006

1.	Michigan	$921.23
2.	Connecticut	834.72
3.	Washington	807.94
4.	Ohio	793.22
5.	Indiana	774.37
6.	Louisiana	771.42
7.	Maine	768.80
8.	Kansas	760.24
9.	New York	751.72
10.	Massachusetts	743.18
11.	West Virginia	738.86
12.	Maryland	725.52
13.	Delaware	723.39
14.	Wyoming	718.53
15.	Minnesota	706.43
16.	Idaho	704.31
17.	New Jersey	696.76
18.	Kentucky	695.41
19.	Virginia	691.78
*	UNITED STATES	690.83
20.	Iowa	687.16
21.	New Hampshire	682.27
22.	Missouri	674.39
23.	Wisconsin	673.18
24.	District of Columbia	669.51
25.	Illinois	658.83
26.	Colorado	649.94
27.	California	644.38
28.	Alabama	636.40
29.	Montana	636.00
30.	Oregon	630.59
31.	Pennsylvania	627.10
32.	Utah	626.78
33.	Vermont	625.28
34.	South Carolina	616.23
35.	Nebraska	615.14
36.	Hawaii	613.35
37.	Florida	612.13
38.	Nevada	609.52
39.	Arizona	604.13
40.	Oklahoma	589.32
41.	North Dakota	583.83
42.	North Carolina	582.80
43.	Georgia	582.23
44.	Alaska	579.15
45.	South Dakota	578.88
46.	Texas	573.01
47.	Tennessee	553.18
48.	New Mexico	551.15
49.	Arkansas	547.35
50.	Mississippi	542.93
51.	Rhode Island	522.04

©2008 Information Publications, Inc.
All Rights Reserved. Photocopying prohibited.
877-544-INFO (4636) or www.informationpublications.com

Comparative Tables

73. Average Annual Pay, 2006

1.	District of Columbia	$70,151
2.	New York	55,479
3.	Connecticut	54,814
4.	Massachusetts	52,435
5.	New Jersey	51,645
6.	California	48,345
7.	Delaware	46,285
8.	Maryland	46,162
9.	Illinois	45,650
10.	Virginia	44,051
11.	Colorado	43,506
12.	Washington	42,897
*	UNITED STATES	42,535
13.	Texas	42,458
14.	New Hampshire	42,447
15.	Minnesota	42,185
16.	Michigan	42,157
17.	Alaska	41,750
18.	Pennsylvania	41,349
19.	Rhode Island	40,454
20.	Georgia	40,370
21.	Nevada	40,070
22.	Arizona	40,019
23.	Ohio	38,568
24.	Florida	38,485
25.	Oregon	38,077
26.	Hawaii	37,799
27.	Tennessee	37,564
28.	North Carolina	37,439
29.	Missouri	37,143
30.	Wisconsin	36,821
31.	Wyoming	36,662
32.	Louisiana	36,604
33.	Indiana	36,553
34.	Alabama	36,204
35.	Kansas	35,696
36.	Vermont	35,542
37.	Kentucky	35,201
38.	Utah	35,130
39.	New Mexico	34,567
40.	Iowa	34,320
41.	South Carolina	34,281
42.	Oklahoma	34,022
43.	Nebraska	33,814
44.	Maine	33,794
45.	West Virginia	32,728
46.	Idaho	32,580
47.	Arkansas	32,389
48.	North Dakota	31,316
49.	Mississippi	31,194
50.	Montana	30,596
51.	South Dakota	30,291

74. Median Household Income, 2006

1.	Maryland	$65,144
2.	New Jersey	64,470
3.	Connecticut	63,422
4.	Hawaii	61,160
5.	Massachusetts	59,963
6.	New Hampshire	59,683
7.	Alaska	59,393
8.	California	56,645
9.	Virginia	56,277
10.	Minnesota	54,023
11.	Nevada	52,998
12.	Delaware	52,833
13.	Washington	52,583
14.	Colorado	52,015
15.	Illinois	52,006
16.	District of Columbia	51,847
17.	Rhode Island	51,814
18.	New York	51,384
19.	Utah	51,309
20.	Wisconsin	48,772
*	UNITED STATES	48,451
21.	Vermont	47,665
22.	Wyoming	47,423
23.	Arizona	47,265
24.	Michigan	47,182
25.	Georgia	46,832
26.	Pennsylvania	46,259
27.	Oregon	46,230
28.	Florida	45,495
29.	Kansas	45,478
30.	Nebraska	45,474
31.	Indiana	45,394
32.	Texas	44,922
33.	Ohio	44,532
34.	Iowa	44,491
35.	Maine	43,439
36.	Idaho	42,865
37.	Missouri	42,841
38.	South Dakota	42,791
39.	North Carolina	42,625
40.	North Dakota	41,919
41.	South Carolina	41,100
42.	New Mexico	40,629
43.	Montana	40,627
44.	Tennessee	40,315
45.	Kentucky	39,372
46.	Louisiana	39,337
47.	Alabama	38,783
48.	Oklahoma	38,770
49.	Arkansas	36,599
50.	West Virginia	35,059
51.	Mississippi	34,473

©2008 Information Publications, Inc.
All Rights Reserved. Photocopying prohibited.
877-544-INFO (4636) or www.informationpublications.com

Comparative Tables

<table>
<tr><th colspan="2">75. Personal Income, in Current Dollars, 2006</th><th colspan="2">76. Personal Income, in Constant (2000) Dollars, 2006</th></tr>
<tr><td>1. District of Columbia</td><td>$55,755</td><td>1. District of Columbia</td><td>$48,671</td></tr>
<tr><td>2. Connecticut</td><td>49,852</td><td>2. Connecticut</td><td>43,518</td></tr>
<tr><td>3. New Jersey</td><td>46,344</td><td>3. New Jersey</td><td>40,455</td></tr>
<tr><td>4. Massachusetts</td><td>45,877</td><td>4. Massachusetts</td><td>40,048</td></tr>
<tr><td>5. Maryland</td><td>44,077</td><td>5. Maryland</td><td>38,476</td></tr>
<tr><td>6. New York</td><td>42,392</td><td>6. New York</td><td>37,005</td></tr>
<tr><td>7. Wyoming</td><td>40,676</td><td>7. Wyoming</td><td>35,508</td></tr>
<tr><td>8. New Hampshire</td><td>39,311</td><td>8. New Hampshire</td><td>34,316</td></tr>
<tr><td>9. Colorado</td><td>39,186</td><td>9. Colorado</td><td>34,207</td></tr>
<tr><td>10. Virginia</td><td>39,173</td><td>10. Virginia</td><td>34,196</td></tr>
<tr><td>11. Delaware</td><td>39,022</td><td>11. Delaware</td><td>34,064</td></tr>
<tr><td>12. California</td><td>38,956</td><td>12. California</td><td>34,006</td></tr>
<tr><td>13. Minnesota</td><td>38,712</td><td>13. Minnesota</td><td>33,793</td></tr>
<tr><td>14. Illinois</td><td>38,215</td><td>14. Illinois</td><td>33,359</td></tr>
<tr><td>15. Washington</td><td>37,423</td><td>15. Washington</td><td>32,668</td></tr>
<tr><td>16. Rhode Island</td><td>37,388</td><td>16. Rhode Island</td><td>32,637</td></tr>
<tr><td>17. Alaska</td><td>37,271</td><td>17. Alaska</td><td>32,535</td></tr>
<tr><td>18. Nevada</td><td>37,089</td><td>18. Nevada</td><td>32,376</td></tr>
<tr><td>19. Pennsylvania</td><td>36,680</td><td>19. Pennsylvania</td><td>32,019</td></tr>
<tr><td>20. Hawaii</td><td>36,299</td><td>20. Hawaii</td><td>31,687</td></tr>
<tr><td>* UNITED STATES</td><td>36,276</td><td>* UNITED STATES</td><td>31,667</td></tr>
<tr><td>21. Florida</td><td>35,798</td><td>21. Florida</td><td>31,249</td></tr>
<tr><td>22. Kansas</td><td>34,743</td><td>22. Kansas</td><td>30,328</td></tr>
<tr><td>23. Wisconsin</td><td>34,701</td><td>23. Wisconsin</td><td>30,292</td></tr>
<tr><td>24. Nebraska</td><td>34,397</td><td>24. Nebraska</td><td>30,026</td></tr>
<tr><td>25. Vermont</td><td>34,264</td><td>25. Vermont</td><td>29,910</td></tr>
<tr><td>26. Texas</td><td>34,257</td><td>26. Texas</td><td>29,904</td></tr>
<tr><td>27. South Dakota</td><td>33,929</td><td>27. South Dakota</td><td>29,618</td></tr>
<tr><td>28. Michigan</td><td>33,847</td><td>28. Michigan</td><td>29,546</td></tr>
<tr><td>29. Oregon</td><td>33,666</td><td>29. Oregon</td><td>29,388</td></tr>
<tr><td>30. Ohio</td><td>33,338</td><td>30. Ohio</td><td>29,102</td></tr>
<tr><td>31. Iowa</td><td>33,236</td><td>31. Iowa</td><td>29,013</td></tr>
<tr><td>32. Missouri</td><td>32,705</td><td>32. Missouri</td><td>28,549</td></tr>
<tr><td>33. North Dakota</td><td>32,552</td><td>33. North Dakota</td><td>28,416</td></tr>
<tr><td>34. Indiana</td><td>32,526</td><td>34. Indiana</td><td>28,393</td></tr>
<tr><td>35. Maine</td><td>32,348</td><td>35. Maine</td><td>28,238</td></tr>
<tr><td>36. Tennessee</td><td>32,304</td><td>36. Tennessee</td><td>28,199</td></tr>
<tr><td>37. North Carolina</td><td>32,234</td><td>37. North Carolina</td><td>28,138</td></tr>
<tr><td>38. Oklahoma</td><td>32,210</td><td>38. Oklahoma</td><td>28,117</td></tr>
<tr><td>39. Georgia</td><td>31,891</td><td>39. Georgia</td><td>27,839</td></tr>
<tr><td>40. Arizona</td><td>31,458</td><td>40. Arizona</td><td>27,461</td></tr>
<tr><td>41. Alabama</td><td>31,295</td><td>41. Alabama</td><td>27,319</td></tr>
<tr><td>42. Louisiana</td><td>30,952</td><td>42. Louisiana</td><td>27,019</td></tr>
<tr><td>43. Montana</td><td>30,688</td><td>43. Montana</td><td>26,789</td></tr>
<tr><td>44. Idaho</td><td>29,952</td><td>44. Idaho</td><td>26,146</td></tr>
<tr><td>45. New Mexico</td><td>29,673</td><td>45. New Mexico</td><td>25,903</td></tr>
<tr><td>46. South Carolina</td><td>29,515</td><td>46. South Carolina</td><td>25,765</td></tr>
<tr><td>47. Kentucky</td><td>29,352</td><td>47. Kentucky</td><td>25,622</td></tr>
<tr><td>48. Utah</td><td>29,108</td><td>48. Utah</td><td>25,409</td></tr>
<tr><td>49. Arkansas</td><td>27,935</td><td>49. Arkansas</td><td>24,385</td></tr>
<tr><td>50. West Virginia</td><td>27,897</td><td>50. West Virginia</td><td>24,352</td></tr>
<tr><td>51. Mississippi</td><td>26,535</td><td>51. Mississippi</td><td>23,163</td></tr>
</table>

458

©2008 Information Publications, Inc.
All Rights Reserved. Photocopying prohibited.
877-544-INFO (4636) or www.informationpublications.com

Comparative Tables

77. Persons Below the Poverty Level, 2006

1.	Mississippi	21.1%
2.	District of Columbia	19.6
3.	Louisiana	19.0
4.	New Mexico	18.5
5.	Arkansas	17.3
6.	West Virginia	17.3
7.	Kentucky	17.0
8.	Oklahoma	17.0
9.	Texas	16.9
10.	Alabama	16.6
11.	Tennessee	16.2
12.	South Carolina	15.7
13.	Georgia	14.7
14.	North Carolina	14.7
15.	Arizona	14.2
16.	New York	14.2
17.	Missouri	13.6
18.	Montana	13.6
19.	South Dakota	13.6
20.	Michigan	13.5
21.	Ohio	13.3
22.	Oregon	13.3
*	UNITED STATES	13.3
23.	California	13.1
24.	Maine	12.9
25.	Indiana	12.7
26.	Florida	12.6
27.	Idaho	12.6
28.	Kansas	12.4
29.	Illinois	12.3
30.	Pennsylvania	12.1
31.	Colorado	12.0
32.	Washington	11.8
33.	Nebraska	11.5
34.	North Dakota	11.4
35.	Delaware	11.1
36.	Rhode Island	11.1
37.	Iowa	11.0
38.	Wisconsin	11.0
39.	Alaska	10.9
40.	Utah	10.6
41.	Nevada	10.3
42.	Vermont	10.3
43.	Massachusetts	9.9
44.	Minnesota	9.8
45.	Virginia	9.6
46.	Wyoming	9.4
47.	Hawaii	9.3
48.	New Jersey	8.7
49.	Connecticut	8.3
50.	New Hampshire	8.0
51.	Maryland	7.8

78. Gross Domestic Product, 2006 (x $1 million)

*	UNITED STATES	$13,149,033
1.	California	1,727,355
2.	Texas	1,065,891
3.	New York	1,021,944
4.	Florida	713,505
5.	Illinois	589,598
6.	Pennsylvania	510,293
7.	Ohio	461,302
8.	New Jersey	453,177
9.	Michigan	381,003
10.	Georgia	379,550
11.	North Carolina	374,525
12.	Virginia	369,260
13.	Massachusetts	337,570
14.	Washington	293,531
15.	Maryland	257,815
16.	Indiana	248,915
17.	Minnesota	244,546
18.	Tennessee	238,029
19.	Arizona	232,463
20.	Colorado	230,478
21.	Wisconsin	227,230
22.	Missouri	225,876
23.	Connecticut	204,134
24.	Louisiana	193,138
25.	Alabama	160,569
26.	Oregon	151,301
27.	South Carolina	149,214
28.	Kentucky	145,959
29.	Oklahoma	134,651
30.	Iowa	123,970
31.	Nevada	118,399
32.	Kansas	111,699
33.	Utah	97,749
34.	Arkansas	91,837
35.	District of Columbia	87,664
36.	Mississippi	84,225
37.	New Mexico	75,910
38.	Nebraska	75,700
39.	Delaware	60,361
40.	Hawaii	58,307
41.	New Hampshire	56,276
42.	West Virginia	55,658
43.	Idaho	49,907
44.	Maine	46,973
45.	Rhode Island	45,660
46.	Alaska	41,105
47.	South Dakota	32,330
48.	Montana	32,322
49.	Wyoming	29,561
50.	North Dakota	26,385
51.	Vermont	24,213

©2008 Information Publications, Inc.
All Rights Reserved. Photocopying prohibited.
877-544-INFO (4636) or www.informationpublications.com

Comparative Tables

79. Annual Payroll for Major Industry Groups, 2006 (x $1,000)

*	UNITED STATES	$4,482,722,481
1.	California	588,450,315
2.	New York	370,842,630
3.	Texas	315,809,126
4.	Florida	239,197,889
5.	Illinois	217,221,786
6.	Pennsylvania	189,692,284
7.	Ohio	168,350,499
8.	New Jersey	166,018,238
9.	Michigan	148,456,286
10.	Massachusetts	140,580,627
11.	Georgia	128,827,270
12.	Virginia	121,801,479
13.	North Carolina	115,740,410
14.	Minnesota	96,992,711
15.	Washington	94,928,122
16.	Maryland	88,964,728
17.	Indiana	88,145,224
18.	Wisconsin	85,781,279
19.	Missouri	82,340,359
20.	Tennessee	80,959,818
21.	Arizona	76,340,525
22.	Connecticut	75,605,605
23.	Colorado	75,525,841
24.	Alabama	53,365,320
25.	Louisiana	50,657,624
26.	Oregon	50,019,294
27.	South Carolina	49,450,267
28.	Kentucky	47,983,162
29.	Iowa	39,420,961
30.	Nevada	39,261,902
31.	Oklahoma	37,620,071
32.	Kansas	36,646,065
33.	Utah	30,970,696
34.	Arkansas	30,185,779
35.	Mississippi	25,796,066
36.	District of Columbia	25,152,741
37.	Nebraska	24,180,753
38.	New Hampshire	21,026,773
39.	New Mexico	18,171,120
40.	Delaware	16,875,311
41.	West Virginia	16,323,457
42.	Hawaii	16,163,137
43.	Maine	15,873,419
44.	Rhode Island	15,756,079
45.	Idaho	15,397,889
46.	Alaska	9,774,285
47.	Montana	8,950,520
48.	South Dakota	8,860,458
49.	Vermont	8,284,548
50.	North Dakota	7,779,322
51.	Wyoming	6,202,411

80. Paid Employees for Major Industry Groups, 2006 (x 1,000)

*	UNITED STATES	116,317,003
1.	California	13,382,470
2.	Texas	8,305,102
3.	New York	7,417,463
4.	Florida	7,107,378
5.	Illinois	5,235,866
6.	Pennsylvania	5,082,630
7.	Ohio	4,762,618
8.	Michigan	3,796,876
9.	New Jersey	3,594,862
10.	Georgia	3,489,046
11.	North Carolina	3,409,968
12.	Virginia	3,060,127
13.	Massachusetts	2,996,347
14.	Indiana	2,610,899
15.	Wisconsin	2,449,114
16.	Minnesota	2,430,853
17.	Missouri	2,425,403
18.	Tennessee	2,378,754
19.	Washington	2,316,296
20.	Maryland	2,167,999
21.	Arizona	2,159,823
22.	Colorado	1,936,264
23.	Alabama	1,667,526
24.	Louisiana	1,617,507
25.	South Carolina	1,584,914
26.	Connecticut	1,529,827
27.	Kentucky	1,514,199
28.	Oregon	1,409,576
29.	Iowa	1,261,108
30.	Oklahoma	1,220,285
31.	Kansas	1,116,216
32.	Nevada	1,089,422
33.	Arkansas	1,017,424
34.	Utah	974,686
35.	Mississippi	926,952
36.	Nebraska	773,082
37.	New Mexico	595,249
38.	West Virginia	565,499
39.	New Hampshire	562,398
40.	Idaho	519,319
41.	Maine	497,387
42.	Hawaii	490,682
43.	Rhode Island	442,291
44.	District of Columbia	439,610
45.	Delaware	392,840
46.	Montana	326,887
47.	South Dakota	310,802
48.	North Dakota	270,479
49.	Vermont	261,656
50.	Alaska	231,088
51.	Wyoming	191,934

©2008 Information Publications, Inc.
All Rights Reserved. Photocopying prohibited.
877-544-INFO (4636) or www.informationpublications.com

Comparative Tables

81. Number of Farms, 2006

* UNITED STATES	2,089,790
1. Texas	230,000
2. Missouri	105,000
3. Iowa	88,600
4. Kentucky	84,000
5. Oklahoma	83,000
6. Tennessee	82,000
7. Minnesota	79,300
8. Ohio	76,200
9. California	76,000
10. Wisconsin	76,000
11. Illinois	72,400
12. Kansas	64,000
13. Indiana	59,000
14. Pennsylvania	58,200
15. Michigan	53,000
16. Georgia	49,000
17. North Carolina	48,000
18. Nebraska	47,600
19. Virginia	46,800
20. Arkansas	46,500
21. Alabama	43,000
22. Mississippi	42,000
23. Florida	41,000
24. Oregon	39,300
25. New York	35,000
26. Washington	34,000
27. South Dakota	31,300
28. Colorado	30,700
29. North Dakota	30,300
30. Montana	28,100
31. Louisiana	26,800
32. Idaho	25,000
33. South Carolina	24,600
34. West Virginia	21,200
35. New Mexico	17,500
36. Utah	15,100
37. Maryland	12,000
38. Arizona	10,000
39. New Jersey	9,800
40. Wyoming	9,100
41. Maine	7,100
42. Vermont	6,300
43. Massachusetts	6,100
44. Hawaii	5,500
45. Connecticut	4,200
46. New Hampshire	3,400
47. Nevada	3,000
48. Delaware	2,300
49. Rhode Island	850
50. Alaska	640
51. District of Columbia	NA

82. Net Farm Income, 2006 (x $1 million)

* UNITED STATES	$59,005.5
1. California	5,905.7
2. Texas	4,866.3
3. North Carolina	3,702.2
4. Iowa	3,274.8
5. Minnesota	2,493.6
6. Georgia	2,387.6
7. Florida	2,340.4
8. Nebraska	2,297.0
9. Arkansas	1,950.9
10. Kentucky	1,741.5
11. Missouri	1,697.3
12. Ohio	1,614.4
13. Kansas	1,614.3
14. Alabama	1,579.8
15. Indiana	1,545.4
16. Pennsylvania	1,516.4
17. Illinois	1,511.0
18. Michigan	1,321.2
19. Mississippi	1,230.3
20. Wisconsin	1,091.4
21. Washington	958.3
22. Oklahoma	876.5
23. Oregon	875.6
24. New York	868.7
25. Arizona	773.7
26. Louisiana	765.7
27. Idaho	758.4
28. South Dakota	741.5
29. Colorado	734.0
30. South Carolina	722.2
31. Tennessee	721.8
32. Virginia	678.0
33. North Dakota	605.9
34. Maryland	594.6
35. New Mexico	423.0
36. Delaware	388.2
37. New Jersey	305.4
38. Utah	263.6
39. Montana	256.8
40. Maine	216.8
41. Connecticut	182.8
42. Massachusetts	115.4
43. Hawaii	105.5
44. Vermont	103.2
45. Nevada	84.6
46. Wyoming	65.2
47. West Virginia	49.7
48. New Hampshire	42.6
49. Rhode Island	26.0
50. Alaska	20.0
51. District of Columbia	NA

©2008 Information Publications, Inc.
All Rights Reserved. Photocopying prohibited.
877-544-INFO (4636) or www.informationpublications.com

Comparative Tables

83. Farm Marketing Receipts, 2006 (x $1 million)

* UNITED STATES	$239,271.9
1. California	31,402.7
2. Texas	16,026.8
3. Iowa	15,108.3
4. Nebraska	12,042.3
5. Kansas	10,335.8
6. Minnesota	9,769.5
7. Illinois	8,635.7
8. North Carolina	8,199.3
9. Florida	6,974.2
10. Wisconsin	6,791.3
11. Arkansas	6,164.1
12. Washington	6,139.0
13. Georgia	6,005.1
14. Indiana	5,973.2
15. Missouri	5,621.3
16. Colorado	5,614.4
17. Ohio	5,479.7
18. Oklahoma	5,093.6
19. South Dakota	4,716.2
20. Pennsylvania	4,691.7
21. Michigan	4,487.8
22. Idaho	4,415.6
23. Kentucky	4,007.2
24. Oregon	3,990.6
25. North Dakota	3,980.7
26. Mississippi	3,788.5
27. Alabama	3,739.1
28. New York	3,509.0
29. Arizona	2,879.2
30. Virginia	2,688.7
31. Tennessee	2,564.9
32. New Mexico	2,463.5
33. Montana	2,349.2
34. Louisiana	2,186.2
35. South Carolina	1,890.7
36. Maryland	1,597.7
37. Utah	1,243.7
38. Wyoming	1,021.1
39. Delaware	969.1
40. New Jersey	923.9
41. Maine	591.7
42. Hawaii	554.6
43. Connecticut	523.6
44. Vermont	500.8
45. West Virginia	449.6
46. Nevada	446.6
47. Massachusetts	433.0
48. New Hampshire	161.8
49. Rhode Island	65.6
50. Alaska	64.2
51. District of Columbia	NA

84. Exports, Total Value, 2006 (x $1 million)

* UNITED STATES	$1,037,320
1. Texas	150,888
2. California	127,746
3. New York	57,369
4. Washington	53,075
5. Illinois	42,085
6. Michigan	40,405
7. Florida	38,545
8. Ohio	37,833
9. New Jersey	27,002
10. Pennsylvania	26,334
11. Massachusetts	24,047
12. Louisiana	23,503
13. Indiana	22,620
14. Tennessee	22,020
15. North Carolina	21,218
16. Georgia	20,073
17. Arizona	18,287
18. Kentucky	17,232
19. Wisconsin	17,169
20. Minnesota	16,309
21. Oregon	15,288
22. Virginia	14,104
23. Alabama	13,878
24. South Carolina	13,615
25. Missouri	12,776
26. Connecticut	12,238
27. Kansas	8,626
28. Iowa	8,410
29. Colorado	7,956
30. Maryland	7,598
31. Utah	6,798
32. Nevada	5,493
33. Mississippi	4,674
34. Oklahoma	4,375
35. Arkansas	4,265
36. Alaska	4,044
37. Delaware	3,890
38. Vermont	3,817
39. Idaho	3,721
40. Nebraska	3,625
41. West Virginia	3,225
42. New Mexico	2,892
43. New Hampshire	2,811
44. Maine	2,627
45. Rhode Island	1,531
46. North Dakota	1,509
47. South Dakota	1,185
48. District of Columbia	1,040
49. Montana	887
50. Wyoming	830
51. Hawaii	706

©2008 Information Publications, Inc.
All Rights Reserved. Photocopying prohibited.
877-544-INFO (4636) or www.informationpublications.com

Comparative Tables

85. Households with Computers, 2003

1.	Utah	74.1%
2.	Alaska	72.7
3.	New Hampshire	71.5
4.	Washington	71.4
5.	Colorado	70.0
6.	Connecticut	69.2
7.	Idaho	69.2
8.	Minnesota	67.9
9.	Maine	67.8
10.	Oregon	67.0
11.	Virginia	66.8
12.	California	66.3
13.	Nebraska	66.1
14.	Maryland	66.0
15.	New Jersey	65.5
16.	Vermont	65.5
17.	Wyoming	65.4
18.	Iowa	64.7
19.	Arizona	64.3
20.	District of Columbia	64.3
21.	Massachusetts	64.1
22.	Kansas	63.8
23.	Wisconsin	63.8
24.	Hawaii	63.3
25.	Rhode Island	62.3
26.	South Dakota	62.1
*	UNITED STATES	61.8
27.	Nevada	61.3
28.	North Dakota	61.2
29.	Florida	61.0
30.	Missouri	60.7
31.	Georgia	60.6
32.	Pennsylvania	60.2
33.	Illinois	60.0
34.	New York	60.0
35.	Michigan	59.9
36.	Indiana	59.6
37.	Delaware	59.5
38.	Montana	59.5
39.	Texas	59.0
40.	Ohio	58.8
41.	Kentucky	58.1
42.	North Carolina	57.7
43.	Tennessee	56.7
44.	Oklahoma	55.4
45.	West Virginia	55.0
46.	South Carolina	54.9
47.	Alabama	53.9
48.	New Mexico	53.9
49.	Louisiana	52.3
50.	Arkansas	50.0
51.	Mississippi	48.3

86. Households with Internet Access, 2003

1.	Alaska	67.6%
2.	New Hampshire	65.2
3.	Colorado	63.0
4.	Connecticut	62.9
5.	Utah	62.6
6.	Washington	62.3
7.	Minnesota	61.6
8.	Oregon	61.0
9.	New Jersey	60.5
10.	Virginia	60.3
11.	California	59.6
12.	Maryland	59.2
13.	Massachusetts	58.1
14.	Vermont	58.1
15.	Maine	57.9
16.	Wyoming	57.7
17.	Wisconsin	57.4
18.	Iowa	57.1
19.	District of Columbia	56.8
20.	Idaho	56.4
21.	Rhode Island	55.7
22.	Florida	55.6
23.	Nebraska	55.4
24.	Arizona	55.2
25.	Nevada	55.2
26.	Hawaii	55.0
27.	Pennsylvania	54.7
*	UNITED STATES	54.6
28.	Kansas	54.3
29.	South Dakota	53.6
30.	Georgia	53.5
31.	New York	53.3
32.	Delaware	53.2
33.	North Dakota	53.2
34.	Missouri	53.0
35.	Ohio	52.5
36.	Michigan	52.0
37.	Texas	51.8
38.	Illinois	51.1
39.	North Carolina	51.1
40.	Indiana	51.0
41.	Montana	50.4
42.	Kentucky	49.6
43.	Tennessee	48.9
44.	Oklahoma	48.4
45.	West Virginia	47.6
46.	Alabama	45.7
47.	South Carolina	45.6
48.	New Mexico	44.5
49.	Louisiana	44.1
50.	Arkansas	42.4
51.	Mississippi	38.9

©2008 Information Publications, Inc.
All Rights Reserved. Photocopying prohibited.
877-544-INFO (4636) or www.informationpublications.com

Comparative Tables

87. Wireless Phone Customers, December 2006

* UNITED STATES	229,619,397
1. California	29,717,334
2. Texas	17,822,230
3. New York	15,261,760
4. Florida	14,761,666
5. Illinois	9,588,517
6. Pennsylvania	8,831,238
7. Ohio	8,380,138
8. Georgia	7,281,724
9. New Jersey	7,207,018
10. Michigan	7,093,721
11. North Carolina	6,626,582
12. Virginia	5,607,350
13. Massachusetts	5,128,860
14. Tennessee	5,126,510
15. Washington	4,799,143
16. Maryland	4,691,026
17. Arizona	4,405,032
18. Missouri	4,322,458
19. Indiana	4,271,412
20. Minnesota	3,701,515
21. Colorado	3,608,209
22. Wisconsin	3,509,528
23. Louisiana	3,492,358
24. Alabama	3,374,701
25. South Carolina	3,208,504
26. Kentucky	2,966,195
27. Connecticut	2,705,023
28. Oregon	2,655,905
29. Oklahoma	2,479,877
30. Kansas	2,046,542
31. Arkansas	2,044,217
32. Mississippi	2,029,916
33. Iowa	2,009,826
34. Nevada	1,990,215
35. Utah	1,774,755
36. New Mexico	1,333,210
37. Nebraska	1,272,067
38. West Virginia	1,040,224
39. Hawaii	1,034,788
40. Idaho	972,825
41. New Hampshire	943,330
42. District of Columbia	880,077
43. Maine	844,537
44. Rhode Island	797,603
45. Delaware	682,636
46. Montana	619,620
47. South Dakota	547,812
48. North Dakota	472,799
49. Alaska	412,112
50. Wyoming	387,164
51. Vermont	358,052

88. FCC-Licensed TV Stations, January 1, 2008

* UNITED STATES	1,716
1. Texas	135
2. California	108
3. Florida	92
4. New York	55
5. Michigan	54
6. Ohio	52
7. North Carolina	50
8. Georgia	47
9. Illinois	47
10. Pennsylvania	46
11. Alabama	43
12. Wisconsin	43
13. Indiana	40
14. Tennessee	40
15. Kentucky	38
16. Louisiana	38
17. Virginia	36
18. Missouri	35
19. Washington	35
20. South Carolina	34
21. Iowa	33
22. Oregon	33
23. Arizona	31
24. Colorado	31
25. Minnesota	31
26. Mississippi	29
27. Arkansas	27
28. Hawaii	27
29. Nebraska	27
30. North Dakota	27
31. Oklahoma	27
32. Montana	26
33. New Mexico	26
34. South Dakota	26
35. Kansas	25
36. Massachusetts	22
37. Idaho	21
38. Nevada	21
39. West Virginia	18
40. Alaska	17
41. Utah	17
42. Wyoming	17
43. Maryland	16
44. Maine	15
45. New Jersey	15
46. Connecticut	13
47. District of Columbia	8
48. New Hampshire	7
49. Vermont	7
50. Rhode Island	5
51. Delaware	3

©2008 Information Publications, Inc.
All Rights Reserved. Photocopying prohibited.
877-544-INFO (4636) or www.informationpublications.com

Comparative Tables

<table>
<tr><th colspan="2">89. Energy Spending,
per capita, 2004</th><th colspan="2">90. Price of Energy,
2004 (per million Btu)</th></tr>
<tr><td>1. Alaska</td><td>$6,339</td><td>1. Hawaii</td><td>$18.05</td></tr>
<tr><td>2. Wyoming</td><td>5,749</td><td>2. District of Columbia</td><td>16.87</td></tr>
<tr><td>3. Louisiana</td><td>5,428</td><td>3. Massachusetts</td><td>16.18</td></tr>
<tr><td>4. Texas</td><td>4,224</td><td>4. Rhode Island</td><td>15.95</td></tr>
<tr><td>5. North Dakota</td><td>4,167</td><td>5. Connecticut</td><td>15.86</td></tr>
<tr><td>6. Montana</td><td>3,435</td><td>6. Vermont</td><td>15.83</td></tr>
<tr><td>7. Iowa</td><td>3,423</td><td>7. New York</td><td>15.65</td></tr>
<tr><td>8. Maine</td><td>3,403</td><td>8. New Hampshire</td><td>15.52</td></tr>
<tr><td>9. Indiana</td><td>3,364</td><td>9. Nevada</td><td>15.43</td></tr>
<tr><td>10. Alabama</td><td>3,360</td><td>10. Arizona</td><td>15.24</td></tr>
<tr><td>11. Kentucky</td><td>3,353</td><td>11. Florida</td><td>15.21</td></tr>
<tr><td>12. Kansas</td><td>3,270</td><td>12. California</td><td>15.12</td></tr>
<tr><td>13. Mississippi</td><td>3,268</td><td>13. Maryland</td><td>14.11</td></tr>
<tr><td>14. West Virginia</td><td>3,228</td><td>14. New Jersey</td><td>14.07</td></tr>
<tr><td>15. Hawaii</td><td>3,207</td><td>15. Delaware</td><td>13.64</td></tr>
<tr><td>16. Oklahoma</td><td>3,200</td><td>16. North Carolina</td><td>13.60</td></tr>
<tr><td>17. South Carolina</td><td>3,194</td><td>17. New Mexico</td><td>13.48</td></tr>
<tr><td>18. Arkansas</td><td>3,174</td><td>18. Pennsylvania</td><td>13.05</td></tr>
<tr><td>19. Vermont</td><td>3,170</td><td>* UNITED STATES</td><td>12.91</td></tr>
<tr><td>20. New Jersey</td><td>3,119</td><td>19. Missouri</td><td>12.89</td></tr>
<tr><td>21. Nebraska</td><td>3,093</td><td>20. Ohio</td><td>12.85</td></tr>
<tr><td>22. Delaware</td><td>3,066</td><td>21. Oregon</td><td>12.85</td></tr>
<tr><td>23. Ohio</td><td>3,049</td><td>22. Maine</td><td>12.80</td></tr>
<tr><td>24. Connecticut</td><td>3,032</td><td>23. Wisconsin</td><td>12.69</td></tr>
<tr><td>25. New Hampshire</td><td>3,026</td><td>24. Virginia</td><td>12.64</td></tr>
<tr><td>26. South Dakota</td><td>3,008</td><td>25. Colorado</td><td>12.54</td></tr>
<tr><td>27. Tennessee</td><td>3,001</td><td>26. South Dakota</td><td>12.54</td></tr>
<tr><td>28. Minnesota</td><td>2,989</td><td>27. South Carolina</td><td>12.53</td></tr>
<tr><td>29. District of Columbia</td><td>2,983</td><td>28. Mississippi</td><td>12.51</td></tr>
<tr><td>* UNITED STATES</td><td>2,961</td><td>29. Illinois</td><td>12.46</td></tr>
<tr><td>30. Nevada</td><td>2,949</td><td>30. Kansas</td><td>12.44</td></tr>
<tr><td>31. Wisconsin</td><td>2,922</td><td>31. Georgia</td><td>12.42</td></tr>
<tr><td>32. Pennsylvania</td><td>2,914</td><td>32. Washington</td><td>12.32</td></tr>
<tr><td>33. Georgia</td><td>2,872</td><td>33. Michigan</td><td>12.24</td></tr>
<tr><td>34. Virginia</td><td>2,850</td><td>34. Oklahoma</td><td>12.24</td></tr>
<tr><td>35. Missouri</td><td>2,846</td><td>35. Nebraska</td><td>12.18</td></tr>
<tr><td>36. Massachusetts</td><td>2,774</td><td>36. Minnesota</td><td>12.17</td></tr>
<tr><td>37. New Mexico</td><td>2,745</td><td>37. Tennessee</td><td>12.16</td></tr>
<tr><td>38. North Carolina</td><td>2,722</td><td>38. Montana</td><td>12.12</td></tr>
<tr><td>39. Michigan</td><td>2,681</td><td>39. Arkansas</td><td>11.89</td></tr>
<tr><td>40. Illinois</td><td>2,680</td><td>40. Idaho</td><td>11.82</td></tr>
<tr><td>41. Idaho</td><td>2,679</td><td>41. Iowa</td><td>11.80</td></tr>
<tr><td>42. Colorado</td><td>2,567</td><td>42. Texas</td><td>11.50</td></tr>
<tr><td>43. Maryland</td><td>2,551</td><td>43. Utah</td><td>11.39</td></tr>
<tr><td>44. Oregon</td><td>2,544</td><td>44. Kentucky</td><td>11.30</td></tr>
<tr><td>45. California</td><td>2,518</td><td>45. Alabama</td><td>11.29</td></tr>
<tr><td>46. New York</td><td>2,514</td><td>46. Alaska</td><td>11.09</td></tr>
<tr><td>47. Washington</td><td>2,508</td><td>47. West Virginia</td><td>10.66</td></tr>
<tr><td>48. Rhode Island</td><td>2,442</td><td>48. Wyoming</td><td>10.29</td></tr>
<tr><td>49. Arizona</td><td>2,398</td><td>49. Indiana</td><td>10.19</td></tr>
<tr><td>50. Florida</td><td>2,367</td><td>50. Louisiana</td><td>10.09</td></tr>
<tr><td>51. Utah</td><td>2,343</td><td>51. North Dakota</td><td>9.18</td></tr>
</table>

©2008 Information Publications, Inc.
All Rights Reserved. Photocopying prohibited.
877-544-INFO (4636) or www.informationpublications.com

Comparative Tables

91. Energy Consumption, per capita, 2005 (x 1 million Btu)

1.	Alaska	1,186.1
2.	Wyoming	898.9
3.	Louisiana	848.9
4.	North Dakota	632.7
5.	Texas	531.6
6.	Alabama	478.1
7.	Indiana	473.3
8.	Kentucky	472.5
9.	West Virginia	453.5
10.	Montana	434.9
11.	Oklahoma	421.8
12.	Mississippi	419.8
13.	Arkansas	413.5
14.	South Carolina	409.4
15.	Iowa	408.2
16.	Kansas	403.0
17.	Tennessee	390.4
18.	Nebraska	373.2
19.	Delaware	367.8
20.	Maine	365.5
21.	New Mexico	359.0
22.	Minnesota	358.5
23.	Idaho	358.4
24.	Georgia	351.5
25.	Ohio	351.0
26.	Virginia	342.4
27.	South Dakota	342.3
*	UNITED STATES	341.5
28.	Wisconsin	336.0
29.	District of Columbia	328.3
30.	Pennsylvania	327.2
31.	Washington	323.1
32.	Missouri	321.5
33.	North Carolina	318.3
34.	Illinois	311.5
35.	Michigan	309.1
36.	Utah	305.7
37.	Oregon	304.7
38.	New Jersey	303.2
39.	Colorado	300.9
40.	Nevada	297.4
41.	Maryland	274.9
42.	Vermont	272.7
43.	Connecticut	264.4
44.	New Hampshire	262.5
45.	Hawaii	256.9
46.	Florida	256.4
47.	Arizona	250.0
48.	Massachusetts	239.7
49.	California	233.4
50.	New York	220.5
51.	Rhode Island	209.8

92. Electricity from Renewable Sources, 2005 (% of net generation)

1.	Idaho	84.2%
2.	Washington	72.8
3.	Oregon	66.1
4.	South Dakota	49.6
5.	Maine	43.3
6.	Montana	34.5
7.	California	31.6
8.	Vermont	28.6
9.	Alaska	22.3
10.	New York	18.9
11.	New Hampshire	11.2
12.	Tennessee	10.2
13.	Alabama	10.1
14.	Arkansas	10.1
*	UNITED STATES	8.8
15.	Nevada	7.4
16.	Minnesota	6.5
17.	Arizona	6.4
18.	Iowa	6.2
19.	North Carolina	5.6
20.	Hawaii	5.5
21.	Oklahoma	5.5
22.	Georgia	5.3
23.	Virginia	5.0
24.	North Dakota	4.9
25.	Wisconsin	4.9
26.	Massachusetts	4.8
27.	South Carolina	4.6
28.	Colorado	4.5
29.	Maryland	4.4
30.	Louisiana	3.8
31.	Connecticut	3.7
32.	Kentucky	3.5
33.	Mississippi	3.4
34.	Michigan	3.3
35.	Wyoming	3.3
36.	Nebraska	3.2
37.	New Mexico	2.7
38.	Utah	2.6
39.	Florida	2.1
40.	Pennsylvania	2.1
41.	Texas	1.7
42.	West Virginia	1.7
43.	New Jersey	1.5
44.	Missouri	1.3
45.	Kansas	1.0
46.	Ohio	0.6
47.	Illinois	0.5
48.	Indiana	0.4
49.	Rhode Island	0.1
50.	Delaware	NA
51.	District of Columbia	NA

©2008 Information Publications, Inc.
All Rights Reserved. Photocopying prohibited.
877-544-INFO (4636) or www.informationpublications.com

Comparative Tables

93. Average Daily Commute, 2006 (minutes each way)

1. New York	30.9
2. Maryland	30.6
3. District of Columbia	29.2
4. New Jersey	29.1
5. Illinois	27.9
6. Georgia	27.3
7. Virginia	26.9
8. California	26.8
9. Massachusetts	26.6
10. Florida	25.9
11. West Virginia	25.6
12. Hawaii	25.5
13. Washington	25.2
14. Louisiana	25.1
15. Arizona	25.0
16. Pennsylvania	25.0
* UNITED STATES	25.0
17. New Hampshire	24.6
18. Texas	24.6
19. Nevada	24.2
20. Connecticut	24.1
21. Mississippi	24.0
22. Colorado	23.9
23. Alabama	23.6
24. Delaware	23.6
25. Tennessee	23.5
26. Michigan	23.4
27. North Carolina	23.4
28. Missouri	22.9
29. South Carolina	22.9
30. Kentucky	22.4
31. Indiana	22.3
32. Maine	22.3
33. Rhode Island	22.3
34. Ohio	22.1
35. Minnesota	22.0
36. Oregon	21.8
37. Vermont	21.2
38. New Mexico	20.9
39. Utah	20.8
40. Wisconsin	20.8
41. Arkansas	20.7
42. Idaho	20.1
43. Oklahoma	20.0
44. Kansas	18.5
45. Iowa	18.2
46. Wyoming	17.9
47. Alaska	17.7
48. Nebraska	17.7
49. Montana	17.6
50. South Dakota	15.9
51. North Dakota	15.5

94. Workers who Drove to Work Alone, 2006

1. Alabama	83.6%
2. Tennessee	83.3
3. Ohio	83.1
4. Michigan	82.9
5. Indiana	82.4
6. Mississippi	82.2
7. Kansas	81.8
8. New Hampshire	81.7
9. Louisiana	81.6
10. Kentucky	81.5
11. Rhode Island	81.1
12. South Carolina	81.1
13. Delaware	80.8
14. Missouri	80.8
15. Oklahoma	80.4
16. Arkansas	80.2
17. West Virginia	80.0
18. Wisconsin	79.9
19. North Carolina	79.8
20. Connecticut	79.7
21. Florida	79.3
22. North Dakota	79.3
23. Nebraska	79.1
24. Iowa	78.5
25. Texas	78.5
26. Georgia	78.2
27. New Mexico	78.2
28. Minnesota	78.1
29. Maine	77.6
30. South Dakota	77.5
31. Idaho	77.2
32. Virginia	77.0
33. Nevada	76.7
34. Pennsylvania	76.4
35. Wyoming	76.0
* UNITED STATES	76.0
36. Utah	75.2
37. Colorado	75.1
38. Vermont	75.1
39. Arizona	74.6
40. Illinois	74.3
41. Massachusetts	73.7
42. California	73.0
43. Maryland	72.8
44. Washington	72.8
45. Montana	72.7
46. New Jersey	71.9
47. Oregon	71.4
48. Alaska	67.7
49. Hawaii	67.0
50. New York	54.4
51. District of Columbia	35.4

©2008 Information Publications, Inc.
All Rights Reserved. Photocopying prohibited.
877-544-INFO (4636) or www.informationpublications.com

Comparative Tables

95. Workers who Carpooled, 2006

1.	Hawaii	16.0%
2.	Arizona	13.9
3.	Utah	13.1
4.	Arkansas	12.9
5.	Alaska	12.7
6.	Texas	12.7
7.	New Mexico	12.5
8.	North Carolina	12.5
9.	Wyoming	12.5
10.	California	12.4
11.	Nevada	12.3
12.	Mississippi	12.1
13.	West Virginia	12.1
14.	Montana	12.0
15.	Washington	11.8
16.	Idaho	11.7
17.	Oregon	11.7
18.	Louisiana	11.6
19.	Oklahoma	11.6
20.	Georgia	11.5
21.	Virginia	11.4
22.	Alabama	11.3
23.	Kentucky	11.3
24.	South Carolina	11.3
25.	Vermont	11.2
26.	Maine	11.0
27.	Florida	10.9
28.	Iowa	10.8
29.	Maryland	10.7
*	UNITED STATES	10.7
30.	Colorado	10.6
31.	Missouri	10.4
32.	Nebraska	10.4
33.	Tennessee	10.2
34.	Indiana	9.9
35.	Pennsylvania	9.9
36.	South Dakota	9.6
37.	Delaware	9.4
38.	Illinois	9.3
39.	Minnesota	9.3
40.	New Jersey	9.3
41.	Kansas	9.2
42.	North Dakota	9.2
43.	Wisconsin	9.2
44.	Michigan	9.1
45.	Rhode Island	8.9
46.	New Hampshire	8.6
47.	Massachusetts	8.5
48.	Connecticut	8.4
49.	Ohio	8.3
50.	New York	7.6
51.	District of Columbia	6.3

96. Workers who used Public Transit, 2006

1.	District of Columbia	39.0%
2.	New York	26.1
3.	New Jersey	10.3
4.	Maryland	8.8
5.	Massachusetts	8.6
6.	Illinois	8.4
7.	Hawaii	5.4
8.	Pennsylvania	5.2
9.	Washington	5.2
10.	California	5.0
*	UNITED STATES	4.8
11.	Oregon	4.4
12.	Connecticut	4.1
13.	Virginia	4.1
14.	Nevada	3.6
15.	Colorado	3.2
16.	Minnesota	3.0
17.	Delaware	2.8
18.	Rhode Island	2.6
19.	Utah	2.6
20.	Georgia	2.4
21.	Arizona	2.1
22.	Florida	2.0
23.	Ohio	2.0
24.	Wisconsin	1.9
25.	Texas	1.7
26.	Missouri	1.4
27.	Wyoming	1.3
28.	Michigan	1.2
29.	Alaska	1.1
30.	Louisiana	1.1
31.	Indiana	1.0
32.	Iowa	1.0
33.	Kentucky	1.0
34.	North Carolina	1.0
35.	West Virginia	1.0
36.	Montana	0.9
37.	New Mexico	0.9
38.	Idaho	0.8
39.	Vermont	0.8
40.	Maine	0.7
41.	New Hampshire	0.7
42.	Tennessee	0.7
43.	Kansas	0.6
44.	South Carolina	0.6
45.	Alabama	0.5
46.	Nebraska	0.5
47.	Oklahoma	0.5
48.	Arkansas	0.4
49.	Mississippi	0.4
50.	North Dakota	0.4
51.	South Dakota	0.4

©2008 Information Publications, Inc.
All Rights Reserved. Photocopying prohibited.
877-544-INFO (4636) or www.informationpublications.com

Comparative Tables

97. Gasoline Consumption, per capita, 2006 (in gallons)

1.	Wyoming	703.1
2.	Louisiana	617.7
3.	South Carolina	590.4
4.	Mississippi	578.8
5.	Alabama	572.3
6.	Iowa	562.9
7.	Vermont	561.0
8.	North Dakota	552.7
9.	Missouri	551.8
10.	New Hampshire	547.1
11.	South Dakota	543.8
12.	Delaware	538.1
13.	Maine	535.7
14.	Georgia	533.3
15.	Kentucky	530.1
16.	Montana	526.3
17.	Virginia	525.0
18.	Oklahoma	522.4
19.	Minnesota	522.2
20.	Arkansas	515.2
21.	Tennessee	515.0
22.	Indiana	511.2
23.	Texas	505.9
24.	North Carolina	500.9
25.	New Mexico	497.5
26.	Maryland	494.6
27.	New Jersey	494.0
28.	Michigan	483.0
29.	Kansas	482.4
30.	Florida	481.4
31.	Nebraska	474.4
32.	Nevada	470.7
*	UNITED STATES	469.7
33.	Arizona	465.6
34.	West Virginia	465.1
35.	Colorado	454.1
36.	Ohio	454.0
37.	Wisconsin	453.6
38.	Idaho	449.5
39.	Connecticut	448.2
40.	Massachusetts	439.3
41.	California	437.1
42.	Alaska	433.0
43.	Washington	428.4
44.	Oregon	427.4
45.	Utah	411.5
46.	Pennsylvania	411.4
47.	Illinois	406.2
48.	Rhode Island	394.1
49.	Hawaii	377.9
50.	New York	300.0
51.	District of Columbia	225.4

98. Automobile Registrations, 2006

*	UNITED STATES	135,399,945
1.	California	19,835,554
2.	Texas	8,805,316
3.	New York	8,528,457
4.	Florida	7,425,148
5.	Ohio	6,438,988
6.	Illinois	5,947,468
7.	Pennsylvania	5,842,819
8.	Michigan	4,765,547
9.	Georgia	4,141,179
10.	Virginia	4,031,355
11.	New Jersey	3,692,966
12.	North Carolina	3,659,926
13.	Massachusetts	3,310,725
14.	Washington	3,087,818
15.	Tennessee	2,878,136
16.	Missouri	2,715,297
17.	Indiana	2,694,901
18.	Maryland	2,656,597
19.	Wisconsin	2,639,984
20.	Minnesota	2,512,491
21.	Arizona	2,189,979
22.	Connecticut	1,999,809
23.	Kentucky	1,969,142
24.	South Carolina	1,964,994
25.	Louisiana	1,950,372
26.	Alabama	1,795,596
27.	Iowa	1,744,519
28.	Oklahoma	1,606,517
29.	Oregon	1,427,597
30.	Mississippi	1,118,200
31.	Utah	1,079,455
32.	Arkansas	958,640
33.	Kansas	872,878
34.	Colorado	858,967
35.	Nebraska	832,511
36.	West Virginia	734,599
37.	New Mexico	699,312
38.	Nevada	679,828
39.	New Hampshire	585,455
40.	Maine	581,797
41.	Idaho	541,487
42.	Hawaii	538,581
43.	Rhode Island	508,389
44.	Montana	447,446
45.	Delaware	432,509
46.	South Dakota	375,760
47.	North Dakota	345,502
48.	Vermont	309,972
49.	Alaska	242,487
50.	Wyoming	228,057
51.	District of Columbia	168,916

©2008 Information Publications, Inc.
All Rights Reserved. Photocopying prohibited.
877-544-INFO (4636) or www.informationpublications.com

Comparative Tables

99. Vehicle-Miles Traveled, per capita, 2006

1. Wyoming	18,361.5
2. Mississippi	14,314.0
3. Oklahoma	13,609.6
4. New Mexico	13,276.5
5. Alabama	13,161.4
6. Vermont	12,616.4
7. North Dakota	12,377.2
8. Georgia	12,152.8
9. Montana	11,898.0
10. Missouri	11,791.4
11. Arkansas	11,750.0
12. South Dakota	11,627.6
13. Tennessee	11,620.9
14. South Carolina	11,593.0
15. West Virginia	11,547.0
16. North Carolina	11,445.5
17. Maine	11,441.1
18. Kentucky	11,355.1
19. Indiana	11,299.2
20. Florida	11,282.9
21. Delaware	11,072.5
22. Nebraska	11,007.7
23. Minnesota	10,964.6
24. Kansas	10,964.1
25. Louisiana	10,703.3
26. Wisconsin	10,658.8
27. Virginia	10,614.2
28. Iowa	10,548.1
29. Idaho	10,382.0
30. New Hampshire	10,377.9
31. Michigan	10,312.9
32. Colorado	10,205.3
33. Texas	10,178.6
34. Arizona	10,131.6
* UNITED STATES	10,088.9
35. Utah	10,065.4
36. Maryland	10,050.3
37. Ohio	9,704.4
38. Oregon	9,613.2
39. Connecticut	9,080.4
40. California	9,033.9
41. Washington	8,865.5
42. Nevada	8,756.1
43. Pennsylvania	8,730.1
44. New Jersey	8,697.2
45. Massachusetts	8,569.0
46. Illinois	8,364.1
47. Hawaii	7,963.2
48. Rhode Island	7,818.1
49. Alaska	7,331.9
50. New York	7,330.6
51. District of Columbia	6,188.3

100. Motor Vehicle Deaths, 2006

* UNITED STATES	42,642
1. California	4,236
2. Texas	3,475
3. Florida	3,374
4. Georgia	1,693
5. North Carolina	1,559
6. Pennsylvania	1,525
7. New York	1,456
8. Arizona	1,288
9. Tennessee	1,287
10. Illinois	1,254
11. Ohio	1,238
12. Alabama	1,208
13. Missouri	1,096
14. Michigan	1,085
15. South Carolina	1,037
16. Louisiana	982
17. Virginia	963
18. Kentucky	913
19. Mississippi	911
20. Indiana	899
21. New Jersey	772
22. Oklahoma	765
23. Wisconsin	724
24. Arkansas	665
25. Maryland	651
26. Washington	630
27. Colorado	535
28. Minnesota	494
29. New Mexico	484
30. Oregon	477
31. Kansas	468
32. Iowa	439
33. Nevada	432
34. Massachusetts	430
35. West Virginia	410
36. Connecticut	301
37. Utah	287
38. Nebraska	269
39. Idaho	267
40. Montana	263
41. Wyoming	195
42. South Dakota	191
43. Maine	188
44. Hawaii	161
45. Delaware	148
46. New Hampshire	127
47. North Dakota	111
48. Vermont	87
49. Rhode Island	81
50. Alaska	74
51. District of Columbia	37

©2008 Information Publications, Inc.
All Rights Reserved. Photocopying prohibited.
877-544-INFO (4636) or www.informationpublications.com

ORDER FORM

Title	Qty	Edition	Price	Extended Price	Standing Order	
State & Municipal Profiles Series					YES	NO
Almanac of the 50 States 2008		Hardcover	$89		☐	☐
Almanac of the 50 States 2008		Paperback	$79		☐	☐
California Cities, Towns & Counties 2008		CD	$119		☐	☐
		Paperback	$119		☐	☐
Connecticut Municipal Profiles 2008		CD	$85		☐	☐
		Paperback	$85		☐	☐
Florida Cities, Towns & Counties 2008		CD	$119		☐	☐
		Paperback	$119		☐	☐
Massachusetts Municipal Profiles 2008		CD	$109		☐	☐
		Paperback	$109		☐	☐
The New Jersey Municipal Data Book 2008		CD	$119		☐	☐
		Paperback	$119		☐	☐
North Carolina Cities, Towns & Counties 2008		CD	$119		☐	☐
		Paperback	$119		☐	☐
Essential Topics Series						
Energy, Transportation & the Environment: A Statistical Sourcebook and Guide to Government Data 2008		Paperback	$77		☐	☐
American Profiles Series						
Black Americans: A Statistical Sourcebook and Guide to Government Data 2008		Paperback	$77		☐	☐
Hispanic Americans: A Statistical Sourcebook and Guide to Government Data 2008		Paperback	$77		☐	☐
Asian Americans: A Statistical Sourcebook and Guide to Government Data 2008		Paperback	$77		☐	☐

Offer and prices valid until 12/31/08

Purchase orders accepted from libraries, government agencies, and educational institutions.

Prepayment required from all other organizations.

Order Subtotal _____

(Required ONLY for shipments to California) CA Sales Tax _____

Shipping & Handling _____

Total _____

Please complete the following shipping and billing information. If paying by credit card or PO please call **(877)544-4636** or fax your completed order form to **(877)544-4635**. To pay by check, please mail this form and your payment to the address below.

Information Publications, Inc.
2995 Woodside Rd., Suite 400-182
Woodside, CA 94062

U.S. Ground Shipping Rates	
Order Subtotal	Shipping & Handling
$0-$89	$7
$90-$119	$9
$120-$240	$14
$241-$400	$19
$401-$500	$22
>$500	Call

Call for Int'l or Express Shipping Rates

Shipping Information (UPS/FedEx tracking number sent via email)

Organization Name			
Shipping Contact			
Address (No PO Boxes, please)			
City	State	Zip	
Email Address (req'd if want tracking #)	Phone #		

Payment Information (mark choice)	☐ **Check**	☐ **Credit Card** ☐ Visa ☐ MC ☐ AMEX	☐ **Purchase Order** (attach PO to this form)
	Check #	CC#	PO #
		Exp Date	

Credit Card Billing Information ☐ Check if same as Shipping Address

Name on Credit Card			
Billing Address of Credit Card			
City	State	Zip	
Signature			

2995 WOODSIDE RD., SUITE 400-182
WOODSIDE, CA 94062

WWW.INFORMATIONPUBLICATIONS.COM

TOLL FREE PHONE 877-544-INFO (4636)
TOLL FREE FAX 877-544-4635

• Since 1980, A Trusted Ready Reference Resource for Easy-To-Use Federal, State and Local Information •

ORDER FORM

Title	Qty	Edition	Price	Extended Price	Standing Order	
State & Municipal Profiles Series					YES	NO
Almanac of the 50 States 2008		Hardcover	$89		☐	☐
Almanac of the 50 States 2008		Paperback	$79		☐	☐
California Cities, Towns & Counties 2008		CD	$119		☐	☐
		Paperback	$119		☐	☐
Connecticut Municipal Profiles 2008		CD	$85		☐	☐
		Paperback	$85		☐	☐
Florida Cities, Towns & Counties 2008		CD	$119		☐	☐
		Paperback	$119		☐	☐
Massachusetts Municipal Profiles 2008		CD	$109		☐	☐
		Paperback	$109		☐	☐
The New Jersey Municipal Data Book 2008		CD	$119		☐	☐
		Paperback	$119		☐	☐
North Carolina Cities, Towns & Counties 2008		CD	$119		☐	☐
		Paperback	$119		☐	☐
Essential Topics Series						
Energy, Transportation & the Environment: A Statistical Sourcebook and Guide to Government Data 2008		Paperback	$77		☐	☐
American Profiles Series						
Black Americans: A Statistical Sourcebook and Guide to Government Data 2008		Paperback	$77		☐	☐
Hispanic Americans: A Statistical Sourcebook and Guide to Government Data 2008		Paperback	$77		☐	☐
Asian Americans: A Statistical Sourcebook and Guide to Government Data 2008		Paperback	$77		☐	☐

Offer and prices valid until 12/31/08

Purchase orders accepted from libraries, government agencies, and educational institutions.

Prepayment required from all other organizations.

Order Subtotal	
(Required ONLY for shipments to California) CA Sales Tax	
Shipping & Handling	
Total	

Please complete the following shipping and billing information. If paying by credit card or PO please call **(877)544-4636** or fax your completed order form to **(877)544-4635**. To pay by check, please mail this form and your payment to the address below.

Information Publications, Inc.
2995 Woodside Rd., Suite 400-182
Woodside, CA 94062

U.S. Ground Shipping Rates	
Order Subtotal	Shipping & Handling
$0-$89	$7
$90-$119	$9
$120-$240	$14
$241-$400	$19
$401-$500	$22
>$500	Call
Call for Int'l or Express Shipping Rates	

Shipping Information (UPS/FedEx tracking number sent via email)

Organization Name		
Shipping Contact		
Address (No PO Boxes, please)		
City	State	Zip
Email Address (req'd if want tracking #)	Phone #	

Payment Information (mark choice)	☐ **Check**	☐ **Credit Card** ☐ Visa ☐ MC ☐ AMEX	☐ **Purchase Order** (attach PO to this form)
	Check #	CC#	PO #
		Exp Date	

Credit Card Billing Information ☐ Check if same as Shipping Address

Name on Credit Card		
Billing Address of Credit Card		
City	State	Zip
Signature		

2995 WOODSIDE RD., SUITE 400-182
WOODSIDE, CA 94062

WWW.INFORMATIONPUBLICATIONS.COM

TOLL FREE PHONE 877-544-INFO (4636)
TOLL FREE FAX 877-544-4635

• Since 1980, A Trusted Ready Reference Resource for Easy-To-Use Federal, State and Local Information •